IMPRESSED BY LIGHT

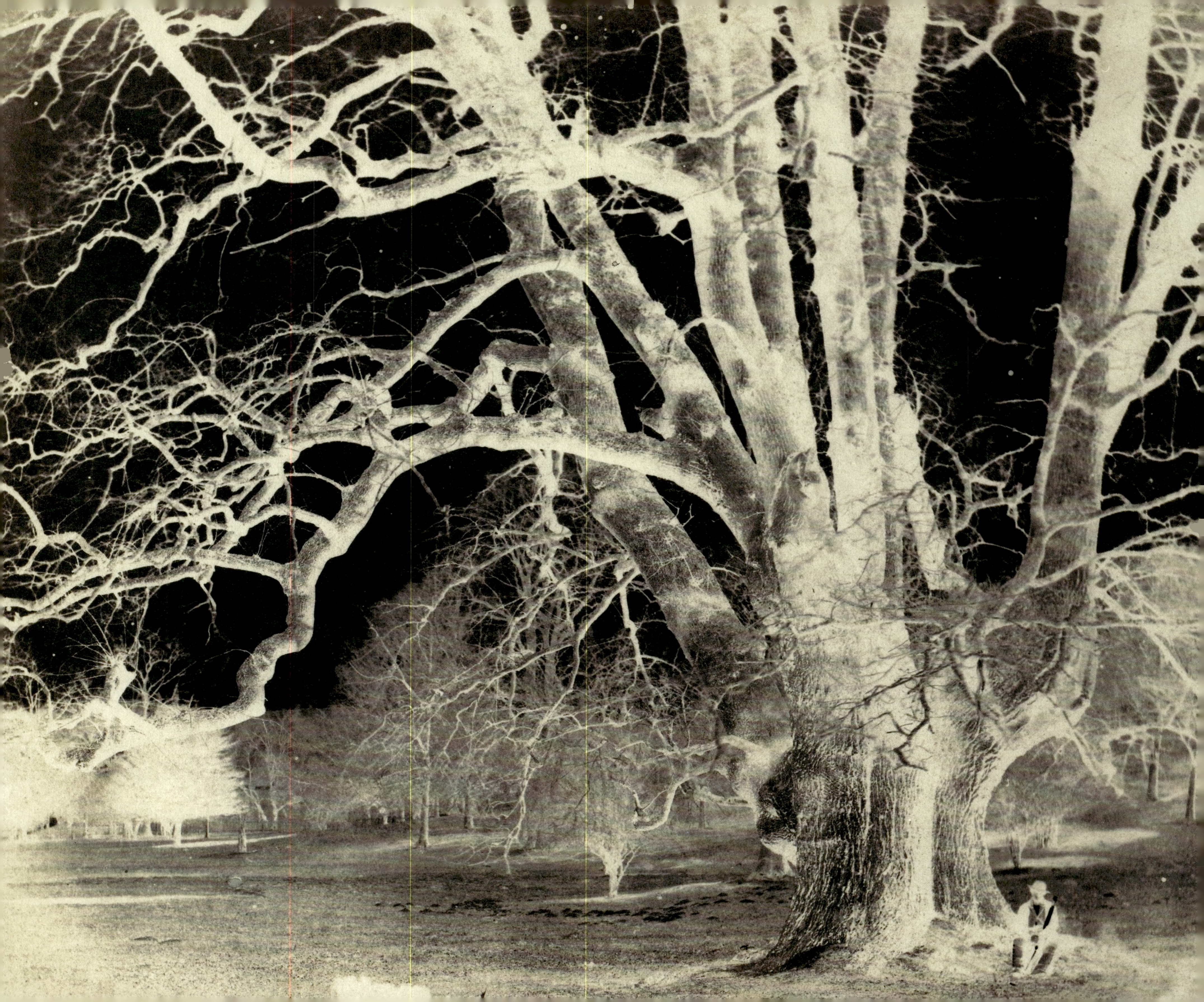

IMPRESSED BY LIGHT

British Photographs from Paper Negatives, 1840–1860

Roger Taylor

Biographical Dictionary by Larry J. Schaaf in collaboration with Roger Taylor

The Metropolitan Museum of Art, New York

National Gallery of Art, Washington

Yale University Press, New Haven and London

This publication accompanies the exhibition "Impressed by Light: British Photographs from Paper Negatives, 1840–1860," held at The Metropolitan Museum of Art, New York, September 24–December 30, 2007; at the National Gallery of Art, Washington, D.C., February 3–May 4, 2008; and at the Musée d'Orsay, Paris, May 26–September 7, 2008.

The exhibition in New York is made possible by The Hite Foundation.

The exhibition in Washington is made possible by the Trellis Fund and The Ryna and Melvin Cohen Family Foundation.

The catalogue is made possible by Howard Stein.

Additional support is provided by the Mary C. and James W. Fosburgh Publications Fund and the Roswell L. Gilpatric Publications Fund.

The catalogue is published with the assistance of The Getty Foundation.

The exhibition was organized by The Metropolitan Museum of Art, New York, and the National Gallery of Art, Washington.

Published by The Metropolitan Museum of Art, New York

John P. O'Neill, Publisher and Editor in Chief
Ruth Lurie Kozodoy, Senior Editor
Jayne Kuchna, Bibliographic Editor
Bruce Campbell, Designer
Peter Antony and Douglas J. Malicki, Production
Robert Weisberg, Assistant Managing Editor
Kathryn Ansite, Desktop Publishing Specialist

New photography by Eileen Travell, the Photograph Studio, The Metropolitan Museum of Art

Typeset in Bell and Centaur
Printed on 115 gsm Gardapat Kiara
Color and duotone separations by Martin Senn
Printed and bound by EBS Editoriale Bortolazzi-Stei s.r.l., Verona

Jacket illustration: John Muir Wood, *Family Group, Leith*, 1847–52, detail (pl. 32)
Frontispiece: Unknown photographer, *Spreading Oak with Seated Figure* (paper negative), 1850s, detail (pl. 17)

Cataloging-in-Publication Data is available from the Library of Congress.
ISBN 978-1-58839-225-1(hc: The Metropolitan Museum of Art)
ISBN 978-0-300-12405-7 (hc: Yale University Press)

Contents

Lenders to the Exhibition

Canada

Montreal, Collection Centre Canadien d'Architecture / Canadian Centre for Architecture: 57, 60, 61, 66–68, 109

Toronto, Art Gallery of Ontario: 20–22

France

Paris, Bibliothèque Nationale de France: 85, 91

United Kingdom

Bradford, National Media Museum: 2–5, 13–15, 25, 48, 54, 72, 74, 79, 83, 84, 86

Edinburgh, Royal Scottish Academy: 69

Edinburgh, Scottish National Photography Collection, National Galleries of Scotland: 9, 10, 12, 24, 28–33, 81

London, The British Library: 104, 108, 111, 113, 114

London, National Army Museum: 100, 101

London, Victoria and Albert Museum: 19, 36–40, 93, 96, 99, 112, 118

Swansea, City and County of Swansea, Swansea Museum: 34, 50

Windsor, The Royal Collection: 47

United States

New York, The Metropolitan Museum of Art: 1, 6, 7, 11, 17, 18, 49, 70, 77, 87–90, 94, 97, 102, 103, 105–107

New York, Museum of Modern Art: 58, 59, 78

Washington, D.C., National Gallery of Art: 8, 23, 51, 73, 80, 115

Private Collections

Robert and Paula Hershkowitz: 82

Lawrence and Sybil Hite: 41, 52

Charles Isaacs and Carol Nigro: 26, 76, 117

Collection Isabelle Jammes: 45, 46, 53

Joy of Giving Something, Inc.: 65

Hans P. Kraus, Jr.: 35, 55

Janet Lehr, Inc.: 62–64

W. Bruce Lundberg: 75

Private collection: 16, 27, 98, 110

Thomas Walther Collection: 44, 56, 71, 95, 116

Stephen White, Collection II: 42, 43

Wilson Centre for Photography: 92

Directors' Foreword

Photography is a young art, and some of the most important chapters of its history have yet to be written. The subject remains a fertile terrain for scholarly exploration and discovery, of which a case in point is the present endeavor: the first major exhibition and the first book-length publication to present the full story of the calotype—the paper-negative photograph—in Britain, the nation of its birth. To be sure, every survey history of photography tells that the medium was invented by the Englishman William Henry Fox Talbot, who devised a process for making a photographic negative from writing paper treated with chemicals and then using the paper negative to produce multiple positive prints—the ancestor of nearly all photography until the digital age. Yet not until now has there been a thorough investigation of how Talbot's invention developed and thrived in the 1840s and 1850s, nor of the social and artistic milieu that contributed significantly to the calotype's rise and eventual decline.

According to most accounts, the calotype flourished in the 1840s, when its only rival was the daguerreotype, but died almost instantly with the introduction in 1851 of the collodion-on-glass negative, which promised the precision of the daguerreotype and the reproducibility of the calotype. Roger Taylor's text in this volume—and the photographs in the exhibition—tell a quite different and altogether fascinating story. In fact, throughout the 1840s calotypes were made chiefly by Talbot, his family, and a close circle of friends, and by a very few other adventurous souls. But during the 1850s, far from dying, the calotype attracted numerous and widespread practitioners. This truth is made abundantly visible by the beautiful and ambitious works displayed in the exhibition and reproduced here, as well as by the inclusion of more than five hundred British calotypists in this volume's biographical dictionary.

Artists who chose to work with paper negatives—even when the more popular, sharper, and faster glass negatives were available—must have done so for good reasons, and those aesthetic, practical, and sociocultural factors are what Mr. Taylor, a noted scholar of Victorian photography, uncovers for us. That this history has long been hidden is not altogether surprising, for, as we find, the calotype was embraced particularly by gentlemen of leisure and learning, who often produced only a small number of prints for friends and fellow photographers or for a family album. They did not seek the widespread distribution and international reputation pursued by their commercial counterparts, nearly all of whom favored glass negatives. As a result, many of these calotype works survive in only a single example. We are therefore especially grateful to the many individual and institutional lenders who have shared their treasures, enabling us to bring them to public view.

We are deeply indebted to Roger Taylor for giving us the benefit of his authoritative scholarship in this immensely readable narrative, and to his co-curators, Malcolm Daniel and Sarah Greenough, for their careful shaping of the exhibition. We thank as well the staffs of our two institutions for their efforts on behalf of the exhibition and publication. We are extremely pleased that the exhibition will also be seen at the Musée d'Orsay, Paris, and thank its director, Serge Lemoine, and curator of photographs, Dominique Planchon-de Font-Réaulx, for their collaboration.

To Howard Stein we express our deep gratitude for ensuring that this catalogue could be produced with the breadth and quality that will make it an invaluable resource for years to come. We are also grateful for the additional support that has been provided by the Mary C. and James W. Fosburgh Publications Fund and the Roswell L. Gilpatric Publications Fund. At the Metropolitan, we offer our sincerest thanks to Sybil and Larry Hite for The Hite Foundation's generous sponsorship of the exhibition; this is the third exhibition devoted to nineteenth-century British photography that The Hite Foundation has helped us bring to the public. At the National Gallery, we express our gratitude to The Getty Foundation for its assistance in making this book possible and extend our deep thanks to Betsy Karel of the Trellis Fund and Ryna and Melvin Cohen of The Ryna and Melvin Cohen Family Foundation for their ongoing support of photography exhibitions.

The early masterpieces presented here—in many instances for the first time in America—demonstrate the newborn medium's artistic accomplishment. For us as for nineteenth-century viewers, they offer a retreat into nature and a meditation on man's place in the universe, a record of the famous and the familiar, an evocation of times past, and an illuminating journey to distant lands.

Philippe de Montebello
Director, The Metropolitan Museum of Art

Earl A. Powell III
Director, National Gallery of Art

Acknowledgments

FROM THE AUTHOR

This project began with a chance remark made in 1989, when Janet Buerger, soon after the publication of her book *French Daguerreotypes*, suggested that I do something along the same lines for British daguerreotypes. I replied that a book on British calotypes might be more appropriate, as British photographers had invented the process. This offhand response became the germ of a research project. I soon discovered that apart from biographies of such significant photographers as William Henry Fox Talbot, David Octavius Hill, and Robert Adamson, little had been written on the subject. Indeed, in photographic histories, whatever was known about the calotype was usually contained in a single chapter at most and was more likely to express criticism of its shortcomings than recognition of its intrinsic beauty.

An early model for my own research was the seminal work by André Jammes and Eugenia Parry Janis published in 1983, *The Art of French Calotype*, which examines the social, economic, and artistic culture surrounding the calotype as it emerged in France between 1845 and 1870. More than twenty years later it remains the standard reference work on the subject. My thanks therefore go to these three photographic historians who in their different ways helped focus my attention on the significance of the British calotype.

With so little known about the history of the calotype, one of my first tasks was to immerse myself in primary source materials. During the course of this research, I became aware of the significance of annual exhibition catalogues from that period, which cite not only the title of a work and its photographer but also the process employed to make the negative. Here at last was a means by which to survey mid-nineteenth-century photography and identify which photographers used the calotype or other paper negative processes. I am deeply indebted to Pam Roberts, then Curator of the Royal Photographic Society collections, Bath, for her generous hospitality and help during these early stages of my research, and to the National Art Library, Victoria and Albert Museum, London, for providing access to these catalogues in its holdings. Of the individuals who encouraged my research none were more supportive than Howard and Jane Ricketts, whose enthusiasm for nineteenth-century photography helped keep me focused; they deserve my special thanks.

The result of these labors was a database containing records of more than twenty thousand individual exhibits in the period 1839–65, which allowed me to identify a significant number of previously unknown calotypists and their works. This was published in 2002 by the National Gallery of Canada, Ottawa, under the title *Photographs Exhibited in Britain 1839–1865*; subsequently it was placed online by De Montfort University, Leicester, as a website at www.peib.org.uk. I owe special thanks to Murray Waddington and Usher Caplan in Ottawa for their patient and careful conversion of my database into a handsome and valuable reference work, and to my colleagues in Leicester, Stephen Brown, Howard Freeman, Dave Gerrard, Robb Ross, and Kelley Wilder, who created the website, which has given researchers and scholars widespread access to this material for the first time.

Early support for the project came as a research fellowship from the Andrew W. Mellon Foundation to study the Gernsheim Collection in the Harry Ransom Humanities Research Center at the University of Texas, Austin, in 1994. Then in 1998 I was awarded a generous Lisette Model/Joseph G. Blum Fellowship in the History of Photography by the National Gallery of Canada, Ottawa, allowing me to devote myself to full-time research. In 2000 I was invited to be a guest scholar in the Department of Photographs at the J. Paul Getty Museum, Los Angeles, where I was able to draw on the extraordinary riches of the collections and those of the Getty Research Institute. Finally, in 2001 I was awarded an Andrew W. Mellon Senior Fellowship by The Metropolitan Museum of Art, New York. This allowed me to draw together the several strands of my research into a coherent exhibition proposal that I presented to the Department of Photographs during my tenure.

A project of this size could never have been realized without the support of these fellowships and awards and of the departments that administer them, and I want to express my heartfelt gratitude for the generous funding and the commitment that fostered my research in a multitude of ways. I also thank my colleagues in these institutions for their friendship and collegial help as they made their collections, files, and departmental records available to me. Special thanks go to Roy Flukinger and David Coleman in Austin; Ann Thomas, Murray Waddington, Jim Borcoman, Lori Pauli, Hazel Mackenzie, Usher Caplan, and Barbara Boutin in Ottawa; and Weston Naef, Gordon Baldwin, Judy Keller, Julian Cox, Annie Lyden, Michael Hargreaves, Frances Terpack, and JoEllen Williamson at the Getty.

Closer to home was the National Media Museum, Bradford, whose collections and archives proved to be a treasure house of images and information, from which I enhanced my understanding of how paper-negative photography developed during the 1850s. I was always made welcome during my frequent research trips there by Brian Liddy, Toni Booth, and Ruth Kitchin, whose intimate knowledge of the collections, especially those of the Royal Photographic Society, made each visit a real pleasure and richly rewarding; my warmest thanks go to them all.

From an early stage, assembling biographical information on photographers was an integral part of this project. While initially there seemed little to add to what was already well documented in photographic histories, the new exhibitions database provided a large number of previously unrecorded names. Around this critical mass of photographers, the Biographical Dictionary of British Calotypists, which forms an essential part of this publication, was created. I am deeply indebted to John Falconer, Michael Pritchard, and Sara Stevenson for generously sharing their own biographical research files, which added significant information. The task of converting all these notes and files into coherent entries fell on the shoulders of my good friend and fellow photographic historian Larry J. Schaaf, Senior Research Fellow and Honorary Professor at the University of the Arts, London, and the leading authority on W. H. F. Talbot. His own research files added significantly to the register, bringing the total to just over five hundred calotypists. My sincere thanks go to him.

By its very nature, photography of the mid-Victorian period carried out by gentleman amateurs was largely a personal occupation, with the results most often circulating only among members of the immediate family. Surviving examples of work are therefore rare, and during the course of my research I visited institutions and individuals throughout Britain, Europe, and America in my search for material. Without the generous support of the many lenders to this exhibition, who are named in the curators' acknowledgments that follow, neither the exhibition nor this catalogue would have become a reality.

Many other individuals also contributed to the project over the years. I would like to thank E. Alkazi, Robin Ansell, Pierre Apraxine, Norma Armstrong, Pam Aucott, Anna Auer, Michel and Michèle Auer, John Balston, Benjamin S. Beck, John Benjafield, Susan Bennett, Kate Best, Denise Bethel, Caroline Bloor, Sjaak Boone, Anthony Burnett Brown, Peter Bower, David Bruce, Gail Buckland, Peter Bunnell, Anne Caiger, Ronnie Capel-Cure, Richard Chamberlaine-Brothers, Edward Chandler, Pamela Clark, Brian Coe, Stephen Croad, Allison Derrett, Janet Dewan, Elizabeth Edwards, Gary Edwards, Paul Elkin, Robert Elwall, Anne Escott, Andy Eskind, Oliver Everett, Lee Fontanella, Geoffrey Foster, Philippe Garner, Michael Gray, Helmut Gernsheim, David Harris, Anthony Hamber, John Hannavy, Mark Haworth-Booth, Ann Heath, Pauline Heathcote, Kathy Henderson, Heinz K. and Bridget A. Henisch, Alan Howell, Iestyn Hughes, Ken and Jenny Jacobson, Jens Jäger, Peter James, Stephen Joseph, Christine Juliat, Nancy Keeler, Gerald F. Kurtz, Julie Lawson, Ian Leith, Natasha Lolljee, Gráinne MacLochlainn, Jay McDonald, Ray McKenzie, Lee Marks, Charles W. Mann, Caroline Marten, Anne de Mondenard, Richard Morris, Mr. and Mrs. John Mounsey, John Munday, Luis Nadeau, Doug Nickel, Mary Nixon, Isabel Ortega, Colin Osman, Richard Pare, Simon Peers, Colin Penman, Sandra Phillips, Valerie Phillips, Michael Pritchard, Timothy Prus, Richard T. Rosenthal, Stephanie Roy, William Rubel, John Sawkill, Keith Scott, Mike Seeborne, Grace Seiberling, Patricia Sheldon, Murray Simpson, Roddy Simpson, Sara Smyth, Paul Stamper, Lindsey Stewart, Sara Stevenson, Peter Stubbs, Rachel Stuhlman, Gareth Syvret, David Taylor, Maria Umali, Edward Wakeling, John Ward, Jennifer Watts, Clive Wilkins-Jones, John Winstone, Sylvia Wolf, and David Zeidberg.

A number of institutions opened their collections and archives to me, and I am immensely grateful for the access provided by the Aberdeen Library; Aberdeen University Library; Art Gallery of Ontario, Toronto;

Biblioteca Nacional de España, Madrid; Biblioteca Real, Madrid; Bibliothèque Nationale de France, Paris; Birmingham Central Library; Bodleian Library, University of Oxford; British Library, London; British Museum, London; Cambridge University Library; Canadian Centre for Architecture, Montreal; Christie's, London and New York; Devonshire Collection, Chatsworth House, Derbyshire; Edinburgh Central Library; Cleveland Museum of Art; Firestone Library, Princeton University; Fox Talbot Museum, Lacock Abbey, Wiltshire; George Eastman House, Rochester; J. Paul Getty Museum, Los Angeles; Gilman Paper Company Collection, New York; Glasgow University Library; Guildhall Library, London; Guernsey Museums and Galleries, St. Peter Port; Houghton Library, Harvard University, Cambridge, Massachusetts; Hulton-Deutsch Collection, London; Huntington Library, Art Collections, and Botanical Gardens, San Marino, California; King's College Library, London; Library of Congress, Washington, D.C.; Leeds Library; Leeds University Library; London Metropolitan Archives; Manchester Central Library; Musée d'Orsay, Paris; Museum of the History of Science, University of Oxford; Museum of Modern Art, New York; National Archives, Kew; National Army Museum, London; National Art Library, Victoria and Albert Museum, London; National Library of Ireland, Dublin; National Library of Scotland, Edinburgh; National Library of Wales, Aberystwyth; Smithsonian National Museum of American History, Washington, D.C.; National Media Museum, Bradford; National Museums of Scotland, Edinburgh; National Monuments Record Centre, Swindon; National Portrait Gallery, London; National Register of Archives, London; New York Public Library; Morgan Library and Museum, New York; Princeton University Art Museum; Public Record Office, London; Public Record Office of Northern Ireland, Belfast; Royal Academy, London; Royal Archives and Collections, Windsor Castle, Berkshire; Royal Commission for the Exhibition of 1851, Imperial College, London; Royal Institute of British Architects, London; Royal Society of Arts, London; Royal Society, London; St. Bride Printing Library, London; San Francisco Museum of Modern Art; Science Museum Library and Archives, London; Scottish National Portrait Gallery, Edinburgh; Scottish Record Office, Edinburgh; Shropshire County Council Archeology Service, Shrewsbury; Société Française de Photographie, Paris; Société Jersiaise, St. Helier, Jersey; Sotheby's, London and New York; Charles E. Young Research Library, University of California, Los Angeles; Victoria and Albert Museum, London; Warrington Museum and Art Gallery; Yeovil Library, Somerset.

Photographic conservators and scientists have come to my aid on more than one occasion as I struggled to understand some unfathomable aspect of photochemistry or the material structure of a paper negative or print. I am especially fortunate in having Mike Ware as a colleague, for his deep understanding of nineteenth-century chemistry and photographic processes has shed light into many dark corners and prevented me from committing serious errors. Others have been equally kind in sharing their knowledge, and I would to thank Lisa Barrow, Susie Clark, Lee Ann Daffner, Nora Kennedy, Jonathon Kline, Hope Kingsley, Connie McCabe, John McElhone, Teresa Mesquit, Doug Munson, Grant Romer, Dusan Stulik, and Roger Watson for their help.

Keeping track of whom to thank over the course of an eighteen-year project has been no easy matter, and if I have inadvertently omitted the name of an individual or institution, I ask for your understanding and remain grateful.

Realizing a project of this magnitude requires a special level of commitment, by all those concerned, to transform the vision into a practical reality. I am especially grateful for the support and encouragement of colleagues at The Metropolitan Museum of Art, the National Gallery of Art, and the Musée d'Orsay. I would like especially to thank Maria Morris Hambourg for her early and decisive support for the project, and Malcolm Daniel and Sarah Greenough, whose genuine enthusiasm for early British photography helped make this a fruitful and happy collaboration. Their curatorial expertise and rigor helped me see the work afresh when we selected works for the exhibition. At the Musée d'Orsay the project found a champion in Dominique Planchon-de Font-Réaulx, whose help and support are greatly valued. Colleagues within the Department of Photographs at the Metropolitan Museum have also lent their effort to the project, notably Judith Hanson, Laura Harris, Lucy von Brachel, and Marta Weiss, who deserve my special thanks.

Publication of this book was managed with great skill by members of the Editorial Department of the Metropolitan Museum. I was especially fortunate in having Ruth Kozodoy as the deft, discerning editor of the work and Jayne Kuchna as its searching and meticulous bibliographic editor. Their perceptive questioning helped clarify both my ideas and the resulting text, and I am deeply grateful to them both. Combined efforts were responsible for bringing the original calotypes onto the printed page so beautifully: I am indebted to Eileen Travell for photographing the majority of the loan objects, Martin Senn for making the color separations, Peter Antony and Douglas Malicki for attending to all details of production with great care and sensitivity to the original works, and Bruce Campbell for his elegant book design. Without Publisher and Editor in Chief John P. O'Neill's unwavering support, such a volume would never have been possible, and I am profoundly grateful for the high standards of editing and production that he has set. Among the many other contributors to this publishing effort I would like to mention Kenneth Conway Benson, Joan Holt, Margaret Chace, Kathryn Ansite, Robert Weisberg, Elizabeth Block, Cynthia Clark, Mary Gladue, Sarah Jean Dupont, and Richard Gallin. Elaine Luthy prepared the fine index.

Since 2003, when I became a Senior Research Fellow at De Montfort University, I have flourished under its sheltering wing. In particular I would like to thank Gerard Moran, Iona Cruikshank, Paul Hill, Stephen Brown, and Robb Ross for shielding me from many other commitments when I was preparing the exhibition and writing this catalogue.

Finally, I would like to thank Rex Lowden, who over fifty years ago set me on this course when he employed me as a photographic apprentice. His insistence that I be formally trained in every aspect of photography laid the practical foundations on which much of my subsequent understanding as a historian has been based. This book is for him.

Roger Taylor

FROM THE CURATORS

As Roger Taylor has done above, we thank the many individuals and institutions who have helped bring this project to completion. Our especial and deep gratitude goes to all those who generously agreed to lend their works for inclusion in this exhibition, both directors and trustees of institutions and private collectors. Many curators, registrars, librarians, and collectors also assisted our research and helped facilitate the loans. We thank them all. In Great Britain, Lady Jane Roberts, Theresa-Mary Morton, Frances Dimond, and Sophie Gordon at the Royal Collections, Windsor Castle; John Falconer and Barbara O'Connor at the British Library, London; Alistair Massie at the National Army Museum, London; Paul Goodman, Russell Roberts, Jane Fletcher, and Colin Harding at the National Media Museum, Bradford; Divia Patel and Martin Barnes at the Victoria and Albert Museum, London; Joanna Soden at the Royal Scottish Academy, Edinburgh; Sara Stevenson and Duncan Forbes at the Scottish National Portrait Gallery, Edinburgh; Bernice Cardy at the Royal Institution, Swansea; Robert Hershkowitz, Cockhaise, Sussex; and Michael G. Wilson and Violet Hamilton at the Wilson Centre for Photography, London. In Canada, Louise Désy at the Canadian Centre for Architecture, Montreal, and Maia Sutnik at the Art Gallery of Ontario, Toronto. In France, Sylvie Aubenas at the Bibliothèque National de France, Paris, and Isabelle Jammes, Paris. In the United States, Peter Galassi and Eva Respini at the Museum of Modern Art, New York; Hans P. Kraus, Shelley Dowell, Russell Lord, and Jennifer Parkinson of Hans P. Kraus, Jr., Inc., New York; Lawrence and Sybil Hite, New York; Charles Isaacs and Carol Nigro, New York; Janet Lehr, New York; Bruce and Dee Lundberg, Guilford, Connecticut; Howard Stein, New York; Thomas Walther, New York; and Stephen and Mus White, Studio City, California.

There are many staff members at the Metropolitan Museum and the National Gallery who have aided immeasurably in the realization of the exhibition and to whom we owe enormous gratitude.

At the Metropolitan Museum, the exhibition has had the vital support of our Director, Philippe de Montebello; Associate Director for Exhibitions, Mahrukh Tarapor; and Manager for Special Exhibitions, Linda Sylling. Nina Maruca and Antonia Moser have handled the complex registrarial aspects of the exhibition. Daniel Kershaw and Emil Micha applied their talents and discernment to the exhibition design and graphics, respectively. Predrag Dimitrijevic brought his skill and artistry to the matting and installation of the works in frames designed by Jed Bark of Bark Frameworks and to the elegant presentation of the show's numerous albums. Conservation aspects of the exhibition have been directed by Nora Kennedy. Other members of the Department of Photographs not yet mentioned have contributed in many ways: Doug Eklund, Mia Fineman, Hanako Murata, Jacqueline Parrott, Nancy Reinhold, Jeff Rosenheim, Deepthi Sasidharan, and Emily Shutt. For their assistance with many other aspects of the exhibition we thank Pamela Barr, Christine Begley, Clint Coller, Christine Coulson, Willa Cox, William Crow, Martha Deese, Vivian Gordon, Elizabeth Hammer, Rebecca Herman, Andrea Kann, Nicole Leist, Rich Lichte, Taylor Miller, Rebecca Noonan Murray, Elyse Topalian, Emily Vanderpool, and John Welch.

We are especially grateful to Sybil and Larry Hite for their support of the exhibition through The Hite Foundation. Their passion for nineteenth-century British photography and their desire to make it more widely known and appreciated have been a great encouragement to our efforts, and their direct support has now been vital in bringing three such exhibitions to the Metropolitan. We likewise acknowledge the Metropolitan's Mary C. and James W. Fosburgh Publications Fund and Roswell L. Gilpatric Publications Fund, whose financial assistance was critical in making the exhibition catalogue possible.

At the National Gallery of Art, we thank the many individuals who supported this endeavor and whose efforts contributed to its success. We are especially grateful to Earl A. Powell III, Director, and Alan Shestack, Deputy Director, for their enthusiastic support of this project from its very inception. Judy Metro in the Publishing Office and Dodge Thompson and Jennifer Cipriano in Exhibitions have lent invaluable assistance, as have Melissa Stegeman of the Registrar's Office and Joseph Krakora, Chris Myers, Carol Kelley, Patty Donovan, Deborah Ziska, and Anabeth Guthrie in Development and External Affairs. Constance McCabe, Hugh Phibbs, Michael Pierce, Jennie Ritchie, and Stephen Muscarella in Conservation, along with Mark Leithauser, Gordon Anson, Jame Anderson, John Olson, Barbara Keyes, and Lisa Farrell in Design and Installation, devoted their considerable expertise to the careful and elegant presentation of the works in the exhibition. Elizabeth Croog offered wise legal counsel. And in the Department of Photographs, we wish especially to thank Sarah Kennel, Molly Bloom, and Yali Lewis for their efficient oversight of all aspects of this complicated exhibition.

We express our gratitude to The Getty Foundation for its support of this volume, and to Betsy Karel of the Trellis Fund and Ryna and Melvin Cohen of The Ryna and Melvin Cohen Family Foundation for their support of the exhibition.

Finally, we three extend our most heartfelt thanks to Howard Stein, whose great generosity ensured that the book could be published with its full scholarly content.

Malcolm Daniel
Sarah Greenough
Roger Taylor

Curators of the Exhibition

Malcolm Daniel
Curator in Charge
Department of Photographs
The Metropolitan Museum of Art, New York

Sarah Greenough
Curator and Head of the Department of Photographs
National Gallery of Art, Washington

Roger Taylor
Professor of Photographic History and Senior Research Fellow
De Montfort University, Leicester
Senior Curator of Photographs, 1985–96
National Media Museum, Bradford, United Kingdom

Note to the Reader

All photographs are from paper negatives unless stated otherwise.

The notes to the essays begin on page 397.

In the Plates and in illustrations to the Biographical Dictionary, titles in *italics* were given by the photographer. Those in roman type are modern descriptive titles.

IMPRESSED BY LIGHT

British Photographs from Paper Negatives, 1840–1860

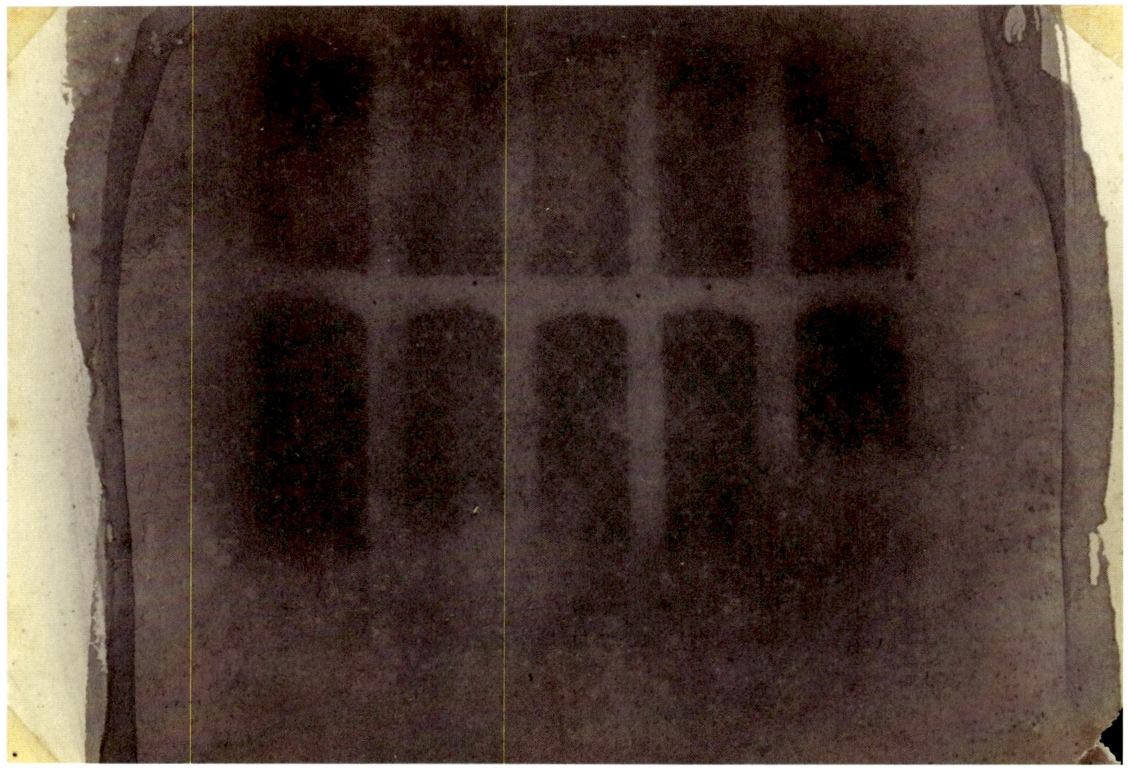

1. *Photography and an Age of Paradox*

PROLOGUE: "ALL THIS IS WONDERFUL"

When William Henry Fox Talbot made his way to bed on the night of Sunday, January 6, 1839, the winds were howling around the chimneystacks and rattling the roof slates of Lacock Abbey, his home in Wiltshire in southern England. Much of Britain was swept that night by a violent storm. In London trees in the parks were brought down, and police officers "could scarcely keep upon their legs."[1] In Manchester roofs were swept away, chimneys toppled, trees uprooted, and lives lost. The port of Liverpool was badly hit, with many vessels driven ashore or capsized as they struggled to reach sanctuary and others feared lost at sea.[2] Not until the momentous storm subsided the following day and "an almost perfect calm" fell across the silent countryside did Britons venture outdoors to inspect the damage and assess the personal cost.[3]

Talbot awoke on January 7 little knowing that his personal world would soon be similarly buffeted and capsized by events about to unfold in Paris. On that morning François Arago, director of the Paris Observatory, rose to his feet at a meeting of the Académie des Sciences to announce that a Monsieur Daguerre had discovered a means of making permanent images with the camera obscura. While his description of the process was deliberately vague, the pictures it produced were characterized as of "unbelievable exactitude and *finesse*."[4] Photography had been launched upon an unsuspecting world.

The news was delayed in reaching Britain by continuing bad weather in the English Channel. Five days later the first sketchy account of the process appeared in the British press, where the invention of Louis-Jacques-Mandé Daguerre, a painter and physicist, was hailed as a "prodigy" that "disconcerts all the theories of science in light and optics." The images, according to the Parisian correspondent, were not merely temporary reflections "but their fixed and durable impress."[5] On January 19 a more detailed account appeared in which the same correspondent struggled to explain their visual qualities, his phrases twisting and turning in wonder at the marvels of what he observed.

> *It is not painting, it is drawing, but drawing carried to a degree of perfection which art can never attain. The facsimile is faultless. . . . What fineness in the strokes! What knowledge of the chiaroscuro! What delicacy! What exquisite finish! How soft is that stuff! How salient those bas-reliefs! There is a Venus crouching down, seen in different points of view. How admirably are the foreshortenings given: it is nature itself. All this is wonderful. But who will say that it is not the work of some able draughtsman? Who will assure us that they are not drawings in bistre or sepia? M. Daguerre answers by putting an eyeglass into our hand. Then we perceive the smallest folds of a piece of drapery; the lines of a landscape invisible to the naked eye . . . we distinguish the smallest details; we count the paving-stones; we see the humidity caused by the rain; we read the inscription on a shop sign.*[6]

Less than two weeks after Arago's announcement, the British public had sufficient information to recognize that what had been revealed by Daguerre was little short of miraculous. It was if a magician's wand had, like the hurricane itself, passed across the heavens, allowing Mother Nature to record herself in infinite detail (fig. 2)—although whether this was accomplished by art, science, or necromancy remained clouded in uncertainty, for details of the method were undisclosed.

The reports of Daguerre's invention dealt Talbot a telling and personal blow, for the process appeared to mirror his own researches in the same direction.[7] Beginning in the summer of 1833, Talbot, a classicist, physicist, and mathematician with wide-ranging interests, had attempted to make images by the agency of light, and he finally succeeded in the

Opposite: Fig. 1. William Henry Fox Talbot, *The Oriel Window, South Gallery, Lacock Abbey*, 1835 or 1839. Photogenic drawing, 8.3 x 10.7 cm (3¼ x 4¼ in.). The Metropolitan Museum of Art, New York, The Rubel Collection, Purchase, Ann Tenenbaum and Thomas H. Lee and Anonymous Gifts, 1997, 1997.382.1

spring of 1834.[8] But whether because of neglect or self-effacement, his early successes had remained in private obscurity, unknown to the scientific establishment and unannounced to the rest of the world (fig. 1). The disconcerting news of Daguerre's achievement raised the all-important question of who could rightfully claim priority for the discovery. The circumstances forced Talbot into the public arena before he was ready. Needing to act immediately and decisively—behavior that was unfamiliar to his character—he gathered examples of his work that he had to hand and sent them to the Royal Institution, London, where they were displayed to the public on January 25, 1839, following a Friday evening lecture by the eminent physicist Michael Faraday.[9]

The working details of Daguerre's invention had still not been published, and thus Talbot could not judge whether it was fundamentally the same as his own process or entirely different. He must have feared the worst. His mother, Lady Elisabeth Feilding, made the point painfully clear: "I shall be very glad if M. Daguerre's invention is proved to be very different from yours. But as you have known it *five years* à quoi bon concealing it till you could by possibility have a competitor? If you would only have made it known *one* year ago, it could never have been disputed, or doubted, and there are many people entirely ignorant of *the details* of the discovery who will run away with the idea that it is the same."[10]

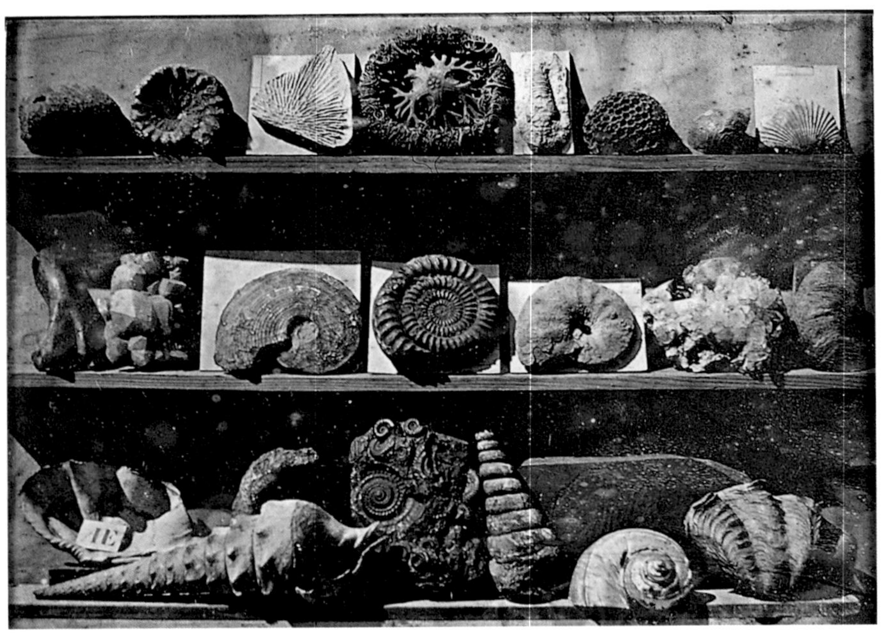

Fig. 2. Louis-Jacques-Mandé Daguerre, *Fossils and Shells*, 1839. Daguerreotype, 16.3 x 21.2 cm (6⅜ x 8⅜ in.). Musée des Arts et Métiers, Paris, 8745-2

In fact, the two processes were conceptually very different, although both began with the capacity of the camera obscura to receive an image. Literally a darkened chamber, the camera obscura had evolved by the early nineteenth century into a portable optical device in which rays of light, reflected by whatever objects the device faces, were projected by a simple lens onto the opposite inner surface, usually a ground glass screen on which the inverted image could be examined or traced.[11] Until the advent of photography, there had been no way to catch that image and hold it permanently.

In Daguerre's new process, metal became the support for a photographic image. He placed in the camera a highly polished sheet of silver-plated copper sensitized in iodine fumes. After exposure the plate was "developed" in mercury fumes, producing a picture that appeared as either a positive or a negative, depending on the circumstances under which the plate was viewed. The image was unique and incapable of being replicated.[12]

On the other hand, Talbot's photogenic drawing, as he called it, began with ordinary writing paper of the kind that would have been readily found at Lacock Abbey. In this chemically elegant process, the paper was made sensitive to light by a two-step process.[13] First it was coated with, or dipped in, a weak solution of sodium chloride (common salt) and left to dry. Next a solution of silver nitrate was applied with a brush to one surface, where it combined chemically with the sodium chloride, creating light-sensitive silver chloride. Once dry, the paper was ready for exposure in a camera. Where strong light hit the paper it darkened to a deep, rich brown—a chemical change brought about by the actinic power of light alone. Frequently Talbot bypassed the camera and simply placed the paper in firm contact with an object such as a leaf or piece of lace, then set them, held in a printing frame, in sunlight. The paper remained light beneath the object but otherwise darkened (fig. 3; pl. 1). Whether an image was produced with the camera or without, once the desired tonality had been reached it was stabilized, or fixed, to prevent any further darkening.[14] As the image produced was a negative, with darks and lights reversed, Talbot placed the paper negative in direct contact with another sheet of sensitized paper and once more exposed both to light. The resulting positive—or re-transfer, as he initially called the second sheet—bore an image that was tonally

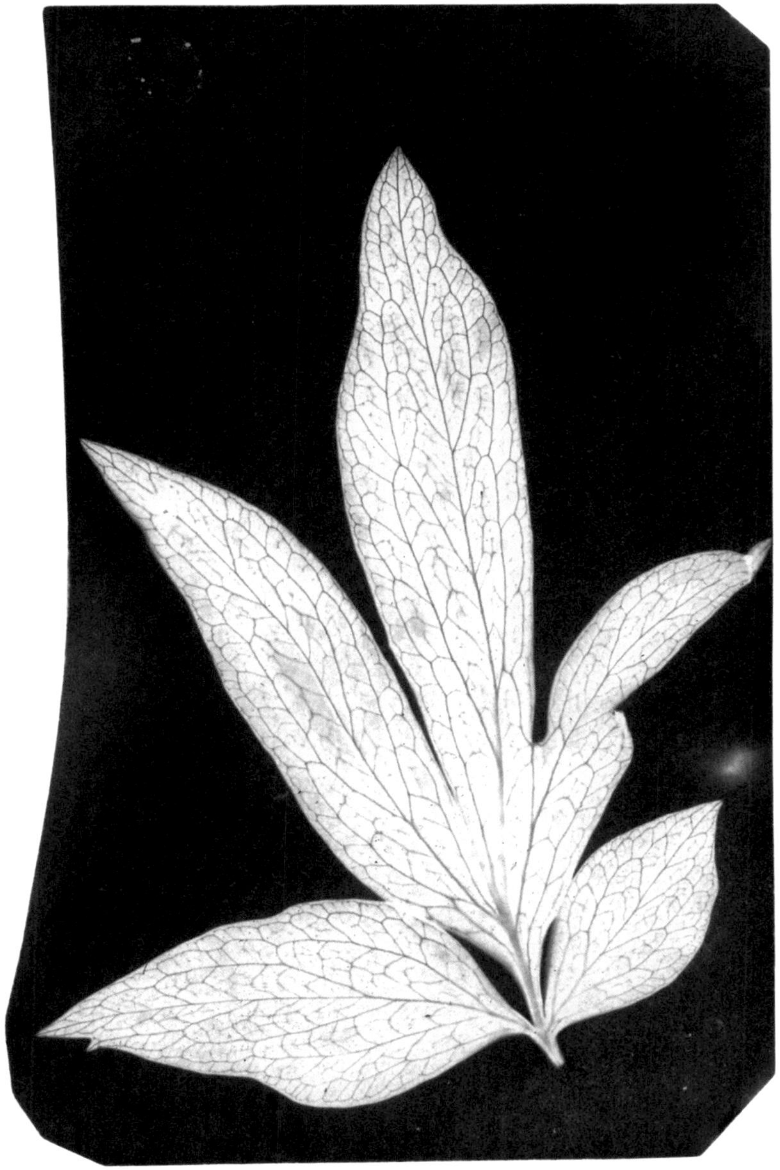

Fig. 3. William Henry Fox Talbot, *Leaves of the Pæony*, 1839. Photogenic drawing contact negative, 18.6 x 12 cm (7⅜ x 4¾ in.). The Metropolitan Museum of Art, New York, Harris Brisbane Dick Fund, 1936, 36.37 (7)

correct; and this process could be repeated indefinitely to make any number of positives.[15] Unlike Daguerre, Talbot had created a system that provided the physical and conceptual framework for photography for the next 150 years.[16]

"THE HUNGRY FORTIES": BRITAIN, 1840–1850

Had photography been announced to the British public not in 1839 but a decade later, its evolution would have been very different indeed. By 1850 the nation stood at the threshold of a period characterized by national harmony, optimism, and the interchange of ideas and skills necessary for economic and cultural progress. But as it was, photography was born into a most unhappy environment. The social misery, discontent, and political upheavals of the 1840s undoubtedly colored the way the new technique was perceived and disseminated.

When Princess Victoria succeeded to the throne on June 20, 1837, she had just passed her eighteenth birthday and was in many respects unequipped for the responsibilities she was about to assume. With the candor and optimism of youth, she declared in her journal, "I am very young and perhaps . . . inexperienced, but I am sure, that very few have more real good will and more real desire to do what is fit and right than I have."[17] Victoria's determination and sense of moral purpose became defining qualities of her long reign.

The power and wealth of the kingdom the queen inherited lay firmly in the grasp of the aristocracy and landed classes, or what one social reformer of the time called "the Lords and Great Proprietors of the soil."[18] Although the Reform Bill of 1832 increased the parliamentary voice of some constituencies—particularly in the rapidly expanding industrial towns and cities, which had been seriously underrepresented—it did little to erode the overall supremacy of landowners.[19] With the franchise still extended to less than 20 percent of the adult male population, the vast majority of people had no real political voice and little chance of exercising any control over their daily lives. At the same time they were feeling the effects of the Industrial Revolution; the tectonic plates of the social order were shifting, traditional patterns of employment were changing.

For centuries, Britain's economy had been predominantly agrarian. Industries, small in scale and distributed according to local resources, had been based on the specific handcraft skills and muscle power of individuals. But by the 1830s, trades like wool combing, framework

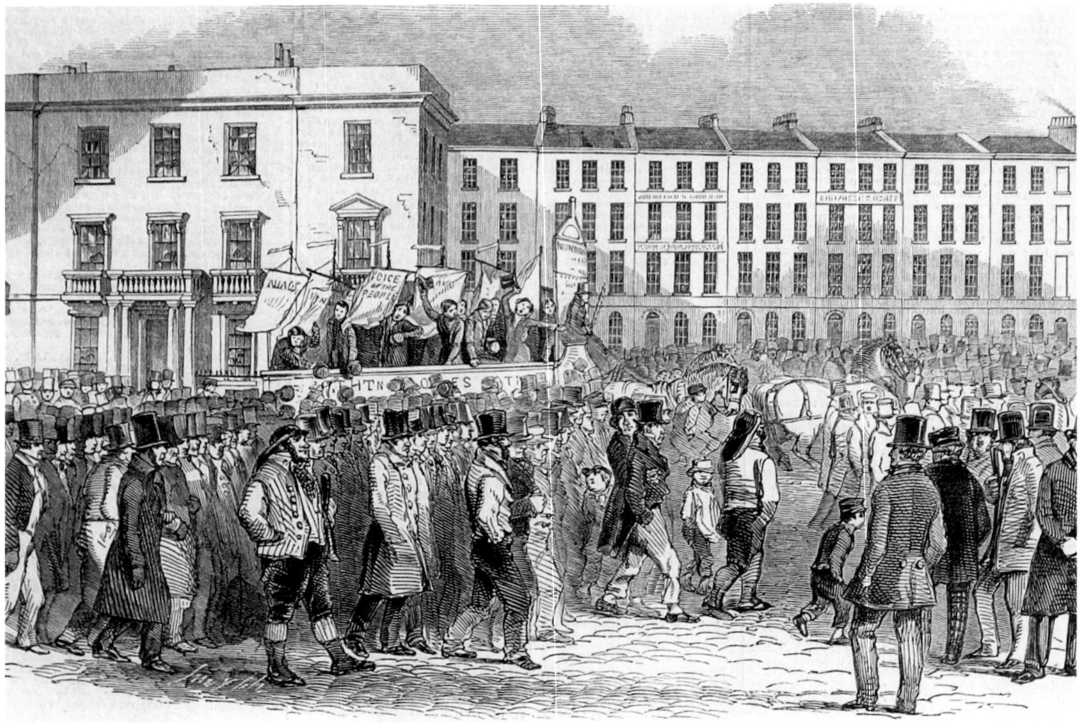

Fig. 4. Unknown artist, *Part of the Procession.—Sketched at Blackfriars-Bridge*, from *Illustrated London News*, April 15, 1848, p. 242. Wood engraving, 13.2 x 22.5 cm (5¼ x 8⅞ in.). Private collection

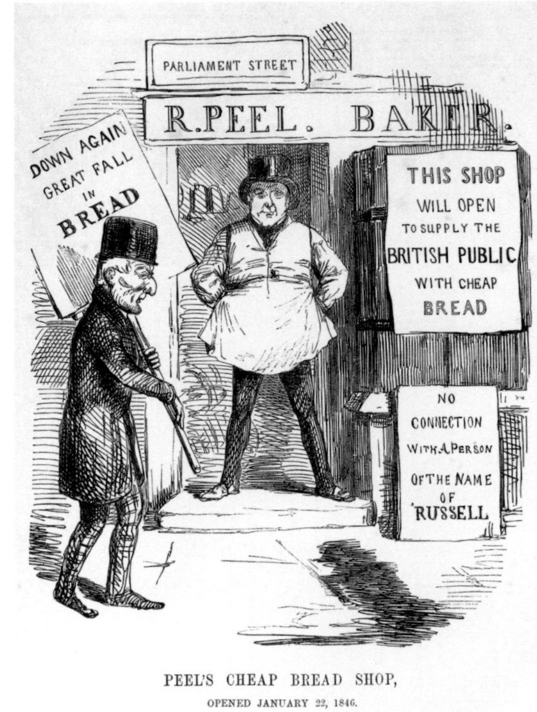

Fig. 5. Unknown artist, *Peel's Cheap Bread Shop*, from *Punch*, January 24, 1846, p. 47. Wood engraving, 24.7 x 18.1 cm (9¾ x 7⅛ in.). Private collection

knitting, and handloom weaving were being replaced by the work of machines and factory systems. With their livelihoods eroded, many families faced poverty, starvation, and the indignity of the workhouse, where husbands were separated from wives and children from their mothers.[20] To escape the trap of poverty, families began in increasing numbers to drift away from the countryside. Some emigrated. Others moved to rapidly expanding industrialized towns adjacent to the coalfields of the Midlands, Lancashire, Yorkshire, and Scotland. Here at least there was always the prospect of employment, although it was frequently menial or degrading.[21] When the census was taken in 1851 it was discovered that, for the first time in the nation's history, more people lived in towns and cities than in the countryside.[22] The gradual decline of agriculture was being offset by the steady growth of manufacturing industries, and capitalism became the relentless force reshaping not just the economy but the class system. Class was no longer based solely on the ownership of land; industry, manufacturing, and the burgeoning ranks of the professional classes were now powerfully transforming the old, established order of society.

The 1840s were characterized by episodes of social unrest, political demonstrations, and a widespread unease about the state of the nation (fig. 6). When Talbot arrived in Birmingham in August 1839 to give an account of his photogenic drawing process at the annual meeting of the British Association for the Advancement of Science, the town was besieged by angry workers demonstrating for the cause of Chartism.[23] The Chartist movement had been founded on the six demands of a "People's Charter" that sought to reform the injustices of the parliamentary system and extend the vote to the working classes.[24] This push for a national political program was fueled by social discontents over local grievances, often having to do with circumstances of unemployment or poor working conditions.

Its petitions rebuffed by Parliament, the movement simmered away for much of the decade to little real effect until 1848, when the political storms that swept across Europe caused British authorities to pay closer attention.[25] During the early months of that year, vivid accounts and woodcut illustrations of the rioting mobs in Berlin and Paris filled the pages of the *Illustrated London News*, heightening public anxiety that similar outbreaks would occur in London. It was widely feared that the Chartists would follow the example of the republican movements of France, Prussia, and Italy, unseat the administration, and overthrow the monarchy. When the Chartists announced a mass meeting for London on April 10, 1848, these fears were further aroused. But the meeting passed without incident, largely because of careful strategic planning by the Duke of Wellington, who kept the entire body of Chartists south of the Thames, well away from Parliament, Whitehall, and Buckingham Palace (fig. 4).[26] Thereafter, British Chartism diminished in force, and by the close of the decade the movement had faded into obscurity.

Further social unrest centered around opposition to the Corn Laws of 1815, which had imposed a duty on the import of foreign grain in order to stabilize prices in the wake of the Napoleonic Wars. A series of bad harvests further squeezed the grain supply, and during the early 1840s these laws were seen increasingly as protecting the interests of the landed classes by keeping the price of wheat and other grain artificially high. The effects were dire among the poor and the working classes, whose diet was in large part bread.[27] Manufacturers also opposed the protectionist Corn Laws. The duties were keeping the cost of living high, they argued, and creating a demand for higher wages that was hindering economic expansion and national progress. Manufacturers joined forces with social reformers and established the Anti-Corn-Law League, which was a vocal and effective force for change in the 1840s and enjoyed great popularity in manufacturing towns and cities. The Corn Laws were suspended in 1846 in response to the famine in Ireland brought about by the failure of the potato crop (fig. 5).

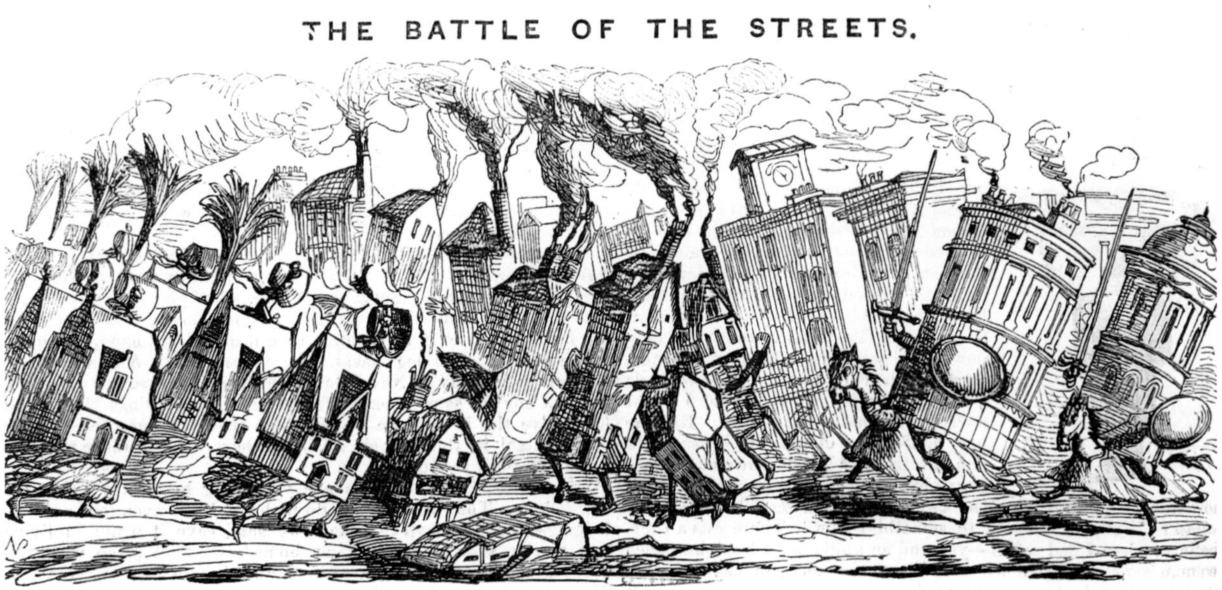

Fig. 6. Unknown artist, *The Battle of the Streets*, from *Punch*, August 9, 1845, p. 64. Wood engraving, 7.5 x 18 cm (3 x 7⅛ in.). Private collection

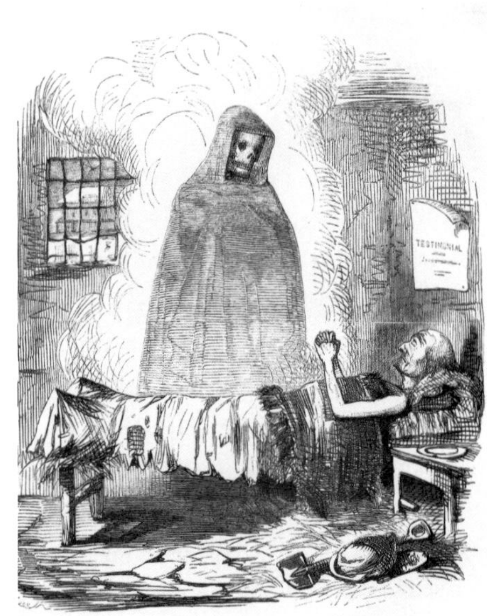

Fig. 7. John Leech, *The Poor Man's Friend*, from *Punch*, February 22, 1845, p. 97. Wood engraving, 24.7 x 17.9 cm (9¾ x 7 in.). Private collection

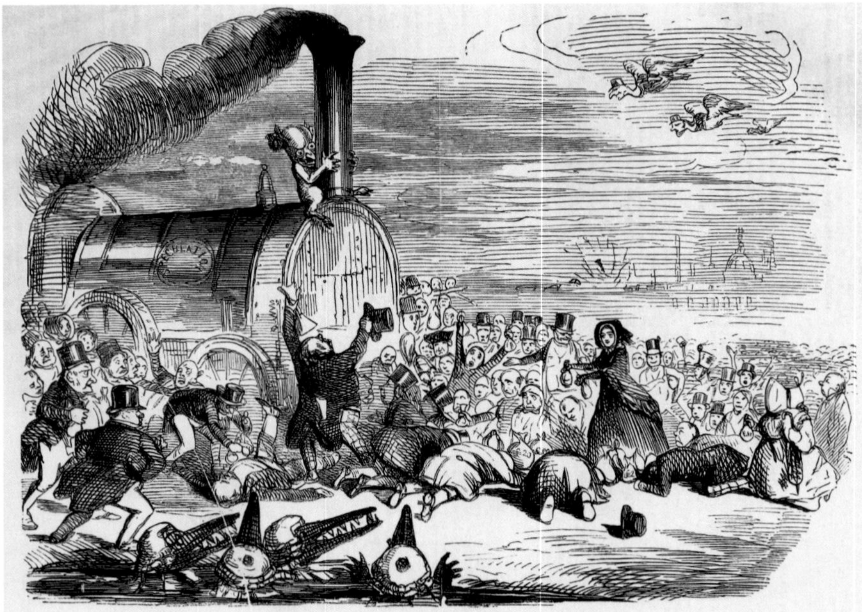
THE RAILWAY JUGGERNAUT OF 1845.

Fig. 8. Unknown artist, *The Railway Juggernaut of 1845*, from *Punch*, July 26, 1845, p. 46. Wood engraving, 17.9 x 25 cm (7 x 9⅞ in.). Private collection

The campaigns of the Anti-Corn-Law League belonged to the wider free trade movement that quickly gained ground following the institution of financial reforms in 1842 by the prime minister, Sir Robert Peel. Peel introduced an income tax and simplified import duties, and these measures among others proved so successful that by 1845 the national debt had been replaced by a budget surplus; this in turn would do much to pave the way for sustained economic growth in the early 1850s. Free trade, and everything associated with it, was being adopted as a national ideology; anything that stood in its way was seen as a threat to progress.

These political struggles, a predominant feature of the 1840s, were not the only issues preoccupying a public increasingly conditioned to expect bad news. The steady migration from countryside to town created problems of housing and hygiene. Street after street of relentlessly drab jerry-built houses had been thrown up in record numbers to accommodate the influx. A government report of 1842 is an indictment of the uncontrolled way such places had been allowed to develop. In Derby, one doctor testified, "Three elevated parts of the town . . . are hardly ever exempt from fever"; another doctor told of eight thousand cellar dwellings in Liverpool that housed an estimated thirty-five to forty thousand inhabitants in squalid conditions. In Manchester many of the streets were "so covered with refuse and excrementitious matter as to be almost impassable from depth of mud, and intolerable from stench."[28] Given this "contagion of numbers," it was little wonder that cholera, typhus, whooping cough, tuberculosis (the "white death"), influenza, scarlet fever, measles, and countless other frequently fatal diseases swept through the densely packed communities like violent storms.[29] Of them all, cholera was the most feared for its virulence and capacity to take life; during the "visitation" of 1849, between June and October, it caused more than thirteen thousand deaths in London alone (fig. 7).[30]

Despite the darkness of the period, lurking in the shadows were glimpses of optimism and personal happiness. The introduction in 1840 of the Penny Post, for example, greatly eased the means by which individuals could exchange a few words.[31] The rapid expansion of the railway network throughout the 1840s—by midcentury, 6,084 miles of track were in use—forever transformed national travel and vastly expanded intercommunication and trade among the various parts of Britain.[32] To the Victorian sensibility the railway network was a cause for wonder, as conceptually liberating as the Internet to a later generation. Practically, railways invigorated trade and commerce by opening new markets, revived the fortunes of declining market towns, and linked the metropolis of London swiftly and efficiently to the rest of the nation. They not only revitalized the economy but helped forge a newly coherent sense of national identity.

The railway's development also created new investment opportunities for those with capital.[33] Speculation grew apace and share prices rose rapidly, enabling railway companies to raise more than forty million pounds in share capital between 1820 and 1844—an impressive sum at the time (fig. 8). When the bubble burst in 1848, the losses were equally spectacular.[34]

THE ROLE OF ROYALTY

Queen Victoria took her first railway trip, from Windsor to Paddington Station, London, in 1842. She was so delighted by the smooth ride and the speed of the journey that she and her family became enthusiastic train travelers.[35] Her example gave the railways a new respectability and helped establish them as fashionable. Passenger numbers grew

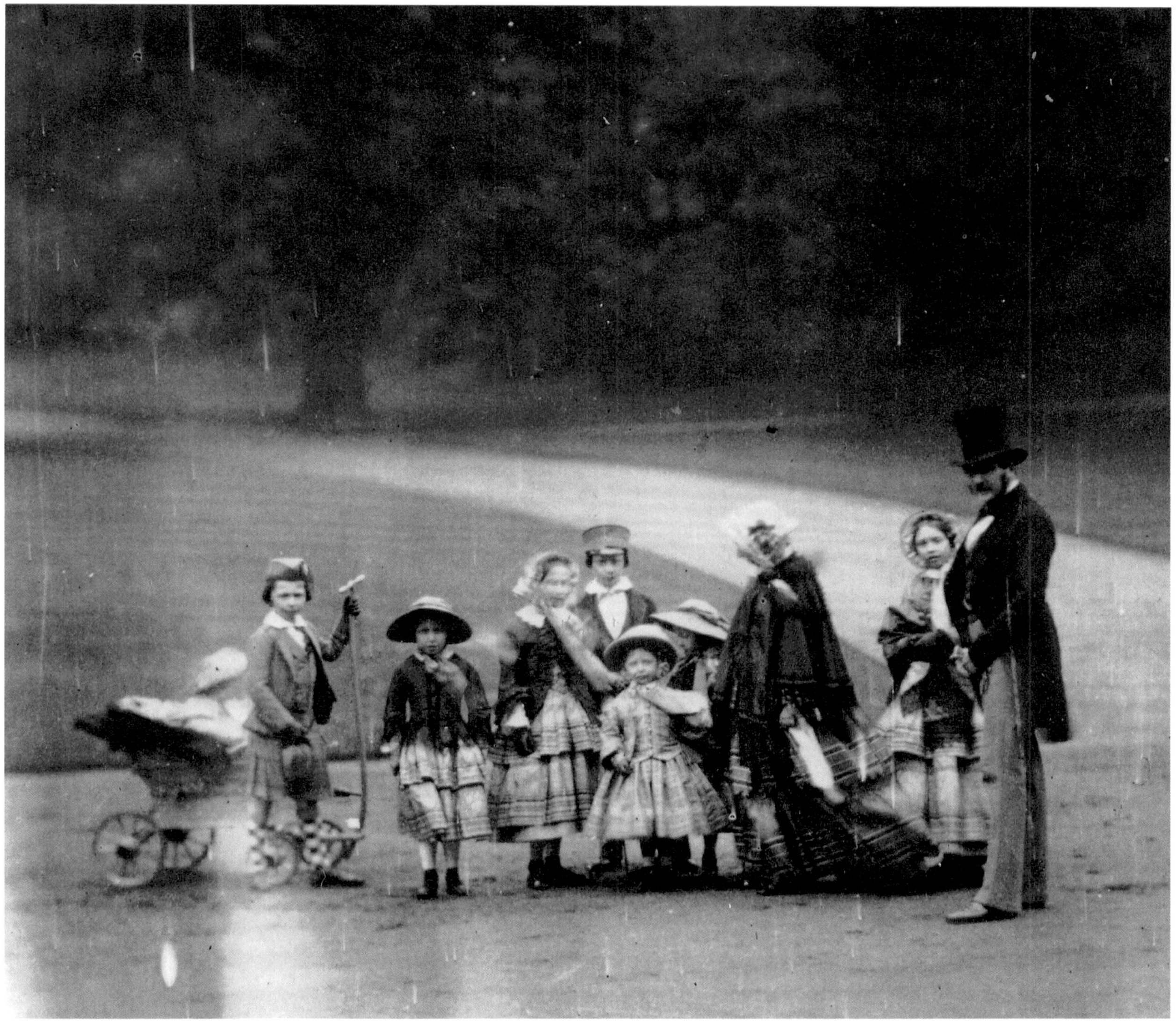

Fig. 9. Roger Fenton, *The Royal Family in the Gardens of Buckingham Palace, 22 May, 1854*, detail. Albumen silver print from glass negative, 11.9 x 10 cm (4¾ x 4 in.). The Royal Collection © 2007, Her Majesty Queen Elizabeth II, RCIN 2906086

rapidly—indeed, during 1850 some sixty-seven million passenger journeys were made.[36]

During this period the popularity of the monarchy rose as well. At Victoria's coronation in 1838, the sight of the diminutive young woman, barely out of childhood, emerging from Westminster Abbey as their new queen deeply touched the hearts of the people.[37] Two years later her marriage to the dashing young Prince Albert of Saxe-Coburg and Gotha proved irresistible to a nation that could still recall the excesses of her predecessor, George IV, whose profligate ways and debauchery had undermined the authority of the monarchy. Anxious not to be cast in this mold, the young couple did everything to regain the high moral ground by demonstrating the virtues of marriage and constancy. During the first decade of their marriage the young queen was constantly pregnant; she had borne seven children by the close of 1850 (fig. 9). Rather than astonishing the nation her fecundity won admiration, and the large family became a model widely adopted throughout the century.

Despite the royal couple's matrimonial happiness, Albert met with considerable opposition from the aristocracy and members of Parliament. They regarded him as an upstart German princeling who should not be allowed to meddle in British policy and affairs of state. While he worked alongside the queen each day, the prince was never allowed to read state papers or government correspondence, which traditionally were the sole concern of the sovereign and not to be shared with anyone, let alone a foreigner. When ministers came for an audience they met the queen alone, and although she may have related snippets of information to her husband, the opinion of the prince was never sought by the state. The situation was especially dispiriting for the queen, who idolized her husband and valued his opinions; yet the procedures could not be changed without the support of the prime minister and members of his cabinet, which initially was not forthcoming. However, when Robert Peel became prime minister in 1841, a new

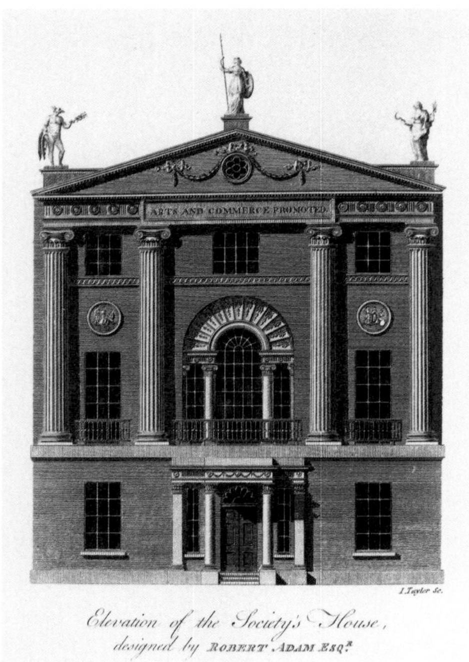

Fig. 10. Unknown artist, *Elevation of the Society's House, designed by Robert Adam, Esq*ʳ. Copperplate engraving, 19 x 13.1 cm (7½ x 5⅛ in.). Frontispiece from Henry Trueman Wood, *A History of the Royal Society of Arts* (London, 1913)

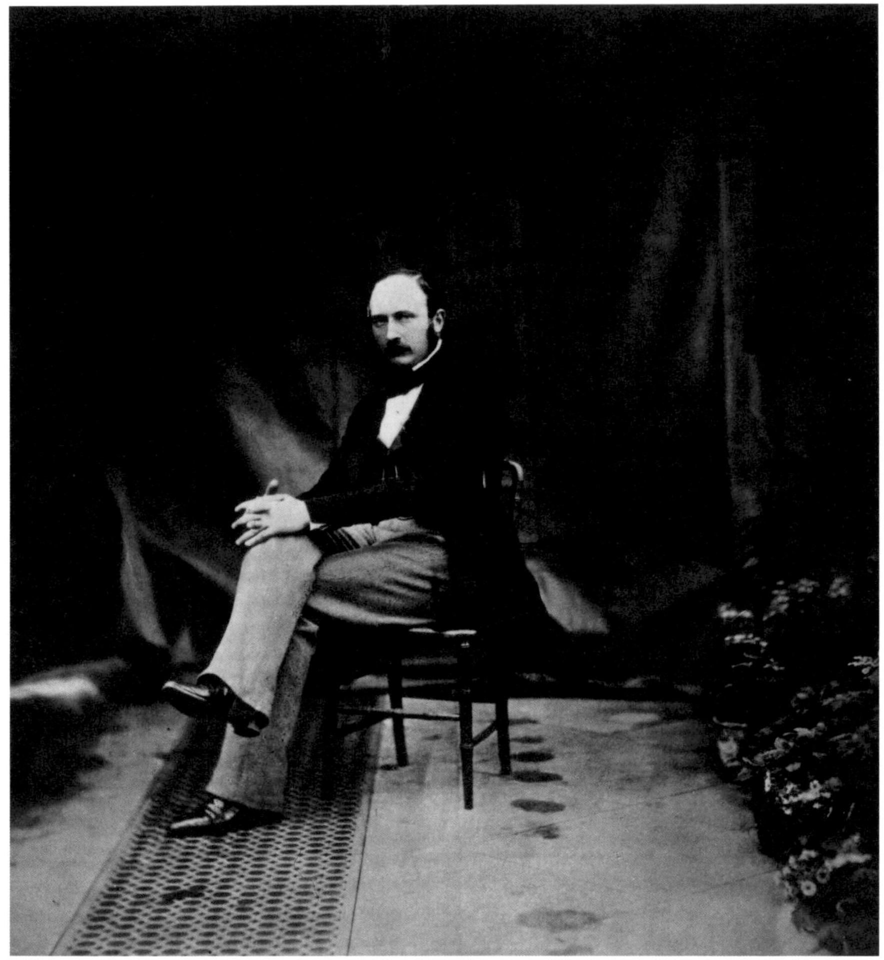

Fig. 11. Roger Fenton, *The Prince, Buckingham Palace, May 1854*. Carbon print made ca. 1865 from collodion negative, 16.2 x 14.5 cm (6⅜ x 5¾ in.). The Royal Collection © Her Majesty Queen Elizabeth II, RCIN 2906511

attitude came with him. Peel's background as the son of a Lancashire cotton manufacturer and capitalist, significantly different from that of most prime ministers, who were drawn from the landed classes, made him unusually sensitive to the prince's predicament. With Peel's encouragement, Albert became increasingly involved in the political life of the nation.

When the government established a royal commission in October 1841 to encourage the fine arts in Britain,[38] Peel invited the prince to lead the inquiry and report on the rebuilding of the Palace of Westminster, and Albert's performance in this capacity allowed him to be initiated gracefully into public life. The secretary of the commission was Charles Lock Eastlake—a painter, royal academician, translator of Goethe's *Theory of Colors*, and admirer of the German art historian Johann Passavant, whose biography of Raphael had been published in 1839.[39] With their common interests in science, art—especially Raphael—and German art scholarship, Eastlake and Prince Albert worked in a harmonious alliance that won the prince a reputation as conscientious and fair-minded. Fears that he would favor German artists over British artists were soon dispelled. Albert settled into his new role, displaying a capacity for hard work that would characterize all his undertakings (fig. 11).

In April 1843 the Society of Arts, London, invited the prince to become its next president. Founded in 1754 for the sole purpose of encouraging arts and manufactures in Britain, the society rewarded innovation and endeavor by bestowing cash prizes and medals (fig. 10).[40] For the first ninety years of its existence it was instrumental in promoting activities in areas that ranged from the textile industry and iron shipbuilding to lithography, fire prevention, and the curing of herring.[41] By 1842, however, years of mismanagement had brought the society's funds to the point of crisis. When the prince was approached, moves were already afoot to secure a long-term future. Nothing pleased Albert more than the challenge of reform, and upon assuming leadership he became actively engaged in the management of the society, endearing himself to its powerful and influential members in the process. Under his energetic presidency, direction and a sense of purpose were regained. In 1847 the society was granted a royal charter and became the Royal Society of Arts. (It continued to be known as the Society of Arts and is so called throughout this volume.)

Guided by Albert, the society adopted a policy of encouraging the application of art and science to industrial and manufacturing purposes. The success of the industrial exhibitions held in Europe, especially in Paris, brought home a realization that such events created a competitive climate in which aesthetic standards were raised and trade stimulated. The idea of holding a national exhibition in London was first discussed as early as 1845, but it took years for the proposal to find sufficient support beyond its immediate backers in the metropolis. The turning point came in June 1849, when the society formally established a subcommittee to look into the feasibility of holding an exhibition and the prince became closely and actively involved. By 1851, when the Great Exhibition opened (see chapter 3), the undertaking had become forever associated with his name.[42] It transformed British attitudes toward Albert. More important, the exhibition marked a significant turning point in the history of Britain, one that shaped its cultural, economic, and imperial destiny.

There were few regrets for the 1840s as they drew to a close. Although in much of Europe the political upheavals of 1848 still reverberated, Britain had emerged relatively unscathed; and from this the public took comfort, especially since so much of the last decade had been marked by disquiet and despair. The editor of the *Illustrated London News* gave voice to the hopes of the nation when he suggested, "For individuals and for the country, for manufacturers, for commerce, and for agriculture—for all interests in the State—let us hope that the new year will be better than the old—that employment will increase, and pauperism diminish; and that 1850 will shine brightly in history, when compared with 1849."[43]

In fact, 1850 heralded an extraordinary decade and a fundamentally transformed emotional tone. Britons seemed collectively to put the past behind them and move forward with a newfound optimism and sense of purpose. For photography, all the necessary factors for long-term development were in place, and only some external stimulus was needed to bring about the realization of its latent potential. Before embarking on that story, however, we need to retrace our steps, look more carefully at the circumstances surrounding the discovery and development of the calotype process, and examine how photography fared during the 1840s.

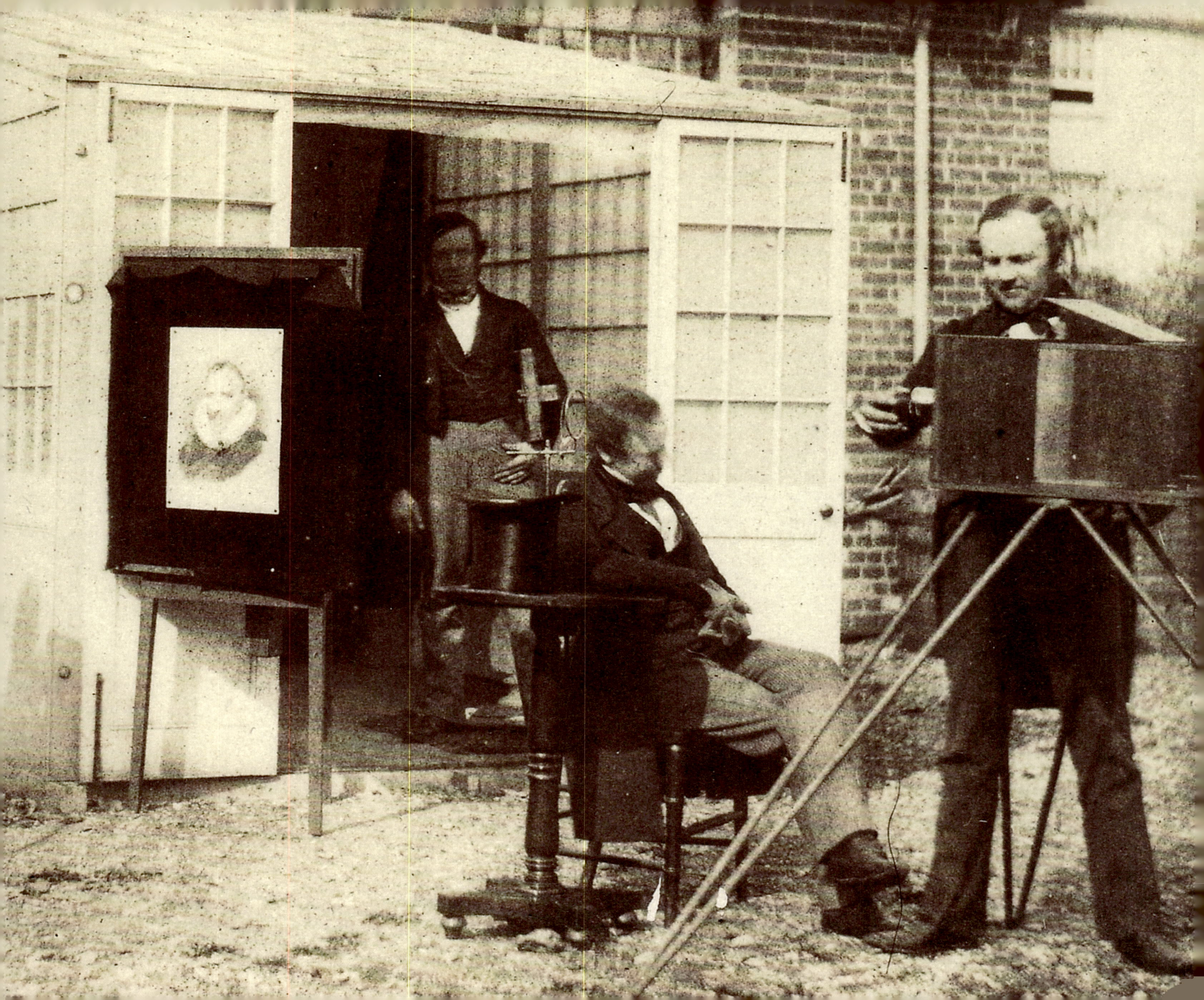

2. The Formative Years: The Calotype in the 1840s

THE INVENTION OF THE CALOTYPE

From the very outset, Daguerre's process had received the widest attention and warmest praise from the press—not just in Britain but throughout Europe and in America. Unhappy that his own invention was being overshadowed, Talbot worked diligently to improve it. The photogenic drawing process that he had introduced in 1839 relied entirely upon the actinic power of light to convert the silver chloride trapped in the fibers of the paper into fine particles of black silver. Even in direct sunlight, this conversion took place slowly—especially so when the exposure was made in a camera, which admits only a limited amount of light. The tediously long exposure times required by the process made it impractical for most commercial applications.[1]

Throughout 1839 and 1840, Talbot's notebooks reveal a wide-ranging series of investigations into the efficacy of different chemicals and metallic salts for registering and fixing photographic images. On September 20, 1840, he began a series of experiments that fundamentally altered the course of photography. After three days of research Talbot recorded that "some very remarkable effects were obtained,"[2] and, describing the sequence of events in greater detail a few months later, he recalled the moment of revelation.

> *One day, last September, I had been trying pieces of sensitive paper, prepared in different ways, in the camera obscura, allowing them to remain there only a very short time, with the view of finding out which was the most sensitive. One of these papers was taken out and examined by candlelight. There was little or nothing to be seen upon it, and I left it lying on a table in a dark room. Returning some time after, I took up the paper, and was very much surprised to see upon it a distinct picture. I was certain there was nothing of the kind when I had looked at it before; and, therefore (magic apart), the only conclusion that could be drawn was, that the picture had unexpectedly* developed itself *by a spontaneous action.*[3]

Opposite: Fig. 12. Detail of William Henry Fox Talbot and Nicolaas Henneman, *The Reading Establishment*, 1846 (see pl. 6)

Talbot's wonder at what he had observed is easily imagined. Being a scientist, he sought a rational explanation for the appearance of this "kind of latent picture" and undertook a further series of chemical experiments to identify the cause. In the course of these he tried in the camera obscura another sheet of treated paper, which, "when taken out of the camera, presented hardly any thing visible; but . . . I continued to observe it by candlelight, and had soon the satisfaction of seeing a picture begin to appear, and all the details of it come out one after the other."[4]

Talbot soon realized that he had stumbled upon two phenomena: the fact that a latent, or hidden, image is registered in light-sensitive silver salts after a comparatively short exposure to light; and the ability of chemicals to "develop" that image into visible existence. Although the principle of the latent image had already been utilized in the daguerreotype process, where it was "developed" into visibility by mercury fumes, its significance was not fully appreciated at the time. Talbot, however, because of his systematic approach and deductive reasoning, was immediately able to recognize the full implications of what he had discovered. In his hands the bringing out of a latent image through chemical development became a winning formula, on the basis of which a workable system of negative/positive photography would be created (figs. 13a, 13b).

Initially Talbot kept the working details of his method secret. On February 8, 1841, he was issued a patent for "Improvements in Obtaining Pictures, or Representations of Objects."[5] Having thus established his claim to the process, he felt comfortable revealing his discovery the next week in a letter to the *Literary Gazette*, describing the new approach as a "chemical process by which paper may be made far more sensitive to light than by any means hitherto known" so that "a better picture can now be obtained in *a minute* than by the former process in *an hour*." While the new process had many advantages over photogenic drawing, nothing had been sacrificed; on the contrary, the resulting negatives were "more easily and perfectly fixed" than before, and "a

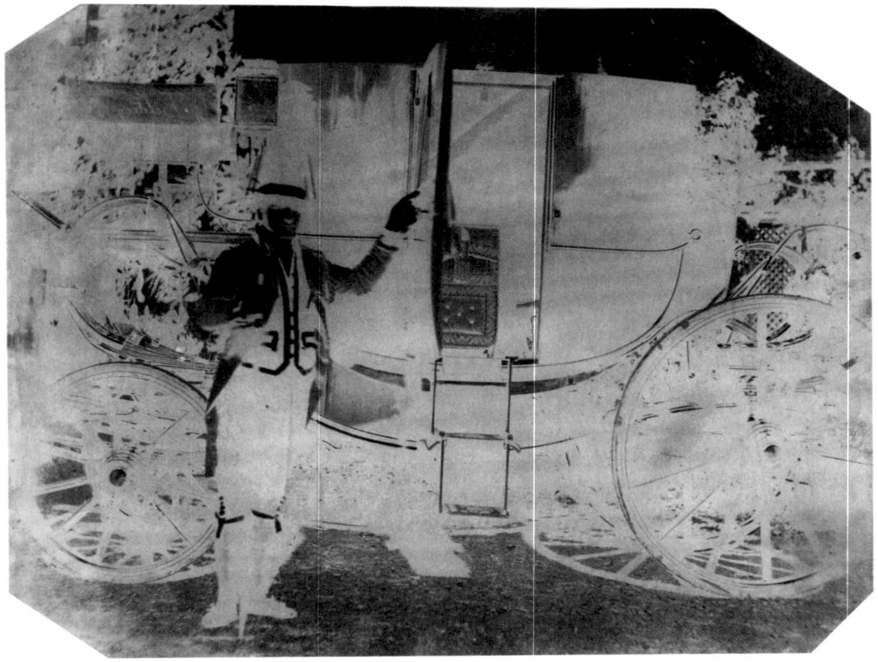

Fig. 13a. William Henry Fox Talbot, *The Footman,* October 14, 1840. Waxed calotype negative, 16.3 x 21 cm (6⅜ x 8¼ in.). Hans P. Kraus, Jr., New York

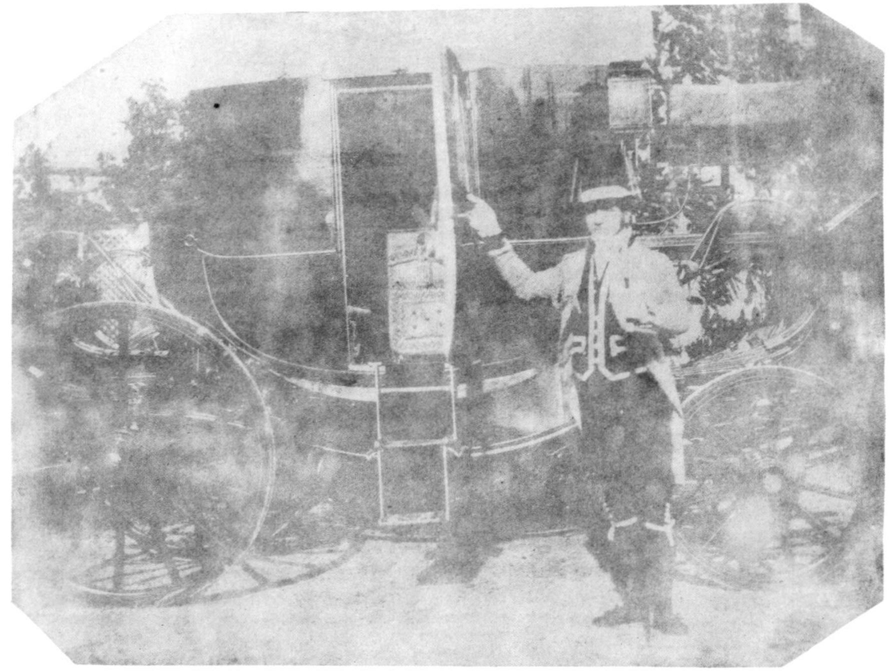

Fig. 13b. William Henry Fox Talbot, *The Footman,* October 14, 1840. Salted paper print, 16.3 x 21 cm (6⅜ x 8¼ in.). William B. Becker Collection

great many copies may be made from them, and thus the original view can be multiplied with facility."[6]

The confident tone of Talbot's letter suggests delight with his process. "The new kind of photographs," he announced, "I propose to distinguish by the name of *Calotype*; a term which, I hope, when they become known, will not be found to have been misapplied."[7] Fastidious in his use of words, Talbot had drawn on the Greek word *kalos,* meaning beautiful, to impart to his term the connotation he desired. Not everyone approved the choice. His mother would "have liked a name more referable to *you,* more individualized."[8] Well-meaning friends thought he should follow Daguerre's example and name the process Talbotype, but the self-effacing Talbot used that term rarely.[9]

The introduction of the calotype opened a new chapter for Talbot. The process was his alone; no struggle was needed to establish his priority, as there had been with Daguerre in 1839. And, although the daguerreotype had meanwhile been adapted and chemically enhanced to reduce its exposure times to under a minute, making its use for portraiture a viable proposition, this time Talbot at least understood what he was up against. The success of his own process would rest on persuading others to adopt it. In his letter to the *Literary Gazette,* Talbot pointed out two important purposes to which the calotype could be put: recording topography and making portraits.

> *How many travellers are almost ignorant of drawing, and either attempt nothing, or bring home rude unintelligible sketches! They may now fill their portfolios with accurate views, without much expenditure of time or trouble; and even the accomplished artist will call in sometimes this auxiliary aid, when pressed for time in sketching a building or a landscape, or when wearied with the multiplicity of its minute details.*
>
> *One of the most important applications of the new process, and most likely to prove generally interesting, is, undoubtedly, the taking of portraits. I made a trial of it last October, and found that the experiment*

readily succeeded. Half-a-minute appeared to be sufficient in sunshine, and four or five minutes when a person was seated in the shade, but in the open air.[10]

By stressing topography, Talbot was appealing to individuals of his own class and level of education who enjoyed traveling in search of the antiquarian or picturesque. Sketching and experiencing the landscape belonged to that portfolio of talents expected of cultured individuals. The idea of taking portraits would appeal to an even wider audience—travelers or not—and the news that exposure times of half a minute were a reality might tempt even the most hesitant to try their hand.

The final point in Talbot's campaign was an assertion of the cultural value of calotype photography. In closing his letter he offered what is perhaps the first artistic manifesto about the unique transforming power of photography:

I remember it was said by many persons, at the time when photogenic drawing was first spoken of, that it was likely to prove injurious to art, as substituting mere mechanical labour in lieu of talent and experience. Now, so far from this being the case, I find that in this, as in most other things, there is ample room for the exercise of skill and judgment. It would hardly be believed, how different an effect is produced by a longer or shorter exposure to the light, and, also, by mere variations in the fixing process, by means of which almost any tint, cold or warm, may be thrown over the picture, and the effect of bright or gloomy weather may be imitated at pleasure. All this falls within the artist's province to combine and to regulate; and if, in the course of these manipulations, he, nolens volens, *becomes a chemist and an optician, I feel confident that such an alliance of science with art will prove conducive to the improvement of both.*[11]

In a period when machines were revered for their capacity for endless replication, Talbot suggested that photography was predisposed to human intervention, a welcome alternative to the idea of the camera as merely another mechanical contrivance. In emphasizing the way in which exposure times and chemical procedures alter the appearance of a picture he was underlining a distinction between the calotype and its competitor, the daguerreotype, whose popular success largely relied on the creation of faultless facsimiles. Talbot's belief that his calotype process was a happy union of science and art emerged from the wider cultural context of the late eighteenth and early nineteenth centuries, in which science was seen as a discipline perfectly suited for understanding the natural world (fig. 14).[12] In the 1840s, scientists were still called natural philosophers and their apparatus "philosophical instruments."

In a second letter to the *Literary Gazette* published two weeks after the first, on February 27, 1841, Talbot offered new specifics about the advantages of the calotype. Its negative was more "strongly fixed" than in photogenic drawing and did not "readily become altered" by exposure to the sun. Even were it to fade, the negative's image could be chemically "*revived* . . . to its pristine strength"—and during the process of revival fresh details that had lain dormant within the paper often appeared. This "invaluable property of the calotype" allowed "the artist to correct the error of his judgment, in case he has made too faint a picture at first."[13] In describing these redemptive qualities Talbot

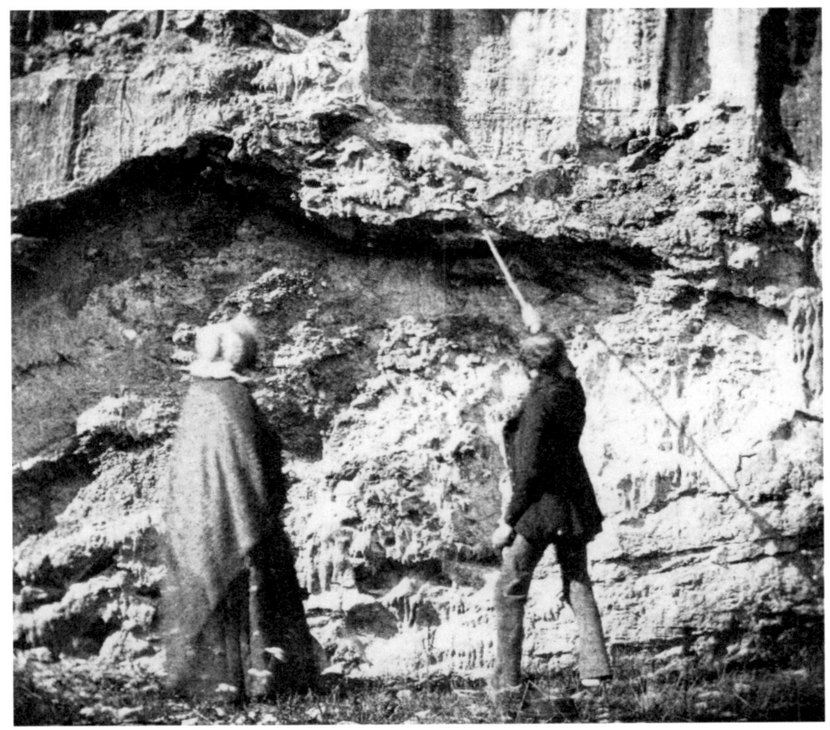

Fig. 14. William Henry Fox Talbot, *"The Geologists," Chudleigh, Devon*, ca. 1843. Salted paper print, 9.7 x 11.3 cm (3⅞ x 4½ in.). National Media Museum, Bradford, 1937-1612/2

doubtless intended to reassure the uncertain beginner for whom the business of taking a photograph, let alone developing and fixing the image, was shrouded in mystery.

Actual working details of the process, however, were not offered; Talbot studiously avoided disclosing them in either letter. He was mindful of his unhappy experiences of 1839, when the Royal Society repeatedly thwarted his attempts to establish the priority of his photogenic drawing process because information had already been made public.[14] This time Talbot's caution paid off, and his paper describing the chemistry and working manipulations of the calotype process was accepted and read at a meeting of the society on June 10, 1841.[15] Two days later a brief outline was published in the *Literary Gazette*; a full and detailed account appeared early the following month in the *Athenaeum*.[16] The era of the calotype had begun.

Two contrasting images convey something of the excitement and wonder that photographers must have experienced during the early years of working with the calotype process. One (pl. 4), a tiny image Talbot made in 1842, is a contemplative study with the mysterious self-reflective overtones of German high Romanticism;[17] the second (pl. 5), taken some three years later by Calvert Jones during a visit to Lacock Abbey, strikes an altogether more confident note and demonstrates that photography was already being used with increasing assurance, especially by those with artistic training or sensibilities.

THE TECHNIQUE OF TALBOT'S CALOTYPE PROCESS

In his account published in the *Athenaeum*, Talbot described several distinct operations that went into making a calotype negative, most of them part of the process of sensitizing the paper.

Iodizing: A smooth-textured writing paper, such as Whatman's Turkey Mill, was brushed with a weak solution of silver nitrate and allowed to dry, then immersed in a solution of potassium iodide, causing silver iodide to form within the paper fibers. Next the sheet was rinsed by immersing briefly in water, and dried. The timing of the last two stages was critical: too long an immersion in potassium iodide could redissolve the silver iodide, and prolonged rinsing could wash out the silver iodide, in either case leading to poor results. Once successfully produced, the iodized paper was insensitive to light and could be kept indefinitely.

Exciting: The iodized paper was made sensitive to light, or excited, by brushing it with a mixture containing silver nitrate, acetic acid, and gallic acid, which Talbot called "gallo-nitrate of silver." Gallic acid helped increase sensitivity, and acetic acid inhibited a spontaneous decomposition of the chemical mixture. Nevertheless the solution was notoriously unstable and had to be used when freshly made. The excited paper was briefly rinsed, blotted, and sometimes dried.

Exposing: The excited paper was most often exposed in the camera while still moist, since in this state its sensitivity was enhanced. Vulnerable to light, the paper was housed in a specially designed holder that was fitted snugly into the back of the camera immediately prior to exposure. This dark slide, as it was known, often held the paper behind a sheet of glass to prevent its drying out; it also held the paper firmly in place, minimizing the risk that large-size negatives would ripple or move.

Bringing out: The exposed negative was developed, or "brought out," by the application of more "gallo-nitrate of silver," which reacted with the sensitized silver iodide, reducing it to silver, and deposited additional silver onto the exposed areas, increasing the density of the darks in the negative.

Fixing: After being developed, the negative was washed in water to remove all traces of soluble chemicals. This did not fix the negative in the conventional sense but made it reasonably stable and insensitive to light.[18] Not until 1843 did Talbot recommend fixing negatives in a bath of hot, strong sodium thiosulphate, the solution known today as "hypo."

Printing: Strictly speaking, printing does not belong to the calotype process,[19] but as the necessary final step in producing a photographic image, it is included here. A print was made by placing the negative in direct contact with a sheet of paper made sensitive to light using the formulation for Talbot's original photogenic drawing process (soaking in a solution of common salt, drying, and brushing with a solution of ammonio-nitrate of silver). After the negative and the paper had been exposed together, preferably to direct sunlight, the negative was removed, revealing a positive with dark areas of rich, brownish black. The positive was then fixed by the same method as the negative.[20]

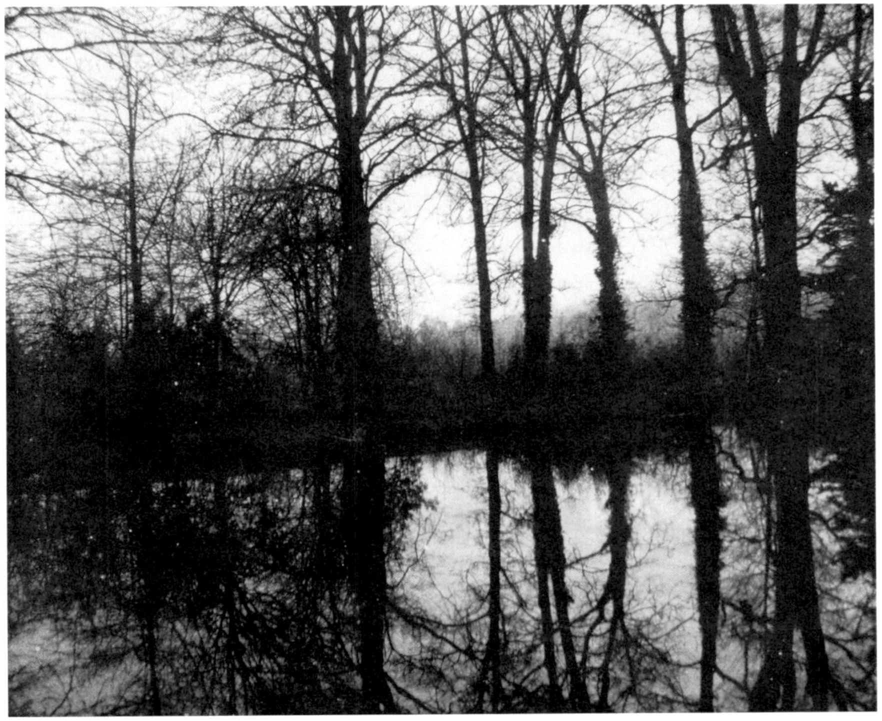

Fig. 15. William Henry Fox Talbot, *Winter Trees Reflected in a Pond*, ca. 1842. Salted paper print, 16.5 x 19.2 cm (6½ x 7½ in.). National Media Museum, Bradford, 1937-2050/3

Today, prints made by this method are called salt prints or salted paper prints (fig. 15).

EARLY CALOTYPES

In his search for heightened sensitivity and a correspondingly shorter exposure time, Talbot had unwittingly devised formulae that pushed the chemistry to the very limits of its stability, where the slightest miscalculation caused the paper to turn brown. For the process to have any hope of success, the chemicals had to be freshly made and all the equipment scrupulously clean, and even then the procedure remained wayward and difficult to control. Among amateurs it acquired a mixed reputation. Although all who saw Talbot's own photographs praised their beauty and perfection, those who followed his formulae and procedures were often dissatisfied with their results.[21] As was later remarked, "Mr. F. Talbot's directions, though sufficient for his own pre-instructed hand, were too vague for the tyro."[22]

The calotype was nevertheless a great advance over Talbot's original photogenic drawing process and, with its reduced exposure time, could present a serious challenge to the daguerreotype—which by the late summer of 1841 had been adopted everywhere for commercial portraiture. The first to establish daguerreotype studios in London were Richard Beard and Antoine Claudet; others elsewhere in Britain soon followed their example.[23] Sensing an opportunity to launch the calotype into this new area of enterprise, Talbot added advice on making portraits to his patent specifications. He recommended focal lengths, lens apertures, and taking a portrait "in the open air, under a serene sky, and without sunshine," which required an exposure time of only half a minute—hoping that emphasis on the exposure's brevity would show that the process was a viable alternative to the daguerreotype (fig. 16).[24]

The first person to receive a license from Talbot was Henry Collen, a miniaturist who began making calotypes commercially sometime during the summer of 1841.[25] Then, in the spring of 1842, Talbot was approached by Beard and subsequently Claudet; each of them sought a license to use the calotype as an alternative to the daguerreotype in his portrait studio. Beard wanted exclusive use of the process in London and, since Talbot was unable to grant this because of his prior commitment to Collen,[26] ultimately withdrew his request.[27]

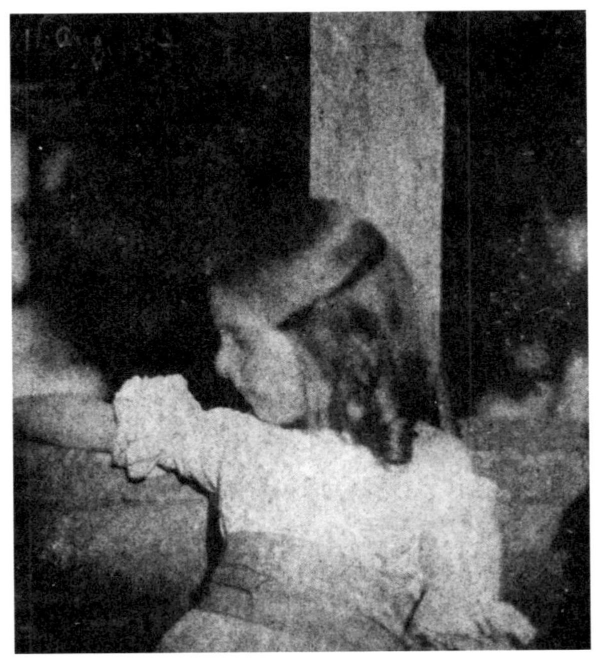

Fig. 16. William Henry Fox Talbot, *Rosamond Constance Talbot*, August 11, 1843. Salted paper print, 8.9 x 7.8 cm (3½ x 3⅛ in.). National Media Museum, Bradford, 1937-3476/3

Claudet, on the other hand, grew close to Talbot, and an extensive correspondence between the two men shows that they shared many interests. Leisurely negotiations beginning in April 1842 culminated in a licensing agreement signed in the spring of 1844. Claudet then began advertising his "Talbotype (or Calotype) portraits" with characteristic showmanship (fig. 17). A portrait cost one guinea, with further copies from the negative costing five shillings each.[28] This was an auspicious beginning.[29]

But in fact, neither venture in commercial calotype portraiture proved successful. Collen, an artist rather than an entrepreneur and without the means to advertise, received commissions for only slightly more than two hundred portraits during his first year. The license entitled Talbot to 30 percent of his takings,[30] and with the additional cost of chemicals, materials, and overhead, Collen is likely to have operated at a loss. Although he hung on for several years, in May 1844 he wrote that unless his circumstances changed, "calotype portraiture will fail as a profitable affair."[31] Claudet, despite an extensive advertising campaign, fared no better. In the summer of 1845 he confided to Talbot, "So far, the Talbotype has brought me nothing but losses. The entire takings do not even cover an assistant's salary."[32]

Meanwhile, the business of daguerreotype portraiture was thriving. Compared to the sharp, jewel-like image of a daguerreotype, portraits taken by the calotype process simply lacked appeal. One reviewer of a display of calotype portraits found "a rough air of truth about them" but thought the results no better than "a decent artist might produce with a burnt stick."[33] The paper fibers of the calotype negative created a more textured appearance, size-for-size, than the daguerreotype; a larger negative could produce a sharper picture, but few sitters were willing to pay the additional cost. While today the calotype's "rough air of truth" and the charcoal qualities of the salted paper print are highly valued, in the 1840s they found few admirers.

Other factors contributed to the discrepancy in popularity between the two methods. Proprietors of daguerreotype portrait studios, chiefly interested in turning a profit, invested money in making their products attractive. Adopting the form of presentation used in the preceding era to house delicate portrait miniatures, they set their daguerreotypes into pinchbeck frames and compact morocco leather cases. These enhanced the work's appearance and helped portraitists justify their higher prices. Many painters of miniatures, displaced by the arrival of the new method, turned their hand to coloring daguerreotypes with finely powered pigments, creating images that were convincingly lifelike. All these factors contributed to the rise of an entirely new market for family portraits—until then a luxury reserved for wealthy patrons of the more traditional arts.[34]

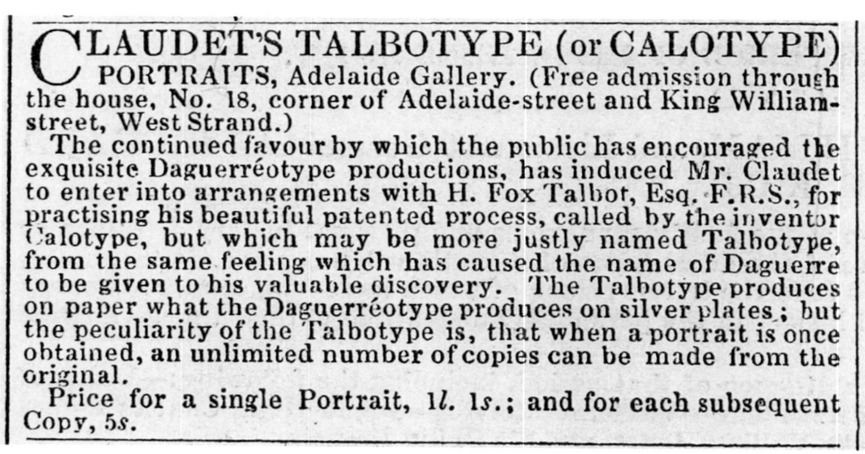

CLAUDET'S TALBOTYPE (or CALOTYPE) PORTRAITS, Adelaide Gallery. (Free admission through the house, No. 18, corner of Adelaide-street and King William-street, West Strand.)

The continued favour by which the public has encouraged the exquisite Daguerréotype productions, has induced Mr. Claudet to enter into arrangements with H. Fox Talbot, Esq. F.R.S., for practising his beautiful patented process, called by the inventor Calotype, but which may be more justly named Talbotype, from the same feeling which has caused the name of Daguerre to be given to his valuable discovery. The Talbotype produces on paper what the Daguerréotype produces on silver plates; but the peculiarity of the Talbotype is, that when a portrait is once obtained, an unlimited number of copies can be made from the original.

Price for a single Portrait, 1*l.* 1*s.*; and for each subsequent Copy, 5*s.*

Fig. 17. Advertisement for Claudet's Talbotype (or Calotype) Portraits, from *Athenaeum*, July 6, 1844, p. 609. Private collection

NICOLAAS HENNEMAN AND THE "READING ESTABLISHMENT"

Undoubtedly discouraged by the commercial failure of calotype portraiture, Talbot was struggling as well with other photographic enterprises that he hoped would promote both the calotype and his name. Central to these activities was Nicolaas Henneman (or Nichole, as he was known to the Talbot family). Born in Holland in 1813, he had joined the Talbot household sometime before 1838 and had soon become Talbot's valet, effectively taking charge of his domestic arrangements. After 1839, Henneman worked closely with Talbot on his photographic projects and from firsthand observation grew ever more knowledgeable about the practical workings of the process. As Talbot increasingly came to rely on this help, Henneman's role transmuted from valet to photographic assistant. By 1844 he had acquired sufficient ability and assurance to leave his post and begin work independently as a calotypist for subjects of all types (fig. 18): now his relationship to Talbot was that of a photographic contractor.

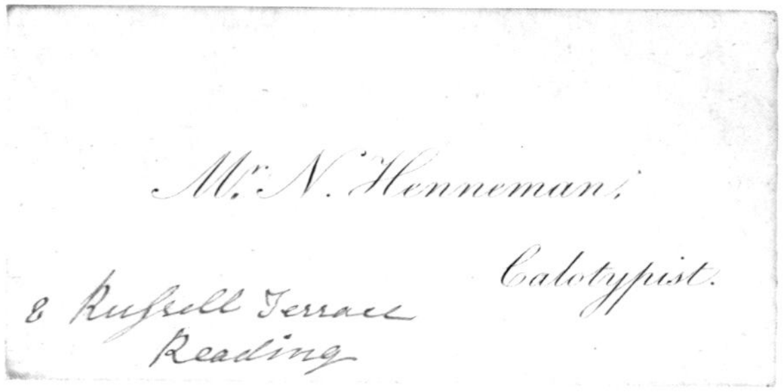

Fig. 18. Nicolaas Henneman's calling card, ca. 1845. Printed card, 3.7 x 7.4 cm (1½ x 2⅞ in.). Hans P. Kraus, Jr., New York

Henneman set himself up in the ancient market town of Reading, located on the banks of the Thames in Berkshire, some twenty miles from Lacock, some forty miles west of London, and a boomtown ever since it had been made a principal station on the line to Bristol by the Great Western Railway. He chose for his premises a former schoolhouse with outbuildings and a little garden to the rear. Here he erected a small glasshouse for use as a daylight studio and built trestles on which he set out his printing frames in the sun.[35] A two-part photograph of the Reading Establishment must show it especially set up to demonstrate the range and scope of work undertaken there (fig. 12; pl. 6). We see works of art being photographed for reproduction, portraits being made, and negatives being printed—all reminding us that photography was at heart very much a handicraft activity based on the skills of individuals rather than the humming machinery of industry. The talented Henneman turned his hand to whatever photographic work came his way, taking portraits, undertaking private commissions, supplying printsellers, and giving instruction to those wanting to take up photography. Essentially, however, it was work as Talbot's photographic printer that kept him most fully occupied during the next two years.[36]

Talbot was issued a second patent for the calotype process in December 1843; he intended to bring the calotype up to date by specifying new chemical formulae and working methods that he hoped would enlarge its practical applications.[37] In a journal article he made a telling reference to "photographic publication; that is, producing a number of positive photographic copies of a picture or print, for the purposes of sale."[38] For publishing in commercial quantity Talbot stressed the importance of making all the prints consistent in exposure, color, and permanency. Achieving such an objective is taken for granted in our age of infinite reproducibility but in 1843 was immensely difficult, with subtle differences in the chemistry, paper, water supply, or manipulation working against uniformity. Seeking to overcome this problem, Talbot adopted a systemized approach to each of the four stages of print production and codified it in this second patent—even though some skeptics felt that by adding patents he was "rather overdoing it" for "what is at best an amusing, rather than valuable art."[39]

There was no better place to carry on the commercial production and distribution of photographs than at the Reading Establishment. Next to Talbot himself, Henneman was perhaps the most competent calotypist in Britain and certainly the most experienced; moreover, he was used to carrying out Talbot's orders. Indeed, it could be argued that Henneman's move to Reading was Talbot's way of furthering his own ambition to engage in what he called a "branch of manufacture" without undermining his status as a gentleman. It was acceptable for a valet to set himself up in trade—Charles Fortnum of the luxury comestibles firm Fortnum & Mason had done much the same thing—but would have been quite another matter for Talbot to do so under his own name.[40]

THE PENCIL OF NATURE

Whatever the precise nature of the business relationship, it was Henneman and the Reading Establishment that provided Talbot with a practical means of realizing his most ambitious and significant publication, *The Pencil of Nature.* It is hard to imagine how giant a leap of faith—or naïveté—was involved in this ambitious undertaking. Talbot's original conception called for the issuing of monthly parts, or fascicles, each with "Five Photographic Plates"; the whole was "To be completed in Ten or Twelve Numbers."[41] Such publication in installments had been widely adopted for books containing expensive illustrations, since it enabled costs to be recouped through sales along the way. It was also preferred by connoisseurs and collectors because it allowed them to spread the cost of acquisition over several months or, in this instance, an entire year.[42]

The first two fascicles of *The Pencil of Nature,* published in June 1844 and January 1845, contained six and seven photographs, respectively, making them the most ambitious of the six installments eventually published.[43] Accounts record the sale of 463 copies of these first two fascicles. Although this is perhaps an insignificant number by modern standards, more than 72,000 discrete and time-consuming steps were needed to complete the 6,019 prints contained in them (fig. 19).[44]

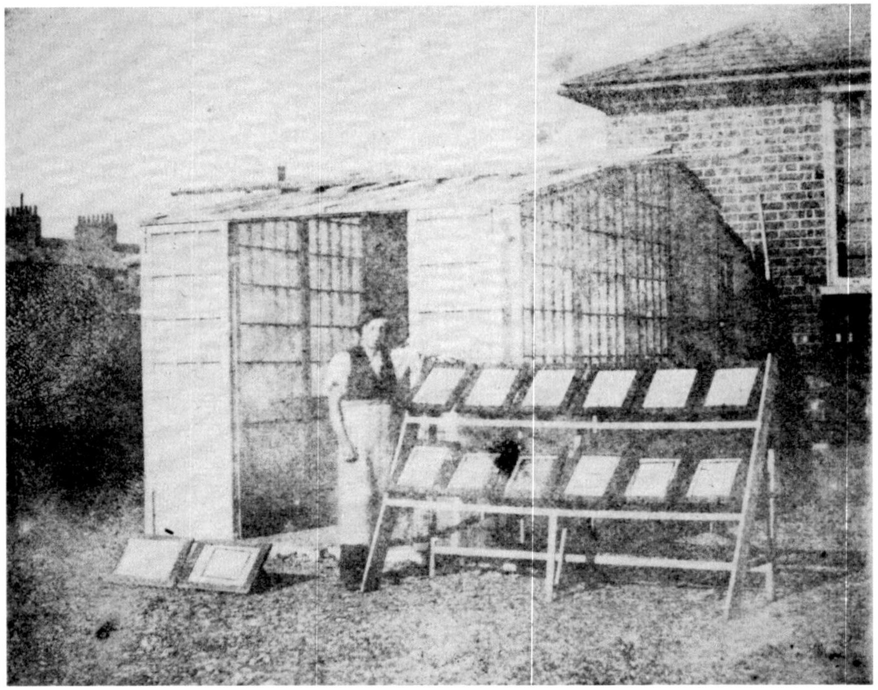

Fig. 19. Nicolaas Henneman, *Boy with Printing Frames, Reading Establishment*, ca. 1844. Salted paper print, 9 x 11.1 cm (3½ x 4⅜ in.). National Media Museum, Bradford, 1937-3127/1

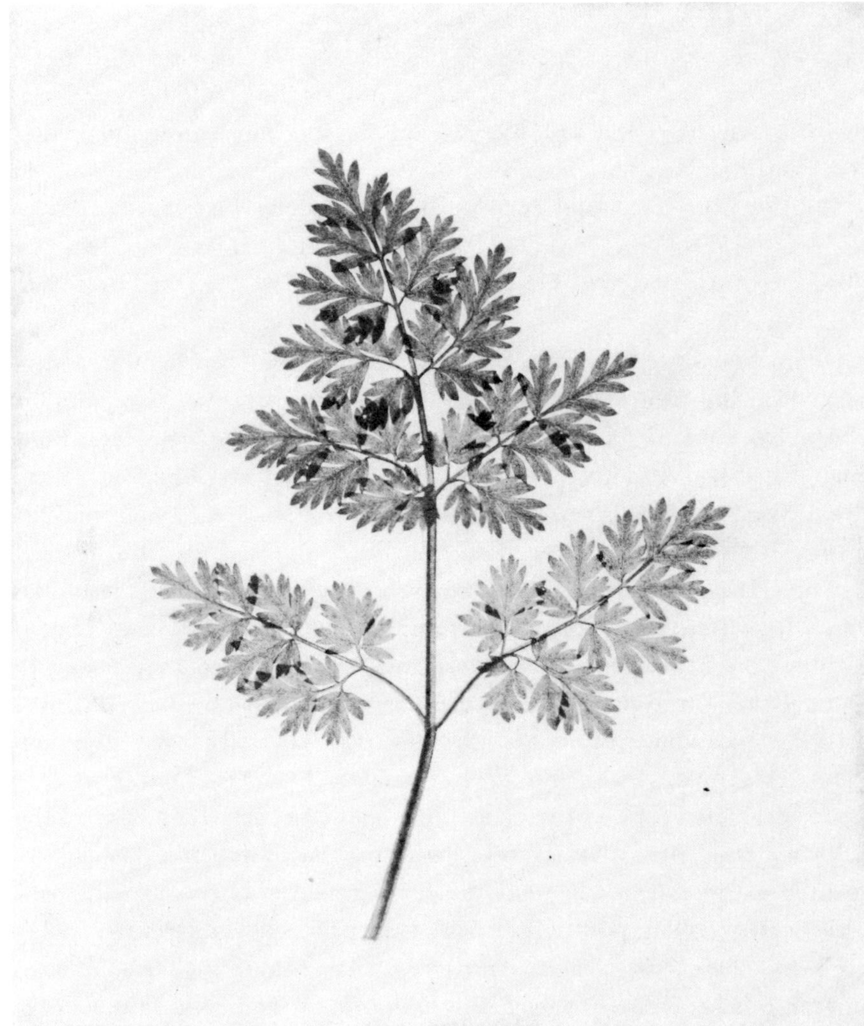

Fig. 20. William Henry Fox Talbot, *Leaf of a Plant*, ca. 1843–44, from *The Pencil of Nature*, plate 7. Salted paper print, 22 x 17.5 cm (8⅝ x 6⅞ in.). The Metropolitan Museum of Art, New York, Gift of Jean Horblit in memory of Harrison D. Horblit, 1994, 1994.197 (7)

Fascicles issued thereafter each contained just three prints, seeming to suggest that Talbot was facing up to the difficulties encountered by Henneman in sustaining so high an output. With each new fascicle sales continued to dwindle, until it was no longer economically possible to continue—at which point, in April 1846, this groundbreaking and ambitious photographic publishing project finally came to an end.[45]

Conceptually and artistically, *The Pencil of Nature*—with its combination of images and text—allowed Talbot to express his faith in the potential of the photographic medium. His choice of subjects was eclectic, and each was selected to illustrate a particular capability. Among the images were architectural studies, a botanical study of a leaf (fig. 20), still lifes of china and glass, a facsimile of an ancient printed page, and copies of a lithographic print. One of the most striking is Talbot's study *The Haystack*, which he included to demonstrate that his calotype process rendered "a multitude of minute details" with perfect accuracy (pls. 2, 3).[46] Not just an example of photographic verisimilitude, the image is also a tribute to the perfection of the stack itself, with its straw-thatched roof, projecting eaves, and inward-sloping sides all designed to limit the damage caused by rain. This haystack belongs to a careful, fastidious landowner; it is something to be proud of and a reassuring fact of life for anyone caring for livestock over the winter. In this context the study takes on another meaning of singular resonance for those of Talbot's class and landowning responsibilities, who would have appreciated it as a thing of joy, a pleasure to behold, and a heartening reminder of ancestral values.

Production of Talbot's grand vision must have been an enormous challenge for Henneman and the Reading Establishment—not only to achieve the consistency that Talbot sought but also to maintain reasonable levels of output despite British weather, seasonal dwindling of daylight hours, and dim wintry light. Moreover, while the last four parts of *The Pencil of Nature* were still in production, Talbot further compounded Henneman's problems by embarking on two ambitious new projects.

OTHER PUBLISHING VENTURES

Sun Pictures in Scotland, published in July 1845, was conceived as a photographic portfolio. Its twenty-three images, inspired by the writings of Sir Walter Scott, were Talbot's personal contribution to a veritable cult that thrived in the mid-Victorian era, transforming the public attitude toward Scotland and the Scots.[47] *Ivanhoe, Rob Roy,* and Scott's other lavishly romantic novels touched the imagination of the educated classes, many of whom headed north, guidebook in hand, in search of the locations so lovingly and accurately described—escaping for a while the realities of the uneasy present to see themselves as part of a historic tableau peopled with heroes, heroines, and villains. In *Sun Pictures* Talbot takes his viewers on a visual pilgrimage to scenes intimately associated with Scott's life and writings. Entirely devoid of text or explanation, the publication contains only photographs and titles. The sequence begins in Edinburgh and takes in Abbotsford, Melrose, Dryburgh, Loch Katrine, and Doune, closely following the itineraries offered by the latest edition of *Black's Picturesque Tourist of Scotland* (fig. 21).[48]

One admiring reader of Scott was Queen Victoria, who with Prince Albert made her first visit to Scotland in 1842. The royal couple fell in love with the land and the sturdy character of its people; here, far from the formalities of court life in London, they could enjoy an altogether simpler life. Their acquisition of the Balmoral estate six years later established a fashion among high society for the Highlands and all things Scottish—including baronial castles, deer stalking, salmon fishing, and tartan plaids.

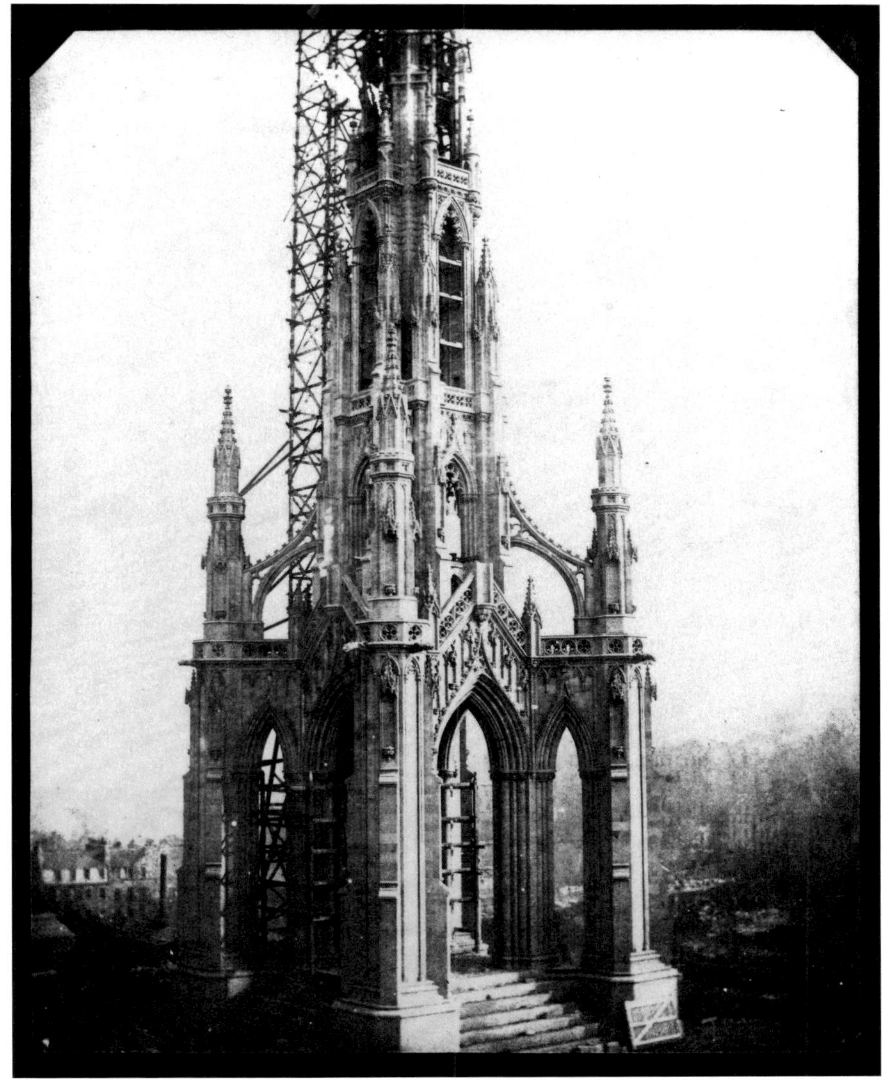

Fig. 21. William Henry Fox Talbot, *Sir Walter Scott's Monument, Edinburgh; as it appeared when nearly finished, in October 1844.* Salted paper print, image 19.7 x 15.8 cm (7¾ x 6¼ in.). The Metropolitan Museum of Art, New York, Gilman Collection, Museum Purchase, 2005, 2005.100.746

From the outset, *Sun Pictures in Scotland* was planned to appeal to friends, acquaintances, and relations in the fashionable circle of Lady Elisabeth Feilding, Talbot's mother. It was her self-appointed task to persuade them to subscribe in advance to the publication, and surviving lists give some sense of this society. Notable subscribers included the Duke of Devonshire, the Duchess of Bedford, and Lord Dudley

Stuart (who bought twelve copies), as well as the eminent collector and amateur landscape gardener Robert Henry Cheney and Edward King Tenison, both of whom later became well-known calotypists.[50] *Sun Pictures* served a very different function from *The Pencil of Nature*, being mostly intended to bring Talbot's achievements to notice among high society.

Unremarked by the wider world, the book disappeared without a trace into the libraries and drawing rooms of its aristocratic subscribers.[51] With its narrowly focused goal and limited number of copies distributed only to subscribers, *Sun Pictures in Scotland* remains one of the most enigmatic of all Talbot's photographic ventures. Nevertheless, it can reasonably claim to be the first photographic essay in the history of the medium.

Talbot's final venture into photographic publishing with the Reading Establishment was an ambitious scheme to provide some seven thousand prints for inclusion in the periodical the *Art-Union*. Beginning modestly in 1839, the journal had grown steadily from a circulation of 750 to about 7,000 copies per issue and had become an influential, authoritative source on the fine arts in Britain.[52] Initially its illustrations were few and of poor quality, but in 1844 high-quality engravings and lithographs began to be incorporated as "inserts"; most often they were plates from already published works submitted to illustrate a new process or to encourage book sales.[53] It was in this context that Talbot agreed to supply examples of his photographs.

In contrast to *The Pencil of Nature* or *Sun Pictures in Scotland*, whose circulations were strictly limited by their high cost, the *Art-Union* sold for a shilling. Through it Talbot would be able to reach a completely new audience, one that he hoped would appreciate seeing an original photograph and reading a detailed explanation of its making. His financial investment in the project was considerable—he later calculated the cost as not "less than a hundred pounds."[54] What he had not taken fully into account were the demands of making such a large number of prints on a short schedule. This prodigious undertaking placed a severe strain on the rudimentary facilities of the Reading Establishment and probably necessitated the cutting of corners to save time. The disastrous result became evident shortly after the journal was published in June 1846, when all seven thousand prints began to fade. As the editor of the *Art-Union*, Samuel Carter Hall, reflected some years later, "They are faded and gone—pieces of slurred paper, nothing more."[55] What had begun as a promotional opportunity for Talbot quickly turned into damaging publicity for him and his process, from which neither fully recovered.

RECEPTION OF THE CALOTYPE PROCESS

Given the popularity of the daguerreotype in the early 1840s, Talbot's attempt to make the calotype as commercially successful as its competitor by patenting "improvements" and moving toward mass production was perfectly understandable. However, converting the edicts of a patent into a workable manufacturing procedure was beyond him. Living in a world narrowly circumscribed by the conventions of his social class, Talbot had little experience of business matters. Throughout his life he remained a scholar, whose forays into the world of capitalism, manufacturing, and free trade invariably met with disappointment. A more knowing individual or one from a different social context might have better understood the nature of competition and perceived the shortcomings of his own process more objectively. But Talbot's view of his photographic discoveries was conditioned by his education and social expectations rather than by the entrepreneurial spirit that helped create the enterprises and fortunes of many Victorians. Things could have turned out very differently for the calotype had Talbot been more like, for instance, his near contemporary Thomas Holloway, a manufacturer of patent medicine, whose shrewd commercial skill fueled his meteoric rise from humble origins to a position as one of the great patrons and benefactors of the nineteenth century.[56]

To be fair, part of Talbot's difficulties stemmed from the nature of the photographs themselves. While the sharp, metallic realism of daguerreotypes set them apart from any kind of image seen before, calotypes, with their warm tones and textured image on a paper support, seemed to belong in the territory of mezzotint engravings or lithographs, which were made by the hand of an artist. To viewers lacking the terms of reference that we now take for granted when looking at photographs, this ambiguity must have been confusing. Talbot took care to spell out the differences in the opening paragraphs of *The Pencil of Nature*, where he explained,

> *The little work now presented to the Public is the very first attempt to publish a series of plates or pictures wholly executed by the new art of Photogenic Drawing, without any aid whatever from the artist's pencil.*

The term "Photography" is now so well known, that an explanation of it is perhaps superfluous. . . .

It may suffice, then, to say, that the plates of this work have been obtained by the mere action of Light upon sensitive paper. They have been formed or depicted by optical and chemical means alone. . . . They differ in all respects, and as widely as possible, in their origin, from plates of the ordinary kind, which owe their existence to the united skill of the Artist and the Engraver.[57]

A brief "Notice to the Reader" slipped into the second fascicle made the point once again (fig. 22). These reminders were necessary, for the complete absence of explanatory text in *Sun Pictures in Scotland* apparently left subscribers wondering about the true nature of the illustrations. As Talbot's mother was quick to point out, "It would have saved me a world of trouble if you had appended an explanation . . . to the Scotch views, & had made use of the word *representations* instead of *Plates* which misleads 'that ineffable Goose the Public' most woefully."[58]

When Talbot's photographs appeared in the *Art-Union* in June 1846, his editor wrote in an introduction, "These 'sun pictures' are still misapprehended . . . we shall accordingly . . . show what they are not, and endeavour to explain what they are, as it is yet far from generally accepted that they result from the action of light alone, and are not produced by some *leger-de-main* of Art." The photographs, he asserted, were "not extensively known in proportion to the importance of the discovery,"[59] a phrase that neatly summarizes Talbot's own struggle for wider recognition.

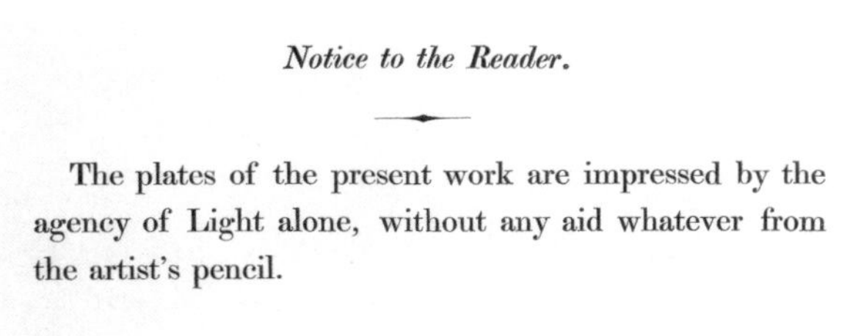

Notice to the Reader.

The plates of the present work are impressed by the agency of Light alone, without any aid whatever from the artist's pencil.

Fig. 22. Notice to the Reader, from William Henry Fox Talbot, *The Pencil of Nature*, fascicle 2, 1844. Printed slip, 8.5 x 19.5 cm (3 ⅜ x 7 ⅝ in.). The Metropolitan Museum of Art, New York, Gift of Jean Horblit in memory of Harrison D. Horblit, 1994, 1994.197

It is clear that many of Talbot's difficulties throughout the 1840s arose because of the struggle for dominance between the two photographic processes. Had the daguerreotype not existed, both photogenic drawing and the calotype process would have been extraordinarily successful. Time and money would have been invested in their improvement; people would have sat patiently for their portraits and delighted in the results. As we have seen, the reality was somewhat different, with the calotype struggling to have any meaningful impact in the public sphere. Such is the nature of competition, especially in the world of commerce.

But the calotype did not belong solely to that world. Because it involved visual judgment and skill, as Talbot had pointed out, and for other reasons as well, those who admired the arts and practiced them as amateurs found paper-negative photography appealing, and in their hands the process began to flourish during the 1840s. They belonged to the social class possessing education and financial independence, which gave them the intellectual and temporal freedom to take up photography as a recreation. Furthermore, as amateurs they were not constrained by Talbot's patents, which strictly required licensing if the process were to be used for commercial purposes. On the contrary, as Talbot explained about his patent, "I do not wish it to interfere with amateurs practising the art for their own amusement."[60]

COLLEGIAL ASSOCIATION

In the 1840s London was home to numerous learned societies devoted to such disciplines as archaeology, chemistry, ethnology, or paleontology, whose members—both professionals and those merely interested—convened, heard lectures, exchanged information, and generally kept abreast of the latest developments in their field. Similar societies were scattered across Britain wherever interest and numbers permitted.[61] Photography amateurs enjoyed none of these benefits, for photography's existence as a discipline was little recognized. It surfaced occasionally at meetings of literary and philosophical societies, where a lecture or practical demonstration on the subject might occupy an evening, but neither the idea nor the practice of photography had more than a diffuse presence in educated society.

The practice of photography in Scotland took its own course quite independent of that in England. Its development was influenced by the distinctive nature of Scottish society, which had a thriving educational

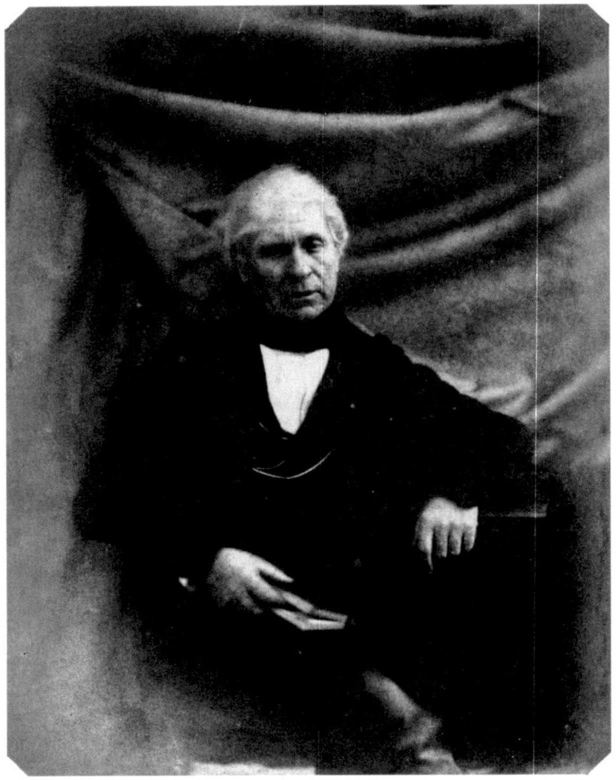

23

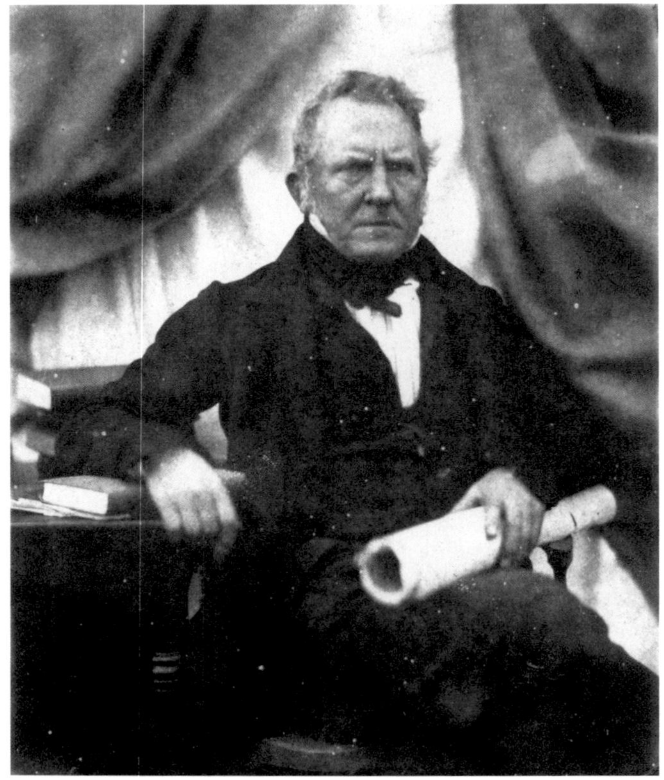

24

Fig. 23. Hugh Lyon Playfair, *Sir David Brewster*, early 1840s. Salted paper print, 19.2 x 14.5 cm (7½ x 5¾ in.). Item 8, vol. 2, Albums of Edinburgh Calotype Club. Edinburgh City Libraries and Information Services

Fig. 24. Unknown photographer, *Hugh Lyon Playfair*, early 1840s. Salted paper print, 17.5 x 14.3 cm (6⅞ x 5⅝ in.) Item 40, vol. 1, Albums of Edinburgh Calotype Club. National Library of Scotland, Edinburgh

Fig. 25. James Francis Montgomery, *George Heriot's Hospital, Edinburgh, North-East Corner of Quadrangle*, early 1840s. Salted paper print, 15.5 x 20.3 cm (6⅛ x 8 in.). Item 21, vol. 2, Albums of Edinburgh Calotype Club. Edinburgh City Libraries and Information Services

Fig. 26. Unknown photographer, *Sailing Vessel at Granton with Steamer in the Background*, early 1840s. Salted paper print, 15.6 x 20.4 cm (6⅛ x 8 in.). Item 105, vol. 2, Albums of Edinburgh Calotype Club. Edinburgh City Libraries and Information Services

Fig. 27. Hugh Lyon Tennant and Robert Tennant, *John Cay, a Member of the Edinburgh Calotype Club, with His Sons Robert and Edward*, early 1840s. Salted paper print, 11 x 14.6 cm (4⅜ x 5¾ in.). Item 14, vol. 1, Albums of Edinburgh Calotype Club. National Library of Scotland, Edinburgh

Fig. 28. Unknown photographer, *Miss M. E. Hunter*, early 1840s. Salted paper print, 14.8 x 18.5 cm (5⅞ x 7¾ in.). Item 64, vol. 2, Albums of Edinburgh Calotype Club. Edinburgh City Libraries and Information Services

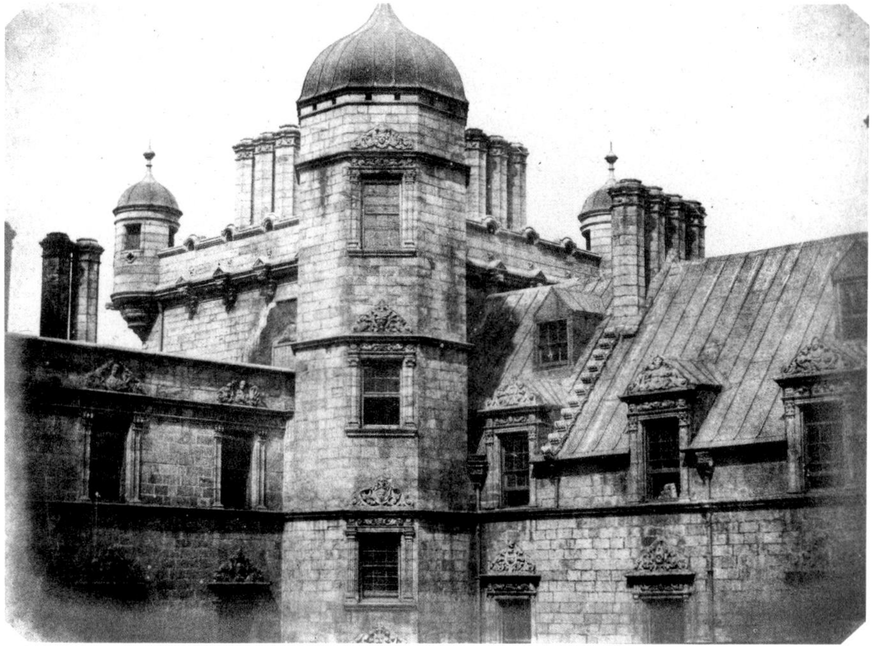

25

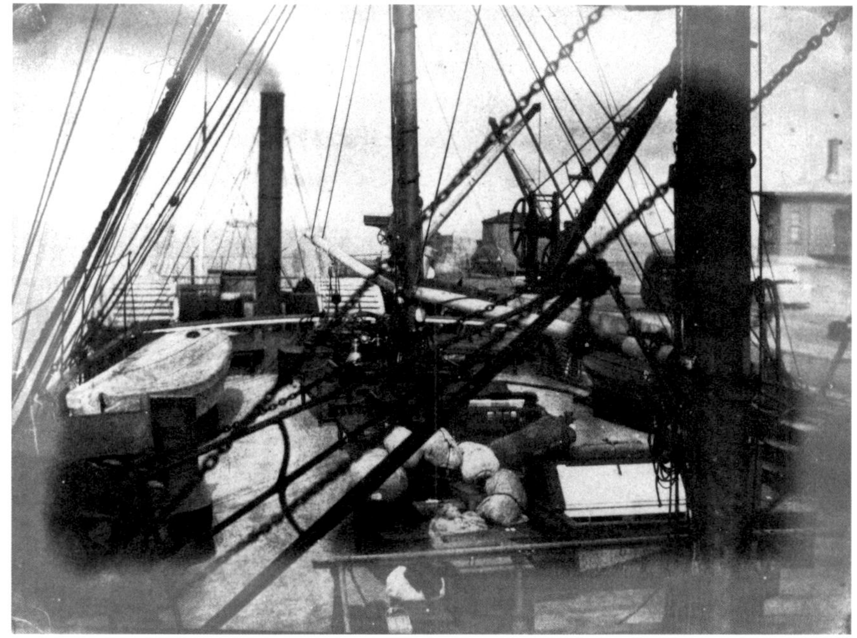

26

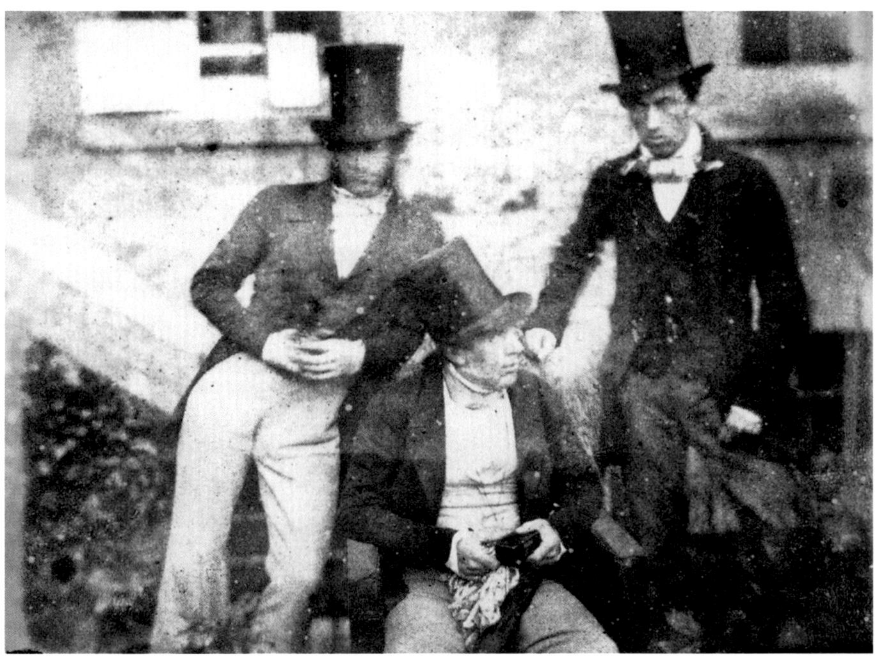

27

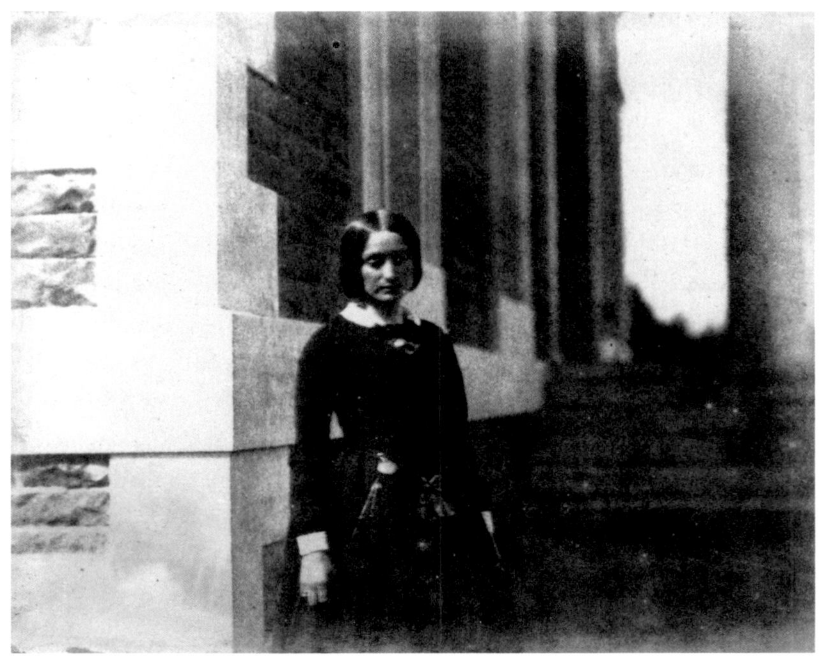

28

system serving a broader cross section of the populace than was the case elsewhere in Britain.[62] A more specific factor was the absence of patent restrictions on the calotype in Scotland. Because separate patent legislations applied in England, Scotland, and Ireland, protection throughout the British Isles could only be obtained by taking out a separate patent in each of the "kingdoms." The complexity and cost of this were nearly prohibitive,[63] and when Talbot filed his patent for the calotype in 1841 he decided against taking a separate patent in Scotland.[64]

Still, freedom from patent issues in Scotland would have affected only commercial exploitation of the process, not its use by amateurs. It was not really the absence of patent restrictions but rather the presence of the eminent physicist Sir David Brewster (fig. 23; pl. 7), an old friend of Talbot's, that kindled Scots' interest in photography. Brewster's active encouragement made the university town of St. Andrews into the "headquarters . . . of the Talbotype" in Scotland.[65] From the outset Brewster had taken a keen interest in Talbot's photographic discoveries and had worked to promote his interests. By the fall of 1841 he had recruited three "disciples" to take up the cause of photography,[66] one of whom, William Holland Furlong, an assistant to the professor of chemistry at the university, in April 1843 proposed a new method for iodizing calotype paper that eliminated many of the problems associated with Talbot's method.[67] When Furlong's paper was read at a meeting of the St. Andrews Literary and Philosophical Society, its significance was fully appreciated by members and not least by Robert Adamson and his brother Dr. John Adamson, both keenly interested in photography.

Just a few weeks later came a momentous event: the signing of the Deed of Demission on May 18, 1843, that established the Free Church of Scotland. The painter David Octavius Hill, who had received a commission to portray the church's founders, at Brewster's suggestion entered into a photographic partnership with Robert Adamson. It is estimated that during their brief and extraordinary collaboration (from July 1843 until Adamson's premature death in January 1848), the two men made several thousand calotype negatives of consistently high technical and aesthetic quality (pls. 7–12), well beyond that of other early photographs.[68]

While best known for portraiture, they took on a range of subject matter—from architectural studies to an enigmatic picture of a diminutive tree at Colinton, some four miles from Edinburgh. *The Fairy Tree* (pl. 9) stands apart from other work of the period for the choice and treatment of its subject. Few photographers would have thought an ordinary tree worthy of their attention; few photographers were confident enough to photograph against the light, knowing it would create a difficult-to-manage contrast in the negative. But here these factors are turned to advantage. The shimmering light transforms the inconsequential limb into an image of startling modernity.

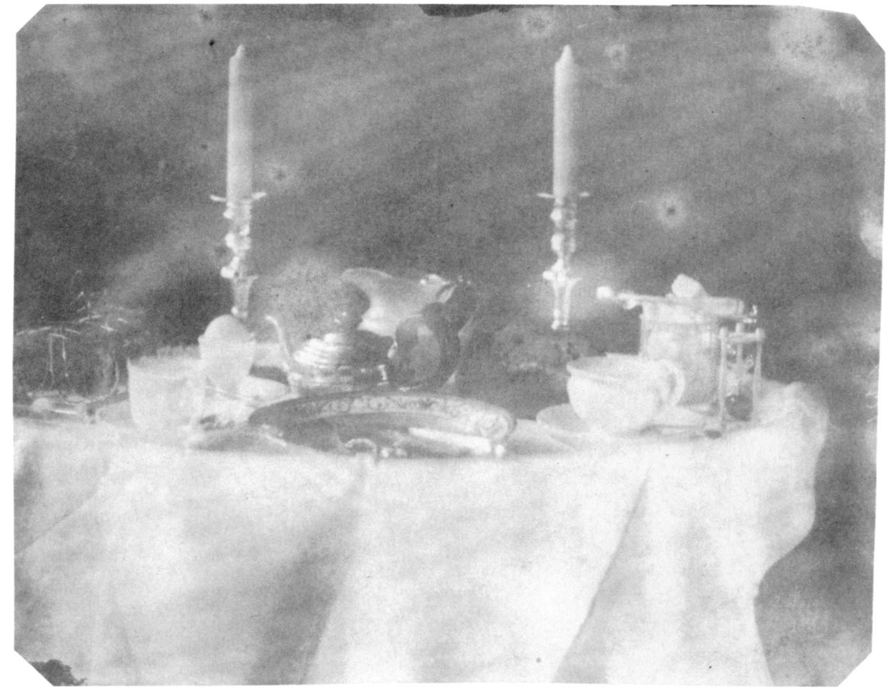

Fig. 29. William Henry Fox Talbot, *"A Breakfast Table," Set with Candlesticks*, March 2, 1840. Salted paper print from photogenic drawing negative, 17.5 x 21.5 cm (6⅞ x 8½ in.). British Library, London, Lacock Abbey Collection, LA 2263/NB6

The energetic example of St. Andrews, where a small group of like-minded individuals came together in the pursuit of their common interest,[69] became a model for Edinburgh. In the early 1840s, possibly as early as 1843, a group of "keen experimentalists" formed the Edinburgh Calotype Club—the first association in Britain specifically for photographers. It was an informal gathering of only a dozen members, with no need for "laws, office bearers, or formalities of any kind."[70] The more than three hundred photographs that survive reveal the membership's overriding interest in architecture, topography, and family portraiture[71] (figs. 23–28).

During the early 1840s there had been no comparable association in London, the nearest equivalent being the Graphic Society, a prestigious assembly of royal academicians who met informally each month at the Thatched House Tavern on St. James Street. Its membership of one hundred was made up exclusively of painters, sculptors, architects, and engravers.[72] In February 1839 they had become the first group of artists in Britain to see examples of photography, and two presentations of Talbot's photogenic drawings followed in 1840. A considerable advance was evident: while in 1839 they had seen smudgy impressions, a year later Talbot's early studies in photographic composition—which included "Various views of Lacock Abbey, the seat of Mr. Talbot; of Bowood; of trees; of old walls and buildings, with implements of husbandry, of carriages; of tables covered with breakfast things; of busts and statues; and, in short, of every matter from a botanical specimen to a fine landscape"—suggested something of the artistic potential of the medium (fig. 29).[73]

In subsequent years photographs may only occasionally have been submitted to the Graphic Society for viewing,[74] but in 1847 examples of both daguerreotypes and calotypes were regularly presented.[75] In 1848 Talbot was elected an "honorary visitor," along with the engineer/inventor Isambard Kingdom Brunel, the mathematician Charles Babbage, and Edward Hawkins, Keeper of Antiquities at the British Museum.[76] Talbot's nomination signaled the respect with which he was by then viewed and demonstrates that photography no longer posed a threat to the artistic community.

At about the same time a portfolio of works taken by the calotype process, which included studies of Dutch towns, rivers, and shipping and a series of architectural views of cathedrals, was submitted to the Graphic Society by Joseph Cundall, a publisher of children's books who had recently been elected a member of the Society of Arts.[77] Cundall belonged to a small gathering of colleagues who called themselves the Calotype Society. A journalist from the *Athenaeum*, invited to one of their early meetings in London, described the "society composed of a dozen gentlemen amateurs associated together for the purpose of pursuing their experiments in this *art-science*" who "keep up a constant communication with each other, detailing their several improvements and discoveries, and interchanging the repetitions of such sun-pictures as each may have produced." As for the pictures themselves, "Many a building subject and many a landscape" vied with "brilliant specimens from the needle of a Rembrandt" in "richness, power and colour."[78] Here at last, in December 1847, eight years after photography was first announced, are beginning signs of an organizational structure, or "center of union," for the medium, with regular meetings, correspondence, and the exchange of prints between members.

It was quite naturally assumed that the Calotype Society's members were "gentlemen amateurs." A gentleman was one "whose education, occupation, or income raises him above menial service or an ordinary trade . . . a man of good breeding, politeness, and civil manners."[79] It is no accident that these gentlemen adopted the calotype process in preference to the daguerreotype. Amateur photographers of the 1840s were responsive to the soft detail and rich tones of the calotype process—which resembled those of drawings and prints—and were intrigued by the artistic potential of the medium. The daguerreotype, on the other hand, thrived in the domain of the commercial portrait studio, where its brilliant charms proved seductive and appealing to a clientele. Daguerreotypists belonged to trade and calotypists to society.

GATHERING MOMENTUM: THE TECHNIQUE EXPANDS

Making a calotype was technically challenging, and at an early stage, amateurs enthralled with the new medium set about devising improvements to Talbot's original, wayward formulation. Some of the enhancements came from individuals with a professional background in chemistry; others were the product of firsthand experience and common sense.[80] One practitioner, George Smith Cundell, summarized the feelings of many in his 1844 essay on the calotype:

> *Had Mr. Talbot thought fit to publish directions for the details and refinements of his process, as minute and explicit as those given by M. Daguerre, his invention, it is probable, would now have stood in a very different position . . . I hope I may without impropriety do that which he has omitted to do, by furnishing plain directions, from my own experience, by which calotype pictures* may *be produced, without much difficulty and with tolerable certainty and success.*[81]

What followed was the first practical set of instructions for making a calotype to be published in Britain. Systematic and straightforward, they were quite unlike Talbot's vaguer descriptions. Crucially, Cundell pointed out that Talbot's solution of "gallo-nitrate of silver" was "unnecessarily strong, and unless skillfully handled . . . apt to stain or embrown the paper," and recommended diluting it with an equal volume of water.[82] The publication of Cundell's treatise proved to be a turning point for the practice of the calotype, giving "the fresh stimulus that was needed."[83]

Whatever the responsible factors were beyond Cundell's essay, the second half of the 1840s saw manufacturing chemists, opticians, and makers of philosophical (i.e., scientific) instruments turning their attention toward the field of photographic manufacturing. Many of these were old, well-respected businesses with enviable reputations. Encouraged by the free trade environment and this new commercial opportunity, they extended the range of their goods to include photographic chemicals, papers, cameras, lenses, and the assorted paraphernalia of early photography. Advertisements appeared in leading periodicals in growing numbers; manufacturers published illustrated catalogues and price lists detailing a full range of products; and, most significantly, some manufacturers commissioned handbooks and instruction manuals to help the novice deal with the myriad complexities of the process. Thomas and Richard Willats, an important optical firm, in 1845 issued the first of a long line of Scientific Manuals, *Plain Directions for Obtaining Photographic Pictures*, in which a debt to Cundell for his "many practical suggestions" was acknowledged.[84] The firm of Horne, Thornthwaite, and Wood, manufacturer of high-quality philosophical instruments, moved into the field of photography and named one of its calotype cameras after Cundell.[85]

These various types of activity continued to expand throughout the late 1840s, and although London remained the center, manufacturers applied themselves with equal enthusiasm in such cities as Birmingham, Cardiff, Edinburgh, Glasgow, Manchester, and Sheffield. Nor were these developments confined to Britain.

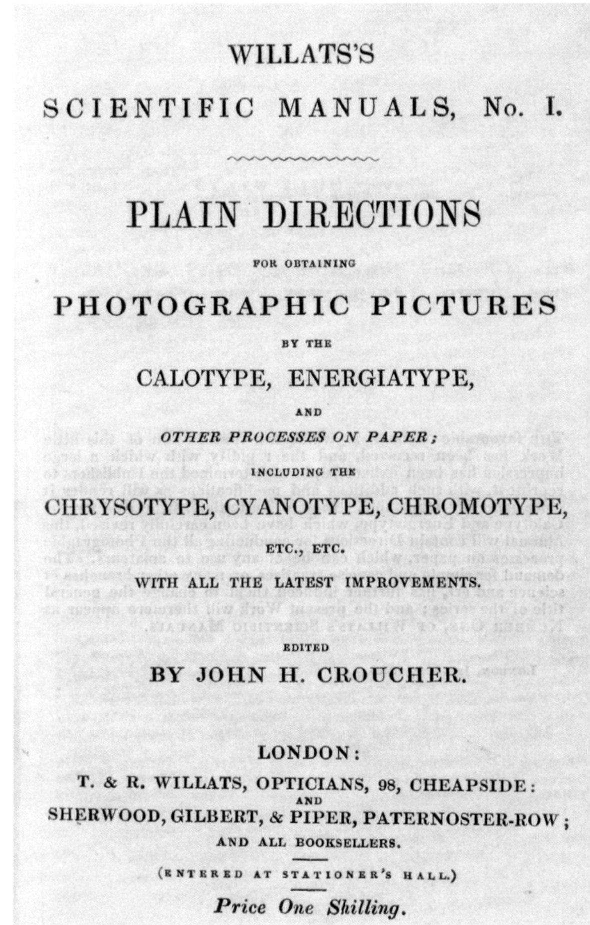

WILLATS'S

SCIENTIFIC MANUALS, No. I.

PLAIN DIRECTIONS

FOR OBTAINING

PHOTOGRAPHIC PICTURES

BY THE

CALOTYPE, ENERGIATYPE,

AND

OTHER PROCESSES ON PAPER;

INCLUDING THE

CHRYSOTYPE, CYANOTYPE, CHROMOTYPE,

ETC., ETC.

WITH ALL THE LATEST IMPROVEMENTS.

EDITED

BY JOHN H. CROUCHER.

LONDON:

T. & R. WILLATS, OPTICIANS, 98, CHEAPSIDE:

AND

SHERWOOD, GILBERT, & PIPER, PATERNOSTER-ROW;

AND ALL BOOKSELLERS.

(ENTERED AT STATIONER'S HALL.)

Price One Shilling.

Fig. 30. *Plain Directions for Obtaining Photographic Pictures by the Calotype, Energiatype, and Other Processes on Paper*, ed. John H. Croucher, Willats's Scientific Manuals, no. 1 (London, 1845). Title page, 17.5 x 10.3 cm (6 ⅞ x 4 in.). Gernsheim Collection, Harry Ransom Humanities Research Center, University of Texas at Austin

THE ROLE OF FRENCH PHOTOGRAPHERS

Talbot had patented his calotype process in France, home of the daguerreotype, in 1841, and had made attempts to establish it in Paris; however, the French remained largely uninterested, and his name was little associated with the process. Only in the late 1840s did what was called "photography on paper" begin to find favor in France. This was principally due to the efforts of Louis-Désiré Blanquart-Evrard, a cloth merchant and amateur photographer from Lille, who published his *Procédés employés pour obtenir les épreuves de photographie sur papier* in 1847.[86] The first detailed discussion of calotype to appear in French, it was warmly received. Although his method closely mirrored Talbot's, Blanquart-Evrard claimed the process as his own and did not acknowledge the accomplishments of any precursor. This omission became the basis of contention between British and French photographers that would last until the early 1850s.[87]

Two other French photographers suggested additional modifications that profoundly affected the future direction of calotype photography. The first proposal came from Dr. Guillot-Saguez, an amateur photographer and doctor of medicine at the Faculté de Paris, who in late 1847 published his *Méthode théorique et pratique de photographie sur papier.*[88] Rather than using silver nitrate in the first stage of the process as Talbot did, Guillot-Saguez employed a strong solution of aceto-nitrate of silver in the second, "exciting" stage, so that iodizing—the formation of silver iodide—occurred then. This radical approach simplified the underlying chemistry and offered far greater control than had been possible previously.

Guillot-Saguez's improvements paved the way for the final significant adaptation in the evolution of the calotype process. That was Gustave Le Gray's waxed-paper process, which—although invented in 1851, slightly later than the period covered in this chapter—is best introduced here.[89] An artist and committed practitioner, Le Gray was one of the most eminent photographers to emerge in France at this time.[90] At his premises in Paris, which became known as a "university" for photography, Le Gray taught photography, experimented with its chemistry, and published a number of treatises. In the most important of these, *Nouveau Traité théorique et pratique de photographie sur papier et sur verre* of 1851,[91] he described his innovative use of pre-waxed paper for making negatives. While Talbot's process used for the substrate a sheet of plain paper (which after exposure and development could either be waxed or left plain), Le Gray waxed the paper *before* the application of any chemicals.[92] The lightweight Canson and Lacroix papers preferred by French photographers lacked gelatin sizing and thus were difficult to handle and vulnerable to tearing when saturated. Impregnating the paper with wax strengthened the fibers and allowed them to be immersed in the chemicals for prolonged periods. The thin waxed-paper negative yielded an image of markedly enhanced sharpness and resolution, making Le Gray's process an elegant refinement of the traditional calotype process.

The first English account of the waxed-paper process, a translation of Le Gray's treatise, was published in 1851 in a new volume of Willats's Scientific Manuals (fig. 30).[93] The following year Roger Fenton published a description of the process as adapted for use with English materials, based on his own experience.[94] His essay spearheaded the transfer of Le Gray's process into British photographic practice, where it was taken up with enthusiasm and widely used for well over a decade—especially in hot climates like India's, where its tolerance to extreme temperatures made it the process of choice.

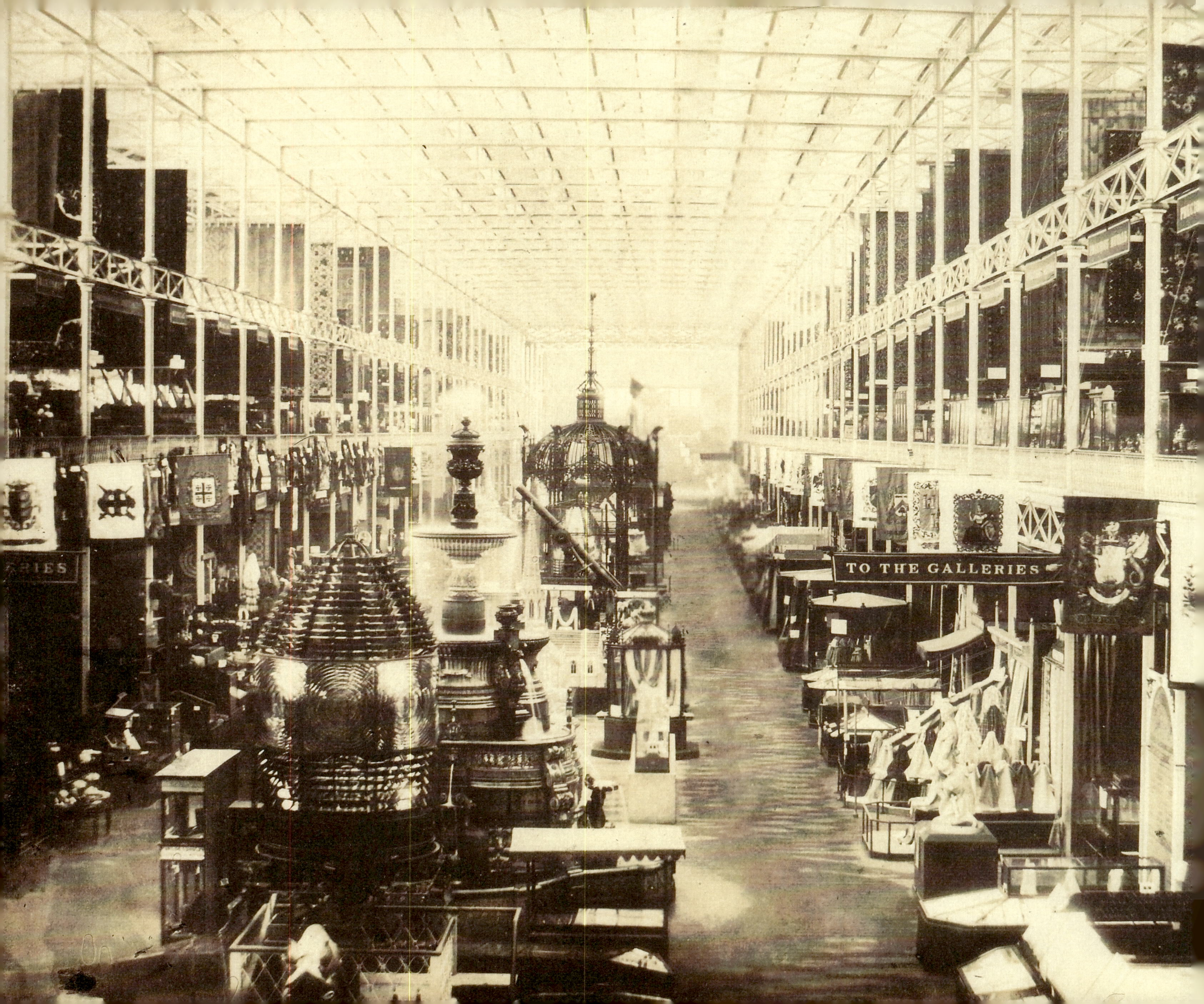
TO THE GALLERIES

3. The Great Exhibition of 1851

> *The Exposition of 1851—the great experiment of modern times, at first an idea, at last a reality—now stands before us, gigantic and sublime, commanding the admiration, and challenging the criticism of the civilized world. Commingling its crystal canopy with the azure vault which surrounds it, and stretching its magic corridors beyond our visual range, we are at once startled by its colossal magnitude, and enchanted with its fairy trellis work. In its moral and political, more than in its physical aspect, it is instinct with deep instruction. . . . Thus has the Palace of the Arts become a cosmopolitan gymnasium for the instruction of the world.*[1]

This wonderfully emotional passage appeared in the *North British Review*, a sober nineteenth-century periodical not usually given to flights of rhetoric or awestruck effusions. Despite the elevated language, it probably encapsulates as well as any published response the sentiments of the many thousands who visited the Great Exhibition.

THE GREAT MEETING PLACE

In every major survey of the nineteenth century, 1851 stands as the decisive turning point for British society in cultural, economic, scientific, and artistic realms. Unlike the 1840s, the decade of the 1850s began optimistically, a major component being newfound confidence built on the notable success of the Great Exhibition. A collective feeling of goodwill transcended social and economic boundaries—a phenomenon rare in the history of the nation. The exhibition was a palace for the people, to which all and sundry came, traveling, sometimes at great cost, from the farthest corners of the kingdom. Thomas Cook offered special excursion trains. Outings for employees were organized by benevolent industrialists. Special days were set aside when the cost of admission was reduced to a shilling so that all but the very poorest had the opportunity to visit (fig. 32).

The idea of holding national exhibitions was not new.[2] In France they had occurred since 1798. In the spring of 1849, the eleventh National Exposition of the Products of Industry, Agriculture, and Manufacture had opened in Paris in a specially built Palace of Industry on the Champs Élysées. By far the largest and most significant of exhibitions until that date, with almost 4,500 exhibitors, it had been substantially funded with some 750,000 francs by the French government, in the hope that it would contribute to restoring a sense of national equilibrium after the grievous events of 1848. The expectation proved correct, and huge crowds drawn from all ranks of society had attended for the duration of the six-month exhibition. Samuel Carter Hall, by

Opposite: Fig. 31. Claude-Marie Ferrier, *View of Western Nave* (of the Great Exhibition), 1851, detail. Salted paper print from glass negative, 16 x 21.9 cm (6¼ x 8⅝ in.). From *Reports by the Juries* 1852, vol. 4, frontispiece. Promised gift to the Art Gallery of Ontario, Toronto, from Archive of Modern Conflict, London © Art Gallery of Ontario

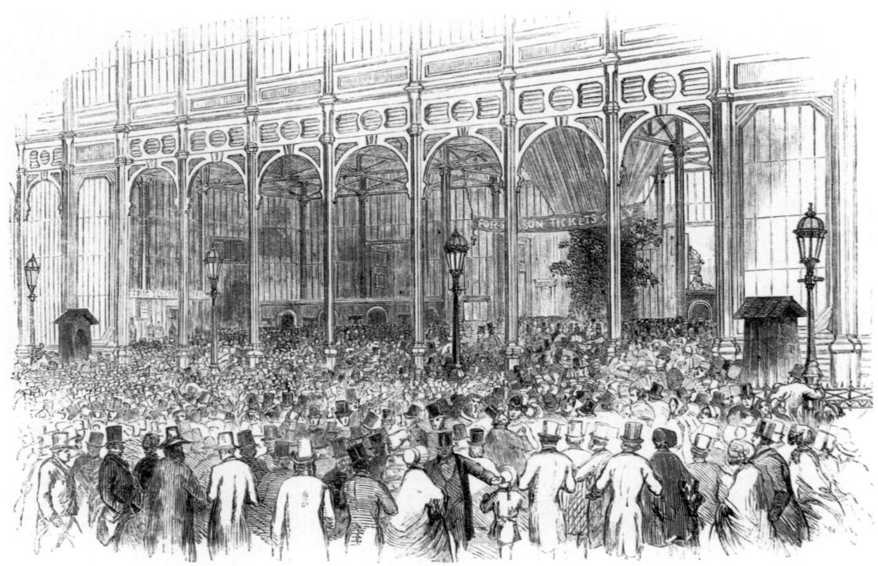

Fig. 32. Unknown artist, *The Shilling Day—Exterior of the Exhibition.* Wood engraving, 15.5 x 23.5 cm (6⅛ x 9¼ in.). From *Illustrated London News*, July 19, 1851, p. 100. Private collection

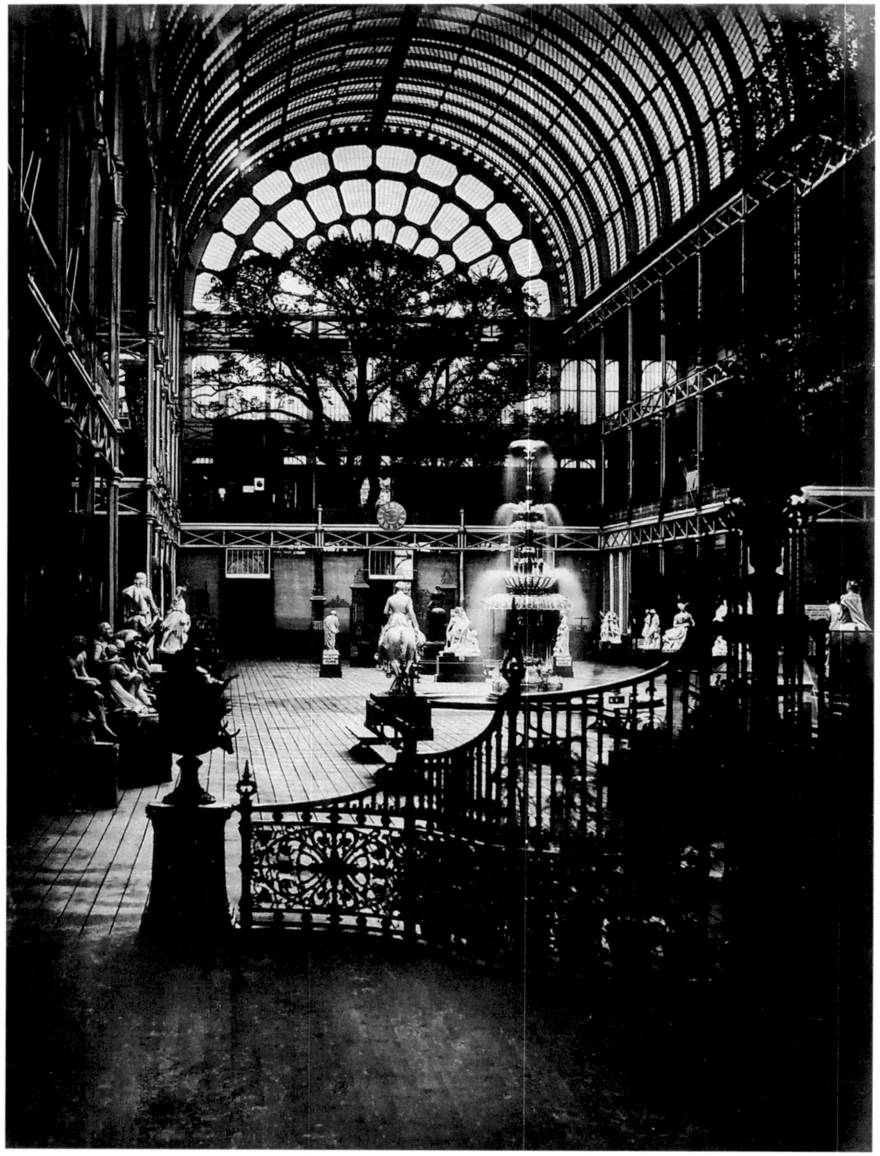

Fig. 33. Claude-Marie Ferrier, *View of Transept Looking South*, 1851. Salted paper print from glass negative, 16.1 x 21.3 cm (6⅜ x 8⅜ in.) From *Reports by the Juries* 1852, vol. 2, facing p. 763. Promised gift to the Art Gallery of Ontario, Toronto, from Archive of Modern Conflict, London © Art Gallery of Ontario

then editor of the *Art-Journal*, suggested that Britain follow the French example and mount its own industrial exhibition in support of the arts, manufacturing, and industry as a whole.[3]

In fact, at a meeting held at Buckingham Palace on June 30, 1849, Prince Albert, president of the Society of Arts, and other interested parties had already launched a scheme for the Great Exhibition.[4] In the months that followed, plans gradually took shape under the vigilant eye of the prince. Representatives visited the manufacturing districts to gather support for the undertaking,[5] and, with the project growing in scale and significance, its management was assigned to a Royal Commission, formally established in January 1850.[6]

But anxieties remained about the wisdom of such an undertaking. British manufacturers were particularly concerned that foreign competitors might steal ideas and plagiarize designs at a time when the domestic market was just starting to emerge from the economic depression of the late 1840s.[7] Others feared that the exhibition would be a magnet to all manner of Continental revolutionaries and malcontents bent on stirring up mischief.[8] The Duke of Wellington had a phobia about the dangers associated with crowds and recommended the use of fifteen thousand men to keep order. Some worried about a risk to public health and the spread of contagious diseases, or even claimed that the exhibition would erode the very structure of British society through the intermingling of the classes.[9] These anxieties were loudly voiced by factions of the press looking to embarrass the administration; however, the disclosure that the entire exhibition would be underwritten by a mixture of subscriptions and guarantees by private individuals to cover any losses, with not a penny coming from government funds, gradually undercut these objections.

The publication of the architect Joseph Paxton's design for the exhibition building—which was soon universally known as the Crystal Palace—did much to capture the public's imagination and win converts to this national cause.[10] Paxton's radical approach, calling for construction entirely of glass and steel, imparted a lightness and grace never before seen in a building of this scale (fig. 33). The structure was vast. Built of prefabricated and standardized components, it displayed none of the Gothic conceits prevalent in many buildings of the period but instead a clean and purposeful outline perfectly in keeping with its function. Charles Dickens described with insight the modernity of Paxton's construction techniques.

His walls and foundations are not simply walls and foundations, but ventilators and drains as well. His roofs are not simply roofs; but, besides being the most extensive of known sky-lights, are light and heat adjusters. His sash-bars do not only hold the glass together, but are self-supporting, and his rafters form perfect drains for both sides of the glass,—for draining off internal, as well as external moisture, whilst the tops of the girders are conduits also. His floors are dust-traps, and aid in ventilation. Lastly, his whole building is, while in course of construction, its own scaffolding. Thus he saves time as well as money.[11]

Londoners watched in wonder as the building gradually rose among the stately elms of Hyde Park. With about two thousand laborers employed on site, it was a spectacle alive with human activity.[12] In constructing the roof, some workers used pulleys, winches, and horsepower to raise the girders, while others, seated on specially designed trolleys and rolling backward, placed sheets of glass into the framework of the huge span. Pronounced by the *Times* "the largest building ever made by human hands, without mortar, brick, or stone," it seemed to be entirely of glass (fig. 34).[13]

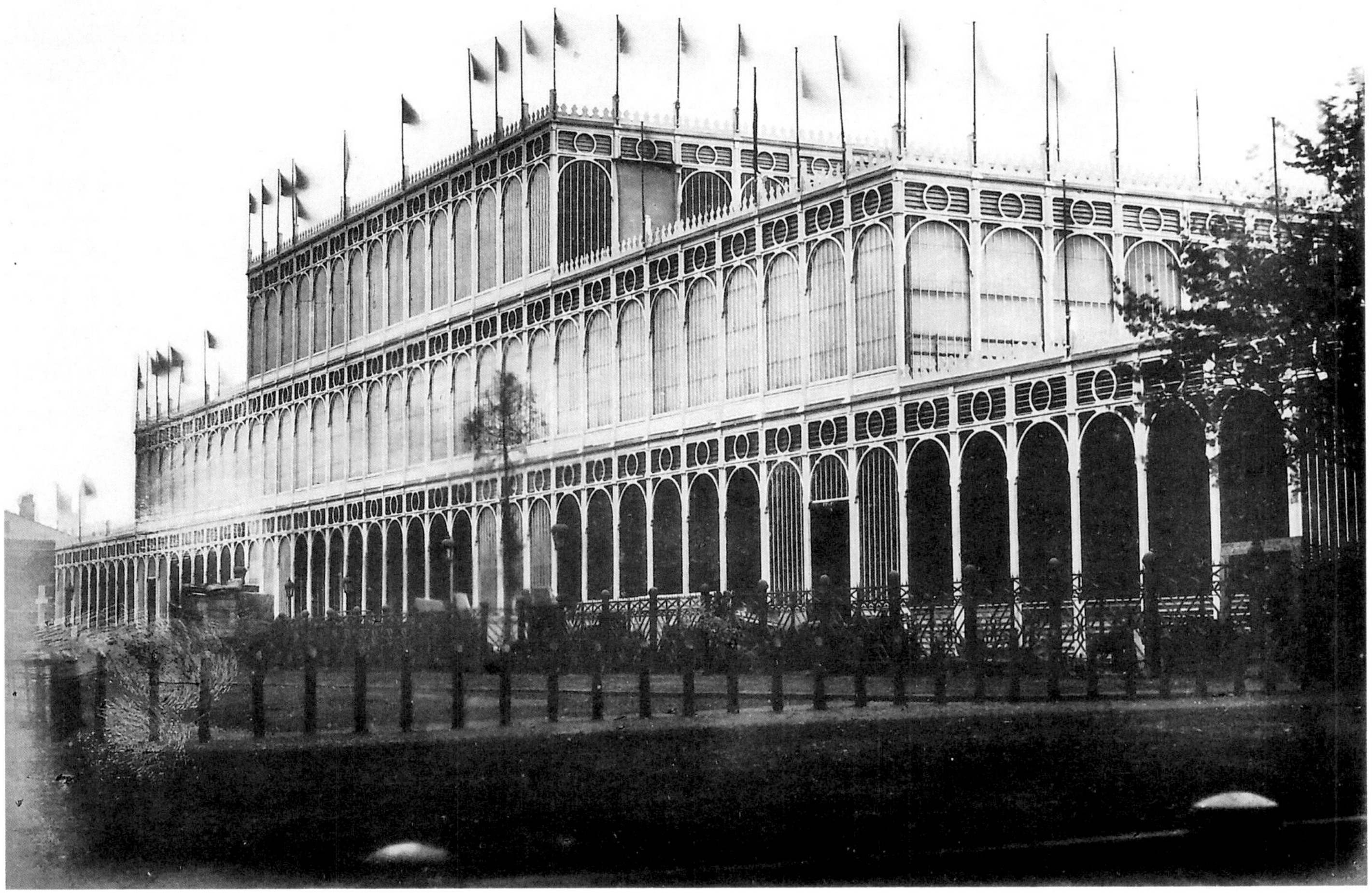

Fig. 34. Claude-Marie Ferrier, *View of East End of the Building*, 1851. Salted paper print from glass negative, 16.1 x 21.3 cm (6⅜ x 8⅜ in.) From *Reports by the Juries* 1852, vol. 2, facing p. 819. Promised gift to the Art Gallery of Ontario, Toronto, from Archive of Modern Conflict, London © Art Gallery of Ontario

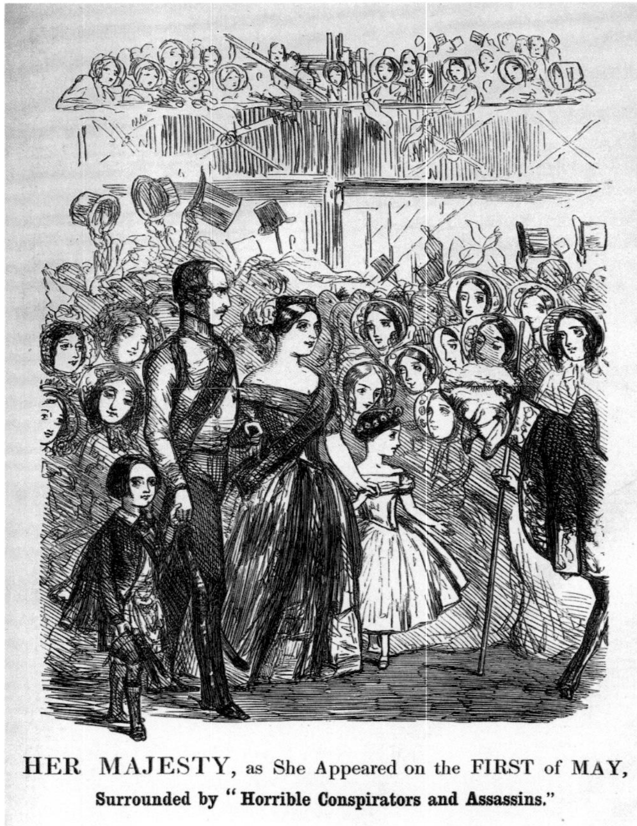

Fig. 35. John Leech, *Her Majesty, as She Appeared on the First of May.* Wood engraving, 24.9 x 19 cm (9¾ x 7½ in.). From *Punch,* May 17, 1851, p. 193. Private collection

The day before the official opening, William Henry Fox Talbot made his way to the site, where, peering through a window, he could see the building's interior along its entire length and marvel at the beauty of the diminishing perspective. Meanwhile, all around him was "a chaotic confusion of packing cases straw and trampled mud" with "crowds of people asking unnecessary questions of impatient policemen." Elsewhere on the site he encountered "foreigners jabbering broken English, goodnatured Englishmen trying to interpret for them, but failing to understand."[14] Contractors, exhibitors, and organizers were rushing to complete their displays, and everything must have seemed disordered and shambolic; but in fact, for months, teams of men had been diligently calculating every tiny detail of the building works, interior decoration, receipt of goods, and allocation of space. A plan was even worked out to deal with troublesome sparrows that had begun roosting throughout the building.[15] With the detailed, almost obsessive precision that characterized everything carried out by Prince Albert, nothing had been left to chance.

The opening ceremony was performed on May 1, 1851, by Queen Victoria, surrounded by her family, court, and ministers, by representatives of other countries, and by the principal managers of the undertaking; it was witnessed by a crowd of twenty-five thousand (fig. 35). Some saw the awe-inspiring ceremony as another, more splendid coronation of their sovereign; others, when Handel's "Hallelujah Chorus" burst out from a choir of six hundred accompanied by mighty organ and orchestra, were reminded of the day they would stand before the throne of their Maker.[16] Talbot, among those taking in the spectacle, felt keenly that he was witnessing history in the making.[17]

The next day and many thereafter, a spellbound nation devoured newspaper articles about the exhibition: its splendor, its significance, its substance in detail. Everything was counted, measured, or calculated. There had been 293,655 panes of glass installed in the building, and 2,147 men employed on site during the last week of construction. Almost 7,000 exhibitors were allocated space to display their goods; 6,039,195 visitors paid admission, making the daily average 42,831 visitors. In the final week, no fewer than 93,224 individuals were reckoned to be in attendance at the same time, a world record for the number of people assembled within a roofed building. Even the food consumed was accounted for: 934,691 bath buns, 28,046 sausage rolls, and 1,092,357 bottles of Schweppes cordials were sold during the 141 days of operation.[18] If nothing else, the Great Exhibition confirmed what had long been suspected but never before established: that such a thing as a mass market existed, whether it was for sheets of glass, sausage rolls, or railway excursion tickets to London (fig. 38).

But the statisticians were defeated when faced with the sheer scale and diversity of the exhibits on display. According to one estimate more than a million things were exhibited, which ranged from single objects to complex arrays of porcelain, cutlery, and the like; true computation proved impossible (figs. 36, 37). Exhibitors were asked instead to calculate the gross value of their goods, and, although only approximations, their results were revealing. Together, British displays were valued at well over 1,000,000 pounds, with "philosophical instruments"—which

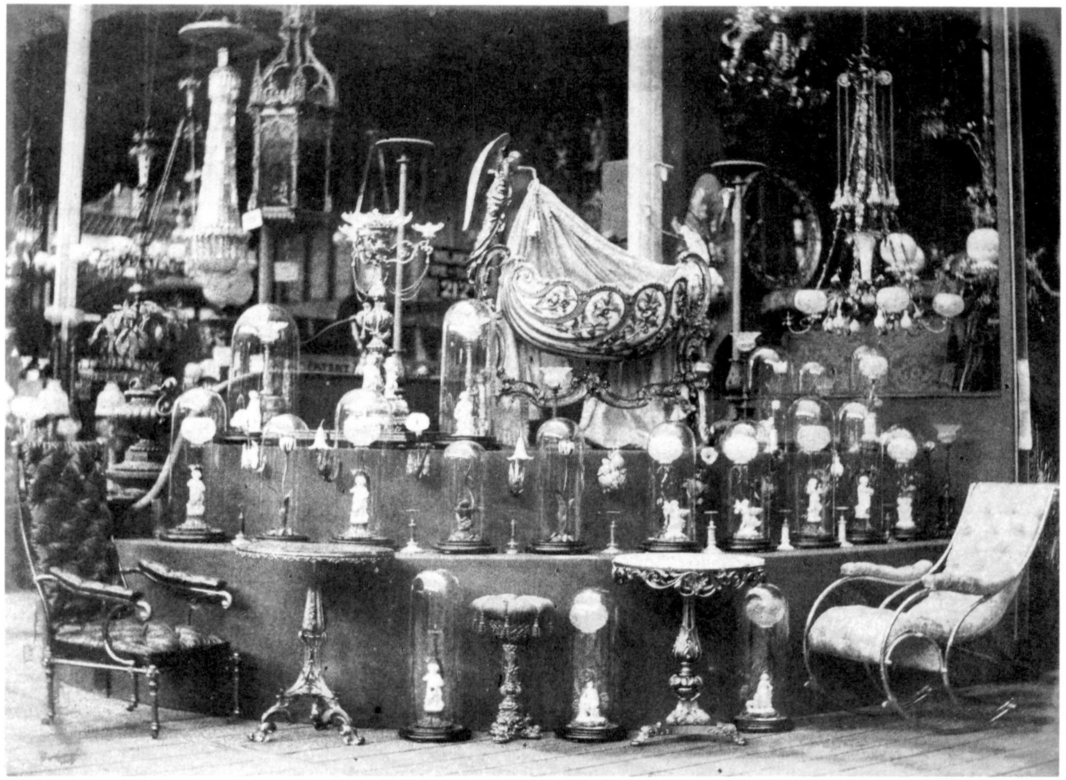

Fig. 36. Hugh Owen, *Metal Work, Lamps, &c,* 1851. Salted paper print, 17.3 x 22.2 cm (6⅞ x 8¾ in.). From *Reports by the Juries* 1852, vol. 3, following p. 1106. Promised gift to the Art Gallery of Ontario, Toronto, from Archive of Modern Conflict, London © Art Gallery of Ontario

Fig. 37. Unknown artist, *Bay of the Fine Art Court.* Wood engraving, 15.2 x 23.5 cm (6 x 9¼ in.). From *Illustrated London News,* July 5, 1851, p. 20. Private collection

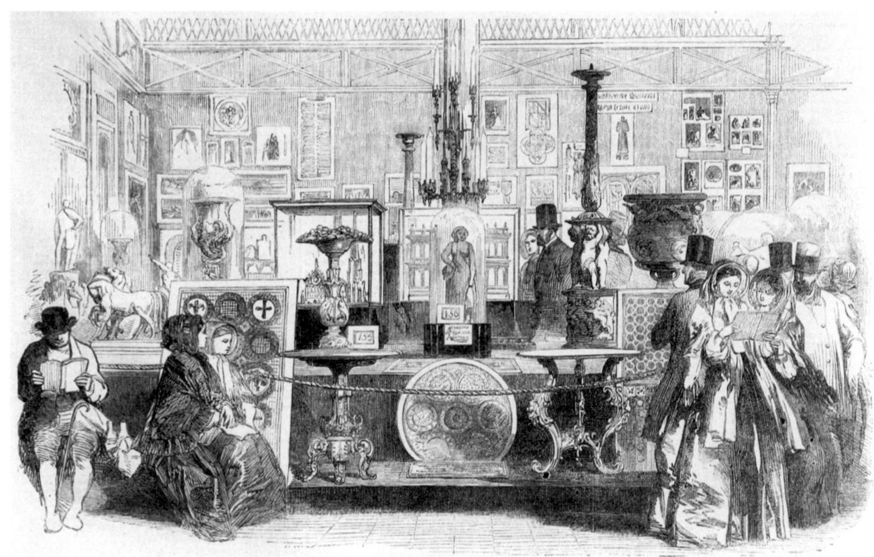

BAY OF THE FINE ART COURT.

included cameras, lenses, and photographic apparatus—having a collective worth of 64,000 pounds (making this the third-most-valuable group).[19] If monetary value can be regarded as a useful index of cultural hierarchy, then what we now call scientific instruments ranked high in mid-Victorian Britain. Photography was becoming an increasingly significant element in this category.

PHOTOGRAPHY COMPETES AT THE EXHIBITION

From the outset of the planning process, the royal commissioners had created a classification system intended to present an explicit rationale for the exhibition and impose a coherent structure on the whole. Thirty classes of object were grouped under four broad headings: Raw Materials, Machinery, Manufactures, and Fine Arts.[20] The British exhibits were all displayed according to this system of classification. Exhibits from foreign countries and British colonies, however, were grouped only according to country and without regard for classification.[21] The category of Fine Arts stood apart as something of an

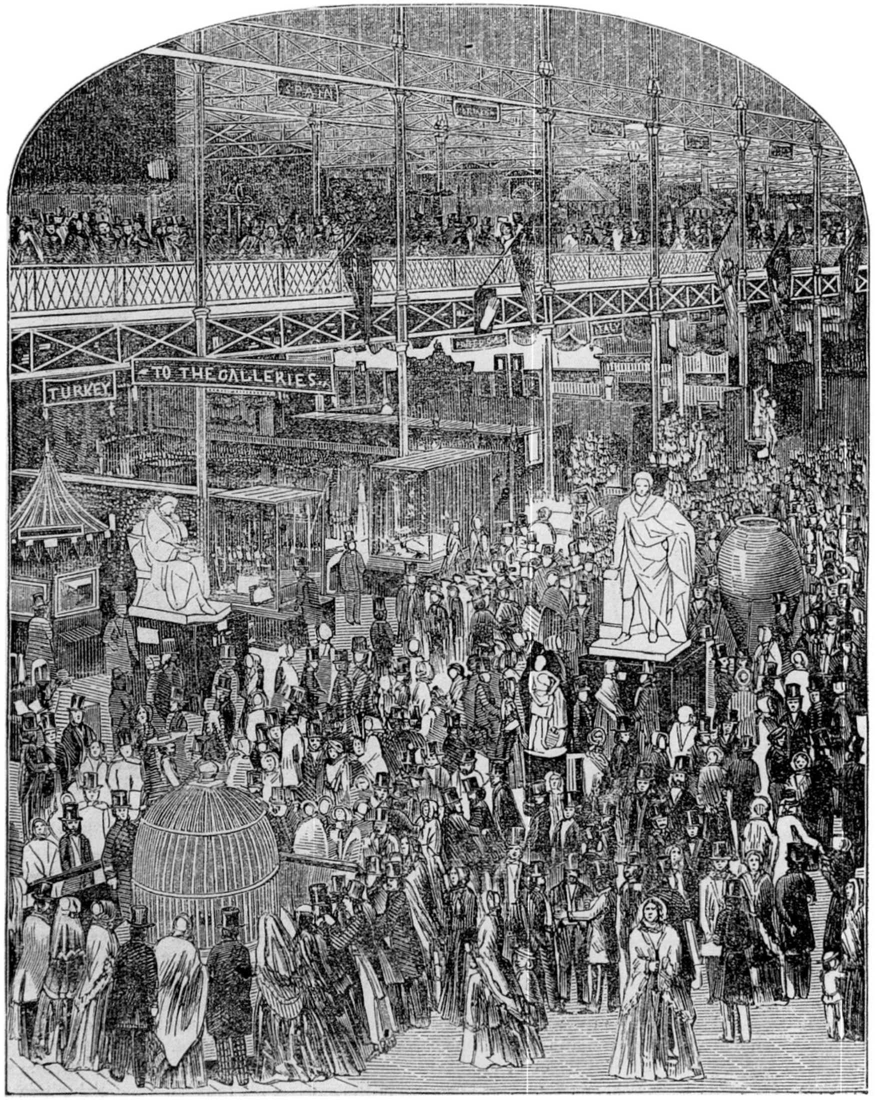

Fig. 38. Unknown artist, *The Great Exhibition on a Busy Day*. Engraving, from a photograph by Emilian Fehrenbach, 16.2 x 12.3 cm (6⅜ x 4⅞ in.). From *Illustrated Exhibitor*, November 1, 1851, p. 393. Private collection

anomaly, with many contradictions in the way the term was applied. For one thing, it constituted a broad grouping but was also, for judging purposes, regarded as a distinct "class," Class 30. Another peculiarity was that sculpture (by living artists) was admitted, but the work of painters and engravers was not. The commissioners later explained that for the exhibition of paintings there were an "abundance of opportunities" elsewhere and that they had feared paintings would be submitted in "such numbers as would have been inconsistent with [the] industrial character" of the exhibition. In keeping with the fundamental purpose of the undertaking, only examples of work that illustrated innovative processes, techniques, and materials were officially admissible.[22] But in truth this category became the repository for many exhibits only distantly associated with art, from specimens of color printing, chromolithography, and fresco painting to samples of penmanship and eggshells perforated to resemble Dresden china.[23]

In such a context, the categorization of photography proved troublesome. Its relative immaturity and the variety of its applications worked against ready classification. In the end, the commissioners admitted photographs as exhibits in two distinct classes. As part of Class 30, Fine Arts, the photographs were presumably meant to illustrate a new process—although this criterion was never strictly applied, and a significant number of photographers exhibited in this class without claiming any originality of process. Photographs were also admitted under Class 10, Philosophical Instruments and Processes Depending Upon Their Use, alongside the cameras, lenses, and equipment that had been used to make them. Here, at least, the rationale was unambiguous.

Further problems were posed for photography by the method of selecting exhibits prescribed for the entire exhibition. Responsibility for selection (as well as for fund-raising and other matters) had been assigned to local committees throughout Britain, on the assumption that local dignitaries and manufacturers would best understand and represent their regional interests.[24] Anyone wishing to exhibit had to pass before the regional committee, which decided whether the work was worthy of inclusion—all well and good for a manufacturer of machinery, steam engines, or cutlery seen as contributing to the level of employment or the local economy, but less satisfactory for a solitary photographer whose calotypic renderings had little to do with local commercial interests.[25] Only if a photographer came from a region not dominated by industry and manufacturing might his work stand a reasonable chance of being accepted. This was the case with three amateur calotypists, Samuel Buckle, Thomas Craddock, and Henry Robert Harmer, all of whom lived in rural East Anglia, where agriculture, brewing, and fishing were mainstays of the economy. Although they were relatively unknown, their work nevertheless found favor with the local committee and was sent to London.[26] But many were not so lucky, and there was much room for misunderstanding. Indeed, Talbot seems not even to have sought the advice of his local committee, believing he could not exhibit his work because the exhibition was intended as a showcase for "manufacturers or shopkeepers" rather than individuals like himself.[27]

While foreign countries had selection committees that also took regional concerns into account, they set local considerations within the wider context of national interests.[28] And while British exhibits were grouped throughout the building according to the classification system, it was found impractical to organize foreign exhibits in the same way. Benefiting from this greater freedom, the national exhibits were arranged for effect rather than taxonomy, and this, above all, gave them a coherence sadly lacking in the British displays. As an American visitor described them,

> *Each Nation's Department is furnished with floor room, elevated platforms, pyramidal shelves, counters, tables, glass cases resting against the walls, and whatever else is necessary for the reception and display of any thing and every thing that the world could bring together as the results of labor, skill, taste and science. And the spaces allotted are all occupied. . . . Some of the best daguerreotypes ever seen, are in the American Department—particularly the likeness of some Vermont young ladies, and of several American Statesmen.*[29]

Overall, the entire exhibition and its building were so vast and the exhibits so numerous that there was simply too much for the average visitor to see (fig. 31). It took Queen Victoria thirty-five visits to work her way through, and for most people this was impractical.[30] All manner of handbooks were published to guide the hapless visitor through the building while taking in the most significant exhibits; one recommended setting aside four days to complete the task, each day still filled with a bewildering quantity of detail.[31] The authorized guide was a broad overview called *Hunt's Hand-Book to the Official Catalogues* by Robert Hunt, a well-respected writer on science and photography.[32]

According to Hunt, there were seven hundred photographs displayed at the Great Exhibition; although the number may sound substantial, the works were neither well promoted nor gathered together for easy viewing. To the vast majority of visitors who passed through the exhibition, photography must have appeared an insignificant player on the world stage of industry, manufacture, and applied arts. Competing attractions included, for instance, the fabled Koh-i-noor, then a recent addition to the crown jewels. Most visitors headed for the diamond rather than the daguerreotypes.

In all, Britain fielded twenty-two photographic exhibitors.[33] Exactly half of them were calotypists: Robert Jefferson Bingham, Samuel Buckle, William Collie, R. & L. Colls, William Constable, Thomas Craddock, Robert Field & Son, Henry Robert Harmer, Henneman & Malone, David Octavius Hill & Robert Adamson, and Hugh Owen. (The others either exhibited photographic equipment and lenses or showed photographs made by other processes: daguerreotype or albumen on glass.)[34] With one or two notable exceptions, few of these calotypists are familiar today. As far as the history of the medium is concerned, the Great Exhibition turned out to be something of a missed opportunity for British photographers.

France, on the other hand, exhibited work by some of its foremost photographers: Hippolyte Bayard, Louis-Désiré Blanquart-Evrard, Frédéric Flacheron, Gustave Le Gray, and Henri Le Secq. With their works of high quality, presented in unified displays, these eminent calotypists had stolen a march on British photography. This was a particularly bitter pill to swallow because of Blanquart-Evrard's 1847 claim to have invented the calotype process, an assertion that resurfaced among the French photographic exhibits.[35] By 1851, Blanquart-Evrard's method had become so widely accepted by French practitioners that for him not to have invented the process seemed unthinkable to them.

Hunt, a man extremely knowledgeable about Britain's contribution to photography, believed there was real mischief afoot among the French displays. As a loyal supporter of Talbot he felt he had to challenge these false claims and in his *Hand-Book* departed from his otherwise general approach to write specifically about photography. But, anxious to avoid direct confrontation, he tackled the subject obliquely, noting that one nation "in its desire of extending its fame, [had] forgotten what was commenced before it entered the field."[36] After offering a full and balanced account of the early history of photography on both sides of the Channel, he concluded with the reminder "that photography on paper, in all its varieties, was not only invented but perfected in England."[37]

As Talbot put it in his correspondence, "The French have shown a fixed determination to claim for themselves the invention of photography on

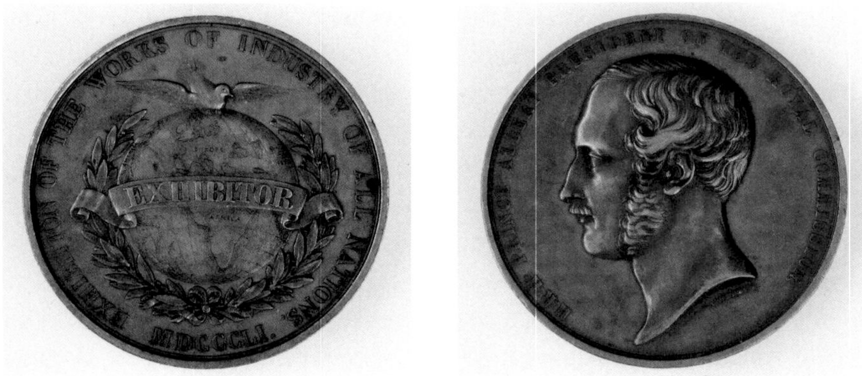

Fig. 39. William Wyon, *Exhibitor's Medal*, recto and verso, 1851. Bronze, diam. 4.4 cm (1¾ in.). Private collection

paper, although purely of English origin from first to last."[38] The situation was not made easier by the French press, large sections of which steadfastly refused to acknowledge Talbot's precedence and occasionally substituted "heliograph" for the term "Talbotype" used in official jury reports.[39] The expression "daguerreotype sur papier" was also employed in France. Talbot dryly remarked, "The English certainly adopted the word Daguerreotype most cheerfully & gave the French inventor every credit, but there is no reciprocity on the other side of the Channel."[40]

The French advantage proved particularly painful for British photographers when the time came for prizes to be awarded. From the very outset the royal commissioners had believed that the exhibition should be competitive, with exhibits from the entire range of nations being judged on their individual merits. Juries for each of the thirty classes were made up of eminent specialists and contained representatives from all the major nations involved. Their task was herculean; collectively they had to inspect the displays of seven thousand exhibitors and examine close to a million items.[41] Beginning work on May 12, they toiled solidly through the duration of the exhibition and announced their decisions only after it closed in October.[42] The two principal types of award were a council medal for work of the highest rank and a prize medal for work of outstanding excellence; additionally, an honorable mention was awarded to exhibitors demonstrating special merit. Altogether, 171 council medals, 2,954 prize medals, and 2,123 honorable mentions were distributed, and every exhibitor was given a bronze medal bearing a portrait of Prince Albert, president of the Royal Commission (fig. 39).[43]

The jury for Class 10, Philosophical Instruments and Processes Depending Upon Their Use, was made up of fifteen authorities from Britain, America, and Europe and chaired by the distinguished scientist Sir David Brewster. This class encompassed an astounding array of instruments, including those used in astronomy, surveying, weighing and measuring, telegraphy, chemistry, and meteorology. (There were even three additional subclasses, each with its own jury, to consider the singular merits of musical instruments, horological instruments, and surgical instruments.) Photography was only a small part of this multifarious whole.[44]

The jury wisely avoided distinguishing between exhibits in the two different classes under which photography had been subsumed, Fine Arts and Philosophical Instruments, and instead considered all things photographic, whether cameras, lenses, apparatus, or images, as belonging to a single category.[45] At the end of the deliberations, four council medals, ten prize medals, and seven honorable mentions were distributed, with a total of four awards going to makers of cameras or equipment and seventeen to photographers. Only five of the photographers were British: Samuel Buckle and Ross & Thomson were awarded council medals, William E. Kilburn received a prize medal, and Henneman & Malone and Hill & Adamson were given honorable mentions.[46] These results were disheartening for Britain, as was the published report of the jury:

> *Let us now turn our attention to the collection before us, in which for daguerreotype portraits, America stands prominently forward;—France, first in order of merit for calotypes, or sun-pictures;—England, possessing a distinct character of her own, and presenting illustrations of nearly all the processes which have as yet been adopted. America stands alone for stern development of character; her works, with few exceptions, reject all accessories, present a faithful transcript of the subject, and yield to none in excellence of execution. France, in her daguerreotypes, of which she has but few, offers bright sunny representations; their effect rather injured than improved by too great masses of sunlight; but in her calotypes she stands unrivalled, and all but rejecting the processes of* Daguerre, *has concentrated all her energies in the further development of those of* Talbot *and his school.*[47]

While many factors had contributed to the inadequate performance of British photography, crucial factors had been the method of selection, which excluded some of the best British photographers, and the system of exhibition, which worked in favor of foreign presentations. The international exhibition had aroused the nation's pride and then, for photographers, wounded it. If British photography was to present itself in a better light in the future, its practitioners had much work to do.

When the amateur photographer Benjamin Brecknell Turner entered the Crystal Palace in the spring of 1852 to photograph the main transept, the place was a hollow shell stripped bare of all exhibits, display cases, banners, and decorations. The iron-and-glass skeleton of the building was revealed in all its intricate detail, and juxtaposed against its rigid geometry was the natural form of an elm tree that during construction had been spared the ax and enclosed within the transept (pls. 18, 19). Shortly after Turner took his photograph, the building was dismantled and removed to Sydenham, where it was reerected to serve as a palace of education and entertainment; nothing of it remained in Hyde Park but the solitary elm.

A BATTLE ROYAL: PHOTOGRAPHY FOR "REPORTS BY THE JURIES"

The Great Exhibition, an extraordinary achievement, proved far more appealing to the British sensibility than had ever been predicted. On the world stage, the dazzling displays of British industry and manufacturing heralded a new age of colonial expansion and worldwide economic dominance. Like a huge magnet, the occasion drew visitors from overseas and others from every corner of the nation.[48] And the exhibition's widening force field spread the belief that the collective good of the nation lay in the hands of countless individuals working in harmony. Mutual collaboration and organized "centres of union" became catchphrases closely associated with notions of economic progress. Social harmony transcendent of class barriers now seemed a real possibility; the working classes, it was recognized, might not pose a threat, since they had proved to be sociable and interested during their "shilling day" visits to the exhibition (fig. 40). This peaceable state was a far cry from the days of Chartism, riots, public disorder, and fears about an overthrow of the monarchy. Indeed, the very opposite was now the case, since the success of the exhibition, heralded as a personal triumph for Queen Victoria and Prince Albert, endeared the royal couple to the nation and firmly established the prince as a leading public figure.

This general feeling of goodwill also extended to international relations between nations and their governments. For instance, to mark the new relationship that had been established between America and Britain, the American investment banker and philanthropist George Peabody held an elaborate dinner with speeches, toasts, and anthems, the whole affair being commemorated in a privately printed book.[49] His gesture mirrored a wider feeling that the success of the exhibition should be celebrated. Indeed, the royal commissioners had discussed this

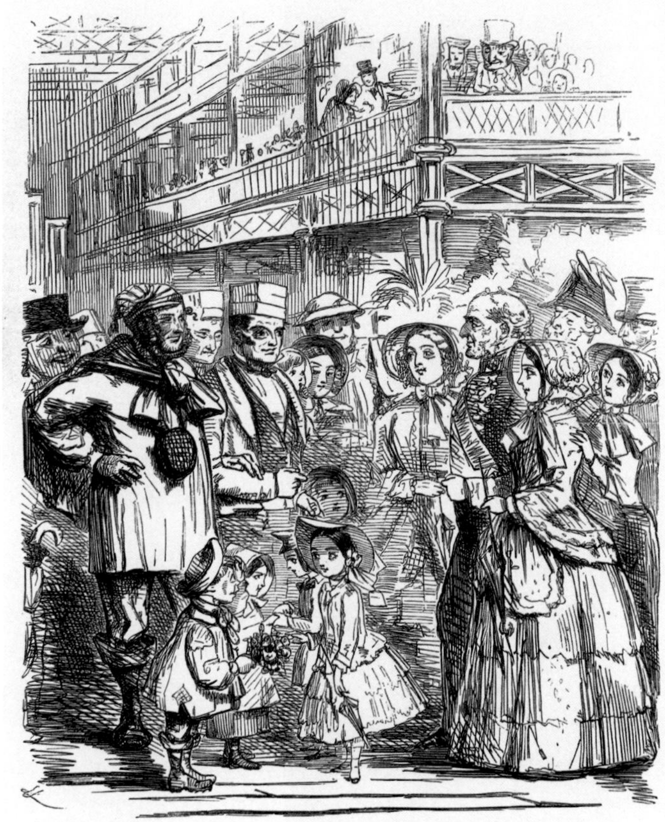

THE POUND AND THE SHILLING.
"Whoever Thought of Meeting You Here?"

Fig. 40. John Leech, *The Pound and the Shilling. "Whoever Thought of Meeting You Here?"* Wood engraving, 24.6 x 18.1 cm (9¾ x 7⅛ in.). From *Punch*, June 14, 1851, p. 247. Private collection subject early on and had decided, before the exhibition began, that instead of marking its closing with a banquet they would distribute a set of presentation volumes to foreign governments and other appropriate recipients. The two exhibition publications ultimately selected for presentation were titled *Official Descriptive and Illustrated Catalogue* and *Reports by the Juries*. They were to be specially printed in large format and reissued in eight volumes, in bindings of red Russian morocco leather with linings of blue silk, by the leading London bookbinder, Robert Rivière. A specially designed case containing a complete set of official exhibition medals completed the ensemble.[50] For the commissioners, the distribution of these presentation sets was an expression of Britain's political might, and no expense was spared in their production, with the cost for each set eventually coming to well over 60 pounds.[51] In the end, 140 sets would be required. Responsibility for carrying out the entire plan was placed in the hands of the Executive Committee.[52]

What really distinguished this venture was the decision to illustrate the *Reports by the Juries* with original photographs, specially mounted and bound into appropriate sections of its four volumes. The Executive Committee had engaged Nicolaas Henneman to photograph exhibits and provide the necessary prints, and a contract had been signed, probably before July 1850.

However, the committee had previously made an informal arrangement with the amateur calotypist Hugh Owen "to make some experiments" photographing the exhibits and supplying prints, for which he was to be paid.[53] It seems likely that Owen had been taught the calotype process by Henneman during the 1840s and, agreeing to restrict his photography to amateur practice in conformity with Talbot's usual licensing requirements, had received from him an amateur's license. However, Owen's financial arrangement with the Executive Committee meant he could no longer claim to be an amateur and therefore would infringe Talbot's patent. When Talbot got wind of the situation he obtained legal advice and then wrote to Henneman asking him to revoke the original licensing agreement and issue a full professional license to Owen, who would need to pay a significant fee.[54] The Executive Committee had little choice but to seek a resolution with Talbot of the situation it had unwittingly created.[55]

The difficulty of determining exactly what separated amateur and professional practice lay at the heart of these licensing problems. Initially Owen had agreed to undertake the work on *Reports by the Juries* for nothing, as an amateur, but when the committee offered to pay for his work, his status changed. But the photographs were never intended for resale, so what was the actual status of this work? Owen was neither an amateur nor a commercial photographer but something in between, an amateur being paid for his professional services.

Talbot was faced with a dilemma. On the one hand, he wanted to protect Henneman's commercial interests; on the other, he wanted to support this nationally important project without upsetting the Executive Committee. He proposed a compromise: allow Owen to take the photographs, but prohibit him from selling the results. The committee members thought differently. They felt that if they purchased a kind of general-use license from Talbot for 20 pounds, they were not required to specify who and how many individuals would undertake the photography and had blanket permission to "engage such assistance as they may find necessary to take the Talbotypes required."[56] Knowing that Henneman had recently appointed his own photographic assistants, Frédéric Martens and "another artist of Paris," to help him undertake the commission, Talbot had little choice but to refuse the Executive Committee such permission, which would have further undermined Henneman's already precarious position.[57]

A month later it had become increasingly clear that the Executive Committee was using the question of a general-use license as a device to distance itself from Henneman and employ its own photographers. Without having reached a formal agreement with Talbot, the committee engaged another photographer, Robert Jefferson Bingham, to work alongside Owen—no doubt hoping to force Talbot into granting the license it sought.[58] To his credit, Talbot did everything he could to resolve this tangle of demands, telling the committee that Henneman had made satisfactory arrangements with Owen and Bingham "to give them assistance in obtaining the photographic views and portraits desired by the Executive Committee." Rather than grant a general-use license he offered to grant licenses free of charge to other photographers if the committee would provide him with names and addresses.[59]

Talbot's efforts at reconciliation proved to be in vain. The committee members decided that Henneman's work did not meet their expectations and the high standards of the publication. At every opportunity they made Henneman's life as difficult as possible, haggling over prices and rejecting all but one of the photographs he submitted for approval.[60]

Further insult was added to injury when they asked him to use a set of Owen's negatives rather than his own and refused to pay him for work he had already undertaken.[61] The grounds for dispute had now shifted from the issue of licensing to the quality of Henneman's photographs.

"The fact is there are endless intrigues among the ranks of the Ex[ve] Comm[ee] they are opposing each other and offending everybody who has the misfortune to have any dealings with them," Talbot wrote to his wife. Once it became clear to him that the Executive Committee was acting mischievously toward Henneman, Talbot actively involved himself in the controversy, even enrolling his old friend Sir David Brewster to intervene on his behalf.[62]

Realizing that they had a fight on their hands, the committee members changed their tack yet again and raised two additional objections with Talbot. The first was the permanence of Henneman's salted paper prints, since it was widely known that these were prone to fading. Talbot responded that to overcome the problem he had recently modified the printing process used. He proposed that two chemists be appointed to oversee every stage of Henneman's printing and certify that all necessary procedures had been carried out.[63]

The second issue was cost. The contract with Henneman stipulated a payment of 2 shillings and 6 pence for each print.[64] Having subsequently discovered that the cost of materials came to just 3 pence per print, the committee argued that this 1,000 percent increase was an unreasonable margin very far beyond the value of Henneman's labor, royalties, and risk entailed.[65] Perhaps the committee had just woken up to the fact that well over 21,000 prints would be required to complete the order, and at Henneman's prices this would surely exceed the projected budget. Moreover, a competitor—most likely Bingham—had proposed to undercut Henneman's price by having the prints made in France.

Talbot's frayed relationship with the French made this suggestion all the more unwelcome. "I can assure you that it would be very painful to me if the Executive Committee of the royal commissioners were to order so important a work as the present [venture] to be executed in France," he wrote to Lyon Playfair, a special commissioner who enjoyed frequent contact with both Prince Albert and the royal commissioners.[66] Doubtless Talbot hoped his plea would reach a sympathetic ear, but to this audience his feelings mattered little. The overriding concern of the commissioners now was to ensure that the work was completed with standards maintained, and they did not trust Henneman to deliver on this, as Henry Cole, a member of the Executive Committee, made abundantly clear:

> *It was the failure of Mr Henneman first in taking satisfactory Paper negatives and next in producing good Positives that have been the immediate causes which led the Executive Committee to ascertain the means by which they could dispense with his services and in making this enquiry they learnt that the Positives could be produced at a much cheaper rate than Mr Henneman proposed. In fact at no price whatsoever would it be worth while having Mr Henneman's Printing. They are too dark, not at all Artistic, and already show serious defects.*[67]

With Bingham now under contract to print the photographs in Versailles, there was little Talbot could do except apply for a legal injunction to stop the infringement of his patent rights.[68] Having foreseen this possibility, the Executive Committee had agreed to indemnify Bingham against any legal action brought against him.[69] Next, Talbot and his lawyer called on Cole and Wentworth Dilke, another committee member, at the Crystal Palace. Cole and Dilke understood that the committee had infringed Talbot's patent rights, especially by contracting with Bingham to make the prints in France, and looked for some way to reach a settlement. When Talbot suggested that in compensation for waiving his patent rights and royalties he receive copies of the *Reports by the Juries*, this was promptly agreed to. Talbot also declared his intention to make a personal gift of 200 pounds to Henneman "as partial indemnity for his disappointment."[70]

"We have settled the matter with the Executive Committee," Talbot wrote to his wife that night.[71] As requested, he drew up a draft contract based on the verbal agreement reached and sent it to the committee that same evening. Hearing nothing, he believed all was well, but experience should have warned him otherwise: three days later the draft contract was repudiated. In desperation Talbot sought a personal interview with Lord Granville, a leading member of the Royal Commission, to explain his difficulties with the Executive Committee.[72] It is not clear what role Granville played, but in the first week of December 1851 the sorry affair was brought to a swift conclusion with a formal letter in which the Executive Committee agreed to provide Talbot with fifteen complimentary copies of *Reports by the Juries.*[73] The five-month battle was over.[74]

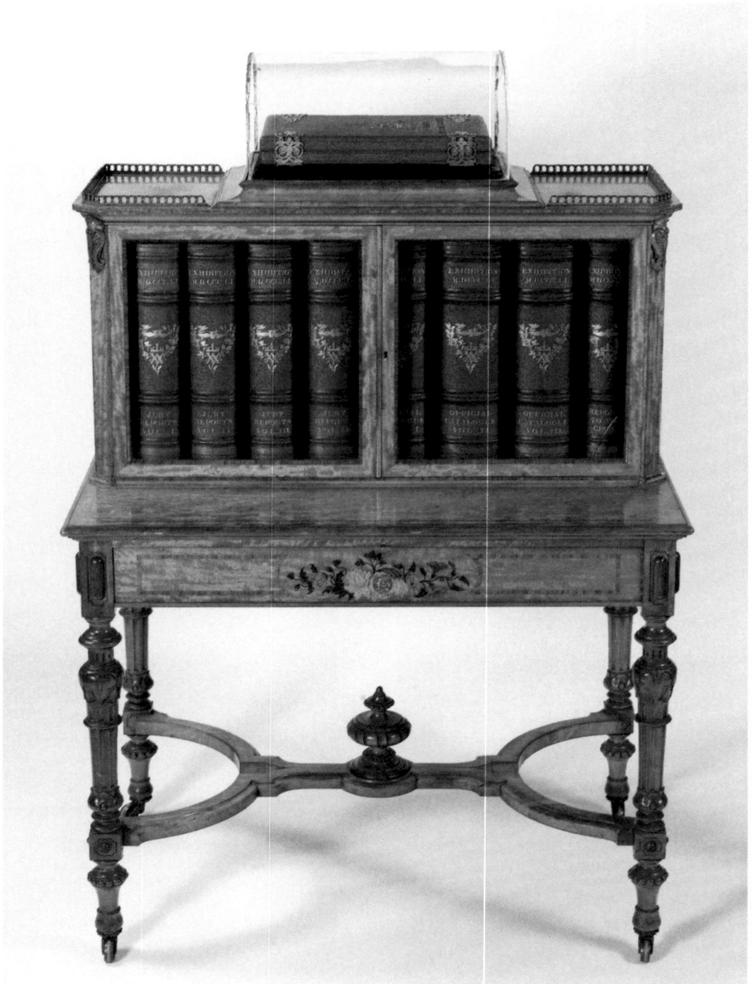

Fig. 41. Vitrine containing a presentation set of *Official Descriptive and Illustrated Catalogue*, *Reports by the Juries*, and *Reports to the Crown*, with the accompanying presentation set of exhibition medals, distributed by the royal commissioners to commemorate the Great Exhibition of 1851. This set belonged to Lieutenant William Crossman, Royal Engineers. Promised gift to the Art Gallery of Ontario, Toronto, from Archive of Modern Conflict, London © Art Gallery of Ontario

The decision by the royal commissioners to illustrate the four volumes of *Reports by the Juries* with photographs was a bold, unprecedented choice that reflected their confidence in Britain's high technological standing. The predictable course would have been to turn to an eminent draftsman for a suite of colored lithographs, a medium that was currently the height of fashion and exemplified advanced printing technology.[75] Instead, the commissioners created one of the most important photographically illustrated books of the early Victorian period and certainly the first large-scale documentary project undertaken on behalf of the nation. Rising to this new challenge, Owen took photographs that are almost completely free of aesthetic artifice—relying rather on the overwhelming presence of the objects, which he framed so that they dominate the image and seize the viewer's attention (pls. 20, 21, 22).

When *Reports by the Juries* finally appeared, its four volumes were illustrated with 154 photographs, 32 from calotype negatives by Hugh Owen and the remaining 122 taken by Claude-Marie Ferrier of France using the albumen-on-glass process. The prints were made on salted paper and mounted on individual sheets that were bound into the volumes.[76] It has always been thought that the entire suite of 21,560 prints was made in France by Bingham, but close examination reveals two distinct types of print and suggests that the prints from Owen's negatives were made in Britain.[77] Perhaps the most telling evidence is the difference in the way the two types of prints have faded; some of the "British" prints are now a pale straw color, while almost all the French prints have retained their density and probably appear as rich as on the day they were made.

The publication and worldwide distribution of these presentation volumes (fig. 41) marked a crucial moment in the history of Britain—and in the history of photography. No longer the dribbling infant of the 1840s, it had through this publication revealed itself as a mature member of society. It had come of age.

Looking back over the events of 1851, the editor of the *Times* offered one expression of the nation's satisfied mood. "England has had her full share in the glories of this world-wide competition. She has effaced the national stigma of inhospitality. She has shown a largeness of conception, a practical talent, a rapidity of performance, a power of organization, a fertility of resources, and even a taste, for which foreigners had hardly given her credit. More conspicuous than all have been her fairness and generosity. All this is gain."[78] But for Talbot, the exhibition had mostly yielded personal disappointment. Having missed the opportunity to exhibit his own photographic accomplishments, he next saw the French photographers claim his calotype process for their own and carry off a significant number of awards. Then came the unpleasant series of dealings over *Reports by the Juries.*

That episode belonged as well to a wider debate about free trade, the protection of inventions, and the place of patents within an industrial society. While some maintained that inventors should be properly rewarded, others argued that patents seriously hindered technological and economic progress and should be abolished. To the royal commissioners, the publication and distribution of presentation volumes to foreign governments were matters of national significance that transcended individual interests. Within this wider context of multiple considerations, Talbot's agreement to surrender his patent rights when faced with overwhelming odds is understandable. Making large sums of money was not a particular priority for him (although he was concerned about protecting Henneman's commercial interests). Talbot valued patents because they established his priority and precedence.

Sadly, the whole incident with *Reports by the Juries* turned out to be little more than a dress rehearsal for what would follow in 1852—when the issue for Talbot would become whether he had a moral obligation to relinquish his patent rights entirely in the service of the nation's interest and photographic progress.

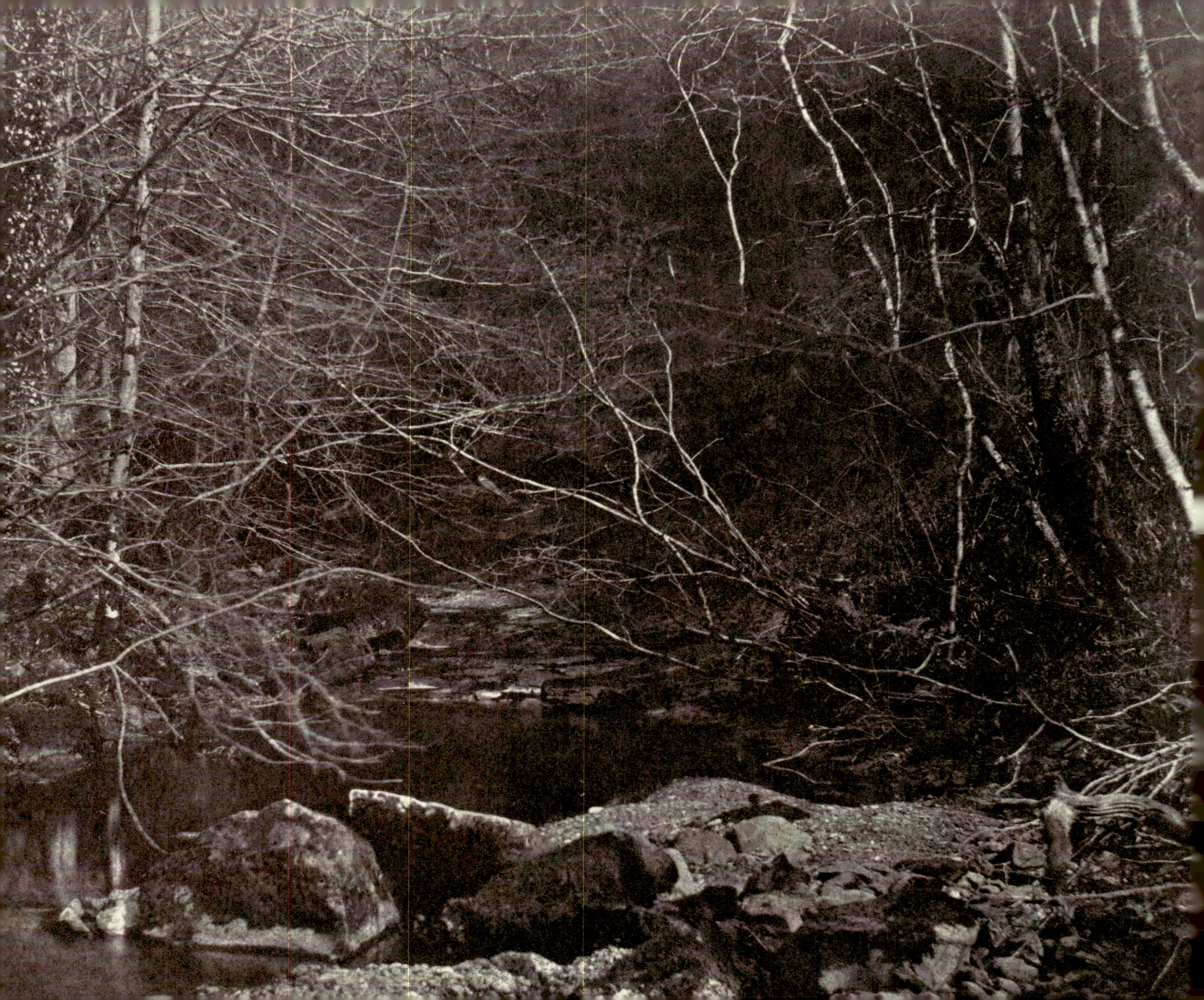

4. Battling Patents and Gaining Legitimacy

The first twenty years of photography's existence witnessed constantly evolving photographic processes and fluctuating relations among their practitioners. The contention over Talbot's patent rights and the Great Exhibition publication had not been the first such skirmish. By the close of the 1840s, Talbot had come under attack on a number of occasions for holding patents that inhibited the progress of photography. At the same time, Daguerre's highly restrictive patents escaped public criticism—perhaps because they were understood to operate within a commercial context, where such matters were regarded as normal. Restricting personal artistic endeavor, which Talbot's patents were mistakenly believed to do, was quite another matter, and criticism in the press continued unabated. In April 1848, Samuel Carter Hall had published an article about the Calotype Society (by then called the Photographic Club) in which, exaggerating for the sake of effect, he deplored the presumed fact that "so beautiful an Art should be shackled, as it is, by the extreme illiberality of the Patentee."[1] With enthusiasm widespread for the free trade that had begun to revitalize the British economy, an ethos flourished of strident opposition to everything that stood in its way—including patents. For the following two years objections to Talbot's patents had remained little more than background noise, but in 1850 these rumblings increased when a new photographic process, albumen on glass, became a working reality.

The albumen-on-glass process had first been published in France: in October 1847 by Claude-Félix-Abel Niepce de Saint-Victor, and then in 1849, in a perfected form that became popular, by Louis-Désiré Blanquart-Evrard (the same man who two years earlier had appropriated Talbot's paper-negative process without acknowledging its source).[2] In this process the support for the light-sensitive emulsion was of glass rather than metal or paper. The glass plate was coated with fresh albumen from the white of eggs, mixed with potassium iodide. Once dried it was immersed in a bath of silver nitrate, which made the albumen sensitive to light. A glass negative had obvious advantages, as it could both capture fine detail, like the daguerreotype, and be used to make multiple prints, like the calotype. A brief report on this improved process appeared in September 1849 in the *Athenaeum*, where the results were claimed "to equal the finest Calotypes."[3]

The idea that the albumen-on-glass process might be subject to British patent laws was first raised by Robert Hunt in 1850 in the *Art-Journal*. In discussing the technique Hunt outlined two possible methods for developing the negative: one, using gallo-nitrate of silver as the developing agent, was photochemically identical to Talbot's calotype process and thus, as Hunt reminded his readers, "subject to the operation of the Patent Laws"; the other, with proto-sulphate of iron as the developing agent, was already in the public domain and therefore "perfectly untrammeled" by Talbot's patents.[4]

It was not Hunt's intention to oppose his friend and colleague Talbot. On the contrary, he wanted to reveal that by adopting the chemistry Talbot had originated, Blanquart-Evrard's albumen process had infringed Talbot's rights. His main purpose was to point out the general inadequacy of the patent laws, which provided "insufficient protection to an inventor, unless he is prepared to incur a large expenditure of money on law." For that reason, he argued, "a reform of our patent laws is much to be desired; the entire practice of the courts is unsatisfactory; and many of the most experienced of our patent agents exclaim against the continued injustice to which real inventors are subjected."[5] However, by citing Talbot's photographic patents as part of his own argument for patent reform, Hunt focused public attention on his friend in a way that would have unwanted consequences.

A major difficulty with patents was their lack of rigor. While the specification itself was clearly defined, no checking was done to determine whether it plagiarized or duplicated an earlier invention—a situation

Opposite: Fig. 42. Detail of John Muir Wood, *Stream in Woods*, 1847–52 (see pl. 28)

that continued until 1883.[6] Furthermore, simply filing a patent gave the inventor little protection. Everything rested on the principle of legal precedent; in order to establish a patent right one had to take the case to court and get a judgment, which then set a "binding precedent." This costly process was beyond the reach of the majority. Talbot, however, could afford to protect his patent interests through a lawsuit and welcomed the opportunity to do so, since this was the only realistic way open to him. To Hunt he wrote, "You will easily understand how unpleasant it is for me to single out any person in particular and subject him to the annoyance of proceedings in Chancery. But if any one would come forward and offer to try the validity of the patent I should be very much obliged to him."[7]

Between 1848 and early 1851, several threads of this already complicated narrative began to knit together into a discernible chain of events. One element was the fact that a dozen or so members of the Photographic Club wanted to establish a more formal photographic society, whose members might extend their photographic activities beyond sheer pastime and would therefore be constrained by having to operate within the terms of Talbot's patents. There was also the public dissatisfaction with an archaic patent system in urgent need of reform, a discontent that was sharpened by Hall's and Hunt's articles in the *Art-Journal* about the long-term future of photography under the existing system.[8] Talbot himself made and in 1849 patented various improvements to the albumen-on-glass process, raising questions about the legitimacy of these new patent claims.[9] Then in March 1851 came the announcement by Frederick Scott Archer of a new process that used a viscous chemical mixture called collodion, rather than albumen, as the transparent substrate coating the glass.[10] Unlike albumen, which had a tendency to frill and lift, the viscous collodion solution adhered well to glass and when still moist readily absorbed photographic chemicals.[11] Would Talbot claim that this process also fell within the scope of his patents? Personal feelings ran high. By late 1851 two campaigns were under way, one to establish a photographic society in London, the second to achieve a complete reform of the British patent system for inventions of all types. In many ways they were deeply intertwined, with the outcome of the first directly influenced by growing belief in the need for the second.

The main difficulties facing the planning group trying to establish a photographic society were Talbot's patents, which would restrict the

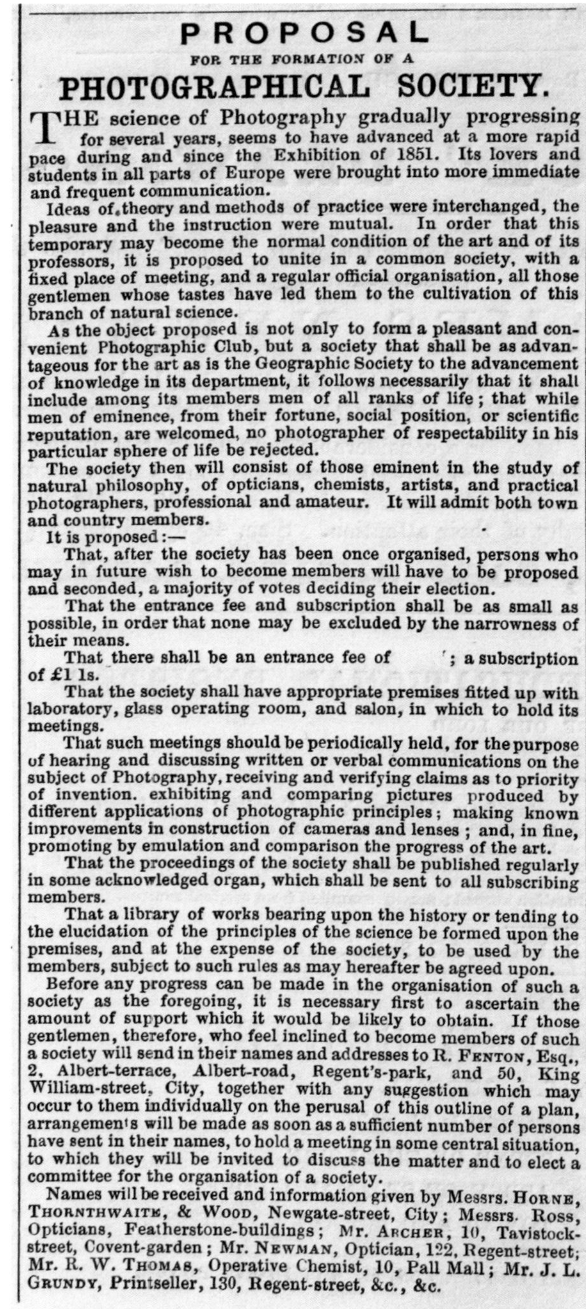

PROPOSAL

FOR THE FORMATION OF A

PHOTOGRAPHICAL SOCIETY.

THE science of Photography gradually progressing for several years, seems to have advanced at a more rapid pace during and since the Exhibition of 1851. Its lovers and students in all parts of Europe were brought into more immediate and frequent communication.

Ideas of theory and methods of practice were interchanged, the pleasure and the instruction were mutual. In order that this temporary may become the normal condition of the art and of its professors, it is proposed to unite in a common society, with a fixed place of meeting, and a regular official organisation, all those gentlemen whose tastes have led them to the cultivation of this branch of natural science.

As the object proposed is not only to form a pleasant and convenient Photographic Club, but a society that shall be as advantageous for the art as is the Geographic Society to the advancement of knowledge in its department, it follows necessarily that it shall include among its members men of all ranks of life; that while men of eminence, from their fortune, social position, or scientific reputation, are welcomed, no photographer of respectability in his particular sphere of life be rejected.

The society then will consist of those eminent in the study of natural philosophy, of opticians, chemists, artists, and practical photographers, professional and amateur. It will admit both town and country members.

It is proposed:—

That, after the society has been once organised, persons who may in future wish to become members will have to be proposed and seconded, a majority of votes deciding their election.

That the entrance fee and subscription shall be as small as possible, in order that none may be excluded by the narrowness of their means.

That there shall be an entrance fee of ; a subscription of £1 1s.

That the society shall have appropriate premises fitted up with laboratory, glass operating room, and salon, in which to hold its meetings.

That such meetings should be periodically held, for the purpose of hearing and discussing written or verbal communications on the subject of Photography, receiving and verifying claims as to priority of invention. exhibiting and comparing pictures produced by different applications of photographic principles; making known improvements in construction of cameras and lenses; and, in fine, promoting by emulation and comparison the progress of the art.

That the proceedings of the society shall be published regularly in some acknowledged organ, which shall be sent to all subscribing members.

That a library of works bearing upon the history or tending to the elucidation of the principles of the science be formed upon the premises, and at the expense of the society, to be used by the members, subject to such rules as may hereafter be agreed upon.

Before any progress can be made in the organisation of such a society as the foregoing, it is necessary first to ascertain the amount of support which it would be likely to obtain. If those gentlemen, therefore, who feel inclined to become members of such a society will send in their names and addresses to R. FENTON, Esq., 2, Albert-terrace, Albert-road, Regent's-park, and 50, King William-street, City, together with any suggestion which may occur to them individually on the perusal of this outline of a plan, arrangements will be made as soon as a sufficient number of persons have sent in their names, to hold a meeting in some central situation, to which they will be invited to discuss the matter and to elect a committee for the organisation of a society.

Names will be received and information given by Messrs. HORNE, THORNTHWAITE, & WOOD, Newgate-street, City; Messrs. ROSS, Opticians, Featherstone-buildings; Mr. ARCHER, 10, Tavistock-street, Covent-garden; Mr. NEWMAN, Optician, 122, Regent-street; Mr. R. W. THOMAS, Operative Chemist, 10, Pall Mall; Mr. J. L. GRUNDY, Printseller, 130, Regent-street, &c., &c.

Fig. 43. *Proposal for the Formation of a Photographical Society.* Advertisement, 15.9 x 6.7 cm (6¼ x 2⅝ in.). From *Art-Journal Advertiser,* April 1, 1852, n.p. Private collection ways members could practice photography and thus discourage growth and experimentation. At an early meeting with Talbot—Hunt acting as intermediary—the gap between the society's expectations for photographic freedom and Talbot's legal rights quickly became apparent.[12] Talbot proposed five conditions designed to protect the interests of his existing licensees, whose commercial success depended upon retaining the exclusive rights they had secured and paid for, as Hunt stressed in a letter to a member of the planning group: "Mr Fox Talbot clearly desires to make no profit by his process where it is used for amusement only or for scientific enquiry. He appears quite disposed to put as few restrictions as possible on the progress of photography. He tells me that he has spent £7,000 in his patents, etc., on the Art, and that he is under engagement to Hanneman [*sic*], Knight and others that prevent his doing more than this."[13]

With no agreement reached, the planning group decided to advertise their intention to form a "Photographical Society" in the national press, perhaps hoping that it would place pressure on Talbot to relax his conditions. The announcement (fig. 43) referred fashionably to ideas of interchange and uniting "in a common society" and proposed a membership of individuals "eminent in the study of natural philosophy, of opticians, chemists, artists, and practical photographers, professional and amateur." The delicate issue of class was also addressed: the society would "include among its members men of all ranks of life," and "while men of eminence, from their fortune, social position, or scientific reputation, are welcomed, no photographer of respectability in his particular sphere of life [would] be rejected." Regular meetings were to be held "for the purpose of hearing and discussing . . . communications on the subject of Photography, receiving and verifying claims as to priority of invention; exhibiting and comparing pictures produced by different applications of photographic principles; making known improvements in construction of cameras and lenses; and, in fine, promoting by emulation and comparison the progress of the art."[14]

At the same time that they published their intentions, the planning group, some of whom were lawyers, decided to test Talbot's determination and the legal validity of his patent claims. They wrote to him that "many gentlemen amateurs will not admit your right to interfere with them in any way—*as they pursue Photography for their own amusement*—and they state they would not belong to a society which admitted your right by any agreement."[15] Upset, Talbot expressed privately

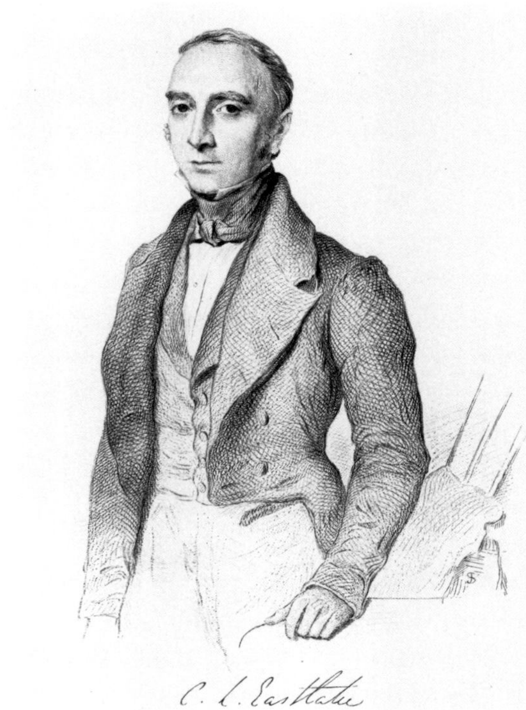

Fig. 44. J. Smyth, *Charles Lock Eastlake, R.A.*, from a photograph by T. Bridgeford. Engraving, 18 x 12 cm (7⅛ x 4¾ in.). From *Art-Union*, March 1, 1847, facing p. 86. Private collection

to Hunt, "I assure you that I have the best wishes for the formation of a prosperous society, but it appears to me that there is not much *reciprocity of feeling* on the part of those who would naturally take a leading part in it. However I have done all that lay in my power."[16] Anxious to find a resolution, he proposed that a "Committee of five gentlemen" be established so that he could meet with them and "arrange everything in a satisfactory manner,"[17] and a provisional committee was duly formed, with Frederick Berger, Roger Fenton, Peter Wickens Fry, Peter Le Neve Foster, Thomas Goodeve, Robert Hunt, and Sir William Newton as members.[18] Discussions at the first meeting revolved around Talbot's interpretation of the patent laws, which remained loosely defined and without legal precedent, and until these issues were tried and tested, it seemed the matter would never be settled. Fenton noted later, "Unfortunately, an independent Society was found incompatible with the existence of the patent, and the committee was therefore adjourned *sine die* [indefinitely]."[19]

However, the real concern of all photographers, and not just those amateurs involved in establishing a photographic society, was Talbot's belief that Archer's collodion process fell under the provisions of his own calotype patent specification and therefore was subject to similar licensing arrangements. Although the two processes were fundamentally different, they both relied on the photographic chemistry that Talbot had specified in his calotype patent, so by extension the collodion process might be thought of as also falling under his claim. As far as the photographic community was concerned, the collodion process was unencumbered by any patent and freely available for use by all.[20] As far as Talbot was concerned, this was not the case; he welcomed the opportunity to test his conviction in the courts and "have the question of my rights finally settled by a competent tribunal."[21] It was not until December 1854 that this matter would finally be resolved in the celebrated case of *Talbot v. Laroche*, which would establish the legally binding precedent that Talbot had no rights whatsoever over the collodion process; it belonged to everyone.[22]

Meanwhile, discussions continued. Foster, a respected member of the Society of Arts,[23] represented the provisional committee, and after careful discussions at several meetings he reported, "the Committee had reason to believe that if Mr. Fox Talbot, the proprietor of the patent rights is called upon by a letter signed numerously and influentially," he would willingly "relinquish his rights and throw them open to the public."[24] The society signaled its approval by allowing the signing of such a letter to take place in its Great Room.[25] The provisional committee was no longer working in a cultural vacuum; it could now count on the support of one of the most influential learned societies in London. Lord Rosse, president of the Royal Society (the premier organization for the sciences), and Sir Charles Eastlake, director of the National Gallery (fig. 44), agreed to be cited as joint authors in the proposed appeal to Talbot. In the minds of the public these two men were the leading representatives of art and science and were generally understood to be speaking on behalf of the nation.

Talbot has often been characterized as a difficult and willful man, eager to prosecute anyone who transgressed his calotype patent. This oversimplification ignores the wider context in which patents operated prior to their reform in 1852. There was nothing odd about Talbot's patenting activities; countless individuals had done the same in other fields and profited thereby. The call for reform was based on the widespread belief that the process of registering a patent should be simpler, cheaper, and more widely available to inventors. Rather than

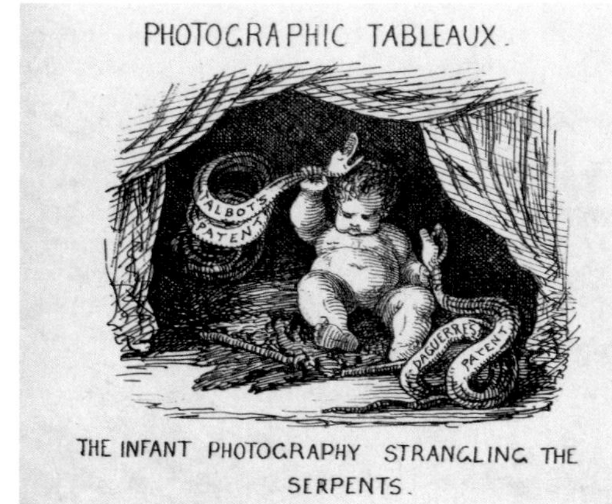

Fig. 45. Cuthbert Bede (pseud. of Edward Bradley), *Photographic Tableaux: The Infant Photography Strangling the Serpents* (of Talbot's Patent and Daguerre's Patent). Lithograph, 7.7 x 8.1 cm (3 x 3¼ in.). From Bede, *Photographic Pleasures* (London, T. McLean, 1855), facing p. 20. Private collection

demonizing Talbot, one can more accurately say that the issue of his hold over his photographic patents was used by opponents as a stalking horse to influence public opinion on patents in general and to hasten change. For his part, Talbot was willing to surrender his rights, in return for two things: full and proper recognition of his role as inventor of the calotype process, and a formal acknowledgment of the contributions the calotype had made to art and science. To Talbot, recognition by his peers mattered far more than financial rewards. This desire had been frustrated since the beginning, when in 1839 the Royal Society refused to publish his paper on the photogenic drawing process, effectively denying him the credit he sought. Thirteen years later, these sentiments still informed his actions. He wrote to Rosse, "I am ready to place myself in the hands of the acknowledged leaders of science and art and to act as they may advise—I made no condition upon the subject not thinking it worthy either of myself to do so nor of those to whom I appeal."[26] These are not the words of a stubborn and litigious man but rather of one seeking approval and respect.

Two months of negotiation finally produced agreement on the form, content, tone, and wording of the letters to be exchanged and published in the national newspapers. While to the unsuspecting reader the exchange appeared spontaneous, with Talbot taking the role of generous benefactor and patron of photography, these letters were the nineteenth-century equivalent of a press release and announced a fundamental change in the status of photography in Britain. They are given here in full.

London, July 1852.
Dear Sir,
In addressing to you this letter, we believe that we speak the sentiments of many persons eminent for their love of Science and Art.

The art of photography upon paper, of which you are the inventor, has arrived at such a degree of perfection that it must soon become of national importance; and we are anxious, that as the art itself originated in England, it should also receive its further perfection and development in this country. At present, however, although England continues to take the lead in some branches of the art, yet in others the French are unquestionably making more rapid progress than we are.

It is very desirable that we should not be left behind by the nations of the continent in the improvement and development of a purely British invention; and, as you are the possessor of a patent right in this invention, which will continue for some years, and which may, perhaps, be renewed, we beg to call your attention to the subject, and to inquire whether it may not be possible for you, by making some alteration in the exercise of your patent right, to obviate most of the difficulties which now appear to hinder the progress of art in England. Many of the finest applications of the invention will, probably, require the co-operation of men of science and skilful artists. But it is evident that the more freely they can use the resources of the art, the more probable it is that their efforts will be attended with eminent success.

As we feel no doubt that some judicious alteration would give great satisfaction, and be the means of rapidly improving this beautiful art, we beg to make this friendly communication to you, in the full confidence that you will receive it in the same spirit—the improvement of Art and Science being our common object.

Rosse.
C. L. Eastlake.
To H. F. Talbot, Esq., F.R.S., &c.,
Lacock-abbey, Wilts.

Lacock Abbey, July 30.
My Dear Lord Rosse,
I have had the honour of receiving a letter from yourself and Sir C. Eastlake respecting my photographic invention, to which I have now the pleasure of replying.

Ever since the Great Exhibition I have felt that a new era has commenced for photography, as it has for so many other useful arts and inventions. Thousands of persons have now become acquainted with the art, and, from having seen such beautiful specimens of it produced both in England and France, have naturally felt a wish to practise it themselves—A variety of new applications of it have been imagined, and doubtless many more remain to be discovered.

I am unable myself to pursue all these numerous branches of the invention in a manner that can even attempt to do justice to them, and, moreover, I believe it to be no longer necessary, for the art has now taken a firm root both in England and France, and may safely be left to take its natural development. I am as desirous as any one of the lovers of Science and Art, whose wishes you have kindly undertaken to represent, that our country should continue to take the lead in this newly-discovered branch of the Fine Arts; and, after much consideration, I think that the best thing I can do, and the most likely to stimulate to further improvements in photography, will be to invite the emulation and competition of our artists and amateurs by relaxing the patent right which I possess in this invention. I therefore beg to reply to your kind letter by offering the patent (with the exception of the single point hereafter mentioned) as a free present to the public, together with my other patents for improvements in the same art, one of which has been very recently granted to me, and has still 13 years unexpired. The exception to which I refer, and which I am desirous of still keeping in the hands of my own licensees, is the application of the invention to taking photographic portraits for sale to the public. This is a branch of the Art which must necessarily be in comparatively few hands, because it requires a house to be built or altered on purpose, having an apartment lighted by a skylight, &c., otherwise the portraits cannot be taken indoors, generally speaking, without great difficulty.

With this exception, then, I present my invention to the country, and trust that it may realise our hopes of its future utility.

Believe me to remain, my dear Lord Rosse,
Your obliged and faithful servant,

H. F. Talbot
The Earl of Rosse, Connaught-place, London.[27]

Talbot's role as the inventor of the calotype process had at last been granted formal recognition within a national context. And members of the provisional committee saw obstacles that once stood in the way of their ambitions disappear at the stroke of Talbot's pen (fig. 45).[28] Those lobbying for reform were gratified when, by happy coincidence, the Act for Amending the Law for Granting Patents for Inventions was passed into law on July 1, 1852.

THE PHOTOGRAPHIC SOCIETY OF LONDON

With the major obstacle of Talbot's patents removed, the provisional committee began making plans in earnest for establishing the Photographic Society. They adopted a constitutional framework with a president, vice presidents, officers, a council of management, and a membership elected by nomination, taking other learned societies as their model.

In 1851 there were estimated to be about a hundred institutions broadly promoting the interests of science and the arts in London, though not all claimed to be learned societies. Many were old and venerated; others had been more recently formed in response to professionalization in such emerging disciplines as engineering, geography, microscopy, medicine, and zoology.[29] One institution with an instructive history was that for chemistry, a field of study that underlay all manner of early nineteenth-century industrial and manufacturing enterprises. In late 1840 a small group of chemists with the idea of forming a chemical society had sought the help and advice of the Society of Arts, and a few months later, in February 1841, they were able formally to establish themselves with all the machinery of a learned society. There were regular meetings, a library, and a collection of chemical preparations and instruments. To establish the new society's credibility within the field, all scientific papers were subjected to peer review prior to publication in its transactions, thus helping raise the standards of the profession. In seven years the society attracted more than two hundred members, and in 1848 it was granted a royal charter of incorporation, a sure indicator of establishment approval. This brought not only social standing but the valued right to formally elect fellows, honorary and foreign members, and associates and to operate as an equal to the Royal Society or any other learned society. Thus chemists had raised their status nationally and had built a newfound confidence for the discipline that reflected its burgeoning significance.[30]

Doubtless the provisional committee of the nascent photographic society hoped to achieve something similar. Its first priority, and also a likely stepping-stone on the way to establishment, was to present an exhibition surveying the current status of photography in Britain and mainland Europe. Already enjoying a close working relationship with the Society of Arts, the provisional committee naturally hoped the exhibition could be held in the rooms of the society, one of the most prestigious venues in London, and this proposal was accepted. On December 22, 1852, a soiree in the Great Room marked the opening of the first exhibition anywhere dedicated exclusively to the art and science of photography.[31] Almost four hundred photographs had been assembled for display. The exhibition was organized by Joseph Cundall and his colleague Philip Henry Delamotte, an artist and amateur photographer.[32] That they were able to bring an extensive range of material together in a short time implies the existence in London of an informal network of photographers and photographic collectors on whom they could call for loans.

Opening at Christmas, the exhibition, called "Recent Specimens of Photography," proved far more popular than anyone had anticipated and as a result was extended for several weeks longer than originally planned.[33] New photographs were added as well, doubling the size of the exhibition to almost eight hundred entries, and a second edition of the catalogue was issued.[34] Thus the exhibition succeeded in bringing a large number of photographs to the attention of a responsive public whose only other such experience had been at the Great Exhibition eighteen months earlier. Now some of the same photographs were being shown, but in a more appropriate setting; at the Society of Arts, individual images could be judged as works of art rather than as products of an industrializing society. Although some were not of high quality, these failings only underlined the urgent need for a photographic society, where interchange would foster progress. Above all the exhibition provided a much-needed showcase for English photographers and did much to restore their self-esteem after the misfortunes of 1851.

A visitor to the exhibition would immediately have been struck by a large, coherent body of work: seventy-two of the photographs of exhibits at the Great Exhibition taken by Claude-Marie Ferrier and Hugh Owen for inclusion in *Reports by the Juries.* Their display underlined the intimate relationship that existed between the Society of Arts and the royal commissioners. It was the first time these photographs had been shown publicly, and they surely captured their viewers' attention—not only because of their subject matter but also for their austere documentary aesthetic, quite unlike the deliberately artistic approach of most of the works.[35]

That artistic quality was exemplified by a group of photographs that Talbot sent at the invitation of the council of the Society of Arts.[36] In addition to six prints of some of his most popular images, among them *The Stable Door*, *The Haystack* (pl. 3), and a *Fruit Piece*, Talbot submitted a small album containing representative examples of his work and that of his colleagues Nicolaas Henneman and Calvert Jones. The fifty-nine pictures ranged widely in subject matter, from *Lace* to *Cloisters of Lacock Abbey*. A label Talbot had pasted on the front cover read, "The specimens sent by H.F. Talbot are intended to exhibit an Early Period of the Art from 1841–1846. None of them are of a more recent date." Planned to be a concise visual history of the calotype process, the album served as an essential benchmark for visitors against which the ambitions of the nascent photographic society could be measured.[37] And, with recent disputes over patents still in the air, it offered a clear perspective on Talbot's contributions to photography.[38]

Seventy-six photographers showed at the exhibition, the majority of them British. One or two, such as Samuel Buckle and Robert Bingham, had previously been seen at the Great Exhibition, but most were practitioners whose work was entirely unknown to the wider world—"gentlemen amateurs" spoken of as a group but rarely, until now, by name. Many are obscure even today. Who, for instance, has heard of Archibald Cocke, Robert Galton, Fallon Horne, and John Spencer, or seen examples of their work? Practitioners whose names are now more familiar also made their first appearance here, among them Delamotte, Hugh Welch Diamond, Fenton, Henneman, Alfred Rosling, William Sherlock, John Stewart, and Benjamin Brecknell Turner (figs. 46, 47; pl. 85). Two lady amateurs also sent in photographs, and these were ladies in the aristocratic sense: the Lady Augusta Nevill and her sister Lady Isabel. Finally, the Europeans were well represented, with examples of work by Maxime Du Camp, Frédéric Flacheron, Gustave Le Gray, Henri Le Secq, Frédéric Martens, and Comte de Montizon (whose photographs of animals and birds at the Zoological Gardens in Regent's Park were among the most enchanting exhibits in the show).[39]

In addition to supplying a valuable list of photographers' names, the exhibition catalogue gives the processes by which the photographs were made and the names of exhibitors providing the works. Among the latter were not only photographers who submitted their own work but also those who lent photographs from their personal collections. Some of these collections reveal specialized interests. Not surprisingly, Antoine Claudet, a French photographer who was a long-standing resident of London, owned a significant number of prints by eminent French photographers of the period. Hippolyte Baillière, a French publisher of scientific and medical books in London, lent twenty-eight European studies.[40] A mysterious Mr. Little[41] owned no less than forty-seven prints by the equally enigmatic French photographer E. Pecquerel. Many British photographers, the list reveals, owned examples of work by others; whether the works were bought or acquired through exchange, it is clear that these early amateur photographers were not working in an aesthetic vacuum. They were actively engaged with the work of others, which is hardly surprising given their education, social status, and especially the new emphasis, in the wake of the Great Exhibition, on interchange as a means of self-advancement.

As for process, taken broadly there were two types exhibited: photographs made by paper processes (noted as either paper or wax paper) and those made on glass (albumen or collodion on glass). The calotype process and its variant, the waxed-paper process, were represented in 460 exhibits, compared with 300 taken on glass. This was the first and last occasion on which the calotype dominated any photographic exhibition. The daguerreotype process was completely excluded. It remained firmly associated with trade and commerce rather than with the higher ideals the provisional committee had in mind for its photographic society. The committee's intention was to position photography in the world of learned societies, not that of trade associations.

With the critical response to the exhibition exceeding all expectations[42] and the *Times* declaring there was "no doubt that England will resume the pre-eminence which she ought never to have lost in an art [that is] the genuine growth of her own soil,"[43] it seemed the perfect moment to launch the Photographic Society. At the inaugural meeting, held at the Society of Arts on January 20, 1853, with Eastlake acting as chair, Fenton read a brief history of the provisional committee's endeavors before Sir William Newton rose to propose the formation of a photographic society. A formal invitation was then issued the

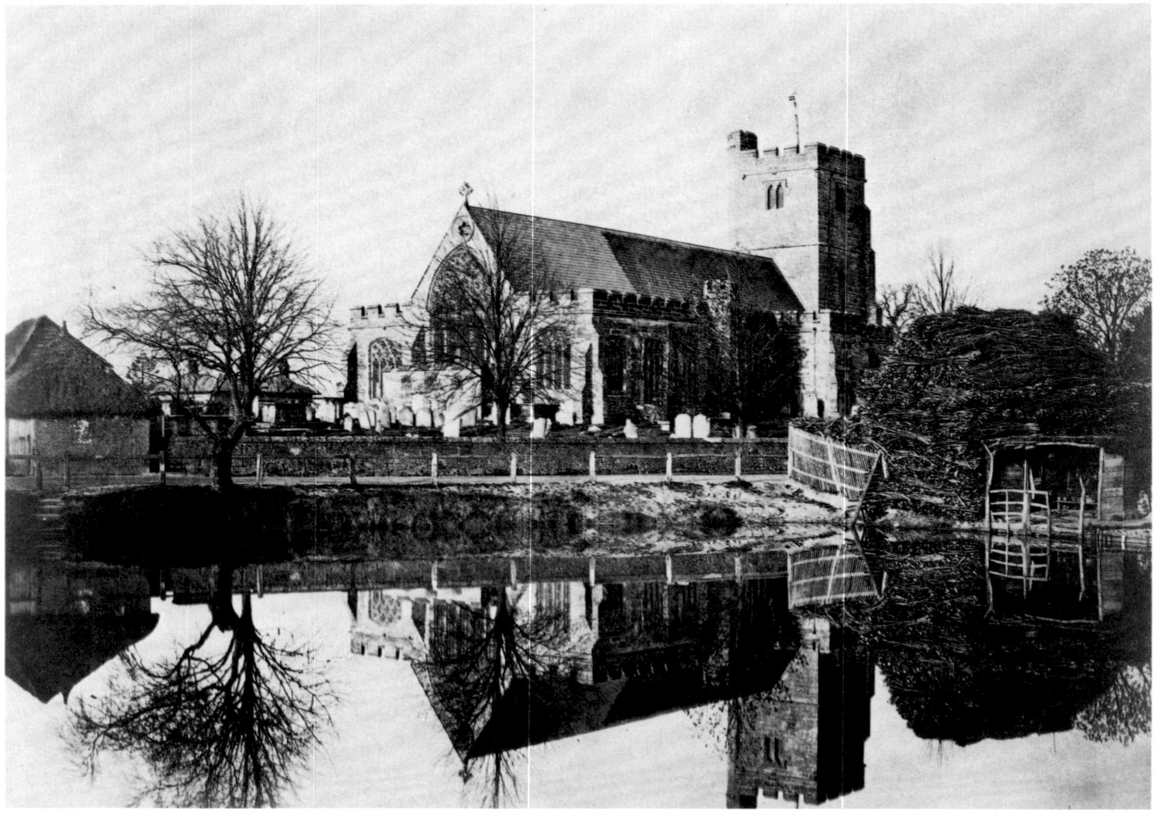

Fig. 46. Benjamin Brecknell Turner, *"A Photographic Truth," Hawkhurst Church, Kent*, ca. 1851. Albumen silver print, 29.8 x 39.8 cm (11¾ x 15⅝ in.). Victoria and Albert Museum, London

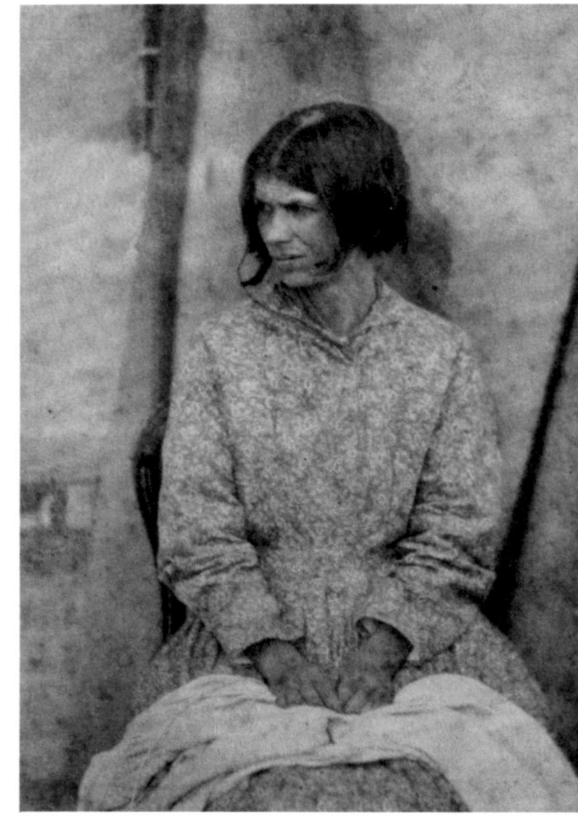

Fig. 47. Hugh Welch Diamond, *Melancholia Passing into Mania*, ca. 1851. Albumen silver print from glass negative, 6.9 x 5.1 cm (2¾ x 2 in.) The Royal Photographic Society Collection at the National Media Museum, Bradford

new group to become a branch of the Society of Arts, which would support them with funds, rooms, and other facilities. After some debate it appeared that a majority believed the long-term future of photography would be better served through "a perfectly independent body," and when this motion was carried, the Photographic Society became a reality.[44]

Like other groups, the Photographic Society wished to signal its status to the outside world through the social standing of its officers. Eastlake was chosen to be president and Earl Somers, Newton, and Charles Wheatstone vice presidents, together impeccably representing art, science, and social circles of influence (fig. 48). The close relationship Eastlake and Somers enjoyed with Queen Victoria and Prince Albert undoubtedly helped raise the status of photography.[45] Members elected to the society's governing council were also prominent men, but here, more than with the officers, enthusiasm for and understanding of photography were what mattered, and nineteen of the twenty-one were committed amateurs whose names now belong to the canon of 1850s photographers.[46] However, a society cannot exist without members or survive without their subscriptions, and within twelve months, 370 individuals had been elected to join.[47] Among their number were members of the clergy, the army, the navy, and the medical profession; also artists, barristers, chemists, professors at London universities, and a fair sprinkling of aristocrats and landed gentry. Thus, apart from those with independent incomes, most members belonged to the professional classes, for whom photography was a recreational pastime and not a way to earn a living. Only two commercial photographers enlisted during the first few months, this imbalance reflecting a distinction between trade and amateur practice that the society sought to maintain.[48]

Among the achievements reported to the first annual general meeting in 1854 was the founding of the *Journal of the Photographic Society*. The first issue had been published on March 3, 1853, with Arthur Henfrey as editor and an initial print run of two thousand copies. Circulation continued to rise, and by early 1854, four thousand copies of each number were being printed.[49] This impressive number of subscribers indicated the widespread interest in photography, not just in London but throughout the country. The undoubted highlight of the year had come in June 1853, when Queen Victoria and Prince Albert agreed to become patrons of the society.[50] Securing royal patronage further elevated the society's standing and by implication enhanced both the respectability and fashionability of photography, significantly advancing its cause through the 1850s.

PHOTOGRAPHS ON TOUR, 1853–1855

One of the immediate consequences of the Great Exhibition was the recognition that Britain lagged far behind its Continental neighbors in matters of design and aesthetic judgment. To sustain its industrial and manufacturing supremacy, it would have to offer better education to artisans and workmen. While this initiative to enhance adult education had been given fresh impetus by the hope of funding from exhibition profits, it was not new.[51] Earlier in the century, numerous mechanics' institutes, literary and philosophical societies, and other such institutions had been established in towns and villages across Britain; in 1853 there were seven hundred of these, with an estimated membership of 120,000.[52] Many had buildings erected for them and endowed by members of the local aristocracy or gentry. Some had significant libraries of several thousand volumes. Others were less privileged and struggled to survive. But all shared the common purpose of adult education through regular courses, special lectures, and the publication of inexpensive tracts and pamphlets.[53] The fortunes of these institutions declined during the difficult years of the 1840s, prompting calls for their reform and revitalization, but it was not until the early 1850s that any tangible steps were taken.

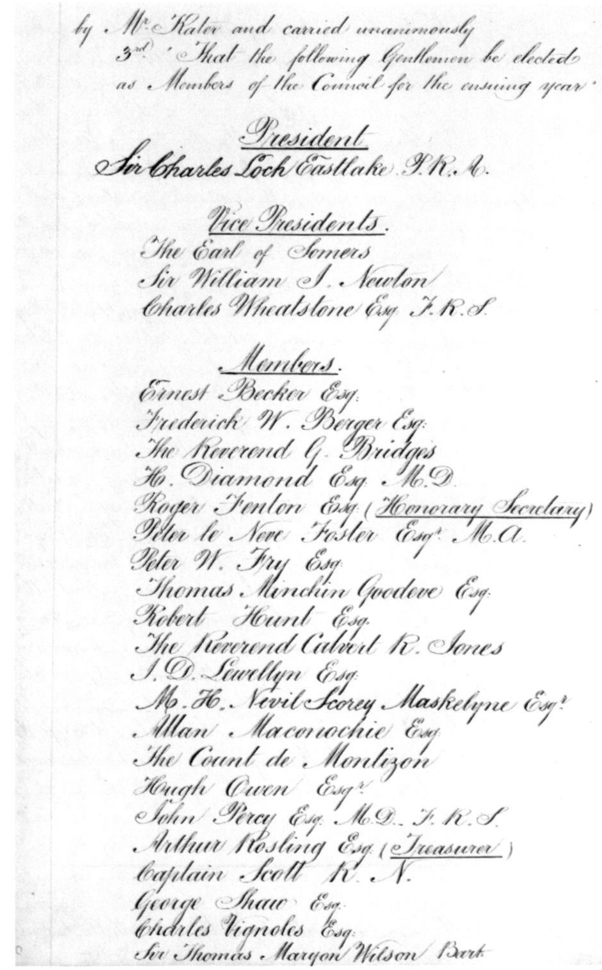
by Mr Kater and carried unanimously
3rd 'That the following Gentlemen be elected as Members of the Council for the ensuing year'

President
Sir Charles Lock Eastlake P.R.A.

Vice Presidents.
The Earl of Somers
Sir William J. Newton
Charles Wheatstone Esq F.R.S.

Members.
Ernest Becker Esq.
Frederick W. Berger Esq.
The Reverend G. Bridges
H. Diamond Esq M.D.
Roger Fenton Esq (Honorary Secretary)
Peter le Neve Foster Esq M.A.
Peter W. Fry Esq
Thomas Minchin Goodeve Esq
Robert Hunt Esq
The Reverend Calvert R. Jones
J. D. Llewellyn Esq
Mr. H. Nevil Storey Maskelyne Esq
Allan Maconochie Esq
The Count de Montizon
Hugh Owen Esq
John Percy Esq M.D. F.R.S.
Arthur Rosling Esq (Treasurer)
Captain Scott R.N.
George Shaw Esq
Charles Vignoles Esq
Sir Thomas Maryon Wilson Bart

Fig. 48. *Members of Council Listed at the Inaugural Meeting of the Photographic Society, January 20, 1853*, manuscript entry from "Minutes of General Meetings." 15.9 x 6.7 cm (6¼ x 2⅝ in.). The Royal Photographic Society Collection at the National Media Museum, Bradford

In November 1851, a proposal for affiliating the literary, philosophical, and scientific societies and mechanics institutes across Britain with the Society of Arts was suggested by Harry Chester, a council member of the society.[54] If these widely scattered institutions were brought under the protective wing of the society, he thought, they would be able to enjoy the benefits of visiting lecturers, exhibitions, discounted library books, and a wide range of educational materials. The scheme was immediately popular, and as soon as it was formally launched in May 1852, well over a hundred organizations from around the country signed up to become an "institution in union."[55] Within four months, some 289 institutions had enrolled.[56] The smaller organizations stood to benefit most from the new privileges; the secretary of one such, the Stafford Mechanics' Institute, thought the affiliation might allow his group to "get up an evening's amusement and instruction in the shape of a scientific conversazione instead of a tea drinking party."[57] It had taken the Society of Arts a little under a year to establish itself as the parent body over an informal network of almost three hundred institutions dedicated solely to adult education. For photography, the timing could not have been better.

When "Recent Specimens of Photography" closed at the end of January 1853, the council of the Society of Arts, recognizing that the exhibition had been "eminently attractive and successful," found themselves "reluctant that the advantages to be derived from such a collection should be allowed to stop here."[58] What they had in mind was to send a small collection of photographs on tour throughout Britain, using their newly established network of institutions as exhibition venues.[59] Letters were sent to photographers asking for the loan or gift of works, and a proposal for the exhibition was circulated to institutions.[60] It was envisioned as a small-scale version of "Recent Specimens of Photography." Eventually, eighty-three prints were selected to represent a broad spectrum of British and French work. It was a tight-knit group of photographs ranging from such works as Talbot's *Gateway, King's College, Cambridge* to ones by Buckle, Delamotte (fig. 49), Fenton, Newton, and Sherlock, who each showed a range of prints. European photographers were well represented and included Domenico Bresolin, Le Gray, Lodoisck, and Paul Pretsch. Ferrier and Owen's studies of entries at the Great Exhibition, lent by the royal commissioners, exemplified the documentary applications of photography, while its scientific usefulness was illustrated by *Specimens of Microscopic Photography,* contributed by Rev. William Kingsley.[61]

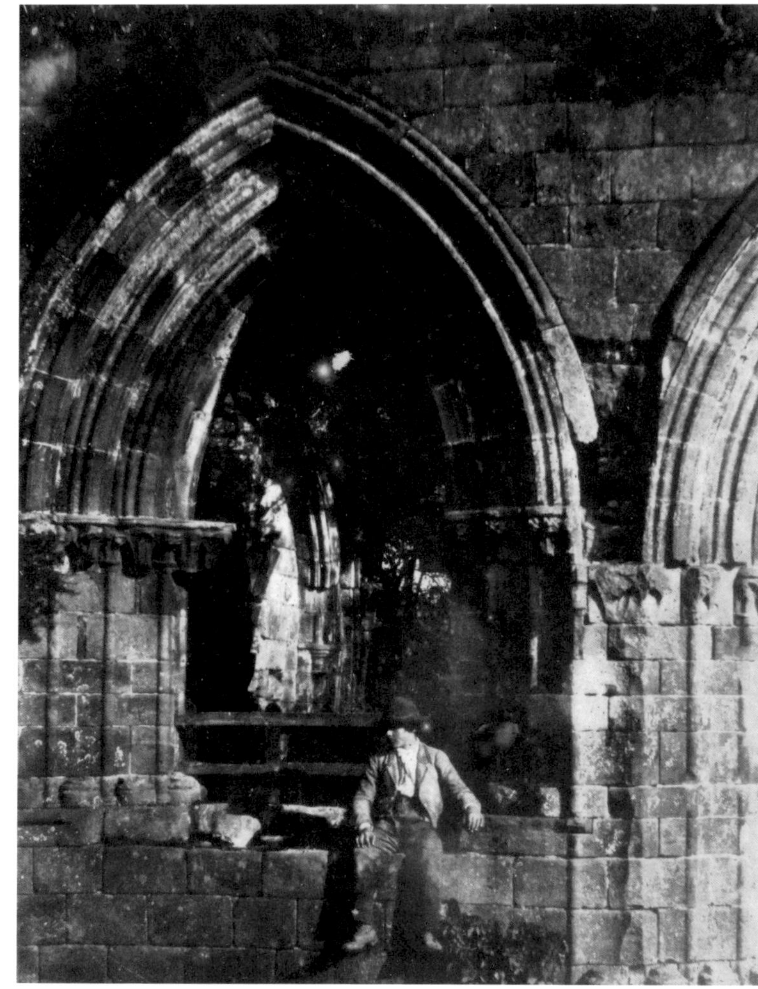

Fig. 49. Philip Henry Delamotte, *Boy in the Arch.* Salted paper print, 12.8 x 9.5 cm (5 x 3¾ in.). Exhibited at the Society of Arts, 1852. Collection Centre Canadien d'Architecture / Canadian Centre for Architecture, Montréal, PH79:528:01

Despite the cost and the burden of work involved in showing the exhibition, enough hosting institutions responded positively to make a national tour viable. By early September 1853 a schedule of eighteen venues had been arranged and the tour had begun.[62] Other than easy access to the rail network, no underlying rationale seems to have determined the route of the exhibition. It first opened at Woburn, near Oxford, and gradually edged its way as far north as Aberdeen, Scotland, before heading south to the Isle of Wight, with stops at other venues en route. A strict timetable was imposed: seven days were allocated for public viewing at each site and three days between venues for packing, transporting, and re hanging the exhibition in its new location. Although Victorian exhibition standards were rather rudimentary and the hanging of the photographs was informal, this was still a demanding schedule with little margin for delay or error. From the outset things went badly, with woeful tales of broken glass, missing photographs, damaged frames, and late deliveries. Perhaps too much had been expected of a railway system more adept at handling coal, iron, and cans of milk; picture the heavy crates of photographs being unloaded at the railway sidings and subsequently hoisted by brute strength onto truck and carrier's wagon. Some institutions dutifully repaired the ensuing damage and absorbed the cost, while others ignored the problem and exhibited the photographs behind cracked glass. There were disputes about whether the railway companies should be forced to pay compensation for the repeated damage and disruptions of schedule.[63] When the tour closed in April 1854, the assembled works must have looked exceedingly careworn.

The leadership of the Society of Arts took their responsibilities toward the "institutions in union" very seriously. Despite the setbacks and problems, they understood that difficulties with transport and broken glass were of little significance when set against the wider benefits of bringing photographs to the widest possible audience. Thus the decision was made to organize for 1854 a second, even more ambitious tour, which was supplemented by a selection of "nature prints"[64] and other examples of the latest printing technologies. To meet the increased demand, two almost identical exhibitions were circulated, one in the north and one in the south.[65] They toured between April and November 1854 and altogether were seen in thirty-three venues.[66] A third tour, also in two parts, took place in 1855.[67]

It is difficult to gauge the influence these exhibitions had upon public sensibilities. We know from newspaper reports that they were well received and appreciated, but, lacking a firsthand account from a visitor, we have to turn to the responses of the institutions. As ever, these varied by locale. Some of the larger, well-established institutions organized supplementary exhibitions of their own displaying photographs, works of art, or scientific equipment. In Aberdeen, for instance, a thriving community of photographers already existed, and a complementary exhibition of the work of colleagues in the region was created. Entries were judged and awarded prize medals; the jury was impressed by the "high intellectual treat" the photographs provided.[68] In Stirling, also in Scotland, the arrival of the exhibition triggered a whole series of lectures, the first dealing with the history of photography and its current applications. A local journalist could barely contain his enthusiasm (or his language) when he reported, "The benefits which would be conferred on posterity by the agency of the newborn and beautiful art of photography, were eloquently alluded to by the lecturer in a brief and effective peroration. The lecture was received with repeated manifestations of applause."[69] At King's Lynn, Norfolk, the organizing committee arranged an opening soiree at which 'several members of the society . . . consented to enliven the evening with selections of vocal and instrumental music."[70] One can only imagine what that was like.

Every local organizing committee welcomed the opportunity to publicize the exhibition in its town. While most simply placed advertisements announcing the dates of the event, the coal-mining town of Wrexham went one better, listing the title and process of every photograph on the front page of the local newspaper.[71] The titles alone—*Kremlin, Moscow*; *Tours Cathedral*; *Baths, Nismes, France*; *Sulimaniyeh, Constantinople*—conjured romantic visions of places far removed from daily existence in northern Wales (pls. 79–80). In the cotton-manufacturing town of Burnley, Lancashire, the directors of the Mechanics' Institute adopted a more pragmatic approach by offering visitors the opportunity to have their portraits taken during the exhibition's run.[72]

These few examples alone suggest that the arrival of a photographic exhibition was greeted with enthusiasm. It is easy to forget that even as late as 1853–54, few people in Britain had seen a photograph. They may have read about them in newspaper articles or even understood the principles involved from a textbook, but photographs were not a part of everyday experience, especially in many of the market towns and villages that hosted the exhibitions. The traveling exhibitions fulfilled an important role by presenting photographs to an audience of the widest possible range both geographically and socially. The exhibitions also indirectly promoted the ideals and aesthetic values of the Photographic Society, encouraging photographers up and down the country both to emulate the works displayed and to establish their own associations to serve local needs.

The role of the Society of Arts in promoting photography during the years 1852–55 has been largely overlooked in favor of the activities of the Photographic Society. However, without the active intervention and support of the older society, photography would likely have followed another route and perhaps arrived at a different outcome. The commitment of the Society of Arts to supporting "institutions in union" shifted the balance of power away from London by stimulating photographic activity in the regions. By 1855, photography had become widely established throughout Britain, and responsibility for its development lay in the hands of practitioners nationwide.

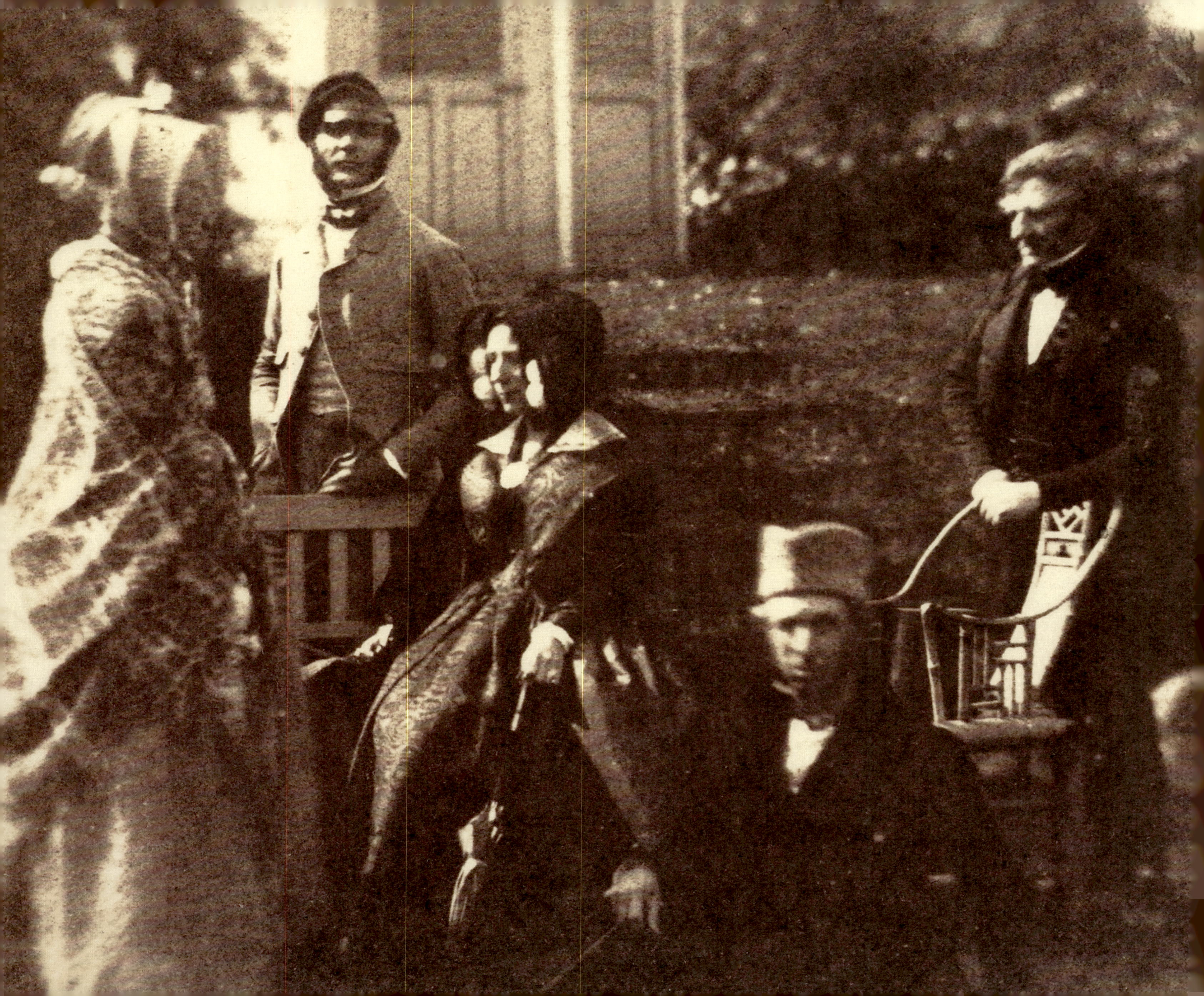

5. The Calotype Finds Its Place

The impetus given photography by the Great Exhibition "had so increased the number of photographers," Roger Fenton suggested at the 1853 inaugural meeting of the Photographic Society, that the art was entering "a new phase of its history."[1] Nonetheless, in the context of the manufacturing ambitions on display at the exhibition, the standing of photography was modest. It was still mostly a personal pastime, small in scale and ideally suited to members of the leisured classes, who liked nothing better than to be diligently occupied with some sort of "rational recreation" whether it be fossil hunting, egg collecting, or botany.

How would such an individual make a start in photography? To understand what was involved, let us follow an imaginary novice, an absolute beginner in search of information and advice. There were questions galore. Was it best to buy one of the many handbooks advertised in the national press? What kind of camera and lens should one acquire to achieve the best results, and where did one buy the chemicals and accompanying paraphernalia? And then, what process should one choose: the cumbersome collodion process that produced wonderfully detailed images, or the lightweight calotype process whose results were appealingly artistic? Should one join a local philosophical or scientific society and attend monthly meetings in the hope of hearing an experienced photographer explain the mysteries of the craft? It was all perplexing—yet, with the promise that one would soon expertly handle a gleaming camera of mahogany, brass, and polished glass, perfectly thrilling.

One beginner who signed himself A.H.R., an amateur antiquarian who wished to photograph some relics, turned for advice to the erudite readership of *Notes and Queries*, a journal of information exchange. "What system would be most convenient, most easily acquired, and best adapted for the purpose I have in view? If any gentleman will kindly enlighten me on this point, he will perhaps be good enough also to inform me where the best portable apparatus can be obtained, and what treatise most clearly explains the process he may recommend to me?"[2] A detailed response was quickly forthcoming. Its author wrote seriously and in detail, perhaps realizing that his reply would be read attentively by a wide audience with a potential interest in photography.

Photography requires much care, nicety of manipulation, cleanliness; and, I may add, some little knowledge of chemistry is useful. Even with all these, some amount of practice is requisite; but, unfortunately, people have generally an idea that they have only to make or to buy some prepared paper or plates, to carry them in a small black box, to expose them to light, and the sunshine will then do all the rest for them, and produce magnificent pictures. Never was there a greater fallacy; . . .

Some shop-keepers who deal in the apparatus make a point of telling a novice that "It's very easy;" "It's so simple;" "This picture was done in ten seconds;" "Our apparatus is so improved," and so on; but they omit saying that it requires care. . . . They induce the uninitiated to purchase a quantity of chemicals, camera, &c., and then, finding it not so easy as he was led to expect, he looks upon it as a piece of humbug.

. . . When I first began, I did not get a picture to my own satisfaction for the whole of one summer; this was very discouraging, but sticking to it I mastered the principle, and can now do pretty well.

. . . Supposing that A.H.R., after reading the above, is still determined to try it, I now come directly to his Queries:—

The Daguerreotype is perhaps the easiest mode of obtaining pictures, but it has serious inconveniences: the pictures are on metal plates, and must be kept covered by a glass. The calotype will be much better for A.H.R., as the pictures may be on glass or paper; and in the latter case, they may be kept in a book or folio.

Opposite: Fig. 50. Detail of John Muir Wood, *Family Group, Leith,* 1847–52 (see pl. 32)

A dark room or tent is not necessary in the calotype; I am doing without one myself, and can make long excursions from home; all I want is a little clean water. The apparatus varies very much by different makers, and mine was made under my own superintendance.

Lastly—this may seem ill-natured—don't believe all that people write or say on this subject; and don't trust too much to opticians and chemists, but first see some one take a picture and complete it in the open air before your eyes.[3]

Notes and Queries, a biweekly established in 1849 as "A Medium of Inter-Communication for Literary Men, Artists, Antiquaries, Genealogists, Etc.," functioned very much the same way as an Internet message board, with letters on a rich variety of subjects flying back and forth.[4] When the editor decided to include photography as a topic—despite having some doubts about "the propriety of introducing the subject of Photography into our columns"[5]—no other publication was fulfilling this role. He certainly tapped into a reservoir of eager and anxious correspondents with inquiries large and small. Answers were supplied by individuals widely regarded as early authorities, such as Hugh Welch Diamond, who became the foremost contributor on photography, and William Crookes, whose description in those pages of Gustave Le Gray's waxed-paper process was among the first to be published in the British press.[6] A spirited letter from Frederick Scott Archer defending his claim as the inventor of the collodion process is evidence that the journal enjoyed a wide and increasingly informed readership.[7] It is surely no coincidence that the announcement of photography as a topic for *Notes and Queries* coincided almost exactly with Talbot's relaxation of his calotype patent and the planning of a photographical society in London. After well over a decade of waiting in the wings, photography emerged center stage during the closing months of 1852, and from then on it played an increasingly important role in the cultural life of Britain.

PHOTOGRAPHIC ASSOCIATIONS

It took a little while for the burgeoning interest in photography to express itself organizationally. Beyond the one in London, only two photographic societies were formally established in this period, both in northern England, in Leeds in 1852 and in Liverpool in 1853; and their similarities and differences are revealing. If our novice had lived in Yorkshire, he may well have turned to the Leeds Photographic Society,

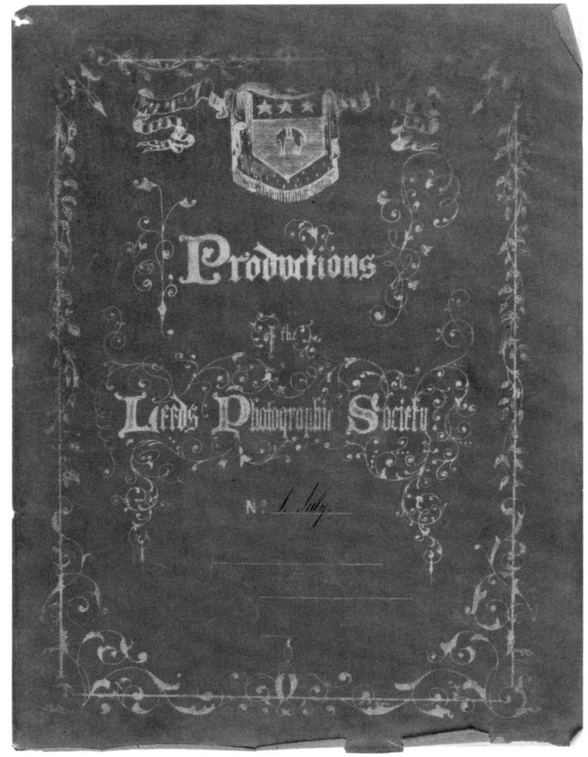

Fig. 51. "Productions of the Leeds Photographic Society," July 1852. Printed cover of first issue, designed by J. A. Hope, 38 x 28.4 cm (15 x 11⅛ in.). The Metropolitan Museum of Art, New York, The Elisha Whittelsey Collection, The Elisha Whittelsey Fund, 1960, 60.554.11

which was formed when amateur photographers joined forces with members of the Philosophical and Literary Society to create an independent group for photography.[8] In comparison with the Photographic Society of London it had few rules and regulations,[9] but despite its modest size the society had grand ambitions, and one of its first actions was to begin distribution of multiple copies of a monthly album, "Productions of the Leeds Photographic Society." The opening issue, assembled in July 1852, was illustrated with ten salted paper prints made from paper negatives. Each image was presented within a ruled border, on its own page, with the title and the name of the photographer hand-inscribed beneath. A handsome production with bright blue-and-gilt paper covers (fig. 51), "Productions" offers a coherent visual record of the society's early activities.[10]

The Leeds Photographic Society was established in a middling-sized town whose importance and economic success were conspicuously based on manufacturing rather than intellectual accomplishments. In 1851 Leeds had a population of just over 170,000, and the vast majority of those employed were manual workers in a thriving textile industry.

As in other manufacturing towns across north and central England, productivity and prosperity were creating an increasingly large middle class, made up mostly of mill owners, manufacturers, capitalists, and bankers who prided themselves on being independent-minded and who were likely to find spiritual fellowship at one of the many Dissenting churches that flourished in the northern industrial regions.[11] This manufacturing context undoubtedly gave the Leeds Photographic Society a distinctive regional character quite unlike that of its more illustrious counterpart in London.[12]

Images in the three surviving issues of "Productions of the Leeds Photographic Society" reflect something of this difference. Apart from the usual sprinkling of antiquarian and ecclesiastic subjects, there are studies of an industrial school and almshouses (fig. 52) and, most notably, several views of shop fronts and other buildings in the city center. Almost all the views were taken in Leeds or its immediate neighborhood, the most distant subject being the Birmingham town hall. Although Leeds is surrounded by beautiful countryside, with Bolton Abbey and the river Wharfe within easy reach to the north and west, there is not a single landscape composition to be seen in these albums. Compared to the extraordinary range of the photographs exhibited at the Society of Arts in December 1852, the aesthetic ambitions and geographic scope of works published by the Leeds Photographic Society seem decidedly constricted. This contrast reflects not only the commercial orientation of Leeds but also the complete lack of interchange at this early date between metropolitan and provincial photographers.[13] None of the photographers from the Leeds society showed work at that 1852 exhibition, and it is likely that the existence of a community of practitioners almost two hundred miles to the north remained unknown to those preparing the London exhibition.

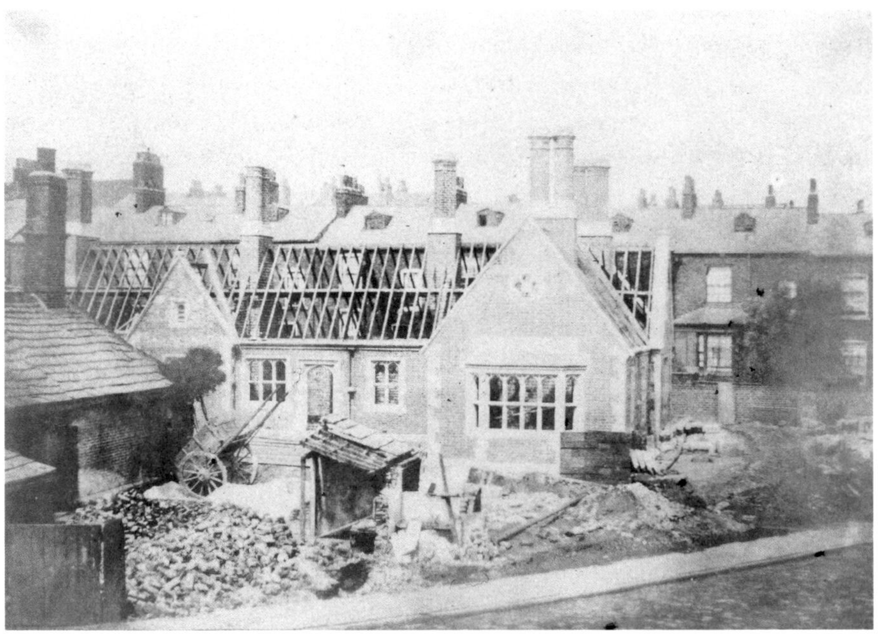

Fig. 52. Thomas Henry Briggs, *Jenkinson's Almshouses, Leeds*, 1852. Salted paper print from calotype negative, 15 x 20.5 cm (5⅞ x 8⅛ in.). From "Productions of the Leeds Photographic Society," issue no. 3, September 1852, pl. 2. The Metropolitan Museum of Art, New York, The Elisha Whittelsey Collection, The Elisha Whittelsey Fund, 1960, 60.554.11.3 (2)

A similar story was unfolding some seventy miles to the west on the other side of the Pennines, in the mercantile port of Liverpool. Here a group of enthusiasts came together under the auspices of the Liverpool Royal Institution to form a photographic society.[14] Although Liverpool was significantly larger than Leeds, the two cities had been linked commercially ever since 1816, when the opening of a canal between them gave textile merchants in Leeds a way to ship goods to American markets. If anything, Liverpool took an even more direct and down-to-earth approach to photography than Leeds. The speaker at the inaugural meeting of the society on March 1, 1853, a well-respected local architect, spoke of photography's "great utility" and "usefulness"; it offered, he believed, the only "universal language which had . . . long been sought after" by those seeking objective information.[15] By the end of the society's first year, 155 Liverpudlians had been recruited as members.[16]

The first issue of the (unillustrated) *Liverpool Photographic Journal*, published on January 14, 1854, not only was available in Liverpool but also was sent to leading photographic retailers and printsellers in London, Manchester, Edinburgh, and Glasgow.[17] The society began to draw national attention, which then further consolidated its importance in Liverpool. One London reviewer concluded, "Liverpool has taken a high place in the cultivation of the art."[18] Reports of the Liverpool Photographic Society's activities began appearing regularly in the journal of London's Photographic Society, and the gesture was reciprocated. This interchange of information established an informal, mutually beneficial axis between the two cities; Liverpool grew in stature from its association with the Photographic Society of London, which in turn reinforced its own standing as the parent society for photography in Britain. Meanwhile, the Leeds society, which had begun with high hopes and the regular issuing of an elaborate photographic record of its activities, was not able to sustain activity at its ambitious initial level and, having established few links outside Leeds, did not achieve the national recognition enjoyed by Liverpool.[19]

Seven new photographic societies were founded during the course of 1854,[20] and in subsequent years more continued to sprout up throughout Britain. Only two could be regarded as having national status: the Photographic Society of Scotland, established in Edinburgh in 1856 with Sir David Brewster as president, and the Photographic Society established in Dublin in 1854 with Lord Otho Fitzgerald as president (it became the Photographic Society of Ireland in 1858).[21] Both mirrored the parent society in London in objectives and constitution. Elsewhere photographic societies were appearing throughout Britain. Some were being established in manufacturing cities: Dundee (1854), Glasgow (1854), Manchester (1855), Birmingham (1856), Nottingham (1858), Leicester (1859), and Bradford (1860); while others served the widespread rural communities indicated in their titles: Devon and Cornwall (1854), Norfolk and Norwich (1854), Brighton and Sussex (1855), Dumfries and Galloway (1856), and Isle of Wight (1859). There were also a number of photographic societies that served smaller communities such as Derby (1854), Blackheath (1857), Chorlton (1857), Greenwich (1857), Paisley (1857), and Macclesfield (1858). Photography was being taken up with remarkable speed during the 1850s, and it has been estimated that between 1852 and 1860 some thirty-one photographic societies were established.[22] Some barely survived for more than a couple of years; others gained wide support both regionally and nationally and became influential voices in the field. Very few of these early societies survived to the 1870s, most either failing to adapt to the rising tide of commercial photography or succumbing to the petty squabbles and heated arguments that inevitably accompanied a rapidly evolving pursuit.

Some practitioners found the collegial atmosphere of a photographic society encouraging and instructive, helping them keep abreast of the latest developments. Others preferred a more independent course and struck out on their own. If our novice had joined one of these newly formed societies, what kind of support would he have found, particularly if he sought advice on materials and equipment for the calotype process? In London he could have heard Dr. Diamond deliver a paper, "On the Simplicity of the Calotype Process," or Dr. John Percy discuss the use of Le Gray's waxed-paper process in hot climates.[23] At one meeting, fourteen different camera models were shown and analyzed; another was devoted to explanations of optics and lens construction.[24] Within a few months, a diligent beginner attending the regular meetings of any of the photographic societies all over Britain would have picked up sufficient practical information and firsthand advice to make a start.

Photographic journals were another important resource. We have seen the value of the photographic correspondence carried by *Notes and Queries* beginning in 1852. Gradually the volume of correspondence on photography appearing in *Notes* diminished and by early 1856 it had all but ceased, this role having been taken over by three specialized photographic journals. Two of these were the journals brought out by the photographic societies of London (1853) and Liverpool (1854), respectively. A third, *Photographic Notes*, appearing in January 1856, was published in Jersey by the photographer Thomas Sutton. His strong opinions often created controversy, despite which, or perhaps because of which, the journal thrived, becoming the official publication for three leading photographic societies.[25] All three publications could be had by subscription or through a specialist local retailer, and thus their influence reached well beyond the immediate boundaries of the local groups responsible for their creation. The authority of these journals and the role they played in directing the course of photography during the 1850s and long after should not be underestimated.

COMMERCIAL CONSIDERATIONS

The attraction of journals was felt not only by their readers but also by a wide range of photographic retailers, publishers, manufacturer-chemists, and other merchants who increasingly used them as a medium to advertise their wares and services.[26] The first advertisement for "photogenic drawing-paper" appeared on the front page of the *Athenaeum* on March 16, 1839, only weeks after Talbot published his account of the process.[27] While some advertisements having to do with photography appeared throughout the 1840s, in the early 1850s the number began to rise sharply as the market for photography became more established. Advertising was increasing partly because of the improved economic climate, but also because manufacturers had learned during the Great Exhibition that there was such a thing as a mass market in Britain, with huge profits to be made from it.[28] Once manufacturers had absorbed this lesson they turned their attention to improving production methods by standardizing components and parts; this in turn laid the foundation of the British camera industry, which thrived through the nineteenth century.

Occupational statistics give some sense of this expansion. In the *Post Office London Directory* of 1853, photographers were lumped together with engravers, painters, etc. under the heading Artists, an indication that photography was not regarded as a distinct trade or occupation. Two years later, in 1855, sixty-six photographers were identified as such by a typographic symbol, although still under the artist heading. Just one year after that, photography had become such a visible presence that two new occupational headings were introduced, Photographic Artists (106 entries) and Photographic Apparatus Makers (30 entries); another, Photographic Material Dealers (19 entries), was added in 1857.[29] Nearly all these photographers and manufacturers directed their attentions to the market for commercial portraits. (Although one enterprise, the Photographic Institution, offered its services to photograph "Works in Progress, Country Houses, Churches, or rural landscapes" at a fee of 3 guineas a day plus expenses, in general commercial photographers did not extend their activities much beyond portraiture.) But this thriving photographic business increased the demand for new equipment, chemicals, and services—all of which benefited the amateur indirectly by lowering costs and broadening the range of goods and materials.[30] However, as we shall see, when these "photographic artists" began to join the photographic societies, whose memberships were attuned to amateur practice, profound differences became evident.

Let us assume that our novice has joined a photographic society, has absorbed what he can from his photographic journals, and now feels confident enough to begin. Despite the modernity of the collodion process, he still feels attracted to the calotype process, which has remained popular with amateur photographers. And there has recently come to his attention a well-regarded handbook on the calotype process by Thomas Sutton (fig. 53) that is to become quite popular.[31]

In the book, Sutton asserted in his preface that he "assumed no previous photographic knowledge whatever on the part of the reader"; if the

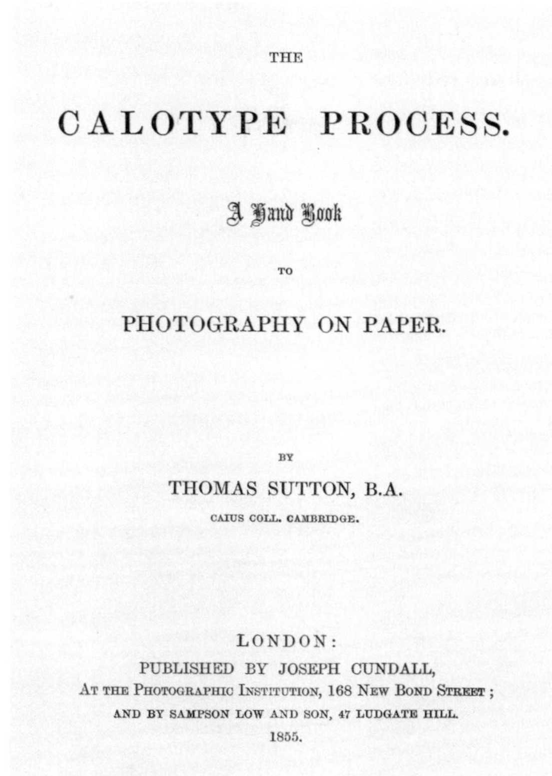
THE

CALOTYPE PROCESS.

A Hand Book

TO

PHOTOGRAPHY ON PAPER.

BY

THOMAS SUTTON, B.A.

CAIUS COLL. CAMBRIDGE.

LONDON:

PUBLISHED BY JOSEPH CUNDALL,

AT THE PHOTOGRAPHIC INSTITUTION, 168 NEW BOND STREET;

AND BY SAMPSON LOW AND SON, 47 LUDGATE HILL.

1855.

Fig. 53. Thomas Sutton, *The Calotype Process. A Hand Book to Photography on Paper* (London, 1855). Title page, 18.3 x 11.3 cm (7¼ x 4½ in.). The Metropolitan Museum of Art, New York, The Joyce F. Menschel Photography Library

detailed instructions were followed carefully, success was "*very nearly*" certain.[32] Sutton's book had been published by Joseph Cundall under the imprint of the Photographic Institution, which was established by Cundall and Philip Delamotte during the spring of 1853 in the wake of their successful organization of the photographic exhibition at the Society of Arts in December 1852.[33] The Photographic Institution was an ambitious, multifaceted enterprise. It had its own portrait studio and a darkroom and offered for the beginner a course of six "lessons in every branch of the Photographic Art."[34] But its main purpose was retail business. It published photographic portfolios and handbooks; it sold equipment and materials. (The book it published by Sutton contained a notice that all the equipment, chemicals, and papers mentioned by the author could be purchased at the Photographic Institution.)

The Photographic Institution also sold photographic studies of landscape and architecture. This was a brave initiative that sought to expand London's traditional, long-established print trade to include, for the first time, photographs. They retailed at correspondingly high prices, ranging from 5 shillings to 2 guineas. By selling their prints at the top end of the market as if they were engravings, mezzotints, or lithographs, photographers of this generation were likely attempting to position themselves with traditional artists, whose works were widely available through leading printsellers such as Agnew and Colnaghi. It would not be long before these well-established art dealers followed the example of the Photographic Institution and included photographs as part of their stock-in-trade.

To promote this side of the business, Cundall and Delamotte mounted the first exhibition devoted exclusively to the sale of photographs. Opening on April 28, 1853, it contained 354 works by leading photographers both British (such as Samuel Buckle, Roger Fenton, Hugh Owen, William Sherlock) and European (Domenico Bresolin, Giacomo Caneva, Frédéric Flacheron, Gustave Le Gray, Henri Le Secq). The two entrepreneurs subsequently represented individual European photographers, importing their portfolios and advertising them in leading periodicals.[35] The Photographic Institution quickly became *the* place to buy photographs in London, and when reports of Prince Albert's visits there began to appear in court circulars, the success of the enterprise was ensured.[36]

Our novice, whom we assume was an unpretentious sort of fellow with a moderate income, may have chosen to start his photographing with the "small but complete set of Apparatus and Chemicals for Beginners, tested and guaranteed" that had as its centerpiece a "Mahogany Sliding CAMERA by *Ottewill*, and Single LENS by *Ross* . . . for Pictures, 8 in. by 6 in. and 5 in. by 4 in."[37] The complete outfit cost

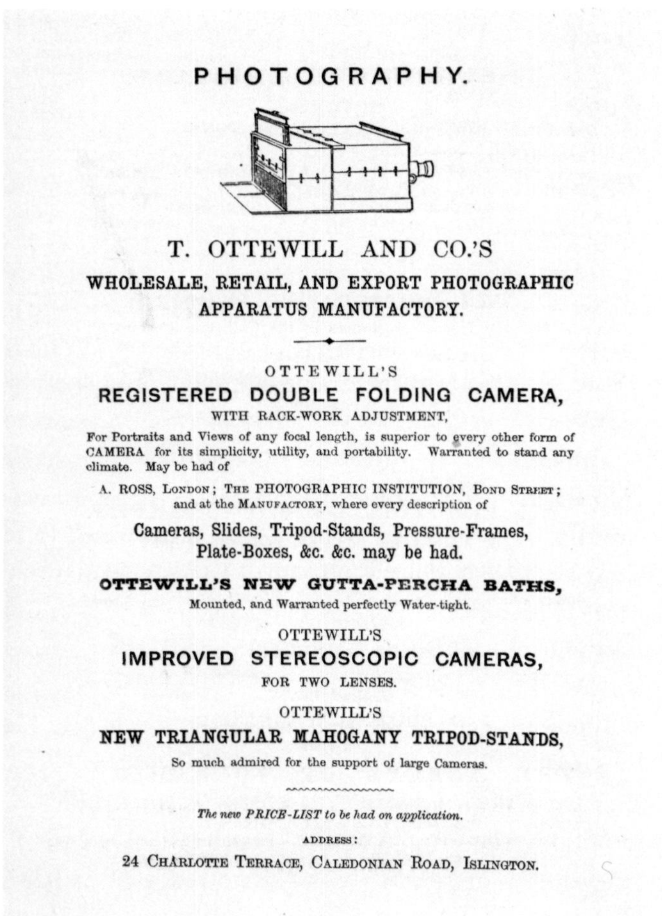

Fig. 54. Advertisement for T. Ottewill's Registered Double Folding Camera. From Thomas Sutton, *The Calotype Process. A Hand Book to Photography on Paper* (London, 1855)., n.p. The Metropolitan Museum of Art, New York, The Joyce F. Menschel Photography Library

Fig. 55. Unknown artist, *A Dark Slide for Holding Sensitized Paper, with letter "a" representing the glass against which the paper is pressed.* Wood engraving, 3 x 3.5 cm (1⅛ x 1⅜ in.). From Marcus Sparling, *Theory and Practice of the Photographic Art* (London, 1856), p. 137, fig. 55. Private collection

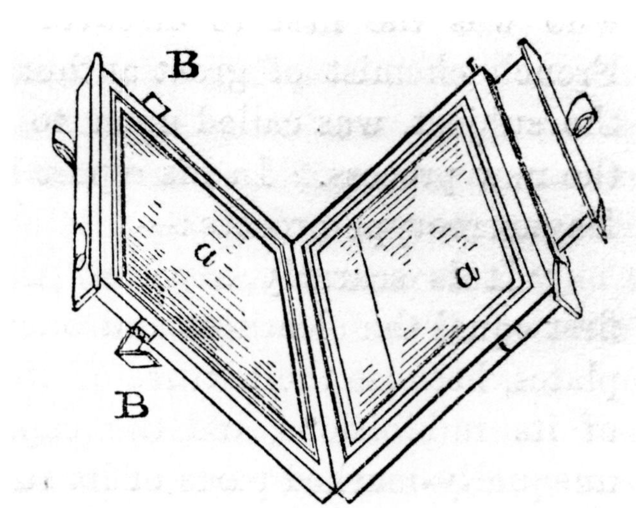

15 pounds, 15 shillings, a modest sum in comparison with the cost of more elaborate outfits offered at 36 pounds. For a beginner the 15-guinea outfit was more than adequate, as the ongoing costs of photography were significant and not for the fainthearted (fig. 54).[38] Far more than the popular pastimes devoted to natural history, it required a serious financial commitment that only a tiny percentage of the population could afford. (For the average workingman, 15 guineas represented many months of labor, while for a domestic servant the possibility of saving such a large sum of money remained a dream throughout the nineteenth century and into the twentieth.)[39]

In the course of the 1850s, photography became a mature discipline practiced with enthusiasm by amateurs and professionals alike, and its results were enjoyed by an ever-widening audience. In this decade the number of commercial portrait studios increased exponentially throughout Britain, so that few towns of any consequence were without their own photographer. The number of recorded photographers rose almost fiftyfold, with 2,534 listed in the 1861 census.[40] As Lady Elizabeth Eastlake, wife of Sir Charles, commented in 1857, "Thus, where not half a generation ago the existence of such a vocation was not dreamt of, tens of thousands (especially if we reckon the purveyors of photographic materials) are now following a new business, practising a new pleasure, speaking a new language, and bound together by a new sympathy."[41]

MAKING A CALOTYPE

Sutton's handbook, *The Calotype Process*, approached its subject straightforwardly. The key to success, Sutton wrote, lay in the making of the negative, a work "requiring considerable thought and study."[42] It was the defining conviction of amateur practice that the negative was the primary object, the print simply its visual manifestation.

The technique had changed little from Talbot's day (see p. 16), although by 1855 the photochemistry had been improved in a number of ways and the process stabilized. There were still six distinct stages for making a calotype negative: iodizing the paper, exciting or sensitizing the paper, exposure in the camera, developing the latent image, fixing the picture to make it permanent, and finishing the negative by washing, drying, and waxing.[43]

Timing was crucial. While iodizing could be "done at home, and at leisure," since the prepared papers kept indefinitely without deteriorating,

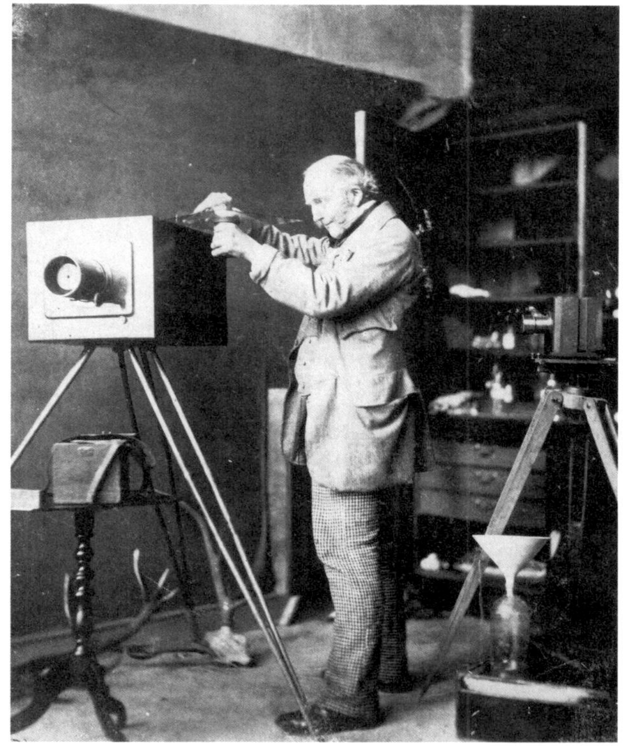

Fig. 56. Henrietta Ross, *A Photographer in His Study* (Horatio Ross), ca. 1858. Albumen silver print from glass negative, 18.9 x 15.2 cm (7½ x 6 in.). The J. Paul Getty Museum, Los Angeles, 84.XM.892.1

sensitizing had to be done with a freshly made solution of gallo-nitrate of silver, which was extremely unstable.[44] This often meant that it was performed "*en route*," perhaps at night in a room illuminated solely by a candle, or in daytime with the windows darkened by a double layer of heavy mackintosh cloth and yellow calico.[45] To prevent spontaneous decomposition of the chemical mix, the equipment had to be scrupulously clean; washing in water was often inadequate, and the recommended method was rinsing in a weak solution of potassium cyanide. This lethal poison could be bought from a pharmacist without difficulty.[46]

To hold the sensitized paper flat, a dark slide was used (fig. 55); some were double-sided and could hold two sheets. Any purposeful amateur carried enough dark slides for a day's work in the out-of-doors. If the format was 12 x 10 inches or larger, the paper was kept motionless by being secured under a sheet of glass or sandwiched between two, but this method carried problems of weight and fragility. When, unknown to the photographer Horatio Ross (fig. 56), a sheet of glass broke in his dark slide prior to exposure, the spider's web of shattered glass created a delicate tracery of radiating lines on his study of Highland cottages

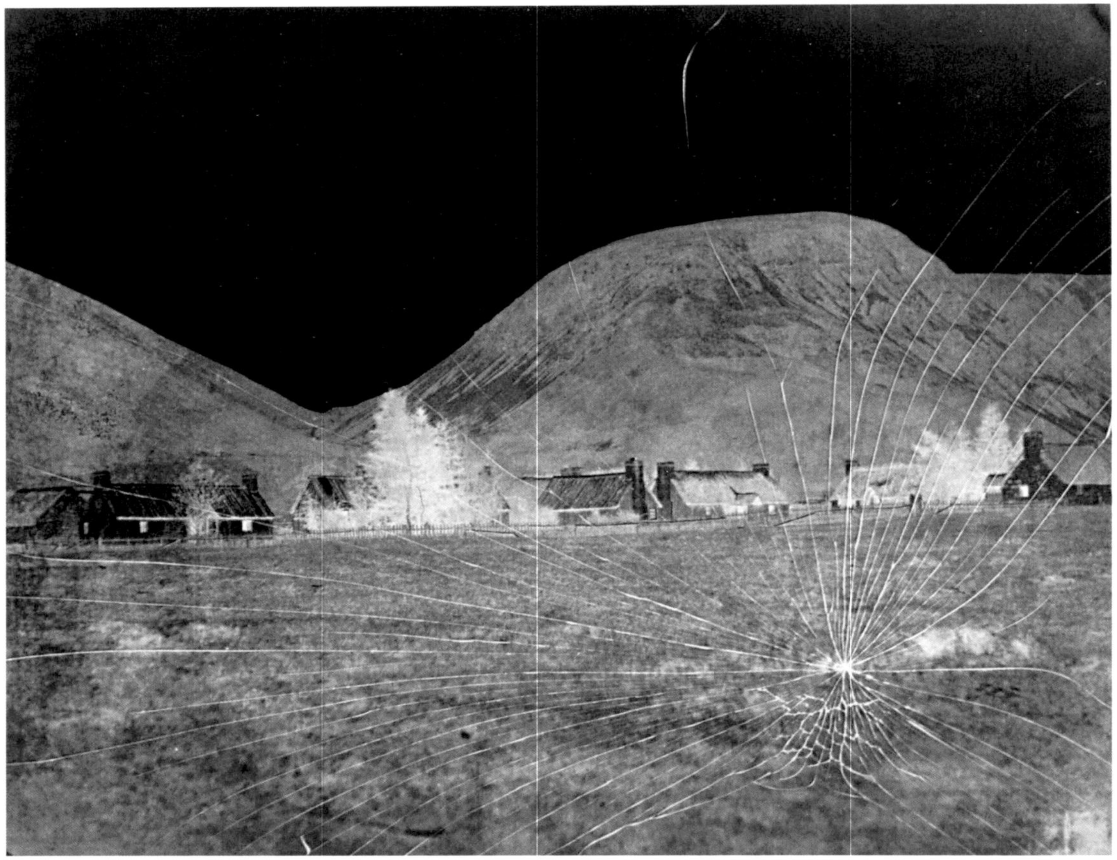

Fig. 57. Horatio Ross, *Cottages in Highland Glen*, showing imprint of glass shattered within dark slide, ca. 1855. Paper negative, 29 x 35.1 cm (11⅜ x 13⅞ in.). Janet Lehr, Inc., New York

(fig. 57). Placing the negative under glass also helped keep it moist and thus reduced the exposure time. However, it also reduced the sharpness of the image—already soft-edged in a paper negative—which did not please all tastes.[47]

Cameras were available in a wide range of designs and formats according to their application. All shared the common feature of a ground glass screen that allowed the photographer to compose and focus the view with the necessary precision. Larger sizes, accommodating a negative of 6½ x 8½ inches (whole plate) and up, were preferred for landscape work, while the smaller half- and quarter-plate sizes were chiefly reserved for portraiture. The negative size dictated the size of the resulting print; there was no practical way to make an enlargement, especially from a paper negative.

A preference for ever-larger formats brought with it the necessity of using lenses with a longer focal length to provide the necessary optical coverage of the negative.[48] But lenses with longer focal length required a significantly longer exposure time to render the negative adequately, and calculating the increase was no easy matter, as Sutton made clear: "Two lenses—one of three inches aperture and six inches focal length, the other of half-an-inch aperture and eighteen inches focal length—are at work together; then the ratio of their times of exposure will be that of 324 to 1. So that if a picture could be taken by the first in one

Fig. 58. Unknown artist, *A Buckle Brush in Use, showing the cotton wool swab [C] used to apply chemicals to a paper negative.* Wood engraving, 2 x 3.5 cm (¾ x 1⅜ in.). From Marcus Sparling, *Photographic Art*, London, 1856, p. 148, fig. 63. Private collection

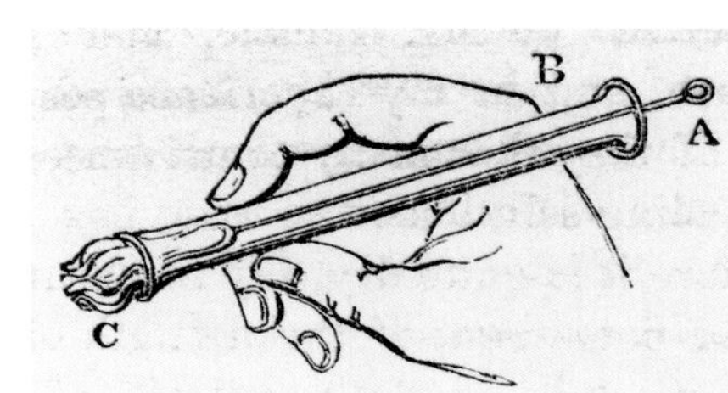

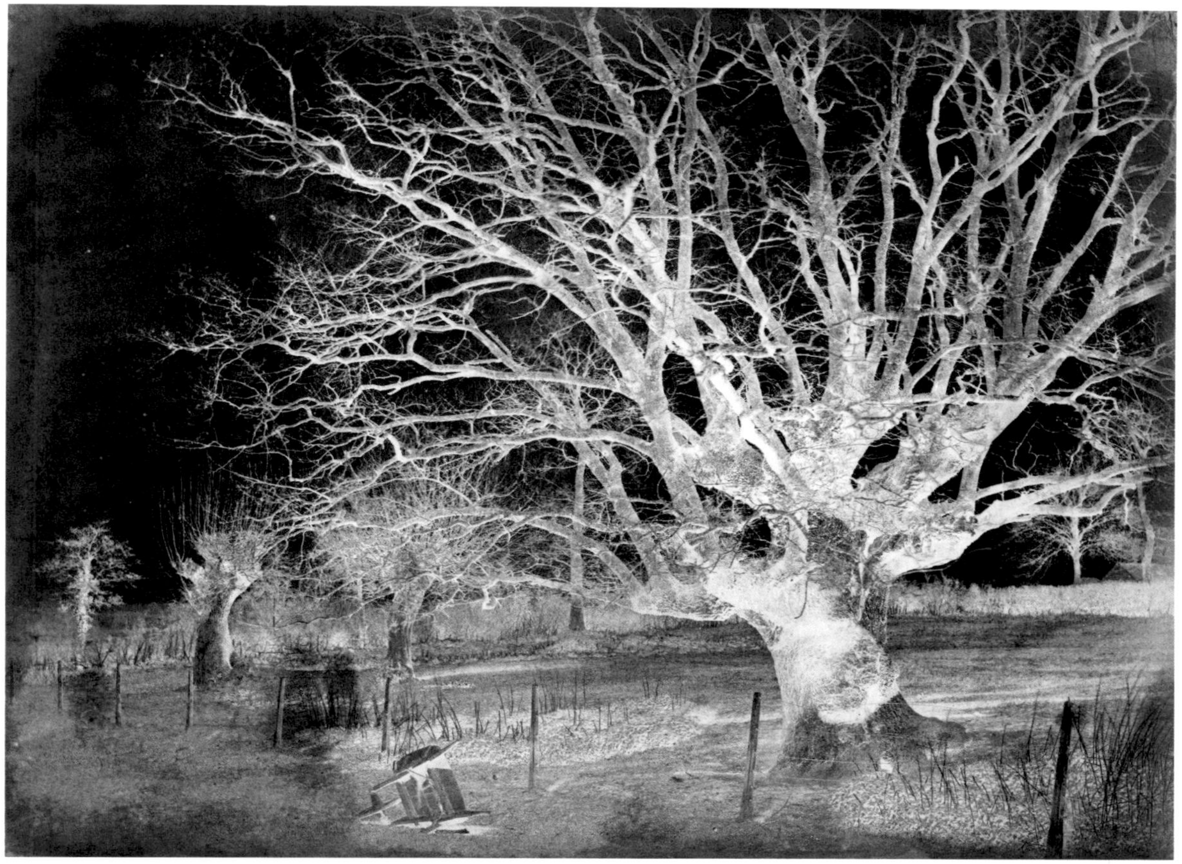

Fig. 59. Benjamin Brecknell Turner (?), *Tree in Winter with Abandoned Wheelbarrow*, ca. 1855. Calotype negative, 29.8 x 40 cm (11¾ x 15¾ in.). The Royal Photographic Society Collection at the National Media Museum, Bradford

second, it would require five minutes and twenty-four seconds by the other,—a difference which could never have been *guessed à priori*, and which will show the importance of rules."[49] For photographers taking large-format landscape views, these exposure times that were minutes longer placed very real constraints on the choice of subject matter. The slightest wind was enough to ruffle foliage and create a distressing blur in the image that would distract the eye and ruin the tranquillity of the scene. Calm weather must have been the dream of all calotypists.

Developing began with removing the exposed negative from the dark slide in the darkroom and examining it by the light of a candle. If there was no visible trace of image, equal proportions of aceto-nitrate of silver and gallic acid were recommended; if the sky area appeared brown through over exposure, the proportion of gallic acid was increased to remedy the problem. The developing solution was applied to the exposed negative using a clean "Buckle" brush "keeping a flowing edge, and not passing over the same place twice, but *bringing the solution gradually down the paper like an advancing tide. Begin with the sky.* . . . The whole picture should be covered in less than a minute" (fig. 58).[50] After a minute's pause for the chemical reaction to begin, the whole surface was copiously swabbed with gallic acid to accelerate and complete the development.

All decisions were based on visual inspection in the yellow light of the darkroom, and knowing when the negative had reached the required density required both experience and judgment. Sutton recommended turning the negative facedown to observe the process through the back of the paper: "When the dark parts of the picture begin to appear through . . . it will be time to lift up the corners and examine the front. *The development should not be arrested until the details in the deepest shadows are fully out.*"[51] The process could take anywhere between ten minutes and an hour. Meanwhile, the back of the negative had to be kept dry to avoid creating unsightly chemical stains that would show up in printing. Once the development was judged to be complete, it was arrested by immersing the negative in a bath of hyposulphite of soda, commonly known as hypo, and keeping it there until every trace of the yellowish silver iodide had dissolved. The fixed negative was clean, white, and utterly insensitive to light (fig. 59).[52]

There were difficulties inherent in the calotype process that Sutton did not mention. Chief among these was weakness of the paper, which often was not robust enough to withstand prolonged immersions, becoming difficult to handle and liable to tear. The addition of a "sizing" compound during manufacture made the paper sturdier, and British papers, sized with animal gelatin, were more robust than French ones sized with starch and resin. The thinner, starch-sized French papers, such as those made by Lacroix and Canson, although extremely weak when wet, were strengthened by Le Gray's waxed-paper process, which filled the pores with wax and gave the paper a strength akin to parchment.[53] The presence of sizing compound influenced the way the paper responded to the photographic chemicals, and it was quickly discovered that while French papers were ideally suited to the waxed-paper process, British papers worked best with the standard calotype recipes.

THE WAXED-PAPER PROCESS

The waxed-paper process was regarded by some as a version of calotype, by others as a closely related but distinct process. According to William Crookes, who wrote the best book on the subject,[54] the waxed-paper process was carried out following the normal photochemical stages of iodizing, sensitizing, developing, and fixing. It differed from the standard calotype process in producing a sharper image and having greater tolerance to extremes of climate, but these advantages were offset by the slowness of every stage of the process.

Assuring the purity of the wax was essential, since it was common for wax to be adulterated with stearin, tallow, rosin, or plaster of paris, all of which impaired its photographic performance.[55] To ensure total saturation the wax had to be molten; Crookes suggested using a kind of photographic bain-marie, a shallow tray in which the wax was kept at a constant temperature by a surrounding bath of boiling water. Copious quantities of best-quality blotting paper and a well-heated smoothing iron were also requisite.

A sheet of ordinary photographic paper (usually French) was briefly immersed in the molten wax, lifted, and carefully drained until the wax congealed on the surface. The paper now contained far more wax than was needed, and the trick was to transfer the excess wax to other sheets of photographic paper. This was achieved by sandwiching the saturated waxed paper between two fresh sheets of photographic paper backed by blotting paper. Heat and pressure were applied with the iron, first to one side and then to the other, until the excess wax from the center sheet was transferred to the sheets of unwaxed paper so they too became saturated. Finally, the waxed sheets were again ironed between clean blotting paper to remove glistening patches of surplus wax. The temperature of the iron at both stages was critical; if too hot the wax decomposed and spoiled, if too cool the excess wax would not transfer. Crookes recommended the Victorian housewife's time-honored test of a drop of water, which should "boil rapidly, but not roll off" the surface of the iron.[56] For those who wanted to avoid this elaborate performance, prewaxed paper had become commercially available during the early 1850s, though at a significantly higher cost than plain paper.[57]

Crookes recommended an iodizing bath with only two main ingredients, potassium iodide and iodine.[58] Getting the waxed paper to absorb the aqueous chemicals of the iodizing bath would seem a physical impossibility, and precisely how it occurred remains an enigma.[59] It took three to four hours for the waxed paper to become completely iodized; by this time the surface of the paper had turned deep purple and was completely smooth and matte.[60] The iodized paper could be stored for long periods without deteriorating—up to ten months, Crookes claimed—which was one of the great attractions of the process.[61] The negative could be sensitized either by floating iodized paper on the surface of the sensitizing bath[62] or, more commonly, by immersing the sheet completely.[63]

Le Gray's waxed-paper negative was far less responsive to light than the calotype, though contemporary opinions on this matter differed widely.[64] For taking a picture, an exposure time of six to eight minutes was quoted as a general rule,[65] but George Fitt, discussing his work in Norfolk, strikes a truer note: "My average exposure, with a good light, is from 16 to 18 minutes; much foliage, and a preponderance of deep shadow, requires a longer time; and light stone buildings in sunshine, much less time. . . . Half an hour . . . is the longest exposure I have ever given a negative out of doors by this process."[66]

The developing and fixing of the exposed waxed-paper negative followed the same procedure as for the calotype. The essential difference between the two finished negatives was that one was on waxed paper, the other on plain paper. They thus imparted differing qualities to their respective prints. The translucent waxed-paper negative gave a sharper, better-resolved image than the calotype, especially if it was of thin, finely structured paper (*homogenous* was the favored term). The heavier and coarser the negative paper, the less the resolution. Not all photographers wanted crisp results, and the choice of paper thickness, like that of a waxed versus an unwaxed negative, became an aesthetic decision.[67]

Easier than making a waxed-paper negative was to make a plain paper negative and then enhance it by "post-waxing." The applied wax allowed more light to be transmitted through the negative, effectively reducing the exposure time necessary for printing. It also heightened the sharpness of the image, although not to the same extent as Le Gray's prewaxed process. But not all photographers pursued this course. Many of Talbot's best-known negatives were never waxed. For instance, in making *The Haystack* Talbot left the negative unwaxed, perhaps preferring the aesthetic relationship between a plain paper negative and a salted paper print. The resulting print, with its fine and intricate detail, disproves the oft-stated belief that the calotype was incapable of such fidelity (pls. 2, 3; see also pls. 18, 19). Exhibition records show that in this period some photographers used the calotype and waxed-paper processes interchangeably, while others remained faithful to one.[68]

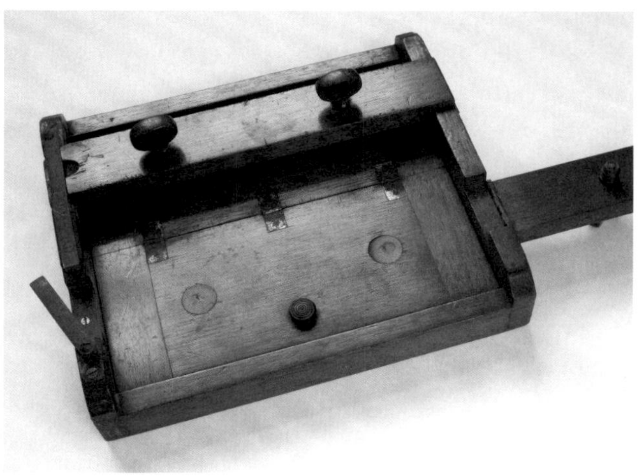

Fig. 60. George Knight, philosophical instrument maker, *Contact Printing Frame for Negatives 10 x 8 Inches*, showing pressure bars and the hinged flap that opened to allow visual inspection of the density during the lengthy exposure, ca. 1855. Wood, iron, and brass, 24.5 x 28.5 cm (9⅝ x 11¼ in.). Private collection

MAKING THE PRINT

The five stages of printing explained in Sutton's handbook, which correspond closely to those originally used by Talbot (see pp. 16–17), were salting or albumenizing and salting the paper; sensitizing it to light with silver nitrate; exposing it to light; fixing and toning the picture; and trimming and mounting the finished picture. Still central to the process was the photochemical conversion of the light-sensitive silver salts by the actinic power of daylight, without the aid of chemical development. Despite requiring significantly longer exposure times (about a million times longer than for modern chemical development), this printing-out process, as it is known today, was preferred for the distinctive warm tones it yielded in comparison with the cooler, more neutral tones of chemically developed prints. For much of the nineteenth century it remained the dominant method of making prints.[69]

Choice of paper for the print also materially affected its appearance. The plain or salted paper print, common throughout the 1840s, was still in general use during the 1850s, but by 1855 it had begun to be superseded and by the end of the decade it had largely dropped out of favor. Distinguished by its matte, nonreflective surface, the salted paper print remained popular with many amateurs because it was thought to "nearly resemble engravings."[70] The contrasting newcomer was albumen paper, which had "a glazed or varnished appearance." Its glossy surface displayed well the fuller tonal range of collodion negatives[71] and was ideal for some of the popular forms of commercial photography, such as photographs viewed in a stereoscope or the diminutive portraits called cartes-de-visite. While the glazed finish did not sit comfortably with calotypists, who prized the "*velvet-like* appearance" of salted paper prints,[72] albumen paper began to dominate public taste during the 1850s, and at that point many amateurs capitulated.

While albumen paper soon became commercially available from photographic retailers, it was of variable quality and dubious freshness, and amateurs were advised to prepare their own. Sutton's instructions read like a classic recipe for meringues: "Into a *very large* basin put: The whites of two dozen fresh eggs. Distilled water . . . half a pint (10 ounces). Common salt . . . one ounce. Beat the whole to a *very stiff* froth with either a *silver* or a *wooden* fork (not an iron one). Cover the basin, and let it stand undisturbed for twenty-four hours."[73] After careful filtering, the salted albumen was placed in a tray and a sheet of plain paper was floated on its surface, then after ten seconds or so lifted off and dried. The albumen acted as a binder, holding the photochemicals on the surface rather than allowing them to be absorbed into the fibers as they would be with plain paper.

Adjustments were possible that offered photographers a measure of control over the print's appearance. Very dilute albumen produced a thin glaze that partially sank into the fibers of the paper, giving a semimatte finish. Conversely, ironing freshly coated paper between sheets of glazed paper hardened the albumen and imparted a smoother gloss. Organic materials other than albumen were frequently used—most notably arrowroot, which produced a different quality and glaze intensity.[74] Although the contrast in appearance between a very matte salted paper print and a fully glossy albumen print is easily recognized, when one process was giving way to the other during the 1850s the transition to higher gloss was gradual, and identifying which type of coating was used for a given print is in some cases almost impossible today.

Whatever the paper used, the basic printing procedures remained the same as it had been: treating the paper in a solution of common salt, drying it, then sensitizing it with a silver nitrate solution. This could be done by floating the paper on the surface of the sensitizing bath (requiring a deft hand), or—more time-consuming but economical and less risky—using a glass rod to roll a tiny wave of sensitizer evenly across the surface.

To make a print, the negative and the sensitized paper were pressed together, and then exposed to daylight. A simple press might be a sheet of plate glass holding the negative and printing paper onto a velvet-covered board. But most photographers employed a specially designed printing frame that firmly held negative and paper together (fig. 60). The whole was then set outdoors: "In the sun, a print may be obtained in from four to ten *minutes*, according to the strength [density or darkness] of the negative; while in the shade, or in diffused daylight, it might require as many *hours*; but if *sufficient* time be allowed, the result will be the same."[75] The only way to tell when a print had reached the required density was by visual inspection, accomplished by opening one half of the hinged flap at the rear of the printing frame while maintaining pressure on the other half. Judging whether a print was ready required experience, since the image would lighten considerably once fixed and toned. As Sutton put it, the print "must not look *too pretty* in this stage, or, when finished, it will appear pale and faded."[76] When deemed ready, the print was removed from the frame and immersed for about ten minutes in a bath of hypo, which dissolved away all unused light-sensitive silver compounds and "fixed" the image permanently.

A final stage was toning the image to enhance its color and depth. The simplest way was to soak the print in a solution of "old hypo" previously used to fix prints.[77] According to one handbook, this would allow the print to "acquire almost any degree of dark tone that may be desired, from red-brown, to violet or black. . . . The time required varies from one hour to three or four days."[78] The results looked impressive, and undoubtedly this method found widespread favor because it recycled what otherwise would have been poured down the drain. It turned out, however, to be a highly damaging treatment that destroyed the color and tonality of prints within a matter of weeks unless they had been repeatedly washed to remove all trace of the chemicals. Doubts about this method of toning first appeared in 1855, when Sutton discovered that many of the prints he had collected from eminent photographers had "either totally perished, or grievously faded!"[79] Others were also concerned, and the council of the Photographic Society established a committee in May 1855 to look into possible reasons for the fading of prints. In its report six months later many causes were adduced, including atmospheric pollution from coal smoke.[80]

A much safer way of toning prints was to employ a solution containing a double hyposulphite of gold and soda, known colloquially as *sel d'or*. During immersion the microscopic particles of silver that make up the image were plated with gold in a fine suspension, which imparted a soft violet tint that was much admired.[81] The procedure was not new, having first been used in 1840 by the physicist Armand-Hippolyte-Louis Fizeau to add warmth and permanence to typically steely-colored daguerreotypes.[82] During the late 1840s it was widely used in France for toning prints but remained relatively uncommon in Britain until 1855. After the public airing of many concerns about old hypo, *sel d'or* toning gradually gained widespread favor.

By 1855, the number of photographers working in paper negative processes had already begun a decline that intensified year by year. Paradoxically, this was part of the calotype's appeal; as one commentator wryly noted, "The *profanum vulgus* keep aloof from it; it is too expensive a pastime for the commonalty."[83] The exclusivity of working with the calotype process made it even more appealing to a social class with deep purses and spare time on their hands. Moreover, the technical matters, which seem endlessly complex and tedious today, were viewed as minor problems that with time and practice could be overcome. Grappling with the issues of chemistry, optics, and light was a welcome challenge for leisured, well-educated minds. Paper negative photography was equally well adapted "for ladies and gentlemen, which cannot be said of the generality of sciences," and this led to its eager adoption by female members of the gentry, for whom silver-black stains on frock and hands were regarded as marks of merit.[84] Whatever their gender, background, and accomplishments, the calotypists of the 1850s were a distinctive group of individuals bound together by a common preoccupation.

PAPER VERSUS GLASS: CONSIDERATIONS OF AESTHETICS AND IDENTITY

Still, it is sometimes hard to fathom the choice of paper-negative photography over one of the glass-based processes. Glass had many advocates. An eminent supporter was the astronomer and meteorologist James Glaisher, who had served as a juror for Class 10, the wide-ranging "Philosophical Instruments" category at the Great Exhibition of 1851.[85] In a paper delivered to the Society of Arts in January 1853, Glaisher expressed admiration for Le Gray's waxed-paper process (see, for example, pl. 20) but preferred the albumen- and collodion-on-glass processes, which rendered subjects of a "smooth and delicate nature" with great clarity.[86] He advised photographers to cultivate and improve the collodion process, which he thought would supersede others in the future.[87]

Glaisher was not alone in this conviction; from the first display of collodion photography at the Great Exhibition, it was seen as a process that would sweep away the disadvantages of both the daguerreotype and the calotype while retaining their best qualities. Collodion fitted the ethos of the period, being modern, unambiguous, bright, and capable of rendering meticulous photographic truths. Above all, it advanced photography commercially. Despite being cumbersome, complex to use, and as demanding of attention as a spoilt child, it was enthusiastically embraced by a whole body of photographers.

The emergence of the glass negative coated with albumen or collodion as a viable photographic alternative coincided almost exactly with

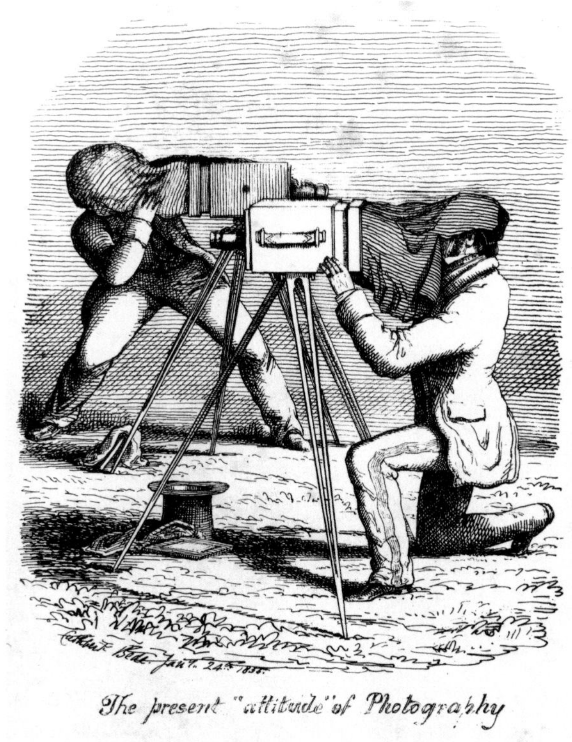

Fig. 61. Cuthbert Bede [pseud. of Edward Bradley], *The present "attitude" of Photography.* Lithograph, 16.5 x 12.2 cm (6½ x 4¾ in.). From Bede, *Photographic Pleasures* (London, 1855), pl. facing p. 80. Two photographers strike "attitudes" when looking through their cameras; the one in the foreground is clearly a studious gentleman, the other perhaps not. Private collection

the introduction into Britain of new methods of making sheet glass. Although this branch of manufacture had been largely dominated by the French, when construction began on the Crystal Palace the British-based firm Chance Brothers won the contract to provide the 300,000 panes of glass needed.[88] The firm had spent six years overcoming the numerous difficulties that beset the process and by 1850 was in a position to mass-produce without any of the bubbles, ripples, and flaws characteristic of glass produced by earlier methods.[89] When ground and polished, the new sheet glass was much prized by photographers. Without these technical advances, the fortunes of paper negative photography and of collodion would likely have followed different courses.

Given the impending dominance of collodion, why did paper processes remain such firm favorites with so many photographers, and for so long? Were their decisions based entirely on aesthetics? Or were they simply conservative and resistant to change? Certainly during the 1840s, the two workable photographic processes were separated by a social divide; the daguerreotype had been adopted by the commercial portrait studios, while the calotype remained the steadfast choice of amateurs who wanted to keep at a distance from anything that hinted of trade. But by the 1850s, new considerations had come to the fore.

Members of the Photographic Society, established in 1853, while basing their individual choices of process on practical considerations and aesthetic preferences, were additionally influenced by the desire to have photography accepted on an equal footing alongside the other fine arts. Although never stated emphatically, this was also an ethos of the Photographic Society itself. Decisions taken by its council clearly suggest that the integration of photography into the fine arts was a principal objective. From the outset, procedures and practices were closer in tone to those of the long-established Royal Academy of Arts (1768) or the more recent Society of British Artists (1823) than to those of a scientifically inclined institution.[90] Securing royal patronage for the Photographic Society at an early stage, an important accomplishment, announced to the numerous skeptics that photography had a legitimate place among the arts. The commitment to mounting annual exhibitions was further indication of the society's artistic ambitions for photography. Indeed, great effort was expended on finding a venue traditionally associated with painting; the first exhibition was held in the rooms of the Society of British Artists, in Suffolk Street, Pall Mall, adjacent to the National Gallery in central London.[91] The printed catalogue was closely modeled on those published by the New Society of Painters in Water Colours, whose galleries were also in Pall Mall.[92] To viewers of the period, these parallels would have been clear. In the Photographic Society's catalogues, the negative process—calotype, albumen on glass, collodion, or something else—was named, establishing that the act of making the negative was more significant than its subsequent printing, and in adopting this approach photographers indicated that their choice of process mattered in the same way that the fact of working in pencil, watercolor, or oil mattered to an artist.

The Photographic Society's artistic ambitions received a significant boost from the private visit Queen Victoria and Prince Albert made to the first annual exhibition in January 1854, at which time the royal party were shown around by leading members of the council.[93] Not only did this give photography the royal seal of approval that in turn encouraged its wider support by fashionable society; it also signaled that the monarchy saw photography as a discipline to be taken seriously, with practitioners worthy of employment and results worthy of acquisition.[94] Previously the royal couple had taken only a passing interest in the new technology, but after 1853 they regularly acquired photographs—as quickly became known—either at the annual exhibitions or from specialized printsellers such as the Photographic Institution.[95]

The 1854 exhibition contained almost a thousand photographs. The British works elicited "expressions of surprise and pleasure . . . at the extreme beauty of the pictures, and the great advance indicated by them, as compared with those produced a year ago."[96] Having been announced as open to contributors from all over, the show also included a strong representation by French photographers, with submissions from Comte Aguado, Édouard Baldus, François Delessert, Auguste Mestral, Henri Le Secq, and others. This diverse range of work presented to the public the wider European context in which British photography could now hold up its head with justifiable pride.[97]

At the Photographic Society's first annual general meeting, self-congratulation seemed in order.[98] However, the mood quickly changed when Matthew Rippingham, accountant and auditor of the society, raised a controversial subject. There was a pressing need to reform the rules by which members were elected to council, he stated, because of the growing number of commercial photographers being admitted to the society. If "the trade once got a footing on the council, the ruin of the society was inevitable," he warned, and therefore he proposed "that no person practising photography professionally, or selling his pictures for profit, nor any dealers in photographic chemicals, materials, or apparatus, should be eligible for election *on the council*."[99] The motion carried by a substantial majority, for no one wanted the society to become the equivalent of a trade association. But the wider question that had been raised was, "Where could the line be drawn between the professional photographer making and *selling his pictures for profit*, and the *amateur* who *sold* his pictures?"[100] Three pillars of the society, Fenton, Foster, and Alfred Rosling, offered their immediate resignations from the council because, although amateurs, they sold their photographs for profit. Indeed, it quickly became clear that if Rippingham's proposition were allowed to stand, the ranks of the council would be decimated and the society left in disarray. After much debate, Eastlake, as president, managed with a few deft moves to get Rippingham's proposal rescinded, the resignations withdrawn, and the status quo restored. But the central question remained unresolved.[101]

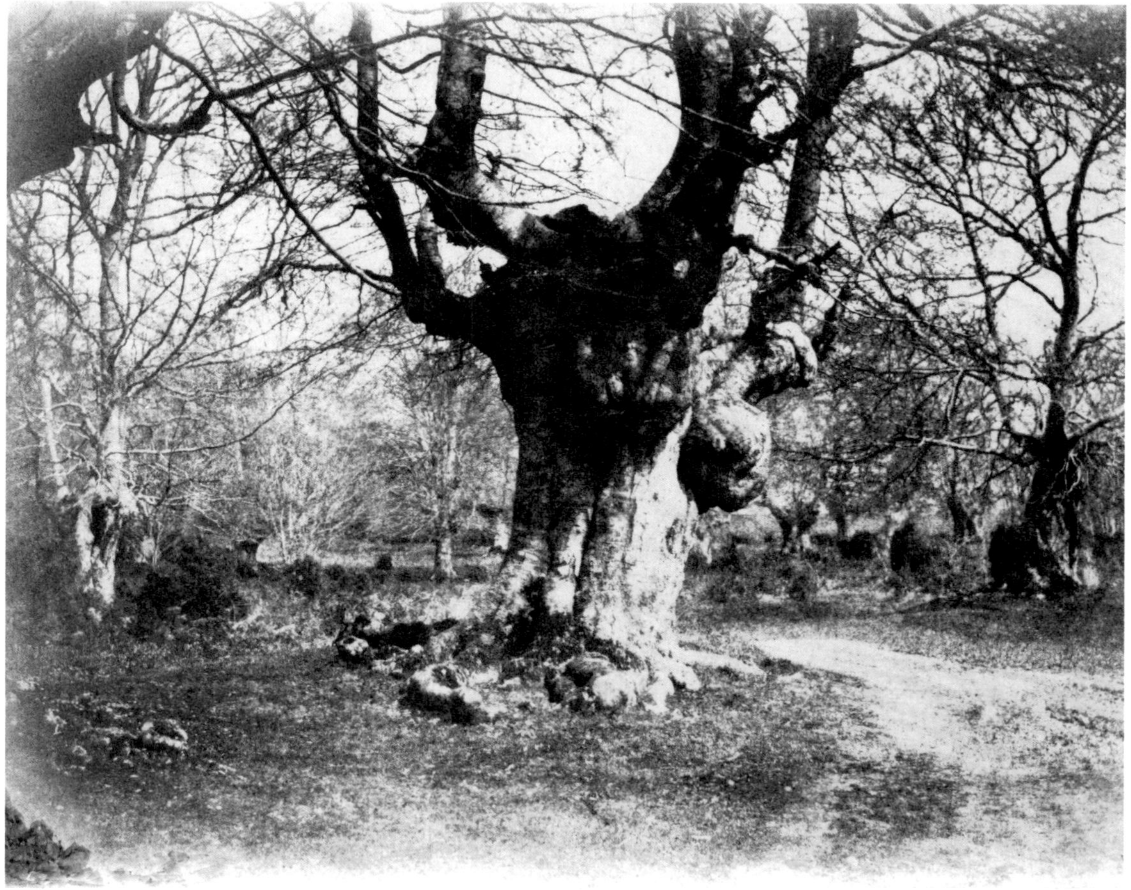

Fig. 62. Sir William Newton, *Burnham Beeches*, ca. 1853. Salted paper print, 16.9 x 21.7 cm (6⅝ x 8½ in.). Princeton University Art Museum, Princeton, N.J., Museum purchase, anonymous gift, 2001-12

This troublesome problem—whether amateurs selling photographs differed from photographers "in trade"—had created difficulties since early in the 1840s, especially for Talbot when amateurs infringed the terms of their licenses by receiving payment for their works. This time, however, the context of the discussion was different. To the council of the Photographic Society, there was no question of artistic recompense being confused with income from trade. Their concern was not, as one might imagine, to preserve class distinctions. It was rather to maintain hold of the elevated status that artists held in society.

The national census taken on March 31, 1851, made use of an improved system of classification designed to account for every known occupation.[102] Fourteen distinct classes were further divided into subclasses according to characteristics of employment. The highest order, class 1, was that of the queen and members of the royal family; in its subclasses were members of the legislature, the civil service, and local governments and officers of the East India Company. Class 2 contained everyone employed in the defense of the realm. In class 3 were practitioners of the three learned professions—the clergy, the law, medicine—and their "irregular assistants of various kinds."[103] Inexorably the system inched downward through the occupations, moving broadly from brain to brawn until it reached the lowest orders of classification, which were reserved for those known collectively as the "labouring classes."[104]

Although originally conceived as a way to comprehend the wide diversity of occupations in the Victorian era within a single classification system, the census scheme inevitably came to be thought of as an index of social status. And anomalies abounded. Relevant to our story is the fact that class 4 was the category of "the poet, the historian, the painter, the sculptor, the musician, the architect, and the natural philosopher, as well as the professors and teachers of literature and science."[105] Class 11, however, was the place for those directly "engaged in the higher class of mechanical and chemical arts," whose daily occupations brought them into close contact with "artists and men of science; from whom they frequently . . . derive materials, direction, or inspiration."[106] They translated works of art into engravings, etchings, or lithographs; they were the musicians, actors, or singers who interpreted compositions. Class 4 created the original, while class 11 performed it.

The decision of the census authorities to place photography in class 4 was undoubtedly correct, for making photographs was closer in spirit to the occupation of poet, painter, and natural philosopher than that of engraver or lithographer. But a contradiction that arose from this decision, becoming especially clear after 1851, when the number of practitioners began to rise, was that many photographers were essentially entrepreneurs and businessmen. Their photographic practice enterprises owed far more to commerce than to artistic self-expression.

In the context of these broader cultural concerns, Rippingham's proposal to the Photographic Society assumes a different complexion. His move to block professional photographers from joining the council becomes an assertion that amateur photography was indisputably a creative endeavor and a plea to clarify the ambiguous status of amateurs selling their work for profit. This was unexplored territory with few precedents to guide the way, and with the benefit of hindsight we can appreciate why Eastlake chose a pragmatic avoidance rather than confrontation. The society, just a year old, was too young to weather fragmentation, which would have undermined its ambitions to secure photography's rightful place among the visual arts.

However, by backing away from conflict, the society also failed to address how it could protect the wishes of amateurs while accommodating the needs of professionals. The issue continued to surface in different guises over the next several years; each time, small concessions were made to the professional photographers, who grew ever more dominant. By the close of the decade, the society's annual exhibitions had virtually become a showcase for commercial portrait studios.[107] This trend was not confined to London. Throughout the country there was no stopping the arrival of commercial photography, and by the mid-1860s the transition would be complete.

To some extent, the choice of glass or paper negative became a proxy for asserting the legitimacy of commercial or amateur photography. But there were genuine artistic allegiances as well. On the one hand was albumen or collodion on glass, whose clarity not only matched the public taste for objective detail but was intrinsically dazzling. Entirely different was the paper negative, whose broad massing of detail and tonal values were most frequently equated with true artistic expression. The distinction between hard and soft, sharp and diffuse, was a topic of debate at meetings of photographic societies throughout the 1850s. Among other things, it divided (although this was never stated openly) those who preferred the traditional realistic mode of art from those sympathetic to the new Pre-Raphaelite style.

An early advocate of soft focus was Sir William Newton, founding member and vice president of the Photographic Society and official miniature painter to Queen Victoria.[108] In a paper he gave to the society he suggested that the foreground of a photograph should be deliberately thrown out of focus to create an artistic effect (fig. 62).[109] While today differential focus is taken for granted as a device to give emphasis to the main subject of the picture, in 1853 optical sharpness was a prized cornerstone of good photographic practice. Newton's championing of selective focusing and soft detail was based on his conviction that photography followed divergent pathways of science and art, the one relying on the laboratory in the pursuit of chemical and optical perfection, the other representing the truths of nature through a more generalized image. It was, he argued, not "necessary or *desirable* for an *artist* to represent . . . every minute detail" but rather to create a broad effect building on "the *suggestions* which nature offers."[110] A committed calotypist, Newton made his proposals in defense of paper negative processes and against the crisp aesthetics of collodion. Not everyone agreed, and the topic continued to generate discussion at meetings of the society and in the correspondence columns of the *Photographic Journal.* Some fifty years later, the deliberate manipulation of focus would reemerge as a central theme of the Pictorialist movement in photography.[111]

Newton also maintained that an artistic approach to photography might include activities beyond strictly photographic ones. Retouching a negative with pigments and chemicals to create a more picturesque effect was, he suggested, a legitimate artistic practice.[112] This was a natural line of thought for someone trained as an engraver and a painter. For makers of paper negatives, Newton was validating an appealing aspect of their practice: the smoothly textured surface of the paper made it easy to retouch a negative, and many photographers

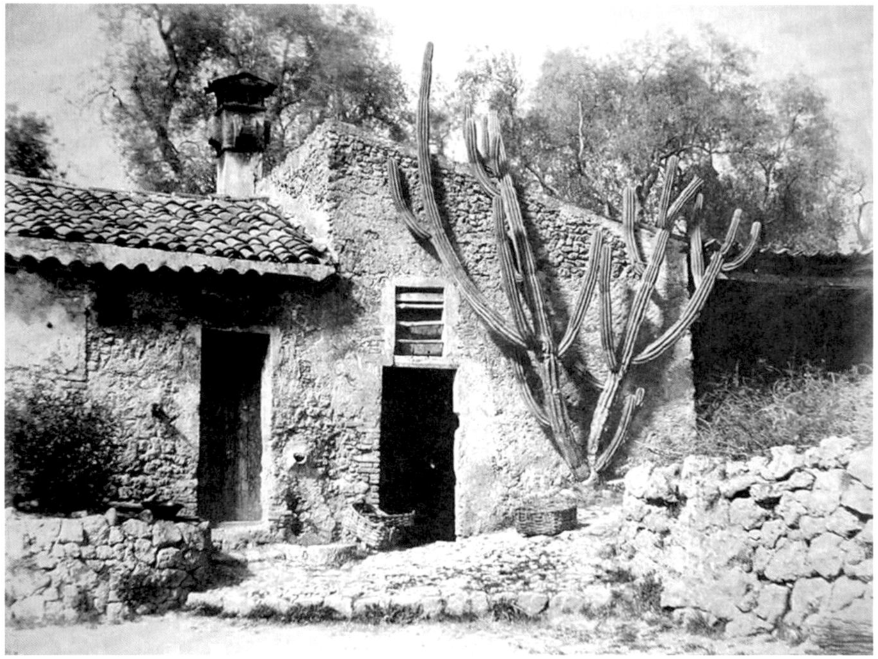

Fig. 63. Alfred Backhouse, *At Nice, 1854.* Salted paper print from waxed-paper negative, 22 x 27.6 cm (8⅝ x 10⅞ in.). Exhibited at the Photographic Institution, 1855. Collection of Jay H. McDonald

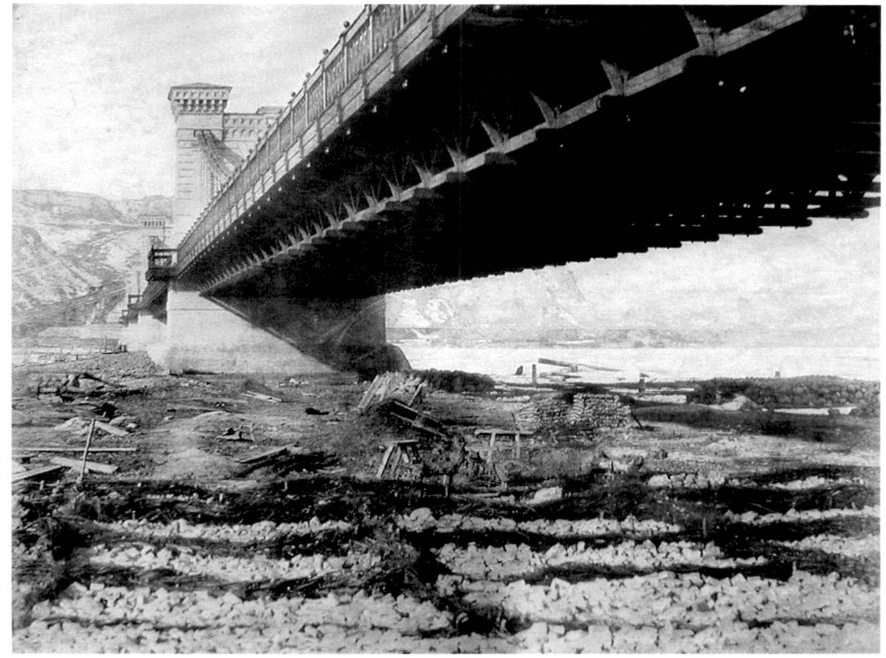

Fig. 64. John Cooke Bourne, *Dnieper Bridge, Looking towards the Lavra Heights, from Water Level,* October 1853. Salted paper print, 40.7 x 53.5 cm (16 x 21⅛ in.). National Museum of the History of the Ukraine, Kyiv

relished the opportunity to intervene artistically with pencil, pigment, and imagination.[113]

Photographers of this period, striving to define themselves, were struggling with the all-embracing nature of the term *photographer.* In the census of 1851 and in post office directories the term was just coming into official use and was broadly used to embrace all manner of photographic activity. If the Photographic Society wanted to plant the flag for photography in the well-established territory of the fine arts, it had to demonstrate a meaningful and legitimate claim. In this context, a choice made by photographers to remain faithful to paper processes became a signal of their artistic intent. When photographs were "sent forth into the world to be placed in similar positions as pictures and engravings," Newton emphasized, "their appearance ought not to be so *chemically,* as *artistically* beautiful."[114] Another commentator put the case against the glass negative succinctly: "Photographic pictures at present are too literal to compete with works of art."[115]

While the choice of calotype or of any paper negative process sprang from the desire to see photography placed among the fine arts and photographers regarded as artists, those following this course were, perhaps without knowing it, swimming against the tide. Photography, with its egalitarian nature, was following the public taste toward sharpness, smoothness, and fidelity. By 1855, when we have our novice taking up photography, the decision to adopt the calotype process would have set him somewhat apart from the mainstream of photographic activity. Before he left the Photographic Institution with his precious new equipment, he may have seen its exhibition of British and European photographs and reflected on the wisdom of his choice. Of all the prints, fewer than 20 percent had been made from paper negatives.[116] He may have taken comfort, however, in the fact that all the British calotypists represented were also members of the Photographic Society and currently exhibiting in London (figs. 63, 64)—reassurance that he now belonged to an exclusive elite.

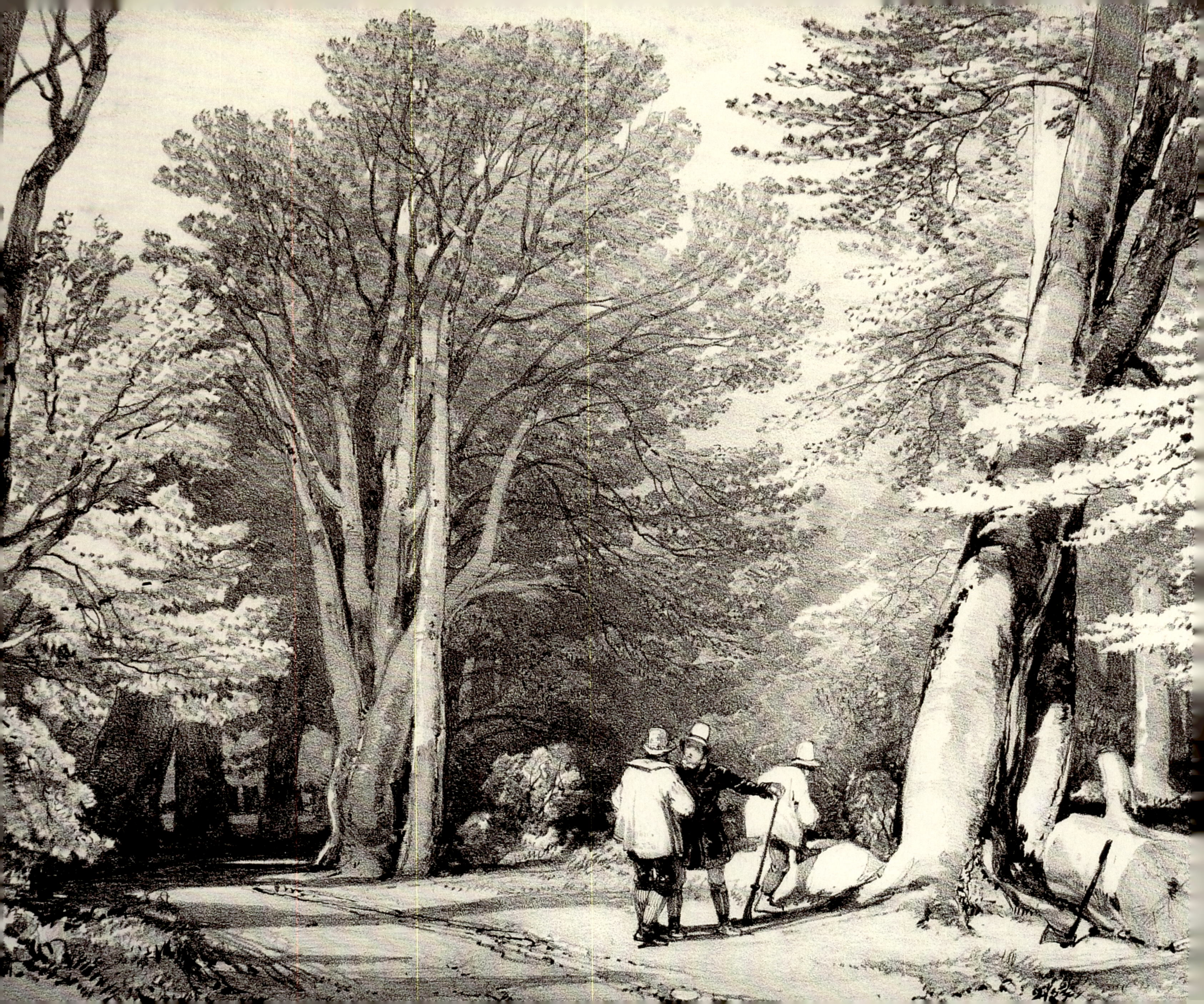

6. *Subjects Fit for the Camera*

The year 1855 opened uncertainly for Britain. She had been at war against Russia in the Crimea for nine months, and the campaign had gone disastrously wrong, with great loss of life. Now the realization was dawning that the army was "overtasked from want of calculation, and underfed from want of foresight," while "Balaklava was a cemetery and Scutari a pesthouse."[1] With the nation uneasy, Parliament was recalled to address the crisis and a committee of inquiry established to investigate the military debacle. In the midst of this national turmoil, Roger Fenton sailed for the site of the war on February 20, taking with him his photographic van, five cameras, seven hundred glass plates, and thirty-six chests of personal effects that included a supply of preserved meats, wine, and biscuits.[2]

Fenton had been making careful preparations in the months leading up to his departure, but this had not prevented him from fulfilling his duties as honorary secretary of the Photographic Society or from submitting a large and diverse body of work to the second annual exhibition that opened in January 1855. Among the forty-five prints he showed was a narrative sequence of five studies made during Queen Victoria's inspection of the fleet at Spithead on the eve of its departure, just days before Britain signed a treaty with France and Turkey that effectively declared war on Russia.[3] Making photographs of this subject seems a natural expression of Fenton's belief in the pluralistic nature of photography. He was, however, the only member of the Photographic Society showing any work that alluded to the war with Russia.[4] The other photographs—more than nine hundred of them—were studies of landscapes and architecture containing no hint that the nation portrayed was gearing up for conflict.

It is not that Britons were ignoring the war. The pages of the *Illustrated London News* had been filled for months with detailed reports of military and naval activity, many accompanied by striking woodcuts designed to stir up patriotic fervor.[5] With men leaving their families to depart for war, commercial photographers most likely experienced a brisk trade in portraiture, their chief business. Amateur photographers preferred to stay with the comforting subject matter of landscapes, woodland glades, and antiquarian architecture.

Why should this have been the case when photography was ideally suited to recording the extraordinary social and structural changes that took place in the mid-nineteenth century? What kept these amateur photographers from breaking with convention to present another side of Victorian life? What ideas about photographic subject matter guided them?

THE LURE OF THE PICTURESQUE

The second annual exhibition of the Photographic Society of London, opening early in 1855, was held in a new location, the Pall Mall galleries of the Society of Painters in Water Colours—a setting that neatly underscored the kinship these photographers felt with the fine arts (and that turned out to be a wise choice, since attendance figures quickly surpassed those for the previous year).[6] The titles in the exhibition catalogue reveal a striking uniformity of subject matter. There are woodland glades, shady pools, cottages, village churches—scenes of rural tranquillity. There are castles, cathedrals, ruined abbeys, ancient trees—subjects suggestive of a distant, more glorious period in Britain's past. Finally, there are scenes of foreign lands; but even here the choice of subject seems largely predetermined, following conventions that now appear conservative (for examples of this aesthetic tendency, see pls. 36–40, 81, 82, 86). To understand how these conventions entered into the visual culture one has to look beyond photography and examine social and artistic forces that shaped the period.

In the mid-eighteenth century, the custom had arisen for members of the British aristocracy and landed gentry to undertake a trip across Europe—the "Grand Tour"—with Italy as their ultimate destination.

Opposite: Fig. 65. James Duffield Harding, *Beech Trees from Buckhurst Park*, detail. Lithograph, 21.5 x 30.6 cm (8½ x 12 in.). From Harding, *Elementary Art; or, The Use of the Lead Pencil*, 1834. Private collection

While this practice began as a means of completing one's education before settling down to manage the family estates, it gradually became transformed into a fashionable pastime.[7] Samuel Johnson's aphorism "A man who has not been in Italy, is always conscious of an inferiority" neatly encapsulates the sentiment of the time.[8] When this regular migration came to a sudden halt late in the century with the onset of the French revolutionary and Napoleonic wars, which closed Europe to peaceful travel, this same group took to their carriages and began to explore the beauties of the British landscape. They were not the first to have done so; for generations, lone individuals had traveled the length and breadth of Britain and reported in detail on the topography and customs of the people they encountered. They had been the exceptions, however, and quite unlike the gentlefolk who now flocked in domestic parties to the countryside, savoring its delights as they journeyed from place to place.

A key figure in shaping public attitudes toward the outdoors was the Reverend William Gilpin, a headmaster, biographer, and writer on art.[9] He had published his first ideas on the Picturesque in 1768, and by 1792 these notions, now fully developed, were elaborated in the influential work *Three Essays: On Picturesque Beauty; on Picturesque Travel; and on Sketching Landscape.* Gilpin proposed a new visual approach, namely, to examine "the scenery of nature" by "the rules of painting."[10] Armed with notebook and sketch pad he journeyed across Britain, identifying locations that he felt conformed to his ideals, and on the basis of these excursions he published, between 1782 and 1809, a series of *Observations* about different regions—in every case "relative chiefly to Picturesque Beauty." In the first of these, *Observations on the River Wye*, Gilpin spells out his intent: "The following little work proposes a new object of pursuit; that of not barely examining the face of a country, but of examining it by the rules of picturesque beauty."[11] Here is his description of the river:

> *The beauty of these scenes arises chiefly from . . . the lofty banks of the river, and its mazy course. . . . From these two circumstances the views it exhibits, are of the most elegant kind of perspective; free from the formality of lines. Every view on a river, thus circumstanced, is composed of four grand parts; the area, which is the river itself; the two side-screens, which are the opposite banks, and mark the perspective, and the front-screen; which points out the winding of the river.*[12]

Having presented the view as if it were a theatrical setting, complete with side screens, foreground, and elegant perspective, Gilpin goes on to analyze the various elements that make an agreeable composition. Nothing escapes his vigilance, from the pictorial value of broken ground and rocky outcrops to the ornamental significance of trees. In his scheme, everything in nature has its place within the vocabulary of the Picturesque. Here is his assessment of rocks:

> *The rock, as all other objects, though more than all, receives its chief beauty from contrast. Some objects are beautiful in themselves. The eye is pleased with the tuftings of a tree: it is amused with pursuing the eddying stream; or it rests with delight on the shattered arches of a Gothic ruin. . . . But the rock, bleak, naked, and unadorned, seems scarcely to deserve a place among them. Tint it with mosses, and lychens of various hues, and you give it a degree of beauty. Adorn it with shrubs, and hanging herbage, and you still make it more picturesque. Connect it with wood, and water, and broken ground; and you make it in the highest degree interesting. Its colour, and its form are so accommodating, that it generally blends into one of the most beautiful appendages of landscape.*[13]

This was persuasive stuff. The reader felt as though accompanied through the countryside by Gilpin himself, who stopped now and then to point out just where the elements of scenery fell into place to create a perfect picture. His careful analysis taught a whole generation how to observe and appreciate landscape as they had never done before. Gilpin gave readers an incentive to explore Britain with fresh eyes, in the hope of discovering some new beauty spot or uncharted view; and he provided a critical language with which to express their response. The eighteenth-century traveler was encouraged to become a tourist in his own country and to savor the delights and emotional rewards of discovery.

> *The first source of amusement to the picturesque traveller, is the pursuit of his object. . . . We suppose the country to have been unexplored. Under this circumstance the mind is kept constantly in an agreeable suspense. The love of novelty is the foundation of this pleasure. Every distant horizon promises something new; and with this pleasing expectation we follow nature through all her walks. We pursue her from hill to dale; and hunt after those various beauties, with which she every where abounds. . . .*

After the pursuit we are gratified with the attainment of the object. Our amusement . . . arises from the employment of the mind in examining the beautiful scenes we have found.[14]

This paragraph demonstrates why Gilpin's theories became so popular among the leisured classes: they offered a purposeful occupation. Appreciation of the countryside now demanded active and imaginative participation. And once the eye had been trained to distinguish a picturesque view, the individual would be amply rewarded by the unfolding panorama of the British landscape, with pleasure at every stage and the ultimate prize the emotional response triggered by locating the faultless view (fig. 66).

Like all new theories, Gilpin's met with serious critical opposition that drew attention to his frequent inconsistencies. However, this did not prevent his ideas from finding widespread acceptance among the intellectual elite who determined fashionable taste;[15] indeed, the controversy surrounding his approach gave it a vitality and currency that ensured its survival well into the nineteenth century. By the 1840s the term *picturesque* had joined the vocabulary of the nation and become widely applied to anything that caught the eye or captured the imagination. But the Victorian impulse to classify, enumerate, and catalogue interacted with Gilpin's broadly set-out scheme to create something altogether more formalized and systematic.

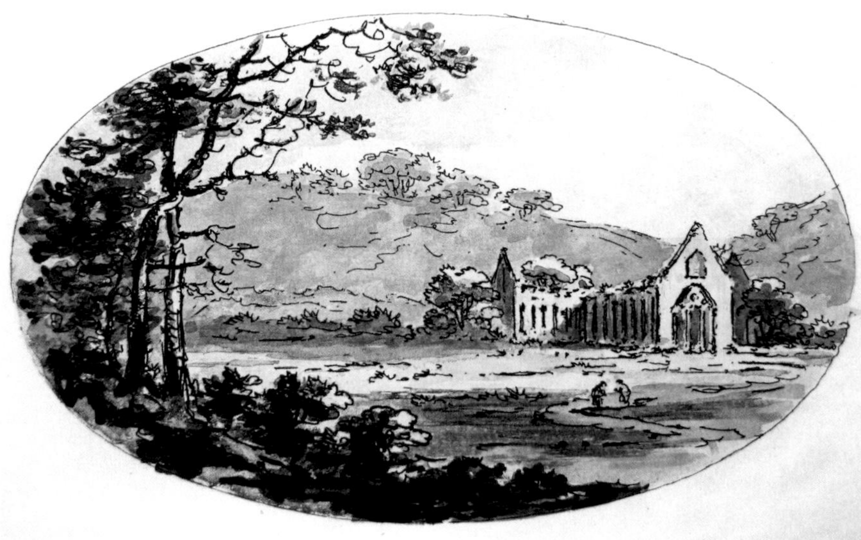

Fig. 66. William Gilpin, *Tintern Abbey.* Etching washed with watercolor, 10.4 x 17.1 cm (4⅛ x 6¾ in.). From Gilpin, *Observations on the River Wye* (London, 1782). The Metropolitan Museum of Art, New York, Purchase, Jeffrey L. Berenson Gift, 2003, 2003.535

Victorians (and their contemporaries on the Continent) took an inventory of picturesque natural phenomena. They categorized mountains, rocks, trees, lakes, rivers, waterfalls, clouds, and sunbeams.[16] All these were thought of not merely as compositional devices but as objects endowed with a metaphoric potential, and pictures were packed with meanings that often elude us today. Trees, for example, were "essential to rural scenery, and their appearance . . . intimately associated with rural and pastoral habits," although in forest scenery their great number implied wildness. An individual tree evoked ideas of strength, protection, and safety, "the leafy roof which shelters . . . from the storm and from the oppressive heat of the sun" (fig. 65).[17] The presence of a picturesque ruin—and all ruins were considered picturesque, no matter how dilapidated—was especially valued, as ruins were intimately associated with "the pleasures of stillness and solitude," making "a delicate allusion to the frailty of human existence."[18]

Instead of merely "feeling" the landscape as Gilpin had suggested, Victorians drew upon a whole portmanteau of sensibilities when experiencing literature, music, and the fine arts. In terms of landscape or pictures of landscape, these emotions were measurable and were categorized as experiences of the Beautiful, the Picturesque, and the Sublime. Each stood at a different plane of intensity. At the lowest pitch came the response to beauty, also generally agreed upon as the most difficult to define. One author quoted the influential eighteenth-century art historian Johann Joachim Winckelmann: "Beauty is a secret of nature: we behold it, and experience its effects; but it is not easy to form a distinct and clear idea of its nature. Its essence is still to be discovered."[19] Still, the idea of beauty was understood by everyone and associated with feelings of tenderness, affection, languor, and inner contentment. At the other extreme was a sense of the Sublime—a state of agitation brought on by the experience of danger, awe, desolation, magnitude, solemnity, and the infinity of nature.[20] It was elicited, for instance, by standing perilously on a cliff, pinnacle, or ledge looking outward across an Alpine vista, especially at sunset or twilight.[21] Somewhere between these two came the Picturesque, which created an emotional response that was neither languorous nor perilous but that pleased the eye and uplifted the soul in a most satisfactory way.

What began as a new way of thinking about the countryside had by the 1840s evolved into a fairly specific course plotted through rural Britain, with regions such as South Wales, the Lake District, the Peak District, and the Lowlands of Scotland identified as areas of outstanding natural beauty. Traveling was no longer merely something to be endured between departure and arrival. The traveler had become a tourist, who took pleasure from exploring, discovering, and absorbing and who moved through the countryside with a sense of anticipation. This transition was supported by the rapid growth of Britain's railway network, which between 1844 and 1850 expanded by an impressive 172 percent. Slightly more than six thousand miles of track crisscrossed the country by 1850, and during the next decade this figure increased to nine thousand.[22] It was now possible to travel from London to the North in comfort and at speeds unimaginable to folk of Gilpin's generation. In 1763, the journey by coach from London to Edinburgh had taken a fortnight. By 1835, improvements in the highways had reduced the travel time to forty-eight hours. In 1849, the same journey by rail took twelve hours.[23] Queen Victoria made her first railway journey in 1842 and found the experience so much to her liking that thereafter she took the train whenever possible. Railway became the fashionable way to travel and, for the prospective tourist based in London, Manchester, or any of the burgeoning industrial cities of the North, the preferred means of escape to the countryside.[24]

Uppermost in the mind of any tourist was the choice of destination, and throughout the nineteenth century answers to this question were supplied by a proliferation of tourist literature.[25] Whether pocket books of local interest or something more sweeping in geographic scope, all provided a detailed interpretation of their chosen territory and suggested itineraries to include the widest possible number of attractions en route. The Edinburgh publishers Adam & Charles Black made their name with a series of *Black's Picturesque Guides* containing "Maps, Charts, numerous Views of the scenery, full particulars regarding Hotels, Inns, Rates of Charges, Distances, and every information likely to prove useful or instructive."[26] Initially such guidebooks only covered the chief beauty spots of Britain, but such was their commercial success that ultimately few regions escaped attention. The situation was similar in Europe, with the German publisher Karl Baedeker and the London publisher John Murray competing to dominate that market.

The guidebooks aimed to enrich the experience of every tourist, often by associating a place with some scene from history or literature belonging to that indeterminate period romantically regarded as a "golden age" by British society. Lengthy quotations from such authors as Wordsworth, Scott, or Shakespeare set the emotional tone, populating the scene with fictional characters made real by mental association.[27]

In many ways these guidebooks were the natural successors to Gilpin's *Observations* published fifty years earlier, for they too encouraged active participation rather than passive observation of the landscape. This was immensely appealing to the Victorian sensibility, which found nothing in life meaningful unless it had a moral value or a specific utility. In the countryside, "rational recreation," or enjoyment with a purpose, included such activities as botanizing, fossil-hunting, collecting birds' eggs and ferns, and sketching and painting.[28] It was as if the portable bits and pieces of nature had to be appropriated, taken home, classified, and placed in display cabinets, aquariums, or terrariums

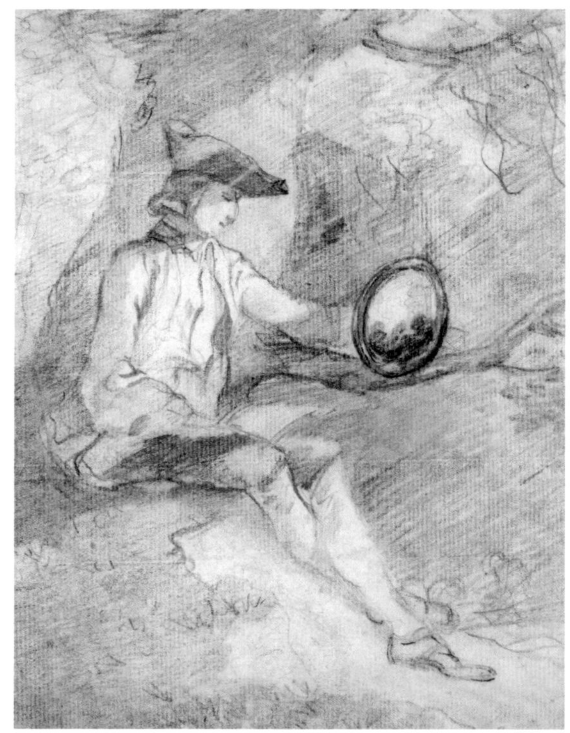

Fig. 67. Thomas Gainsborough, *Study of a Man Sketching Using a Claude Glass*, ca.1750–55. Pencil, 18.4 x 13.8 cm (7¼ x 5⅜ in.). The British Museum, London, Department of Prints and Drawings, 1988.3.5.59. © Copyright The Trustees of The British Museum

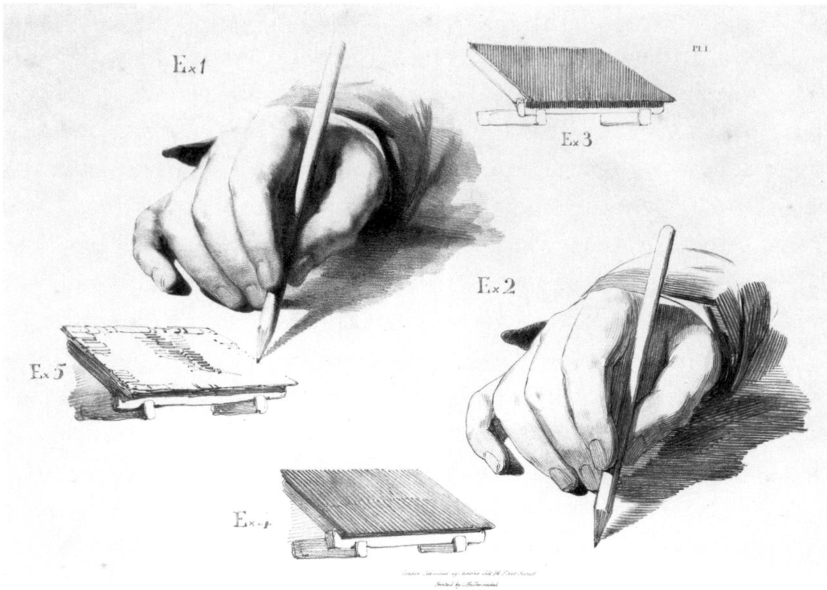

Fig. 68. James Duffield Harding, *Four Illustrations on holding the pencil and applying different types of shading.* Lithograph, 21.5 x 30.6 cm (8½ x 12 in.). From Harding, *Elementary Art; or, The Use of the Lead Pencil,* 1834. Private collection

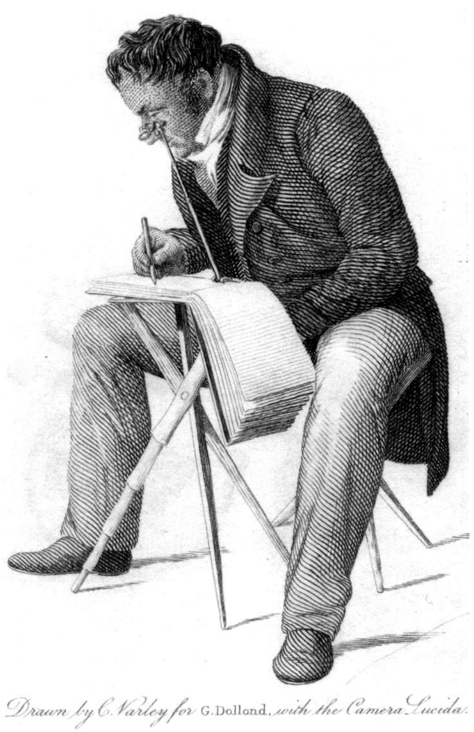

Fig. 69. Cornelius Varley, *Artist Sketching with a Wollaston style Camera Lucida.* From George Dolland, *Description of the Camera Lucida,* 1830. Gernsheim Collection, Harry Ransom Humanities Research Center, The University of Texas at Austin

("Wardian cases") to be fully appreciated.[29] In the rapidly industrializing world of the 1850s, living in an urban environment had become the experience of the majority, and it was comforting to own a little bit of nature in some form.[30]

Of these pastimes, it was sketching and painting that helped pave the way for photography, and for those engaging in them the guidebook proved an invaluable resource. Its directions often led the willing tourist to a specific location where the scenery conformed to the ideals of the Gilpinian Picturesque, with the various elements of the landscape coming together in perfect harmony. Such spots became known as viewing stations (and were the precursors of the little sunburst symbols that enliven tourist maps today).

IMAGING AIDS

Having reached the chosen spot, a visitor could settle down and contemplate the view, either directly or by its reflection in the mirrored surface of an optical device known as a Claude glass. Named for the admired painter Claude Lorraine, this was a framed convex mirror of dark-tinted glass that suppressed the tones of the reflected view. To use it, the viewer usually turned his back on the landscape itself (fig. 67). Miniaturized and muted, the image presented in the Claude glass more closely resembled a painting or print than the bright realities of nature. Containing the view within a frame promoted the proper contemplation of the reflected, transient image, thus fixing it more permanently in the memory.[31]

For in the decades preceding the introduction of photography, tourists who wanted an image that permanently embodied their feelings and sentiments took out their sketch pads, sharpened their pencils, and drew the scene before them.[32] Travel diaries were often enriched with sketches and visual annotations.[33] The ability to sketch and to paint in watercolors was a necessary accomplishment among the leisured classes; one drawing manual of the period asks, "Who is there amongst the numerous classes of men daily leaving our public schools and universities, with leisure and fortune at their command, that would not feel the Art to be an acquisition? It has been called a sixth sense, from the gratification it affords, and the power it gives of fixing scenes, persons, and events to which the memory can refer."[34]

Drawing was taught to both boys and girls from an early age (fig. 68). But making a highly finished drawing or watercolor was a more serious endeavor that required commitment and constant practice. Wealthy families sometimes engaged professional drawing masters to help the tentative beginner master issues of scale, perspective, and detail and ultimately reach the point of being able to translate three-dimensional reality onto a sheet of blank paper. These challenges faced Talbot, who by his own description did not possess a "knowledge of drawing," when he admired the view from the shore of Lake Como during his honeymoon in 1833. Rather than attempt to draw freehand, he employed an optical device with a prism, called a camera lucida, which allowed the user to observe the scene and a sheet of paper simultaneously and to trace a projected outline (fig. 69).[35] It was tricky to use, as Talbot recalled with chagrin.

> *I was amusing myself on the lovely shores of Lake Como, in Italy, taking sketches with Wollaston's Camera Lucida, or rather I should say, attempting to take them: but without the smallest possible amount of success. For when the eye was removed from the prism—in which all looked beautiful—I found that the faithless pencil had only left traces on the paper melancholy to behold.*
>
> *After various fruitless attempts, I . . . thought of trying again a method which I had tried many years before. This method was, to take the Camera Obscura, and to throw the image of the objects on a piece of transparent tracing paper laid on a pane of glass in the focus of the instrument. On this paper the objects are distinctly seen, and can be traced on it with a pencil with some degree of accuracy, though not without much time and trouble.*
>
> *I had tried this simple method . . . but found it in practice somewhat difficult to manage, because the pressure of the hand and pencil upon the paper tends to shake and displace the instrument..*
>
> *Besides which, there is another objection, namely, that it baffles the skill and patience of the amateur to trace all the minute details visible on the paper; so that, in fact, he carries away with him little beyond a mere souvenir of the scene.*[36]

Despite his frustration with the shortcomings that optical devices displayed in the hands of an absolute novice, Talbot badly wanted to make sketches when traveling and persevered for a decade. But in 1833 his repeated failures prompted the thought, "How charming it would be if it were possible to cause these natural images to imprint themselves durably, and remain fixed upon the paper! And why should it not be possible? I asked myself."[37] The idea of capturing light on paper became so intriguing to Talbot that he began to experiment with various light-sensitive silver salts and, in the spring of 1834, succeeded in capturing images of leaves and lace.

It is not his seminal invention of photogenic drawings that we are examining now, however, but the circumstances from which the invention emerged. It was the most natural thing in the world for a person of Talbot's class and education to travel extensively at home and abroad. Being a botanist, he had cultivated powers of observation and a close engagement with the natural world, and these contributed to his keen appreciation of all that was Picturesque and Sublime in the landscape, from the smallest plant to the grand vistas of the Swiss Alps. It was also entirely natural that he should want to sketch when traveling, and own optical devices. When all of these elements, commonplace among his class, came together in the receptive mind of Talbot, struggling to draw on the shores of Lake Como, they created an impulse that led to his invention of photography.

Many of the first generation of calotypists who took up photography in the 1840s, and most of the practitioners who enthusiastically joined the Photographic Society after 1853, would have known how to sketch. It was a part of their existence, like being fluent in Latin or Greek, reading the classics, and visiting art exhibitions during the London season. Probably they were familiar with the most recent debates on the Picturesque and Sublime, had read Byron, Shakespeare, Tennyson, and Wordsworth, and led lives enriched by metaphoric allusion and mental association. For them, photography was not just the latest and most exhilarating method of making pictures but also a medium in which to employ the concepts and ideals instilled in them since childhood by parents and grandparents. The mind-set of the first generation of photographers owed as much to the sensibilities of the previous sixty years as to those of its own Victorian era. And none of these sensibilities directed their attention to the profound social and technological changes that informed their daily lives. Instead they aimed their cameras toward the past, tactfully avoiding the themes of an industrializing society. While the limitations of technology played their part in this avoidance, it is also true that the preference of this social stratum was for a romantically fictionalized view of the world and not the discomforting objectivity offered by photography. Only in a later period, when technology had advanced and attitudes

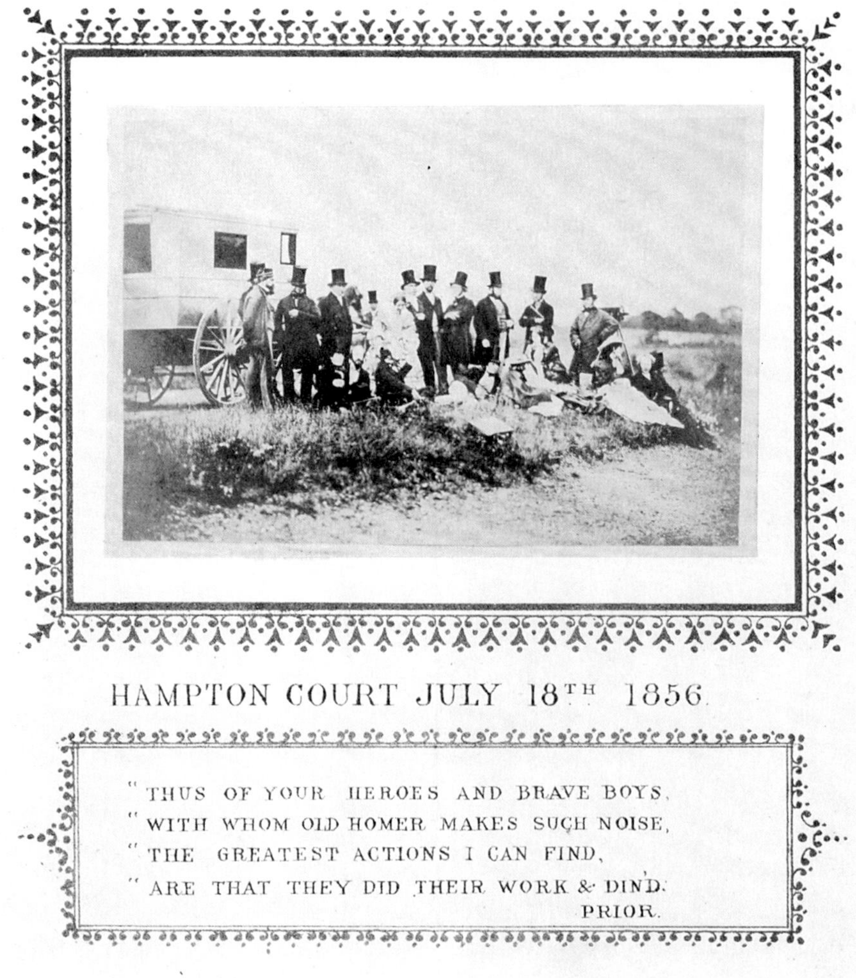

Fig. 70. Roger Fenton, *Meeting of the Photographic Society Club, Hampton Court, July 18, 1856*. Albumen silver print from glass negative, 24.2 x 33.3 cm (9½ x 13⅛ in.). The Royal Photographic Society Collection at the National Media Museum, Bradford, 2003-5000/12787

changed, would photographers begin to explore more socially challenging subject matter.

Historians are often frustrated by the enormous discrepancy between the written record and the material evidence, and this is very much the case for the first decades of photography. Exhibition catalogues that survive from the mid-1850s document more than fourteen thousand photographs submitted to thirty exhibitions by a host of amateur photographers.[38] Reviews in newspapers and journals sometimes offer detailed descriptions, providing insights into certain individual photographs; and when considered collectively, these exhibition reviews help us identify leading practitioners and suggest some generally accepted hierarchy among them. But when it comes to finding the works themselves, the trail generally goes cold. A photographer who exhibited widely and received both praise and prize medals may be represented now by a mere handful of surviving prints.[39] This is not altogether surprising, since amateur photography was a personal pastime, with much of the work remaining within the family and being discarded or mislaid by subsequent generations.

The chances of a photograph's survival improved if it had been preserved in an album, sometimes published as a book—a form that projected more authority than an ephemeral-looking bundle of negatives or prints. Some of these were personal albums assembled by the photographer or his family; others were the collective product of photographic groups. Without doubt some of the most interesting and significant work made in the 1850s by amateurs, especially calotypists, has survived in group albums such as these.

THE PHOTOGRAPHIC SOCIETY CLUB

The Photographic Society flourished during the first two years after its founding in 1853. Its membership had increased to "nearly 400" by February 1856.[40] Exhibitions were held annually, papers were read and duly published, meetings were regular and conducted according to the prevailing rules and protocols. All the characteristics of success did impose a certain level of formality on the society's proceedings, however. Perhaps it was these constraints that led to the creation, sometime during the first half of 1856, of something altogether more relaxed—the Photographic Society Club.

In Britain, a club is very different from a society and tends to operate at a more social level. A community of friends or colleagues joined in a common purpose or interest, it is not encumbered by strict rules and regulations. Moreover, a club can be all these things *and* act as an exclusive clique, keeping out those thought not to belong either socially, educationally, or intellectually. Such seems to have been the case with the Photographic Society Club, which, according to its rules, limited membership to a president and twenty-one members. The secretary took

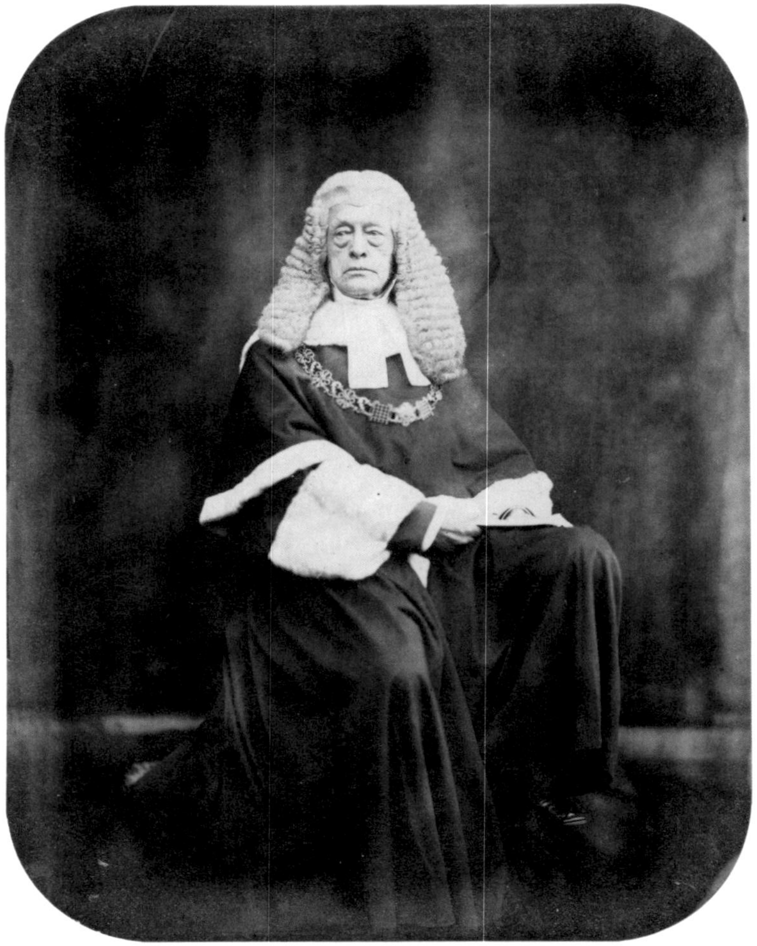

Fig. 71. Unknown photographer, *Sir Frederick Pollock*. Albumen silver print from glass negative, 22.3 x 17.1 cm (8¾ x 6¾ in.). The Royal Photographic Society Collection at the National Media Museum, Bradford, RPS 901.3

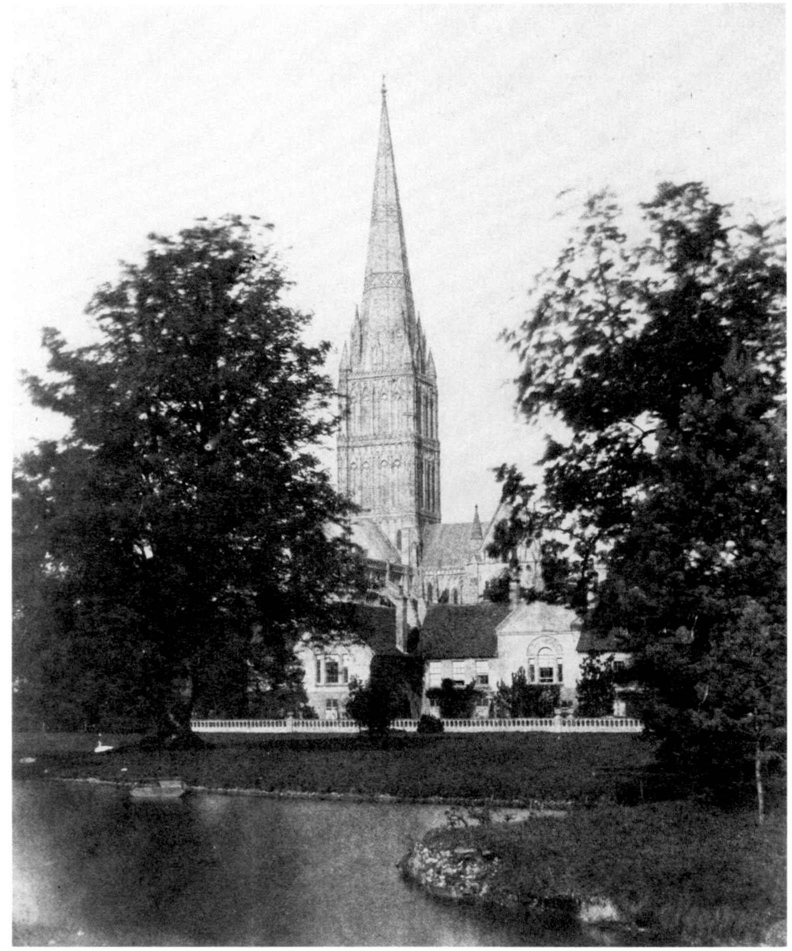

Fig. 72. Robert Wilfred Skeffington Lutwidge, *Salisbury Cathedral*, October 1855. Salted paper print, 19.3 x 15.3 cm (7⅝ x 6 in.). The Royal Photographic Society Collection at the National Media Museum, Bradford, RPS 11464

care of catering arrangements for the five times yearly that the club met and dined together. One of these events always took place out of town, "in some country locality favourable to Photographic Pursuits,"[41] although the emphasis was probably more on conviviality than calotyping (fig. 70).

The twenty-three members of the club were an eclectic mix representing a wide range of social and professional interests, from the president, Sir Frederick Pollock, a senior figure in the British judiciary (fig. 71), to the antiquarian William Thoms, founding editor of *Notes and Queries*, and Joseph Durham, a noted sculptor and a royal academician.[42] All were well-known and distinguished amateurs, and many, such as Hugh Welch Diamond, Philip Delamotte, and Fenton, had been intimately associated with the Photographic Society since its earliest days.[43] One of their first collective acts was to create a handsome volume bound in crimson morocco and grandly titled *Rules of the Photographic Society Club with Portraits of the Members*, which was evidently designed to be a photographic record of its membership. The chief purpose of the club as announced in this volume's pages, "to promote union and friendly feeling amongst the members of the Photographic Society,"[44] does not seem consonant with the strictly limited numbers. Perhaps it was felt that a small club could effectively carry forward schemes that might prove difficult for a larger group.

Other than socializing, the main purpose of the club from the outset was the creation of two photographically illustrated publications entitled, respectively, *The Photographic Album for the Year 1855* and *The Photographic Album for the Year 1857*. Both were lavishly produced in a large format by one of London's most prestigious printers, Charles Whittingham of the Chiswick Press.[45] The 1855 album presented photographs, each mounted on its own page, by forty-four photographers, and the 1857 album works by thirty-nine; in both instances, these numbers far exceeded the membership of the Photographic Society Club. The title page carries the statement "Printed for Members of the Photographic Club." This can be read in a number of ways, but since all of the photographers represented were members of the Photographic Society, the meaning may be that members of the club financially underwrote the publication as their personal contribution to the advancement of photography and of the society.

In a sense, these two albums are microcosms of the annual exhibitions of the Photographic Society, presenting the works between covers rather than on the walls of a gallery. But, unlike the exhibitions, the album contains an accompanying text for each photograph. In some cases it offers nothing beyond technical information about the process, exposure times, and focal length of lens; however, most photographers took the opportunity to insert an appropriate quotation or a personal account relevant to the subject of the work. When we view the club's activities as a whole, then, perhaps we should set aside the notion that it existed principally for social reasons and focus on the significant contribution made by its members to the fuller establishment of photography. These two albums offer the best insights we have into the diverse range of amateur photographic practice during the 1850s (fig. 72). They contain works that reveal the range of photographic processes employed during this period. In subject the photographs also display variety, including, for instance, a conventional study, *Castle of Herstmonceaux, Sussex*, by William Thoms; the more exotic *Hippopotamus at the Zoological Gardens, Regent's Park*, by Count de Montizon; a studio portrait of the newsworthy *Dr. Livingstone* by John Jabez Mayall; and *Still Life and Embroidery*, reflecting the connoisseurship of Robert Skeffington Lutwidge.

PHOTOGRAPHIC EXCHANGE CLUBS

From the very beginning, the Photographic Society believed that one of the most effective ways of communicating about the medium was through the exchange of prints. Ever since the Great Exhibition, interchange had been widely regarded as the key to advancement, and photography was an ideal field for cross-fertilization, since multiple prints could readily be circulated. Participants could examine at their leisure the work of others, learning from their technical example and their aesthetic judgments. Exchanges of prints on a regular basis also became records of individual achievement and collective progress. A notice in April 1853 in the second issue of the *Photographic Journal* announcing the society's ambition to establish an "Exchange of Positive Pictures" explained, "It is evident that Amateurs, who have only a portion of their leisure to devote to Photography, must be content with a limited collection of carefully prepared negatives of their own production. But if the large number of positives capable of being obtained from these negatives can be exchanged among photographers, the portfolios of Amateurs may be enlarged indefinitely, and artists' collections of Photographic studies rendered very complete."[46]

For some reason these good intentions came to naught, and it was not until February 1855 that the Photographic Exchange Club was finally established.[47] Twenty-two members were listed initially, with Rev. John Richardson Major Jr. serving as the honorary secretary and treasurer.[48] Like the Photographic Society Club, the exchange club operated collectively and informally, and there was some overlap between the two, with seven members belonging to both clubs (see the table on pages 86–87).[49]

The first exchange was scheduled to take place in July 1855, with a second optimistically planned for November of the same year and two exchanges yearly intended thereafter. The underlying principle was straightforward, with an equal number of prints required from each member, although a more elaborate system based on print size was subsequently proposed. For various reasons the first exchange was delayed until September, and four members still failed to submit on time.[50] In the end, twenty-three photographers took part in the 1855 exchange,

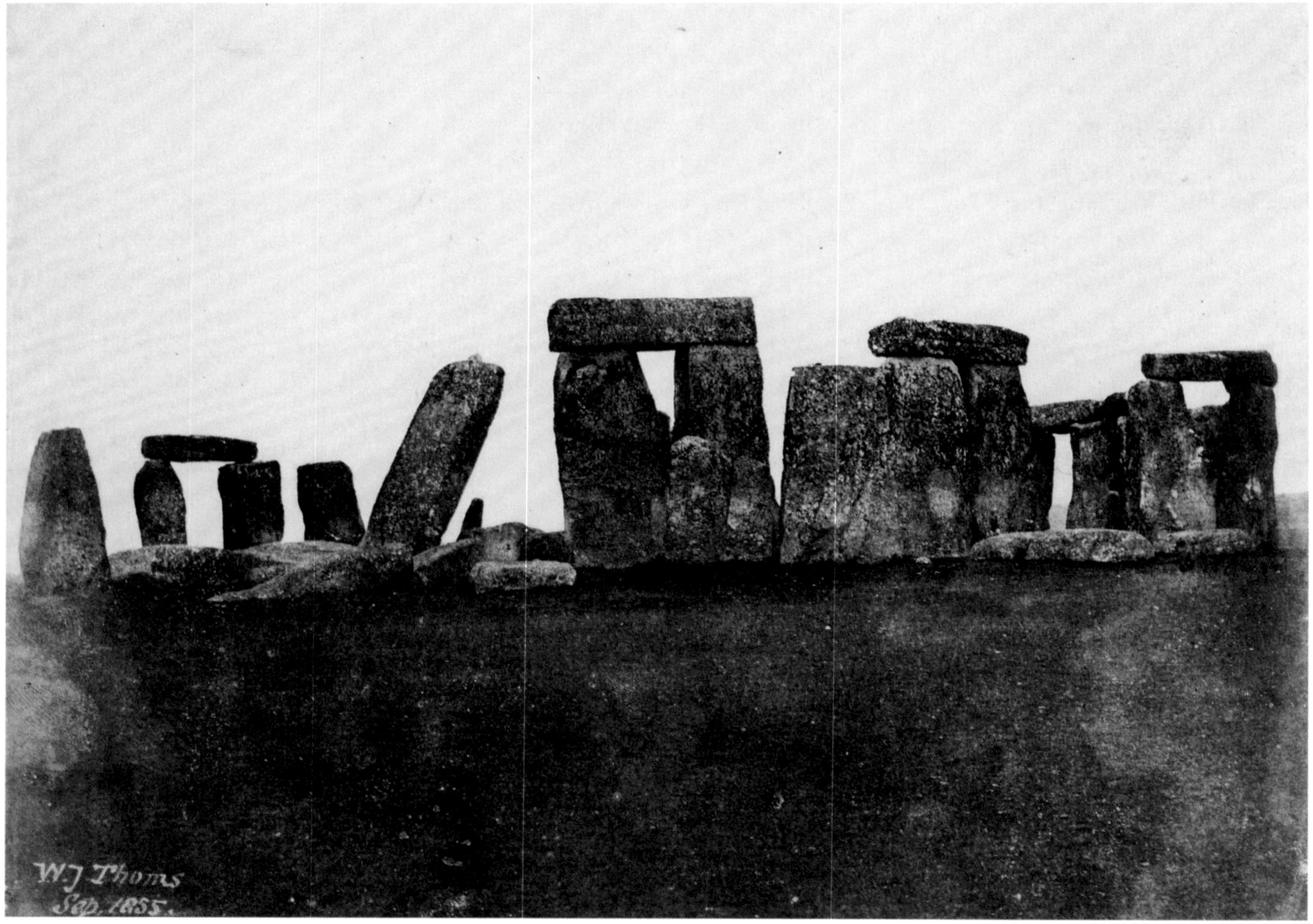

Fig. 73. William John Thoms, *Stonehenge, September 1855.* Albumen silver print, 16.5 x 22.6 cm (6½ x 8 ⅞ in.). The Royal Photographic Society Collection at the National Media Museum, Bradford, 2003-5001-2-21273

all but three sending two prints each; of the total of sixty prints, almost half were made from paper negatives (figs. 73, 74, 75). An elaborate title page and a list of contents were printed and distributed to members to be bound into albums of the exchange that they might personally assemble and further augment with works of their own. There were two further exchanges, in June 1857 and sometime in 1858, both significantly smaller than the first.[51]

Although exchanging photographs according to a strict timetable obviously presented difficulties, the underlying idea remained popular, and further photographic exchanges were established elsewhere.[52] Notable was the Edinburgh Photograph Exchange Club formed in 1859, initially with thirteen members drawn exclusively from the ranks of the Photographic Society of Scotland. The club's operation was similar to that of the London exchange club but on a more modest scale, with one distribution each year timed to coincide with the society's annual exhibition in January.[53]

At first glance, little seems to distinguish London's Photographic Society Club from its Photographic Exchange Club. Both came into existence under the sheltering wing of the Photographic Society, and a core group of seven members belonged to both clubs. Both committed to advancing photography, the two clubs located their ambitions in different arenas, however, and carried them out in different ways. The Photographic Society Club chose to publish, and its two albums preserved the work of the society for future generations. Indeed, its rules stipulated collecting a print from every member of the society each year and further required that "if at any time the Club should come to an end," a book containing the photographs "shall be given to the British Museum."[54] The Photographic Exchange Club, on the other hand, limited the scope of its responsibilities exclusively to the members involved in the exchange. A closely knit group of twenty-two individuals, it neither wined nor dined and published nothing. Its activities were directed toward the mutual benefit of its members, who received valued prints and incorporated them into personal albums. Fortunately, a few of these albums have survived to memorialize the photographic output of this select group.

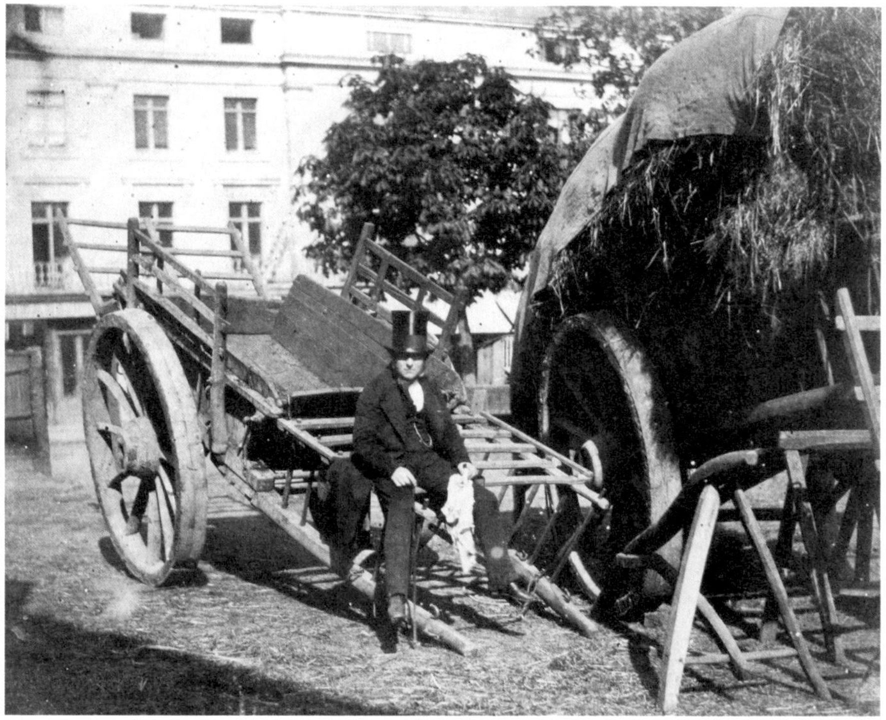

Fig. 74. Edward Kater, *Carts &c*, ca. 1855. Salted paper print, 15.5 x 18.6 cm (6⅛ x 7⅜ in.). The Royal Photographic Society Collection at the National Media Museum, Bradford, 2003-5001-2-21273

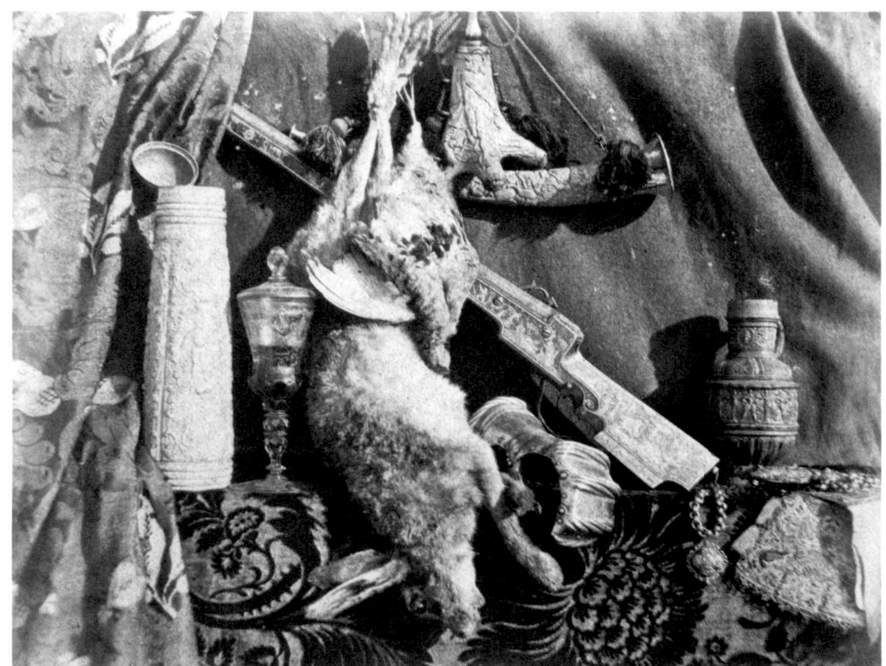

Fig. 75. Rev. Thomas George Mackinlay, *Still Life from Nature*, ca. 1854. Albumen silver print, 17.5 x 22.7 cm (6⅞ x 9 in.). The Royal Photographic Society Collection at the National Media Museum, Bradford, 2003-5001-2-21273

Photographers Associated with the Photographic Society Club and Photographic Exchange Club, 1855–58

	Photographic Society Club member	*In PSC 1855 album*	*In PSC 1857 album*	*Photographic Exchange Club member*	*In 1855 exchange*	*In 1857 exchange*	*In 1858 exchange*	*Contributed calotypes*
Anthony, H. M.			*					
Anthony, J.		*	*					*
Batson, A.		*	*					
Bedford, F.	*	*	*			*	*	
Cotton, A. B.							*	
Campbell, W. G.			*	*	*	*	*	
Coghill, Sir J.		*	*					
Conway, Jr., C.		*	*					
Crace, J. G.			*					
Cundall, J.		*	*					*
Currey, F. E.		*		*	*			
Davies, T.			*					*
Delamotte, P. H.	*	*	*	*	*		*	*
Diamond, Dr. H.	*	*	*	*	*	*	*	*
Downes, G.			*					
Eaton, T. D.				*	*	*		*
Fenton, R.	*	*	*					*
Fitzgerald, Lord O.		*	*					
Forrester, J. J.	*	*	*	*	*	*	*	*
Fry, P. W.				*				*
Gething, G. B.		*	*					
Glossop, Rev. G. G.							*	
Hardwich, F.	*							
Heilmann, J. J.		*						
Hennah, T. H.		*						*
Henry, Capt. R. J.			*					*
Holden, Dr. H.			*					*
Horne, F.		*						*
Howlett, R.		*			*	*	*	*
Kater, E.	*			*	*	*	*	*
Kerr, Hon. A.		*						*
Knight, J.		*						*
Leaf, C.	*							
Llewellyn, J. D.		*	*	*	*			*
Lutwidge, R. W. S.		*	*	*	*	*		*
Lynn, M. E.		*						

	Photographic Society Club member	*In PSC 1855 album*	*In PSC 1857 album*	*Photographic Exchange Club member*	*In 1855 exchange*	*In 1857 exchange*	*In 1858 exchange*	*Contributed calotypes*
Mackinlay, T. G.	*	*	*	*	*	*	*	*
Major, Sr., J. R.	*							
Major, Jr., J. R.	*	*	*	*	*	*	*	*
Mansell, Dr. T. L.		*	*	*	*	*	*	
Marshall, Rev. F. A. S.		*						*
Mayall, J. J.			*					
Montizon, Count de	*	*						
Mostyn, Lady A.					*	*	*	
Nevill, Lady A.				*				
Nevill, Lady C.				*		*		*
Newton, Sir W.				*	*			*
Nicholl, W. H.		*	*					
Parker, J. W.	*							
Percy, Dr. J.	*	*	*	*	*			*
Petley, Lieut.		*						
Plunket, W. C.		*	*					
Pollock, A. J.	*	*	*		*	*	*	
Pollock, Sir F.	*							
Pollock, H.	*	*	*	*	*	*	*	
Price, W. Lake		*		*	*			
Ranking, Dr. W. H.			*					*
Ransome, R. C.			*					*
Rejlander, O. G.		*	*					
Robinson, H. P.						*	*	
Rosling, A.		*	*	*	*		*	*
Shadbolt, G.	*	*	*			*	*	
Stewart, J.		*						*
Stokes, G.		*	*					*
Sturrock, Jr., J.			*					
Taylor, H.		*						*
Thoms, W. J.	*	*		*	*	*	*	*
Turner, B. B.	*	*	*					*
Vignoles, C.	*							
Vivian, W. G.		*						
Watson, H. G.				*		*	*	*
White, H.		*						
Wood, H. T.			*					

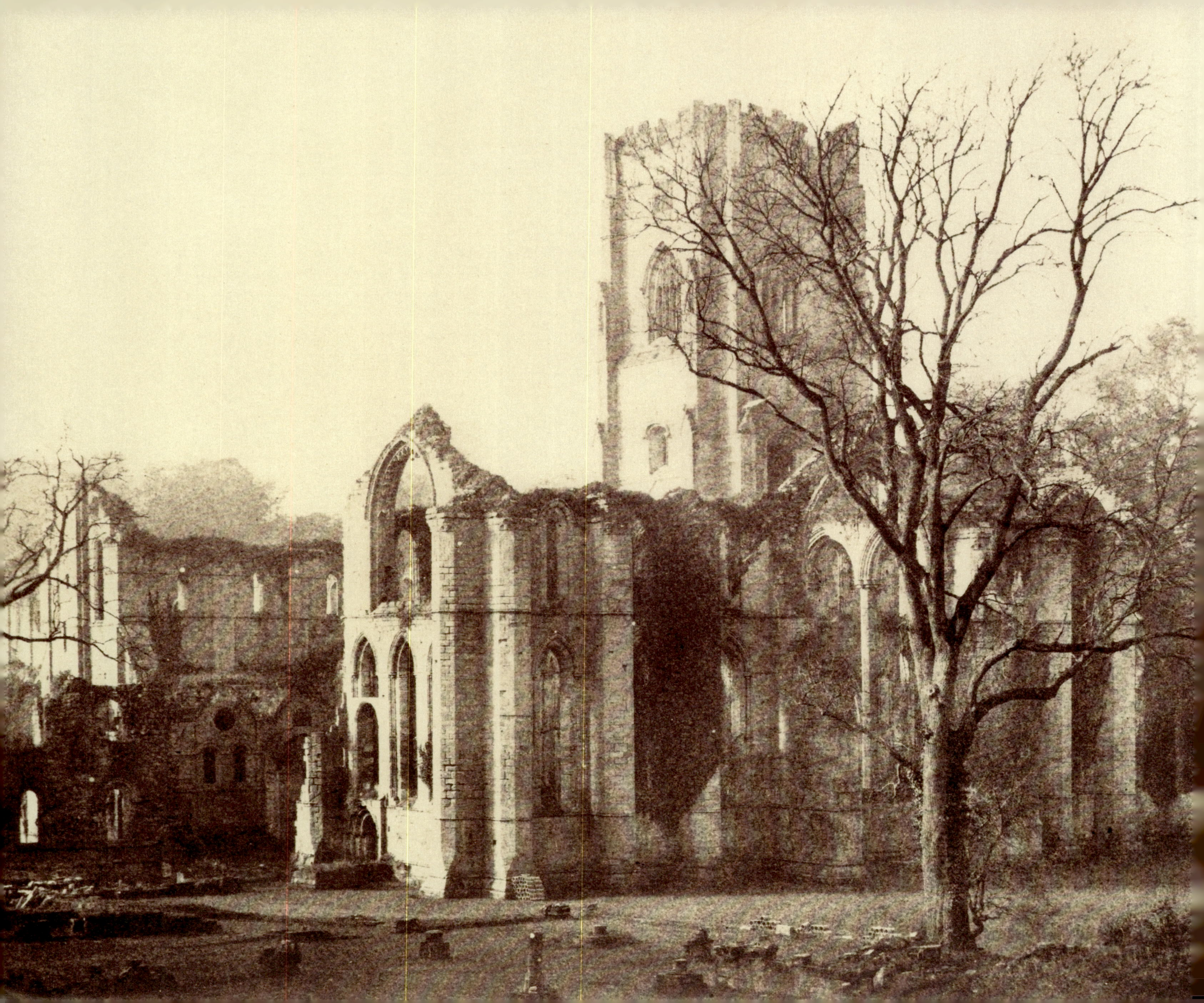

7. British Sensibilities, 1855–1857

Anyone looking through the photographs published by the Photographic Society Club and submitted to the exchanges of 1855, 1857, and 1858 would be struck by both their consistent subject matter and their pervasive mood of dormant solitude. While in the 1850s Charles Dickens and Elizabeth Gaskell were setting before their readers lively and detailed scenes of human activity, these photographic images, one after the other, are peaceful and harmonious, devoid of any suggestion of toil, industry, or, for that matter, pleasure. It is true that capturing photographically the hustle and bustle—what one critic, reviewing a typically crowded painting by William Powell Frith, called "in the midst of the essence"—was still nearly impossible.[1] Exposure times with the waxed-paper process could be as long as ninety minutes. But even in studies made on collodion, for which the exposures required were considerably shorter, figures often appear only as accents in the composition. Although there were certainly technical shortcomings influencing the kind of photography done in this era, one senses that choices about subject matter were driven largely by aesthetic and cultural imperatives.

Beneath the self-confident exterior we see in their portraits, Victorians were deeply anxious, for the threat of disease and sudden death haunted their lives daily. Migration to the industrializing cities, where people lived in dense and unsanitary conditions, had created such a contagion of numbers that few escaped its consequences. In the 1840s, life expectancy at birth for professional men was reckoned to be forty-five, for laborers, just twenty-two; and these figures did not improve substantially for several decades.[2] The majority of families experienced the loss of at least one child, many never reaching the age of five before they were carried away by pneumonia, bronchitis, diarrhea, scarlet fever, or some other childhood disease.[3] Beset by the calamities of life, people turned to their Christian beliefs to carry them through, but when these religious certainties were called into doubt in 1844 by the publication of *Vestiges of the Natural History of Creation*, a widely read book that was something of a precursor to Charles Darwin's *On the Origin of Species*, they felt cast adrift in an increasingly uncertain world.[4]

Undoubtedly, every member of the Photographic Society was affected at some level by the tragedies of life. Roger Fenton lost his eldest daughter in 1850 and his youngest son ten years later.[5] Hugh Owen was a young widower by 1851, with his daughter Betsy in the care of his sister-in-law.[6] Some photographers, among them Robert Adamson and Charles Clifford, died comparatively young, most likely from tuberculosis, then endemic in Britain and elsewhere.[7] It is easy to understand how a sense of vulnerability pervaded all levels of Victorian society.

Photography had drawn considerable interest in London and in rapidly expanding cities such as Liverpool, Leeds, and Manchester, where photographic societies had recently been established. With their sheer aggregation of numbers further increasing the feeling of helplessness,[8] cities were regarded as dangerous places, and the countryside was set in contrast to them as a place where exercise, sunlight, fresh air, and unpolluted water seemed an antidote for numerous ills. At the first hint of an epidemic, those who could abandoned the city for the country or the seaside. Even in relatively unthreatening times, excursion trains allowed people to escape for a day to rural areas, where they could restore their spirits far from the pressures of urban life. Victorians came to ascribe extravagant qualities to the countryside in a way that now seems sentimental or naive.[9] These curative powers of landscapes merged with the idea of the Picturesque. By the 1850s, the Picturesque was no longer simply a fashionable aesthetic but had become the overarching language through which nature was appreciated, informing visual preferences for an entire generation of photographers and their audiences.

Opposite: Fig. 76. Alfred Capel Cure, *Fountains Abbey*, October 22, 1856, detail. Albumen silver print, 21.1 x 27.7 cm (8¼ x 10⅞ in.). The Museum of Modern Art, New York, Gift of Edmund J. McRickard, 88.1983

Henry Taylor lived in Godalming, a small market town of some ten thousand souls set in the heart of the rolling Surrey countryside to the south of London. Beginning in 1855, Taylor contributed regularly to all the major exhibitions, where his landscape pictures and studies of plant forms were widely acclaimed. To accompany his contribution to *The Photographic Album for the Year 1855* he selected a poem, printed beneath the title of the photograph, that opens by contrasting the difficult lives of city dwellers with the honest toil of country folk who rested in such a place and appreciated the beauty of the scene. With this counterpoint of text and image, observers are invited to view the scene through the eyes of the weary laborer and exchange their present concerns for the tranquillity of rural solitude, animated only by the passage of animals and birds (fig. 77).

A Sheltered Nook

Out of this world, a quiet shelter'd nook,
Unknown to those whose anxious lives are pass'd
Within the city walls, or busy town;
But traversed often by the early feet
Of labourer going, and returning tired
From daily toil, along the narrow way,
And resting here: a spot too, known to those
Who love the country's beauties, when the spring
First opens them; or when the summer heat
Is here shadowing trees made temperate;
Or when the leaves hang golden on the boughs,
And, falling on the ground, beneath the tread
Make crackling carpets; or when later still
The unclothed branches cleave the winter sky,
And nothing comes the solitude to break
Save the step of timid hare, or rustling wing
Of passing bird; whose homes are through the year
Around this resting-place. *G. R. T.*

A viewer sensitive to allusion would have found many narratives in Taylor's composition. The low, raking sunlight suggests the onset of eventide and the moment of quiet stillness that precedes twilight. The stile that bars the way, the picket fences that keep the traveler safe from danger, and the upward-leading pathway, which suggestively hints at open spaces and light beyond, all belong to the Victorian vocabulary of anxiety and salvation.

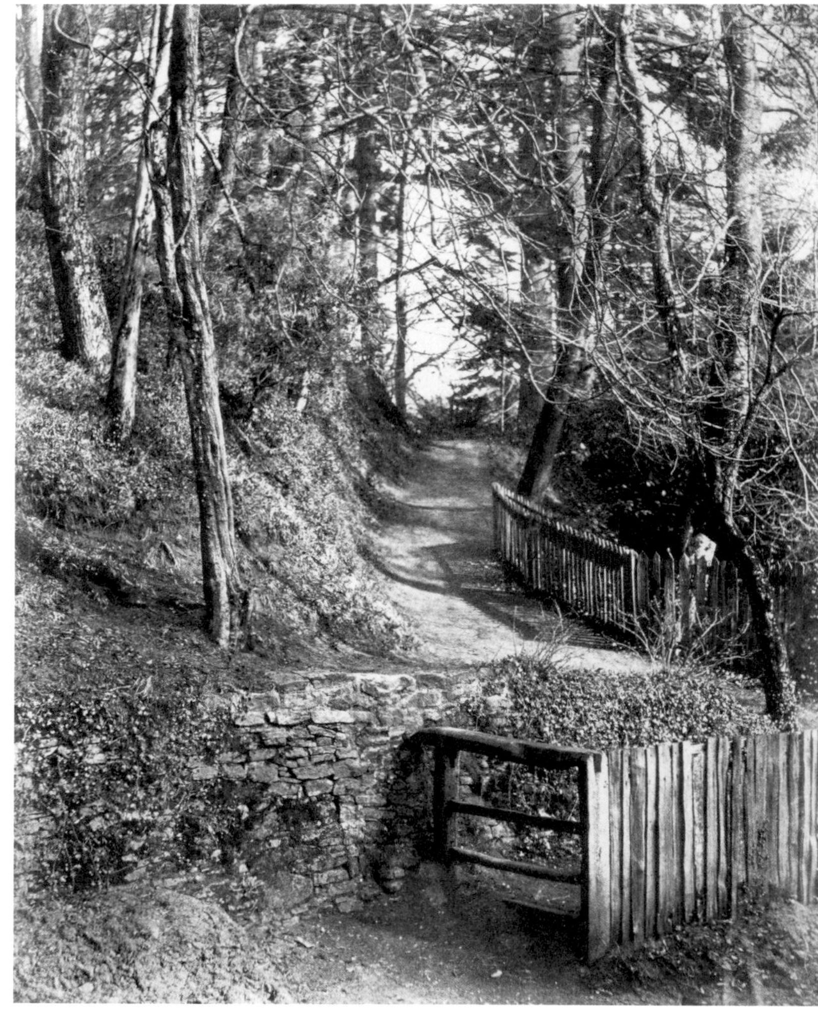

Fig. 77. Henry Taylor, *A Sheltered Nook*, ca. 1854. Salted paper print, 20.7 x 16.4 cm (8⅛ x 6½ in.). The Royal Photographic Society Collection at the National Media Museum, Bradford, RPS 11454

Another study of a woodland glade, by Thomas Davies, appeared in *The Photographic Album for the Year 1857* with a brief quotation from *Endymion* by the much-read poet John Keats, which created a tone of meditative contemplation. These three lines beneath the title of the

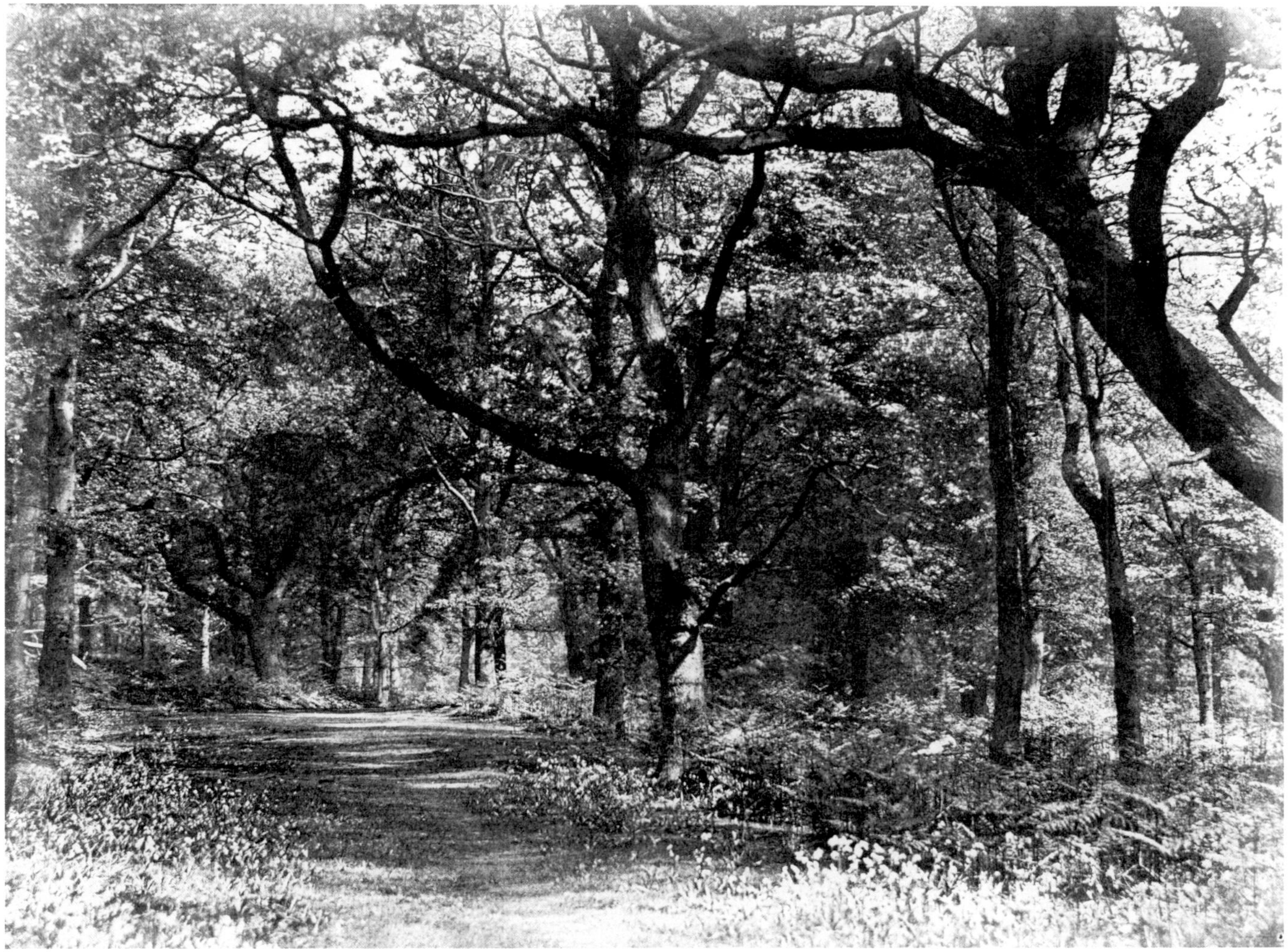

Fig. 78. Thomas Davies, *Wood-Scene, Norton, Cheshire*, May 29, 1856. Albumen silver print, 17 x 22.1 cm (6¾ x 8¾ in.). The Royal Photographic Society Collection at the National Media Museum, Bradford, RPS 905-1074

photograph would have been enough to trigger a recollection of the entire poem in the minds of most mid-Victorian readers.[10]

Wood-Scene, Norton, Cheshire

Through many a woodland dun,
Through buried paths, where sleepy twilight dreams
The summer-time away. *Keats*

The photograph (fig. 78) is thoughtfully composed, with the camera set at eye level and slightly to one side of a woodland track that leads toward a distant patch of light. The path itself appears little used, more animal track than human thoroughfare. It threads invitingly across a woodland floor that, unlike the one in Taylor's composition, is smooth and free of obstacles. To either side, the spring growths of bluebell and bracken reach upward toward the shafts of light that penetrate the overarching canopy of leaves. Both image and text evoke the romantic

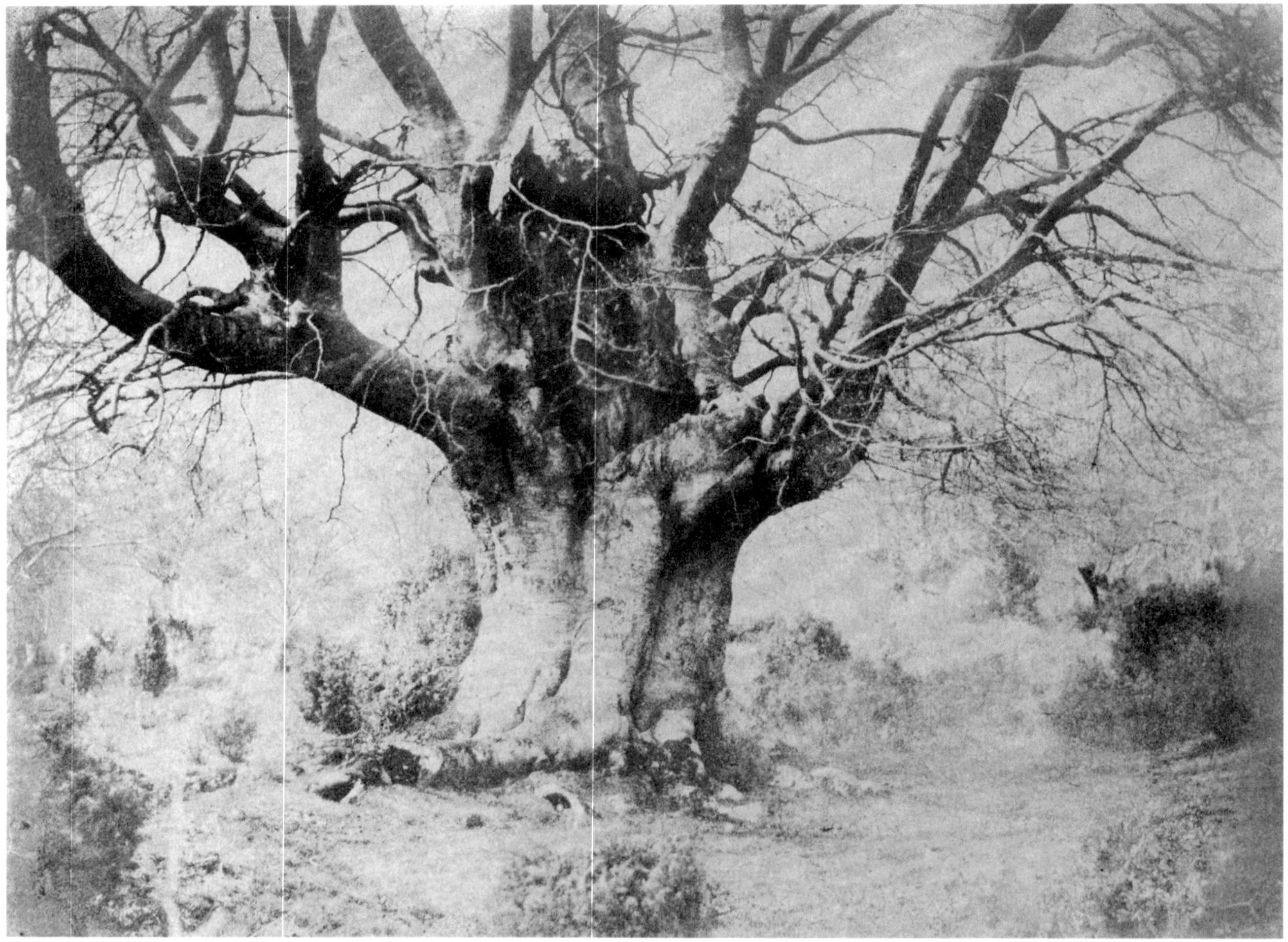

Fig. 79. Sir William Newton, *Burnham Beeches*, ca. 1852. Salted paper print, 17 x 22.3 cm (6¾ x 8¾ in.). The Royal Photographic Society Collection at the National Media Museum, Bradford, RPS 2003-5001-2-21273

sentiment Victorians attached to woods and forests. Places associated with the religious rites and spiritual beliefs of ancient peoples, symbolic of the everlasting cycle of birth, death, and regeneration, they were ideal spots in which to dream the summertime away.

In actuality, the harsh reality of industrial Britain lay closer to hand than is disclosed in the photograph. The Norton Priory wood lay on the outskirts of Runcorn, a port on the banks of the Mersey where Britain's nascent chemical industry was fast becoming entrenched.[11] On a still day such as the one captured in the photograph, the air above the town would have been heavy with noxious chemical compounds and falling soot pumped out by a forest of factory chimneys. For Davies, a sickly young man of twenty-two living nearby, Norton Priory offered both physical and emotional sanctuary from the modern-day industrial world that threatened just beyond the fringes of the wood.[12]

In addition to forests and woodland glades, individual trees occupied a special place within British society and had done so for generations. Living things much older than humans, in many cases hundreds of years old, trees offered a vital link with the distant past. They became objects of veneration and were closely associated with local myth and legends. Some aged trees appeared endowed with the human qualities of individuality, grace, and nobility. To members of the landowning classes, such trees symbolized their own ancient lineage and were carefully preserved as family monuments. To fell an ancient tree was to extinguish the planter's name; in Scotland in former times, when a

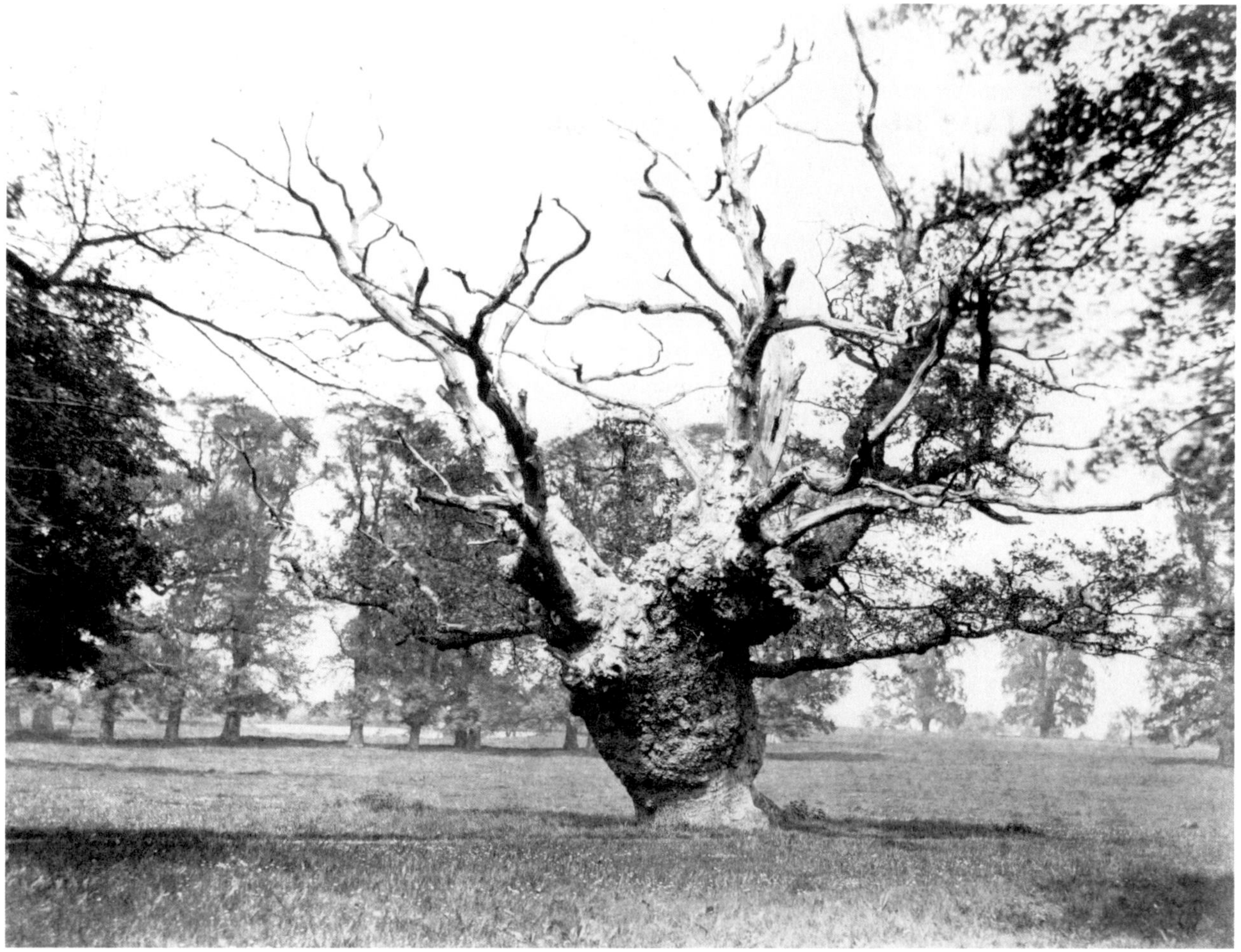

Fig. 80. William John Thoms, *The Very Old Oak, Windsor*, ca. 1856. Salted paper print, 15.8 x 19.7 cm (6¼ x 7¾ in.). The Royal Photographic Society Collection at the National Media Museum, Bradford, 2003-5001-2-200862

family was proved disloyal to the Crown, the finest trees on its estate were cut down as punishment.[13]

Among trees, the oak was "the monarch of its kind," whose vast age and durability of timber placed it above all others. Its forest consort was the ash, or "Venus of the woods," whose delicate foliage and graceful form complemented the rugged oak. But the handsomest of British trees was generally held to be the stately beech, with its smooth gray trunk, massive upswept limbs, and delicate light-green foliage.[14]

Some eighteen miles west of London lay the parish of Burnham, which was close to Eton and Windsor and famous for its woodland tract of ancient beeches that had survived for untold generations. Celebrated for its beauty, Burnham Beeches was cited in contemporary guidebooks. "If the Londoner were to see nothing else," one claimed, he should "come hither for the sake of seeing these Burnham Beeches. He would hardly believe . . . that such a wild spot could be found within an hour's ride of the smoky city."[15]

Members of the Photographic Society were naturally attracted to the place, with Sir William Newton and Fenton among the earliest to capture its majestic trees and untamed, picturesque beauty. Between 1853 and 1856, studies of Burnham Beeches were included in every touring exhibition organized by the Society of Arts and were submitted to numerous exhibitions elsewhere, making this photographic subject one of the most widely seen in those years.[16] It was almost inevitable that Newton would submit one of his celebrated studies of beeches to the first exchange of 1855 (fig. 79). With its softly detailed foreground and general lack of focus, the work exemplifies Newton's ideas of artistic expression and his approach to paper negative photography. The composition, quiet and undramatic, presents the tree as a specimen, with its very heart placed at dead center. Close observation reveals that the aged tree is starting to decay, its central part split and gnarled—to those familiar with the life cycle of the English beech, a sure indication that the tree was pollarded (cut back to the trunk) in olden times to create new growth that could be harvested for timber.[17] Beyond celebrating its subject's age and legendary status, this image of a beech tree pollarded and harvested over countless generations, in an endless, timeless sequence of purposeful regeneration, offered the kind of moral object lesson valued by Victorian society.

Another member of the Photographic Exchange Club was William John Thoms, whose studies of single trees were included in the exchanges of 1857 and 1858. Both photographs were taken in Windsor Great Park, once a great hunting forest and now an extensive deer park lying south of the castle. An antiquarian, Thoms was less interested in the immediate symbolic value of trees than in their great age and literary associations. His study *The Very Old Oak, Windsor* portrays an ancient tree long dead, its naked limbs stripped bare of leaf and twig by countless seasons of decay (fig. 80). Several of these venerable oaks

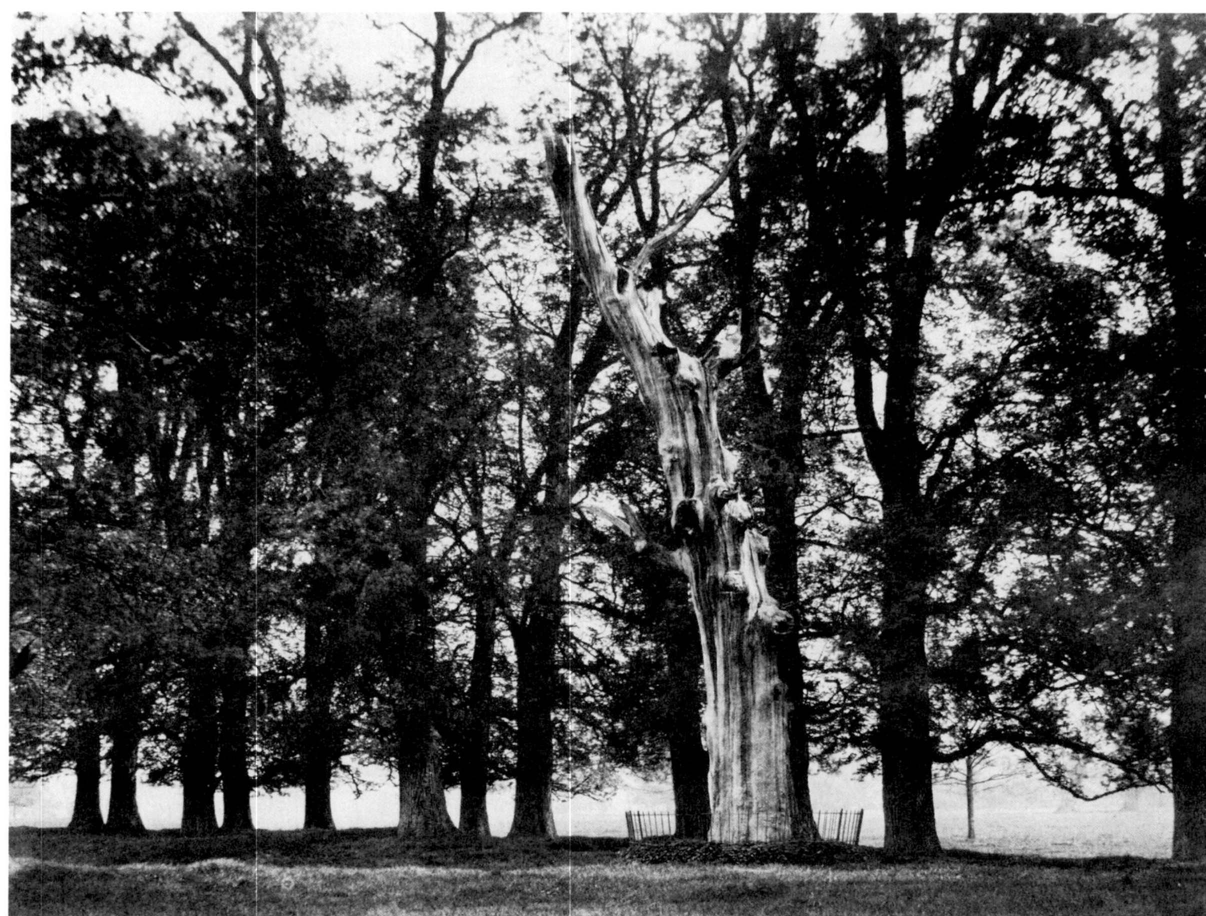

Fig. 81. William John Thoms, ***Herne's Oak, Windsor***, ca. 1857. Salted paper print, 15.4 x 19.6 cm (6⅛ x 7¾ in.). The Royal Photographic Society Collection at the National Media Museum, Bradford, 2003-5001-2-200862

studded the Great Park, and all came under the supervision of Edward Jesse, surveyor of Her Majesty's parks and palaces. Jesse wrote that in looking at the pollarded oaks "my mind is imperceptibly carried back to the many interesting historical facts which have happened since they first sprang from the earth. I can fancy that our Edwards and Henrys might have ridden under their branches,—that they had been admired by Shakespeare; and that Pope, whose early youth was passed in the neighbourhood, had reposed under their shade. At all events, it is impossible to view some of these sires of the forest without feeling a mixture of admiration and wonder."[18] It is not surprising that Jesse left this tree standing as a memorial to the enduring lineage of the British monarchy.

Perhaps the most ancient tree in Windsor Great Park was Herne's Oak, named for the legendary Herne the Hunter—who was thought to haunt, as a spectral vision, the spot where he committed suicide after being dismissed from service by Queen Elizabeth I. The tree was immortalized by Shakespeare in *The Merry Wives of Windsor*, wherein Mrs. Page explains the legend thus:

> *There is an old tale goes that Herne the hunter,*
> *Sometime a keeper here in Windsor forest,*
> *Doth all the winter-time, at still midnight,*
> *Walk round about an oak, with great ragg'd horns;*
> *And there he blasts the tree, and takes the cattle,*
> *And makes milch-kine yield blood, and shakes a chain*
> *In a most hideous and dreadful manner.*[19]

It is not too difficult to imagine the ghostly, ghastly apparition of Herne when looking at Thoms's study of the tree (fig. 81). The oak stands apart, quite dead, like a bleached bone thrust into the earth. Behind, a dark stand of trees loom like sentinels all around, their brooding presence heightening the drama of the image, which begins to meld with Shakespeare's account to create an unsettling impression of the place. Photographs such as these were puzzles with elaborate clues; the viewer needed a receptive and educated mind to decode their meaning.

While Thoms's photographic interests were predominantly scholarly, *Oak Tree in Eridge Park, Sussex*, submitted by Lady Augusta Mostyn to the 1858 exchange, suggests a different objective (fig. 82). The photograph was taken on the grounds of Eridge Castle, the ancestral home of the Nevill family, where Lady Augusta spent her formative years. The tree's massive girth and gnarled appearance indicate an age of several hundred years at least; perhaps it was as old as the Nevill family itself, which traced its lineage back to the Norman Conquest. The Nevills clearly valued the tree, for when it began to decay, a massive iron band had been placed around its girth to support the weight of aging limbs in an attempt to prolong its life for future generations. Perhaps the tree was a favorite place of pilgrimage for the Nevills. Lady Augusta, recently married and living with her husband in London, may have taken the picture in order to have a tangible reminder of childhood days with her family in Sussex. Whatever the specific associations, the photograph was a link between those of her generation and the distant past.

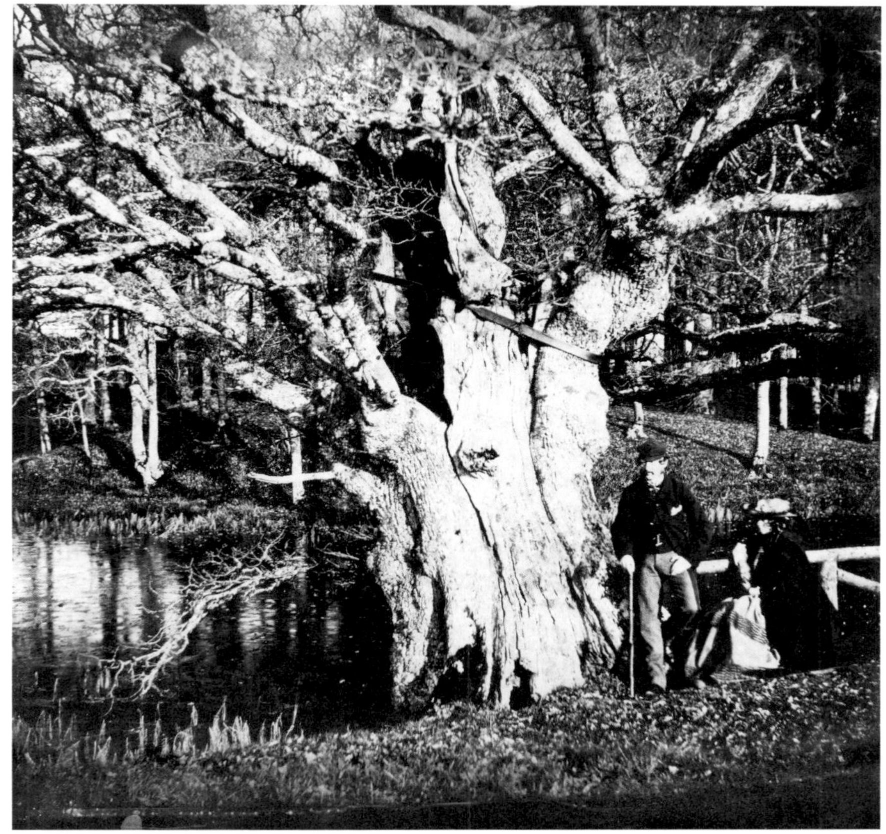

Fig. 82. Lady Augusta Mostyn, *Oak Tree in Eridge Park, Sussex*, ca. 1856. Salted paper print, 18.5 x 19.6 cm (7¼ x 7¾ in.). The Royal Photographic Society Collection at the National Media Museum, Bradford, 2003-5001-2-200862

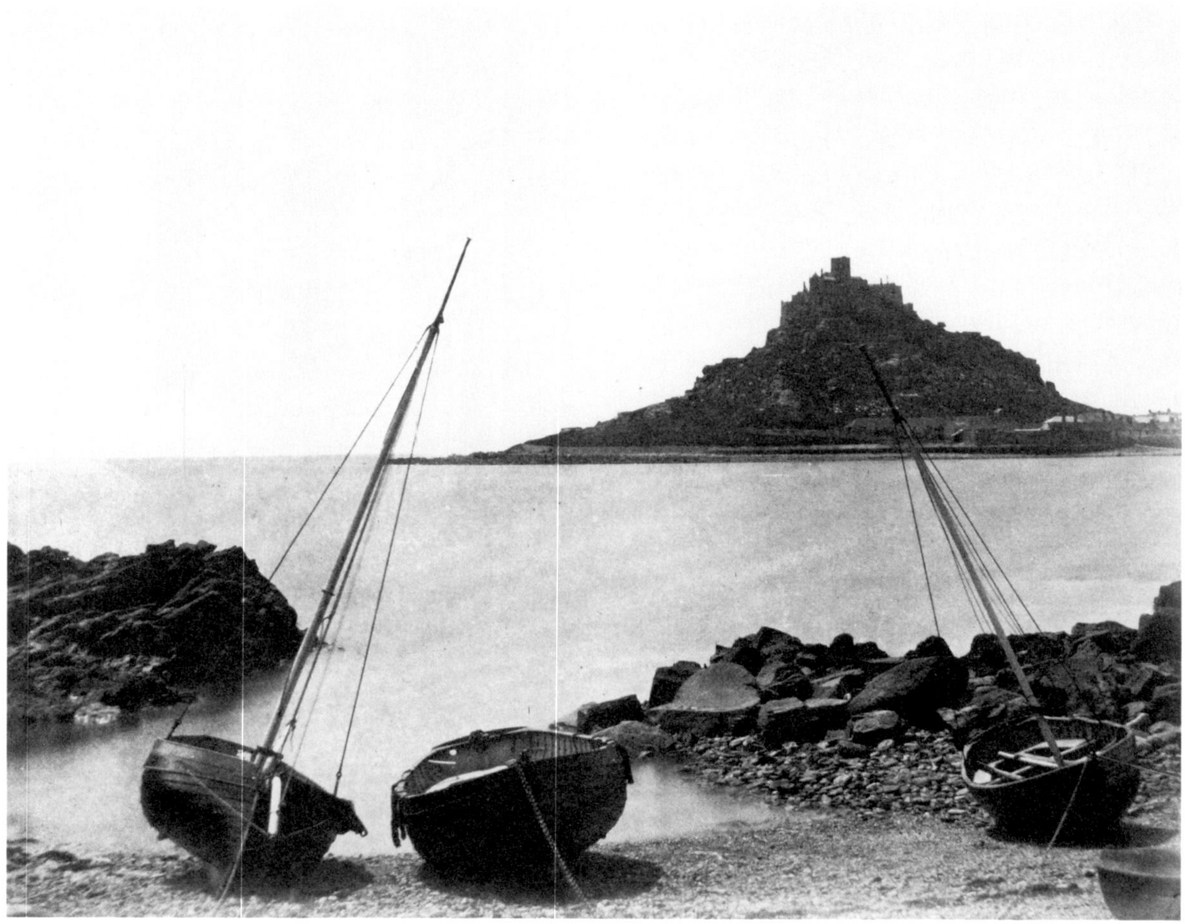

Fig. 83. Robert Wilfred Skeffington Lutwidge, *St. Michael's Mount, Cornwall*, ca. 1856. Salted paper print, 15 x 18.5 cm (5⅞ x 7¼ in.). The Royal Photographic Society Collection at the National Media Museum, Bradford, 2003-5001-2-200862

A SENSE OF PLACE

If ancient trees symbolized the continuity of family ancestry, the richly varied buildings found all across the British countryside offered tangible evidence of the communal history that had shaped the nation. For the photographer these buildings were perfect subjects because, unlike trees, they remained motionless during the long period of exposure required by paper negative processes. No two ever the same, buildings were also interesting because their appearance was affected by age and setting. Architectural studies, with castles, cathedrals, bridges, and picturesque ruins predominating, were a main presence in every photographic exhibition of the 1850s.

One skilled practitioner was Robert Skeffington Lutwidge, a committed photographer whose professional life as secretary to the Lunacy Commission, which oversaw the administration of mental asylums throughout Britain, gave him many opportunities for travel. The few photographs by him that survive display a keen eye for composition and set him apart from his colleagues in the Photographic Exchange Club. In *Knowle, Kent, Taken in the Rain* he chooses for his subject one corner and courtyard of a mansion (with extensive deer park) begun by the archbishop of Canterbury in 1456 and subsequently taken over and enlarged by Henry VIII; it had then, since 1566, been the ancestral home of the Sackville family. It is a "calendar house," with some 365 rooms, 52 staircases, and 7 courtyards, of which Green Court, pictured by Lutwidge, is the largest (pl. 25). Perhaps Lutwidge was sheltering his precious camera from the rain, and if so he certainly made the most of circumstances, incorporating in his composition the uprights of the doorway, which act as framing devices and locate the viewer snugly within the building. He saw how the rain had transformed the flagstones into a ribbon of light that led the eye to the far doorway, where a glimpse of trees and distant parkland might tempt the viewer once the rain had stopped. The strikingly asymmetrical composition succeeds because of Lutwidge's perfectly judged exposure, through which he retained detail and tonality in every area, whether deepest shadow or radiant reflected light.

At St. Michael's Mount, near Penzance in Cornwall, Lutwidge took full advantage of his surroundings once again to overcome the difficulty of photographing a small island set in a restless sea (fig. 83). Only a short distance from the shore, the mount is linked to the mainland by a rocky causeway at low tide. But instead of presenting these elements in what would have been a rather obvious picture, Lutwidge built a more subtle composition around the masts of two boats beached on the rocky shore. He precisely positioned his camera so that the taller mast intersects with the end of the mount's rocky island mass; this visual link flattens the perspective and anchors the island to the foreground. The other mast points toward the castle on the summit. Together, the two masts create a series of triangulations that articulate the whole. The lengthy exposure required blurred the surface of the sea, which carries the visual weight of the bulky isle, and reduced it to a soft tonality that subtly distinguishes it from the sky.

For both these images, the positioning of the camera was paramount. Had Lutwidge moved a step backward or forward at Knowle, the balance of the picture would have been dramatically altered. At St. Michael's Mount, the relationship between mast and promontory was carefully planned. Achieving such compositions required an acute understanding of how an image was presented on the camera's ground glass screen. Not only was the photographer's subject reduced, inverted, and laterally reversed by the lens; additionally, the sense of depth in space perceived by two eyes looking together was lost in the flattened camera image, which is a two-dimensional representation of reality. And prolonged exposure of the negative also altered the result. Humans observe the world as a continuous, linear succession of images, but when photography records these during a lengthy exposure, they blend into a single picture that can differ from the perceived reality.[20] Once they had mastered the basic techniques of the process, early photographers delighted in the medium's capacity to render a three-dimensional subject on a two-dimensional sheet of paper, and used the transforming powers of a prolonged exposure time to explore the world afresh. These possibilities were successfully exploited in many photographs shown in this volume: for example, plates 24, 31, 34, 41, 65, 96, and 118.

ROBERT HENRY CHENEY AND ALFRED CAPEL CURE

Two amateurs who stand apart from others of the period are Robert Henry Cheney (known as Henry) and his nephew, Alfred Capel Cure. Unlike most of the photographers discussed thus far, these two did not belong to any photographic society or exchange club and neither exhibited nor corresponded with the photographic journals. They made pictures entirely for their own pleasure and recreation, but, far from being dabblers, both were accomplished photographers with the technical skills and educated eye necessary to carry off a successful composition.

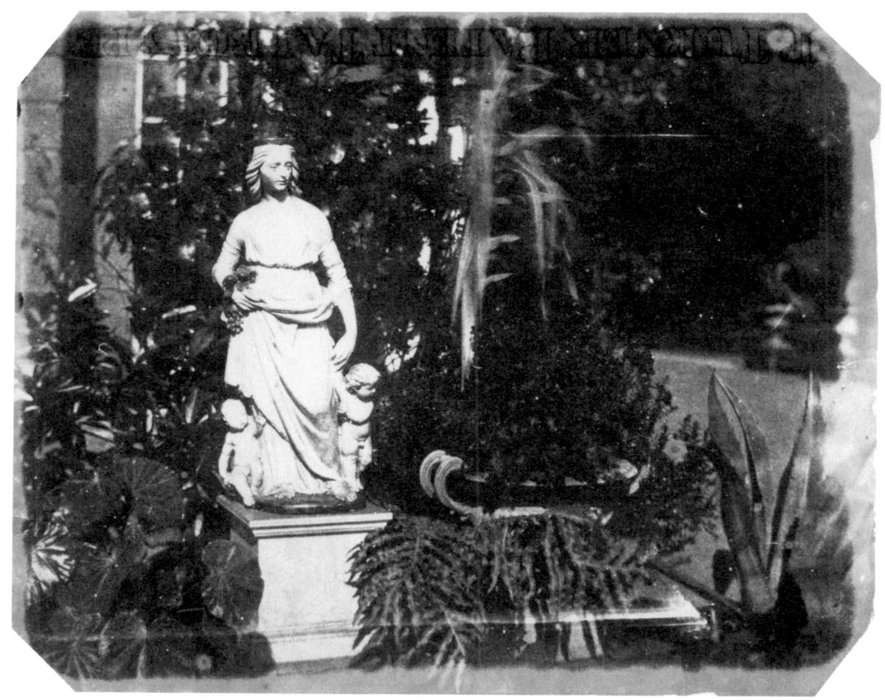

Fig. 84. Alfred Capel Cure, *Statue by Lucca della Robbia, Badger*, ca. 1855. Albumen silver print, 18.3 x 22.6 cm (7¼ x 8⅞ in.). Private collection, courtesy of Hans P. Kraus, Jr., New York

The Cheney and Cure families, while not aristocratic, belonged to what was known as the "upper ten thousand"— members of society's ruling elite by virtue of their standing as members of Parliament or in any of the higher grades of the legal, military, naval, clerical, or colonial services. Such people were usually financially independent, deriving much of their income from their estates and the mineral rights that went with them. The family estate of the Cheneys was Badger Hall, Shropshire; they also held land and manorial rights in the adjoining county of Derbyshire that had come to them through marriage.[21] Lieutenant-General Robert Cheney had had a long and distinguished military career, becoming an aide-de-camp to George III and serving his country with distinction during the Napoleonic Wars.[22] He and Harriet Carr, whom he married in 1799, had three sons and two daughters; Robert Henry, the eldest son, inherited the estates on the death of his father in 1820, while Edward (briefly) and Ralph went into the army.

The Cure family home, Blake Hall in Essex, was a large estate of chiefly agricultural land that they managed and farmed themselves.[23] The Cures could trace their ancestry back to Thomas Cure, member of Parliament for Southwark, London, during the reign of Henry VIII. In 1789 Capel Cure bought Blake Hall, and in 1822 his eldest son, also named Capel, married Harriet Cheney (who carried her mother's given name), the eldest of the five Cheney children and a sister of (Robert) Henry. The couple had many children; Alfred Capel Cure was their next-to-oldest son.[24]

When it came to photography, the elder Cheney brothers, Henry and Edward, were important role models in their nephew Alfred's life, influencing his taste and encouraging him to share their enthusiasm for art, architecture, and landscape gardening. After the death of her husband in 1820, Harriet Carr Cheney moved to Italy and established herself in the Palazzo Sciarra on the Corso in Rome, where she was joined by her sons Henry and Edward in 1825. The Cheneys quickly integrated into the Anglo-Italian social circle that dominated the city's artistic and cultural life. All three were accomplished artists: Harriet and Henry specialized in watercolors, Edward in pen-and-ink drawing[25] (a skill probably developed during his formal training at the Royal Military Academy, Sandhurst, where all officers learned to make topographic drawings and maps).[26] While Henry was considerably occupied with managing the estates at Badger Hall, Edward had the freedom to become a connoisseur of Italian Renaissance art and over the years formed a fine collection of paintings, drawings, stone sculpture, and bronzes, which he kept at Badger and in his London house (fig. 84).[27]

Henry developed an abiding interest in landscape gardening, which was perhaps what led him to photography. Frustrated by the difficulty of recording stages in his landscaping, as he wrote to his friend the artist Thomas Cromek in 1846, he hoped that when "the facility of taking sun pictures is increased" he would have a way to overcome this problem.[28] It seems as though he had only very recently become aware of photography's potential; when he became a subscriber to Talbot's *Sun Pictures in Scotland* he also requested the first fascicle of *The Pencil of Nature*.[29] By 1851 Henry and Edward were living comfortable bachelor lives at Badger, with Henry deeply engaged in his landscape gardening, employing fourteen workers solely for that purpose.[30] He had long sketched and painted in watercolors when he traveled, and his decision in about 1850 to take up photography must have been based on a mixture of pragmatism and the appeal of its possibilities for artistic self-expression.[31]

Alfred Capel Cure was just eighteen when he took the commission of ensign in the 31st Regiment of Foot in 1844. He transferred the following year to the 55th Regiment, then based in Chichester.[32] The next year the regiment was sent to Ireland, where it remained until 1851; then it transferred to Gibraltar and in early 1854 joined other regiments of the British army in the Crimea, under the command of Lord Raglan. Despite a general shortage of troops, however, Cure was not posted to the Crimea until June 5, 1855. There, two days after his arrival, he underwent what one eyewitness called a "*baptême de feu*," leading a contingent of two hundred men in a storming of the quarries at Sebastopol.[33] After the deaths that month of senior colleagues in the field of battle, Cure took temporary command of the 55th until the fall of Sebastopol on September 8, when, severely wounded, he was sent home to recuperate.[34]

It was thus in the course of extended service as an army officer that Cure took up photography during the summer of 1850. An early photograph, made in November 1850, shows his uncles' home, Badger Hall; one is tempted to hypothesize that the photograph was taken with a newly acquired camera and apparatus, perhaps a gift from his uncle Henry, with whom he would share his enthusiasm for photography.[35] Cure was the more productive of the two and remained an active and prolific photographer throughout the 1850s, using paper negatives but experimenting occasionally with collodion.[36] In many ways he had the

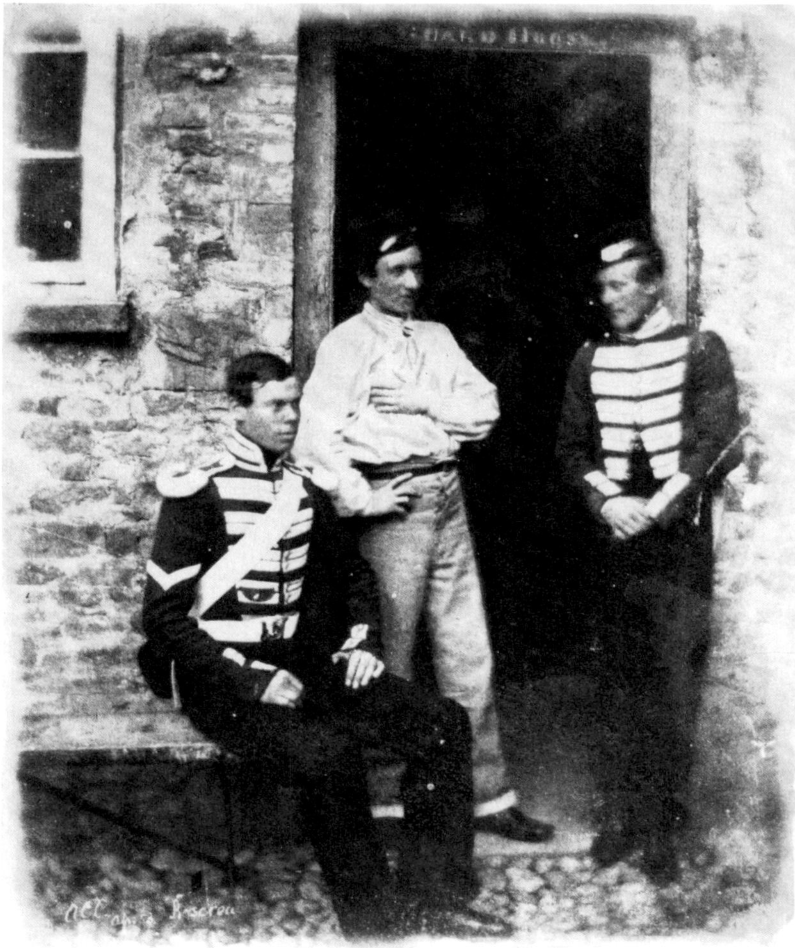

Fig. 85. Alfred Capel Cure, *Guard House, Roscrea*, April 1853. Salted paper print, 21.9 x 18 cm (8⅝ x 7⅛ in.). Private collection, courtesy of Hans P. Kraus, Jr., New York

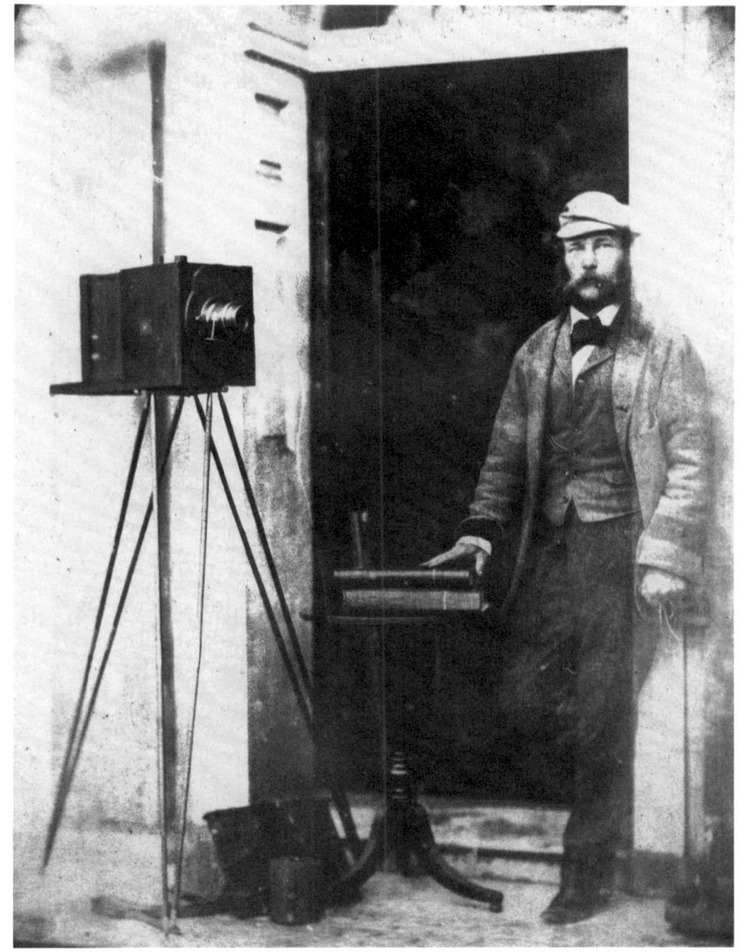

Fig. 86. Alfred Capel Cure, *Self-Portrait*, September 29, 1856. Salted paper print from collodion negative, 21 x 15.8 cm (8¼ x 6¼ in.). Department of Special Collections, Charles E. Young Research Library, University of California, Los Angeles, 94/22

ideal qualities of a novice, being well educated and influenced by the tastes and connoisseurship of his two Cheney uncles, and having (when not seeing war action) sufficient time and income to photograph freely (pl. 78).

Cure's brief but traumatic period of service in the Crimea, June to October 1855, turned out to be a watershed for his photography. Before then his photographs revolved around his life with the regiment at home and abroad—mainly portraits of fellow officers and scenes of new recruits and barracks life (fig. 85). But afterward, once well enough to resume photography, he drew comfort and delight from documenting Britain's castles, cathedrals, ruined abbeys and monasteries, medieval buildings, and country houses. To accomplish this he made a number of extended tours, each concentrated on a particular region. Although technically still an officer, he was no longer formally attached to any regiment and could spend his time as he pleased. He most likely had retained his batman, or orderly, in his employ to serve his personal needs, an ideal arrangement for an invalid who is traveling with all the paraphernalia of photography.

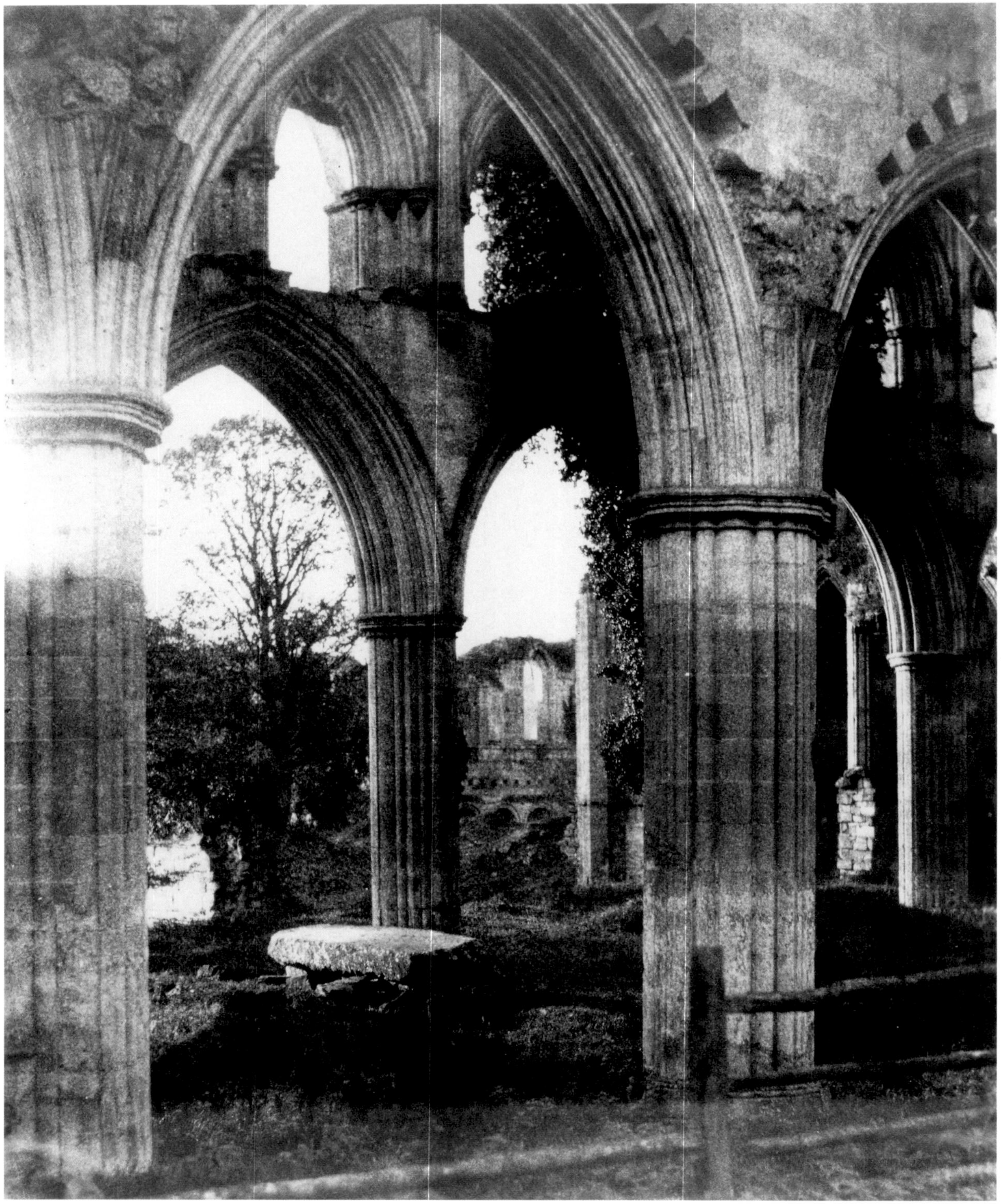

Fig. 87. Alfred Capel Cure, *Rievaulx Abbey*, October 24, 1856. Albumen silver print, 27 x 21.5 cm (10⅝ x 8½ in.). The Museum of Modern Art, New York, Gift of Raymond B. Gary, 91.1983

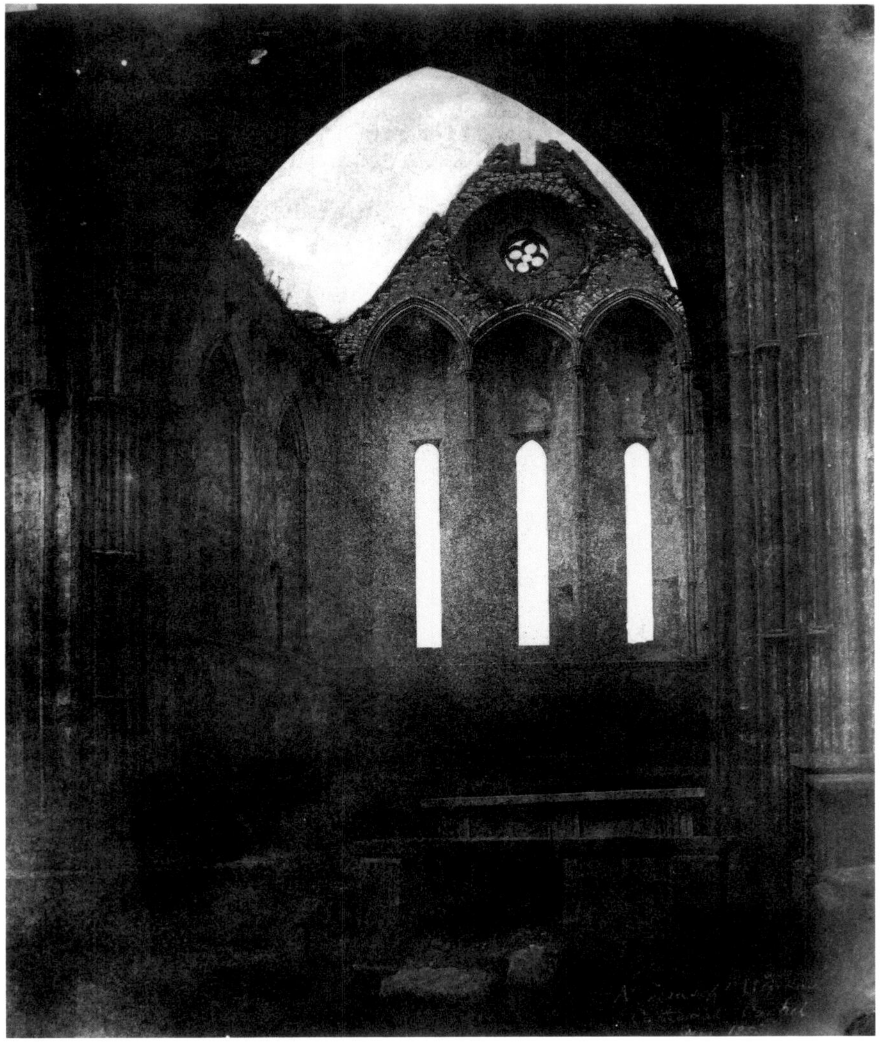

Fig. 88. Alfred Capel Cure, *North Transept, Cathedral of Cashel*, 1853. Albumen silver print, 21.9 x 17.9 cm (8⅝ x 7 in.). Private collection, courtesy of Hans P. Kraus, Jr., New York

A self-portrait made at the close of September 1856 shows Cure the gentleman amateur, with his camera, apparatus, and albums (fig. 86). For someone working alone in the days before shutters and remote controls, the only way to make a self-portrait was to remove the lens cap, walk to the spot framed by the camera, and pose for the long exposure. This sequence of events gives the figure of Cure a ghostly transparency; it suggests a certain transience and contrasts nicely with the solidity of the objects that surround him. Perhaps he made the portrait to mark the anniversary of the battle at Sebastopol, where he nearly lost his life.

Cure's large-format, solidly made mahogany camera was set apart from standard models of the period by the way its lens was mounted on the body. A device, visible in the photograph, made it possible to raise and lower the lens in relation to the negative. This was essential to successful architectural photography, for it allowed the camera to frame the desired view and still remain perfectly horizontal, thereby avoiding the converging verticals that diminish the sense of a building's grandeur when the camera is pointed upward. The circular back plate of this device suggests that the sliding portion could also be rotated, permitting the lens to be shifted diagonally in any direction when the image is composed on the screen. The design of the camera offered a sophisticated degree of control that Cure used to great effect, for example in *Hereford Cathedral from the Northwest* (pl. 59), for which he raised the lens in order to reduce the foreground area and include the whole of the south window and the Norman turrets flanking it. This technical refinement was matched by Cure's sensitivity to the way light describes the character of a building and brings it alive. At Hereford he chose a moment when the early morning sun picked out the buttresses of the nave and bathed the transept in light. By a fortunate coincidence it was also a moment when the shadow of another building in the cathedral close fell across the bishop's porch, adding depth and contrast to the composition.

Waiting for just the right light and weather was a constant occupation of this generation of photographers; for those who had the time, it was worth delaying until conditions were right if the outcome would be a successful photograph. The dates inscribed beneath many of his photographs indicate that Cure kept to a tight schedule, often making several exposures a day before moving to the next place on his itinerary.[37] For example, in mid-October 1856 he began a three-week tour principally of eastern and northern England, making an extended circuit that took in Ely, Peterborough, Temple Newsam House (Leeds), Kirkstall Abbey, Bolton Abbey, Fountains Abbey, Rievaulx Abbey, Byland Abbey, Whitby Abbey, York Minster, Castle Howard, and Lincoln Cathedral—finally returning to Ely, where he ended with a flourish of five exposures. During the three weeks he made no fewer than forty-five negatives, an average of

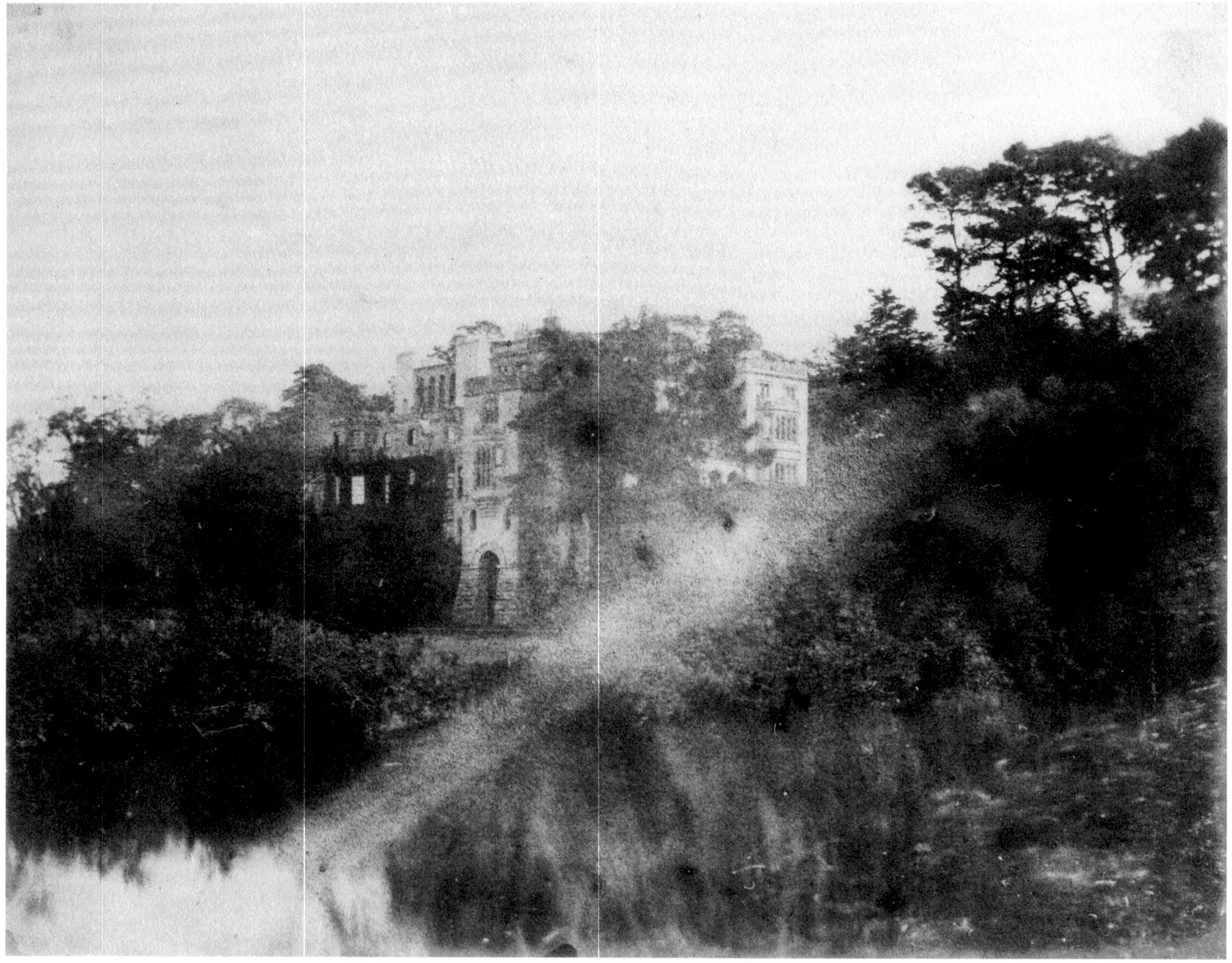

Fig. 89. Alfred Capel Cure, *Guy's Cliff, Effect of Sunbeam*, ca. 1855. Albumen silver print, 17.6 x 21.8 cm (6⅞ x 8⅝ in.). Private collection, courtesy of Hans P. Kraus, Jr., New York

three exposures per day; because waiting for the right light took time, this was a realistic pace for making photographs without compromising the results.

Cure made several exposures at Fountains Abbey, the most evocative of which shows the ruined building bathed in a soft, autumnal light in early morning, when the air was absolutely still (fig. 76). His composition is dominated by a solitary tree whose leafless limbs reach imploringly toward the sky, slender and fragile against the solid masonry of the Cistercian abbey. Somehow the image evokes both the anxieties of the present and a consoling reassurance from the past.

After a couple of days at Fountains, Cure moved on to nearby Rievaulx, where the ruined Cistercian abbey nestled dramatically in a steep-sided and heavily wooded valley. Architecturally, as *Black's Guide* noted, the building was considered the finest "example of the earliest English style . . . to be found in the kingdom," with parts of it "beautifully clothed in ivy" that greatly enhanced its picturesque appearance.[38] Artists had been attracted to this romantic spot for generations, and the site had already been extensively photographed by Joseph Cundall, Francis Bedford, Philip Delamotte, Fenton, and Benjamin Brecknell Turner.[39] Photographs of it by Cundall and Delamotte had been exhibited in the spring of 1855 and published in 1856 in an expensive portfolio entitled *A Photographic Tour among the Abbeys of Yorkshire.*[40]

Of the several studies Cure made at Rievaulx, the most striking looks through the open arches of the presbytery to a massive slab of stone placed where the high altar once stood (fig. 87). As with his study of Hereford Cathedral, he was able to maintain the integrity of the composition by raising the lens, which here allowed him to keep the apex of the foreground arch just visible within the frame. The repeated arch forms create a rhythmic interplay that animates the composition without overshadowing the significance and drama of the altar stone, which has the appearance of being illuminated by a shaft of celestial light. One is tempted to think that Cure removed the top two rails of the fence in the foreground of his picture to prevent them from interfering with his composition.[41] This photograph has an emotional tone very different from his studies at Hereford and Fountains, for here the viewer is being invited to take spiritual and physical sanctuary in the ruined building, to enter and pray.

Cure was a careful, even studious photographer whose appreciation of the technical limitations of photography allowed him to overcome most difficulties. Although he made an occasional mistake, usually he managed to redeem himself. Miscalculating the exposure, which resulted in weak negatives lacking detail and contrast, was perhaps the difficulty most frequently experienced by photographers. At Cashel Cathedral in County Tipperary, Ireland, the difference between the levels of interior and exterior light was so great that all Cure could hope to achieve was a reasonable balance between the two. His precise placement of the camera both vertically and laterally allows the open sky to become a graphic form that visually balances the powerful pattern of the empty windows beneath (fig. 88).

At Guy's Cliff, Warwickshire, Cure's camera developed a problem, leaking light onto the negative during exposure. Most photographers would have discarded the result as a complete failure. But Cure recognized the picture's good qualities and playfully entitled it *Effect of Sunbeam* (fig. 89). The artistic influence of his uncle Henry is perhaps evident in this work, for the print has the feel of a watercolor sketch made rapidly to catch the transient effect of passing light.

Cure's affectionate portrait of his dog asleep among the flowers is a bold and striking composition, with the dog, on a diagonal, tucked into the corner of the frame and nicely set against the lighter ground (pl. 55). The attractive textures and forms of the plants, especially the pale blooms, animate the upper portion of the picture and balance the dark, weighty presence of the animal below. Made hastily before the dog awoke, the photograph has the spontaneity and feel of a snapshot, but this casual appearance owes more to Cure's confidence in handling his camera than to chance.

At the opposite end of the emotional scale is Cure's arresting study of a young oak tree torn apart by lightning during a September storm (pl. 56).[42] Perhaps Cure saw the tree's awkwardly arching limbs and shattered form as an analogue for the agonies he had witnessed in the storming of the quarries at Sebastopol, where so many of his friends and colleagues were torn apart by shot and shell. This death portrait of a tree was made shortly after Cure's self-portrait with camera, almost exactly a year after he was severely wounded and nearly lost his life.[43]

Cure pursued his craft with a dedication and strict routine that set him apart from many amateurs of the period. On his frequent photographic tours around Britain after his return from the Crimea he created a substantial body of work, which informally records many of Britain's foremost architectural treasures. In attaining his high level of skill and judgment he undoubtedly benefited from visits to Badger Hall, where fine paintings and sculpture were to be seen, and from the influence of his uncles. Connoisseurs and accomplished artists, they became his role models; one senses their presence and implicit approval in all his photographic achievements.

After a decade of sustained activity, Cure suddenly abandoned photography. He made his last photograph in 1860 and never took up the camera again.[44] When Henry Cheney died in 1866, the estates at Badger passed to his younger brother Edward. With his death in 1884, they were inherited by his nephew Alfred Capel Cure. Cure lived there until his own tragic death in 1896; as baldly stated in the *Times* obituary, he "was killed . . . by the accidental explosion of dynamite while he was engaged in blasting the roots of trees in his park."[45]

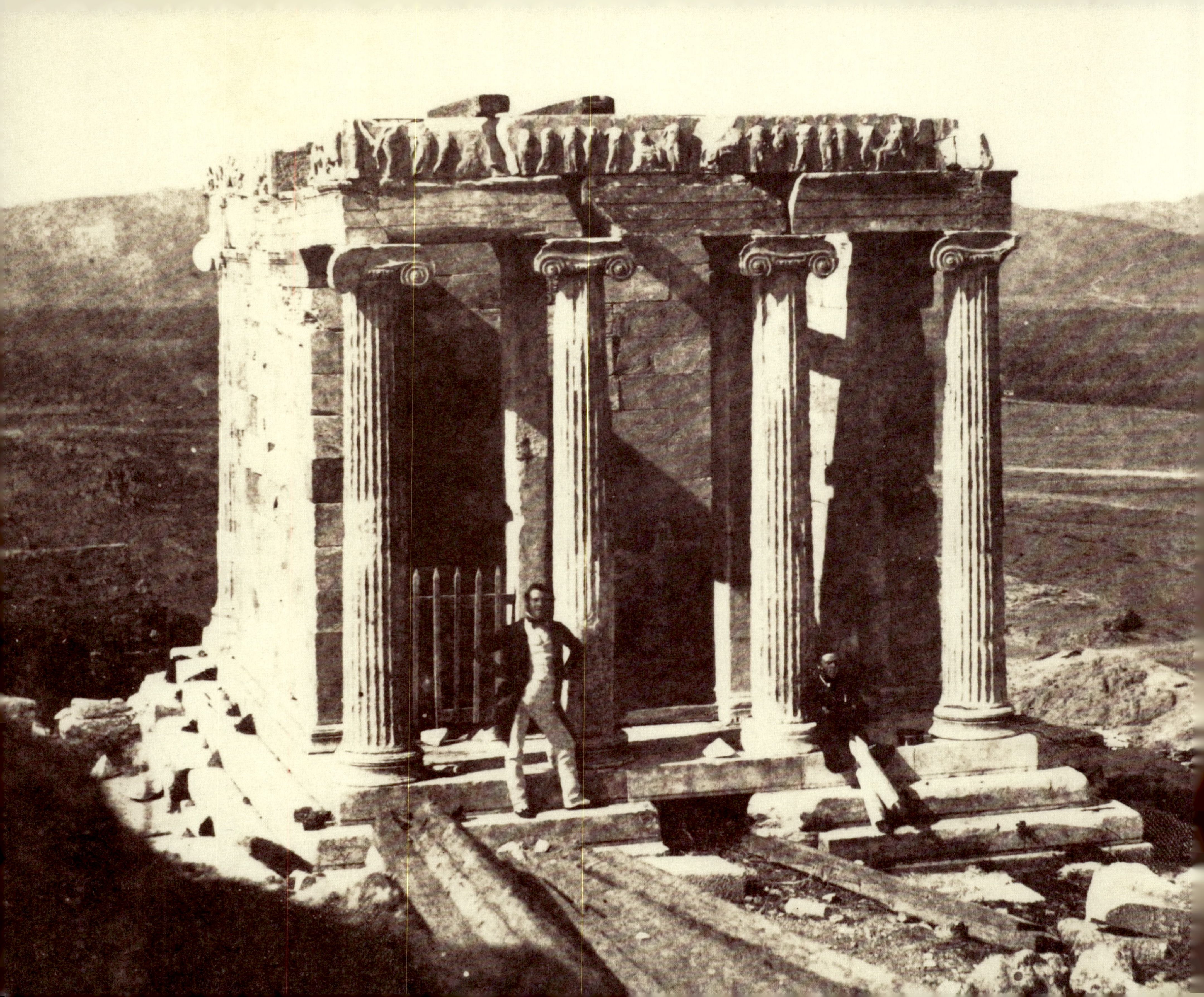

8. *Echoes of the Grand Tour*

Italy is the place to live in, where you get figs & peaches to cool your thirst, instead of the snow.[1]

Talbot's exuberant reaction to the Mediterranean climate and culture was typical for Britons rediscovering the joys of Europe when, after the Napoleonic Wars, it again became accessible.[2] Throughout the 1820s and 1830s, Talbot, his mother, and numbers of their relatives and close friends could often be found somewhere in Europe, traveling alone or in family parties. Cultured and indefatigable, they moved from place to place as their mood or the season dictated, relishing their social and intellectual activities in this milieu. In a letter to Talbot, his half sister, Lady Caroline Mount Edgcumbe, expressed the general sentiment: "How delightful it is to feel oneself once more in Italy! what I have longed for for so many years!"[3]

Indeed, countless British aristocrats and gentry were crisscrossing Europe, rubbing shoulders with their French, German, and Italian counterparts and joining an international upper class that was socially, intellectually, and artistically compatible. Britons were drawn abroad for many reasons: some were following in the footsteps of their forebears, who had made the Grand Tour in the eighteenth century, while others were attracted by the sublimity of the Alps, the romance of Mediterranean civilizations, or the sheer freedom of being abroad. As one author put it, "Whether the pleasure exists chiefly" in the "historical, poetical" associations or "in the pure idea of contemplating the individual beauties of ancient art:—the pleasure *does* exist."[4]

By the early 1840s, this ever-larger band of British tourists had taken the essential features of the eighteenth-century European tour and redefined them according to Victorian tastes and expectations. They still drew, sketched, and made the circuit of major cities taking in the sights, but now with a Murray or Baedeker handbook to point the way and interpret what they saw. Once photography became a workable activity, it was natural to think of using it to record and document one's travels. However, practical matters at first kept most tourists from attempting photography overseas. The biggest problems were the high temperatures and humidity of the Mediterranean climate. Chemicals deteriorated rapidly in the heat; humidity played unexpected tricks when iodizing and sensitizing the paper.[5] Any problems normally associated with photography were multiplied tenfold. Careful planning was essential, and when materials ran out—often because of repeated failures—and letters requesting additional supplies were sent back home, nothing further could be done until the necessary items arrived weeks or even months later. This meant that photographers working abroad during the 1840s were generally members of the leisured classes who could afford to linger while they awaited the arrival of fresh supplies.

Opposite: Fig. 90. Detail of George Wilson Bridges, *Temple of Victory* (Acropolis, Athens), ca. 1848. Salted paper print, 16.5 x 21.2 cm (6½ x 8⅜ in.). The Metropolitan Museum of Art, New York, Gilman Collection, Purchase, Joseph M. Cohen Gift, 2005, 2005.100.846

GEORGE BRIDGES, CALVERT JONES, AND CHRISTOPHER TALBOT

In the spring of 1846, the paths of three such photographers converged on the island of Malta, a British settlement and often the first port of call for tourists sailing the Mediterranean. They were Christopher Rice Mansel Talbot, sometimes known as "Kit" by his family; the Reverend Calvert Richard Jones; and the Reverend George Wilson Bridges. All three knew William Henry Fox Talbot and were connected to him through their interest in photography, although only with Kit, as a relative, was there also a close family connection. Kit Talbot and Jones, both from Swansea, belonged to families that had grown rich through

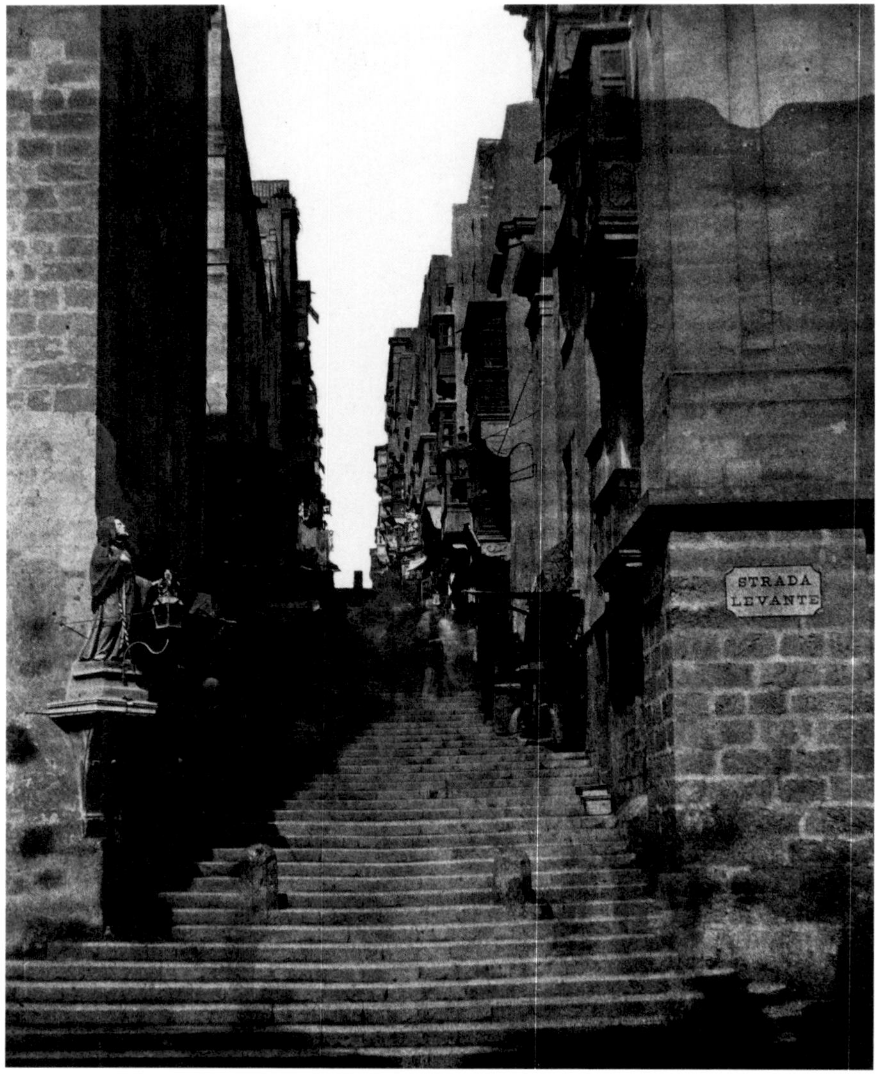

Fig. 91. Calvert Richard Jones, *Strada Levante, Valetta, Malta*, 1850s. Salted paper print, 21.7 x 17.4 cm (8½ x 6⅞ in.). The Metropolitan Museum of Art, New York, David Hunter McAlpin Fund, 1946, 46.1.109

commercial exploitation of the coal and iron industries that dominated this area of South Wales. The vast fortune Kit Talbot inherited on reaching his majority earned him the sobriquet "the wealthiest commoner" and gave him freedom to indulge his taste for foreign travel; he even commissioned the building of a yacht in which to sail around the Mediterranean with his family.[6] He and Jones had been good friends since their university days at Oxford, and both took a keen interest in photography after its announcement in 1839. By the time they arrived in Valletta, the capital of Malta, both men were committed calotypists. Jones, however, was clearly the more experienced of the two, and his belief in the commercial potential of his photographs sets him apart from Kit.[7]

George Bridges came from Essex, where his father was a successful banker and merchant with numerous commercial interests in the surrounding counties.[8] After George's ordination as an Anglican priest he took on a parish in Jamaica, where he moved with his family in 1815 and lived in some comfort for the next twenty years. During this time he wrote a book, *The Annals of Jamaica*, and pamphlets opposing the abolition of slavery.[9] In 1836 his wife and four daughters were drowned in a boating accident. The traumatized Bridges fled Jamaica with his sole surviving son and lived in a series of locations abroad, including the remote backwoods of Canada, before eventually returning to Britain. At that point he got to know the Talbot family through church connections and became interested in photography after seeing the first fascicle of *The Pencil of Nature*.[10] In the spring of 1845, armed with letters of introduction from W. H. F. Talbot and a bundle of his iodized photographic paper, Bridges set off for Malta, pausing first in Paris to commission and receive a camera from the celebrated instrument maker Charles Chevalier.[11] Once arrived in Malta he was taught the calotype process by Jones, at Talbot's request. This occupation so caught Bridges's imagination that he spent the next six years traveling around the shores of the Mediterranean, photographing extensively wherever he went. Driven by a consuming sense of purpose, he produced, by his own reckoning, some 1,700 negatives.[12]

Jones, undoubtedly the most skilled of the three friends, took particular care when selecting his viewpoint and adjusting his camera to achieve an optimal composition on its ground glass screen (fig. 92). He also intuitively understood the expressive value lighting played in creating a successful picture. For Jones, light was not just an element to factor into the exposure but an essential part of the composition; it revealed and described some objects and suppressed others. These effects come together perfectly in *St. Paul's Cathedral, Valetta, Malta, with Bell Tower* (pl. 73), where the soft, raking light plays up the solid roundness of the three Ionic columns while casting the doorway behind into mysterious darkness. The rapidly receding wall leads the eye toward the center of the frame, where it is arrested for a moment by a tiny crescent of light seen through an open archway. This extremely effective composition is achieved by careful positioning; had the camera been farther to the left or right, or closer in, the picture's carefully balanced structure would have been significantly altered. Or imagine the photograph taken at a different time of day, or under different lighting conditions, and it becomes obvious that Jones was keenly aware of these various elements when setting up his camera and making the exposure. The subtle blemishes that occurred when the paper negative was sensitized and developed hint at the difficulties of working abroad, where darkroom conditions and chemical stability often lay beyond immediate control.[13]

Either Jones was a gifted teacher or Bridges a receptive pupil, for within a matter of weeks the latter was writing to Lacock Abbey asking for fresh supplies, and within a month he was taking photographs on his own, proudly sending examples to Talbot to show what he had achieved.[14] But although he mastered the calotype process and learned how to calculate exposure times under a Mediterranean sun, he never succeeded in making prints, despite sustained efforts. He wrote to Talbot, "I am quite in despair—utterly discouraged by my failures . . . and much inclined to give up all attempts in an art which stops short of utility just at the very point when one thinks to have attained it."[15] Frustrated, he sent his negatives to Talbot to have them printed professionally in England. It would have been weeks or even months before he saw the finished prints, and by that time he would likely have moved to a fresh location. The delay between the making of the negative and its realization as a print must have been a real problem for Bridges, since judging the success of a picture solely from the negative required more experience than he had accumulated.

Perhaps the fact that he was always working at one remove from the finished prints accounts for the slightly hesitant look of Bridges's

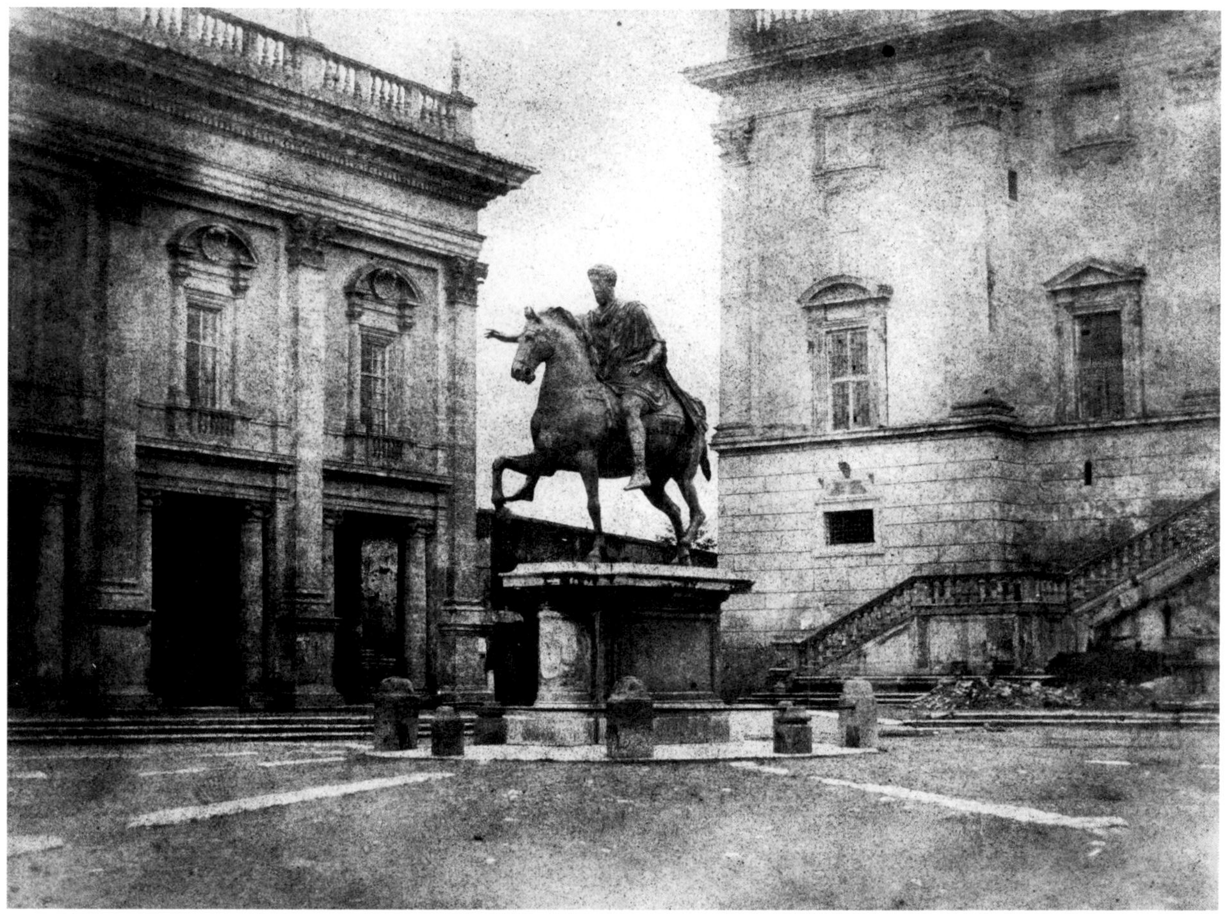

Fig. 92. Calvert Richard Jones, *The Capitoline* (Statue of Marcus Aurelius, Piazza del Campidoglio, Rome), 1846. Salted paper print, 16.2 x 21.2 cm (6⅜ x 8⅜ in.). The Metropolitan Museum of Art, New York, Purchase, Hans P. Kraus, Jr., Gift, and Mrs. Harrison D. Horblit and Joyce and Robert Menschel Gifts, 1992, 1992.5167

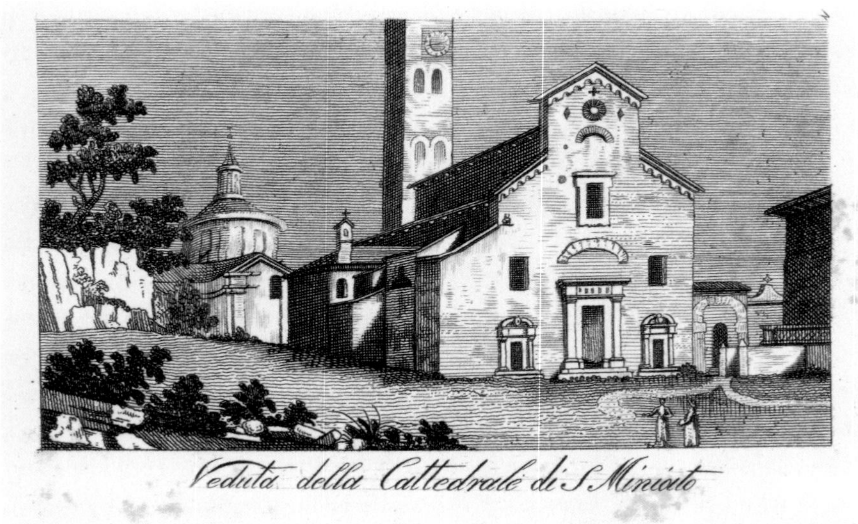

Fig. 93. Unknown artist, *Veduta della Cattedrale di S Miniato*, ca. 1820s. Woodcut, 5.3 x 9.4 cm (2½ x 3¾ in.). Private collection

compositions, which despite their considerable interest lack the assurance and finesse of his mentor's works. In Jones's *House of Sallust, Vesuvius behind, Pompeii*, for instance, the sustained repetition of verticals across the horizontal format creates a satisfying rhythm that is punctuated with great effectiveness by the top-hatted Englishman casually leaning against a wall (pl. 74). Bridges's pictures instead communicate the sense of awe and exhilaration he must have felt when seeing legendary places for the first time (fig. 90). In his hands the camera becomes a tool of exploration, a justification for traveling, and a means of recording every important scene and site along the way. In his *Taormina, the Amphitheater* (pl. 76), is it Bridges himself seated in the amphitheater with a sketchpad balanced on his knee, gazing reflectively at some distant point beyond the frame? One is tempted to think so, and this image, presumably of the "Wayworn Wanderer," as he liked to call himself, suggests the eager curiosity that impelled Bridges to keep moving from place to place around the shores of the Mediterranean for six years, photographing as he went.

Jones, rather differently, was ambitious to achieve recognition for the medium of photography, like his mentor W. H. F. Talbot. He recognized the photographic potential of Malta and felt sure his pictures would "sell extremely well here, as Malta has become a vast recipient of tourists and travelers, who wd all like memorials of it" (fig. 91).[16] Among the negatives of churches, cathedrals, and the Valletta palace that in February 1846 he sent to Talbot to have printed in quantity was an arresting study entitled *Palacea Brig, Hove Down, Malta* (pl. 71). Unlike his other Malta photographs, this is a strikingly abstract image, which isolates the forms of the mast and rigging of a ship careened on its side in the harbor. There is no identifiable subject, other than the cat's cradle of spars, masts, and rigging that intersect the frame in a way that sets our modernist sensibilities alight. What attracted Jones in 1846 beguiles us yet with its apparent randomness, bold conception, and visual power. It is the photograph of an artist.

Photography can work in fascinating ways. In Jones's study of rigging, a prolonged exposure and the optical intervention of the lens together produced an image subtly different from the actual view, and a mundane subject emerged transformed into something quite mysterious. The photographs made by Kit Talbot—an absolute amateur with no need to consider commercial factors—suggest a different sensibility, one principally bent on capturing the essence of a place. The Villa Reale in Naples, a magical estate and park "washed by the sea, with its vases,

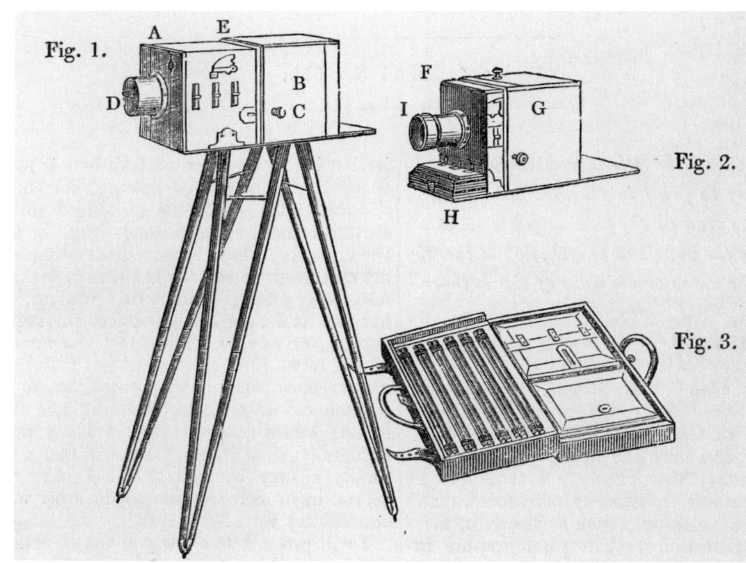

Fig. 94. Charles Knight, *Designs for a folding camera suitable for the photographic tourist*, 1853. Woodcut illustration, 8.5 x 10.5 cm (3⅜ x 4⅛ in.). From *Journal of the Photographic Society of London*, May 2, 1853, p. 46. Private collection

fountains, alleys of acacias, groves of myrtle and orange-trees," was much used as a promenade by gentry and aristocracy.[17] We know from Talbot's inscription on his negative of this subject that it was exposed with the aperture opened to its maximum for five minutes in good sunlight. This combination accounts for the overall lack of definition and the soft spreading form of the light flooding through the trees behind the statue, which together create the shimmering, luminous sense of heat associated with southern Italy (pl. 72). The figure of a young girl posed before the statue's plinth appears as a tiny negative set within positive surroundings. At some point during the long exposure the child lost patience and moved away, leaving an ethereal suggestion of her form impressed upon the image. She may be Kit Talbot's eldest daughter, Emily, dressed in mourning following her mother's death from tuberculosis, in Malta, a few weeks earlier.[18] Why else would a child so young be dressed in black on a sunny Saturday afternoon in Naples?

PHOTOGRAPHING ABROAD

When Bridges, Jones, and Kit Talbot were photographing along the Mediterranean, their choice of the calotype medium was something of a forgone conclusion. The only alternative at the time was the daguerreotype, and although Jones was familiar with that process, the calotype, with its ability to yield multiple prints from a single negative, matched his intent to discover a nascent market for photographs of foreign views. Their beauty and truthfulness would set them far above the pedestrian engravings peddled as tourist souvenirs both at home and overseas (fig. 93). All three photographers sought technical advice from W. H. F. Talbot, whose advice and materials helped sustain their practices over many years.[19] But by the early 1850s a wide variety of processes had been introduced, the chief distinction among them being between paper and glass. Paper negatives could be iodized and sensitized well in advance of exposure and developed long afterward, making the calotype far simpler to handle than the collodion process. For collodion the glass plate had to be coated, sensitized, exposed, and developed in rapid sequence,[20] and therefore required immediate access to a darkroom even when the work was done outdoors. For this purpose portable darkrooms had been ingeniously designed; they made collodion photography a possibility for travelers, although still one involving significantly more paraphernalia and inconvenience than paper processes. Moreover, in the rough-and-tumble of travel a box of glass plates might easily be shattered, whereas paper negatives were less susceptible to damage, light to carry, and capable of being posted home like so many letters.

Climate was also a major factor for the traveler deciding on a process. High temperatures and humidity made the photographic chemistry skittish and difficult to control. During the hot summer of 1852, John Percy found that even in Britain the waxed-paper process proved more stable than the calotype, which failed him repeatedly despite his long experience with it.[21] At the other temperature extreme, Roger Fenton discovered that waxed paper worked well during his trip to Russia in 1854, where on one occasion "the thermometer stood considerably below the freezing point." Like the calotype, the waxed-paper negative could be iodized and sensitized well in advance and "kept for a month without great injury to the result."[22] Fenton saw very little difference between his results with waxed-paper negatives prepared in London prior to his departure and those he sensitized on the spot in Russia.[23] Largely for all these practical reasons, paper negative processes would continue to be used by travelers well into the 1860s, long after they had been replaced by the collodion process back in Britain.[24]

The needs of traveling photographers were also receiving attention from camera manufacturers, who introduced, as an improvement on the usual rigid box form, a variety of folding cameras "highly recommended for tourists, travellers and others requiring a most effective instrument for taking views, portraits, &c, combined with the smallest possible bulk and weight."[25] Some of these were ingeniously constructed with folding side panels that allowed the camera to spring into action like a piece of scenery in a Victorian pantomime (fig. 94). The design was pioneered by Thomas Ottewill,[26] copied widely by other makers, and immortalized by Lewis Carroll in a passage from his satirical "Hiawatha's Photographing."

In its case it lay compactly,
Folded into nearly nothing;
But he opened out the hinges,
Pushed and pulled the joints and hinges,
Till it looked all squares and oblongs,
Like a complicated figure
In the Second Book of Euclid.[27]

Cameras to be used in a British climate were usually of ordinary mahogany, but manufacturers knew from experience that if they were "intended for India or other hot countries, it is necessary they should be constructed of Spanish mahogany, and the sides clamped with brass, so as to ensure their withstanding the effects of climate."[28] While these precautions added to the cost, the expense was justified, since this type of construction preserved the camera's integrity and avoided the frustration of having light penetrate joints distorted by the combination of heat and humidity. Cameras constructed in this way were later known as "tropical" models; their manufacture continued well into the twentieth century.[29]

Thus, by the early 1850s an array of techniques and devices had become available that greatly improved the chances of success for those making photographs in the course of foreign travel. British amateurs began photographing overseas with enthusiasm; indeed, in some instances photography may well have provided the incentive to travel abroad. The travelers ranged widely, photographing new and exciting subjects in Russia, Europe, Mediterranean lands, Egypt, and the Holy Land and submitting their results to exhibitions once back home. The annual exhibitions of the Photographic Society contained, from the very first, a good sprinkling of foreign views made by these peripatetic photographers (although their impact was somewhat diminished by the quantities of pictures sent in by European and especially French photographers).[30]

Unlike the tentative work of traveling Britons in the 1840s, these post-1850 photographs are self-confident and assured. The first to be exhibited were some views of Russia by Fenton, displayed in London at the Society of Arts in December 1852; he showed a larger group of his Russian subjects, more than thirty, at the first annual exhibition of the Photographic Society in January 1854. Some of these were pairs of nearly identical photographs made specifically for viewing through a "Wheatstone's mirror stereoscope," which gave the appearance of three-dimensionality.[31] Since frequently the original relationship between these paired prints has been lost, we cannot be sure whether a given view was intended for the stereoscope. But the way Fenton composed his photographs, with deep perspective and clear, strong forms in the foreground, makes it likely that a number of his Russian views were intended to be viewed three-dimensionally (pl. 80). Seen under these circumstances, the bare branches and their reflection that dominate the foreground in *Banks of the Dnieper, near Kief* are spatially resolved; and the moving boat, which in two dimensions appears to hover over the landing stage, is returned to the surface of the river when viewed three-dimensionally (pl. 79).

EDWARD TENISON AND CHARLES CLIFFORD

Like Fenton, the Irish aristocrat Edward King Tenison, Earl of Kingston, was photographing and exhibiting in the early 1850s. Equally active was his wife, Lady Louisa, daughter of the first Earl of Lichfield, a spirited woman of independent means, who shortly after their marriage in 1838 had traveled extensively in Syria, Egypt, and the Holy Land. Her account of her journeys, *Sketches in the East*, published some years later and lavishly illustrated with lithographs from her own watercolor illustrations, established her reputation as a travel writer and amateur artist.[32] For reasons of health, the Tenisons moved to Spain in 1850 or 1851 and lived there for two years, she sketching in preparation for her next book, he photographing the architecture of Madrid, Segovia, Seville, Toledo, and other sites.[33] His early studies in Granada are modest in scale, but in 1852 he began making pictures in a significantly larger format, 15 x 12 inches, which in this early period set his work apart from that of other British photographers.[34] A selection of his Spanish studies were first seen at the Dublin International Exhibition of 1853, where they were well received, although one critic felt that only their impressive size elevated them above their French counterparts.[35] Tenison also photographed the exhibition itself (pl. 44).

The following year Tenison submitted five of his Spanish studies to the annual exhibition of the Photographic Society (which, with almost a thousand exhibits, was a setting very different from the small-scale photographic display at Dublin).[36] At this first event organized by the society a number of newcomers exhibited for the first time, among them Peter Hinckes Bird, Charles Clifford, and Vicomte Joseph Vigier, all of whom showed studies of Spanish architecture—and of these the critics singled out the work of Clifford and Tenison for special mention.[37] The works of these two men reveal marked differences in their photographic aspirations. Tenison frequently photographed the ordinary scenes of life. Deserted squares where fountains gently play, civic plazas, small shops, apartment buildings where open windows catch the breeze, all suggest the ordered domesticity of the place (fig. 95; pl. 91). His photographs serve a private function, as personal recollections of his extended stay in Spain.

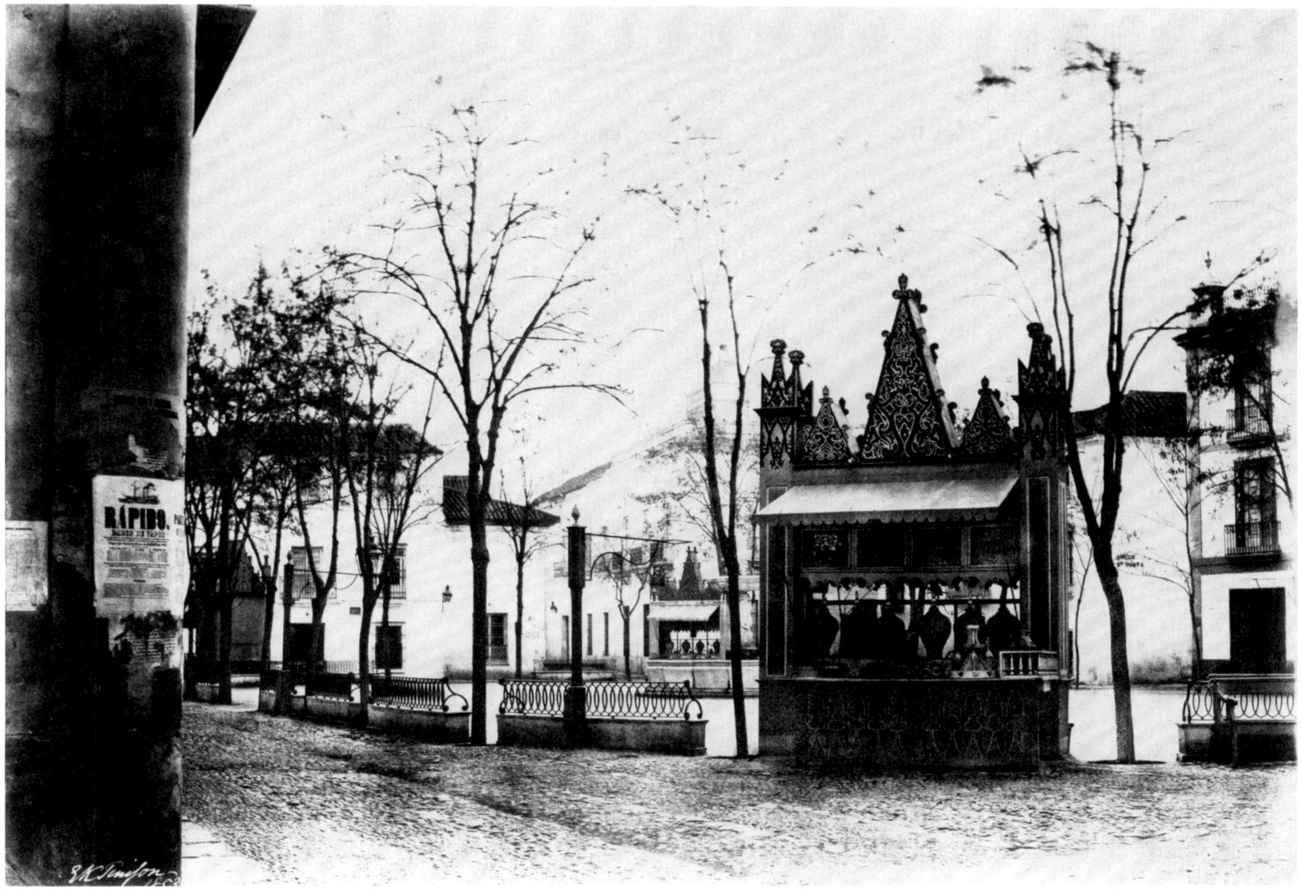

Fig. 95. Edward King Tenison, *Sevilla, Plaza de la Magdelena,* 1853. Salted paper print, 27.8 x 39.9 cm (11 x 15¾ in.). Bibliothèque Nationale de France, Paris, RES VF-268-FOL

Clifford had a different set of purposes. He established himself as a resident photographer in Madrid in 1850, intending to sell his architectural and topographic studies to British tourists, who were just beginning to explore Spain following the establishment of formal diplomatic relations between the two countries that same year.[38] Tourists found the climate impossibly hot and the lack of transport an aggravation, but they persevered because, in comparison with France and Italy, the country and its culture were little known or understood. The challenges of photographing in temperatures of 90 to 100 degrees, and where dust was "the absolute rule and not the exception," led Clifford to choose the calotype process initially, but the public's preference for the faultless definition of collodion soon forced him to switch.[39] The calotypes he made during the brief first period often have an enigmatic quality, despite his stated belief that the purpose of photographs was to be "historically interesting" and "serve as mementos" for the curious visitor.[40]

At the palace of La Granja de San Ildefonso, near Segovia, Clifford's use of the long exposure demanded by the process transforms the fountain into a series of transparent plumes and arcs that joyfully animate his composition (pl. 96). By some photographic magic he makes the decaying ninth-century church of San Miguel de Lillo, near Oviedo, appear to shimmer before his camera like a religious apparition, barely tethered to reality by a column of rocks in the immediate foreground (pl. 95).[41] Many of Clifford's early compositions convey the sense of dramatic expectancy felt when the curtain rises and the stage has yet to fill with life. When he arranged for the lifesize statue of Saint Bruno,

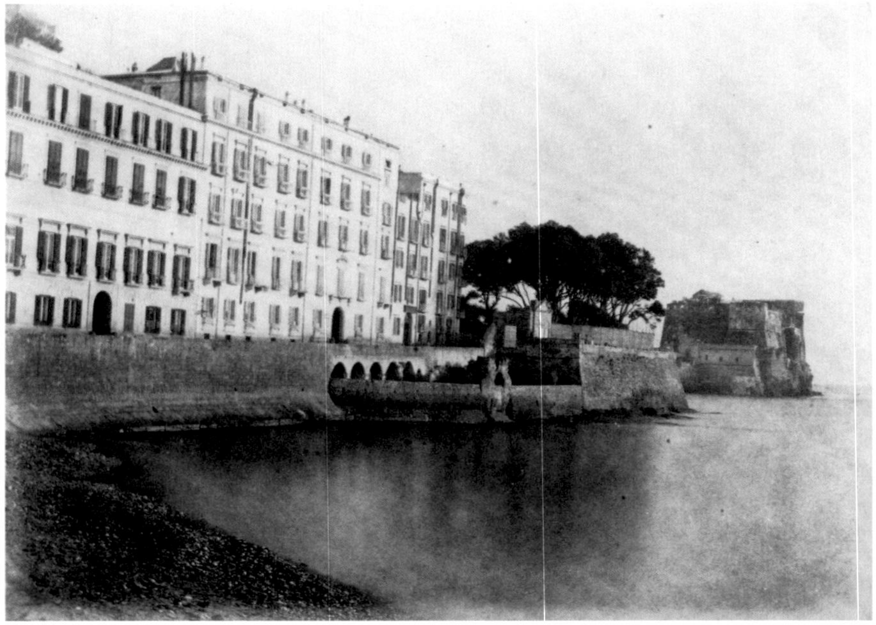

Fig. 96. Jane Martha St. John, *Hotel des Etrangers, Naples,* 1856. Albumen silver print, 18.3 x 24.8 cm (7¼ x 9¾ in.). The J. Paul Getty Museum, Los Angeles, 84.XA.760.14.7

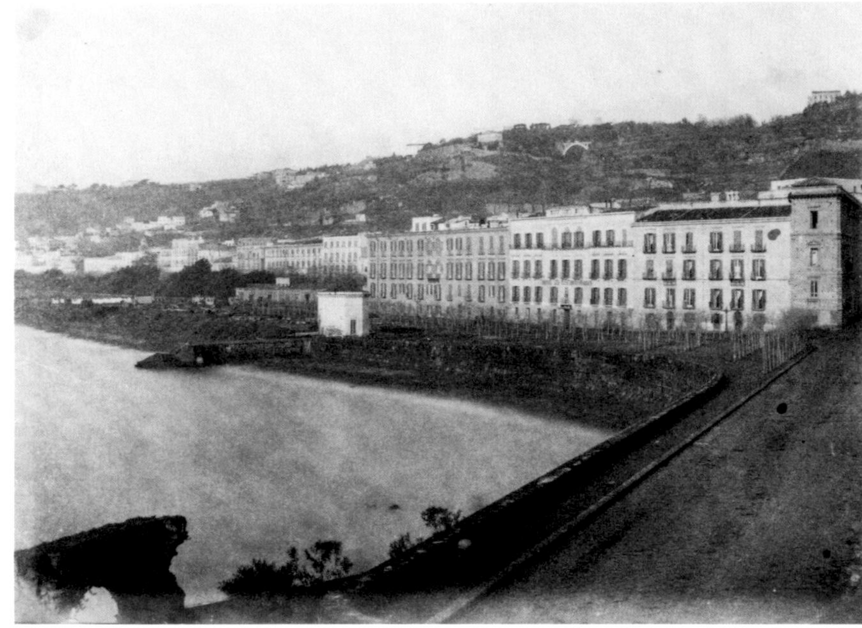

Fig. 97. Jane Martha St. John, *Naples, from our window in the Hotel des Etrangers,* 1856. Albumen silver print, 19 x 24.9 cm (7½ x 9¾ in.). The J. Paul Getty Museum, Los Angeles, 84.XA.760.14.5

the eleventh-century founder of the Carthusian order, to be positioned in the open doorway of the monastery of Our Lady of Miraflores at Burgos, he was consciously creating a theatrical tableau that paid homage to the saint. The pose and expression of the figure are so convincing that one wonders momentarily whether it is a statue or a real monk caught at a moment of private revelation (pl. 97).[42]

JANE MARTHA ST. JOHN

No intention to catch the eye of tourists seeking photographic mementos but rather a desire to make a highly personal record of a foreign tour (rather like Tenison's) motivated the interesting amateur Jane St. John. An indefatigable photographer, she made more than one hundred studies while she and her husband were traveling through Italy in the spring of 1856.[43] She was born in 1803, the second daughter of William Beach, who had estates in Church Oakley, Hampshire, and Keevil, Wiltshire, the latter some eight miles south of Lacock.[44] In many respects the St. Johns were typical members of the landowning classes that loomed so large in the social and cultural landscape of mid-nineteenth-century Britain. Possessing good lineages, impeccable connections on both sides of the marriage, and friendships throughout society, as well as education and economic freedom, they lived a decidedly privileged life. Through these social connections St. John became good friends with the Llewelyns of Penllergare and was affectionately referred to as "Aunt Jane" by Emma Llewelyn, W. H. F. Talbot's cousin.[45] Through them she would also have known the various members of the Talbot family in Wales as well as those at Lacock. It was this spider's web of family and social interconnections, complex, delicate, enduring, and linking many families of the British upper classes, that allowed individuals to build a strong identity and sense of their place within society.

Somewhere, somehow, within this network of friends and relatives, Jane St. John was won over to photography—the most likely person to have influenced and taught her being John Dillwyn Llewelyn, Emma's husband, with whom she seems to have been especially close. Although we know little of her early photography, when she and her husband departed for Italy she was clearly self-confident enough to embark upon the extended photographic project of recording their trip. She was fifty-three.

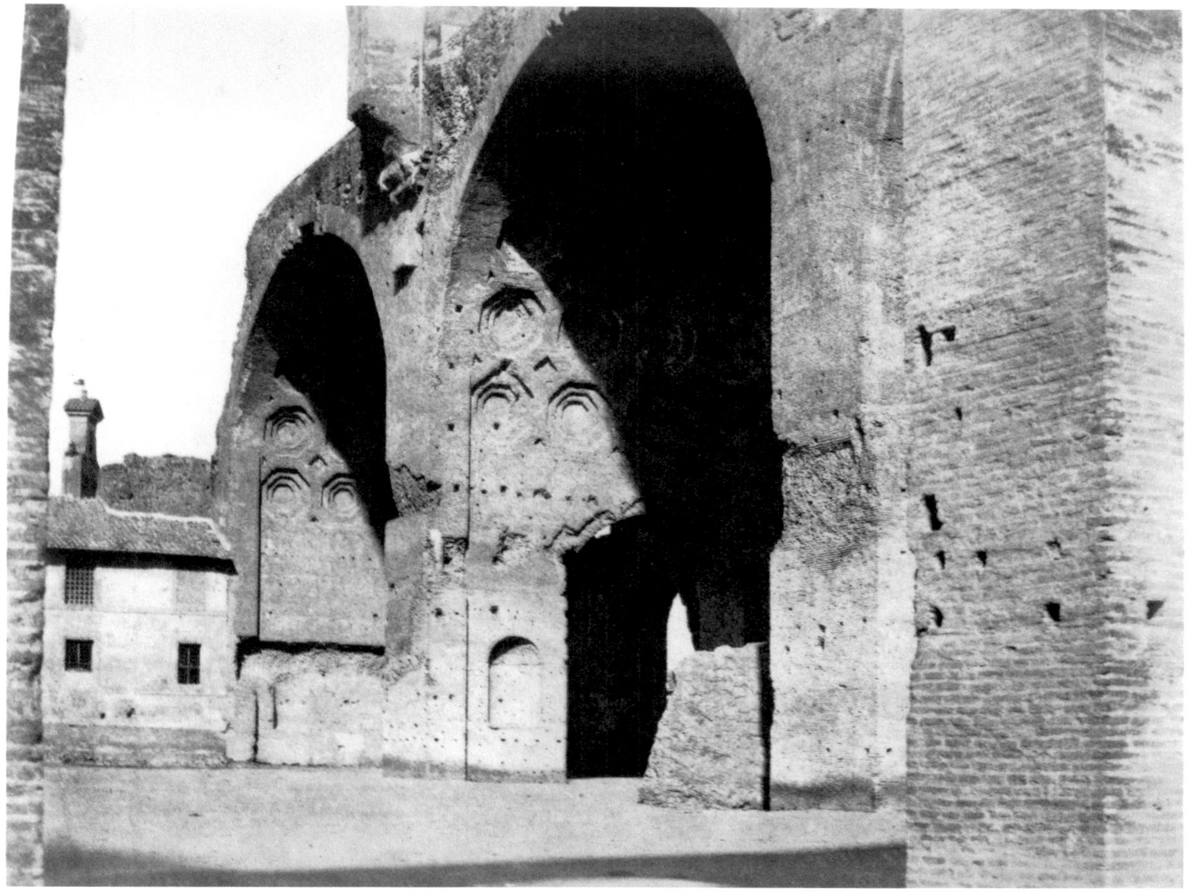

Fig. 98. Jane Martha St. John, *Temple of Peace, Rome*, 1856. Albumen silver print, 19.2 x 24.9 cm (7½ x 9¾ in.). The J. Paul Getty Museum, Los Angeles, 84.XA.760.14.27

No letters or diaries survive to provide a personal account of the trip; the only evidence we have is the album of prints that Jane St. John subsequently assembled as a keepsake. While their Grand Tour most likely followed the favored route through France and across the Swiss Alps, she made photographs only in Italy and in the album sequenced them chronologically.

Unpacking her camera for the first time after their arrival in Genoa, she took a couple of unremarkable photographs, a kind of warm-up. From Genoa they stopped briefly in Pisa before making for Naples, probably by steamship. (One traveler to Naples described steamship passage: "Certainly very useful and convenient; but . . . dull and unpoetical: smoke, noise, dirt, a *restaurant*, a reading-room, like a fragment of Paris floating through the seas.")[46] In Naples their tour began in earnest, and with it her photography. She took a pair of photographs, one looking out from their hotel window at the promenade along the bay, the second from the promenade, looking back at the hotel. Gazing back and forth across the intervening space, these two photographs acquire a conceptual weight of a type that was exceptional for the period (figs. 97, 96).

They are also the pictures of a tourist eager to record the individual experiences of travel. As the couple explored the Naples area, visiting Salerno and Paestum, before making their way steadily northward to Rome, Florence, Venice, and Como, photography provided St. John with a means of responding at a personal level to settings and incidents she found appealing. Unlike the work of Talbot or Jones, with which she was surely familiar, many of her compositions display the unstudied approach of an observer more concerned with capturing the moment than conforming to reigning artistic principles. This gives her

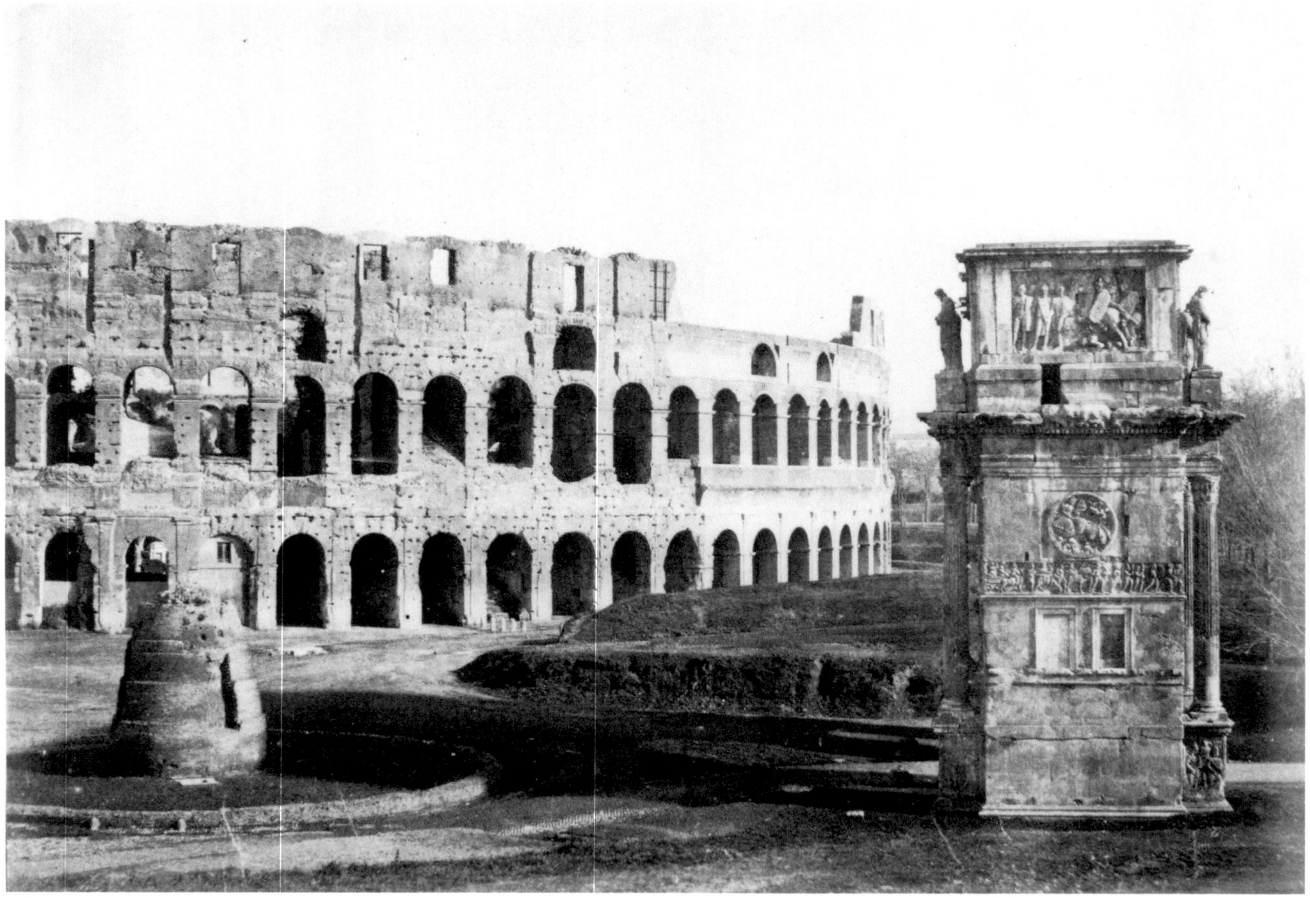

Fig. 99. Jane Martha St. John, *Colosseum, Meter Sudans & Arch of Constantine, Rome*, 1856. Albumen silver print, 17.7 x 24.9 cm (7 x 9¾ in.). The J. Paul Getty Museum, Los Angeles, 84.XA.760.14.24

work a refreshing freedom closer in spirit and gesture to that of Alfred Capel Cure than, for example, Clifford or Tenison, whose compositions owe more to convention than to spontaneity. Still, she could structure a picture as skillfully as any, and clearly took the time to compose her photographs carefully on the ground glass screen of the camera when the occasion demanded. This is evident in *Temple of Peace, Rome*, where her inclusion of brickwork down the left side of the frame successfully contains an otherwise unbalanced composition (fig. 98). Often she sought out a less-than-obvious view that presented its subject in a new light. How often has one seen the Colosseum pictured in relation to the Arch of Constantine and the remains of the first-century imperial fountain known as the Meta Sudans?—or, from a shaded side street, the Colosseum suddenly looming up close, its massive form dominating the composition (fig. 99; pl. 89)? After photographing the main front of the mighty basilica Santa Maria Maggiore, St. John made her way to the back of the building, where she positioned her camera so that the pattern of the cobblestone pavement directs the eye toward the church, while avenues of trees frame it on either side (figs. 100, 101). The first view resembles traditional representations of the monument found in engravings; the second arises from an imaginative seizing of the opportunity to explore freely through photography. In the hands of the right person, a camera was a liberating device that could be used to satisfy the visual curiosity of the photographer.

When a buffalo cart parked before an ancient Roman gateway caught St. John's eye, she set up her camera as best she could and, with little regard for the formal rules of composition, made her exposure. She

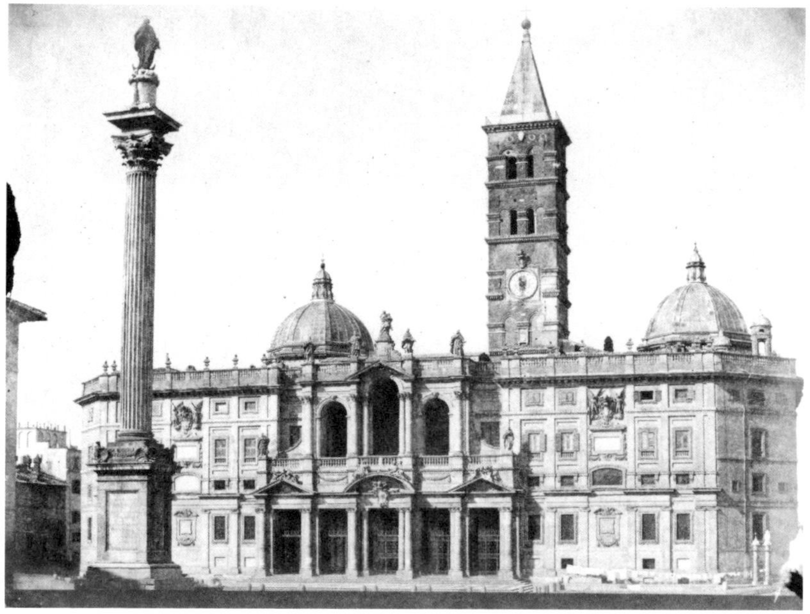

Fig. 100. Jane Martha St. John, *Church of Santa Maria Maggiore, Rome* (front), 1856. Albumen silver print, 19.4 x 24.9 cm (7⅝ x 9¾ in.). The J. Paul Getty Museum, Los Angeles, 84.XA.760.14.34

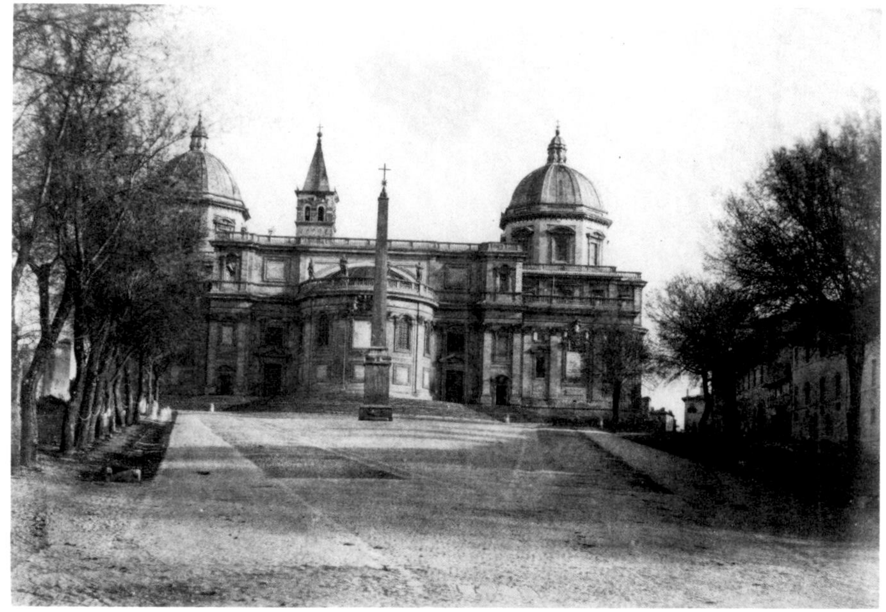

Fig. 101. Jane Martha St. John, *Church of Santa Maria Maggiore, Rome* (back), 1856. Albumen silver print, 17.9 x 25 cm (7 x 9⅞ in.). The J. Paul Getty Museum, Los Angeles, 84.XA.760.14.35

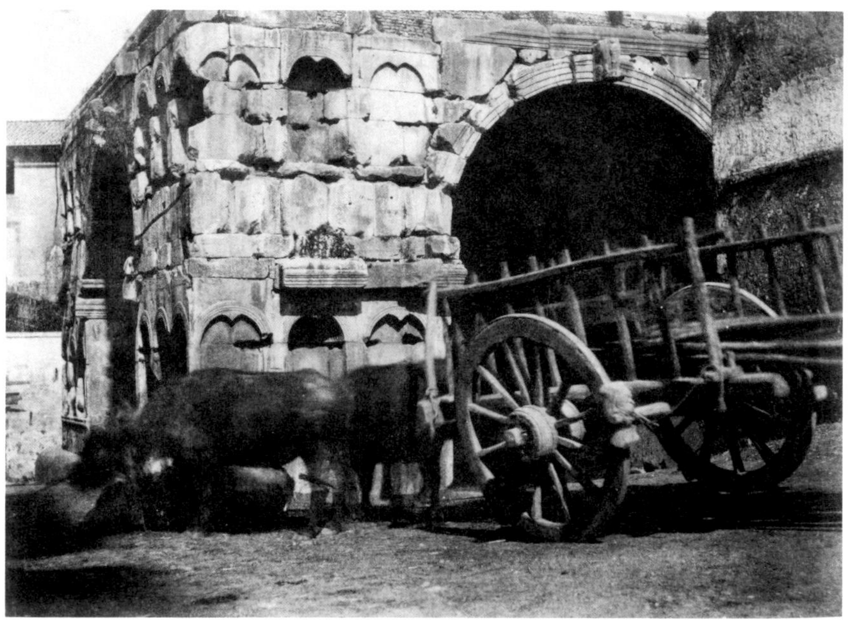

Fig. 102. Jane Martha St. John, *Buffalo Cart, Rome,* 1856. Albumen silver print, 18.4 x 22.5 cm (7¼ x 8⅞ in.). The J. Paul Getty Museum, Los Angeles, 84.XA.760.14.57

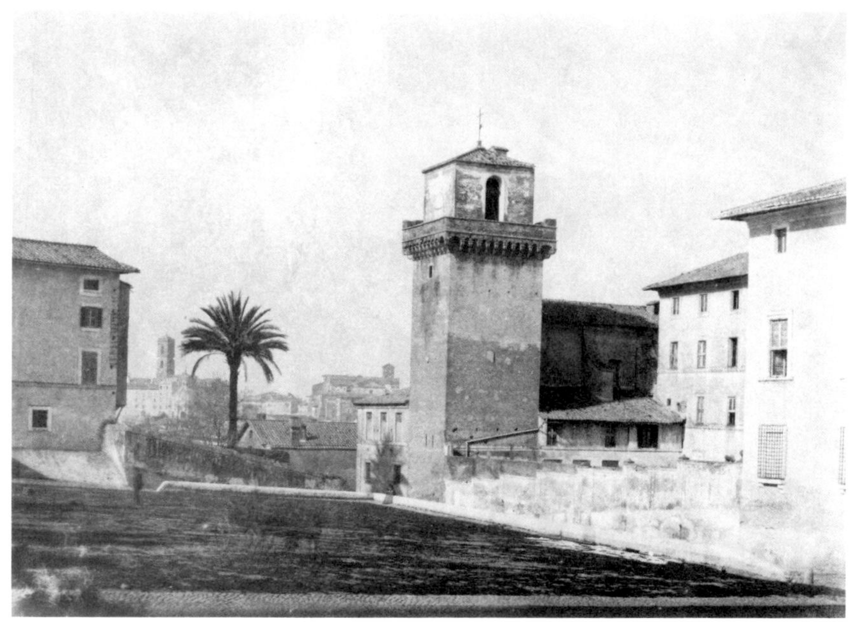

Fig. 103. Jane Martha St. John, *Palm Tree, from St. Pietro in Vincoli, Rome,* 1856. Albumen silver print, 18.2 x 24.8 cm (7⅛ x 9¾ in.). The J. Paul Getty Museum, Los Angeles, 84.XA.760.14.70

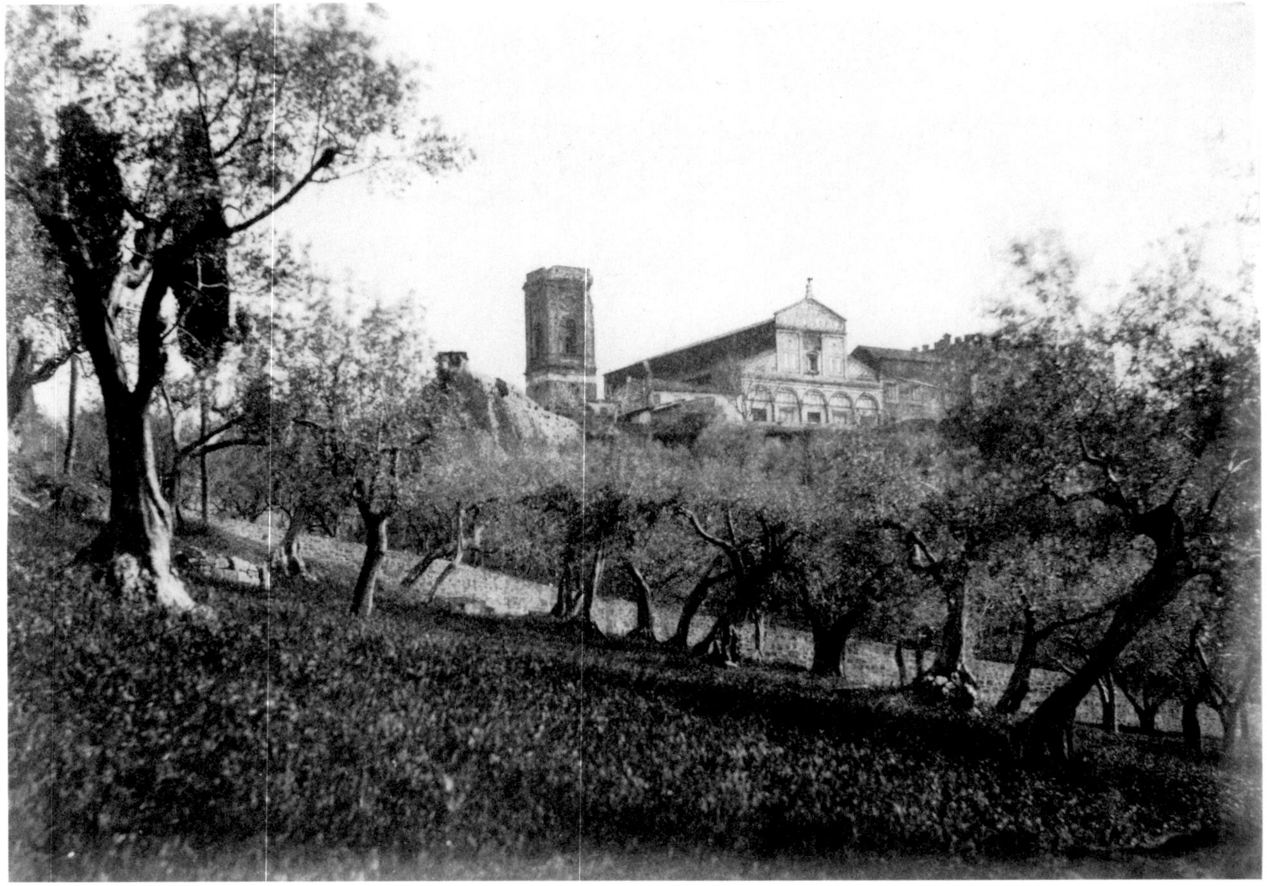

Fig. 104. Jane Martha St. John, *St. Miniato, Florence,* 1856. Albumen silver print, 17.9 x 24.8 cm (7 x 9¾ in.). The J. Paul Getty Museum, Los Angeles, 84.XA.760.14.79

must have decided not to worry about the technical limitations of a necessarily long exposure, although she doubtless hoped the beasts would remain motionless (fig. 102). The result has the immediacy of photographs taken several decades later, when the introduction of faster emulsions and handheld cameras made this type of image more commonplace. She adopted a similar approach when visiting the church of San Pietro in Vincoli, where she was attracted not so much by the building as by the sight of a single palm tree silhouetted against the sky—an ostrich feather duster contrasting with the angular geometry of its surroundings (fig. 103). In the 1850s it was rare for this kind of impulsive self-expression to find its way into an image.

The couple reached Florence toward the end of their journey northward; by this time St. John had already taken almost eighty photographs en route. She took the long walk from her hotel near the Ponte Vecchio up the steep pathway to the hilltop church of San Miniato al Monte and, perhaps exhausted by the climb—made more difficult by the heavy enveloping dress she was surely wearing—paused in the shade of an olive grove. From here she photographed the church, rising behind the trees, and instead of setting up her camera on a high tripod in the normal way, she placed it beside her in the long grass, where the low vantage point and out-of-focus foreground create the impression that the photograph was taken by someone resting (fig. 104). It is a peaceful, almost drowsy study, evoking thoughts of weary pilgrims stopping beneath the trees before the final ascent to their destination.

Few photographers of her generation made photographs like this. At a time when composition and technical mastery were often valued more highly than self-expression, many photographers either suppressed

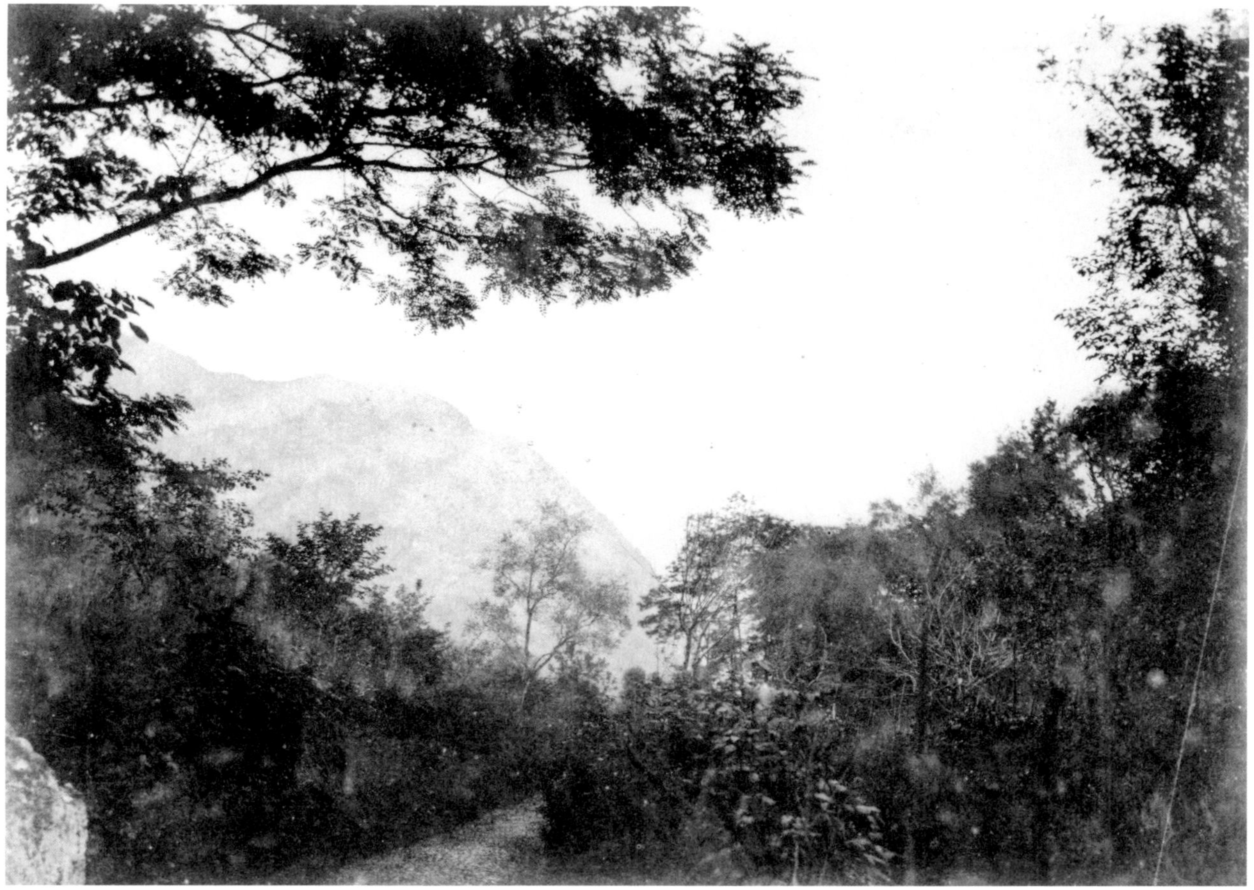

Fig. 105. Jane Martha St. John, *Acacia, Como*, 1856. Albumen silver print, 18.3 x 24.7 cm (7¼ x 9¾ in.). The J. Paul Getty Museum, Los Angeles, 84.XA.760.14.100

their feelings or channeled them into works of the kind that sat comfortably with established pictorial conventions. For Jane St. John, however, such matters were of little concern, for she neither belonged to a photographic society nor exhibited but rather made her photographs for the eyes of immediate family and friends. Moreover, one senses that her maturity endowed her with a certain spirit and confidence to act, freeing her from the inhibitions that might have constrained the imagination of someone younger and more self-conscious. She was unquestionably assured behind the camera and, when circumstances demanded it, seemed to care little about formal composition, preferring to catch the picture come what may. Fortunately, her technical grasp of the fundamentals, such as the proper sensitizing of waxed paper and the judging of exposure times, allowed her to make these rapid-decision photographs, which would have eluded the grasp of someone less competent. Although she is unlikely ever to be considered a great photographer, St. John was certainly one of the more interesting amateurs of the mid-nineteenth century, not only because she was a woman but because her attitude toward picture making and photography was highly original (fig. 105).

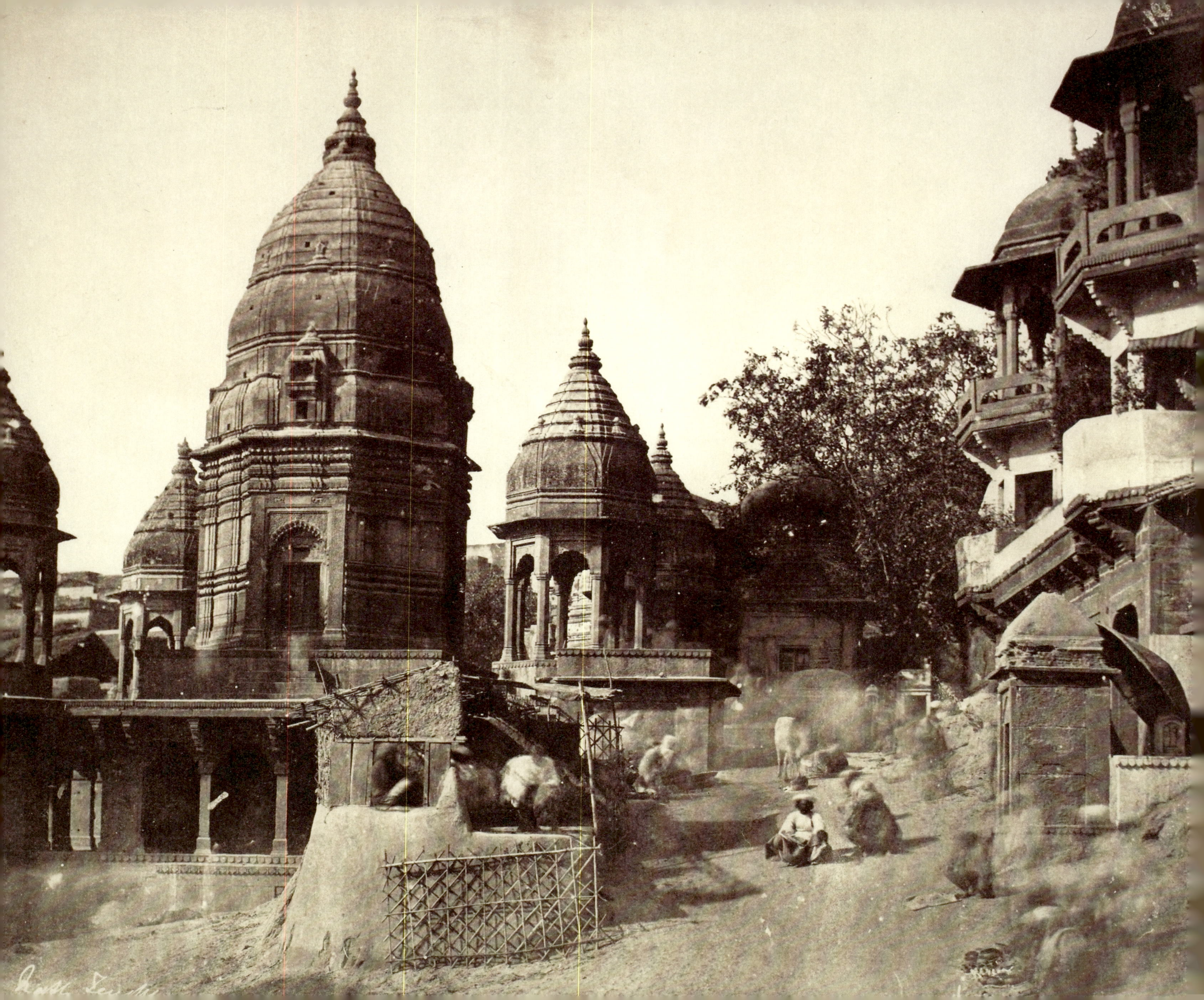

9. *Under an Indian Sky*

Taking photographs in India was a challenge. The difficulties that bedeviled travelers photographing in Europe—climate, wayward chemicals, and an absence of ready supplies—were in India multiplied tenfold. Here extreme heat in summer and saturating humidity during the monsoon season distorted equipment and evaporated chemicals. An atmosphere filled with insects and dust penetrated everywhere at all times, often with ruinous consequences. Nothing could be taken for granted, since processes that worked well in Britain failed dismally in India; every aspect of the operation had to be modified and adapted to local conditions.[1] Under these circumstances, photography required a brave heart and a dedicated sense of purpose.[2] Little wonder that British photographers in India were a muscular lot, drawn almost exclusively from the army and government administration and well equipped both by training and by disposition to deal with the "causes and effects" of living "under an Indian sky."[3]

MOMENTOUS EVENTS; BRITISH INDIA IN THE 1850S

In the course of India's long history, many regional empires had formed and dissolved; foreign merchants had arrived for trade; invaders had conquered and held parts of the vast land for years or centuries. The Mughal empire was at its height, extending over much of the subcontinent, when the British arrived in the closing decades of the sixteenth century. Britain was one of several European powers eager to use their recently expanded navigational expertise to gain access to the rich resources of the East. Its relationship with India began with traders visiting the country in search of the exotic spices and luxury commodities for which there was growing demand at home.[4] In 1600, the British Crown having granted traders a royal charter carrying monopoly commercial rights, they formed themselves into a joint stock company, the Company of Merchants of London Trading into the East Indies, more commonly known as the East India Company. This commercial body would acquire great wealth and in time become a sovereign power in all but name.

As it prospered, the company attracted the attention of aristocratic families seeking lucrative appointments to bureaucratic and administrative positions for their younger sons. Initially operating through trading agreements with the Mughals, the company soon occupied territories in India and expanded them at every opportunity, successfully opposing local resistance with the well-organized military force and superior weaponry supplied by British troops. The simultaneous waning of the Mughal empire facilitated this regional conquest. By the close of the eighteenth century, however, it was clear that the company's reach had exceeded its ability effectively to govern its now-vast territories, and the British government introduced a series of economic and administrative reforms, gradually establishing control over the company. By the 1830s, the East India Company, while still a commercial enterprise, was managing the country on behalf of the British government.

For administrative purposes the country was divided into three "presidencies," those of Bengal, Madras, and Bombay, which controlled, roughly speaking, regions in the northeast, south, and east, respectively.[5] Each had its own standing army with artillery, infantry, cavalry, engineers, and medical staff. Together these totaled almost a quarter of a million individuals by 1830, the vast majority of them Indian recruits.[6] In addition the company employed an extensive bureaucracy of judges, civil servants, customs officials, tax collectors, and assorted administrators, clerks, and scribes. By the mid-1850s, according to the *Illustrated London News*, the three presidencies wielded administrative control over almost 840,000 square miles of territory, the equivalent of "France, Austria, Prussia, Spain, Portugal, Holland, Belgium, Switzerland, and Federal Germany," with an aggregate population of some 102 million, or four times that of Great Britain and Ireland.[7]

Opposite: Fig. 106. Detail of John Murray, *Bishessur Nath Temple, Benares*, 1858 (see pl. 108)

For most Britons, India lay well beyond their concerns or comprehension. It conjured "vague notions of a great Mogul, turbaned Nabobs, black soldiers, Cashmere shawls, Trichinopoly chains,[8] elephants' teeth, curry-powder, cadetships and liver complaint" (fig. 107).[9] These distorted and unexamined perceptions were actively encouraged by the directors of the East India Company, largely for commercial reasons; condoned by Parliament; and widely accepted by a public led to think of India as a country of inexhaustible wealth and the brightest jewel in the Imperial Crown. During the first half of the nineteenth century, the East India Company, riding a series of successes, was at the height of its powers.[10]

From an Indian perspective, however, these same years were characterized by challenges to the power of Indian princes and landed classes, the overturning of traditional customs, further British annexation of territories, and a series of punitive wars that suppressed one region after another.[11] The growing dissatisfaction came to a head in early 1857, when a group of sepoys (Indian soldiers) in the Bengal Army mutinied. They were immediately joined by the Indian garrison at Delhi (New Delhi), and then the whole valley of the Ganges from the east coast to Delhi rose in open rebellion against British rule in what became known as the Indian Mutiny (fig. 108).[12] Fighting raged for more than a year, with bloody acts of vengeance committed by both sides, before British forces prevailed. At the same time the British government dissolved the East India Company, transferring its assets and authority to the Crown, and assumed full responsibility for the government of India.[13]

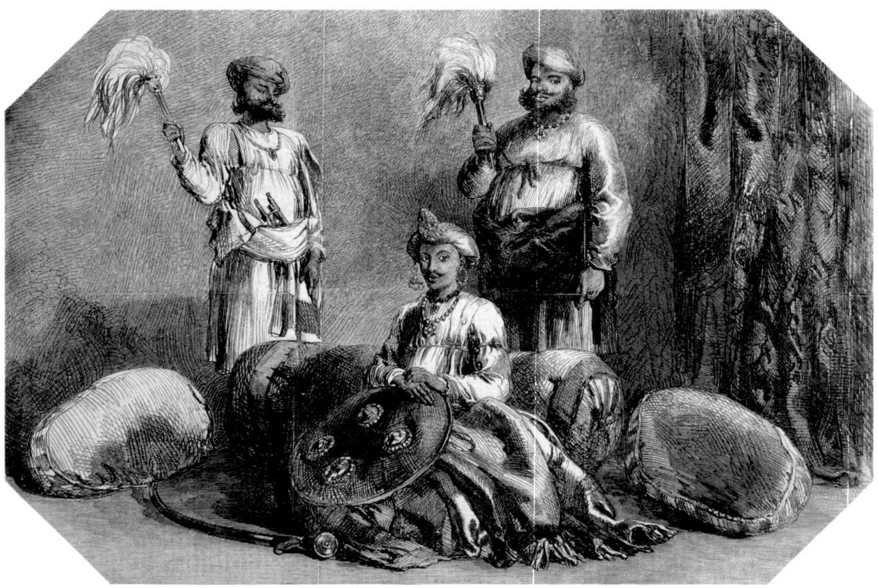

Fig. 107. William Carpenter, *Tookajee Rao Indore.* Wood engraving of a drawing by Carpenter, 23.4 x 34.4 cm (9¼ x 13½ in.). From *Illustrated London News,* October 10, 1857, p. 360. Private collection

Public opinion in Britain was deeply outraged by the events of the mutiny, especially the slaughter of innocent British women and children caught up in the conflict. Paradoxically, however, the general feeling of revulsion was matched by an upsurge of interest in India. The popular press responded with articles describing the progress of the mutiny and, alongside them, detailed descriptions of the country and its people. The *Illustrated London News,* with its lavish use of line illustrations, delivered images of India into homes throughout Britain in an unprecedented way. The hazy perceptions of the past were transformed during the course of 1857 into a concrete and educated interest in the country, and this increased the public's curiosity to see photographs of India when they were first exhibited in London in November 1857.[14]

Almost two decades before the mutiny, when news of the development of photography reached the distant shores of India, it might have been expected that the educated, upper-class Britons in the employ of the East India Company would take an interest in the new invention. One early experimenter was William O'Shaughnessy, an assistant surgeon in the Indian Medical Service (Bengal). In the late summer of 1839 he created an innovative photographic process based on chloride of gold and showed his results at a meeting of the Asiatic Society of Bengal in October of that year.[15] And the enigmatic amateur Alfred Huish quietly worked at making pictures (pl. 98). But there are few others whose names have survived; the record of photography in India during the 1840s is almost completely blank.[16] Those connected with the East India Company seem to have been, at this early date, singularly uninterested in photography and its potential—perhaps discouraged by the difficulty of obtaining reliable chemicals and photographic supplies and the unavailability of experienced instruction.

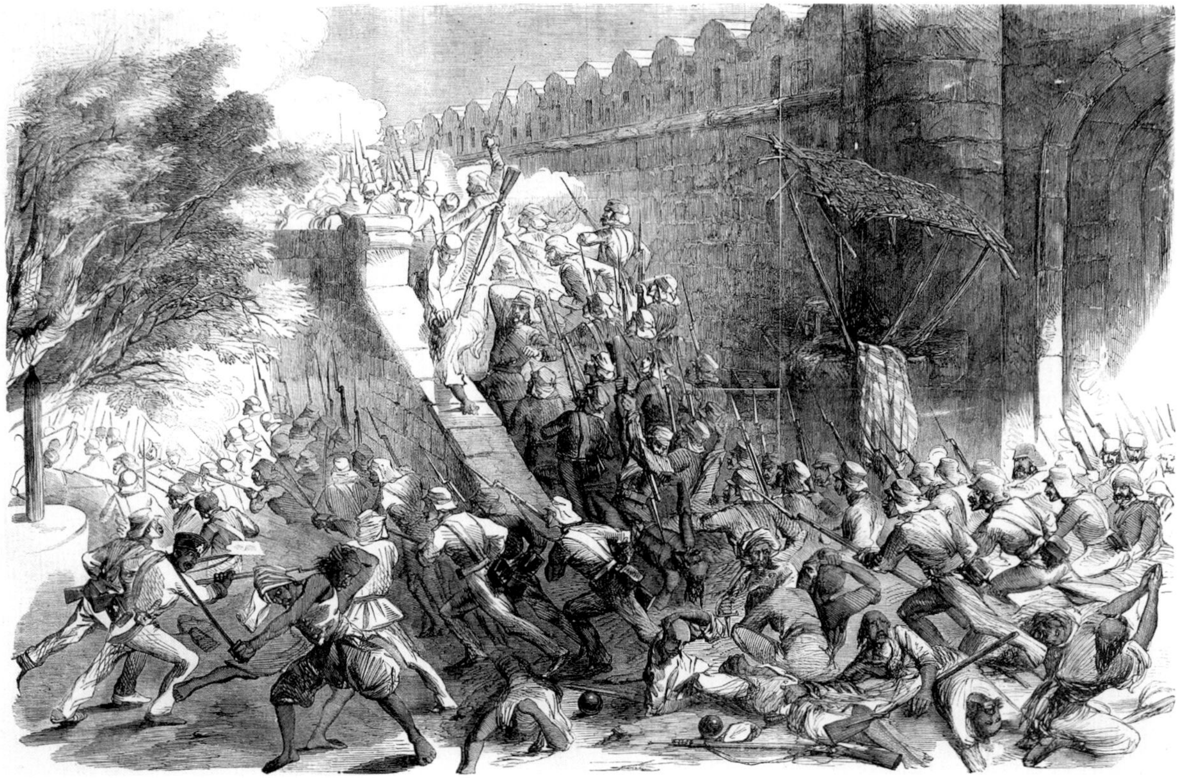

Fig. 108. Unknown artist, *The Storming of Delhi.—The Cashmere Gate*, 1857. Wood engraving, 23.9 x 34.5 cm (9⅜ x 13⅝ in.). From *Illustrated London News*, November 28, 1857, p. 552. Private collection

JOHN McCOSH

A notable exception was John McCosh, who had joined the Indian Medical Service (Bengal) as an assistant surgeon in 1831.[17] After a decade of active service punctuated by bouts of severe illness and warfare, he returned to Edinburgh in 1841–42 for further training as a surgeon. His interest in photography may well have begun during this spell in Edinburgh, for in the same period David Brewster and his "disciples" in St. Andrews were conducting their photographic experiments and devising modifications of the calotype process. It is tempting to think that some informal, personal link between this group and McCosh encouraged him to take up photography—perhaps through Sir Hugh Playfair and his family, who had intimate connections with India, Edinburgh, photography, and medicine.[18] In any case, by the time McCosh returned to Bengal and the Indian Medical Service in 1843, he was an accomplished photographer with a telling eye for tightly framed compositions and the technical self-confidence to carry them off.[19]

His duties as a surgeon meant that McCosh traveled widely with his regiment, the 31st Bengal Native Infantry. He was sent to Almora, in the foothills of the Himalayas, and later to Jalandhar Doab in the Punjab, also in the north, when headquarters were established there. He saw action in the Punjab in the Second Sikh War of 1848–49, and later in Burma (Myanmar) in the Second Burma War of 1852–53. Everywhere McCosh was busy with his camera. He was intrigued by the ability of photography to record people and places associated with the British rule in India, and although most of his portraits were of fellow officers, administrators, and their wives and daughters, he also photographed natives. When the war in Punjab had ended he sought permission to take portraits of Maharaja Dalip Singh and other Sikh leaders, but this was refused; however, he managed to photograph Diwan Mulraj, governor of Multan, who had been a key leader of the Sikh nation against the British (fig. 109).[20]

Three years later, during the Second Burma War, now attached to the 5th Battery, Bengal Artillery, McCosh saw active service in

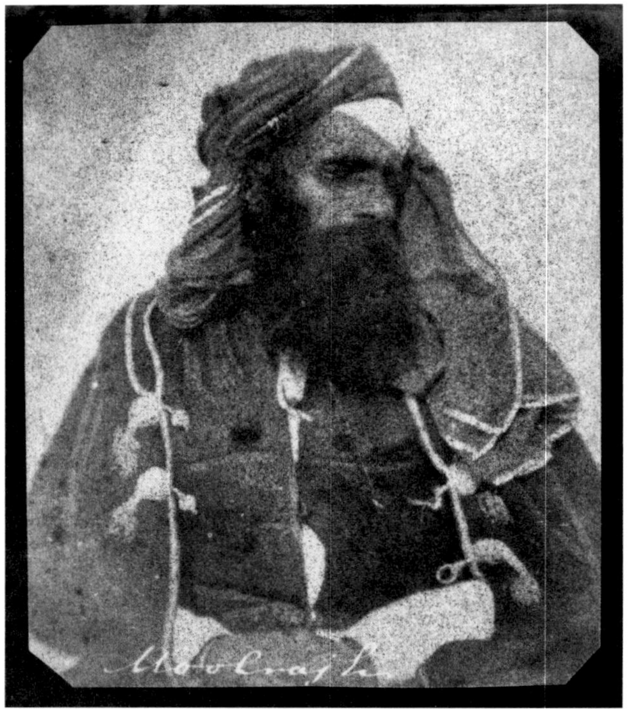

Fig. 109. John McCosh, *Diwan Mulraj, Governor of Multan,* ca. 1848. Salted paper print, 10 x 8.5 cm (4 x $3\frac{3}{8}$ in.). Courtesy of the Council of the National Army Museum, London, NAM 1962-04-3-3

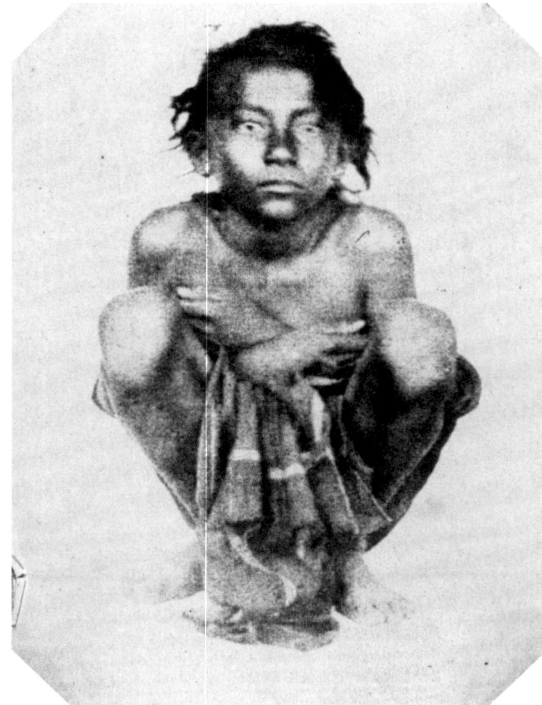

Fig. 110. John McCosh, *Burmese Boy,* 1852. Salted paper print, 13 x 8 cm ($5\frac{1}{8}$ x $3\frac{1}{8}$ in.). Courtesy of the Council of the National Army Museum, London, NAM 1962-04-3-120

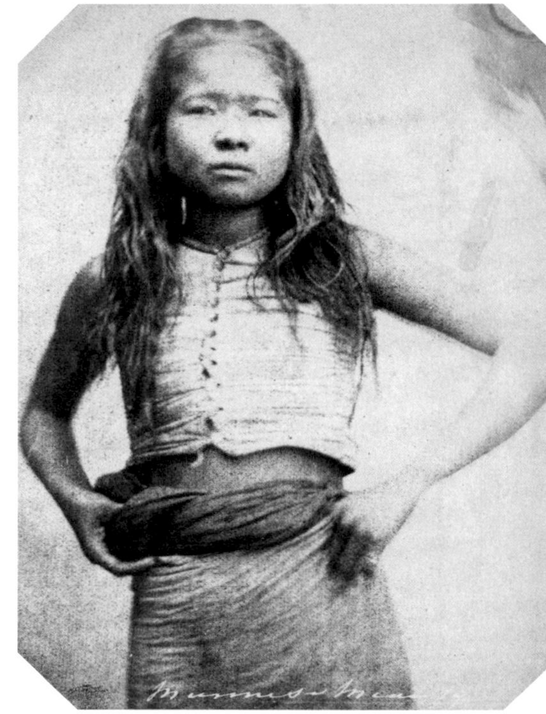

Fig. 111. John McCosh, *Burmese Beauty,* 1852. Salted paper print, 13.3 x 10.1 cm ($5\frac{1}{4}$ x 4 in.). Courtesy of the Council of the National Army Museum, London, NAM 1962-04-3-287

Rangoon (Yangon) and Prome, where he made an extensive series of portraits and photographs relating to the conflict (pl. 99). There are studies of captured guns, temple architecture in Rangoon, and colleagues; also sensitive portraits of Burmese as they stood or squatted before his camera. Lowering his camera to match the height of people hunkered down on their heels and thus face them directly, he flouted the conventions adopted by anthropologists, in which people were portrayed as specimens. Clearly what fascinated McCosh was the individual person, whose dignity was revealed before his camera (figs. 110, 111). This is especially evident in his studies of "African Croomen," who stand before his camera with a self-possessed poise that transfixes our attention (pl. 101). (The "Croomen" must be Krumen, individuals from the Kru region in eastern Liberia, who were known throughout the nineteenth century as hardworking migrant laborers.)[21]

For practical reasons most of McCosh's portraits were made in a small format, averaging about $4\frac{1}{2}$ x 3 inches. In most instances the corners of the paper negatives were neatly cut away and the resulting prints carefully trimmed to retain a fine black border, creating a strong, well-defined frame that McCosh used to great advantage in the composition of his studies. The treatment works especially well in his portraits of Burmese natives, where the crisp black line emphasizes the fluid outlines of their torsos (figs. 112, 113). With fully clothed Europeans he also used the black frame effectively, for instance his portrait of a colleague with a walking stick and hat whose figure fills the available space with a geometric precision that captivates the eye (fig. 114). Instead of attempting to compose his portraits meticulously on the screen of his camera, McCosh trimmed his negatives subsequently, establishing a sensitive relationship between the contours of his subject and the edge of the frame. With this unusual method and the high degree of control

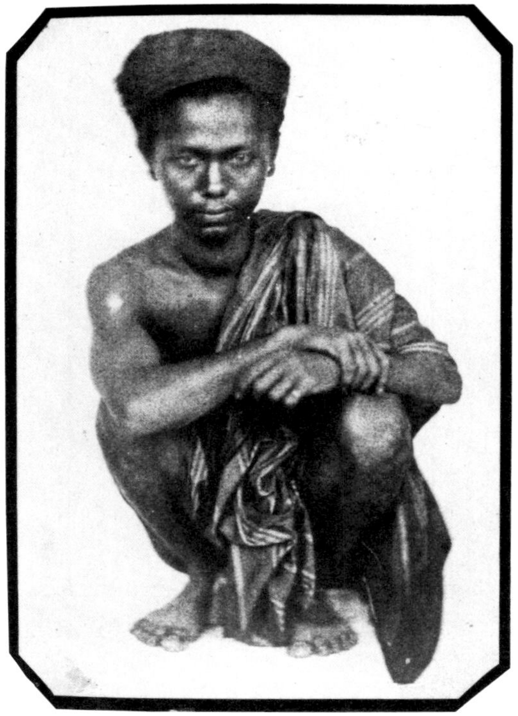

Fig. 112. John McCosh, *Burmese Man*, 1852. Salted paper print, 12.1 x 8.4 cm (4¾ x 3¼ in.). Courtesy of the Council of the National Army Museum, London, NAM 1962-04-3-127

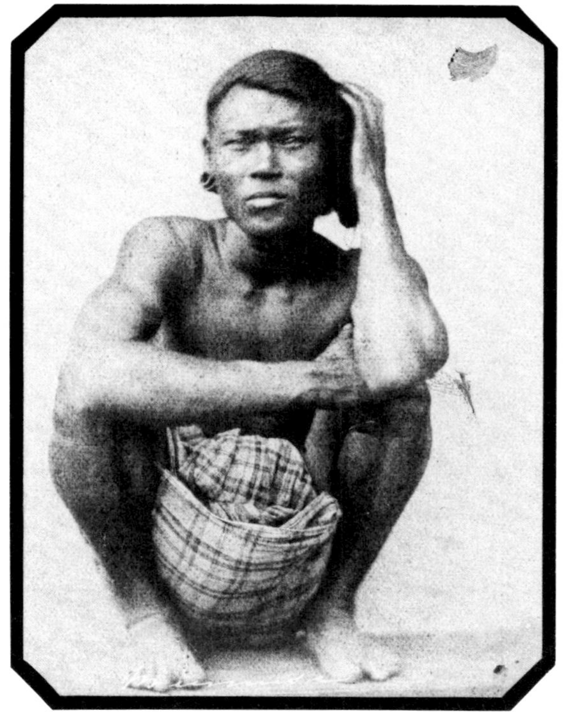

Fig. 113. John McCosh, *Burmese Man*, 1852. Salted paper print, 10.7 x 7.9 cm (4¼ x 3⅛ in.). Courtesy of the Council of the National Army Museum, London, NAM 1962-04-3-128

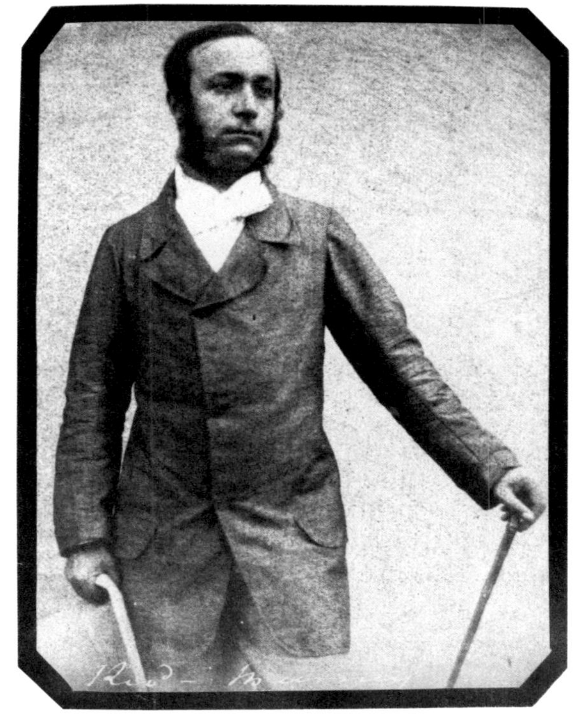

Fig. 114. John McCosh, *Rev'd Murray*, ca. 1852. Salted paper print, 10.7 x 7.9 cm (4¼ x 3⅛ in.). Courtesy of the Council of the National Army Museum, London, NAM 1962-04-3-130

it afforded, McCosh fashioned compositions that were exceptional for the period.

In Burma, too, the desire to record history was never very far away. Although there are no portraits of Burmese kings or rebel leaders, McCosh's portraits of two rather anxious-looking "Italian Priests" tell a story. The British advance toward Prome triggered a revolution in Amarapura, then the capital, in which the old king, Pagan Min, was deposed and replaced by his half brother, Mindon Min. A devout Buddhist, the new king was anxious to avoid further bloodshed and to mark his accession released all Europeans held in captivity. He sent two of them, the Italian priests Father Domingo Tarolly and Father Abbona, to meet the British commander leading troops toward Prome and inform him that he wished to discuss a peace settlement.[22] It seems likely that the anonymous priests photographed by McCosh were Abbona and Tarolly, peace envoys to the Burmese royal court (pl. 100).[23]

Before he retired from army service in 1856, McCosh published a handbook entitled *Advice to Officers in India*. In it he suggested taking up a hobby while in India, to "take a quiet canter along the monotonous high-ways and bye-ways of tropical existence."[24] Not surprisingly, he "would strongly recommend every assistant-surgeon to make himself a master of photography in all its branches," an ideal occupation because an officer could create pictures that would be "a welcome contribution to any museum."[25] The idea of the photographer as a hunter-gatherer, navigating the pathways of foreign lands in search of new subjects to bag and preserve for posterity, was not new; however, McCosh's discussion reveals something particular about the significance that he placed on his own photography. In his hands, photography was not merely a pastime but became the means of recording history. About an album of his own Indian and Burmese studies McCosh wrote in 1859, "These photographs have no pretensions to merit. The negatives were taken on paper before the present process of collodian [*sic*] was known. Their fidelity will however make amends for their sorry imperfection. Like fragile remains of lost ages their value is enhanced because the originals are no longer forthcoming."[26] Not only did photography have the power to evoke memories of past events and old friends; as McCosh realized, it could also acquire the gravitas that comes from serving as witness to a pivotal moment in history.

PHOTOGRAPHIC SOCIETIES

Among other things, McCosh's example shows how the emergence of amateur practice in India echoed the route taken back home. It did not take long for the cultural impulses and influences that swayed the course of photography in Britain to reach the shores of India, and in October 1854 the Photographic Society of Bombay was formed, with societies in the presidencies of Bengal and Madras following its example shortly afterward. All three were constituted along lines similar to those of their counterpart in London, with a president, a vice-president, a council, regular meetings, an annual exhibition, and monthly journals, and were formed "for the interchange of ideas and experience with reference especially to many amateurs in the interior."[27] The society in Bombay (Mumbai) undertook to enlist the "experience and co-operation of the cleverest and most scientific Photographers in the world" by inviting leading practitioners belonging to the photographic societies in London and Liverpool to become honorary members.[28] This connected members with fellow photographers in England on whom they could call for advice through correspondence and "never be at a loss for the solution of any problem however difficult"[29]—a move undoubtedly designed to allay the sense of isolation that many photographers in India felt.

By way of encouragement to his members, the president of the Photographic Society of Bombay reminded them of the exceptional opportunities that lay before them:

> *India, I need hardly point out to you, offers a vast field to the Photographer. Its magnificent Scenery – its Temples – Palaces – Shrines – and Ruins, dating back, as many of them do, to the remotest antiquity – the varied costumes, characters, and physiognomies of its millions of inhabitants; its religious and other processions, and all the other endless objects of attraction or of curiosity which present themselves to us – each and all should incite us to the practice of an Art, of which the beauty and utility are only surpassed by its truthfulness; and where, I would ask, can that art be more advantageously studied than under the sunny skies of Ind?*[30]

This simple, self-evident proposal became almost a manifesto guiding the practice of photography in India for the next fifty years and beyond (see pls. 106, 109, 110). Whether undertaken by an amateur out of personal interest or more formally as a government commission, nearly all photography presented, in one form or another, subjects of this nature. After the mutiny, however, photographic work changed in mood and intent, for a while becoming graver and more topical. Photographers had also grown more assured in their command of the medium, and two of them, John Murray and Linnaeus Tripe, are notable for the quality and scope of their work.

JOHN MURRAY

Dr. John Murray belonged to that hardy breed of Scottish individualists who helped Britain uphold its colonial ambitions overseas throughout the nineteenth century. Despite his humble upbringing as a farmer's son, he was educated at Aberdeen University and then at Edinburgh, where he qualified as a doctor in 1831. In 1832 he was appointed an assistant surgeon by the East India Company and posted to Calcutta (Kolkata), and he served the next thirteen years there attached to various regiments. He came to the notice of authorities during the First Sikh War of 1846, when in his capacity as a field surgeon he took responsibility for all medical and surgical care during the battle of Aliwal. After a brief spell serving with the residency, or administrative center, at Indore in central India, he was appointed civil surgeon of Agra in 1848 and distinguished himself in his practice there for the next twenty years, specializing in the prevention and treatment of cholera and later serving as superintendent and deputy inspector of hospitals.[31]

Murray had taken up photography in 1849 and by 1856 had become an accomplished photographer, showing his work to fellow members of the Photographic Society of Bengal in May 1856 and exhibiting a group of prints at its annual exhibition in March 1857. The prints were on an imposing scale, for by this date he was using a large-format camera that could make negatives of up to 19 x 15 inches. When Murray and his wife returned to Britain in April 1857 for a six-month leave, they brought with them some eight hundred negatives depicting Indian subjects made between 1849 and 1857. These likely included large images, many smaller-format ones, and some made especially for the stereoscope.[32]

In London, a number of printsellers and publishers had begun to explore the commercial potential of photography. In January 1857, one of them, Joseph Hogarth, invited members of the London Photographic Society to send lists of "their productions with the size and price" from which he could prepare a catalogue of their works for sale—a shrewd proposal calculated to tempt photographers to take him on as their agent.[33] With his background as a publisher and retailer of prints, Hogarth was well placed to enter the photographic market. During his leave Murray got in touch with Hogarth, and the timing was auspicious, for India was then an overriding preoccupation of the British public. By early October a contract had been drawn up giving Hogarth a free hand to choose and publish whichever of the photographs he thought proper without consulting Murray, who by now was about to depart for India. His wife remained in London and handled his photographic affairs.[34]

Within a matter of weeks Hogarth had selected thirty negatives taken in Agra, Secundra (Sikandra), Futtehpore Seekree (Fatehpur Sikri), Brindaban (Vrindavan), and Nynee Tal (Nainital) showing scenes connected in one way or another with the mutiny. Before the year was out the set had been exhibited at his premises and subsequently published as a folio entitled *Photographic Views in Agra and Its Vicinity*. Fresh news was arriving from India by telegraph every day, and a reviewer for the *Art-Journal* pointed out that Murray's photographs presented "localities that must hereafter be regarded with an interest far beyond that which ordinary historical events communicate." The prints were not only topical but, also, by virtue of their impressive size, revelatory: "They are very large, being each eighteen by fifteen inches, but, nevertheless, it is only on examination with a glass that the ornamental detail of Indian palatial architecture becomes visible; and great indeed is the contrast between these sumptuous edifices and the squalid habitations by which they are so often surrounded."[35]

Until now, the public had satisfied its thirst for images of India with the line engravings in the *Illustrated London News*, which mostly offered generalized artistic interpretations of events. Even in the few instances when woodblock engravings were based on photographs, their treatment was necessarily broad and omitted many details.[36] Now, for the first time, the public could examine through a magnifying glass the minute detail in Murray's large-format prints and gain some sense of India's infinite texture and diversity. The experience must have been extraordinary (see pls. 104, 105, 108; fig. 106).

By the time Murray returned to India in November 1857, his reputation as a photographer was established in government circles. Viscountess Canning, wife of the governor-general of India, wrote to Queen Victoria from Calcutta, "I think it is possible that Your Majesty has lately seen some photographs of Dr Murray of Agra. He left 800 negatives with Hogarth to print & has just returned here. I hope he will be immediately employed to photograph everything to be demolished at Delhi."[37] (Many of the buildings were no longer safe, having been severely damaged by rebel gunfire; see pl. 111.) Her expectations were fulfilled. In early January 1858 Murray had been commissioned and, with some four hundred pounds of apparatus and baggage, was ready to leave Calcutta for Benares (Varanasi), Allahabad, Cawnpore (Kanpur), Agra, and Delhi in order to photograph scenes directly associated with the mutiny. He had instructions from Lord Canning to make photographs showing the British entrenchments, forts, and other military defenses, as well as sites under reconstruction, and to capture "as clear and complete an impression of the works as possible."[38] To a modern eye, many of these commissioned photographs seem to be the usual studies of Indian architecture and dusty landscapes with little to distinguish them from other pictures by Murray. Seen through the historical prism of the mutiny, however, the same images take on an emotional charge and poignancy that for contemporary viewers were palpable.

Of all the atrocities that occurred during the mutiny, nothing shocked or appalled the British public more than the twin massacres in Cawnpore, a city on the Ganges. The mutiny had been spreading rapidly in early 1857 and broke out in Cawnpore on June 7. Besieged by the rebels under the leadership of a nobleman named Nana Sahib, Major General Hugh Wheeler, his small detachment of troops, and the entire European population of the town took refuge in the army barracks. With food, water, and ammunition scarce, they nevertheless hung on for three weeks while conditions continued to deteriorate. On June 24, Nana Sahib sent a message offering the besieged British safe passage to Allahabad if they surrendered their stores, treasury, and barracks, and, choosing the safety of the civilians over honor in battle, Wheeler reluctantly consented. Two days later the British made their way unmolested to the landing place known as Suttee Ghat on the banks of the Ganges, boarded boats, and cast off; but suddenly the rebels opened fire from hidden positions ashore, indiscriminately killing both soldiers and civilians, who were easy targets in the boats drifting downstream. Still, some survived. They were recaptured and led back to Cawnpore, where the men were shot and the women and children placed under house arrest. Then, on hearing that a column of British under General Henry Havelock were marching toward Cawnpore, Nana Sahib ordered the two hundred women and children to be murdered and their naked bodies thrown down a well.

When news of this atrocity reached Britain, every newspaper reported the scenes in graphic, gory detail. The massacre became a defining moment of the mutiny. These events, wrote the editor of the *Times*, "engrossed the attention of the whole country . . . for, whatever the issue of this rebellion, and whatever other prodigies and horrors it may bring forth, the Massacre of Cawnpore and the name of NENA SAHIB will hold rank among the foulest crimes and the greatest enemies of the human race to the end of the world."[39] From then on, national attitudes toward India hardened, and all residual notions of great Moguls, turbaned nabobs, and cashmere shawls were swept away.[40]

When Murray photographed the Suttee Ghat in February 1858, just seven months after these terrible and traumatic events, his mind must have been filled with images of death and slaughter. As a surgeon he was doubtless somewhat immured to the pain and suffering of warfare, but hardly to acts of gratuitous brutality inflicted upon innocents. His study of the ghat is a stark and graphic composition that reveals the grimy bleakness of the spot (pls. 102, 103). Nothing softens the impact; even the trees appear as deformed stumps harshly backlit against the beaten earth. There is something ineffably sad about the two native figures sitting with their knees drawn up under their chins. Their solitude no longer conveys human scale but rather the physical and emotional distance that had come to separate the Indians from the British.

Many months of guerilla resistance by the rebels followed, but by the end of August 1858 the mutiny had finally been suppressed. On September 1 the directors of the East India Company met for the last time, their authority having been transferred to the Crown by Parliament. A new chapter of Indian history began.

In Agra, Murray resumed his post as civil surgeon. In July 1858 he was appointed superintendent and deputy inspector general of hospitals, a post that gave him the time and freedom to continue photographing with the undiminished energy of earlier days. He remained active until 1865, although much of his later work was made between 1858 and 1862, when, among many other subjects, the Taj Mahal became a major preoccupation.[41]

Built by the great ruler Shah Jahan between 1630 and 1652 in memory of his wife Mumtaz Mahal, who died in childbirth, the mausoleum, constructed of white marble and richly decorated by carving and mosaics within and without, was as much a destination for visitors to northern India in the nineteenth century as it is today. Murray visited the site repeatedly and photographed its buildings and gardens from every conceivable angle. Clambering along the banks of the Yamuna River, from which he carefully composed many of his pictures, he paid special attention to the foreground, whose crumbled ruins and rank vegetation contrasted perfectly with the pristine forms of the Taj itself (pl. 107). For these riverbank scenes, he waited until the rainy season provided enough water to lap the shore so that its gently zephyred surface could reflect the buildings, lending depth and animation to the empty river expanse. Too much water, however, and the sandbanks would be lost to view, spoiling the balance of the composition. Local knowledge and ready access were clearly important to Murray's photographic success.

Of all the photographs he made of the Taj, the most impressive are his triptych panoramas, taken from the roof of the high entrance gate and looking down and across the formal gardens to the mausoleum beyond. After his return to Agra in 1858, Murray had first experimented with diptych panoramas, coming to terms with the optical and technical difficulties involved in framing, exposing, and developing two negatives so that they could be joined in an apparently seamless result.[42] Photographers from the very earliest period on, recognizing the limitations of their cameras and lenses, had made diptych panoramas, and Calvert Jones designed a special camera for the task that produced a pair of negatives suitable for joining (pl. 77).[43] Even with a diptych, the difficulties of making a satisfactory panorama were formidable; for a triptych they were more complex still, and overcoming them required a practiced competence. The technique did not work well with all subjects, and Murray, understanding this, used it only when photographing architecture, making diptychs of the smaller buildings and triptychs of the Taj Mahal.

Perched high above the heavily wooded gardens, whose foliage is rendered even darker by the poor sensitivity to green of the waxed-paper process, the pale building appears almost translucent in the early morning sunlight (pl. 106). So often described as a tribute to feminine beauty, the monument itself becomes an architectural odalisque reclining against dark silky billows. Murray's visual poems to this loveliness, his triptychs of the Taj, have now become his signature pieces. His last recorded photograph of the subject is dated March 25, 1864—surely one of the last great huzzahs for paper negatives!

Before going on leave to Britain in February 1857, Murray had prepared a set of twenty-seven prints for inclusion in the exhibition of the Photographic Society of Bengal to open in Calcutta on March 4.[44] The brief catalogue entries suggest that he chose the same views as those subsequently selected by Hogarth for publication in *Photographic Views in Agra and Its Vicinity*. Almost five hundred photographs were on display, many taken by members of the society but also a good number by European photographers and drawn from personal collections. Lady Canning, a keen supporter of photography, lent prints by the French photographers Bisson Frères and Louis-Cyrus Macaire, and the British aristocrat and banker Lord Somers. Others sent in views of Italy, Turkey, Egypt, and the Crimea. The scope of these loans demonstrates that even when living in isolated regions like Bengal, people kept collections of photographs with them for their personal enjoyment and instruction.

The Bengal Presidency, with Calcutta as its administrative capital, was the center of British power in India. From his residency there the governor-general, directing legions of secretaries and bureaucrats, oversaw the government of India. The Photographic Society of Bengal, also based in Calcutta, was closely, if informally, linked with government; it enjoyed the patronage of Lady Canning, and most of its members were associated with the government in one way or another. This relationship with officialdom is one of the features that distinguished Indian photography from its counterparts elsewhere and accounted for much of its direction during the 1850s and 1860s.

LINNAEUS TRIPE: PHOTOGRAPHING IN BURMA

Lady Canning would have been familiar not only with Murray's work but with that of Linnaeus Tripe, who exhibited a series of nineteen Burmese views in the Calcutta exhibition.[45] Tripe had been appointed photographer to the British delegation sent in 1855 to negotiate the terms of a treaty with the king of Burma after the Second Burmese War ended in 1853. McCosh had been in Burma in a quasi-official capacity to photograph during that conflict, which arose principally for commercial reasons and ended with the East India Company's annexation of the province of Pegu and thus its control over all of southern Burma. But this had never been formally ratified, and two years later the British sent a diplomatic mission to the royal court, known as the Court

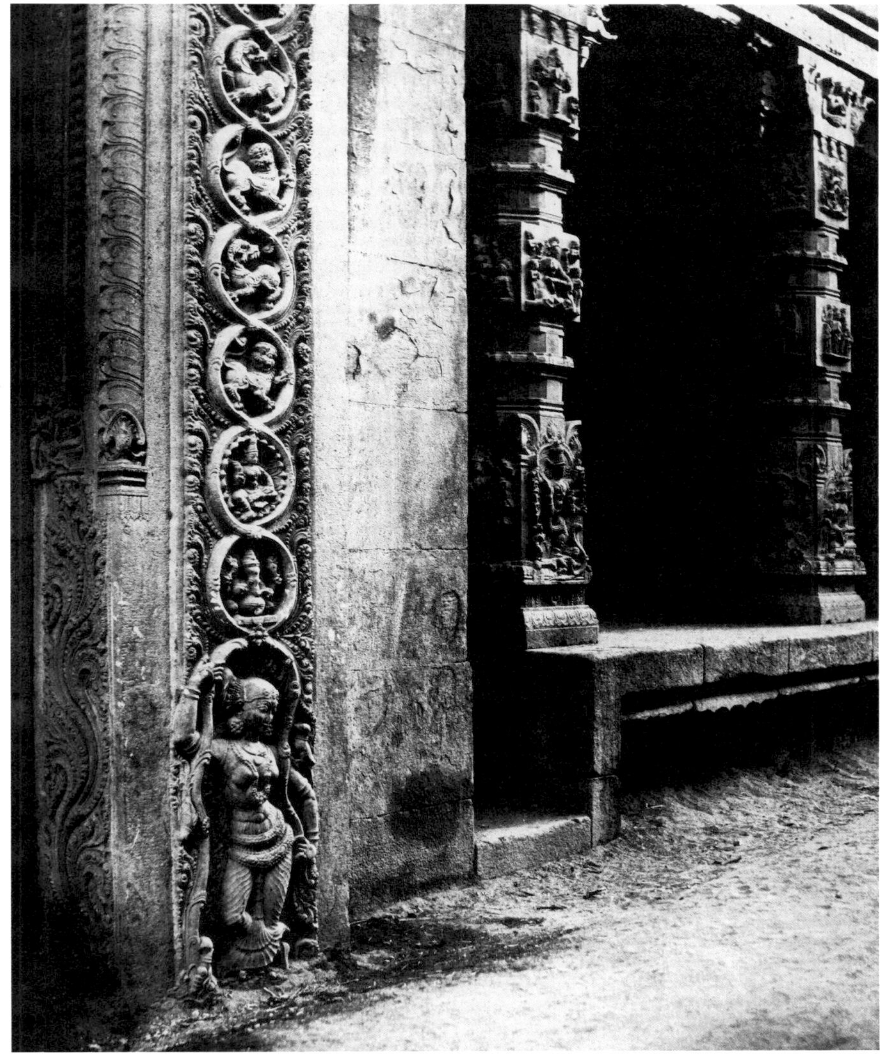

Fig. 115. Linnaeus Tripe, *Madura. Pillars in the recessed portico in the roya gopurum with the base of one of the four sculptured monoliths*, January–March 1858. Albumen print from waxed paper negative, 37.4 x 31.5 cm (14¾ x 12⅜ in.). The Metropolitan Museum of Art, New York, Gilman Collection, Purchase, Cynthia Hazen Polsky Gift, 2005, 2005.100.381.1.9

of Ava, in an attempt to get a treaty signed by the Burmese king, Mindon Min.[46] At the very last minute, the governor-general, Lord Dalhousie, decided that the party should be accompanied by a photographer, whose documentation could complement that of the official artist, Colesworthy Grant.[47]

Like many of his colleagues in the Photographic Society of Bengal, Tripe had come to India to join the army of the East India Company. He arrived in Madras (Chennai) in December 1839, joined the infantry, and served for eleven years before returning to Britain for a two-year furlough. While there, perhaps encouraged by the emerging influence of photography in 1851, he decided to take it up. By October 1853 he had become an accomplished and self-confident practitioner, taking large-format views of the dockyards and naval shipping in his home town of Devonport. In June 1854, now promoted to the rank of captain, he returned to India, bringing his camera and photographic paraphernalia with him.

Tripe first came to the attention of the authorities after making a photographic expedition in December 1854 with a fellow amateur, Dr. A. C. B. Neill of the Indian Medical Service, to the three temple sites of Halebid, Belur, and Sravanabelagola in the south Indian state of Mysore (Karnataka). Together they made a comprehensive survey of the sites, with Tripe taking one hundred negatives of the temple buildings showing their architecture, the rich carving on their exteriors, and individual statues. In February 1855 he exhibited sixty-eight of these at the Exhibition of Raw Products, Arts, and Manufactures of Southern India held in Madras; the jury recommended that a set be purchased and forwarded to the directors of the East India Company in London.[48] As it happened, the directors had been thinking that it was time to move the company into the modern era and, in addition to employing artists and draftsmen as in the past, employ photographers "where it may be considered desirable by the Government to obtain representation of objects of interest."[49] And so Lord Dalhousie appointed Tripe "Artist in Photography" to accompany his political delegation to the Burmese court.

The mission departed from Rangoon on August 1, 1855, and traveled by steamer up the Irrawaddy River toward the territories of northern Burma, stopping briefly at Prome, Thayetmyo, and Pagan before reaching Amarapura in the north a month later. Beyond the underlying diplomatic purpose of the mission was the opportunity this offered the British authorities in India to gather intelligence about the region. Burma north of Prome was little known to the outside world, including the East India Company, which was intent on annexing part of it. Tripe, as a photographer, was one of a group of experts who had been attached to gather information on the culture, religion, topography, geography, architecture, and natural resources of the region.[50] As part of their military training they had been schooled in the art of detailed observation, including sketching, surveying, mapping, and setting down on paper whatever lay before them.

The mission lasted three months. By the time of its return to Rangoon in November 1855, Tripe had made well over two hundred large-format paper negatives, each approximately 12 x 15 inches and the vast majority portraying Buddhist temples, shrines, and other buildings.[51] Although Grant was undoubtedly a skilled and efficient artist, his sketches offered nothing to match the documentary precision of photography, which in this large format rendered the finely carved details of Burmese religious architecture with impressive accuracy.[52] However, Tripe's photographs are not merely documentation. Although he worked with the discipline of an army officer and in some instances had little choice but to set the camera down foursquare, especially when a building occupied a visually sterile space, the dullness of those photographs was outweighed by the artistry evident in others. Even under these testing circumstances, Tripe's aesthetic sensibility was rapidly developing.

When the British mission arrived in Amarapura they were given quarters a little to the south on a peninsula surrounded by a large lake, which effectively isolated them from the city. Their only means of access was a wooden bridge that ran for three-quarters of a mile, a solid and impressive piece of civil engineering. At one end of it stood the British residency and at the other a small cluster of temples dominated by a colossal statue of Gautama, the Buddha.[53]

Had Tripe been nothing more than a documentary photographer he would have moved in close and placed the massive figure in the center of the frame, where it would dominate the composition. Instead, he moved away and viewed the statue from a distance, permitting the surrounding shrines and slender palms to emphasize its impressive size (pl. 114). Meandering pathways cross the foreground and, in the absence of the usual perspective cues, allow the eye to wander freely toward the crumbling stairway, then approach the base of the figure itself. In this deliberately asymmetrical composition, the solid form of the statue is offset by the three palm trees—a framing done with such lightness of touch that the underlying serenity of the subject is fully conveyed.

Rotating his camera 180 degrees, Tripe turned away from the statue to look back across the lake toward the British residency on the far horizon, reached by the celebrated wooden bridge. Here he adopted a rigorous compositional approach. Using the dark shadows to divide the picture horizontally and the twin wooden pillars of the bridge to partition the space vertically, he created a series of discrete rectangles, each containing a very different image. Most visually arresting is the space between the pillars, where the bridge's commanding perspective draws the eye far out over the water until it reaches the point where the bridge veers left and strikes out for the distant shore. The other sections of the composition appear dormant and two-dimensional by comparison, but their presence is essential to carrying off the inviting spatial illusion of the whole (pl. 118). The picture follows none of the generally accepted rules of nineteenth-century composition; perhaps Victorians found its dissonance unsettling, or even overwhelming. But it was no accident—rather a photograph deliberately framed to exploit to the full the optical ambiguity of the medium.

Tripe knew full well that his efforts would be closely scrutinized by the governor-general and by the directors of the East India Company in London, and two further examples from his Burma series are evidence of his growing self-confidence behind the camera. Attracted in Tsagain Myo (Sagaing) by a *tazaung*, or chapel, that had fallen into disrepair, he positioned himself so that the statue of Buddha seated in its protective niche would be revealed, and photographed the building with straightforward respect, even reverence. The perfect symmetry of the chapel's upper tiers contrasts effectively with the ramshackle disorder of the shrine beneath, its roof boards lost and its very survival threatened by rampant undergrowth (pl. 112). Some weeks later he photographed, in a very different mode, the most important Buddhist shrine in Burma, the impressive Shwedagon Pagoda that overlooks Rangoon. Instead of being left to decline gracefully, the building was undergoing restoration, and its upper portion was clad in a latticework of bamboo scaffolding in preparation for regilding of the massive dome and spire. The scale, setting, and importance of the pagoda clearly impressed Tripe, who made a number of studies, surveying the site with his camera from every quarter. Photographing a tall building set within a confined space is challenging, and often it is difficult to include the apex, but here Tripe found a spot that allowed him to capture the pagoda's entire spire and nicely show the *sein-phoo*, or symbolic bud, that adorns the vane (pl. 113).

To the right, an overhanging tree fluttered in the breeze during the long exposure needed for the waxed-paper process, creating a dense, dark blur of leaves that if left alone would have distracted the eye. To remedy this Tripe worked on the paper negative with black pigment, dabbing his brush in rapid downward strokes to create a patterning that visually lightened the heavy mass of foliage. This kind of artistic intervention was widely performed by photographers making paper negatives, although with differing degrees of success. Faced with the featureless skies of India, both Murray and Tripe retouched their negatives to suggest the presence of clouds. Skies were tricky things to photograph; because of their brightness they were often overexposed on the negative, and under certain conditions this produced an unsightly mottled or grainy texture. In that case the only way to save the negative was to paint out the offending sky, painstakingly outlining whatever buildings stood against it. This required a delicacy and sureness of touch that came only with practice, which, to judge from their surviving negatives, both Murray and Tripe possessed to a high degree.

When Tripe embarked with the mission to Burma as its official "artist in photography," he was a relatively inexperienced photographer with only one self-initiated project to call his own. By the time he returned to Bangalore at the end of his three-month trip he had made more than two hundred negatives under testing circumstances of climate and location, as well as of his own photographic naïveté. His surviving negatives bear witness to difficulties with overexposure and wayward chemicals.[54] When he distributed fifty sets of *Burma Views*, he thought a word of explanation was needed to account for their shortcomings:

> *The accompanying Views . . . should not be looked upon as a challenge to Photographic criticism; but as a series of views of subjects interesting on account of their novelty; many having been retained solely on that account when they would certainly have been otherwise discarded. As excuses, too, for these defective photographs he would wish it known, that he was working against time; and frequently with no opportunities of replacing poor proofs by better. Also that, from unfavourable weather, sickness, and the circumstances unavoidably attending such a mission, his actual working time was narrowed to thirty six days.*
>
> *If criticism be provoked, it is trusted that her chidings will be mild.*[55]

Fig. 116. Linnaeus Tripe, *Madura. West front of the roya gopurum*, January–March 1858. Albumen print from waxed paper negative, 29.3 x 36.8 cm (11½ x 14½ in.). The Metropolitan Museum of Art, New York, Gilman Collection, Purchase, Cynthia Hazen Polsky Gift, 2005, 2005.100.381.1.10

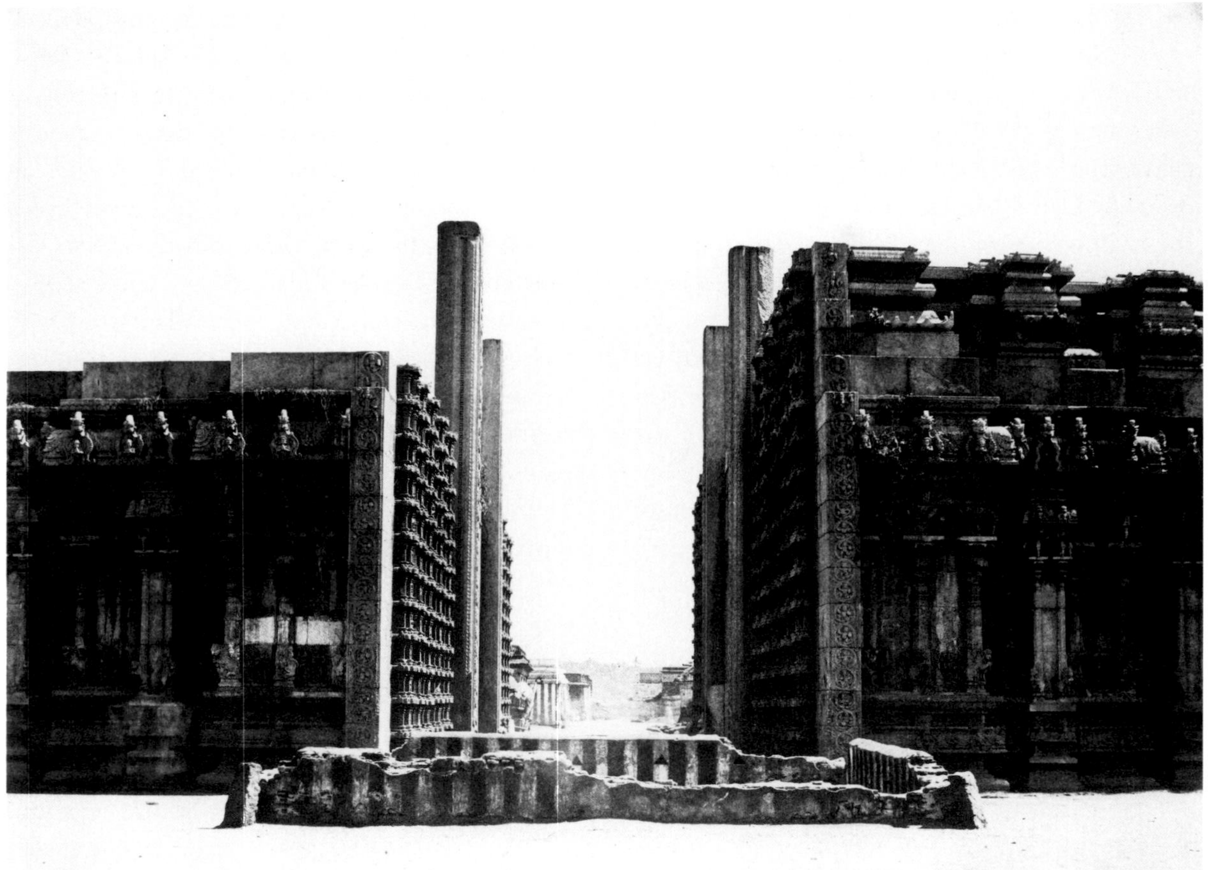

In fact, these comments underline Tripe's newfound proficiency, for despite myriad adversities he managed to take an average of six negatives each working day. The experience helped transform him from a gentleman amateur into a professional photographer.

Whatever his private doubts, Tripe's *Burma Views* were well received, and in 1856 he was appointed official photographer to the Madras Presidency. Asked how he intended to apply himself, he replied that he would document "the objects in the Presidency that are interesting to the Antiquary[,] Architect, Sculptor, Mythologist and Historian" and that it was also important to "obtain Illustrations of the Races" living within the presidency along with their "arms, implements, musical instruments &ca . . . deemed worthy of being represented." He added, "The Picturesque may be allowed perhaps, supplementally."[56]

For the next four years Tripe applied himself tirelessly to these self-appointed tasks, photographing extensively throughout the huge region, issuing nine portfolios in a series called *Photographic Views*, and managing the photographic establishment, where his foreman and four assistants were kept busy printing and publishing his pictures (figs. 115, 116).[57] This brief period of enormous activity was brought to an end after government was transferred from the East India Company to the Crown and Sir Charles Trevelyan was appointed governor of the presidency in March 1859. Trevelyan was known as a zealous watchdog of government expenditure, and in Madras he trimmed costs and questioned long-standing arrangements. Tripe became an early victim of his scrutiny when Trevelyan asked "whether the Government Photographic Establishment is not an article of high luxury which is unsuited to the present state of our finances."[58] In June 1860, strained and exhausted by this scrutiny, Tripe submitted his final accounts, left the employ of the government, and returned to the army, where he was promptly placed on sick leave to convalesce. By November the government had closed the photographic establishment, ending one of the most productive episodes in the history of photography in India (pls. 115, 116, 117).[59]

The kind of work done by McCosh, Murray, and Tripe was echoed in a wide pattern of photographic activity throughout India, and in many ways these three can be regarded as role models to whom others looked for inspiration. In their hands, paper negative photography continued to flourish long after its popularity had begun to wane back home. Their deliberate decision to stick with paper owed as much to aesthetic preferences as to its practical utility in an Indian setting. (Although both Murray and Tripe used the sharper collodion from time to time, when making large-format negatives both returned to paper, knowing that at large scale the process was capable of rendering even the finest details.) Few photographers in the calotype era came close to matching the sustained output of these three, and in visual sensitivity and technical bravado they remain unequaled.

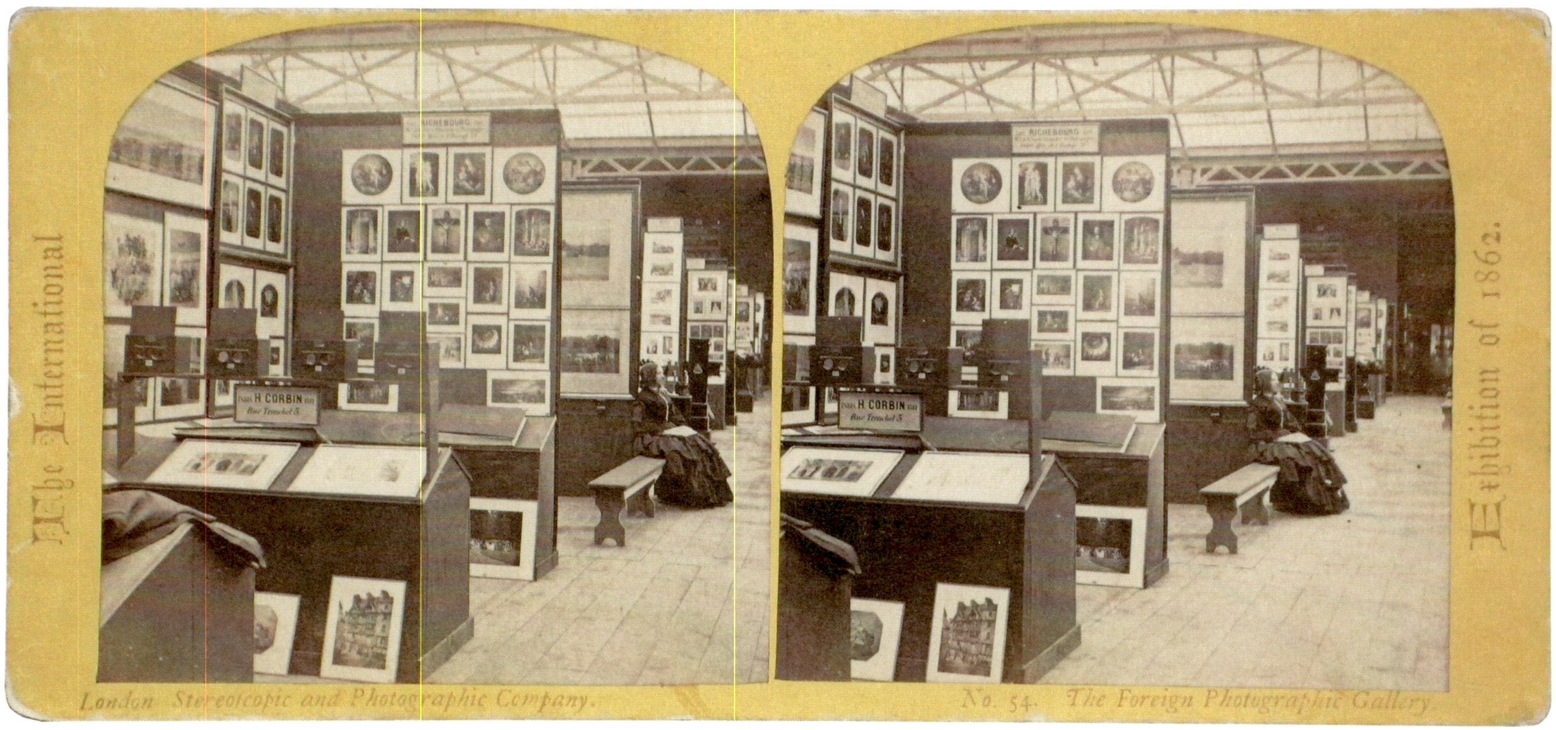
The International
Exhibition of 1862.
H. CORBIN
Rue Tronchet 5
RICHEBOURG
London Stereoscopic and Photographic Company.
No. 54. The Foreign Photographic Gallery.

10. *Commercialism Advances, the Calotype Declines*

Photography has become a household word and a household want; is used alike by art and science, by love, business, and justice; is found in the most sumptuous saloon, and in the dingiest attic—in the solitude of the Highland cottage, and in the glare of the London gin-palace—in the pocket of the detective, in the cell of the convict, in the folio of the painter and architect, among the papers and patterns of the millowner and manufacturer, and on the cold brave breast on the battle-field.[1]

This extract from an article published in 1857 was written by Lady Elizabeth Eastlake (wife of Sir Charles, the first president of the Photographic Society). While only half a generation earlier, she emphasized, "the existence of such a vocation was not dreamt of," now "tens of thousands" were "following a new business, practising a new pleasure, speaking a new language, and bound together by a new sympathy."[2] Photography had arrived with headlong swiftness, taking Victorian society by surprise as it transformed itself from the subject of experimentation by a privileged few into a commodity available to all (fig. 118).

The new universality of photography distinguished it from other pastimes and occupations, Lady Eastlake pointed out, for "when before did any motive short of the stimulus of chance or the greed of gain unite in one uncertain and laborious quest the noblemen, the tradesman, . . . the artist, the manservant, the general officer, the private soldier, the hard-worked member of every learned profession, the gentleman of leisure . . . and, though last, not least, the fair woman whom nothing but her own choice obliges to be more than the fine lady?"[3] As Eastlake seems to have sensed very well, photography reflected in microcosm broader changes in society, among them the challenges that commercial expansion was posing to the old class structures.

Opposite: Fig. 117. William England, *The Foreign Photographic Gallery, The International Exhibition of 1862.* Stereoscopic albumen silver prints from glass negatives, each image 7.8 x 7.6 cm (3⅛ x 3 in.). Private collection

CHANGES IN THE PHOTOGRAPHIC SOCIETY

The institutional embodiment of photography continued to be the Photographic Society, through whose encouragement other societies, like "branches from the parent tree," had spread across the nation.

By 1857, the society was riding high. With membership growing, sales of the journal increasing, and critically successful exhibitions, for the first time the society seemed to have sufficient funds to secure its long-term future by acquiring a permanent home. This would enable it to follow the example of the Chemical Society and apply for a charter of incorporation, which, once royal assent was granted, would formally acknowledge the national significance of its work and elevate it to the high status of other learned societies in London.[4] Finding a suitable building in central London was then as now no easy matter, but after

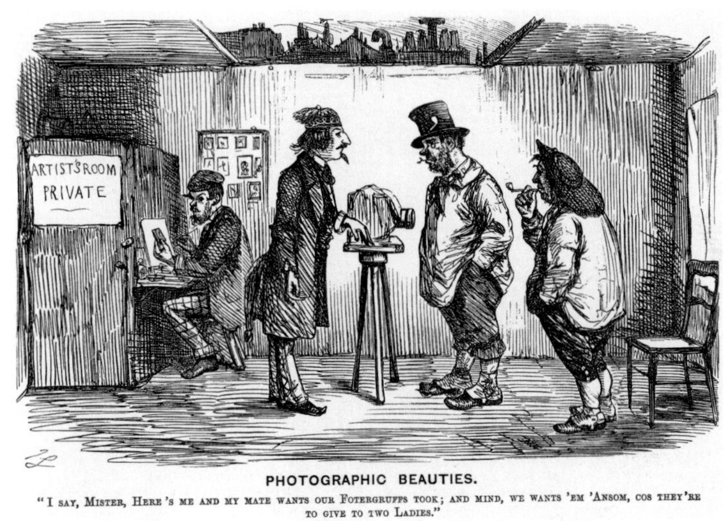

Fig. 118. John Leech, *Photographic Beauties.* "I say, Mister, Here's me and my mate wants our Fotergruffs took; and mind, we wants 'em 'Ansom, cos they're to give to two Ladies." Wood engraving, 13 x 17.6 cm (5⅛ x 6⅞ in.). From *Punch*, June 19, 1858

months of searching, rooms were found above a bank in New Coventry Street, Piccadilly, in the very heart of the city. The lease was signed, the premises renovated at considerable expense, and, in the fall of 1857, the rooms occupied.[5]

However, internal problems were brewing despite this seeming success. An organization in which "slight improvements in processes, and slight varieties in conclusions, are discussed as if they involved the welfare of mankind,"[6] the society was focused on matters increasingly distant from the everyday concerns of photographers struggling to get ahead. At its founding in 1853 the Photographic Society had directed its attention to the needs of gentlemen amateurs, then the dominant presence in the world of photography. Within the space of four years, however, the context had changed completely, as photography became a viable commercial endeavor and the number of photographers increased exponentially. Instead of adapting to the changing situation, the Photographic Society had grown ever more aloof.

In 1854, as discussed earlier, fear that the presence of photographers "in trade" would change the character of the society had led to an attempt to bar them from serving on its council.[7] This underlying attitude remained, and a similar anxiety now surrounded the society's annual exhibitions. These were open to all photographers, amateurs and professionals alike, in the belief that work of every genre should be represented, and initially this policy had not presented any problems. However, when a number of portrait studios began exhibiting prints that had been heavily retouched to enhance their appearance, doubts were raised about the wisdom of including such work, and some members called for its outright rejection.[8] The council subsequently introduced rules designed to hinder (but not prohibit) the exhibition of retouched work.[9]

In 1858, driven once again by the impulse to protect the society from the undignified intrusion of trade, the council introduced a rule rejecting all photographs submitted for exhibition "that have been exposed in shop windows or otherwise publicly exhibited in this country."[10] "A picture seen in a shop-window is not hung in the Royal Academy" was the justification offered.[11] However, the ruling also inadvertently excluded work previously exhibited at regional societies. An uproar followed in which criticism came not only from members but also from the wider photographic community, which recognized in the ruling another strategy to keep commercial practitioners at bay.

CHANGES IN PHOTOGRAPHY

In a sense it was understandable that the society felt beleaguered. By 1857, photographic wares had become ubiquitous. There was, in Eastlake's phrase, a "legion of petty dabblers, who display their trays of specimens along every great thoroughfare in London,"[12] while printsellers and photographic retailers sought to attract customers by filling every inch of their shop windows with extravagant displays of their latest photographic stock (fig. 119). The public's appetite for stereoscopic views was insatiable, and photographic publishers (such as George Washington Wilson and the London Stereoscopic Company) responded by issuing catalogues of their latest offerings. A network of independent retailers sprang up in cities, towns, and tourist resorts, wherever a commercial opportunity, no matter how small, was present (fig. 120). After 1858, the carte-de-visite, a small photographic portrait

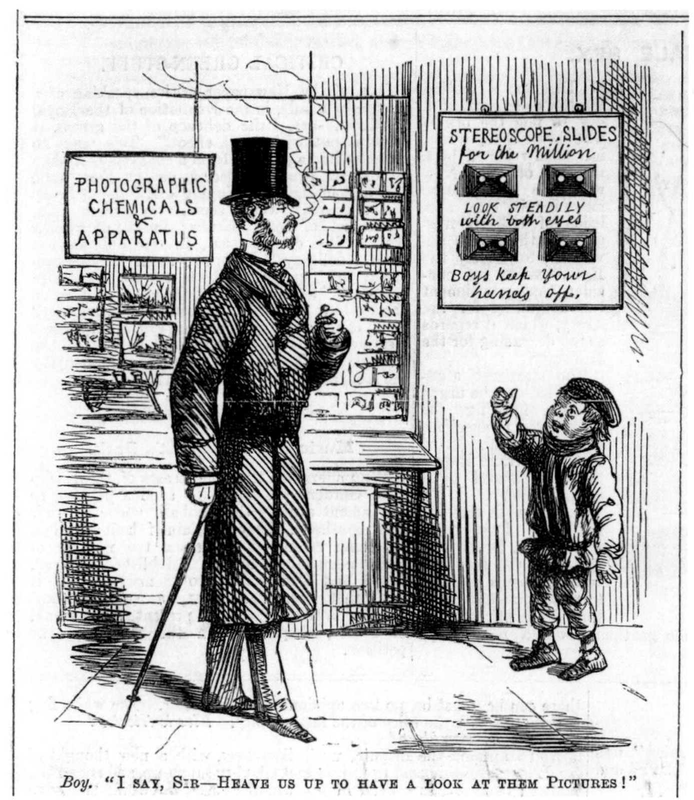

Fig. 119. John Leech, *Boy: "I say, Sir—Heave us up to have a look at them Pictures!"* Wood engraving, 12.5 x 10.3 cm (4⅞ x 4 in.). From *Punch*, May 17, 1856. Private collection

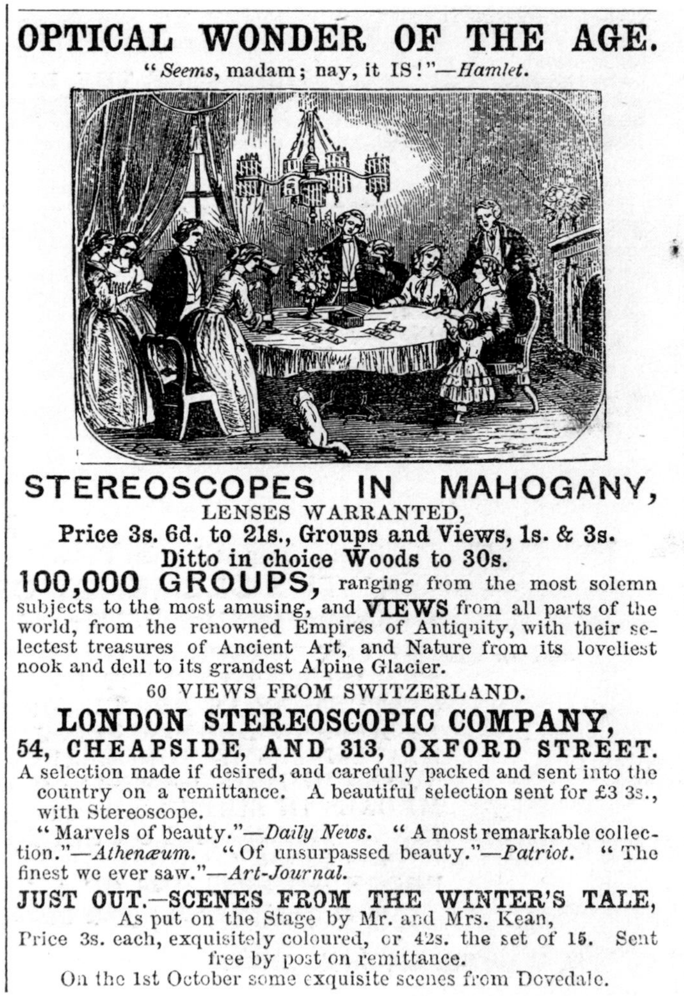

Fig. 120. *Optical Wonder of the Age*, advertisement for the London Stereoscopic Company. 10.8 x 7 cm (4¼ x 2¾ in.). From *Art-Journal Advertiser*, October 1856. Private collection

pasted onto a mount the size of a calling card, began to establish itself as the preferred format for portraiture. Cartes-de-visite became wildly popular, especially those that portrayed royalty or celebrities, and were collected and kept in albums. The combined cultural impact of just these two formats—the stereoscopic view and the carte-de-visite—was considerably greater than that created by any annual exhibition, especially among the emergent middle classes.

Of growing concern was a completely new class of photography that grew up in response to the public demand for stereoscopic genre pictures, in which a lively domestic scene something like a cartoon by George Cruikshank or John Leech was reenacted for the camera (fig. 121). Many of the pictures were in dubious taste; one, for example, showed "a woman in bed, with a man in his night-cap and night-shirt seated in a chair nursing a baby," a composition that one journalist thought displayed a "coarse brutality of taste and sentiment."[13] Such images easily offended the delicate sensibilities of Victorians, for whom the sanctity of home and marriage were paramount. A quick stroll down the Strand, the same author continued, revealed "numerous shop-windows—in other particulars of the most respectable character—which are studded with stereoscopic slides, representing women more or less naked, and generally leering at the spectator" (fig. 122).[14]

With each passing year, sales of prints rose and the influence of popular photographic publishers was further consolidated. Perhaps just as important as the sheer volume of photographs sold was the way this market intensified the public's taste for highly finished albumen prints made from collodion-coated negatives. From the early 1850s, some photographers who had their eyes firmly fixed on the business potential of photography, including Roger Fenton and Philip Delamotte, had gradually abandoned paper negatives and the matte surface of salted paper prints in favor of this glossier, sharper, and more fashionable combination.[15] Those amateurs for whom the sale of exhibited prints was not a financial necessity were almost the only ones to remain faithful to paper negatives. Even they often printed on albumen paper or some variant of it.

During this period of changeover—from paper to collodion, from amateur to professional, from high art to popular taste—the Photographic Society underwent its own transformation. The optimism that in 1857 was still driving things forward began to evaporate rapidly. The first crisis came in 1858 with the fifth annual exhibition. The society had been persuaded to install it in the new South Kensington Museum, to which it was hoped the public would flock in droves. However, the museum's location a little outside central London made it seem inaccessible, attendance was poor, and the exhibition was losing money. In an attempt to reverse this the society reinstalled the exhibition at its new headquarters, but members then discovered, to their horror, that the venue was "too small, and altogether inadequate to the requirements of exhibitors."[16] Faced with the blunt reality that

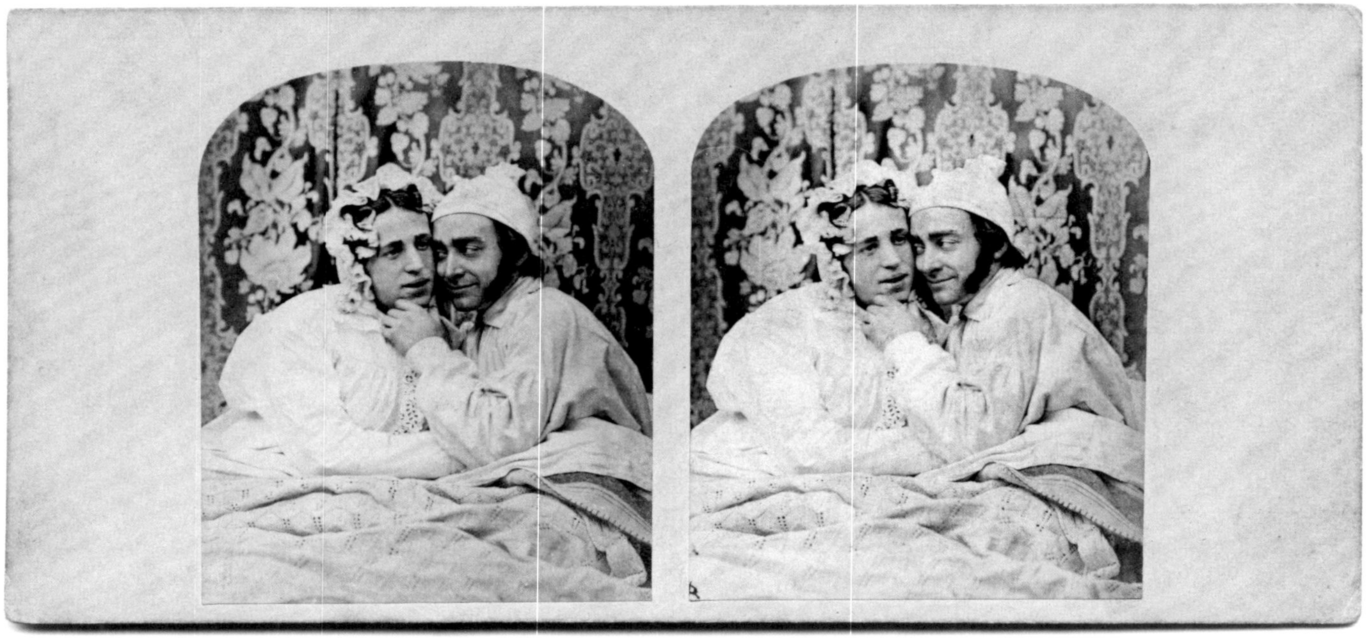

Fig. 121. J. Elliott, *Mr. & Mrs. Caudle*, ca. 1855. Stereoscopic albumen silver prints from glass negatives, each image 7.1 x 6.4 cm (2¾ x 2½ in.). Collection of Brian May, London

its new premises had been a costly mistake, the society decided to cut its losses. In the summer of 1860 it terminated its lease in New Coventry Street and gratefully accepted the temporary accommodation for meetings offered by King's College in central London.[17] Its funds had been seriously depleted by the heavy expenses of the original move to New Coventry Street, and the society now found itself more vulnerable than at any previous stage of its existence. Gone were the hopes of incorporation and a royal charter, for without permanent premises and adequate funds to secure one, the application would very likely fail. Gone, too, within the space of three years, was the mood of optimism. Membership was falling, the deficit grew ever larger, and the annual exhibitions were all financial failures. By the early 1860s the society teetered on the brink of collapse, its sense of purpose confused and its resolve confounded by circumstance.[18]

With photographic commerce burgeoning and the fortunes of the Photographic Society waning, amateur photographers became increasingly marginalized; for those dedicated to the aesthetics of paper negatives, the ever-spreading preference for collodion was ominous. Amateur calotypists outside London seem to have maintained their position longer, although essentially they faced similar issues. A tabulation of selected exhibition records for the period 1854–60 shows the number of displayed photographs made from paper negatives steadily declining each year, with the falloff in the regions outside London more gradual but steady (see table 1).[19] These figures should be interpreted with caution, however, for they do not give the numbers of participating photographers. The forty-two prints from paper processes shown at the London Photographic Society in 1859 were the work of just eight photographers, and the nine shown the following year came from just six die-hard practitioners, one of them Thomas Raven (see pl. 83).

Whatever photographic medium they chose, for gentlemen amateurs their early aspirations to see photography regarded as an artistic profession no longer seemed possible. They sought to occupy a place at the upper end of the fine-art print market; but a multitude of photographic publishers, by applying the economics of mass production, had driven prices for photography in the opposite direction, bringing them within the reach of a general public. Even the creative intention of amateurs was undercut, when phrases like "artistic subjects" and "photographic artist" were freely applied for commercial purposes. By the close of the decade these terms had been so debased as to become meaningless.

Finally, the annual exhibition, that bastion of artistic photography, succumbed. No longer an academy show for photography, it had become an event where the dominant presence was photography

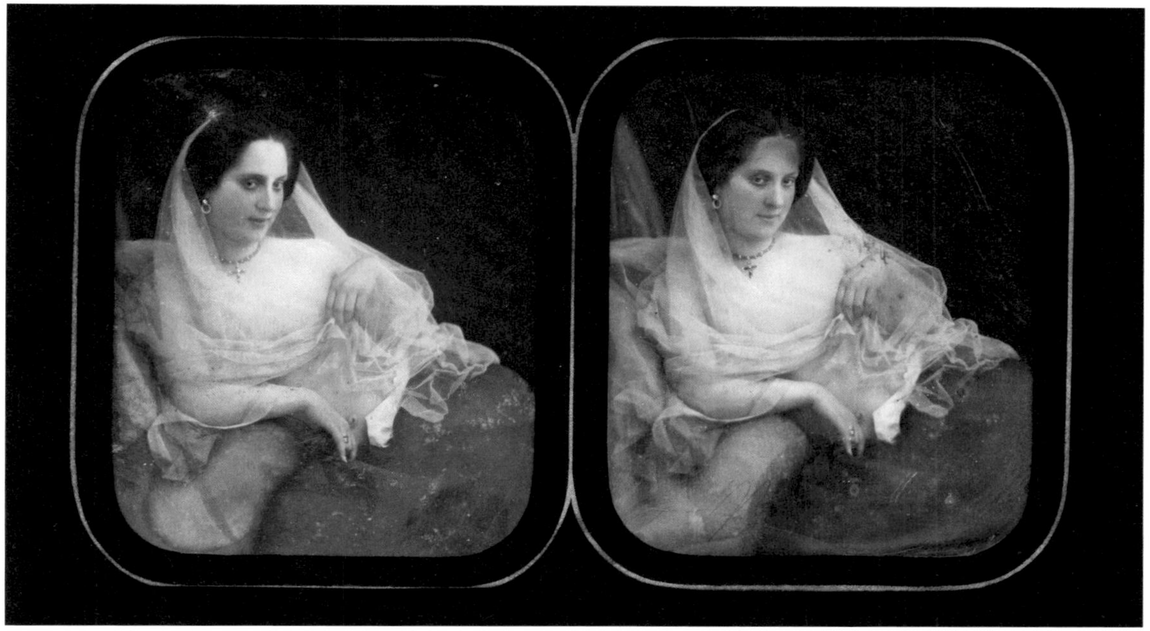

Fig. 122. Unknown photographer, *Woman with Veil,* ca.1850s. Stereoscopic daguerreotypes, each image 7.1 x 6.4 cm (2¾ x 2½ in.). Collection of Brian May, London

applied to commerce and trade. With these demoralizing conditions, the meetings of the Photographic Society—which earlier boasted all the fizz and pop of novelty—had by 1859 become "desultory," containing "little that was useful or interesting" to members.[20] The 1850s had seen photography pass from the hands of a few privileged individuals into the homes of the nation.

THE INTERNATIONAL EXHIBITION, 1862

As the decade ended, many lovers of photography looked to the International Exhibition planned for the summer of 1861 in London, in the hope that it would rekindle the same spirit of mutual collaboration and enterprise that had earlier emerged from the Great Exhibition. This initiative for mounting an exhibition in London on the tenth anniversary of the Great Exhibition of 1851 had begun with the Society of Arts, which began planning the event in the summer of 1857. But when political turmoil erupted in Italy and seemed it might draw most of Europe into war, preparations were interrupted.[21] By early 1861, with timing already out of sync, responsibility for the exhibition was passed to the royal commissioners of the 1851 world fair[22] and plans were made to open the exhibition in the summer of 1862, despite worrying news of impending civil war in America.[23]

Table 1. Photographs from Paper Negatives in Selected Photographic Society Exhibitions, 1854–60

Exhibition	*Total of photographs exhibited*	*Total from paper*	*Percentage from paper*
1854, London	980	405	41
1855, London	918	266	29
1856, London	757	167	22
1856, Edinburgh	935	260	28
1856, Manchester	739	218	29
1857, London	831	98	12
1857, Birmingham	524	117	22
1858, London	1,009	92	9
1858, Edinburgh	967	153	15
1859, London	759	42	5.5
1860, London	595	9	1.5

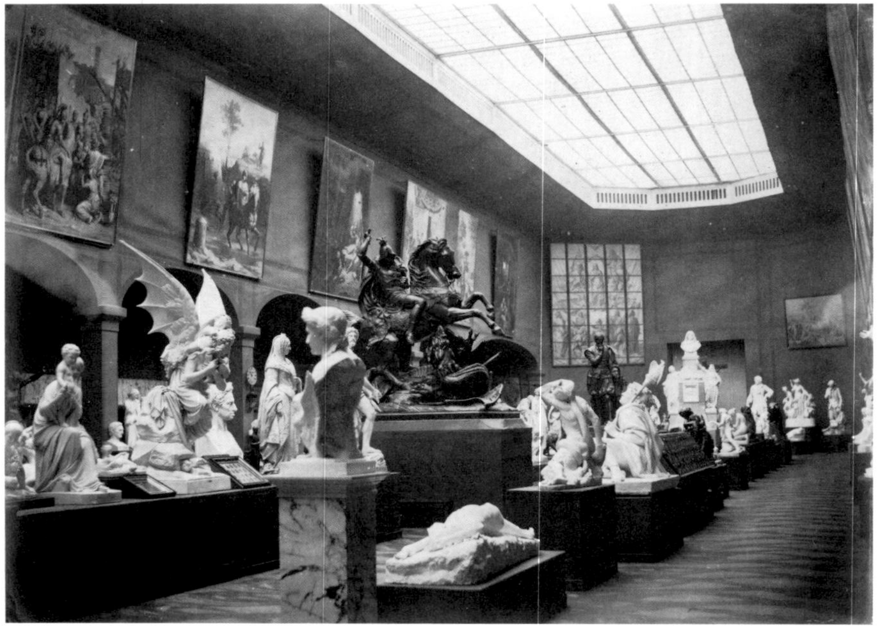

Fig. 123. Unknown photographer, *Grand Galerie de Sculpture, Exposition Universelle, Paris, 1855.* Albumen silver print from glass negative, 37 x 50 cm (14⅝ x 19¾ in.). The J. Paul Getty Museum, Los Angeles, 84.XA.832

The exhibition was organized along the same general lines as its predecessor. In the sections dedicated to materials, machinery, and manufacture there were thirty-six classes of exhibits; national committees administered these, while locally appointed committees made the selections; and specialist juries were appointed to award prize medals and honorable mentions.[24]

In the area of the arts, however, the exhibition departed from the precedent of a decade ago, when the work of living artists had been excluded. In the intervening period, the Universal Exposition, held in Paris in 1855, had incorporated a Palace of Fine Arts displaying paintings, sculpture, architectural drawings, and engravings from every major European nation, with Britain alone contributing almost eight hundred works (fig. 123).[25] The addition of arts to an industrial exhibition was popular with visitors, who sought refuge from the muscularity of manufacturing among pictures and statuary. This success for France and booster for the status of British art[26] argued powerfully for the inclusion of a fine arts section in the 1862 London exhibition. Therefore the commissioners created a new section, "Modern Fine Arts," and four new classes: architecture; paintings in oil and watercolors; sculpture, die sinking, and intaglio; and etchings and engravings.[27]

As it had in 1851, the question of how best to accommodate the new profession of photography proved troublesome. The commissioners decided to create a new heading, Class 14, Photographic Apparatus and Photography. It was to be positioned alongside Class 13, Philosophical Instruments and Processes Depending on Their Use, and both were to be displayed in the section dedicated to machinery. While photography had indeed enjoyed a long and close relationship with philosophical instruments, the decision to locate it with machinery was incongruous to say the least. Those in the Photographic Society community, deeply offended, insisted on a reclassification. The current arrangement was, wrote the society's president, Sir Frederick Pollock, "as if architecture were placed along with trowels and scaffolding, or Humboldt were put among commercial travellers."[28] In their reply the commissioners sought to reassure Pollock, offering to provide a separate exhibition space for photography adjacent to the fine arts exhibitions, but they declined to address the question of reclassification. Angered by this response, Pollock adopted the strategy of refusing to assist the commissioners with the formation of a committee to oversee Class 14 and deal with installation of the photographs.

The issue rumbled on for several months, drawing wide attention, especially in the photographic world. Regional societies debated the matter and sent letters of support, while in Paris, the Société Française de Photographie criticized the commissioners for their "philosophical error."[29] Public opinion seems to have been sharply divided, and even among photographers the arguments went back and forth. What had begun as an issue of wrongful classification developed into a philosophical dispute about the intellectual and artistic nature of photography.

Many factors played into the debate, not least the commercialization of photography, which in its sweep now embraced photographers of every persuasion and ability. As the photographer Antoine Claudet suggested, was it not nonsense to imagine "that every photographer of landscapes and rural sceneries is a Fenton, a Maxwell Lyte, a Lake Price, an Aguado, a Montizon, a Bedford, a Legray, a Ferrier, a Bisson—that every photographer of portraits can produce pictures of the most perfect kind—and that there are no such portraits as those the price of sixpence for which is a fair remuneration for the talent and taste displayed in their composition?" (fig. 124). But, he continued, "If it is acknowledged that a photographer of talent and refined mind can impart to his works a peculiar character, can compose pictures with taste and feeling . . . is not this a proof that there is something more in photography than the use of a mere machine?"[30] Claudet avoided discussing the swelling ranks that occupied photography's middle ground. Distinguishing between a superior photographer and a hack was relatively easy; it required the wisdom of Solomon, however, to classify the remainder with proper artistic judgment. One can appreciate why the commissioners desperately needed a committee to advise them about photographic matters, on which they simply lacked competence.

Independent of these concerns but not unrelated to them was the issue of the artistic copyright of photographs, which were being offered protection for the first time in a bill making its way through Parliament in the spring of 1861. In 1857 the Society of Arts had taken the initiative in tackling the broader subject of artistic copyright, questioning whether the existing legislation offered sufficient protection, and by early 1858 it had drawn together a powerful committee to consider the matter. Significantly, photography had been included in its deliberations and Fenton invited to represent the interests of photographers. The committee's recommendations had been sent to Parliament,[31] and it now seemed likely that copyright protection would indeed be extended to photographs.[32] At just the same time, the row about the status of photography at the International Exhibition was reaching a crescendo. How was it possible, photographers argued, for the commissioners to deny the artistic status of photography when the government was about to include photography under its proposed artistic copyright legislation? It was a persuasive argument.[33]

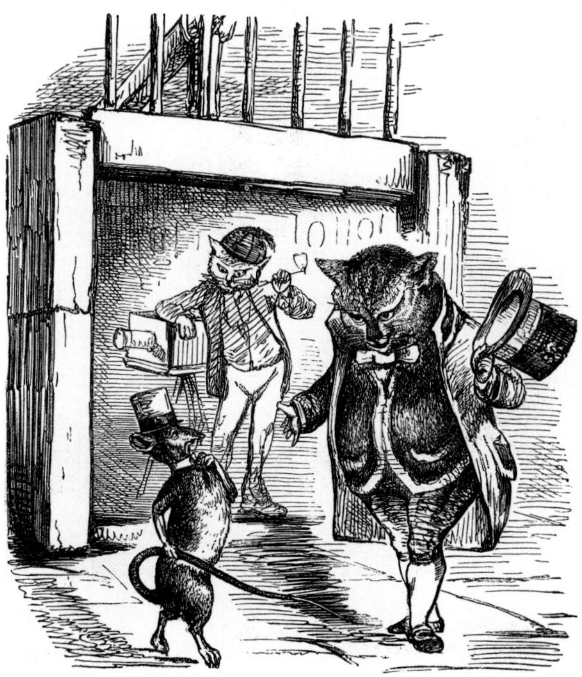

Fig. 124. Unknown artist, *"Step in, and be done, Sir!"* Wood engraving, 11.2 x 8.8 cm (4⅜ x 3½ in.). From *Punch*, September 29, 1860. Private collection

Nevertheless, the stalemate between the commissioners and the Photographic Society continued. In August 1861 the society reiterated its demand: "If the Commissioners are prepared to receive Photography as a branch of the Fine Arts, the Council are willing to appoint a Committee and afford every assistance in their power."[34] No meaningful response was forthcoming. Individual photographers now felt torn between standing by their principles and supporting the society, or sacrificing them and exhibiting their work. Many blamed the Photographic Society for committing a tactical error. There was great concern that unless they made a strong showing, British photographers would be overwhelmed once again by French and other European practitioners (who exhibited with their individual countries and were not affected by these classification controversies). The editor of the *Photographic News* put the matter in a certain perspective:

> *All minor considerations should be now laid aside. Photographers have made their protest. If their works be pronounced as worthy of the niche in the Temple of the Fine Arts which they claim for it, no mistaken arrangement in classifying will prevent its taking its proper position in the minds of the educated public. Let us admit for the present that the art does occupy a novel position: it is young, and has yet to . . . prove its claims; but a representation at the present exhibition of overwhelming excellence, will be one of the most important steps that can be taken to that end, and no matter how catalogued, let us be content to await the world's verdict.*[35]

Finally, the South London Photographic Society independently suggested to the commissioners a middle way that allowed both sides to proceed without loss of face.[36] Within weeks, the commissioners announced at last the appointment of an official photographic committee; it was made up of the Earl of Caithness (James Sinclair), Edward Kater, Hugh Welch

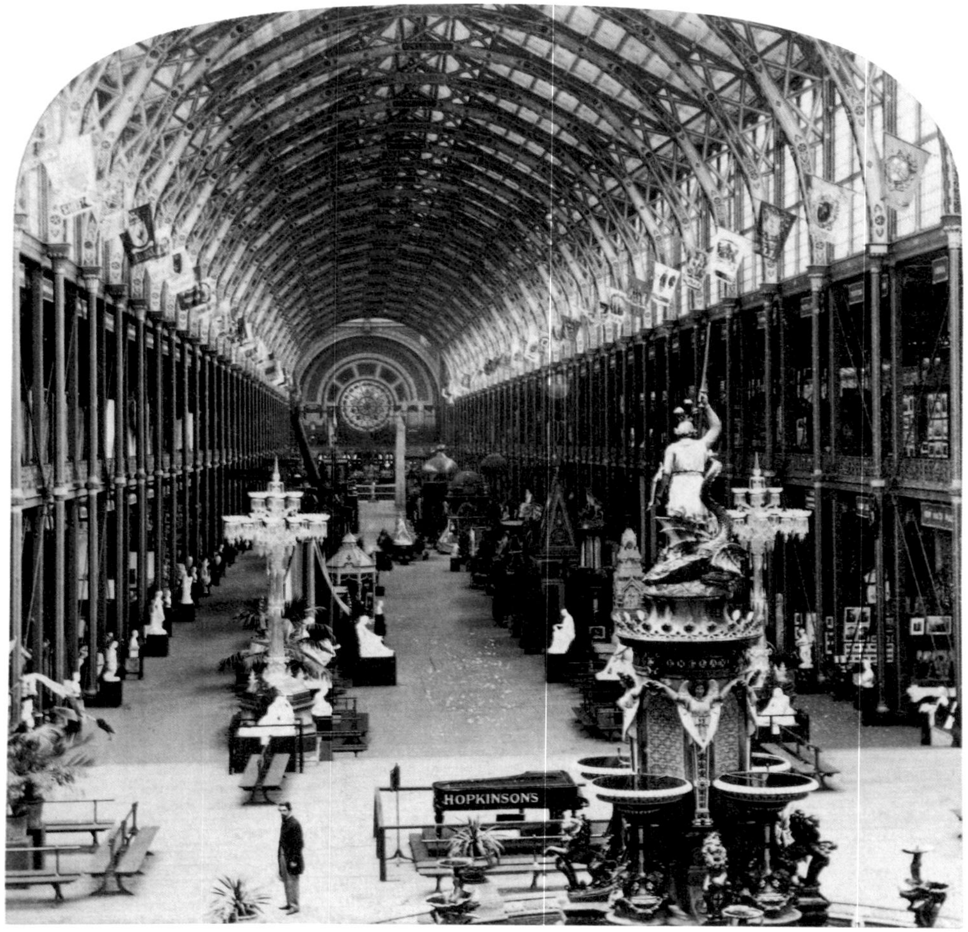

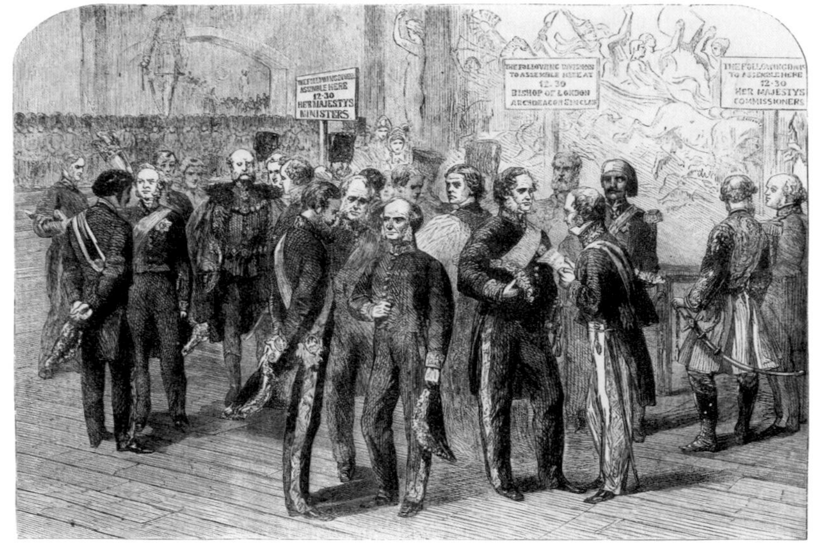

Fig. 126. Unknown artist, *Opening of the International Exhibition: The Procession Forming in the South Central Court.* Wood engraving, 24 x 34.1 cm (9½ x 13⅜ in.). From *Illustrated London News*, May 10, 1862, p 482. Private collection

Fig. 125. William England, *The Nave, from the Eastern Dome, The International Exhibition of 1862.* Single image from stereoscopic pair, albumen silver print from glass negative, 7.8 x 7.6 cm (3⅛ x 3 in.). Private collection

Diamond, and Peter Le Neve Foster as superintendent. British photographers would not have to take their place in the International Exhibition's machinery court "among the ploughs, harrows, and watering cans"; they had been promised their own, separate department.[37]

But all too late, it was discovered that the newly allocated space was at a remote distance from the main displays, in the central tower over the entrance to the building, where it could be reached only by a long and winding staircase. Moreover, instead of photography's promised placement alongside engravings, it would occupy a large room together with Class 29, Educational Works and Appliances, whose displays of school desks, orthographic projections, and diatonic harmoniums created an overall air of self-righteous propriety. According to the *Times*, photography had been placed in "the most inaccessible and unfavourable spot to which it could be banished"[38]—confined, like a naughty child, to its room, far from the international gathering below (fig. 125).

The ceremonial opening of the International Exhibition on May 1, 1862, was a grand affair, with choirs massed, anthems sung, and the usual dignified procession of royalty, commissioners, dignitaries, and worthies (fig. 126). But it lacked the sparkle of its predecessor in the Crystal Palace; the sudden illness of Prince Albert and his death in December 1861 had plunged the nation into mourning. The thrones on the grand dais stood empty, and solemnity characterized the formal addresses.[39] With his sound judgment, common sense, and devoted work, Prince Albert had won the hearts of the nation. His death came

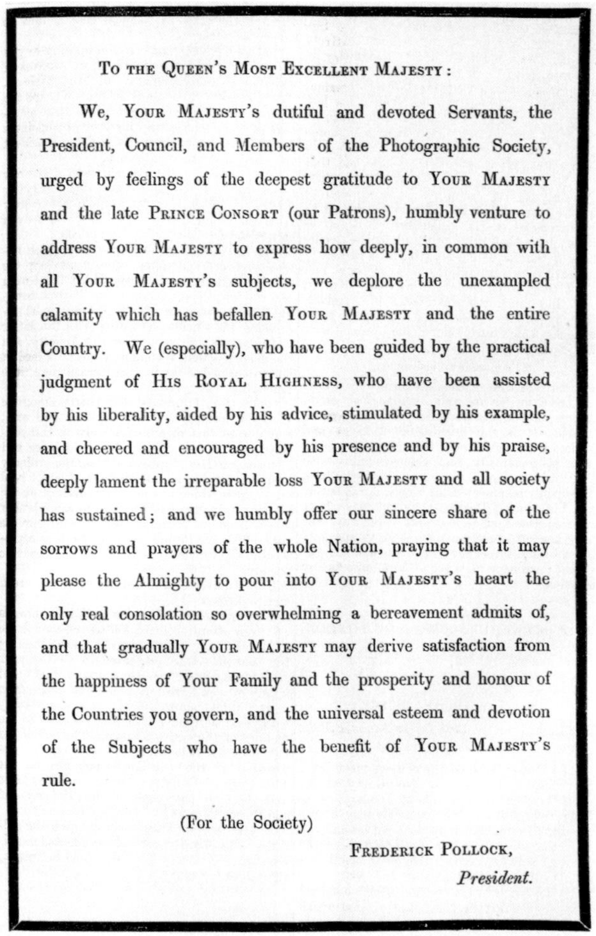

To the Queen's Most Excellent Majesty:

We, Your Majesty's dutiful and devoted Servants, the President, Council, and Members of the Photographic Society, urged by feelings of the deepest gratitude to Your Majesty and the late Prince Consort (our Patrons), humbly venture to address Your Majesty to express how deeply, in common with all Your Majesty's subjects, we deplore the unexampled calamity which has befallen Your Majesty and the entire Country. We (especially), who have been guided by the practical judgment of His Royal Highness, who have been assisted by his liberality, aided by his advice, stimulated by his example, and cheered and encouraged by his presence and by his praise, deeply lament the irreparable loss Your Majesty and all society has sustained; and we humbly offer our sincere share of the sorrows and prayers of the whole Nation, praying that it may please the Almighty to pour into Your Majesty's heart the only real consolation so overwhelming a bereavement admits of, and that gradually Your Majesty may derive satisfaction from the happiness of Your Family and the prosperity and honour of the Countries you govern, and the universal esteem and devotion of the Subjects who have the benefit of Your Majesty's rule.

(For the Society)

Frederick Pollock,

President.

Fig. 127. Frederick Pollock, Address of condolence to Queen Victoria. 20.6 x 12.6 cm (8⅛ x 5 in.). From *Journal of the Photographic Society*, January 15, 1862

as a severe blow to the Photographic Society, for throughout the 1850s his patronage had helped make photography widely acceptable to polite society, while his visits to the annual exhibitions gave encouragement to members and his commissions raised the status of individual photographers (fig. 127). Albert's death came at a time when the Photographic Society was undergoing a crisis of confidence that seemed impossible to shake off.

With all the controversy surrounding its classification at the International Exhibition, did British photography rise to the occasion? Did it find its niche in the temple of fine arts and win its spurs in the face of European competition? And what kind of a showing did paper negatives make in a field dominated by collodion?

For any attempt to find answers to these questions, a few statistics about Class 14 provide a useful context. Some can be gleaned from *Catalogue of the Photographs Exhibited in Class XIV*, a special, independent catalogue uncharacteristically issued by the commissioners, which lists titles of the British photographs exhibited in the manner of a traditional art exhibition catalogue.[40] It contains no information about cameras or equipment. The catalogue reveals that 131 photographers were represented and some 1,100 works displayed, a significant increase over the number of British photographs on view at the Great Exhibition.[41] Of these, the majority came from photographers with commercial or publishing interests. The exhibiting needs of amateurs were better served by a *salon des refusés* organized by the South London Photographic Society and held at the Crystal Palace in Sydenham.[42]

There are no similarly detailed catalogues for photographers of other nationalities, but we know that the French were the next most numerous exhibitors. The official catalogue lists 119 entrants, of which 26 were manufacturers of equipment and materials.[43] Other foreign nations were less well represented, and America, deeply preoccupied with the Civil War, sent almost no photographic entries. In 1851 the United States had been represented by some five hundred exhibitors and had swept the field with her daguerreotypes; in 1862 the nation could only muster a total of 95 exhibitors, chiefly manufacturers of agricultural machinery and the like, with photography represented by a single, rather lifeless display.[44]

Table 2. 1862 Exhibition Awards for Photography Showing Top Five Nations

	Number of Exhibitors	*Medals*	*Honorable Mentions*
Great Britain	150	27	53
France	119	32	47
Austria	12	4	7
Italy	9	2	1
Belgium	8	1	4

In reality, the competition lay between the British and the French. The commissioners appointed a jury that reflected national interests, its seven members being four British, two French, and a Belgian.[45] After careful deliberation they awarded 85 prize medals and 150 honorable mentions. Britain and France won the most awards, with Austria, Italy, and Belgium heading the list of runners-up (see table 2).[46]

It may seem that the French won proportionally more awards than their British counterparts, but in its report the jury explained otherwise: the entries for British photographic apparatus had been found to be of such "thorough excellence" that rather than present medals to a chosen few, the judges awarded honorable mentions to all.[47] This curious decision was perhaps an attempt to compensate for the appalling conditions in the central tower, where damp walls and wildly fluctuating temperatures wrought their special havoc on British equipment and photographs alike. According to one damning report, "Polish has been cracked; collodion bottles have exploded; dark tents and boxes of pine have warped and twisted in all ways; cameras have been stuck together in their sliding bodies." Photographs were similarly affected by the "combined action of damp and gases exhaled from the materials of the newly made walls."[48] First affected were "those tinted in water colours, which rapidly showed blotches of discoloration from some change in the pigments used." When these were removed by their owners, "a sorry display of patches of bare wall began to disfigure the room," and soon many of the "plain prints began to show signs of fading and yellowness."[49] Finally, "a portion of the skylight fell in, and dashed to fragments one of Mr. Breese's tables, containing his stereoscopes and exquisite transparencies."[50]

By the time the International Exhibition closed its doors to the public on November 1, 1862, it was reckoned that just over six million visitors had attended, a turnout broadly equivalent to that for the Great Exhibition of 1851. This time there was no large financial surplus;[51] reasons cited included the death of the prince consort and the effect of America's war on British pocketbooks and purses, especially in the cotton-manufacturing districts of the north.[52] Nevertheless, the exhibition, widely believed worthwhile, had clearly demonstrated how much the British economy had prospered since the previous exhibition (between 1850 and 1860 the value of British exports had risen, it was estimated, by 80 percent).[53]

A similar economic expansion had occurred with photography. By 1862 there were well over 2,500 professional photographers throughout Britain, and those employed in associated trades and occupations took this number even higher.[54] Photographic mass-production and retailing of the kind Talbot had dreamed during the 1840s was firmly established and thriving by 1860, with large sums of capital being invested in it. For example, when bids were invited for the exclusive right to photograph the displays and exhibits of the 1862 exhibition, the London Stereoscopic Company won the contract with a bid of 1,500 guineas, an unprecedented sum at the time.[55] The company then issued "nearly a million" prints, of which the vast majority were stereoscopic views (fig. 117). Requiring 70 reams of paper, 2,400 ounces of silver nitrate, and 200 gallons of albumen for production, this venture was photography raised to the level of factory production—a far cry from amateur practice.[56]

Amateur photographers, who in recent years had seen their ambitions all but evaporate in the heat and glare of commercial practice, had been hoping to regain ground through the exhibition, but both general trends and the unhappy display circumstances had worked against them. As for the dwindling band of photographers still dedicated to using paper negatives, only a few examples of their work were included in the exhibition, most likely to serve as illustrations of former achievements. If nothing else, the International Exhibition drew out the fact that now, unlike in 1851, there were two distinct constituencies of photographer: the amateur for whom self-expression and personal fulfillment were all, and the professional for whom survival meant catering to the broadest possible taste.[57]

AMATEURS REORGANIZE

Seeing commercial factors upend their chosen field and throw the Photographic Society into conflict, a group of photographers had come together in the summer of 1861 to form the Amateur Photographic Association.[58] Its main purpose was to "impart an interest and a stimulus to amateur photography."[59] Professional photographers were barred from joining, but membership was open to all amateurs, at home and overseas. The only requirement, apart from payment of the annual subscription, was for a member to submit "as many good negatives as he conveniently can," and from these the association made prints that it retailed on a commercial basis. Members were entitled to claim prints up to the value of their subscription; "subscribers," who did not submit negatives, could claim up to half that amount. The goal of the association

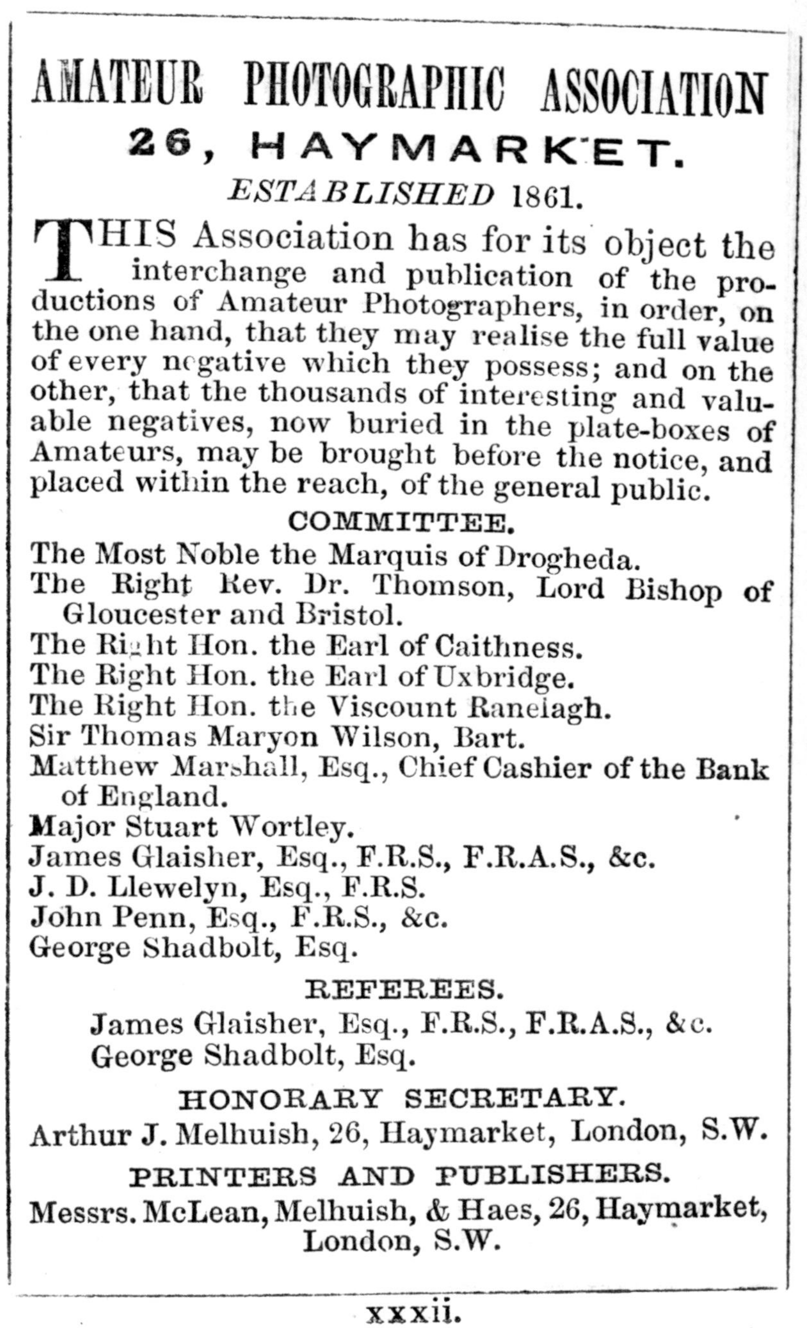

AMATEUR PHOTOGRAPHIC ASSOCIATION

26, HAYMARKET.

ESTABLISHED 1861.

THIS Association has for its object the interchange and publication of the productions of Amateur Photographers, in order, on the one hand, that they may realise the full value of every negative which they possess; and on the other, that the thousands of interesting and valuable negatives, now buried in the plate-boxes of Amateurs, may be brought before the notice, and placed within the reach, of the general public.

COMMITTEE.

The Most Noble the Marquis of Drogheda.
The Right Rev. Dr. Thomson, Lord Bishop of Gloucester and Bristol.
The Right Hon. the Earl of Caithness.
The Right Hon. the Earl of Uxbridge.
The Right Hon. the Viscount Ranelagh.
Sir Thomas Maryon Wilson, Bart.
Matthew Marshall, Esq., Chief Cashier of the Bank of England.
Major Stuart Wortley.
James Glaisher, Esq., F.R.S., F.R.A.S., &c.
J. D. Llewelyn, Esq., F.R.S.
John Penn, Esq., F.R.S., &c.
George Shadbolt, Esq.

REFEREES.

James Glaisher, Esq., F.R.S., F.R.A.S., &c.
George Shadbolt, Esq.

HONORARY SECRETARY.

Arthur J. Melhuish, 26, Haymarket, London, S.W.

PRINTERS AND PUBLISHERS.

Messrs. McLean, Melhuish, & Haes, 26, Haymarket, London, S.W.

xxxii.

Fig. 128. *Amateur Photographic Association.* Advertisement, 9 x 5.3 cm (3½ x 2⅛ in.). From *British Journal Photographic Almanac,* 1862

was, in the words of its advertisement, to create for "Amateur Photographers an 'Exchange Club' of the most comprehensive kind, a bond of union, and a medium of communication, such as no mere Society however excellent, can hope to offer" (fig. 128).[60]

Despite pointed criticism in the photographic press, the association quickly gathered momentum, especially after the Prince of Wales agreed to become its president. Other members of the aristocracy were then pleased to accept positions as vice presidents and members of council.[61] In social class and status the new association far outranked the Photographic Society. This exclusivity apparently gave it great appeal, and within a short time it could boast of having received 1,500 good negatives for printing and distribution. Offering substantial prizes each year for the best photographs also drew many participants, and by the time of the International Exhibition the association was self-assured enough to submit works in a collective entry, for which it won a prize medal. Having confounded doubters and established its credentials, the association received credit for the fact that "an additional impetus has been given to the operations of a large number of amateurs, the first love revived, and the waning zeal of many quickened, by finding a public for their productions."[62]

This was both a retrenchment and the beginning of a new epoch for amateur photography. Technically, collodion reigned supreme. In terms of approach, there was finally an unambiguous, clearly acknowledged distinction between amateur and professional practice. The old era had passed and another had begun.

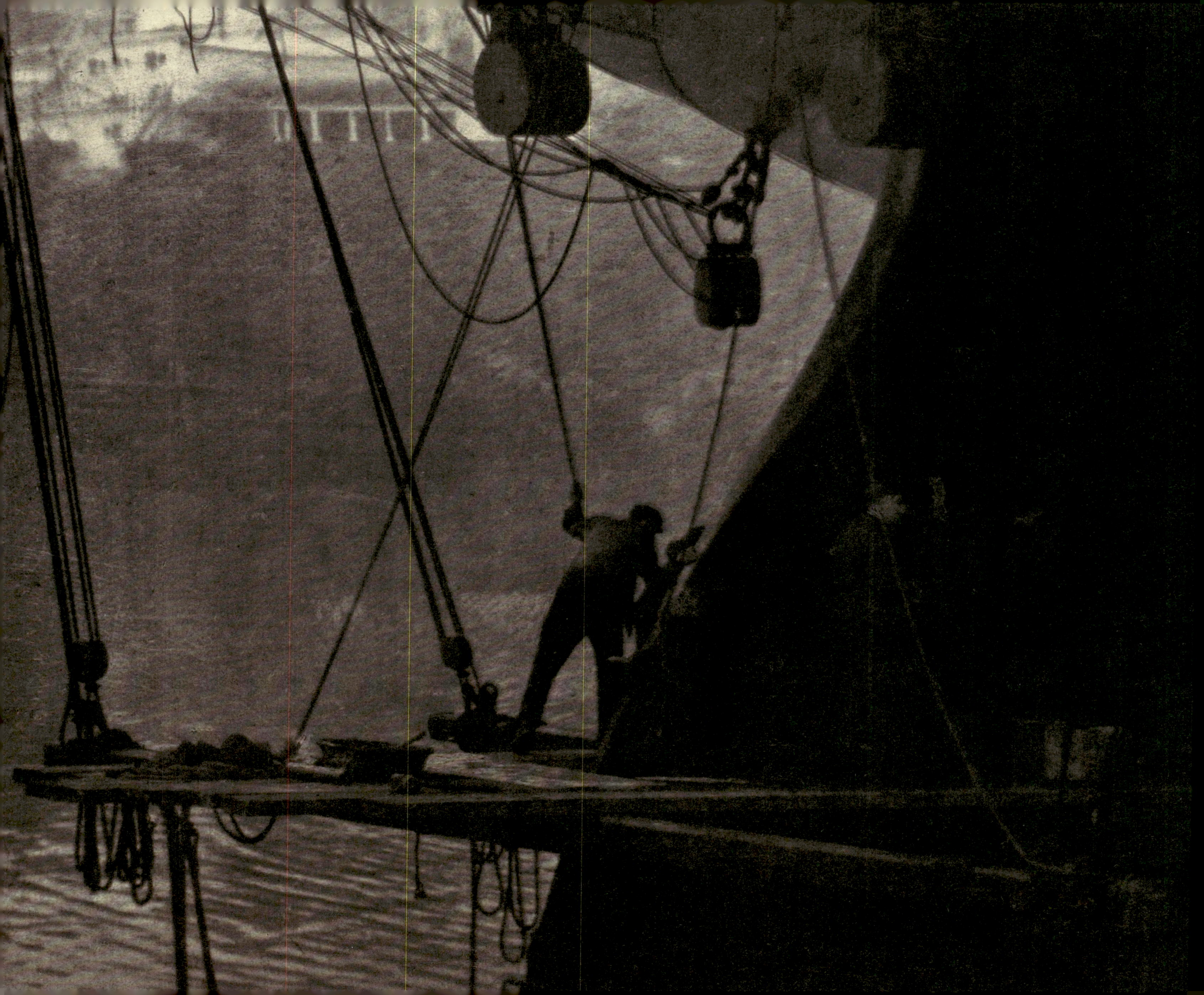

Epilogue: Revivals of the Paper Negative after the 1860s

For most of the 1860s, the Photographic Society was a shadow of its former self and constantly on the verge of bankruptcy. Its annual exhibitions declined in both quality and number of submissions, and after 1865 the society abandoned them for a number of years.[1] During the same period, the Amateur Photographic Association went from strength to strength. An international fraternity of amateurs was drawn to its annual competition, where handsome and expensive prizes were awarded. By 1867, more than a thousand images had been submitted from India alone.[2] The association's success was built on demanding little of its members while giving them much in return.

No records were kept of the kinds of negatives sent in to the association, so we do not know whether paper negatives still held any appeal for members,[3] but it is unlikely. A look through its surviving albums suggests overwhelmingly that collodion was the preferred medium.[4] With the Photographic Society, one suspects that the situation was similar.[5] By the mid-1860s, the collodion process had reached into every corner of photographic practice. In clarity, detail, tonal gradation, and utility it had been so greatly improved and refined that it was possible to achieve brilliant images with exposure times unimaginable a decade earlier. The days of the paper negative appeared to be over.

However, just at what seemed like the moment of demise for these archaic processes, interest was revived in the use of paper for making negatives. Frustrated by the elaborate procedures required for the wet-collodion process and weary of the weight and expense of glass, photographers began to cast about for viable alternatives. First, they sought to perfect a dry process (i.e., one that would not have to be exposed while still moist), using gelatin as a substitute for collodion. Then they began to experiment with paper as a support for these new emulsions.

Opposite: Fig. 129. Detail of Alvin Langdon Coburn, *The Rudder, Liverpool*, 1906 (see fig. 133)

In 1870, George Dawson, professor of photography at King's College, London, described the ease with which he had carried "several dozens of sheets of sensitised waxed paper" on his summer wanderings in Scotland, and expressed surprise that few attempts had been made to revive the process using modern materials.[6] After months of experimentation with different types of paper and collodion emulsions, however, he reluctantly admitted that much remained to be done "before the process can be pronounced anything like perfect."[7] Dawson was defeated by the impracticality of coating paper with collodion, but his ambition to reintroduce paper negatives proved to be an important marker in the gradual evolution of photographic chemistry away from the era of glass.

At around the same time another amateur photographer, Richard Leach Maddox, began experimenting with collodion and gelatin emulsions in an attempt to create a dry process on glass. His research, an account of which was published in the *British Journal of Photography* in September 1871, is now thought of as having heralded a whole new direction for photography, the dry-plate era.[8] His process, notoriously complex, was well beyond the reach of the average amateur photographer working in a darkroom at home, but his success in creating a workable dry process encouraged others to experiment in the "comparatively neglected field" of gelatin emulsions.[9]

Throughout the 1870s, gelatin increasingly featured in new photographic processes, which were being introduced with unfailing regularity as the market continued to expand. The turning point came in 1885. As one writer summarized, "The year may be considered almost revolutionary, for, . . . both in positive and negative work gelatino-chloride or gelatino-bromide papers seem destined to gain a footing in the place of processes and materials previously in vogue. . . . It is now some years since negatives were taken, experimentally, on the same paper. At the present time, however, . . . there appears every probability that paper will shortly, to a very large extent, replace glass for negative work."[10]

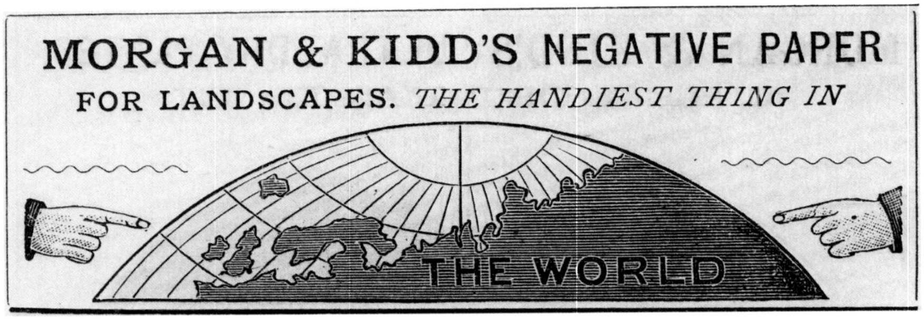

Fig. 130. *Morgan & Kidd's Negative Paper.* Advertisement, 2.9 x 8.9 cm (1⅛ x 3½ in.). From *British Journal Photographic Almanac,* 1888, p. 556.

These new paper negatives with gelatin silver emulsions found favor with amateurs for a number of reasons (fig. 130). They were significantly cheaper, lighter, and sturdier than glass plates of equivalent size and, once waxed or impregnated with castor oil to make them transparent, yielded splendid results. One amateur observed that with the new negatives he could work directly on the surface of the paper, "adding effect and suppressing undesirable and obtrusive detail," with a degree of finesse that was impossible with glass plates. This kind of handwork, he asserted, when done with skill, enabled a photographer to fashion works of great breadth and simplicity that were more worthy of the name of art than the mechanical prints of sharply focused negatives.[11]

Also in 1885 the American entrepreneur and inventor George Eastman introduced his "American film" system to the British public, setting in motion events that would profoundly affect the future direction of amateur photography. When Eastman's American film and roll holder were shown at the International Inventions Exhibition held in London that summer, even the *Times,* that most dignified and staid of British newspapers, ran an editorial predicting that the film would bring about "a revolution in out-of-door photography." The quality of its results could not "be distinguished from those made from glass negatives."[12] The *Times* was not alone in this judgment, for the exhibition jury awarded the Eastman Dry Plate and Film Company a silver medal for its apparatus and films.[13] Like the negative papers being introduced by British manufacturers, the American film employed paper as a support for a silver gelatin emulsion. But the principle was quite different: in Eastman's system the paper was a vehicle to carry the light-sensitive silver gelatin emulsion prior to exposure, and once the "film" had been developed was stripped away. This left a transparent negative that was mounted directly onto a sheet of glass and printed by contact in the normal way.[14]

Eastman's stated objective was to perfect "a system of film photography that would supplant the use of glass dry plates,"[15] and his 1885 success was merely an intermediate step along the way to his most memorable and significant invention, a small handheld camera loaded with a roll of American film that was capable of taking one hundred exposures. Everything about the camera was kept as simple as possible, and it was not even possible to adjust the focus or the exposure. The fact that the camera could be used by anyone regardless of experience proved to be an enormous attraction. Eastman christened it the "Kodak," and under this banner an entirely new branch of amateur photography was launched.[16] Instead of composing a picture by carefully maneuvering the camera and tripod, the new breed of snapshooter merely aimed his Kodak at his subject and fired the shutter. No understanding was required of either photography or picture making.[17] Even the tricky business of developing and printing was taken care of by Eastman at his factories—in Harrow in Britain, and in Rochester in the United States. The act of taking a photograph had been reduced, in Eastman's immortal advertising slogan, to "You push the button and we do the rest" (fig. 131).[18]

The revolution launched by the arrival of the Kodak camera was far more profound than anything the *Times* had prophesied. Photography had been placed in the hands of the uninitiated. While a novice of the 1850s needed a working understanding of chemistry, optics, and exposure, the Kodaker needed none of these. Photography branched off in an entirely new direction, turning from the ideologies and aesthetics that had sustained much of amateur practice to embark upon a love affair with the snapshot.

This widening of the range of photographic practitioners gave new vigor to the British photographic industry, as ever more manufacturers entered the field hopeful of finding a niche in the amateur market. The number of camera owners swelled, and scarcely a year went by without a new photographic society being formed. By 1892 there were 240 scattered throughout Britain, ranging in size and intent from the parent body, now renamed the Photographic Society of Great Britain (it became the Royal Photographic Society two years later), to the

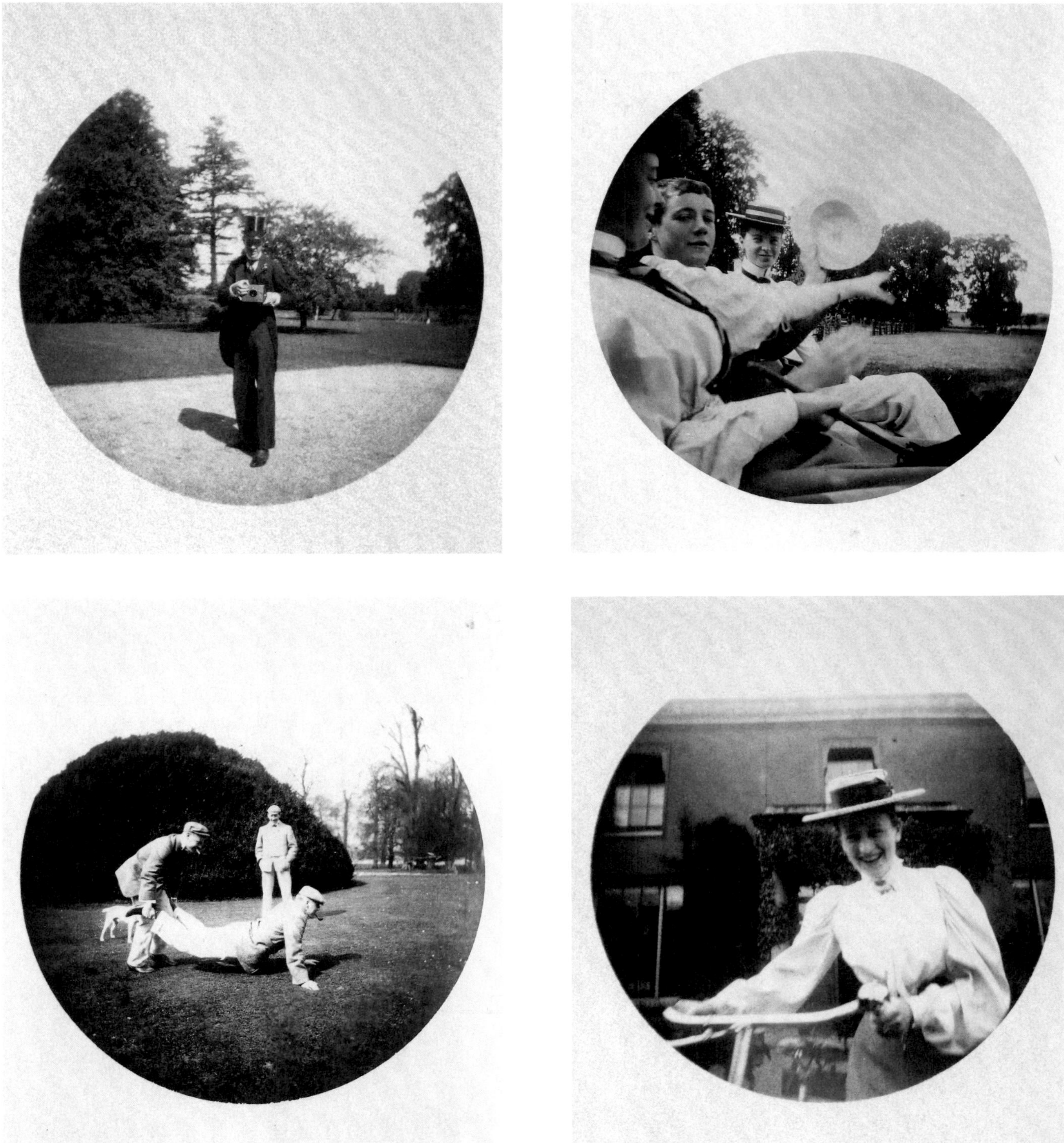

Fig. 131. Unknown photographer, Four snapshots taken with a Kodak camera, 1895. Each, diam. 8.5 cm (3⅜ in.). Private collection

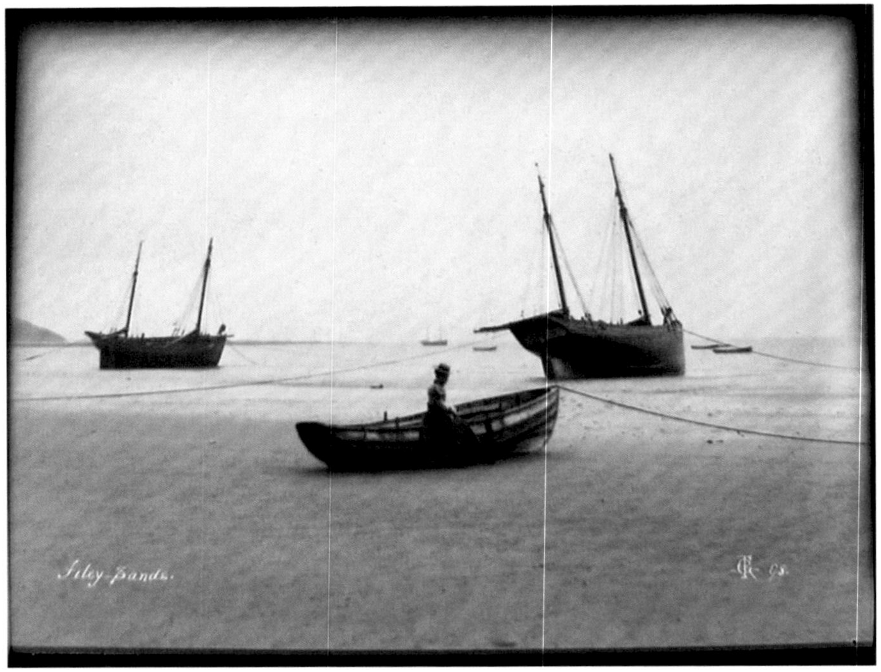

Fig. 132. George Fowler Jones, *Filey Beach, 1898.* Image digitally created from a paper negative, 16.5 x 21.5 cm (6½ x 8½ in.). The Royal Photographic Society Collection at the National Media Museum, Bradford

Light and Truth Postal Photographic Club based in Plymouth.[19] Annual exhibitions became mainstays of the calendar, with many photographers working steadfastly throughout the summer season in hope of winning a coveted prize medal for excellence.[20] Much of what was exhibited now appears pedestrian, with greater emphasis placed on technical perfection than aesthetic judgment. Nearly every town of consequence had its specialist retailer offering equipment and materials for every need and pocketbook. From the earnest amateur with a field camera to the Kodak snapshooter happily clicking away, photography had entered the mainstream and become a national pastime (fig. 132).

Against this background of mass activity and widespread mediocrity, it was inevitable that certain photographers would rebel and appropriate the high ground. Interest in the new approach, called Pictorialism, transcended national boundaries, with activity in many parts of Europe and in the United States. In May 1892 a small number of well-respected and influential British photographers broke away from the Photographic Society of Great Britain to found the Linked Ring Brotherhood, an informal society "without any constitution, entrance fee, or subscription" and open by election to "anyone of good reputation who has shown marked artistic ability and conscientious work."[21] The formation of the Linked Ring, with its annual salon, marked the effective beginning of Pictorialism in Britain. Internationally, the movement ultimately included such notable photographers as Alvin Langdon Coburn, George Davison, F. Holland Day, Theodor and Oskar Hofmeister, Heinrich Kühn, Edward Steichen, Alfred Stieglitz, and Clarence H. White.[22] Eager to reassert the artistic potential of the medium, the movement drew inspiration from the artistically pioneering photographs of the 1850s and 1860s. Coburn, for example, was a great admirer of Hill & Adamson and Thomas Keith, collecting examples of their negatives. In his quest for self-expression he adopted the aesthetic qualities of the calotype in his own work, massing light and shade and softening detail (figs. 129, 133).[23] As one modern historian characterized the movement: "Pictorialism is at once more sophisticated than the Picturesque, and more nuanced in its exploitation of the technical resources of the medium. But above all it shifts the balance finally and decisively away from the traditional concern with the medium's mimetic efficiency, towards the photographer's own more private and subjective needs."[24] Among photographers with these common goals there were then differences of preference, "straight versus manipulated, naturalistic versus impressionist, sharp versus 'fuzzy' modes of working."[25]

The impressionistic look that we now associate with Pictorialism was frequently achieved by manual intervention on the surface of the negative, prior to printing, with a pencil, stump or brush. Because applying pigment directly onto glass or film is difficult, some Pictorialists used paper negatives, which offered an ideal surface for their handiwork. The process worked particularly well with a large negative, which could be made in one of two ways. Some were made directly in the camera, using a large-format camera, but this meant long exposures and the kind of cumbersome equipment familiar from the 1850s. The other possibility was to start with the negative taken in a hand camera, as this was more manageable and required a shorter exposure. The negative was then printed using an enlarger, a device that was just coming into more general use by some of the more progressive photographic establishments at about this time.[26] The resulting positive print was then placed in contact with a further sheet of paper and exposed to create an enlarged, paper negative. It was a long

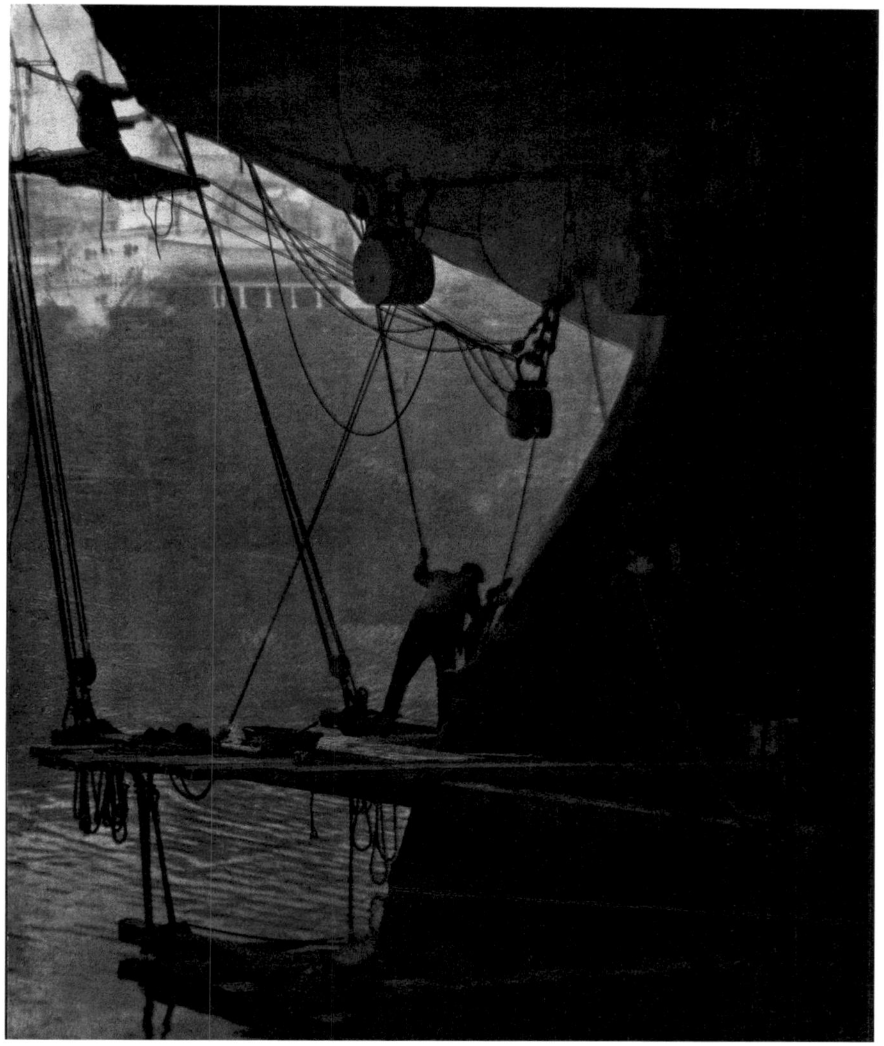

Fig. 133. Alvin Langdon Coburn, *The Rudder, Liverpool*, 1906. Gum bichromate over platinum print, 36.2 x 28.6 cm (14¼ x 11¼ in.) The Metropolitan Museum of Art, New York, Alfred Stieglitz Collection, 1933, 33.43.199

and tedious process, but for the Pictorialist committed to achieving artistic results, the additional stages of darkroom work were no deterrent.

The overriding concern now was the appearance of the finished print, and to achieve desired effects, old processes were revived and new ones introduced.[27] Talbot's plain salted paper process was found to produce admirable results when applied to the rough-textured drawing papers much favored by those wishing to suppress the finer details of the image.[28] The carbon pigment process, a method explored in the 1850s, was revived, modified, and widely adopted by Pictorialists, who delighted in mastering its elaborate procedures and using it to create finished prints likened to charcoal drawings.[29]

Platinum papers, added to the repertoire of photographic printing processes in 1878, were slow working and expensive but much favored for their soft, neutral tonality, which remained in vogue for many years.[30] In comparison with other printing papers in more general use, these specialized papers were notoriously insensitive to light. When paper negatives came into their own once more for large-format exhibition prints, they could not be successfully printed on platinum papers by enlargement; the only effective way was by direct contact in a printing frame.

During the first quarter of the twentieth century, widespread enthusiasm for the aesthetic values of Pictorialism and the resurgence of annual photographic exhibitions introduced a whole new generation to the benefits of paper negatives. Although this was far removed from the calotype process, the fact that photographers were using paper negatives to make fine exhibition prints linked them ideologically to that first generation of photographers who had struggled to establish the medium as a fine art during the 1850s. And so it was that when photography celebrated its seventy-fifth anniversary in 1914,[31] paper negatives were still being used to create artworks of a high order.[32]

PLATES

Early Years of the Calotype, 1840–1850

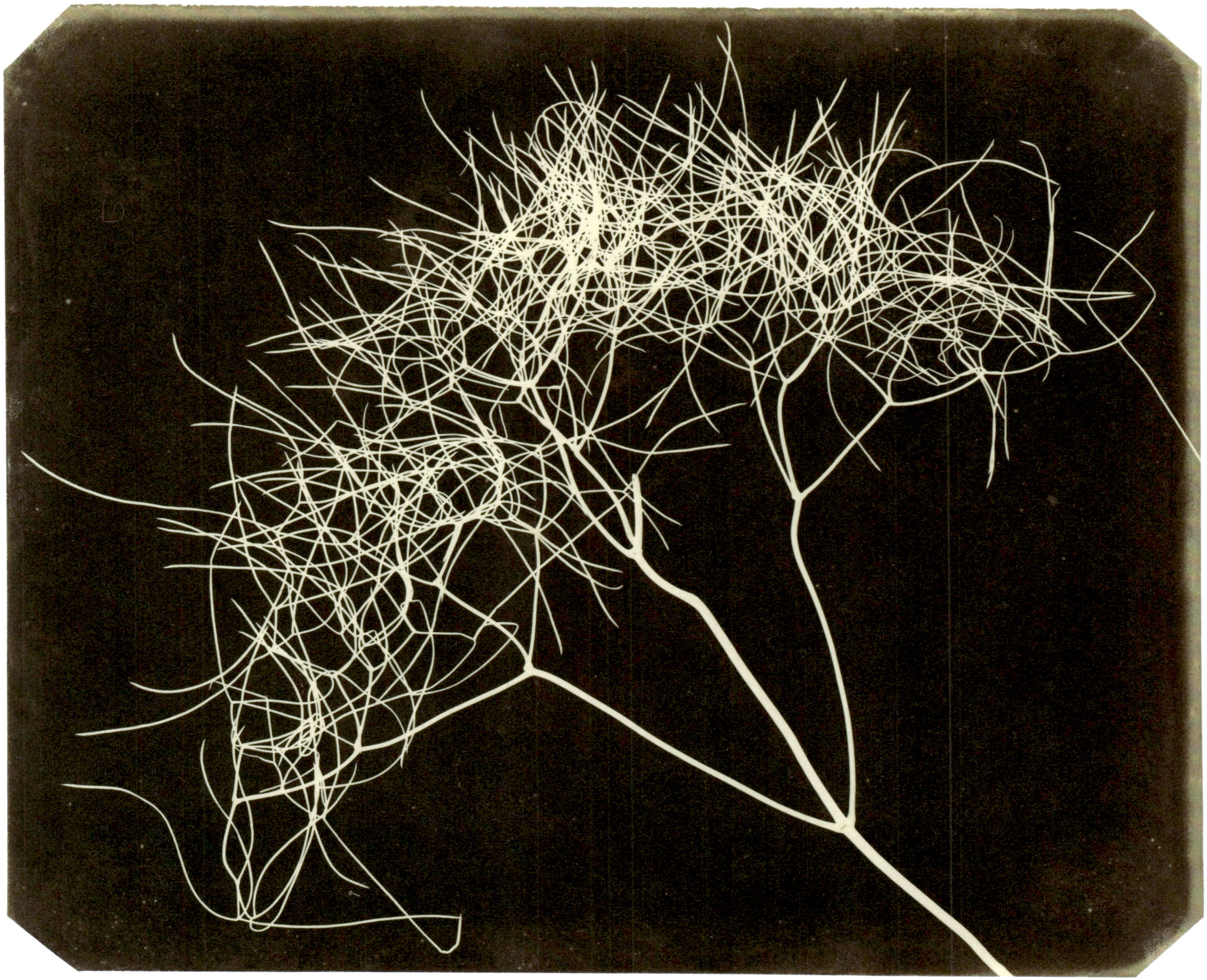

1. William Henry Fox Talbot, Wild Fennel, 1841–42

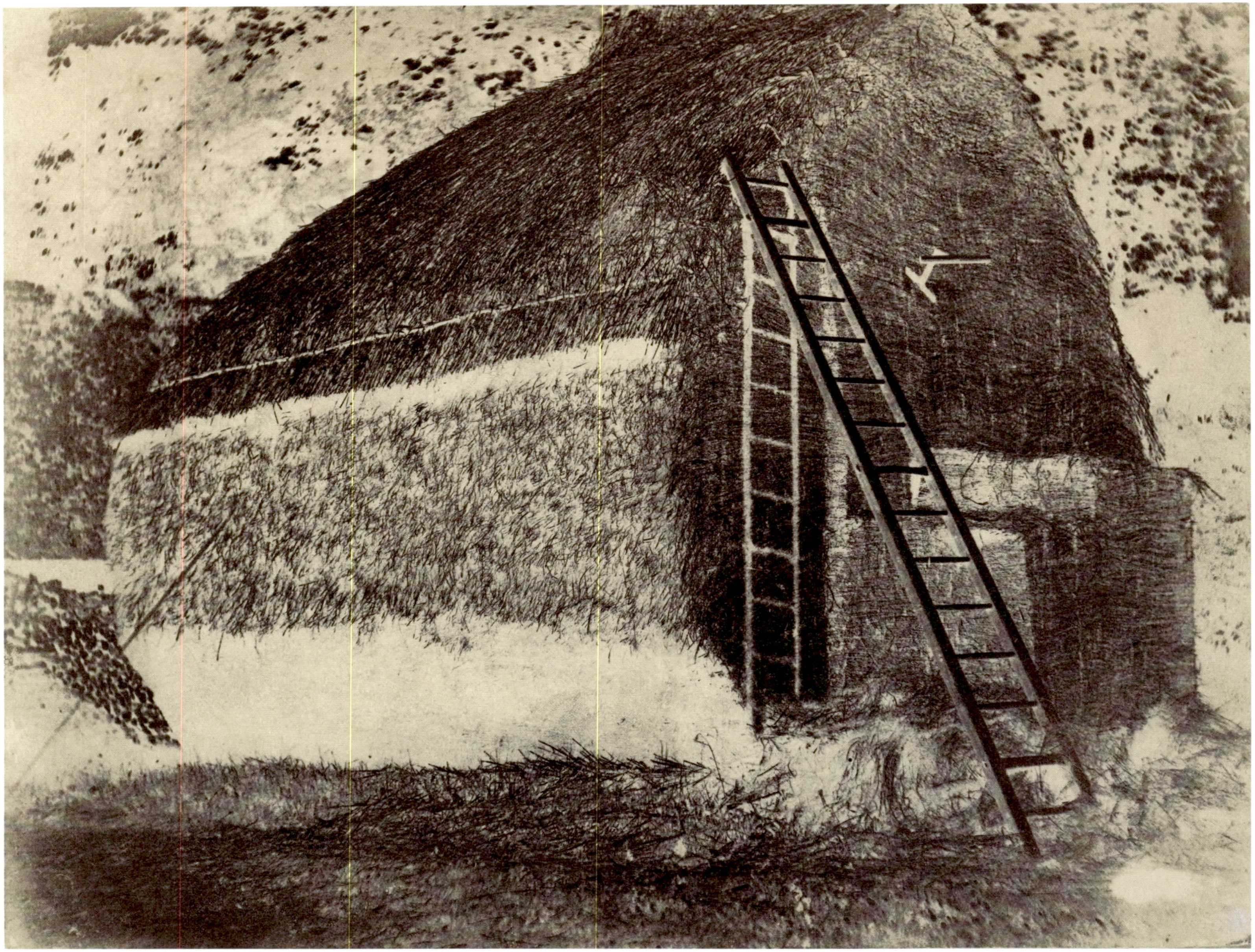

2. William Henry Fox Talbot, *The Haystack* (negative), April 1844

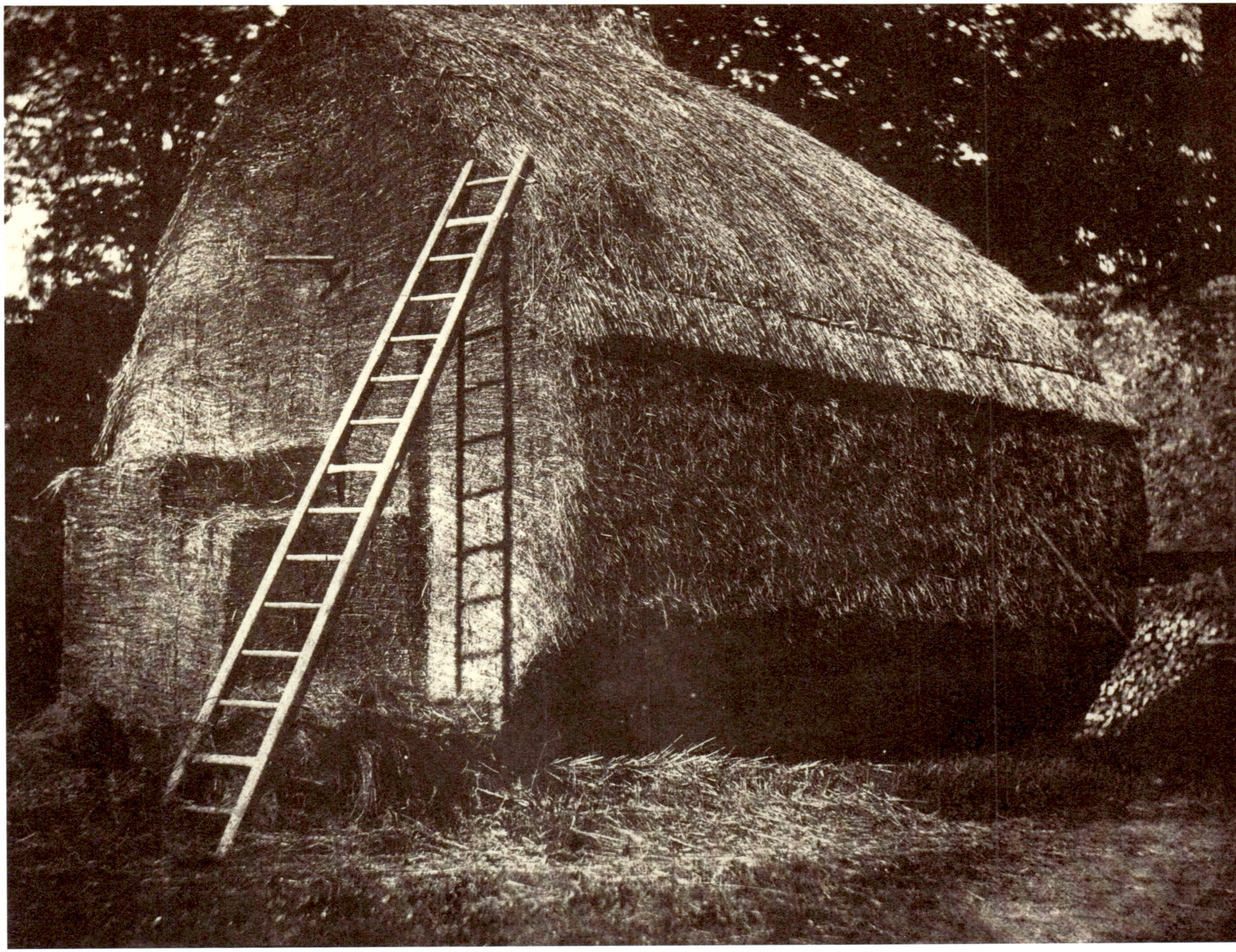

3. William Henry Fox Talbot, *The Haystack*, April 1844

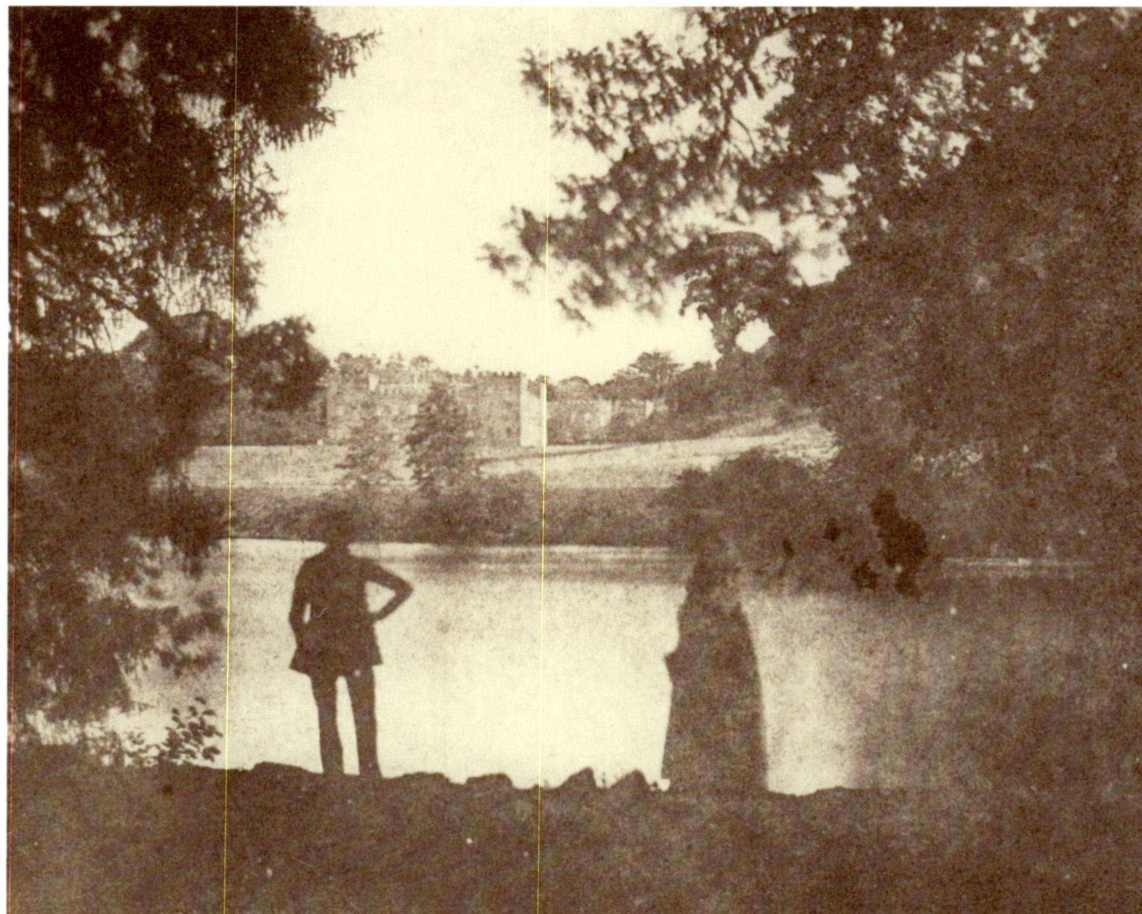

4. William Henry Fox Talbot, *Ugbrook Park,* 1842

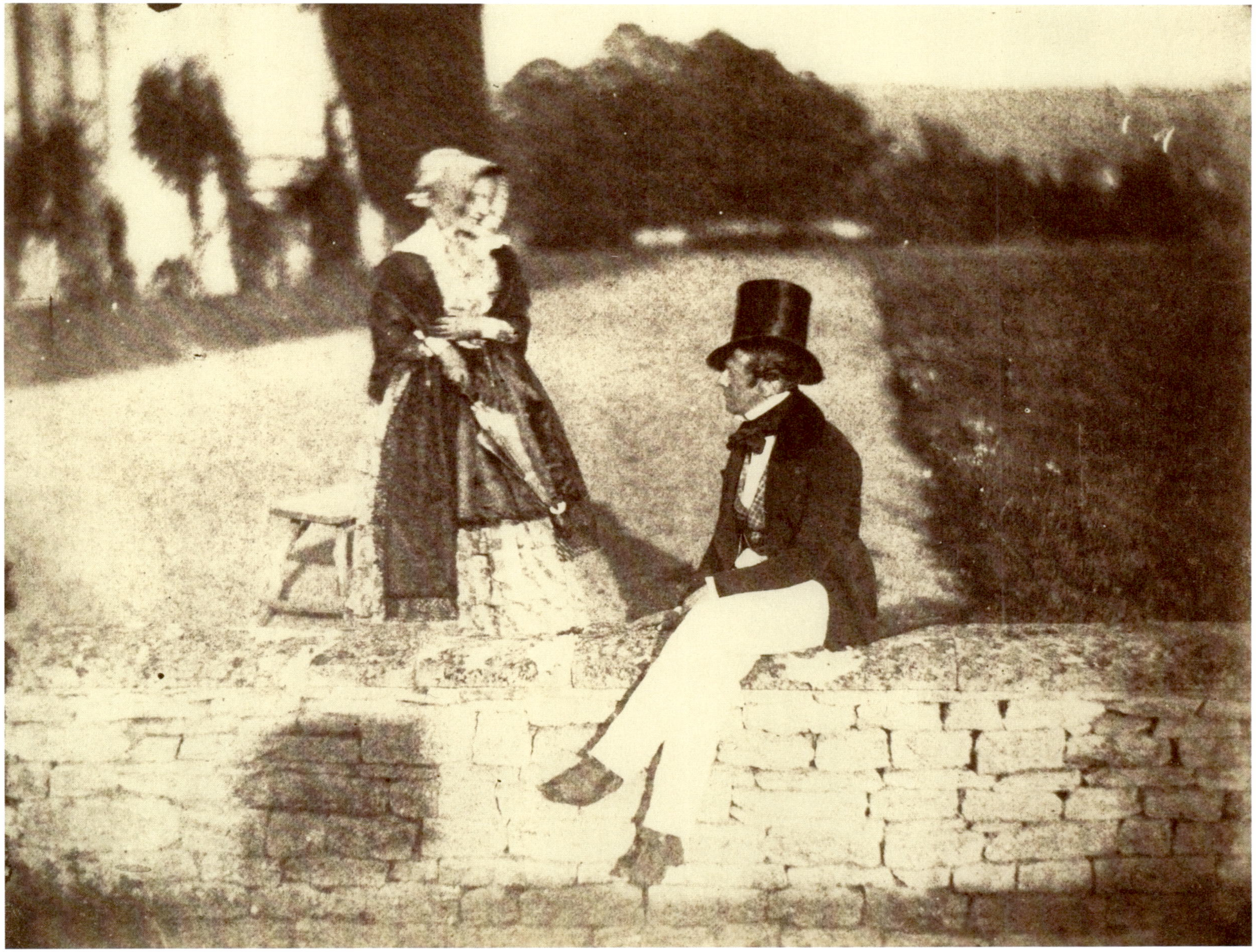

5. Calvert Richard Jones, Two Figures on the Terrace at Lacock Abbey, ca. 1845

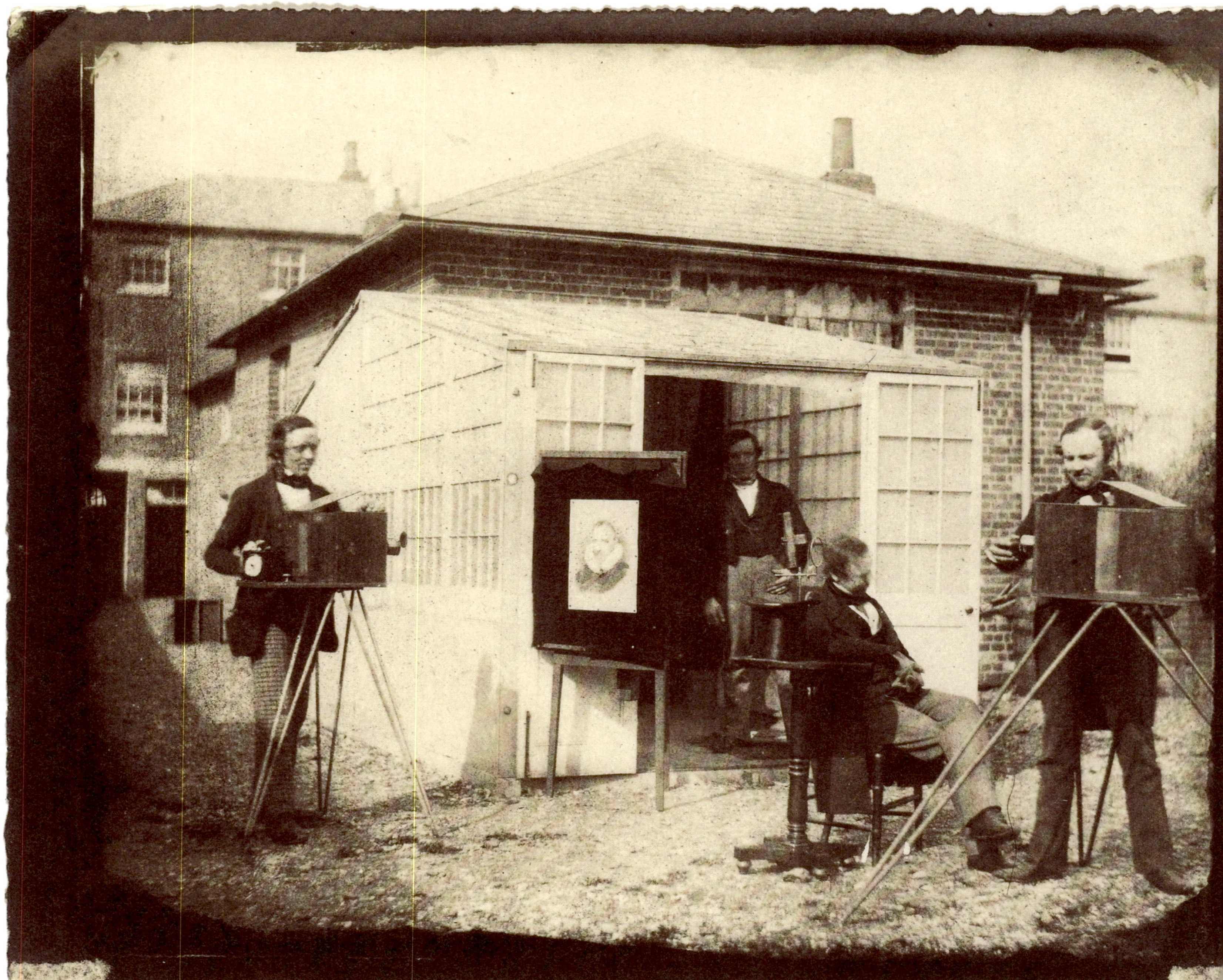

6. William Henry Fox Talbot and Nicolaas Henneman, The Reading Establishment, 1846

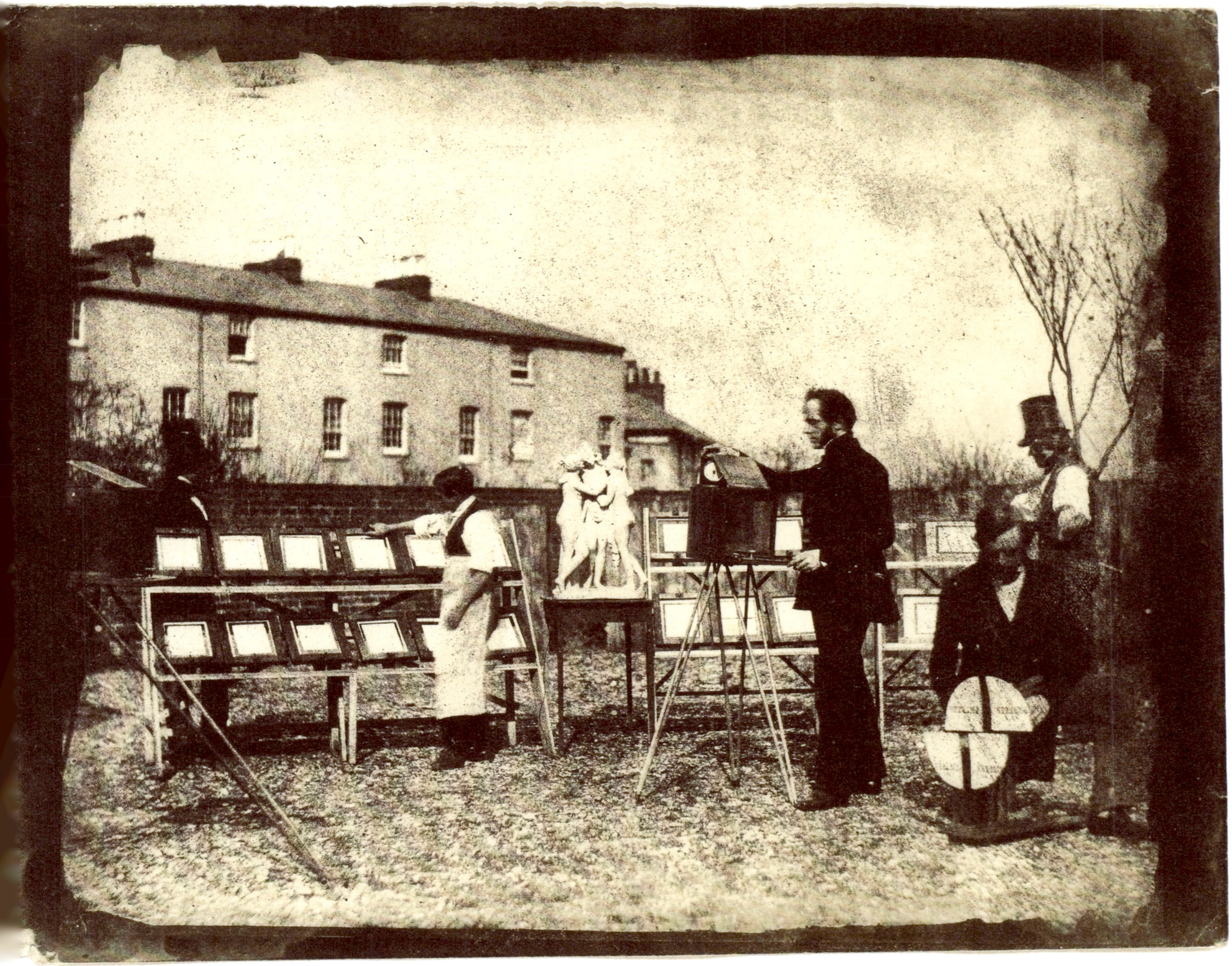

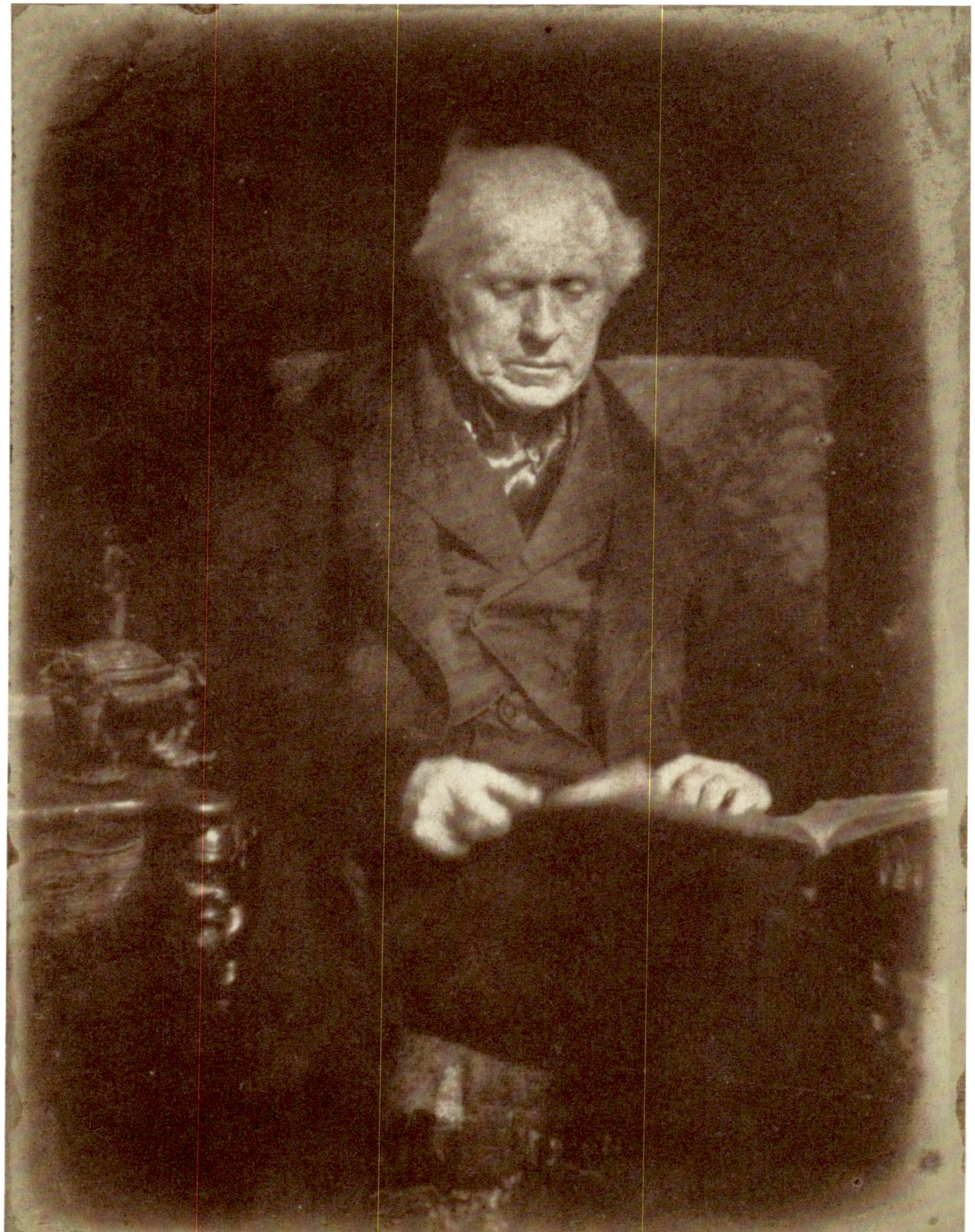

7. David Octavius Hill and Robert Adamson, *Sir David Brewster*, ca. 1844

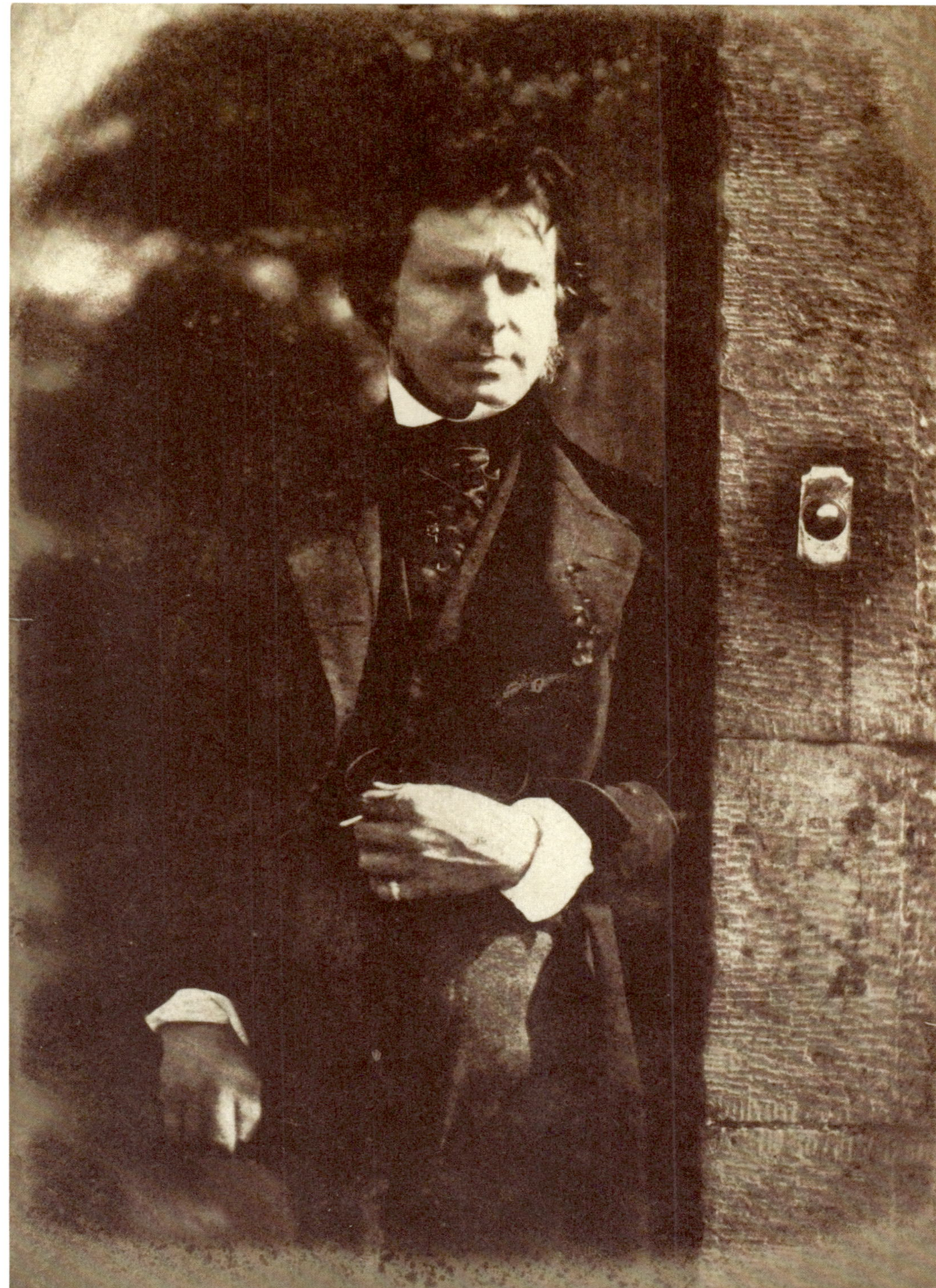

8. David Octavius Hill and Robert Adamson, David Octavius Hill at the Gate of Rock House, ca. 1845

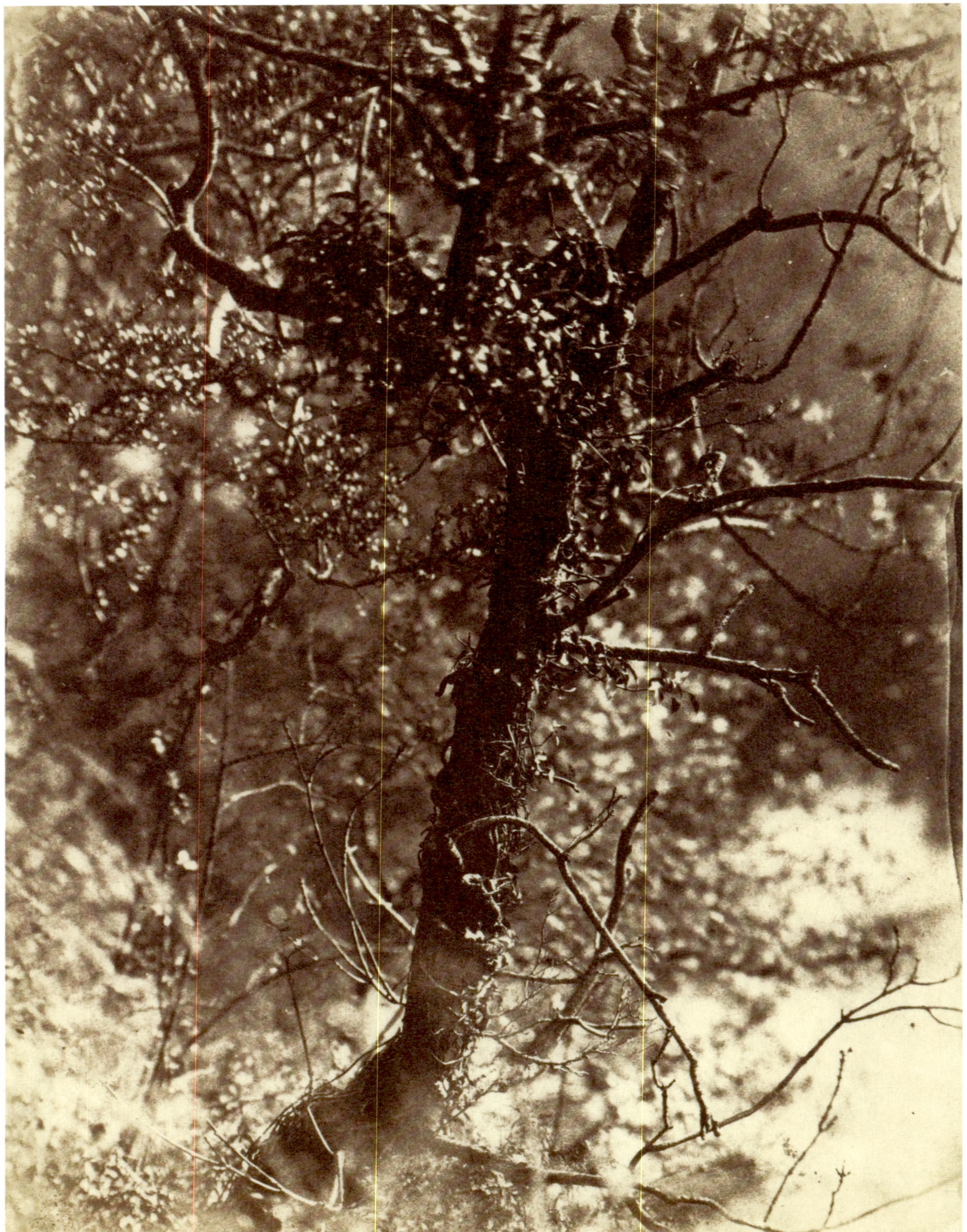

9. David Octavius Hill and Robert Adamson, *The Fairy Tree, Colinton*, late 1846

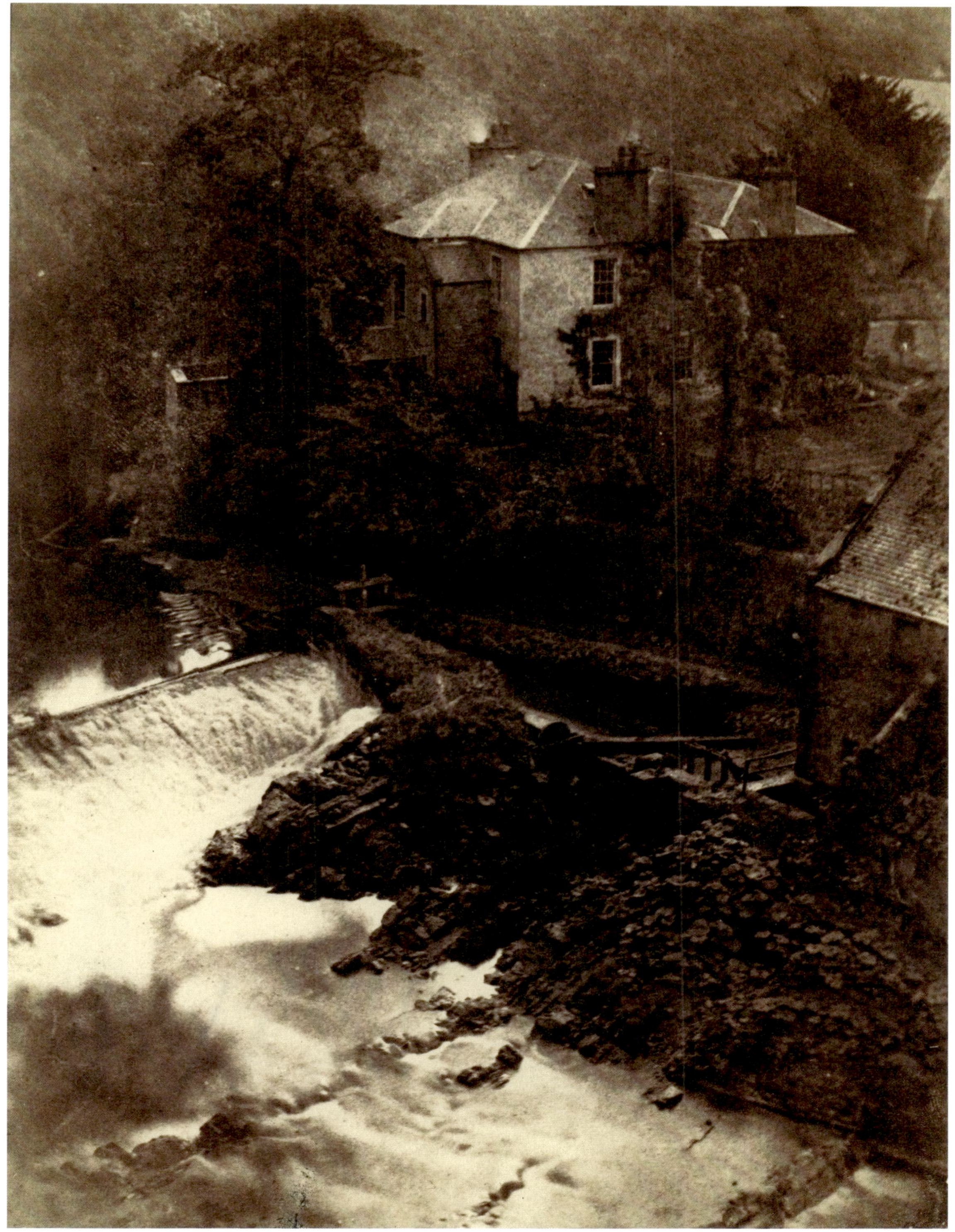

10. David Octavius Hill and Robert Adamson, Colinton Manse and Weir, late 1846

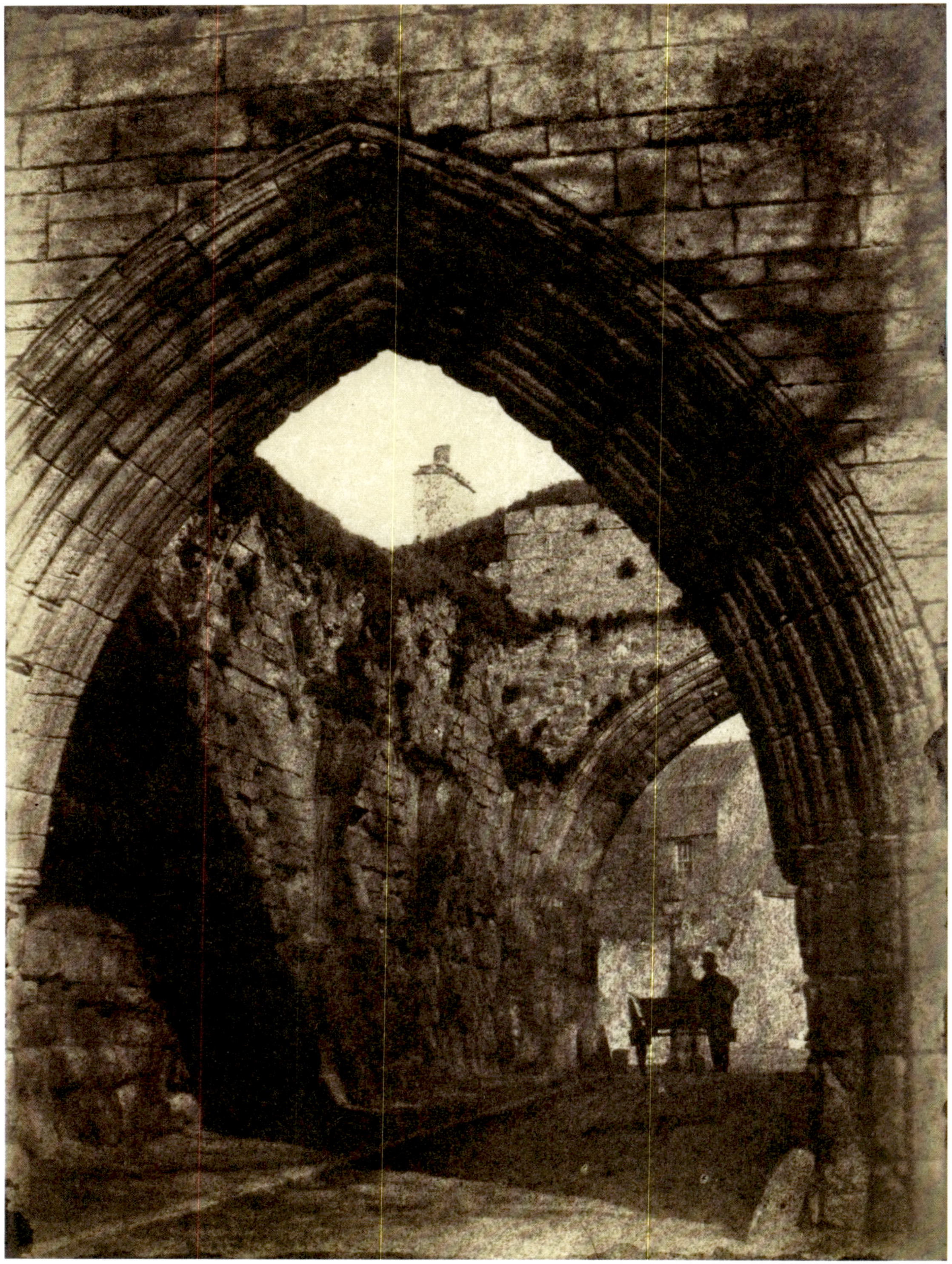

11. David Octavius Hill and Robert Adamson,
The Pends, St. Andrews, ca. 1844

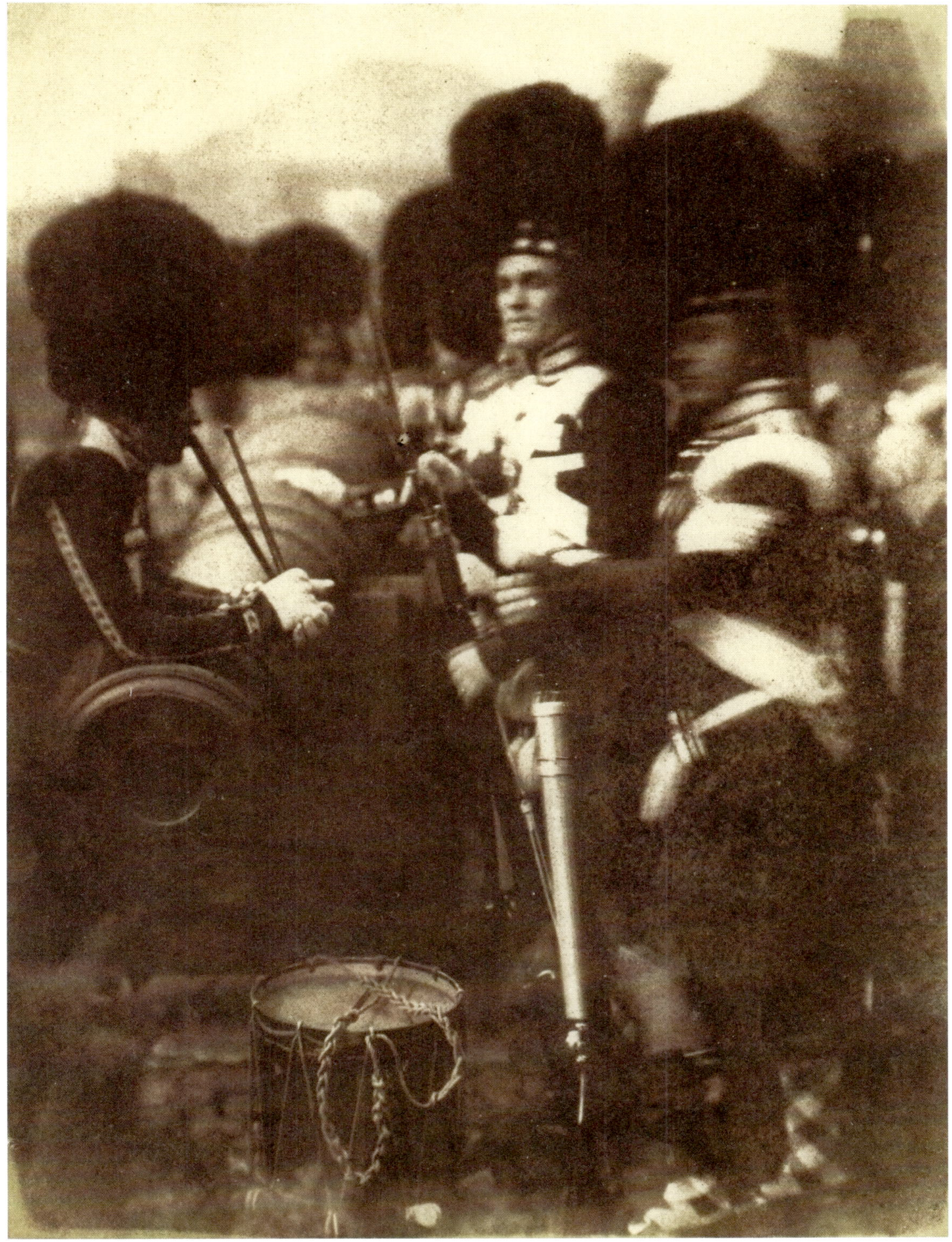

12. David Octavius Hill and Robert Adamson,
92nd Gordon Highlanders at Edinburgh Castle, April 1846

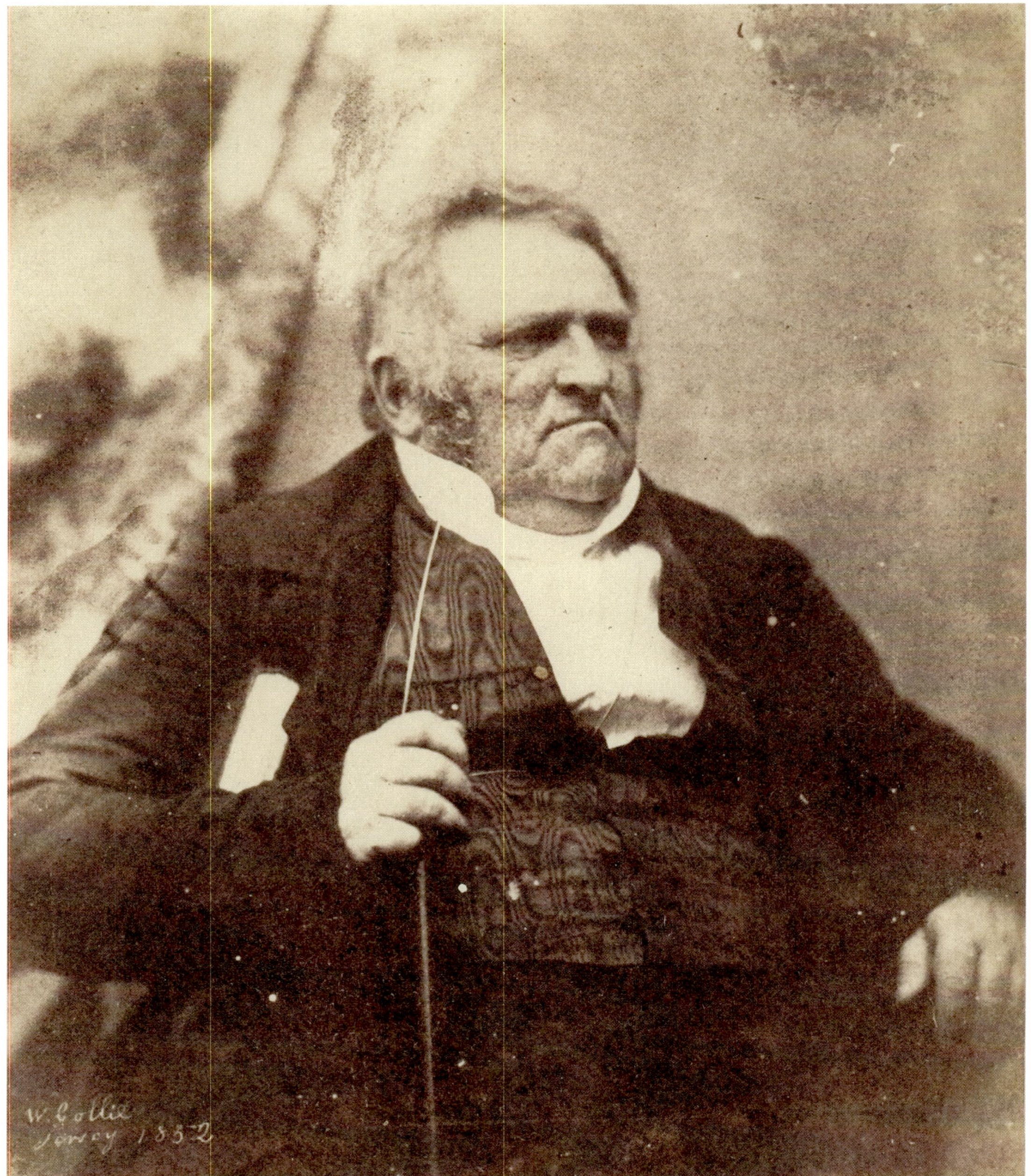

13. William Collie, *Dr. Wolfe*, 1852

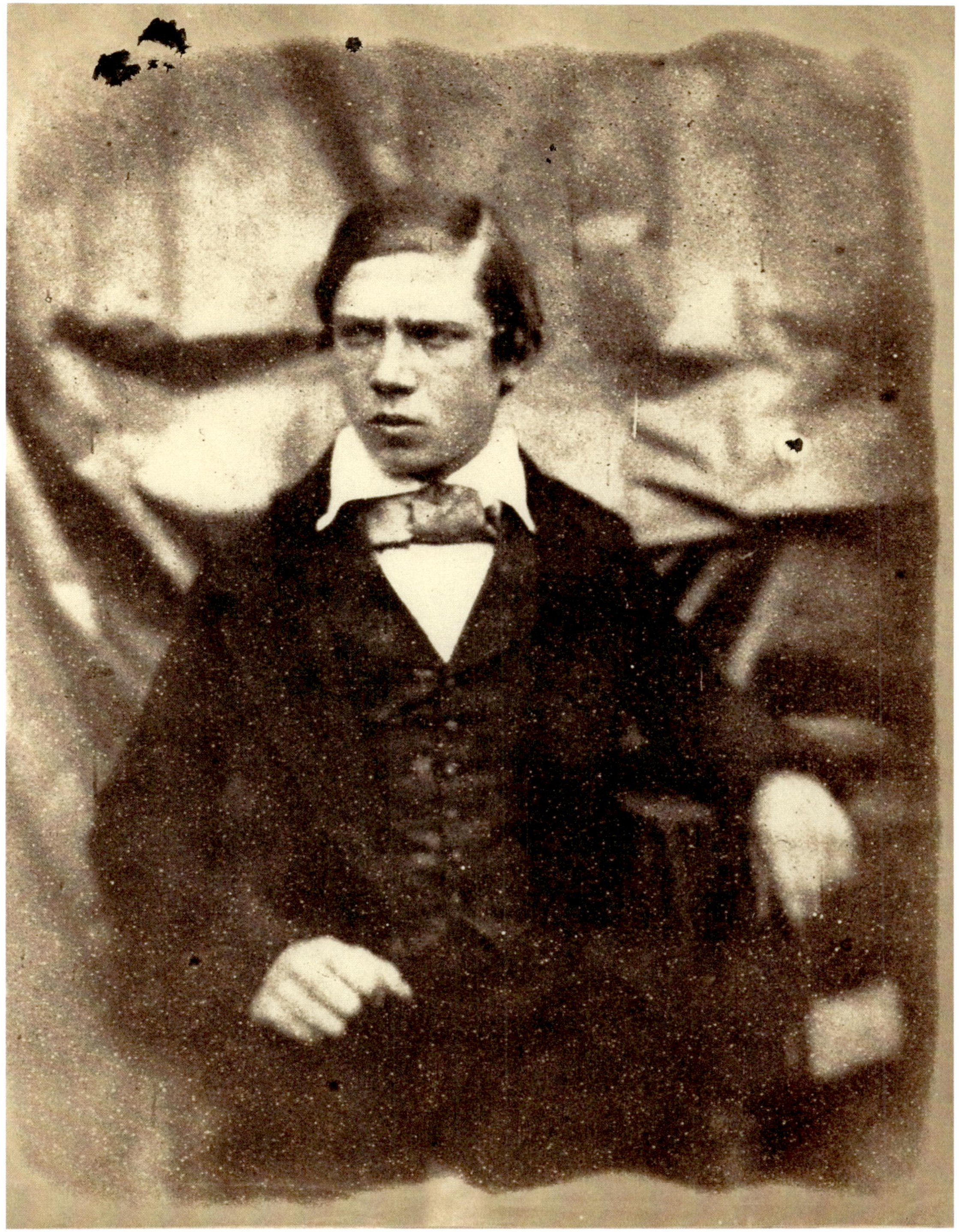

14. William Collie, Young Man, Seated, late 1840s

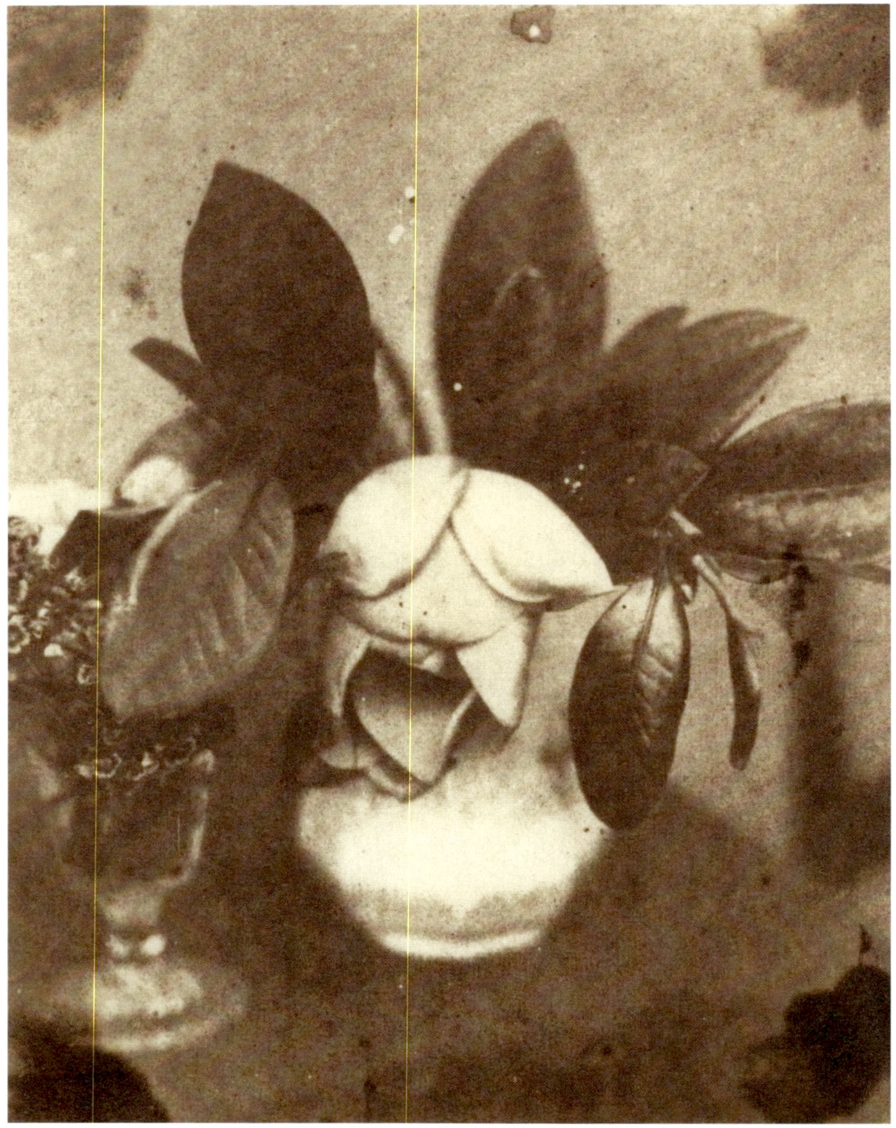

15. William Collie, Camellia, late 1840s

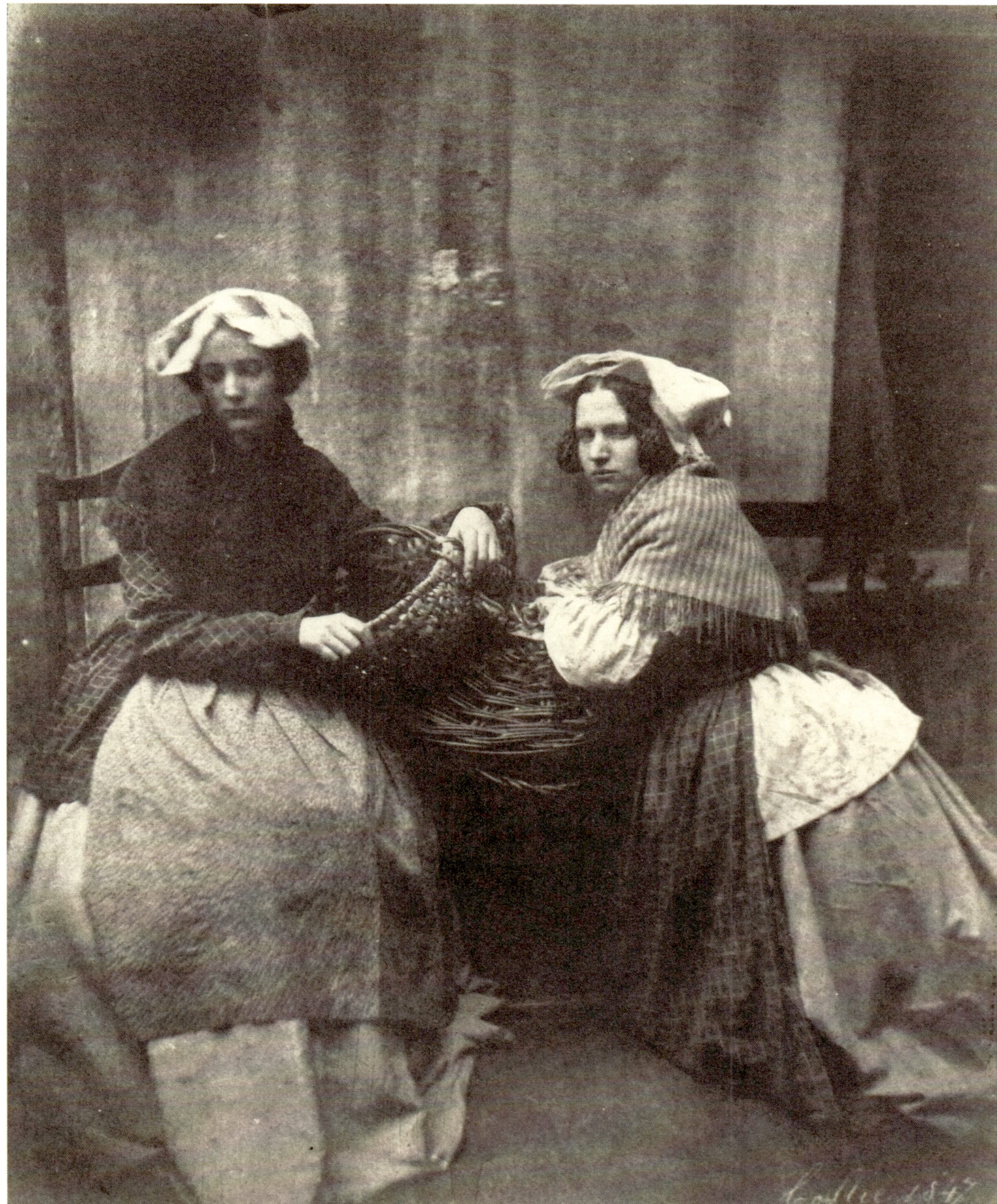

16. William Collie, Market Women, St. Helier, Jersey, 1847

The Calotype in Great Britain

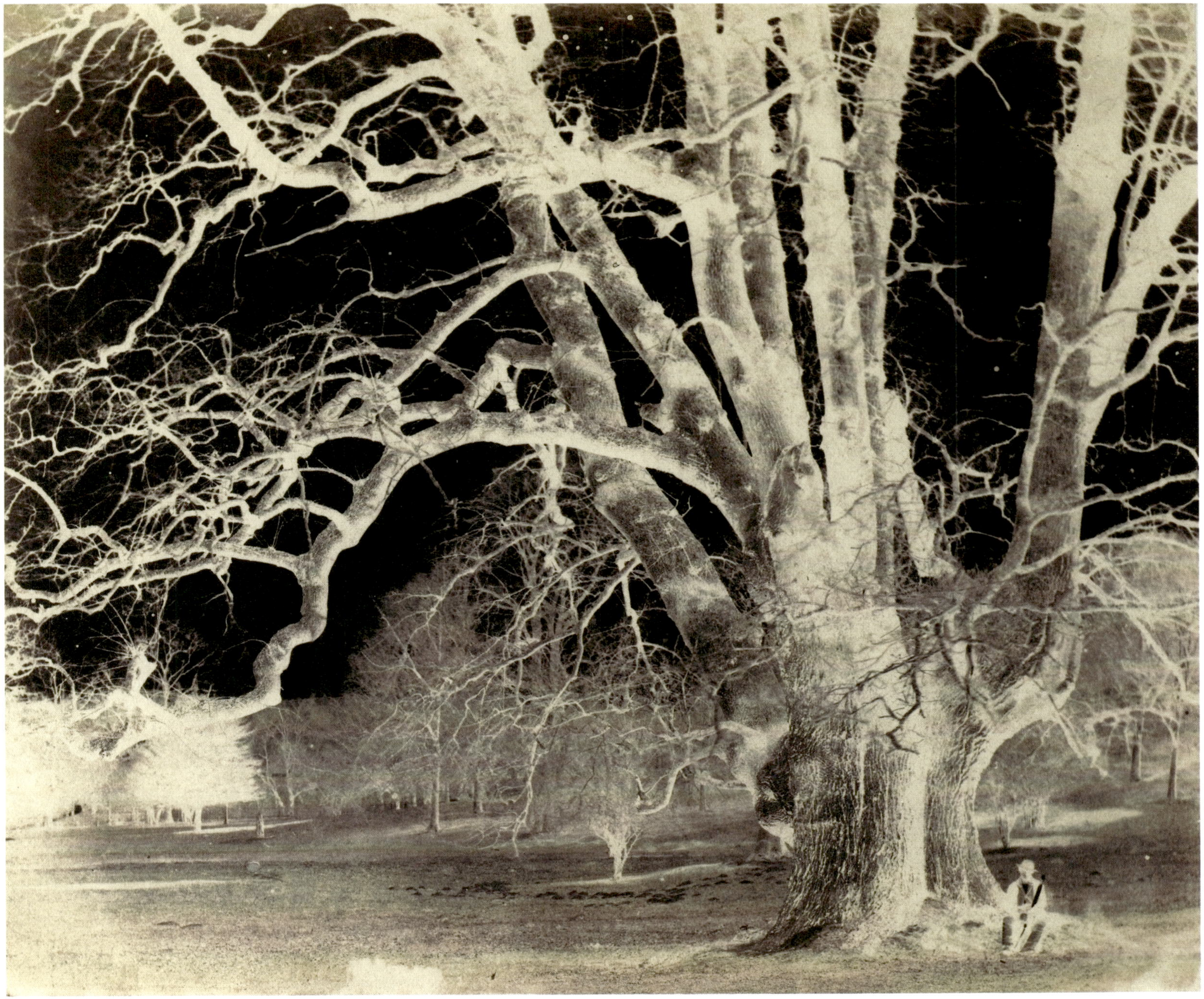

17. Unknown photographer, Spreading Oak with Seated Figure (negative), 1850s

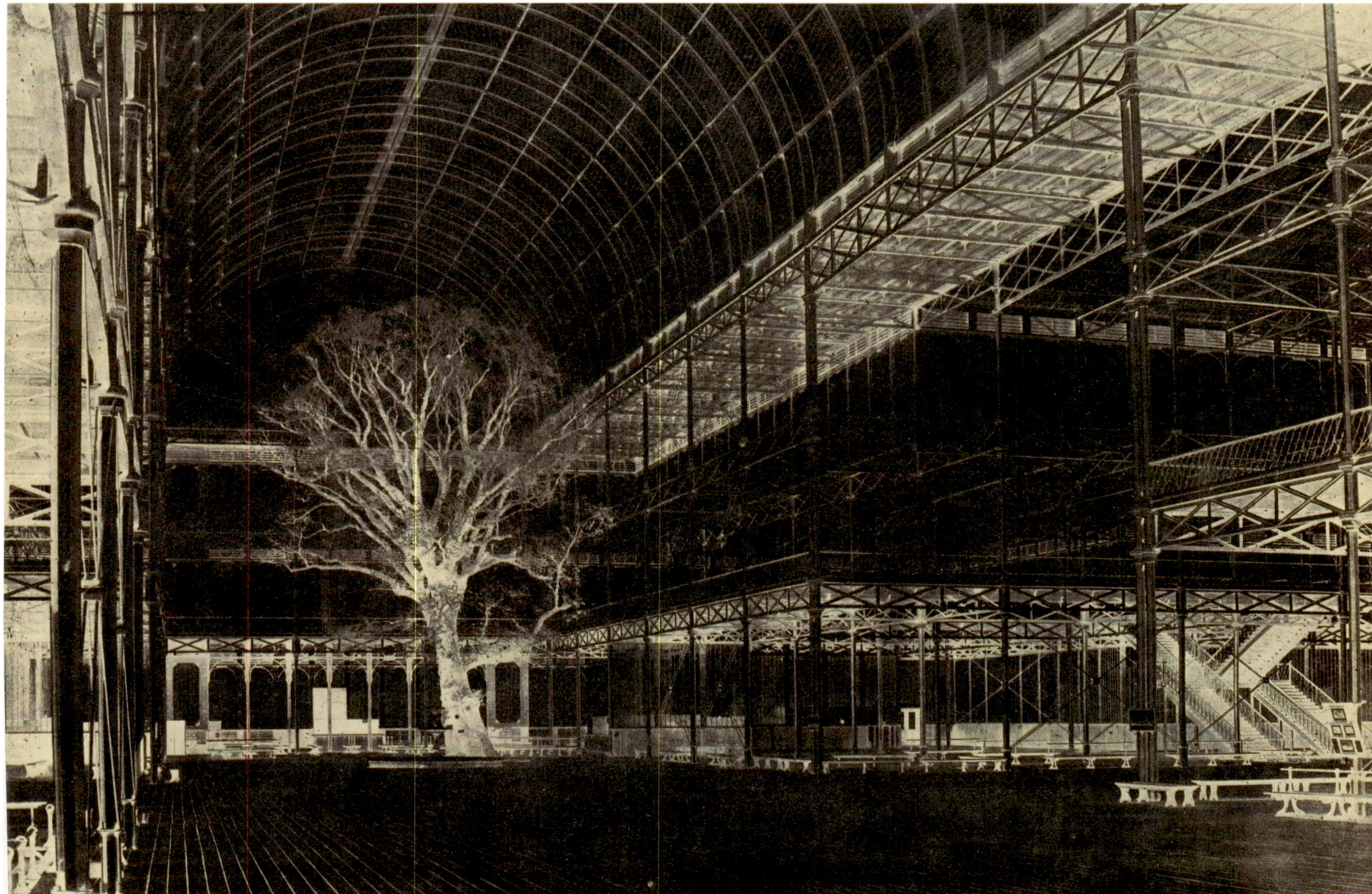

18. Benjamin Brecknell Turner, *Crystal Palace, Hyde Park, 1852, Transept* (negative)

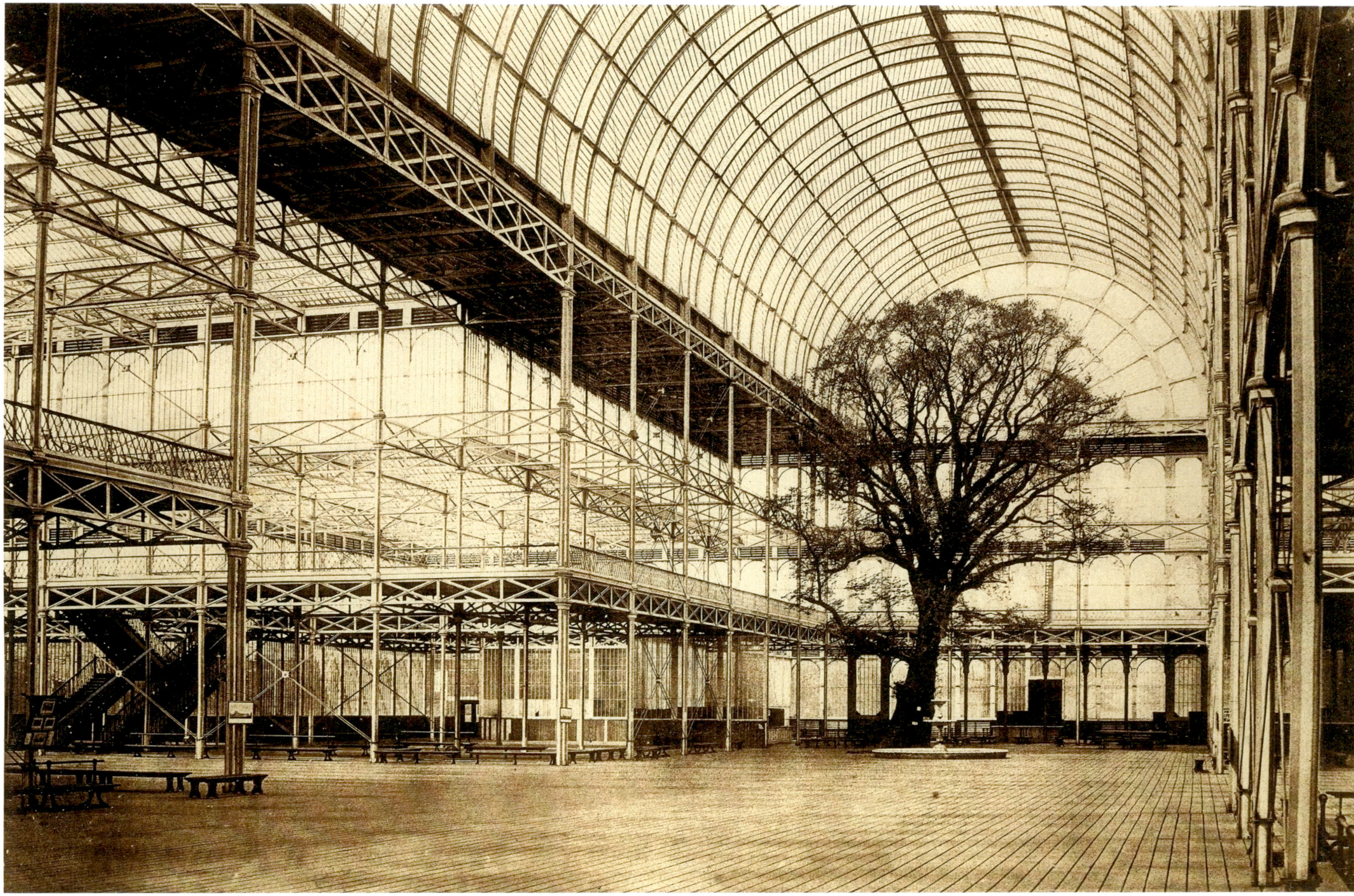

19. Benjamin Brecknell Turner, *Crystal Palace, Hyde Park, 1852, Transept*

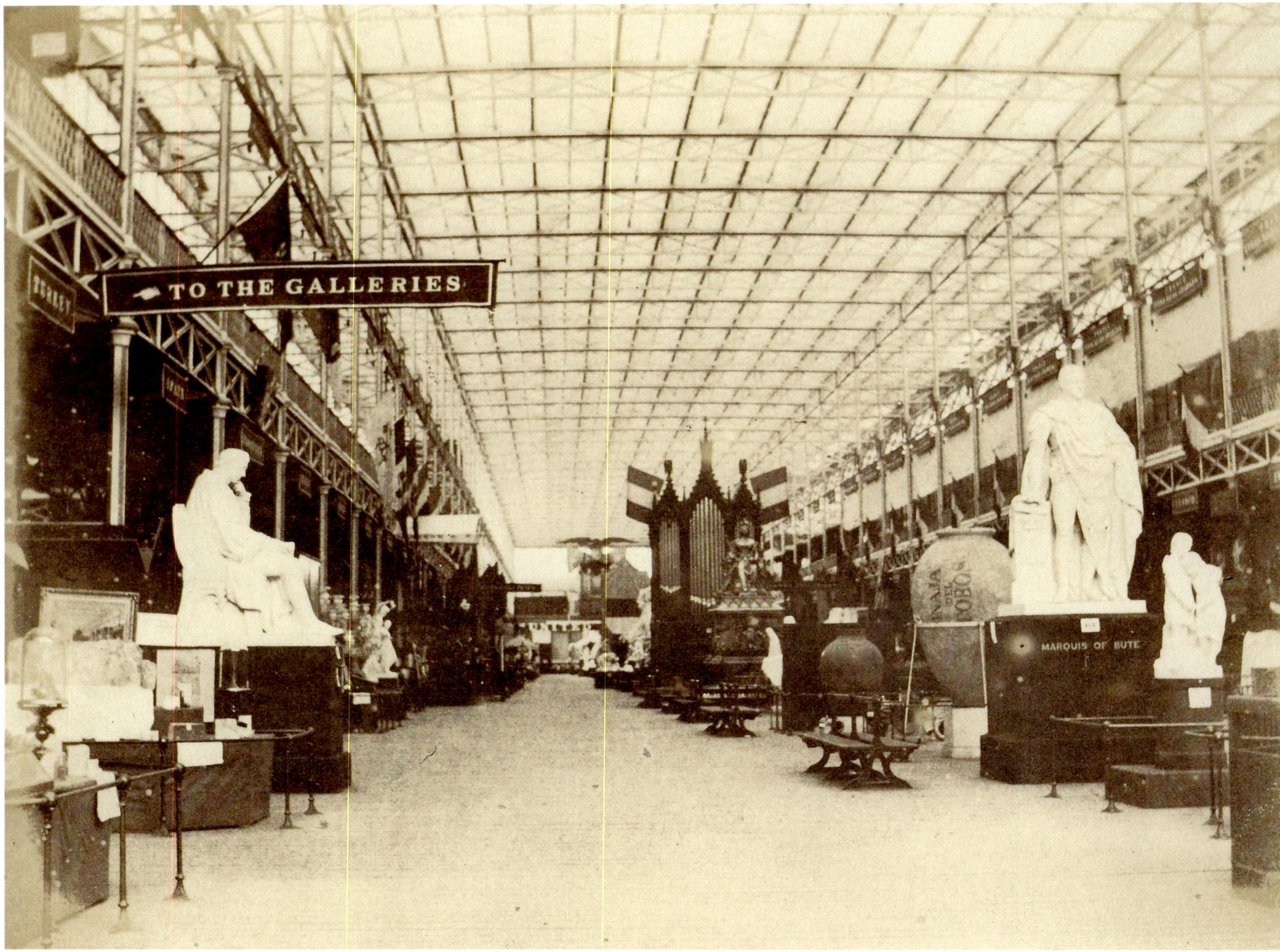

20. Hugh Owen, *General View from Transept, Looking East,* 1851

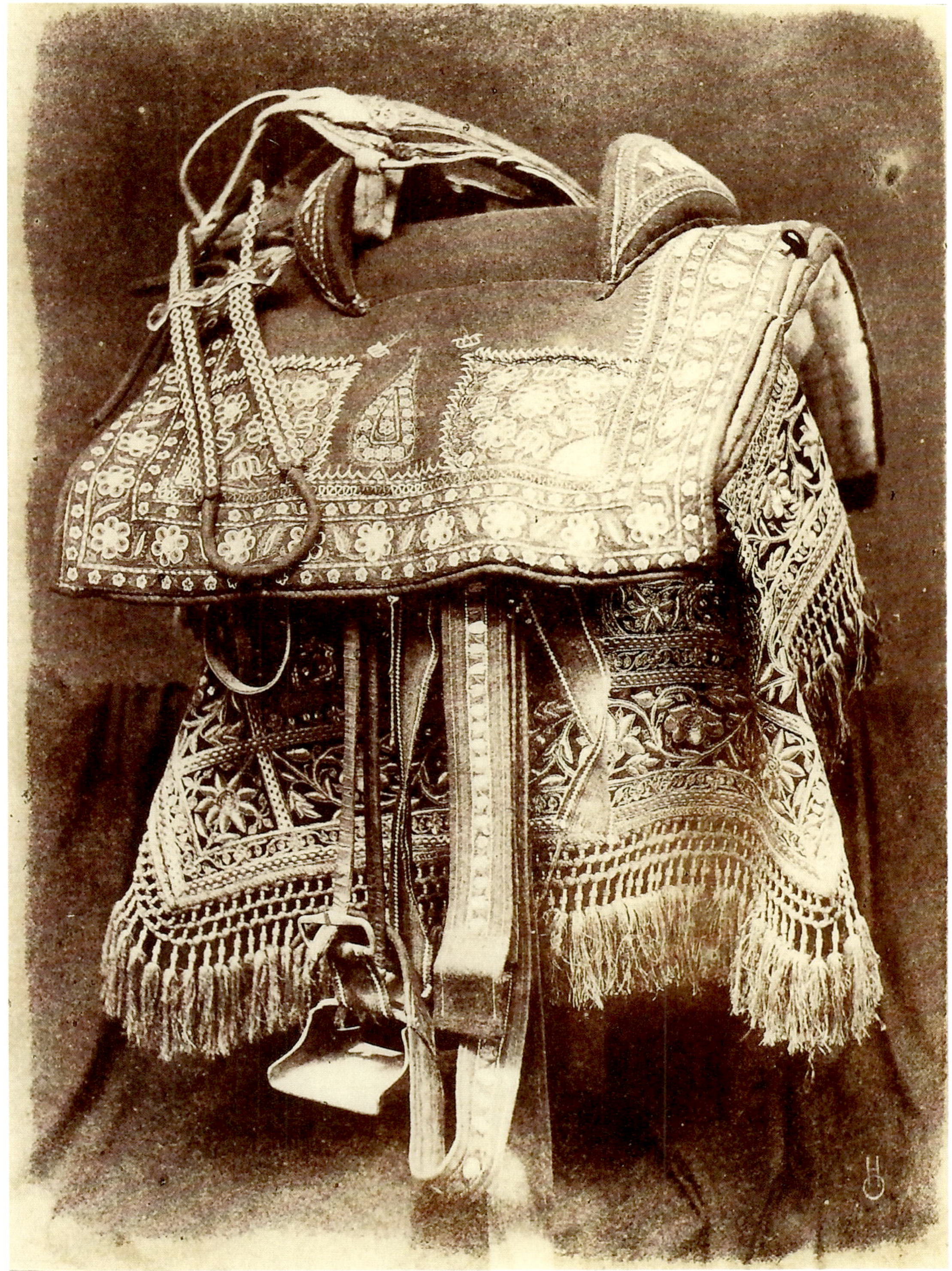

21. Hugh Owen, *Embroidered Saddle*, 1851

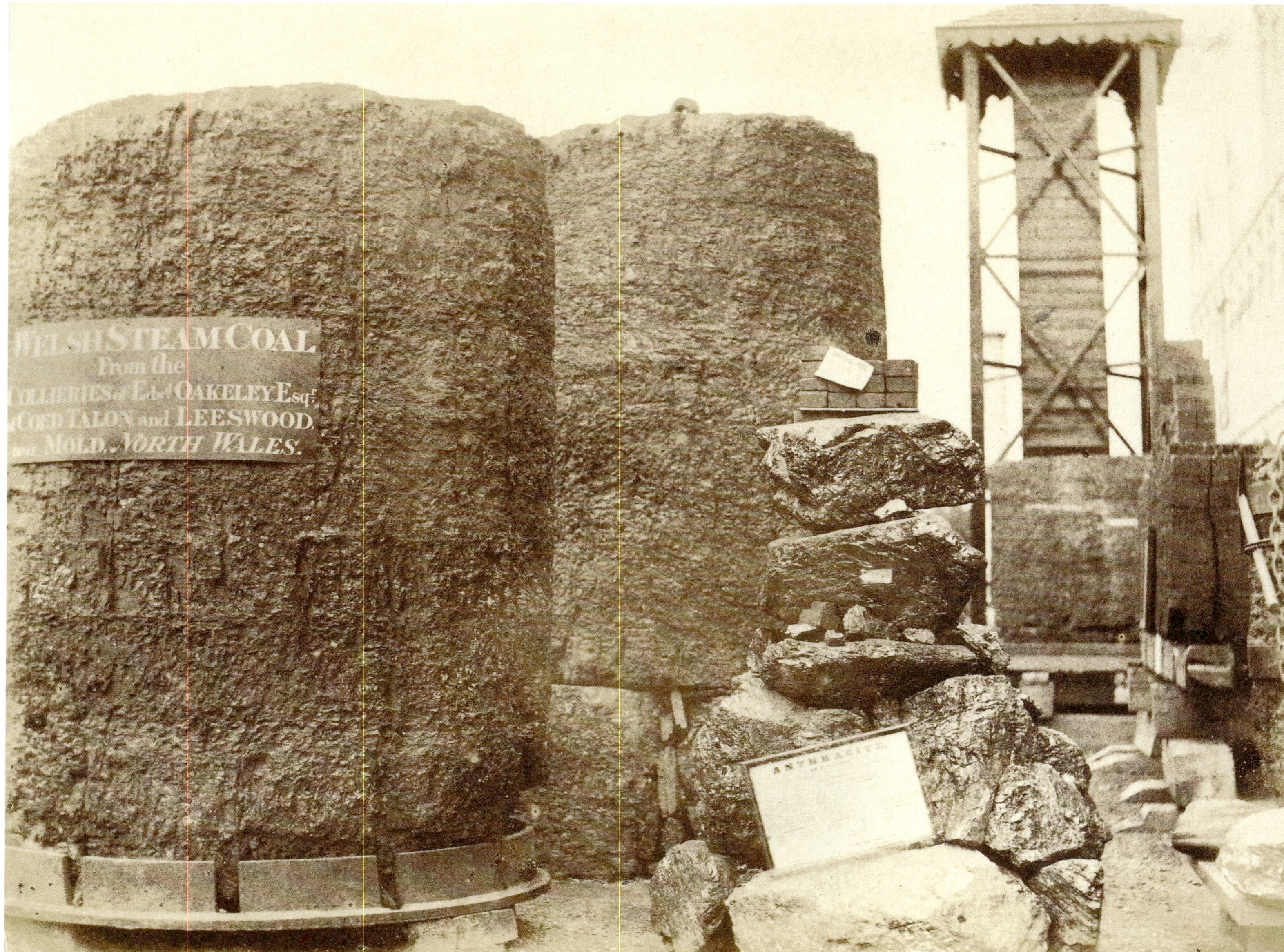

22. Hugh Owen, *Large Blocks of Coal*, 1851

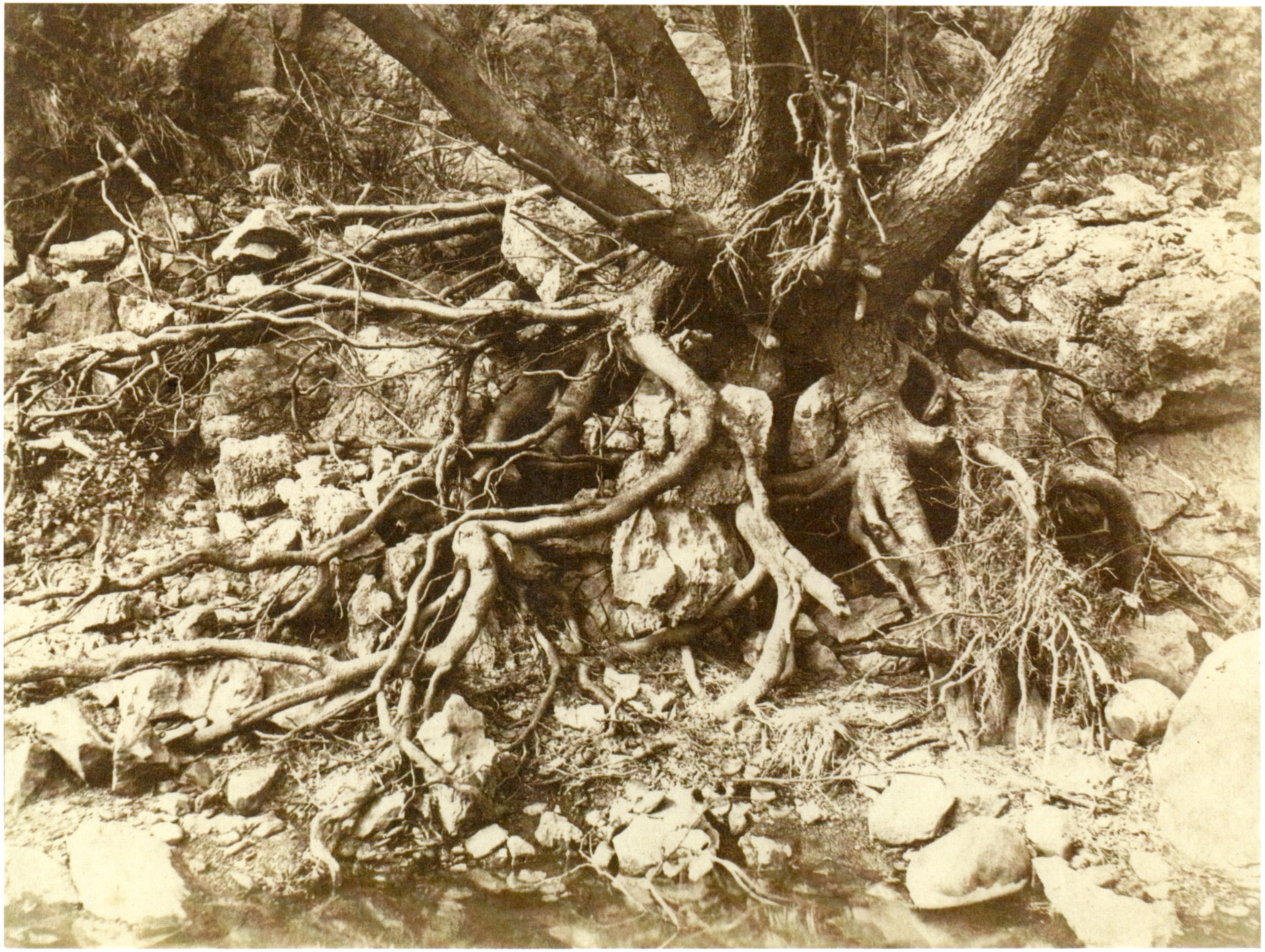

23. Hugh Owen, Tree with Tangled Roots, 1853

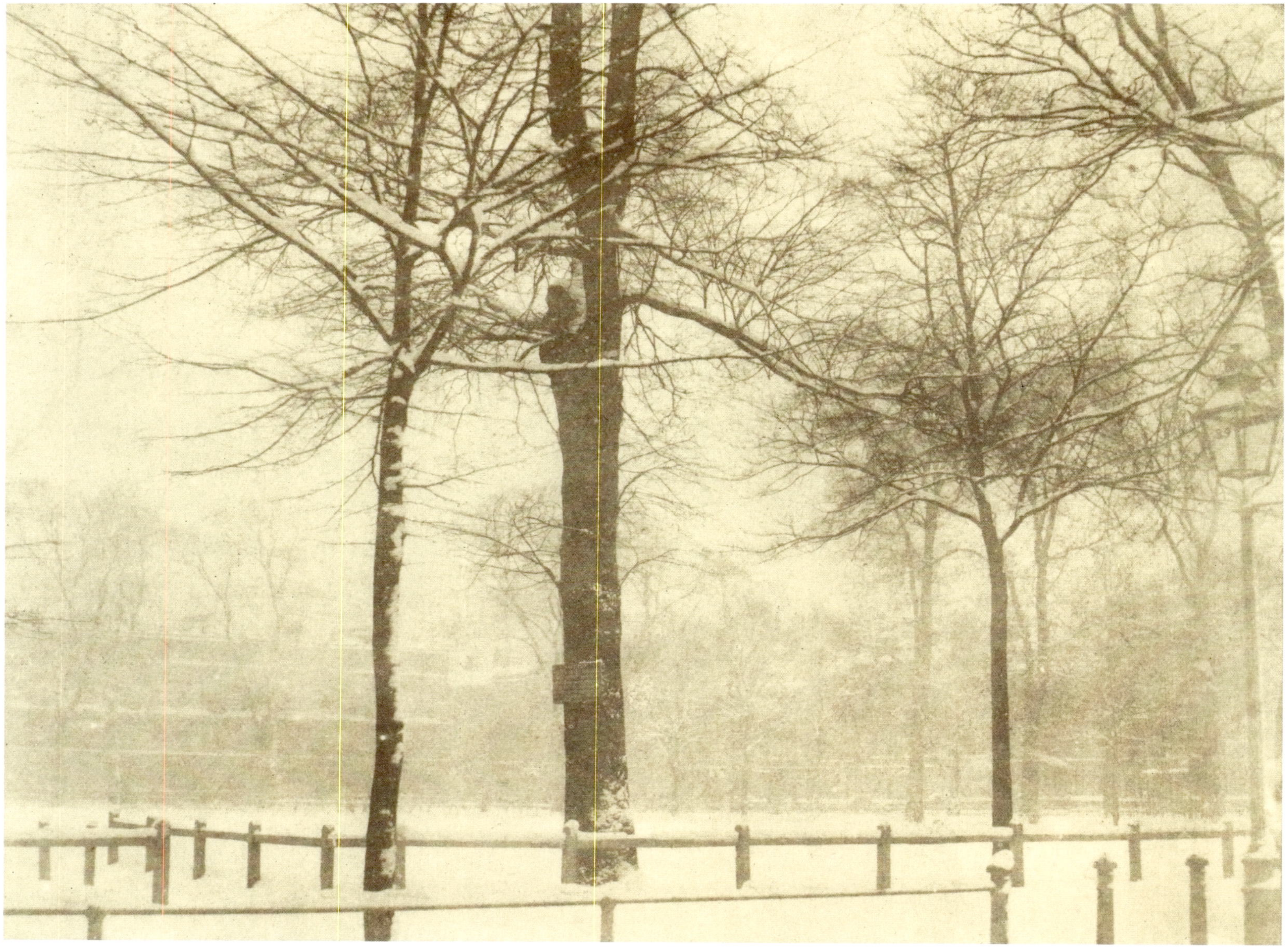

24. Hugh Owen, *Queen Street, Bristol*, 1853

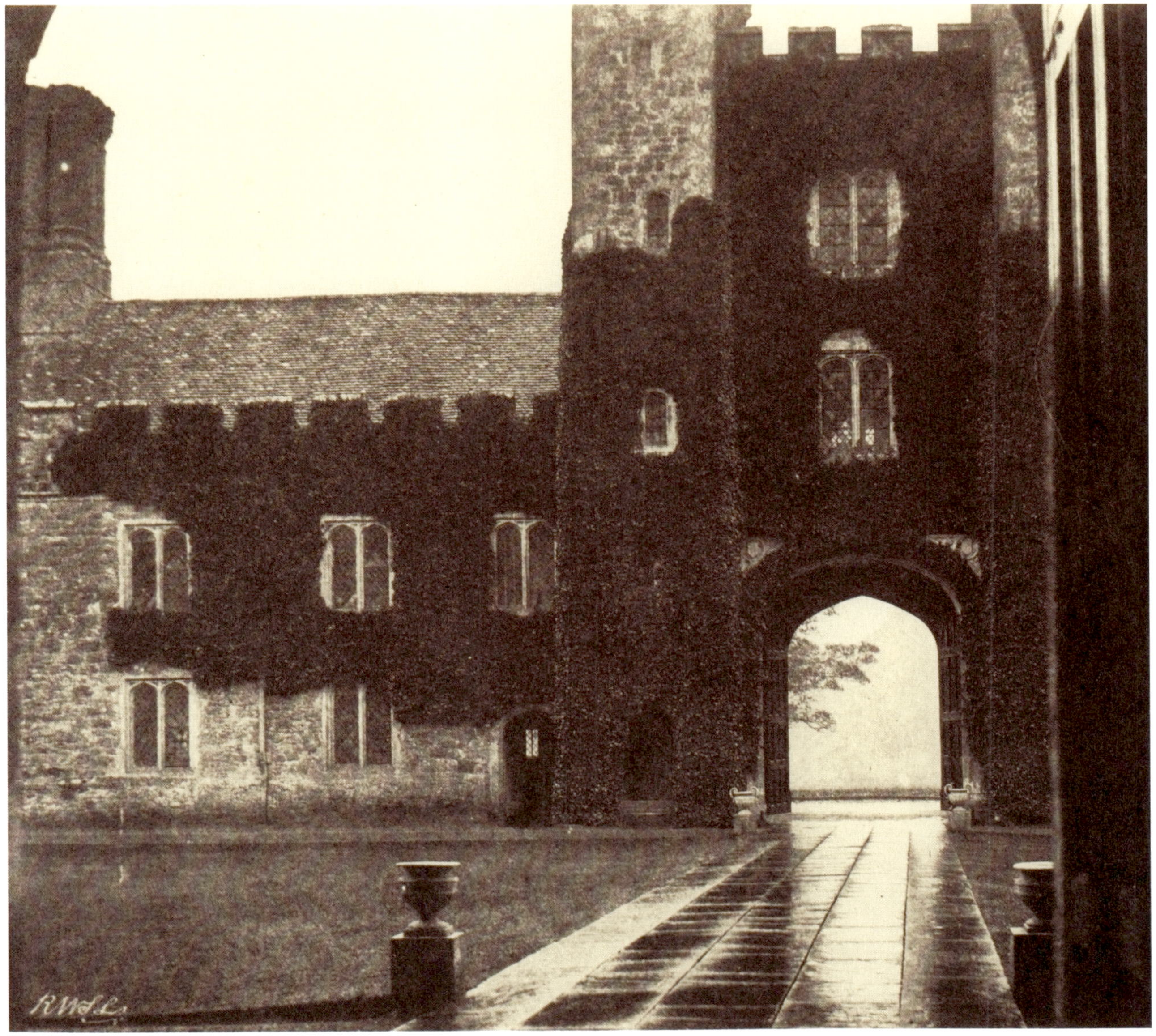

25. Robert Wilfred Skeffington Lutwidge, *Knowle, Kent, Taken in the Rain*, 1855

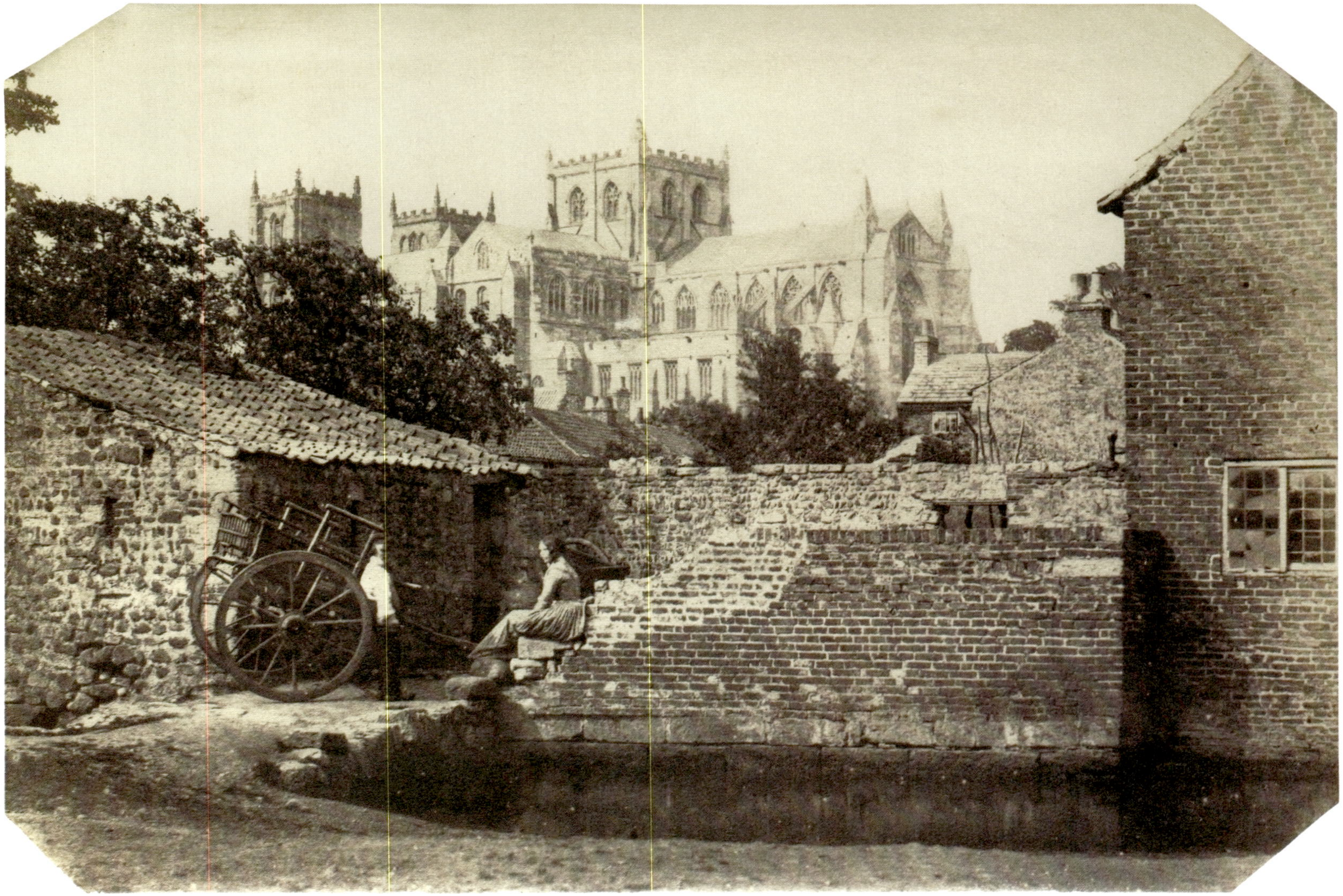

26. William A. Pumphrey, *Ripon Cathedral from the Southeast adjacent to the River Skell*, ca. 1855

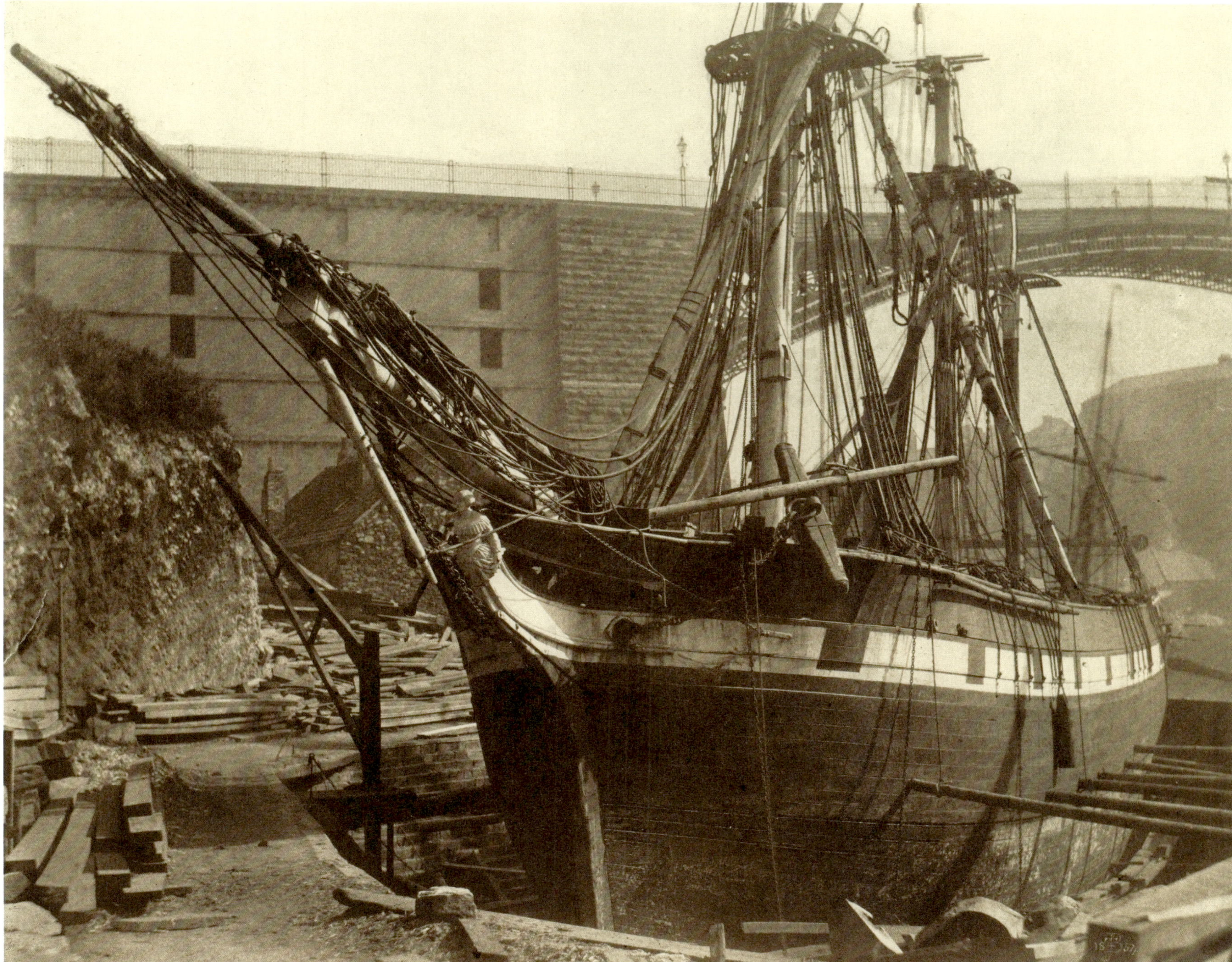

27. Thomas James Backhouse, *At Sunderland*, 1854

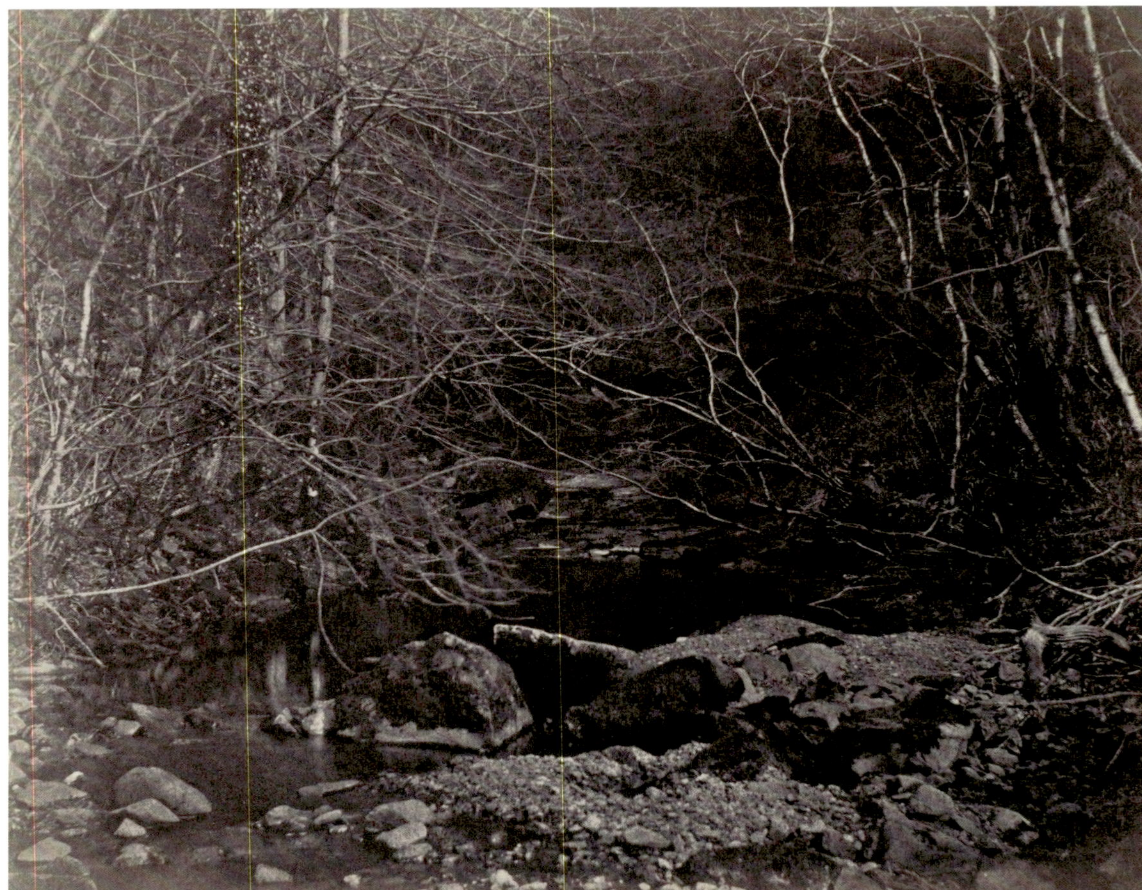

28. John Muir Wood, Stream in Woods, 1847–52

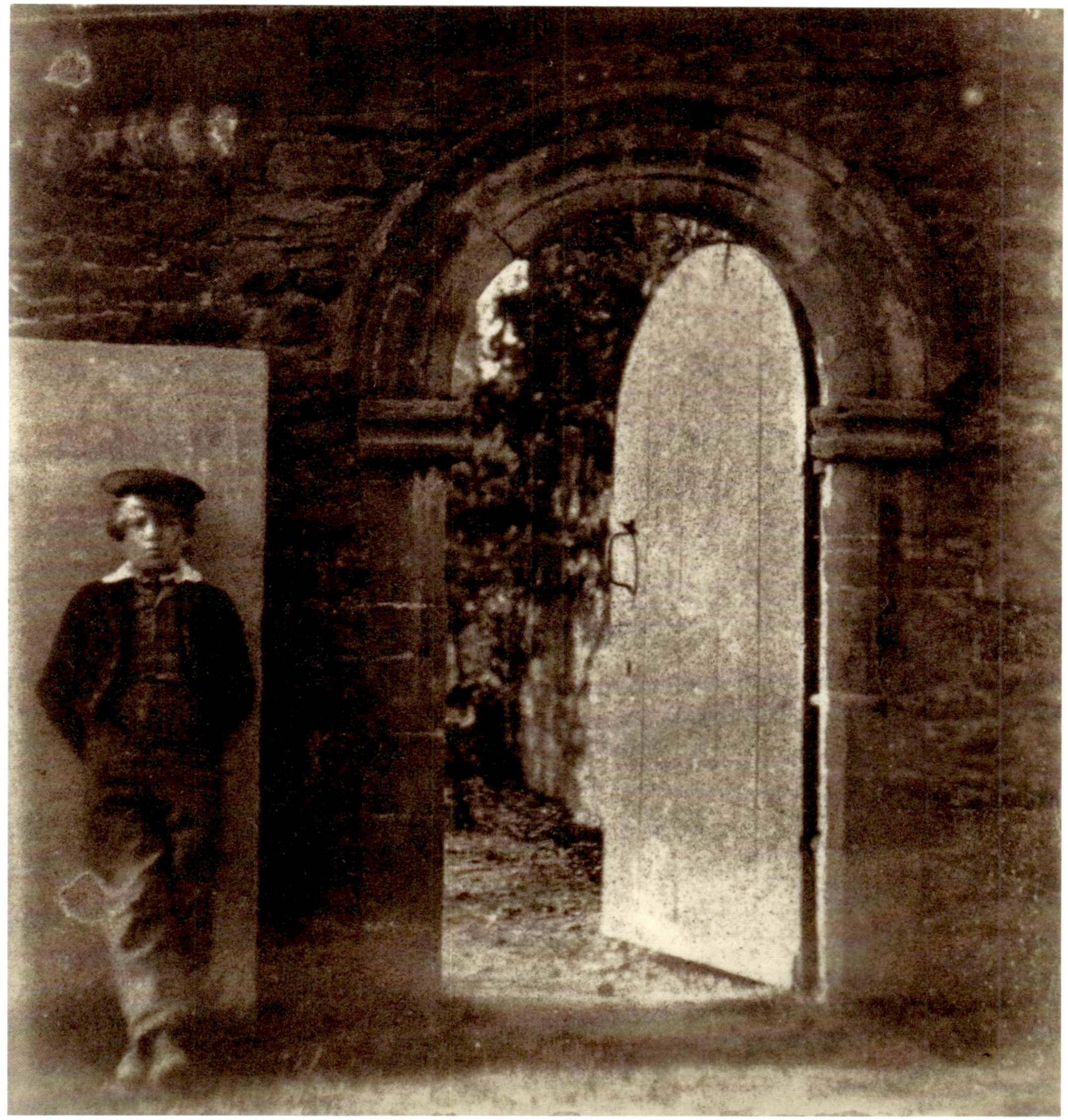

29. John Muir Wood, Boy by Open Door, 1847–52

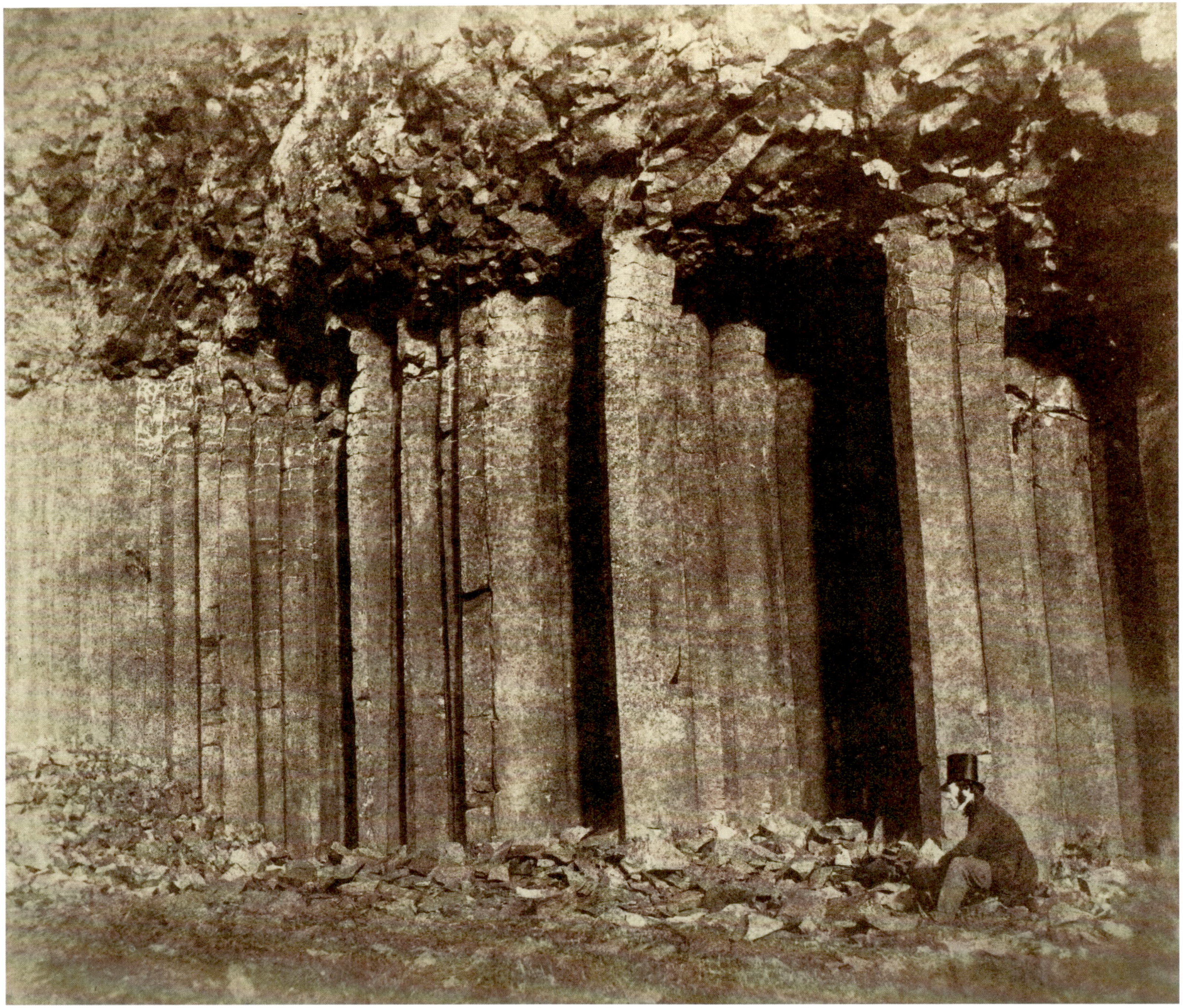

30. John Muir Wood, Columnar Basalt, possibly near Fingal's Cave on Staffa, in the Hebrides, 1847–52

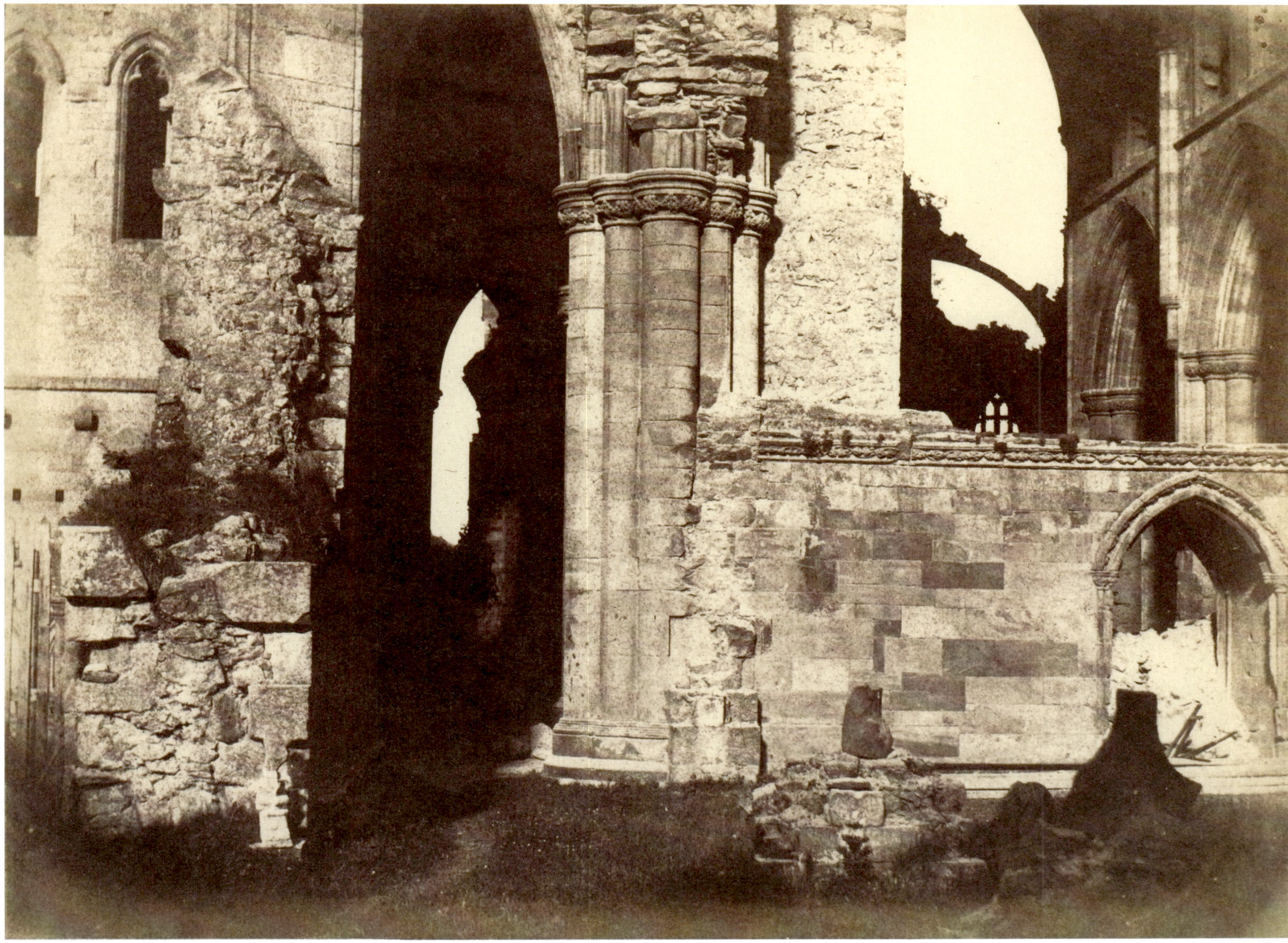

31. John Muir Wood, Melrose Abbey, 1847–52

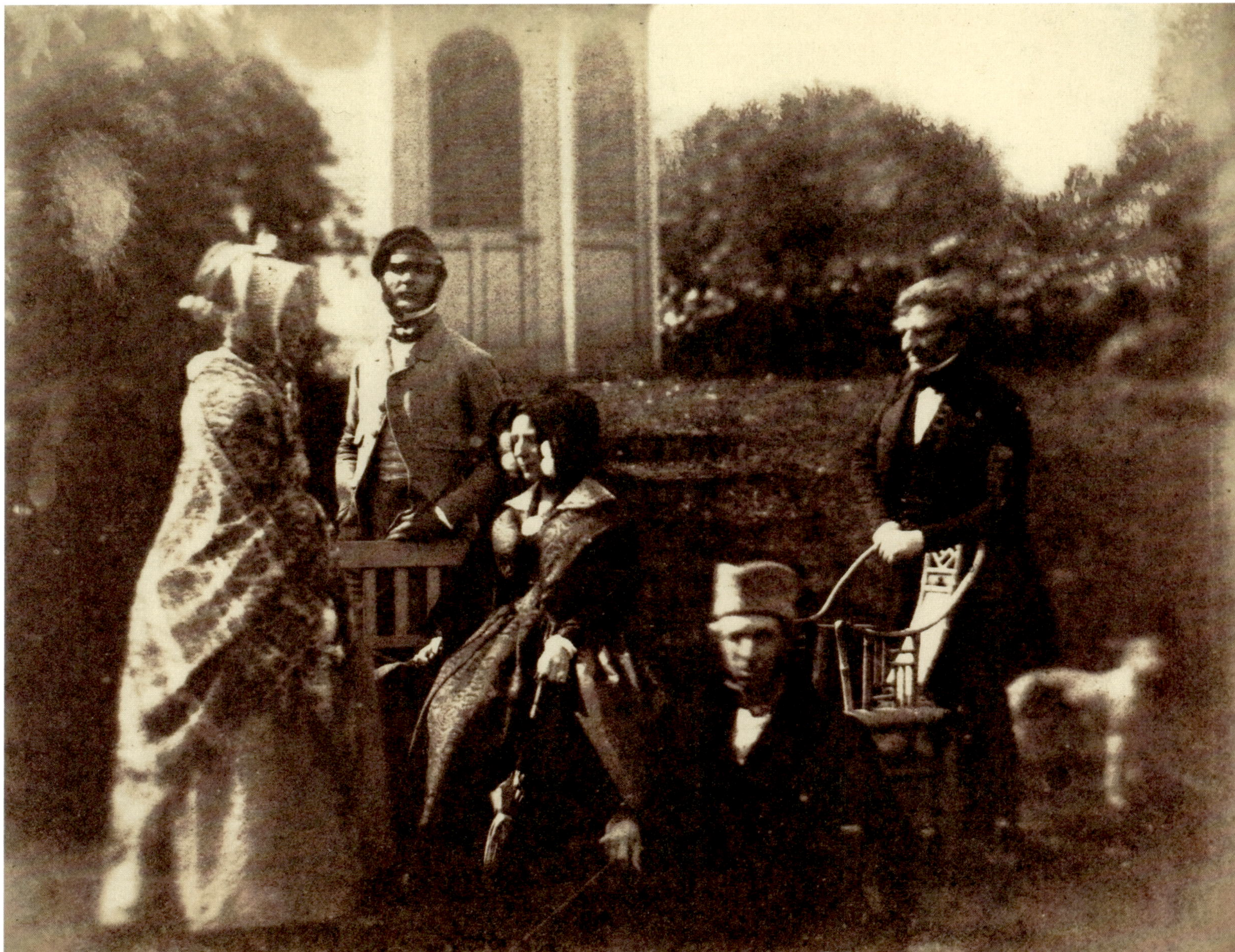

32. John Muir Wood, Family Group, Leith, 1847–52

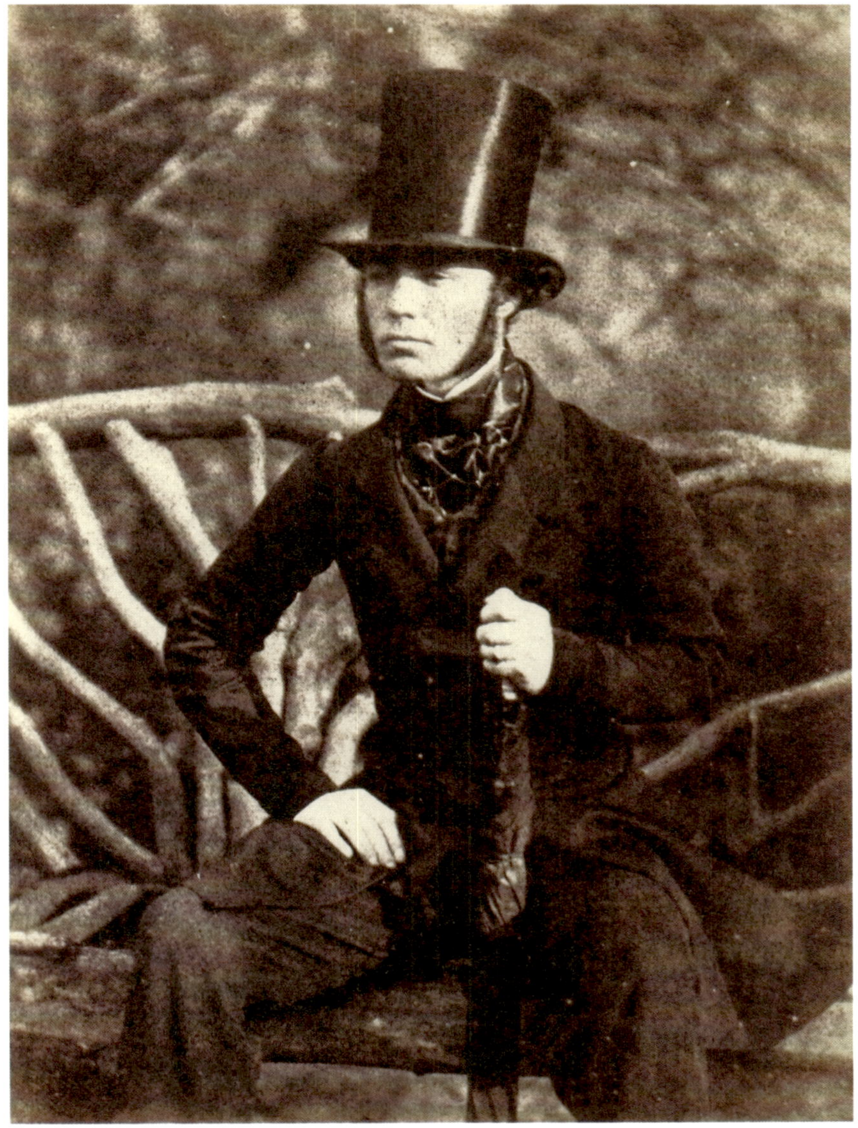

33. John Muir Wood, *George Wood*, 1847–52

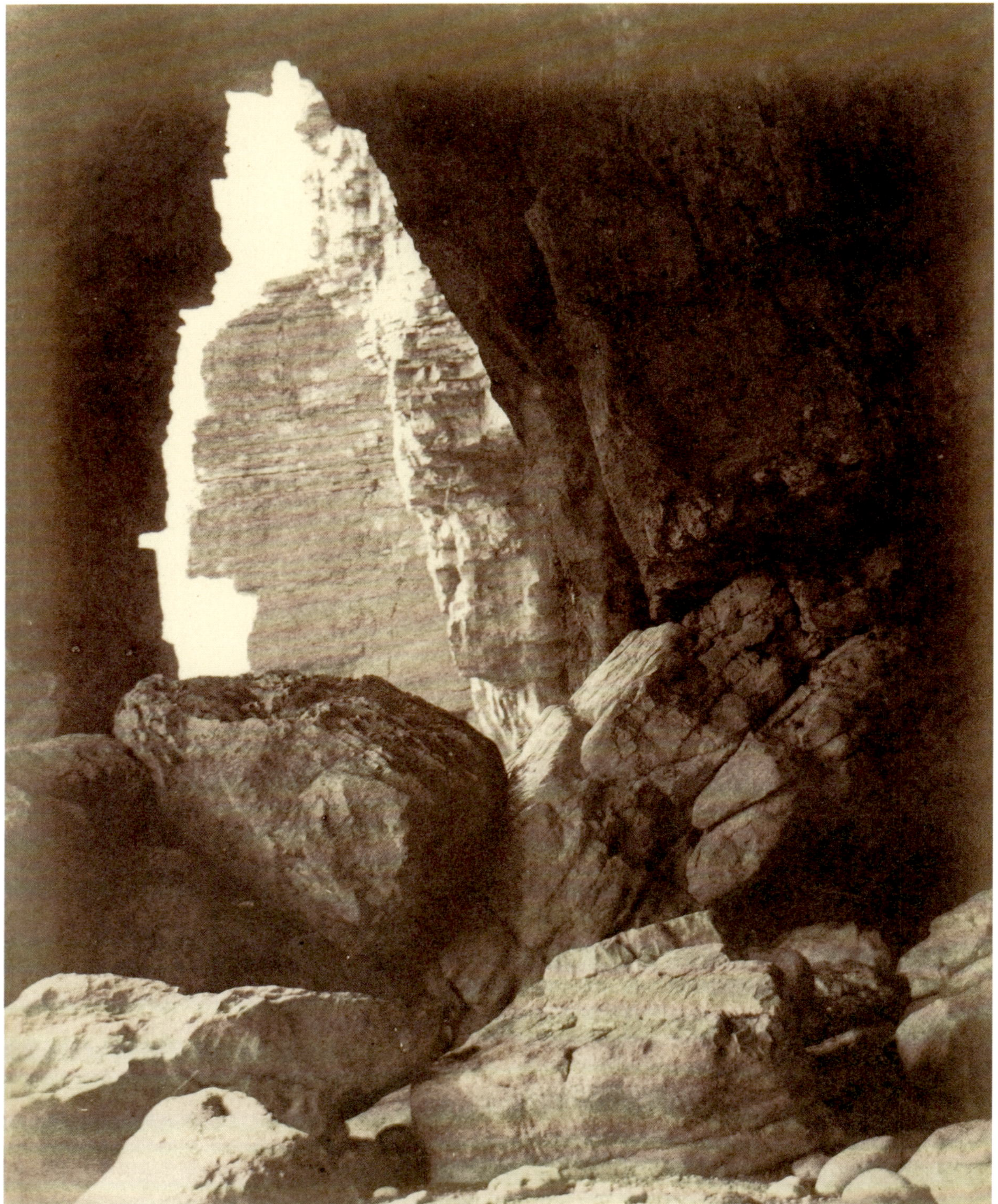

34. John Dillwyn Llewelyn, *Inside the Great Cave, Dunraven*, 1854

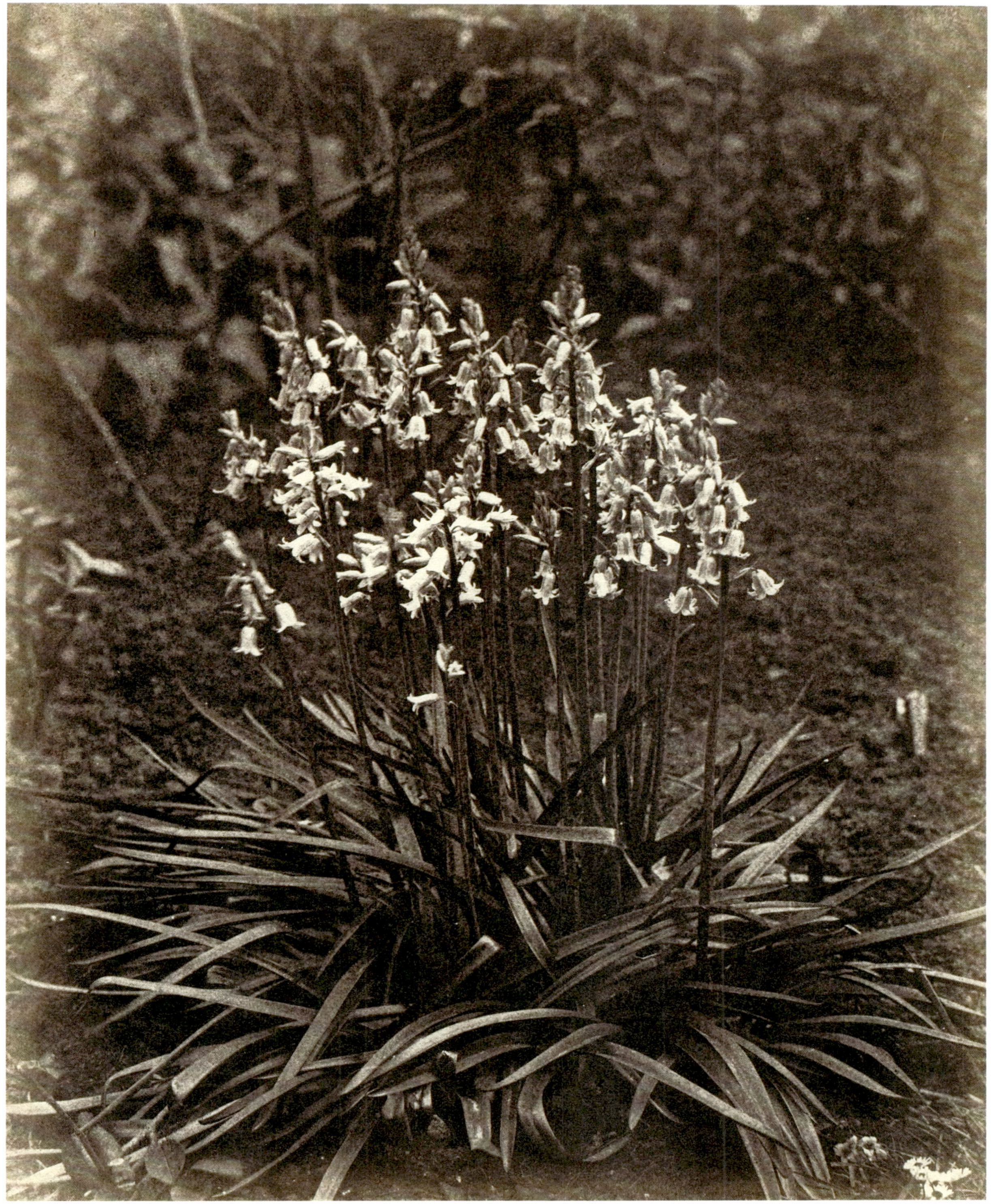

35. John Dillwyn Llewelyn, *Blue Squills,* ca. 1852

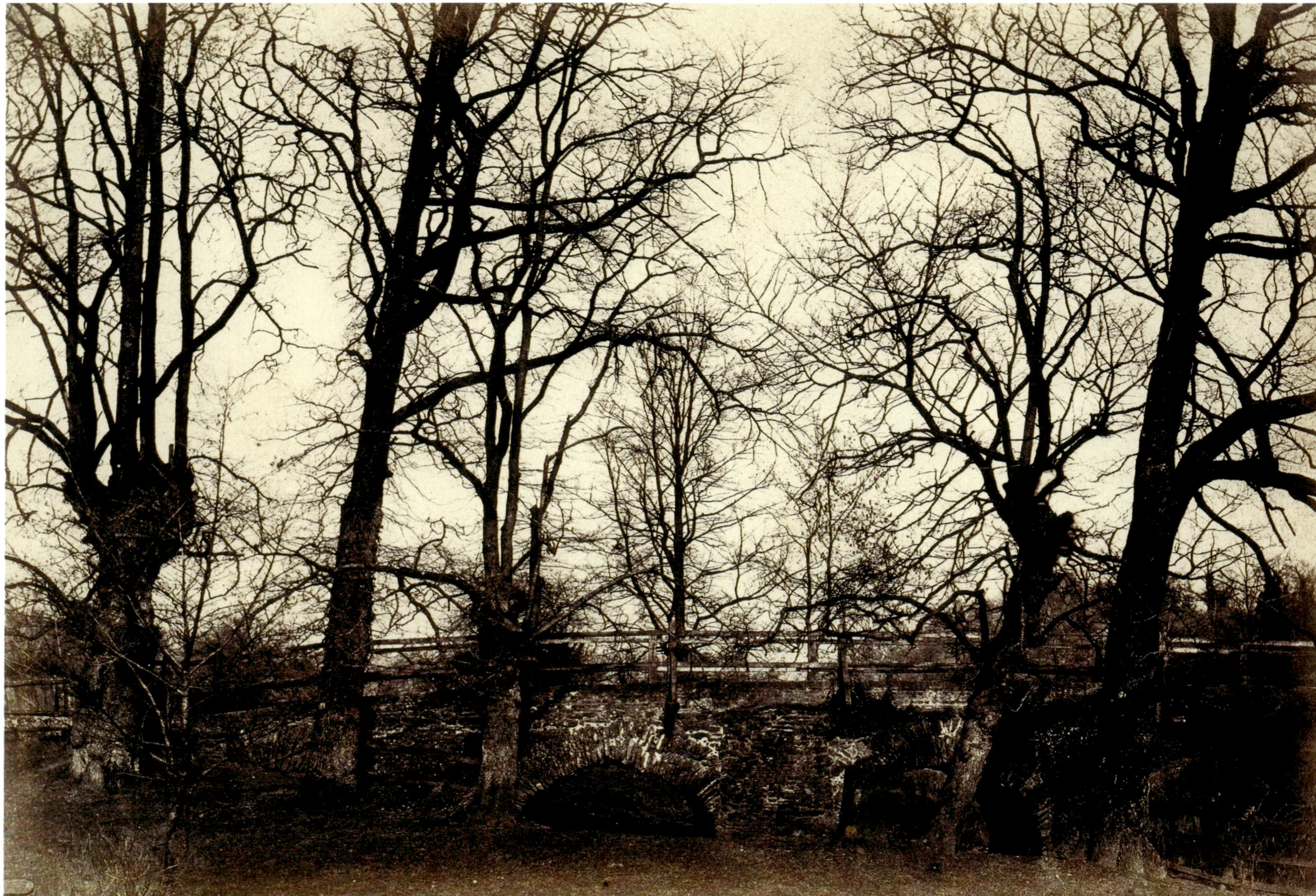

36. Benjamin Brecknell Turner, *Eashing Bridge, Surrey*, 1852–54

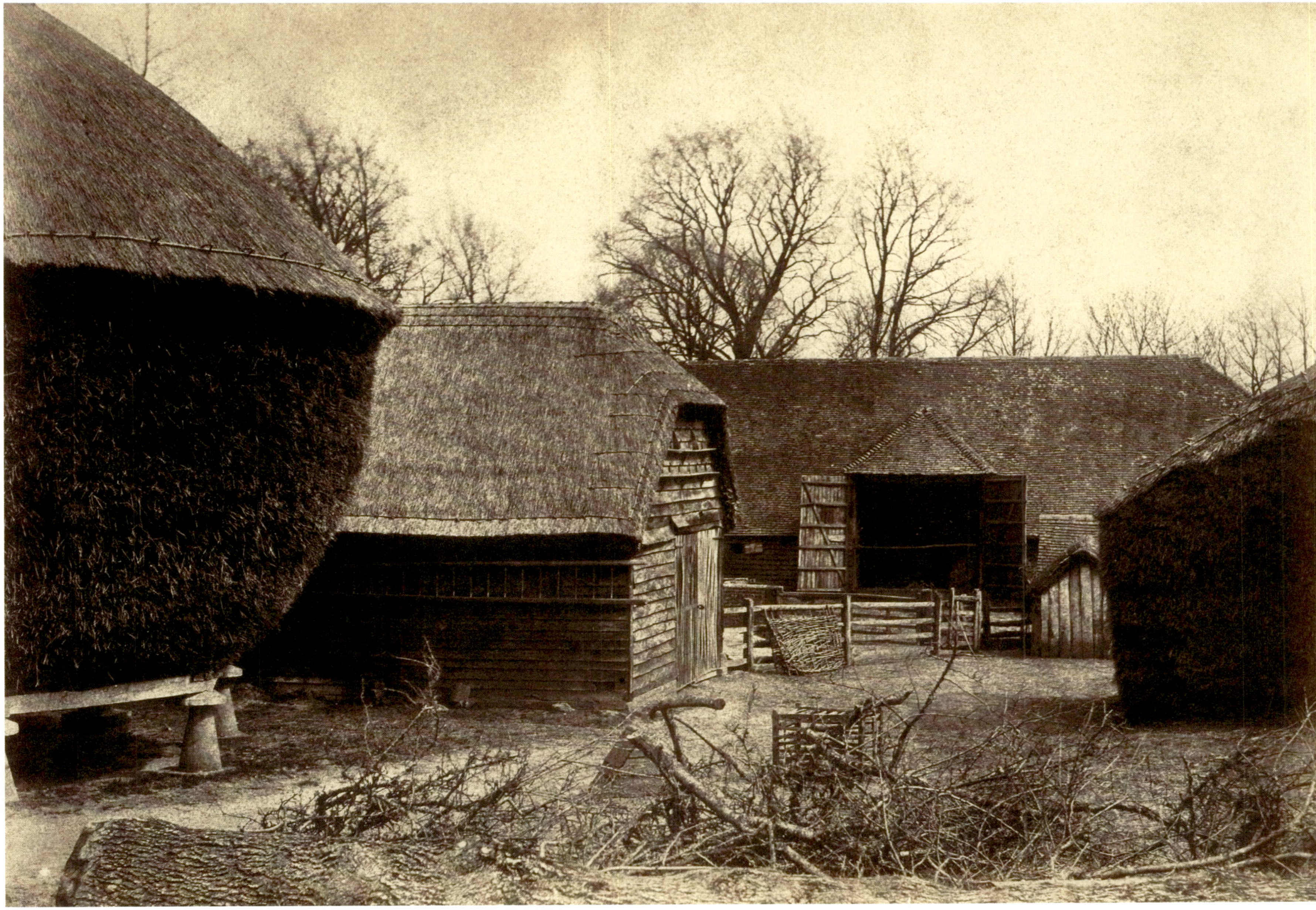

37. Benjamin Brecknell Turner, *At Compton, Surrey*, 1852–54

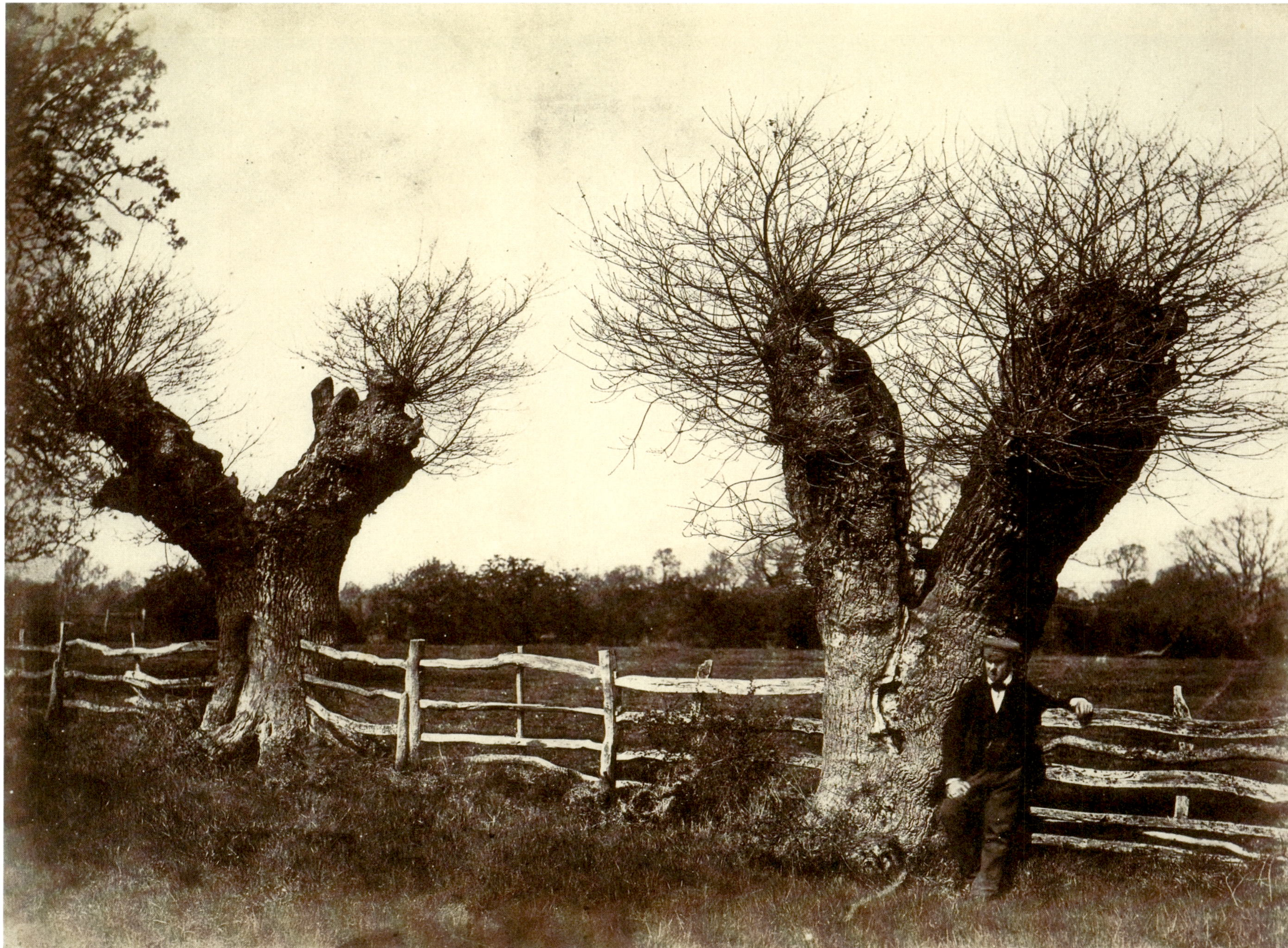

38. Benjamin Brecknell Turner, *Hedgerow Trees, Clerkenleap, Worcestershire,* 1852–54

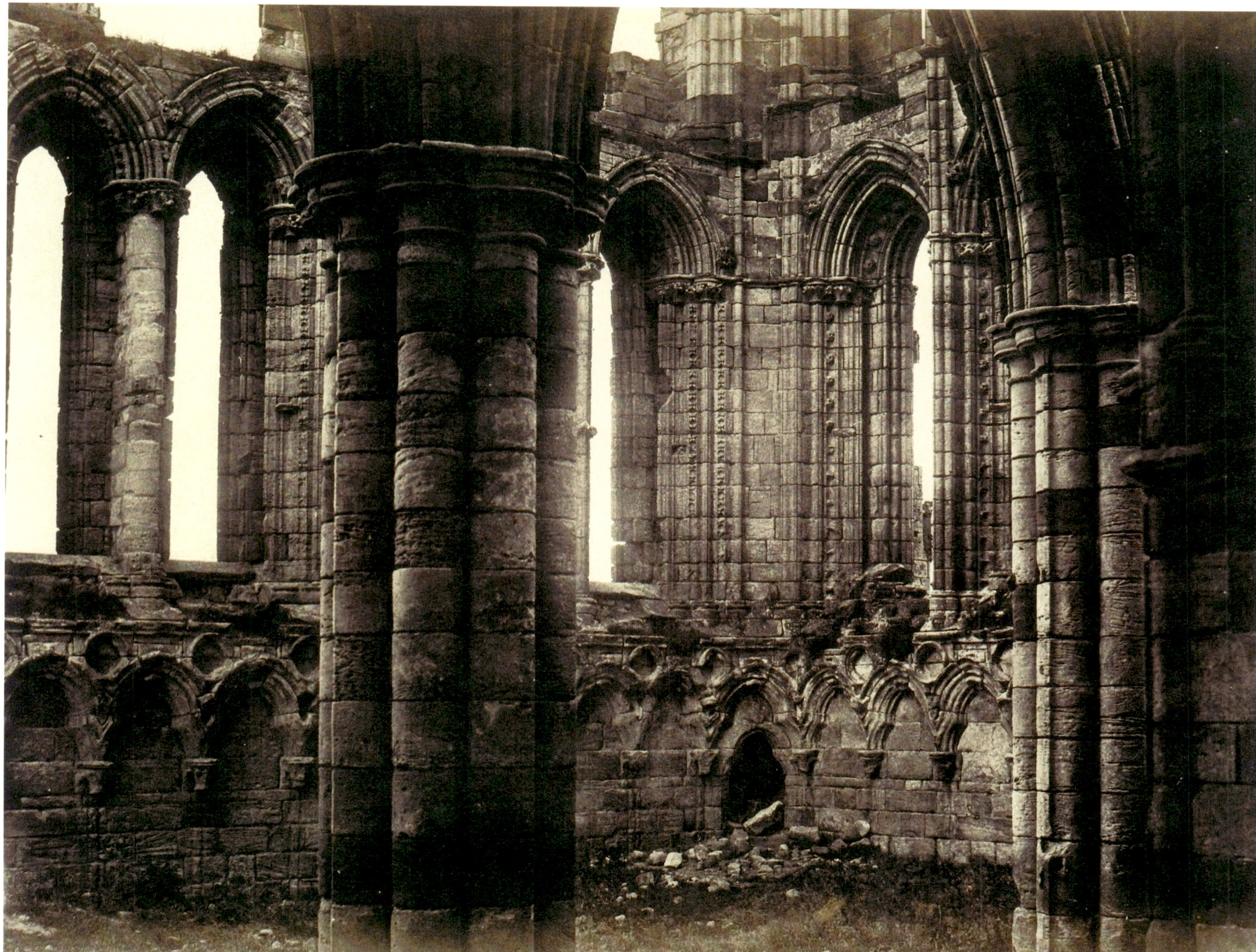

39. Benjamin Brecknell Turner, *Whitby Abbey, Yorkshire, North Transept,* 1852–54

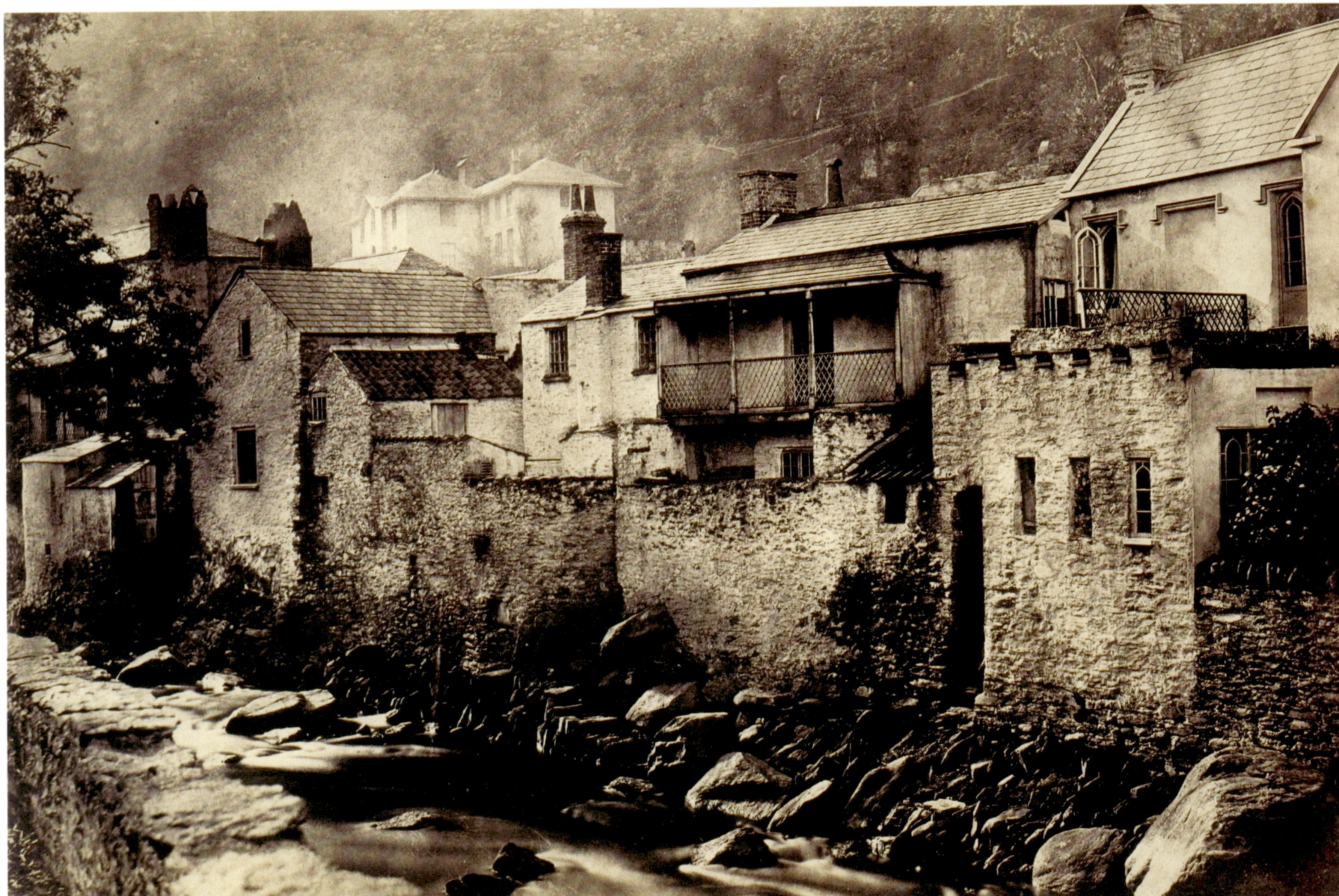

40. Benjamin Brecknell Turner, *Lynmouth, North Devon*, 1852–54

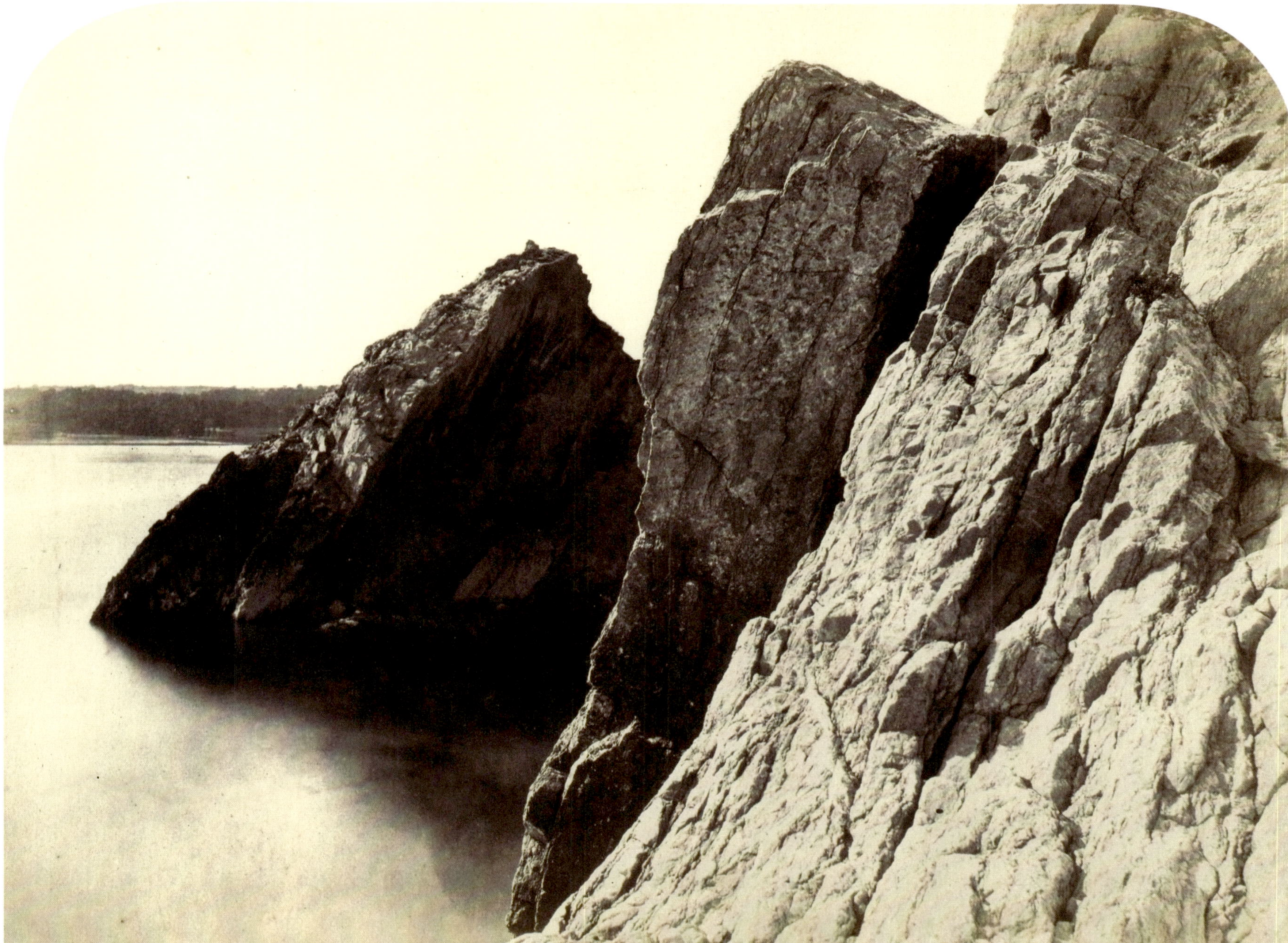

41. Benjamin Brecknell Turner, Anstey's Cove, Torquay, 1861

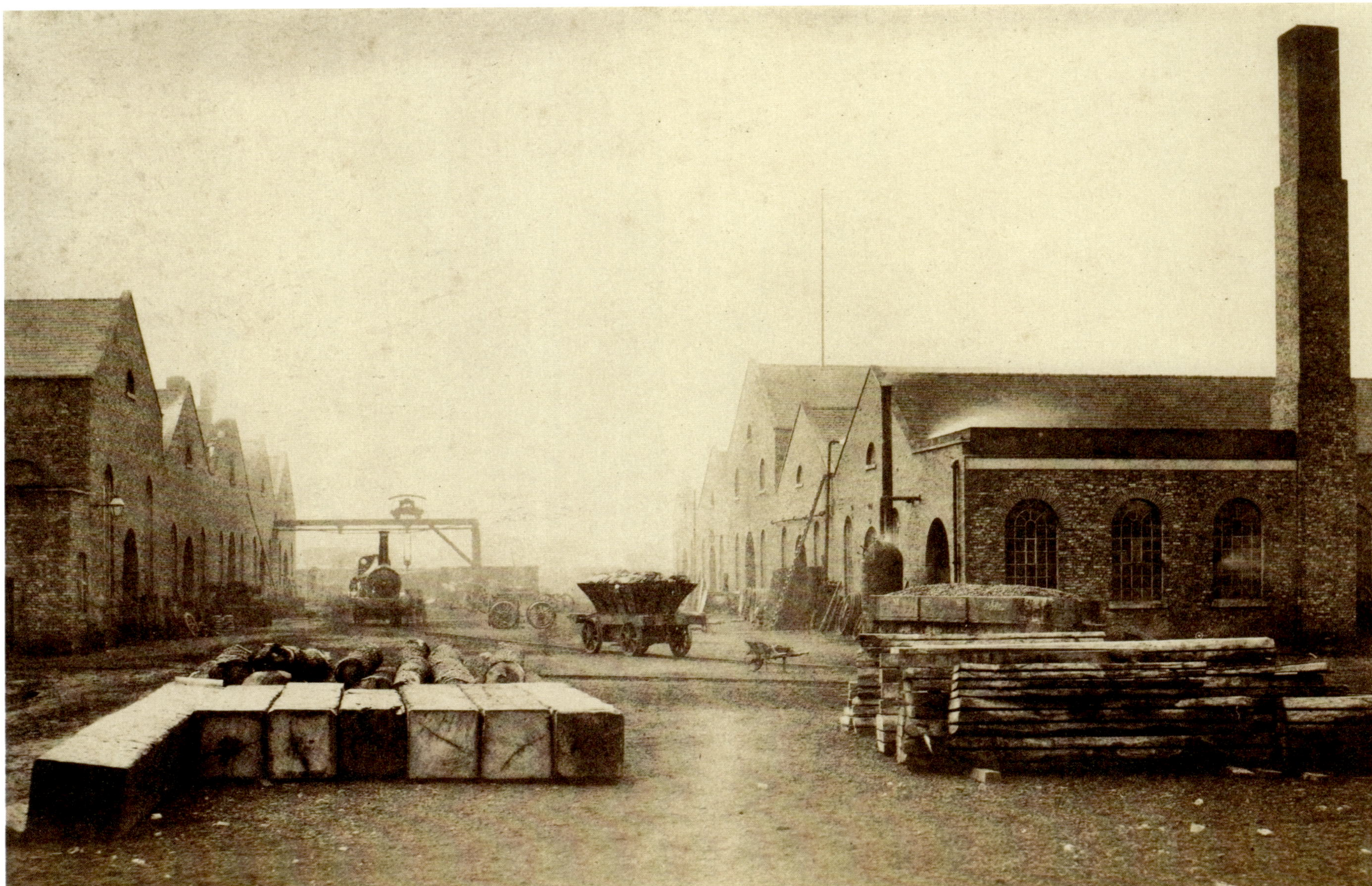

42. James Mudd, The Yard of Beyer Peacock Railway Engine Manufacturers, Gorton, Manchester, ca. 1855

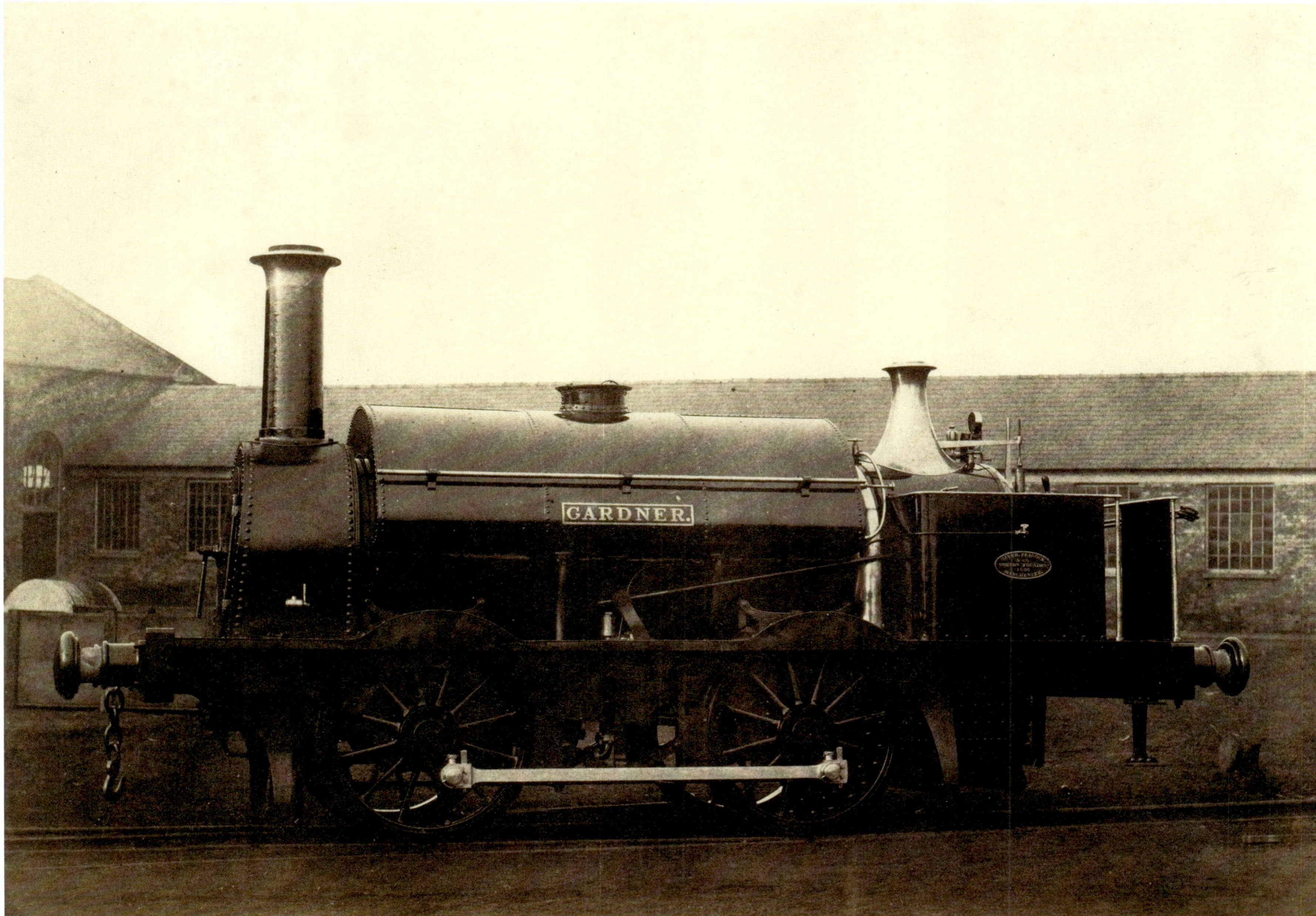

43. James Mudd, Steam Locomotive "Gardner" at Beyer Peacock's, 1856

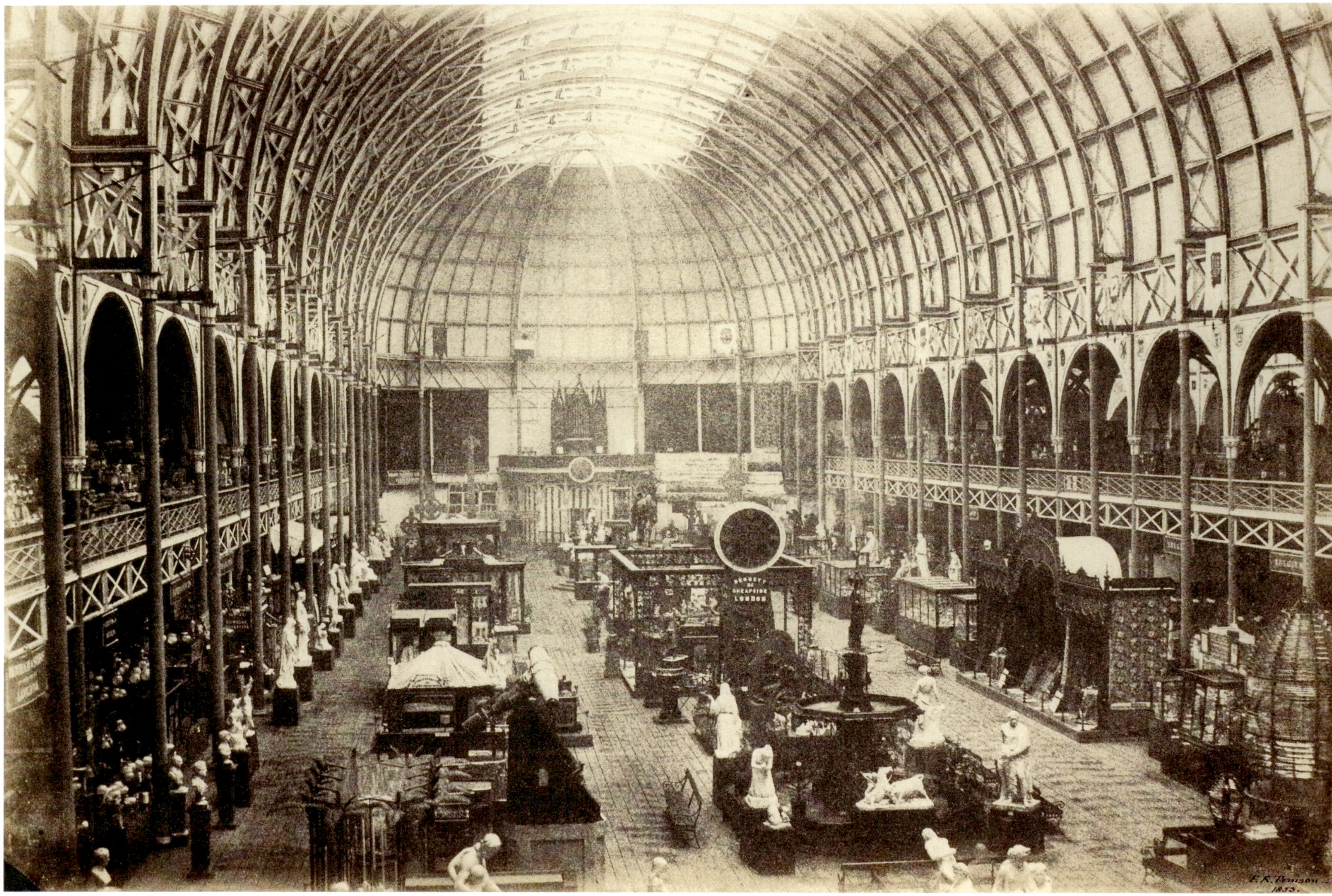

44. Edward King Tenison, Dublin International Exhibition, 1853

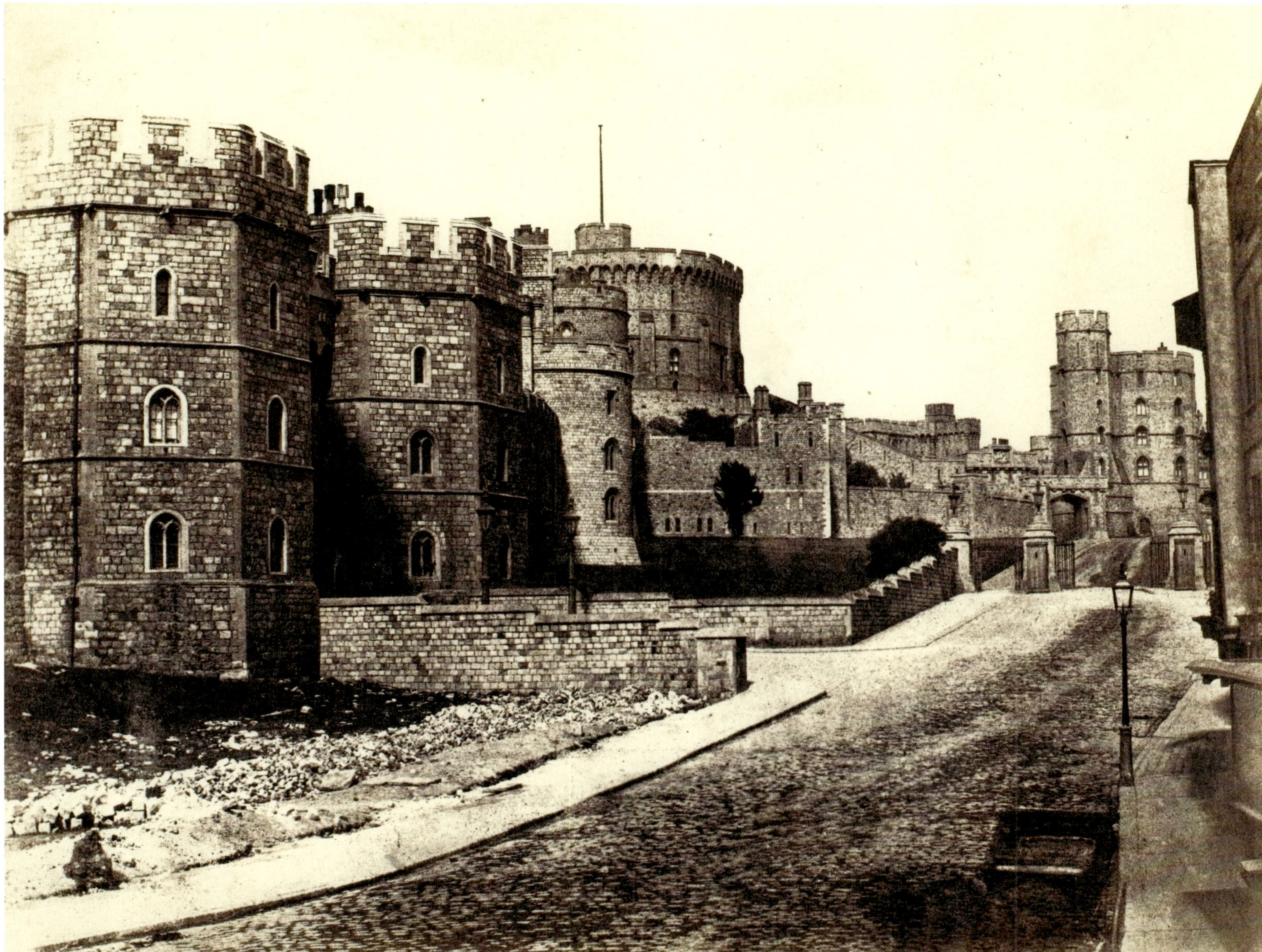

45. Arthur James Melhuish, *View of the Henry VIII Gate, Windsor Castle,* 1855

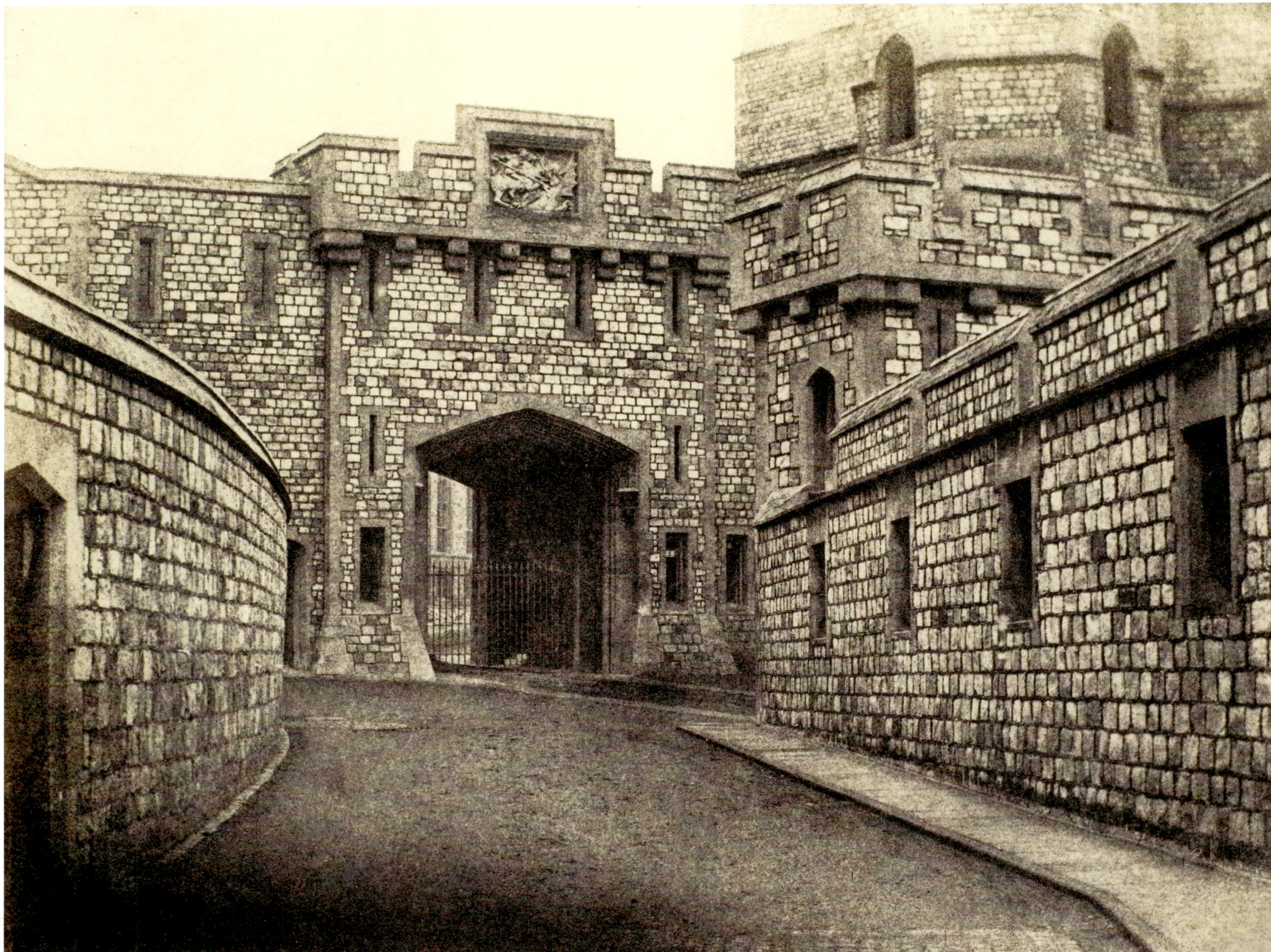

46. Arthur James Melhuish, *St. George's Gate, from the Moat Path*, 1855

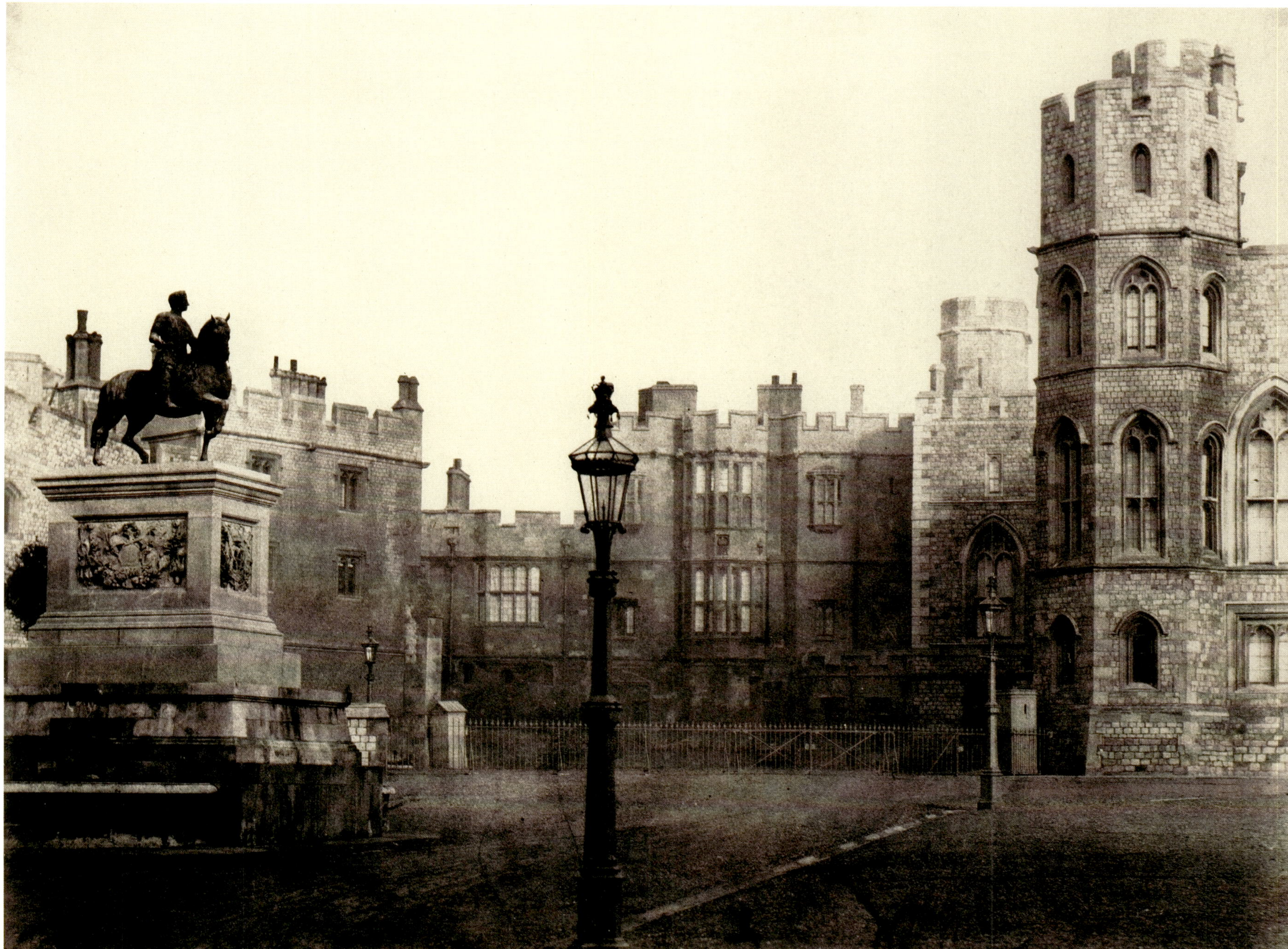

47. Arthur James Melhuish, *Statue of Charles II and the Entrance to the Quadrangle, Windsor Castle,* 1856

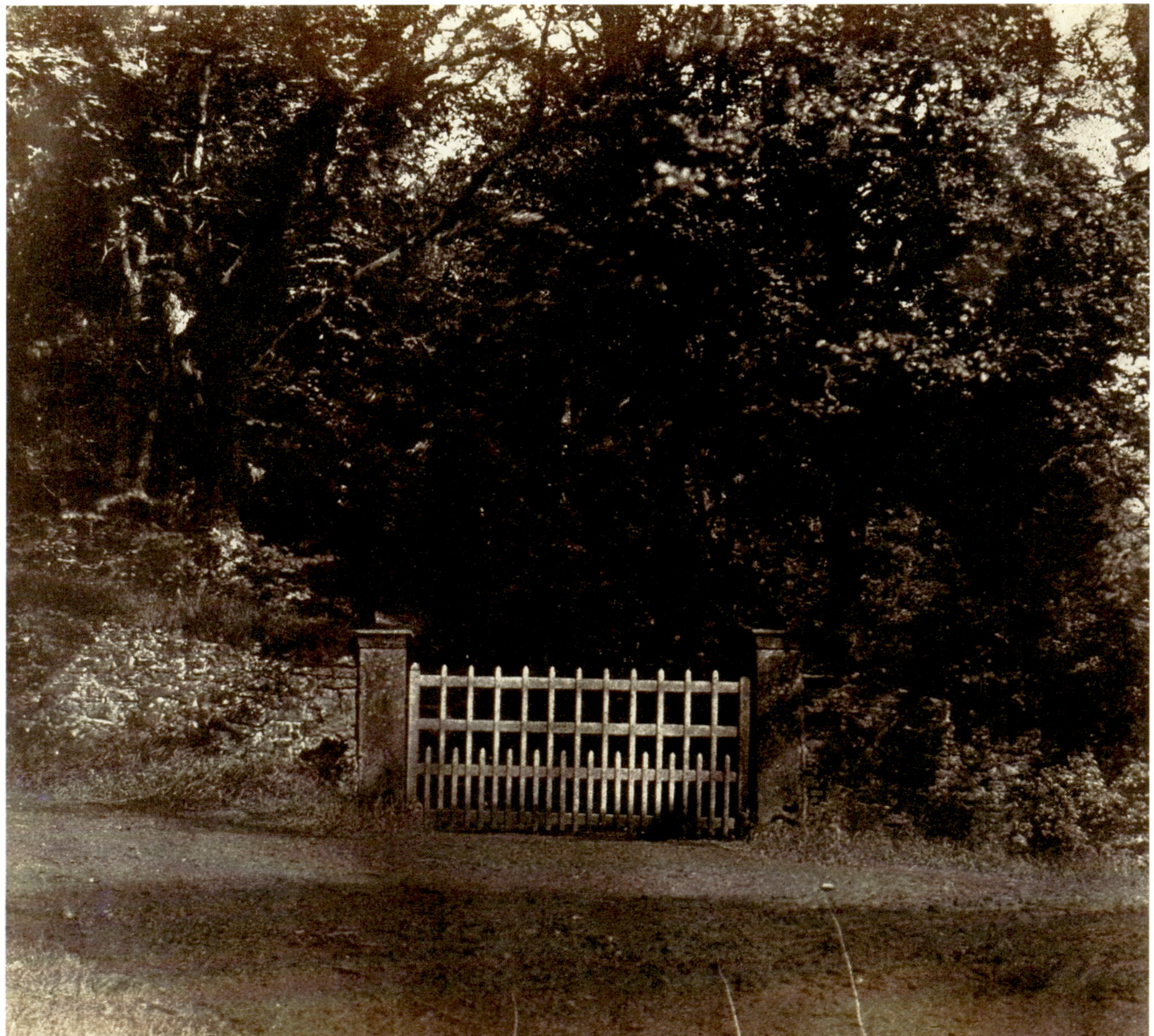

48. George Moir, *At Arniston*, ca. 1855

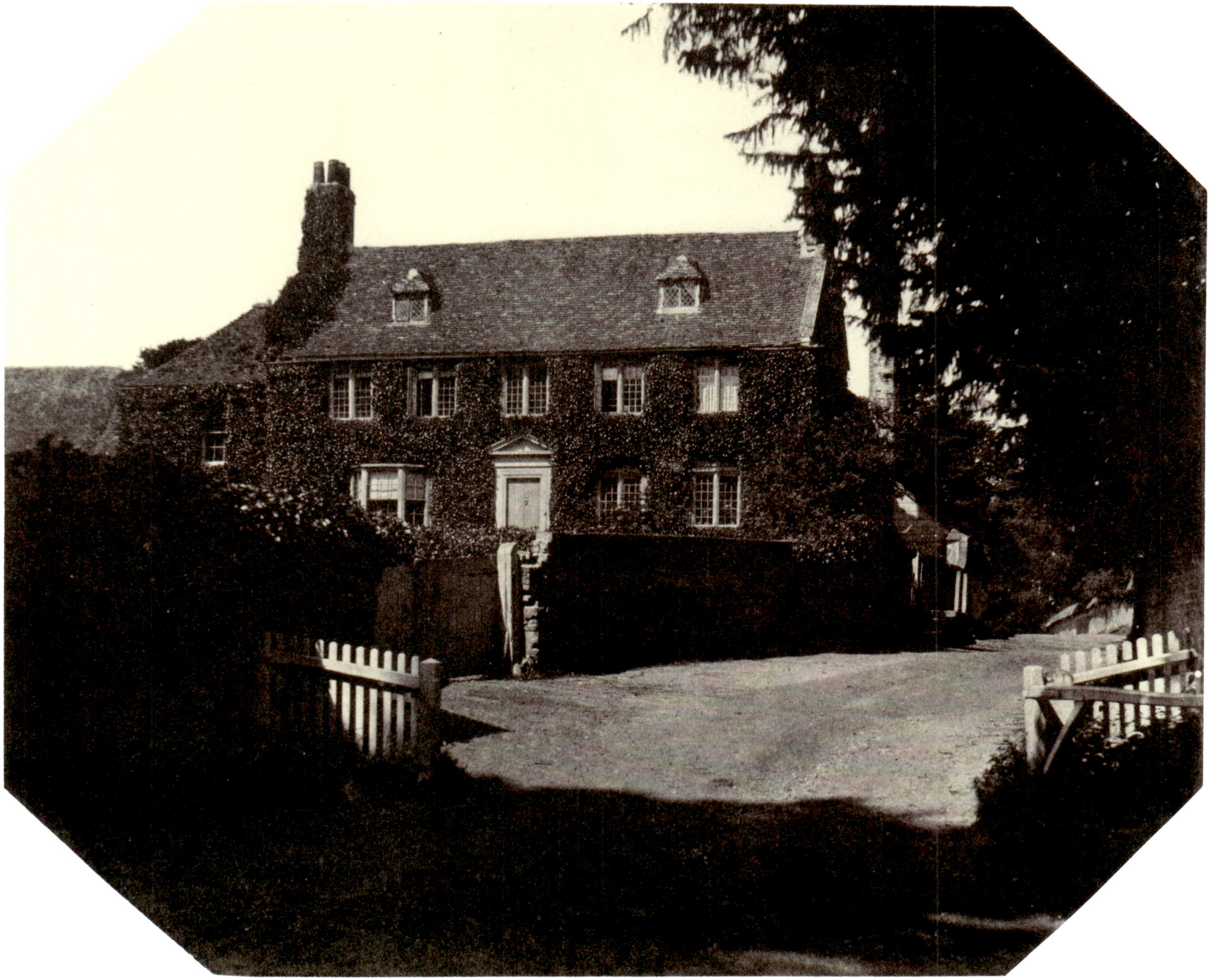

49. Unknown photographer, House and Picket Fence, 1850s

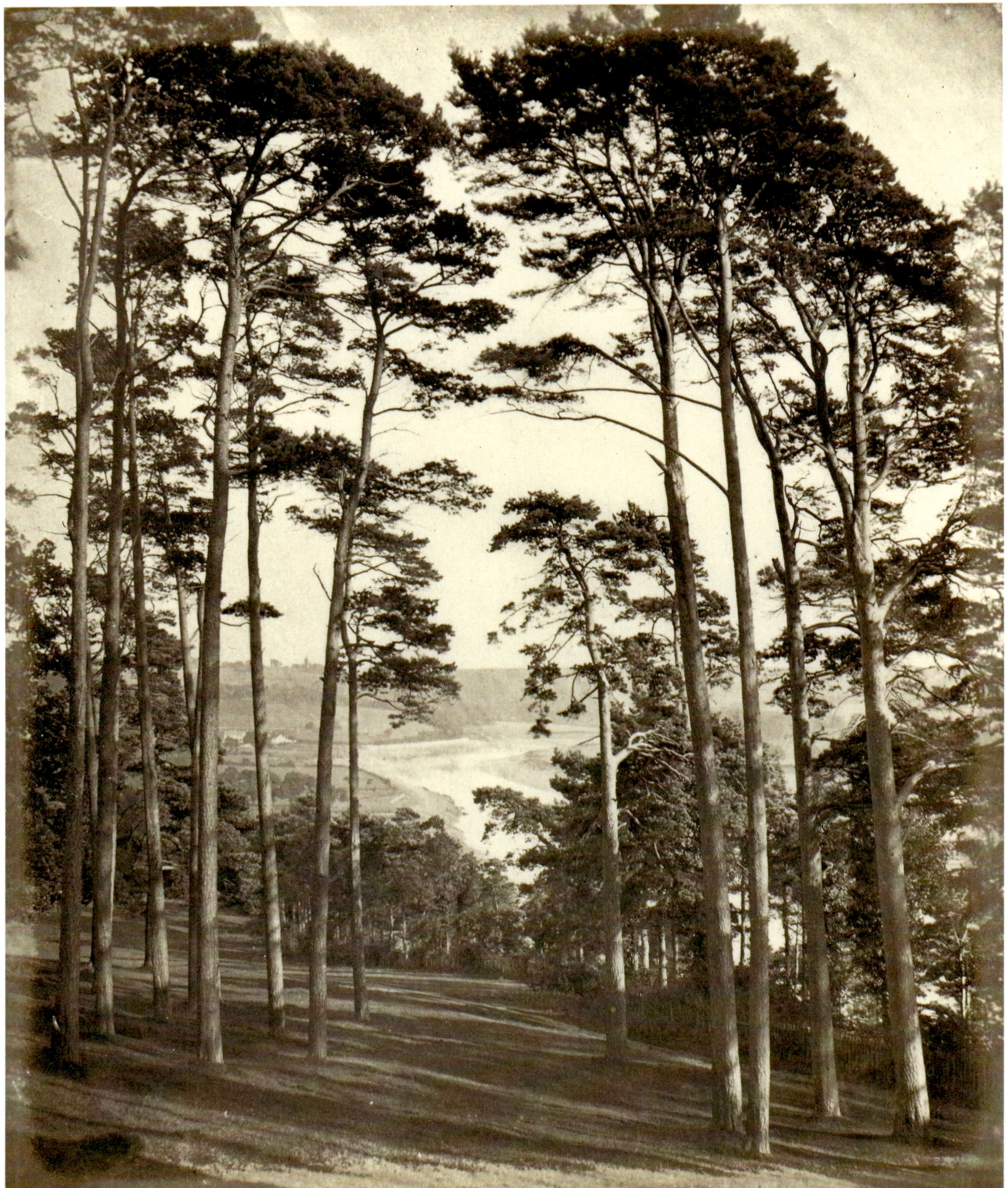

50. John Hill Morgan, *In King's Weston Park, Bristol,* ca. 1855

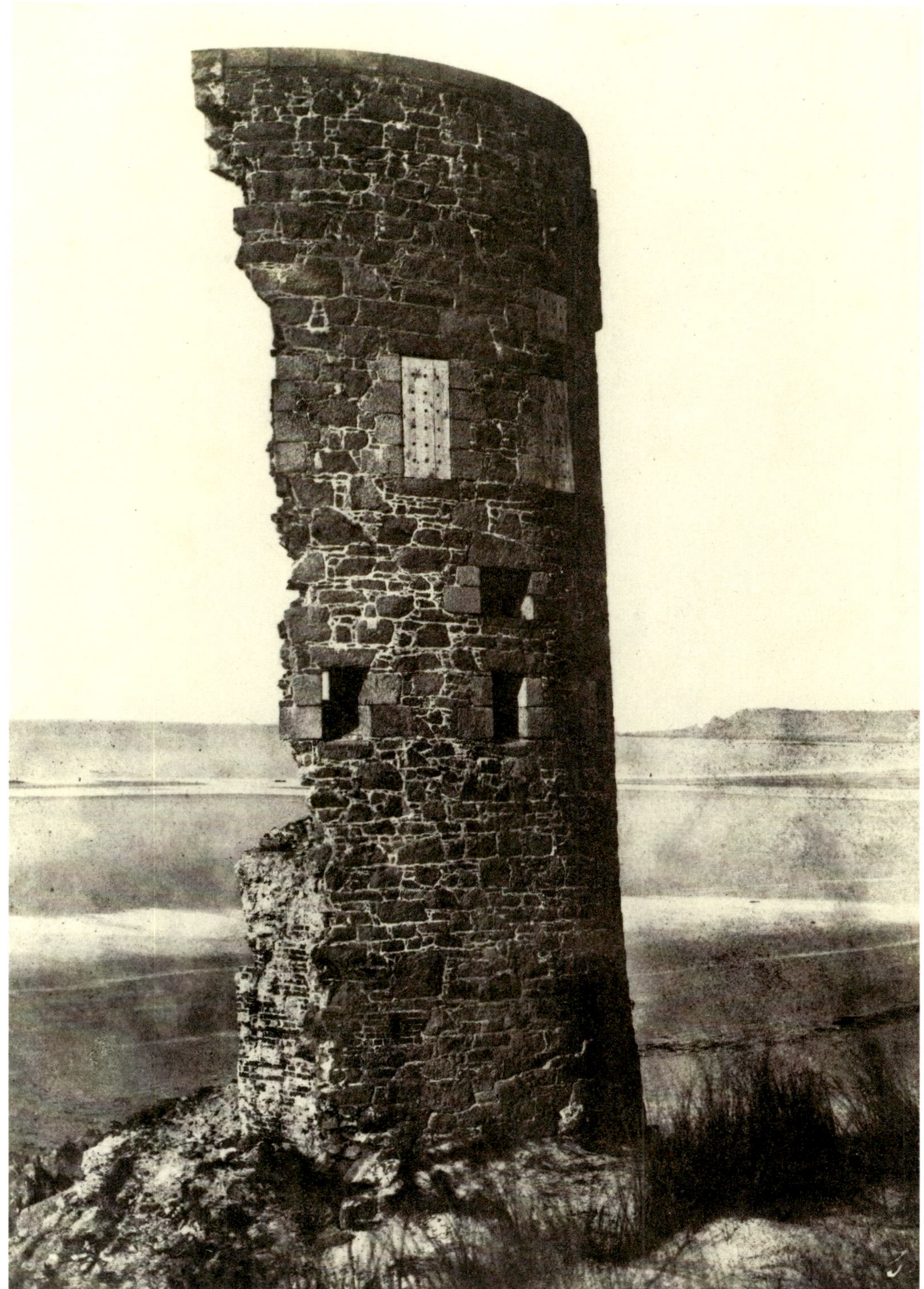

51. Thomas Sutton, *Tower Struck by Lightning, Saint-Ouen Bay*, 1854

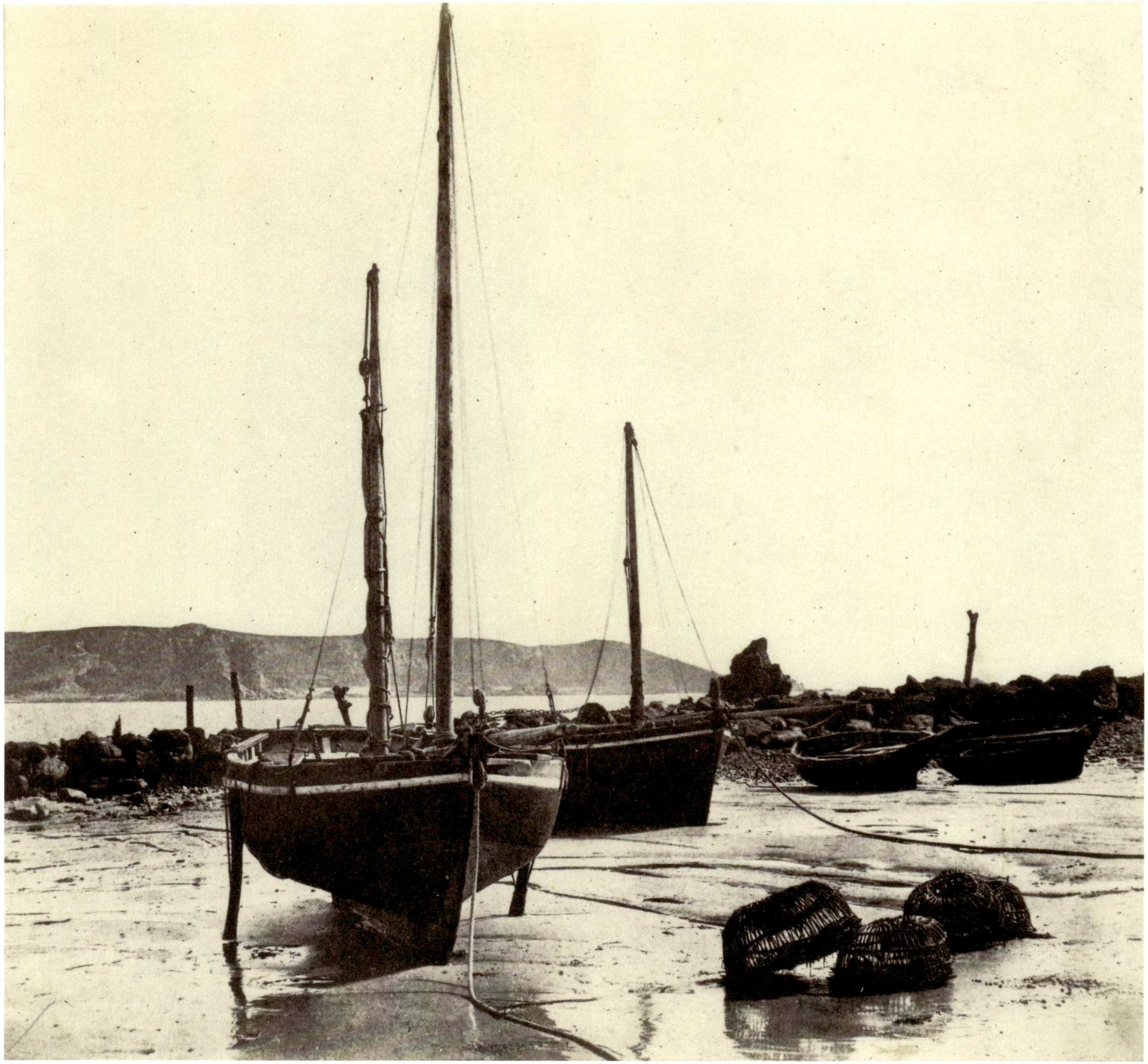

52. Thomas Sutton, *Fishing Boats, Saint Brélade Bay*, 1854

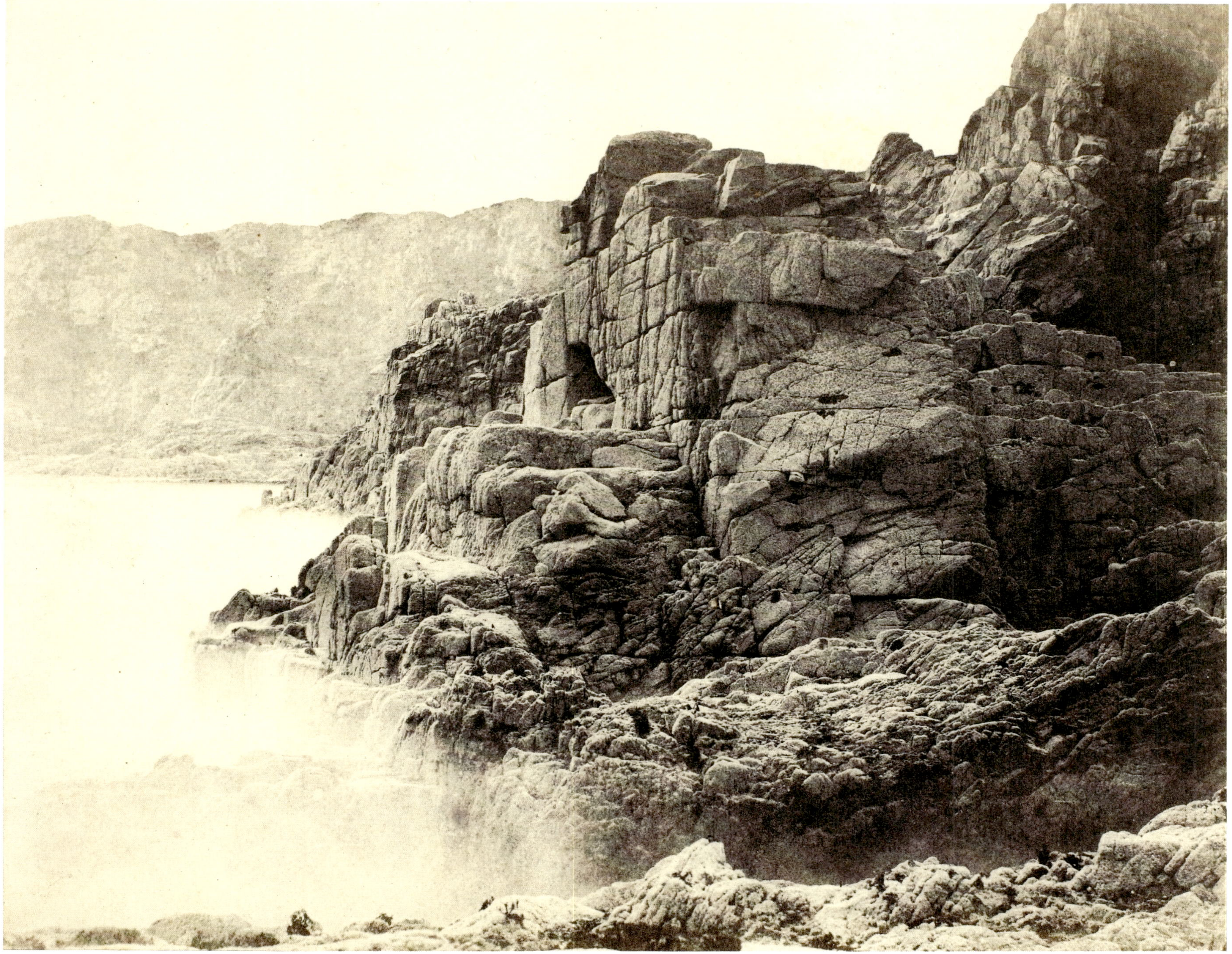

53. Thomas Sutton, *Rising Tide, Fiquet Bay*, 1854

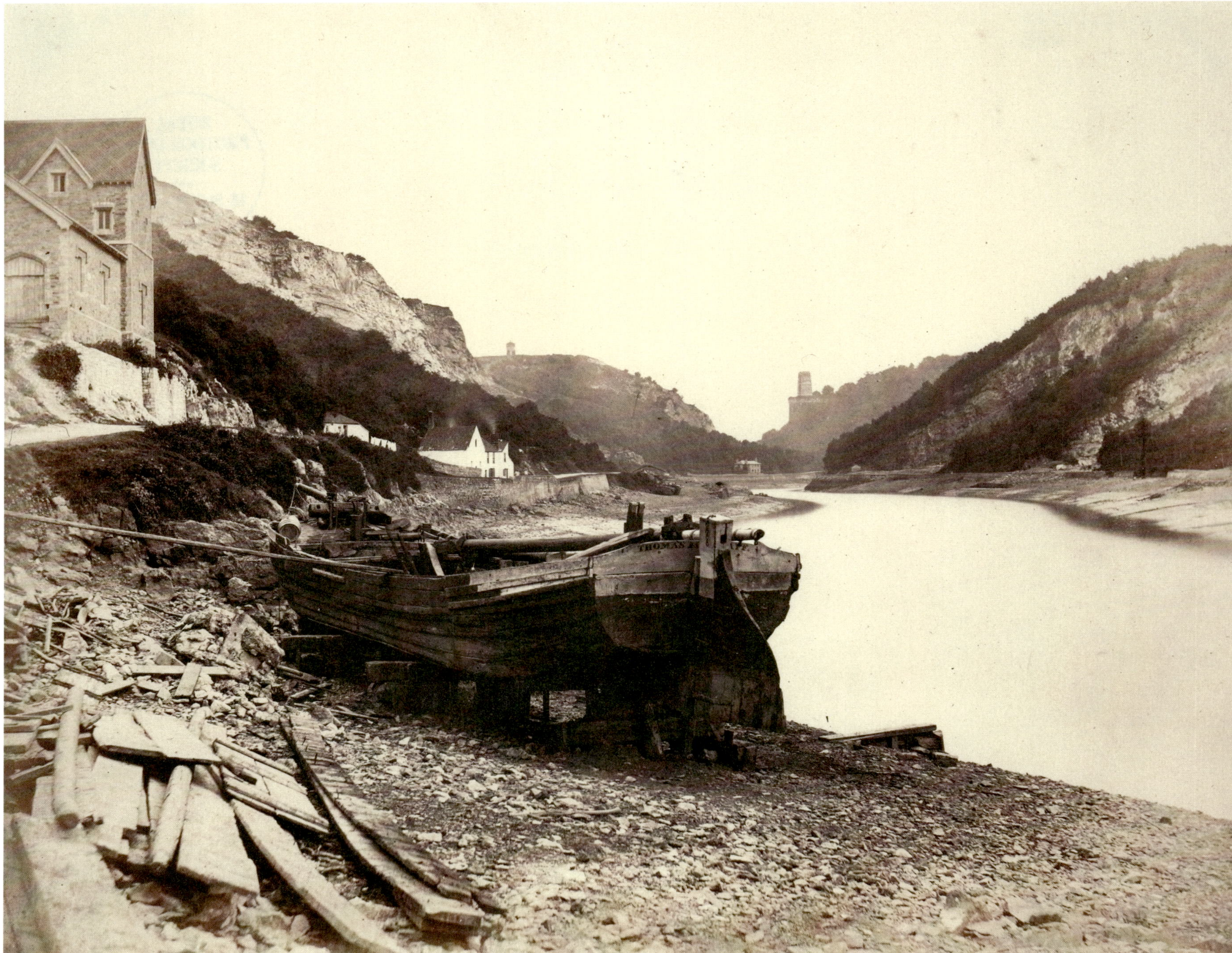

54. Charles Brittan, *Clifton Gorge*, 1853–54

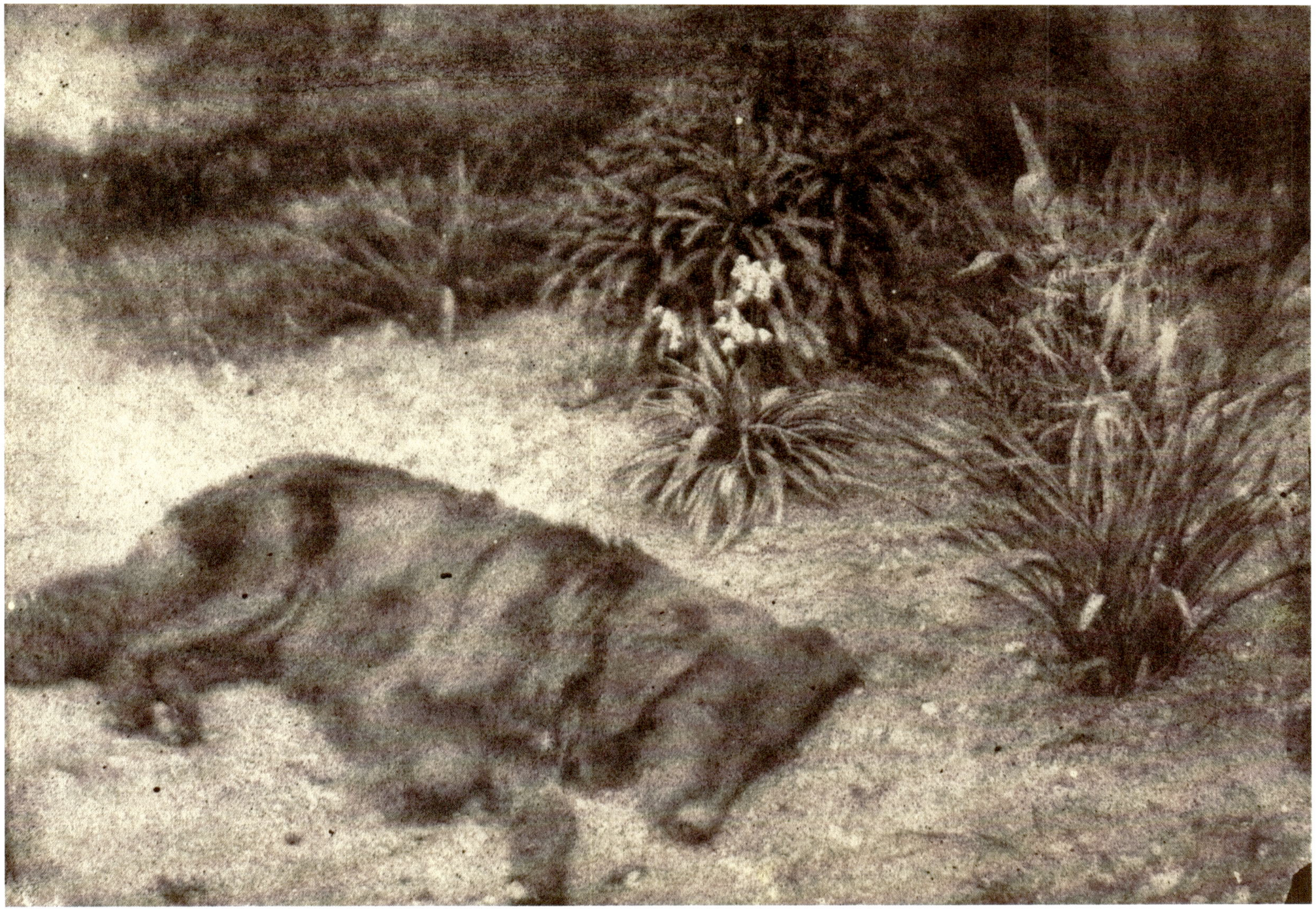

55. Alfred Capel Cure, *"Nigger" Asleep—Roscrea,* 1850s

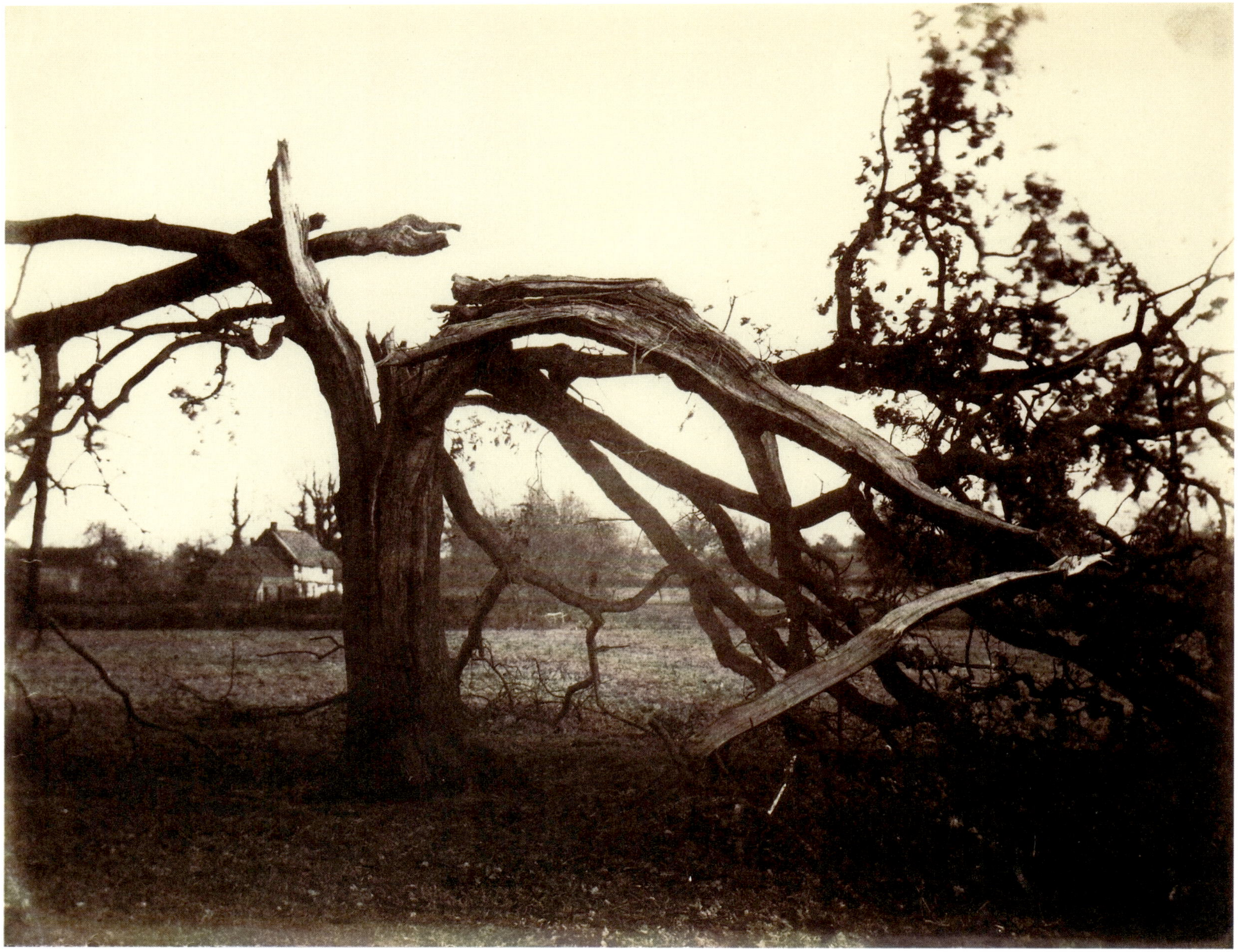

56. Alfred Capel Cure, *Blasted Tree at Badger*, 1856

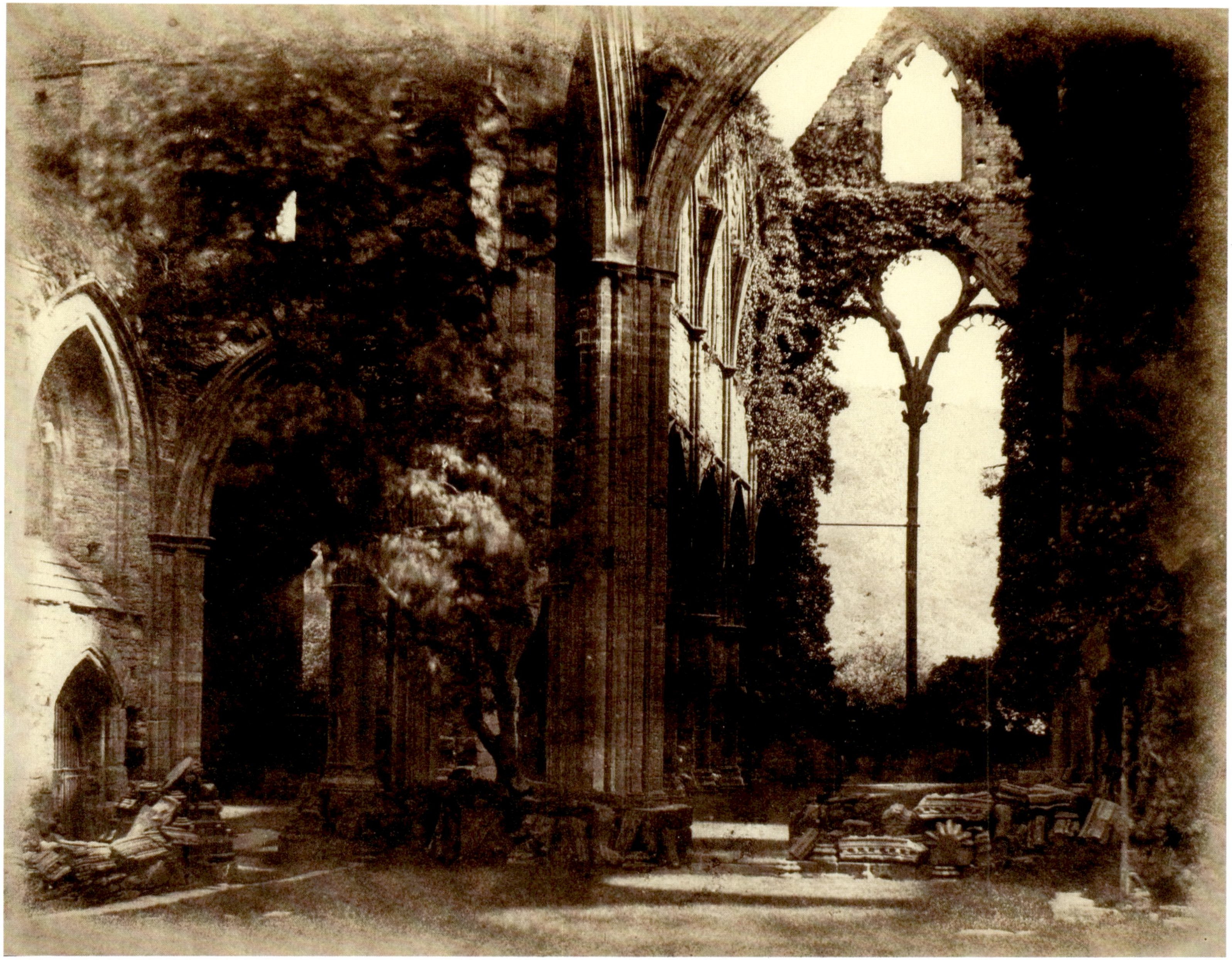

57. Alfred Capel Cure, *East Window, Tintern,* August 17, 1857

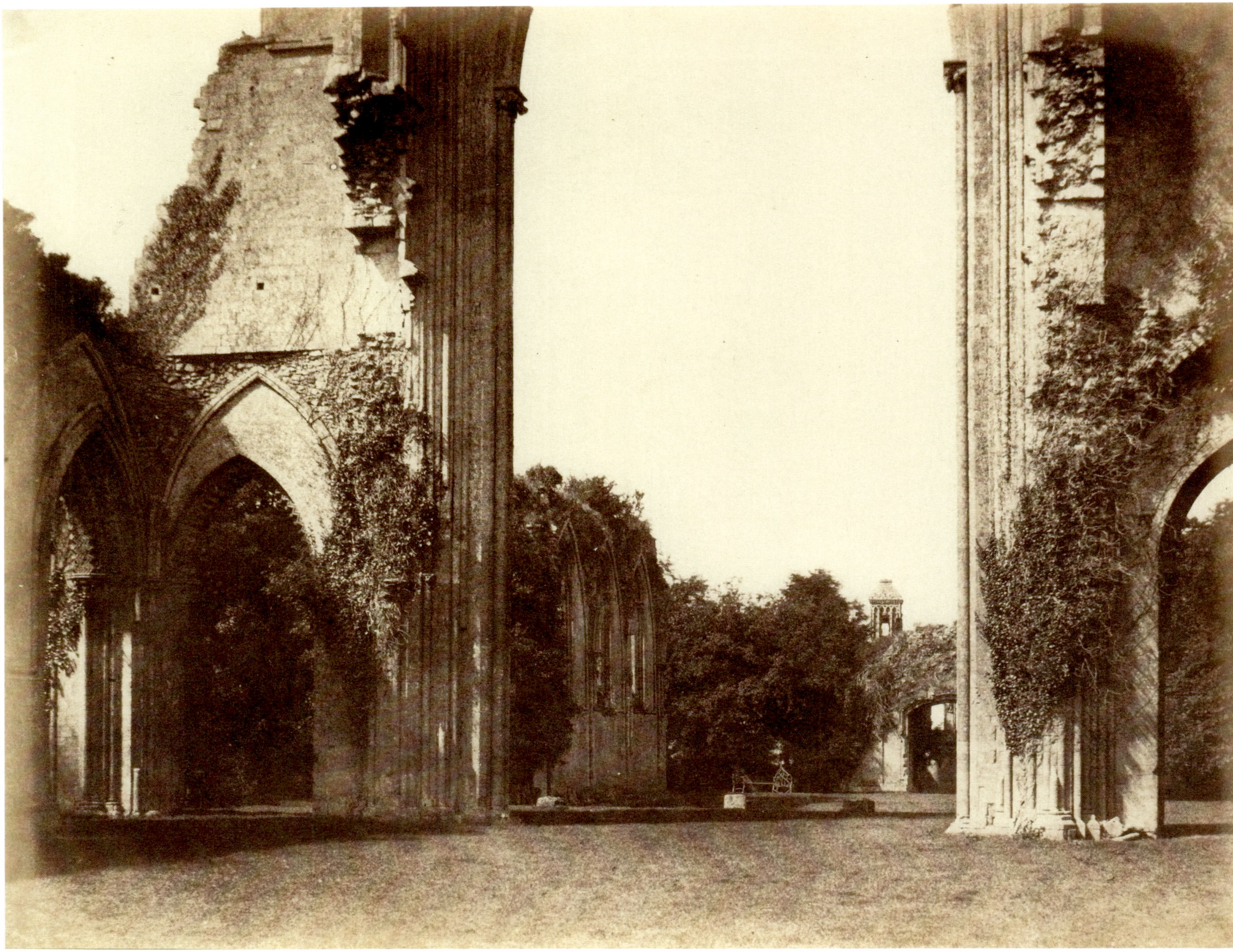

58. Alfred Capel Cure, *Glastonbury Abbey, Looking West,* 1857

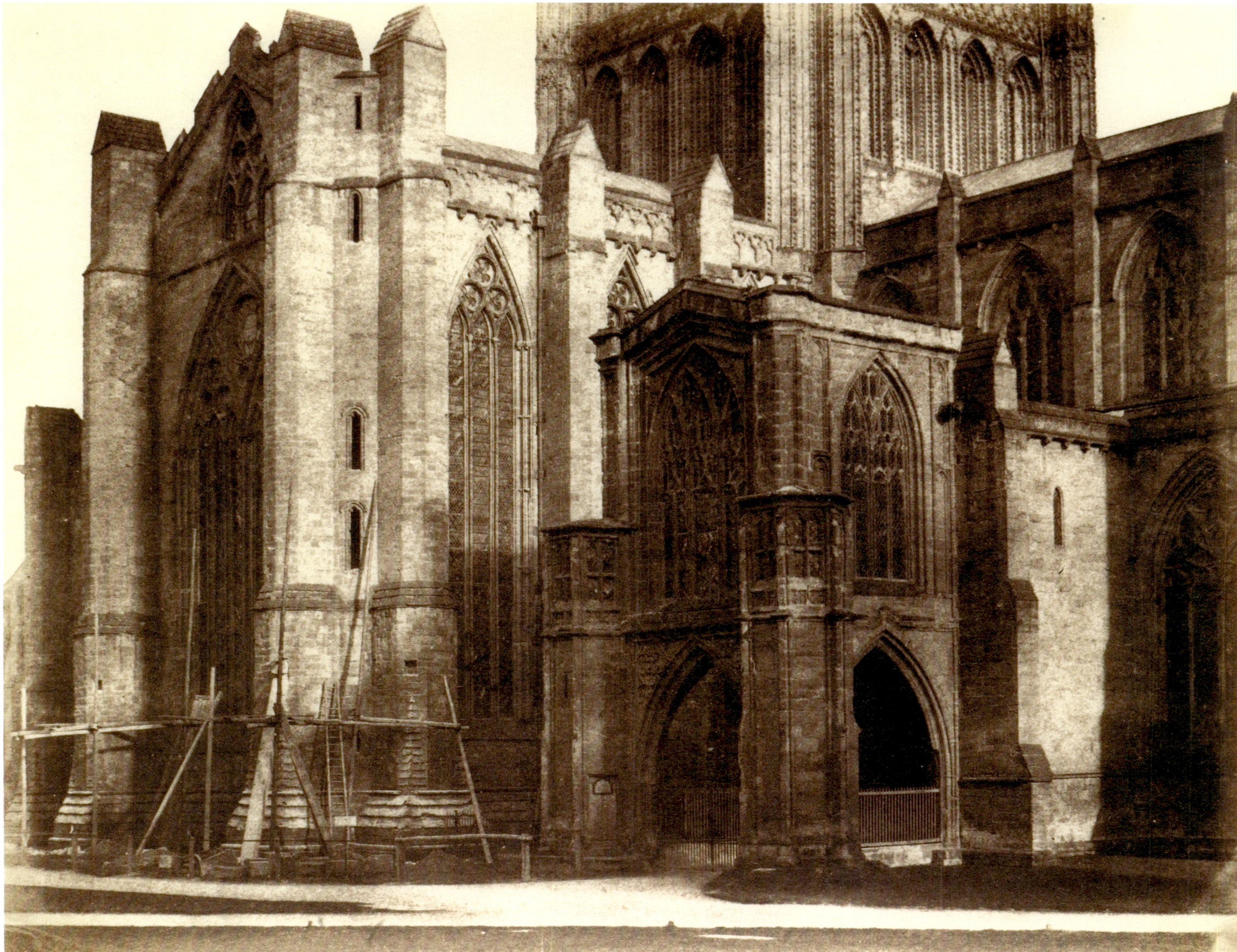

59. Alfred Capel Cure, *Hereford Cathedral from Northwest*, 1858–60

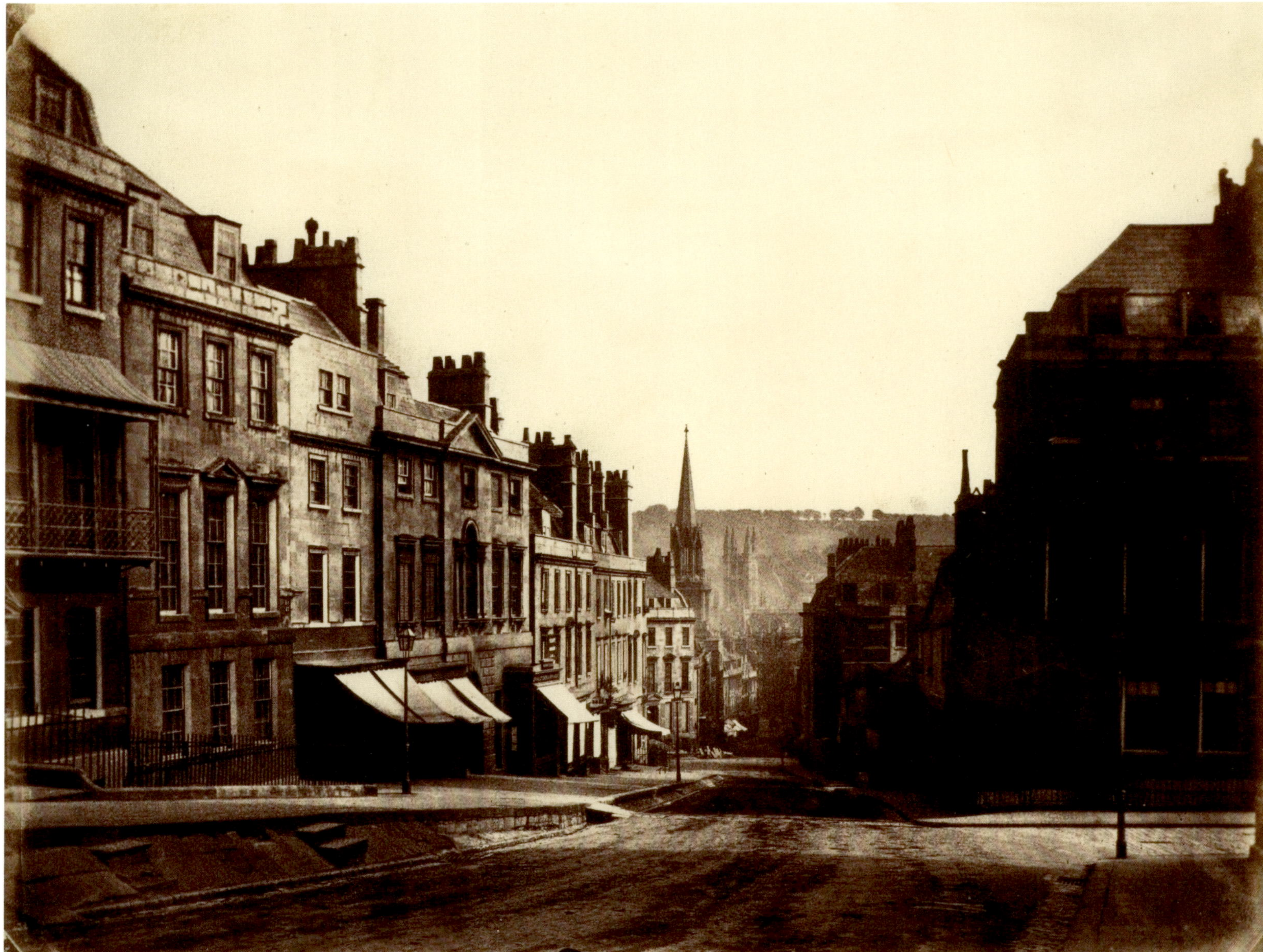

60. Robert Henry Cheney, *Belmont, Bath,* 1850s

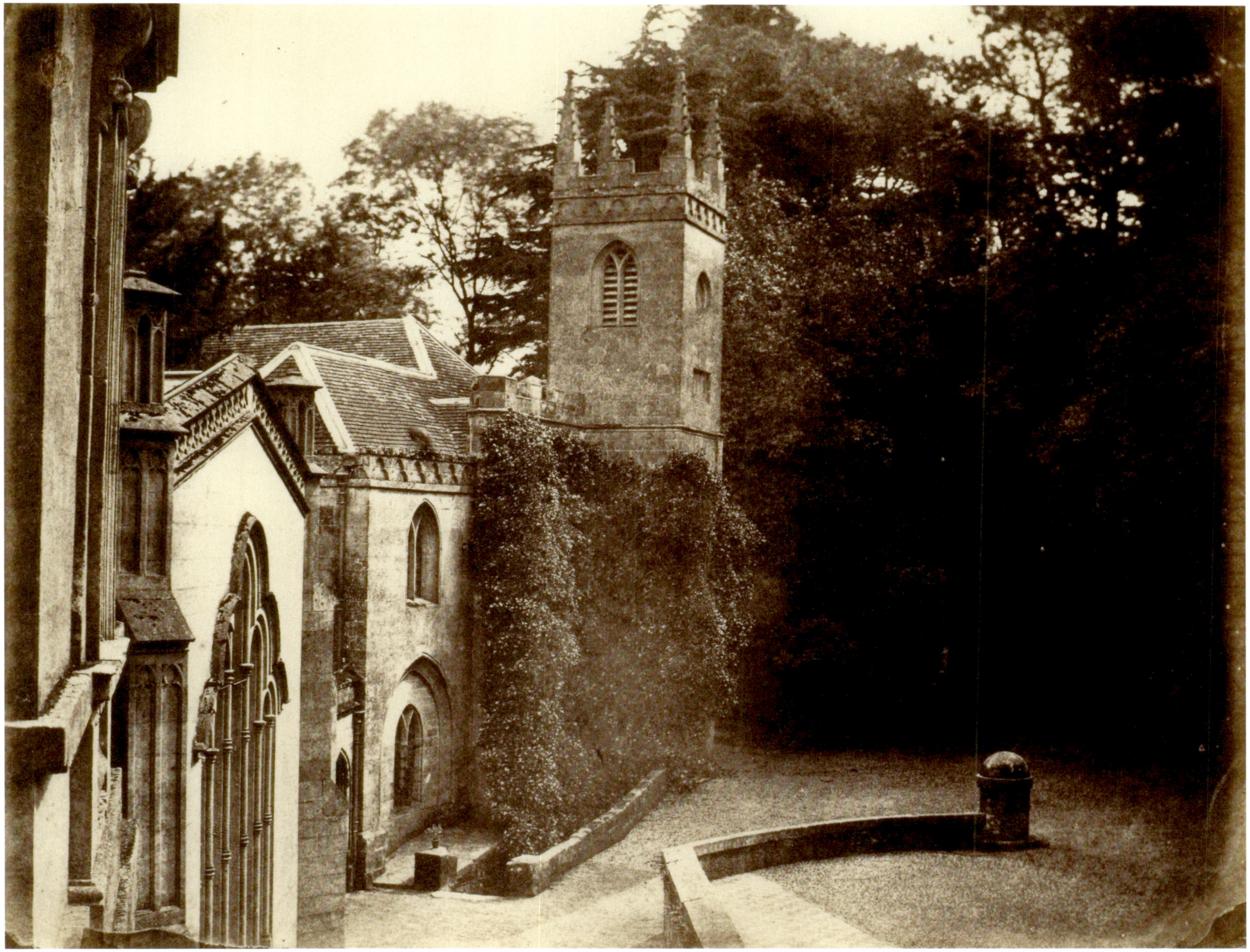

61. Robert Henry Cheney, *Guyscliffe*, 1850s

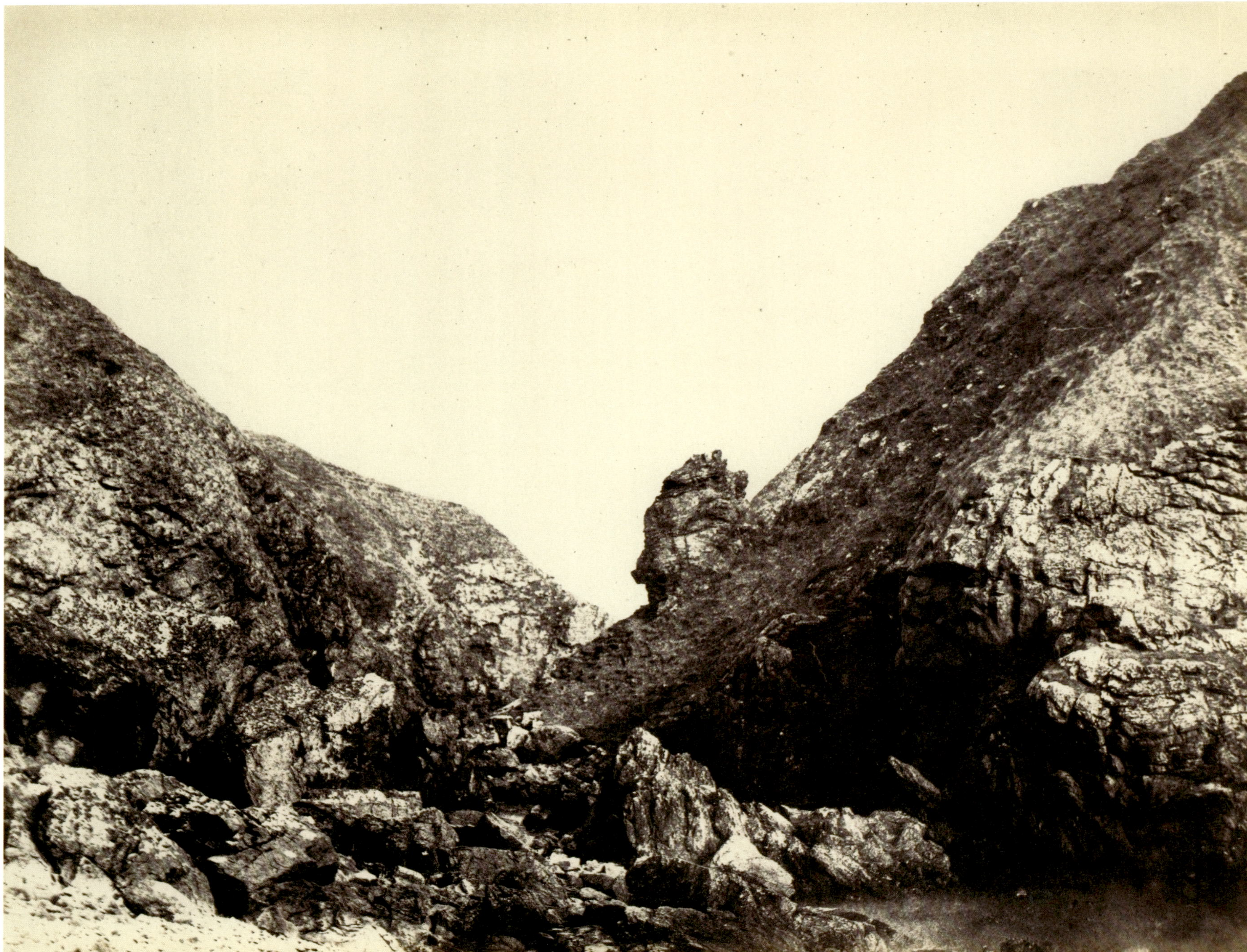

62. Horatio Ross, *Sea Coast near Netherley*, mid-1850s

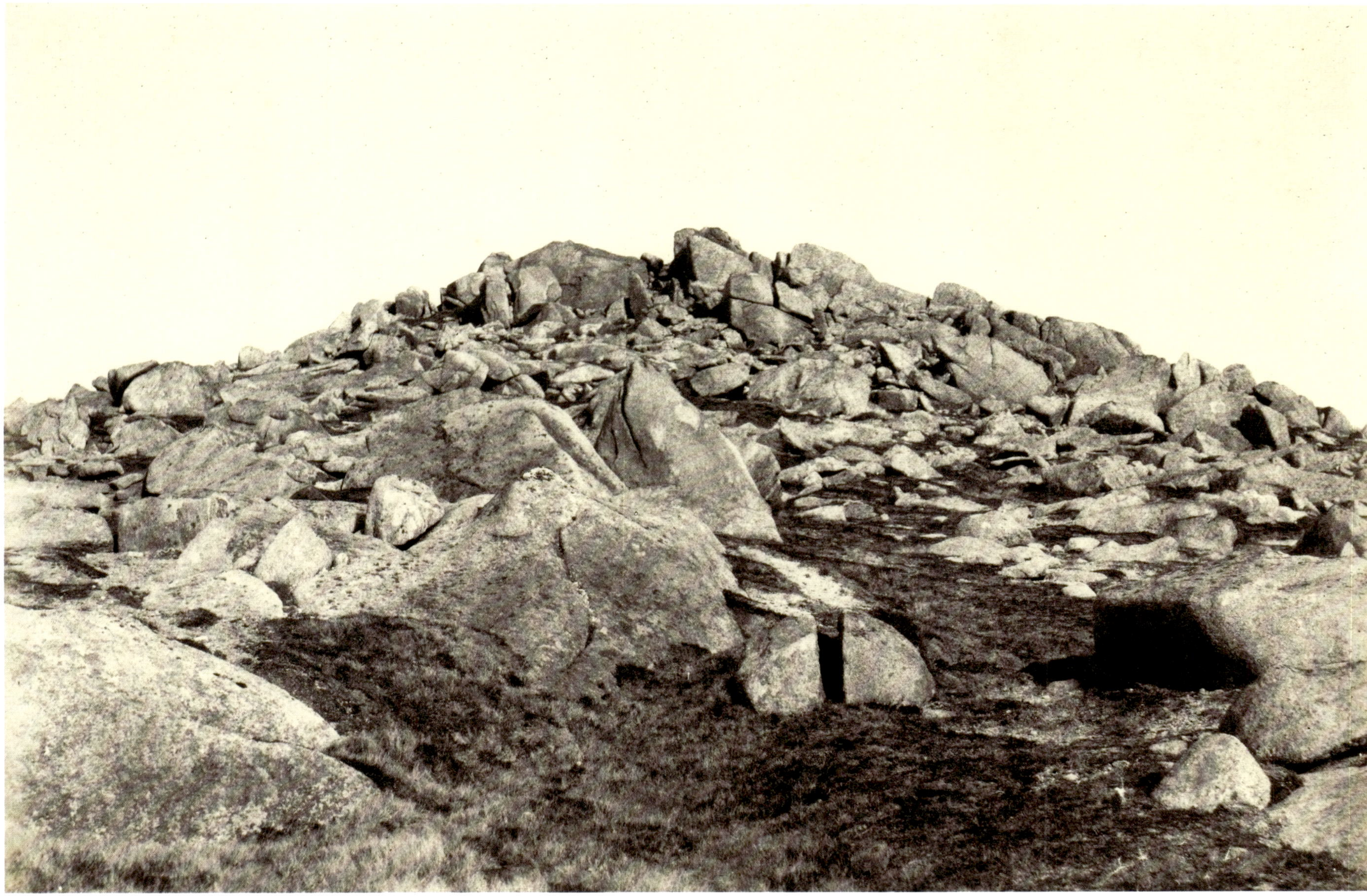

63. Horatio Ross, Rocky Landscape, mid-1850s

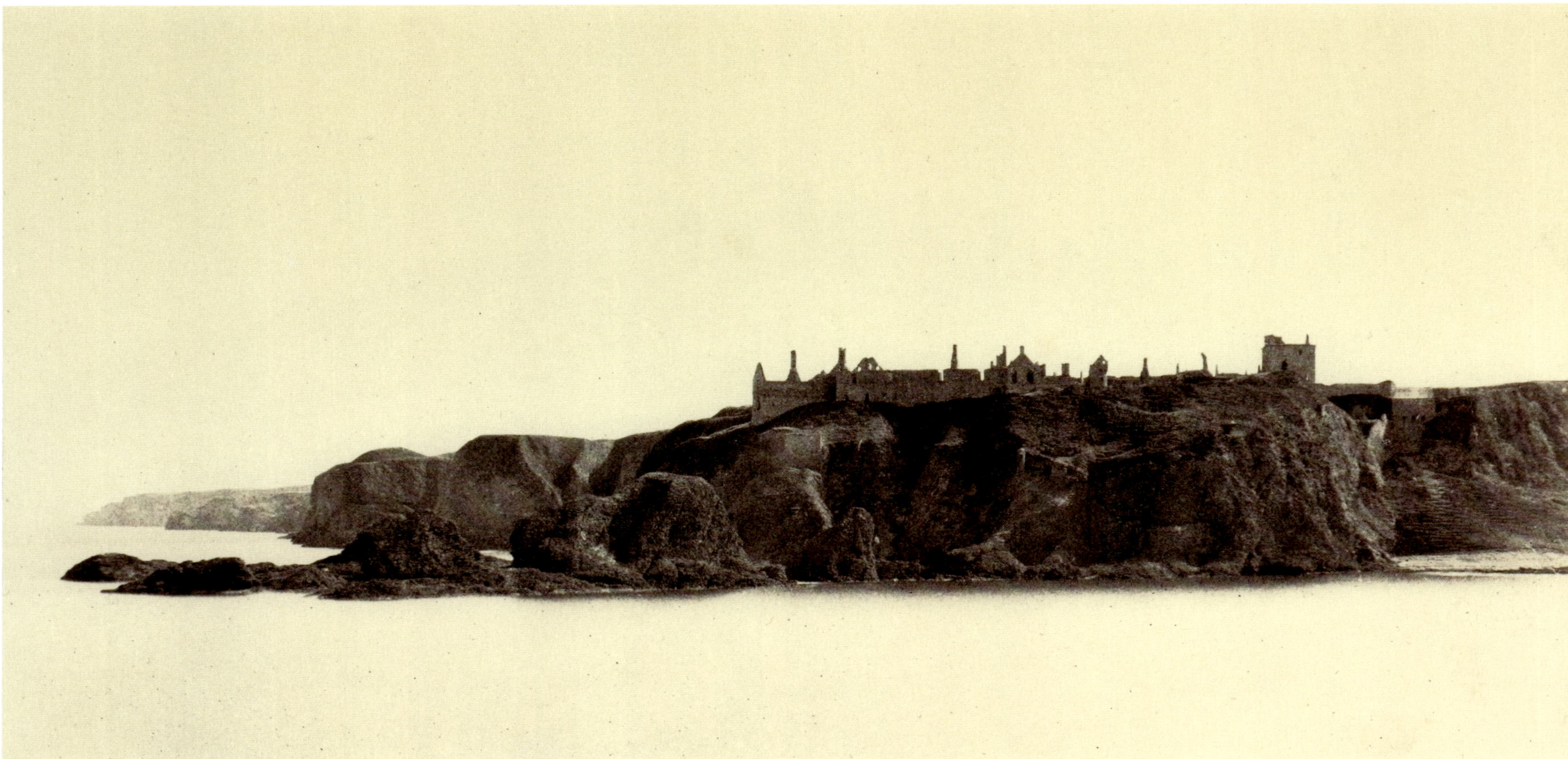

64. Horatio Ross, *View of Dunottar Castle,* mid-1850s

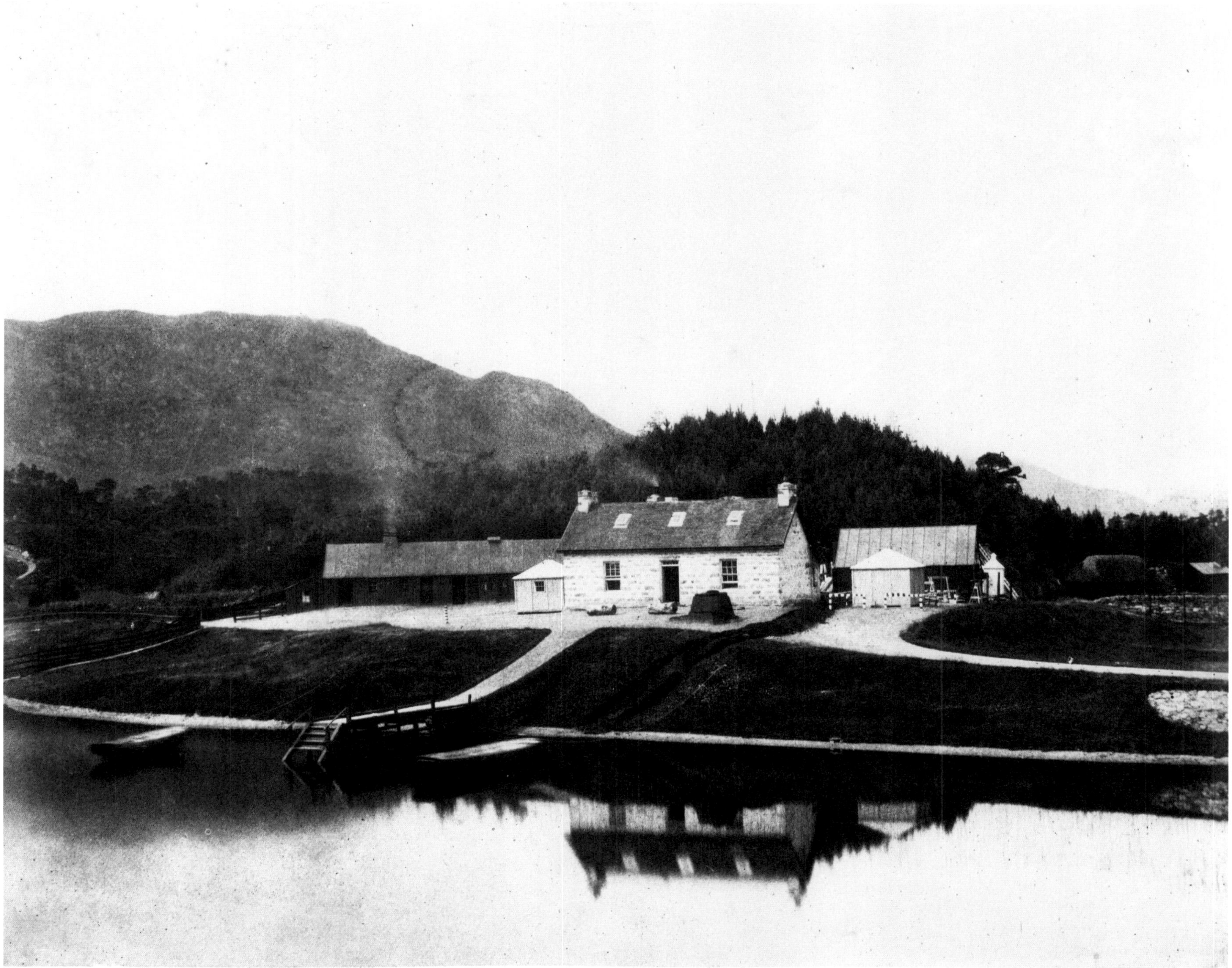

65. Horatio Ross, *Affaric Lodge*, mid-1850s

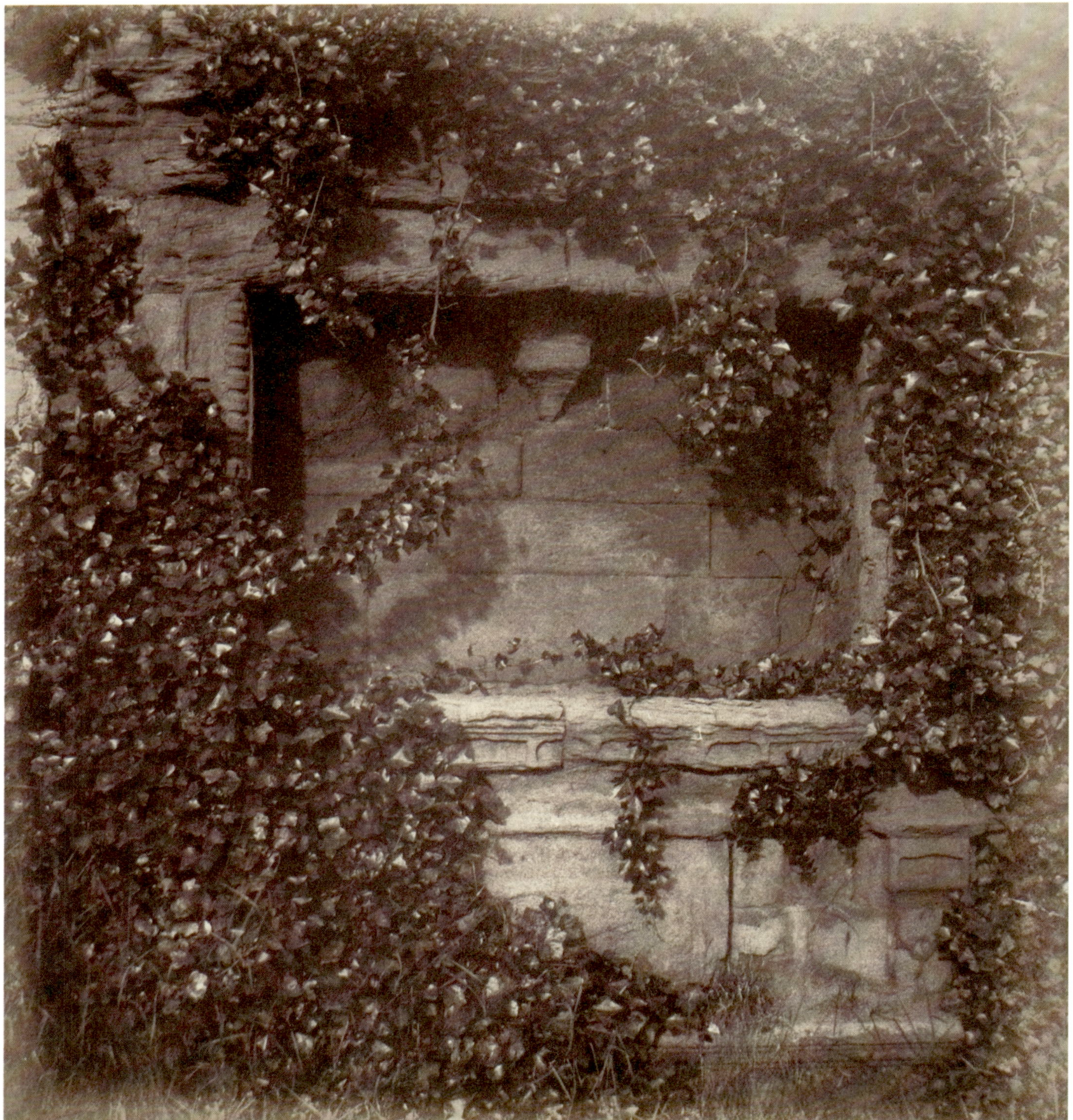

66. Thomas Keith, *Greyfriars Churchyard, Monument to Provost Archibald Tod, Edinburgh*, 1854–57

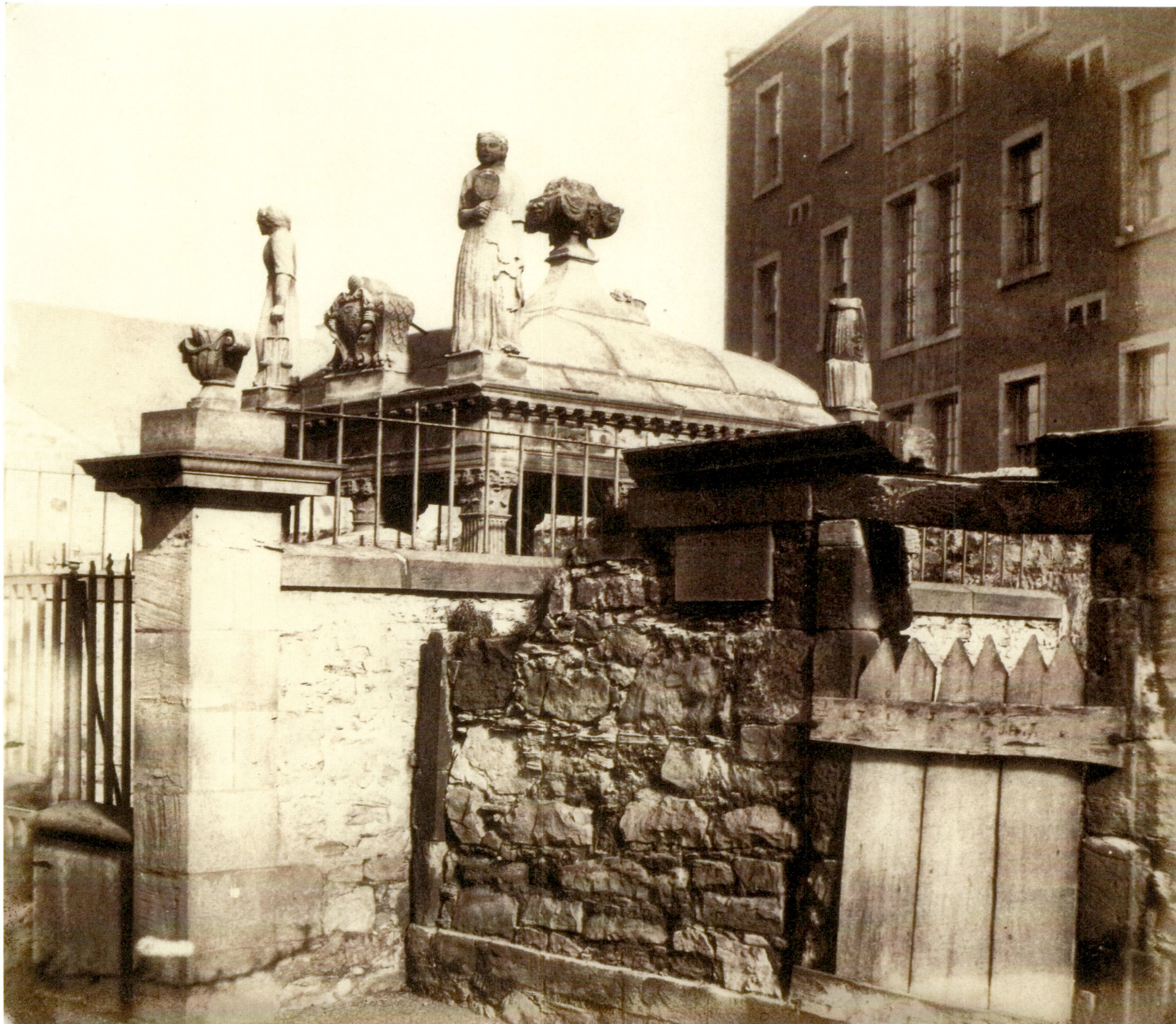

67. Thomas Keith, *Greyfriars Churchyard, Monument to Provost William Little of Liberton, Edinburgh*, 1854–57

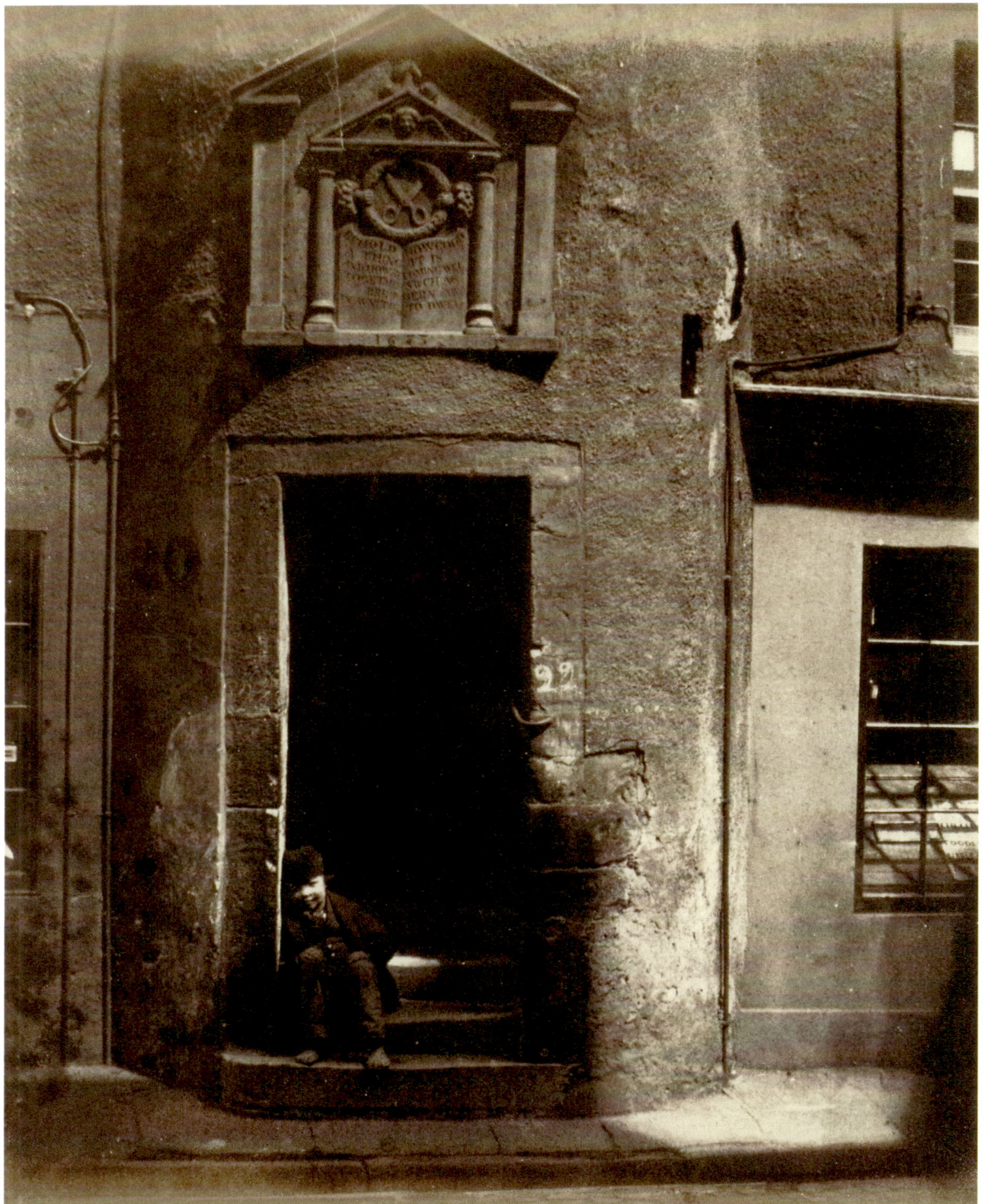

68. Thomas Keith, *Doorway of Tailor's Hall, Potterrow, Edinburgh*, 1854–57

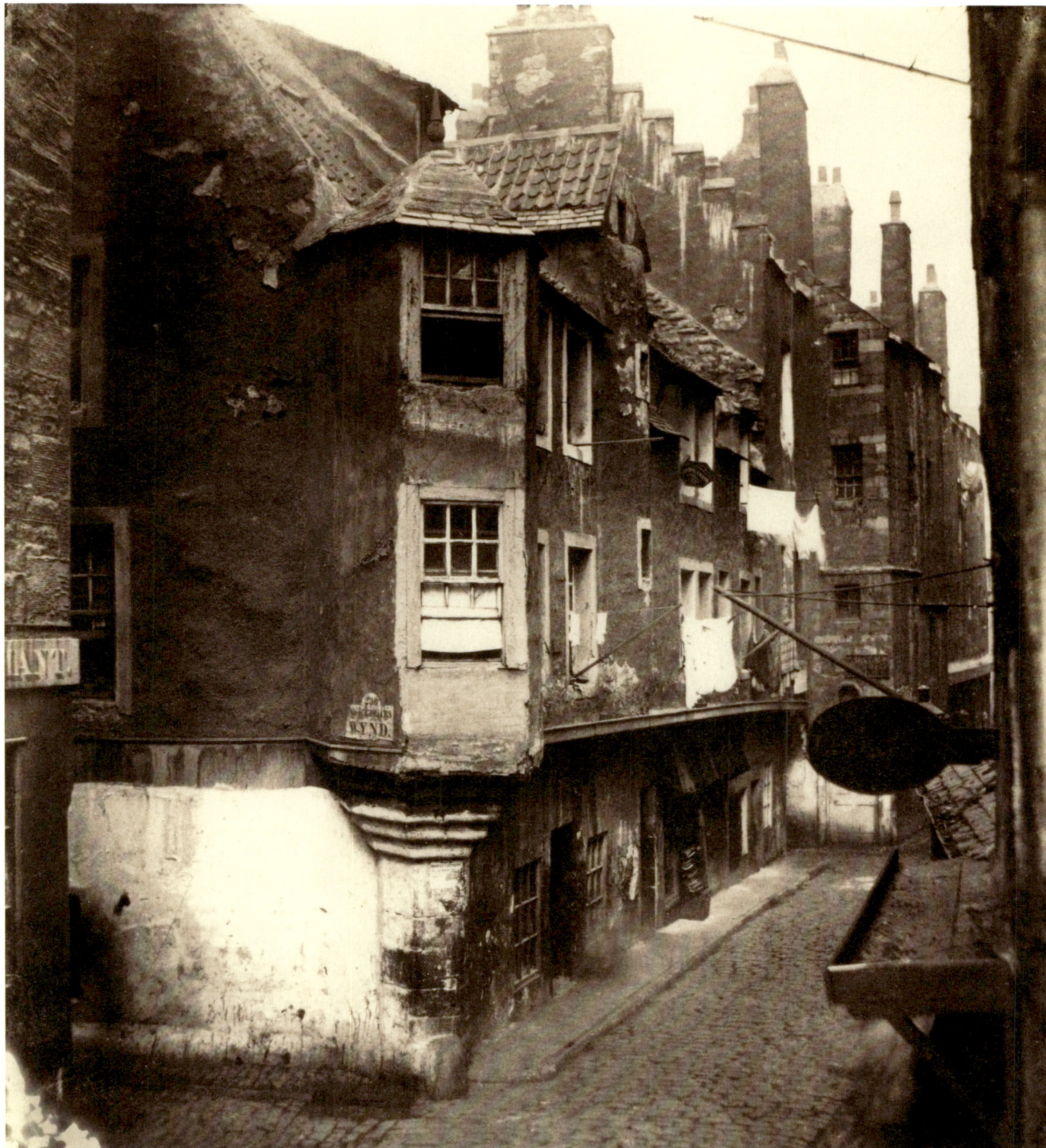

69. Thomas Keith, *Cardinal Beaton's House, Edinburgh*, 1854–57

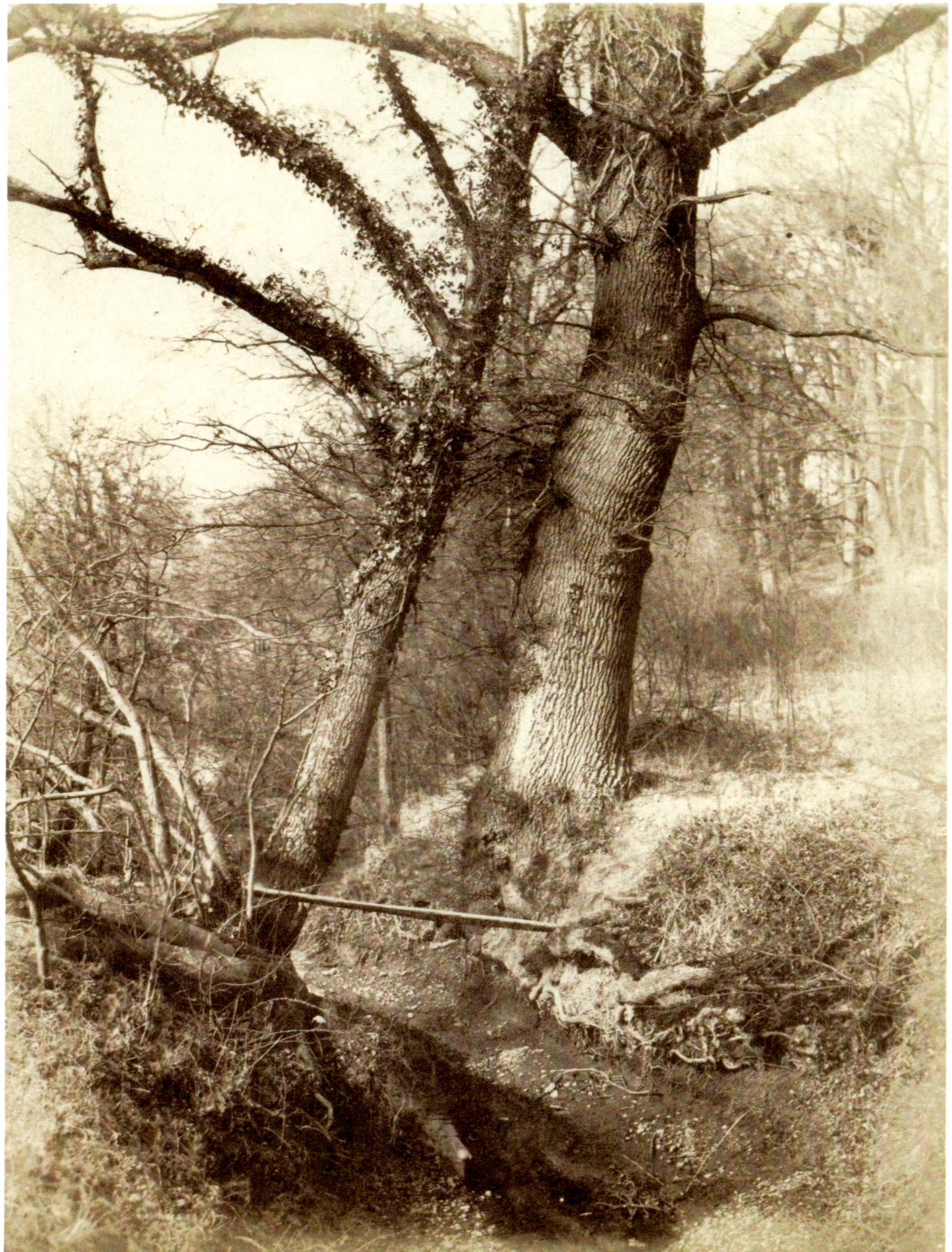

70. Thomas Keith, Trees, 1854–57

British Calotypists Abroad

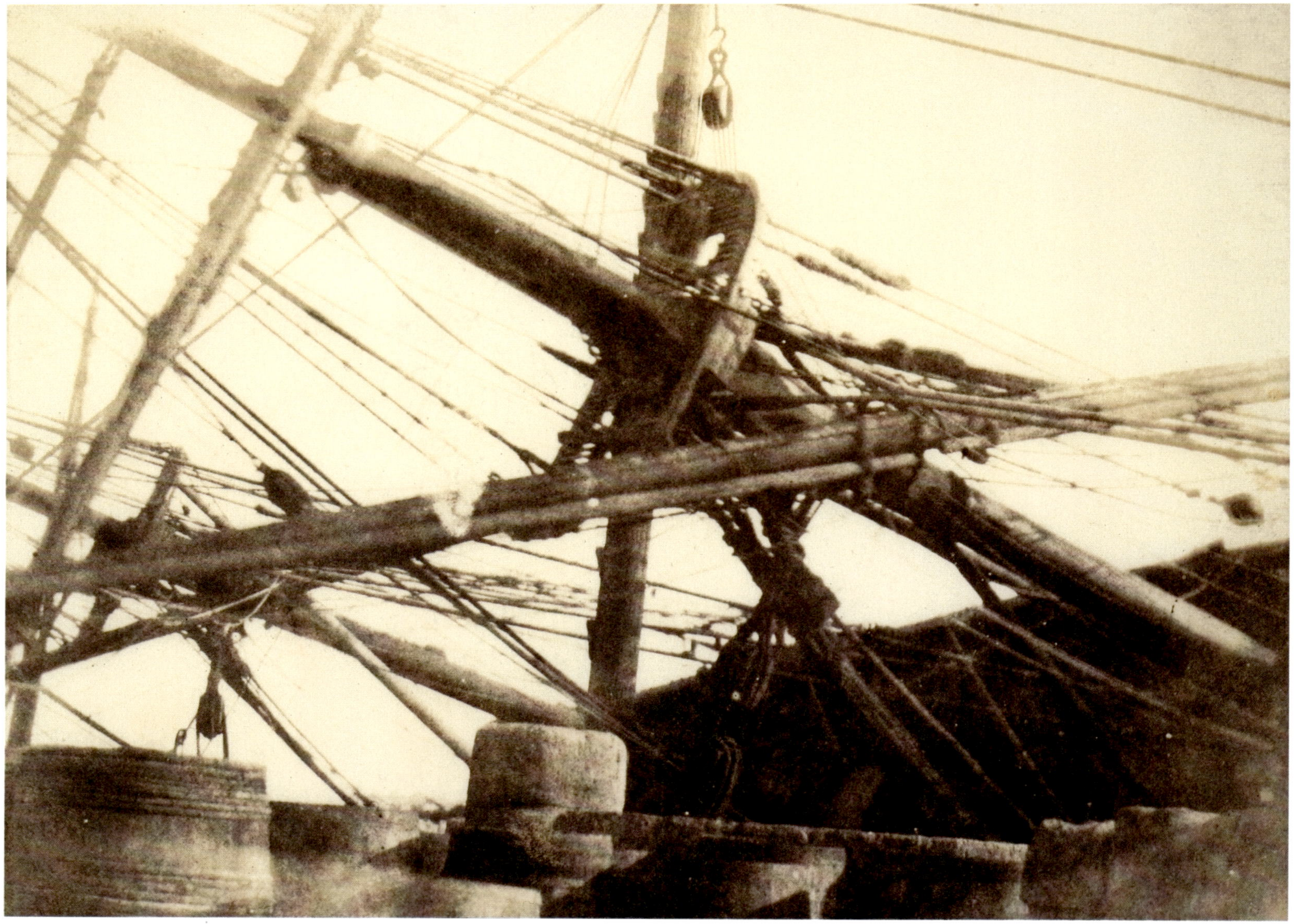

71. Calvert Richard Jones, *Palacea Brig, Hove Down, Malta,* December 1845–January 1846

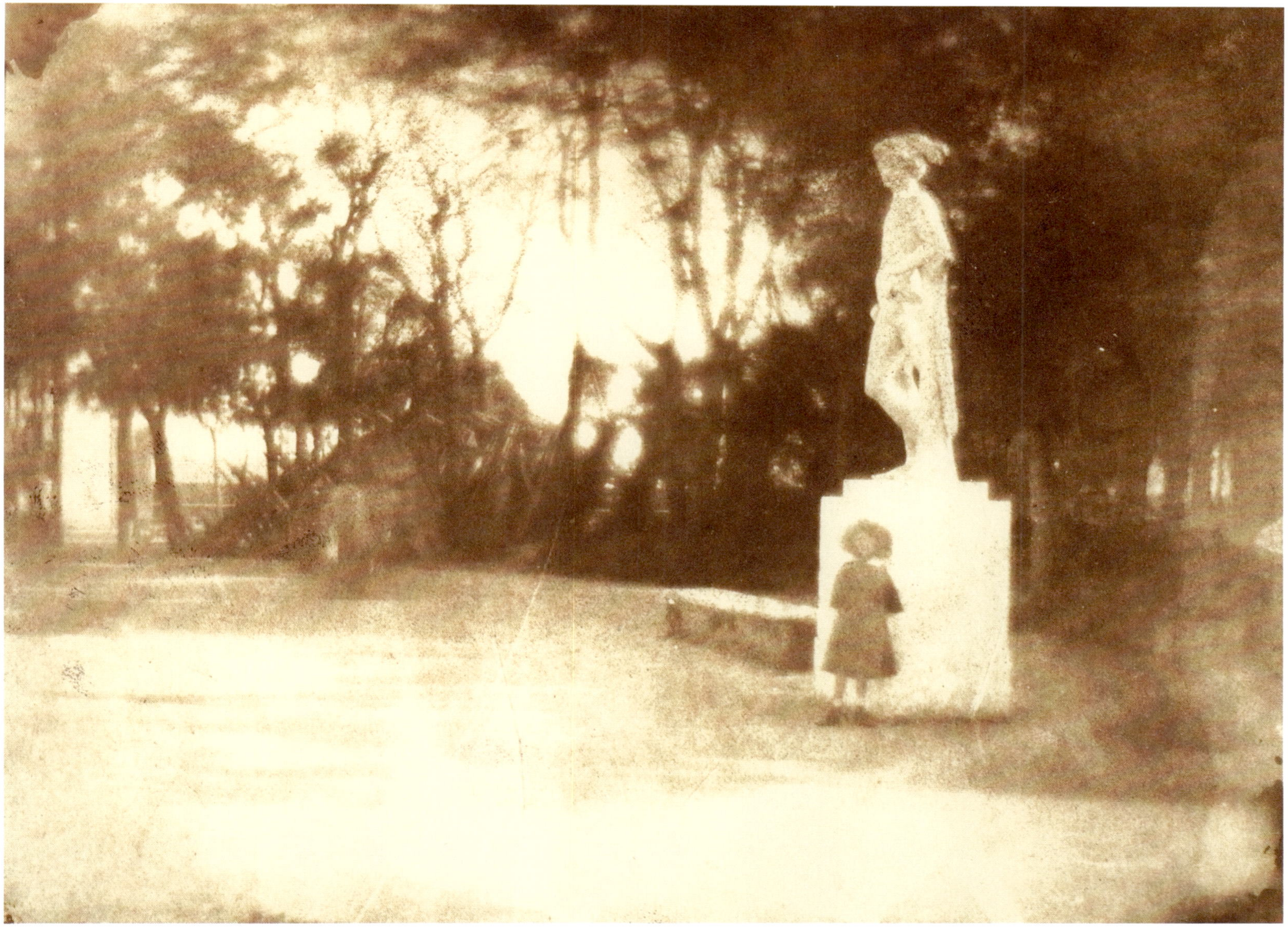

72. Christopher Rice Mansel Talbot, *Villa Reale, Naples*, 1846

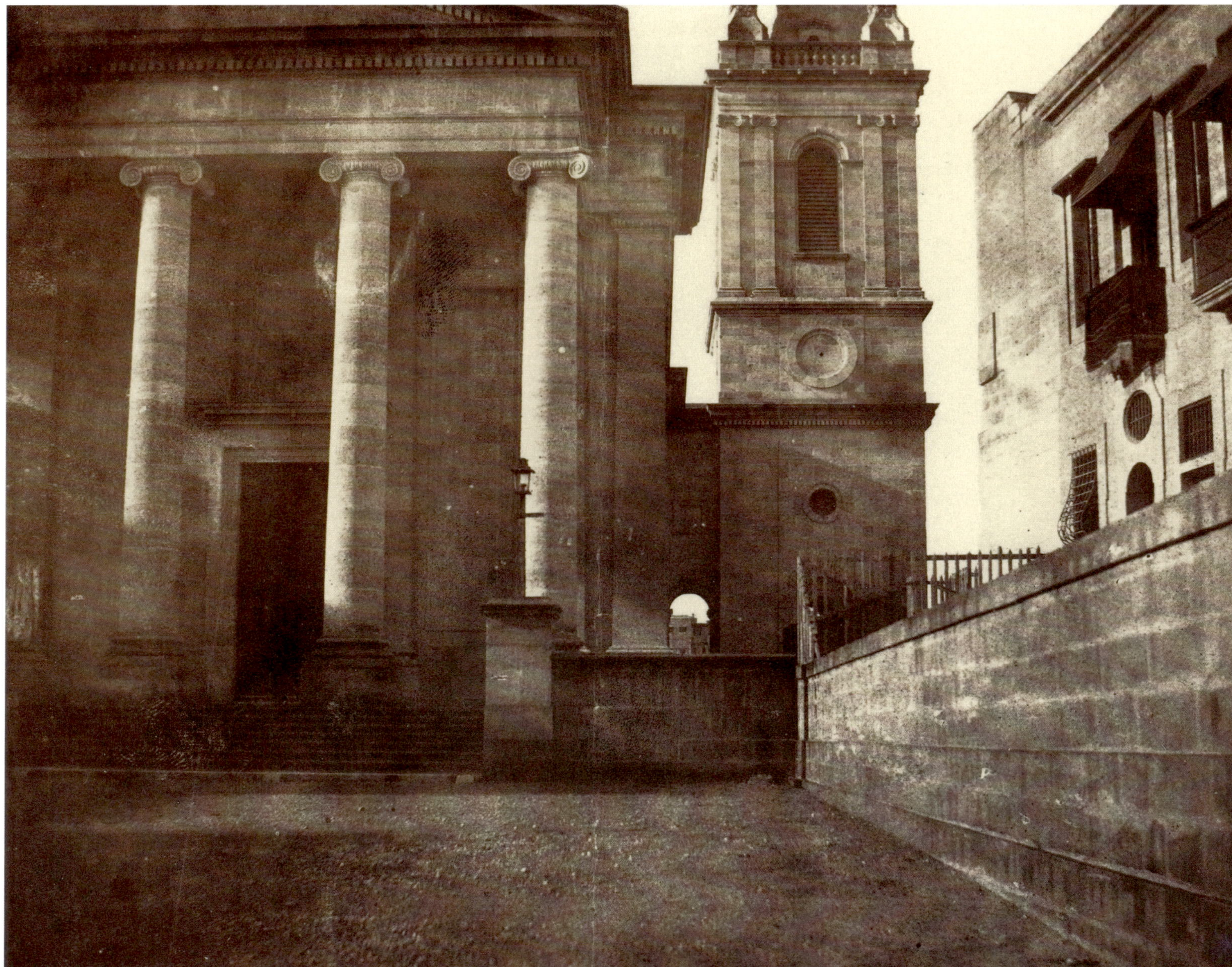

73. Calvert Richard Jones, *St. Paul's Cathedral, Valetta, Malta, with Bell Tower,* 1846

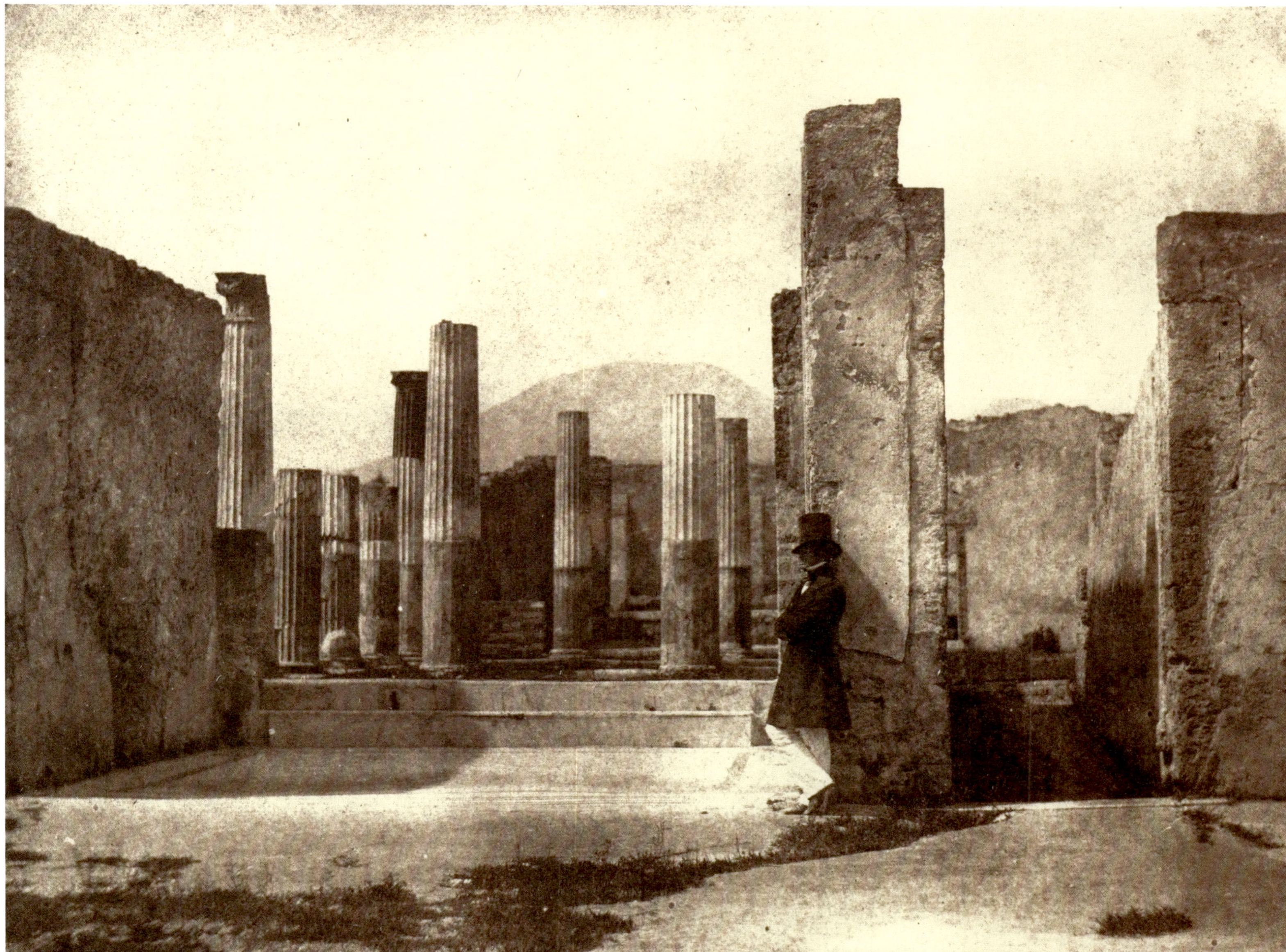

74. Calvert Richard Jones, *House of Sallust, Vesuvius behind, Pompeii*, spring 1846

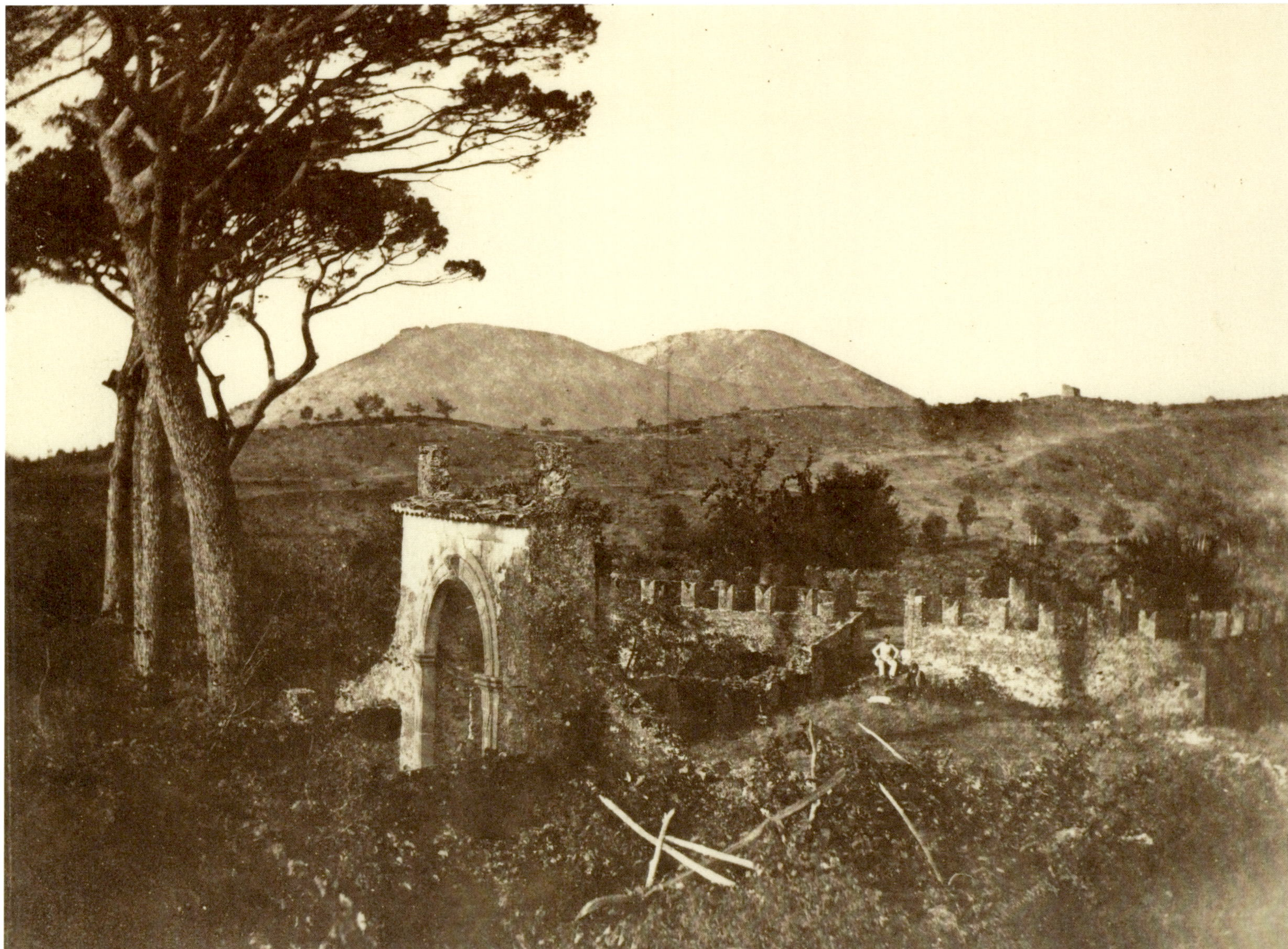

75. George Wilson Bridges, View of Mount Aetna, 1846

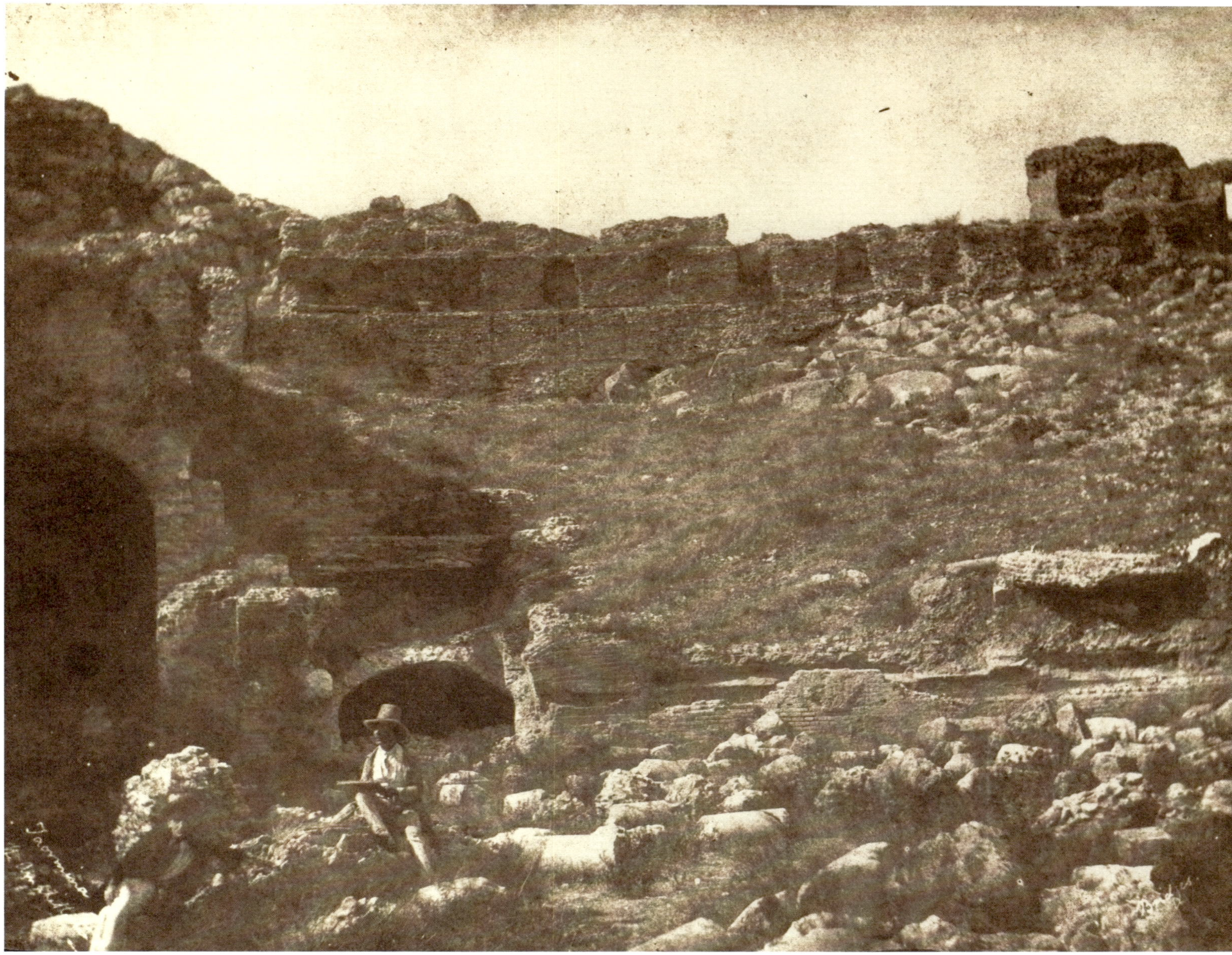

76. George Wilson Bridges, *Taormina, The Amphitheater,* 1846

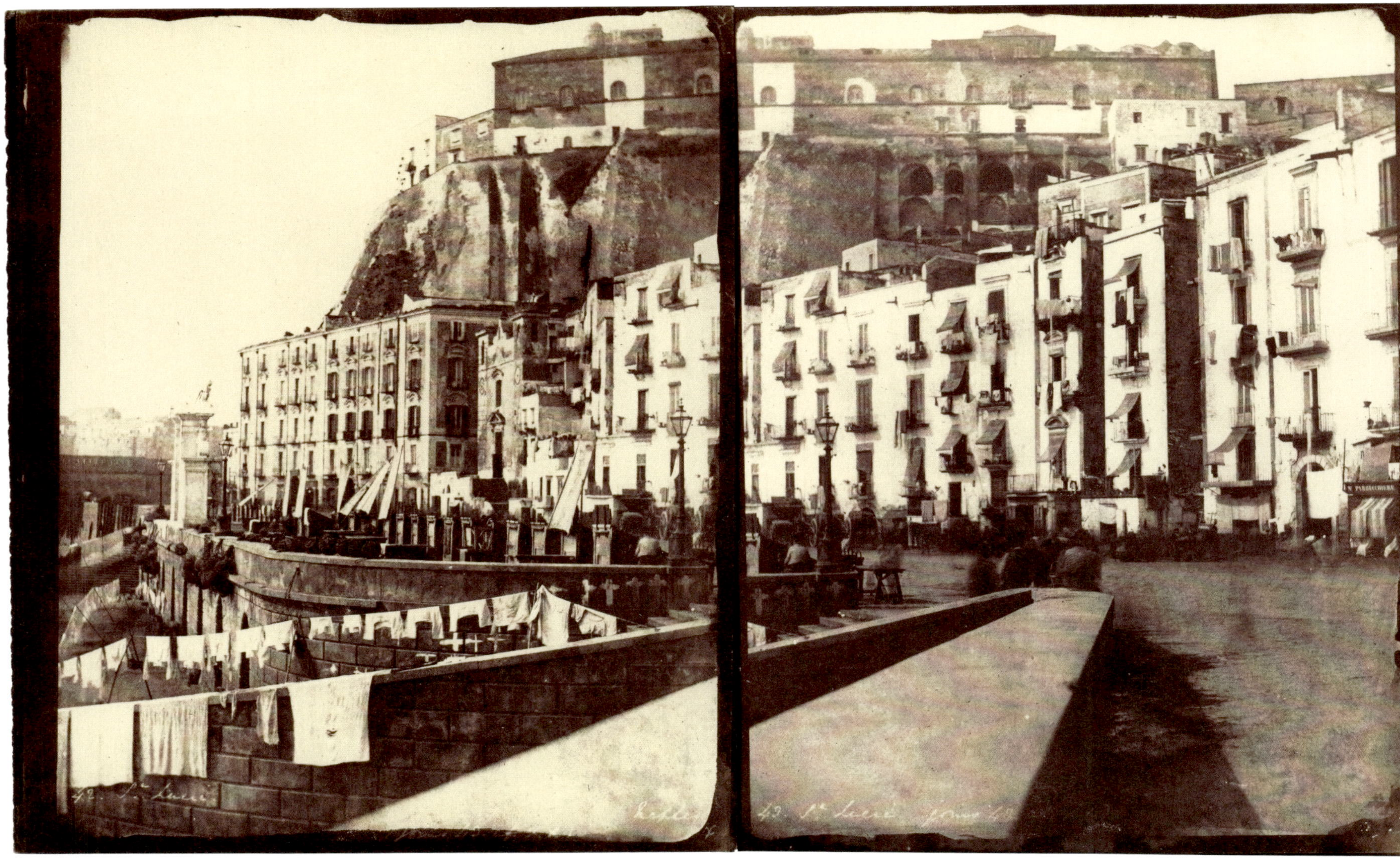

77. Calvert Richard Jones, *Santa Lucia, Naples*, 1845–46

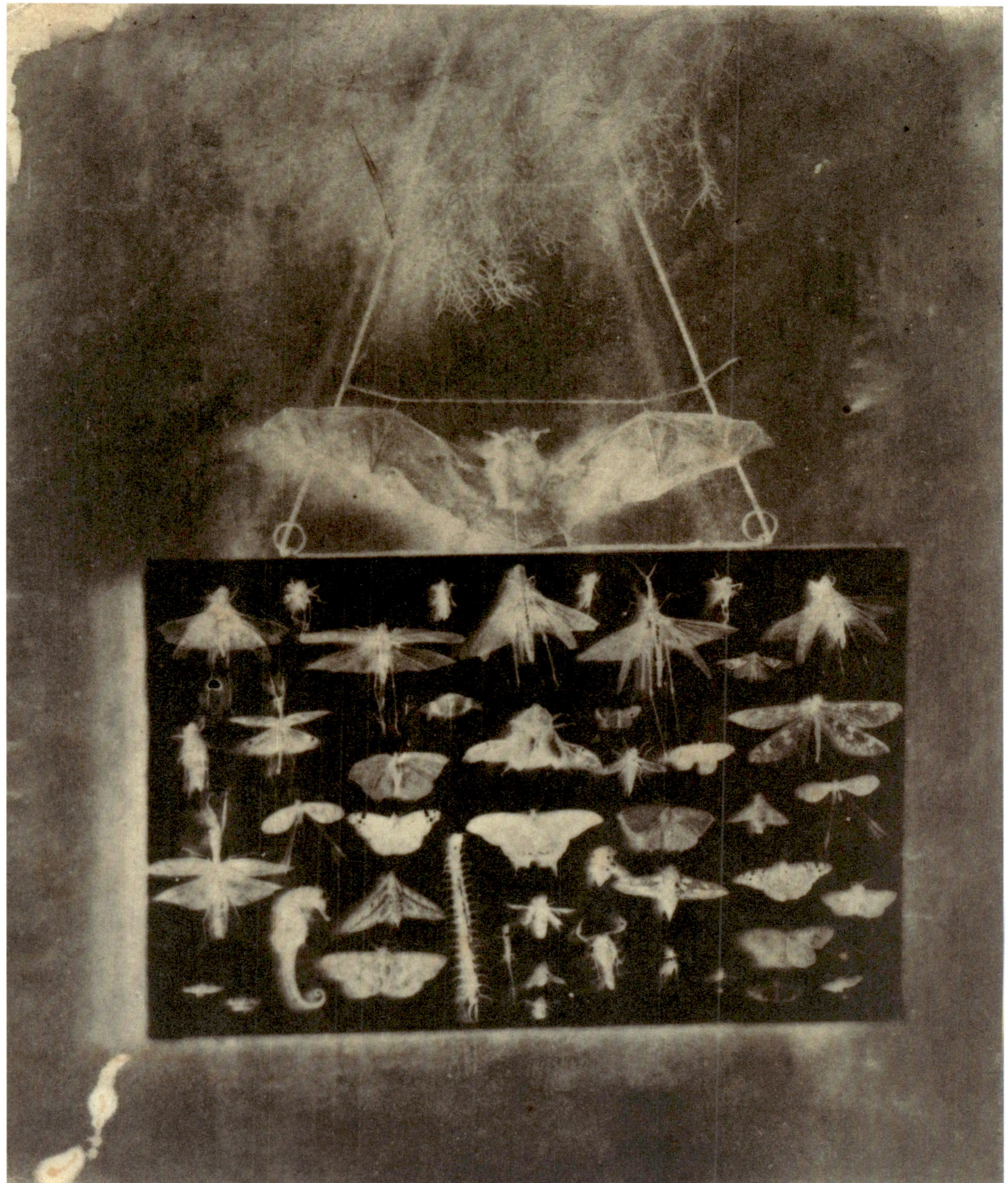

78. Alfred Capel Cure, *My Beasts* (negative), February 1, 1852

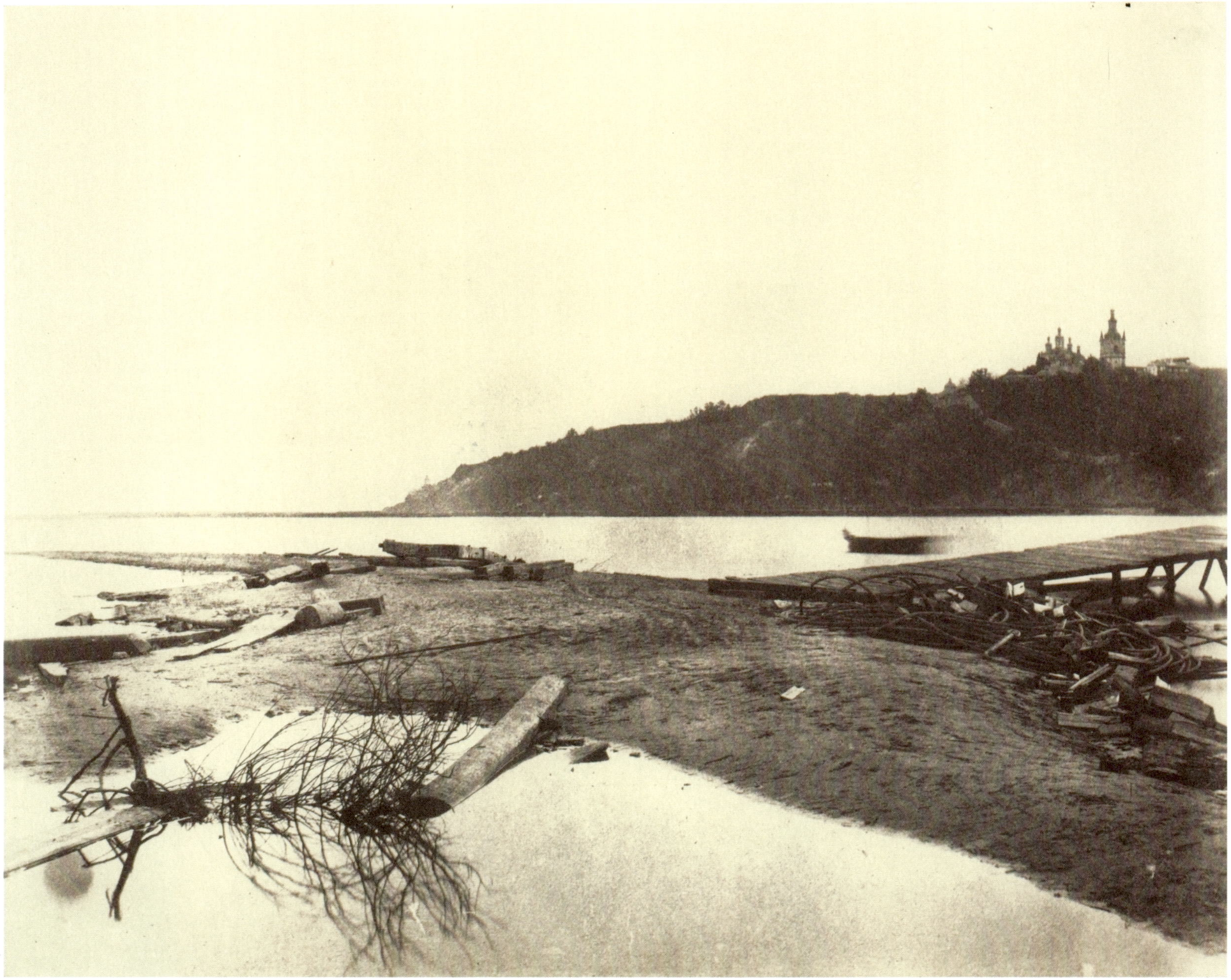

79. Roger Fenton, *Banks of the Dnieper, near Kief,* fall 1852

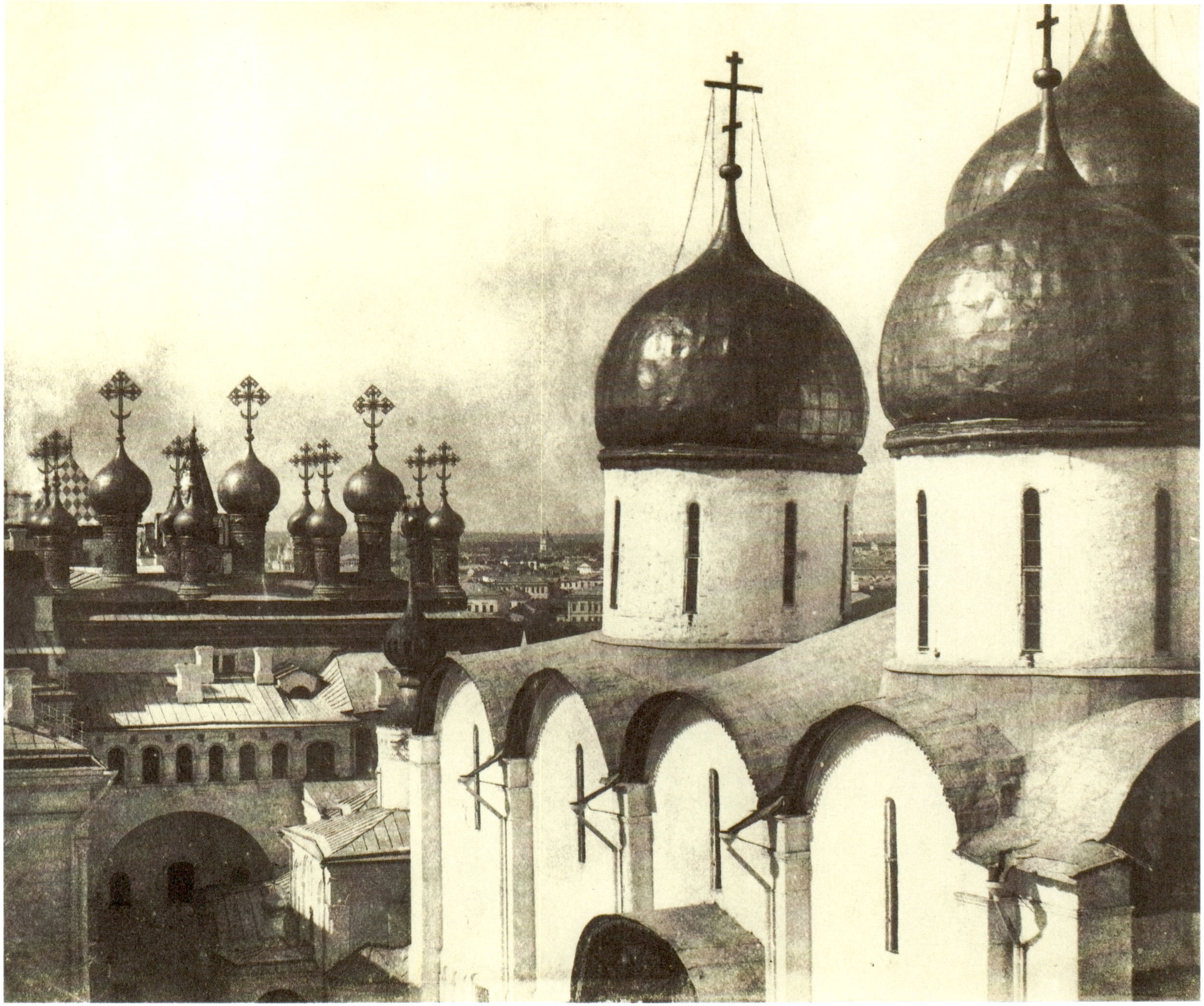

80. Roger Fenton, *Moscow, Domes of Churches in the Kremlin*, fall 1852

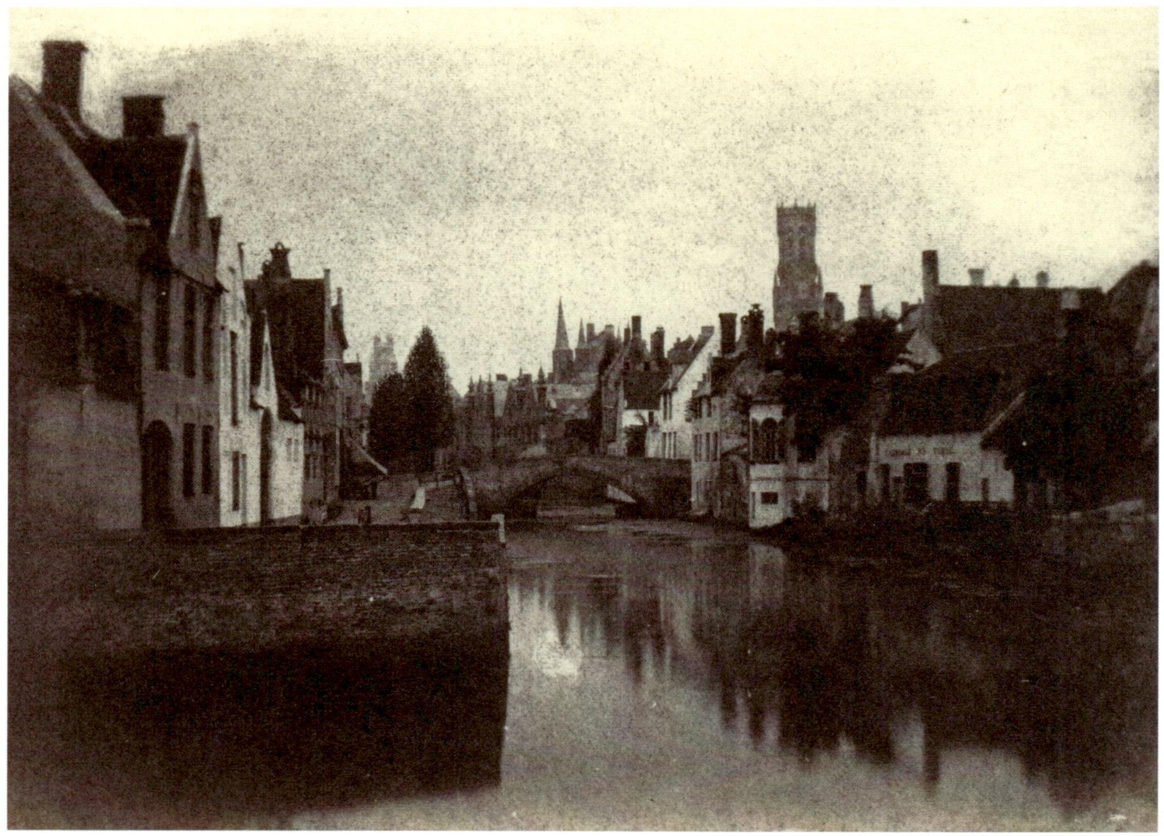

81. John Muir Wood, Groene Rei, Bruges, July 1847

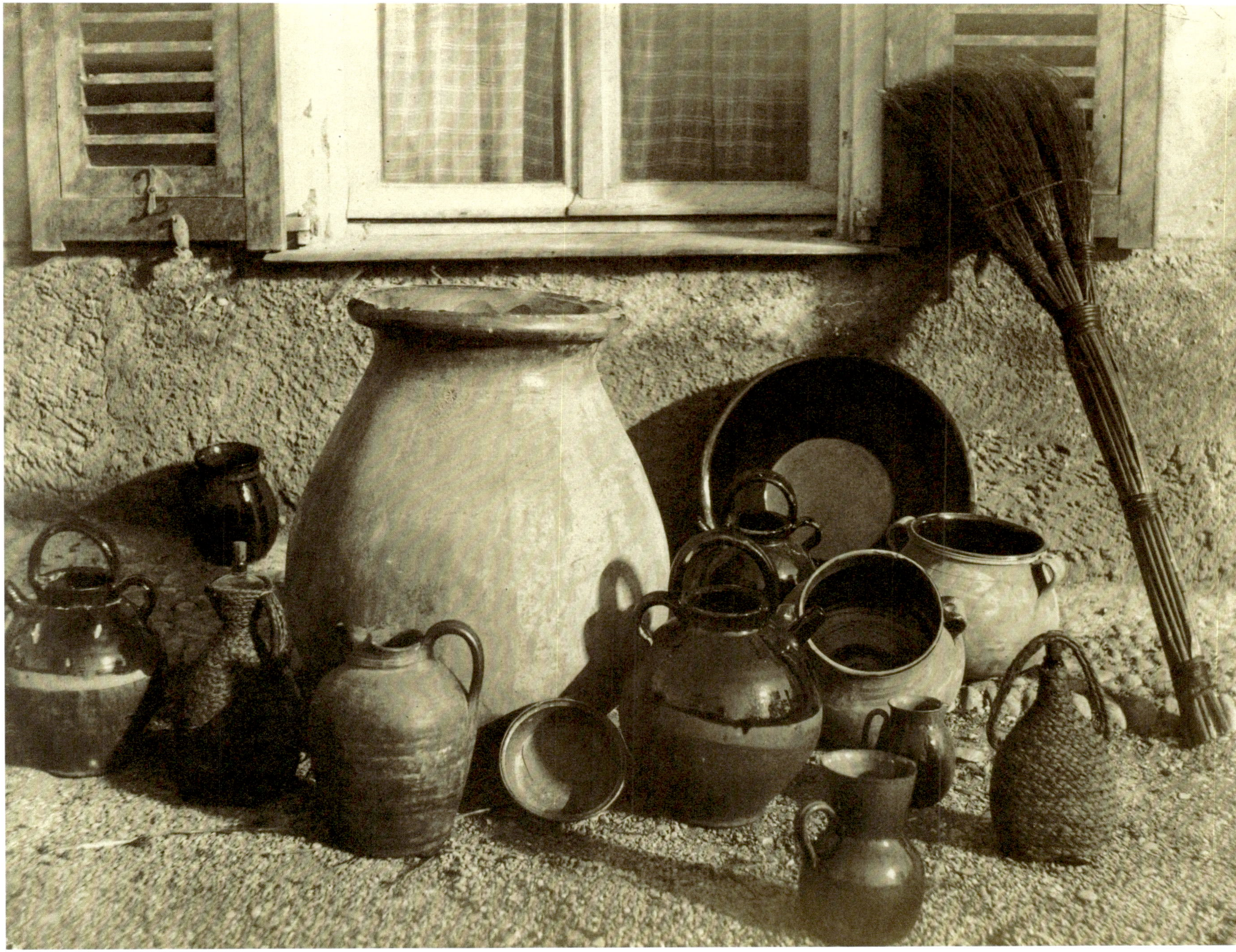

82. Alfred Backhouse, *Pots and Pans at Nice*, 1855

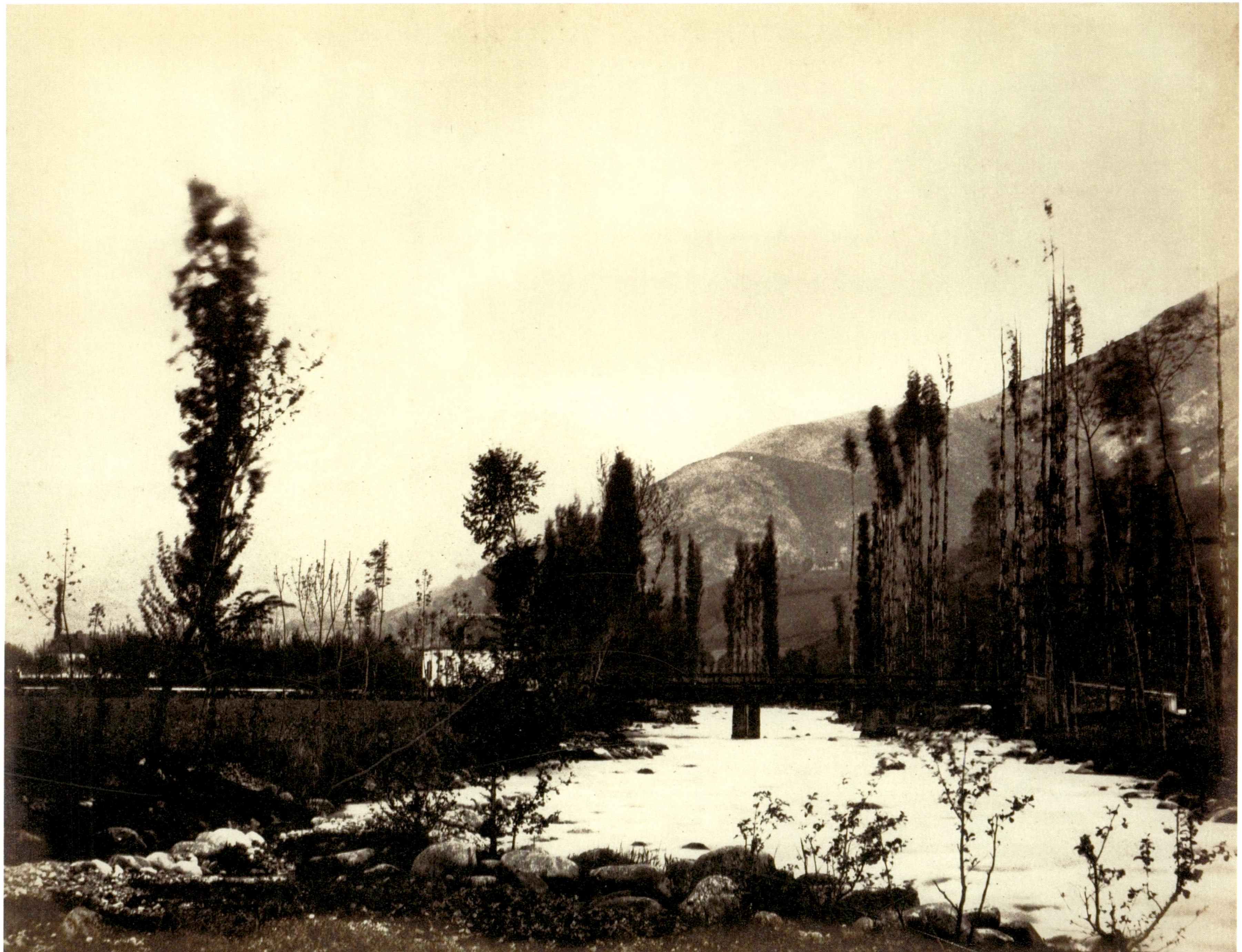

83. Thomas Milville Raven, *Near Bagnières de Bigorre*, 1856–57

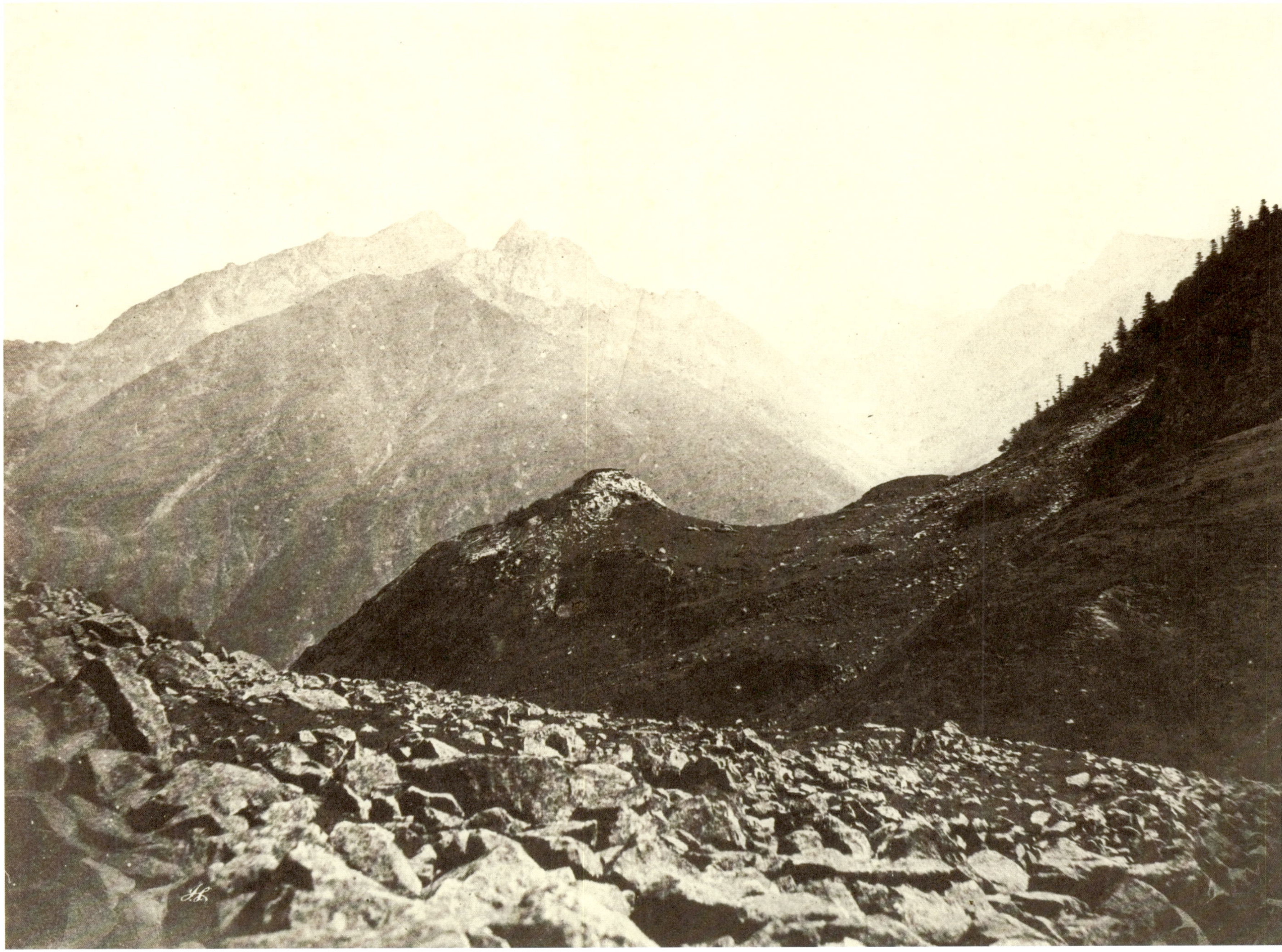

84. John Stewart, *View of the Arruns Pass and Peak from the Pont de Soubé*, 1852

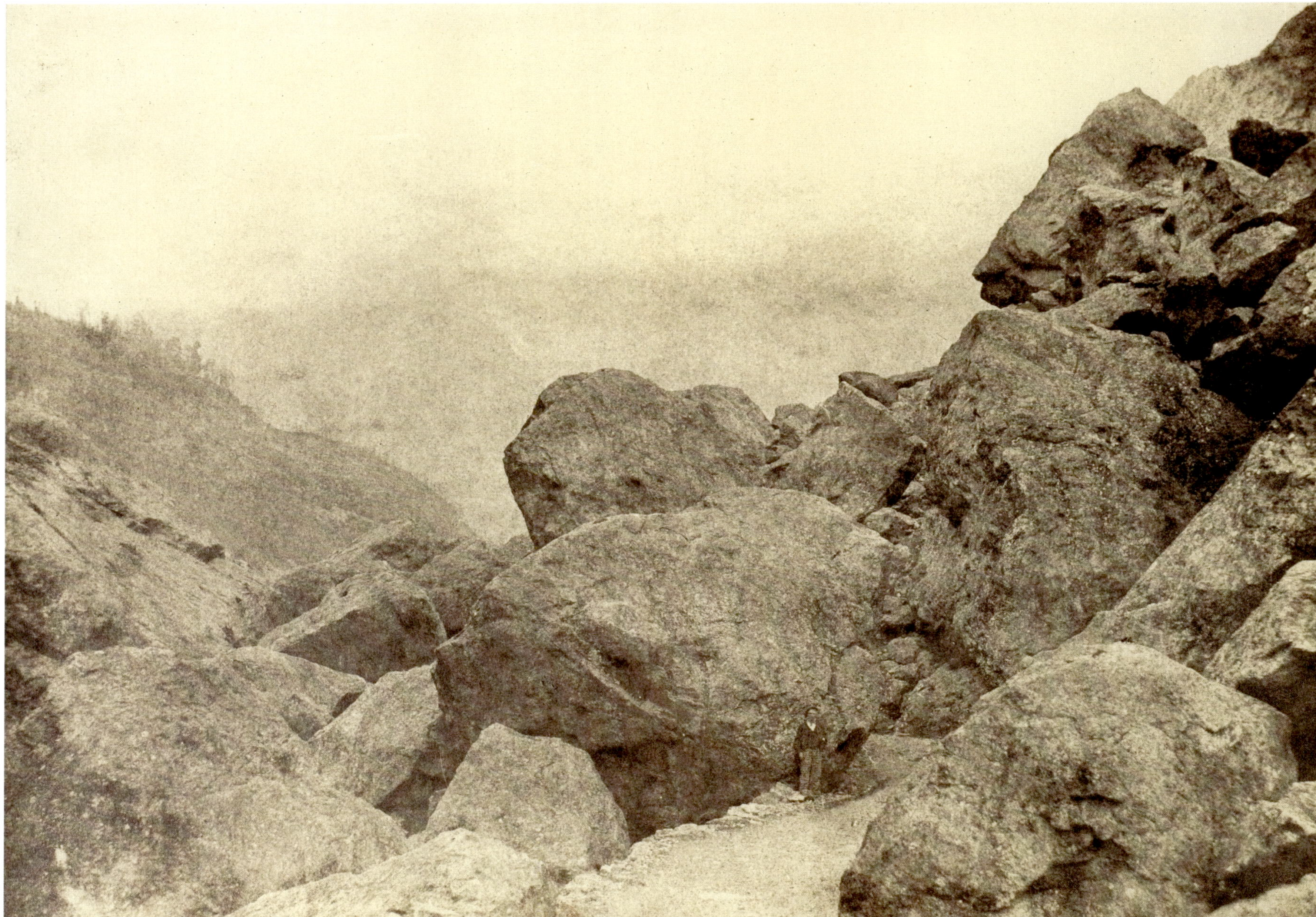

85. John Stewart, *Chaos de Gavarnie*, 1852

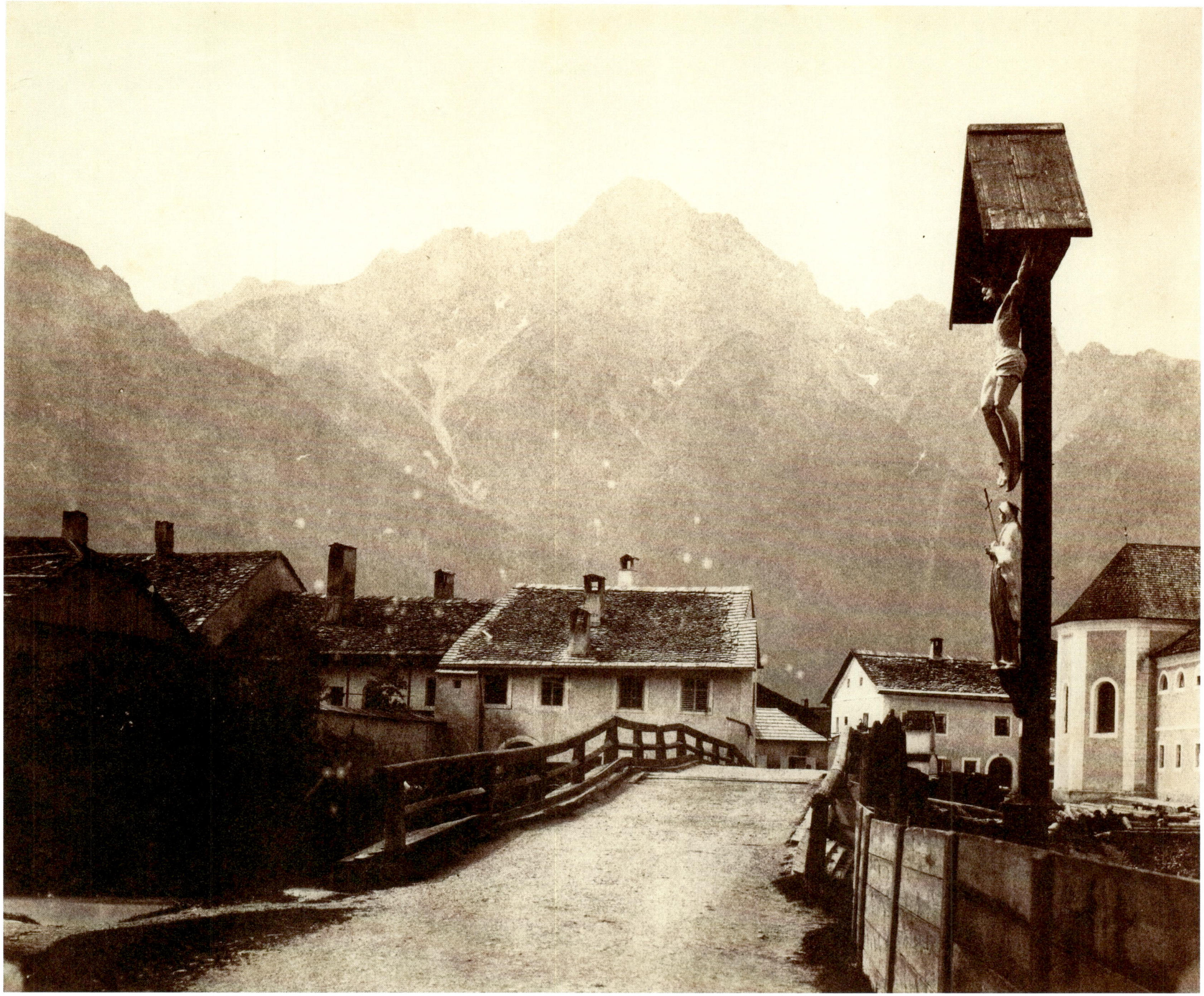

86. William Robert Baker, Roadside Crucifix in Alpine Village, ca. 1855

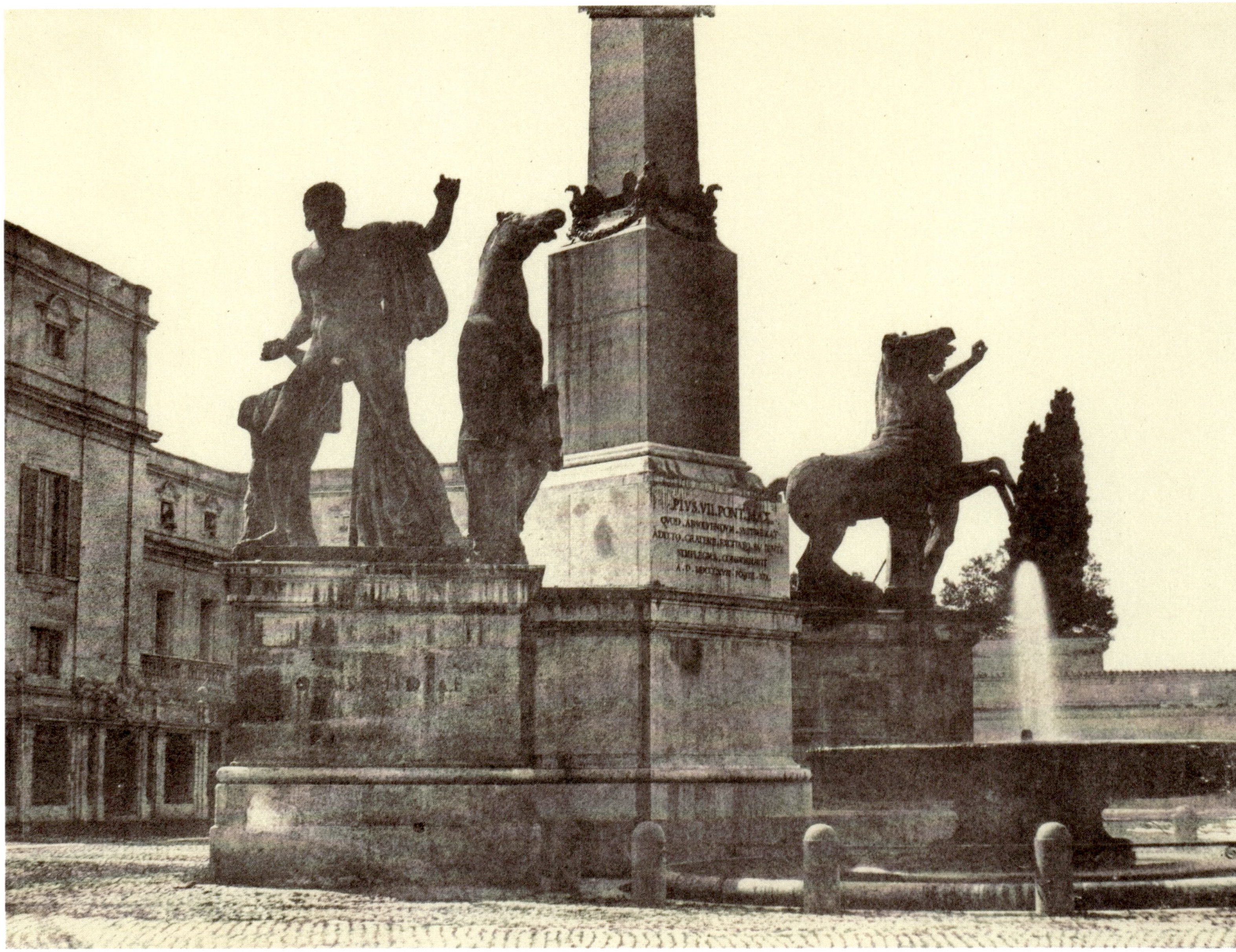

87. Unknown photographer, *Rome, Quirinale*, ca. 1855

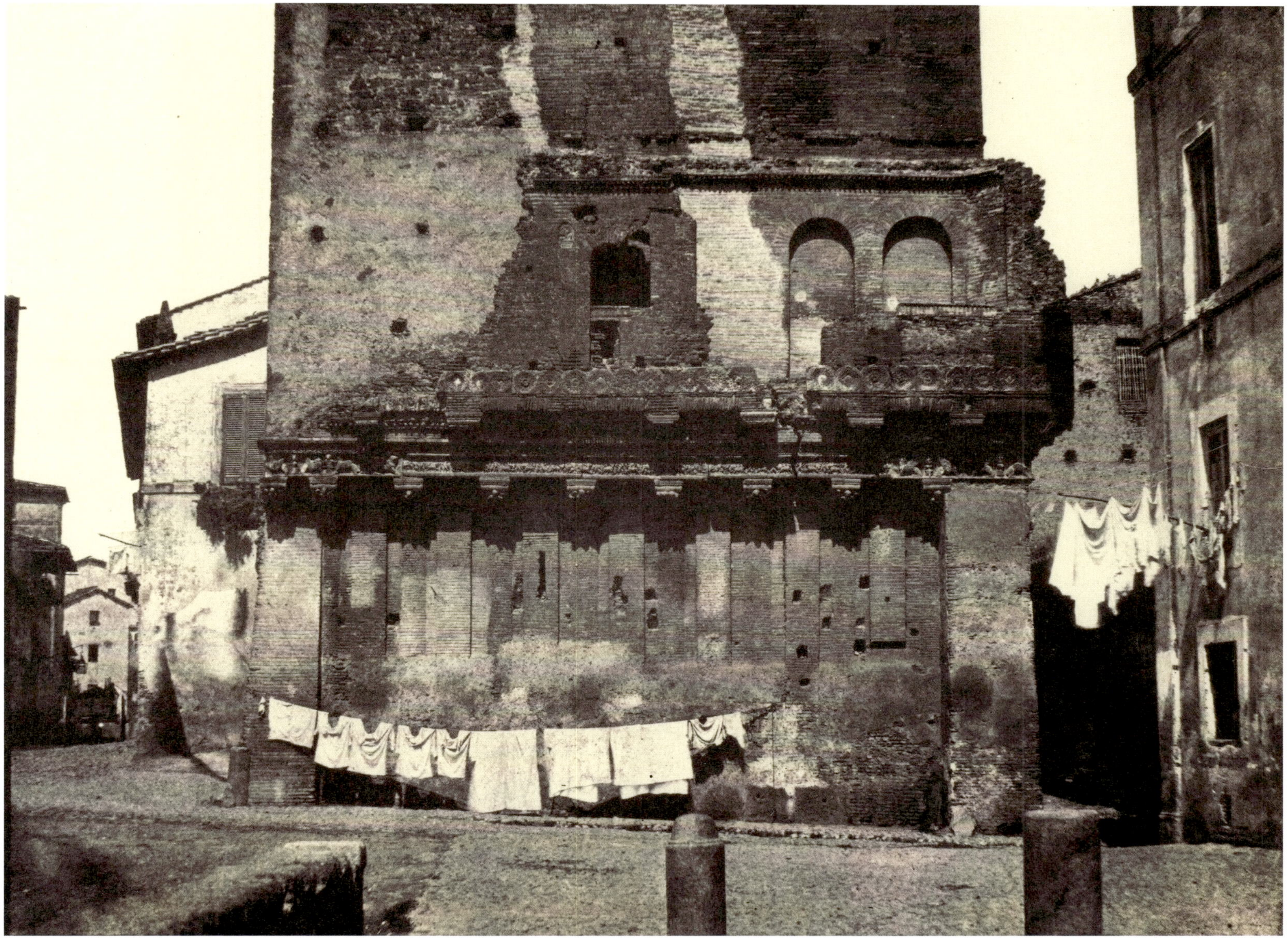

88. Unknown photographer, *Rome, So-Called Casa di Rienzi, the Oldest Medieval Private House,* ca. 1855

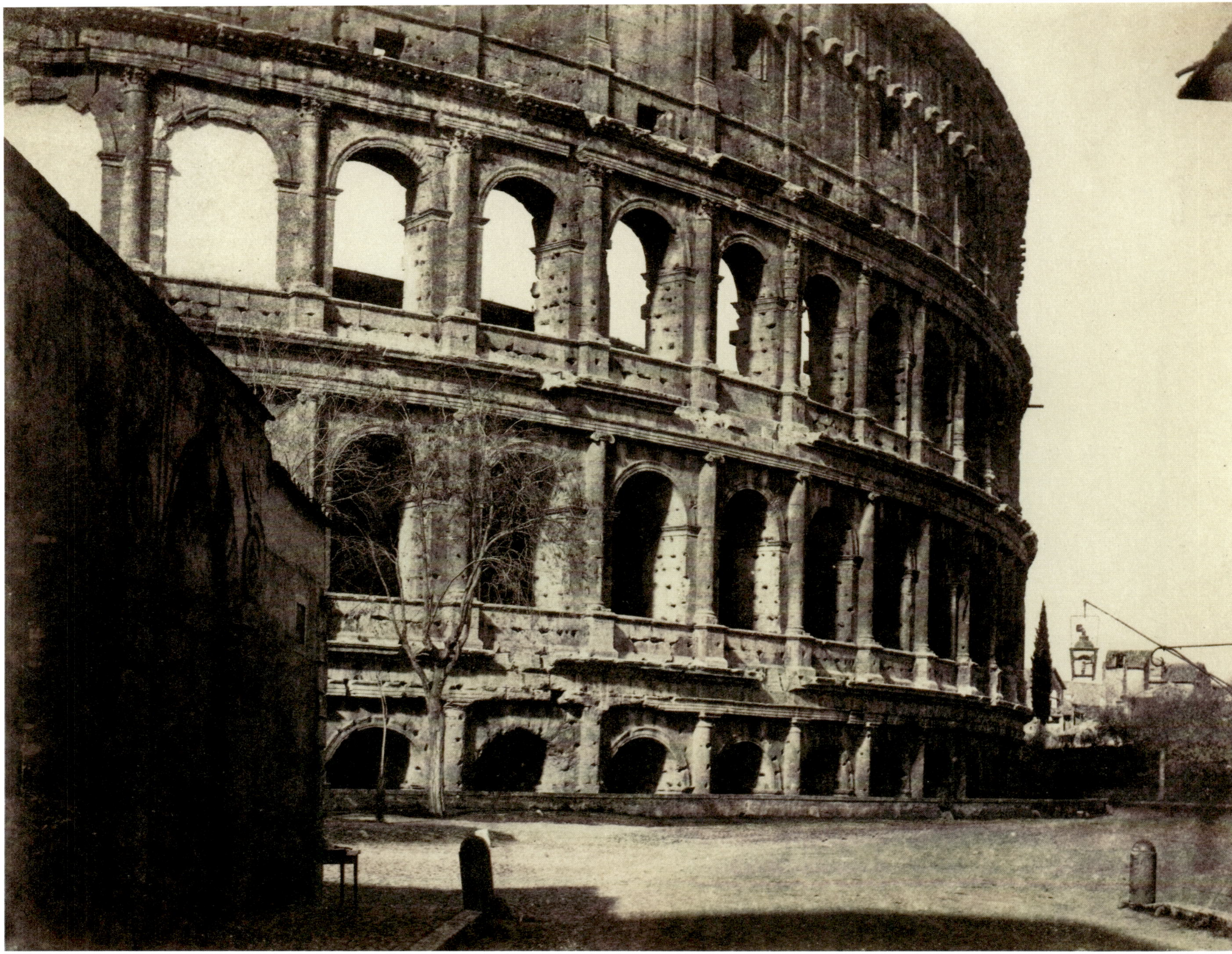

89. Jane Martha St. John, *The Colosseum*, 1856

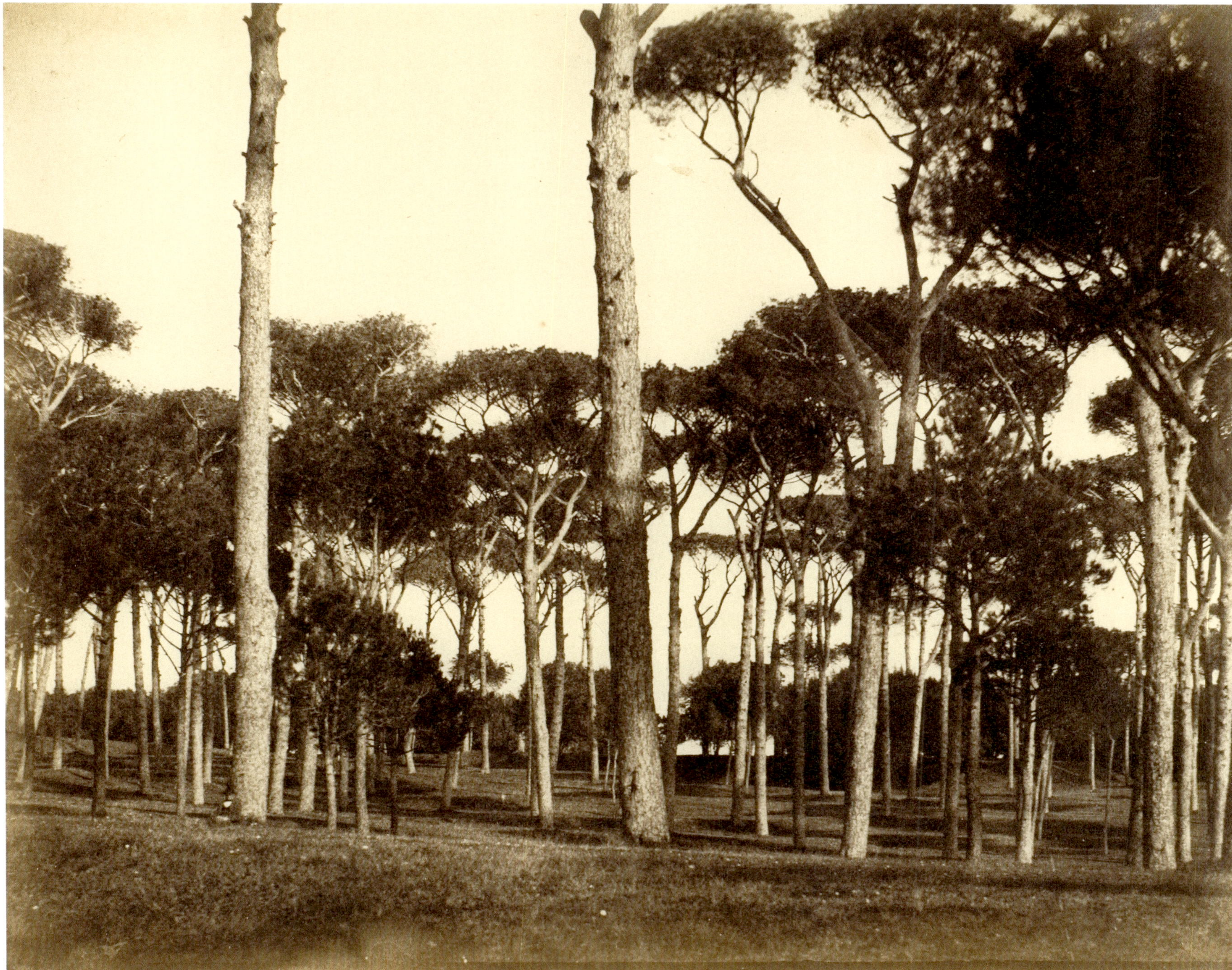

90. Jane Martha St. John, *Stone Pines, Villa Pamfili Doria, Rome,* 1856

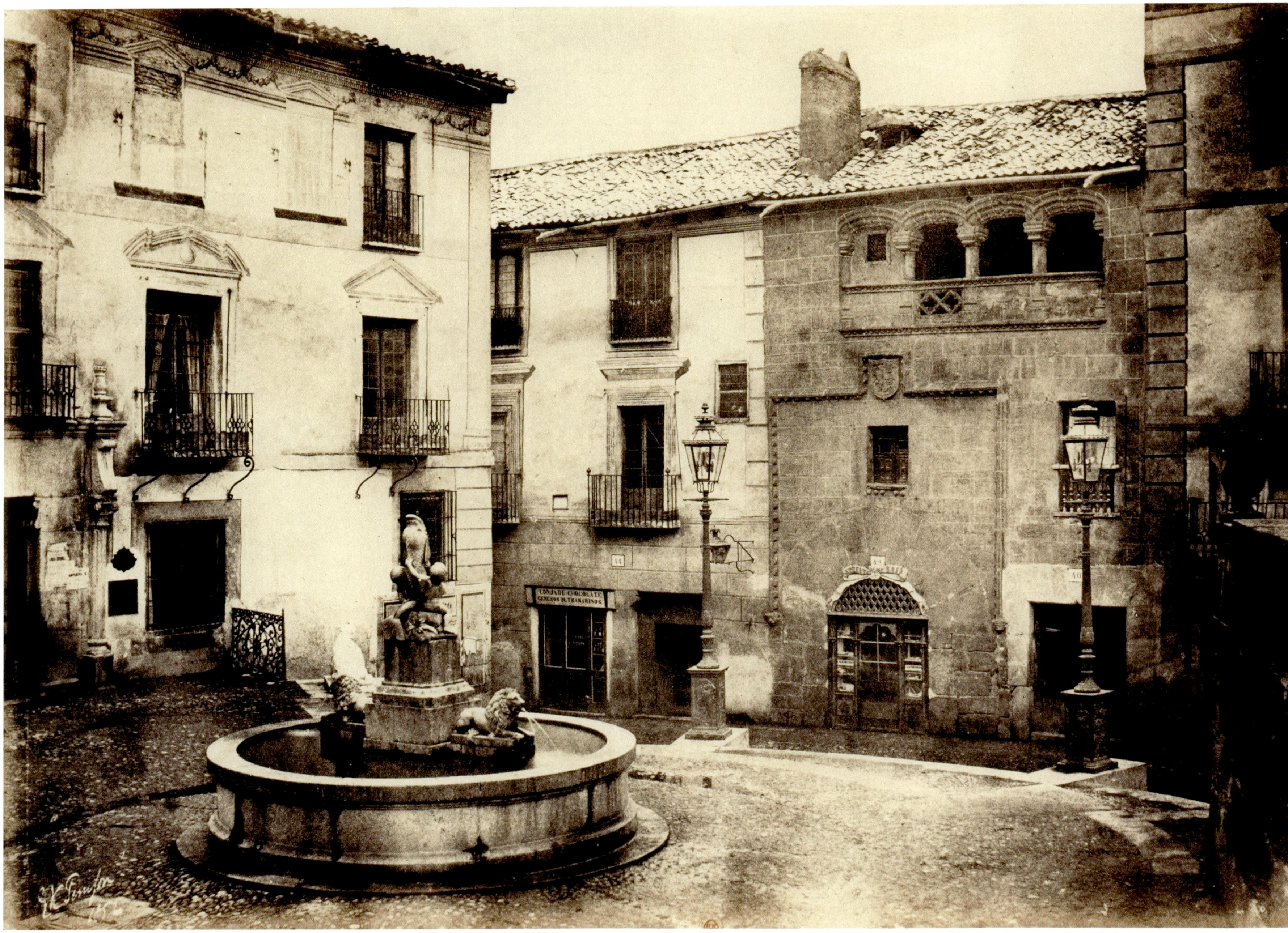

91. Edward King Tenison, *Segovia,* 1852

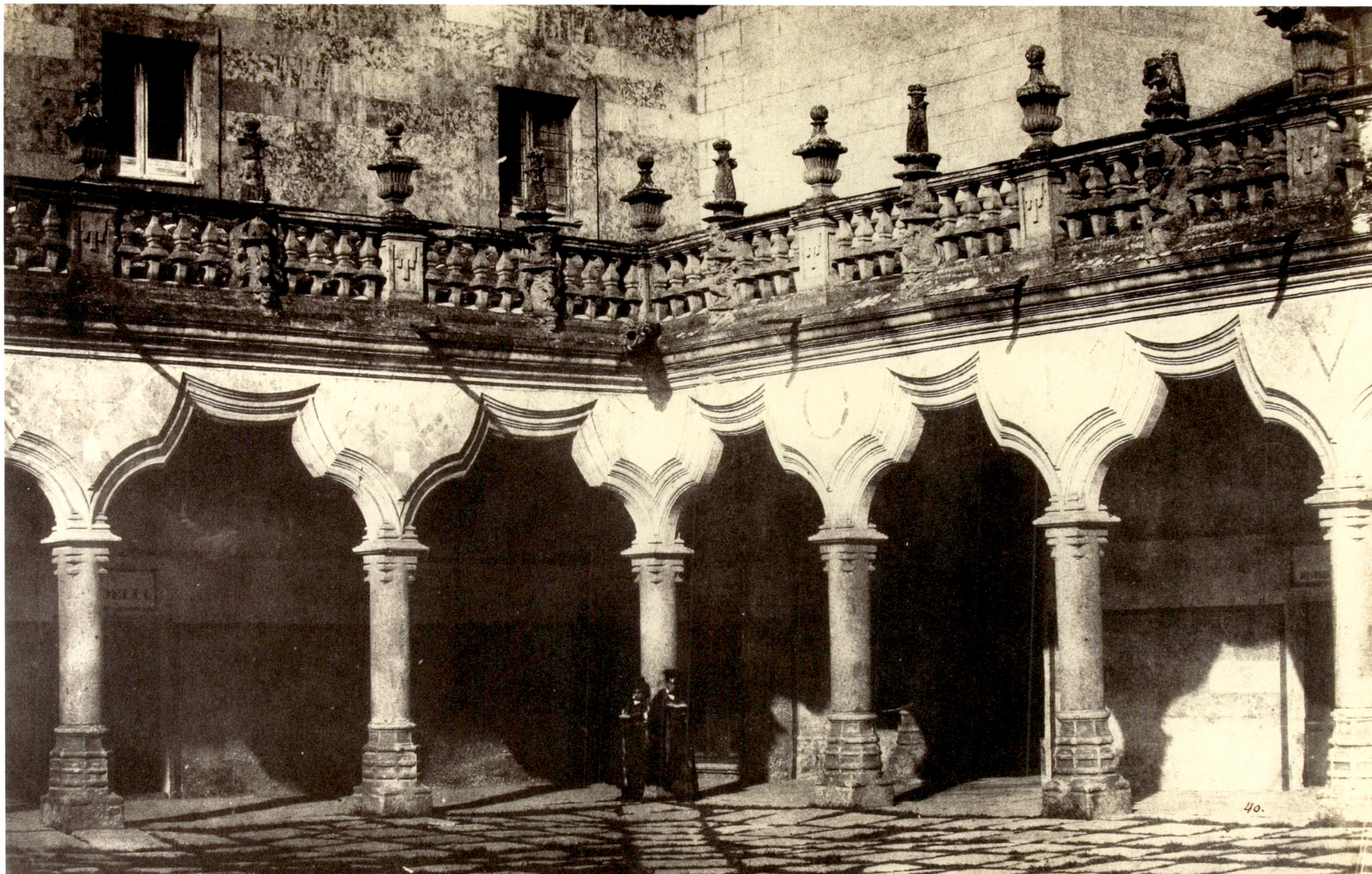

92. Charles Clifford, *Courtyard of the Lower School, Salamanca*, 1853–54

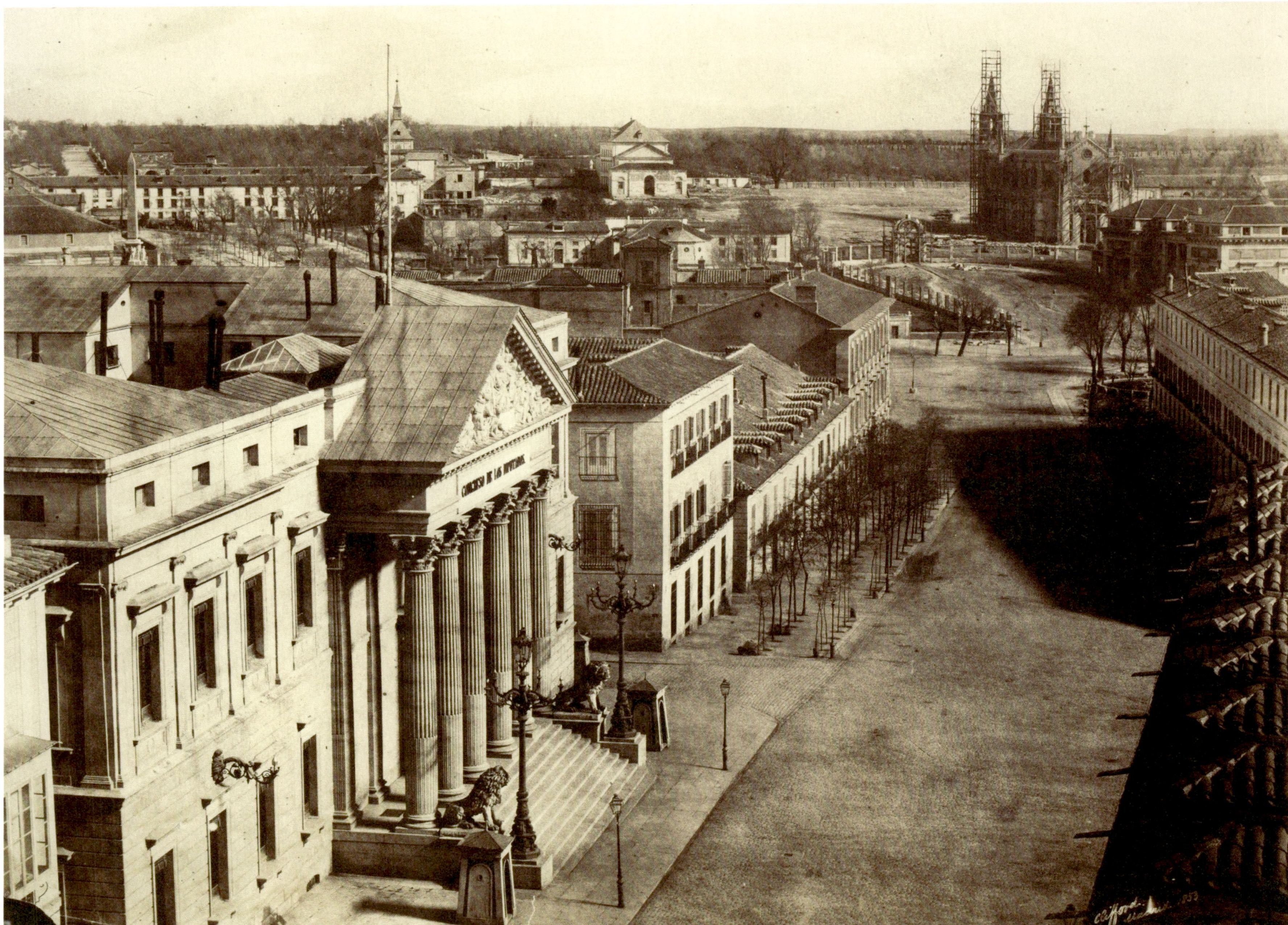

93. Charles Clifford, Carrera de San Jerónimo, Madrid, 1853

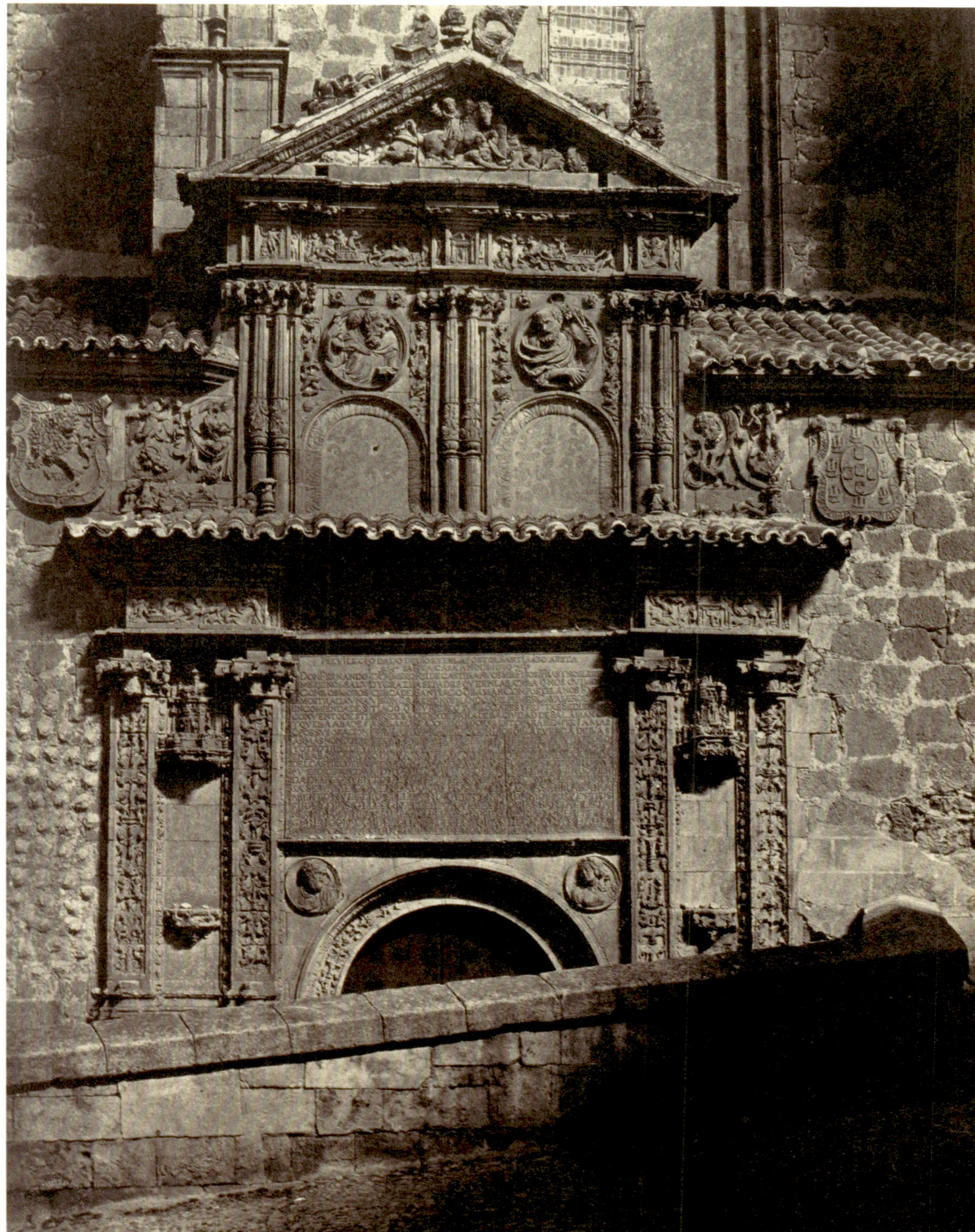

94. Charles Clifford, *Portal of the Convent of Sancti Spiritu, Salamanca,* 1853

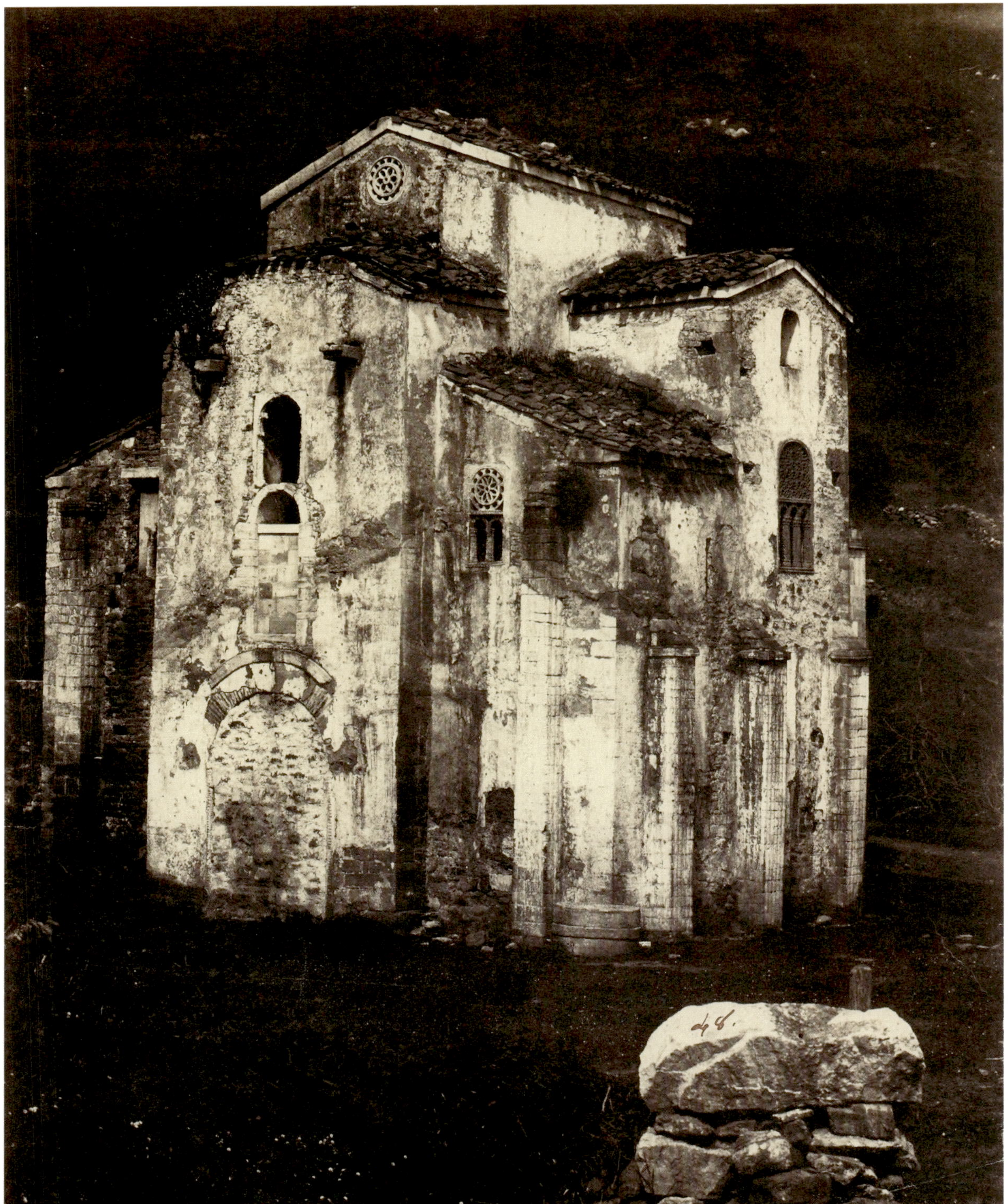

95. Charles Clifford, Church of San Miguel de Lillo, near Oviedo, 1854

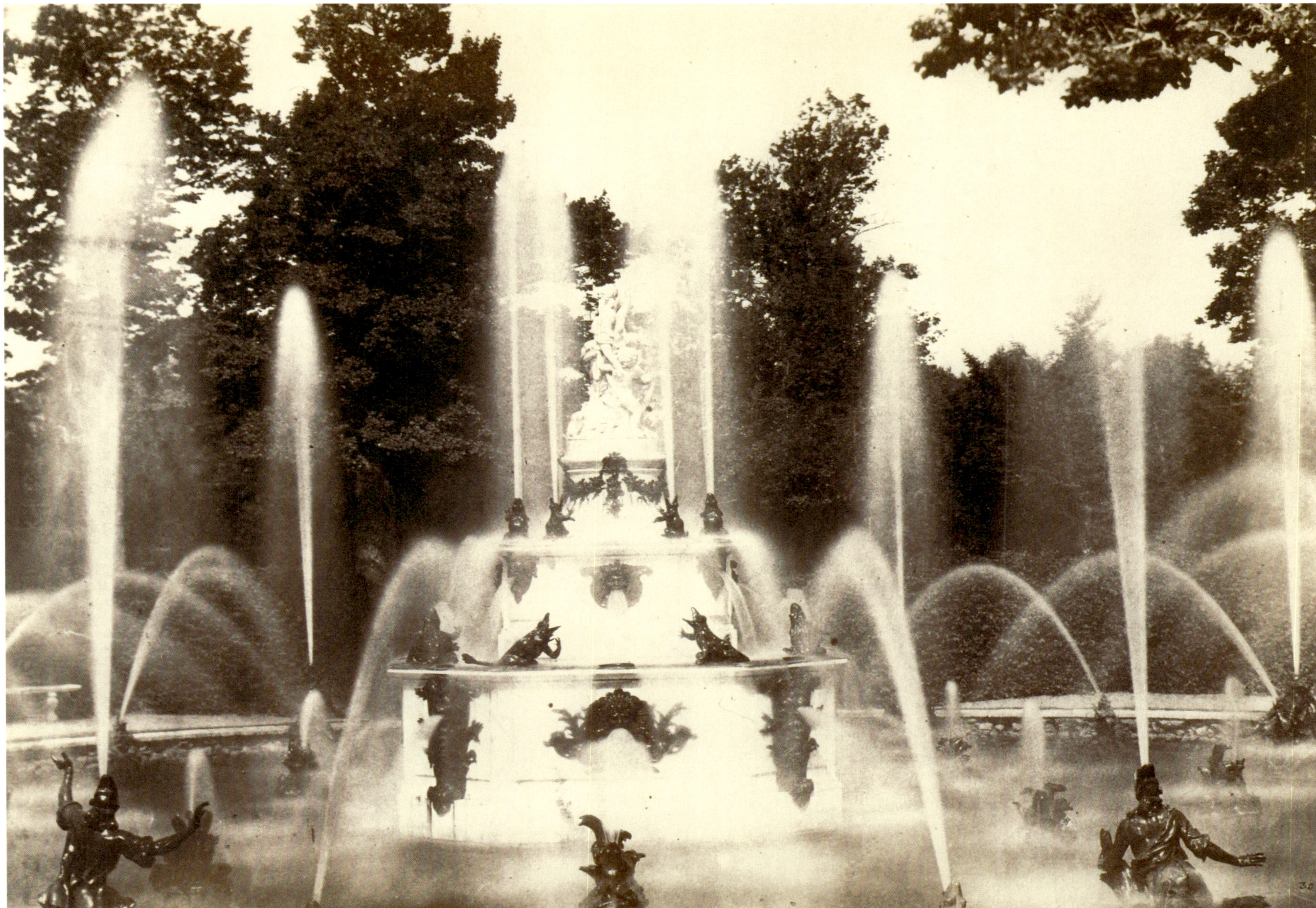

96. Charles Clifford, *Latona Fountain in the Gardens of La Granja, Segovia,* 1853

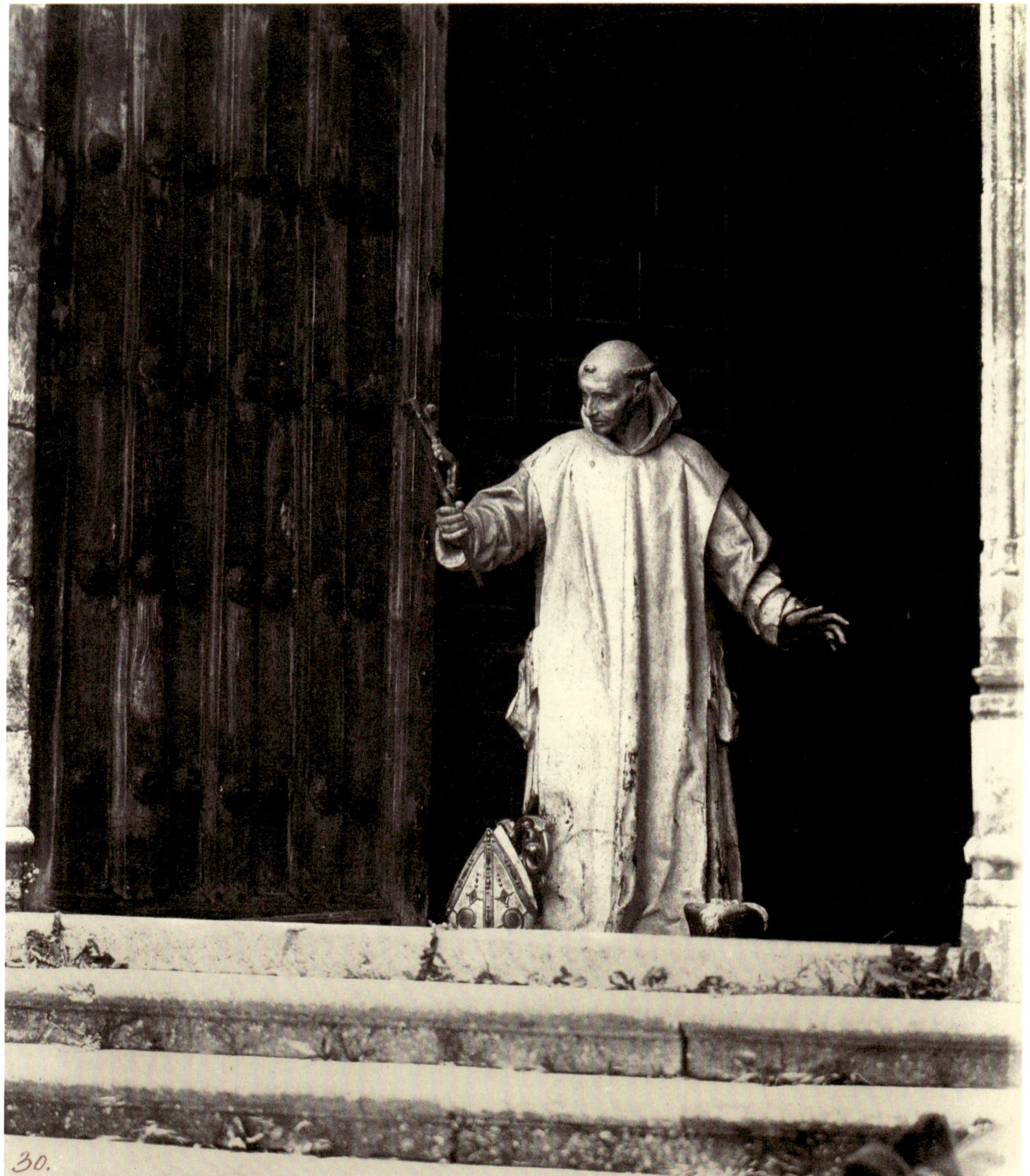

97. Charles Clifford, *Principal Doorway of the Carthusian Monastery, Burgos*, 1853

The Calotype in India and Burma

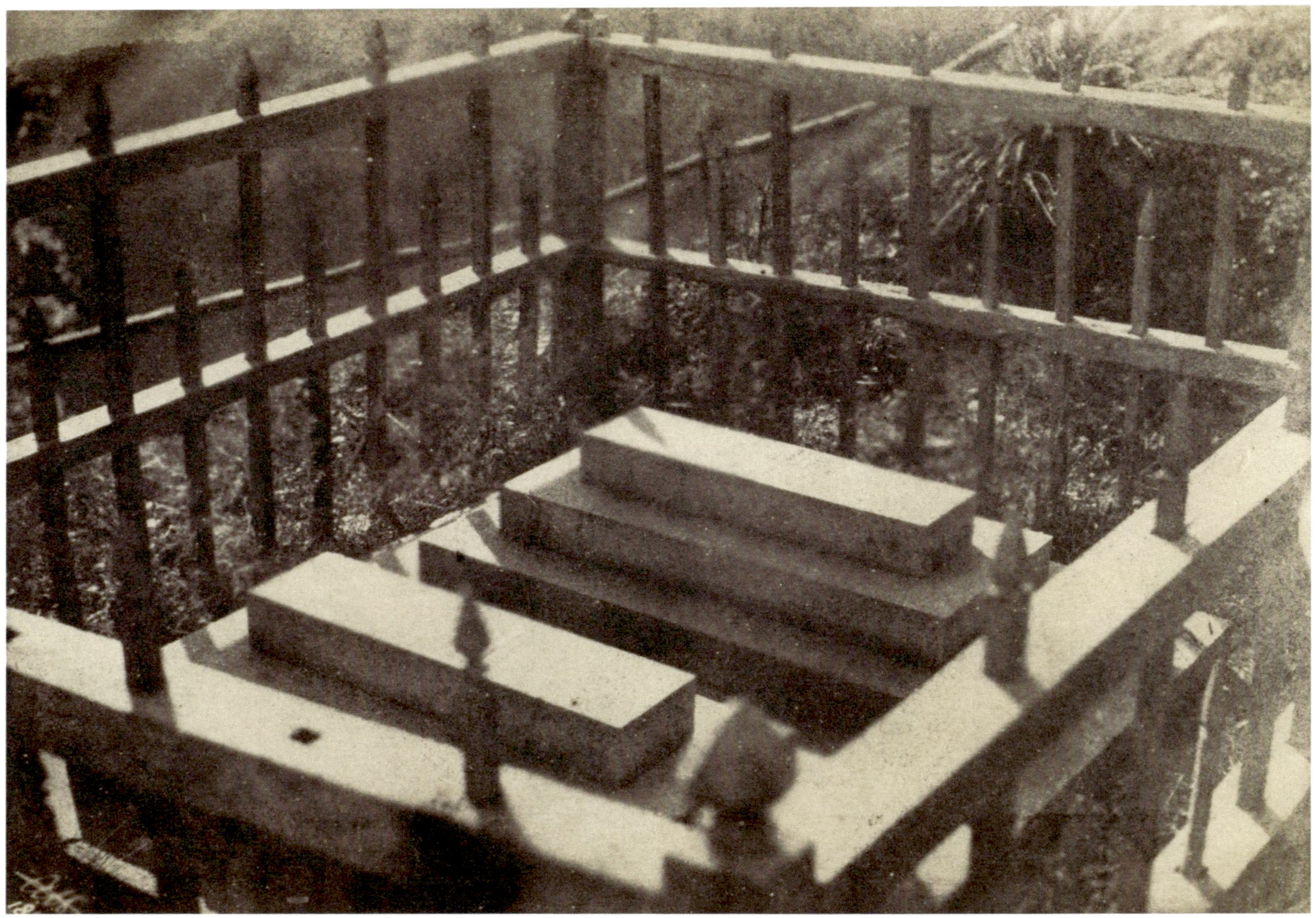

98. Alfred Huish, Children's Graves, India, 1848

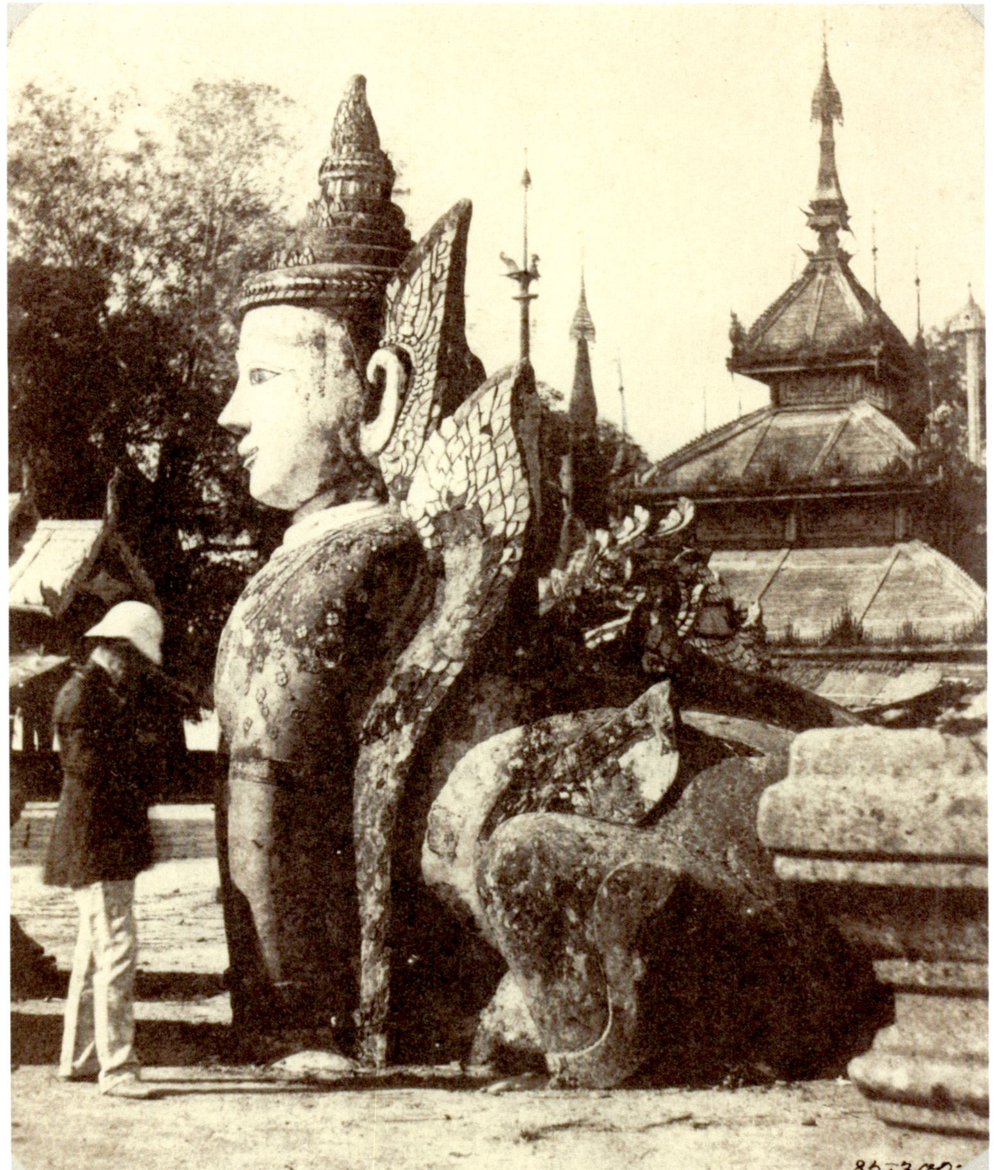

99. John McCosh, Englishman at the Entrance to a Pagoda, 1848–50

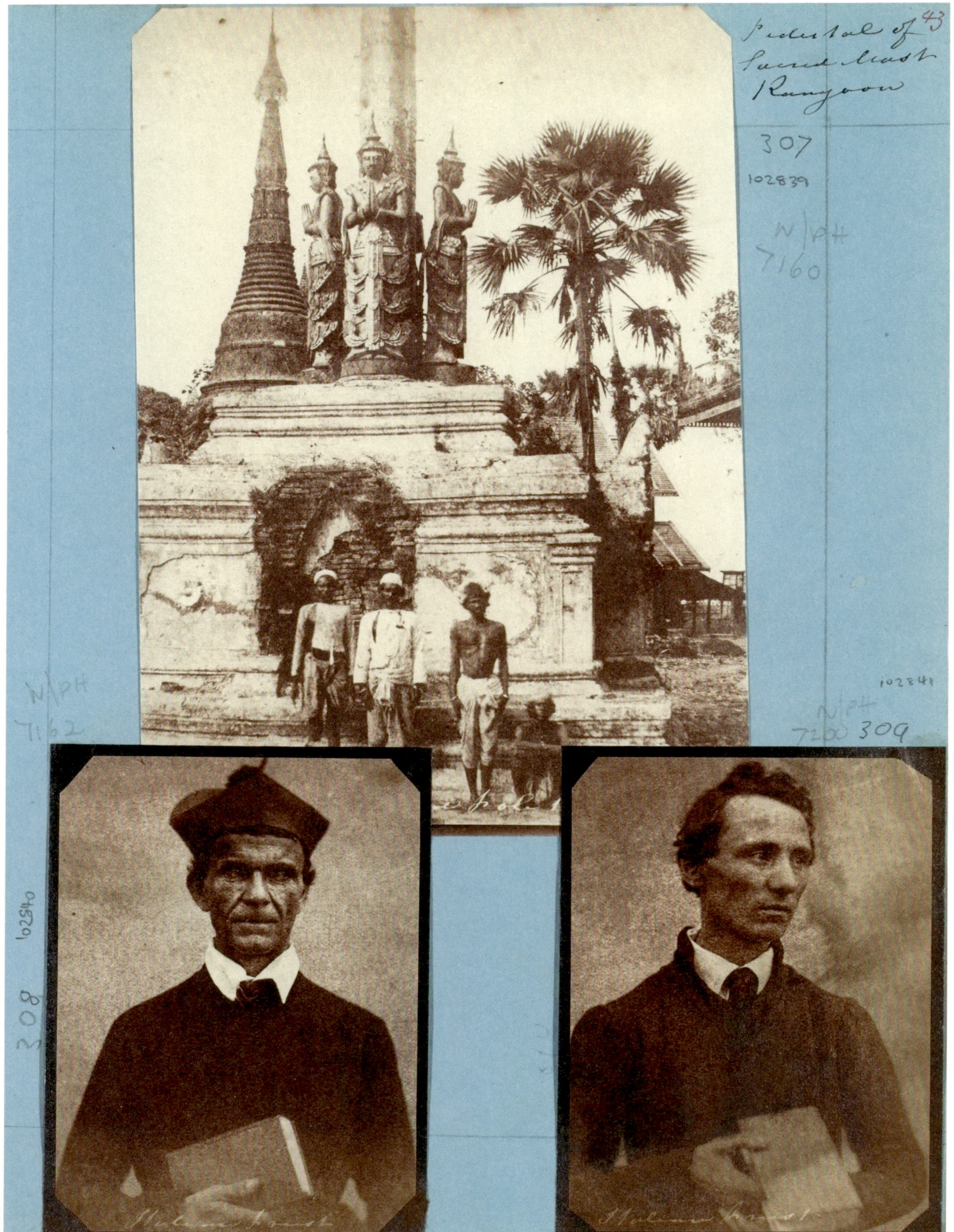

100. John McCosh, *Pedestal of the Sacred Mast, Rangoon; Italian Priest; Another Italian Priest*, 1848–50

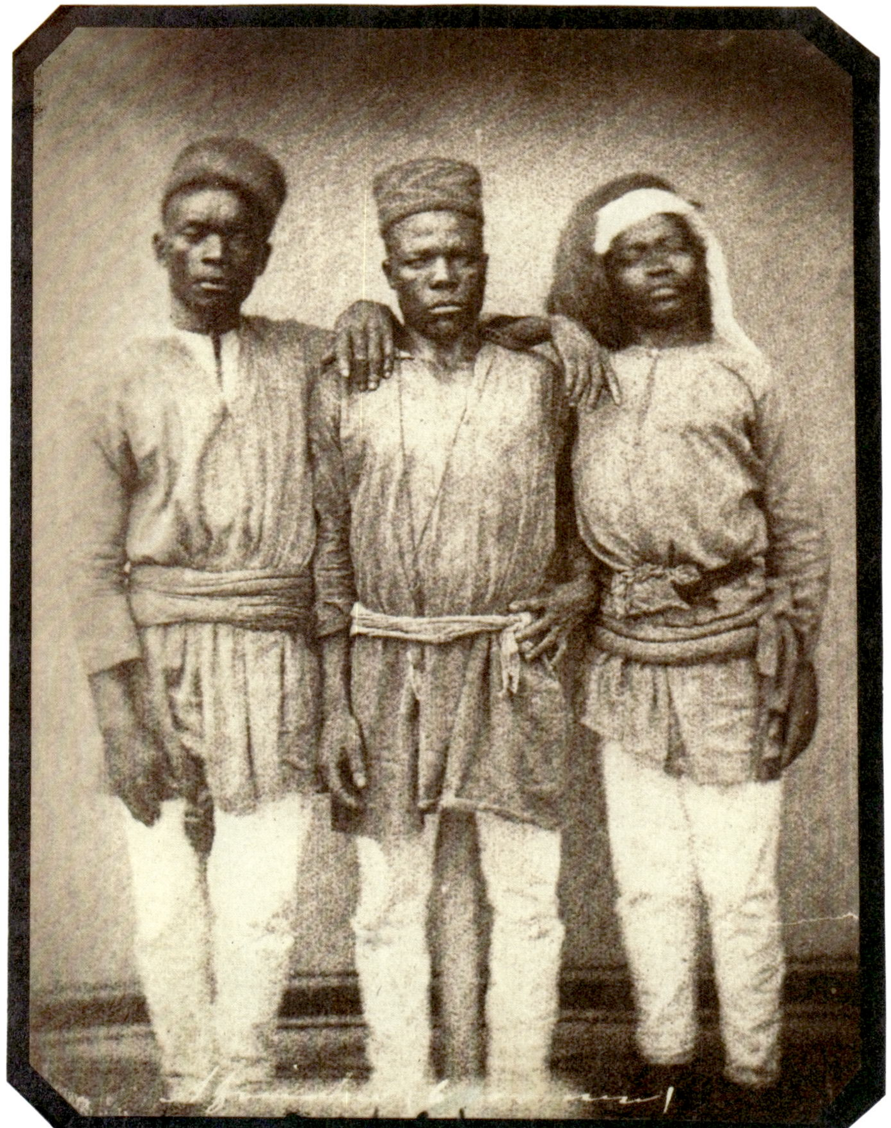

101. John McCosh, *African Croomen*, 1848–50

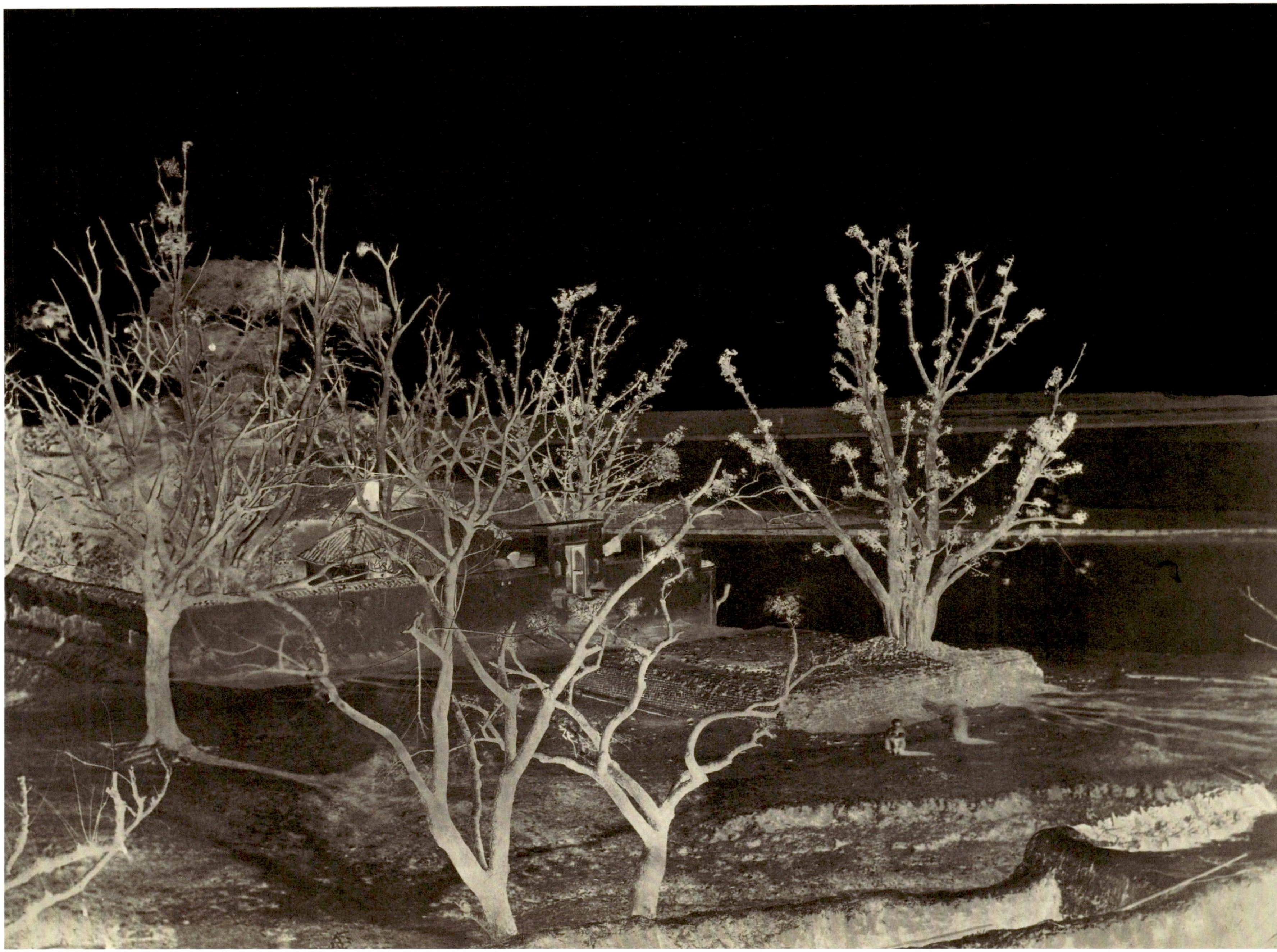

102. John Murray, *Suttee Ghat, Cawnpore* (negative), 1858

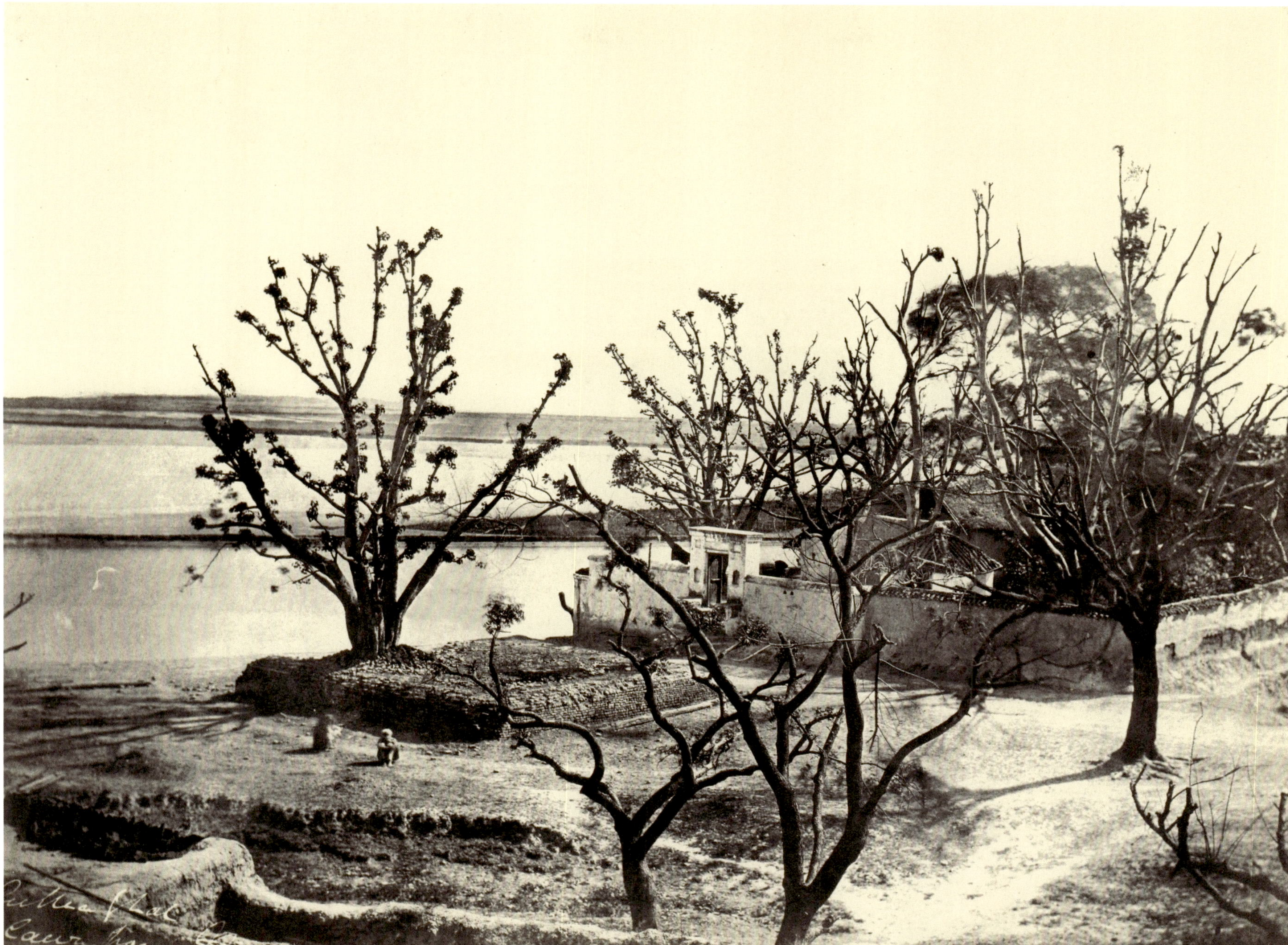

103. John Murray, *Suttee Ghat, Cawnpore*, 1858

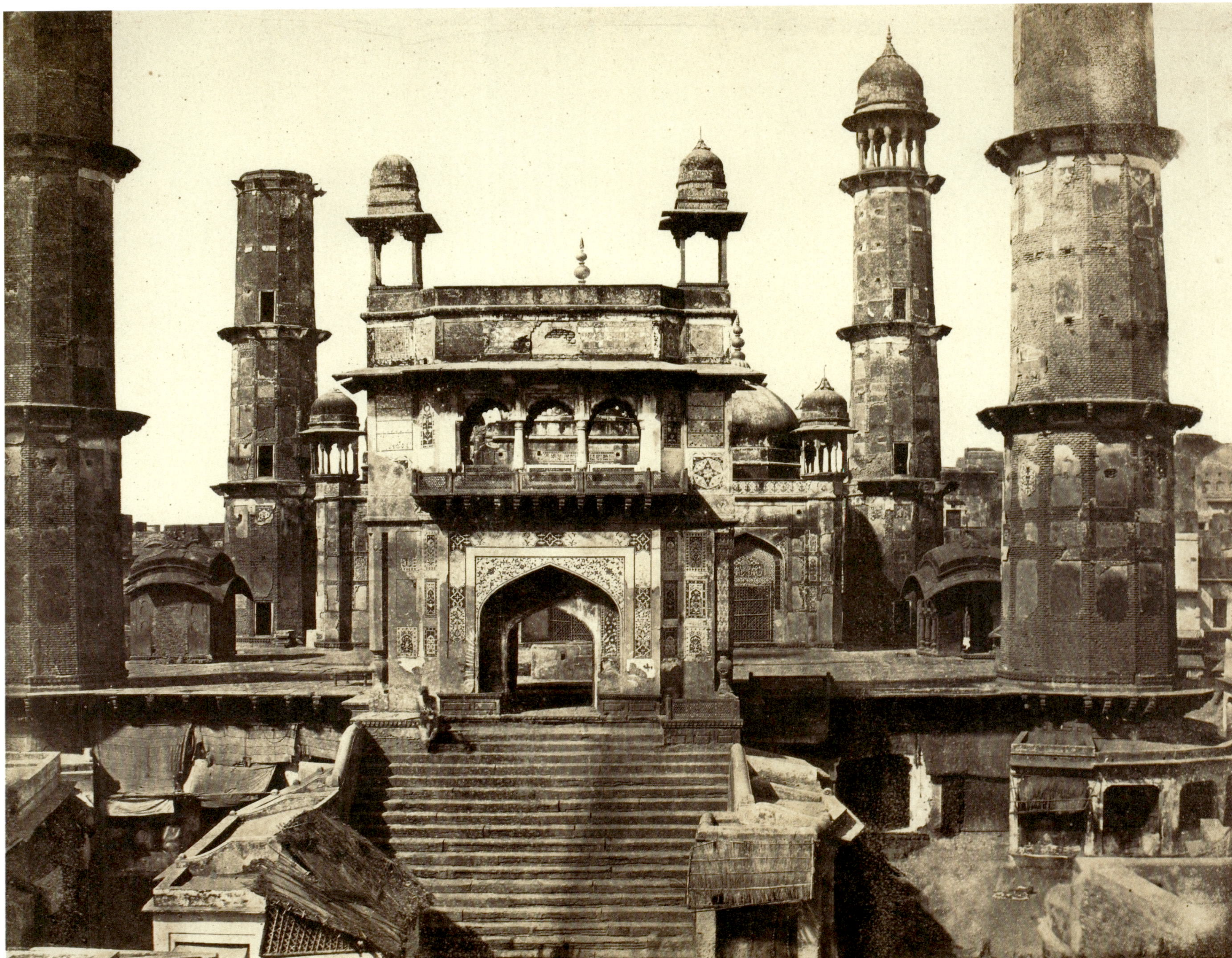

104. John Murray, *Auringzebe's Mosque*, 1856–57

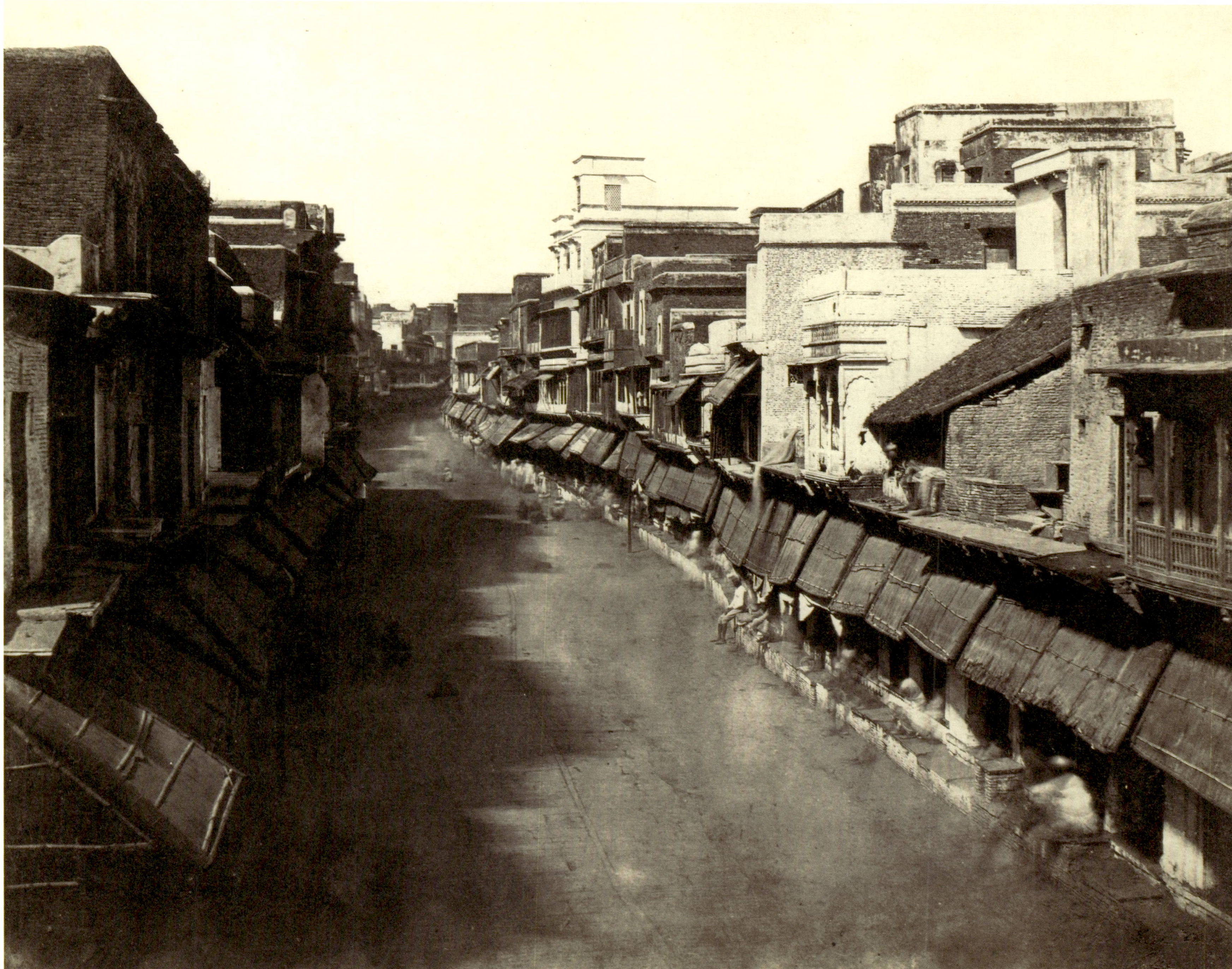

105. John Murray, *The Chowk*, 1856–57

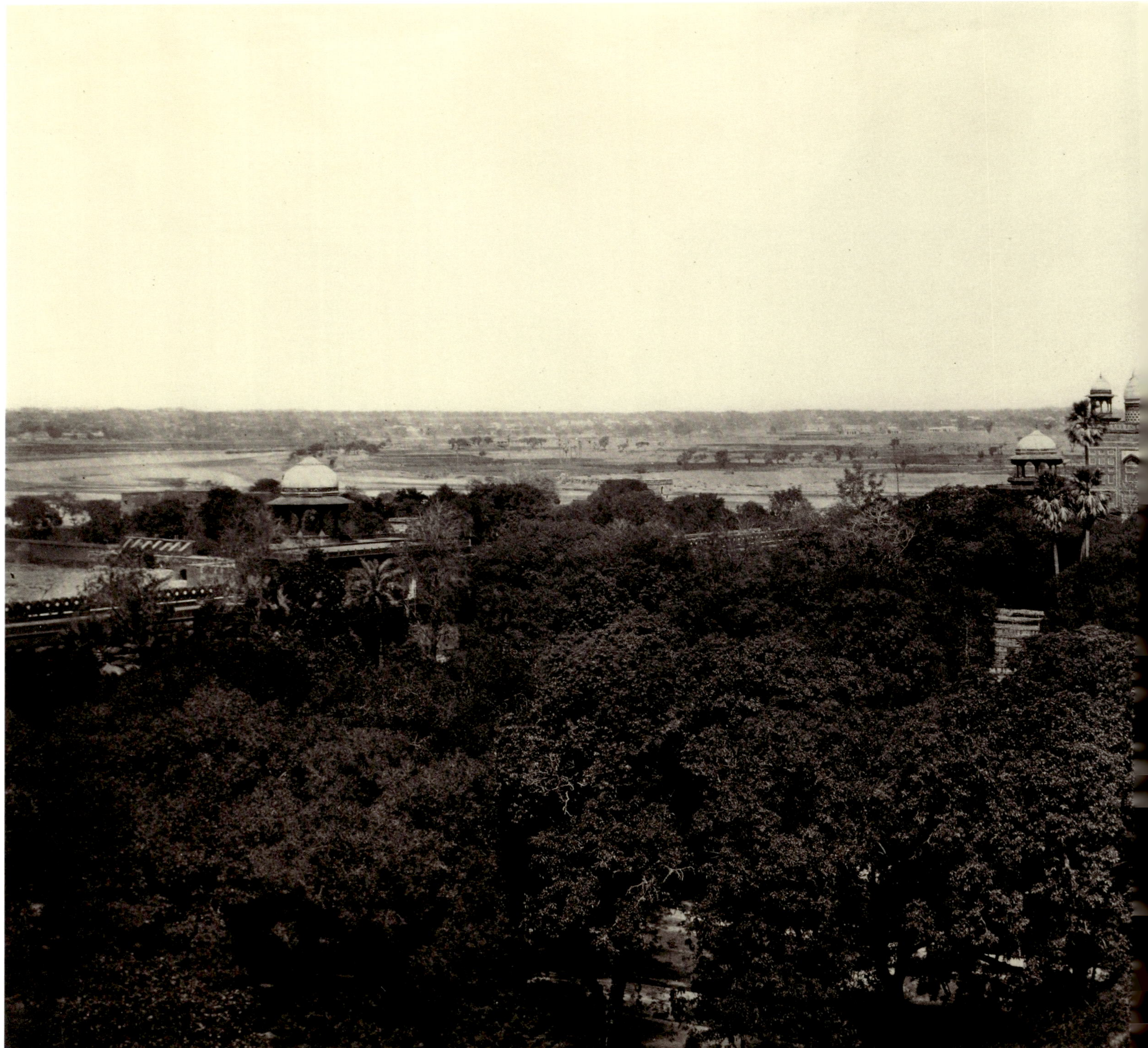

106. John Murray, The Taj Mahal from the Gateway, January–March 1864

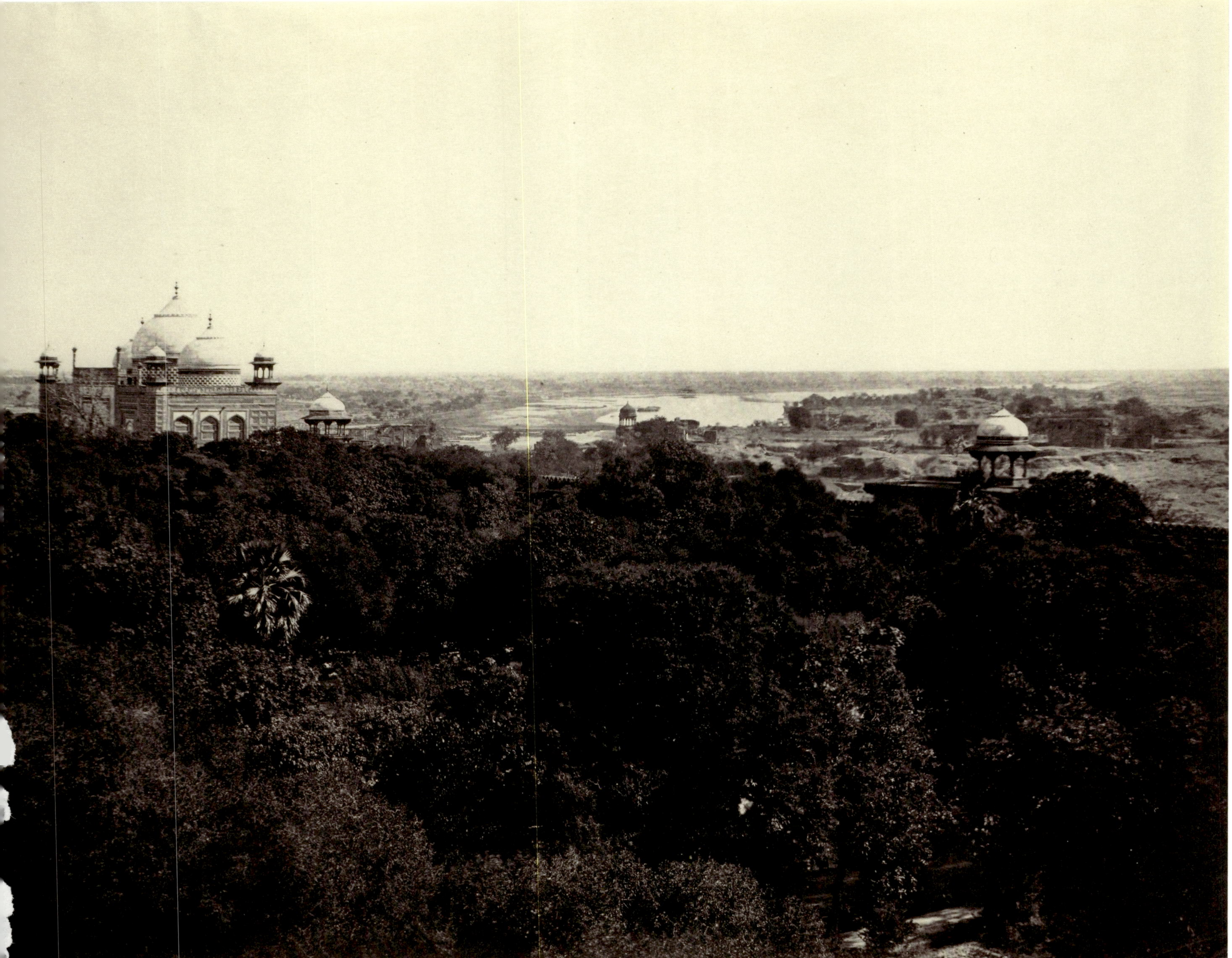

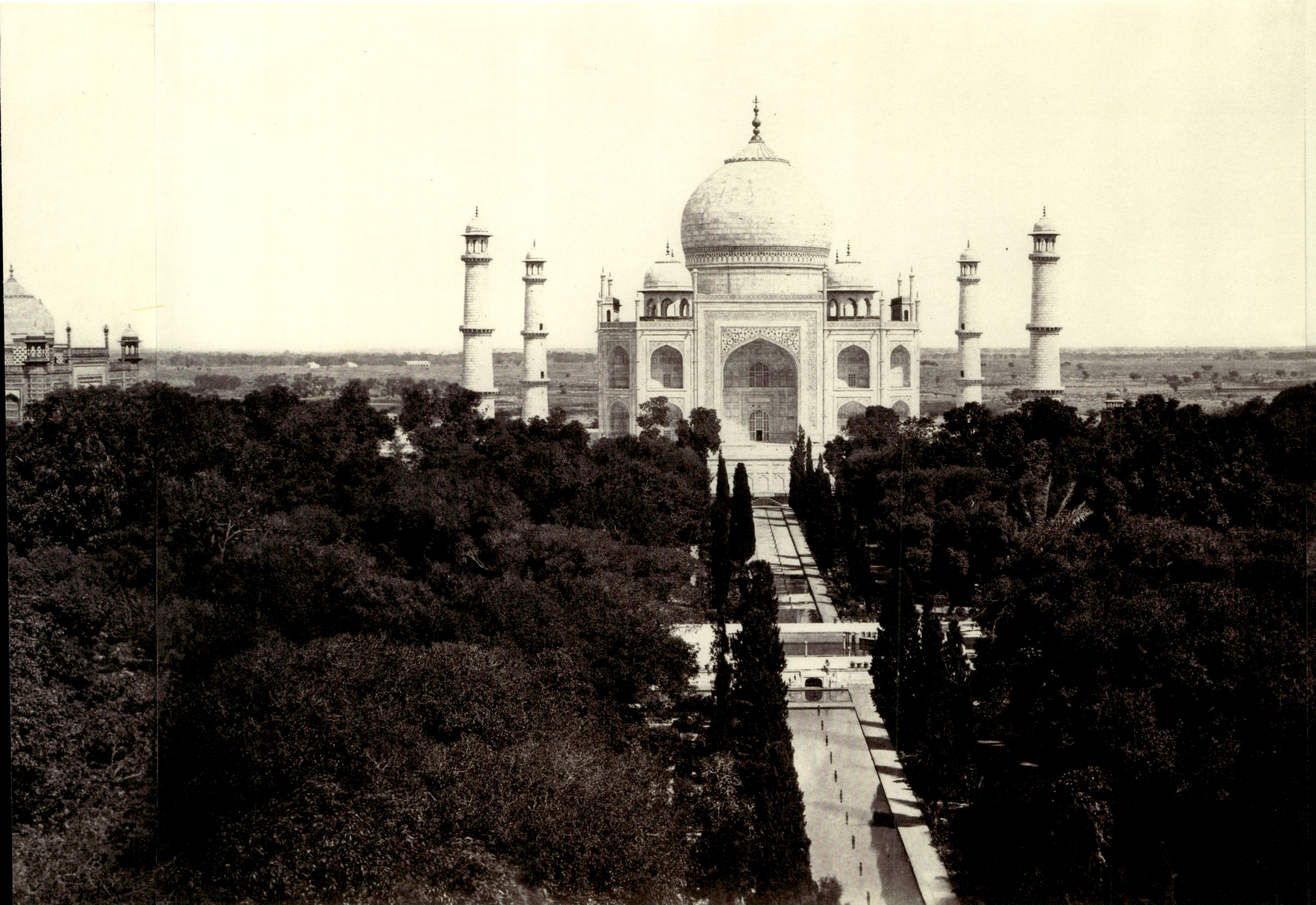

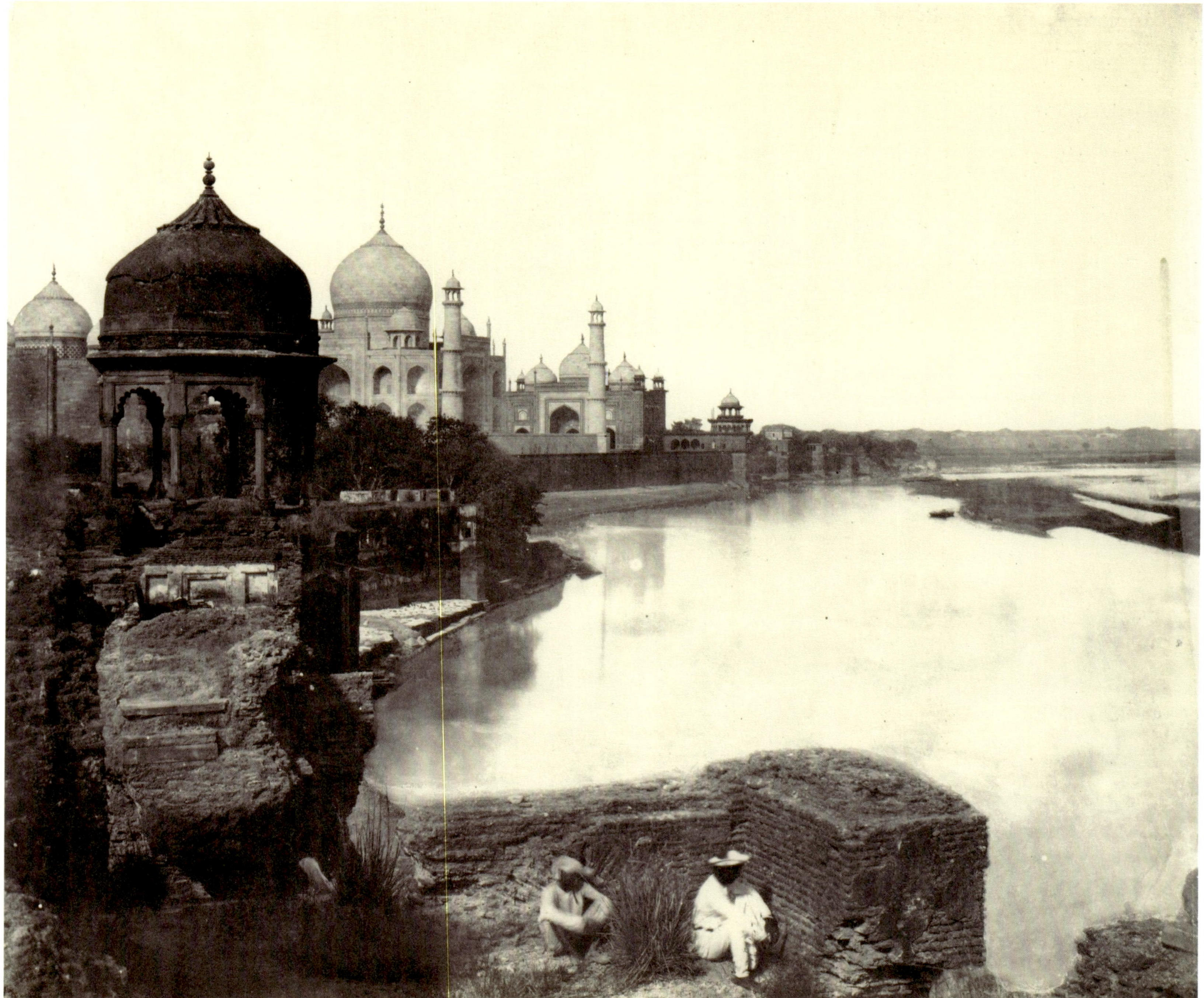

107. John Murray, The Taj Mahal from the Banks of the Yamuna River, 1858–62

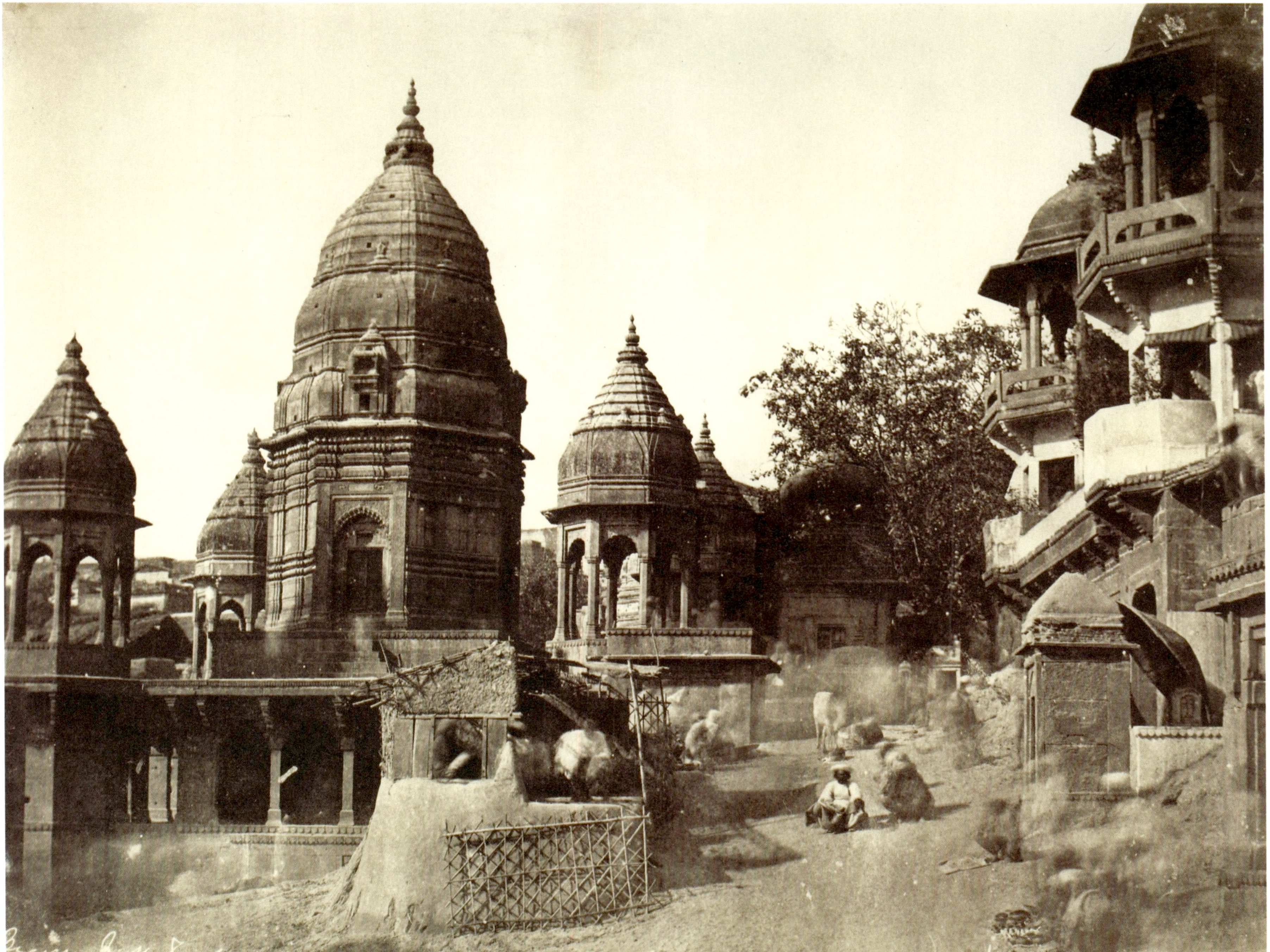

108. John Murray, *Bishessur Nath Temple, Benares,* 1858

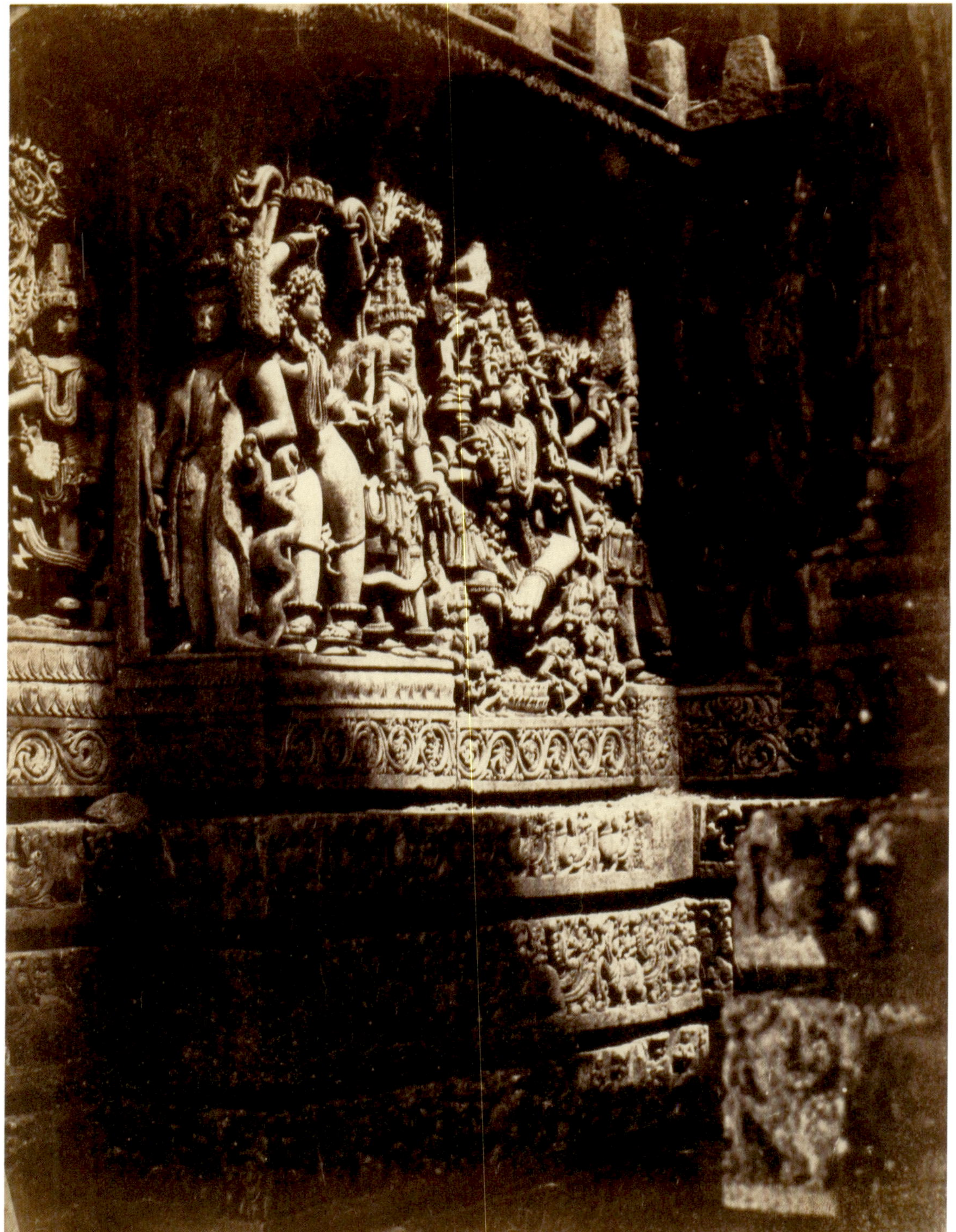

109. Richard Banner Oakeley, *Group of Apsaras*, 1856

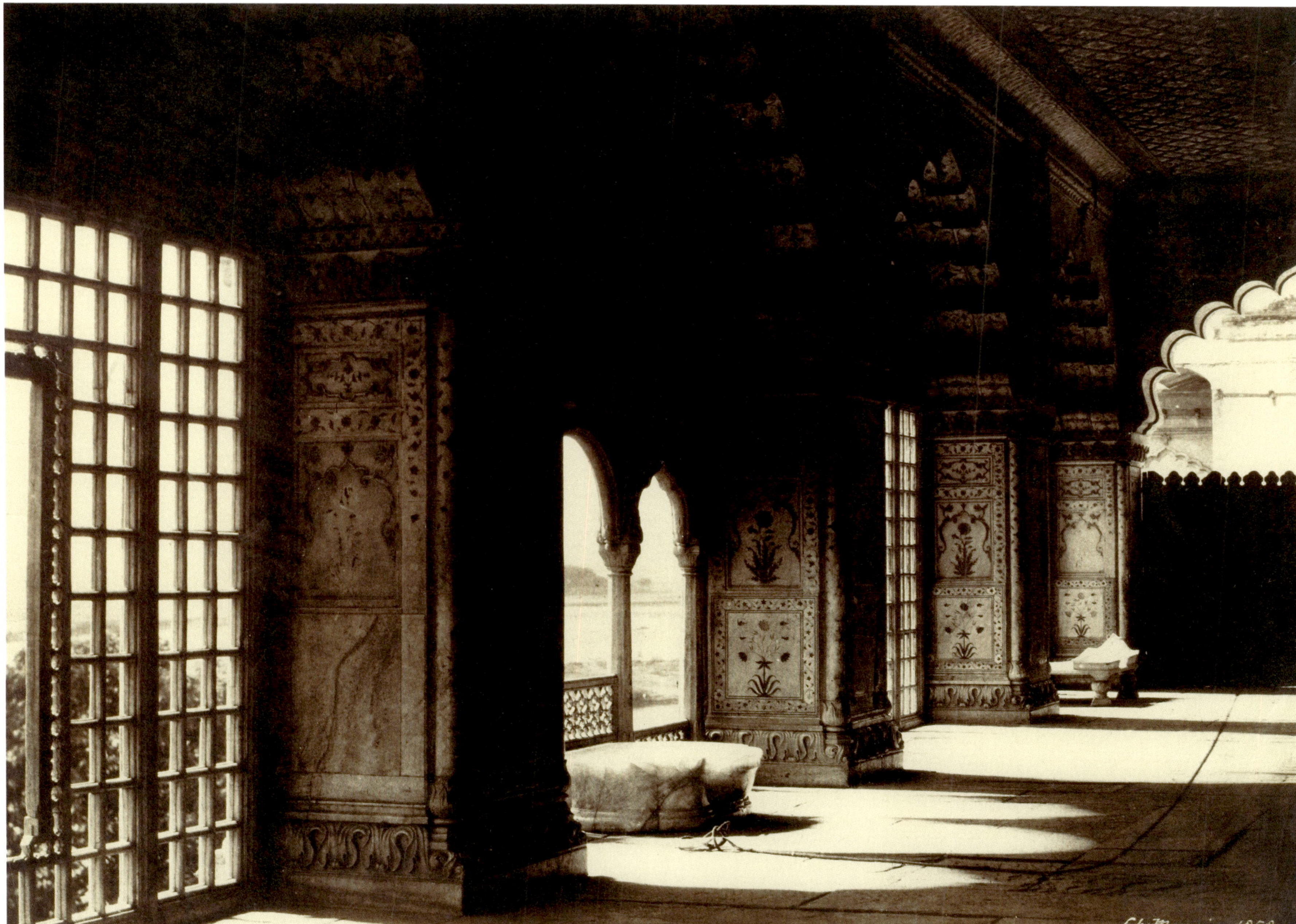

110. Charles Moravia, The Crystal Throne in the Diwan-i-Khas, Delhi, 1858

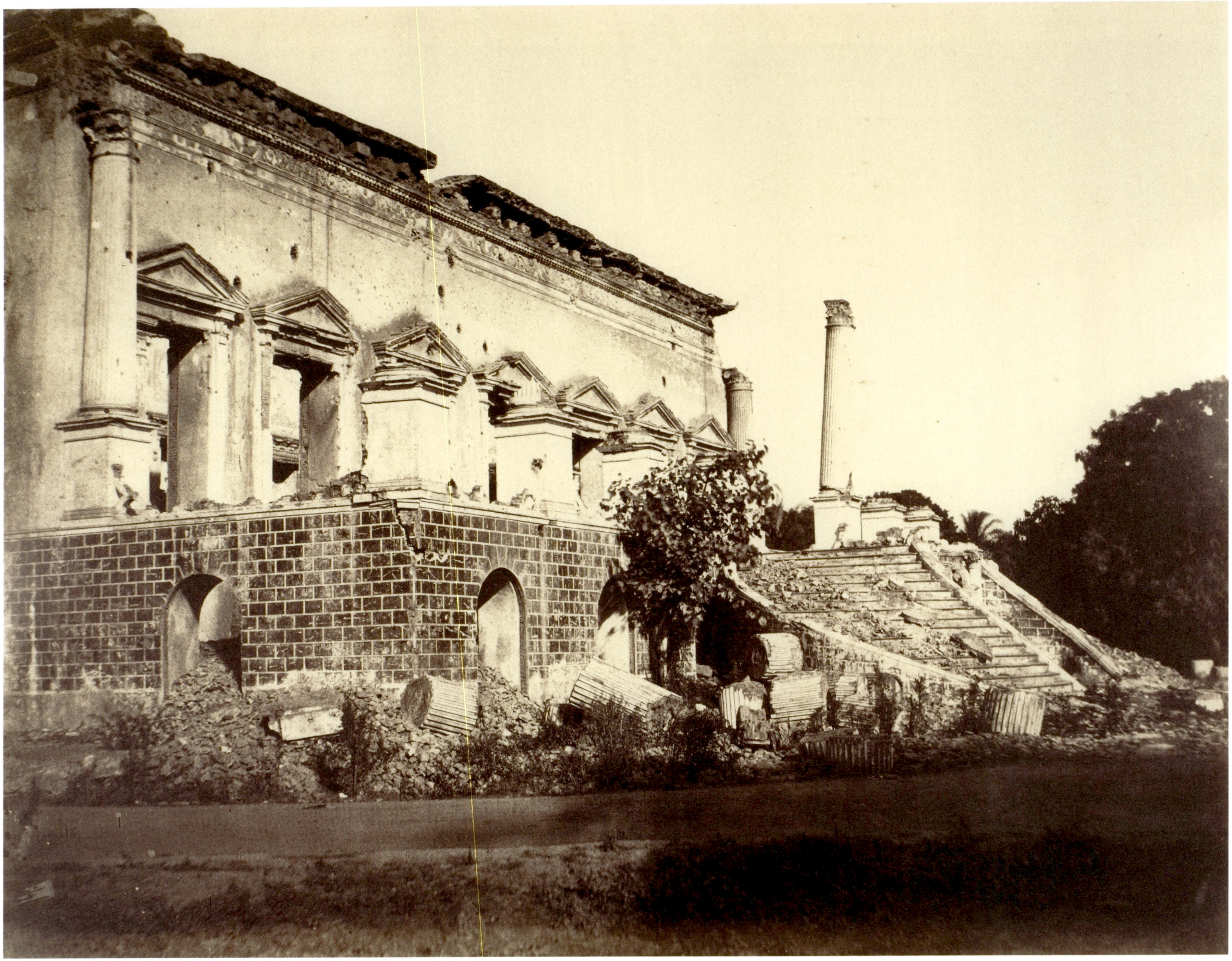

111. Robert Christopher Tytler and Harriet Christina Tytler, *The Bank of Delhi*, 1857–58

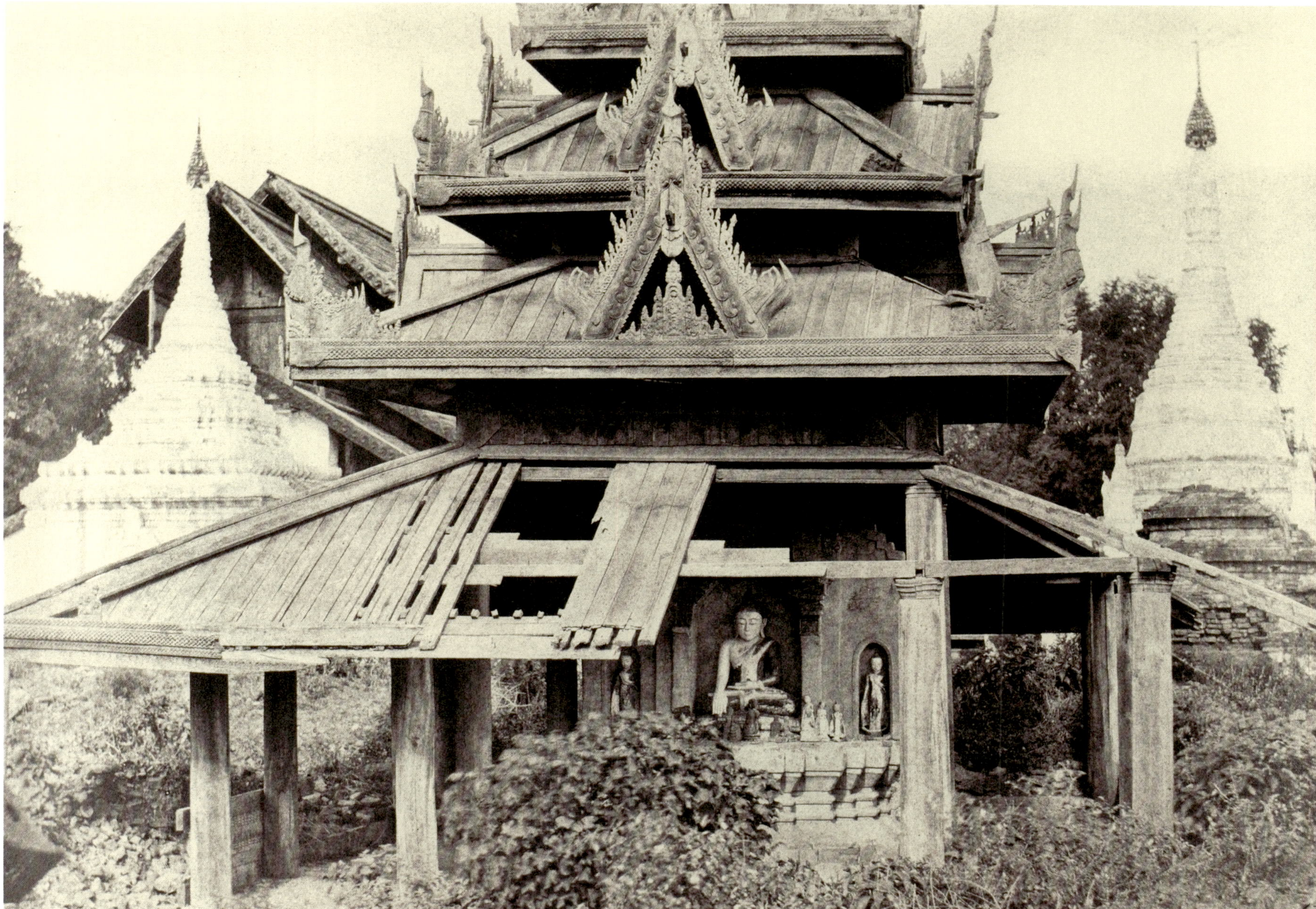

112. Linnaeus Tripe, *Ruined Tazoung, Tsagain Myo*, September–October 1855

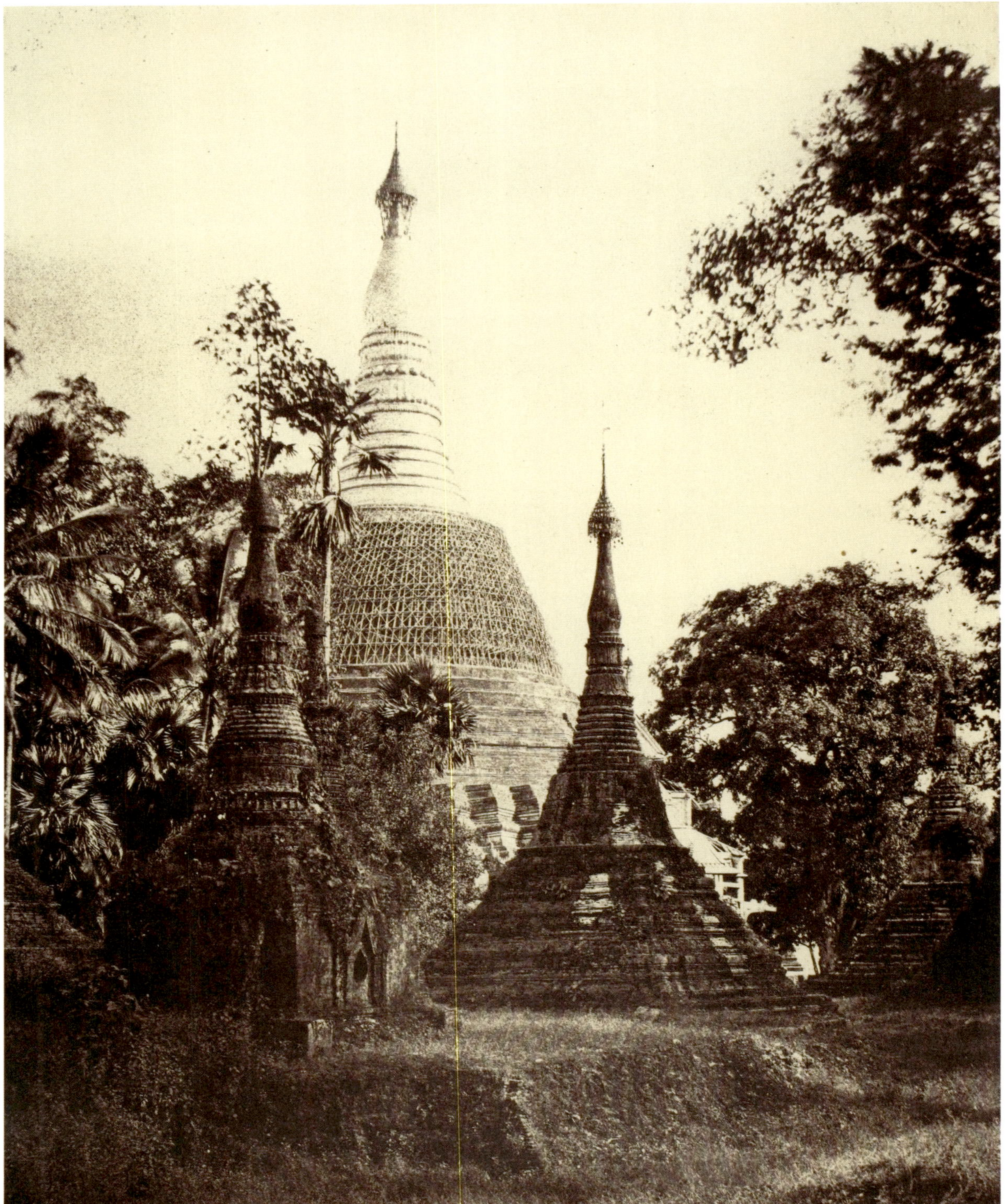

113. Linnaeus Tripe, *Near View of the Pagoda, Rangoon,* November 1855

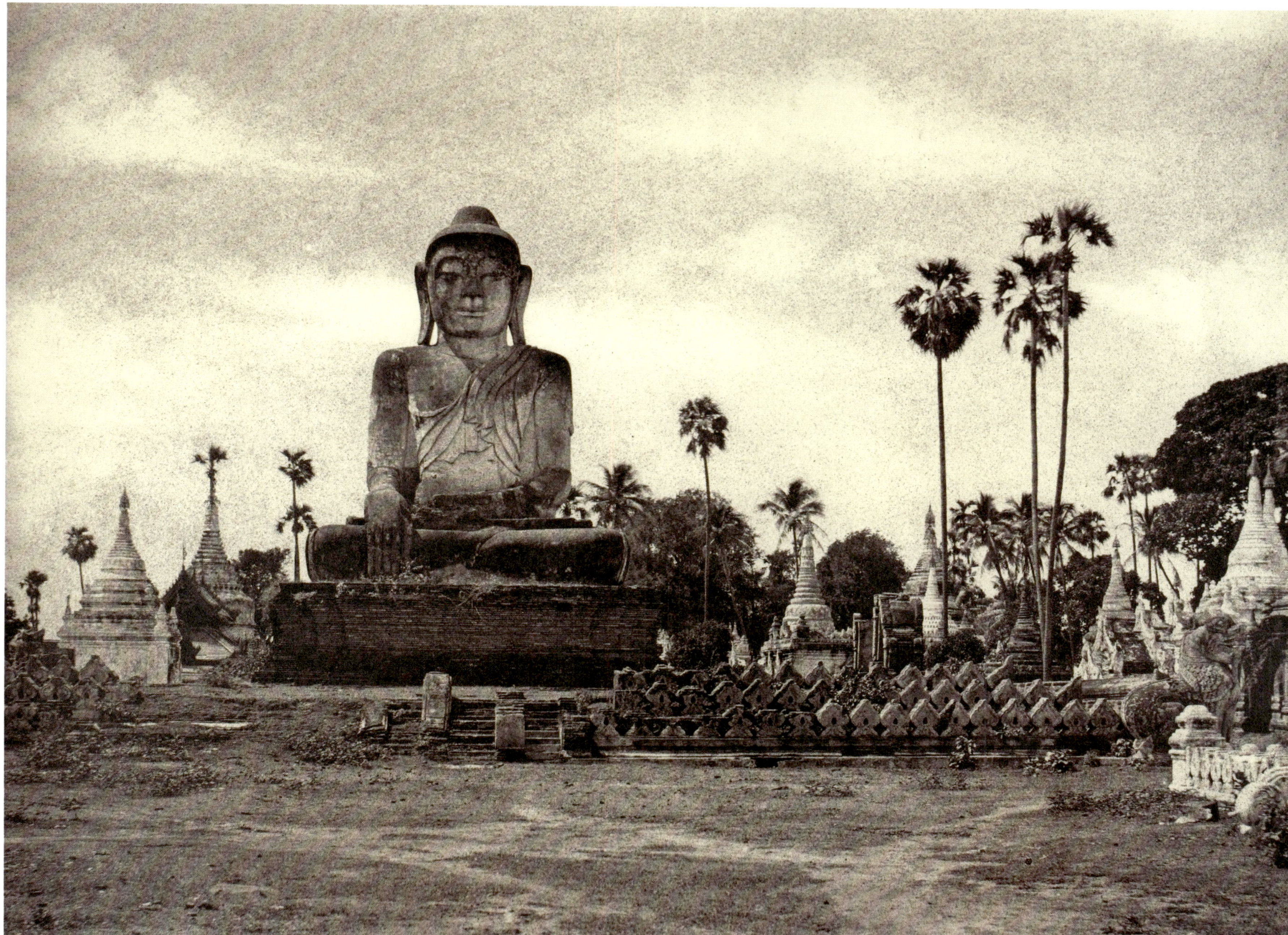

114. Linnaeus Tripe, *Colossal Statue of Gautama Close to the North End of the Bridge, Amerapoora,* September–October 1855

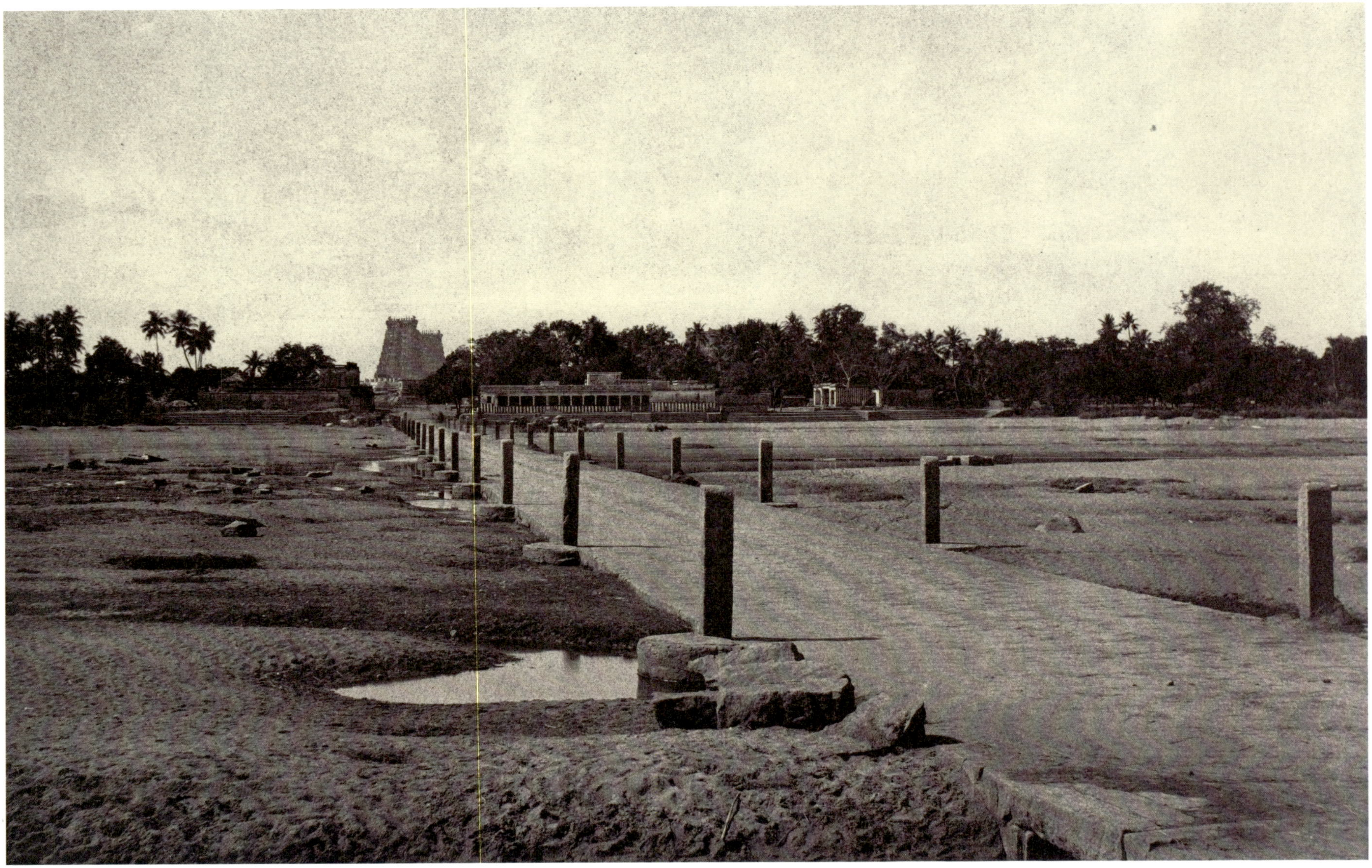

115. Linnaeus Tripe, *The Causeway across the Vaigai River, Madura,* January–March 1858

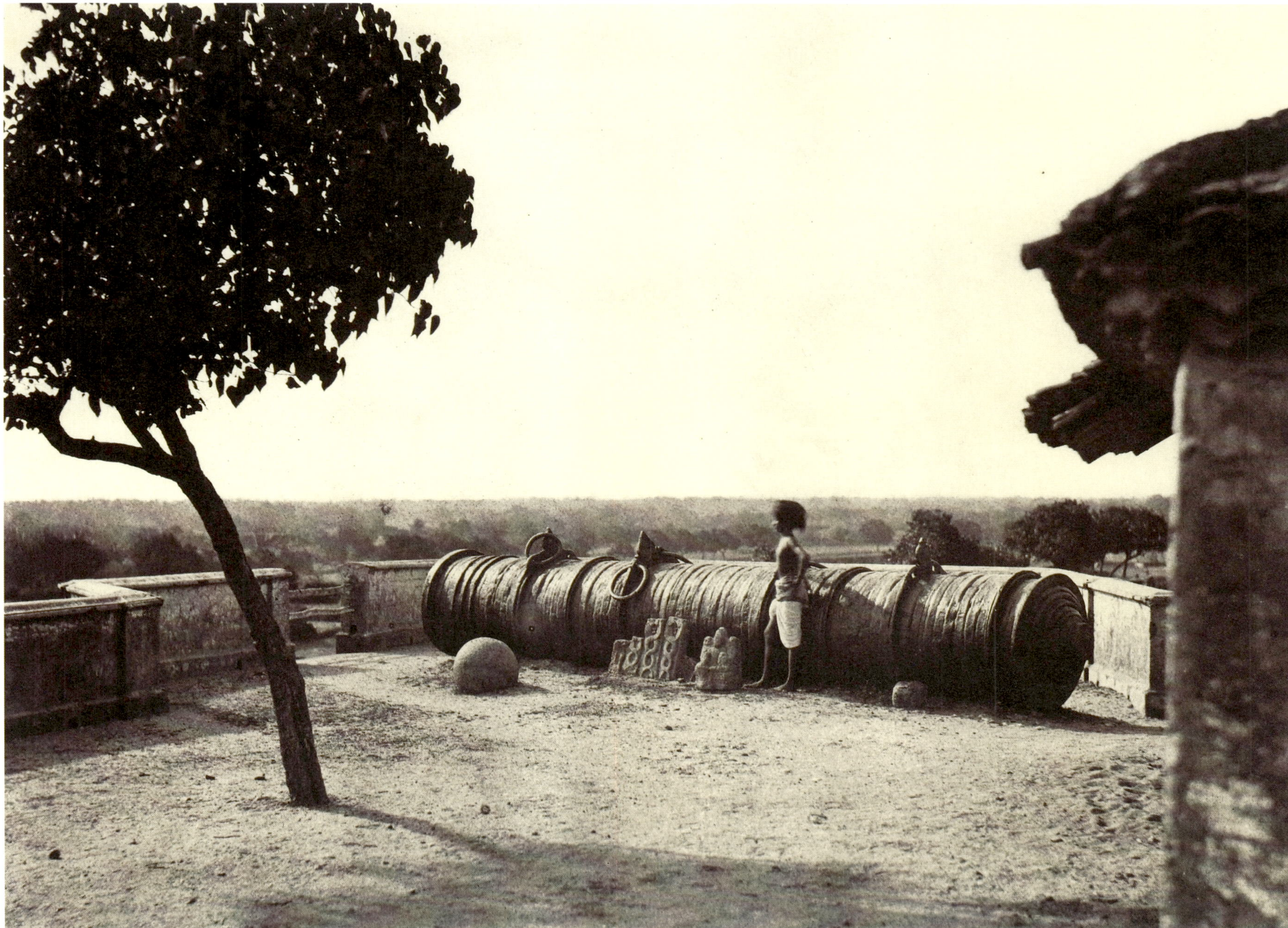

116. Linnaeus Tripe, *The Monster Gun of Tanjore*, March–April 1858

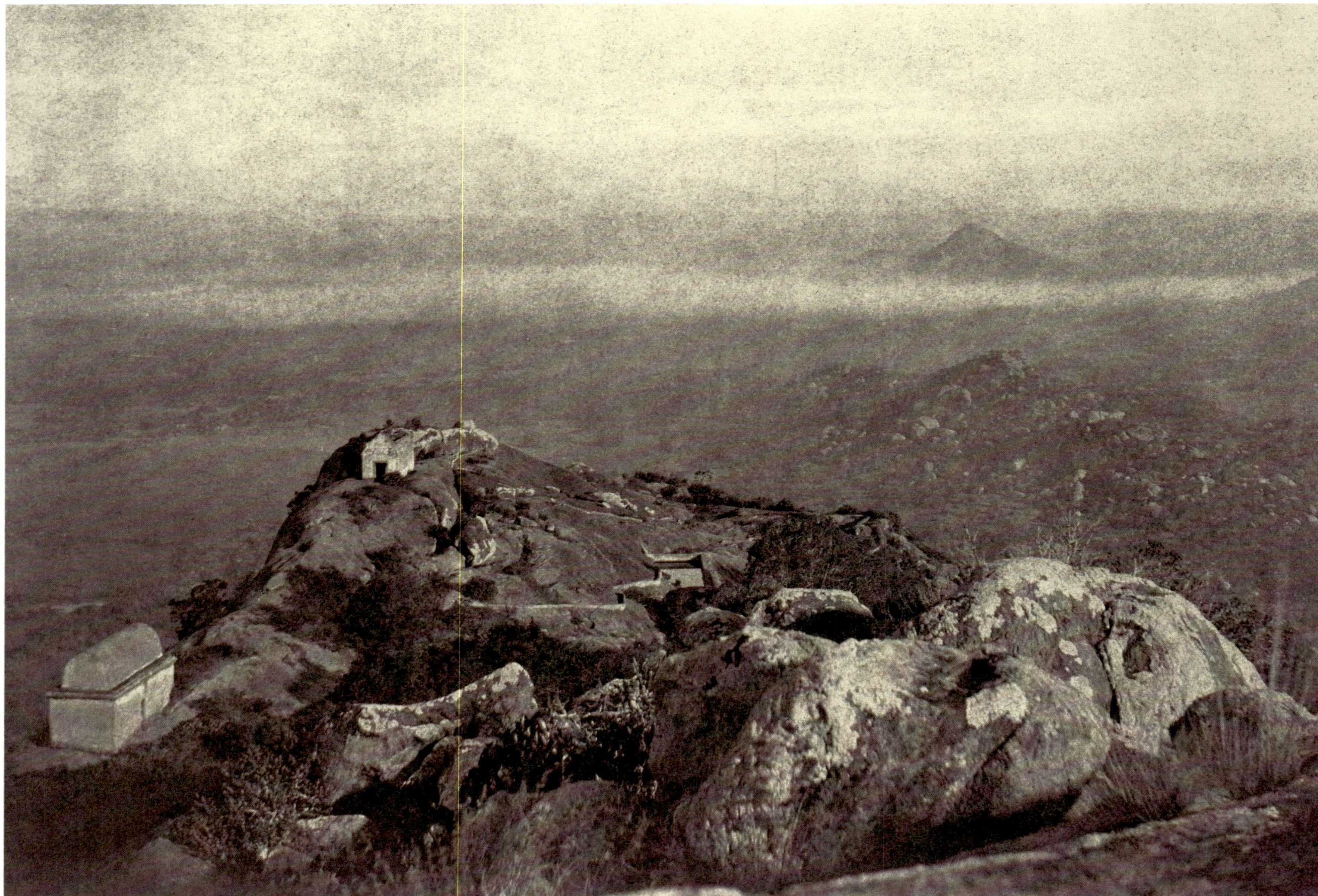

117. Linnaeus Tripe, *View of the Country Looking N.N.W. from the Top of the Ryakotta Hill,* December 1857–January 1858

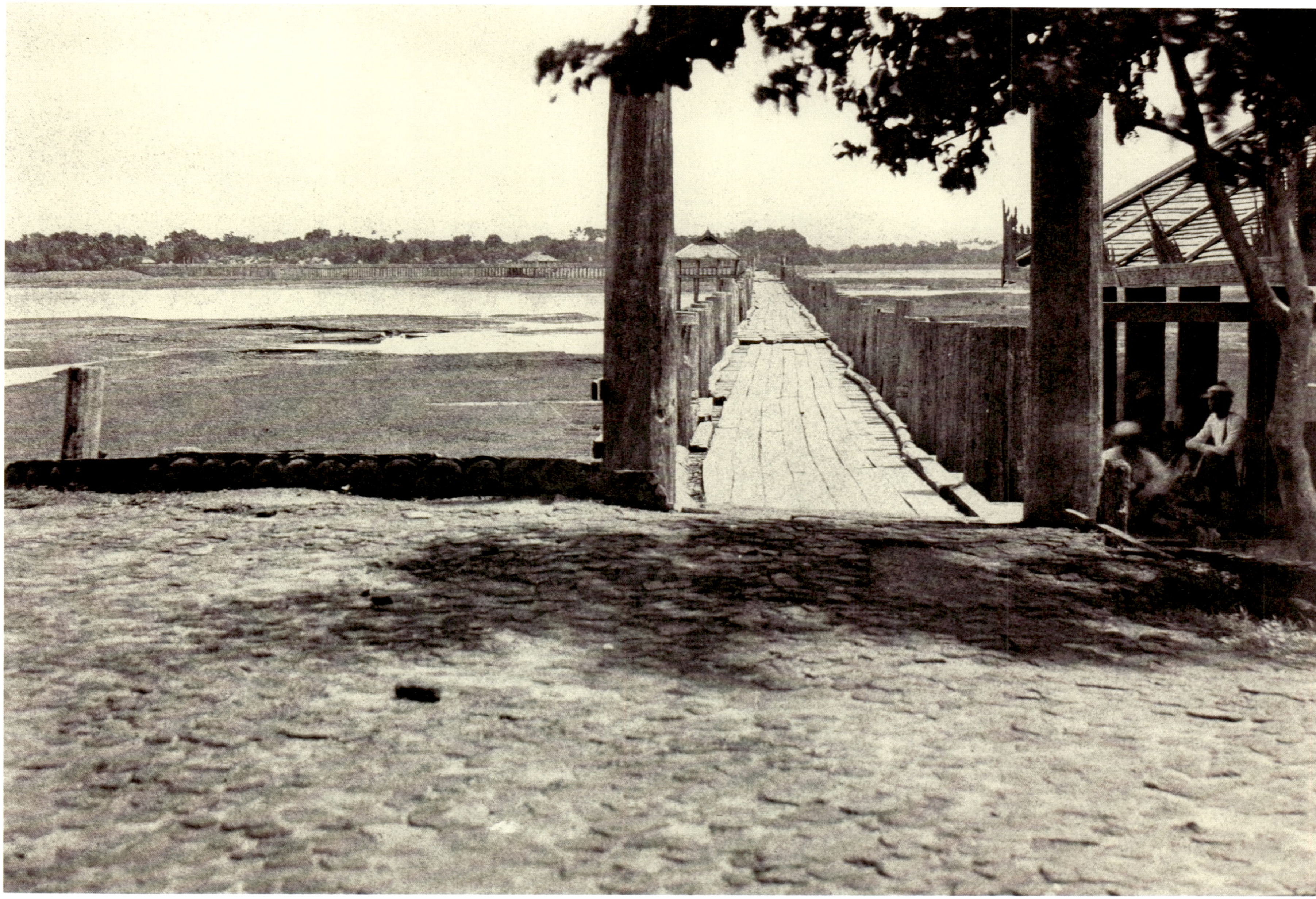

118. Linnaeus Tripe, *Wooden Bridge, Amerapoora,* September–October 1855

List of Plates

Titles in *italics* were given by the photographers and were usually inscribed on the print or mount, printed on a label affixed to the mount, or published in exhibition catalogues of the period. Those in roman type are modern descriptive titles. All prints are from paper negatives.

1. William Henry Fox Talbot (English, 1800–1877)
Wild Fennel, 1841–42
Salted paper print
18.7 x 22.7 cm (7⅜ x 9 in.)
The Metropolitan Museum of Art, New York, Gilman Collection, Purchase, Mr. and Mrs. Andrew W. Saul Gift, 2005
2005.100.260

2. William Henry Fox Talbot (English, 1800–1877)
The Haystack, April 1844
Paper negative
16.2 x 21 cm (6⅜ x 8¼ in.)
National Media Museum, Bradford
1937-1248

3. William Henry Fox Talbot (English, 1800–1877)
The Haystack, April 1844
Salted paper print
15.9 x 21 cm (6¼ x 8¼ in.)
National Media Museum, Bradford
1937-1251/2

4. William Henry Fox Talbot (English, 1800–1877)
Ugbrook Park, 1842
Salted paper print
8 x 9.8 cm (3⅛ x 3⅞ in.)
National Media Museum, Bradford
1937-4796/3

5. Calvert Richard Jones (Welsh, 1802–1877)
Two Figures on the Terrace at Lacock Abbey, ca. 1845
Salted paper print
17.6 x 22.7 cm (6⅞ x 9 in.)
National Media Museum, Bradford
1937-4489

6. William Henry Fox Talbot (English, 1800–1877) and Nicolaas Henneman (Dutch, 1813–1898)
The Reading Establishment, 1846
Salted paper prints
19.9 x 48.1 cm (7⅞ x 19 in.) overall
The Metropolitan Museum of Art, New York, Gilman Collection, Gift of The Howard Gilman Foundation, 2005
2005.100.171

7. David Octavius Hill (Scottish, 1802–1870) and Robert Adamson (Scottish, 1821–1848)
Sir David Brewster, ca. 1844
Salted paper print
20.2 x 15.1 cm (8 x 6 in.)
The Metropolitan Museum of Art, New York, Rubel Collection, Purchase, Lila Acheson Wallace Gift, 1997
1997.382.9

8. David Octavius Hill (Scottish, 1802–1870) and Robert Adamson (Scottish, 1821–1848)
David Octavius Hill at the Gate of Rock House, ca. 1845
Salted paper print
19.6 x 13.8 cm (7¾ x 5⅜ in.)
National Gallery of Art, Washington, Paul Mellon Fund
2007.29.27

9. David Octavius Hill (Scottish, 1802–1870) and Robert Adamson (Scottish, 1821–1848)
The Fairy Tree, Colinton, late 1846
Salted paper print
21.3 x 15.4 cm (8⅜ x 6⅞ in.)
Scottish National Photography Collection, National Galleries of Scotland
PGPHA426

10. David Octavius Hill (Scottish, 1802–1870) and Robert Adamson (Scottish, 1821–1848)
Colinton Manse and Weir, late 1846
Salted paper print
20.6 x 15.5 cm (8⅛ x 6⅛ in.)
Scottish National Photography Collection, National Galleries of Scotland
PGPHA584

11. David Octavius Hill (Scottish, 1802–1870) and Robert Adamson (Scottish, 1821–1848)
The Pends, St. Andrews, ca. 1844
Salted paper print
19.4 x 14.2 cm (7⅝ x 5⅝ in.)
The Metropolitan Museum of Art, New York, Rubel Collection, Promised Gift of William Rubel
L.1997.84.4

12. David Octavius Hill (Scottish, 1802–1870) and Robert Adamson (Scottish, 1821–1848)
92nd Gordon Highlanders at Edinburgh Castle, April 1846
Salted paper print
19 x 14.1 cm (7½ x 5½ in.)
Scottish National Photography Collection, National Galleries of Scotland
PGPHA347

13. William Collie (Scottish, 1810–1896)
Dr. Wolfe, 1852
Salted paper print
17 x 14.2 cm (6¾ x 5⅝ in.)
The Royal Photographic Society Collection at the National Media Museum, Bradford
2003-5001_2_23571_108

14. William Collie (Scottish, 1810–1896)
Young Man, Seated, late 1840s
Salted paper print
19.4 x 14.8 cm (7⅝ x 5⅞ in.)

The Royal Photographic Society Collection at the National Media Museum, Bradford
2003-5001_2_23571_062

15. William Collie (Scottish, 1810–1896)
Camellia, late 1840s
Salted paper print
12.1 x 9.5 cm (4¾ x 3¾ in.)
The Royal Photographic Society Collection at the National Media Museum, Bradford
2003-5001_2_23571_065

16. William Collie (Scottish, 1810–1896)
Market Women, St. Helier, Jersey, 1847
Salted paper print
20.9 x 17.1 cm (8¼ x 6¾ in.)
Private collection

17. Unknown photographer
Spreading Oak with Seated Figure, 1850s
Paper negative
17.7 x 20.7 cm (7 x 8⅛ in.)
The Metropolitan Museum of Art, New York, Gift of Hans P. Kraus, Jr., 2007
2007.234

18. Benjamin Brecknell Turner (English, 1815–1894)
Crystal Palace, Hyde Park, 1852, Transept
Paper negative
30.2 x 40.1 cm (11⅞ x 15¾ in.)
The Metropolitan Museum of Art, New York, Gilman Collection, Purchase, The Horace W. Goldsmith Foundation Gift through Joyce and Robert Menschel, 2005
2005.100.259

19. Benjamin Brecknell Turner (English, 1815–1894)
Crystal Palace, Hyde Park, 1852, Transept
Albumen silver print
26.3 x 39.5 cm (10⅜ x 15½ in.)
Victoria and Albert Museum, London
Ph2-1982

20. Hugh Owen (English, 1808–1897)
General View from Transept, Looking East, 1851
Frontispiece to *Reports by the Juries*, vol. 2
Salted paper print
17.4 x 22.8 cm (6⅞ x 9 in.)
Promised gift to the Art Gallery of Ontario, Toronto, from Archive of Modern Conflict, London
AGO ID 102894

21. Hugh Owen (English, 1808–1897)
Embroidered Saddle, 1851
In *Reports by the Juries*, vol. 3
Salted paper print
22.3 x 17.1 cm (8¾ x 6¾ in.)
Promised gift to the Art Gallery of Ontario, Toronto, from Archive of Modern Conflict, London
AGO ID 102871

22. Hugh Owen (English, 1808–1897)
Large Blocks of Coal, 1851
In *Reports by the Juries*, vol. 4
Salted paper print
17.2 x 22.4 cm (6¾ x 8⅞ in.)
Promised gift to the Art Gallery of Ontario, Toronto, from Archive of Modern Conflict, London
AGO ID 102893

23. Hugh Owen (English, 1808–1897)
Tree with Tangled Roots, 1853
Salted paper print
17.5 x 22.8 cm (6⅞ x 9 in.)
National Gallery of Art, Washington, The Horace W. Goldsmith Foundation through Robert and Joyce Menschel
2007.25.1

24. Hugh Owen (English, 1808–1897)
Queen Street, Bristol, 1853
Salted paper print
15.6 x 20.5 cm (6⅛ x 8⅛ in.)
Scottish National Photography Collection, National Galleries of Scotland
PGPW252

25. Robert Wilfred Skeffington Lutwidge (English, 1802–1873)
Knowle, Kent, Taken in the Rain, 1855
Albumen silver print
15.6 x 17.3 cm (6⅛ x 6⅞ in.)
The Royal Photographic Society Collection at the National Media Museum, Bradford
2003-5001_2_21723_21

26. William A. Pumphrey (English, 1817–1905)
Ripon Cathedral from the Southeast adjacent to the River Skell, ca. 1855
Salted paper print
14.4 x 20.9 cm (5⅝ x 8¼ in.)
Collection of Charles Isaacs and Carol Nigro

27. Thomas James Backhouse (English, 1810–1857)
At Sunderland, 1854
Salted paper print
20.2 x 24.9 cm (8 x 9¾ in.)
Private collection

28. John Muir Wood (Scottish, 1805–1892)
Stream in Woods, 1847–52
Salted paper print
12.3 x 15.2 cm (4⅞ x 6 in.)
Scottish National Photography Collection, National Galleries of Scotland
PGPW96

29. John Muir Wood (Scottish, 1805–1892)
Boy by Open Door, 1847–52
Salted paper print
10.4 x 9.6 cm (4⅛ x 3¾ in.)
Scottish National Photography Collection, National Galleries of Scotland
PGPW91

30. John Muir Wood (Scottish, 1805–1892)
Columnar Basalt, possibly near Fingal's Cave on Staffa, in the Hebrides, 1847–52
Salted paper print
17 x 19.3 cm (6¾ x 7⅝ in.)
Scottish National Photography Collection, National Galleries of Scotland
PGPW70

31. John Muir Wood (Scottish, 1805–1892)
Melrose Abbey, 1847–52
Salted paper print
15.8 x 21.6 cm (6¼ x 8½ in.)
Scottish National Photography Collection, National Galleries of Scotland
PGPW67

32. John Muir Wood (Scottish, 1805–1892)
Family Group, Leith, 1847–52
Salted paper print
11.3 x 14 cm (4½ x 5½ in.)
Scottish National Photography Collection, National Galleries of Scotland
PGPW55

33. John Muir Wood (Scottish, 1805–1892)
George Wood, 1847–52
Salted paper print
11.5 x 8.4 cm (4½ x 3¼ in.)
Scottish National Photography Collection, National Galleries of Scotland
PGPW46

34. John Dillwyn Llewelyn (Welsh, 1810–1882)
Inside the Great Cave, Dunraven, 1854
Albumen silver print
16.9 x 19.9 cm (6⅝ x 7⅞ in.)
City and County of Swansea: Swansea Museum
SM LIB JDL Album 3

35. John Dillwyn Llewelyn (Welsh, 1810–1882)
Blue Squills, ca. 1852
Albumen silver print
21 x 16.9 cm (8¼ x 6⅝ in.)
Hans P. Kraus, Jr., New York

36. Benjamin Brecknell Turner (English, 1815–1894)
Eashing Bridge, Surrey, 1852–54
Albumen silver print
26.9 x 38.4 cm (10⅝ x 15⅛ in.)
Victoria and Albert Museum, London
Ph32-1982

37. Benjamin Brecknell Turner (English, 1815–1894)
At Compton, Surrey, 1852–54
Albumen silver print
27 x 38.6 cm (10⅝ x 15¼ in.)
Victoria and Albert Museum, London
Ph34-1982

38. Benjamin Brecknell Turner (English, 1815–1894)
Hedgerow Trees, Clerkenleap, Worcestershire, 1852–54
Albumen silver print
28.8 x 38.8 cm (11⅜ x 15¼ in.)
Victoria and Albert Museum, London
Ph13-1982

39. Benjamin Brecknell Turner (English, 1815–1894)
Whitby Abbey, Yorkshire, North Transept, 1852–54
Albumen silver print
26.6 x 34.4 cm (10½ x 13½ in.)
Victoria and Albert Museum, London
Ph5-1982

40. Benjamin Brecknell Turner (English, 1815–1894)
Lynmouth, North Devon, 1852–54
Albumen silver print
26.7 x 38.7 cm (10½ x 15¼ in.)
Victoria and Albert Museum, London
Ph3-1982

41. Benjamin Brecknell Turner (English, 1815–1894)
Anstey's Cove, Torquay, 1861
Albumen silver print
28.9 x 38.6 cm (11⅜ x 15¼ in.)
Lawrence and Sybil Hite

42. James Mudd (English, 1821–1906)
The Yard of Beyer Peacock Railway Engine Manufacturers, Gorton, Manchester, ca. 1855
Salted paper print
17.2 x 25.8 cm (6¾ x 10⅛ in.)
Stephen White, Collection II

43. James Mudd (English, 1821–1906)
Steam Locomotive "Gardner" at Beyer Peacock's, 1856
Salted paper print
24.5 x 34.2 cm (9⅝ x 13½ in.)
Stephen White, Collection II

44. Edward King Tenison (Irish, 1805–1878)
Dublin International Exhibition, 1853
Salted paper print
26.6 x 40.4 cm (10½ x 15⅞ in.)
Thomas Walther Collection

45. Arthur James Melhuish (English, 1829–1895)
View of the Henry VIII Gate, Windsor Castle, 1855
Salted paper print (Blanquart-Evrard process)
21 x 27 cm (8¼ x 10⅝ in.)
Collection Isabelle Jammes

46. Arthur James Melhuish (English, 1829–1895)
St. George's Gate, from the Moat Path, 1855
Salted paper print (Blanquart-Evrard process)
20.8 x 27 cm (8 ¼ x 10 ⅝ in.)
Collection Isabelle Jammes

47. Arthur James Melhuish (English, 1829–1895)
Statue of Charles II and the Entrance to the Quadrangle, Windsor Castle, 1856
Salted paper print (Blanquart-Evrard process)
36.6 x 48.8 cm (14 ⅜ x 19 ¼ in.)
The Royal Collection
2100361

48. George Moir (Scottish, 1800–1870)
At Arniston, ca. 1855
Albumen silver print
15.8 x 16.8 cm (6¼ x 6⅝ in.)
National Media Museum, Bradford
1990-5131_1_4

49. Unknown photographer
House and Picket Fence, 1850s
Salted paper print
15.8 x 19 cm (6¼ x 7½ in.)
The Metropolitan Museum of Art, New York, David Hunter McAlpin Fund, 1946
46.1.64

50. John Hill Morgan (English, 1833–?)
In King's Weston Park, Bristol, ca. 1855
Salted paper print
20.5 x 20.2 cm (8⅛ x 8 in.)
City and County of Swansea: Swansea Museum
SM LIB JDL Album 8

51. Thomas Sutton (English, 1819–1875)
Tower Struck by Lightning, Saint-Ouen Bay, 1854
Salted paper print (Blanquart-Evrard process)
28.8 x 19.5 cm (11⅜ x 7⅝ in.)
National Gallery of Art, Washington, The Horace W. Goldsmith Foundation through Robert and Joyce Menschel
2006.15.2

52. Thomas Sutton (English, 1819–1875)
Fishing Boats, Saint Brélade Bay, 1854

Salted paper print (Blanquart-Evrard process)
21.7 x 22.8 cm (8½ x 9 in.)
Lawrence and Sybil Hite

53. Thomas Sutton (English, 1819–1875)
Rising Tide, Fiquet Bay, 1854
Salted paper print (Blanquart-Evrard process)
21.8 x 27.2 cm (8⅝ x 10¾ in.)
Collection Isabelle Jammes

54. Charles Brittan (English, 1832–after 1881)
Clifton Gorge, 1853–54
Salted paper print
20.2 x 25.4 cm (8 x 10 in.)
The Royal Photographic Society Collection at the National Media Museum, Bradford
2003-5001_2_23565

55. Alfred Capel Cure (English, 1826–1896)
"Nigger" Asleep—Roscrea, 1850s
Salted paper print
13.1 x 18.1 cm (5⅛ x 7⅛ in.)
Private collection, courtesy of Hans P. Kraus, Jr., New York

56. Alfred Capel Cure (English, 1826–1896)
Blasted Tree at Badger, September 19, 1856
Albumen silver print
17.8 x 22.5 cm (7 x 8⅞ in.)
Thomas Walther Collection

57. Alfred Capel Cure (English, 1826–1896)
East Window, Tintern, August 17, 1857
Albumen silver print
22 x 27.4 cm (8⅝ x 10¾ in.)
Collection Centre Canadien d'Architecture / Canadian Centre for Architecture, Montréal
PH1983:0491:109

58. Alfred Capel Cure (English, 1826–1896)
Glastonbury Abbey, Looking West, 1857
Albumen silver print
21 x 27 cm (8¼ x 10⅝ in.)
The Museum of Modern Art, New York. Gift of Peter Steil, 1983
110.1983

59. Alfred Capel Cure (English, 1826–1896)
Hereford Cathedral from Northwest, 1858–60
Albumen silver print
21.6 x 27.4 cm (8½ x 10¾ in.)
The Museum of Modern Art, New York. Gift of Peter Steil, 1983
126.1983

60. Robert Henry Cheney (English, 1800–1866)
Belmont, Bath, 1850s
Albumen silver print
17.4 x 22.5 cm (6⅞ x 8⅞ in.)
Collection Centre Canadien d'Architecture / Candian Centre for Architecture, Montréal
PH78:103:34

61. Robert Henry Cheney (English, 1800–1866)
Guyscliffe, 1850s
Albumen silver print
17.7 x 22.3 cm (7 x 8¾ in.)
Collection Centre Canadien d'Architecture / Canadian Centre for Architecture, Montréal
PH78:103:30

62. Horatio Ross (Scottish, 1801–1886)
Sea Coast near Netherley, mid-1850s
Albumen silver print
25.6 x 32.4 cm (10⅛ x 12¾ in.)
Janet Lehr Inc., New York

63. Horatio Ross (Scottish, 1801–1886)
Rocky Landscape, mid-1850s
Albumen silver print
22.3 x 33.4 cm (8¾ x 13⅛ in.)
Janet Lehr Inc., New York

64. Horatio Ross (Scottish, 1801–1886)
View of Dunottar Castle, mid-1850s
Albumen silver print
16.4 x 33 cm (6½ x 13 in.)
Janet Lehr Inc., New York

65. Horatio Ross (Scottish, 1801–1886)
Affaric Lodge, mid-1850s
Salted paper print
26.7 x 32.9 cm (10½ x 13 in.)
Joy of Giving Something, Inc.

66. Thomas Keith (Scottish, 1827–1895)
Greyfriars Churchyard, Monument to Provost Archibald Tod, Edinburgh, 1854–57
Salted paper print
25.9 x 23.9 cm (10¼ x 9½ in.)
Collection Centre Canadien d'Architecture / Canadian Centre for Architecture, Montréal
PH1993:0428:030

67. Thomas Keith (Scottish, 1827–1895)
Greyfriars Churchyard, Monument to Provost William Little of Liberton, Edinburgh, 1854–57
Salted paper print
24.4 x 27.2 cm (9⅝ x 10¾ in.)
Collection Centre Canadien d'Architecture / Canadian Centre for Architecture, Montréal
PH1993:0428:020

68. Thomas Keith (Scottish, 1827–1895)
Doorway of Tailor's Hall, Potterrow, Edinburgh, 1854–57
Salted paper print
27.2 x 21 cm (10¾ x 8¼ in.)
Collection Centre Canadien d'Architecture / Canadian Centre for Architecture, Montréal
PH1993:0428:012

69. Thomas Keith (Scottish, 1827–1895)
Cardinal Beaton's House, Edinburgh, 1854–57
Salted paper print
27.9 x 24.8 cm (11 x 9¾ in.)
Royal Scottish Academy, Edinburgh
1994.04

70. Thomas Keith (Scottish, 1827–1895)
Trees, 1854–57
Salted paper print
The Metropolitan Museum of Art, New York, Gilman Collection, Purchase, Harriette and Noel Levine Gift, 2005
2005.100.5

71. Calvert Richard Jones (Welsh, 1802–1877)
Palacea Brig, Hove Down, Malta, December 1845–January 1846
Salted paper print
15.4 x 21.1 cm (6⅛ x 8¼ in.)
Thomas Walther Collection

72. Christopher Rice Mansel Talbot (English, 1803–1890)
Villa Reale, Naples, 1846
Salted paper print
15.7 x 21.2 cm (6⅛ x 8⅜ in.)
National Media Museum, Bradford
1937-4558

73. Calvert Richard Jones (Welsh, 1802–1877)
St. Paul's Cathedral, Valetta, Malta, with Bell Tower, 1846
Salted paper print
18.6 x 22.4 cm (7⅜ x 8⅞ in.)
National Gallery of Art, Washington, The Carolyn Brody Fund and The Horace W. Goldsmith Foundation through Robert and Joyce Menschel
2007.27.1

74. Calvert Richard Jones (Welsh, 1802–1877)
House of Sallust, Vesuvius behind, Pompeii, spring 1846
Salted paper print
16.2 x 21 cm (6⅜ x 8¼ in.)
National Media Museum, Bradford
1937-4589/6

75. George Wilson Bridges (English, 1788–1863)
View of Mount Aetna, 1846
Salted paper print
16.2 x 21.7 cm (6⅜ x 8½ in.)
W. Bruce Lundberg

76. George Wilson Bridges (English, 1788–1863)
Taormina, The Amphitheater, 1846
Salted paper print
16.9 x 21.5 cm (6⅝ x 8½ in.)
Collection of Charles Isaacs and Carol Nigro

77. Calvert Richard Jones (Welsh, 1802–1877)
Santa Lucia, Naples, 1845–46
Salted paper prints
22.4 x 36.2 cm (8⅞ x 14¼ in.) overall
The Metropolitan Museum of Art, New York, Gilman Collection, Purchase, The Horace W. Goldsmith Foundation Gift through Joyce and Robert Menschel, 2005
2005.100.947.1,.2

78. Alfred Capel Cure (English, 1826–1896)
My Beasts, February 1, 1852
Paper negative
19.7 x 15.9 cm (7¾ x 6¼ in.)
The Museum of Modern Art, New York. Gift of Paul F. Walter, 1986
SC1986.77

79. Roger Fenton (English, 1819–1869)
Banks of the Dnieper, near Kief, fall 1852
Salted paper print
17.3 x 21.4 cm (6⅞ x 8⅜ in.)
The Royal Photographic Society Collection at the National Media Museum, Bradford
2003-5000/3285

80. Roger Fenton (English, 1819–1869)
Moscow, Domes of Churches in the Kremlin, fall 1852
Salted paper print
18.2 x 21.2 cm (7⅛ x 8⅜ in.)
National Gallery of Art, Washington, Paul Mellon Fund
2005.52.1

81. John Muir Wood (Scottish, 1805–1892)
Groene Rei, Bruges, July 1847
Salted paper print
11.1 x 15.2 cm (4⅜ x 6 in.)
Scottish National Photography Collection, National Galleries of Scotland
PGPW62

82. Alfred Backhouse (English, 1823–1888)
Pots and Pans at Nice, 1855
Albumen paper print
21.5 x 27.6 cm (8½ x 10⅞ in.)
Paula and Robert Hershkowitz

83. Thomas Milville Raven (English, 1828–1896)
Near Bagnières de Bigorre, 1856–57
Albumen silver print
22.9 x 28.7 cm (9 x 11¼ in.)
National Media Museum, Bradford
1990-5131_1_47

84. John Stewart (Scottish, 1814–1887)
View of the Arruns Pass and Peak from the Pont de Soubé, 1852
Salted paper print (Blanquart-Evrard process)
22.1 x 29.4 cm (8¾ x 11⅝ in.)
National Media Museum, Bradford
1990-5036_11242

85. John Stewart (Scottish, 1814–1887)
Chaos de Gavarnie, 1852
Salted paper print (Blanquart-Evrard process)
22.1 x 31.2 cm (8¾ x 12¼ in.)
Bibliothèque Nationale de France, Paris
EO227/P5

86. William Robert Baker (English, 1810–1896)
Roadside Crucifix in Alpine Village, ca. 1855
Albumen silver print
25.6 x 29.6 cm (10⅛ x 11⅝ in.)
National Media Museum, Bradford
1990-5036_11241

87. Unknown photographer
Rome, Quirinale, ca. 1855
Salted paper print
16.7 x 21.4 cm (6⅝ x 8⅜ in.)
The Metropolitan Museum of Art, New York, David Hunter McAlpin Fund, 1946
46.1.48

88. Unknown photographer
Rome, So-Called Casa di Rienzi, the Oldest Medieval Private House, ca. 1855
Salted paper print
16.4 x 21.3 cm (6½ x 8⅜ in.)
The Metropolitan Museum of Art, New York, David Hunter McAlpin Fund, 1946
46.1.54

89. Jane Martha St. John (English, 1803–1882)
The Colosseum, 1856
Albumen silver print
19.5 x 25 cm (7⅝ x 9⅞ in.)
The Metropolitan Museum of Art, New York, Gilman Collection, Gift of The Howard Gilman Foundation, 2005
2005.100.382 (68)

90. Jane Martha St. John (English, 1803–1882)
Stone Pines, Villa Pamfili Doria, Rome, 1856
Albumen silver print
20 x 24.8 cm (7⅞ x 9¾ in.)
The Metropolitan Museum of Art, New York, Gilman Collection, Gift of The Howard Gilman Foundation, 2005
2005.100.382 (66)

91. Edward King Tenison (Irish, 1805–1878)
Segovia, 1852
Salted paper print
27.4 x 37.8 cm (10¾ x 14⅞ in.)
Bibliothèque Nationale de France, Paris
RES VF 268-FOL

92. Charles Clifford (Welsh, 1819–1863)
Courtyard of the Lower School, Salamanca, 1853–54
Albumen paper print
27.4 x 41.2 cm (10¾ x 16¼ in.)
Wilson Centre for Photography
98.5991

93. Charles Clifford (Welsh, 1819–1863)
Carrera de San Jerónimo, Madrid, 1853
Salted paper print
31.9 x 42.8 cm (12½ x 16⅞ in.)
Victoria and Albert Museum, London
X739G/40001

94. Charles Clifford (Welsh, 1819–1863)
Portal of the Convent of Sancti Spiritu, Salamanca, 1853
Albumen silver print
39.9 x 31.4 cm (15¾ x 12⅜ in.)
The Metropolitan Museum of Art, New York, Purchase, The Horace W. Goldsmith Foundation Gift through Joyce and Robert Menschel, 1994
1994.519

95. Charles Clifford (Welsh, 1819–1863)
Church of San Miguel de Lillo, near Oviedo, 1854
Albumen silver print
36.7 x 29.3 cm (14½ x 11½ in.)
Thomas Walther Collection

96. Charles Clifford (Welsh, 1819–1863)
Latona Fountain in the Gardens of La Granja, Segovia, 1853
Albumen silver print
28.7 x 40.8 cm (11¼ x 16⅛ in.)
Victoria and Albert Museum, London
X795H/35695

97. Charles Clifford (Welsh, 1819–1863)
Principal Doorway of the Carthusian Monastery, Burgos, 1853
Albumen silver print
33.9 x 28.4 cm (13⅜ x 11⅛ in.)
The Metropolitan Museum of Art, New York, Gilman Collection, Purchase, Alfred Stieglitz Society Gifts, 2005
2005.100.65

98. Alfred Huish (English, 1811–?)
Children's Graves, India, 1848
Salted paper print
12.5 x 17 cm (4⅞ x 6¾ in.)
Private collection

99. John McCosh (Scottish, 1805–1885)
Englishman at the Entrance to a Pagoda, 1848–50
Salted paper print
15.8 x 12.6 cm (6¼ x 5 in.)
Victoria and Albert Museum, London
85300

100. John McCosh (Scottish, 1805–1885)
Pedestal of the Sacred Mast, Rangoon; Italian Priest; Another Italian Priest, 1848–50
Salted paper prints
18.7 x 13.3 cm (7⅜ x 5¼ in.); 10.7 x 7.8 cm (4¼ x 3⅛ in.); 10.7 x 7.9 cm (4¼ x 3⅛ in.)
Courtesy of the Council of the National Army Museum, London
6204-3/307–309

101. John McCosh (Scottish, 1805–1885)
African Croomen, 1848–50
Salted paper print
15.3 x 9.3 cm (6 x 3⅝ in.)
Courtesy of the Council of the National Army Museum, London
6204-3/298

102. John Murray (English, 1809–1898)
Suttee Ghat, Cawnpore, 1858
Paper negative
38 x 48 cm (15 x 18⅞ in.)
The Metropolitan Museum of Art, New York, Gilman Collection, Purchase, Cynthia Hazen Polsky Gift, 2005
2005.100.946

103. John Murray (English, 1809–1898)
Suttee Ghat, Cawnpore, 1858
Albumen silver print
33 x 43.1 cm (13 x 17 in.)
The Metropolitan Museum of Art, New York, Gilman Collection, Purchase, Cynthia Hazen Polsky Gift, 2005
2005.100.945

104. John Murray (English, 1809–1898)
Auringzebe's Mosque, 1856–57
Salted paper print
36.5 x 46 cm (14⅜ x 18⅛ in.)
The British Library, London
Photo 101/25

105. John Murray (English, 1809–1898)
The Chowk, 1856–57
Salted paper print
37.4 x 46.5 cm (14¾ x 18¼ in.)
The Metropolitan Museum of Art, New York, Gilman Collection, Purchase, Cynthia Hazen Polsky Gift, 2005
2005.100.70

106. John Murray (English, 1809–1898)
The Taj Mahal from the Gateway, January–March 1864
Albumen silver prints
35 x 127 cm (13¾ x 50 in.)
The Metropolitan Museum of Art, New York, Gilman Collection, Purchase, Cynthia Hazen Polsky Gift, 2005
2005.100.315a–c

107. John Murray (English, 1809–1898)
The Taj Mahal from the Banks of the Yamuna River, 1858–62
Albumen silver print
39.9 x 44 cm (15¾ x 17⅜ in.)
The Metropolitan Museum of Art, New York, Gilman Collection, Purchase, Joseph M. Cohen Gift, 2005
2005.100.71

108. John Murray (English, 1809–1898)
Bishessur Nath Temple, Benares, 1858
Salted paper print
33.4 x 42.9 cm (13⅛ x 16⅞ in.)
The British Library, London
Photo 52/42

109. Richard Banner Oakeley (English, active 1850s)
Group of Apsaras, 1856
Albumen silver print
27.8 x 20.5 cm (11 x 8⅛ in.)

Collection Centre Canadien d'Architecture / Canadian Centre for Architecture, Montréal
PH1985:0676

110. Charles Moravia (British, 1821?–1859)
The Crystal Throne in the Diwan-i-Khas, Delhi, 1858
Albumen silver print
26.1 x 35.6 cm (10¼ x 14 in.)
Private collection

111. Robert Christopher Tytler (British, 1818–1872) and Harriet Christina Tytler (British, 1828–1907)
The Bank of Delhi, 1857–58
Albumen silver print
40.9 x 51.7 cm (16⅛ x 20⅜ in.)
The British Library, London
APAC Photo 193 (12)

112. Linnaeus Tripe (English, 1822–1902)
Ruined Tazoung, Tsagain Myo, September–October 1855
Albumen silver print
24.1 x 34.3 cm (9½ x 13½ in.)
Victoria and Albert Museum, London
1511-1909

113. Linnaeus Tripe (English, 1822–1902)
Near View of the Pagoda, Rangoon, November 1855
Albumen silver print
34.3 x 27.6 cm (13½ x 10⅞ in.)
The British Library, London
Photo 61/1 (115)

114. Linnaeus Tripe (English, 1822–1902)
Colossal Statue of Gautama Close to the North End of the Bridge, Amerapoora, September–October 1855
Albumen silver print
24.7 x 33.3 cm (9¾ x 13⅛ in.)
The British Library, London
Photo 61/1 (46)

115. Linnaeus Tripe (English, 1822–1902)
The Causeway across the Vaigai River, Madura, January–March 1858
Albumen silver print
23.1 x 35.4 cm (9⅛ x 14 in.)
National Gallery of Art, Washington, The Carolyn Brody Fund and Funds from an Anonymous Donor
2006.6.1

116. Linnaeus Tripe (English, 1822–1902)
The Monster Gun of Tanjore, March– April 1858
Albumen silver print
28.8 x 38.1 cm (11⅜ x 15 in.)
Thomas Walther Collection

117. Linnaeus Tripe (English, 1822–1902)
View of the Country Looking N.N.W. from the Top of the Ryakotta Hill, December 1857–January 1858
Albumen silver print
26 x 35.6 cm (10¼ x 14 in.)
Collection of Charles Isaacs and Carol Nigro

118. Linnaeus Tripe (English, 1822–1902)
Wooden Bridge, Amerapoora, September–October 1855
Albumen silver print
22.8 x 38 cm (9 x 13 in.)
Victoria and Albert Museum, London
1526-1909

Biographical Dictionary of British Calotypists

LARRY J. SCHAAF

IN COLLABORATION WITH ROGER TAYLOR

Names in SMALL CAPITAL LETTERS are those of calotypists for whom an entry exists in this dictionary. The name of William Henry Fox Talbot has been shortened to TALBOT.

"Exhibited" references include only those exhibitions at which the photographer's works from paper negatives were shown.

The following abbreviations are used in the references:

BJP	*British Journal of Photography*
BJPA	*The British Journal Photographic Almanac and Photographer's Daily Companion*
ILN	*Illustrated London News*
JPS	*Journal of the Photographic Society*
LMPJ	*Liverpool and Manchester Photographic Journal*
LPJ	*Liverpool Photographic Journal*

See also the headnote to the Bibliography, p. 414.

A primary source of information on many of these calotypists is the large number of letters written to and by William Henry Fox Talbot. The principal repositories for these documents are the British Library, London, and the National Media Museum, Bradford. Transcriptions are available on the Talbot Correspondence Project website (http://foxtalbot.dmu.ac.uk).

Much information on exhibitions and their catalogues can be found in Roger Taylor, *Photographs Exhibited in Britain, 1839–1865: A Compendium of Photographers and Their Works / Photographies exposées en Grande-Bretagne de 1839 à 1865: Répertoire des photographes et de leurs oeuvres* (Ottawa: National Gallery of Canada, 2002), and at http://www.peib.org.uk.

A useful source for sale records is Gary Edwards, *International Guide to Nineteenth-Century Photographers and Their Works: Based on Catalogues of Auction Houses and Dealers* (Boston: G. K. Hall, 1988).

Abbot, Benjamin

Abbot's known photographic output is represented by a single waxed-paper study, *Ickleford, Hertfordshire*, shown in the 1856 exhibition of the Norwich Photographic Society. To date, no other clues about his identity have emerged. A likely candidate is Benjamin Abbott of Hitchin (1793–1870), a Quaker teacher friendly with the scientist Michael Faraday. Although the surnames differ slightly, this might easily be due to a typographical error, for Hitchin is only a mile away from Ickleford.

EXHIBITED: 1856, Norwich, Photographic Society

Abbot, James

1822–1898

Even while apprenticed as a mechanic, the youthful Abbot displayed an intense interest in the study of works of art. One of the earliest to practice photography in Scotland, Abbot designed and built his own cameras and made his first lens by grinding down the bottom of a water tumbler. The *Practical Photographer* remembered him for devising "other ingenious arrangements when materials were less readily obtainable." Abbot set up as a portrait photographer in Dundee in 1858, advertising himself solely as a calotypist, a title perpetuated on the backs of his carte-de-visite mounts through the 1850s, although he did turn to wet collodion and albumen paper. Abbot was a member of the Edinburgh Photographic Society and a close friend of the St. Andrews photographer THOMAS RODGER.

REFERENCES: *Practical Photographer* 9 (May 1898), p. 150 (obituary); *BJPA*, 1899, pp. 655–56 (obituary)

Abney, William de Wiveleslie

1843–1920

Abney, born just a year before TALBOT began issuing *The Pencil of Nature*, at first would seem to be an unlikely practitioner of paper negative photography. He was a lieutenant in the Royal Engineers serving in Bombay, an instructor in chemistry, a fellow of the Royal Society, and a prolific author. Always a keen traveler, Abney was appointed to head the expedition to Egypt to observe the 1874 transit of Venus. With wide photographic experience, he nevertheless chose to work with waxed-paper negatives on this important occasion, and for many of the same reasons that made the process appealing to British photographers in India in the 1850s. While neither wet collodion nor the emerging factory-made dry plates were stable in the extreme heat, Abney accomplished excellent results with this archaic process, producing 12 x 15 inch negatives. In 1883 he was awarded the Royal Society's Rumford Medal for his achievements in spectral analysis, an effort that led to the practical development of an infrared-sensitive emulsion. Having worked tirelessly throughout his career to bring about greater practical and theoretical understanding of the mechanisms of photography, Abney was knighted in 1900. He was also instrumental in establishing the photographic collection for the Science Museum in London, now the core of the photography collection of the National Media Museum, Bradford.

REFERENCES: *BJP* 47 (December 10, 1920), pp. 755–56 (obituary); W. B. Ferguson, in *Photographic Journal* 61 (January 1921), pp. 44–46 (obituary); Chapman Jones, "Sir William de Wiveleslie Abney, K.C.B., D.C.L., D.Sc., F.R.S., Hon F.R.P.S., etc., 1843–1920," *Photographic Journal* 61 (July 1921), pp. 296–310

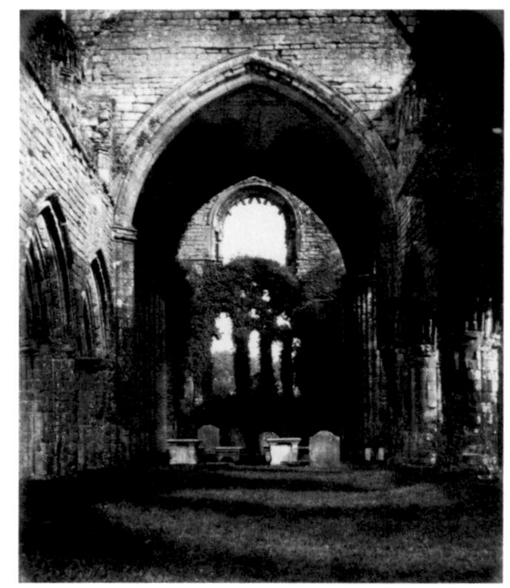

1. Alexander Forsyth Adam

Adam, Alexander Forsyth *ill. 1*

1822–1881

An Edinburgh lawyer and member of the Edinburgh Photographic Exchange Club, Adam was one of the founders of the Photographic Society of Scotland in 1856. He practiced the waxed-paper process as an amateur and undertook photographic trips to France in search of picturesque subjects, at least once with colleagues from the society, including his brother JAMES ADAM and CHARLES KINNEAR. Adam photographed ancient architecture in Monmouthshire and modern villages in Devon. He took a particular interest in Isambard Kingdom Brunel's suspension bridge over the Tamar in Cornwall. In his capacity as the society's honorary secretary from 1860 to 1862, Adam corresponded with TALBOT, whose photoglyphic engravings he would exhibit at one of the society's meetings.

Exhibited: 1857, 1858, and 1859, Edinburgh, Photographic Society of Scotland

Reference: Charles George Hood Kinnear, "Abstract of an Account of an Architectural and Photographic Tour in the North of France," *JPS* 4 (December 21, 1857), pp. 116–20

Adam, James, Jr.
b. 1825
An Edinburgh lawyer and member of the Photographic Society of Scotland, James was the younger brother of fellow member ALEXANDER FORSYTH ADAM. Their father, also James, was a solicitor. The two brothers shared a 9 x 11 inch Ottewill folding camera when they joined CHARLES KINNEAR in a photographic tour of the north of France in 1857, all three using the waxed-paper process during the journey. No other photographic activity by Adam is known.

Reference: Charles George Hood Kinnear, "Abstract of an Account of an Architectural and Photographic Tour in the North of France," *JPS* 4 (December 21, 1857), pp. 116–20

Adamson, John *ill. 2*
1809–1870
Dr. Adamson received his education in his hometown of St. Andrews, continued his medical education in Edinburgh, and became a physician in 1829. Following additional medical training in Paris he was a ship's surgeon in the China seas before returning to St. Andrews to establish a medical practice. When Sir DAVID BREWSTER founded the St. Andrews Literary and Philosophical Society in 1838, Adamson became not only a member but also the curator of its museum. It was through Brewster's close friendship with TALBOT that photography flourished in St. Andrews during the early 1840s. Adamson, HUGH LYON PLAYFAIR, and THOMAS RODGER were some of the chief advocates for the new art. Using the calotype process exclusively, Adamson took studies of the landscape, topography, and notable worthies of St. Andrews, and is credited with having taken the first calotype portrait in Scotland, sometime during the early months of 1842. He is most remembered for introducing his younger brother ROBERT ADAMSON to photography, which would lead to the remarkable partnership of Hill & Adamson. John Adamson may have been the author of the photographs, dating from 1842 to 1845, which document his efforts to clean up the typhoid-ridden Fishergate area of St. Andrews. In the 1854 exhibition of the Royal Infirmary Fund in

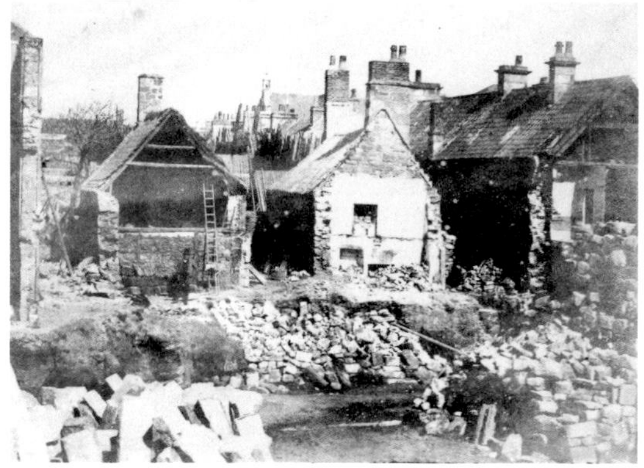

2. John Adamson

nearby Dundee, Adamson showed a collodion portrait. He expanded his collodion work for the 1855 exhibition of the British Association for the Advancement of Science, displaying both scientific and artistic work, but, significantly, also displaying calotypes he had made in 1842. He once again showed calotype portraits, apparently freshly made, in the 1856 exhibition of the Photographic Society of Scotland in Edinburgh. Even as photography matured as an art, his antityphoid efforts and his medical practice increasingly demanded Adamson's time. It was not until 1864 that he once again contributed some collodion photographs to the Photographic Society of Scotland exhibition.

Exhibited: 1856, Edinburgh, Photographic Society of Scotland

References: John Adamson, "Photography," in *Chambers's Information for the People*, new ed. (Edinburgh: William and Robert Chambers, 1857), vol. 2, pp. 777–85; *Edinburgh Medical Journal* 16 (September 1870), pp. 286–88 (obituary); Alison Morrison-Low, "Dr. John and Robert Adamson: An Early Partnership in Scottish Photography," *Photographic Collector* 4 (Autumn 1983), pp. 199–214; Graham Smith, "John Adamson, Sanitary Reform and the St Andrews Fishing Community," *History of Photography* 25 (Summer 2001), pp. 180–89; Larry J. Schaaf, *Sun Pictures, Catalogue Eleven: St. Andrews and Early Scottish Photography, including Hill & Adamson* (New York: Hans P. Kraus, Jr., 2002)

Adamson, Robert *ills. 52, 53*
1821–1848
The son of a tenant farmer at Burnside, in his youth Adamson excelled at mathematics in nearby St. Andrews. His facility with mechanics indicated a promising career in engineering, but fragile health barred this path. In 1839 his older brother JOHN ADAMSON eagerly took up photography with Sir DAVID BREWSTER, and Robert soon followed into the rapidly developing world of this new art. By the summer of 1842 Brewster reported to TALBOT that the young man was becoming highly accomplished in calotypy. On May 10, 1843, Robert established Scotland's first calotype studio, in Rock House on the side of Edinburgh's Calton Hill. The timing proved fortuitous, for nine days later the Disruption took place in the Church of Scotland, when more than four hundred ministers were separated from their livings for forming the Free Church of Scotland. It was through DAVID OCTAVIUS HILL's ambition to commemorate this event in a painting that calotypy took its first real foothold in the public consciousness. With Hill facing the impossibility of rapidly recording hundreds of ministers before they dispersed throughout Scotland, Brewster suggested Adamson's photography as a facile way to make preliminary "sketches" of the clergymen. The partnership of Adamson and Hill blossomed from this initial collaboration, and their calotypes, originally intended only as drafts, began to take on a life of their own. The partners' reputation grew rapidly and their subject matter soon extended into general portraiture, architecture, and social documentation. Within a year, Rock House had become the aesthetic center of paper negative photography in the mid-1840s, certainly in Britain, perhaps in the world. The pair completed at least three thousand calotypes before Adamson's chronic ill health finally asserted itself. He died in St. Andrews on January 14, 1848, at the age of twenty-seven. Hill continued in photography, but he never again achieved the creative heights that he had in his work with Adamson.

Exhibited: 1859, Aberdeen, British Association for the Advancement of Science (posthumously)

References: Alison Morrison-Low, "Dr. John and Robert Adamson: An Early Partnership in Scottish Photography," *Photographic Collector* 4 (Autumn 1983), pp. 199–214; Alison Morrison-Low, "Robert Adamson, 1821–1848," *Studies in Photography*, 1998, pp. 2–4

Alexander, G.
Nothing has been discovered of Alexander's personal circumstances, not his profession, his residence, or even his given name. An "Alexander" started exhibiting prints from paper negatives in 1854 and most likely is one and the same as the "G. Alexander" who exhibited in 1855, including a study, *Fishing Smacks in Yarmouth Harbour*, which was incorporated into three touring exhibitions organized by the Society of Arts. Alexander's other subjects were architectural and topographic, and by 1856 he was working in the collodion process.

Exhibited: 1854, London Photographic Society; 1854, second touring exhibition, Society of Arts (London); 1855, London, Photographic Society; 1855–56, third touring exhibition, Society of Arts (London)

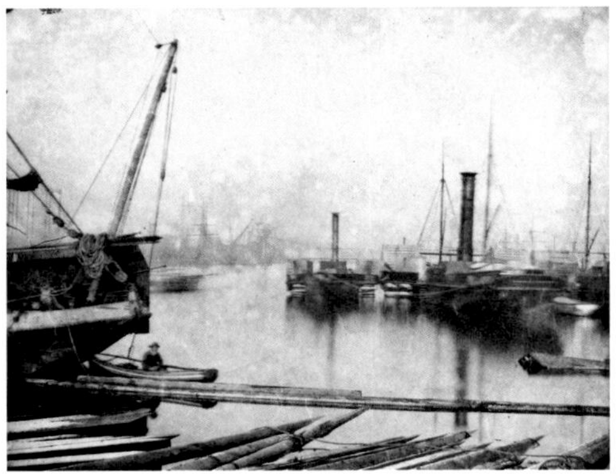

3. Richard Dykes Alexander

Alexander, Richard Dykes *ill. 3*

1788–1865

Alexander was probably lured into photography through the influence of close family members. His nephew was the photographic pioneer JOHN DILLWYN LLEWELYN, who married TALBOT'S cousin EMMA THOMASINA LLEWELYN, herself a photographer. By the time Alexander took up photography in the 1850s he was a well-established member of Ipswich society, having founded a hospital and a temperance hall. Elected a member of the Photographic Society in London in 1853, Alexander used both calotype and collodion processes, although he publicly exhibited only works made from glass plates. A substantial body of his work was dispersed at auction at Sotheby's, London.

References: Joseph Smith, *A Descriptive Catalogue of Friends' Books* (London: Joseph Smith, 1867), vol. 1, p. 10; sale cats., Sotheby's, London, June 28, 1978, lots 241, 242, 244, 260, and October 27, 1978, lot 195

Allen, John Allen

b. 1834

To date, very little is known about Allen, but there is a realistic hope of learning more. He was born in England and by 1851 was living at Errol Park House, in Perthshire, with his mother and stepfather. No other trace of Allen's life has been found except for a critical album of his photographic work sold in 1980 and at present unlocated. What little information we have is drawn from the auction description, which was possibly incomplete. The calotypes in the album were dated in the negative 1852 (when Allen was only eighteen) and had manuscript notations. One image was of Peebles Church, a well-known structure on the Scottish borders. A possible association with James Nasmyth, the famous engineer who took an early interest in photography, was indicated by some of the pictures in the album. Allen took portraits of Mrs. Nasmyth besides a large telescope (possibly Lord Rosse's?) and of Mr. and Mrs. Nasmyth with a microscope. There were also three photographs either of drawings or of a model of the moon; Nasmyth was famous for his detailed moon model. Curiously, Allen is not mentioned in Samuel Smiles's 1883 edition of Nasmyth's *Autobiography*.

Reference: Sale cat., Sotheby's, London, June 27, 1980, lot 243

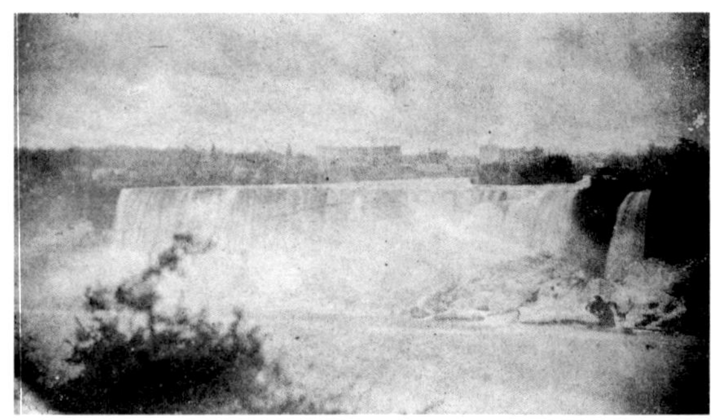

4. Alexander Todd Anderson

Anderson, Alexander Todd *ill. 4*

b. 1822

What little is known of Dr. Anderson suggests that he was an unusually adventurous calotypist. Irish by birth, he received his medical training in Edinburgh and entered the service of the East India Company. For unknown reasons, probably medical, he was furloughed in 1848, traveling to Canada three years later. Anderson took the first known calotypes of Niagara Falls, prints of which are preserved in St. Andrews and in New South Wales, where he retired.

References: Graham Smith, "The First American Calotypes?" *History of Photography* 6 (October 1982), pp. 349–52; Larry J. Schaaf, *Sun Pictures, Catalogue Eleven: St. Andrews and Early Scottish Photography, including Hill & Adamson* (New York: Hans P. Kraus, Jr., 2002), p. 34

Anderson, William Coussmaker

1822–1893

The son of a Hereford solicitor, Anderson received a classical and mathematical education at Abingdon School, Oxfordshire. In 1839, the year photography was introduced, he was accepted as a cadet in the Bengal Army. Passing his examination in the Hindustani language, he was appointed as an interpreter and assigned to the Revenue Survey. In spite of his relatively innocent-sounding position, Anderson was cited for bravery in frontline action and saw service against piratical tribes on the Persian coast. By 1852 he had been raised to the rank of superintendent of the Revenue Survey and presumably then found time to take up photography as an amateur, becoming a corresponding member of the Photographic Society of Bombay. For its meeting of March 11, 1856, the *Liverpool Photographic Journal* reported that "Captain Anderson produced a portfolio of negatives in Talbotype and waxed paper, some of very excellent character, also a number of prints of the same, well developed and of a fine rich tone." Anderson was ultimately promoted to the rank of general.

Reference: "Bombay Photographic Society," *LPJ* 3 (October 11, 1856), p. 140

Archer, Frederick Scott

1813–1857

A sculptor by profession and possessed of an active imagination on practical matters, Archer is best known for his invention of the wet-collodion negative on glass, the very process that displaced the paper negative (especially quickly in the commercial world). Archer's interest in photography dated back to its earliest days. He was a daguerreotypist and invented an economical water-filled lens. This, like most of his ventures, proved unsuccessful commercially. One of Archer's trades in the 1840s was as a Talbotype portraitist. In 1875 the *British Journal of Photography* described such works as "portraits possessing great vigour and undoubted merit, although devoid of delicacy." While his daguerreotypes "fulfilled the highest requirements of sharpness and delicacy," Archer was keenly aware of the advantage of TALBOT's negatives, from which multiple prints could be obtained. Perhaps for his portrait work, or perhaps to achieve smooth and full-toned prints of his sculptures, Archer worked to combine the merits of the two processes and succeeded with glass negatives using collodion. He published the wet-collodion method freely, continuing to work as a photographer and inventor. Archer died in great poverty not long afterward. In a belated effort spearheaded by M. Digby Wyatt, architect and secretary to the executive committee of the

Great Exhibition of 1851, and widely supported by a grateful photographic community, a subscription was raised to support his widow and children.

REFERENCES: M. Digby Wyatt and Jabez Hogg, "The Archer Fund: The Report of the Committee of the Archer Testimonial," *JPS* 4 (July 21, 1858), pp. 261–63; "Frederick Scott Archer," *BJP* 22 (February 26, 1875), pp. 102–4

Atkins, Anna
1799–1871
TALBOT immediately saw the intimate connection between photography and the printed page; his 1844 publication of *The Pencil of Nature* was a vivid demonstration. Nearly a year before this, however, Anna Atkins had begun publishing the first book illustrated with actual photographs, *British Algae: Cyanotype Impressions*, which would be issued in parts over a span of ten years. Its thousands of plates were actual blueprint photograms; each was an original cyanotype negative, printed directly from dried seaweed at her home of Sevenoaks, near London. An illustrator and serious amateur botanist, Atkins was a friend of Sir JOHN HERSCHEL and his family. Her father, John George Children, chaired the Royal Society meeting at which Talbot first disclosed the working details of photogenic drawing. Atkins and her father received a tutorial and examples of calotypes directly from Talbot. None of Atkins's calotypes are known to have survived, but thousands of her original cyanotype photograms are still in fine condition, most in copies of *British Algae*; more diverse subject matter is preserved in albums. A few of these are still intact, but others have more recently been broken up.

REFERENCES: Anna Atkins, *British Algae: Cyanotype Impressions* (Sevenoaks, 1843–54); Larry J. Schaaf, *Sun Gardens: Victorian Photograms by Anna Atkins* (New York: Aperture, 1985)

Ayling, Charles
1825–1894
Ayling was born the son of a bricklayer in a small village in West Sussex. Largely self-taught, he flourished locally as a poet, newspaper contributor, and village schoolmaster. By 1860 Ayling was advertising himself as a photographer, taking Talbotypes "only by appointment." No surviving examples of his work are known.

REFERENCE: *West Sussex Gazette*, March 15, 1860 (advertisement)

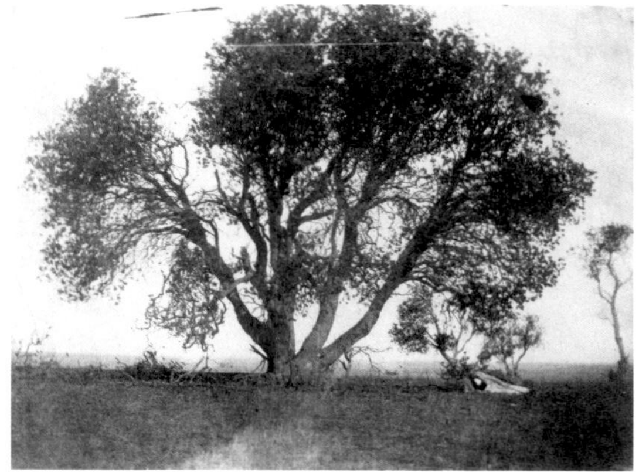

5. Benjamin Herschel Babbage

Babbage, Benjamin Herschel *ill. 5*
1815–1878
Babbage's namesake was Sir JOHN HERSCHEL, the closest friend of his father, the eccentric computer pioneer Charles Babbage. It was undoubtedly through these connections that Benjamin Babbage first met TALBOT. After working for Isambard Kingdom Brunel on the Great Western Railway, Babbage traveled to South Australia in 1851 to conduct a geological and mineral survey. Active in gold mining, he would go on to build the first railway in the county. It seems certain that he began his calotyping while still in England, for Babbage observed that "the great heat makes it much more difficult to obtain good paper photographs" in Australia. In 1857 he proposed calotyping on an expedition for the government, suggesting in his application for funding that he "should take a photographic apparatus to bring back faithful representations of the country traversed by the expedition, and pictures of any rare animals, birds, or vegetable productions that may be met with." The commissioner approved, and in a report to the Philosophical Society of Adelaide after his return, Babbage confirmed the value of the calotype process for field use, detailing a complex system of nine different iodizing approaches by which to cope with the effects of extreme heat. Near the end of his life Babbage became a pioneer in the fledgling South Australian wine industry.

REFERENCES: Dawn Gill, *Iron Tracks and Dusty Trails: The Life of Benjamin Herschel Babbage* (Henley Beach, South Australia: Seaview Press, 2002); Larry J. Schaaf, *Sun Pictures, Catalogue Eleven: St. Andrews and Early Scottish Photography, including Hill & Adamson* (New York: Hans P. Kraus, Jr., 2002), pp. 17, 36–40

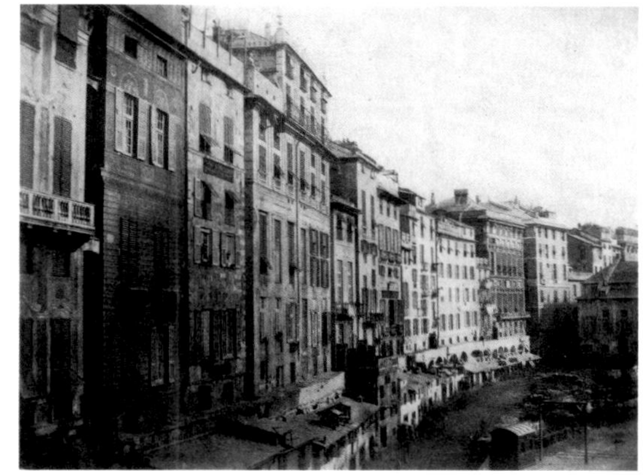

6. Alfred Backhouse

Backhouse, Alfred *ill. 6*
1823–1888
The photographic outputs of the three Backhouse brothers, from a family of naturalists, horticulturalists, and bankers, are intriguingly intertwined. Alfred (identified incorrectly as Arthur in some auction catalogues) was elected a member of the Photographic Society in 1855. Supported by his coal earnings, he actively exhibited prints from waxed-paper negatives. In 1854–55, Venice, Strasbourg, and Nice supplied his subjects, including architectural details and more comprehensive views. In 1857 his exhibited photographs were all from Switzerland, ranging from Lucerne's monument to the Swiss Guards to images of glaciers and Mont Blanc; the exhibition catalogue revealed that in one of these, the "sky of negative [is] slightly touched" (i.e., retouched).

EXHIBITED: 1855 and 1857, London, Photographic Society

REFERENCE: Joseph Foster, *The Descendants of John Backhouse, Yeoman, of Moss Side, near Yealand Redman, Lancashire* (London: Privately printed at the Chiswick Press, 1894)

Backhouse, Edward, Jr. *ill. 7*
1808–1879
Like his younger brother ALFRED BACKHOUSE, Edward Jr. initially made his fortune from coal holdings, but other interests kept him busy. An accomplished lithographer by the 1830s, he was also a historian. A group of waxed-paper architectural studies was attributed at auction to an Elizabeth Backhouse, but the signature was "E. Backhouse," and to date no Elizabeth has been traced. Another auctioned print from a waxed-paper negative was signed "EB Jr., 1854." In family lore, Edward was described as

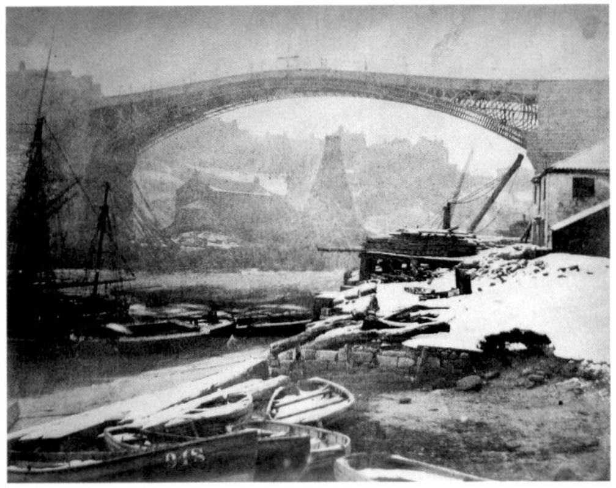

7. Edward Backhouse, Jr.

the most active photographer of the three brothers, but his only known exhibited work is an 1857 portrait taken by collodion. There is evidence to show that he was taking stereo portraits at least as late as 1859. Later in life Backhouse became a philanthropist. His best-known work is the posthumously published *Early Church History to the Death of Constantine* (1884).

REFERENCES: Joseph Foster, *The Descendants of John Backhouse, Yeoman, of Moss Side, near Yealand Redman, Lancashire* (London: Privately printed at the Chiswick Press, 1894); sale cat., Sotheby's, London, October 24, 1979, lot 330

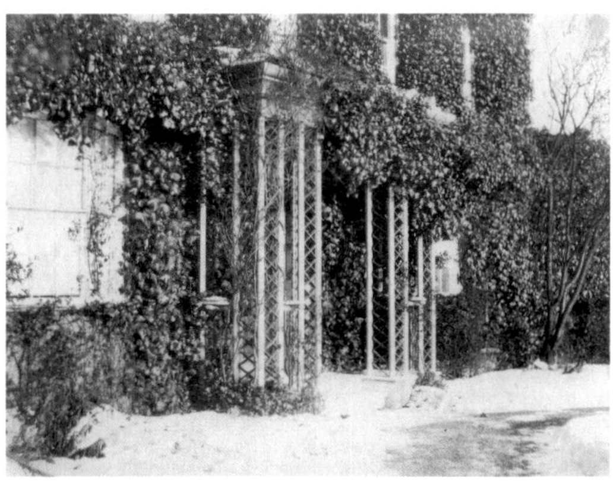

8. Thomas James Backhouse

Backhouse, Thomas James *ill. 8*

1810–1857

The middle of the three Backhouse brothers, Thomas derived his income as a proprietor of coal mines in Durham. He exhibited prints from waxed-paper negatives in 1855, including views of Sunderland harbor and Windermere. Architectural studies by Backhouse have turned up at auction. His son, Thomas William, earned a reputation as an outstanding meteorologist and astronomer.

EXHIBITED: 1855, London, Photographic Society

REFERENCES: Joseph Foster, *The Descendants of John Backhouse, Yeoman, of Moss Side, near Yealand Redman, Lancashire* (London: Privately printed at the Chiswick Press, 1894); sale cat., Sotheby's, London, October 24, 1979, lot 330

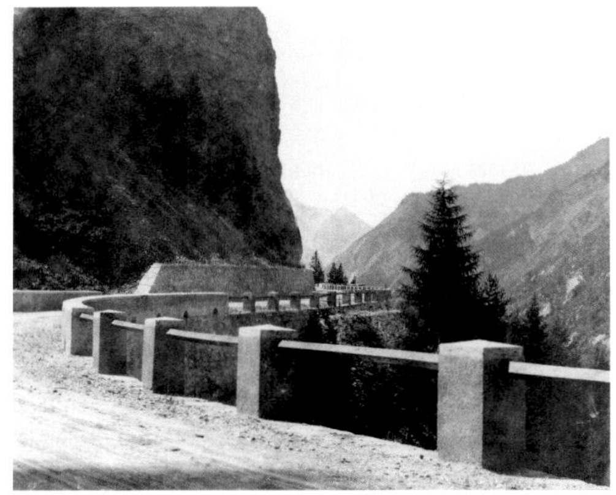

9. William Robert Baker

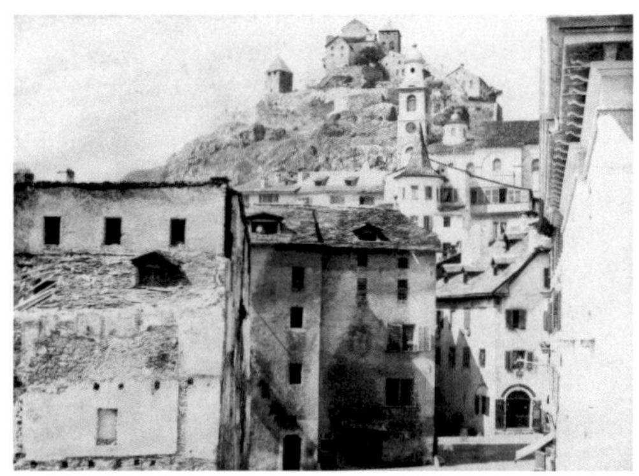

10. William Robert Baker

Baker, William Robert *ills. 9, 10*

1810–1896

At the tender age of fourteen Baker inherited Bayfordbury Manor, Hertfordshire, and its associated wealth from his paternal grandfather. His maternal grandfather was the British consul to Sicily and Malta. Educated at Eton, Oxford, and Cambridge, Baker never received a degree, instead devoting himself to running his extensive estates. He held a particular interest in landscaping and especially trees, and at some point he took up photography, apparently for his own pleasure and not for public exhibition. Baker traveled widely in Europe, taking the Grand Tour and also documenting landscape and architecture much as he had done for the English countryside. A few of Baker's calotype negatives are preserved, but most of his work was in the waxed-paper process. Only a portion of his extensive output, mostly negatives, is known to have survived after the estate and family home were sold in 1947.

REFERENCE: Robert E. Lassam and Michael Gray, *The Romantic Era: Reverendo Calvert Richard Jones, 1804–1877, Reverendo George Wilson Bridges, 1788–1863, William Robert Baker di Bayfordbury, 1810–1896*, exh. cat. (Florence: Alinari, 1988)

Barker, George

Virtually nothing is known of Barker's personal details—surprisingly, since he was one of the most prolific exhibitors of photographs in the period from 1852 to 1857. Working with both glass and paper photography processes, he took some still lifes and also made copies of engravings. However, portraits and architecture were clearly his favored subjects. Most of Barker's known landscape and architectural views were made in Britain, but he did at least some work at Tivoli. His portrait subjects point both to ties with Ireland and to an interest in archaeology; they include Lord Talbot de Malahide and the Earl of Belmore, an outstanding collector of Egyptian antiquities. In the 1856 exhibition of the Photographic Society in London, Barker included a portrait of William Boutcher, an artist and important archaeologist specializing in Assyria. According to the catalogue, Barker outfitted Boutcher "in Arab dress" and displayed his portrait with photographic copies of Assyrian sculpture.

EXHIBITED: 1852 and 1855, London, Photographic Society

Barr, Henry James

1851–1881

The son of a lieutenant colonel in the Indian army, Barr was born in Bombay and educated in England at Addiscombe Military Seminary; he entered the Bombay Native Infantry in 1833. He was proficient in Hindustani and became an interpreter. Holding a number of largely administrative posts, Barr took two leaves of absence to visit Egypt and seemed to be doing well in the army until 1852, when, according to his service record, he showed "great want of energy, decision and accuracy of recollection." Perhaps photography proved a welcome release, but one at least hopes that Barr's newly found passion for the camera was not a detriment to his military career. How and when he got his start in amateur photography are not known, but Barr was elected president of the Photographic

Society of Bombay in 1856 and subsequently served on its council. He contributed both calotypes and waxed-paper views to the society's 1856 exhibition. His was obviously an appointment of merit; according to the *Journal of the Photographic Society of Bombay*, fellow members felt that Barr "excels in Talbotype," and his calotypes of "the wood scenery about Bombay . . . were very beautiful, both as regards execution as photographs, tone as prints, and in artistic effect, and were deservedly admired by all." Barr remained in military service in India for his entire career.

References: Henry James Barr, records of military service, India Office Records, British Library, London; "Cursory Notes Taken at the Exhibition of Photographs, Bombay, February 1856," *Journal of the Photographic Society of Bombay*, nos. 13–17 (February–June 1856), pp. 26, 27

Barry, Charles, Jr.
1823–1900
As part of a calotyping journey to the Continent, John Muir Wood visited Belgium, finding himself in Ghent on July 30, 1847. He recorded in his diary (now in a private collection): "Met with 3 *agreeable* Englishmen, Snell, Charles and Wm H Barry, all architects apparently: the first sketching the 2nd Calotyping; got detail of his process & showed mine; his w[or]k sharp but bad in colour & would not print out well." It is tempting to think that Wood had met up with Sir Charles Barry, the famous architect whose Victorian Gothic Houses of Parliament are one of the most prominent features of London. However, this project was behind schedule and greatly over budget in 1847, and it is unlikely that the beleaguered senior architect would have chosen this period for his holiday. On the other hand, his son, Charles Jr., also an architect, was forced to travel that year for reasons of health, and it is he who must have been the experimenting calotypist. None of his work is known to have survived.

Reference: Sara Stevenson, Julie Lawson, and Michael Gray, *The Photography of John Muir Wood, 1805–1892: An Accomplished Amateur* (Edinburgh: Scottish National Portrait Gallery; London: Dirk Nishen, 1988), p. 13

Barton, Alfred
Little is known of Barton beyond the fact that he joined the Manchester Photographic Society in 1856, rising to become a member of their council the following year. He exhibited harbor and architectural views, all made on waxed-paper negatives, in the society's 1856 exhibition. No examples of Barton's work are known to have survived.

Exhibited: 1856, Manchester, Photographic Society

Baxter, William Raleigh
1812–1875
In 1842, at an early period when Talbot's instructions were brief and little understood, Baxter published his popular *The Calotype, Familiarly Explained*, interpreting Talbot's directions in a clear manner and supplementing them with practical tips from Dr. John Ryan's series of lectures at the London Polytechnic Institution. Prior to the publication of George Smith Cundell's 1844 article "On the Practice of the Calotype," Baxter's *Calotype* was one of the few clear and concise descriptions of how both to prepare the necessary materials and to take a photograph. Irish by birth, shortly after publishing his manual Baxter graduated from Aberdeen University and became a surgeon, serving first in the Osmanli horse artillery in Turkey in 1854 and later as a volunteer surgeon major to the French army at Constantinople. In later life he was the editor of the *Medical Record*. Baxter did not exhibit, and no examples of his work are known to have survived.

Reference: W. Raleigh Baxter, *The Calotype, Familiarly Explained: Being a Treatise on Its Objects and Uses, and the Methods of Preparing the Sensitive Paper, and Taking Pictures by the Agency of Light* (London: H. Renshaw, 1842)

Beatty, Francis Steward
1807–1891
Beatty's name is closely associated with daguerreotypy, and he is credited with producing the first ones made in Ireland. He was a well-known engraver possessed of the social conscience then emerging in Ireland. In 1832 Beatty became the first secretary of the Belfast Co-operative Society, putting him in the vanguard of efforts to address the sweeping social tensions of the day. About 1840 he traveled to London to learn more under the eminent daguerreotypist Richard Beard. Beatty set up the first of his various daguerreotype studios in Belfast in the early 1840s. He had already begun working with paper negatives, however; in September 1839 he wrote to the *Belfast News-Letter* that he "was somewhat surprised to find that in using silver paper the effect was different from silver plated on copper . . . namely, the light parts of the subject are dark, and the dark shades are in a proportionate degree light." The fact that Beatty relocated his studio almost annually throughout the 1840s, alternating between Belfast and London, implies that commercial success eluded him. His engraving skills led him back to paper, and he offered calotypes as well as daguerreotypes. He took great interest in photomechanical processes, particularly photolithography, and opened a correspondence with Talbot in 1859, receiving examples of photoglyphic engraving from the inventor. Beatty exhibited these in Dublin and took pride in the newspaper reviews. Talbot gave him a free license to practice the new art, but not commercially. In March 1860 Beatty exhibited his own photoglyphic engravings made by Talbot's process to the members of the Photographic Society of Scotland, who were charmed, especially by the miniature copy of the business program for the evening, a plate capable of making many impressions. Like Talbot, Beatty instinctively saw that photography rendered in printer's ink was the future, but also like Talbot, he never made a commercial success of the venture. He died a pauper, and few of his photographs are known to have survived.

References: Francis Steward Beatty, letter in *Belfast News-Letter*, September 20, 1839; Beatty, "Some Historical Recollections of Photography," *Photographic News* 23 (August 8, 1879), pp. 382–83; W. A. Maguire, *Century in Focus: Photography and Photographers in the North of Ireland, 1839–1939* (Belfast: Blackstaff Press, 2000), pp. 2–5; Edward Chandler, *Photography in Ireland: The Nineteenth Century* (Dublin: Edmund Burke, 2001), pp. 4–9

Bell, Christopher
Bell reminisced in the *Liverpool Photographic Journal* that he was in Mexico in 1840 or 1841 when he first became aware of photography and purchased his first lens, a simple spectacle glass. But when he returned to England, Bell "left it behind me, and had even entirely forgotten and cast off the once loved subject, photography, not then so named, or so much talked of or thought about; but a friend among his heaps of rubbish found my old boxes, and kindly brought them home with him." He recalled this when he began comparing modern lenses in 1855. Bell's movements are not documented, but by 1853 he was a wine merchant in Liverpool, an ideal place to rekindle an interest in the art of photography. Bell was soon using both Frederick Townshend's and James How's waxed-paper formulas. In 1856 he was appointed treasurer of the Liverpool Photographic Society, contributing four waxed-paper views of Malvern to their scrapbook the next year. In 1856 he also became the chairman of the Liverpool and National Photographic Exchange Club. Brimming with enthusiasm for the art, Bell joined up with James Alexander Forrest and James Newlands as proprietors of the new *Liverpool Photographic Journal*.

References: Christopher Bell, "On the Comparative Results of Using Large and Small Lenses," *LPJ* 2 (April 14, 1855), pp. 48–50; James Alexander Forrest, "Historical Notes of What Liverpool Has Done in the Art-Science of Photography," *BJP* 35 (February 3, 1883), pp. 72–74

Bell, Thomas
1792–1880
Encouraged by his mother's keen interest in natural history, Bell became equally important as an amateur scientist as in his chosen profession of dental surgery. Bell established his practice in London and was appointed professor of zoology at King's College and lecturer on anatomy at Guy's Hospital. He held a number of positions in learned societies, always promoting the emerging field of zoology. The first president of the Ray Society, Bell was named president of the Linnean Society in 1859, and by this time his interest in photography had become apparent. Bell explained in the *Photographic Journal* his special method for handling paper negatives once they had been exposed and developed: "Having completed the waxed-paper negative as usual," he trimmed the negative a little smaller than a sheet of glass. A starch solution was then used to adhere the negative to the glass and next the paper was varnished. Bell observed that "the negative will now be found to possess a transparency and sharpness such as it had not before, and in the printing the positives will have an intensity and definition far superior to those taken from the unprepared waxed paper." None of his photographs are known to have survived.

REFERENCES: Thomas Bell, "Method of Mounting Waxed-Paper Negatives on Glass, and Varnishing Them," *Photographic Journal (JPS)* 5 (January 8, 1859), pp. 141–42; *Times* (London), March 17, 1880, p. 7, col. G (obituary)

Bennett, William
1811–1871
Bennett was a landscape artist, exhibiting prolifically from 1842 to 1871. He was described by the *Illustrated London News* as a "painter of considerable ability in the simpler manner of the earlier water-colourists" who excelled in "suggesting rather than realising details." This stood him in good stead when working with paper negative photography. In 1848 Bennett joined the New Water Colour Society, and at some point later in life he studied under the popular watercolorist David Cox. In the period of 1856–58 Bennett exhibited numerous studies of trees and landscapes done in the waxed-paper process, reserving his use of collodion for portraiture, which an 1857 catalogue revealed he "coloured from the back." At the time of Bennett's death, the *Art-Journal* observed: "A few years ago his drawings bore far greater similarity" to Cox "than his later works show; especially in the treatment of foliage. His works of all periods bear evidence of close study of nature, and, consequently, of truthfulness."

EXHIBITED: 1856, 1857, and 1858, London, Photographic Society

REFERENCES: *ILN*, March 25, 1871, p. 294 (obituary); *Art-Journal*, May 1, 1871, p. 139 (obituary); *Bryan's Dictionary of Painters and Engravers*, vol. 1 (London: G. Bell and Sons, 1918), p. 118

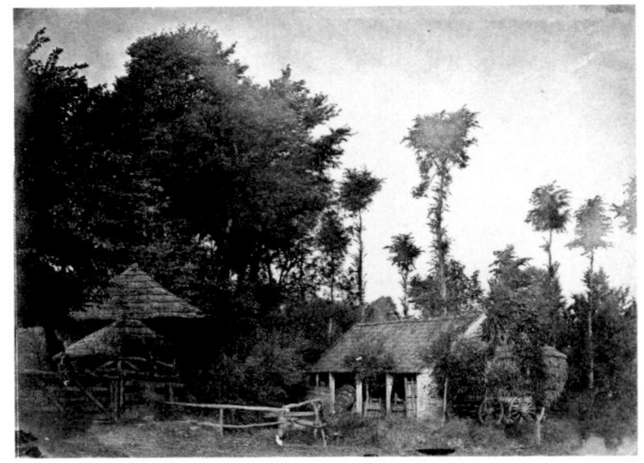
11. Arcangelo Corelli Collard Bere

Bere, Arcangelo Corelli Collard *ill. 11*
1822–1891
Born in Somerset, a property developer by profession but a keen amateur photographer from the start, Corelli Bere (as he was known to his many friends in the photographic community) delighted in introducing newcomers to the art of photography. With his experience in the art dating back to the 1840s, and having mastered virtually every process, Bere was described in the *British Journal of Photography* as "a living encyclopedia of photographic lore . . . imbued with keen artistic abilities, and his studies always formed the most beautiful type of pictures." His early calotypes were a prized bequest to the Royal Photographic Society after his death.

REFERENCES: H. E. Davis, "The Late Corelli Bere," *BJP* 38 (June 5, 1891), p. 368; R. Child Bayley, "Calotypes," *BJP* 43 (August 21, 1896), p. 537

Berry, George Robert
1818–1863
A chemist and dealer in photographic supplies, Berry was one of the founding members of the Liverpool Photographic Society and would become its secretary. So enthusiastic and dedicated was he that in 1855 the chairman observed that it "had already been called, 'a Berry Society.'" As a professional photographer and photographic dealer with a specialist laboratory, Berry was admired by his longtime friend CHARLES COREY for being "in possession of attainments in chemical science of no ordinary character." Shortly after he had defended the collodion process before the society, Berry was captivated by the simplifications and reliability that FREDERICK TOWNSHEND had brought to the waxed-paper process, writing in 1854, "Such is the certainty of the process that no one ought to have a single failure." Although none of his photographs are known to have survived, photographers today still owe Berry a special debt, as he was the direct inspiration for one of the longest-running and most influential photographic journals. Frustrated that the Liverpool Photographic Society was rarely noticed in the journal of London's Photographic Society, Berry, as quoted by Corey, insisted: "We would have a Gazette of our own." The *Liverpool Photographic Journal*, established in 1854, quickly grew in influence and in 1860 became the *British Journal of Photography*. Corey, also an early member of the Liverpool Photographic Society, recalled that Berry "passed his time in painstaking search after truth in the arcana of our art; and his leisure, when he could command any, was fully taken up in visiting and comforting the poor."

REFERENCES: George Robert Berry, "Townshend's Process," *LPJ* 1 (October 14, 1854), pp. 130–31; Charles Corey, in *BJP* 10 (June 1, 1863), p. 233 (obituary); George Good, *The History of the Liverpool Amateur Photographic Association from 1853 to 1953* (Liverpool, 1953), pp. 6–15

Beverley, M.
Beverley has yet to be identified, but his or her photographic reputation has been preserved by a small group of paper negatives and prints in a private collection. Undated, they are all from Norfolk and Suffolk and include images of Brook Hall, Rushmere Church, Mettingham Castle, and Costessy Hall (also known as Cossy, Cossey, or Costessey).

Biggs, Thomas *ill. 12*
1822–1905
The son of a minister, Biggs was educated in classics and mathematics at Guildford Grammar School in Surrey. In 1840, just at the dawn of photography, he entered Addiscombe Military Seminary, the training establishment of the East India Company. Two years later he was in the Bombay Artillery, but the following year he proved proficient in Hindustani and was made an interpreter. Biggs was assigned to the Revenue Survey and may have met WILLIAM COUSSMAKER ANDERSON during that service. He passed his examination on the Canarese language of South India "in a very credible manner" in 1845. Like many military men in India, Biggs became fascinated

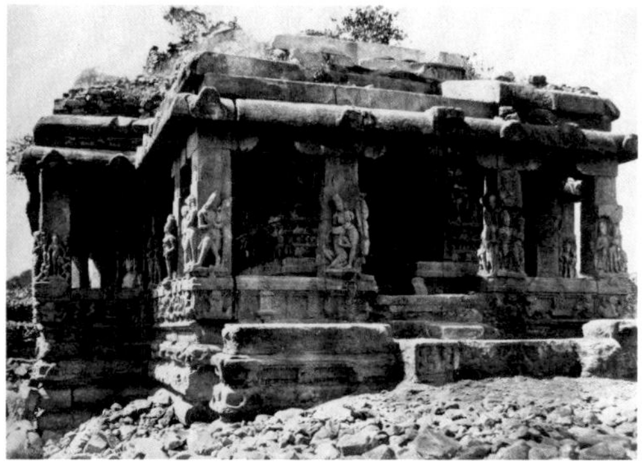

12. Thomas Biggs

with archaeology, but he soon discovered the difficulty and uncertainty of sending manual copies of stone inscriptions back to London. Biggs was furloughed on sick leave in England starting in 1850. As he recalled in the *British Journal of Photography* more than three decades later, he watched his brothers practicing photography and it struck him "that it would be a perfect method of copying the sculptures and inscriptions." He considered wet collodion, but after studying chemistry and visiting the laboratories of Andrew Ross and Noël-Marie Paymal Lerebours, he realized that paper negatives were far more practical for the Indian climate. Biggs took lessons from SAMUEL BUCKLE and then presented his plan to the directors of the East India Company, who were so impressed that they traded him a complete new photographic outfit in exchange for his first album. He was appointed "Government Photographer, Bombay," and was the first person to officially assume that position. But the outbreak of the Persian War forced his return to the Bombay Artillery, and in 1855 Biggs was replaced by another calotypist, WILLIAM HARRY PIGOU. Biggs remained loyal to the original calotype process, observing that he had never achieved a good negative by the waxed-paper process, and, as far as he had seen, neither had anyone else. In the 1856 exhibition of the Photographic Society of Bombay, his 15 x 18 inch views of the ruins and inscriptions of Beejapoor, done with Buckle's version of the calotype, "carried off the palm." In 1866 Biggs was a major contributor to the exhibition of the Amateur Photographic Association in England. In 1866 he supervised the publication in England of three volumes of photographs of Ahmedabad, of which only forty copies were issued.

EXHIBITED: 1856, Bombay, Photographic Society

REFERENCES: Thomas Biggs, records of military service, India Office Records, British Library, London; Biggs, letter of April 13, 1855, in *Journal of the Photographic Society of Bombay*, no. 5 (May–June 1855), pp. 82–83; "Awards of Prizes," *Photo News* 10 (November 30, 1866), pp. 572–73; "Cursory Notes Taken at the Exhibition of Photographs, Bombay, February 1856," *Journal of the Photographic Society of Bombay*, nos. 13–17 (February–June 1856), p. 26; James Fergusson, *Architecture at Ahmedabad, the Capital of Goozerat* (London: John Murray, 1866); Biggs, "A Retrospect of Photographic Experiences," *BJP* 29 (April 21, 1882), pp. 231–32; Janet Dewan, "Captain Biggs and Dr Pigou: Photographers to the Bombay Government, 1855–1858," *Photoresearcher*, no. 5 (December 1993), pp. 6–13

Bingham, Robert Jefferson

1824–1870

Beyond the fact that he was born in Leicester, nothing is known of Bingham until the early 1840s, by which time he was a chemical assistant and lecturer at the London Institute. When the author of the popular book *Photogenic Manipulation* died unexpectedly in 1847, Bingham was asked to take over the new edition, and he steadily revised and expanded the book through the fifth edition in 1854. Bingham exhibited calotype landscapes in the Great Exhibition of 1851 and continued actively exhibiting calotypes in Britain through 1854. His larger connection with the exhibition was in printing many of the photographs used to illustrate the *Reports by the Juries*; previously unsuccessful in negotiating a license from TALBOT, Bingham eventually became a foe of the inventor, producing the prints in France in order to circumvent the patent. He moved to Jersey in 1851, but soon made Paris the base of his operations. Bingham was the first to fully recognize the emerging commercial market for photographic copies of works of art. He purchased copyrights and became the preeminent reproduction artist of his day, proudly exhibiting his copies in Parisian exhibitions and winning much praise. In the period of 1857–64, Bingham also exhibited dozens of art reproductions (all done in collodion) in his native Britain. In 1862 Prince Albert commissioned him to photograph the Raphaels in the Louvre. Bingham died suddenly in Brussels. He is remembered more fondly in France than in the country of his birth.

EXHIBITED: 1851, London, Great Exhibition; 1852, London, Society of Arts; 1853, London, Photographic Institution; 1854, London, Photographic Society

REFERENCES: Robert J. Bingham, *Photogenic Manipulation Containing the Theory and Plain Instructions in the Art of Photography* (London: George Knight and Sons, 1848) (and later editions); *Bulletin de la Société Française de Photographie* 16 (March 1870), p. 58 (obituary); *Photographic News* 14 (March 4, 1870), p. 107 (obituary); Stephen Bann, *Parallel Lines: Printmakers, Painters and Photographers in Nineteenth-Century France* (New Haven: Yale University Press, 2001), pp. 118–25

Birch, John

b. 1823

Little is known about Birch except that he was one of the founding members of the Leeds Photographic Society. His only recorded photograph is a single calotype, *Bowling Hall, near Bradford*, included in *Productions of the Leeds Photographic Society* for 1852, an apparently unique publication now in the collection of The Metropolitan Museum of Art. The photographer is listed simply as "J. Birch," so the identification must remain speculative, but there was a John Birch who was born and lived in Bowling. His occupation as an iron refiner implies a familiarity with chemistry. The oldest part of the original "Bouline Haul" has been standing since the fifteenth century; this rambling stone house, known as Bowling Hall in Birch's time, survives today as Bolling Hall.

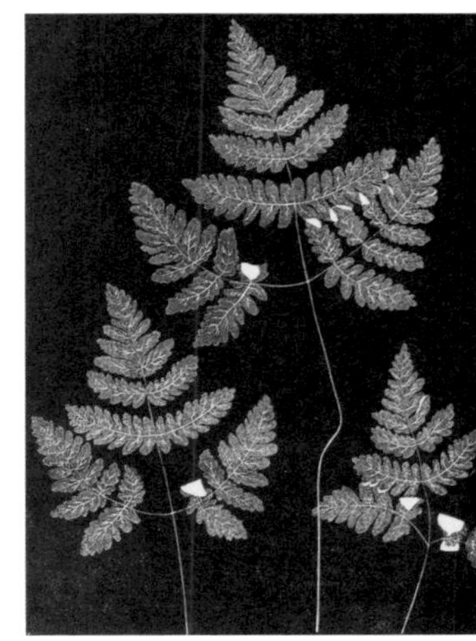

13. Golding Bird

Bird, Golding

ill. 13

1814–1854

Dr. Bird displayed his chemical prowess as a child, regularly lecturing and demonstrating on chemistry to his fellow schoolmates. He became an exceptional physician and invented the flexible stethoscope still familiar today. In 1836 Bird was appointed to the chair of natural philosophy at Guy's Hospital, London. It was in a letter dated March 25, 1839, and published in the *Magazine of Natural History*, "Observations on the Application of Heliographic or Photogenic Drawing to Botanical Purposes," that Bird revealed his insight into the new art. A month later, in the *Mirror*, his text was illustrated by one of the icons of early photography, a woodcut facsimile of a photogenic drawing of ferns, printed in brown ink and as a negative. Bird had displayed interest in the action of light in the 1839 edition of his popular *Elements of Natural Philosophy*, written before the announcement of photography. In the second edition of 1844, he devoted an entire chapter to photography, expanding this in subsequent editions. Although he never exhibited and none of his own photographs are known to have survived, Puttick and Simpson's 1856 auction of Bird's library included not only photographic equipment but also many photographs "by artists of the first eminence," including ROGER FENTON, JAMES D. ROBERTSON, PHILIP HENRY DELAMOTTE, and HUGH OWEN.

REFERENCES: Golding Bird, "Observations on the Application of Heliographic or Photogenic Drawing to Botanical Purposes," *Magazine of Natural History*, n.s., 3 (April 1839), pp. 188–92; "Fac-Simile of a Photogenic Drawing," *Mirror*, April 20, 1839, p. 241 (with reprint of Bird's article in *Magazine of Natural History*); Golding Bird, *Elements of Natural Philosophy: Being an Experimental Introduction to the Study of the Physical Sciences*, 2nd ed. (London: John Churchill, 1844) (and later editions); Frederic Bird, "The Late Dr. Golding Bird," *Association Medical Journal*, January 5, 1855, pp. 1–6

Bird, Peter Hinckes

1827–1891

A physician, Bird was interested in children's hygiene and especially in public sanitation issues and was the author of numerous medical treatises. Shortly after the formation of the Photographic Society in London, Bird was elected a member. Waxed paper was his favored negative process, although on occasion he employed calotype, albumen, and collodion negatives. Bird exhibited actively from 1854 through 1862. His most adventurous series, exhibited in 1854–55, derived from an archaeological tour of Egypt and architectural studies in Spain. Only one print from Bird's extensive body of work is known to have survived, held in the collection of the Society of Antiquaries, London.

EXHIBITED: 1854, London, Photographic Society; 1854, Dundee, Royal Infirmary Fund; 1855, Glasgow, British Association for the Advancement of Science; 1862, London, International Exhibition

REFERENCE: Eugène Bouchut, *Practical Treatise on the Diseases of Children and Infants at the Breast; including the Hygiene and Physical Education of Young Children*, trans. and ed. Peter Hinckes Bird (London: John Churchill, 1855)

Bishop, Robert

b. 1821

In 1857 the veteran Scottish photographer JAMES ROSS recalled: "My attention was first drawn to this subject from the circumstance of the very first calotype I ever had in my hand vanishing from my sight while admiring it. It had been merely washed, probably in common salt. This took place some fourteen or fifteen years ago, when in conjunction with Mr. Bishop, a very able chemist, I made my first experiments in the art. We soon, or rather I should say my fellow worker soon, mastered the negatives completely." No chemist or pharmacist by the name of Bishop has been traced in the Edinburgh directories. However, the 1844–45 directory shows a Robert Bishop, an engraver on wood, sharing No. 23 Lauriston Place with James Ross, portrait painter and future photographer. It would not be surprising for someone involved in the printing industry, such as this engraver, to also be an able amateur chemist.

REFERENCE: "The Substance of a Paper Read by Mr. J. Ross before the Photographic Society of Scotland, April 14th, 1857," *Photographic Notes* 2 (October 1, 1857), pp. 361–64

Blair, William

1817–1871

The triumph of collodion on glass was complete by 1870, but many remembered the convenience of paper negatives to the tourist and other travelers. One who sought to merge these worlds, with more success than others, was William Blair. In September 1871 the *Photographic News* recalled that "as an experimentalist, Mr. Blair was distinguished by rare ingenuity, care, and perseverance, added to a large inventive faculty." Keenly interested in permanent printing processes, Blair freely published in the *Photographic News* his process for coating collodion onto paper to use in making a negative. While this did preserve the portability and convenience of paper, the images were recorded in a fundamentally different way. With calotypes and waxed-paper negatives, the image was embedded in the fibers of the paper; in Blair's process it was made in the surface coating, a process conceptually similar to modern emulsions. In a subsequent communication with the journal in February 1871, Blair wrote of his disillusionment with modern papers, finding that he succeeded "best with some very old prepared paper that I had had lying past for some years." (He was probably unaware that three decades earlier, TALBOT had also sought out old paper.) After Blair died saving one of his sons from drowning, a grateful photographic community took up a subscription for his family in recognition of all that he had done to advance the art.

REFERENCES: William Blair, "Suggestions for a Negative Paper Process," *Photographic News* 14 (November 25, 1870), pp. 556–57; Blair, "Paper Negative Process," *Photographic News* 15 (February 24, 1871), p. 88; *Scotsman* (Edinburgh), September 4, 1871, p. 2 (obituary); *Photographic News* 15 (September 8, 1871), pp. 421–22 (obituary)

Blowers, John

b. 1798

Blowers was the land agent for Lord Stafford's Gothic Revival fantasy Costessy Hall (also known as Cossy, Cossey, or Costessey) in Norfolk, and a member of the Norwich Photographic Society. He was identified by the society as "the oldest of our local amateurs." Blowers's work is known today mainly through salt prints from calotype negatives, some of which were sold in recent years at auction, including a view of Norwich Castle and a portrait of a young man (the latter print associated with a group of calotypes, including one by GEORGE HARPER and one by WILLIAM HOWES HUNT). In the 1856 exhibition of the Norwich Photographic Society, Blowers showed several photographs of Costessy Hall, the negative process not identified. However, *At Halesworth* was listed in the catalogue as having been "printed ten years ago," which must have been from a calotype negative, so it is likely the others were as well. The reviewer for the *Norfolk News* was happily surprised that Blowers's photographs showed no "signs of deterioration, and are worthy to be placed side by side with similar productions of the present day."

EXHIBITED: 1856, Norwich, Photographic Society

REFERENCES: *Norfolk News*, January 3, 1857; sale cat., Sotheby's, London, June 25, 1985, lot 123; Richard Denyer and Andrew Moore, eds., *A Period Eye: Photography Then and Now*, exh. cat. (Norwich: Norfolk Museums and Archaeology Service, 2003), pp. 39–40

Bolding, William Johnson Jennis

1815–1899

As an amateur artist Bolding favored a monochromatic brown watercolor for his landscapes and silhouettes for his portraits. One must assume that these preferences set the stage for his later enthusiasm for the inherent tones of photography. A wealthy shipowner and landowner in Weybourne, Bolding made most of his income as a brewer and maltster. An amateur archaeologist with friends in the Norwich School of artists, he traveled widely throughout Britain, making sketches as he went, and in 1850 he visited Switzerland. Two of his oil paintings were exhibited in 1853. We do not know exactly when his interest in photography bloomed, but Bolding benefited from the tutelage of HUGH WELCH DIAMOND, and in 1856 he joined the Norwich Photographic Society. His first exhibited prints were local architectural studies produced from waxed-paper negatives, and in 1857 the *Norfolk News* praised them as "perhaps the finest proofs we have seen from waxed paper, on account of the unusual transparency of the shadows." After this, using collodion negatives, Bolding produced an extensive series of "country types," photographing the local people around him. In order to facilitate these portraits he had large windows installed in one of his malt barns so it could be used as a photographic studio.

Exhibited: 1856, Norwich, Photographic Society

References: *Norfolk News*, January 3, 1857, p. 15; C. S. Middleton, "W. J. J. Bolding: A Country Photographer, 1815–1899," *Norfolk Fair*, September 1977, pp. 23–26; C. S. Middleton, "The Country Portraits of William Bolding," *Norfolk Fair*, October 1977, pp. 25–26; Richard Denyer and Andrew Moore, eds., *A Period Eye: Photography Then and Now*, exh. cat. (Norwich: Norfolk Museums and Archaeology Service, 2003), pp. 15–16, 24–25

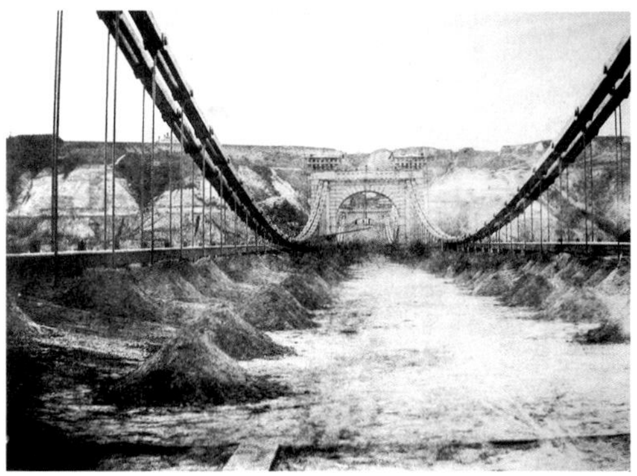

14. John Cooke Bourne

Bourne, John Cooke *ill. 14*

1814–1896

The son of a London hatter, Bourne was emerging by the 1830s as a draftsman of unusual skill. A chance meeting with the author and antiquary John Britton brought about his involvement in a project to document the construction of the London and Birmingham Railway. Published in four volumes in 1839 and extensively illustrated with tinted lithographs made from Bourne's camera lucida drawings, this work was the first documentation of British railways. By 1847 Bourne was in the employ of the engineer Charles Blacker Vignoles, working in Russia documenting a series of civil works projects. In September 1852 Bourne was joined by Roger Fenton to document Vignoles's grand suspension bridge over the Dnieper River at Kiev. Bourne had experimented with the daguerreotype and by then was taking calotypes to supplement his drawings; Fenton was invited along to contribute large-format stereo photographs for the Wheatstone stereo viewer. Fenton and Vignoles were instrumental in founding the Photographic Society in London. Elected a member in May 1853, Bourne contributed nineteen calotype and waxed-paper images of Russia to the society's 1854 exhibition, and he would go on to design and patent a camera with a built-in darkroom for developing wet-collodion negatives in the field.

Exhibited: 1854 and 1855, London, Photographic Society

References: John Britton, *Drawings of the London & Birmingham Railway* (London: Bourne and Ackermann, 1839); John Cooke Bourne, "Description of a New Patent Portable Camera, with Separate Dark-Chamber . . . ," *JPS* 2 (January 21, 1856), pp. 283–84; John Hannavy, "John Cooke Bourne, Charles Blacker Vignoles and the Dnieper Suspension Bridge," *History of Photography* 28 (Winter 2004), pp. 334–47

Bramwell, J.

In 1843 the Durham Mechanics' Institute held a Polytechnic Exhibition, displaying a typically wide range of material. In the Fine Arts section, Bramwell exhibited *Rebecca*, medium unspecified, and a "Photogenic Portrait." The first sounds like a painting and therefore implies a profession as an artist, but a likely contender has not yet been identified. Possible candidates include: John Bramwell, Esq.; J. Bramwell, a surgeon; J. Thomson Bramwell, a local agent of the London Indisputable Life Policy Company; and Joseph C. Bromwell, a druggist in the 1851 census.

Exhibited: 1843, Durham, Mechanics' Institute

Brewster, David

1781–1868

Irrepressible in his enthusiasm but irascible in temperament, the Scotsman Sir David Brewster was one of the most visible and respected scientists of the Victorian era. He was groomed for pastoral duties and served as a literary assistant to a clergyman-scholar in his youth. Uncomfortable in the pulpit because of his stammer, he would make his living not through saving souls but rather with his pen. As a scientific journalist, Brewster had access to all the latest ideas as well as a platform from which to project his own reputation. While today he is best known as a historian of science, Brewster was esteemed by his peers as a scientist and inventor, and was credited with the invention of the kaleidoscope and the stereoscope. Introduced to Talbot by Sir John Herschel, Brewster became one of the inventor's few intimate friends. Writing to her mother-in-law, Lady Elisabeth Feilding, Talbot's wife was "quite amazed . . . that scarcely a momentary pause occurs in their conversation" between the two normally shy men, and that during Brewster's visits her husband "seems to possess new life." In 1839 Talbot turned almost immediately to Brewster to share his discovery of photography, and Sir David plunged into the new art with the greatest of enthusiasm. In the early days of photography, when Daguerre seemed to receive all the credit and Talbot at times despaired of the viability of photography on paper, the support of friends like Brewster and Herschel was critical. Brewster made his own calotype negatives and took equal pleasure in printing those made by others. His real significance in the history of photography, however, derives from his position at St. Andrews. He was central to the calotype movement there, inspiring first John Adamson and his younger brother Robert Adamson, who in turn enabled David Octavius Hill to accomplish what he did; it was James Francis Montgomery's visit to St. Andrews to consult with Brewster on photography that led to the formation of the Edinburgh Calotype Club. Brewster was not a great photographer himself, but his influence in lending credibility to the new art was essential. In 1847 he confessed to Talbot: "I do not believe that a Child ever received a Toy with more pleasure than I do a Sun-Picture. It is a sort of monomania which my dealings with light have inflicted upon me."

References: Constance Talbot to Elisabeth Feilding, August 15, 1836, Talbot Collection, British Library, LA36-58; David Brewster to Talbot, November 13, 1847, National Media Museum, Bradford, 1937-4963 (Talbot Correspondence Project, http://foxtalbot.dmu.ac.uk, doc. no. 06048); *Proceedings of the Royal Society* 17 (1868–69), pp. lxix–lxxiv (obituary); "A Reminiscence of the Calotype Club," *BJP* 21 (August 14, 1874), p. 385; Alison Morrison-Low, "Sir David Brewster and Photography," *Review of Scottish Culture*, no. 4 (1988), pp. 63–73

Brewster, Henry Craigie

1816–1905

The fourth and youngest son of Sir David Brewster, Henry Craigie Brewster served as a captain in the 76th Regiment, Royal Scots. He shared his father's scientific interests and was given an honorary corresponding membership in the St. Andrews Literary and Philosophical Society. In 1842 Sir David canceled a meeting with Talbot when the opportunity arose to spend time with his son, who was on leave from military service. In her biography of Sir David, her father, Margaret Gordon recalled his passion for calotypy, writing that his "youngest son, when at home on leave, practised it under his superintendence, and it was one of his father's means of relaxation from heavier work, to take positives from the negatives of his son and others." In October 1842 Sir David wrote to Talbot that his son's calotyping was going well and that he had purchased a camera from the Edinburgh optician Thomas Davidson in order to photograph his regiment when they were assigned to Cork. Captain Brewster left very few clues about his work, but we know from Sir David's letter that his son oiled his calotype negatives to make them print faster. The largest surviving group of his photographs, depicting his fellow soldiers and the architecture of Cork, was taken before the regiment transferred out in May 1843. These may have been his last photographs, for Brewster was then posted to Plymouth, and therefore faced some uncertainty over Talbot's calotype patent. While on subsequent postings to Corfu and Cephalonia, he sent home pen-and-ink sketches. Brewster rose to the rank of major-general. In his obituary he was remembered as an enthusiastic golfer with a wide circle of friends.

References: David Brewster to Talbot, October 22, 1842, National Media Museum, Bradford, 1937-4912 (Talbot Correspondence Project, http://foxtalbot.dmu.ac.uk, doc. no. 04628); Margaret Gordon, *The Home Life of Sir David Brewster* (Edinburgh: Edmonston and Douglas, 1869); *Times* (London), September 21, 1905, p. 7, col. D (obituary); Alison Morrison-Low, "Sir David Brewster and Photography," *Review of Scottish Culture*, no. 4 (1988), pp. 63–73; Graham Smith, "Captain Brewster: Calotypist," in *Photography—Discovery and Invention: Papers Delivered at a Symposium Celebrating the Invention of Photography* (Malibu: J. Paul Getty Museum, 1990), pp. 71–80

Bridges, George Wilson *ills. 15, 16*

1788–1863

Of all the alliances in the early days of photography, none would seem more improbable than that of the Rev. George Wilson Bridges and Talbot. A minister in Jamaica, Bridges watched helplessly as all four of his daughters drowned in a boating accident. Already a widower, he fled in distress from the West Indies with his only remaining son to the farthest place on earth he could find, the backwoods of Canada. After seven years of living in a quirky pentagonal log cabin crowned by an observatory, Bridges returned to England. It appears that he considered becoming the curate at Lacock and in the process came to the attention of Talbot's formidable mother, Lady Elisabeth

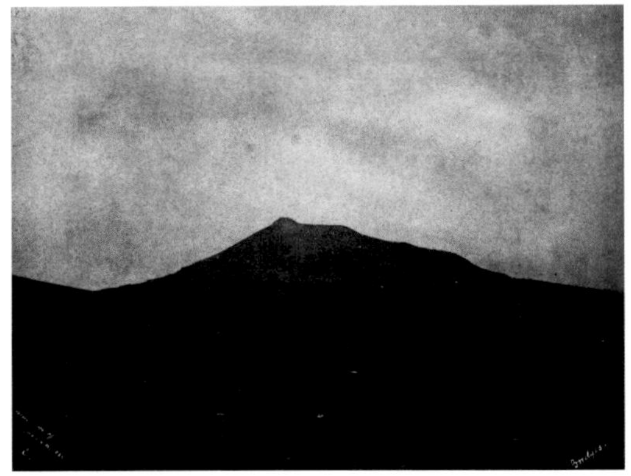

15. George Wilson Bridges

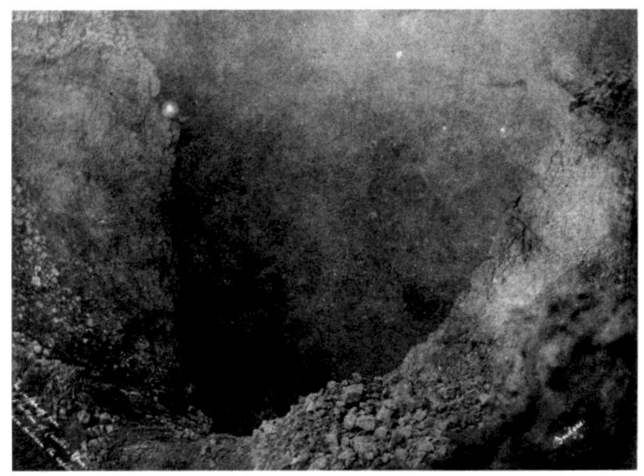

16. George Wilson Bridges

Feilding. Somehow they all became friends, and Nicolaas Henneman gave Bridges lessons in the calotype in preparation for his return to the life of a traveler. In 1846 Talbot's cousin Christopher Rice Mansel Talbot ("Kit") and Calvert Richard Jones embarked on a Mediterranean voyage. Bridges met up with the party in Malta, and his nascent calotyping passion was ignited by their shared enthusiasm for the new art. From that point forward he was an adventurous and fearless photographer, making hundreds of paper negatives as he toured the Holy Land and the Mediterranean. In 1852, under the appropriate epithet of the "Wayworn Wanderer," Bridges began to issue *Selections from Seventeen-Hundred Genuine Photographs . . . Taken around the Shores of the Mediterranean between the Years 1846–52*. In 1858 J. Hogarth proposed publishing his *Palestine as It Is: In a Series of Photographic Views Illustrating the Bible*. But none of Bridges's publications would prove to be a commercial success. While not a scientific man, through tireless efforts Bridges mastered the calotype negative, even managing to photograph down into the fiery vent of Mount Etna between explosions. However, his printing let him down, and most of his work survives today as seriously faded salt prints. In many ways, the eccentric Bridges embodied Talbot's dream that photography would become a useful illustrative tool in the hands of other artists; and as for so many others since, the creative act of photography helped to return a sense of meaning to Bridges's troubled life.

Reference: George Wilson Bridges, *Selections from Seventeen-Hundred Genuine Photographs: (Views—Portraits—Statuary—Antiquities.) Taken around the Shores of the Mediterranean between the Years 1846–52. With, or without, Notes, Historical, and Descriptive. By a Wayworn Wanderer* (n.d., [ca. 1852])

Briggs, Thomas Henry

b. 1833

In 1852, at the age of nineteen, Briggs became a founding member of the Leeds Photographic Society. He contributed three calotypes to the society's albums, his only known productions. By 1856 Briggs was a photographic chemist in Leeds in partnership with John William Ramsden, and by 1861 he had become a general manufacturing chemist.

Reference: Adrian Budge, *Early Photography in Leeds, 1839–1870*, exh. cat. (Leeds: Leeds Art Galleries, 1981), p. 9

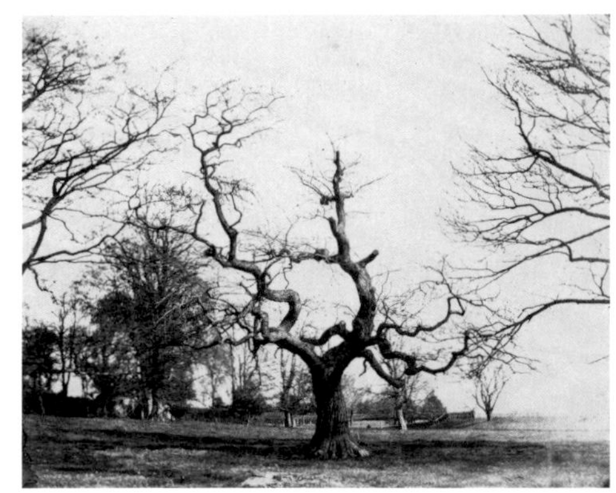

17. Charles Brittan

Brittan, Charles *ill. 17*

1832–after 1881

A substantial group of Dr. Brittan's calotypes is preserved in the Royal Photographic Society Collection at the National Media Museum, Bradford, but little is known about him beyond their testimony. Born in Clifton, the son of an attorney, Brittan studied at St. John's College, Cambridge. About 1854 he returned to the Clifton area to photograph in the region, also venturing into Wales. Nearly all of his productions were landscapes (one inscribed "taken in very heavy rain"), with one portrait and one copy of a drawing surviving. By 1871 he was chaplain of the gaol, Bristol.

Reference: Reece Winstone, *Bristol's Earliest Photographs*, with a preface by Hugh Casson, 2nd ed. (Bristol: Printed by R. J. Acford, 1974)

Brodie, Mr.

Nothing is known about Brodie, save for a substantial group of calotype portraits and genre studies preserved in the richard willats album in the collections at Princeton University, all of which seem to be from Jersey. At least 21 of the 255 prints in the album are positively attributed to Brodie and more than 40 others are tentatively so, making up a fourth of this critical early record of photography. There was a William Brodie (*not* the William Brodie whose story inspired Stevenson's Jekyll and Hyde story) who made a stereoscopic ambrotype of statuary in the Crystal Palace, but the connection seems remote. But while the subject matter and the Jersey location argue against the attribution, the chemist Sir Benjamin Brodie, whom mervyn herbert nevil story maskelyne credited as his first teacher in photography, also remains a possibility.

Reference: Richard Willats Photograph Album, Princeton University Library

Brooks, William

1838–1916

A group of waxed-paper "views in the village of Willian, Hertfordshire" was shown by a "W. Brook" in the 1861 exhibition of the Photographic Society in London. Since no individual can be linked to this record, a slight typographical error can be suspected, and William Brooks emerges as the most likely candidate. The details of Brooks's early life are contradictory, but we know that he was born in Kent and that he was an engineer's pattern maker by 1861. In 1916 the *British Journal Photographic Almanac* recalled that in "his early twenties Brooks had become a competent *plein-air* photographer." In the 1860s Brooks took up stereo photography in Penzance, first as an amateur but soon as a professional; by the time of the 1871 census he was listing himself as a "landscape photographer." By 1875 Brooks had established himself in London as a photographer and photographic inventor, becoming vice president of the South London Photographic Society. He continued to lecture on photography at the Royal Cornwall Polytechnic Society until 1882 and died in Reigate, Surrey.

Exhibited: 1861, London, Photographic Society

References: George Clement Boase, *Collectanea Cornubiensia: A Collection of Biographical and Topographical Notes Relating to the County of Cornwall* (Truro: Netherton and Worth, 1890), p. 110; *BJPA*, 1916, p. 417 (obituary); Charles Thomas, *Views and Likenesses: Early Photographers and Their Work in Cornwall and the Isles of Scilly, 1839–1870* (Truro: Royal Institution of Cornwall, 1988), pp. 37–42

Brothers, Alfred

1826–1912

The son of a chemist, the eight-year-old Brothers was so captivated by the appearance of Halley's Comet that astronomy remained a fascination throughout his life. Discovering photography when he was sixteen, he made his own photographic paper. Brothers followed a somewhat uncertain path after that, working in a bookseller's shop and then as a railroad surveyor and an insurance agent. In 1855 he moved to Manchester, a city rife with amateur photographers, and joined the photographic society. Brothers purchased a photographic studio and by the 1861 census was listing himself as a "photographic artist." Between 1856 and 1865 he participated in many major photographic exhibitions, showing wet collodion, and was well known as the inventor of a magnesium ribbon for photographic lighting. Brothers applied photography to many different scientific undertakings, and his *Photography: Its History, Processes, Apparatus, and Materials*, first published in 1892, enjoyed wide popularity. None of his early paper negative photographs are known to have survived, but in 1898 Brothers wrote to Charles Henry Talbot, the inventor's son, proudly noting that he owned photographs signed, "From Nature, 1844, H. F. T."

References: Alfred Brothers, *Photography: Its History, Processes, Apparatus, and Materials; Comprising Working Details of All the More Important Methods* (London: C. Griffin, 1892); Brothers to Charles Henry Talbot, July 6, 1898, Wiltshire Record Office; *Times* (London), August 27, 1912, p. 7, col. e (obituary); "The Late Mr. Alfred Brothers," *Penrose's Pictorial Annual: The Process Year Book* 18 (1912–13), pp. 181–84

Brown, Duncan

1819–1897

In 1861, thinking back to the days before his own hair had turned gray, Brown recalled: "It was, I think, about the year 1848, that I first thought of trying my hand at photography. A young acquaintance of mine had made a box, and we purchased a lens, which cost only a few pence, fitted it to the box with a paper tube, and set to work with great glee. But my partner, who was engaged all day, could spare no time except in the evenings." Brown had more time during the day and first tried the calotype, following a formula given in the 1846 *Art-Union*, but without satisfactory results. He finally secured "a quarter-plate camera, with a good lens, which had been used by a lady for taking Daguerreotypes" in Glasgow. Brown read some of the books that were just then emerging in photography and finally "arrived at great success" with waxed-paper negatives. "An exposure of from one to two minutes, in the sun's rays, was then necessary," he explained to the Glasgow Photographic Society in 1861, and "you will see by one of the specimens that I had the cruelty to make the gentleman sit in the full blaze of the sun!" Brown was at the time the janitor but later rose to the position of administrative superintendent of the Glasgow School of Art.

References: Duncan Brown, "On the Collodion Process: Its Pursuit under Difficulties," *BJP* 8 (May 1, 1861), pp. 166–67; John Hannavy, *A Moment in Time: Scottish Contributions to Photography, 1840–1920*, exh. cat. (Glasgow: Third Eye Centre, 1983), p. 70

Brown, John

1838–1874

The son of a landscape painter in Kilmarnock, Scotland, Brown was a precentor, the human voice that led the congregation in song in the era before church organs became common. By the time of the 1871 census Brown identified himself as a "student of photography." This was a peculiar declaration for an experienced artist, for a decade before, in 1861, he had first advertised as a "photographer and calotypist" in Kilmarnock, a rapidly industrializing Ayrshire town. The following year he expanded into a "commodious portrait gallery," and a local newspaper announced in 1865 that Brown had opened "a first class establishment (wooden) in Bank Street, Kilmarnock." (In nineteenth-century Scotland, wooden buildings were often allowed by the authorities for temporary businesses and exhibitions where a permanent stone structure would not be permitted.) By 1872 Brown was advertising the novelty of "enlarged photographs (untouched) by the new photo-crayon process"; two years later, he succumbed to typhus. Although his death certificate described him as a city missionary, that might not have been Brown's real passion, for when his wife died twenty years later she was listed as the widow of a photographer.

References: *Ardrossan & Saltcoats Herald*, April 29, 1865; *Ardrossan & Saltcoats Herald*, January 13, 1872

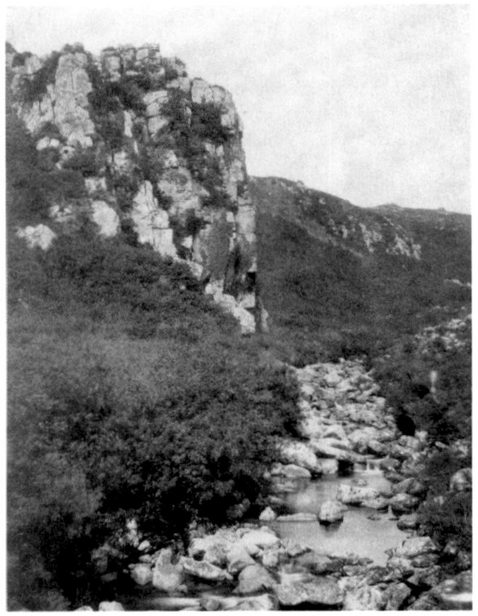

18. Benjamin Browning

Browning, Benjamin *ill. 18*
b. 1799
Educated at Glasgow University, Browning became a Royal Navy surgeon. Little is known about him, but modern auction records hint at an extensive photographic output. He used waxed-paper negatives and often annotated them with exposure times and other technical information. Some are industrial scenes, such as his 1856 *Keyham Steam Factory*, which required 1½ hours exposure. Another, *Trees in Mount Edgcumbe Park*, required 2½ hours (Mount Edgcumbe was the home of TALBOT's half sister Caroline). Other views reflected the industrialization of Britain. In one diverse album containing views by Maxwell Lyte and others, Browning's work makes up a substantial portion, including subjects in Rome, Gibraltar, Australia, Sevastopol, and Suez. This geographical diversity strongly suggests that Browning's naval travels also served as photographic jaunts.

Buckle, Samuel *ill. 19*
1808–1860
Many modern practitioners of old photographic processes have used the Buckle Brush—a wad of cotton wool caught on a glass tube—most likely without knowing anything about the photographer behind this invention. Buckle was a brewer by trade. His entry into the world of photography was heralded by the large group of prints he exhibited at the Great Exhibition of 1851, where they caught the attention of the official jury, who felt they were "characterized by great delicacy of tint and exquisite *cleanness* of execution, and deserve to be ranked among the finest specimens of photography in the Exhibition." He was awarded the Council Medal, the jury's highest honor. Amateur activities gave way to professionalism two years later, when Buckle sold his brewery and established himself in Leamington, Warwickshire, as a photographer and retailer of photographic apparatus. Buckle long remained loyal to TALBOT's process, being one of the most prolific exhibitors of calotypes from 1851 to 1856. He also gave lessons in Talbot's process to many other photographers. In 1857 Buckle suddenly converted to collodion, but he then gave up photography entirely, dying soon after at the relatively young age of fifty-one.

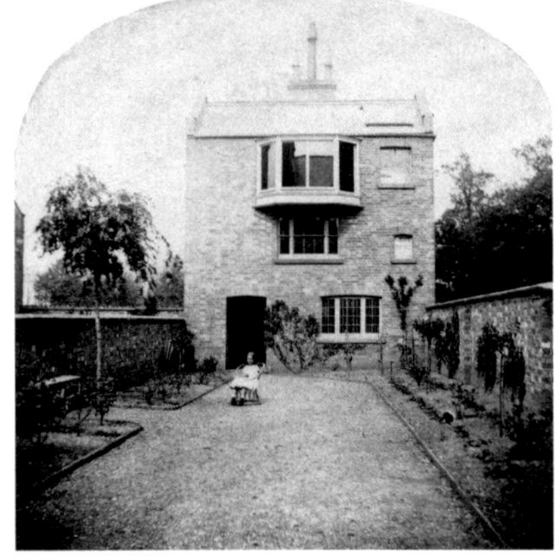

19. Samuel Buckle

EXHIBITED: 1851, London, Great Exhibition; 1852, London, Society of Arts; 1853, London, Photographic Institution; 1853–54, first touring exhibition, Society of Arts (London); 1854, London, Photographic Society; 1854, Dundee, Royal Infirmary Fund; 1854, second touring exhibition, Society of Arts (London); 1855, London, Photographic Society; 1855, Glasgow, British Association for the Advancement of Science; 1855–56, third touring exhibition, Society of Arts (London); 1856, London, Photographic Society

REFERENCES: James Glaisher, "Class X," in *Reports by the Juries on the Subjects in the Thirty Classes into which the Exhibition Was Divided* (London: Printed for the Royal Commissioners, William Clowes & Sons, 1852), p. 278; *BJP* 7 (June 15, 1860), p. 183 (obituary)

Buckler, Alexander
b. 1826
Like his father before him, Buckler became a shorthand writer. He worked in Cornwall in the 1850s but then returned to his native London. Buckler was probably intimately familiar with the characteristics of paper and perhaps sought an escape in amateur photography. In 1861 he wrote to *Photographic Notes* suggesting that "a good Negative Paper Process, which shall be uniform in its results, is to my mind one of the greatest necessities of photography. . . . With this in view I have made great many experiments, with various degrees of success, and have, I believe, tried every paper process that has come out." Buckler turned to THOMAS SUTTON's albumenized calotype paper, a commercially prepared base normally employed in making prints but just as easily usable for producing his negatives. The paper had to be sensitized in the hours just before use, for it did not keep long, but Buckler had a very practical idea. Instead of wasting already sensitized paper if it could not be used, "in the event of a wet day, at an hotel, the papers already prepared can be used for printing positives."

REFERENCE: Alexander Buckler, "Paper Processes," *Photographic Notes* 6 (February 1, 1861), p. 48

Bull, W. J.
All three of the photographs contributed by Bull to the 1860 exhibition of the Photographic Society in London, one of them a calotype, were taken in Harrow, outside London, later the British home of the Eastman Kodak Company. They were apparently the happy outcome of some years of effort, for in 1855 Bull wrote to the *Liverpool Photographic Journal* asking for help with failed negatives that he had made using FREDERICK TOWNSHEND's version of the waxed-paper process. Nothing else is presently known of Bull or his work.

EXHIBITED: 1860, London, Photographic Society

REFERENCE: W. J. Bull, letter in *LPJ* 2 (October 13, 1855), p. 132

Burke, J. or T.
Photographic exhibition catalogues often contain errors, sometimes from an editor misreading a handwritten label, sometimes from typographical lapses. A "J. Burke" exhibited a photograph of Waltham Abbey, Essex, in the 1855 exhibition of the Photographic Society in London, and a "T. Burke" exhibited one of the same subject, listed as being done in waxed paper, in the society's 1857 exhibition. This might be a coincidence, but it is more likely that the handwritten J. or T. was misread by a cataloguer. T. Burke also exhibited a collodion image of Willesden Station in 1857, slightly tipping the balance toward him.

EXHIBITED: 1855, London, Photographic Society; 1857, London, Photographic Society

Burnett, Charles John
1820–1907
Burnett, best known for his application of uranium to photography, came from an old Aberdeenshire family. He was educated privately and was still living with his mother in Edinburgh by 1851. Well aware of the cyanotype process, and perhaps inspired by ANNA ATKINS, Burnett exploited the natural color of cobalt compounds to photographically reproduce the *Floridae*, or red seaweeds. He exhibited examples of these and other photograms in the exhibition that accompanied the 1855 meeting of the British Association for the Advancement of Science in Glasgow. When Burnett became one of the founding members of the Photographic Society of Scotland in 1856, he exhibited more cobalt seaweeds in the society's first exhibition. In the 1859 exhibition of the Photographic Society in London, Burnett's series of "pictures exhibited to show chemical actions" was tied to his article in the *Photographic Journal*. Burnett then moved to Australia, becoming a sheep farmer, and later in life returned to Aberdeen. A leader in the Primrose League, a conservative political movement, Burnett was described in his obituary as a "man of fine literary tastes."

REFERENCES: Charles John Burnett, "On the Application of Uranium and Other Matters to Photography," *Photographic Notes* 2 (March 15, May 1 and 15, 1857), pp. 97–101, 160–64, 181–84; "Description of Mr. Burnett's Pictures in the Photographic Exhibition, Suffolk Street," *Photographic Journal* 5 (February 5, 1859), pp. 182–83; Burnett, "Proposed Contrivance for Keeping Waxed or Plain Paper Pictures Longer than Usual before Development," *Photographic Journal (BJP)* 6 (August 15, 1859), p. 200; Burnett, *Photographic Negative Processes on Waxed and Plain Papers, and on Glass* (London: J. Sanford, 1859); *Scotsman* (Edinburgh), August 13, 1907, p. 4 (obituary)

Burrow, Frederic
A collection of photographs "taken and processed by an amateur experimenter" emerged in an otherwise routine auction in 1986. This richly varied grouping included negative and positive Talbotypes, cyanotypes, and examples by many other processes, mostly copies of prints and photographs. Dating from the 1850s and 1860s, the collection was accompanied by a 106-page manuscript with notes on the various processes. The collection has not been traced, and nothing further is known of the photographer, cited as Frederic Burrow. The most likely candidate by this name is a Westmoreland artist in stained glass, born about 1816, who is known for one of the windows in Chester Cathedral.

REFERENCE: Phillips, London, April 23, 1986, lot 315

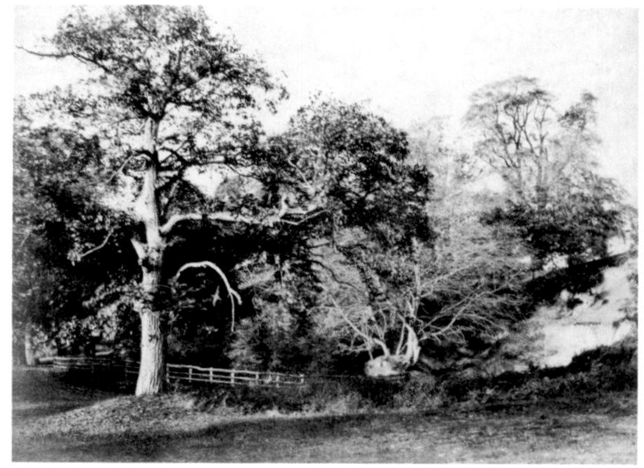
20. Robert Burrows

Burrows, Robert *ill. 20*
1810–1883
Burrows filled a number of roles in Ipswich, listing himself in the 1855 gazetteer as a silversmith, pawnbroker, insurance agent, music teacher, artist, and town councilor. As a painter, he exhibited in London at the Royal Academy and the British Institution in the period 1851–55. In common with many others, Burrows took up photography during the 1850s, perhaps as an aid to his painting. He used the waxed-paper process and never seems to have exhibited; but there is an indication that he sold his work, for some of his photographs appear on printed mounts, such as "George and Joseph Lott (Late Burrows)." Several of his prints have passed through the auction rooms, and a large album of his photographs from the period 1850–70 survives.

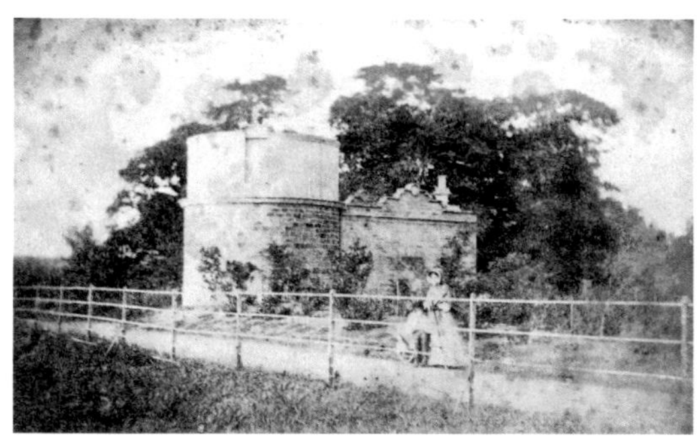
21. Miss Bush

Bush, Miss *ill. 21*
The identity of Miss Bush is nearly a complete mystery. Her involvement with photography is represented by a single competent and clearly credited example in a Llewelyn family album thought to have been compiled by Emma Charlotte, the daughter of JOHN DILLWYN LLEWELYN and EMMA THOMASINA LLEWELYN (TALBOT's cousin). Taken at the Llewelyn family estate of Penllergare, *The Observatory* is a salted paper print made from a paper negative, probably dating from the early to mid-1850s. Miss Bush is not mentioned in any known Llewelyn family records. She may have been a one-time visitor to Penllergare, perhaps given the opportunity to experiment with a camera there, or perhaps she was already accomplished in the art.

REFERENCE: Emma Charlotte Dillwyn Llewelyn's Album, The Metropolitan Museum of Art, Gilman Collection, Gift of The Howard Gilman Foundation, 2005, 2005.100.382

Butterfield, Charles
b. 1835
Born to Scottish parents in the booming Yorkshire city of Bradford, Butterfield took full advantage of his student days. While still in his teens, he was an older pupil who was granted the privilege of perusing the headmaster's library. One of the volumes that intrigued him most was the *Mechanics' Magazine*, reminiscing in 1861 that "it was through this medium I first became possessed of the knowledge that such a thing as photography existed." Butterfield started out with MUNGO PONTON's cheap photographic process using bichromate of potash paper, which allowed him to make simple contact negatives of leaves and other natural objects. He built his first camera out of a cigar box fitted with a spectacle glass, but found Ponton's paper insufficiently sensitive for the camera. He struggled with various paper processes until discovering the ease of the collodion process in achieving successful negatives. Butterfield was so prosperous as a wool merchant that he was able to retire in his thirties, and this gave him leisure time to pursue his photography. Although the rapidity of glass negatives was appealing, he never lost track of his early roots in paper. As Butterfield observed in the *British Journal of Photography*: "Wax paper is very good for reproducing views of old ruins, rustic cottages, &c., where required of extra large size; but I certainly cannot recommend it generally, in consequence of the length of exposure required, and its inability to give any amount of sharpness to views embracing distant objects."

REFERENCE: Charles Butterfield, "A Photographic Retrospect," *BJP* 8 (January 15, 1861), pp. 30–31

Cameron, James
1800–1875

Cameron chose not to follow his father as the taxman in Dunkeld, Scotland, instead becoming self-taught in science. Trained as an artisan missionary, he was sent to Madagascar in 1826. When the missionaries were expelled in 1835, Cameron moved to Cape Town and became a surveyor. He was also a pioneer in the supply of water to the town, something that stood him in good stead when he started making calotypes as an amateur in 1848. Cameron's additional interest in electrotyping almost certainly led him to work with silvered metal plates, and by 1850 he had set himself up as a professional daguerreotypist. In 1853 Cameron returned to Madagascar, accompanying the Rev. WILLIAM ELLIS as a photographer, possibly taking calotypes but learning the new collodion process as well, and he also built a timber residence for Queen Rasohèrina—the first European-style house in the country. Cameron died in Madagascar and was given an elaborate public funeral.

REFERENCE: Marjorie Bull and Joseph Denfield, *Secure the Shadow: The Story of Cape Photography from Its Beginnings to the End of 1870* (Cape Town: Terence McNally, 1970), pp. 190–91

Campbell, Dr.
We know nothing of Dr. Campbell save for his two calotype views of Egypt, which were shown in the 1853 exhibition of the Mechanics' Institution in Aberdeen. These were contributed by an A. Ewing, Esq., whose identity is also a mystery, although we know that he displayed some views by Maxime Du Camp as well.

EXHIBITED: 1853, Aberdeen, Mechanics' Institution

Campbell, J. M. S.
Campbell contributed a single view of Kirkstall Abbey, near Leeds, made by the waxed-paper process to the 1856 exhibition of the Photographic Society in London. Another waxed-paper view of Kirkstall Abbey was shown in the same exhibition by the equally unknown F. W. CAULFIELD.

EXHIBITED: 1856, London, Photographic Society

Campbell, William George *ill. 22*
1810–1881

It is unclear what drove so many photographers to the study of the insane, but both Campbell and ROBERT SKEFFINGTON LUTWIDGE were commissioners of the Lunacy Commission. Described in his *Times* obituary as a "most genial and accomplished gentleman," he was a London

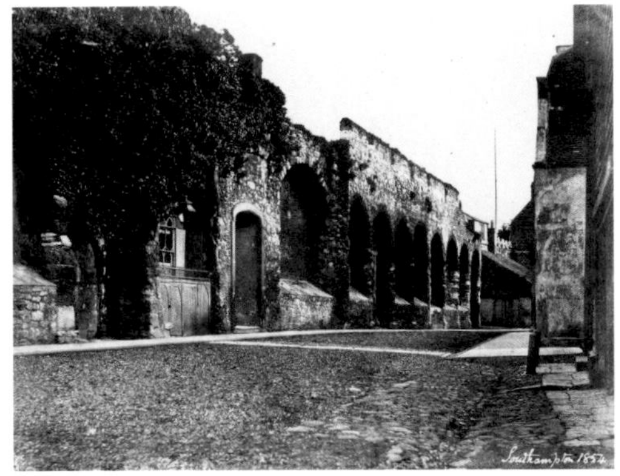

22. William George Campbell

lawyer holding the position of professional commissioner when he became interested in photography. Campbell contributed two views to the Photographic Exchange Club's 1855 album: *Part of the Old Walls, Southampton*, a silver salt print made from a calotype negative dated 1854, and *On the Mole, at Burford Bridge*, an albumen print also made from a calotype negative. The following year he contributed two albumen prints made from calotype negatives to the club's album: *Sandwich, Kent* and *Windsor Locks*.

REFERENCE: *Times* (London), June 16, 1881, p. 10, col. E (obituary)

Cartwright, Samuel
b. 1803

A solicitor in Preston, Lancashire, Cartwright may possibly have been influenced by the photographic circle in nearby Liverpool. He showed one calotype, *The Fire Station, Preston*, in the 1854 photographic exhibition at the Royal Institution in Liverpool. Retiring about this time, he kept up photography as an amateur pursuit. For the 1855 exhibition of the Photographic Society in London, Cartwright continued to photograph the architecture around Preston, but by then had converted to collodion.

EXHIBITED: 1854, Liverpool, Photographic Society

Caulfield, F. W.
Nothing is known at present of Caulfield's background, profession, or personal circumstances. He contributed a single view of Kirkstall Abbey, near Leeds, made by the waxed-paper process and shown in the 1856 exhibition of the Photographic Society in London. Another waxed-paper view of Kirkstall Abbey was shown in the same exhibition by the equally mysterious J. M. S. CAMPBELL.

EXHIBITED: 1856, London, Photographic Society

Cay, John
1790–1865

According to the *Scotsman*, in his four decades as sheriff of Linlithgow, West Lothian, Scotland, Cay was admired for "his decisions being invariably sound, which, together with his amiable qualities, made him extremely popular." Cay was a lawyer based in Edinburgh, one of an extended and influential family abounding in artists and scientists, including his nephew, the brilliant physicist James Clerk Maxwell. He was an active member of the Royal Scottish Society of Arts. In 1843 Cay banded together with a number of like-minded souls to form the Edinburgh Calotype Club, swapping information and techniques and sharing their new photographic images. Cay and members of his family were calotyped by Hill & Adamson during the mid-1840s. In 1856 Cay became a member of the governing council of the new Photographic Society of Scotland. Only one surviving Cay photograph was known (attached to a letter in the National Library of Scotland) until 2003, when a trove of them emerged as the Cay Gift, donated by his descendants to the city of Toowoomba, Australia. Cay's two sons had emigrated to Australia in 1841. They preserved a wide range of nineteenth-century photographs, but one album compiled in 1852 is of particular interest. Its thirty-seven salt prints from calotype negatives are headed with the title, "The Crown Jewels, by Sheriff Cay."

REFERENCES: *Scotsman* (Edinburgh), December 14, 1865, p. 2 (obituary); "A Reminiscence of the Calotype Club," *BJP* 21 (August 14, 1874), p. 385; Desmond MacAuley, *Hemispheres of Light: Extraordinary Lives in Britain and Australia—The Cay Gift Exhibition* (Toowoomba, Queensland: Regional Art Gallery, 2003)

Chattock, Richard Samuel
1825–1906

Chattock was a well-established solicitor in Birmingham, eventually becoming a justice of the peace, but he was as widely known in the artistic community as in legal circles. He studied at Rugby and exhibited at the Royal Academy and the New Water Colour Society. Little is known of Chattock's photography save for the four studies he made by the waxed-paper process in North Wales and showed at the 1855 exhibition of the Photographic Society in London. Given his talents and zeal in other areas one would expect that his photographs were brilliant, but sadly none are known to have survived. Not content with the accomplishment of a lifetime of practicing the law, once he retired Chattock became one of the revivers of the nearly lost art of copperplate etching.

EXHIBITED: 1855, London, Photographic Society

REFERENCE: *Times* (London), February 3, 1906, p. 10, col. D (obituary)

Cheney, Robert Henry
1800–1866
The eldest son of a Shropshire military family whose fortune was built on coal and iron, Cheney had every opportunity and encouragement to develop his artistic tastes. While his youngest brother carried on the family's military tradition, the middle brother, Edward, became the best-known member of the family, a literary figure who built a significant and unusual collection of art while residing in Venice. In the 1820s Robert (often known as Henry) and Edward were living in Rome, along with their mother and their sister Harriet. All were watercolorists and all were interested in art. About 1830 Cheney returned to Badger Hall, the family home in Shropshire, to run the estate, becoming justice of the peace and sheriff. Cheney first showed an interest in photography in 1845, when he approached TALBOT's printer offering to subscribe to *Sun Pictures in Scotland* if a copy of *The Pencil of Nature* could be located for him. Just when interest turned to active participation is unknown, but about 1850 Cheney took up amateur photography, although he never exhibited or openly participated in photographic circles. He was a prolific and highly accomplished photographer nonetheless. His known works are almost exclusively architectural, concentrating on grand country houses but also including more unusual subject matter such as seascapes and the British Museum under construction. His sister Frederica's second son, ALFRED CAPEL CURE, was to figure significantly in Cheney's photographic life. Born in 1826, Cure took up photography at about the same time as his uncle; one may have taught the other, or, more likely, they learned the art together. Many of the albums that survive consist of albumen prints made by Cure from Cheney's paper negatives, apparently mostly printed in the late 1850s, and as a result of their close collaboration, it is sometimes difficult to attribute authorship to specific images within the albums.

REFERENCE: *Watercolours of the Grand Tour from a Private Collection*, sale cat., Christie's, London, October 12, 2005 (sale of drawings and paintings by the Cheney family)

Clark, William Donaldson
1813–1873
Born in Ayr and described by the *Scotsman* as "a man of exquisite taste and fine perception," Clark sadly had his life cut short by a tramway accident in Edinburgh. At a time when chemical knowledge was essential to industry, he became a prosperous calico printer in Derbyshire. Then, according to his obituary in the *British Journal of Photography*, Clark set up house in Edinburgh, gathering "round him a circle of friends interested in art and photography." It was during this early retirement that Clark took up a second career, buying the print shop of Alexander Hill (brother of DAVID OCTAVIUS HILL) and expanding the stock with a "higher class of articles of virtu." He was secretary of the Photographic Society of Scotland and a vice president of the Edinburgh Photographic Society. A prolific exhibitor, Clark was contributing photographs taken by the waxed-paper process as late as 1858. His largest single body of work is an extensive stone-by-stone photographic documentation of Melrose Abbey. For this project, Clark rented a large furnished house nearby, welcomed his photographic friends, and engaged workmen to erect scaffolding to secure the best points of view for photographing the abbey.

EXHIBITED: 1858, Edinburgh, Photographic Society of Scotland

REFERENCES: *Scotsman* (Edinburgh), April 24, 1873, p. 4 (obituary); *BJP* 20 (May 9, 1873), pp. 220–21 (obituary); Julie Lawson, *William Donaldson Clark, 1816–1873* (Edinburgh: National Galleries of Scotland, 1990)

Clarke, Edward Marmaduke
d. 1859
An optician, machinist, and engineer based on The Strand in London, Clarke made photographic cameras and lenses by hand in the days before industrial suppliers took over the business. THOMAS SUTTON recalled that in the early 1840s he bought his first daguerreotype apparatus from Clarke, the complete outfit costing a then-astonishing 30 pounds. Sutton was not entirely happy with his purchase, reminiscing in the *British Journal of Photography* that "a more wretchedly planned affair can hardly be conceived." To address his concerns, he called on Clarke, who "showed me a large calotype portrait which he had himself taken, and which induced me to abandon silver plates in favour of paper." No surviving photographs by Clarke are known.

REFERENCE: Thomas Sutton, "Reminiscences of an Old Photographer," *BJP* 14 (August 30, 1867), p. 413

Clifford, Charles
1819–1863
Clifford, a Welshman, made his whole photographic career in Madrid, where he started at least by 1850, calling himself the "Photografito inglés." He primarily photographed the architecture of Spain and by 1858 had been appointed the official photographer to Queen Isabel II. In this capacity Clifford documented her journeys and the massive building projects undertaken during her reign. Clifford's wife, Jane, photographed the holdings of the Royal Armory and other precious royal objects. Most of this work was on collodion, but early in his career Clifford made both daguerreotypes and calotypes. In the 1854 exhibition of the Photographic Society in London, Clifford submitted ten views of Spanish architecture, three of them specifically identified as calotypes. Clifford disappeared from Spain in 1854, and the most likely explanation is also an intriguing one. There exists a group of waxed-paper negatives taken in the Crimea—not of the action of war, which because of the long exposure times required would have been impossible, but rather studies of the battlefields—and these can probably be attributed to Clifford. They are particularly poignant, some showing orderly rows of men and equipment before an engagement, others depicting turmoil and disarray in the aftermath of battle. Clifford also photographed in Istanbul, most likely on his way to or from the Crimea, and in 1855 he visited Paris and began exhibiting there. Clifford died an early death, at the height of his photographic powers.

EXHIBITED: 1854, London, Photographic Society; 1856 and 1863, Paris, Société Francaise de Photographie

REFERENCES: Lee Fontanella, *Clifford en España: Un fotógrafo en la corte de Isabel II* (Madrid: Ediciones El Viso, 1999); Larry J. Schaaf, *Sun Pictures, Catalogue Ten: British Paper Negatives, 1839–1864* (New York: Hans P. Kraus, Jr., 2001), pp. 92–101

Cocke, Archibald Lewis
b. 1824
Already described in the 1854 *Art-Journal* as "one of the oldest photographers" whose "landscape subjects on paper are unsurpassed for truth and beautiful detail," Cocke must have started early indeed. The son of a surgeon and the brother of another artist, he was one of the most prolific exhibitors of calotypes. His fifteen entries in the 1852 exhibition of the Society of Arts included views of the Great Exhibition of 1851, landscapes, architecture, and *Pines Uprooted by a Flood*. In 1853 his work mostly reflected the natural world, but starting with the 1855 exhibition at the Photographic Institution in London, Cocke took an increasing interest in historic buildings. In 1855 his waxed-paper views "elicited considerable admiration" from the Liverpool Photographic Society; they were, according to their journal, "exceedingly sharp, and presented a peculiar softness of tone, with a completeness of detail seldom accomplished." Working sometimes with his brother Arthur, Cocke established the Institute of Photography at the prestigious London address of 179 Regent Street. He moved his studio to Hammersmith and

participated in the 1861 Architectural Photographic Exhibition, contributing a series on Exeter Cathedral, but the following year Cocke was declared bankrupt.

Exhibited: 1852, London, Society of Arts; 1853 and 1855, London, Photographic Institution; 1855, Liverpool, Photographic Society; 1856, London, Photographic Society

References: "Photography," *Art-Journal*, October 1, 1854, p. 315; "Liverpool Photographic Society," *LPJ* 2 (December 8, 1855), p. 147

Codington, T.

The still mysterious Codington, assumed by the surname to be British, is known to have exhibited waxed paper only once: in the 1858 exhibition of the Photographic Society in London, his entries were *Falaise Castle, Normandy* and *Spire of Hotel de Ville, Brussels.*

Exhibited: 1858, London, Photographic Society

Cogan, John Daniel

1818–1912

On the eve of World War I, the *British Journal of Photography* lamented the loss of one of the earliest professional photographers. Cogan was a lecturer in experimental science in Bath, obviously well trained to undertake photography, who also "took advantage of his nearness to Fox Talbot at Lacock Abbey to make himself acquainted with the Talbotype process and to commence the taking of photographs on paper." Cogan is not mentioned in Talbot's correspondence, although of course he may have called on the inventor in person. Cogan supplemented his lecture fees with other activities; at one time he was a dentist, and he also established a photographic studio on Milsom Street in Bath, which he sold in 1866. None of his early paper photographs are known to have survived.

Reference: "Death of a Photographic Pioneer," *BJP* 59 (August 9, 1912), p. 611

Coghill, John Joscelyn

1826–1905

Sir John Joscelyn Coghill, 4th Baronet, and typically known as Sir Joscelyn Coghill, came from a long-established and wealthy Yorkshire family. His second marriage brought him ties to Ireland. When or how he became interested in photography is not known, but Coghill began taking paper negatives by the early 1850s or even before. His photographs reflect the interests of a wealthy amateur and include family portraits, idyllic country scenes, and architectural studies. Coghill became briefly active in photographic circles in 1857, contributing a view to *The Photographic Album for the Year 1857*; showing nine landscapes in the "Manchester Art Treasures" exhibition; and presenting a paper to the Dublin Photographic Society that detailed his second major photographic tour, a trip through Switzerland in the summer of 1856. He had by then established a strong preference for wet-collodion negatives, perhaps having been cautioned by a colleague who had lost several weeks worth of work when his waxed-paper photographs failed to develop properly. As far as we know Coghill exhibited only one other time, twelve Irish views in the Dublin International Exhibition in 1865.

References: "Dublin Photographic Society," *JPS* 4 (November 21, 1857), pp. 92–93; James Henry Coghill, *The Family of Coghill, 1377 to 1879* (Cambridge: Riverside Press, 1879)

Coles, James

Elected a member of the Photographic Society in London in 1854, Coles worked in waxed paper, showing three views in the society's 1858 exhibition, ranging from Canterbury to Ventnor to Llangollen. His residence, occupation, and other personal details are at present unknown.

Exhibited: 1858, London, Photographic Society

Collen, Henry *ill. 23*

1798–1875

A well-established miniature painter in London, Collen enjoyed social connections that helped him overcome his modest artistic achievements, becoming a miniature painter to Queen Victoria. Always possessed of an experimental bent, in 1841 he published his experiments on electrotyping a daguerreotype plate. But on seeing one of Talbot's calotype portraits in February 1841, Collen was hooked. Working with the inventor, he sought to perfect his photographs on paper and by the spring was laying plans for a photographic studio. In August of that year Collen acquired the first commercial license issued by Talbot. He also commissioned the eminent London optician Andrew Ross to make the first photographic lens designed in Britain. A reporter for the *Morning Post* who went to Collen to get his portrait taken in 1842 had obviously already been daguerreotyped, since he observed that for the sitter the experience was the same. He found the calotype results "very satisfactory . . . there is a rough air of truth about them, which reminds one of the first, and sometimes the best, sketches of an artist—a sort of free sepia, or rather lithotint drawing, full of broad effects

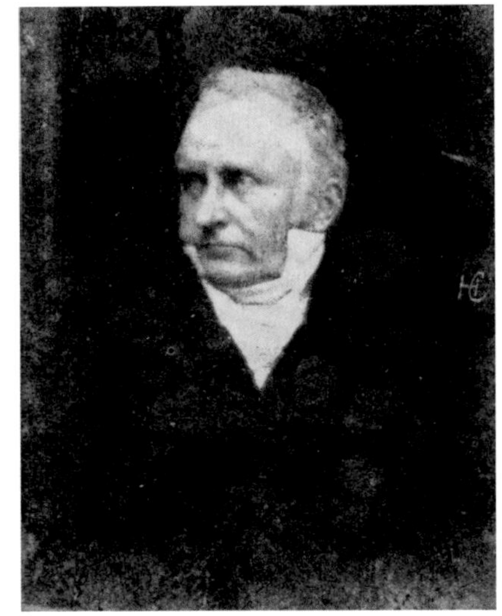

23. Henry Collen

and vigour. One of the advantages of the art is, that, from the original portrait, any number of fac-simile copies may be taken." A writer for the *Chemist* was also attracted to Collen's work: "Nothing can be more admirable than the extreme accuracy of the likenesses: they are free from the defect which constitutes the common objection to this kind of portraiture, namely, the ghastly corpse-like hue given to the complexion." As an artist, Collen was free in his retouching, something praised by his contemporaries, among them Sir David Brewster. However, this has undermined his modern reputation, since the photographic images have faded while the retouching ink has not, leading to what look like grotesque caricatures. Collen produced stereo portraits for Charles Wheatstone, but perhaps his most unusual commission was one he carried out for the Foreign Office on Christmas Day 1842. The Treaty of Nanking, ceding Hong Kong to British control, had just arrived in London, but there were no scribes who could copy the unfamiliar characters. Both as a record of the original and as a way to impress the Chinese with Western technological skills, Collen made photographic copies of the scroll. One was given to the queen and another sent back to China.

The daguerreotype captured the public's imagination in a way that calotype copies on paper could not, and Collen began to lose both money and Talbot's confidence. The relationship between the two men temporarily came under strain and Collen finally abandoned his calotype portrait business in 1844, but he and Talbot stayed in touch and possibly photographed together afterward. Collen never lost his interest in photography, assisting the Kew Observatory with daguerreotyping in 1846. In 1865 he proposed a color system, one which the American inventor and pioneer of color printing Frederic Eugene Ives acknowledged in his own work more than twenty years later. In common with many other photographers of the time, including Sir Arthur Conan Doyle, Collen became more and more engaged in spiritualism later in life, convinced, in his case, that "odic" light—spiritual emanations—could be recorded on photographic plates.

REFERENCES: "Calotype Portraits," *Morning Post* (London), March 11, 1842; "The Calotype Process," *Chemist* 3 (April 1842), p. 122; Larry J. Schaaf, "Henry Collen and the Treaty of Nanking," *History of Photography* 6 (October 1982), pp. 353–66; Schaaf, "Addenda to Henry Collen and the Treaty of Nanking," *History of Photography* 7 (April–June 1983), pp. 163–65; Rupert Derek Wood, "The Treaty of Nanking: Form and the Foreign Office, 1842–43," *Journal of Imperial and Commonwealth History* 24 (May 1996), pp. 181–96

Collie, William *ills. 24, 25, 26*

1810–1896

Born in Aberdeen, Collie trained as an artist and established himself as a painter and teacher of drawing in Jersey. Exactly when he became interested in photography is not known, but Collie clearly considered his first significant accomplishments to be the series of calotypes that he began in 1847. Formal calotype portraits were then rare, and studio portraits of ordinary people were even more uncommon. In 1847 the *Art-Union* was very impressed with Collie's calotypes of Channel Islands market women, "whose expressions, countenances, and picturesque costumes, are well suited for the purpose." The editor had "seen nothing at all comparable to them, except those of Mr. D. O. Hill, of Edinburgh," pointing out that both Hill and Collie were artists and that their photography benefited from this. Collie's portraits do recall the Newhaven series by Hill & Adamson, but differ from having been staged in a studio. Collie was well aware of the singularity of his portraits, explaining how difficult it was to achieve such naturalism with exposures of twenty seconds, the best he could manage. He contributed a group of photographs of "French and Jersey Market-women" to the Great Exhibition of 1851, and this seems partly to have been his undoing. For although his work had few parallels in Jersey, when hung next to the best work of Britain and the Continent, his prints appeared, according to the *Reports by the Juries*, "not all equally good; many of them are blotty and wanting in depth." Collie also incurred TALBOT's wrath when he started offering his unlicensed calotypes for sale in England. Turning to collodion, whose exposure times were more

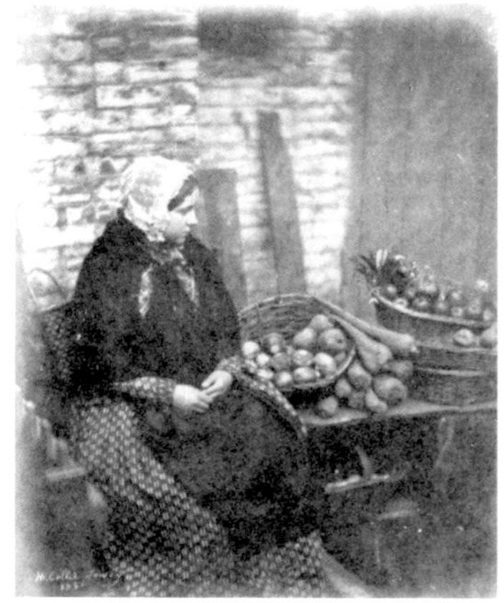

24. William Collie

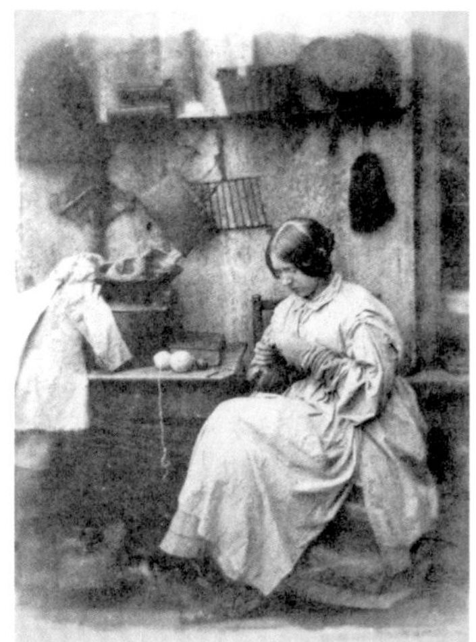

25. William Collie

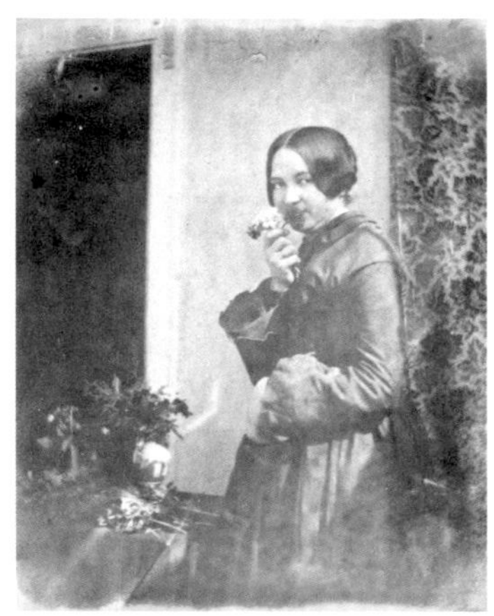

26. William Collie

suited to his subject matter and which was free from licensing problems, Collie continued with a long career in photography and painting in Jersey. He bequeathed his collection of paintings (now untraced) to a newly formed art gallery in his native Aberdeen.

EXHIBITED: 1851, London, Great Exhibition

REFERENCES: "Calotypes," *Art-Union* 9 (June 1, 1847), p. 231; James Glaisher, "Class X," in *Reports by the Juries on the Subjects in the Thirty Classes into which the Exhibition Was Divided* (London: Printed for the Royal Commissioners by William Clowes & Sons, 1852), p. 279; "Early Calotypes," *Photographic Journal* 6 (February 15, 1860), pp. 166–67; Jonathon Carter, "'A Theft from the Heavens': The Beginnings of Photography in Jersey," *127th Annual Bulletin* (Société Jersiaise, Saint Helier, Jersey) 28, pt. 2 (2002), pp. 226–33

Collings, F.

In the 1854 exhibition of the Royal Infirmary Fund in Dundee, Collings displayed several waxed-paper studies and a calotype, *Early English Capital Walls.* No personal details are known of him (or her) and no tie has been established to the photographer WILLIAM THOMAS COLLINGS.

EXHIBITED: 1854, London, Photographic Society; 1854, Dundee, Royal Infirmary Fund

Collings, William Thomas

1823–1882

Rev. Collings came from a wealthy and extended Guernsey family. His marriage to the daughter of a famous Guernsey archaeologist made him a relative of Dr. THOMAS LUKIS MANSELL. He briefly served as a curate at Wells Cathedral, and it is from this period that his known waxed-paper photography dates. In the 1854 exhibition of the Photographic Society in London, Collings showed numerous views from Wells, submitting many of them again to the Royal Infirmary Fund exhibition in Dundee the same year. His waxed-paper negatives, which he sensitized in the morning before setting out to photograph, were an impressive 24 x 18 inches. Nothing more is known of his photography, but he spent his considerable inheritance wisely for the defense and improvement of Guernsey. When the island's silver mines failed, Collings became quite active in promoting the new industry of tourism, undoubtedly relying on photography to present Guernsey's glories.

EXHIBITED: 1854, London, Photographic Society; 1854, Dundee, Royal Infirmary Fund

Reference: T. L. Mansell, "Gravelly Wax Negatives," *Notes and Queries*, May 13, 1854, p. 456; L. James Marr, *Guernsey People* (Chichester: Phillimore, 1984), pp. 37–38

Colls, Lebbeus
1818–1897
The photographs of Lebbeus Colls are largely unknown, but RICHARD WILLATS preserved a calotype taken near Windsor in his album, credited to "Mr. A. Cocke and Mr. Colls, London." With his brother RICHARD COLLS he exhibited "several sun-pictures on paper" in the Great Exhibition of 1851; according to the *Reports by the Juries*, the "views of Windsor Castle and Stoke Church deserve high commendation." After TALBOT secured an injunction against Richard Colls in early 1852, his brother continued to work with JOSEPH CUNDALL, who had taken over Richard Colls's Gallery of Modern Art, rechristening it the Photographic Institution. Lebbeus Colls continued as a dealer of fine art.

Exhibited: 1851, London, Great Exhibition

Reference: James Glaisher, "Class X," in *Reports by the Juries on the Subjects in the Thirty Classes into which the Exhibition Was Divided* (London: Printed for the Royal Commissioners by William Clowes & Sons, 1852), p. 278; Richard Willats Photograph Album, Princeton University Library

Colls, Richard
1802–1880
Colls was a calotypist only briefly, if at all, and his photographs are unknown today, but there is no doubt that it was the Talbotype that got him into difficulty. A London artist and picture dealer, Colls displayed with his brother LEBBEUS COLLS "several sun-pictures on paper" in the Great Exhibition of 1851. The judges were not overly impressed; in the *Reports by the Juries*, the pictures were described as "rather blotty in appearance, but . . . good in colour." In 1848 Colls applied to TALBOT for a calotype license to be shared with his brother and ROBERT BINGHAM. The price was deemed too high, but Colls and Bingham proceeded without a license nevertheless. Eventually, in January 1852, Talbot secured an injunction against Colls and his Gallery of Modern Art, prohibiting them from producing or selling photographs on paper. Although Bingham was a pioneer in glass-negative photography, it is likely that at this early date Colls and Bingham were still employing the calotype. The Colls injunction would be the legal basis for the later, better-known action against Sylvester Laroche.

Exhibited: 1851, London, Great Exhibition

References: James Glaisher, "Class X," in *Reports by the Juries on the Subjects in the Thirty Classes into which the Exhibition Was Divided* (London: Printed for the Royal Commissioners by William Clowes & Sons, 1852), p. 278; Rupert Derek Wood, "J. B. Reade, F.R.S., and the Early History of Photography, Part II: Gallic Acid and Talbot's Calotype Patent," *Annals of Science* 27 (March 1971), pp. 52–53, and passim

Compton, Joseph, Jr.
b. 1821
Compton was a calico printer for the firm of Thomas Hoyle & Sons in Manchester, well placed both professionally and in location to learn about photography. In the 1856 exhibition of the Manchester Photographic Society, he placed six calotypes, three of which were studies of Haddon Hall and its grounds, while the other three were architectural views in Surrey and in Derbyshire. To date, no other record of Compton's photographic activity has been found.

Exhibited: 1856, Manchester, Photographic Society

Contencin, James
1814–1879
Serious amateur photographers often regarded their art to be the making of the negative, and left the printing to specialists. As a stationer in London, Contencin was ideally positioned to observe the increasing demand for papers intended for photographic use, and he became a professional photographic printer during the 1850s. Although most of his extensive exhibition work was in collodion, he contributed a calotype copy of a monumental tablet to the 1854 exhibition of the Photographic Society in London. In 1860, even as Contencin published photographic views of Streetley Church in Derbyshire, he was already aware of the changes looming for photography. Three years earlier he had begun experimenting with producing photographic woodblocks, in which the image was created by the sun but the final engraving was done by hand. He contributed three of these to the 1858 exhibition of Photographic Society in London. Contencin also displayed several photolithographic copies of drawings in the 1862 International Exhibition in London.

Exhibited: 1854, London, Photographic Society

References: James Contencin, "Photography on Wood for Engraving," *Photographic News* 5 (March 1, 1861), pp. 100–102; Anthony Hamber, "Photography and the Ecclesiological Society," *Ecclesiology Today*, no. 28 (May 2002), pp. 33–44

Cook, Mr.
In an 1857 meeting of the Liverpool Photographic Society, "Mr. Cook presented, for insertion in the Society's album, a number of well-executed prints from wax-paper negatives. The prints, which were passed round for examination, and generally admired, included views of Furness Abbey, Conway Castle, and old Bidston Church." Cook employed GEORGE ROBERT FITT's formula for waxed-paper negatives but then printed them on albumen paper. In reply to a question from James Alexander Forrest, Cook explained his feeling that "the English paper made infinitely better pictures than the French paper, the tone being so much superior." Although references to him are numerous, they always refer simply to "Mr. Cook," and no details of his personal life are known.

Reference: "Liverpool Photographic Society," *LMPJ* 4 (December 1, 1857), p. 256

Copland, Edward A.
b. 1806
A lawyer in Essex, Copland took up photography as a hobby. During a tour of South America in 1855, he modified the process developed by JOHN STEWART (1814–1887) of using a vacuum pump to prepare paper for negatives. This insured a more complete penetration of the chemicals into the fibers, and Copland adopted it to meet the special demands of working in a hot climate. Nothing else is known of his photographic work or his travels.

Reference: Edward A. Copland, "Process for a Hot Climate," *JPS* 3 (May 21, 1856), p. 52

Corey, Charles
b. 1811
In 1855 Corey was a surgeon and dentist in Liverpool when he delivered a paper, "The Waxed Paper Process," to the Liverpool Photographic Society. In addition "he illustrated by performing very successfully" during the meeting all the operations involved by developing two negatives that he had taken earlier in the day. Corey was a good friend of GEORGE ROBERT BERRY, the undisputed driving force of the society, and he became editor of the *Liverpool Photographic Journal* and was later secretary of the Liverpool Photographic Society. He displayed examples using FREDERICK TOWNSHEND's process in the 1854 exhibition at the Royal Institution in Liverpool. Despite all this activity, by the time of the 1861 census he had returned to dentistry, in Oswestry, Shropshire.

Exhibited: 1854, Liverpool, Photographic Society

References: "The Waxed Paper Process," *LPJ* 2 (May 12, 1855), pp. 60–61; James Alexander Forrest, "Historical Notes of What Liverpool Has Done in the Art-Science of Photography," *BJP* 35 (February 3, 1883), pp. 72–74

Cowley, H. C.

Cowley left few traces of his life, but those clues that do exist indicate a serious interest in photography in India. In 1855, he wrote from the outpost of Cawnpore (Kanpur) that "Indian photographers would do well to turn more of their attention to the 'calotype' process, which is so simple and certain in its effects, and far less expensive than any of the waxed-paper ones." Two years later, during the rebellion of 1857, Cawnpore came under siege, leading to a massacre, which Cowley obviously survived, for in 1860 he published a tract of practical instructions for photography in India.

Reference: H. C. Cowley, "Photography in India," *JPS* 2 (May 21, 1855), p. 173

Cox, William Joseph

b. 1819

Elected a member of the Photographic Society in their inaugural year of 1853, Cox belonged to a family of opticians active in Devonport, near Plymouth. In the 1854 photographic exhibition at the Royal Institution in Liverpool, Cox's waxed-paper views were praised by the reviewer for the *Liverpool Photographic Journal* as "wonderfully minute and distinct." In the 1856 exhibition of the Photographic Society in London, Cox displayed waxed-paper scenes of Devonport and Port Eliot, along with a view of the gardens and the cliffs at Mount Edgcumbe. This was the home of Caroline Mount Edgcumbe, Talbot's artistic half sister, who had so greatly influenced his early efforts in photography. In 1853 Cox's father, also a William and also an optician, was commissioned to make a special camera for the Royal Yacht.

Exhibited: 1854, Liverpool, Photographic Society; 1856, London, Photographic Society

Reference: "Photographic Exhibition at the Royal Institution," *LPJ* 1 (October 14, 1854), p. 139

Craddock, Thomas

b. 1812

A private tutor in Cambridgeshire, Craddock displayed an impressive group of photographs in the Great Exhibition of 1851, including views of Peterborough Cathedral, new iron and wooden railway bridges, and copies of prints and paintings. Although his photographic process was not specified, a hint of his working methods and zeal was given in the *Cambridgeshire Directory* for that year: "Mr. Craddock has been honoured with the correspondence of Sir David Brewster, from the superior talent and chemical research displayed by him in the Calotype process applied to the production of pictures by the Talbotype system." Craddock was interested in the application of illustration to publications. In 1849 he expanded his 1833 *History of Wisbech* into a fourteen-part series heavily illustrated with engravings. In the 1855 exhibition of the London Photographic Institution, Craddock showed views of Peterborough, Cambridge, Ely, and Wisbech done by a "paper-process." He continued his activity in the 1856 and 1857 exhibitions of the Photographic Society in London, showing numerous Talbotypes, mostly of ecclesiastical architecture.

Exhibited: 1851, London, Great Exhibition; 1855, London, Photographic Institution; 1856 and 1857, London, Photographic Society

References: Neil Walker and Thomas Craddock, *The History of Wisbech and the Fens* (Wisbech: Richard Walker, 1849); *History, Gazetteer, and Directory of Cambridgeshire* (Peterborough: R. Gardner, 1851), p. 649

Crake, William Hamilton

b. 1825

With his multiple responsibilities as a director of the Bank of Madras, a committee member of the Madras Chamber of Commerce, and an East India merchant, Crake traveled often between India and England. Crake's first public showing of photographs was a group of three prints from waxed-paper negatives displayed in the 1857 exhibition of the Photographic Society of Bengal. In the 1859 exhibition of the Photographic Society in London, his extensive showing of "plain-paper process" views was drawn from his work in India, including not only architectural and archaeological views, but also the wreck of the barque *Alhambra* on the beach at Madras. In the 1860 exhibition of the Madras Photographic Society, Crake's large waxed-paper views from nature were so impressive that the council of the society chose one for distribution to subscribers that year. By the time of the 1871 census, Crake was back living in London.

Exhibited: 1857, Calcutta, Photographic Society; 1859, London, Photographic Society

Crawford, William Henry Stanley

1823–1883

A partner in a Bombay shipping firm, Crawford operated a daguerreotype studio there from 1854, and later a photographic business. In 1853 he was involved in a spirited debate with Antoine Claudet over who could claim priority for an improvement to the Daguerreotype process. By 1855 Crawford's interest had begun to turn toward paper negatives and he showed a large group before the Photographic Society of Bombay, of which he was secretary. The prints he showed in the society's 1856 exhibition were so admired that the negatives were examined, bringing pleasure to the council, which, according to the *Journal of the Photographic Society of Bombay*, had "no hesitation in saying they are, as a whole, the finest and best collection we ever saw," also noting that Crawford had "long borne a high name as a Daguerreotypist, and . . . some of his best specimens were on view." In 1859 Crawford detailed his approach to making waxed-paper negatives in hot climates, pointing out "that the various processes recommended by a variety of practitioners in England, present each and all some serious obstacle to the Indian amateur." After a brief period of teaching photography classes at the Elphinstone Institute in Bombay, Crawford appears to have abandoned photography, managing a steam navigation company and later becoming a coffee planter.

Exhibited: 1856, Bombay Photographic Society

References: William Henry Stanley Crawford, "A New Mode of Conducting the Daguerreotype Process," *JPS* 1 (September 21, 1853), pp. 105–6 (for the response by Claudet, see "On the Introduction of Mercurial Vapour into the Camera in Daguerreotypy," *JPS* 1 [October 21, 1853], pp. 117–19); Crawford, "On the Waxed Paper Process," *Journal of the Photographic Society of Bombay*, no. 2 (February 15, 1855), pp. 29–33; "Cursory Notes Taken at the Exhibition of Photographs, Bombay, February 1856," *Journal of the Photographic Society of Bombay*, nos. 13–17 (February–June 1856), pp. 26, 27, 29–30; Crawford, "The Waxed Paper Process for Hot Climates," *Photographic News* 2 (August 5, 1859), pp. 254–56

Crawley, Charles and/or Catherine

Several nature prints of leaves, inscribed "C. Crawley" on the verso, were offered in a 1985 auction and are now in a private collection. Accompanying these was a solitary salted paper print, made from a calotype negative and inscribed "Group in Vicarage Garden, Hartpury, August, 1846"; it is monogrammed "C. C." and is heavily retouched in ink. From 1838 to 1856, the vicar of Hartpury, Gloucester, was the Reverend Charles Crawley-Boevey (1780–1856), who was also a justice of the peace. With their flexible work schedules and enthusiasm for investigating the natural world, clergymen like Rev. Crawley often took up pursuits such as photography. On the other hand, the vicar's wife was Catherine, née Yonge (b. 1789), and photograms of leaves were particularly attractive to women photographers. Either "C. C."—husband or wife—is thus a possible identification, and perhaps they even worked together as a team.

Reference: Sale cat., Christie's, London, October 31, 1985, lot 168

Critchett, Charles
b. 1837
As the surprisingly young assistant secretary of the Society of Arts, Critchett was ideally placed to monitor the progress of photography. He started out by contributing a single collodion photograph to the 1855 exhibition of the Photographic Society in London. The following year, Critchett exhibited three calotypes and three collodion images, but shortly after this he took an interesting turn. Most photographers moved with the times, eventually phasing out paper negatives in favor of glass. Instead, at the society's 1857 exhibition, Critchett showed only waxed-paper photographs, all views of Cambridge architecture. At the 1862 International Exhibition in London, Critchett was still showing architectural views from waxed-paper negatives.

Exhibited: 1856 and 1857, London, Photographic Society; 1862, London, International Exhibition

Crookes, William
1832–1919
The only one of twenty-one siblings to display the slightest interest in science, Sir William Crookes emerged as one of the most influential scientists and scientific writers of his generation. As an assistant to William Hoffman at the Royal College of Chemistry, he met Charles Wheatstone and Michael Faraday, whose combined influence directed the young man toward the study of chemical physics. According to Fournier d'Albe's biography, late in life Crookes recalled: "I was working at photography in 1848, and not long after I had the privilege of being shown the Talbotype process by the master himself. One of my most highly prized relics is a copy of Talbot's *Pencil of Nature*." Crookes worked in Nicolaas Henneman's London studio, taking some of the earliest stereo photographs for Wheatstone. In 1852 he published his own adaptation of Gustave Le Gray's waxed-paper process, specially adapted for rapid exposures in the field, in *Notes and Queries*. As he wrote on page 1 of his *Hand Book* in 1857, Crookes believed that "the Waxed Paper Process appears to me to be more particularly applicable to the ordinary requirements of the tourist or amateur in general than any other paper process whatever." In 1854 Crookes became director of the meteorological department at the Radcliffe Observatory in Oxford, using waxed-paper negatives to continuously record the findings of instruments. He also took some of the first photographs of the moon. Although Crookes probably took few photographs for himself, he was enthusiastic about the possibilities of the art and in 1857 published *A Hand Book to the Waxed Paper Process in Photography*. The next year, as editor of the *Photographic News*, Crookes recalled his early contacts with Talbot and included actual examples of the inventor's photoglyphic engraving process, understanding that the future of photographic reproduction lay in printer's ink. Crookes was a mass of contradictions, often as interested in business as he was in science. He lost a brother at sea in the 1870s and became increasingly convinced not only that séances were genuine but that the spiritual "auras" conjured up by mediums could be measured scientifically. Despite the discomfort this new enthusiasm caused among his scientific friends, Crookes did not abandon serious scientific research, and his work on cathode-ray tubes led to the discovery of X-rays and ultimately a complete shift in our understanding of chemistry and physics.

Exhibited: 1858, London, Photographic Society

References: William Crookes, "The Wax-Paper Process," *Notes and Queries* 6 (November 6, 1852), p. 443; Crookes, "Description of the Wax-Paper Photographic Process, Employed for the Photo-Meteorographic Registrations at the Radcliffe Observatory, Oxford," *LMPJ*, n.s., 1 (July 1, 1857), pp. 138–40; Crookes, *A Hand Book to the Waxed Paper Process in Photography* (London: Chapman and Hall, 1857); Crookes, "On the Calotype Process," *Photographic News* 1 (October 1 and 8, 1858), pp. 38, 51; Crookes, "Simplicity of the Talbotype Process," *Photographic News* 1 (November 12, 1858), pp. 119–20; *BJP* 66 (April 11, 1919), p. 189 (obituary); *BJPA*, 1920, pp. 339–40 (obituary); E. E. Fournier d'Albe, *The Life of Sir William Crookes, O.M., F.R.S.* (London: T. Fisher Unwin, 1923), p. 389

Croucher, John Honour, Jr.
b. 1811
One can never be certain whether the authors of early manuals on photography were actually practicing photographers. Six of Croucher's energiatype negatives (done by Robert Hunt's process) were preserved by Richard Willats in his album, almost certainly indicating that Croucher, a schoolmaster in London, practiced what he preached. In 1845 Willats published Croucher's *Practical Hints on the Daguerreotype*, which quickly went into a second edition. Even more lasting was its companion volume, *Plain Directions for Obtaining Pictures by the Calotype, Energiatype, and Other Processes on Paper*, which went through several editions in Britain and the United States, supplemented in 1853 with a chapter by Gustave Le Gray. Other than those preserved in the Willats album (in the collections at Princeton), no other surviving photographs by Croucher are known, but he undoubtedly produced many.

Reference: John Honour Croucher, Jr., *Plain Directions for Obtaining Pictures by the Calotype, Energiatype, and Other Processes on Paper, including the Chrysotype, Cyanotype, Chromatype, etc., etc., all the Latest Improvements* (London: T. & R. Willats, 1845)

Cumine, George
b. 1815
In the 1856 exhibition of the Photographic Society of Scotland in Edinburgh, Captain Cumine showed eight calotypes of Bruges (half with the sky retouched); the *Scotsman* pronounced them "admirable views of the picturesque houses of Bruges." He also displayed two calotypes of Edinburgh Castle and one view taken near Cheltenham. Scottish by birth, Cumine was a member of the society and is known to have lived both in Edinburgh and in Jersey. His daughter was born in India, so at some point he may have benefited from the intense interest in the waxed-paper process shown by photographers in that hot climate.

Exhibited: 1856, Edinburgh, Photographic Society of Scotland

Reference: *Scotsman* (Edinburgh), July 12, 1856, p. 3

Cumming, John
b. 1828
A native of Ayr, Cumming first showed his photographs in the 1852 exhibition of the Society of Arts, employing calotype negatives to present views of Tunbridge Wells. By 1854 Cumming's paper negatives shared billing with his collodion work, and by 1861 he was established as an artist and photographer in Edinburgh, soon opening a professional portrait gallery on Princes Street. His "Cumming's Patent Automatic Photo Delivery Machine" was advertised as capable of mass-producing views in a carte-de-visite format, but there is no record that it was ever patented or even used. His son, W. Skeoch Cumming, became a well-known painter.

Exhibited: 1852, London, Society of Arts; 1853–54, first touring exhibition, Society of Arts (London); 1854, London, Photographic Society; 1854, second touring exhibition, Society of Arts (London)

Cundall, Joseph
1818–1895
Trained as a printer in Norfolk, Cundall came to London at the age of sixteen. The young man took an interest in illustrated children's books, first as an author, soon as a printer and publisher. He worked with Henry (later Sir Henry) Cole and many other budding artists who would later become royal academicians. Cundall is perhaps best known for his invention of the Christmas card in 1846. With his interest in book illustration, it is not surprising that Cundall would turn to photography. At a meeting of London's Graphic Society in 1847, his photographs were displayed to great effect. The *Athenaeum* declared: "Nature was seen vieing with Art in the Portfolio of Calotypes, or Talbotypes, contributed by Mr. Cundall—containing views of Exeter, Canterbury, and other cathedrals—and displaying all the beauty of Gothic detail with the solemnity of effect which their time-stained fronts wear. Views of some Dutch towns and rivers, and transcripts of shipping and other craft, gave a good idea of the fidelity with which such matters are representable by the powers of this art. In the landscapes we saw a great advance." Cundall joined the Calotype Society in 1847 and the Photographic Society in 1854. He exhibited regularly, sometimes with partners, usually in collodion but also displaying works in waxed paper in 1854, and he took part in the Great Exhibition of 1851.

Cundall was a pioneer in photographic book illustration, a venture fraught with peril in the days when print stability was far from assured. THOMAS SUTTON, the outspoken editor of *Photographic Notes*, said in 1857: "Mr. Cundall has been the most spirited adventurer in this line, and he has contrived, by sun printing . . . to illustrate two editions of Mr. Delamotte's 'Practical Photography.' The negatives were superb. . . . Nothing could be finer. But what has become of the prints? That in my copy has turned so yellow that it makes one sick to look at it." Active in photography throughout his career, Cundall accepted the post of supervisor of publications at the South Kensington Museum, London, in 1866, continuing in this civil service position until close to the end of his life.

EXHIBITED: 1853, London, Photographic Institution; 1853–54, first touring exhibition, Society of Arts (London); 1854, second touring exhibition, Society of Arts (London); 1856, Manchester, Photographic Society

REFERENCES: "The Graphic Society," *Athenaeum* (December 11, 1847), p. 1278; [Thomas Sutton], in *Photographic Notes* 2 (March 15, 1857), p. 104; *Times* (London), January 21, 1895, p. 6, col. c (obituary); Ruari McLean, *Joseph Cundall, a Victorian Publisher: Notes on His Life and a Check-List of His Books* (Pinner: Private Libraries Association, 1976)

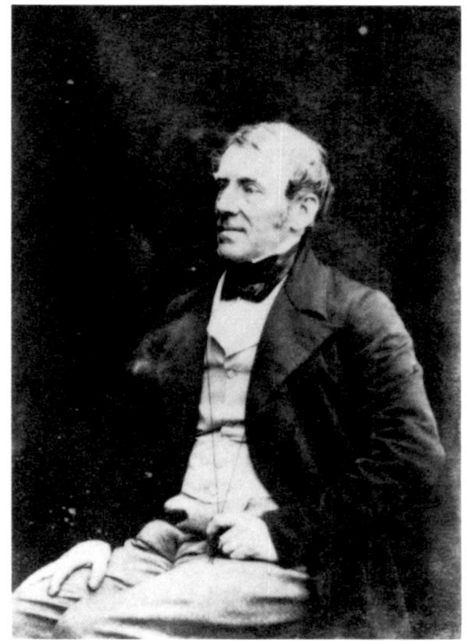
27. Portrait of George Smith Cundell

Cundell, George Smith *ill. 27*
1798–1882
Born in Scotland and reverently addressed as "Most Worthy Master" by the great engineer James Nasmyth, Cundell was not only a pioneering calotypist but also critically shaped the direction of paper photography in its early days. A banker, keen politician, and agent for West Indian estates, Cundell was based in London while maintaining important connections in Edinburgh. The most scientific of the Cundell brothers, he published a number of articles on photography, none more influential than "On the Practice of the Calotype Process of Photography" in 1844. TALBOT did not intend to shroud the practice of calotypy in obscurity, indeed just the opposite. However, he was not aware of how his own unconscious and habitual traits entered into his expertise, and many who tried to follow his deceptively simple instructions were frustrated in their attempts. In his 1844 article Cundell explained the creation of a calotype negative in a clear, practical, and complete manner. We will never know how many calotypists owed their success to this article, but the testimonials are plentiful. One contemporary quoted in *Humphrey's Journal* stated that "Amateurs date their success from the time Mr. Cundell published." Cundell's instructions were based on extensive practical experience, for he had produced hundreds of calotype negatives and was a member of the original Edinburgh Calotype Club. Unlike his brother, HENRY CUNDELL, he never participated in public exhibitions. Nevertheless, George Cundell had a major impact on the early history of photography as one of the driving forces behind the groundbreaking and enormous exhibition of photographs at the Society of Arts in 1852.

REFERENCES: George Smith Cundell, "On the Practice of the Calotype Process of Photography," *London, Edinburgh, and Dublin Philosophical Magazine and Journal of Science* 24 (May 1844), pp. 321–32; Cundell, "On the Gallo-Nitrate of Silver of Mr. Fox Talbot, and Its Action upon Iodised Paper," *London, Edinburgh, and Dublin Philosophical Magazine and Journal of Science* 29 (August 1846), pp. 101–3; "Progress of Photography," *Humphrey's Journal* 6 (August 15, 1854), p. 133; Sara Stevenson, Julie Lawson, and Michael Gray, *The Photography of John Muir Wood, 1805–1892: An Accomplished Amateur* (Edinburgh: Scottish National Portrait Gallery; London: Dirk Nishen, 1988)

Cundell, Henry
1810–1886
Cundell shared a passion for calotypy with his older bachelor brother, GEORGE SMITH CUNDELL, and like him was born in Scotland but made his living as a banker in London. Both brothers were prolific creators of calotype negatives, but whereas George greatly influenced the field with his writings, Henry Cundell was a major contributor to the photographic exhibitions of the day. In the 1852 exhibition of the Society of Arts in London, for which his brother was a driving force, Henry showed a dozen views of landscape and architecture in England and Wales. An entry in the 1853 exhibition of the Photographic Institution in London was *St. Paul's Cathedral, from the River*, while the next year Cundell contributed views of Wales to Society of Arts touring exhibitions.

EXHIBITED: 1852, London, Society of Arts; 1853, London, Photographic Institution; 1853–54, first touring exhibition, Society of Arts (London); 1854, second touring exhibition, Society of Arts (London)

REFERENCE: Sara Stevenson, Julie Lawson, and Michael Gray, *The Photography of John Muir Wood 1805–1892: An Accomplished Amateur* (Edinburgh: Scottish National Portrait Gallery; London: Dirk Nishen, 1988)

Cunningham, James
b. 1817
A solicitor in Dunse, Scotland, Cunningham contributed photographs to the 1854 exhibition at the Architectural Institute in Edinburgh. He joined the Photographic Society of Scotland at its founding in 1856. In the society's exhibition that year Cunningham showed ten works (all waxed paper save for one collodion), mostly views around his home of Briary Bank, Dunse. By the time of the society's 1858 exhibition, Cunningham had apparently

abandoned collodion entirely, exhibiting a wider variety of subjects in waxed paper only, ranging from views of Berwick to his *Study of an Old Dog Kennel.* Although Cunningham maintained his membership in the society until his resignation in 1864, these were his last exhibited works. In exhibition listings his name was sometimes given the traditional spelling of Cunninghame.

Exhibited: 1856 and 1858, Edinburgh, Photographic Society of Scotland

Reference: "Photographic Exhibition," *Scotsman* (Edinburgh), March 8, 1854, p. 3

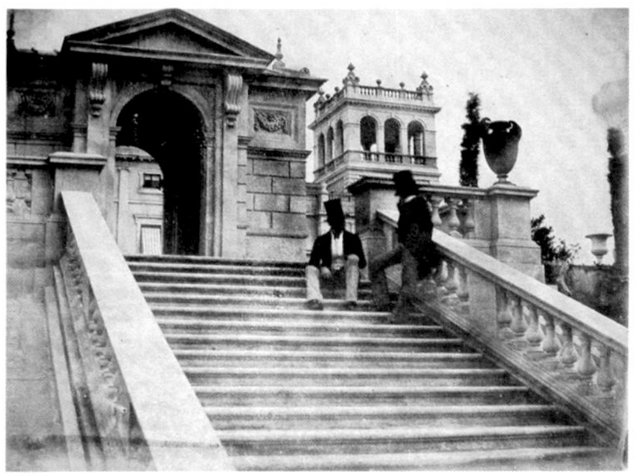

28. Alfred Capel Cure

Cure, Alfred Capel *ill. 28*
1826–1896
Cure joined the army at the age of eighteen, rising through the ranks in active service to the level of major in 1855. By the time he bought himself out of the army in 1867 he was a colonel in the Grenadier Guards, and thereafter he generally styled himself Col. Capel Cure. His earliest known photographs, dated 1850, are calotypes preserved in an album titled "Photographic Experiments." Cure briefly experimented with the collodion process in March 1854, but during his extensive tours of duty with the army he remained faithful to the calotype. Many of his photographs were occasioned by his military assignments. He made panoramic studies of Gibraltar's harbor and in Ireland photographed not only its antiquities but also fellow officers, while on nonmilitary travels he recorded ecclesiastical architecture and country houses throughout Britain and northern Europe. Some of these tours may have been made in the company of his uncle ROBERT HENRY CHENEY. They collaborated so closely and their work is so intermixed in surviving albums that assigning specific authorship is sometimes difficult. While it is clear that the two men learned and practiced photography together, and that Cheney had at least an intellectual interest in photography by 1845, Cure was more likely the instigator and certainly was the more prolific photographer. His preferred method of displaying his work was in albums, and it appears that he never exhibited publicly. His last known photograph is dated 1860, a time when amateur photography in general was in decline. But perhaps Cure simply gave up photography about the same time his aging uncle abandoned the art. Some decades later, Cure accidentally killed himself while dynamiting the roots of trees in his park.

Reference: *Times* (London), July 31, 1896, p. 5, col. F (obituary)

Currey, Francis Edmund
1814–1896
Born in England, Currey was called to the bar in 1838 and the following year succeeded his father as the agent of Lismore Castle in Ireland, owned by the Duke of Devonshire. With the duke largely absent from the estate, Currey was treated as lord of the manor, with ample time to practice photography as an amateur, a pursuit he took up in the latter part of the 1840s. Currey was an experimentalist, taking full advantage of the resources and production facilities of a country estate. Much of his early work was in calotype, with the subjects mostly local, including the people whose work Currey supervised and the land over which he had stewardship. He also built a glasshouse studio on the estate. In 1853 Currey was elected one of the first members of the Photographic Society in London. He became a member of the Photographic Exchange Club two years later, having by this time converted to wet collodion, and in 1862 was elected to membership in the Amateur Photographic Association. Between 1856 and 1865 Currey submitted wet-collodion views to exhibitions in London and Dublin, and he maintained an interest in photography until late in life.

References: *Photographic Journal,* n.s., 21 (October 31, 1896), p. 46 (obituary); Edward Chandler, *Photography in Ireland: The Nineteenth Century* (Dublin: Edmund Burke, 2001)

Curwen, Robert Ewing
A resident of St. Andrews, Curwen became a member of the Photographic Society of Scotland in 1859. An album compiled by him that emerged at auction in 1976 contained not only his own prints, which were made from waxed-paper negatives, but also a significant collection of works by others, ranging from views of the Great Exhibition of 1851 to later carbon prints of the Middle East. It also included an extensive series of portraits by the St. Andrews calotypist THOMAS RODGER. Nothing is known of Curwen's occupation or any other personal details, but he was possibly the Robert Ewing Curwen born in 1841 whose father of the same name died in 1854.

Reference: Sale cat., Sotheby's, London, October 29, 1976, lot 49

Daubeny, Charles Giles Bridle
1795–1867
The professor of botany, chemistry, and rural economy at Oxford, Dr. Daubeny was, according to *The History of the Daubeney Family,* "very clever with his head but awkward with his hands," the latter perhaps not the most promising attribute for a photographer. Nevertheless, he took an immediate interest in the scientific possibilities of photography. Daubeny was a cofounder of the British Association for the Advancement of Science, the annual meeting of amateur scientists that would provide such an important forum for photography in its earliest days. By the time the association met in August 1839, Daubeny had already invented a self-registering photometer, using photogenic paper to measure solar output. TALBOT presented his second and largest exhibition of photography at this 1839 meeting, and subsequently he and Daubeny became friends. Thereafter Talbot visited the professor often at Oxford, photographing the laboratory in the Botanic Gardens, a facility built on the ancient Physic Garden that Daubeny had only recently persuaded the reluctant dons at Magdalen to accept. In 1842 Talbot sent him examples of his work to show during the professor's chemistry lectures. A great traveler who was widely known in scientific circles, Daubeny undoubtedly did much to promote photography, even if it was not an art he practiced very often himself.

References: "Ninth Meeting of the British Association for the Advancement of Science," *Athenaeum,* August 31, 1839, p. 643; *Proceedings of the Royal Society* 17 (1868–69), pp. lxxiv–lxxxiv (obituary); Giles Daubeney, *The History of the Daubeney Family* (Pontypool: Griffin Press, 1951)

Davey, Morris Fatima
b. 1820
An Essex surgeon, Dr. Davey seems to have been a typical example of a highly accomplished amateur who practiced photography largely for his own pleasure. In 1853 he described his "simple method" of iodizing paper in the *Journal of the Photographic Society.* JOHN STEWART

(1814–1887) had promoted the use of a vacuum pump to ensure that the paper fibers thoroughly imbibed the chemicals, but Davey felt that a simple presoak in distilled water or rainwater promoted iodizing nearly as effectively. It is clear from this that Davey had thoroughly mastered the waxed-paper process, although he apparently never exhibited his photographs.

Reference: Morris Fatima Davey, letter in *JPS* 1 (October 21, 1853), p. 127

29. Thomas Davies

Davies, Thomas *ill. 29*

1832–1880

An author and glass manufacturer in Warrington, Davies was also an enthusiastic contributor to the photographic exhibitions. According to the *Warrington Gazette,* he died prematurely, but "had it not been for his delicate health, it is possible that he might have taken rank amongst the scientific men of the century, for he was possessed of an acute intellect and had considerable mathematical and analytical power." Davies combined the powers of science with those of aesthetics, perhaps influenced in the latter by his older brother William, a poet and painter. Shortly after the calotype was released from patent restrictions in 1852, Davies took up the process, improving its working methods to the point where he was able to make a significant contribution to the *Liverpool Photographic Journal* in 1854. In addition to local exhibitions in Warrington, he displayed large numbers of calotype studies of architecture and nature in the 1856 exhibitions of the Photographic Society of Scotland and the Manchester Photographic Society. Davies also contributed a calotype to *The Photographic Album for the Year 1857,* a wood scene with, as the caption stated, an "exposure twenty-five minutes (usually five) owing to the foliage." By 1858 he had switched over to collodion albumen negatives and continued to exhibit extensively. Perhaps influenced by his early experience in the glass trade, Davies also became a pioneer in the photography of crystals under the influence of polarized light.

Exhibited: 1856, Manchester, Photographic Society; 1856, Edinburgh, Photographic Society

References: "Liverpool Photographic Society," *LPJ* 1 (June 10, 1854), pp. 72–74; *Warrington Gazette,* January 17, 1880, p. 5 (obituary)

Davis, Thomas Sebastian

When a newcomer to photography wrote in to the *Photographic News* in 1858 expressing bewilderment at how to keep the sensitive paper supported in the camera, Davis came to the rescue. Speaking with the confident voice of experience, he suggested a series of pins rather than the more common glass pressure plate. None of Davis's work has yet come to light, perhaps, as he confessed to the *Photographic News,* because "for some time past my ardour for talbotype experiments has vanished before the fascinations of collodion." The published version of his letter revealed neither his residence nor his occupation.

Reference: Thomas Sebastian Davis, "To Hold the Sensitive Calotype Paper in the Dark Slide," *Photographic News* 1 (November 5, 1858), p. 107

Dawson, George

1821–1897

Dawson was widely known among his peers, not only because of his long-standing position as the professor of photography at King's College, London, but also as an editor of the *British Journal of Photography.* His numerous publications on photography remain standard reference works on the period to this day. In 1857 Dawson exhibited considerable personal expertise in the waxed-paper process in a talk given to the North London Photographic Association. He was particularly active in the quest for a method of preventing the fading of photographic prints.

References: George Dawson, "The Waxed-Paper Process," *JPS* 4 (October 21 and November 21, 1857), pp. 53–56, 95–96; Dawson, *A Manual of Photography Founded on Hardwich's Photographic Chemistry,* 8th ed. (London: J. & A. Churchill, 1873)

Delamotte, Philip Henry

1821–1889

Born into a Huguenot family, Delamotte was inspired by his father, the drawing master at the Royal Military College at Sandhurst. His two brothers were also artists, and he quickly became a skilled illustrator and engraver, contributing engravings to the Society of Arts. His watercolor landscapes are picturesque, yet still realistic and not overly stylized. Photography eventually emerged as Delamotte's major passion and artistic outlet. With truth to nature the goal, the new art also comfortably complemented the range of his artistic endeavors. In 1850 Delamotte, as described in a publication that year, "availed himself of that ingenious invention the Talbotype" to reproduce copies of Roman art newly discovered in Cirencester. Soon after, the writer and architect M. Digby Wyatt called upon Delamotte to produce watercolors of the Great Exhibition of 1851, and Delamotte also made calotypes of the construction of the Crystal Palace, where Wyatt was superintendent building works. Delamotte secured a license from talbot and began to offer calotypes, becoming the first truly successful commercial calotypist in England. One of the most prolific contributors to photographic exhibitions in Britain, beginning with the pivotal exhibition at the Society of Arts in 1852, he worked primarily in collodion. However, his contributions to the society's 1855–56 exhibition marked a return to the paper negative. His subject here was again the Crystal Palace, now reerected at Sydenham, and perhaps Delamotte turned to paper to avoid the halation problems that were endemic with glass negatives. Commissioned by the Crystal Palace Company, these are his finest photographs. He continued to exhibit through 1861, sometimes in conjunction with his business partners, robert howlett and, later, George Downes, but only once more in paper negative—a calotype view of a lake in Wales for the 1856 exhibition of the Manchester Photographic Society. Always interested in teaching, in 1853 Delamotte published *The Practice of Photography,* which would be a starting point for many new to the art. In 1855 he was appointed the professor of drawing and perspective at King's College, London. One of Delamotte's most important contributions to photography was his promotion of the oxymel process, which was invented by his friend john dillwyn llewelyn. A mixture of honey and vinegar, oxymel made it possible to use a collodion glass plate in a dry condition, thus enabling a photographer to prepare plates in advance. The portability of the paper negative was thereby combined with the detail of the glass, and Delamotte's 1856 *The Oxymel Process in Photography* helped to popularize the new approach, a harbinger of the factory-made dry plates that began to arrive a few decades later.

Exhibited: 1855–56, third touring exhibition, Society of Arts (London); 1856, Manchester, Photographic Society

REFERENCES: James Buckman and C. H. Newmarch, *Illustrations of the Remains of Roman Art, in Cirencester, the Site of Antient Corinium* (London: George Bell, 1850), p. vi; Philip Henry Delamotte, *The Practice of Photography: A Manual for Students and Amateurs* (London: Joseph Cundall, 1853); Delamotte, *The Oxymel Process in Photography* (London: Chapman and Hall, 1856); *BJP* 36 (March 1, 1889), p. 138 (obituary); *Times* (London), March 1, 1889, p. 13, col. c (obituary) *Art-Journal*, April 1889, p. 126 (obituary); Alec Stirling, "Philip Henry Delamotte: Artist and Photographer," *RSA Journal*, June 1990, pp. 491–95

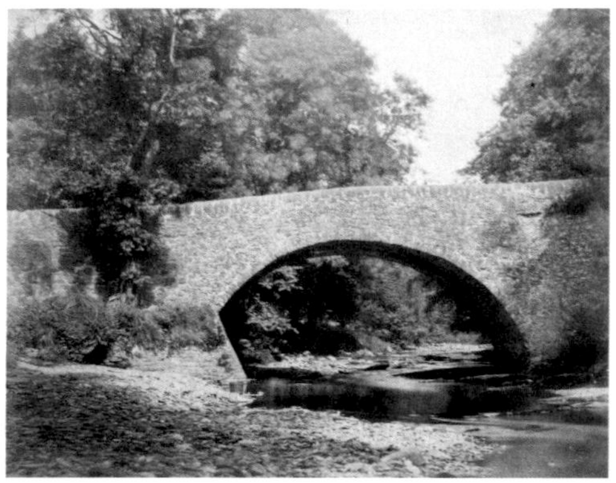

30. Hugh Welch Diamond

Diamond, Hugh Welch *ill. 30*

1809–1886

In 1853 Diamond wistfully observed, "There has been lately such a desire for something new, that we all have more or less run away from a steady wish to improve if possible the original details of Mr. Fox Talbot." Later in the century, Diamond was remembered as one of the most influential figures in the formative days of photography. Like his father he became a surgeon, making his reputation battling an outbreak of cholera in 1832, but then turned to the study of mental disorders. A keen antiquarian and a collector not only of ceramics but also of prints and printed materials, Diamond sold collections of prints to the British Museum in 1838 and 1851. He made his first photogenic drawing in April 1839 and by 1847 had joined the Calotype Society, an informal gathering of a dozen friends with like interests. He was a master of TALBOT's process, eloquent in his landscapes and particularly earnest about making archaeological studies. Diamond published his techniques and insights freely, thereby becoming a critical tutor to many in the first wave of photographers. By the time of the seminal photographic exhibition at the Society of Arts in London in 1852, he had begun to meld his professional and amateur interests, taking insightful portraits of the insane; this would emerge as a major preoccupation. Because these portraits required relatively short exposure times, often under difficult conditions, Diamond became a pioneer in the use of the wet-collodion negative. He was elected the first secretary of the Photographic Society in London in 1853 and the next year was named honorary photographer to the Society of Antiquaries. It was during this period that Diamond's work in calotypy and wet collodion happily coexisted, with each process applied where it would be most effective. In the 1854 exhibition of the Royal Infirmary Fund in Dundee, and in the 1854, 1855, and 1856 exhibitions of the Photographic Society in London, Diamond displayed calotype landscapes, archaeological subjects, and architectural studies. In later exhibitions, collodion portraits of the insane and of amateur photographers (if such a distinction can be made!) predominated. Diamond was widely admired by his photographic contemporaries and was paid tribute to in public testimonials. In 1867 the Photographic Society (later the Royal Photographic Society) fittingly presented its first medal to Diamond, not only for his "eminent services to the art generally" but also out of the council's "own regard and esteem personally." Times changed rapidly after that, and two decades later, when Diamond's effects were auctioned after his death, the correspondent for the *Photographic News* was struck both by the rapid evolution of the art and the lackluster response to the artifacts of its history. Notably, one of Diamond's "ancient" lenses, signed by Daguerre himself, realized a mere eleven shillings from the unsentimental buyers.

EXHIBITED: 1854, London, Photographic Society; 1854, Dundee, Royal InWrmary Fund; 1855 and 1856, London, Photographic Society; 1856, Norwich, Photographic Society

REFERENCES: Hugh Welch Diamond, "On the Simplicity of the Calotype Process," *Notes and Queries*, December 17, 1853, pp. 596–600; Hugh Welch Diamond, "Photography and Photographic Apparatus," in *The Record of the International Exhibition, 1862* (Glasgow: William MacKenzie, 1862), pp. 564–78; "Presentation to Dr. Diamond," *Photographic News* 11 (February 15, 1867), p. 73; "To Be Sold at Auction. By a Photographic Patriarch," *Photographic News* 31 (April 22, 1887), p. 243; Carolyn Bloore, *Hugh Welch Diamond: Doctor, Antiquarian, Photographer*, exh. cat. (Twickenham: Orleans House Gallery, 1980)

Diamond, John R.

b. 1832

Dr. Diamond's reputation is overshadowed by the more widely known work of Dr. HUGH WELCH DIAMOND (no known relation). An apothecary in London, he presented a Talbotype of the west window of Hadley Church in the 1856 exhibition of the Photographic Society in London, along with a collodion portrait, but at present nothing else is known of Diamond's photographic work.

EXHIBITED: 1856, London, Photographic Society

Dickins, Charles Spencer Scrase

1833–1884

It is not surprising that Dickins, a justice of the peace in rural Kent, took an interest in photography. His uncle, the Duke of Northampton, was the president of the Royal Society when photography was announced to the public, and the duke's soirees provided an important platform for the new art. Dickins traveled to Italy in the early 1850s and his earliest known photographs date from 1854. Working in waxed paper, he took as his most frequent subjects his home of Coolhurst and the surrounding countryside of Kent.

REFERENCE: Larry J. Schaaf, *Sun Pictures, Catalogue Four: The Harold White Collection of Historical Photographs from the Circle of Talbot* (New York: Hans P. Kraus, Jr., 1987), p. 17

Dickson, John Burnie

1806–1884

Born in Scotland, Dickson entered the Indian Medical Service (Bengal) in 1825, rising to the rank of surgeon by 1845. He saw service in both the First Sikh War and the Indian Mutiny. By 1862 Dickson had become inspector general of hospitals, a position he held until he retired to London two years later. Dickson joined the Photographic Society of Bengal in 1856, showing a portfolio of portraits and copies of paintings photographed in Gustave Le Gray's waxed-paper process. He collaborated with Lieutenant Alexander Simpson in photographically copying paintings for the geologist Sir Henry Yule's *A Narrative of the Mission Sent by the Governor-General of India to the Court of Ava in 1855*, a major contribution to Burmese historical studies. No other photographs by him are known to have survived.

REFERENCE: Henry Yule, *A Narrative of the Mission Sent by the Governor-General of India to the Court of Ava in 1855, with Notices of the Country, Government, and People* (London: Smith, Elder and Co., 1858)

Dixon, Thomas
b. 1818
A dental surgeon in Leeds, Dixon never exhibited, but he was the largest single contributor to the "Productions of the Leeds Photographic Society," lending a varied repertoire to the albums, including architectural studies, street scenes, still lifes, and portraits. He may have been the Thomas Dixon who was elected to the Photographic Society in London in 1853.

Domville, William Thomas
1822–1879
Dr. Domville was a man of many talents but is best remembered as the surgeon on HMS *Resolute*, one of the ships that traveled to the Arctic in 1852 in search of Sir John Franklin, whose expedition to find the Northwest Passage had disappeared in 1845. Domville's journals from the period are profusely illustrated with his sketches and watercolors, but he also used a camera during the journey. Several calotype negatives made by him survive, providing eloquent testimony to the frigid conditions that trapped the rescue party. In addition to providing medical and photographic services, Domville organized theatrical entertainment for the stranded men. (The *Resolute* was trapped in the ice and abandoned, but subsequently broke free and was salvaged. The president's desk in the Oval Office, a present from Queen Victoria to President Rutherford B. Hayes, is made from the ship's timbers.) Domville Point in Wellington Channel in the Arctic is named in his honor. Domville was later put in charge of Haslar Naval Hospital in Hampshire and was named honorary surgeon to the queen. No other photographs of his are known.

Dove, John
b. 1811
A Glaswegian by birth, Dove was the editor of the *Parliamentary Gazetteer* and a contributor to *Chambers's Journal*. He also knew quite a few Scottish scientists, and it is perhaps through these connections that his interest in photography was born. In May 1842 Dove wrote to TALBOT about "your ingenious invention, the Calotype," wondering if Talbot wanted to see it established in Glasgow or in Edinburgh. The inventor's reply has not been traced, but by then Talbot had been informed by Sir DAVID BREWSTER of ROBERT ADAMSON's progress in calotypy. It is not known whether Dove actually proceeded with his plans, or even if he ever took any photographs himself.

REFERENCE: John Dove to Talbot, May 11, 1842, Talbot Collection, British Library, London (Talbot Correspondence Project, http://foxtalbot.dmu.ac.uk, doc. no. 04502)

Dredge, J. J. (or T., or John Ingle?)
Rev. J. J. Dredge contributed three waxed-paper views of Southwell Cathedral to the 1857 exhibition of the Photographic Society in London. In the inaugural exhibition of the Nottingham Photographic Society in 1859, his 10 x 12 inch calotype view, *West Door, Southwell Minster*, taken in 1856, was awarded first prize out of two thousand entries from around the world. The next year, a "T. Dredge," possibly a relative, contributed a collodion view taken in Nottinghamshire to the society's exhibition. No Rev. J. J. Dredge has been identified, and of course it is easy to confuse the initials of handwritten signatures. Was this photographer perhaps the Rev. John Ingle Dredge (1818–1897), a Wesleyan minister today highly regarded by genealogists for his extensive transcriptions of Devonshire parish records?

EXHIBITED: 1857, London, Photographic Society; 1859, Nottingham Photographic Society

REFERENCE: A. G. Grant, "Nottingham Photographic Society," *Photographic News* 1 (January 14, 1859), p. 226

Drummond, James
1816–1877
It is not certain at this point whether Drummond was an active photographer himself, but his enthusiasm for collecting and exhibiting calotypes is clear. His merchant father was an avid historian of old Edinburgh, and this influenced the young artist. Elected an academician of the Society of Arts, Drummond is known for genre paintings firmly grounded in historical studies. A painter and a scholar, he was also a collector of artworks in many fields. In 1848 he was elected a fellow of the Royal Scottish Society of Antiquaries, becoming curator of the society's museum. Drummond's collection of Hill & Adamson calotypes and THOMAS KEITH's "Old Edinburgh" series remains a key resource to this day.

Drummond, William Henry
1810–1886
In 1844, when the young Queen Victoria and her husband Prince Albert made their second visit to Scotland, the Duke of Atholl turned over Blair Castle to the royal entourage. Drummond, who had taken up calotypy in the early 1840s, was invited and took a number of calotypes to mark the occasion, assembling them into a commemorative album, including an early self-portrait, perhaps one of his first works. No other photographs by Drummond are presently known.

Dudgeon, Miss (Elizabeth Jane?)
b. 1816
Dudgeon is a common name in Scotland, so attempts to identify a "Miss Dudgeon of Edinburgh" are fraught with difficulty. The Royal Scottish Academy received a donation of salt prints from waxed-paper negatives, landscapes of Dunkeld and Birnam taken in 1853. They are initialed "JWD ф" and are additionally annotated as having been taken by Miss Dudgeon of Edinburgh. "JWD" is almost certainly JOHN WILLIAM DUDGEON, a Scottish-born calotypist who was based in London. Patrick Dudgeon of Kailzie Mansion House had three sisters, and of these, the unmarried Elizabeth Jane lived with her father, retired general PETER DUDGEON, in Edinburgh. Nothing further is known of Miss Dudgeon or her photographs.

Dudgeon, John William
d. 1865
Born in Scotland, Dudgeon was a merchant in London. Two of his calotype landscapes were hung in the 1853 exhibition of the Mechanics' Institution in Aberdeen. They were presented by a local resident, presumably a friend of Dudgeon's. In the 1855 exhibition at the Photographic Institution in London, "Dudgeon" contributed three studies of trees and the "Bank of a Pool." This may have been John William Dudgeon. The Royal Scottish Academy received a donation of salt prints from waxed-paper negatives, landscapes of Dunkeld and Birnam taken in 1853, initialed "JWD ф" and additionally annotated as having been taken by MISS DUDGEON of Edinburgh, who was most likely his sister Elizabeth Jane Dudgeon.

EXHIBITED: 1853, Aberdeen, Mechanics' Institution; 1855, London, Photographic Institution

Dudgeon, Peter
For the 1853 exhibition of the Mechanics' Institution in Aberdeen, Dudgeon gave his address as Kailzie, in the Scottish border country on the River Tweed. The ambitious nature of his entries indicates that he was certainly keen if not accomplished. Working exclusively in the calotype process, Dudgeon covered a remarkable range, from conventional portraits to pictures of a sleeping dog, to studies of trees, and calotypes of snowy streets—the last a challenge with its low contrast in the weak winter

light. Perhaps he was the retired general Peter Dudgeon (b. 1786), whose daughter (MISS DUDGEON) lived with him in Edinburgh about this time and whose son Patrick lived at Kailzie Mansion House. None of Dudgeon's photographic work is known to have survived.

EXHIBITED: 1853, Aberdeen, Mechanics' Institution

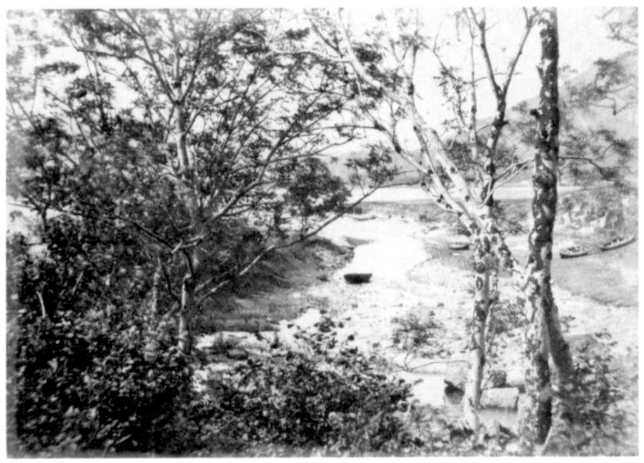

31. James Matthews Duncan

Duncan, James Matthews *ill. 31*
1826–1890
In some circles, Dr. Duncan is best known for being the first person rendered insensible by chloroform, a distinction he had the opportunity to gain as the private assistant to the pioneering Scottish obstetrician Sir James Young Simpson. Born in Aberdeen, Duncan studied medicine in Edinburgh and Paris and earned distinction in both scientific theory and actual practice. With this brace of skills, it is not surprising that he took up photography. A member of the Edinburgh Photographic Exchange Club, Duncan contributed four waxed-paper photographic landscapes to the 1858 exhibition of the Photographic Society of Scotland.

EXHIBITED: 1858, Edinburgh, Photographic Society of Scotland

REFERENCES: *Times* (London), September 3, 1890, p. 7, col. F (obituary); *Lancet* (London), September 13, 1890, pp. 594–96 (obituary); *British Medical Journal*, September 13, 1890, pp. 655–66 (obituary); *Edinburgh Medical Journal* 36 (1890–91), pp. 392–97 (obituary)

Dundas, John F.
b. 1811
Dundas was a civil engineer based in Edinburgh, a city bound to inspire an interest in photography. In the 1858 exhibition of the Edinburgh Photographic Society, he contributed a calotype, *Doorway of Dalmeny Church*. No other photographic activity by Dundas has been established thus far. However, an album titled "Aug 1852–1856," associated with James Dundas of Dundas, a financially unsuccessful inventor who was to become the last of the Dundas family, was sold at auction in 1985. It is possible that there was a distant relationship between these two men, and therefore a mutual influence.

EXHIBITED: 1858, Edinburgh, Photographic Society of Scotland

REFERENCE: Sale cat., Sotheby's, London, June 21, 1974, lot 107

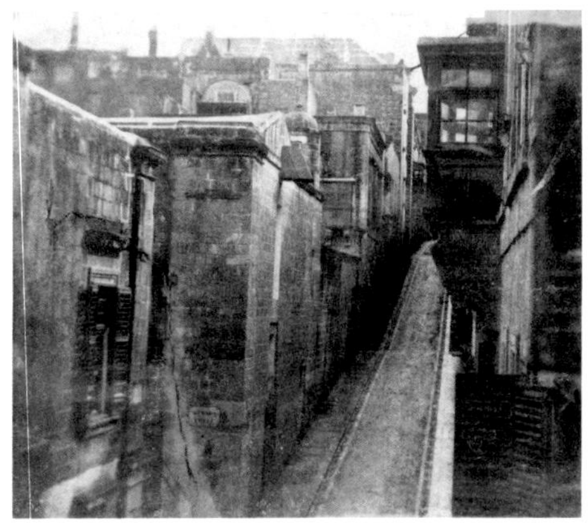

32. James Dunlop

Dunlop, James *ill. 32*
1830–1858
Dunlop was only nine years old when he succeeded to his father's title. The young Sir James probably learned photography as a teenager from his aunt, the calotypist FRANCES WALLACE MONTEITH. During a Continental tour in about 1847, Dunlop took calotypes in Malta and Italy that are preserved in various albums, including one once owned by Sir DAVID BREWSTER. Dunlop entered the Coldstream Guards in 1849 and served with distinction in the Crimean War. While there is no record that he was wounded, apparently his health was undermined. In 1857 Dunlop sold the ancient family estate in Ayrshire and moved to the south of France, where he died unmarried the following year.

REFERENCES: *Scotsman* (Edinburgh), February 17, 1858 (obituary); Julie Lawson, "Sir James Dunlop: A Photographic Prodigy?" *Scottish Photography Bulletin*, Autumn 1986, pp. 11–13

Durnford, Frederick A.
b. 1816
Based in London, Durnford was a parliamentary agent, one of the small group of lawyers who specialize in shepherding private bills through the legislature. In the 1854 exhibition of the Photographic Society in London, Durnford showed six waxed-paper views of Ilfracombe and one of Hampton Court Bridge, the choice of subjects implying that he was an amateur taking advantage of holiday trips.

EXHIBITED: 1854 and 1856, London, Photographic Society

Dutton, John
Dutton is a complete mystery save for a useful paper he read before the North London Photographic Association in 1858 outlining his "Experiments on the Waxed-Paper Process." In this presentation he spoke of using a stereo camera with a Ross landscape lens, but none of his photographs have been traced. The year before, a Miss Dutton had submitted collodion portraits to the Photographic Society exhibition in London; she was likely Miss Jane Dutton, a commercial photographer from 1856 to 1862, and perhaps she and James Dutton were related.

REFERENCE: John Dutton, "Experiments upon the Waxed-Paper Process," *JPS* 4 (May 21, 1858), pp. 215–17

Dyball, Robert Henry
1819–1883
A draper in Cambridgeshire who somehow became interested in photography, Dyball showed two waxed-paper views in the 1855 exhibition of the Photographic Society in London. He began exhibiting collodion views the following year and by 1859 had established himself as a photographer in London. In 1865 Dyball was cheered by the photographic press for successfully chasing down the thief who had coolly carried his camera out of the studio. He remained a professional photographer until his death.

EXHIBITED: 1855, London, Photographic Society

REFERENCE: "Look after Your Lenses," *Photographic News* 9 (May 26, 1865), p. 251

Eastham, John
1821–1889
In 1888, S. L. Dobie wrote to the *British Journal of Photography* that a friend had a collection of Talbotypes, kept since 1857 in India: "The series consists of ten 10 x 8 portraits, and one group. They are by John Eastham,

Photographer to the Queen, 22, St. Ann's-square, Manchester." The editor agreed from the description that these sounded more like calotypes printed on plain salted paper than albumen prints from glass negatives. This is the only known reference to Eastham's work in the calotype. Originally based in Manchester, he was an accomplished portraitist. In 1859 Eastham went into a short-lived partnership with Alexander Bassano in London, and by 1871 he was bankrupt.

References: "Portraits of Roger Fenton, by J. Eastham, Manchester," *BJP* 12 (March 17, 1865), p. 143; S. L. Dobie, "Talbotypes? A Query," *BJP* 35 (July 13, 1888), p. 446

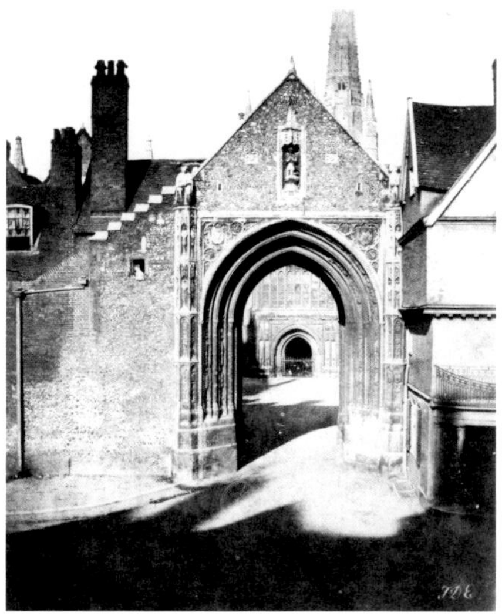

33. Thomas Damant Eaton

Eaton, Thomas Damant *ill. 33*

1800–1871

Born in Norwich, where he spent his entire life, Eaton was a successful if unenthusiastic silk merchant. According to a local paper, "In music he was a genius, an accomplished flautist, a composer and a widely-respected critic." He retired from business in 1846, which allowed him time to pursue his scientific, literary, and artistic interests, as well as his passion for chess. Eaton discovered photography around 1843 and was initially drawn to the daguerreotype but was soon won over to the calotype, perhaps because, with his generous nature, he enjoyed being able to share prints with his friends. Eaton traveled extensively, but all of his photography was done in and around Norwich, and he was at the center of the group of amateur calotypists who formed the Norwich Photographic Society. His friend Hugh Welch Diamond submitted one of Eaton's calotypes to the 1852 exhibition of the Society of Arts in London. Eaton was the driving force behind the 1856 exhibition of the Norwich Photographic Society, to which he contributed two calotypes and one collodion view, but as photography became more commercialized, he took progressively less interest in the art. Nevertheless, his well-documented albums are a rich trove of photography in its earliest days.

Exhibited: 1852, London, Society of Arts; 1856, Norwich, Photographic Society

References: *Norfolk News*, April 1 and 15, 1871 (obituaries); Grace Seiberling, with Carolyn Bloore, *Amateurs, Photography, and the Mid-Victorian Imagination* (Chicago: University of Chicago Press, 1986), p. 130; Richard Denyer and Andrew Moore, eds., *A Period Eye: Photography Then and Now*, exh. cat. (Norwich: Norfolk Museums and Archaeology Service, 2003), pp. 21–22

Edgeworth, Michael Pakenham

1812–1881

The son of a novelist and an inventor and the youngest half brother of the enormously popular novelist Maria Edgeworth, Michael Edgeworth (also Edgworth) was born in Ireland and studied botany and Oriental languages in Edinburgh. He taught briefly at the East India College and went out to India in 1831, holding a series of administrative posts. His sister was a friend and correspondent of Sir David Brewster's, and it was perhaps through this connection that Edgeworth first learned of photography. Returning to Britain on leave in 1842–46, Edgeworth worked with Sir David on photography and also photographed with Henry Craigie Brewster. He was elected a fellow of the Linnean Society while on leave and conducted botanical studies during his return trip to India. Retiring in 1859, Edgeworth moved to London; he died while on a visit to the Outer Hebrides.

Reference: Alison Morrison-Low, "Sir David Brewster and Photography," *Review of Scottish Culture*, no. 4 (1988), pp. 63–73

Elliot, William Scott

1811–1901

A member of the Photographic Society of Scotland and on its council in 1864, Elliot was a justice of the peace at his home of Arkleton, near Dumfries. In the society's 1858 exhibition, he displayed mostly collodion portraits, ranging from several called *Old Man* to two of "Professor MacDonald." The landscapes and architectural views that Elliot exhibited, however, were all done in calotype or waxed paper, with locales ranging throughout Scotland, from Aberdeen to Fife to Glasgow.

Exhibited: 1858 and 1864, Edinburgh, Photographic Society of Scotland

Elliott, Robert

b. 1806

Elliott owned the Pensher Iron Works, a foundry supplied by the plentiful coal mines near Durham, which benefited from the boom in industrialization of the 1840s. Undoubtedly already familiar with industrial and chemical processes, Elliott began his experiments in photography at least by 1852, initially thinking of creating a special tent under which to operate. He failed in his first attempts at employing Gustave Le Gray's waxed-paper process, largely due to difficulties in development, but like most photographers, Elliott soon modified the process to suit his own working habits. Within a few months he had become sufficiently confident with the process to start offering advice to others, including recommending the use of French glass developing trays in order to avoid contamination, and by 1855 he had succeeded in reducing his exposure times with waxed paper to those of the calotype. By 1857 Elliott was experimenting with a dry collodion on glass process for his outdoor work. He is not known to have exhibited any of his photographs, and apparently none of them have survived.

References: Robert Elliott, letter in *Notes and Queries*, November 6, 1852, pp. 442–43; Elliott, "Difficulties in Photographic Practice," *Notes and Queries*, March 5, 1853, p. 245; Elliott, "On Developing in the Waxed Paper Process," *JPS* 2 (November 21, 1855), pp. 261–62

Ellis, Joseph Jr.

1815–1891

Ellis inherited the Star & Garter Hotel in Richmond from his father but in 1845 moved to Brighton and took over the Bedford Hotel, the finest accommodation in the seaside resort. Exactly when photography piqued his interest is not known, but in 1842 he wrote a poem, "Photography," hailing "Niepce, and Daguerre, and Talbot, and Claudet!" A dedicated amateur, Ellis was a close friend of Antoine Claudet, from whom he learned about photography and whose eulogy he would write. In 1847 he published *Photography: A Popular Treatise*, which he introduced as a "labour of love," inscribing a copy to Talbot, and later he expanded a lecture given at the Literary and Scientific Institution of Brighton into *Progress of Photography—Collodion, the Stereoscope* (1856). From his large personal collection, Ellis generously shared his own work and that of other photographers with interested amateurs. A life member of the British Association for the Advancement of Science, he was in later years a wine merchant and served on Brighton's town council. At a meeting of the Photographic Club in 1862, Ellis displayed one of his proudest possessions. Since his Richmond days he had been intrigued by the 1827 visit of Joseph Nicéphore Niépce, the French inventor of photography, to nearby Kew. His friend Benjamin Cussell, a hotel proprietor, had been presented by Niépce with a precious heliograph, one of a handful to have survived. Cussell died suddenly and the heliograph was almost melted down for scrap before Ellis tracked it down and purchased it. After the 1862 meeting, nothing more is known of this precious artifact. Perhaps Ellis lent it to his friend Claudet and it perished in the disastrous fire at Claudet's studio in 1868. Or perhaps it remains to be found.

REFERENCES: Joseph Ellis Jr., *Photography: A Popular Treatise, Designed to Convey Correct General Information Concerning the Discoveries of Niepce, Daguerre, Talbot, and Others* (Brighton: Robert Folthorp, 1847); Ellis, *Progress of Photography—Collodion, the Stereoscope: A Lecture by Joseph Ellis* (London: Bell & Daldy, 1856); "The Oldest Existing Photographs," *Photographic News* 6 (July 11, 1862), p. 336; *Brighton Gazette & Sussex Telegraph*, June 13, 1891, p. 5 (obituary); *ILN*, August 1, 1891, p. 135 (obituary)

Ellis, Robert

Ellis contributed at least two detailed studies of the properties of the proto-nitrate of iron that were of importance in the early history of photography. He found the process of photographic development to be both uncertain and a hindrance, and closely studied the work of TALBOT and of his Irish nemesis, Dr. THOMAS WOODS. As he wrote in the *Athenaeum*, Ellis modified Woods's Catalysotype iron process "to apply the art of photography to some interesting geological examinations." He doubted that most photographers would want to go to the trouble he did, in taking "a geological ramble over the rocks of the Channel Islands, with a camera under one arm, and a portable dark tent, in which I prepared paper on the spot, under the other." Ellis stressed that he was "anxious that the paper-photography of England may receive a due illustration in all its varieties at the forthcoming Exhibition, and may present as favourable an evidence of the progress of that art in our country, where it is our boast that perfect photography has had its birth, as doubtless the exquisite Daguerreotypes of our neighbours will of their success in that department of photography in France." With this tie, it seems probable that he was the same Robert Ellis whose skills were called upon for the "scientific revision and preparation" of the entries in the official *Catalogue* of the Great Exhibition of 1851. A fellow of the Linnean Society and a member of the Royal Chemical Society, Ellis was also the author of *The Chemistry of Creation*, a popular work first issued in 1850 and continued through several editions. No surviving examples of his photography are known.

REFERENCES: Robert Ellis, "The Process of 'Development' in Photography," *Athenaeum*, February 22, 1851, pp. 224–25; *Official Descriptive and Illustrated Catalogue (of the Great Exhibition of 1851)* (London: Spicer Brothers and W. Clowes, 1851), 3 vols.; Ellis, "The Proto-Nitrate of Iron in Photography," *Athenaeum*, January 10, 1852, pp. 55–56

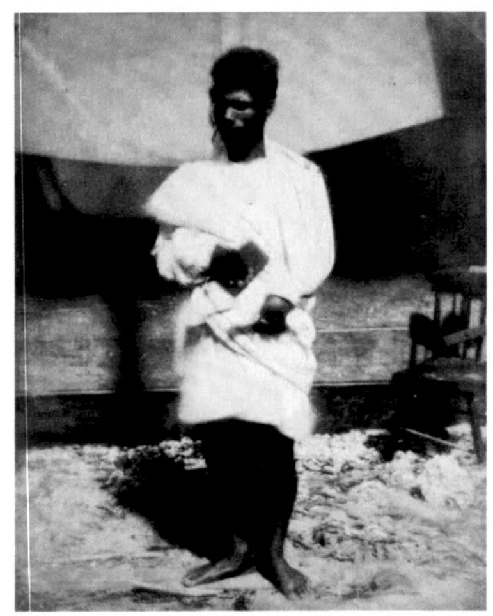

34. William Ellis

Ellis, William *ill. 34*

1794–1872

Disparaged as a "political missionary" by the Foreign Office, Rev. Ellis took an activist approach in his work for the London Missionary Society. The souls he sought to convert were as much in England as among the native populations to which he ministered. Ellis believed that science could be of service in his work, and when he prepared to go into the newly opened country of Madagascar, photography was one of his tools. Not a young man and already a seasoned traveler when he took up photography, Ellis sought the help of ROGER FENTON, perhaps his first contact in the field, probably when he joined the Photographic Society in London in 1853. His son later recalled that in "the interval between receiving the appointment and leaving England [he] was diligently employed in preparation. . . . That the collateral advantages of the journey might be fully secured, Mr. Ellis made himself practically familiar, as far as limited time would allow, with the principles and manipulations of photography, and provided himself with the requisite apparatus and chemicals." In Mauritius, "from Dr. Powell, the superintendent of the lunatic asylum, who was an accomplished chemist, he gained much valuable information, and improved his practical knowledge of photography." Ellis at first used both waxed-paper and collodion negatives, although later he would turn mostly to glass. Part of the reason for this is that much of his work was portraiture, at first intended to win over local leaders and later to record the indigenous peoples. Ellis's *Three Visits to Madagascar* (1858) was illustrated with woodcuts based on his photographs. The *Journal of the Photographic Society* found it to be of "intense interest" and the most important book of travel photography since CHARLES PIAZZI SMYTH's *Teneriffe*.

REFERENCES: William Ellis, *Three Visits to Madagascar, during the Years 1853-1854-1856, including a Journey to the Capital* (London: John Murray, 1858); review of *Three Visits to Madagascar*, by Ellis, *JPS* 5 (December 21, 1858), pp. 117–19; *ILN*, June 29, 1872, p. 630 (obituary); John Eimeo Ellis, *Life of William Ellis: Missionary to the South Seas and to Madagascar* (London: John Murray, 1873), pp. 215, 221; Simon Peers, "William Ellis: Photography in Madagascar, 1853–65," *History of Photography* 21 (Spring 1997), pp. 23–31

Elmore, Thomas

b. 1823

Born in Ireland, Elmore was the vice-counsul at Algiers when he mastered not only the technique of calotypy but also the spirit of photography. As the *Literary Gazette* reported in December 1850, in his annual exhibition of recent watercolors and paintings, the London printseller Joseph Grundy displayed recent calotypes by the "expert amateur, Mr. Elmore (not the painter),—they represent Moors, Arabs and Algerines, in their various costumes, and with the accessories of dwelling-places, furniture, arms, pipes and other things that convey the peculiar truth and accuracy of the picture, which would only be obtained by visiting the spot, and even then but seldom, if ever, by any of the ordinary methods of sketching. These specimens of such an interesting art are particularly worthy of a visit." In an enthusiastic 1851 review of glass negatives recently brought from Paris by John Mayall, the *Athenaeum* observed, "Some calotypes from the hands of Mr. Thomas Elmore that we have examined privately made the nearest approach to excellence here reached." Elmore retired to Brighton in the 1870s, and, sadly, none of his of calotypes are known to have survived.

REFERENCES: "Sun Pictures," *Literary Gazette*, December 28, 1850, p. 976; "Photography on Glass," *Athenaeum*, March 15, 1851, p. 304

Evans, Susan Eliza
1834–1891
The daughter of a British civil servant, Susan Eliza Evans (née Gisborne) was born in Russia. Her grandfather the Reverend Thomas Gisborne was a well-known and popular poet and naturalist, and it was perhaps from him that she acquired the inclination to pursue a pastime like photography. Gisborne's closest friend was Joseph Wright of Derby, and the two of them often took their paint boxes into the countryside together; his butler was James Fox, who later emerged as an important toolmaker who sold to Russia. In 1854, Susan married WALTER EVANS of Darley Abbey. They both became photographers. Only one example of her photography is known to have survived, an undated view of Snelston Church in Derbyshire; made from a paper negative, it is preserved in an album assembled by either ROBERT HENRY CHENEY or, more likely, ALFRED CAPEL CURE. Signed "Mrs. W. Evans," it might have been made before her marriage and later inserted into the album, but it is more likely that she and her husband learned photography together.

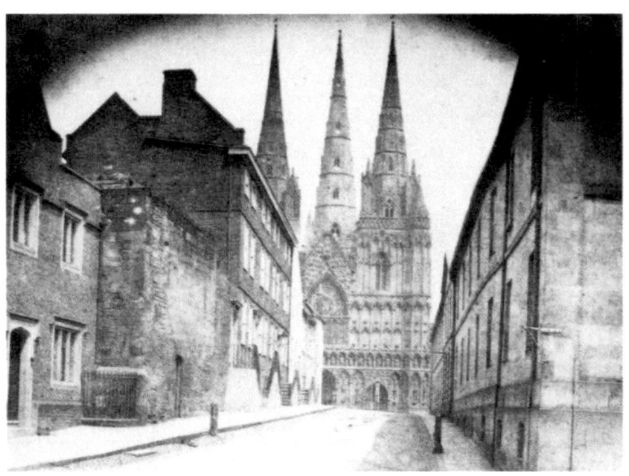

35. Walter Evans

Evans, Walter *ill. 35*
1827–1903
Walter Evans came from a well-connected Derbyshire family. His home, Darley Abbey, was close to Markeaton Hall, the estate of the Mundy family and the childhood home of TALBOT's wife Constance. Evans presided over many commercial undertakings, including banking, cotton spinning, and papermaking, and he became a justice of the peace. Many examples of his paper negative photography are preserved in albums assembled by either ROBERT HENRY CHENEY or his nephew ALFRED CAPEL CURE. Undated but almost certainly from the mid-1850s, the photographs are primarily views of Derbyshire. It appears that Evans took up photography at about the same time that he married Susan Gisborne in 1854. With her family's interests in natural philosophy and painting, she was perhaps the one who inspired her husband to take up the art. Evans remarried after the death of SUSAN EVANS, his first wife and fellow photographer, who left a substantial fortune.

Farmer, Robert
1823–1859
Farmer's occupation as a chemist undoubtedly brought him photographers as customers in search of supplies. In 1853 he established the Daguerreotype Rooms on North Street in Brighton. While metal plates were suitable for portraiture, tourists visiting the seaside resort would also want keepsakes for their albums. By November, Farmer was advertising in the *Brighton Gazette* that he was "exhibiting . . . his CALOTYPE views of the Pavilion, the Railway Terminus, &c taken by Gustave le Gray's new waxed-paper process."

Fenton, Roger *ill. 36*
1819–1869
No photographer of his generation was more important to the field than Roger Fenton. Born into a freethinking and prosperous Lancashire family, Fenton entered University College, London, in 1836. Three years later he began the study of law, becoming a London barrister in 1851; but Fenton had broader ambitions than the law and by that autumn was in Paris studying art. In October Gustave Le Gray demonstrated the waxed-paper process to him, and by the next February Fenton was making his own photographs. In 1852 he also wrote the section on waxed paper for the new edition of Thornthwaite's popular *Guide to Photography*. Fenton began to speak out in favor of establishing a society of photographers based on the one he had visited in Paris, and by 1853 his efforts had paid off with the founding of the Photographic Society (later the Royal Photographic Society) in London. Through his campaigning Fenton met the brilliant engineer Charles Blacker Vignoles, then engaged in building Europe's largest suspension bridge over the Dnieper River at Kiev. Vignoles engaged Fenton to photograph the work in large-format stereo negatives, and in August

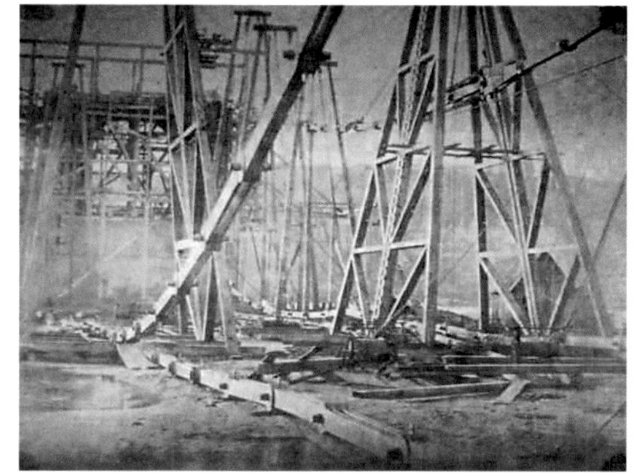

36. Roger Fenton

1852 the two departed for Russia. Fenton succeeded brilliantly, submitting a selection of these photographs to the Society of Arts exhibition that opened in London at the end of the year—some of the more than forty waxed-paper works he contributed to the exhibition. These included architectural views, landscapes, and one study, *Dead Stag, Zoological Gardens*. Fenton's success was immediate and no one could match his impressive exhibition record. Every one of the major exhibitions in Britain was underpinned by Fenton's extensive and beautiful displays. He became the model photographer. In 1854 Fenton began to use wet collodion, at first selectively, then exclusively. His well-known Crimean photographs were all done in collodion, sensitized and developed in a converted wine merchant's van. After his return to Britain, Fenton worked exclusively with enormous glass negatives, a process at which he excelled. Through exhibitions and his active role in the Photographic Society, Fenton helped popularize the art of photography in the 1850s. Fenton's last public showing was in the 1862 International Exhibition in London. Stunning the photographic world by announcing the sale of all of his photographic equipment and negatives in October, Fenton returned to the practice of law.

EXHIBITED: 1852, London, Society of Arts; 1853, London, Photographic Institution; 1853–54, first touring exhibition, Society of Arts (London); 1854, London, Photographic Society; 1854, Dundee, Royal Infirmary Fund; 1854, second touring exhibition, Society of Arts (London); 1855, London, Photographic Institution

REFERENCES: *BJP* 16 (August 20, 1869), pp. 400–401 (obituary); Gordon Baldwin et al., *All the Mighty World: The Photographs of Roger Fenton, 1852–1860*, exh. cat. (New York: The Metropolitan Museum of Art; Washington, D.C.: National Gallery of Art; New Haven and London: Yale University Press, 2004)

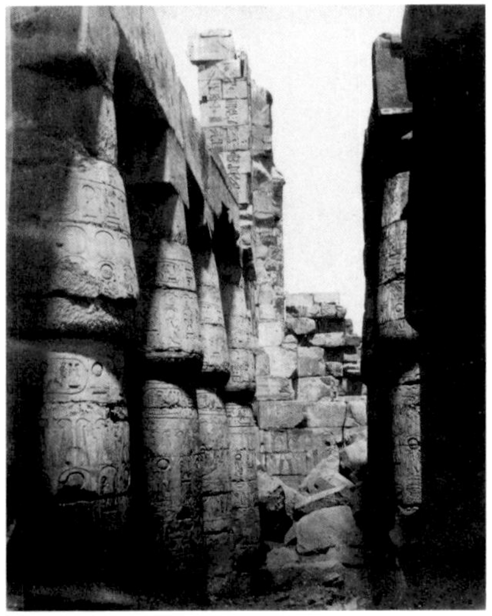

37. Thomas Hatton George Fermor

Fermor, Thomas Hatton George *ill. 37*
1832–1864
Fermor was the son of Thomas, 4th Earl of Pomfret, of Easton House in Northamptonshire, who served with distinction in the Peninsular War. The son's connection with photography is firmly established through several identical albums titled *Ancient Egypt in 1853 & 1854, Being Illustrations in Photography.* The prints were made from paper negatives, but little else is known about the albums. Fermor joined the 2nd Life Guards, part of the Household Cavalry, in 1850. A lieutenant by 1855, he was a corporal at the time the photographs were made. The 2nd Life Guards were eventually posted to Egypt, but not until 1882, so the photographs must have been made while Fermor was on leave, and as they show a reasonably high degree of accomplishment, he must have had some experience in the art before leaving England. However, no other photographic work by Fermor has been traced. Fermor predeceased his older brother and thus never acceded to the distinguished family title.

Reference: Thomas Hatton George Fermor, *Ancient Egypt in 1853 & 1854, Being Illustrations in Photography by the Honble. T. H. B. Fermor, 2nd Life Guards* (London: Printed by J. C. Sanford, n.d.)

Field, Robert, Jr.
b. 1828
The Birmingham firm of Robert Field & Son, philosophical instrument makers, would have been drawn naturally into photography. The son who joined his father in partnership was the younger one, also Robert. Two 1845 portraits made by the son are preserved in the Richard Willats album (now at Princeton University), at least one of them a rare practical implementation of Dr. Thomas Woods's Catalysotype process. During the Great Exhibition of 1851, in addition to photographic lenses, the Fields displayed "Calotype pictures: Scene, Forest of Arden, Warwickshire; staircase, Haddon Hall, Derbyshire; and Wych Elm, Packington churchyard, Warwickshire." Perhaps these were their own photographs, or perhaps they anticipated the later promotional efforts of George Eastman, who distributed cameras to photographers of the day in order to secure examples for advertising his wares.

Exhibited 1851, London, Great Exhibition

Fieldhouse, William
b. 1795
An ironmonger and cut nail manufacturer in Leeds, Fieldhouse had reached the age of semiretirement when the Leeds Photographic Society was formed in 1852. Elected the society's first president, he contributed calotypes to the three issues of their publication "Productions of the Leeds Photographic Society" (1852), including architectural studies and one portrait.

Reference: "Correspondence," *JPS* 1 (June 21, 1854), p. 224

Finn, Elizabeth Anne
1825–1921
Elizabeth Anne Finn, née McCaul, was born in Warsaw, the daughter of an English Christian missionary to the Jews of Poland. The family returned to England in 1841 and her father was appointed professor of Hebrew at King's College, London. This was both the right time and the right place to learn of new developments in photography. In 1846 Elizabeth married James Finn, a scholar of Hebrew and Arabic, setting out with him for Palestine, where her husband took up the post of British consul for Jerusalem. It was here, in 1849, that Finn met George Wilson Bridges, who was by then an enthusiastic calotypist. Years later, she recalled: "We had an interesting visitor in an old English clergyman named Bridges . . . he was the first to take anything like photographic views in Jerusalem. These were called 'talbottypes,' invented by his friend Mr. Fox Talbot, and he explained to me as much as he could about photography. I therefore wrote to my friends, and photographic apparatus was sent out to me." Strongly devoted to the small enclave of Jews in Jerusalem, Finn set up a workshop for Jewish women artisans, but, mired in controversy over their active support of the local population, she and her husband returned to Britain in 1861. A prolific writer, Finn was also a founding member of the Palestinian Exploration Fund. None of her photographs are known to have survived.

References: Elizabeth Anne Finn, *Reminiscences of Mrs. Finn: Member of the Royal Asiatic Society* (London: Marshall, Morgan and Scott, 1929); Nissan N. Perez, *Focus East: Early Photography in the Near East (1839–1885)* (New York: Harry N. Abrams, 1988), p. 162

Fitt, George Robert
1809–1893
A banker's clerk by trade but an amateur watercolorist by passion, Fitt helped found the Norwich Photographic Society in 1854. He exhibited waxed-paper photographs that the *Norwich Chronicle* considered "very sharp and spirited, and the most successful attempts by that process that have been made in this city." In 1855 Fitt became a commercial photographer in Norwich, not only promoting "Mr. Fitt's Collodion" but also providing instructions in the waxed-paper process. In November of that year he visited the Liverpool Photographic Society and passed around prints made from his waxed-paper negatives, moving the chairman to observe in the society's journal of November 10 that the photographers of Norwich "were no laggards in the practical application of the art." At a later meeting, as reported on December 8, Fitt's waxed-paper negatives were praised as having "produced some of the most pleasing and effective pictures ever exhibited to the Society." The prints Fitt entered in the 1856 exhibition of the Edinburgh Photographic Society were drawn from negatives made in Norfolk, but the ones he displayed at the Norwich Photographic Society's exhibition that year began to reflect the photographer's growing interest in Edinburgh subjects. In reviewing these, the *Norfolk News* lauded Fitt, to "whose instruction and example the society was much indebted in its infancy, and whose skill in all the processes is universally acknowledged."

Exhibited: 1856, Norwich, Photographic Society; 1856, Edinburgh, Photographic Society of Scotland

References: "Liverpool Photographic Society," *LPJ* 2 (November 10, 1855), p. 135; "Liverpool Photographic Society," *LPJ* 2 (December 8, 1855), p. 147; George Robert Fitt, "Mode of Working the Wax-Paper Process," *LPJ* 3 (January 12, 1856), pp. 4–10; Fitt, "On Waxed Paper," *Photographic Notes* 1 (September 1, 1856), pp. 160–61; Fitt, letter in *Photographic*

Notes 1 (December 1, 1856), p. 258; *Norfolk News*, January 3, 1857 (reprinted in *Notices of the First Exhibition of the Norwich Photographic Society* [Norwich: Norwich Photographic Society, 1857])

Fitzgerald, Patrick Gerald
1820–1910
Dr. Fitzgerald rose through the ranks of the Indian Medical Service, starting as an assistant surgeon in 1846 and becoming deputy surgeon general by 1875. A devoted amateur photographer, loyal to the waxed-paper process (as were many in India), Fitzgerald displayed his waxed-paper views of Bengal in the 1860 exhibition of the Madras Photographic Society. In another off-duty avocation, Fitzgerald wrote a series of manuscript diaries covering the period from 1844 to 1867. Much of his writing recorded the carnage he was forced to witness, but, more pleasantly, photography was a favorite subject, as well as his travels home to Dublin through the Continent.

Exhibited: 1860, Madras, Photographic Society

Flower, Frederick William
1815–1889
Through an accident of timing, Flower was born in Scotland. His father, the sheriff of Hull, was transporting French prisoners to Edinburgh and had taken his pregnant wife along with him. The thriving trade in port wine at Leith must have influenced Flower, for at the age of nineteen he moved to Oporto, Portugal, to become a shipping clerk for a wine merchant. The calotype was then virtually unknown in Portugal, but somehow Flower became a master of the process, perhaps based on information that he received from Edinburgh. The majority of his negatives were made on paper watermarked "Whatman's Turkey Mill 1849," and also on R. Turner Patent Talbotype Paper, which was available from 1854. In 1853 Flower entered into his own wine business, and his temporary relocation to Bristol in 1859 seems to have put an end to his photographic pursuits. Although he did not exhibit and very few of his prints survive, a substantial archive of Flower's calotype negatives has been preserved.

Reference: Vitória Mesquita et al., *Frederick William Flower: A Pioneer of Portuguese Photography*, exh. cat., Museu do Chiado (Lisbon: Lisboa 94; Milan: Electa, 1994)

Foard, James Thomas
b. 1833
Foard gained significant commercial experience in photography at an early age. He worked for some months in a room built for a Mr. Constable on the Marine Parade, Brighton, and also spent some time at the Polytechnic Institution, London. It was the latter experience, when he worked with the daguerreotypist Richard Beard, that most shaped his career, and by the 1850s, Foard was Beard's agent in Manchester and Liverpool. At some point he met Roger Fenton, later remembering that Fenton told him that the negative papers he took with him to Russia in 1852 had been presensitized in London. Foard joined the Liverpool Photographic Society, which is where he first revealed his own extensive experience in waxed paper, and his simplified and effective formula was circulated to all members of the society. In 1888 the *British Journal of Photography* recalled that Foard "did great work in the Society by supplying it with papers of high-class merit," presumably referring to his communications to the society rather than to actual paper. Some daguerreotypes by Foard have been identified, but none of his paper photography is known to have survived.

References: "Liverpool Photographic Society," *LPJ* 1 (March 11, 1854), pp. 37–39; James Thomas Foard, "Correspondence" [giving formula], *LPJ* 1 (April 8, 1854), pp. 54–55; James Alexander Forrest, "Historical Notes of What Liverpool Has Done in the Art-Science of Photography," *BJP* 35 (February 3, 1888), pp. 72–74

Forrester, Joseph James *ill. 38*
1809–1861
Born in England to Scottish parents, Forrester moved to Oporto, Portugal, in 1831 to join his uncle in the port wine business. He had ample leisure time to work in watercolors and chalk (he was an unusually accomplished amateur artist), and particularly to pursue his passion for cartography. Forrester's map of the Douro River, completed in 1843 and based on his own survey, became the standard for navigation. In 1844 his gently titled *A Word or Two on Port Wine* shook up the industry and led to necessary reforms. Forrester took lessons in photography from Hugh Welch Diamond, probably growing out of their shared interest in archaeological photography. Like Diamond he preferred a close variation of Talbot's original calotype process that involved waxing after the negative was developed. In 1854 Forrester wrote to the *Journal of the Photographic Society* that he was "about to plant my camera amongst the mountain scenery of Portugal, which I am desirous graphically to describe, and photographically to illustrate." The French photographic critic and historian Ernst Lacan recalled that Forrester had been "accused of exaggeration and inexactitude" in his descriptions of Portugal and desired a "means to prove he had told the truth," but, whatever the motivation, his output was prodigious. Introducing his contribution to *The Photographic Album for the Year 1855*, Forrester said his *Margins of the Douro* was but one of a series of 220 negatives. He showed a similar view in the 1855 exhibition of the Photographic Society in London, but otherwise contributed primarily to exchange club albums. Also in 1855, the queen of Portugal, reflecting the gratitude of a nation, made Forrester a baron. Charles Piazzi Smyth stopped by Oporto on his way to Tenerife to take lessons from Forrester in the new stereo photography. In 1861 the very river that Forrester had mapped claimed his life when his boat was smashed on the rocks, the Douro never yielding up his body.

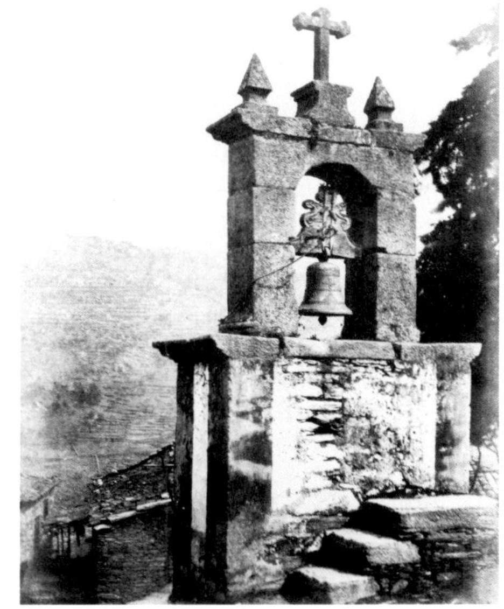
38. Joseph James Forrester

Exhibited: 1855, London, Photographic Society

References: Joseph James Forrester, "Waxed Positives," *JPS* 2 (August 21, 1854), p. 25; Ernst Lacan, "La Photographie en Angleterre," *La Lumière* 5 (June 20, 1855), p. 1001; João de Brito e Cunha, *Barão de Forrester; Exposição comemorativa do centenário da sua morte, 1861–1961*, exh. cat. (Vila Nova de Gaia: Instituto do Vinho do Porto, 1961); Grace Seiberling, "The Photographs of Joseph James Forrester," *History of Photography* 7 (January 1983), pp. 51–61

Forster, Percival

Forster, who seems to have had a particular interest in cathedrals, displayed calotypes of Hereford, Wells, Peterborough, and Durham in the 1857 and 1858 exhibitions of the Photographic Society in London. In the 1858 exhibition he also included a view of trees in Richmond Park, but nothing further is known of him or his work.

Exhibited: 1857 and 1858, London, Photographic Society

Forster, Ralph W.

b. 1834

Forster was an analytical chemist, which certainly stood him in good stead for practicing photography. In the 1856 exhibition of the Edinburgh Photographic Society, his three calotypes were of scenes in and around Ennerdale, near his home of Whitehaven in Cumberland. In 1857 Forster lamented the onslaught of collodion, publishing a passionate defense of the calotype process, which he emphasized was "*the* process for the tourist." However, by the time of the society's 1858 exhibition, Forster had converted to collodion albumen negatives and had switched his focus to Scottish architecture, possibly indicating that he had relocated to Scotland.

Exhibited: 1856, Edinburgh, Photographic Society of Scotland

Reference: Ralph W. Forster, letter in *LMPJ* 4 (April 15, 1857), p. 86

Foster, Peter Le Neve

1809–1879

Foster's family was long involved with the Society of Arts, and after becoming a lawyer he was elected into the society. After a brief stint as treasurer, Foster (over the strenuous objections of ROBERT HUNT) was elected secretary of the society in 1853, a full-time position that gave him considerable influence over matters of art and science. In 1847 Foster joined with PETER WICKENS FRY and a few others in an informal group popularly known as the Calotype Club, the first indication of his interest in the new art. He began producing calotypes in the late 1840s, many of which survive today. Foster helped plan the Great Exhibition of 1851, which brought photography to a wide public for the first time, and even more importantly the groundbreaking exhibition at the Society of Arts in 1852. While he did not himself exhibit in the latter, Foster took an active role in the formation of the Photographic Society in London the following year, later gracefully conceding defeat in his attempts to have it remain a part of the Society of Arts. Foster first began showing his waxed-paper views in the 1854 exhibitions of Photographic Society and the Royal Infirmary Fund, and was instrumental in setting up Society of Arts touring exhibitions from 1854 to 1856, contributing waxed-paper views. For the Photographic Society's 1860 exhibition, Foster turned to the turpentine waxed-paper process for his "untouched" view of the Chelsea Suspension Bridge. At the 1862 International Exhibition in London two years later, he again used the turpentine process to depict a suspension bridge, this time at Battersea. Foster's last known contribution to an exhibition was a group of twelve portraits in the 1865 Dublin International Exhibition; the process was not specified but was almost certainly collodion. Throughout the 1850s Foster served as a critical link between the long-established Society of Arts and the youthful Photographic Society. He maintained an interest in photography until the end of his life, most notably photographing the erection of Cleopatra's Needle on the Thames embankment the year before he died.

Exhibited: 1854, London, Photographic Society; 1854, Dundee, Royal Infirmary Fund; 1854, first touring exhibition, Society of Arts (London); 1855–56, third touring exhibition, Society of Arts (London); 1860, London, Photographic Society; 1862, London, International Exhibition

References: *Photographic Journal*, n.s., 4 (February 20, 1880), p. 56 (obituary); *BJP* 26 (February 28, 1879), p. 97 (obituary); *ILN*, March 8, 1879, p. 224 (obituary); Arthur T. Gill, "Peter Le Neve Foster and Cleopatra's Needle," *History of Photography* 3 (October 1979), pp. 289–94; Alec Stirling, "Peter Le Neve Foster and Photography," *RSA Journal*, November 1994, pp. 67–70

Fox, Edward, Jr. *ill. 39*

1823–1899

Fox's father was a decorative painter before becoming an artist, eventually exhibiting with regularity at the Royal Academy. His son also started as a decorative painter but sometime in the late 1850s moved on to photography as his means of visual expression. The younger Fox adopted the waxed-paper process, taking landscape and architectural photographs, mostly around his home of Brighton. By the early 1860s he was copyrighting his images for sale, including stereo views taken "instantaneously," with a strong leaning toward subjects that would be of study interest to artists. It was in the winter of 1864–65 that Fox began a project echoing one undertaken by TALBOT two decades earlier. This was a series of views of trees, specifically aimed at student artists. In order to show their structure (and to avoid the blurring of leaves that his long exposures encouraged), Talbot had photographed trees in winter. Fox expanded on this idea, photographing the same tree in both winter and summer, in order to

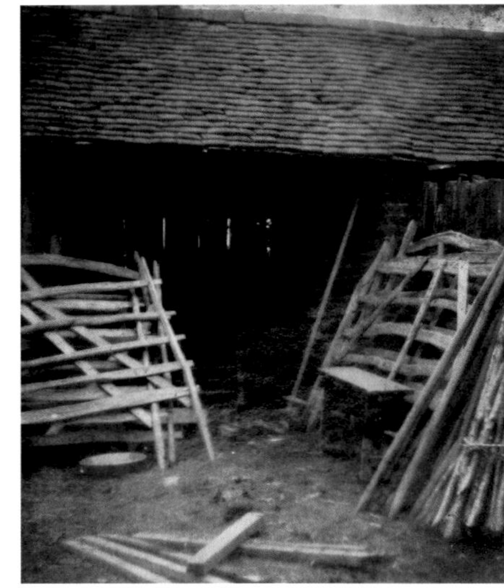

39. Edward Fox, Jr.

reveal to the student the structure underlying the foliage. Although much of Fox's serious work was in waxed paper, his contributions to the 1863 and 1864 exhibitions of the Photographic Society in London were taken on collodion. Fox disposed of his entire collection of photographs and paintings in 1892, mostly to friends, but a significant photographic archive survives to this day.

Reference: Philippe Garner, *A Seaside Album: Photographs and Memory* (London: Philip Wilson, in association with the Royal Pavilion, Libraries and Museums, Brighton, 2003), pp. 39–54

Francis, W. B.

Nothing is known of Francis beyond his membership in the Norwich Photographic Society and the two waxed-paper views of Beccles Church that he placed in their 1856 exhibition. Beccles was a Suffolk market town known widely for its extensive clockmaking and watchmaking traditions. Another waxed-paper view, titled simply *Paysage*, by a photographer named only as "Francis," was loaned to the 1856 exhibition of the Manchester Photographic Society by R. P. Greg, Esq.

Exhibited: 1856, Norwich, Photographic Society

Fraser, William

Based in Aberdeen, Fraser became intrigued with photography early on, and his "Remarks on Photographic Drawing" (1840) was one of the first papers on the new art presented to the Society of Arts in Edinburgh. Later that year he submitted a "Description of a Method of Photographic Printing, with Specimens." Here, Fraser's vision for the potential uses of photography was wide-ranging, and he produced examples of photographically decorated paper and of how photography could replace the conventional printing press. No examples of his work are known to have survived, but Fraser was corresponding with photographic journals at least as late as 1857.

Reference: William Fraser, "Description of a Method of Photographic Printing, with Specimens," November 23, 1840, manuscript, Society of Arts, Edinburgh

Freeman, T. J. (or T. F., or Thomas Tripp?)
According to the catalogue of the 1856 exhibition of the Norwich Photographic Society, a T. J. Freeman presented a calotype view, *Stranded Vessels on Kessingland Beach.* Then, the following year in Birmingham, a T. F. Freeman exhibited a view (process unspecified), *Somerleyton Hall, near Lowestoft, the Seat of Sir M. Peto, M.P.* Kessingland is near Lowestoft, and such a coincidence seems less likely than that we are dealing with a typographical error and hence the same photographer. (There was also a Thomas Frederick Freeman, later a justice of the peace in the area, but nothing has been found to connect him with photography.) Although neither of these photographs is known to have survived, their subject matter suggests one other possibility. Thomas Tripp Freeman (b. 1812), the keeper of the lighthouse at Lowestoft, would have had an obvious interest in shipping and would also have had his daytimes free to pursue an avocation like photography.

Exhibited: 1856, Norwich, Photographic Society

Fry, Peter Wickens *ills. 40, 41*
1798–1860
Fry's well-deserved reputation as one of prime movers behind the promotion of photography sometimes overshadows his own considerable attainments in the art. We do not know when he first became interested in photography, but, according to the *British Journal of Photography*, after his death it was said that he had begun with photogenic drawing even before Talbot announced his discovery of the calotype process in 1841, and also that he visited Robert Hunt in Falmouth to share information. A solicitor in London who was always known as a kind-hearted fellow and a good companion, Fry founded the Calotype Club, a loosely organized gathering of a dozen amateurs, in 1847. When the Photographic Society was being formed in 1853, the controversy concerning Talbot's patent rights had still not been resolved, with

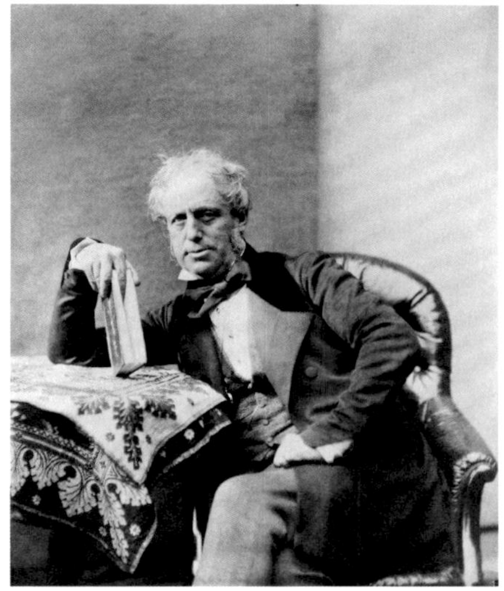

40. Portrait of Peter Wickens Fry

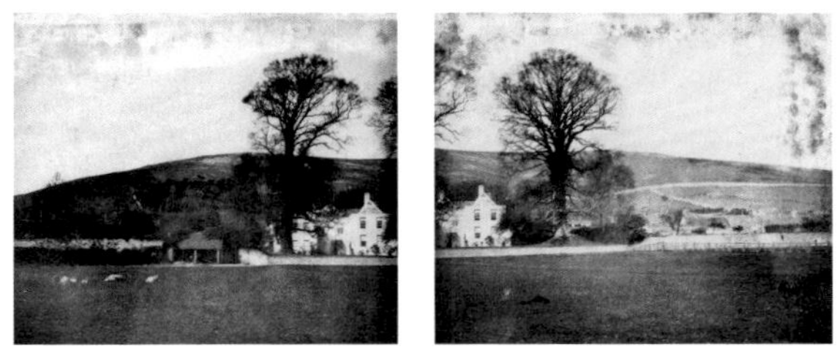

41. Peter Wickens Fry

Fry leading the battle to reject the inventor's offer of a special license. He was also the zealous defense lawyer for Sylvester Laroche in the action that eventually overturned Talbot's patent in 1854. Fry participated regularly in exhibitions between 1852 and 1856; most of his work was in paper negatives, predominantly architectural views; there were also some portraits rendered in collodion. Fry was one of the first to learn of Frederick Scott Archer's wet-collodion process and he urged the young sculptor to publish his invention, which he did in 1851. Not long after this, during a visit to Italy, Fry set up his camera to photograph a work of art in collodion. A student had been engaged for a week in making a copy of the work in oils, but on seeing how rapidly Fry was able to make his exactingly faithful photographic copy, the hapless artist smashed his canvas across his knee. Perhaps Fry had inadvertently created one more convert to photography.

Exhibited: 1852, London, Society of Arts; 1854, London, Photographic Society; 1854, second touring exhibition, Society of Arts (London); 1855–56, third touring exhibition, Society of Arts (London)

References: *BJP* 7 (October 1, 1860), p. 280 (obituary); "Photographic Society of London. Annual General Meeting. Report," *Photographic Journal* 7 (February 15, 1861), p. 99

Fry, Samuel Herbert
1833–1890
A Quaker, Fry was an assistant with the London School of Photography in 1857, his first known connection with photography. By 1860 he had established himself as a portrait photographer in Brighton, issuing an enticing promotional leaflet, *Talbotype Portraits in the Highest Style of Art*; however, no surviving examples of his calotype work are known. Fry relocated his portrait studio to London's East End by 1862, also venturing into the manufacturing of the newly popular dry collodion plates, an uncertain business in its early days. Fry joined the Photographic Society in 1873 and later became recording secretary of the Photographic Club. He continued operating photographic studios in London until late in life. In 1890, the *British Journal of Photography* remembered Fry as "a trenchant writer, and a man of active business habits."

References: *BJP* 37 (October 3, 1890), p. 628 (obituary); *BJPA*, 1891, p. 476 (obituary)

Furlong (or Furlonge), William Holland
b. 1826
Only a handful of calotypes taken by Furlong have been identified, but his influence on the young art of photography was enormous. Born in Ireland, he and his brother moved to St. Andrews at an early age, apparently without other immediate family members. He must have already been a promising young man, for in 1840, at the age of fourteen, Furlong secured a position as an assistant to Arthur Connell, professor of chemistry at the University of St. Andrews. It was through this connection that he met Sir David Brewster, the Scottish conduit to Talbot's inventiveness. (Brewster soon grouped Furlong along with John Adamson and Robert Adamson, describing them as Talbot's "three ardent disciples.") Furlong himself entered into correspondence with Talbot in order to better understand the fundamentals of the calotype process. In 1843 he made a critical breakthrough, simplifying Talbot's iodizing method and thereby making the process much more certain in its results. Furlong returned to Ireland sometime in the 1840s, and frustratingly little is known about him after that. He contributed to photographic journals in the 1850s, obviously maintaining his interest in the art and in an 1855 article tellingly praising "the *truly beautiful* calotype process," which "perhaps from old friendship, is certainly *my* favourite process." In 1876

Furlong renewed his correspondence with Talbot, by then spelling his name as *Furlonge* (perhaps in a return to the traditional Irish spelling). Although he reminisced about their photographic discussions of the early 1840s, by then Furlong shared a very different passion with Talbot, namely, the scholarly study of Assyriology.

REFERENCES: Sir David Brewster to W. H. F. Talbot, October 27, 1841, National Media Museum, 1937-4891 (Talbot Correspondence Project, http://foxtalbot.dmu.ac.uk, doc. no. 04349); William Holland Furlong, "Preparation of Iodized Paper by One Solution Only," *JPS* 2 (March 20, 1855), pp. 135–36; Furlong, "The Calotype Process," *Photographic Notes* 1 (January 1, 1856), pp. x–xiii; Graham Smith, "W. Holland Furlong, St Andrews and the Origins of Photography in Scotland," *History of Photography* 13 (April–June 1989), pp. 139–43

Fyfe, Andrew

1792–1861

At the March 1839 meeting of the Society of Arts in Edinburgh, Dr. Fyfe gave a speech on "Mr. Talbot's Process of Photogenic Drawing." A lecturer in chemistry and professor of medicine at Edinburgh University, Fyfe went beyond a mere lecture to demonstrate the production of an actual photograph, using oxyhydrogen light as a source. This was the first of three active demonstrations of photography that he presented to the society that year, and he would go one to be awarded an honorary silver medal for their combined effect. In the earliest years of photography, Fyfe was both an enthusiastic reporter and a participant, inventing his own direct positive process on paper and analyzing the daguerreotype, but his interest was always more in scientific understanding than in creative expression, and none of his photographs are known to have survived.

REFERENCE: Alison Morrison-Low, "Photography in Edinburgh in 1839: The Royal Scottish Society of Arts, Andrew Fyfe and Mungo Ponton," *Scottish Photography Bulletin*, no. 2 (1990), pp. 26–35

Galton, Robert Cameron

1830–1902

Born in Switzerland, Dr. Galton was a British national. By 1851 he was studying medicine in Cambridge while staying with a watchmaker. In the 1852 exhibition of the Society of Arts, Galton, barely twenty-one years old, exhibited a wide range of Swiss and British views taken on paper, including architecture, landscapes, and railway viaducts. In the 1854 exhibition of the Photographic Society in London he showed studies of trees done in both calotype and waxed paper, as well as a view of wagon horses taken by collodion. Galton became a Harley Street physician, a prestigious and demanding, if lucrative position. It was a decade before Galton would once again exhibit, and by then he had turned to collodion.

EXHIBITED: 1852, London, Society of Arts; 1854, London, Photographic Society

Gardam, William

b. 1826

Gardam was a mathematical instrument maker in Bradford when he joined the Leeds Photographic Society in 1852. He contributed one calotype to the society's collection, a view in Leeds, and while this is his only known photograph, it is likely that he produced a larger body of work. Gardam relocated to Leeds at this time, establishing himself as an optical and mathematical instrument maker. In about 1870 Gardam moved to New York, where he set up in partnership with his son as a maker of surveying instruments.

REFERENCES: *Brooklyn Standard Union*, April 14, 1907 (obituary); Adrian Budge, *Early Photography in Leeds, 1839–1870*, exh. cat. (Leeds: Leeds Art Galleries, 1981)

Gastineau, William

1821–1872

Gastineau was born in London of a Huguenot family. His father, Henry, was a landscape painter who originally apprenticed as an engraver. Art pervaded the family (so much so that his younger sister Maria died after falling off a mountain while completing a painting). William exhibited five calotypes and one waxed-paper study of garden scenes and views from chalk quarries in the 1857 exhibition of the Photographic Society in London. No other photographic work of his is known, but in the 1871 census, a year before his death, Gastineau still listed his profession as photographer.

EXHIBITED: 1857, London, Photographic Society

Giberne, George

b. 1798

A retired Indian civil servant and judge living in Epson, Giberne contributed thirteen photographs to the 1857 exhibition of the Photographic Society in London: the six portraits were done on collodion, presumably to take advantage of its shorter exposure time, while for the seven landscape and architectural views, Giberne chose the waxed-paper process. No other work of his is known.

EXHIBITED: 1857, London, Photographic Society

Gill, Robert

1804–1874

The son of a London stockbroker, Gill joined the Madras Native Infantry at the age of twenty and was to spend most of his life in India. "An excellent draughtsman," Gill was "entrusted with the duty of making drawings of the architectural and Pictorial remains in the Caves of Adjunta [Ajanta]" starting in 1844, according to his military service record, and this type of assignment would later inform his photographic work. In twelve years of highly dedicated labor, Major Gill, although hobbled by illness and impeded by strife in the region, produced a fine series of documentary paintings. Tragically, many of them were destroyed in a fire at the Crystal Palace in London in 1866; the few survivors are now in the Victoria and Albert Museum. Gill became a photographer in the mid-1850s and was a corresponding member of the Photographic Society of Bombay. Although his initial work was in collodion, he exhibited a series of calotype views before the society in 1856. The competition was stiff, but, as the society's journal pronounced in the same year, Gill had "the most on view, and all, without exception, perfect," the society said, calling it "very evident" that he "not only understands the details of photographic manipulation, but evinces very high artistic skill." For one important set of views, Gill had written in the journal the previous year, he could "think of no plan other than anchoring a Balloon whence to operate in front of the cave, when it happens to be on the side of a steep hill" (the society opined that perhaps he could try an extra wide-angle achromatic lens). Gill battled the government over payment and delays but finally completed his work on the Ajanta paintings in 1863. He was buried in India, his spirit living on in his son, who became an important traveler.

REFERENCES: Robert Gill, records of military service, India Office Records, British Library, London; *Journal of the Photographic Society of Bombay*, no. 9 (October 1855), p. 159; "Cursory Notes Taken at the Exhibition of Photographs, Bombay, February 1856," *Journal of the Photographic Society of Bombay*, nos. 13–17 (February–June 1856), pp. 26, 29; G. Thomas, "Major Robert Gill in the Nizam's Dominion of Berar," *History of Photography* 7 (October–December 1983), pp. 323–27

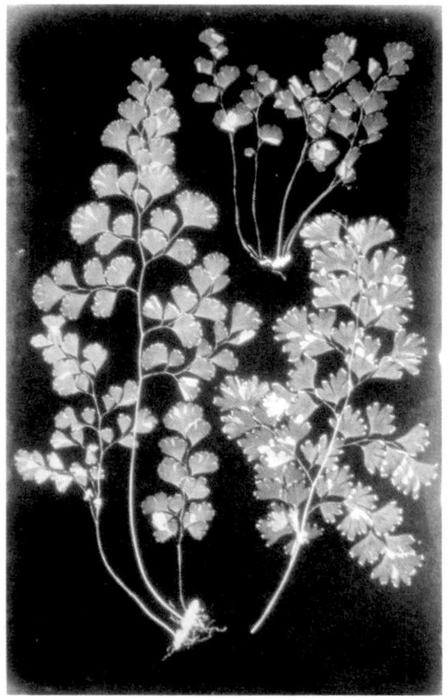

42. Cecilia Louisa Glaisher

Glaisher, Cecilia Louisa *ill. 42*

1828–1892

Cecilia Belville was the daughter of an assistant at the Royal Observatory. Little is known of her early life except that she started drawing lessons at the age of thirteen. In 1843, at the age of fifteen, she married James Glaisher, the superintendent at the observatory, who would become one of the best-known people in the photographic circles of the day, heading various societies and participating in research. Cecilia, who made illustrations of snow crystals that her husband employed in his publications, was probably drawn into photography through her husband's interests and may also have been influenced by various photographers that she would have met at Hartwell House, the home of Dr. John Lee, astronomer, mathematician, and philanthropist. In 1855, at the exhibition held in conjunction with the British Association for the Advancement of Science meeting in Glasgow, Glaisher displayed her large photogenic drawings of ferns. Meticulously done, they so impressed the natural history publisher Edward Newman that he hoped to enter them into the highly competitive botanical print market. But Glaisher's health was broken in childbirth not long after this, and nothing is known of any subsequent photographic work on her part.

Exhibited: 1855, Glasgow, British Association for Advancement of Science

Glynn, William

b. 1821

Glynn served with the Great Trigonometrical Survey of India from 1840 to 1846, continuing on in other administrative posts in the country. He may have first begun photography in 1855 while on an excursion through Tibet and Kashmir taken for his health. The next year Glynn was elected to the Photographic Society of Bengal, where he displayed a series of photographs of Agra and Kashmir that were much admired for their sharpness of detail and subtlety of tone. Glynn and Dr. John Murray exhibited waxed-paper views at the society in 1857; its *Journal* observed in the May 20 issue that "in point of size if not in quality the paper process had the advantage of the Collodion views." The article also noted that "the difficulties in the preparation and preservation of the materials" for wet collodion, along with the cumbersome and fragile glass plates, "have prevented its being yet applied with that success to the more interesting classes of Indian subject."

Reference: *Journal of the Photographic Society of Bengal*, no. 2 (January 21, 1857), p. 27; *Journal of the Photographic Society of Bengal*, no. 3 (May 20, 1857), p. 67

Goble, Harvey

1822–1867

Goble took an early interest in photography and in 1850 delivered two lectures on the "Science of the Sunbeam" before the Hastings Mechanics' Institution, illustrating these with his own examples of the Talbotype and the daguerreotype. While he did not participate in any national exhibitions, around 1857 Goble established a photographic studio in Worthing, advertising not only the common collodion portrait, but Talbotype and vignette portraits as well. To date, no examples of Goble's work have come to light.

Goddard, John Frederick

1797–1866

Goddard and Talbot shared many interests. In 1838, right on the eve of photography's introduction to the public, Goddard's work on the polarization of light was rewarded with the prestigious silver medal from the Society of Arts. Goddard's polariscope and Talbot's photogenic drawings were shown side by side in Edinburgh in December 1839. Goddard went to work for the London daguerreotypist Richard Beard and in 1840 discovered the applicability of bromine in sensitizing daguerreotype plates, which so greatly increased the sensitivity of the plates that portraiture immediately became practical. In 1842 Goddard visited Talbot at Lacock Abbey, photographing with both him and Nicolaas Henneman. He returned to London brimming with enthusiasm for the paper negative process, fitting out a special room to conduct further experiments. Although few details of this period are known, something apparently did not work out, and Goddard wound up a minor daguerreotypist in the provinces. In 1863, overenthusiastic supporters credited Goddard with introducing bromine into photography, prompting Talbot to prove that in fact he had done this first with bromine on paper. But Goddard's application of bromine to the daguerreotype would prove to be a critical underpinning of its commercial success, and a grateful photographic community raised a subscription to provide Goddard with an annuity in his old age.

Reference: Larry J. Schaaf, *Sun Pictures, Catalogue Nine: William Henry Fox Talbot—Friends and Relations* (New York: Hans P. Kraus, Jr., 1999), pp. 22–29

Goodeve, Thomas Minchin

b. 1821

It is likely that Goodeve first came into contact with photography during his stint as a mathematical lecturer and tutor at King's College, London, for the lively interest of Professor Charles Wheatstone and others at King's would have been inescapable. In the 1852 exhibition of the Society of Arts, Goodeve showed some portraits done on collodion but also views of statuary, landscapes, and the interior of the Great Exhibition of 1851, all done on albumenized paper (this was apparently the negative process, an unusual choice but not an impossible one). He appears to have left for France after this, marrying in Dieppe in 1873, and returning to London by 1876. Goodeve became a prolific author, issuing books on mechanisms, steam engines, and especially patent laws.

Exhibited: 1852, London, Society of Arts

Graham, James *ill. 43*

1806–1869

A native of Scotland, Graham arrived in Jerusalem in 1853 as the lay secretary of the London Society for Promoting Christianity Amongst the Jews. Already proficient in the calotype, he turned his energies to providing visual evidence of biblical sites. While in Jerusalem and without any commercial motivation, Graham, most of whose negatives are dated 1854 and 1855, freely taught others to calotype. He befriended the Pre-Raphaelite painters William Holman Hunt and Thomas Seddon, both of whom based paintings on his photographs. Hunt

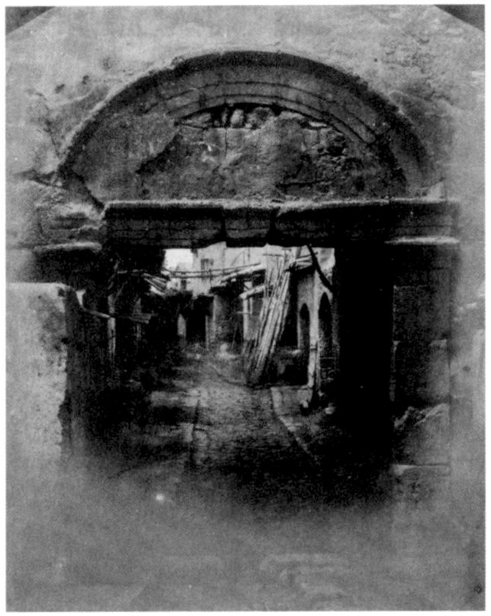

43. James Graham

especially relied on him, mentioning Graham's photography in his journals, and Seddon even confessed to his fiancée that he used Graham's photographs "to supply my own want of sketches." In 1856 he took a journey of several months to Egypt, returning to Jerusalem to meet criticism from his religious associates, who accused him, as one wrote in a letter on June 6, of indulging "too much in the society of worldly people" (such as Hunt and Seddon). Graham returned to Britain in 1857. He showed his photographs in the 1859 Exhibition of Fine Arts in Paris and displayed more than twenty waxed-paper views of Jerusalem in the 1862 International Exhibition in London. Among Graham's accomplishments are two calotype panoramas of Jerusalem, one in six parts and one in ten parts.

Exhibited: 1859, Paris, Société Francaise de Photographie; 1862, London, International Exhibition

References: James Graham to Maria Gobat, June 6, 1856, in *Fifth Annual Report of the Jerusalem Diocesan Missionary Fund* (London, 1858), p. 43; John Pollard Seddon, *Memoir and Letters of the Late Thomas Seddon, Artist* (London: J. Nisbet, 1858), p. 111; Michael Bartram, *The Pre-Raphaelite Camera: Aspects of Victorian Photography* (Boston: Little, Brown and Co., 1985), pp. 110–13; Carney E. S. Gavin and Nitza Rosovsky, "Mendell John Diness of Jerusalem and Cincinnati," *History of Photography* 19 (Autumn 1995), pp. 224–28

Gray, J. J.

A planter in Maldah, Bengal, Gray took up photography as an amateur sometime in the mid-1850s. In 1855 he gave a paper, "On a Simple Method of Manipulation in the Calotype Process," to the Photographic Society of Bengal, which would be published in *Journal of the Asiatic Society of Bengal*. Gray was resourceful, working out a method of making silver nitrate by dissolving rupees in acid, and he exhibited photographs made by calotype and waxed paper as well as the air-pump process developed by John Stewart (1814–1887). As reported in the *Journal of the Photographic Society of Bengal*, in 1857 he exhibited "excellent views about the ruins of Gour [Gaur]," the ruined ancient Muslim city in West Bengal. That same year, Gray asked advice of the society concerning a new process that he intended to use to supply prints to Lady Charlotte Canning, a former lady-in-waiting to Queen Victoria and the wife of the governor-general of India. He finally joined the Photographic Society of Bengal in 1862 and continued to photograph. In 1868 W. Le F. Robinson, the commissioner of the Rajshahi Division, recommended Gray as "a very good photographer" who would be willing to take additional photographs of Gaur.

References: *Journal of the Asiatic Society of Bengal* 24 (1855), pp. 287–90 "At Their Monthly and Annual Meeting," *Journal of the Photographic Society of Bengal*, no. 3 (May 20, 1857), p. 54; W. Le F. Robinson, Officiating Commissioner of Rajshahi Division, letter of November 26, 1867, Bengal General Proceedings, no. 110, June 1868, British Library, London

Grazebrook, J. T.

Grazebrook was almost certainly a member of the prominent Staffordshire family of iron founders and glassmakers. In 1858, he or she wrote from Audnam, near Birmingham, to the *Photographic Notes* complaining of a persistent problem of red-colored skies in calotype negatives (this was not uncommon, and was sometimes caused by overexposure). The editor suggested applying a gallic acid solution as soon as the image started to appear, as well as prolonging the development. Grazebrook continued photographic activity but apparently was still having problems the next year.

References: *Photographic Notes* 3 (June 15, 1858), p. 151; *Photographic Notes* 4 (August 1, 1859), p. 197

Green, John

The only personal information we have about Green is his banker's address, and with such a common name, his exact identity remains elusive. He showed work in the 1854, 1856, and 1857 exhibitions of the Photographic Society in London, including portraits, figure studies, still lifes, and views. Although Green normally employed collodion, he displayed at least one Talbotype in the 1856 exhibition.

Exhibited: 1856, London, Photographic Society

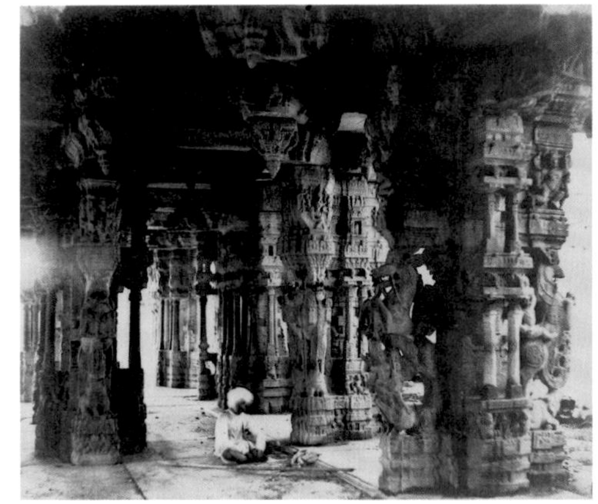

44. Alexander John Greenlaw

Greenlaw, Alexander John *ill. 44*

1818–1870

Greenlaw entered the East India Company as a cadet in 1834 and quickly rose through the ranks. He married in India in 1841 and made captain in the Madras Native Infantry by 1850. Exactly when Greenlaw began to practice photography as an amateur is not known, but it must have been in the early 1850s, for he showed works in an 1855 exhibition in Madras and was awarded a second-class medal for his "great variety of head size portraits, half-lengths, and groups," as later cited in *Reports by the Juries*. Like many other British photographers in India, Greenlaw was drawn to its architecture, landscape, and ruins, and negatives on paper were the most practical way to obtain the best results. In order to cope with the heat, Greenlaw ordered a special camera from Richard Williams Thomas in London. For the 1857 exhibition in Madras, the *Reports by the Juries* concluded: "It would be supposed from the nature of Photography that all pictures executed by its means must possess a similarity of style . . . this is not the case." Of the "the best Indian photographs in the Exhibition . . . the views by Capt. Tripe excel in finish and delicacy—those by Capt. Greenlaw in boldness, freedom and effect, the former are perhaps the best photographs, but the latter are the best pictures." Had Greenlaw done nothing more in his life than make better "pictures" than the famous Linnaeus Tripe, that would have been quite an accomplishment, but in fact his influence would prove to be much wider and longer lasting. Adapting methods from several others, he greatly simplified the calotype process, reducing it to its essentials, mostly in order to cope with the heat of India. In 1869 Greenlaw freely published his method, and it was reported under his name in both Abney's and Towler's influential manuals. The last of the original practitioners to publish on the calotype, Greenlaw had tuned the process to perhaps its finest potential, and it was his process that was cited well into the twentieth century.

Exhibited: 1856, Madras, Photographic Society; 1857, Madras, Madras Exhibition of Raw Products, Arts, and Manufactures of Southern India

References: *Madras Exhibition of Raw Products, Arts, and Manufactures of Southern India, 1855: Reports by the Juries on the Subjects in the Thirty Classes into which the Exhibition Was Divided* (Madras: General Committee of the Madras Exhibition, 1856); *Madras Exhibition of Raw Products, Arts, and Manufactures of Southern India: Reports by the Juries* (Madras, 1858); "Calotype Process," *Photographic News* 13 (January 15, 1869), pp. 28–29; John Towler, "The Calotype Process—by Col. A. G. Greenlaw," in *The Silver Sunbeam: A Practical and Theoretical Text-Book on Sun Drawing and Photographic Printing*, 8th ed. (New York: E. and H. T. Anthony, 1873), pp. 527–30; Janet Dewan, *Photographs of Linnaeus Tripe: A Catalogue Raisonné* (Toronto: Art Gallery of Ontario, 2003), p. 726

Gregory, J.

Nothing is known about Gregory, who listed his or her address simply as Peckham (a part of the Southwark area of London). Gregory showed seven waxed-paper copies of engravings in the 1858 exhibition of the Photographic Society in London. Interestingly, in the 1859 exhibition he exhibited additional copies of prints, but these were done in the "wet waxed-paper" process. Engravings were typically copied by superimposition, directly in contact with the sensitive photographic paper. However, calotypes were commonly used in a damp state to maintain sensitivity, and "wet waxed-paper" seems to have been a variant of this process. Since the wet chemicals would have adversely affected the original engravings if placed in direct contact, perhaps Gregory took the unusual step of copying his in the camera.

Exhibited: 1858 and 1859, London, Photographic Society

Grey, Stephen

1823–1891

Grey bought a Talbotype license for the town of Brighton in 1854, briefly had his own studio, and later that year went into partnership with William Hall. Grey & Hall advertised "large size" Talbotype portraits mounted in a gilt frame for fifteen shillings. Daguerreotypes were also offered, but it is not known how long the pair remained loyal to the paper negative. They parted ways in 1859, and Grey continued in the photographic business with his sons until the end of his life.

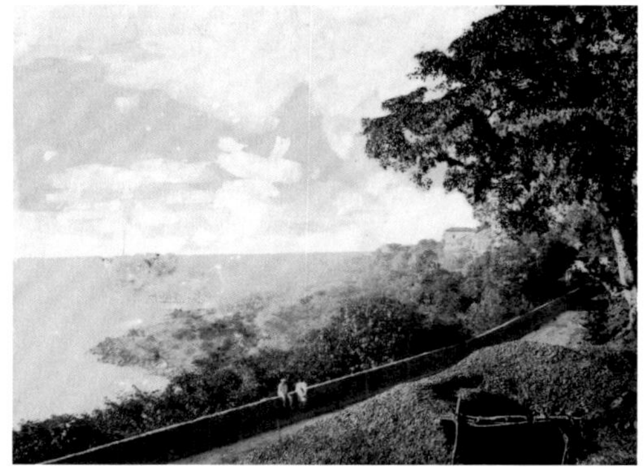

45. Francis Robert Griffith

Griffith, Francis Robert *ill. 45*

1828–1901

Griffith was a native of Corsley, Wiltshire, not far from Talbot's Lacock Abbey. However, he spent most of his career as a civil engineer in India. Very little is known about Griffith personally, but it seems most likely that he practiced photography as an amateur, and he photographed the architecture, archaeology, and landscape of India extensively. Griffith signed and titled many of his negatives, substantial groups of which were sold at auction in the 1970s and 1980s. Although these were identified as waxed paper, many of them carried the watermark of "R. Turner's Patent Talbotype" paper. This was a fairly thick paper, most suitable for Talbot's original calotype process, but of course it could be waxed after development for purposes of printing. Most of Griffith's work has been assigned to the 1850s, but at least one negative is dated 1861 and another 1863.

References: Sale cats., Sotheby's, London, March 8, 1974, lot 148; October 18, 1974, lot 148; June 26, 1975, lot 208, October 24, 1975, lot 247, June 29, 1979, lots 84–87, October 24, 1979, lots 107–12, March 21, 1980, lots 116–21, June 6, 1980, lots 67–73; October 29, 1980, lot 28

Griffiths, Lewis Richard Cook

b. 1826

Griffiths was curate of Hitcham in 1851 and rector of Swindon by 1861. When he started in photography is not known, but he contributed six calotypes to the 1855 exhibition of the Photographic Society in London, including views of bridges and ecclesiastical architecture and two landscapes. In 1857 Rev. Griffiths published his thoughts on removing iron spots from paper, a problem that had dogged photographers from the days of Talbot. Paper, then made by chopping up rags, sometimes included bits of metal buttons or tiny fragments of the machinery. These metallic spots were not apparent when the paper was used for writing, but they played havoc with the chemistry of the photographic process.

Exhibited: 1855, London, Photographic Society

Reference: Lewis Richard Cook Griffiths, "Calotype Process," *JPS* 3 (February 21, 1857), p. 225

Grove, William Robert

1811–1896

The son of a magistrate, Grove was born in Glamorgan and studied classics at Oxford. Preparing for a legal career, he moved to London, and was called to the bar in 1835. His interests in electricity and natural philosophy were possibly inspired by his tutor at Oxford, Baden Powell. Grove joined the Royal Institution in 1835 and that same year was one of the founding members of the Swansea Literary and Philosophical Society. He was probably first exposed to photography in Paris in the summer of 1839, where he read a paper on his new and powerful battery to the Académie des Sciences and undoubtedly also had an opportunity to examine Daguerre's early works. And that August, when attending the British Association for the Advancement of Science (BAAS) meeting in Birmingham, he would have seen Talbot's largest exhibition of photogenic drawings. In 1841 Grove read a paper at the London Electrical Society, "On a Voltaic Process for Etching Daguerreotype Plates" (the meeting was summarized in the *Times* on August 20th). In January 1843 he wrote to Henry Collen that he was giving a lecture the following week at the London Institution and hoped to borrow some examples of photographs of letters and prints, especially Collen's photographic copy of the Treaty of Nanking. At the 1844 BAAS meeting Grove read a paper, "On Photography," which detailed the experiments he had undertaken to perfect methods of direct positive photography on paper, including the conversion of negatives. He was particularly interested in copying lithographs, but unfortunately none of his photographs are known to have survived. Grove made many important contributions to science, including establishing the basis for the theory of the conservation of energy. Returning to the law in 1871, he became a judge and was knighted the following year.

References: "Important Combination of the Electrotype with the Daguerreotype Process," *Times* (London), August 20, 1841, p. 5, col. d; Grove to Henry Collen, January 13, 1843 (private collection); "On Photography. By Professor Grove," *Annual Report of the British Association for the Advancement of Science*, 1844, p. 37

Grubb, Thomas
1800–1878
Born into a Quaker family in Dublin, Grubb separated from the Society of Friends to marry in 1826. Little else is known about his early days, but by 1830 he had established himself as a very clever mechanical engineer. His system for supporting large mirrors was critical to the success of Lord Rosse's gigantic telescope, "The Leviathan," completed at Parsonstown in 1845. He almost certainly would have met Dr. THOMAS WOODS while working there. Grubb's interest in photography grew naturally out of his manufacture of fine optics, and in 1854 he was one of the founding members of the Dublin Photographic Society. He displayed his achromatic photographic lenses in the Dublin International Exhibition in 1853, but his achievements were not all technical. Four years later he showed some of his own photographs in the exhibition of the Photographic Society in London. All done in waxed paper, these included architectural views around Ireland, studies of foliage and a cedar of Lebanon, and the *Telescope of Lord Rosse*, the very instrument that Grubb's mechanical genius had made possible. Grubb published extensively on photography, usually on lenses and cameras, and his 1858 "aplanatic" lens was important to the development of landscape and wide-angle photography. Later in his career he was appointed engineer to the Bank of Ireland. Confined to a sickbed at the end of his life, Grubb designed and had built a swing bench that pivoted over his bed, and he died with his tools in his hands.

EXHIBITED: 1856, Paris, Société Francaise de Photographie; 1857, London, Photographic Society

REFERENCES: *BJP* 25 (September 27, 1878), p. 458 (obituary); John Burnett and Alison Morrison-Low, *Vulgar and Mechanick: The Scientific Instrument Trade in Ireland, 1650–1921* (Edinburgh: National Museums of Scotland, 1989), pp. 94–117; Ian S. Glass, *Victorian Telescope Makers: The Lives and Letters of Thomas and Howard Grubb* (Bristol: Institute of Physics Publications, 1997)

Gulliver, Thomas
b. 1822
Other than the fact that he was a native of Oxfordshire, nothing is known about the first decades of Gulliver's life. By the late 1850s he was resident in Swansea and was apparently already an experienced photographer. Gulliver was a fan of paper negatives because of their practical value and wrote to *Photographic Notes* in 1858 that he "was engaged to take 14 views in the town of Cardiff, to be used as evidence before a Committee of the House of Commons, in order to obtain a local act for the improvement of the Town." Glass negatives failed him, but, Gulliver revealed, the "Paper process . . . is quite a *Pet* process of mine." He interleaved the sensitized paper with damp towels, asserting, "The papers prepared this way will keep near a week. They can be easily changed in a small portable tent made to fit over the camera stand." How long Gulliver remained loyal to his "pet" process of paper negatives is not known, but he continued as an active professional photographer in Swansea at least into his eighties.

REFERENCES: Thomas Gulliver, letter in *Photographic Notes* 3 (July 15, 1858), p. 171; Gulliver, letter in *Photographic Notes* 4 (January 15, 1859), p. 32

Guppy, Amelia Elizabeth
1808–1886
A mercurial, high-spirited, and striking woman, Amelia Guppy (née Parkinson) first learned to love painting from her mother and then under the personal tutelage of the English landscape painter David Cox. In 1834 she eloped from her comfortable family home in Hertfordshire to marry Robert Guppy, a lawyer whose father and mother had made a fortune in copper cladding British warships. One new brother-in-law was a partner of Isambard Kingdom Brunel and another was the owner of Trinidadian sugar plantations. In 1839, the very year that photography was announced to the public, the Guppys moved to Trinidad to assist in the emancipation of the slaves. Guppy cut a striking figure on her mule, going out to paint the flora and the landscape, but she looked forward to her return visits to England. Her first known photograph is an 1847 portrait of her son Robert Lechmere Guppy (namesake of the popular aquarium fish). Back in London, she donated a negative taken in Trinidad to the Photographic Society in June 1853. That same year she calotyped various items in the vast collections of the mad bibliophile Sir Thomas Phillipps, a relative by marriage, her paper negatives including copies of ancient seals from Utrecht, Babylonian urns, and modern books. In 1854 Guppy displayed four calotypes of British architecture and landscape in the Photographic Society's exhibition in London, and she became a member of the society five years later, listing her address in Trinidad. In 1871, at the age of sixty-three, Guppy set off on her own to explore the upper reaches of the Orinoco River in Venezuela, intent on painting and collecting the region's rare orchids. We may never know the full extent of her photographic work, for most of Guppy's paintings and other artifacts were destroyed by the effects of storage during World War II.

EXHIBITED: 1854, London, Photographic Society

REFERENCES: Yseult Bridges, *Child of the Tropics: Victorian Memoirs*, edited and completed by Nicholas Guppy (London: Collins and Harvill Press, 1980); Larry J. Schaaf, "'Splendid Calotypes': Henry Talbot, Amelia Guppy, Sir Thomas Phillipps, Photographs on Paper," in *Six Exposures: Essays in Celebration of the Opening of the Harrison D. Horblit Collection of Early Photography* (Boston: Houghton Library, Harvard University, 1999), pp. 21–46

Gutch, John Wheeley Gough
1809–1862
The son of a publisher and antiquarian in Bristol, Gutch was educated at the infirmary there and practiced as a private physician in Florence for two years. Returning to England, he was a physician in Swansea and London until 1850, becoming a fellow of the Linnean Society and a member of the Meteorological Society. After consulting ROBERT HUNT, Gutch wrote to TALBOT about his difficulties in mastering the calotype, and Talbot replied in September 1841, supplying hints, examples of his own work, and even a sheet of iodized paper. Gutch's opportunities to travel were much enhanced when he was appointed a queen's messenger in 1850, charged with bearing dispatches to embassies throughout Europe, and the earliest known surviving print from one of his paper negatives is a view of a fountain in Madrid, dated May 21, 1851. He soon turned to wet collodion. Gutch contracted paralysis during a trip to Constantinople, forcing his retirement from the queen's service but giving him more time to pursue photography. He recalled in 1858 that "from ill-health and lameness, I was on the point of giving up Photography, when, in the early part of 1856, I was shown, for the first time, an 'Archer's Camera,' which appeared to me so thoroughly to combine all that could be desired." FREDERICK SCOTT ARCHER, better known as the inventor of the wet-collodion negative, also designed a portable camera incorporating a built-in darkroom. Gutch exhibited regularly from 1856 to 1861, primarily landscapes and views of ancient architecture, but also geological studies. Additionally, Gutch edited *The Literary and Scientific Register*, an annual encyclopedia, which highlighted photographic formulas in its 1857 edition, and at one point almost became editor of the *British Journal of Photography*.

REFERENCES: John Wheeley Gough Gutch, "Recollections and Jottings of a Photographic Tour, Undertaken during the Year 1856," *Photographic Notes* 3 (March 1 and April 1, 1858), pp. 66–69, 89–90; *BJP* 9 (June 2, 1862), p. 218 (obituary); *Gentleman's Magazine* 213 (July 1862), p. 113 (obituary); David Wooters, "John Wheeley Gough Gutch 'In Search of Health and the Picturesque,'" *Image* 36 (Spring 1993), pp. 3–15

Haes, Frank
1833–1916
Haes was a native of London but spent some of his youth in Australia. In fragmentary "photographic recollections" (first published by the *British Journal of Photography* to accompany his obituary), Haes recalled: "My first attempts in the black art began when I was not more than eleven years old, with the calotype process for copying leaves, etc., but I soon wanted a camera, and having never seen one, tried to make it with pasteboard and the field-glass of a shilling telescope." About 1852 he acquired a proper French camera, taking collodion positives "of no merit. After flirting with the Daguerreotype, about 1855 I was so pleased with the waxed paper process that I worked hard at it." Haes was then living in Blackheath and practicing as a photographer, showing waxed-paper views of English architecture in the 1855 and 1856 exhibitions of the Photographic Society in London. He then returned to Australia for two years, submitting seven waxed-paper views from there to the 1858 Photographic Society exhibition. Haes also teamed up with ARTHUR JAMES MELHUISH to devise a roller mechanism for the camera; joining up ten or twelve sensitized sheets of waxed paper as large as 12 x 15 inches, he was able to stock a whole day's shooting in his camera. Haes made a reputation in photographic circles for his photographs of zoo animals and, as secretary and treasurer of the Jewish Historical Society, he was often called upon to photograph historical objects. Haes was also one of the first photographic collectors. In the 1890s, his Fridays were spent at the Islington Cattle Market, looking for photographic artifacts. Perhaps it was to feed his collecting habit that Haes took an active interest in the stock market.

EXHIBITED: 1855, 1856, and 1858, London, Photographic Society

REFERENCES: *BJP* 63 (January 14, 1916), p. 24 (obituary); *Photographic Journal* 56 (January 1916), p. 11 (obituary)

Hall, Robert W.
In 1856 Hall was struggling with the waxed-paper process. Writing to the *Photographic News* two years later, he claimed: "I am an old hand at calotype, and, like all who know that simple and beautiful process, still entertain a strong regard for it, in spite of the numerous dry glass processes." Hall wrote from Baglan House, a historic property near Neath, Wales, owned by the Llewelyn family. In the same year, Richard Hall, a justice of the peace, was living there, and the two men were almost certainly related. Nothing else is at present known of Hall or his photographs.

EXHIBITED: 1858, London, Photographic Society

REFERENCES: Robert W. Hall, "Query on Woolliness in Wax-Paper," *JPS* 3 (April 21, 1856), p. 35; Hall, "Browning of Calotype Paper," *Photographic News* 1 (October 29, 1858), p. 94

Hall, William
b. 1827
Born in Scotland, Hall went into partnership in 1854 with STEPHEN GREY in Brighton to produce "large sized" Talbotype portraits, mounted in a gilt frame for fifteen shillings. Grey had purchased a Talbotype license for Brighton. Grey & Hall also offered daguerreotypes, but it is not known how long they remained loyal to paper negatives. Hall left the firm in 1859, Grey continuing the business with his sons. Hall did well on his own and by 1871 was employing three men, four women, and two boys in his photographic firm.

Harding, James Duffield
1797–1863
Harding was tutored in art by his father, the engraver John Harding, and showed such talent that he was accepted into exhibitions at the Royal Academy from the age of thirteen, winning a silver medal from the Society of Arts at nineteen. Harding vividly recalled that as a young man he had approached an artist in a park with some questions; nastily brushed off, he then and there vowed to share his knowledge whenever he could. Harding made good on his promise both as a teacher and, especially, through numerous influential publications, including his *Elementary Art; or, The Use of the Lead Pencil Advocated and Explained.* An early master of lithography, he was surely aware of photography from its start. In 1847 CALVERT RICHARD JONES wrote to WALTER CALVERLEY TREVELYAN: "I lately received a note from my Drawing master J. D. Harding whom I initiated into the Talbotype, and he is enraptured with its capabilities and promised to send me a specimen of some amplifications of it which he has devised; in such hands it is sure to prosper." In 1850 Harding approached Henneman & Malone, hoping they could produce twenty-five thousand photographic prints 12 x 10 inches in size for an intended publication, but Malone wisely confessed to TALBOT that an order of this magnitude would be impossible for the fledgling firm. None of Harding's calotypes are known to have survived.

REFERENCES: Calvert Richard Jones to Walter Calverley Trevelyan, December 13, 1847, Special Collections, Newcastle University Library, WCT 157-1; Malone to Talbot, April 27, 1850, Talbot Collection, British Library, London, LA50-20 (Talbot Correspondence Project, http://foxtalbot.dmu.ac.uk, doc. no. 06316)

Harmer, Henry Robert
b. 1823
A solicitor in Great Yarmouth, Harmer was elected a member of the Photographic Society in 1854, already an experienced photographer. The *Reports by the Juries* for the Great Exhibition of 1851 praised his entries, and he was awarded a medal. He "exhibited two calotype pictures, one a landscape; the reflections as shown in the water are excellent. The fluctuation of the reflections caused by the ripple of the water is very beautiful, and true to nature. The execution of the picture is good, and the tints are clear and delicate." Harmer exhibited calotypes regularly between 1854 and 1856, but he had started to use collodion as well and after 1856 seems to have switched completely to the glass process. Fellow photographer THOMAS LOUND proudly showed Harmer's "series of beautiful views in North Wales" to a meeting of the Norwich Photographic Society in 1857. After this, nothing further is known of his photographic work. Harmer was elected alderman for Yarmouth in 1880.

EXHIBITED: 1851, London, Great Exhibition; 1854, London, Photographic Society; 1854, second touring exhibition, Society of Arts (London); 1855, London, Photographic Society; 1855–56, third touring exhibition, Society of Arts (London)

REFERENCES: James Glaisher, "Class X," in *Reports by the Juries on the Subjects in the Thirty Classes into which the Exhibition Was Divided* (London: Printed for the Royal Commissioners, William Clowes & Sons, 1852), p. 278; "Norwich Photographic Society," *JPS* 3 (May 21, 1857), p. 281

Harper, George
b. 1821
Harper was a chemist in Norwich on Bank Plain, with a substantial business employing four men by 1851, but very little else is known about him. At least two of his calotypes survive. One, of a house under repair, is in fellow photographer THOMAS DAMANT EATON's 1845 "Camera Sketches" album. The other was sold at auction in 1985 as part of a small group that also included the work of JOHN BLOWERS and WILLIAM HOWES HUNT, and was described as "Bank Plain, (July 1845), Norwich, street scene with scaffolding."

REFERENCES: Sale cat., Sotheby's, London, June 28, 1985, lot 123

Harris, Mary
b. 1810
A landed proprietor at Long Sutton, Somerset, Harris wrote to the *Journal of the Photographic Society* in 1854. She had tried using the procedure developed by JOHN STEWART (1814–1887) for iodizing paper with a vacuum pump, hoping that, as promised, the paper would last "for months or even *years*." However, after two months her papers were losing sensitivity. Harris felt Stewart's "pictures speak so strongly in favour of his process" that she wanted to emulate them. None of her photographs are known to have survived.

REFERENCE: Mary Harris, "Mr. Stewart's Process," *JPS* 1 (January 21, 1854), p. 164

Hartshorne, Charles Henry
1802–1865
Rev. Hartshorne was a reluctant clergyman who had been introduced to bibliomania while still in his university days. His marriage to the daughter of the librarian at Cambridge brought him both a compatible soulmate and immense wealth. A move to Northamptonshire in 1838 positioned Hartshorne to pursue both antiquarian studies and photography. At an Architectural Society meeting in Northampton in 1850, Hartshorne "delivered a viva voce account of the Calotype," exhibiting not only the apparatus involved but also "some of these sun-pictures, the results of his own experiments." He cautioned his audience that "the calotypist must reckon upon scores and scores of failures for a single instance of tolerable success." No further reference to Hartshorne's patient calotyping has been traced, but he went on to be a significant author and an active member of several societies. His library was sold at Sotheby's after his sudden death, but the sale was a disappointment, as many of the items had been water damaged in a fire, and Hartshorne's own photographs might well not have survived this double calamity.

REFERENCES: Summary of Charles Henry Hartshorne's talk to the Architectural Society, explaining his own work with the calotype, in *Northampton Mercury*, October 2, 1850; *Dictionary of National Biography*, s.v. "Hartshorne, Charles Henry (1802–1865)"; Arnold Hunt, "A Study in Bibliomania: Charles Henry Hartshorne and Richard Heber," *Book Collector*, Spring–Summer 1993, pp. 250–83

Hay, John, Jr.
Hay was a partner with his father in a frame-making and picture-restoring business in Aberdeen; J. & J. Hay sold artists' materials and a range of scientific and optical instruments. Undoubtedly the young man had taken notice of customers coming in asking for supplies for the new art of photography, because sometime before 1853 John Jr. opened a calotype portrait studio. The new calotypist seems to have attracted a steady flow of interested customers, for he soon received a testimonial from John Philip, a prominent local painter, who opined in the *Aberdeen Journal* that Hay's portraits "are most faithful—so true to nature, and the treatment admirable as to tasteful arrangement, &c. Indeed, as far as I am able to judge, many of them are equal to Delamotte, and other noted London practitioners of this delightful and most useful art." In September 1853 Hay approached his old friend George Washington Wilson, and a partnership was soon formed. Wilson & Hay contributed to the 1853 exhibition of the Aberdeen Mechanics' Institution, displaying calotype portraits, some hand colored, and landscapes. In March 1854, Queen Victoria commissioned the firm to photograph the construction of Balmoral Castle. With royal patronage, the business flourished, the firm offering portraits, landscapes, views of "Gentleman's Seats," and stereo views, as well as chemicals, cameras, and lessons in photography. By the time of the 1854 exhibition of the Royal Infirmary Fund in Dundee, Wilson & Hay had converted completely to wet collodion. Hay's family went bankrupt in January 1855, prematurely ending his partnership with Wilson, and as far as is known Hay took no more photographs.

EXHIBITED: 1853, Aberdeen, Mechanics' Institute

REFERENCES: *Aberdeen Journal*, September 10, 1853 (advertisement); Roger Taylor, *George Washington Wilson: Artist and Photographer, 1823–93* (Aberdeen: Aberdeen University Press, 1981), pp. 16–19, 23

Hazard, John Bevan
b. 1831
Hazard presents some mysteries, for he worked closely with HUGH OWEN in Bristol and their calotypes are frequently commingled in albums. Studies of trees, shipping, and architecture seemed to be his favorites, and his work, which dates mostly from the 1850s, is quite accomplished. Hazard clearly initialed many of his negatives "J.B.H.," and yet one wonders, when did he find the time to photograph? In the 1851 census, at about the time he would have entered photography, Hazard was an apprentice in his father's mastmaking and blockmaking firm in Bristol. Even allowing for family indulgence, apprentices in such trades normally applied every daylight hour to their work. Hazard was unmarried and still filling this position in his father's firm in 1861, by which time he seems to have given up photography. He next appears in the 1891 census as a widower managing a brewery in Bristol.

REFERENCE: Reece Winstone, *Bristol's Earliest Photographs* (Bristol: Reece Winstone, 1970)

Heath, Robert Vernon
1819–1895
Known invariably as Vernon Heath, the young man was plunged into the art world in 1841 when he became secretary to his uncle, Robert Vernon, the respected art collector and major donor to the National Gallery in London. In his *Recollections*, published near the end of his life, Heath recalled attending one of Michael Faraday's lectures at the Royal Institution in London, on January 25, 1839, the very evening that TALBOT first displayed his new art of photogenic drawing. In 1842 Heath secured a license from Talbot (only the third one issued), purchased his first calotype camera from the famous London optician Andrew Ross, and gathered together the proper chemicals, obtaining "results with these which then afforded me the greatest pleasure and gratification." He photographed his uncle's estate at Ardington, Berkshire, exhibiting these views as late as 1874, and finally summoned up the courage to ask his famous uncle to sit for his camera. The portrait's exposure was eight minutes, with the subject sitting in a garden chair; Heath remembered that "he did as he was told. I obtained a capital result, for it was the most characteristic portrait that had ever been done of him." His new passion brought him many new contacts, and in 1854 Heath opened a photographic studio in London, accepting "engagements at country houses" and giving lessons in photography. He took in ROBERT MURRAY as a partner in 1855, by which time he had abandoned calotypy for wet collodion. From 1857 to 1865 Heath contributed regularly to various photographic exhibitions, and his views of Burnham Beeches were considered some of the finest photographs of the time. But despite his artistic success and the respect of his peers, Heath found himself in constant financial difficulty. He first filed for bankruptcy in 1865 and was in legal trouble throughout the 1870s and 1880s. He attempted suicide in the river Thames in 1891 but fortunately survived, completing his illuminating *Recollections* the following year.

REFERENCES: Vernon Heath, "The Early History of Photography," *Photographic News* 30 (October 29, 1886), pp. 701–2; Heath, *Vernon Heath's Recollections* (London: Cassell & Co., 1892); *BJP* 42 (November 1, 1895), p. 699 (obituary)

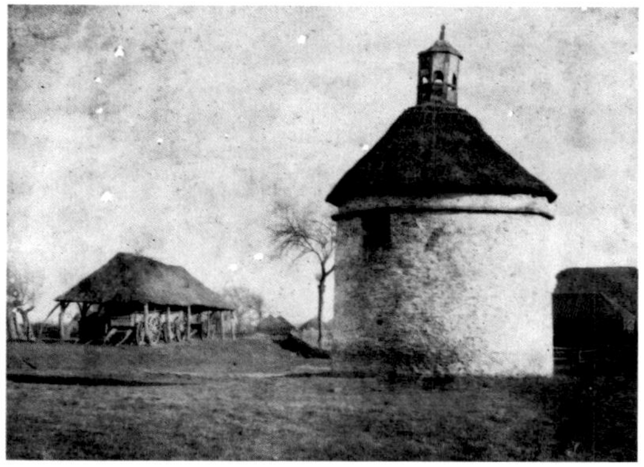

46. John Moyer Heathcote, Sr.

Heathcote, John Moyer, Sr. *ill. 46*
1800–1892
Heathcote had a son of the same name who became the finest tennis player of his generation. The son (1834–1912) was a man of many interests and an amateur artist, so it is tempting to think that in fact he was the photographer. However, a personal memory by Cuthbert Bede (the pen name of Edward Bradley), whose 1855 *Photographic Pleasures* was a critical if amusing record of the period, makes it clear that the older Heathcote was the photographer with whom he worked. Heathcote, of Conington Castle, Norfolk, was a justice of the peace and a watercolor artist as well as both a patron and an amateur pupil of the English landscape painter Peter De Wint. He worked extensively in the waxed-paper process, and many of his negatives survive and are annotated. Heathcote was an antiquarian who used photography to document architecture and scenes; one important album is his 1853 "Anglia Illustrata." Although his features cannot be made out, Heathcote is pictured in a dynamic pose in Bede's humorous cartoon, "The Present 'Attitude' of Photography," first published in *Punch* and later in *Photographic Pleasures.*

References: Cuthbert Bede [Edward Bradley], *Photographic Pleasures: Popularly Portrayed with Pen and Pencil* (London: T. McLean, 1855); *Sun Pictures, Catalogue One: Early British Photographs on Paper* (New York: Hans P. Kraus, Jr., 1984), no. 27; Bridget A. Henisch and Heinz K. Henisch, *The Photographic World and Humour of Cuthbert Bede* (Lewiston, N.Y.: Edwin Mellen Press, 2002)

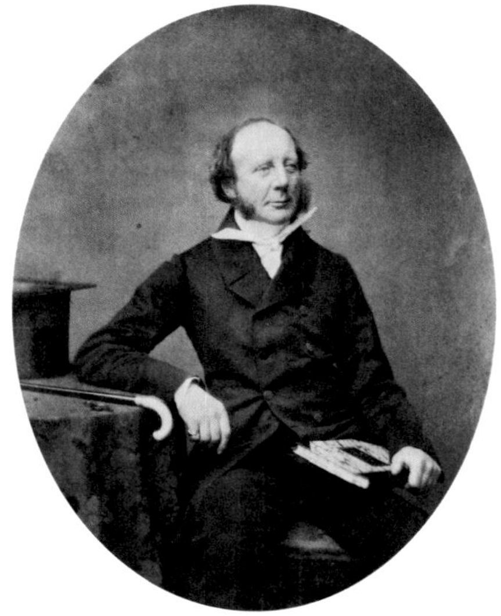

47. Portrait of Charles Heisch

Heisch, Charles *ill. 47*
b. 1821
Lecturer in chemistry at Middlesex Hospital in London and a forensic consultant, Heisch would have had no difficulties in mastering the physical intricacies of photography. His 1851 *Plain Directions for Obtaining Photographic Pictures* demonstrated an easy mastery of paper processes, one expanded in his 1862 *Elements of Photography.* When VERNON HEATH retired from ROBERT MURRAY's firm in 1862 to devote himself to photography, Heisch was chosen as his replacement. A fellow of the Chemical Society, Heisch was appointed gas examiner for the City of London in the 1880s and was instrumental in bringing gas lighting to the city. None of his photographs are known to have survived.

Exhibited: 1856, 1857, and 1859, London, Photographic Society

References: Charles Heisch, *Plain Directions for Obtaining Photographic Pictures upon Waxed and Albumenised Paper and Glass by Collodion and Albumen* (London: R. Willats, 1851); "Mr. Vernon Heath," *Photographic News* 6 (February 14, 1862), p. 84; Heisch, *Elements of Photography* (London: Murray and Heath, 1862)

Hele, Henry Herbert
b. 1804
A surgeon in Ashburton, Devon, in November 1854 Hele credited HUGH WELCH DIAMOND in *Notes and Queries* for "having given me the first impulse in the art." He was active in calotypy at least by 1853, writing that "the season is fast advancing for the calotypist." However, the idea of fine details intrigued him, and he confessed that he had become "a wax-paper man to the back-bone." Photography must have taken over his life, for Hele admitted to "devoting my whole time to the work," but he started having trouble with his negatives, which suffered from a granular surface mottling. One day, in the course of making wax casts of fruits (for unexplained reasons), he observed that the common wax he was working with had been adulterated. After that, Hele used beeswax that he personally melted from the comb for both his wax casting and his photography. By 1856, however, he had succumbed to the lure of collodion photography, writing to *Photographic Notes* of its desirability "on account of the greater sharpness of its proofs, together with its capabilities of admitting living figures in its foregrounds, life-giving desiderata to all pictures." In spite of his continuing enthusiasm in the press, Hele appears never to have exhibited, and none of his photographs are known to have survived.

References: Henry Herbert Hele, "Photographic Unanimity," *Notes and Queries* (November 18, 1854), p. 410; "Correspondence," *LPJ* 2 (November 10, 1855), pp. 142–43; Hele, "On Waxed-Paper," *Photographic Notes* 1 (September 15, 1856), pp. 176–77

Henderson, James (of Edinburgh)
Henderson was a commercial photographer in Edinburgh with a studio on Princes Street. He first participated in an exhibition showing collodion works, both portraits and copies of prints, and by 1858 he was experimenting with coloring photographs. Henderson joined the Photographic Society of Scotland in 1856, and perhaps it was through its influence that he turned to waxed paper. In the society's 1864 exhibition, he presented nineteen portraits done in waxed paper. Henderson joined the Edinburgh Photographic Society in 1869.

Exhibited: 1864, Edinburgh, Photographic Society of Scotland

Henderson, James (of London)
b. 1824
A London native, Henderson set up his first Talbotype and daguerreotype studio in 1848. He moved to the more prestigious Strand, but must have known events were taking a bad turn when the facade of his new studio collapsed into the street in September 1853. In May of the next year, TALBOT sued Henderson for infringing on his patent. The suit was later abandoned when Talbot lost to Sylvester Laroche; nevertheless, Henderson relocated to Brighton in August 1855 and then to Launceston,

Cornwall, a month later. His subsequent photographic activities are unknown.

Henderson, William

Henderson first appeared in Bombay in 1840 as a clerk in the Military Board Office, continuing on in a number of clerical and bookkeeping positions. In 1856 he became a member of the Photographic Society of Bombay and exhibited waxed-paper views in their exhibition that year. Henderson held his last known clerical position in 1857, and the next year the photographic firm of Johnson & Henderson was listed. In 1859 this became the Henderson & Co. Photographic Depot, which lasted at least until 1866. William Henderson's involvement in this firm or its predecessor has yet to be established.

Exhibited: 1856, Bombay, Photographic Society

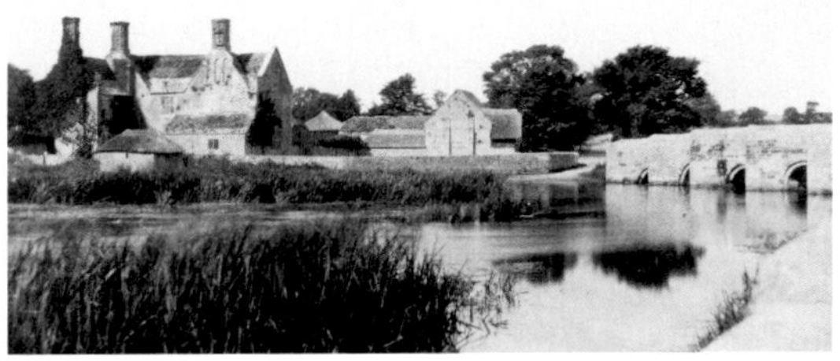

48. Thomas Henry Hennah

Hennah, Thomas Henry *ill. 48*

1826–1876

Hennah and his partner, WILLIAM HENRY KENT, purchased a Talbotype license in 1852 and established a Talbotype Portrait Gallery above William Mason's print shop on King's Road, Brighton. Hennah's reputation is based foremost on his practical handbook on wet-collodion photography, first published in 1853 and enlarged through several subsequent editions. However, he was an accomplished calotypist from the beginning. In reviewing the first (1854) exhibition of the Photographic Society in London, the *Builder* enthused: "Mr. Hennah's portraits are faultless: one would not begrudge a journey to Brighton for no other purpose than to be Calotyped by him." In the society's 1855 exhibition, Hennah supplemented his studio collodion work with six landscape and architectural views of Sussex, all done on waxed paper. It may be that the original paper negative process continued to command Hennah's respect, for the Talbotype Portrait Gallery kept its name until 1884, long after the calotype process had been abandoned.

Exhibited: 1855, London, Photographic Society

References: Thomas Henry Hennah, *Plain and Practical Directions for Obtaining Both Positive and Negatives Pictures upon Glass by Means of the Collodion Process* (London: George Knight and Sons, 1853); "Photography and the Photographic Exhibition," *Builder* 12 (January 21, 1854), p. 28; *BJP* 23 (January 28, 1876), p. 47 (obituary); Philippe Garner, *A Seaside Album: Photographs and Memory* (London: Philip Wilson, in association with the Royal Pavilion, Libraries and Museums, Brighton, 2003), pp. 25–28

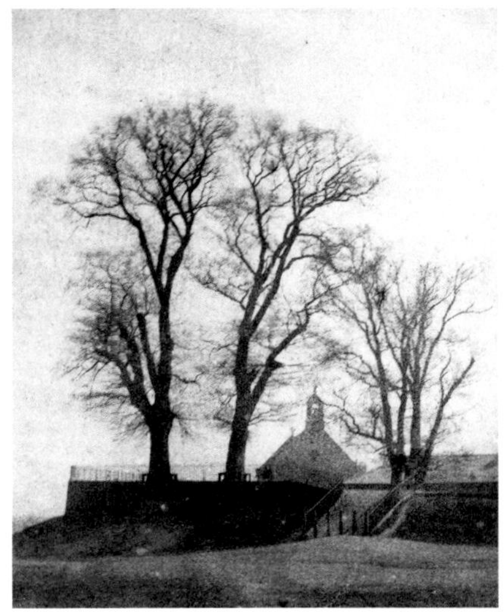

49. Nicolaas Henneman

Henneman, Nicolaas *ill. 49*

1813–1898

No one was more important to TALBOT's introduction of photography on paper than Nicolaas Henneman. Born in Holland and polished in Paris, Henneman was a clever and dedicated worker. As valet to Talbot at Lacock Abbey, he assisted in preparations, experiments, and printing, and he took many photographs himself, some of which are undoubtedly credited to Talbot. More importantly, Henneman's loyalty and enthusiasm buttressed Talbot's spirits and resolve during the early days, when it appeared that the triumph of the daguerreotype might, so to speak, reverse the British victory at Waterloo. Clearly Henneman played a critical role, but, ironically, he was himself quite an underwhelming photographer. He accompanied Talbot on photographic expeditions around Britain, and in 1843 the pair ventured into France, securing important photographs later published in *The Pencil of Nature*. Later that year, in an act of great confidence and courage, especially for one of his social standing, Henneman left Talbot's employ to set up the world's first dedicated photographic printing works, in the town of Reading, proudly declaring himself a "Calotypist." (The operation was never called The Reading Establishment, nor was it owned and operated by Talbot—both common misconceptions.) Henneman printed the plates for *The Pencil of Nature* at Reading, including the one of Westminster Abbey that he took himself. Later in 1844 he accompanied Talbot north to assist in the photography for *Sun Pictures in Scotland*. Print permanence remained a crippling problem, and Henneman was unable to sustain his operation in Reading. By 1847 he was forced to approach the larger market of London, this time in a business largely owned by Talbot but called Nicolaas Henneman's Sun Picture Rooms. In 1848 he was joined by the young chemist THOMAS AUGUSTINE MALONE, and by the next year Henneman & Malone were billing themselves as "Photographers to the Queen." The firm made every attempt to be innovative, advertising photography by electric light (crucial in the smog-ridden capital) and exhibiting a wide range of photographs in the Great Exhibition of 1851, including works not only on paper but also on silk and other materials. Originally Henneman was commissioned to make the prints for the exhibition's *Reports by the Juries*, but he was brutally pushed aside. At the point when amateurs began to seriously embrace the calotype, the process was in fact on the wane commercially. Henneman planned to greatly expand his printing works at Kensal Green, London, but Talbot warned him that mass photographic printing in silver would have no future once he had perfected his photographic engraving process (this took some decades, but Talbot was eventually proven correct). While Henneman taught many successful photographers at Lacock, Reading, and London, he never achieved true artistry himself, and in the increasingly competitive photographic world of the 1850s he was more and more out of step with the times. By 1859 financial difficulties had overwhelmed him and he shut down his business. In the 1860s Henneman worked as an operator for other photographers in Scarborough and Birmingham. He considered becoming a photographer in Portugal but instead returned to London in 1868, operating a rooming house. Throughout all this, he and Talbot remained loyal to each other, never forgetting the unusually close photographic bond they had established in the 1840s. Henneman's service to photography on paper was of crucial importance to Talbot and hence to the early development of the new art.

Exhibited: 1851, London, Great Exhibition

Reference: Arthur Gill, "Nicholas Henneman, 1813–1893 [*sic*]," *History of Photography* 4 (October 1980), pp. 313–22

Henry, Robert John

Captain Henry was attached to the 4th Royal Irish Dragoon Guards, based variously in Dublin and in London. A member of the Photographic Society in London from its start in 1853, Henry showed six waxed-paper views of landscape and topography in England, Ireland, and Scotland at the 1856 exhibition of the Société Française de Photographie in Paris. He also contributed to *The Photographic Album for the Year 1857* but by then had turned to collodion.

Exhibited: 1856, Paris, Société Francaise de Photographie

Hering, Henry

1814–1893

Hering started as a bookbinder in London and progressed through print selling and other related trades, becoming a publisher by 1851. How he first became involved in photography is not known, but Dr. HUGH WELCH DIAMOND called on him to photograph inmates at an insane asylum between 1852 and 1862. Herring's varied experience in the commercial end of the visual arts stood him in good stead when he opened his first photographic studio in London in 1856. In that year's exhibition at the Photographic Society, he displayed three Talbotype views; probably representing a larger body of paper negative photography by him, they are all that are known to have survived. In the same exhibition Hering showed a framed group of engravings copied in the collodion process, a harbinger of the copies of engravings and paintings that he would exhibit regularly through 1862. After winning an honorable mention for artistic excellence in the 1862 International Exhibition in London, Hering began to move away from photography. Two years later he sold his print shop and retired to Reigate.

Exhibited: 1856, London, Photographic Society

Herries, Alexander Young *ills. 50, 51*

1827–1918

Herries, also known as the younger, of Spottes, Scotland, was an advocate in Edinburgh. When and how he became interested in photography are not known, but he was a member of the Edinburgh Photographic Exchange Club. Herries was married in Guernsey and perhaps that

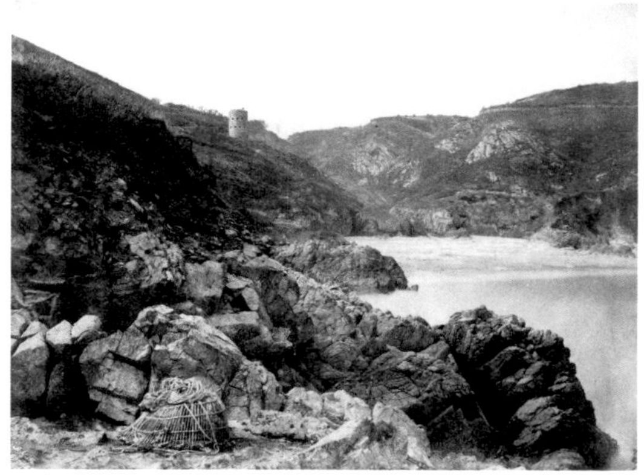

50. Alexander Young Herries

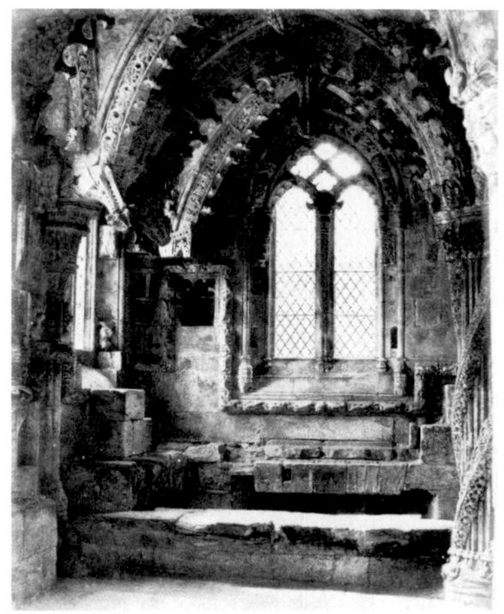

51. Alexander Young Herries

explains his first exhibited waxed-paper views, all taken in Guernsey, which were included in the 1856 exhibition of the Photographic Society of Scotland. In the society's 1858 exhibition and in the 1859 exhibition of the Glasgow Photographic Society, Herries showed waxed-paper architectural and landscape views, all from Scotland. In his last known public exhibition, for the Photographic Society of Scotland in 1864, he remained loyal to waxed paper, showing a range of views from England, Guernsey, and Scotland. A member of the Photographic Society of Scotland until it folded in 1873, Herries inherited the ancient mansion of Spottes in Kirkcudbright, Scotland. Locally, he took an interest in archery and was friends with fellow photographer Patrick Dudgeon and the scientist James Clerk Maxwell.

Exhibited: 1856 and 1858, Edinburgh, Photographic Society of Scotland; 1859, Glasgow, Photographic Society; 1864, Edinburgh, Photographic Society of Scotland

Herries, R.

R. Herries showed waxed-paper views of Kirkcudbright, Scotland, in the 1859 exhibition of the Glasgow Photographic Society. No identifying information was given, but both a Richard Herries and a Robert Herries were living in Kirkcudbright at the time.

Exhibited: 1859, Glasgow, Photographic Society

Herschel, John Frederick William

1792–1871

TALBOT had few important sources of support in the early days of photography on paper, but among these the commanding scientific figure was Sir John Herschel. The name Herschel was known throughout the world, not only because of the family's achievements in astronomy but also as a model of the modern scientific man. Separated by a generation, the critical one that bridged the eighteenth and nineteenth centuries, Herschel and Talbot first met in Munich in 1824. It was Herschel who introduced Talbot to Sir DAVID BREWSTER, and the two became fast if improbable friends. When Talbot was forced to hurriedly disclose his invention of photography in January 1839 after the announcement of daguerreotypy, Herschel was one of the first colleagues he contacted. Taking the newly laid railway out to Slough to see Herschel, Talbot discovered that the scientist had independently invented his own photographic process in less than a week! From that point on, Herschel's immediate and far-ranging series of experiments set a pace that Talbot was only too happy to meet. Their correspondence during 1839 brims with excitement, creativity, and enthusiasm. Applying a concept he had first explored in 1819, Herschel used hypo (sodium thiosulfate) as a fixer in the photographic process, a critical advance. He was also concerned with regularizing the advance of photography, inventing not only the word "photography" but also the terms "positive" and "negative." Herschel produced numerous paper negatives using variations of his own processes during 1839, and by that autumn he had even succeeded in making negatives on glass. Over the next few years he explored hundreds of different processes on paper, his 1842 cyanotype process proving the most influential. Herschel had little interest in actually producing images with the photographic processes he explored; his real quarry was an understanding of light. However, this did not reflect a rejection of either aesthetics or practical applications. Herschel had long been a master of the camera lucida (the instrument that had so frustrated Talbot that he was forced to invent photography). He preferred the analytical process of drawing to the extractive process of photography (but, indeed, it was also Herschel who coined the term "snap-shot" in 1860). He greatly influenced the photographers around him, including his brother-in-law, JOHN STEWART (1814–1887), and especially Julia Margaret Cameron, who considered him "my first Teacher & to you I owe all the first experiences & insights" in the art. Acting on his philosophy of self-sacrifice and devotion to country, Herschel reluctantly accepted the position of master of the mint in 1851 and accomplished major and necessary reforms to Britain's financial system, but at a cost to his health and scientific endeavors.

REFERENCES: Julia Cameron to John Frederick William Herschel, December 31, 1864, in *The Cameron Collection: An Album of Photographs by Julia Margaret Cameron Presented to Sir John Herschel* (Wokingham: Van Nostrand Reinhold, in association with the National Portrait Gallery, London, 1975), pp. 140–41; "The Late Sir John F. W. Herschel, F.R.S.: His Discoveries in Photography," *BJP* 18 (May 19 and 26, 1871), pp. 229–31, 241–43; Charles Pritchard, *Monthly Notices of the Royal Astronomical Society* 32 (1872), pp. 122–42 (obituary); Günther Buttman, *The Shadow of the Telescope: A Biography of John Herschel*, ed. David S. Evans and trans. B. E. J. Pagel (London: Lutterworth Press, 1974); Larry J. Schaaf, *Out of the Shadows: Herschel, Talbot, & the Invention of Photography* (New Haven and London: Yale University Press, 1992)

Higgin, Thomas

b. 1827

Higgin was a substantial merchant in Liverpool, employing fifty men and specializing in salt. He was an advocate of the pure calotype, writing in 1855 of "being impressed with the conviction that by the Talbotype process, much delicacy, beauty, and softness is obtained, especially in foliage, which cannot be found in pictures taken by the waxed-paper process." Higgin was on the council of the Liverpool Photographic Society. In 1888 the *British Journal of Photography* noted that Higgin "has devoted his efforts to the department of microscopic photography with great ardour and enthusiasm, and produced works of the highest possible merit, which have not been excelled." Higgin's firm later became an important exporter of salt to South Australia.

REFERENCES: Thomas Higgin, "On the Application of Mr. Townsend's Process to Un-Waxed Paper," *LPJ* 2 (January 13, 1855), pp. 6–7; *LPJ* 2 (February 10, 1855), pp. 15–16; James Alexander Forrest, "Historical Notes of What Liverpool Has Done in the Art-Science of Photography," *BJP* 35 (February 3, 1888, pp. 72–74

Hilditch, George

1803–1857

The son of a silk merchant, Hilditch even in boyhood took a keen interest in drawing and painting from nature. From the time of his first contribution in 1823 until his early death, he exhibited regularly in the Royal Academy. Hilditch, widely known as "The Richmond Painter," was fascinated with the landscape of this important town near London. With his devotion to truth to nature, it is not surprising that photography would capture his interest. In the groundbreaking 1852 exhibition at the Society of Arts in London, Hilditch contributed thirteen architectural and landscape views done with paper negatives, along with collodion portraits. In 1854 Hilditch still favored the calotype but also contributed a few waxed-paper views to the exhibitions of the Royal Infirmary Fund in Dundee and the Photographic Society in London. By the time of the society's 1855, 1856, and 1857 exhibitions, Hilditch was doing all of his architectural work on waxed paper, concentrating on London and its environs. To the end, Hilditch approached his subject matter with the same skill using his camera as he did his paints.

EXHIBITED: 1852, London, Society of Arts; 1853–54, first touring exhibition, Society of Arts (London); 1854, London, Photographic Society; 1854, Dundee, Royal Infirmary Fund; 1854, second touring exhibition, Society of Arts (London); 1855, 1856, and 1857, London, Photographic Society

REFERENCE: *From Canvas to Camera: George Hilditch, 1803–1857*, exh. cat. (Richmond: Museum of Richmond, 2000)

Hill, David Octavius

ills. 52, 53

1802–1870

The Edinburgh partnership of Hill and ROBERT ADAMSON represented the absolute high point of the earliest days of calotypy. Born in Perth, Hill published his first serious lithographs while still a teenager. Moving to Edinburgh, he quickly established a reputation as an accomplished landscape artist. Hill was a highly attractive figure, both in physique and personality, and with his talent and bonhomie he built a wide circle of artistic friends. In 1829 he was a founding member of the Society of Artists, which later became the Royal Scottish Academy (he would be its secretary throughout his lifetime). When the Disruption took place in the Church of Scotland in 1843, Hill was so moved by the courage of the breakaway ministers that he publicly vowed to record the more than four hundred of them in a giant portrait. Fortunately, Adamson had just established his calotype studio on Calton Hill, and Sir DAVID BREWSTER put the two men in touch, resulting in a

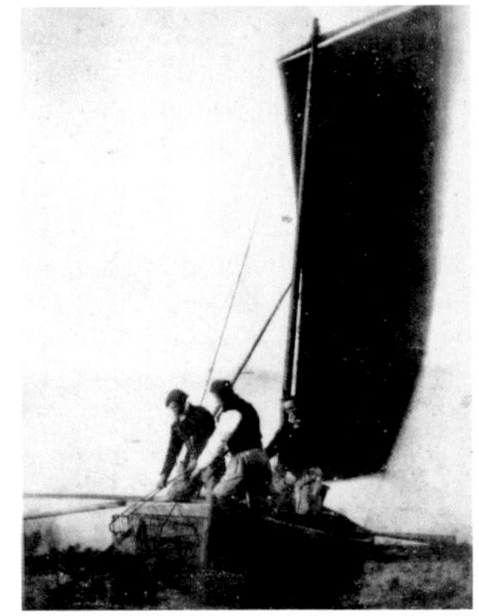

52. David Octavius Hill and Robert Adamson

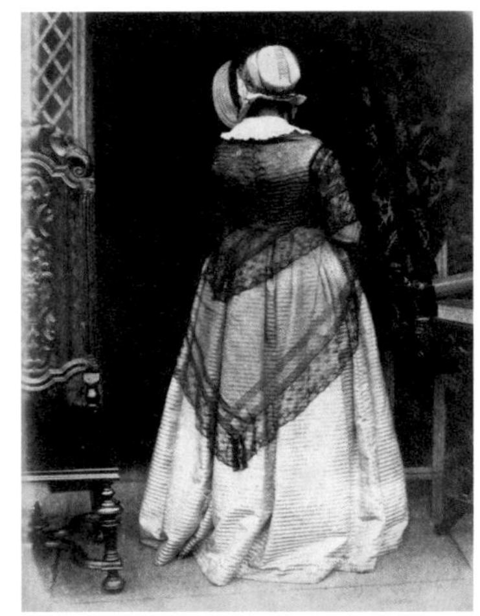

53. David Octavius Hill and Robert Adamson

truly symbiotic partnership that almost immediately began to produce calotype portraits of great eloquence, sensitivity, and good humor. The firm's reputation grew rapidly, and their clientele soon included the society of Edinburgh. Although known primarily for their portraiture, Hill & Adamson also produced important landscapes, architectural views, and studies of the fishing community of Newhaven. Adamson's tragic early death brought an end to the partnership, which had lasted only a little over three years, nevertheless producing thousands of significant photographs. Hill remained active in the artistic community, but his photographic work following Adamson's death is of little interest. He entered Hill & Adamson's calotypes in the Great Exhibition of 1851, giving full credit to his late friend, as well as the 1854 exhibition of the Royal Infirmary Fund in Dundee; the 1856 exhibition of the Photographic Society of Scotland in Edinburgh; the 1857 exhibition of the Birmingham Photographic Society; and the 1859 exhibition at the British Association for the Advancement of Science meeting in Aberdeen. At the 1862 International Exhibition in London, Hill displayed the enigmatically titled *Contributions to Photography*, his final showing in a photographic exhibition. In their very brief collaboration, Hill & Adamson proved beyond a doubt that photography was an art.

Exhibited: 1851, London, Great Exhibition; 1854, Dundee, Royal Infirmary Fund; 1856, Edinburgh, Photographic Society of Scotland; 1857, Birmingham, Photographic Society; 1859, Aberdeen, British Association for the Advancement of Science; 1862, London, International Exhibition

References: *Edinburgh Evening Courant*, May 18, 1870, p. 8 (obituary); *BJP* 17 (May 27, 1870), p. 250 (obituary); Sara Stevenson, *The Personal Art of David Octavius Hill* (New Haven: Published for the Paul Mellon Centre for Studies in British Art by Yale University Press, 2002)

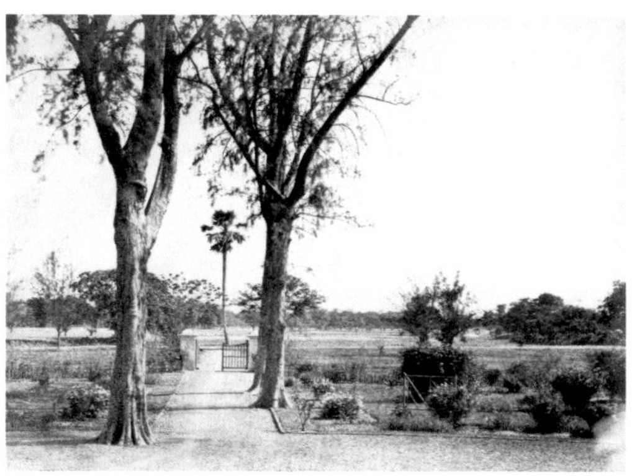

54. Richard Barton Hill

Hill, Richard Barton *ill. 54*

b. 1835

The son of a Gloucestershire surgeon, Hill studied classics and mathematics and became a cadet in the Bengal Army in 1853. Very little is at present known about his photographic work, but it included at least one paper negative, a *View from Himalayas*, that probably represents a larger body of work. In the 1864 exhibition of the Photographic Society of Bengal, his efforts were noticed: "Capt. R. B. Hill has some good Barrackpore sketches. No. 744, a pretty view in the station, is a pretty good picture, well taken; the perspective is excellent, but the photograph is not well vignetted, and an inch on each side with half an inch from top and bottom might have been cut off with advantage; it would then form a sweet little picture."

Exhibited: 1864, Calcutta, Photographic Society of Bengal

Reference: *Journal of the Photographic Society of Bengal* 2 (March 1864), p. 83

Hinton, J. G. Henry

Variously known as H. Hinton, Henry Hinton, or J. G. Henry Hinton, he was a schoolmaster in Bombay, where his wife taught at a seminary. In 1856 Hinton joined the Photographic Society of Bombay, whose members tried to be encouraging, recognizing that Hinton had previously "devoted much of his time and practice to daguerreotype, and although his specimens are not of the first order, yet we have no doubt it needs only a little more experience to place him in the first rank of the devotees of this beautiful branch of the art." Hinton fared little better with the waxed-paper views he entered into the society's 1856 exhibition: "Mr Hinton's negatives, judging from the uneven skies of his prints, are deficient in density." In 1857 his work *was* accepted in the *Indian Amateurs Photographic Album*. Although his merits as an educator are not recorded, perhaps he was better at photography, for in spite of the discouragement, Hinton began to style himself in the directories as a "schoolmaster and photographer." Under the name of Henry Hinton, he operated a photographic studio in Bombay until 1872.

Exhibited: 1856, Bombay, Photographic Society

Reference: "Exhibition of Photographs at Bombay," *LPJ* 3 (October 11, 1856), pp. 141–42

Hogg, Jabez

1817–1899

For most of his professional career, Dr. Hogg was a surgeon of ophthalmology, a fellow of the Linnean Society, and an influential microscopist. However, as a young man, as soon as he could escape the drudgery of his apprenticeship to a medical practitioner, Hogg turned to writing, perhaps inspired by his schoolboy association with Charles Dickens. Hogg's 1845 *Practical Manual of Photography* went through several editions, promising "photography made easy." In 1895, by which time photographs in print were becoming commonplace, *Men and Women of the Time* recalled the late Herbert Ingram, founder of the *Illustrated London News*, having "had a great idea that Photographic Art could be made available for the purposes of the newspaper, but after many trials, this, for the time being, proved a failure, although it has of late years become a great factor in newspaper as well as in book work." For these pioneering attempts, Ingram had turned to Hogg, who would also go on to edit *The Illustrated London Almanack* for fifty years. After he obtained his surgeon's diploma in 1850, Hogg became increasingly involved in ophthalmology. Although obviously experienced in photography, Hogg exhibited only once that we know of, in the 1854 exhibition of the Royal Infirmary Fund in Dundee, to which he contributed copies of engravings.

References: Jabez Hogg, *A Practical Manual of Photography* (London: E. Mackenzie, Cleave, Clark, 1845); *Men and Women of the Time: A Dictionary of Contemporaries*, 14th ed. (London: G. Routledge, 1895), pp. 425–26; *American Monthly Microscopical Journal* 20 (1899), p. 259 (obituary); *Nature* 59 (1899), p. 612 (obituary); *Lancet* (London), May 6, 1899, p. 1263 (obituary); *Times* (London), April 26, 1899, p. 8, col. b (obituary); *ILN*, April 29, 1899, p. 604 (obituary)

Holden, Henry

1814–1909

Considered the greatest headmaster in the history of the prestigious Catholic School in Durham, the Reverend Dr. Holden was a long-remembered inspiration to his charges. As one former student reminisced in the *Dunelmian* about his days with Holden nearly a quarter of a century earlier, recollections of Greek lessons and school traditions were almost crowded out by the strong memory of the headmaster's photographs lining the Long Room, bringing images "vague, shadowy, and mysterious upon us from the prehistoric age." When Holden was invited to join the Photographic Club in 1857, he worried, with typical reserve, that "I am to be such a very young member." In fact, he had already shown dozens of photographs in the 1856 exhibitions of the Photographic Society of Scotland, the Norwich Photographic Society, and the Photographic Society in London. All of these had been by collodion, but then a very interesting thing happened. In the summer of 1857, Holden took a six-week vacation in Italy. Tossing off the burden of working with glass plates, he took waxed-paper views in Venice and Milan. Holden must have already been experienced in waxed paper, for these were good enough to be accepted into the 1857 exhibitions of the Birmingham Photographic Society and the Photographic Society in London. It is not known if Holden continued in waxed paper, for all of his subsequent exhibited work through 1862 was done in collodion.

Exhibited: 1857, London, Photographic Society; 1857, Birmingham, Photographic Society

Reference: Henry Holden, letter of July 3, 1857, Royal Photographic Society Collection, National Media Museum, Bradford; "Olim Meminisse Juvabit," *Dunelmian* 7 (July 24, 1909), pp. 40–41 (reprint of an article originally published in *Dunelmian* in 1882)

Holder

Captain Holder was attached to the Scots Fusilier Guards and thus would have had opportunities to travel. In the 1855 exhibition of the Photographic Society in London he contributed two waxed-paper views taken in France. Holder also exhibited in 1859 and 1860, but by then he was using collodion for views in England. No other photographic work by him is known.

EXHIBITED: 1855, London, Photographic Society

Holliday, E. (Emma?)

In the 1852 "Productions of the Leeds Photographic Society," there is a single paper negative photograph, *Bust of Locke*, which was contributed by E. Holliday. The only possible candidate traced to date is Emma Holliday, an unmarried thirty-year-old bookbinder in Leeds, of whom nothing further is known.

Hooper, William

With addresses in Bradford and Manchester, Hooper was unanimously elected a member of the Manchester Photographic Society in 1860 and was elected a vice president the next year. He was clearly an enthusiastic experimenter, describing in the *British Journal of Photography* an 1859 presentation to the Chorlton Photographic Association as having been undertaken "after long experiment on nearly all the paper processes which have been published." Hooper's first public showing of work was in the 1859 exhibition accompanying the British Association for the Advancement of Science meeting in Aberdeen. His five entries were all architectural, taken at various places in England, and all were done on turpentine waxed paper. Hooper had already published on a variation of Taupenot's process in 1856, demonstrating it to the members of the Liverpool Photographic Society, and in 1859 he offered further information on waxed paper. Hooper planned to present a paper, "On the Production of Large Waxed-Paper Negatives," to the Chorlton Photographic Society late in 1859, but held off pending some additional experiments involving albumen, which must have eventually disappointed him. He contributed a waxed-paper view of Furness Abbey to the Amateur Photographic Association, and this was shown in the 1863 exhibition of the Photographic Society in London. Hooper's interest in photography was long-standing, and he felt that his experience might be useful to a younger generation of photographers who were rediscovering the facility of paper negatives in fieldwork. He wrote in the *British Journal Photographic Almanac* in 1889: "To those who are now using paper instead of glass my plan of waxing may be useful . . . I have negatives waxed as above over thirty years since, and they are as good as when first prepared."

EXHIBITED: 1859, Aberdeen, British Association for the Advancement of Science; 1863, London, Photographic Society

REFERENCES: William Hooper, "Modifications of Taupenot's Process," *LPJ* 3 (August 9, 1856), pp. 104–5; Hooper, "Turpentine Waxed Paper Process," *Photographic Journal (BJP)* 6 (March 1, 1859), pp. 55–56; Hooper, "On the Turpentine Waxed-Paper Process," *BJP* 7 (February 1, 1860), p. 40; Hooper, "Waxing Paper Negatives," *BJPA*, 1889, pp. 446–47

Hope, Thomas Alfred

b. 1834

The son of a carver and gilder (i.e., a picture frame maker), Hope was a very young engraver when photography came to his hometown of Leeds. He joined the Leeds Photographic Society and contributed a paper view, *Briggate, Leeds*, to their 1852 *Productions*, signing the ornately designed gilt-stamped cover of the album. There were six engraving firms located on Briggate in Leeds at the time, but only one, Samuel Brown Jr., that specialized in gold lettering, and Hope may well have designed and manufactured the album there. Hope was still in the printing business in Leeds by the time of the 1901 census, but any further photographic work of his is unknown.

Horne, Fallon

1814–1858

Horne was one of the principals of Horne, Thornthwaite, and Wood, the most prominent London firm specializing in photographic apparatus and chemicals. The firm's wholesale and retail business was substantial by at least 1848, but in spite of its success, Horne was first praised by the *Journal of the Photographic Society* as "an amiable man" who "had rendered good service to photography," "liked and respected by all who had transactions with him." The editor of *Photographic Notes* remembered him more specifically as "an exceedingly clever practical photographer in every branch of the art, but more particularly as a Calotypist." When ARTHUR NEILD showed some of Horne's calotypes at the Manchester Photographic Society in 1856, according to *Photographic Notes* of that year, he wanted to "express the obligation I am under to that gentleman for the information and assistance he has . . . given me in this beautiful art, as well as for the loan of specimens." The *Journal of the Photographic Society* recalled that Horne, working with PETER WICKENS FRY, "was the chief person who aided Mr. Archer to bring his collodion process into general use. He is a man, therefore, to whom every practical photographer is more or less indebted, and deserving a record in a journal devoted to the chronicles of a science which he loved and advanced." Very little of Horne's own photography is known, although he did exhibit a calotype portrait in the pioneering 1852 exhibition at the Society of Arts in London, as well as two Buckinghamshire landscapes in the 1855 exhibition at the London Photographic Institution. He also exhibited many collodion views during this period. In the Great Exhibition of 1851, Horne's firm displayed a complete daguerreotype apparatus, but also a folding calotype camera and an improved printing frame suitable for printing calotype negatives and for making photogenic drawing photograms. Horne died at the age of forty-four while visiting the Isle of Thanet in Kent, where he was born.

EXHIBITED: 1852, London, Society of Arts; 1855, London, Photographic Institution

REFERENCES: A. Nield [Arthur Neild], "On the Calotype Process," *Photographic Notes* 1, 2nd ed. (January 1–25, 1856), p. xvi; Fallon Horne, "On the Calotype Process," *Humphrey's Journal* 8 (July 15, 1856), pp. 88–92; Horne, "Waxed Paper Process," *Humphrey's Journal* 8 (August 1, 1856), pp. 102–5; *JPS* 5 (October 21, 1858), p. 36 (obituary); *Photographic Notes* 3 (November 1, 1858), p. 252 (obituary)

How, James

1821–1872

How was known to generations of photographers as the manager of George Knight & Sons, an important London supplier of cameras and photographic materials. On his death he was remembered by the *Photographic News* "for his connection with photography as an early calotypist" and by the *British Journal of Photography* for his "method of producing negatives by the waxed-paper process—a process which he simplified to a very great extent, and by which he produced many fine photographs." How had originally presented his techniques before the Chemical Discussion Society in London, but his influence spread much further when his papers were printed in *Notes and Queries* in 1853 and in the *Chemist* in 1854. In the first, he suggested the use of a hot iron to get the wax to penetrate the paper fibers. In the second, How revealed his method of immersing, rather than floating the paper on the sensitizing solution. How is not known to have participated in the major exhibitions, but he was an active participant in the South London Photographic Society and undoubtedly showed his work informally. How died unexpectedly from a fast-growing tumor.

References: James How, "Simplification of the Wax-Paper Process," *Notes and Queries*, January 22, 1853, pp. 93–94; How, "On the Production of Waxed Paper Negatives," *Chemist*, n.s., 1 (1864), pp. 529–36; *BJP* 19 (December 13, 1872), pp. 588–89 (obituary); *Photographic News* 16 (December 20, 1872), p. 611 (obituary)

Howes, James

A committee member of the Norfolk Photographic Society, Howes contributed several works to their inaugural exhibition in 1856, including collodion portraits and the waxed-paper studies *Dead Game* and *Hare's Foot Fern*. No further mention of him has been traced, and the name was a common one in Norfolk. The most likely candidate is the printer James Howes (b. 1821), who was prosperous enough to employ three men at the time of the 1851 census.

Exhibited: 1856, Norwich, Photographic Society

Howie, James, Jr.

b. 1819

Howie started as a miniature portrait painter in Edinburgh, undoubtedly influenced by his father, James Sr., an animal and portrait painter. In 1840 the father established the first commercial daguerreotype gallery in Scotland. He was remembered as a "great character," and Ebsworth's well-known 1845 engraving clearly shows his rooftop open-air portrait studio, a perch whose precariousness must have at least contributed to the "frozen" character of some of his early portraits. His wife Mary and daughters Ann and Julia were all involved in the photographic trade, but it was James Jr. who was the most active. His professional career can be traced through years of advertising in the *Scotsman*. Howie apparently started in his father's studio, for in later years he dated the beginning of his involvement in photography to 1840, and by 1850 he had his own photography salon on Princes Street in Edinburgh. Three years later he moved to 71 Princes Street, directly opposite the National Gallery, and advertised both photographic and daguerreotype portraits. The studio was renamed the American Photographic Gallery in 1854 (the American connection has never been explained), offering portraits in a choice of daguerreotype, collodion, or calotype. By 1859 Howie could boast that he had been in business for eighteen years, having expanded his gallery to offer all the latest improvements, adding glass and leather photographs to his daguerreotype and calotype lines; and advertisements he ran in 1860 show that he was one of the first to promote the novelty of night portraits, taken with the aid of "his new and astonishing Artificial Light."

References: *Scotsman* (Edinburgh), August 22, 1859, p. 1 (advertisement); *Scotsman*, December 28, 1860, p. 3 (advertisement)

Howlett, Robert W.

1830–1858

Born in London, Howlett came of age just as photography was beginning to, and it would be his only career. Little is known of how he began, but Howlett traced his first photographic work back to 1852. Within three years he was in partnership with Joseph Cundall and Philip Henry Delamotte at the Photographic Institution on New Bond Street. Howlett contributed three calotypes to the 1856 exhibition of the Manchester Photographic Society and became involved with the Photographic Society in London, rapidly developing a reputation as a solid experimentalist. As T. Frederick Hardwich observed, "Rarely did I leave him without feeling that I had carried away something which I could set down in my note-book as a genuine experimental fact." Howlett was a versatile photographer, doing portraits, landscapes, and even the character studies that William Powell Frith would use as a basis for his celebrated painting *The Derby Day*. Among his contemporaries, Howlett was most admired for his large reproductions of artworks, but today he is best remembered for his iconic portrait of the great British engineer Isambard Kingdom Brunel. Howlett exhibited prolifically, nearly always offering his work for sale, but in 1858, less than three weeks after an enthusiastic report to the Photographic Society, he succumbed to typhus. Howlett's shocked colleagues blamed his premature death on the fact that, trying to do the work of three men, he had caught a severe cold while working in his new and damp darkroom.

Exhibited: 1856, Manchester, Photographic Society

References: Robert W. Howlett, *On the Various Methods of Printing Photographic Pictures upon Paper, with Suggestions for Their Preservation* (London: Sampson Low, 1856); *Photographic Notes* 3 (December 15, 1858), p. 290 (obituary); T. Frederick Hardwich, "Remarks on the Death of Mr. Howlett," *JPS* 5 (December 21, 1858), pp. 111–12

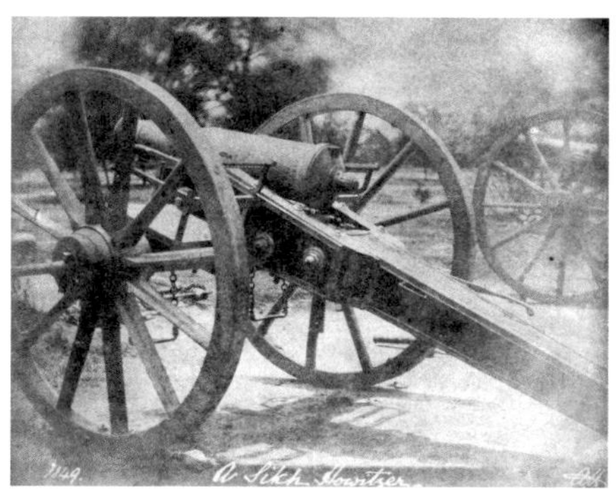

55. Alfred Huish

Huish, Alfred

ill. 55

b. 1811

Born in Devon, Huish attended Addiscombe Military Seminary, the training school for East India Company cadets, entering the Bengal Horse Artillery in 1827. Nothing is known of how he became interested in photography, but Huish's salt prints made from paper negatives between 1848 and 1852 are among the earliest surviving images from the Indian subcontinent.

Reference: John Falconer, *India: Pioneering Photographers, 1850–1900* (London: British Library, 2001), p. 138

Hunt, Robert

1807–1887

Even if Hunt had never taken a photograph, he would engage our interest as the first historian of photography, for he was both a documenter of that history and an active creator of it. Hunt's early life was a tangled struggle against adversity, and this shaped his later response to success. His father, a ship's carpenter, died before he was born. Unhappily apprenticed to a surgeon at the age of twelve, Hunt fell into the frozen Thames in 1827 while trying to see the funeral procession of the Duke of York, compromising his health. He alternated between London and Penzance throughout his youth, somehow preserving his true ambitions as a poet and lover of literature. His widowed mother remarried into the family of Sir Humphry Davy, the pioneering English scientist, and through this connection Hunt was able to establish himself as a chemist in Penzance. He was an active member of the Penzance Literary and Scientific Society, but his chemist's business failed. Hunt returned to London, trying his hand at playwriting, but by the time of the invention of photography was employed as a druggist again, this time in Devonport. Hunt contributed articles to diverse publications, including the *Philosophical Magazine* and the *Art-Journal*, and began a correspondence with Sir John Herschel. In 1845, through Herschel's influence, Hunt obtained the position of Keeper of the Mining Record Office, and from here on his career blossomed. This diverse background, an awkward mixture of literature, science, and poverty, informed all of Hunt's actions and helped to secure for him a unique if controversial role within the photographic community. After attending a meeting of the British Association for the Advancement of Science in Glasgow in 1840, Hunt published his *Popular Treatise on the Art of Photography*, the first of several engagingly written and ever-more sophisticated books on the interaction of light, physical objects, and aesthetics. His 1844 *Researches on Light* went through several editions. Hunt made it a personal challenge to master every photographic process before including it in one of his publications. Most of the processes were on paper, but Hunt was also a confident master of the calotype. He invented a wide range of photographic processes, few of which attained widespread use; but the totality of his practical efforts and his theoretical understanding of the new art gave him great credibility and stature in the field. In 1847 Hunt joined the Calotype Club, and in 1854 he was elected vice president of the fledgling Photographic Society in London. However, as he advanced further and further from his difficult beginnings, Hunt became increasingly estranged from old friends and benefactors, including Herschel. He became deeply involved in mining and in 1854 was named a fellow of the Royal Society. When TALBOT's patents were first challenged in the early 1850s, Hunt became a vicious (and often anonymous) critic of the inventor, once his friend and correspondent, alienating himself even more from his early supporters. Nevertheless, Hunt's professional reputation continued to grow until his retirement in 1883. He was a prolific and widely published author on many subjects, scientific and not. By 1865 Hunt was confident enough of his professional standing to return to his earliest interests, publishing the first of his *Popular Romances of the West of England*, which preserved the stories and folktales of his childhood. Hunt's massive 1884 *British Mining* is perhaps his most substantial and today best-remembered work; but his role as an active participant, not only in shaping the progress of photography but in recording its earliest history from the standpoint of a contemporary, remains an unparalleled achievement.

REFERENCES: Robert Hunt, *A Popular Treatise on the Art of Photography, including Daguerréotype, and All the New Methods of Producing Pictures by the Chemical Agency of Light* (Glasgow: Richard Griffin, 1841; facsimile ed., with an introduction by James Yingpeh Tong, Athens: Ohio University Press, 1973); Hunt, *Researches on Light: An Examination of All the Phenomena Connected with the Chemical and Molecular Changes Produced by the Influence of the Solar Rays; Embracing All the Known Photographic Processes and New Discoveries in the Art* (London: Longman, Brown, Green, and Longmans, 1844); Hunt, *Researches on Light in Its Chemical Relations; Embracing a Consideration of All the Photographic Processes* (London, Longman, Brown, Green, and Longmans, 1854); *BJP* 34 (October 21, 1887), p. 661 (obituary); *Athenaeum*, October 22, 1887, pp. 541–42 (obituary); *Times* (London), December 1, 1887, p. 8, col. A (obituary)

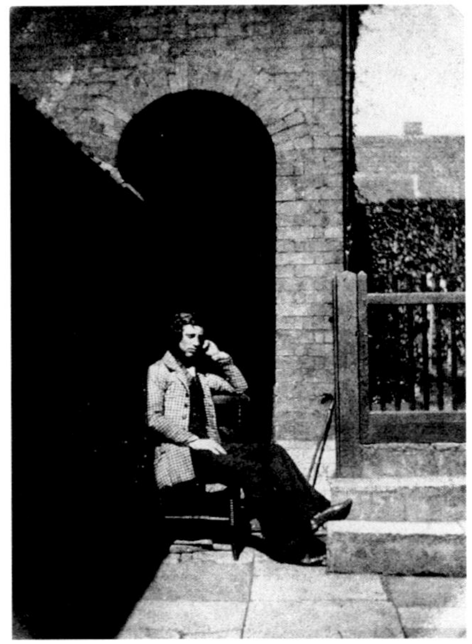

56. William Howes Hunt

Hunt, William Howes *ill. 56*

1806–1879

There is the possibility of a confusion of identities here, for the name William Hunt turns up in a variety of photographic contexts. However, it seems most likely that these various personalities all belong to a linen draper from Leeds who enjoyed painting in Great Yarmouth. WASHINGTON TEASDALE credited him with developing a rice water–based waxed-paper negative process but questioned his use of a common meniscus lens, feeling this hurt the quality of his photographs, while acknowledging Hunt's "connected series of carefully made experiments on the use of the bromides." In 1854 a frustratingly unidentified "well-known amateur" wrote to WILLIAM JOHN THOMS, the editor of *Notes and Queries*. Looking at his first photograph, made in 1845, the writer praised the contribution of GEORGE SMITH CUNDELL, who clarified the operation of the calotype to the amateur, adding: "Mr. William Hunt, of Yarmouth, was my first friend and instructor in the art; and *if* there be any merit in the pictures I did before I knew you, the credit is due to *him entirely*." Some of Hunt's photographs survive, including in one of THOMAS DAMANT EATON's albums.

REFERENCES: Washington Teasdale, "Photographic Processes," *JPS* 1 (January 21, 1854), pp. 161–62; "Progress of Photography," *Notes and Queries*, June 10, 1854, p. 549; Richard Denyer and Andrew Moore, eds., *A Period Eye: Photography Then and Now*, exh. cat. (Norwich: Norfolk Museums and Archaeology Service, 2003), p. 44

Hutchinson, Charles Waterloo

1824–1890

Born in Scotland, the son of a major in the Bengal Native Infantry, General Hutchinson was educated at the College for Civil Engineers, Putney, and joined the Bengal Engineers in 1843. Although he saw some military action, including the 1857 mutiny, Hutchinson primarily supervised the building of roads and canals, providing him with ample opportunities for travel within India. When Hutchinson first took up photography is not known, but in 1857 he wrote to the Photographic Society of Bengal that he was returning from a campaign in the hills with forty large paper negatives. The society's council was obviously already familiar with his work, calling him "one of their best photographers at Lahore." None of Hutchinson's work is known to have survived, but an engraving based on one of his photographs is reproduced in J. Cave-Browne's *The Punjab and Delhi in 1857* (1861). Hutchinson continued in service in India until at least 1873 and died in London.

REFERENCE: *Journal of the Photographic Society of Bengal*, no. 3 (May 20, 1857), p. 67; J. Cave-Browne, *The Punjab and Delhi in 1857: Being a Narrative by which the Punjab Was Saved and Delhi Recovered during the Indian Mutiny* (London: William Blackwood and Sons, 1861)

Huxley, Thomas Henry

1825–1895

"Darwin's Bulldog," Huxley is best known for helping to establish and defend the theory of evolution. In 1846 he was a brilliant but disillusioned young surgeon still trying to make his way in the world when he obtained the position of scientific assistant surgeon on HMS *Rattlesnake*, under the command of Captain Owen Stanley. The main purpose of the expedition was to locate a safe passage through the Great Barrier Reef, in preparation for the screw steamers that would be coming from Sydney. It was during this voyage that Huxley defined his scientific life. He wrote to his sister Eliza on October 6, 1846: "Again, I have learnt the calotype process for the express purpose of managing the calotype apparatus, for which Captain Stanley has applied to the Government." Although successful in his lessons, it is not known how many, if any, calotypes Huxley was able to make during the expedition. John MacGillivray's two-volume narrative of the voyage (1852) includes lithographs based on Huxley's drawings but makes no mention of his photography.

REFERENCE: Leonard Huxley, ed., *Life and Letters of Thomas Henry Huxley* (New York: D. Appleton and Co., 1900), p. 29

Ibbetson, Levett Landen Boscawen
1799–1869
Among the hundreds of contributions to the 1852 exhibition of the Society of Arts, only two albums were shown. One was made up by TALBOT, according to the handwritten label he affixed to its cover, to memorialize "an early period of the art." The other, "Le Premier Livre imprimé par le soleil," was a book handmade by Ibbetson in 1839, with not only photogenic drawing illustrations but also a photographically printed title page and preface. Further tying together the new art of photography with the traditional world of the book, Ibbetson published a pioneering engraving on a daguerreotype plate in the *Westminster Review* in 1840. Working at the Royal Polytechnic Institution, he used oxyhydrogen light to project a photographic image. Ibbetson also showed a new process of photolithography to James D. Forbes and Sir JOHN HERSCHEL. In 1842 he corresponded with Talbot, thanking him for the iodized paper he had sent and discussing his own experiments with the calotype. Robert J. Longbottom reported that Ibbetson was "going on with the experiments daily." None of Ibbetson's photographic work is known to have survived, nor, seemingly, have any details of his early life. It is known that he was born in Peterborough and that in 1849 the queen gave him permission to wear the insignia of the Royal Prussian Order of the Red Eagle. Within months, Ibbetson was part of the deputation from the Society of Arts charged by Prince Albert with laying the foundations for the Great Exhibition of 1851 (Ibbetson wrote the official report on the exhibition's toilets, a new public innovation and a matter of no small interest). His gift of his collection of fossils was an important contribution to the Museum of Practical Geology, but Ibbetson lived in Prussia in his later years, and after his death, his effects were dispersed.

EXHIBITED: 1841, London, Royal Polytechnic Institution; 1852, London, Society of Arts

REFERENCES: "Fossils, Engraved on a Daguerreotype Plate," *Westminster Review* 24 (September 1840); Robert J. Longbottom to W. H. F. Talbot, March 18, 1842, Talbot Collection, British Library, London, LA42-14 (Talbot Correspondence Project, http://foxtalbot.dmu.ac.uk, doc. no. 04457); "The Educational System in Germany and Its Advantages," in *Essays upon Educational Subjects Read at the Educational Conference of June 1857* (London: Longman, Brown, Green, Longmans, & Roberts, 1857), pp. 114–24; *Quarterly Journal of the Geological Society*, 1870, p. xli (obituary)

Ingleby, Clement Mansfield, Jr.
1823–1886
The son of a highly respected Birmingham solicitor, Ingleby entered the family law firm, as was expected of him, but his spare time was filled with the study of mathematics, literature, and metaphysics. Another of Ingleby's ways of escaping the law was photography: in the 1857 exhibition of the Birmingham Photographic Society, he showed two Talbotypes, both architectural views. In 1859, two events happened that encouraged Ingleby to follow his true interests: he received a doctorate in literature from Cambridge, and his father died. Quitting the law, he moved with his wife to her childhood home, Valentines Mansion in Ilford, Essex. Now free to pursue his philosophical studies, Ingleby spent much time in the library of the British Museum, making his reputation as a Shakespearean scholar. It is not known if he continued to pursue photography after leaving the active photographic circle in Birmingham, but one of his last books was illustrated with Autotype prints.

EXHIBITED: 1857, Birmingham, Photographic Society

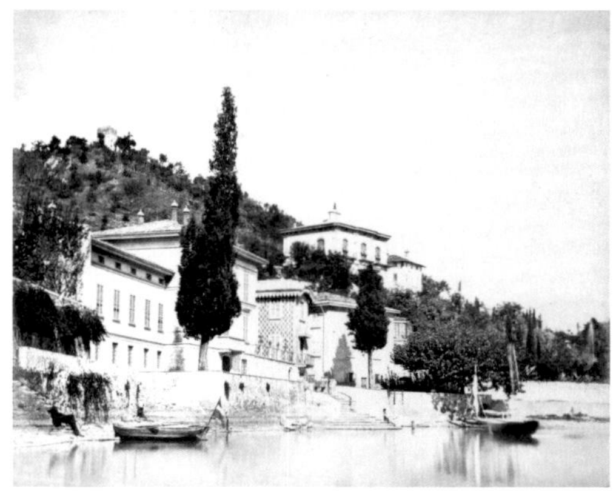
57. Cosmo Nelson Innes

Innes, Cosmo Nelson *ill. 57*
1798–1874
A professor of history at Edinburgh University and an antiquarian, Innes had contempt for mere bookworms, feeling that "more was to be learnt outside books than in them." As a lawyer and an antiquarian, however, he was a formidable intellect. As he recalled in 1863, his motivation for entering photography was simple: "To myself, who cannot draw at all, it is too vexatious to pass through striking scenes, fine cities, quaint or curious buildings, without being able to take away the faintest memorial to help the recollection." Innes joined the Edinburgh Calotype Club in the 1840s and was a friend of TALBOT's friend Sir WALTER CALVERLY TREVELYAN. In 1856 he joined the newly formed Photographic Society of Scotland, becoming a vice president. His six entries for that year's exhibition were all calotypes of architecture in Scotland. Although this was the only exhibition that he was to enter, Innes continued to photograph on his annual trips to the Continent, amusing and instructing the society's audiences with the photographs that accompanied his talks. In the days of collodion, Innes remained an unrepentant calotypist, still claiming in 1863 that "my process is the ancient unwaxed paper—the Talbot, in short, unmodified," which, he modestly pointed out, "has some advantages for wandering photographers."

EXHIBITED: 1856, Edinburgh, Photographic Society of Scotland

REFERENCES: *Scotsman* (Edinburgh), March 19, 1856, p. 2; *Scotsman*, July 12, 1856, p. 3; Cosmo Nelson Innes, "Short Notes of Photographic Tours," *Photographic Journal* 8 (February 16, 1863), pp. 231–32; *Scotsman*, August 3, 1874, p. 5 (obituary); *British Journal of Photography* 21 (August 7, 1874), p. 376 (obituary); "A Reminiscence of the Calotype Club," *BJP* 21 (August 14, 1874), p. 385; Katherine Burton, *Memoir of Cosmo Innes* (Edinburgh: William Paterson, 1874); *Proceedings of the Royal Society of Edinburgh* 8 (1875), pp. 453–60 (obituary); *Oxford Dictionary of National Biography*, s.v. "Innes, Cosmo Nelson (1798–1874)" (by W. W. Wroth, rev. H. C. G. Matthew)

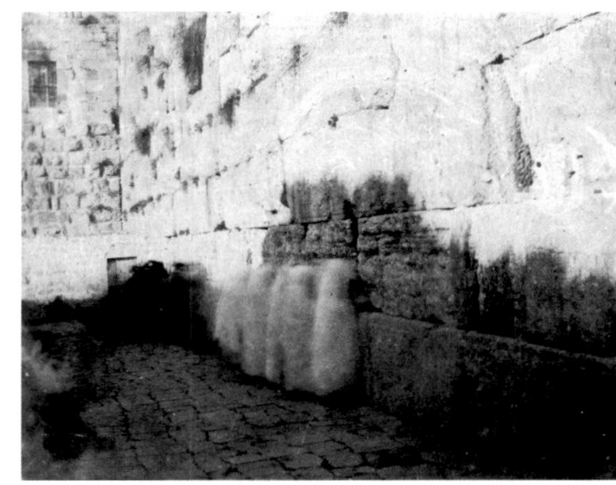
58. Albert Augustus Isaacs

Isaacs, Albert Augustus *ill. 58*
1826–1903
Isaacs was born in Jamaica, educated at Cambridge, and died in Düsseldorf; the well-traveled reverend was known as "the Jew of Leicester" for his efforts in the conversion of Jews to Christianity. It is not known when he first took an interest in photography, but when Isaacs made a pilgrimage to the Holy Land in 1856, the camera was to be his witness. As he explained in his 1857 travelogue, *The Dead Sea*: "We well know how often *the pencil* is proved to be treacherous and deceptive; while on the other hand the *fac simile* of the scene must be given by the aid of the *photograph*. This consideration induced me to determine that . . . I would visit these places, and not only judge for myself, but endeavour likewise to give the public the best

means of arriving at a just conclusion." Isaacs did most of his work with waxed-paper negatives, well suited to the hot climate and extended travels that he faced. At some point, the reverend himself underwent a sort of conversion. As Isaacs recalled late in life in a letter to John Ruskin: "I can speak of this authoritatively, having been the first person (1856) to take any photographs of importance in the Holy Land—and indeed the first who had taken any by the then new and beautiful collodion process."

References: Albert Augustus Isaacs, *The Dead Sea: or, Notes and Observations Made during a Journey to Palestine in 1856–7 on M. de Saulcy's Supposed Discovery of the Cities of the Plain* (London: Hatchard and Son, 1857) ("Illustrated from Photographs taken on the spot by the Author"); *A Pictorial Tour in the Holy Land* (London: Wertham, MacIntosh, & Hunt, 1862); description of his photography in Isaacs, *The Fountain of Siena: An Episode in the Life of John Ruskin, L.L.D.* (London: S. W. Partridge, 1900); *Times* (London), November 19, 1903, p. 9, col. F (obituary)

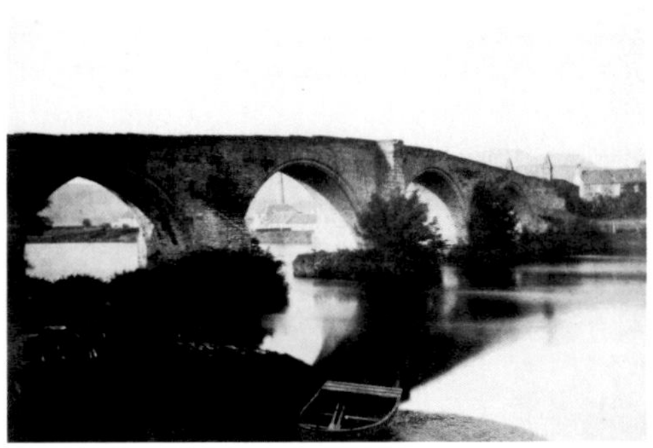

59. Thomas Brumby Johnston

Johnston, Thomas Brumby *ill. 59*

1814–1897

A native of Perth, David Octavius Hill's birthplace, Johnston was one of the founding members of the Photographic Society of Scotland in 1856. His entries that year were all in collodion; in 1858 he entered only waxed-paper views; and by 1864, a mixture of paper and glass. Johnston participated in the Edinburgh Photograph Exchange Club and was a member of several learned societies. In 1871, on the death of his father, he became head of the family firm of geographical publishers, and in 1877 he was appointed geographer to the queen for Scotland.

Exhibited: 1858 and 1864, Edinburgh, Photographic Society of Scotland

References: Thomas Brumby Johnston, "Stereoscopic Angles," *Notes and Queries*, August 13, 1853, p. 157; *Geographical Journal* 10 (1897), pp. 446–47 (obituary)

Johnstone, John

Johnstone's entry in the 1857 exhibition of the Birmingham Photographic Society was both atypical and revealing. His first four calotypes, of Kenilworth Castle and Tintern Abbey, received particular notice in the catalogue for demonstrating "the permanency of good Photographs having been printed more than 11 years." This places Johnstone's start in calotyping at least as far back as the mid-1840s, when he was an active daguerreotypist in Birmingham, but also demonstrates that he was unusually adept at printing. Two of his calotype portraits were included in the Richard Willats album, taken "by his modification of Calotype Process on Paper." According to *Photogram*, Johnstone was known among his colleagues as a painstaking worker "who knew that he was always right," and who took a particular interest in the electro-disposition of metals. In the catalogue for the 1857 exhibition he advertised Johnstone's Photographic Establishment in Birmingham, stressing that his portraits were "highly finished, Artistic, Permanent, and at Reasonable prices." Johnstone was also a friend of the London photographer John Mayall.

Exhibited: 1857, Birmingham, Photographic Society

Reference: W. H. Garbutt and E. C. Middleton, "The History of Photography in Birmingham," *Photogram* 7 (1900), pp. 164–68

Jones, Mr.

At a November 1856 meeting of the Liverpool Photographic Society, "Mr. Jones, of Birkenhead, made some experiments by dipping various kinds of negative paper in iodised serum solution, for the purpose of shewing that some were more liable to the defect of spotting than others." He also "produced several pictures taken with the wax-paper process." Unfortunately, the Cheshire parish of Birkenhead was then rich in Joneses, frustrating any attempt at identification.

Reference: "Liverpool Photographic Society," *LPJ* 3 (November 8, 1856), p. 151

Jones, Baynham, Jr.

1806–1890

Looking around the Jubilee Convention of Photography in 1889, the pioneering photohistorian John Werge had begun to think that he "was the oldest photographer present, when I espied Mr. Baynham Jones . . . certainly the oldest amateur of photography living." Werge recalled that in 1839 Jones "made himself a camera out of a cigar-box and the lens of his opera glass, and, being unable to obtain a Daguerreotype plate in the country, he cut up a silver salver." Jones, a lawyer in Cheltenham, soon turned from silver to paper as a base, and from 1854 was an active exhibitor of calotypes in various exhibitions through 1860. In 1861 he turned to collodion, yet he still exhibited a calotype in the 1862 International Exhibition in London. When Jones died the year following the Jubilee Convention, the editor of the *British Journal Photographic Almanac*, John Traill Taylor, called him "a veritable veteran," while Werge remembered him as from the first "an enthusiastic photographer."

Exhibited: 1852, London, Society of Arts; 1853–54, first touring exhibition, Society of Arts (London); 1854, London, Photographic Society; 1854, Dundee, Royal Infirmary Fund; 1854, second touring exhibition, Society of Arts (London); 1855, 1856, 1857, 1858, and 1860, London, Photographic Society; 1862, London, International Exhibition

References: *Photographic News* 34 (July 4, 1890), pp. 526–27 (obituary); John Werge, *The Evolution of Photography* (London: Piper & Carter, 1890), pp. 123–24; *BJPA*, 1891, p. 476 (obituary)

Jones, Calvert Richard

1802–1877

Jones was the most artistically accomplished of the photographers in Talbot's circle. While taking a first class degree in mathematics at Oxford he formed a close friendship with Talbot's cousin, Christopher Rice Mansel Talbot ("Kit"), initially based on their mutual love of mathematics and music. In 1829 Jones entered unenthusiastically into holy orders in Wales, near Penllergare, the home of John Dillwyn Llewelyn. His friendship with Kit Talbot blossomed along with their shared passion for travel and fast yachts, the funding being supplied by Talbot and the artistic underpinning by Jones, who emerged as a gifted dilettante, adept with the camera lucida and a close observer of the marine subjects of his native Swansea. Jones was one of the first to learn of Talbot's photogenic drawing in 1839, but initially he was more drawn to daguerreotypy, which he practiced with enthusiasm and success. He served as a bridge between Hippolyte Bayard in France and Talbot in England, helping to forge the first bonds between photographers on paper from the rival camps. In 1844 Jones was stunned by the prints in Talbot's *The Pencil of Nature* and was immediately seduced by the prospect of creating photographs on paper, a medium he was intimately familiar with through his work in watercolors. While traveling around the Mediterranean with Kit Talbot, moving about Britain, and residing in Swansea, Jones produced hundreds of calotype negatives. Architecture, shipping, and the romance of the common workingman were his favored subjects, as they were in his paintings.

Jones sometimes waxed his negatives after development but never strayed far from Talbot's original formula, of which he was an undisputed master. Ever conscious that his financial state fell short of supporting his desired lifestyle, he began producing and selling negatives to Talbot for use at NICOLAAS HENNEMAN's printing establishment. This mirrored a practice already common among print sellers, but the presence of Jones's original negatives within Talbot's archive has led to much confusion of attribution. In 1847 Jones was on the verge of entering into a more serious commercial photographic arrangement with Talbot but changed his mind when he unexpectedly came into an inheritance with the death of his father. Relations were strained for a while, but Jones and Talbot were soon friends again, the younger man never forgetting who had given him a new art, and the inventor seeing in his artistic acolyte the very best realization of his ambitions for photography. The obligations of his new estate preoccupied Jones during the late 1840s, leading to a lapse in his photographic work, but about 1850 he and his artist wife Anne once again began to travel, and Jones returned to the camera. In 1853 he became a member of the council of the Photographic Society in London, but he never participated in the society's exhibitions. Later that year Jones moved to Brussels, where he greatly increased his photographic activity. On Anne's premature death Jones returned to Britain, taking up residence in Bath and in 1858 marrying a much younger woman. After his death his estate was dispersed, and very little is known about his artistic activities after the mid-1850s. Jones's photographic legacy is largely preserved within Talbot's archives, perhaps a fitting conclusion for one of the most successful symbiotic relationships in the history of early photography.

REFERENCES: Rollin Buckman, *The Photographic Work of Calvert Richard Jones* (London: H.M.S.O. for the Science Museum, 1990); Larry J. Schaaf, *Sun Pictures, Catalogue Five: The Reverend Calvert R. Jones* (New York: Hans P. Kraus, Jr., 1990)

Jones, George Fowler *ill. 60*

1819–1905

Born in Inverness, Scotland, Jones was an architect in York and appears to have used photography to document his work from the first. He contributed a calotype to the "Productions of the Leeds Photographic Society" in 1852, suggesting that he was a member. As an architect, Jones was much in demand for his ecclesiastical architecture, and his photographs reflected that expertise. Starting in

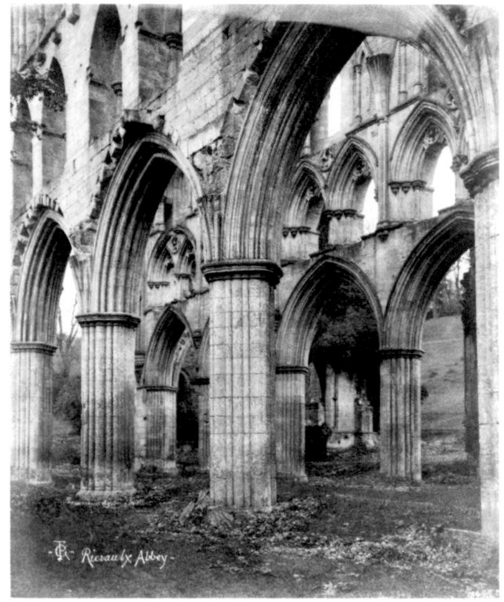

60. George Fowler Jones

1897, at the end of his long career, Jones donated a remarkable collection of 2,100 negatives to the Royal Photographic Society, the earliest from 1848 and reflecting every conceivable photographic process, including many paper negatives dating into the early twentieth century, and many of which were dated and monogrammed by him. Jones collected the works of other photographers as well and also donated several large negatives he thought were by TALBOT and one very early calotype by Sir DAVID BREWSTER. Jones was also an amateur watercolorist, so accomplished that after his death his collection was sold at Christie's.

REFERENCE: "Ordinary Meeting," *Photographic Journal*, n.s., 21 (May 31, 1897), p. 215

Jones, Owen

1809–1874

The exuberant chromolithographed cover of TALBOT's *The Pencil of Nature* is unmistakably the work of Owen Jones. On a Grand Tour made after completing his architectural studies, Jones was deeply moved by the architecture of Islam and devoted six months to studying the Alhambra. In 1834 he began preparing a lavish publication on this complex architectural masterpiece and was quickly frustrated by the limitations of the existing color printing technology. Therefore, he mastered chromolithography and color block printing, producing many of the plates in the book, which was issued between 1836 and 1845. Other works followed, none more influential than his 1856 *The Grammar of Ornament*. Jones was responsible for the controversial but highly successful interior of the Crystal Palace for the Great Exhibition of 1851, one of the first industrial applications of color theory. Not surprisingly he took an interest in photography, but very little is known about his efforts in this area, for later in his career his design style fell out of favor and his widow disposed of his estate. Jones contributed six photographs to the 1856 exhibition of the Norwich Photographic Society: five collodion views of colleges in Cambridge and a waxed-paper study of the New Bridge at St. John's College, almost certainly indicators of a much more substantial photographic output.

EXHIBITED: 1856, Norwich Photographic Society

REFERENCES: *Architect* 11 (April 25, 1874), pp. 235–36 (obituary); *Builder* 32 (May 9, 1874), pp. 383–85 (obituary)

Jones, R. L.

In the mid-1850s, JOHN TRAILL TAYLOR published extracts from his "Manuscript Photographic Journal," a compendium that circulated among his friends (until the original was stolen in a burglary). Taylor obviously knew Jones, a contributor to the extracts, but did not otherwise identify him, and his background and residence remain a mystery. In 1857 Jones contributed his design for a portable camera for paper negatives; looking forward to a summer holiday tour, he had come up with a camera that would hold any number of prepared sheets within its confines. With his 1858 contribution, however, Jones left no doubt about his photographic loyalties: "Were I in a South Sea Island I should be tabooed; were I in India I should be a Pariah, but being in England I feel my position as degraded as if I were both. I, nothing but waxpaper, while all around me rejoice in the Brahminism of collodion." If any of his photographs survive, none have been identified.

REFERENCE: John Traill Taylor, ed., "'The Photographer,'" *Photographic Notes* 2 (June 15, 1857), p. 222, and 3 (September 1, 1858), p. 205

Jordan, C. J.

In 1855 the *Journal of the Photographic Society* reprinted a formula for sensitizing papers from a man it styled as "one of the oldest friends of Photography." Jordan had originally published his formula in the *Mechanics' Magazine* and the *Pharmaceutical Times* in 1848, writing that "for a considerable length of time I have employed an expeditious method of preparing iodized papers for the calotype and other photogenic processes." In addition to his chemical formula, Jordan gave hints on how to use a glass rod to evenly distribute chemical solutions over the entire surface of the paper. Such a familiarity with materials and techniques suggests that Jordan was almost certainly a chemist, but, unfortunately, none of his three publications revealed his full name or even his place of residence, and none of his photographs have been traced.

REFERENCES: C. J. Jordan, "Preparation of Iodized Papers by One Solution Only," *Mechanics' Magazine* 49 (August 5, 1848), pp. 134–35, and *Pharmaceutical Times*, August 5, 1848, pp. 595–96 (reprinted in *JPS* 2 [January 22, 1855], pp. 111–12)

Jordan, Thomas Brown
1807–1890
Born in Bristol but a resident of Cornwall, Jordan was a teacher of painting who was irresistibly drawn to all things mechanical. Already a fine philosophical instrument maker, he became the secretary of the Royal Cornwall Polytechnic Society (TALBOT's uncle, Sir Charles Lemon, was the president). Immediately on the publication of Talbot's invention of photogenic drawing in 1839, Jordan found a way to combine his two loves, art and science. Part of his duties as secretary was to keep local meteorological records, and in March 1839 he demonstrated his self-registering barometer, a device that used Talbot's sensitive paper to track an hour-by-hour record; he also invented a heliograph, which kept a daily record of the intensity of the sunlight at Falmouth. In 1840 Jordan moved to London and was replaced as secretary by ROBERT HUNT, a friend of his who ran a chemist's shop in Penzance. Hunt soon emerged as the most important historian of early photography and helped to ensure Jordan's reputation. For his part, Jordan continued as an inventor deeply interested in photographers and photography.

REFERENCE: Charles Thomas, *Views and Likenesses: Early Photographers and Their Work in Cornwall and the Isles of Scilly, 1839–1870* (Truro: Royal Institution of Cornwall, 1988), pp. 81–82

Kater, Edward *ill. 61*
1816–1866
Kater's father was the scientist Henry Kater, famous for his precision in designing instruments, and his mother, Mary, was a well-known author. Kater grew up in a household that welcomed scientific visitors such as Mary Somerville and William Hyde Wollaston. He himself became a fellow of the Royal Society in 1840; he was also

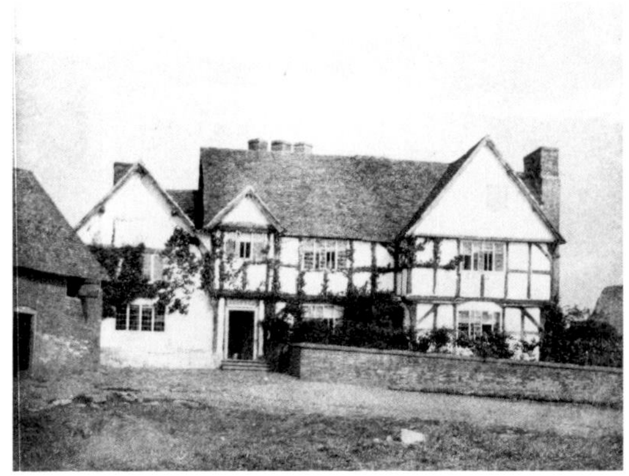

61. Edward Kater

a fellow of the Statistical Society and a member of the Royal Institution. A landed proprietor in Mexborough, Yorkshire, Kater enjoyed the means to pursue a life of scientific and literary pursuits. He joined the Calotype Club in the 1840s, becoming a vice president of the Photographic Society when it was formed. In 1852 Kater's "Proof of the Value of Photography to the Archaeologist" appeared in *Notes and Queries*. He had recently returned from photographing the ancient ruins of Paestum in southern Italy, anxious to preserve the subtlest features of the site, including carvings barely discernible to the naked eye, before they were lost to the passage of time. Kater's guide pointed him to the carved effigy of "the Sirena Paestana," but try as he might, he could not make out the faded portrait of a woman holding a rose. However, when he developed his calotypes back in Salerno, he could see the figure distinctly: "By aid of a glass, the doll-like figure, worn and much obliterated, was very apparent. I believe that many interesting little morceaux would be detected by archaeologists during a quiet study of their photographs at home which escaped them in the originals." Kater advised the government on the use of photography by the military and tried mightily to salvage the position of photography in the 1862 International Exhibition in London. Kater died suddenly at the age of fifty while on a visit to Cambridge, a loss keenly felt in the scientific and photographic communities.

EXHIBITED: 1854, Dundee, Royal Infirmary Fund

REFERENCES: Edward Kater, "Proof of the Value of Photography to the Archaeologist," *Notes and Queries*, November 6, 1852, p. 443; *Photographic News* 10 (July 13, 1866), p. 335 (obituary); *Photographic Journal* 11 (July 16, 1866), pp. 86–87 (obituary)

Keith, Thomas *ill. 62*
1827–1895
Dr. Keith saved the lives of a higher proportion of his female patients than any of his contemporaries, wielding his surgeon's knife with such speed and precision that, simply, fewer of them went into shock. His photographic eye was no less adept. Born near Aberdeen, Keith came

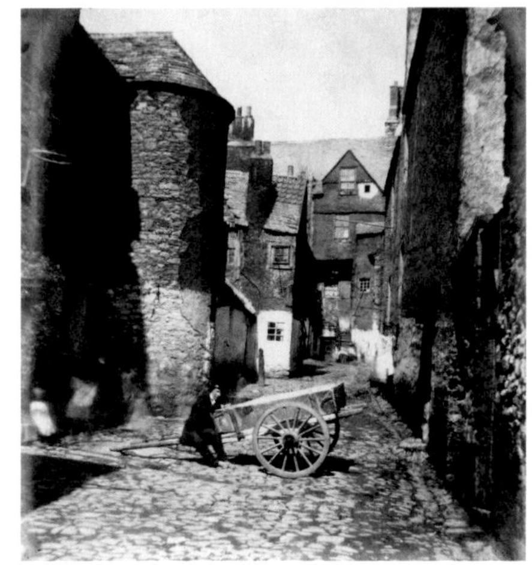

62. Thomas Keith

from a family of high accomplishment: his grandfather was an authority on weights and measures; his uncle was the gardener to the Duke of Orleans; his father, Dr. Alexander Keith, made daguerreotypes in the Holy Land; and his brother, Rev. Alexander Keith, took part in the 1843 Disruption and was calotyped by Hill & Adamson. Keith teamed up with his friend JOHN FORBES WHITE, probably in the summer of 1853, to take waxed-paper views, which they entered into that year's exhibition of the Aberdeen Mechanics' Institution. The only other time Keith participated in a major public exhibition was at the 1859 meeting of the British Association for the Advancement of Science, held in his native Aberdeen. During the 1850s Keith mastered the waxed-paper negative like no one else, producing views of architecture in Scotland and urban studies of Edinburgh that had no equal, then or since. Light itself was his most formidable tool, and in 1856 he confessed to *Photographic Notes*: "I never expose my paper, unless the light is first-rate. This I have made a rule, and nothing ever induces me to deviate from it." Keith was elected to the council of the Photographic Society of Scotland in 1856 and 1858, but was rarely able to attend meetings, for the demands of his medical practice crowded out his beloved hobby of photography. At the time of his death the *Scotsman* described Keith as "decidedly picturesque" in personal appearance, adding, "no one could see him without recognising that he was in the presence of a man of unique power." For Alvin Langdon Coburn, writing in the *Century Illustrated Monthly Magazine* in 1915, Keith's "Old Edinburgh" series stood out "as his most remarkable achievement with the camera," and he included fifteen of Keith's photographs in a pivotal exhibition at the Albright Art Gallery in Buffalo that year.

EXHIBITED: 1853, Aberdeen, Mechanics' Institution; 1859, Aberdeen, British Association for the Advancement of Science

REFERENCES: Thomas Keith, "Dr. Keith's Paper on the Waxed Paper Process," *Photographic Notes* 1 (July 17, 1856), pp. 101–4; *Times* (London), October 12, 1895, p. 6, col. A (obituary); *British Medical Journal* 2 (October 19, 1895), pp. 1003–5 (obituary); *Scotsman* (Edinburgh), October 10, 1895, p. 5 (obituary); Alvin Langdon Coburn, "The Old Masters of Photography," *Century Illustrated Monthly Magazine* 90 (October 1915), p. 912; C. S. Minto, *Thomas Keith, 1827–1895, Surgeon and Photographer: The Hurd Bequest of Photographic Paper Negatives* (Edinburgh: Libraries and Museums Committee, 1966); Larry J. Schaaf, *Sun Pictures, Catalogue Six: Dr. Thomas Keith and John Forbes White* (New York: Hans P. Kraus, Jr., 1993)

Keith, William
1829–1883
As a young chemist Keith was intrigued by photography, joining the Liverpool Photographic Society and soon becoming its secretary. In an 1854 presentation to the society "Mr Keith described the calotype process, in which he had been very successful," but he soon turned away from paper negatives. That same year Keith sent a collodion-on-glass view to Prince Albert, receiving a reply from Mr. Ernst Becker, librarian to the prince and a founding member of the Photographic Society, and at an 1855 meeting of the society he demonstrated his apparatus for enlarging by gaslight. Keith began offering "Photographic Chemicals of known purity" and in 1857 introduced "Keith's Collodion," offering testimony that the chemicals were "prepared exclusively by himself, and have in the course of his extensive practise produced the most splendid pictures." In the 1861 and subsequent censuses Keith listed himself as "Photographer."

REFERENCES: William Keith, "Photography: Past, Present, and Prospective," *Photographic Journal (BJP)* 6 (March 1, 1859), pp. 58–60; George Good, *The History of the Liverpool Amateur Photographic Association from 1853 to 1953* (Liverpool, 1953), p. 14

Kent, William Henry
1827–1897
In 1852 Kent and his partner THOMAS HENRY HENNAH purchased a Talbotype license and opened the Brighton Talbotype Portrait Gallery above William Mason's print shop on King's Road in Brighton. Born on the Isle of Wight, Kent had previously established himself in Brighton as an artist. Kent and Hennah often exhibited jointly, and Hennah was more active in exhibiting under his own name, but of Kent we know only that he contributed a series of six daguerreotype portraits to the 1863 exhibition of the Photographic Society in London. Although none of his independent work has yet been identified, it is reasonable to assume that he as well as his partner took Talbotype portraits. After Hennah's death in 1876 Kent continued the business until 1884, maintaining the "Talbotype" gallery long after the process itself had become obsolete.

Kerr, Arthur Schomberg *ill. 63*
1820–1856
Born in London and related to the marquess of Lothian, Kerr was the youngest son of a vice admiral. He was taught photography by SAMUEL BUCKLE and was apparently an apt pupil, exhibiting four calotypes in the 1854 exhibition of the Photographic Society in London. The *Liverpool Photographic Journal* wrote that Kerr "takes a distinguished position" in the exhibition "with a view of the High-street, Guildford, and three other views in Surrey, from Talbotype negatives, which are first-rate." The next year Kerr showed some collodion portraits as well as three calotype views, but by 1856 all of his entries to the Photographic Society exhibition were calotypes. Kerr died of tuberculosis at the age of thirty-six. Looking back many years later, HENRY D. TAYLOR remained "indebted to the Hon. Arthur Kerr for my introduction to photography. In the year 1853 he was staying in my neighborhood (Godalming), and as he had just been taking lessons from Mr. Buckle, of Leamington, in calotype, he offered to instruct me in its mysteries."

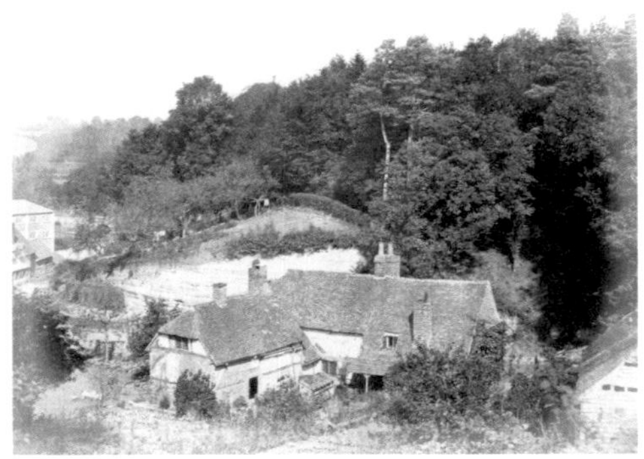
63. Arthur Schomberg Kerr

EXHIBITED: 1854, 1855, and 1856, London, Photographic Society

REFERENCES: "The Exhibition of Photographs and Daguerreotypes, by the London Photographic Society," *LPJ* 1 (February 11, 1854), p. 19; Henry D. Taylor, "The Calotype Process, and How We Photographed in the 'Fifties,'" *International Annual of Anthony's Photographic Bulletin*, June 1889, pp. 242–43

King, Henry
Captain King remains a tangled mystery. His calotype group portrait of the Maitland family of Ramornie, Fife, survives in an album that once belonged to Sir DAVID BREWSTER, who was himself related to the Maitlands. Another album belonging to the Maitlands includes a series of large calotype views, including one of Ramornie, along with watercolors attributed to Captain King. Isabella Louisa Heriot Maitland married a Henry King in 1850, but the most likely candidate for our photographer entered the Royal Navy in 1795 and in 1814 participated in the sack of Washington, an episode in the War of 1812. Captain Henry King was then promoted but he never again saw service at sea. Retiring from the navy in 1852, he was later a police magistrate in New Zealand, where a branch of the Maitland family had established a new Ramornie.

REFERENCE: Graham Smith, *Disciples of Light: Photographs in the Brewster Album* (Malibu: J. Paul Getty Museum, 1990), pp. 110, 120, n. 216

Kingsley, William Towler
1815–1916
Rev. Kingsley was a relatively young fellow and tutor at Sidney College, Cambridge, when he took up photography in the 1850s. His first public showing was in the 1853–54 Society of Arts touring exhibition; remarkably diverse, his work included photographs taken through a microscope (photomicroscopy) and examples of photolithography. Between 1854 and 1856 he exhibited dozens of images, the majority examples of photomicroscopy. Kingsley also employed the daguerreotype and wet collodion, but most of his photographs were accomplished in waxed-paper negatives, and the process was always carefully specified. Reviewing the 1855 exhibition of the Photographic Society in London, the *Liverpool Photographic*

Journal declared that "the most remarkable specimens are those taken from the microscope by the Rev. Mr. Kingsley, the whole of whose collection from collodion and waxed-paper negatives are exquisitely delineated, and appear to me the most successful, especially of semi-opaque objects, that have yet been taken." The 1855 exhibition also revealed Kingsley's new interest in architectural views, also done in waxed paper. A series of his studies of Cambridge colleges emerged at auction in the 1970s; of an extraordinarily large size, these averaged 33.5 x 43 centimeters. In 1859 Kingsley (who lived to be 101 years old) became rector at South Kilvington, Yorkshire, and nothing is known of his photographic activity after this point.

EXHIBITED: 1853–54, first touring exhibition, Society of Arts (London); 1854, London, Photographic Society; 1854, second touring exhibition, Society of Arts (London); 1855, London, Photographic Society; 1855–56, third touring exhibition, Society of Arts (London)

REFERENCES: "Correspondence from J.B.E.," *LPJ* 2 (March 10, 1855), p. 43; sale cat., Sotheby's London, July 1, 1977, lot 277

Kinnear, Charles George Hood *ill. 64*

1832–1894

From an influential Fife family, Kinnear was a highly sought after Edinburgh architect and an early member of the Edinburgh Photographic Exchange Club. A founding member of the Photographic Society of Scotland in 1856, he was elected the society's honorary secretary. Kinnear designed a sturdy folding camera, which he had constructed by Robert Bell, an Edinburgh woodworker. He first used the camera in 1857 while on an architectural and photographic tour of the north of France, an area not yet opened up by the railroad. Early cameras were mostly sliding boxes, although bellows cameras had begun to appear in 1851. While in early models the bellows was square, Kinnear recognized that a "conical" or tapered bellows would make possible a much smaller field camera. In his camera the bellows was full size at the negative end tapering to a much smaller size at the lens end and it was able to collapse in on itself. Kinnear's innovation set the pattern for nearly all subsequent cameras. Between 1856 and 1859 Kinnear exhibited dozens of waxed-paper views of architecture in Scotland, Germany, Italy, France, and England. A reviewer of the 1860 exhibition of the Photographic Society of Scotland regretted the growing prominence of his commercial work, lamenting in the *Photographic Journal*: "We miss the fine architectural wax-paper studies of Mr. Kinnear, who is probably too much occupied with erecting building[s] *terra firma* to find much time for delineating them on paper." (In 1856

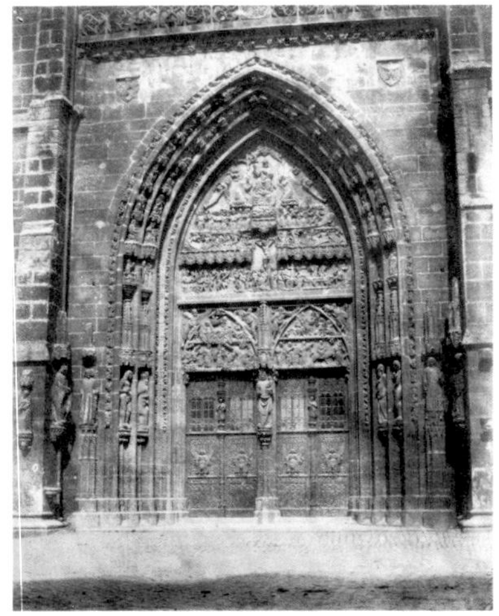

64. Charles George Hood Kinnear

Kinnear had joined the thriving practice of John Dick Peddie, one of the most prolific Scottish architects of his time.) Kinnear's final public showing was at the 1864 exhibition of the Photographic Society of Scotland, by which time he had abandoned waxed paper for Dr. Hill Norris's dry-collodion plates. Just days before his death in 1894 Kinnear visited the editor of the *British Journal of Photography*, who was struck by the fact that "his love for photography had suffered no diminution, but that he was, if possible, still more attached to it than ever." The next year the *British Journal Photographic Almanac* remembered Kinnear primarily for his influential camera design.

EXHIBITED: 1856 and 1858, Edinburgh, Photographic Society of Scotland; 1859, 1859, Glasgow, Photographic Society; 1859, Aberdeen, British Association for the Advancement of Science

REFERENCES: Charles George Hood Kinnear, "Abstract of an Account of an Architectural and Photographic Tour in the North of France," *JPS* 4 (December 21, 1857), pp. 116–20; "Mr. Kinnear's Portable Camera," *JPS* 4 (February 22, 1858), pp. 165–66; "Exhibition of the Photographic Society of Scotland," *Photographic Journal* 6 (February 15, 1860), pp. 157–58; *BJP* 41 (November 16, 1894), p. 723 (obituary); *BJPA*, 1895, p. 572 (obituary); Rob Niederman, "Kinnear Cameras: Large Format in a Small Size," *Photogram* 34 (September–October 2006), pp. 3–7

Kirk, John *ills. 65, 66*

1832–1922

Scottish by birth, Kirk was elected a fellow of the Edinburgh Botanical Society while still an undergraduate. Taking his medical degree in 1854, he then volun-

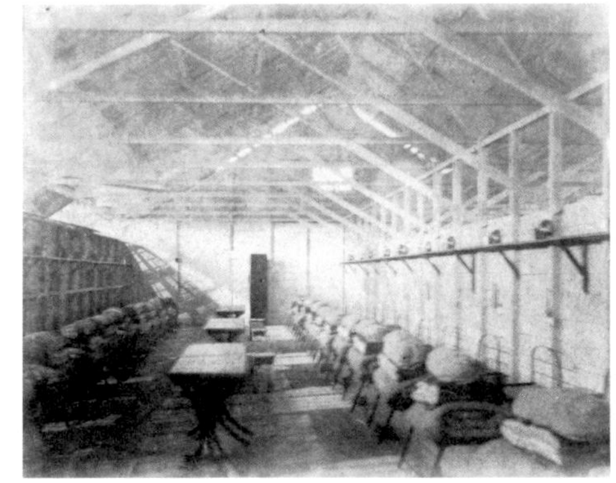

65. John Kirk

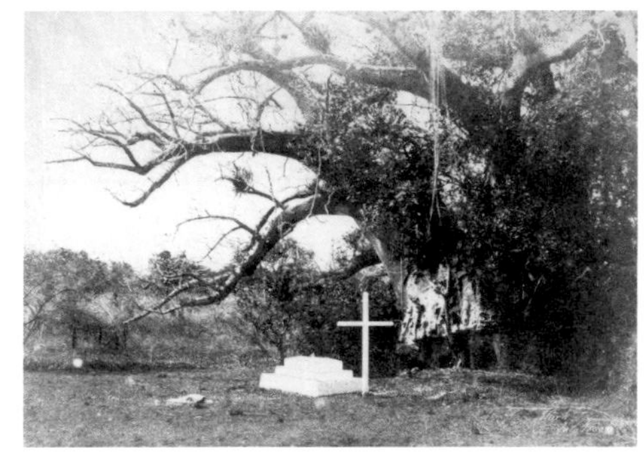

66. John Kirk

teered for medical service in the Crimean War. He probably had begun photographing during his student days, for while in the Crimea Kirk took calotype negatives of a hospital ward at Renkioi and the various amenities of camp life. Following his return in 1857 he was on the verge of moving to Canada when he was offered the position of medical officer and botanist for Dr. David Livingston's second expedition to Zambezi. Livingston's brother Charles was the official photographer, but Kirk considered him hopeless, especially in his choice of the wet-collodion process. Observing the noxious fumes emanating from Charles Livingston's dark tent, Kirk wrote in his journal on July 8, 1858: "I don't anticipate much to come of the Photography. I certainly believe, as I said in London, that the paper process is the only one which at present is worth taking on an expedition such as this." And he was correct, for virtually none of Charles Livingston's photographs were successful. Kirk took numerous waxed-paper negatives during the expedition, including the first significant views of the interior of Africa and studies of unusual botanical specimens, but he was also impressed with Dr. Hill Norris's new dry plates. He remained loyal to waxed paper as late as 1862, finding it even more forgiving in difficult circumstances than he had previously thought. Dr. Kirk moved to Zanzibar in 1866, serving there as a medical officer for two decades, but nothing is known of his photographic activity during this period.

Exhibited: 1856, Edinburgh, Photographic Society of Scotland

References: Reginald Foskett, ed., *The Zambesi Journal and Letters of Dr. John Kirk, 1858–63* (Edinburgh: Oliver & Boyd, 1965), pp. 50–51; Julie Lawson, "Dr. John Kirk and Dr. William Robertson: Photographers in the Crimea," *History of Photography* 12 (July–September 1988), pp. 227–41

Kirkman, Joseph

After training in Richard Beard's London daguerreotype studio, Kirkman moved to Cape Town, South Africa, to start a stationer's business and in 1859 opened his first photographic studio. At first he practiced collodion photography, the standard process for the period, but in December 1861 Kirkman made a surprising decision: he began advertising Talbotype photography, surely making him one of the last professionals anywhere to take up calotypy. Kirkman is best remembered for his 1860 photographs of Prince Alfred tilting the first truckload of stones for the building of the Cape Town Breakwater.

Reference: Marjorie Bull and Joseph Denfield, *Secure the Shadow: The Story of Cape Photography from Its Beginnings to the End of 1870* (Cape Town: Terence McNally, 1970), pp. 200–201

Knight, James Peter

ills. 67, 68

1826–1897

Often confused with John Prescott Knight, the respected portrait painter, James Peter Knight was an artist and drawing master in Cheltenham and a friend of John Dillwyn Llewelyn. Llewelyn family tradition has it that Knight lived for some time in Glamorganshire, acting as a tutor to the Llewelyn children (Thereza Llewelyn, who became Thereza Story Maskelyne, recorded in her diary that "Mr. Knight" accompanied the boys on an 1856 trip to Switzerland). In the 1857 exhibition of the Photographic Society in London, James Knight entered *View from the Windows of the Hotel Bellevue, at Thurn, Switzerland,* almost certainly one and the same photographer as the J. Knight who had submitted a calotype view of Caswell Bay to the society's 1854 exhibition. James Knight contributed two calotype views of Llewelyn's home of Penllergare to the 1855 exhibition; the next year he showed nearly three dozen views, most in collodion but also two in calotype, with Penllergare and its vicinity again the subject, as well as Christopher Rice Mansel Talbot's Welsh home of Margam Castle. Knight participated in the 1857 Manchester Art Treasures exhibition and the 1857 and 1859 Photographic Society exhibitions, by then working primarily in collodion or in Llewelyn's oxymel process. Named headmaster of the Government School of Art in Cheltenham in 1858, he published seven years later *The Practical Guide to Perspective,* codifying the observations that clearly informed his own photographic work. Later in life Knight was again an artist and private teacher in Cheltenham.

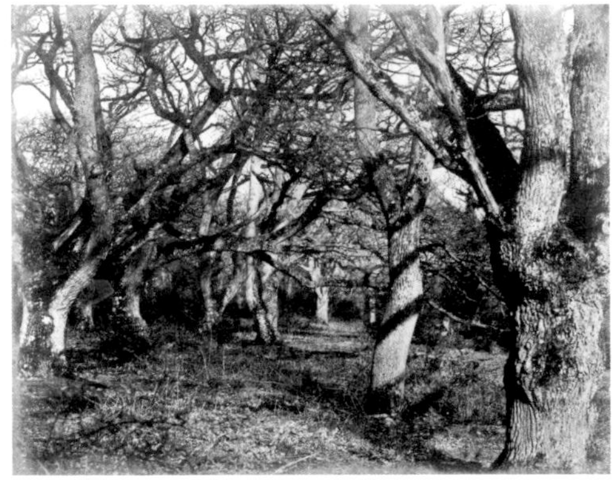

67. James Peter Knight

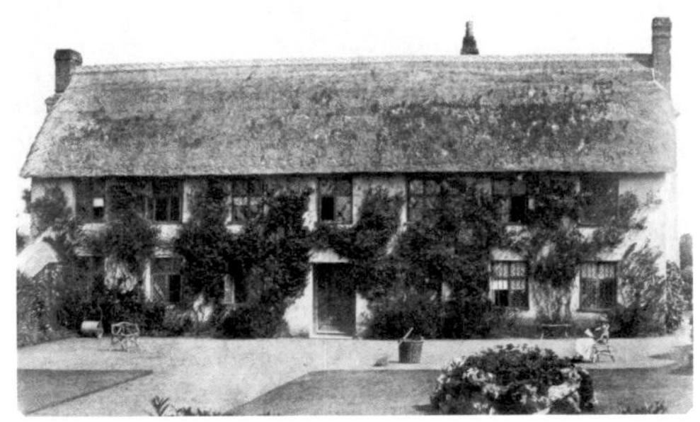

68. James Peter Knight

Exhibited: 1854, 1855, and 1856, London, Photographic Society

References: James P. Knight, *The Practical Guide to Perspective* (London: Simpkin, Marshall & Co., 1865); Larry J. Schaaf, *Sun Pictures, Catalogue Two: Llewelyn, Maskelyne, Talbot—a Family Circle* (New York: Hans P. Kraus, Jr., 1986), pp. 6, 31

Knight, John Prescott

1823–1881

While Knight's portrait paintings are familiar and well documented, the extent of his photographic endeavors is not as clear, and he is often confused with James Peter Knight. J. P. Knight, R.A., was a member of the loosely knit Calotype Club started in London by Peter Wickens Fry in 1847. In the 1854 exhibition of the Photographic Society in London the calotypists J. Knight, Esq., and John Knight were carefully distinguished. The former entered a view of Caswell Bay, near John Dillwyn Llewelyn's home of Penllergare (so this was surely James Peter Knight), and the latter submitted a calotype of Blenheim Palace. Nearly four out of five of John Prescott Knight's paintings are portraits, but early in his career he was less specialized. The son of a popular comedian, Knight occasionally mounted the London stage himself. From 1839 he taught at the Royal Academy and was later professor of perspective, a post he maintained until 1860. Knight may have given up photography once his reputation as a portrait painter began to flourish; in any case his calotype of Blenheim Palace remains to date his only documented photograph.

Exhibited: 1854, London, Photographic Society

Lamb, John

b. 1828

Lamb was a plumber, brass founder, and gas fitter in Aberdeen, employing several men. He established himself as a "Photographic Artist" in 1851 and was a major contributor to the 1853 exhibition of the Aberdeen Mechanics' Institution, showing a number of calotypes, including street views and portraits. An experimenter, Lamb showed collodion portraits on both glass and talc-coated paper, his calotype *View from George Street* winning the bronze medal. The French photographic critic and historian Ernst Lacan singled out Lamb's work at the 1855 Exposition Universelle in Paris, citing its experimental nature and remarking on the "great power" of the views. (Lacan was particularly struck by the Byron quotation attached to Lamb's *Brig of Balgounie.*) In later exhibitions Lamb displayed work solely in collodion. Ever the experimenter, at the 1862 International Exhibition in London he showed a number of chemically developed prints, which was unusual for the time, along with specifically identified salted paper prints.

Exhibited: 1853, Aberdeen, Mechanics' Institution

Reference: Ernest Lacan, *Esquisses photographiques à propos de l'Exposition Universelle et de la guerre Orient* (Paris: A. Gaudin et Frère, 1856), pp. 103–4

Lambly, John

Nothing is known of Lambly save for the fact that he was living in Kilburn, London, at the time of the 1859 and 1860 exhibitions of the Photographic Society in London and contributed two Talbotypes to each exhibition, all of them views from Cornwall.

Exhibited: 1859 and 1860, London, Photographic Society

Lane, William

1818–1889

The son of orange merchants in Brighton, Lane was a servant to William Mason, a well-respected local print seller, and perhaps this is how he first became interested in photography. In 1852 Mason opened his new Repository of Arts, inviting Thomas Henry Hennah and William Henry Kent to set up a Talbotype establishment. Lane set up his own business that year, Lane's Photographic Depot, making picture frames and selling photographic apparatus. In 1853 he began taking portraits, initially by daguerreotype, two years later advertising "Talbotype portraits on paper." Lane worked as a photographer in Brighton until 1879.

Laverty, John Nicolas

b. 1818

A native of Jersey, Laverty became a naval instructor in 1841. He devised a system of determining a ship's position at sea by a projection on a Mercator chart, an ingenious innovation traditionally ascribed to Capt. Thomas Sumner of the U.S. Navy. None of his photographs are known to have survived, but his photographic reputation would be secured by the influential Thomas Sutton's reminiscences about him published in 1867. Sutton was deeply impressed by Laverty's calotypes, which he had seen displayed in a shop window in the Jersey town of St. Helier about 1850. To the normally critical Sutton, Laverty appeared "very intelligent," and he put down a guinea to take Laverty's six-lesson course in calotypy. Most of Laverty's dozen students were successful, none more so than Sutton. (After his course of instruction Sutton considered himself an "established calotypist" who "went in at it with great enthusiasm.") Laverty survived service in the Crimea, but none of his subsequent photographic activity has been traced.

Reference: Thomas Sutton, "Reminiscences of an Old Photographer," *BJP* 14 (August 30, 1867), pp. 413–14

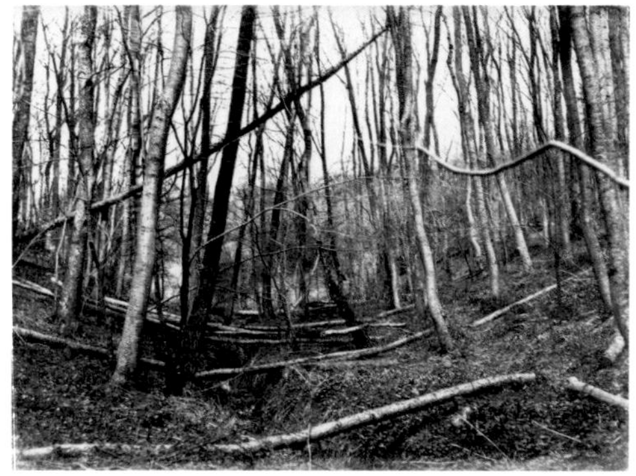

69. William Law

Law, William *ill. 69*

1812–1900

Corresponding with *Photographic Notes* in February 1857, Rev. Law was addressed by the editor as one of the "photographers of old standing." His earliest known works are daguerreotypes and collodion negatives of his family made in 1853, but he was producing calotypes by at least 1855 and soon turned to waxed paper. Taking a lively interest in all matters photographic, Law subjected a print created with one of Thomas Sutton's processes to a torture test by suspending it for many months against a damp wall. He was an experimentalist who believed, as he wrote in "Waxed Paper Process," that "the grand secret . . . of success in photographic operations is the disposition and ability to trace failures to their causes." Law participated in the newly formed Northamptonshire Photographic Society, expressing the hope in the *Northampton Mercury* that the society's monthly meetings would "blend the practical and instructive with the theoretical and the descriptive." Law exhibited only once, but his contribution was significant. Of the twenty-seven photographs that he submitted to the 1857 exhibition of the Birmingham Photographic Society, the majority were done in waxed paper; four were by Talbotype and two in collodion. He also experimented with the albumen-on-glass negative process. Law read a detailed account of his waxed-paper process before the Birmingham Photographic Society in 1857, expanding on his remarks in the journals. Late that year he was attracted to collodion, but unlike most photographers he eschewed the heavy and fragile glass and instead turned to paper coated with collodion. Writing in *Photographic Notes* in December, Law observed somewhat ruefully that this approach "will bear off the palm from the Calotype, which is certainly saying a great deal." In 1897 the local paper noted that Rev. Law was still active, photographing the May Queen and her entourage.

Exhibited: 1857, Birmingham, Photographic Society

References: William Law, "On Calotype Paper, Doubly Iodized," *Photographic Notes* 1 (February 25, 1856), pp. 7–8; "Photographic Society," *Northampton Mercury*, November 3, 1856; "Correspondence. Printing by Development," *Photographic Notes* 2 (February 15, 1857), p. 71; Law, "Waxed Paper Process," *LMPJ*, n.s., 1 (October 1, 1857), pp. 210–12; Law, "Remarks on the Wax Paper Process," *LMPJ*, n.s., 1 (October 15, 1857), pp. 221–22; Law, "Collodion on Paper," *Photographic Notes* 2 (December 1, 1857), pp. 444–45

Leather, William Henry

b. 1819

A manufacturing chemist in Leeds, Leather would have been familiar with photographers seeking supplies. In 1860 he presented a paper (subsequently published in the *British Journal of Photography*) to the Bradford Photographic Society, introducing his presentation with an apology: "As the Waxed-Paper may now be considered an old process, I will simply give in detail my present practice." Leather's thorough instructions betray a long experience in the art, but unfortunately none of his photographs are known to have survived.

Reference: William Henry Leather, "On the Waxed-Paper Process," *BJP* 7 (December 15, 1860), p. 365

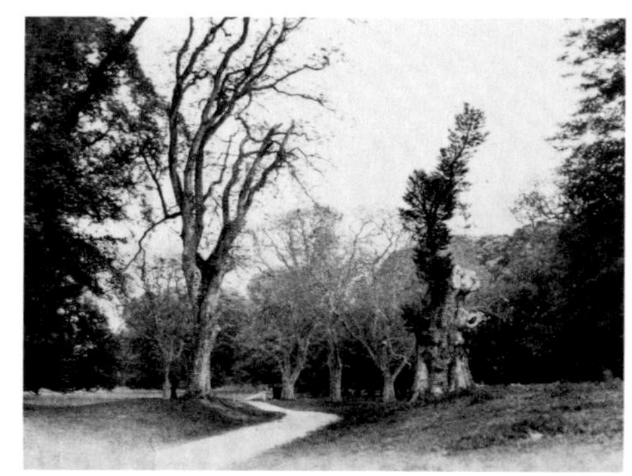

70. Henry Ledger

Ledger, Henry *ill. 70*

In the 1970s several albums emerged at auction that were attributed to Ledger by his grandson. The majority of them were titled and monogrammed. One album, "A Month with the Camera in the North Highlands of Scotland by an Amateur–August 1854," contained several calotypes, almost certainly by Ledger. Nothing further is known of his work.

REFERENCE: Sale cat., Sotheby's, London, June 26, 1975, lots 204, 205, 207

Leverett, Henry F.

b. 1816

A landlord and property owner in Ipswich, Leverett requested membership in the Photographic Society in London in 1854 and was elected that December. He contributed to the society's exhibition the next year in the first known public display of his work. Of his three waxed-paper views, all taken in Suffolk, the reviewer for the *Liverpool Photographic Journal* asserted: "Waxed paper is upheld by Mr. Leverett." In the 1856 exhibition Leverett displayed six similar views. He contributed four photographs to the 1857 Manchester Art Treasures exhibition, the process unspecified but probably waxed paper, since he was still loyal to waxed paper at the 1859 British Association for the Advancement of Science meeting in Aberdeen.

EXHIBITED: 1855 and 1856, London, Photographic Society; 1857, Manchester, "Art Treasures Exhibition"; 1859, Aberdeen, British Association for the Advancement of Science

Levi, Georges Montefiore

1832–1906

Born in London to a Jewish family with extensive international business interests, Levi was educated primarily in Belgium. Much of his personal fortune came from his invention of phosphor bronze, a corrosion-resistant bronze used in manufacturing. Levi was elected a member of the Photographic Society in London in May 1853 and later that year exhibited his new rapid-acting shutter, this at a time when a top hat usually served that purpose. When Levi began in photography is not known, but his earliest surviving photographs, taken in 1854, were salt prints from paper negatives documenting the hydraulic machine he had invented for bringing fresh water to Brussels. That same year he adapted an invention by a Liège daguerreotypist to fashion a device for taking a series of waxed-paper negatives; it allowed him to shoot from ten to fifteen paper negatives in succession without opening the camera. In 1857 Levi wrote to the *Journal of the Photographic Society* from Piedmont describing, and illustrating, a tent he had devised for processing collodion negatives in the field. He exhibited only once, a group of collodion views submitted to the 1858 exhibition of the Photographic Society in London. Later moving to Belgium, he was elected president of the Association Belge de Photographie in 1877 and became a naturalized Belgian citizen five years later. President of the International Monetary Conference in 1892, Levi endowed the Montefiore Institute, one of the first electrical engineering schools in the world, now part of the University of Liège.

REFERENCE: Georges M. Levi, "Description of a Frame for Taking a Series of Waxed-Paper Negatives," *JPS* 1 (March 21, 1854), pp. 181–84; Levi, "Portable Tent for Out-Door Work," *JPS* 4 (September 21, 1857), pp. 43–44

Llewelyn, Emma Thomasina

1808–1881

We will probably never know the full extent of her photographic contributions, not through any attempt to write women out of history but rather because Emma Thomasina Llewelyn, née Talbot, fit naturally and comfortably into the larger context of a photographic family. Emma and her brother CHRISTOPHER RICE MANSEL TALBOT ("Kit") were Welsh cousins of W. H. F. TALBOT. Wed to JOHN DILLWYN LLEWELYN, she took justifiable pride in their daughter Thereza, who would marry MERVYN HERBERT NEVIL STORY MASKELYNE in 1858 (becoming THEREZA STORY MASKELYNE). An active and no doubt influential participant in the scientific projects of her family, Llewelyn is known to have taken at least some paper photographs in the 1840s, but very few are separately identified in family collections. As a photographer she is most closely identified with her cousin W. H. F. Talbot's second major career in photography, when in 1852, realizing that the future of photography was in printer's ink, he laid the groundwork for the process of photogravure. Llewelyn indeed became one of the earliest and most enthusiastic practitioners of Talbot's photographic engraving process as well as his later (1858) photoglyphic engraving process.

REFERENCES: Emma Charlotte Dillwyn Llewelyn's Album, The Metropolitan Museum of Art, Gilman Collection, Gift of The Howard Gilman Foundation, 2005, 2005.100.382; Larry J. Schaaf, *Sun Pictures, Catalogue Two: Llewelyn, Maskelyne, Talbot—a Family Circle* (New York: Hans P. Kraus, Jr., 1986); Richard Morris, *Penllergare, a Victorian Paradise: A Short History of the Penllergare Estate and Its Creator, John Dillwyn Llewelyn (1810–82)* (Llandeilo: Friends of Penllergare, 1999)

Llewelyn, John Dillwyn *ill. 71*

1810–1882

Some photographers are historically important as much for the central role they played in a nexus of activity as for their own photographic work. In a sense Llewelyn married into photography, for his wife Emma was a cousin of W. H. F. TALBOT and their first daughter, Thereza, married MERVYN HERBERT NEVIL STORY MASKELYNE (becoming THEREZA STORY MASKELYNE). Llewelyn's Welsh estate Penllergare was a regular stopping-off point for Talbot and his cousin CHRISTOPHER RICE MANSEL TALBOT ("Kit"), as well as WILLIAM HENRY NICHOLL, CALVERT RICHARD JONES, and others. The son of a botanist who grew up surrounded by both wealth and amateur scientific industry, Llewelyn was already a fellow of the Royal Society and the Linnean Society when he became a member of the Photographic Exchange Club and the Amateur Photographic Association. His daughter recalled sitting for a daguerreotype portrait by her father in about 1841 or 1842, and his wife corresponded regularly with her cousin about photography. A wonderfully accomplished landscape photographer, Llewelyn was certainly taking photographs on paper by the mid-1840s. A love of botany informed his sensitive reactions to nature in his work, while his intimate acquaintance with the comfortable life of country houses resulted in a gentle vision of that privileged world. Photography was both a scientific and an aesthetic tool for him, recording both the beauty of the landscape and the archaeological ruins in Wales. For the 1854 exhibition of the Royal Infirmary Fund in Dundee, Llewelyn contributed fifteen calotypes, mostly of Penllergare and its surroundings, including studies of rocks and shells and a seaside view, *Sea Shore—Breaking Waves (Taken on a dull sunless November day)*. His work covered a similar range, again in calotype, in that year's exhibition of the Photographic Society in London. Studies of trees made up most his paper-negative contributions to the 1855 exhibition of the London Photographic Institution. In 1856 a reviewer for the *Norfolk News* observed that Llewelyn carefully employed selective development of his calotype negatives, thereby saving "many pictures that must otherwise have been lost" and obtaining "a higher degree of excellence than would have

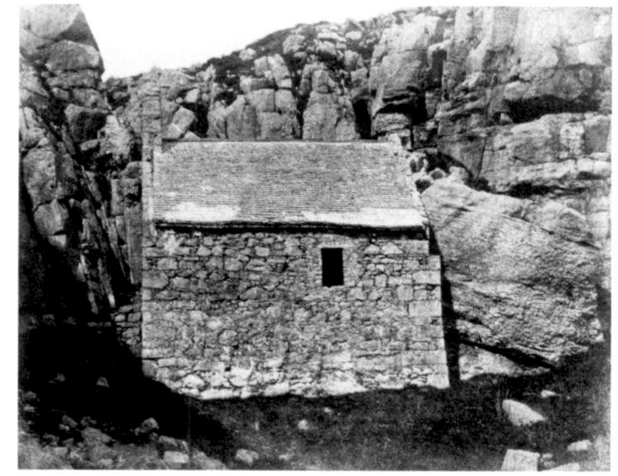

71. John Dillwyn Llewelyn

been practicable under any other treatment." After 1855 Llewelyn remained a steady contributor to exhibitions, primarily showing views of Wales done from glass negatives. Most of his work is known through his wet-collodion negatives, but here too he made a signal contribution to the art. The necessity of coating the glass plate in the field, exposing it while wet, and then developing it while it was still wet imposed a great burden on the photographer. To deal with this difficulty Llewelyn devised the oxymel process. This involved adding a commercially available mixture of honey and vinegar to the plate, which preserved it in a moist state, thus allowing the photographer to prepare sensitive plates at home and even to defer development until the end of the day. Oxymel's strongest advocate would be PHILIP HENRY DELAMOTTE.

EXHIBITED: 1854, London, Photographic Society; 1854, Dundee, Royal Infirmary Fund; 1855, London, Photographic Institution

REFERENCES: John Dillwyn Llewelyn, "Calotype Process," *JPS* 1 (April 21, 1854), pp. 194–96; Larry J. Schaaf, *Sun Pictures, Catalogue Two: Llewelyn, Maskelyne, Talbot—a Family Circle* (New York: Hans P. Kraus, Jr., 1986); Richard Morris, *Penllergare, a Victorian Paradise: A Short History of the Penllergare Estate and Its Creator, John Dillwyn Llewelyn (1810–82)* (Llandeilo: Friends of Penllergare, 1999)

Lockey, Francis
1794–1869
With flexible hours and a duty to observe nature, clergymen often took up the practice of photography, and Rev. Lockey was an unusually devoted member of this corps of amateurs. Born in Reading, where NICOLAAS HENNEMAN would establish his pioneering photographic printing works in 1843, Lockey began photographing as early as 1849, using TALBOT's calotype process, apparently without a license. At least two of his negatives are of nearby Lacock Abbey, so it is possible that he knew Talbot or someone else connected with the village. Working in both calotype and waxed paper, Lockey photographed the area around his home, Swainswick Cottage, outside Bath, as well as ranging through the surrounding countryside. While architecture and city views were his favorite subjects, trees and other scenes from nature also appealed to him. Lockey seems never to have exhibited or joined a photographic society, but he was so keen on the art that he added a photographic printing studio as a wing to his house. His last known photographs date from 1861. A few years after his death, Lockey's house was auctioned, advertised in the *Times* as featuring "an excellent photographic studio." Swainswick Cottage still stands today, largely unchanged.

REFERENCES: "Sales by Auction," *Times* (London), August 27, 1874, p. 15, col. E; David McLaughlin and Michael Gray, *Shadows and Light, Bath in Camera, 1849–1861: Early Rare Photographs—Calotypes by the Rev. Francis Lockey, LLD, 1796–1869* (London: Dirk Nishen, 1989)

Long, Charles Albert
b. 1828
In the 1851 census the young Mr. Long described himself as a "Student of Natural Philosophy." Three years later he had established the fast-emerging London partnership of Bland and Long, which, in a February 21, 1856, advertisement, styled itself as a firm of "Opticians, Mathematical, Philosophical, Photographic & Chemical Instrument Makers, & Operative Chemists." Long took a particular interest in photography, publishing helpful instructions on the calotype process as well as a handbook, *Practical Photography on Glass and Paper.* He was an active participant in the Photographic Society in London and in 1856 spoke on paper negative processes, publishing his remarks in the society's journal that December. Long said he did not want to "raise the old war-cry of paper *versus* collodion, but . . . to state my conviction, that for most subjects of landscape and allied subjects the paper stands pre-eminent." He continued, "for subjects where texture, gradations of tint and distance are required, there is nothing . . . to compare with a good picture from a calotype or waxed paper negative," and pointed out that the original calotype process "has had many votaries . . . some of the most beautiful and charming pictures in our last Exhibition were taken from calotype negatives." Observing that of all the paper processes "there is none other that has yielded such certain results in the hands of the uninitiated, as that of waxed paper," Long noted that yet "there is no other process which bears on the face of it so much complication." His directions were simple and practical, taking into account the materials available and the skills that an amateur might possess. Exactly what happened to Long after his 1856 presentation to the Photographic Society is currently a mystery. In 1885 he reappears again as a photographer in London. For the 1891 census he gave his occupation as electrician, apparently continuing to apply his interest in natural philosophy to an emerging scientific field. Long worked as a photographer in London until at least 1894 and later set himself up in Brighton. No obituary has been traced.

REFERENCES: Charles Albert Long, *Practical Photography on Glass and Paper* (London: Bland and Long, 1854); "Mr. Long on an Easy Calotype Process," *Notes and Queries,* July 1, 1854, pp. 14–15; *JPS* 2 (February 21, 1856), n.p. (advertisement); Long, "On Some Modifications of the Paper Process," *JPS* 3 (December 22, 1856), pp. 174–79

Lound, Thomas
1802–1861
Lound held an undemanding position in his family's Norwich brewery, the source of his personal fortune, but his true passion was art. A pupil of John Sell Cotman, he exhibited his watercolors and oils in Norwich regularly between 1820 and 1833. Views of Norfolk, including the eighteen watercolors he exhibited at the Royal Academy from 1845 to 1857, were his special forte. An enthusiastic amateur painter, gregarious and well liked, Lound also emerged as an important collector of works by his friends in what would come to be known as the Norwich School. He contributed five watercolors to the 1856 exhibition of the Norfolk and Norwich Fine Arts Association; this was a special occasion, for that year the association welcomed a companion exhibition by the newly formed Norwich Photographic Society. Already a member of the new society, Lound showed four waxed-paper views: two of Ely Cathedral, one of Bromholm Priory, and one of the fish market in Norwich. Any subsequent photographic work by him has yet to be discovered. Lound died suddenly in 1861. As documented in *A Period Eye: Photography Then and Now,* at the sale of his collection the auctioneer observed: "Mr. Lound's attractive social qualities procured him a widely extended circle of friends; whilst his indefatigable and eminently successful application to art—in which a correct knowledge of chiaro-oscuro, and perfect truthfulness to nature in color, united with innate genius, were especially remarkable—earned for him a celebrity that many professional men might have good reason to envy."

EXHIBITED: 1856, Norwich, Photographic Society

REFERENCES: Harold A. E. Day, *The Norwich School of Painters* (Eastbourne: Eastbourne Fine Arts, 1979), pp. 246–59; Richard Denyer and Andrew Moore, eds., *A Period Eye: Photography Then and Now,* exh. cat. (Norwich: Norfolk Museums and Archaeology Service, 2003), p. 18

Lousada, Percy Martingdale
d. 1859
Lousada was associated with the extended colony of Sephardic Jews of Spanish descent settled in Devonshire who derived their fortunes from holdings in Jamaica. Resident in London, he converted to Christianity and

married in 1848, and became a clergyman. Nothing is known of his artistic training, but in 1853 he was elected a member of the newly formed Photographic Society in London. His first known public showing was in the society's 1855 exhibition; he used collodion to copy both a Raphael and a Landseer and also to make a view of his wife's native Sidmouth. However, like many of his peers, Lousada recognized that the waxed-paper process was far more adaptable to the needs of the traveler. He showed nearly two dozen architectural views taken in Spain and Germany in the 1858 exhibition of the Architectural Photographic Association and the same year contributed two "wet paper process" studies of the Alhambra to the Photographic Society's exhibition. His sudden death the following year meant the loss of an enthusiastic, if today little-known photographer. In a book containing sermons he had preached, published the year after his death, it is recorded that Rev. Lousada observed as he was dying "how shadows and realities separated themselves clearly now."

Exhibited: 1858, London, Photographic Society; 1858, London, Architectural Photographic Association

Reference: Richard Cowley Powles, *Sermons Preached at St. John's Chapel, St. John's Wood, by the Late Rev. Percy Lousada* (London: J. T. Hayes, 1860)

Lowdon, George, Jr.
1825–1912
An optician, philosophical instrument maker, and fishing rod maker in Dundee, Lowdon (sometimes Lowden) vividly recalled having been drawn to science at an early age. "I was," he reminisced in the *Dundee Advertiser*, "aided considerably by my father, who, though a grocer to trade, was a good mechanic and had many mechanical tools which he was able to use cleverly in making various articles. Hence I may say that I was born with tools at my finger-ends and a turning-lathe at my bedside. Even at that time my father had successfully ground and polished lenses of different kinds; so naturally I took to . . . making scientific instruments." After working in a flax factory, Lowdon opened an optician's business in 1849, just as photography was poised to become a major artistic and commercial phenomenon. Meeting Sir David Brewster through Lord Kinnaird, he was selected to manufacture Brewster's newly invented stereoscope. Lowdon also imported a daguerreotype apparatus from Paris and was the first to show examples of the process in Dundee. He would have had plenty of opportunities to learn about calotypy in nearby St. Andrews, but Lowdon confessed that, perhaps surprisingly, his initial attempt at paper photography in 1846 was a failure. Three years later he tried again, this time successfully, recalling in the *Dundee Advertiser* that "since that period I have taken pictures and made many cameras and given instruction to a large number of professionals and amateurs." Lowdon was commissioned to build a "jumbo microscope" for the Great Exhibition of 1851; standing four feet high and incorporating a "photographic slide for Fox-Talbot paper," it unfortunately arrived too late to be displayed. His only recorded public showing of his photographs was in the 1854 exhibition of the Royal Infirmary Fund in Dundee, for which he contributed seven waxed-paper views of the Dundee area and waxed-paper negative copies of thirty-two engravings. While it cannot be confirmed, Lowdon claimed that he was the first to teach photography to George Washington Wilson, the Aberdeen photographer who developed an enormous business in views of Scotland.

Exhibited: 1854, Dundee, Royal Infirmary Fund (as by "Louden")

References: "George Lowdon, Optician and Scientist, Dundee: Sketch of His Reminiscences and Career," *Dundee Advertiser*, February 3 and 6, 1906; T. N. Clarke, Alison D. Morrison-Low, and Allen D. C. Simpson, "George Lowdon of Dundee," in *Brass & Glass: Scientific Instrument Making Workshops in Scotland* (Edinburgh: National Museums of Scotland, 1989), pp. 146–49

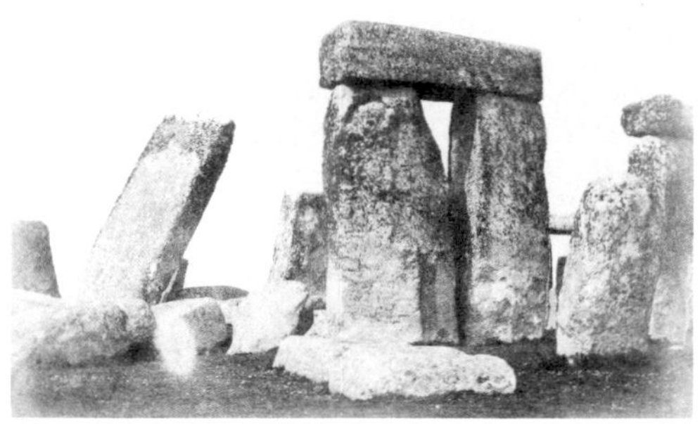

72. Robert Wilfred Skeffington Lutwidge

Lutwidge, Robert Wilfred Skeffington *ill. 72*
1802–1873
Lutwidge attended Cambridge, was admitted to Lincoln's Inn in 1822, and became a barrister in London in 1827. He began what would be a lifelong career with the Lunacy Commission in 1842, filling the post of commissioner from 1855 until his death. His sister married a Dodgson and the two families became quite close. A favorite nephew of Lutwidge's was Charles Lutwidge Dodgson, better known as the author and photographer Lewis Carroll. While his nephew specialized in portraiture, appropriately using the wet-collodion process, Lutwidge focused on landscape and the architecture of grand buildings. Although he did not participate in public exhibitions, he was an avid member of the Photographic Exchange Club, contributing to its albums in 1855 and 1857 as well as to the Photographic Society's albums of the same years. A master of light and shade with a superb sense of composition, Lutwidge did his finest work with calotype negatives. But in time his professional responsibilities appear to have taken precedence over what had been a consistently fine and ever-more promising photographic avocation.

Mackinlay, Thomas
Giving addresses in Paisley and Edinburgh, Mackinlay exhibited a mixture of collodion and calotype work in the 1858 exhibition of the Photographic Society of Scotland, his only known public showing. Two possible candidates for the photographer emerge from the 1861 census. One was a Renfrewshire native, born in 1834, who lodged in Edinburgh and listed himself as an "Artist, painting." The other contender, born the year before, was an investor in Anstruther, Fife. While the artist might appear to be the more obvious choice, the exhibitor's calotypes were all taken in Crail, a village very near Anstruther. Two of Mackinlay's calotypes were of the wreck of the *Queen*, a steamer that crashed into North Carr Rock in the North Sea in the early morning of April 19, 1857. Filling rapidly with water, she made for the lights of Crail Harbour, but it was low tide and she struck a sandbar four hundred yards offshore. Mackinlay would have had a relatively short period to calotype the wreck, which was sold on May 26. A Fife resident would have been well placed to capture the wreck of the *Queen* with his camera.

Exhibited: 1858, Edinburgh, Photographic Society of Scotland

Mackinlay, Thomas George
1809–1865
A music publisher in London, Mackinlay was also a keen amateur scientist. When he married the daughter of the famous chemist Andrew Ure he gained both a devoted wife and a very useful father-in-law. Mackinlay purchased a camera directly from Daguerre, but, frustrated with the results, he turned to the eminent London optician and lens maker Andrew Ross for assistance. According to the *Photographic Journal* his first photographs were taken "at

such an early date that, in an assembly of several highly educated persons, the general question asked was, what the productions were." His friends remembered that Mackinlay was taking photographs even before the publication of TALBOT's *The Pencil of Nature* in 1844. While most paper-negative photographers concentrated on landscape and architecture, *Photographic News* observed that "some of the earliest and finest portraits ever produced by the calotype process were taken by Mr. Mackinlay, who, as an amateur, excelled in this branch of the art." A member of the Photographic Society in London from its founding, Mackinlay submitted three calotypes to the society's 1856 exhibition, including one taken on the Rhine. He contributed two calotypes to the Photographic Exchange Club album in 1855 and one to the following year's album. By the time of the Exchange Club's 1857 album, Mackinlay had turned to collodion; his contributions to the 1858 exhibition of the Photographic Society of Scotland in Edinburgh were a mixture of collodion and calotype. Mackinlay was also an early practitioner of electrotyping, reproducing works from Horace Walpole's art collection "with a degree of excellence that has never been surpassed," in the opinion of the *Photographic Journal*. His obituary in *Photographic News* recorded that Mackinlay, a fellow of the Society of Arts, "was well known to and highly respected by the early photographers, and by the members of many learned societies and clubs of which he was a member."

EXHIBITED: 1856, London, Photographic Society

REFERENCES: *Photographic News* 9 (July 7, 1865), p. 324 (obituary); *Photographic Journal* 10 (July 15, 1865), pp. 102–3 (obituary)

Maconochie, Allan Alexander Welwood

1806–1885

Descended from an old Scottish family, Maconochie practiced law from 1829 until his appointment as professor of Roman and Scots law at Glasgow University in 1842. "He was an enthusiastic professor, who took much interest in his students and endeavoured to assist them in other ways than by lectures," according to a memoir about the school published in 1927. One of his many interests was chemistry, and by May 1839 Maconochie was able to show photogenic drawing negatives and positives to his friends Sir WALTER CALVERLEY TREVELYAN and his wife, Lady PAULINE TREVELYAN. Writing to Sir Walter on January 7, 1843, Maconochie advised that he had "made great strides in the Photographic art" the previous summer, always striving to shorten the exposure time to better capture action. Working in the weak Glasgow sunlight of the dead of winter, he eventually managed to reduce the exposure times for his calotype negatives to as little as seventeen seconds. Maconochie attended the first meeting of the Photographic Society in London in 1853, showing instantaneous photographs taken on glass. No one knew him, but as the *British Journal of Photography* recalled some years later, the images "were at once recognised as wonderful; and it seemed as if the producer of them had dropped from the clouds he so faithfully depicted." Maconochie began a correspondence with ROGER FENTON in which he analyzed the properties of collodion and suggested ways to make it more stable. He was particularly excited by the shortened exposures he was able to achieve. Obviously impressed, Fenton published extracts of Maconochie's letters in the *Journal of the Photographic Society*, which led the firm of W. E. & F. Newton to write to the journal in August 1853 about a "Method of Deepening Negatives," which had been communicated to them by the professor "some time since." By allowing the correction of problems caused by too short an exposure, Maconochie's method helped make it possible to obtain instantaneous photographs, and it seems unlikely that he ever returned to the slower paper negative. Succeeding his father to the family estates in 1861, he became Allan Alexander Maconochie-Welwood, 3rd Lord Meadowbank.

REFERENCES: Allen Alexander Welwood Maconochie to Walter Calverley Trevelyan, January 7, 1843, Special Collections, Newcastle University Library, WCT185; "On a Normal Collodion, and on Iodide of Iron," *JPS* 1 (July 21, 1853), pp. 87–88; W. E. and F. Newton, "Method of Deepening Negatives," *JPS* 1 (August 22, 1853), p. 104; B. Marc, "Instantaneous Photography," *BJP* 8 (July 15, 1861), p. 251; *Scotsman* (Edinburgh), June 1, 1885 (obituary); David Murray, *Memories of the Old College of Glasgow* (Glasgow: Jackson, Wylie and Co., 1927), p. 230

MacOwen, Peter

b. 1831

In the first of two communications published in *Photographic Notes* in 1860, MacOwen (misspelled MacOwan) noted that "the peculiar sin of photographers is, working in a blind rule-of-thumb style, without any attempt at logical sequence in their doings." He proposed a "Paper Magazine," for which he was willing to serve as secretary, "in which each correspondent may tell his quarterly tale of success or failure." This would result in "reflection and consecutive experiment substituted for isolated trials." MacOwen wrote from the laboratory of Huddersfield College, but his actual photographic experience may have been limited; encouraged by the editor, in his second communication he confessed that "photography being to me a sort of romance of chemistry, a relief from the daily routine of demonstration and analysis, I am less of a picture producer than of an experimentalist." The clearly talented MacOwen was soon named professor of chemistry and physics at London University.

REFERENCES: Peter MacOwen, letter in *Photographic Notes* 5 (November 15, 1860), p. 302 (for the journal's response to MacOwen's proposal, see pp. 302–4); MacOwen, "The Paper Club," *Photographic Notes* 5 (December 1, 1860), p. 323

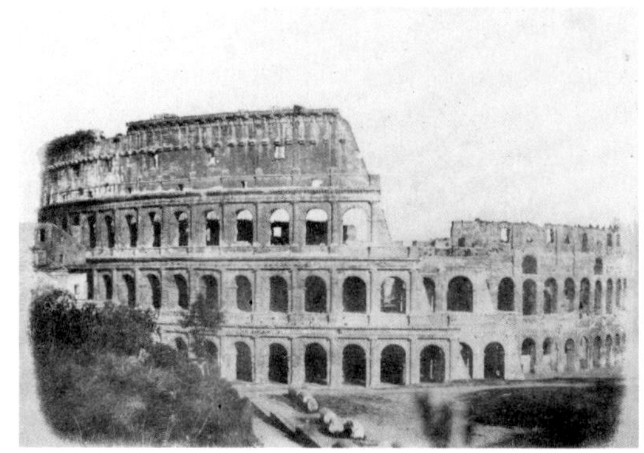

73. James Calder Macphail

Macphail, James Calder *ill. 73*

1821–1908

A minister in the Free Church of Scotland, Macphail participated in the Disruption, but we do not know if he was photographed by Hill & Adamson, although he certainly had every opportunity to meet the calotypists. An authority on Gaelic literature, Macphail was an active advocate for developing a Gaelic-speaking ministry. Until recently, his only known photographic work documented a tour of the Holy Land late in life. However, four of Macphail's photographs have been identified in a newly discovered Edinburgh Calotype Club album. Salt prints from calotype negatives, they show the Colosseum and St. Peter's in Rome, the Temple of Serapis in Naples, and the Quarantine Hospital in Valletta, Malta, and were all possibly taken when he traveled with his friend JAMES DUNLOP in the 1840s.

Macpherson

Nothing is at present known of Dr. Macpherson except for his contributions to the 1856 exhibition of the Photographic Society of Scotland in Edinburgh: three albumen-on-glass works and four calotypes, all landscapes taken in the Dunoon area.

EXHIBITED: 1856, Edinburgh, Photographic Society

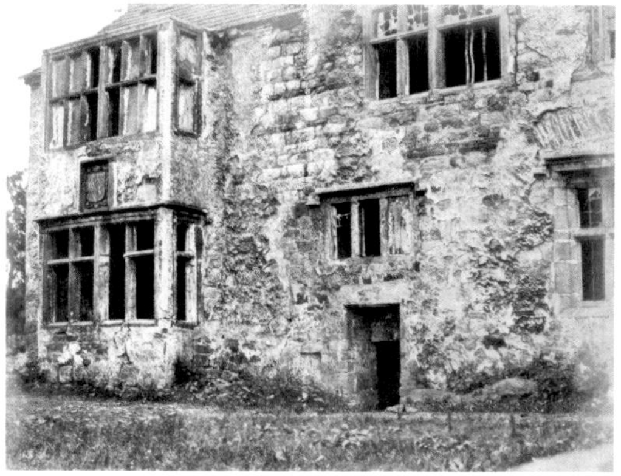

74. John Richardson Major, Jr.

Major, John Richardson, Jr. *ill. 74*
b. 1822
Rev. Major is easily confused with his distinguished father, headmaster at King's College School, London, where the son would serve as a master. Born in Thetford, Norfolk, and resident there most of his life, Major was actively involved in photography in various official capacities, but it is not known when he first became interested in the medium. He was honorary secretary of the Photographic Exchange Club and contributed a calotype to the club's 1855 album, an architectural study taken in Lancashire. The next year he contributed two calotypes, but by 1857 Major had converted to collodion. Named secretary of the Photographic Society in London in 1856, he was also editor of the *Photographic Journal* in 1856–57. For the society's 1856 exhibition Major displayed one photograph that was clearly labeled a calotype, the last time, as far as we know, that he participated in a photographic exhibition.

Exhibited: 1856, London, Photographic Society

Reference: F. J. C. Hearnshaw, *The Centenary History of King's College, London, 1828–1928* (London: George Harrap & Co., 1929), pp. 154, 191

Malden, Henry Charles S.
1829–1907
Malden was a headmaster and justice of the peace in Brighton and Godalming. He entered an assortment of collodion portraits as well as calotype and waxed-paper architectural views in the 1855 exhibition of the Photographic Society in London, the range of subjects and processes being those of an amateur photographer who was already a seasoned experimenter. Malden submitted calotype views to the society's 1856 exhibition and a mixture of calotype and waxed-paper work the next year, but by the time of the 1858 exhibition, like many other amateurs, he had become enamored of stereoscopic views taken with collodion.

Exhibited: 1855, 1856, and 1857, London, Photographic Society

Malone, Thomas Augustine
1823–1867
Malone was born in London but his family came from Reading. He had just started in partnership with Nicolaas Henneman in their London studio when he listed himself as a "Talbotype artist" in the 1851 census. The story of his early years in photography is somewhat unclear, but he was an active presence in photographic society meetings in the 1850s and later reminisced about Talbot and Henneman, often inserting himself into the narrative. (One story has him working as an apprentice in the chemist's shop where Henneman purchased his supplies.) He first turns up in Talbot's correspondence in September 1844, when Henneman mentions that Malone is interested in a position with Antoine Claudet, with whom he was soon working. Near the end of 1846 he encouraged Talbot to open a London studio; within a couple of years the two were writing regularly, trying to solve the problem of permanence in prints. In 1849 and 1851 Malone and Talbot took out joint photographic patents. Malone was working in a supporting role at Henneman's establishment in 1847 and by the next year the business was known as Henneman & Malone. Lasting through the Great Exhibition of 1851, the firm then became Henneman & Co., and Malone moved back to Reading. He entered the Royal College of Chemistry in 1852 and the following year began teaching photography courses (to both men and women, although separately) at the Royal Polytechnic Institution. Later a commercial photographer in London, Malone never exhibited but was an active photographer on paper from the earliest days. He maintained a friendly professional relationship with Talbot over a span of many years. He was made a fellow of the Chemical Society and also edited the *Liverpool and Manchester Photographic Journal* in 1857–58. Malone later returned to work as an operative in a chemist's shop. According to the death certificate, he died of "acute melancholia."

References: Thomas Augustine Malone, "Photography on Glass," *Athenaeum*, June 1, 1850, p. 589; Malone, "Amateurs' Column," *LMPJ*, n.s., 1 (December 15, 1857), p. 270

Mann, Miss (Jessie?)
1805–1867 (?)
Writing to David Octavius Hill on March 27, 1847, the great engineer James Nasmyth inquired: "How goes on the divine solar art? and how does that worthy artist Mr. Adamson the authentic contriver & manipulator in art of light and darkness? and thrice worthy Miss Mann the most skillfull and zealous of assistants." That she was some kind of assistant to Hill and Robert Adamson in their calotype studio is all that is known of Miss Mann, who was very likely one of the three Mann sisters: either Margaret (1795–1861), Elizabeth (1799–1872), or Jessie (baptized Janet; 1805–1867). The sisters had grown up near Hill in Perth and their brother was his solicitor. By the early 1840s they all lived on Leopold Place in Edinburgh, very close to the Hill & Adamson studio. If the "most skillful and zealous" assistant was indeed one of these three, as seems almost certain, Jessie, the youngest, emerges as the most likely candidate.

Reference: James Nasmyth to David Octavius Hill, March 27, 1847, Royal Observatory, Edinburgh

Mansell, Thomas Lukis
1809–1879
The son of an admiral, Dr. Mansell completed his medical studies in Dublin and took an active interest in science, distinguishing himself particularly in the study of meteorology. Through marriage he was related to William Thomas Collings. Mansell was initially frustrated by the calotype process, for the photographs he took by the seaside were overly rich in blue light, burning out the sky. However, in the autumn of 1852 he discovered a means of overcoming this problem. Like many early photographers, Mansell was acutely aware of the important differences between individual batches of paper. His personal favorites, he wrote in *Humphrey's Journal*, were Whatman's 1849 and Turner's Chafford Mills, that is, "if two or three years old." Mansell published his techniques for producing waxed-paper negatives in 1853–54. Beginning in 1856 his considerable contributions to the exhibitions were all made using collodion, as were the works he included in the Photograph Exchange Club's 1855 album and *The Photographic Album for the Year 1857*. An ardent horticulturalist, Mansell later became a magistrate.

References: Thomas L. Mansell, "Photographic Paper," *Athenaeum*, March 5, 1853, p. 298; Mansell, "The Calotype on the Sea-Shore, *Humphrey's Journal* 5 (March 15, 1854), pp. 371–73; Mansell, "Gravelly Wax Negatives," *Notes and Queries*, May 13, 1854, p. 456; *The Mansell Family: A Brief Sketch of the Career of Some of Its Members* (N.p., [ca. 1895]), pp. 19–22

Mantell, Edward W.
b. 1830
Dr. Mantell was both a surgeon and, curiously, an architect at King's College, London. A member of the Photographic Society in London, he exhibited four collodion views and one calotype in the society's 1857 exhibition.

Exhibited: 1857, London, Photographic Society (as by "E. W. Mansell")

Marriott, Montague
b. 1820
A barrister in London, Marriott informed the *Liverpool Photographic Journal* in 1854 of his extensive experiments in waxed paper. No other record of his photography has been found, and he may have simply returned to the more mundane demands of his law practice. Indeed, as late as 1883 Marriott was the editor of *Willich's Tithe Commutation Tables.*

Reference: Marriott Montague, letter in *LPJ* 1 (November 11, 1854), pp. 151–52

Marshall, Frederick Anthony Stansfield
b. 1818
As he wrote in his 1855 *Photography*, Rev. Marshall, like many others, owed his mastery of the art of calotypy to the published instructions of "one of its earliest Amateurs, George Cundell." Another early calotypist, HENRY D. TAYLOR, remembered Marshall as one of his colleagues. Based in Peterborough, Marshall showed eight Talbotypes, mostly views in Kent, in the 1854 exhibition of the Royal Infirmary Fund in Dundee and a similar group that year at the Photographic Society in London. In 1855 his subjects were Peterborough Cathedral and Canterbury for the exhibition at the Photographic Institution in London, while at the Photographic Society he displayed fifteen calotypes as well as a group of four collodion views. Marshall's *Photography* was an impassioned plea for the importance of photography for preserving the memory of the architectural fabric of the nation. Echoing thoughts expressed earlier in Talbot's *The Pencil of Nature*, Marshall exclaimed: "What would we not give for such memorials of those noble piles of buildings formerly connected with our Cathedral . . . but which have fallen into ruin and decay by the ravages of Time, and the still more destructive hands of wanton violence or ignorant innovation? Photography, had it been known, would have rescued from oblivion such valuable records, and no longer left it to the uncertain light of conjecture whereby to trace out the foundation walls, and, from the ivyed arch and broken column scattered here and there, to restore as we may, in our imagination, those edifices."

Exhibited: 1854, London, Photographic Society; 1854, Dundee, Royal Infirmary Fund; 1855, London, Photographic Society; 1855, London, Photographic Institution

References: Frederick Anthony Stansfield Marshall, *Photography: The Importance of Its Application in Preserving Pictorial Records of the National Monuments of History and Art* (London: Hering and Remington, 1855); Henry D. Taylor, "The Calotype Process, and How We Photographed in the 'Fifties,'" *International Annual of Anthony's Photographic Bulletin*, June 1889, pp. 242–46

Martin, G.
Four related groups of waxed-paper negatives emerged at auction in 1976: more than fifty in number and measuring 16 x 21 centimeters each, they were all taken in Dover, a coastal town in Kent. About half are architectural and town views while the rest are, unsurprisingly, studies of shipping and harbor views. (Restored by a royal commission in the late 1840s, the harbor would have been a rich subject.) The dated negatives were taken predominantly in 1851.One is further inscribed "G. Martin, Market Pl., June 17-51," providing a tempting clue, but to date the exact identity of the photographer has not been confirmed.

Reference: Sale cat., Sotheby's, London, March 19, 1976, lots 126, 127

Maskelyne, Mervyn Herbert Nevil Story
1823–1911
Born into science, Maskelyne was the eldest son of the astronomer royal, Nevil Maskelyne. (Through an inheritance the family became the Story-Maskelynes in 1845.) Maskelyne was born at Basset Down House in Wiltshire, not far from TALBOT's Lacock Abbey. When and how he first came to photography are unrecorded, but as a youth he made photogenic drawings in what he called "My Laboratory," and as a student at Oxford in the 1840s he was in correspondence with Talbot over matters photographic. The chemist Benjamin Brodie successfully deflected Maskelyne's original progression toward the law, luring him into a life of chemistry and in the process becoming his first formal teacher of photography. By 1846 Maskelyne had devised his own variation of the calotype based on bromide of silver; this offered additional sensitivity to the green portion of the spectrum, thus rendering foliage more true to nature. His main interest in calotypy, however, seems to have been architectural, and he often recorded the houses of friends and the places that he visited. In support of his lectures, Maskelyne was given a laboratory below the Ashmolean Museum at Oxford in 1850; he used it as much for photography as for mineralogy. He remained an experimentalist, notably developing a method of producing negatives on sheets of mica. Maskelyne married Talbot's niece Thereza Llewelyn (who became THEREZA MARY DILLWYN STORY MASKELYNE) in 1858, completing a photographic circle, but he never strove to exhibit his photographs publicly. Sharing a love of minerals with his friend John Ruskin, Maskelyne went on to become a member of Parliament and a collector of gems.

Reference: *Times* (London), May 22, 1911, p. 13, col. c (obituary)

Maskelyne, Thereza Mary Dillwyn Story
1834–1926
Few were born into the aristocracy of photography, as was Thereza Llewelyn, but fewer still were equipped to take real advantage of that privileged state. When she was about seven or eight Thereza sat for a lengthy daguerreotype exposure for her father, JOHN DILLWYN LLEWELYN. It was not the first time she had assisted in his amateur scientific endeavors. At the family estate of Penllergare, everyone—family, friends, and visitors—was making photogenic drawings and calotypes in the 1840s, and the scientifically minded young lady joined in with enthusiasm. By the time of her marriage to MERVYN HERBERT NEVIL STORY MASKELYNE (later Story-Maskelyne), the center of interest for photographers had moved to the wet-collodion plate, a process in which Thereza Story-Maskelyne excelled as an amateur—mostly for her own enjoyment and never for exhibition.

References: Larry J. Schaaf, *Sun Pictures, Catalogue Two: Llewelyn, Maskelyne, Talbot—a Family Circle* (New York: Hans P. Kraus, Jr., 1986); Richard Morris, *Penllergare, a Victorian Paradise: A Short History of the Penllergare Estate and Its Creator, John Dillwyn Llewelyn (1810–82)* (Llandeilo: Friends of Penllergare, 1999)

Matthew, T. E.
Matthew showed four calotypes in the 1858 exhibition of the Photographic Society in London, three views of Whitby Abbey and a study of shipbuilding in Scarborough Harbour. Both the abbey and the harbor were popular tourist destinations, so it is possible that he was a visitor to the area, but in any case no further information about Matthew or his photographic work has been traced.

Exhibited: 1858, London, Photographic Society

Mawson, John
1816–1867
Mawson was a newly established druggist and chemical supplier in Newcastle just as photography was gaining in popularity. In the summer of 1854 he announced in the *Journal of the Photographic Society* that he held the sole license from Talbot for photographic portraiture in Newcastle and its neighborhood. "Having obtained the assistance of a skillful artist from London, he is now able to carry on every branch of the Photographic Art," the advertisement pointed out, including "Talbotype photography on paper and glass." Mawson had taken on the young Joseph Swan, whose sister he would marry, as an assistant in about 1847. (Swan was later an important photographic inventor and even owned a copy of TALBOT's *The Pencil of Nature*, but there is no evidence that he ever made paper negatives.) Mawson's active period as a Talbotypist was brief, for while he continued to stock materials for the paper art, Mawson & Swan emerged as one of the foremost suppliers of collodion products. In 1867, Mawson, in his role as sheriff, was called in to dispose of barrels of nitroglycerin found in the basement of a pub in the heart of Newcastle. Tragically, he and seven others were killed in the process. Mawson was well remembered by the photographic community; four decades later, on the death of his widow, the history of his untimely demise was recounted in the *British Journal of Photography.*

REFERENCES: *JPS* 2 (July 21, 1854), n.p. (advertisement); "Terrible Explosion at Newcastle," *Times* (London), December 19, 1867, p. 9, col. E; "Death of Mrs. Mawson," *BJP* 52 (August 11, 1905), p. 636

Maynard, Mr. (Capt. Edmund Gilling?)
Writing in 1896, R. Child Bayley pointed out that as the art of photography matured, "an increasing interest manifests itself in the memorials and relics of the earlier stages of its career." He was especially interested in the calotypes in the collection of the Royal Photographic Society, noting that "of this beautiful process there are many specimens extant." After outlining the collection, which ranged from TALBOT to ANGELO CORELLI COLLARD BERE, Bayley singled out in particular "some prints by the process of scenes in the neighbourhood of the Crimea by Mr. Maynard." These prints still survive: apparently dating from the 1850s, the views either were taken in the field under the stress of war or were, perhaps, simply the beginning efforts of an amateur. Bayley identified a Mr. Maynard as the photographer, but in a later account they were listed as having been donated by "Maynard Esq." Assuming that Maynard was indeed the photographer, the only logical candidate would be Capt. Edmund Gilling Maynard of the 88th Regiment, who was in the Crimea at the time, had already expressed an interest in the history and topography of the region, and was recovering from wounds and therefore had time on his hands. Moreover, he would not have had far to look for either supplies or tutelage in the art, for Maynard was the brother-in-law of ROGER FENTON.

REFERENCES: *Photographic Journal*, n.s., 20 (October 25, 1895), p. 36; R. Child Bayley, "Calotypes," *BJP* 43 (August 21, 1896), pp. 535–57

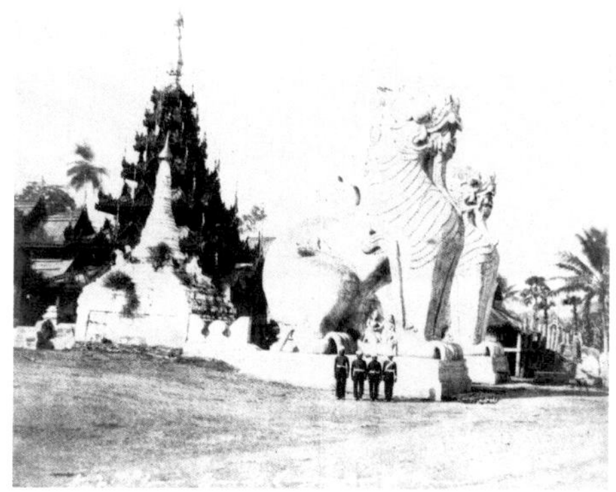

75. John McCosh

McCosh, John *ill. 75*
1805–1885
The son of a Scottish surveyor, McCosh (also MacCosh) studied medicine in Edinburgh and joined the Indian Medical Service in 1831. Returning to India from Tasmania, where he had been on sick leave with jungle fever, he was the sole survivor when his ship was wrecked off the desolate island of Amsterdam in 1833. Stationed in the foothills of the Himalayas, he took up photography in 1844. McCosh is best known for the small calotype negatives, mostly portraits, which he took during the Second Sikh War in 1848, today recognized as the earliest war photographs. He again turned to photography for the Second Burmese War in 1852, this time using a larger camera. McCosh was not only an early photographer but one always aware of artistic considerations. He submitted hand-colored photographs to the 1855 exhibition of the Photographic Society of Bombay. In the revised edition of his *Advice to Officers in India* (1856), McCosh urged "every assistant-surgeon to make himself master of photography in all its branches, on paper, on plate glass, and on metallic plates. I have practised it for many years, and know of no extra professional pursuit that will more repay him for all the expense and trouble (and both are very considerable) than this fascinating study . . . during the course of his service in India, he may make such a faithful collection of representations of man and animals, of architecture and landscape, that would be a welcome contribution to any museum." For the humid climate he recommended French paper, rather than English, as well as a substantial mahogany camera, observing that "it is a great mistake to make things light and portable for Indian use, as if the owner himself had to carry them. Carriage for every piece of apparatus is cheap, safe, and abundant." McCosh later turned to travel and poetry, bringing to the latter more enthusiasm than talent.

EXHIBITED: 1858, Bombay, Photographic Society

REFERENCES: John McCosh, *Advice to Officers in India* (London: Allen, 1856); Peter R. Russell-Jones, "John MacCosh's Photographs of the 2nd Sikh War, 1848–49, and the 2nd Burma War, 1852–53," *Photographic Journal* 108 (January 1968), pp. 25–27; Ray McKenzie, "'The Laboratory of Mankind': John McCosh and the Beginnings of Photography in British India," *History of Photography* 11 (April–June 1987), pp. 109–18

McGregory, J.
McGregory showed four waxed-paper photographs in the 1856 exhibition of the Manchester Photographic Society, all views in Cheshire, of either Disley or Strines, where fellow photographer JOSEPH SIDEBOTHAM established his calico printing business. No further identification has been traced.

EXHIBITED: 1856, Manchester, Photographic Society

Melhuish, Arthur James *ill. 76*
1829–1895
After a brief stint as a pawnbroker, Melhuish entered the world of photography, perhaps stimulated by his widowed mother's 1846 marriage to JOHN BUCHANAN SMITH. His first public showing was in the 1855 London exhibition of the Photographic Society, where his seven waxed-paper architectural studies included one interior. In 1856 Melhuish sent nearly twenty architectural views to the society's exhibition. By 1857 he had begun to work with collodion, although he showed two waxed-paper views at the society. He continued to exhibit there annually through 1860, submitting some waxed-paper photographs in 1859. His last participation in major exhibitions was at the 1861 Architectural Photographic Association in London. Melhuish was an inveterate inventor, although none of his inventions found a wide market. In 1856 he patented

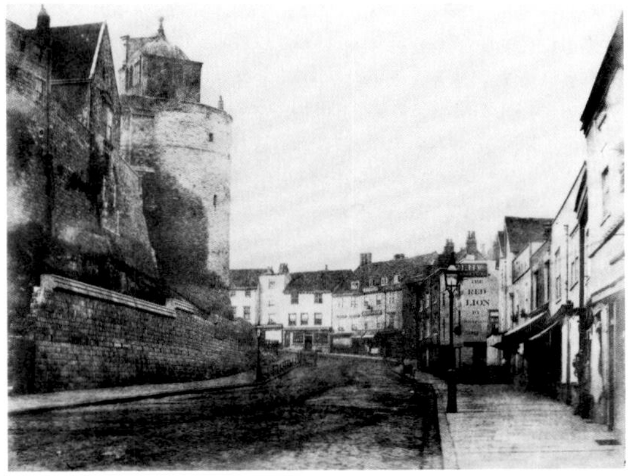

76. Arthur James Melhuish

his design for a roller slide that permitted the photographer to carry a number of sheets of sensitized paper and change them in the camera without the need for a darkroom. His 1860 metal camera was promoted as being one-third lighter than wooden ones and twice as strong. Melhuish was more successful at building a photographic printing business, employing several assistants, but he had some economic reversals and by 1871 was listed as a picture dealer, operating out of his mother's house. He was declared bankrupt by 1882. Melhuish rebuilt his reputation, becoming Photographer Royal and by the 1890s hosting a British Museum of Portraits at his Pall Mall studio. He was secretary of the Photographic Association from 1861 to 1889 and was elected a fellow of the Royal Astronomical Society in 1863. Melhuish was born and registered as a Nonconformist Protestant, which perhaps explains why his later contributions to the literature ventured away from photography to include *The Geology of the Bible* and *The Truth about Ghosts.* In the 1881 census he listed himself an "artist," but by the 1891 census, near the end of his life, Melhuish proudly claimed to be a "Photographic Artist." At least two of his sons and three of his daughters became photographers.

EXHIBITED: 1855 and 1857, London, Photographic Society; 1858, London, Photographic Society; 1858, Edinburgh, Photographic Society of Scotland; 1859, London, Photographic Society

REFERENCES: Arthur J. Melhuish, "Melhuish's Roller Slide," *JPS* 3 (April 21, 1856), p. 28; *Monthly Notices of the Royal Astronomical Society* 16 (February 1896), p. 206 (obituary); *BJPA,* 1897, p. 622 (obituary); Neal Rhind, *Blackheath Village and Environs, 1790–1870* (Blackheath: Bookshop Blackheath, 1983), vol. 2, p. 87

Middleton, J.

Middleton was the principal of Agra College in northern India and a friend of JOHN MURRAY's. His involvement in calotypy is known only through an 1854 letter he wrote to the Photographic Society in London, but from that it seems to have been an early and significant one. About 1851 he had taken a daguerreotype of the college while with Murray, and they both observed that colors distinctly appeared but then sadly disappeared on fixing; Murray had corroborated these events in a separate letter. Middleton ran out of daguerreotype plates soon afterward and gave up that process. Since that time, he wrote, he had "been chiefly engaged, during the little spare time I can command, in making a collection of Calotype negatives of places and things about here." Middleton wrote the introduction to Murray's 1857 *Photographic Views in Agra and Its Vicinity* and appears to have taken the calotype view of the cenotaph of the Mughal emperor Akbar's tomb at Sikandra.

REFERENCE: J. Middleton, "Natural Colour in Daguerreotypes," *JPS* 2 (February 21, 1855), p. 121 (letter dated "Agra, December 7, 1854"; published along with testimony from John Murray)

Middleton, John

1827–1856

Middleton was born in Norwich; his father was a painter-decorator and his mother an exhibitor of flower pieces. He was influenced by the Norwich school of painting and was the youngest of the group. Middleton had a passion for sunlight and greenery, and unlike some of his contemporaries mastered the use of watercolors to bring out their beauty. Of delicate health, Middleton traveled little outside his native Norwich. It was a fortunate location, for Norwich had not only its school of painters but also a very active photographic community centered around THOMAS DAMANT EATON. Middleton used waxed-paper negatives for some Norfolk landscapes in about 1852, only a few of which are known. He was a prolific exhibitor of paintings but is not known to have entered any major photographic exhibitions. Middleton's photographic and painting careers were cut short by his early death from consumption.

REFERENCES: Derek Clifford, *Watercolours of the Norwich School* (London: Cory, Adams & Mackay, 1965), pp. 75–78; Harold A. E. Day, *The Norwich School of Painters* (Eastbound: Eastbourne Fine Art Society, 1979), pp. 268–78

Miles, John Augustin

b. 1818

Miles was a banker's clerk in Norwich. He is not known to have exhibited, but in 1855 he contributed his thoughts on "Waxed Paper v. Calotype," to the *Journal of the Photographic Society.* Miles had tried the calotype, waxed-paper, and collodion processes and recognized the advantages of paper negatives. However, he felt that calotype was limited and that "the waxed-paper process is as certain in its results as any other at present known, when in the hands of a practised and skilful operator." Few of Miles's photographs are known, but some were preserved by fellow Norwich photographer THOMAS DAMANT EATON.

REFERENCE: John Augustin Miles, "Waxed Paper v. Calotype," *JPS* 2 (May 21, 1855), pp. 164–65

Mitchell, Jesse

Little is known about the life of Mitchell, except that he was an adjutant in the 1st Native Veteran Battalion of the Indian Army. When he showed his photographs at a meeting of the Photographic Society of Bengal in 1857, they were praised in the *Madras Journal of Literature and Science* as "splendid subjects in architecture and old Hindu buildings and temples taken by the wax paper process." In 1858 he displayed some of his negatives at a meeting of the Photographic Society of Madras. The *Madras Journal* noted that his "large negatives on paper, views lately taken . . . were exceedingly clearly brought out and delicate in the half tints. It was thought that they would yield fine impressions." Although Mitchell experimented with photomicrography and even gave a paper on the subject, it is clear that his passion was photographing the ancient architecture of India. His approach was so sensible and his advice so clear that in England the *Photographic News* published a three-part series on his method. Like many others, Mitchell had initially based his work on the waxed-paper process of Gustave Le Gray, but he found, as reported by the *News,* that his photography was "equally suited to unwaxed papers. As the manipulation of unwaxed paper is much the easiest, and the results so much alike that the operator himself cannot, after a time, say which was taken on waxed, which on plain paper." Although he worked with special imported Canson negative paper, Mitchell found that the sheets varied in density, having thin spots that would let the chemicals soak through to the wrong side. He triaged his new batches of paper, holding each up to the light. The most uniform ones were destined for his favored calotype negatives; those with minor imperfections could be salvaged by waxing; and the least uniform were used to make prints. His practical approach paid off, for in 1858 the Madras Photographic Society judged that Mitchell's more than two dozen 15 x 11 inch views of the Seven Pagodas were, according to the account in the *Madras Journal*, "fully the equal to any Photographs which have been produced in India."

Exhibited: 1857, Calcutta, Bengal Photographic Society

References: *Madras Journal of Literature and Science*, n.s., no. 3 (May 20, 1857); "Proceedings of the Photographic Society," *Madras Journal of Literature and Science*, n.s., no. 7 (April–September 1858), pp. 163, 166, 172; Jesse Mitchell, "Description of a Plain or Waxed Paper Process in Photography," *Photographic News* 2 (September 2, 1859), p. 302, and 3 (September 9 and 16, 1859), pp. 5, 15–16

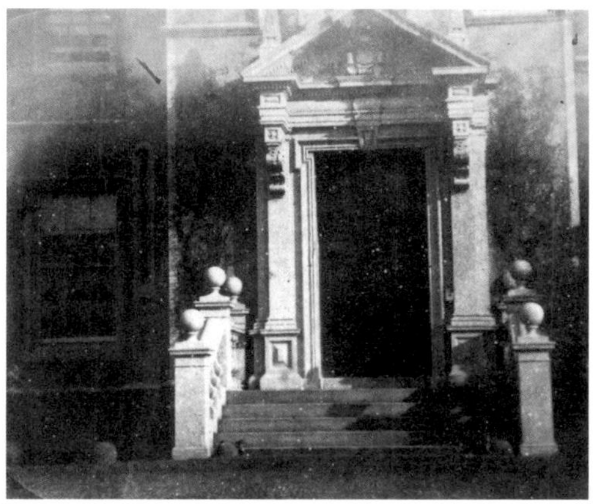

77. George Moir

Moir, George *ill. 77*

1800–1870

Moir, one of the finest lawyers in Edinburgh, was highly regarded for his clarity and force at the bar. But in its obituary of him, the *Scotsman* noted "that he was better known as a literary man than as a lawyer." A prolific author, he took the post of professor of Rhetoric and Belles Lettres at Edinburgh University in the late 1830s. His special passion was poetry. Moir knew a wide range of people in Edinburgh, and it is not surprising that photography became his interest. He joined the Calotype Club in the 1840s and contributed to the Edinburgh Photograph Exchange Club album. In 1856, Moir, one of the founding members of the Photographic Society of Scotland, was elected a vice president. Some of his photographs were taken in Ghent. At what would be late in professional life for many lawyers, Moir was appointed chair of Scots Law for the Faculty of Advocates. Ill health prevented him from giving his lectures, and he decided to move to London, but he died in Edinburgh the day he was to depart.

Exhibited: 1853, Aberdeen, Mechanics' Institution (as by "George More")

References: *Scotsman* (Edinburgh), October 21, 1870, p. 2 (obituary); "A Reminiscence of the Calotype Club," *BJP* 21 (August 14, 1874), p. 385

Monson, Edward

b. 1822

Monson was a land surveyor in Northamptonshire when photography captured his interest. He became a master of the daguerreotype and contributed a number of papers to the *Journal of the Photographic Society*, outlining his experiences with that process. Monson was versatile, however, realizing that the metal plates were limiting, and acknowledged the value of paper photography. When the Northamptonshire Photographic Society held its first exhibition in 1856, he contributed not only examples of daguerreotypes and collodion photographs but also work from waxed-paper negatives. He had called on his younger brother, Charles (b. 1831), a portrait painter, to assist, exhibiting what the Norfolk papers called "some portraits of a large size in which photography lays the foundation on which the artist works his colours. These were painted very effectively in oil by Mr Monson's brother, who is an artist of talent." In order to allow the viewers to compare the results, some "untouched positives from waxed paper were also exhibited by way of comparison." There is no evidence that Charles Monson took any paper photographs, but in the 1861 census Edward listed himself as a "Photographic Artist" and Charles called himself an "Artist & Photographer." By 1871 Edward had returned to civil engineering, but Charles continued as an artist and in the 1891 census listed himself a "Portrait Painter & Photographer."

Exhibited: 1856, Northampton, Photographic Society

References: Edward Monson, "Modification of the Daguerreotype," *JPS* 2 (December 21, 1855), pp. 279–80; Monson, "Method of Cleaning Daguerreotype Plates," *JPS* 3 (July 21, 1856), pp. 86–87; Monson, "The Daguerreotype Process," *JPS* 3 (October 21, 1856), pp. 142–44

Monteith, Frances Dunlop Wallace

b. 1813

Frances Dunlop married Alexander Earle Monteith, an Edinburgh advocate who, according to Conolly's *Biographical Dictionary*, "kept well up with the reading of the day in literature, science, and art." Perhaps indirectly encouraged by this influence, she took up calotypy. Her work is known through portraits preserved in an album by Sir David Brewster. Inexplicably, they replaced on the pages images by Brewster's friend Talbot. One of her portraits was of her nephew James (later Sir James Dunlop), who, perhaps influenced by her, became a photographer.

References: Matthew Forster Conolly, *Biographical Dictionary of Eminent Men of Fife of Past and Present Times* (Edinburgh: Inglis & Jack, 1866), p. 366; Julie Lawson, "Sir James Dunlop: A Photographic Prodigy?" *Scottish Photography Bulletin*, Autumn 1986, pp. 11–13; Graham Smith, *Disciples of Light: Photographs in the Brewster Album* (Malibu: J. Paul Getty Museum, 1990), pp. 113, 114, 122

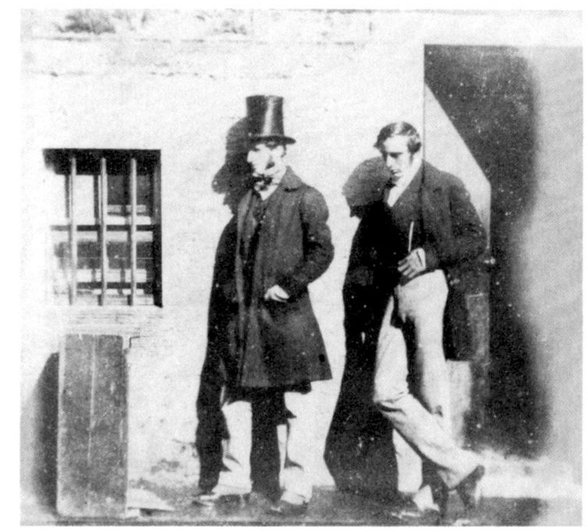

78. James Francis Montgomery

Montgomery, James Francis *ill. 78*

1818–1897

Montgomery, descended from an old Scottish family, was called to the Scottish bar in 1840, and it was during his service as a lawyer in Edinburgh that his interest turned to photography. At some point in the 1840s, as recalled in an 1874 "Reminiscence," "Mr. Montgomery . . . along with some others, visited Sir David Brewster, at St. Andrews, and being immediately smitten with the photographic mania, set about the work as if their very existence depended on success. On their return to town the results were shown and the manipulation explained, and Edinburgh was for some time in a state of *furore* and excitement." They formed a Calotype Club, an informal group of "keen experimentalists" eager to share their advancing knowledge and to examine each others' results.

Montgomery's growing deafness began to pose insurmountable problems for his law career, and he decided to take holy orders. After a brief stint in Dorset from 1856 to 1858, he returned to Edinburgh as curate of St. Paul's, eventually becoming dean of the diocese there. While Montgomery is not known to have participated in formal exhibitions, he served history well, presenting an important collection of calotypes to the Society of Antiquaries of Scotland and compiling a valuable album of early Scottish calotypes.

References: "A Reminiscence of the Calotype Club," *BJP* 21 (August 14, 1874), p. 385; *Times* (London), September 22, 1897, p. 7, col. F (obituary); *ILN*, October 2, 1897, p. 445 (obituary)

Moravia, Charles Barclay Woodham
1821?–1859
Frustratingly little is known about Moravia, an executive engineer with the British Army in India. He was involved in the demolition of dangerously damaged buildings in Delhi after the 1857 mutiny, the very threat that motivated fellow photographer HARRIET TYTLER to try to preserve the scene through a painted panorama. Moravia photographed in Delhi, using waxed-paper negatives in 1858. Nothing further is known of his photography.
In 1859 he was appointed principal of the Engineering School in Lahore but succumbed to smallpox shortly after he arrived.

Reference: John Falconer, *India: Pioneering Photographers, 1850–1900* (London: British Library, 2001), p. 139

More, George
More displayed but did not enter for competition "3 Calotype Views" in the 1853 exhibition at the Mechanics' Institution in Aberdeen. He listed his address as Edinburgh, so he was possibly the George More at 20 India Street who was a Writer to the Signet, that is, a member of a venerable society of Scottish solicitors. Nothing further is known of him. More is perhaps the same person as GEORGE MOIR.

Exhibited: 1853, Aberdeen, Mechanics' Institution

Morecroft, John Johnston Hilton
b. 1813
Morecroft lived in West Derbyshire but worked in Liverpool as an attorney. He was already experienced in photography when the Liverpool Photographic Society was formed in 1854. Morecroft "sent a number of negatives taken, with wonderful success and judgment, by Buckle's process on paper, of which impressions are to be printed by Mr. G. R. Berry, for the purpose of distribution to the Society—two prints to each member." Morecroft also contributed "positives printed from them for the stereoscope as arranged by Professor Wheatstone." In the 1854 exhibition at the Royal Institution, Liverpool, Morecroft showed three calotypes done by Buckle's process: *Quarry Bank, Country Inn,* and *View on the Avon.* None of his work is known to have survived.

Exhibited: 1854, Liverpool, Photographic Society

Reference: *LPJ* 1 (January 14, 1854), p. 2

Morgan, John Hill
b. 1833
Morgan's father died while he was young, enabling him to live off the income of the family's property in the Clifton area throughout his life. Photographically, Morgan made excellent use of these resources, becoming one of the most prolific exhibitors in England and Scotland from 1856 through 1864. His last known public showing was in the 1865 Dublin International Exhibition. All of his works were done from collodion negatives. Presumably they were conventional negatives except for a frame of four views of the Avon submitted to the 1858 Photographic Society exhibition in London. These were done with "John H. Morgan's Sugar Process." Sugar, honey, and other culinary substances were used to retain moisture on the plate, a technique more versatile for use in the field than the conventional wet process. Although he does not seem to have exhibited these, some of Morgan's early work was from paper negatives and was highly accomplished. Where he started practicing photography is uncertain, but Morgan's work was known within the Welsh photographic circle of JOHN DILLWYN LLEWELYN.

Moss, W. Boyd
Moss showed four calotypes in the 1855 exhibition of the Photographic Society in London. His subjects were architectural and views in Kent and on the Isle of Wight. Nothing else is known about him.

Exhibited: 1855, London, Photographic Society

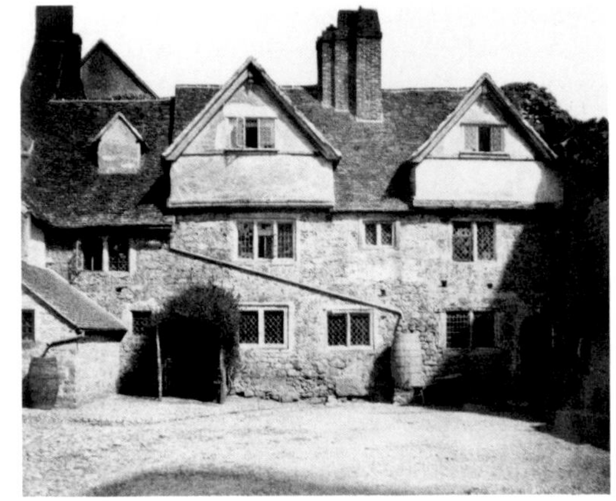

79. Henrietta Augusta Mostyn

Mostyn, Henrietta Augusta *ill. 79*
1830–1912
Henrietta Augusta was the next youngest sister of Lady CAROLINE NEVILL; daughters of William Nevill, 4th Earl of Abergavenny, both were given every encouragement and resource to develop their accomplishments. Caroline and Augusta (as she was known) turned to photography, perhaps stimulated by a family friend, WILLIAM THOMS, editor of the lively journal *Notes and Queries*, who took a great interest in the new art. Much of their work was portraiture of their aristocratic family done with collodion negatives. In the 1854 exhibition of the Photographic Society in London, the sisters exhibited jointly under the name "The Ladies Nevill." They must have been stung by the review in the *Athenaeum*, which sniped that their portraits "report to us the improved employment of their leisure by some members of the aristocracy of the present day." Having exhibited under the name Lady Henrietta Nevill before her marriage in 1855 and afterward as Lady Augusta Mostyn, Lady Augusta contributed to the albums of the Photographic Exchange Club in 1855 and 1856. For these pictures of architecture in Sussex and in Kent, she used waxed-paper negatives.

References: "Photographic Society," *Athenaeum*, January 7, 1854, p. 23; Grace Seiberling, with Carolyn Bloore, *Amateurs, Photography, and the Mid-Victorian Imagination* (Chicago: University of Chicago Press, 1986), p. 139

Moultrie, F. R.
Moultrie is a mystery. He showed two calotypes in the 1856 exhibition of the Photographic Society in London, views of Chiselhurst Church and of a wood barn at

Dutchworth Rectory, both in Kent. In the 1857 exhibition Moultrie again showed two calotypes, one of Elizabeth Castle and one of the Hermitage, both in Jersey. Moultrie does not appear in any census, but when he joined the Photographic Society in 1859, he listed his address as in care of G.W. Moultrie, Bank, Bengal.

Exhibited: 1856 and 1857, London, Photographic Society

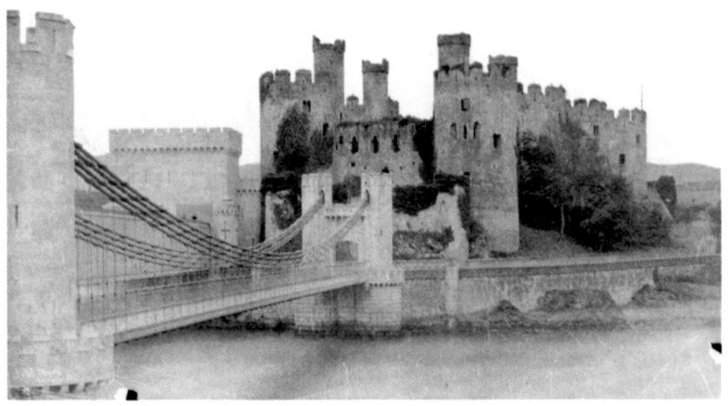

80. James Mudd

Mudd, James *ill. 80*

1821–1906

By about 1847, Mudd was established in Manchester as a master pattern designer in silk, working in conjunction with his brother Robert. He began taking calotypes about 1850, influenced by his friend Joseph Sidebotham. By 1854 James and Robert had added photography to their calico design business. In the 1856 exhibition of the Manchester Photographic Society the Mudds' talents became clear. In addition to two collodion views they exhibited the astonishing number of nearly fifty waxed-paper architectural and landscape photographs. These were widely admired for both their composition and their technical excellence. By 1857 the Photographic Establishment of J. & R. Mudd was prepared not only to take photographs and make prints but also to supply cameras and supplies. In an advertisement in the *Journal of the Photographic Society*, they announced that since the "chemicals and papers in stock are constantly used in the establishment, they are enabled to recommend . . . those materials which, from experience, they know to give the best results." The two brothers exhibited jointly through 1864, usually in their own glass-negative process of albumen-collodion. Little is known about Robert, but every indication is that James was the master of the calotype and waxed-paper negatives. From 1857 to 1859, their prints were embossed with both names. Prior to that, when paper negatives dominated their work, only James Mudd's manuscript signature is found. After 1859 the embossed markings are for James Mudd alone until 1875, when he began sharing credit with his son, James Willis Mudd. By 1863 the elder Mudd was listing himself separately as a photographer and as a pattern designer. He had begun to exhibit under his own name starting in 1858, always in the albumen-collodion process, a practice he continued at the 1865 Dublin International Exhibition.

Exhibited: 1856, Manchester, Photographic Society; 1857, Manchester, "Art Treasures" Exhibition; 1858, London, Photographic Society

Reference: *JPS* 4 (July 21, 1857), n.p. (advertisement); James Mudd, "A Photographer's Dream," *BJP* 12 (April 21, 1865), pp. 202–5; Jenny Wetton, "James Mudd, Photographer (1821–1906)," *Scottish Photography Bulletin*, 1990, pp. 13–20

Mullens, Joseph

1820–1879

After attending divinity school in London and Edinburgh, Mullens was appointed a missionary and sailed for Calcutta in 1844. He became active in photography in the mid-1850s, offering a paper on the applications of photography in India to the Photographic Society of Bengal in 1856. In its 1857 exhibition, Mullens showed five calotype views of Calcutta and Bhowanipore (Bhabanipur). He was appointed a fellow of the Senate of Calcutta University in 1857. None of Mullens's photographic work is known to have survived.

Exhibited: 1857, Calcutta, Photographic Society of Bengal

Muller, C. J.

Virtually nothing is known of Muller's life, not even his citizenship. In 1851 he wrote to the *Athenaeum* from "Patna in the East Indies." Under the control of the East India Company since the eighteenth century, Patna was a major trading center hosting a variety of nationalities, including Dutch and Danish. Muller offered no explanation of why he was there, but the photographic process that he had developed impressed not only the editor but also the "experienced photographer" that the editor consulted. Muller's was a modification of Talbot's calotype process and closely related to Dr. Thomas Wood's variant Catalyssotype, on which it was judged to be an improvement. By 1857 Muller resided in London and wrote to the *Journal of the Photographic Society*, hinting that he had abandoned his experiments in India because of ill health. Muller referred to his 1851 process and noted that he had improved it by simplifying the chemistry. He kept the image on the surface of the negative paper rather than letting it embed in the fibers; this not only produced a sharper image but also resulted in a paper that was self-developing. Muller had experimented with various French and English papers, finding promise in some of the latter, but he felt that the sizing in all of them was a problem. He argued for the adoption of an Indian paper made from the *Daphne cannabina*, which had very fine fibers and was "highly transparent." He added: "It is also exceedingly strong, and it behaves admirably with photographic chemicals. I think it a promising fibre for photographic paper." An evergreen, the plant is better known today as *Daphne papyracea* and is the principal source of handmade papers in Nepal. All parts of the plant are highly poisonous, and perhaps it was the source of his ill health in India. None of Muller's photographs are known to have survived.

References: C. J. Muller, in "New Photographic Process," *Athenaeum*, November 22, 1851, p. 1234; Muller, "New Self-Developing Negative Process," *JPS* 3 (April 21, 1857), pp. 262–64

Murray, John

1809–1898

Born in northern Scotland, Murray received his M.D. from Edinburgh University in 1831. He then studied in Paris and toured the Continent. Murray accepted a medical posting with the East India Company and sailed to Calcutta in 1833. He remained in India for the next four decades, serving in a number of positions and leading the fight against cholera. Shortly after his promotion to surgeon in 1849, Murray took up amateur photography and soon formed a friendship with another doctor, John McCosh. By 1853 Murray was producing highly accomplished 13 x 17 inch waxed-paper negatives of Agra in great quantity. He began participating in the Photographic Society of Bengal in 1856. In 1857, during a visit to Britain, he took along a portfolio of four hundred of his negatives. By September of that year, the London publisher J. Hogarth was offering prints from them, individually or in sets of thirty. The introduction was written by his old friend J. Middleton, who also contributed at least one of the plates. On his return to India Murray experimented briefly with dry collodion and with stereo photography, but his favorite continued to be large waxed-paper negatives. His last exhibition at the Bengal society was in 1862, when it refused to give him a medal for his most recent calotypes. Although the society admitted that they were "very superior examples of the art," it noted that "the process itself cannot compete with the results of more recent discoveries in clearness, sharpness, and artistic effect." Murray ignored their rejection and continued to do some of his finest work. His last known photographs were taken in 1865, and he retired in 1870. Some of Murray's photographic work was done on commission and is preserved in public archives. Fortunately, the family until recently retained an extensive group of his works. Now his glorious waxed-paper negatives are distributed widely in both private and public collections. Most appear to be as fresh as the day they were made, and collectively they serve as a fitting testimony not only to Murray's passion and artistic talent but also to the suitability of the waxed-paper negative for use in India.

EXHIBITED: 1856, Calcutta, Photographic Society of Bengal; 1858, London, Photographic Society; 1861, London, Architectural Photographic Association; 1862, Calcutta, Photographic Society of Bengal

REFERENCES: John Murray, *Photographic Views in Agra and Its Vicinity*, with an introduction by J. Middleton (London: J. Hogarth, 1857); *Journal of the Photographic Society of Bengal* 1 (September 1862), pp. 40–41; John Fraser, "Dr John Murray of Agra," *Photohistorian*, no. 132 (November 2000), pp. 13–15; *Early Photographs of India*, sale cat., Sotheby's, London, June 18, 1999 (sale of the archives of Dr. John Murray)

Murray, J. M.

Murray's connection with photography was significant but is at present documented only by a single letter of 1856 published in *Photographic Notes*. Writing from Drogheda, a port town outside Dublin, Murray was "just starting to the North on a photographic tour." His letter concerned the proper paper for calotype, and he was "glad to be able to add my testimony, as well as that of my partner, to the goodness of Hollingworth's paper. We can speak from our own experience as well as that of several of our customers who have shown us their results on paper bought from us." Murray related that he started calotypy as an amateur, following GEORGE SMITH CUNDELL's 1844 directions. In common with many amateur photographers, Murray gave up calotype when the supply of suitable papers dried up, noting that those papers "would never have come into such general use if good Talbotype paper had been procurable." In 1856 Murray had on hand papers that he had prepared in 1849 and 1850 still in usable condition. With the Hollingworth's paper, Murray judged his results as good as any on waxed paper, with less trouble and expense. He expressed the hope that with newer papers "the Talbotype process, or some modification of it, will obtain that attention it so well deserves." No further communications from Murray have been traced. The initials "J. M." are clearly printed under the text of his letter. If it were not for the initials, one would be tempted to think that the author was ROBERT MURRAY, the London-based Irish chemist, who entered into the partnership of the photographic suppliers Murray & Heath in 1855 and who died suddenly in 1857.

REFERENCE: J. M. Murray, "On Calotype Paper," *Photographic Notes* 1 (December 1, 1856), pp. 257–58

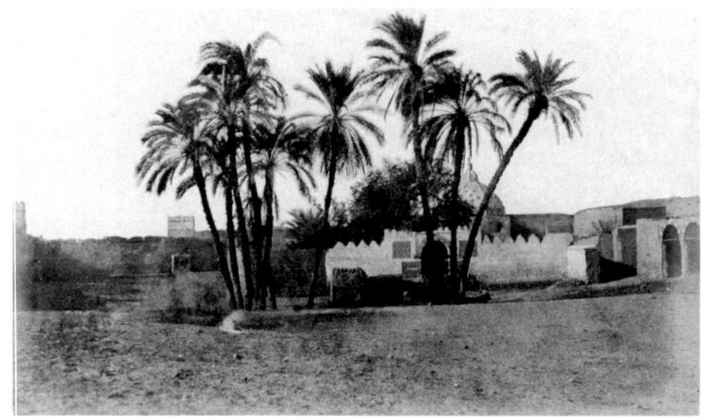

82. Robert Murray

Murray, Robert *ill. 81*

1822–1893

Coming from an Edinburgh family of lawyers and military men, Murray patterned himself after his older brother and entered the world of engineering. In the 1840s and early 1850s he spent time in Russia and at least three years in Malta. Why he went to Egypt in the early 1850s is not known, but the viceroy's efforts to improve the transportation systems there provided ample opportunities for engineers. In 1880 Murray recalled, in the *British Journal of Photography*, that he taught himself photography "entirely from a shilling guide book (published by Messrs. Horne and Thornthwaite), while residing on the banks of the Nile, far from professional assistance." He taught himself well. In 1856 J. Hogarth offered an extensive portfolio of Murray's views in Malta and Egypt, accompanied by a text by Joseph Bonami, the prominent Egyptologist. The published views were albumen prints made from Murray's negatives, although he is known to have made salted paper prints from them himself. A second edition was offered in 1858, this time including only views from Egypt. The *Athenaeum* was ecstatic, saying, "All previous photographs of Egypt 'go down' before the large and finely-wrought views published by Robert Murray, late chief engineer to the Viceroy of Egypt. . . . He has engraved them, by the aid of sunbeams." Lamenting the loss of antiquities that time and man were continuing to wreak, the reviewer praised "this Vishnu of Art," who "came in due time, and came to save and to record." Back in England Murray was elected to the Amateur Photographic Association in 1862. In his inaugural meeting, as reported by the *Photographic Journal*, he displayed "some very fine Egyptian negatives . . . which were much admired. The negatives are by the Calotype process, and almost rival in sharpness and half-tone the finest collodion plates." Murray returned to England and became the principal officer for the Board of Trade. He maintained his interest in photography, communicating with the photographic journals into the 1880s. By then mature in his practice, he had concluded, as he wrote in his 1880 article, that "excellence of the resulting negative . . . depends greatly upon an infinity of *little things*, which can be learnt and appreciated only by an intelligent and thoughtful practice." Murray died in Plymouth during an influenza epidemic.

EXHIBITED: 1856, Edinburgh, Photographic Society

REFERENCES: "Fine-Art Gossip," *Athenaeum*, June 5, 1858, p. 727; A. J. Melhuish, "Amateur Photographic Society," *Photographic Journal* 8 (October 15, 1862), p. 148; Robert Murray, "A Few Hints to Amateur Landscape Photographers," *BJP* 27 (February 13, 1880), pp. 77–78; "Robert Murray of Edinburgh (1822–1893)," *Photoresearcher*, no. 6 (March 1997), pp. 7–11

Napier, Mark

1798–1879

An advocate in Edinburgh who came from a distinguished family, Napier was known mostly for his writings on Scottish law and history. His views were staunchly conservative and unpopular but widely respected, and his obituary noted that "he had a great fund of humour." Just as photography was being introduced into Scotland, Napier became the sheriff for Dumfriesshire. He had his portrait taken by DAVID OCTAVIUS HILL and ROBERT ADAMSON. Intrigued by the process, he promptly joined the Edinburgh Calotype Club. In 1856 Napier became one of the founding members of the Photographic Society of Scotland. It is unclear whether he was really a calotypist or simply a very interested bystander to the new art.

REFERENCES: "A Reminiscence of the Calotype Club," *BJP* 21 (August 14, 1874), p. 385; *Scotsman* (Edinburgh), November 24, 1879, p. 4 (obituary); *Journal of Jurisprudence* 23 (December 1879), pp. 652–55 (obituary; reprinted from the *Edinburgh Courant*)

Neild, Arthur
b. 1829
A cotton manufacturer, magistrate, and eventually captain of the Rifle Volunteers, Neild was typical of many amateur photographers who had both manipulatory skills and the blocks of free time that, surprisingly, seem to come to particularly active people. A vice president of the Manchester Photographic Society in 1856, he had an excellent understanding of all the processes in use. Neild singled out the calotype for his presentation to the society, modestly claiming that perhaps his was not the best method but stressing that it was based on experience and successful for him. He favored Turner's paper for being the most uniform in texture, critical for calotype negatives, and used TALBOT's first method of brushing on the coatings. More than many of his colleagues who thought they could compensate for poor exposure in developing, Neild understood the importance of proper timing in the camera. Overexposed negatives acquired "a dull red appearance . . . destitute of vigor and sharpness." When underexposed, "the high lights are hard and black with neither middle tints nor detail in the shadows." Neild displayed nine calotypes, all of architecture, in the 1856 exhibition of the Manchester Photographic Society. He had the unusual but very sensible advice that often "there are very strong shadows with fine and interesting detail; but if we give sufficient time to bring out the dark parts of the picture, the sky and light parts will be heavy and devoid of beauty and interest." Neild cautioned, "take care of the shadows." Opaquing would correct the sky, "whereas nothing will restore half tones and detail which may have been sacrificed to obtain" a uniform sky.

EXHIBITED: 1856, Manchester, Photographic Society

REFERENCE: A. Nield [Arthur Neild], "On the Calotype Process," *Photographic Notes* 1, 2nd ed. (January 1 and 25, 1856), pp. xiii–xvi

Neill, Andrew Charles Brisbane *ill. 82*
1814–1891
Neill, born in Scotland and a doctor attached to the Indian Medical Service in Madras, was a good friend of RICHARD BANNER OAKELEY. In the 1855 exhibition of the Photographic Society of Madras he exhibited calotypes, which one reviewer felt could be compared to the work of LINNAEUS TRIPE. During the 1856–57 mutiny at Lucknow, Neill took portraits and photographed the scenes of destruction. At a meeting of the Photographic Society of Bengal in 1857 he showed twenty architectural views in the waxed-paper process. Neill's photographs were used to illustrate the 1866 *Architecture in Dharwar and*

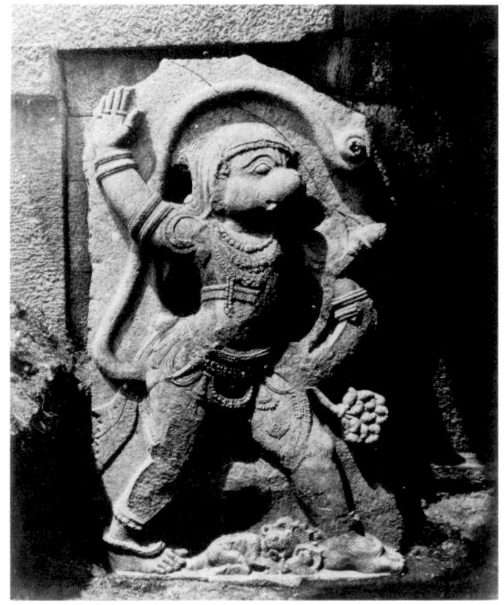
82. Andrew Charles Brisbane Neill

Mysore and the 1869 *Illustrations of Various Styles of Indian Architecture.*

EXHIBITED: 1855, Madras, Photographic Society

REFERENCES: *Madras Exhibition of Raw Products, Arts, and Manufactures of Southern India, 1855: Reports by the Juries on the Subjects in the Thirty Classes into which the Exhibition Was Divided* (Madras: General Committee of the Madras Exhibition, 1856); Meadows Taylor and James Fergusson, *Architecture in Dharwar and Mysore* (London: John Murray, 1866); James Fergusson, *Illustrations of Various Styles of Indian Architecture* (London, 1869)

Neill, James George
1810–1857
Neill was a cousin of the photographer ANDREW NEILL. He was born in Ayrshire, and after a brief education in Glasgow he went to India and joined the Madras Fusiliers, rising rapidly through the ranks. In spite of poor health, he served in the Crimea. Little is presently known of his photography beyond his two waxed-paper views of the Hindu temple at Mysore (Karnataka) shown at the 1856 Photographic Society of Scotland exhibition in Edinburgh. The views may have been some of his last and were contributed not by Neill but by JOHN MCCOSH, a surgeon in the Indian service and himself an early calotypist. Neill became a brigadier general, "the pride and idol of the Army." He fell in battle during the relief mission to Lucknow on September 25, 1857.

EXHIBITED: 1856, Edinburgh, Photographic Society of Scotland

REFERENCE: *Times* (London), November 17, 1857, p. 10 (obituary)

Nelson, Duckworth John
1816–1870
Born in Dublin, Nelson, a doctor, practiced in Norfolk before moving to London in the 1850s. His only known surviving photograph is a calotype negative of a village, possibly in the Norfolk area. One of his sons was Edward Milles Nelson (1851–1938), an eminent microscopist.

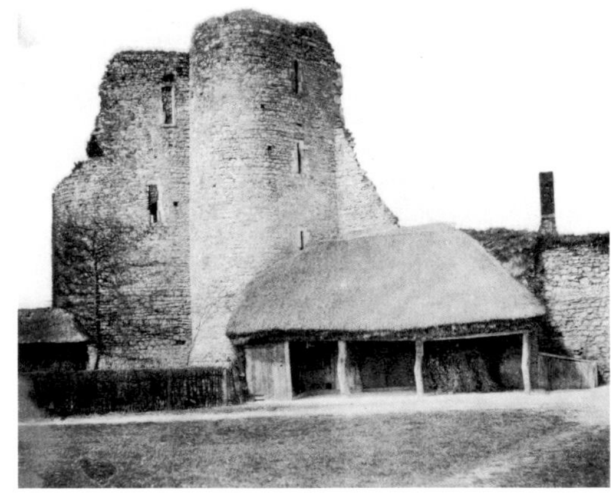
83. Caroline Emily Nevill

Nevill, Caroline Emily *ill. 83*
1829–1887
Lady Nevill was the eldest of three sisters, daughters of William Nevill, 4th Earl of Abergavenny, known in photographic circles as "The Trio." All three of them, Caroline, HENRIETTA AUGUSTA (later MOSTYN), and Isabel, took an interest in photography. When the sisters exhibited in 1854 at the Photographic Society in London, the *Athenaeum*'s observation was that aristocratic ladies "taking sun pictures is certainly as useful and beautiful an occupation as crochet and Berlin-work." Caroline, however, became a pioneering member of the Photographic Exchange Society when it was founded in 1855. She contributed architectural views of Kent, all done with waxed-paper negatives, to the albums of the Photographic Exchange Club from 1855 to 1858 and to the Amateur Photographic Association after 1859. Caroline Nevill never married.

REFERENCES: "Photographic Society," *Athenaeum*, January 7, 1854, p. 23; "Photographic Exchange Society," *Notes and Queries*, February 24, 1855, p. 151; Grace Seiberling, with Carolyn Bloore, *Amateurs, Photography, and the Mid-Victorian Imagination* (Chicago: University of Chicago Press, 1986), p. 139

Newall, Robert Stirling
b. 1813
Born in Dundee, Scotland, known for its manufacture of hemp ropes for ships, Newall became a patent wire rope manufacturer in Durham. In the 1848 Exhibition of Arts, Manufactures, and Practical Science at Newcastle-upon-Tyne, he showed a daguerreotype portrait, perhaps the medium to be expected given his expertise in metals. Surprisingly, Newall exhibited beside it a calotype portrait for comparison. This is the only known instance of Newall's interest in photography. He went on to be a chemical manufacturer and a figure in society.

Exhibited: 1848, Newcastle, Mechanics' Institute

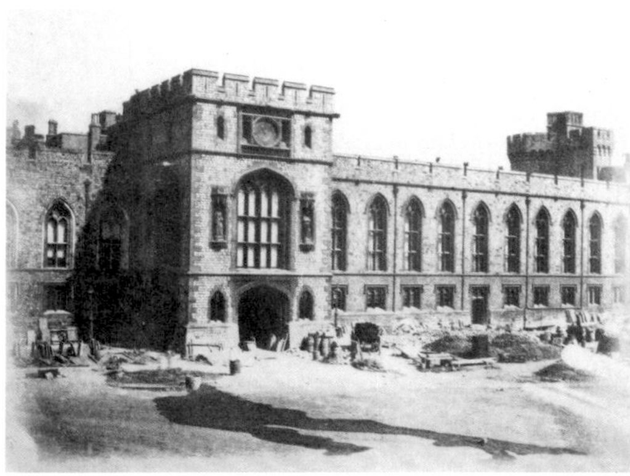

84. William John Newton

Newton, William John *ills. 84, 85*
1785–1869
Newton built a substantial reputation as a miniaturist before the advent of photography and in 1837 was appointed Painter in Ordinary to Her Majesty. His early participation in the Photographic Society bolstered its claims for admission into the London art scene. He became vice president of the society and led the efforts to overturn Talbot's patent restrictions. Sir William became a member of the Calotype Club in 1847, but nothing is known about his early photography. He was an active contributor to exhibitions, starting with six paper negative views in the 1852 Society of Arts exhibition in London. Newton's series on the Burnham Beeches, first shown in 1853, boosted his photographic reputation. He contributed to exhibitions every year, remaining loyal to the calotype through the 1856 Manchester Photographic Society exhibition. He also contributed calotypes to the Photographic Exchange Club. In 1852 Newton devised a

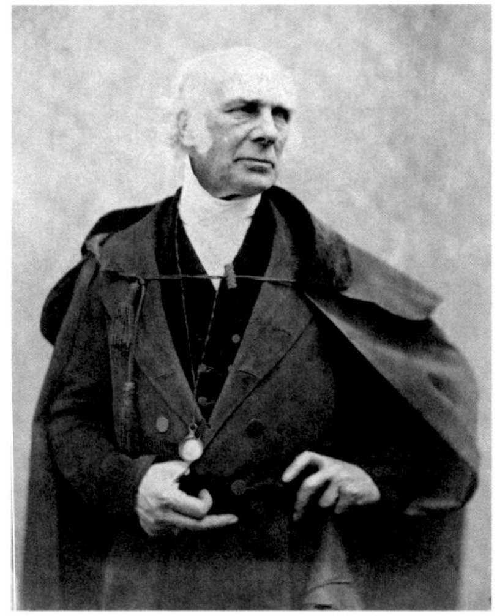

85. Portrait of William John Newton

method of coating his calotype paper with barium chloride, isolating the silver salts from the vagaries of the paper fibers and yielding a more consistent negative. Newton was a leading advocate of soft-focus photography, an anathema to the more strictly scientific participants in the emerging world of photography but a further step in the forays of photography into the world of art. His 1853 lecture on photography in relation to art, published in the very first issue of the *Photographic Journal* and reprinted in the *Civil Engineer and Architect's Journal*, was an influential survey and commentary. Newton's photographic colleagues were disappointed when, during the planning for the 1862 International Exhibition in London, he sided with those who reclassified photography as a science rather than as an art.

Exhibited: 1852, London, Society of Arts; 1853–54, first touring exhibition, Society of Arts (London); 1854, London, Photographic Society; 1854, second touring exhibition, Society of Arts (London); 1855, London, Photographic Society; 1855–56, third touring exhibition, Society of Arts (London); 1856, London, Photographic Society; 1856, Manchester, Photographic Society

References: William J. Newton, "Sir W. Newton's Process," *Notes and Queries*, February 5, 1853, pp. 140–41; Newton, "Sir William Newton's Process: Further Explanations," *Notes and Queries* 7 (February 19, 1853), p. 187; Newton, "Upon Photography in Its Artistic View, and in Its Relations to the Arts," *JPS* 1 (March 3, 1853), pp. 6–8; *BJP* 16 (January 29, 1869), p. 48 (obituary); *Times* (London), January 26, 1869, p. 9, col. f (obituary); Linda Goforth Zillman, *Sir William Newton: Miniature Painter and Photographer, 1785–1869* (Tempe: School of Art, Arizona State University, 1986)

Nicholl, William Henry
1819–1874
Nicholl was the third son of the high sheriff of Glamorgan and lived off his family's fortunes. His earliest recorded photograph was an ambrotype of his brother made in October 1852. Nicholl joined the Photographic Society in 1853 and must have met Roger Fenton at its meetings: One of his ambrotypes carries an additional inscription: "RF has seen this and approves highly, July 5/1853." Nicholl contributed a calotype of the Crymlyn Viaduct to the society's *Photographic Album*. His contribution to the 1857 *Photographic Album* was taken by collodion.

Nicholson, Mr.
Among the treasures preserved by Richard Willats in his early album is a calotype view, *Goring Church, n^{r.} Reading*. This location was so near to Nicolaas Henneman's pioneering photographic establishment that one wonders if there was a connection. Even more intriguing are two calotypes in the album showing the stained glass at Winchester Cathedral, one, *Winchester West Window—from the Interior*, inscribed "by Mr. Nicholson, London—an early *interior* on paper if not the first." Although there were professional London photographers by the name of Nicholson in later years, none are known this early. He could have been an amateur or, perhaps, someone that Willats knew through his professional contacts. Peter Nicholson (1765–1846) was a well-known optician, author, and teacher. If he is the Nicholson in question, the date of his death would explain why no other work is known by this innovative photographer.

Nightingale, James Edward
1817–1892
In the 1858 exhibition of the Photographic Society in London, Nightingale showed two calotypes of cedars taken near his home in Wilton Park, Wiltshire, and two taken in France. These are his only known photographs. A gentleman of independent means, Nightingale was an accomplished antiquarian and was the discoverer of the lost eighteenth-century porcelain factory of Longton Hall. He was the author of numerous books and became a fellow of the Society of Antiquaries. On his death the society remembered Nightingale as "a man of kindly disposition and of accurate knowledge, and the ceramic collections in the British Museum are indebted to his liberality for several acquisitions."

Exhibited: 1858, London, Photographic Society

Reference: *Proceedings of the Society of Antiquaries*, 2nd ser., 14 (1892), p. 136 (obituary)

Norman, George

Norman was an enthusiastic exhibitor for two years, but nothing else is known about him. In the 1854 exhibition for the Royal Infirmary Fund in Dundee he showed one Talbotype, of an elm tree in Yorkshire, and a number of collodion views of Yorkshire. His contribution to the Photographic Society exhibition in London that same year was more complex. Norman identified his work as two Talbotypes and nine calotypes, without explaining the difference in his use of the terminology, along with four collodion views. All were of architecture and scenery in Yorkshire, with several taken in the Kingston-upon-Hull area. In the 1855 London exhibition of the Photographic Society, Norman had eight calotypes and four waxed-paper views (no collodion), all of Yorkshire scenes. His name was not an uncommon one, and there are no obvious candidates for his identity.

EXHIBITED: 1854, London, Photographic Society; 1854, Dundee, Royal Infirmary Fund; 1855, London, Photographic Society

Nowell, Benjamin Jonathon

Nowell was living in Bedford, apparently on independent means, when he took up amateur photography. His contribution to the 1855 Photographic Society exhibition in London included not only a frame of microscopic objects, taken in collodion, but also four waxed-paper views of bridges and cottages in Bedford. In the 1856 and 1857 Photographic Society exhibitions in London, Nowell showed waxed-paper views, all from Bedfordshire. Nothing further is known of his work.

EXHIBITED: 1855, 1856, and 1857, London, Photographic Society

Oakeley, Richard Banner

Of the various photographers of archaeology in India, Oakeley stands out as one of the finest. Near the end of 1856, advised by his friend ANDREW NEILL, he paid a visit to the ruins at Halebid in southwestern India. Oakeley took a number of waxed-paper negatives, later published as albumen prints in his *The Pagoda of Hallibeed, Illustrated by Fifty-six Photographic Views*. In spite of a broken apparatus and servants who were ill with rheumatic fever, he did an extraordinary job. His text reveals that he had previously visited "a great number of the most celebrated Pagodas in the South of India," but that "this was my first attempt at Photographing in a hot climate. I was compelled to reject the formulae I had used in England." He was a fellow of the Royal Geographical Society, and Sir Henry Rawlinson, praising his photographs, made the library of the Royal Asiatic Society freely available to him. Amazingly, beyond these details and the visual testimony of his photographs, we know almost nothing about Oakeley. He obviously traveled a great deal, missing all the censuses in the nineteenth century. In 1859, when he married Mary Ann Field of Shrewsbury, he was living at Oswaldkirk Hall in Yorkshire. In 1859 and 1862 Oakeley stood as the parliamentary candidate for Shrewsbury, both times unsuccessfully, and was a resident of Oswaldkirk, Yorkshire, in 1862. In 1863 he was one of the directors of the Stafford and Uttoxeter Railway and by 1864 also a director of the Opera Company in London. Oakeley's largest claim to fame is as the plaintiff in a three-year trial that started in 1859. He was duped out of a 6,500-pound loan by the ambassador for the king of the Indian province of Oudh, who claimed to need the money to build an embassy in England.

REFERENCES: Richard Banner Oakeley, *Oakeley v. Ooddeen . . . Printed from Mr. Tolcher's Short-Hand Notes of the Proceedings* (London: Thomas Scott, 1859); Oakeley, *The Pagoda of Hallibeed, Illustrated by Fifty-six Photographic Views, with Descriptive Letter-Press* (London: Thomas M'Lean, 1859)

Oakes, Thomas George Alexander

d. 1878

In 1856, the Northamptonshire Photographic Society was formed with the hope that its monthly meetings would "blend the practical and instructive with the theoretical and the descriptive." In its first exhibition that year, one professional, EDWARD MONSON, and two amateur photographers showed work from paper negatives. Of these two, WILLIAM LAW had the more extensive showing, but Oakes displayed "superior calotypes." Thomas was the only Captain Oakes in the army or navy during this period and must have been the photographer. He fought bravely in the Kaffir War in South Africa from 1851 to 1853 and distinguished himself during the Crimean campaign in the siege of Sebastapol and the battle of Eupatoria. He almost certainly would not have been present during the exhibition, but a friend or family member might have submitted his work. If this is the correct Captain Oakes, he was one of the finest cavalry officers in the British Army, rising eventually to the rank of major general and serving as the inspecting officer of the Yeomanry Calvary. He retired to Farnham, Surrey, and was remembered in his obituary in the *Annual Register* "for his liberal mind and many amiable qualities." At least one waxed-paper negative produced by Oakes survives, a view of Brigstock Church in Northamptonshire.

EXHIBITED: 1856, Northampton, Photographic Society

REFERENCES: "Naval and Military Intelligence," *Times* (London), August 30, 1878, p. 8, col. A (obituary); *Annual Register*, 1878, p. 165 (obituary)

Owen, Hugh

1808–1897

By day a Bristol-based cashier for Isambard Kingdom Brunel's Great Western Railway, Owen first became an amateur daguerreotypist in the early 1840s. In March 1845, about to give a lecture on photography to the Bristol Mechanics Institute & Philosophical Society, he wrote to TALBOT. Owen had not yet tried the calotype and asked Talbot for some examples to illustrate his lecture. These must have won him over, for within two years Owen had became a master of the paper negative. In 1847, after seeing an exhibition by the members of the Calotype Society in London, the *Athenaeum* drew particular attention to Owen, the "gentleman of Bristol well known for his talent in his art . . . whose various views . . . justified the reputation which [he] has earned." Owen entered a series of calotypes in the 1851 Great Exhibition, so impressing the commissioners that they engaged him to make photographs of some of the displays. In the 1852 Society of Arts exhibition, views from the Crystal Palace were included in Owens's group of more than forty calotypes. After this exhibition, he joined the founding council of the Photographic Society. In 1853 JOSEPH CUNDALL published two volumes of Owens's *Photographic Pictures*. The *Athenaeum* felt they showed the "shortcomings of the Sun's work," but admired "the delicate touch of the ivy" in his view of the gate of Farleigh Castle. By 1854 Owen felt compelled to defend his favorite negative process in the *Journal of the Photographic Society*: "Although I dislike controversy on matters of taste, I must be permitted to remonstrate against the tone assumed by some of the Photographists of the New School with regard to the paper process. . . . For the delineation of nature, however, I . . . assert the superiority of paper, both for force and effect, as well as convenience." His views from Portugal were in the 1855 exhibition, where he continued to be one of the most prolific exhibitors of the period. In 1856 Owen finally succumbed to the dominance of collodion on glass. His exhibitions stopped, and he seems to have had little to do with photography after that. By the time of his death he was forgotten by the photographic fraternity to which he had contributed so bountifully.

EXHIBITED: 1851, London, International Exhibition; 1852, London, Society of Arts; 1853, London, Photographic Institution; 1853–54, first touring exhibition, Society of Arts (London); 1854, London, Photographic Society; 1854, Dundee,

Royal Infirmary Fund; 1854, second touring exhibition, Society of Arts (London); 1855, London, Photographic Society; 1855, London, Photographic Institution; 1855–56, third touring exhibition, Society of Arts (London)

REFERENCES: Hugh Owen to Talbot, March 4, 1845, Talbot Collection, British Library, London (Talbot Correspondence Project, http://foxtalbot.dmu.ac.uk, doc. no. 05202); "The Calotype Society," *Athenaeum*, December 18, 1847, p. 1304; "New Publications," *Athenaeum*, December 24, 1853, p. 1559; Owen, "Collodion *versus* Paper," *JPS* 2 (December 21, 1854), p. 100; Reece Winstone, *Bristol's Earliest Photographs* (Bristol: Bristol's History, 1970); Nancy B. Keeler, "Illustrating the 'Reports by the Juries' of the Great Exhibition of 1851: Talbot, Henneman, and Their Failed Commission," *History of Photography* 6 (July 1982), pp. 257–72; James Belsey, *A Small Light in the Far West: Victorian Photographers in Bristol* (Bristol: City Museum and Art Gallery, 1996)

Oxley, Thomas

Oxley was referred to as "a teacher" in one communication, but little else is known about him. He was a frequent contributor to the *Kaleidoscope* and to the *Liverpool Mercury* during the 1820s and 1830s. Oxley was extensively involved in scientific and technological circles in Liverpool and claimed, with some substantiation, to have suggested in 1823 the use of silver salts to capture the images in the camera obscura. His claim appeared to be better witnessed and less improbable than many that emerged in 1839. When photography was announced to the public in 1839, Oxley set to work to accomplish his sixteen-year-old dream. He published various formulas for photographic papers that were clearly based on his own experience.

REFERENCE: "Mr. Oxley's Processes for Preparing Photogenic Paper, &c.," *Mechanics' Magazine* 30 (March 30, 1839), pp. 455–56

Parkes, Bessie Raynor *ill. 86*

1829–1925

Parkes's mother was an American-born descendant of Joseph Priestley, the controversial Quaker scientist involved in the prehistory of photography. Her father was a radical lawyer in Birmingham, and the family had many connections in scientific and artistic circles. In 1847 she taught herself the photogenic drawing process and used it to photograph New Zealand ferns she had received from her uncle, the illustrator Edwin Swainson. For a period in 1847, photography was her consuming passion. In 1858 she purchased the *Englishwoman's Journal*, a feminist publication that promoted the stories of professional women. In 1867 she married Louis Belloc and moved to France. Parkes's photograms made as a teenager are her only known photographs.

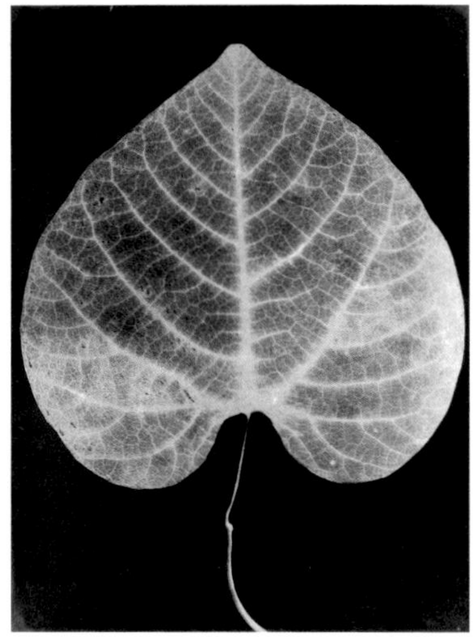

86. Bessie Raynor Parkes

REFERENCE: Larry J. Schaaf, *Sun Pictures, Catalogue Ten: British Paper Negatives, 1839–1864* (New York: Hans P. Kraus, Jr., 2001), pp. 36–41

Parry, John

Parry was elected vice president of the Manchester Photographic Society in 1861. Nothing else is known about him. When he chaired its meeting on March 7, 1860, he "exhibited several very beautiful paper negatives taken by him about six years ago, which were much admired for their sharpness, &c.: they were on Canson's plain paper, and waxed afterwards. . . . He hoped that more attention would be given to waxed-paper, as he believed the process to be capable of more than was generally supposed. He intended to give it a trial next summer." No record of that following summer's work has been traced.

REFERENCE: "Manchester Photographic Society," *BJP* 7 (March 15, 1860), pp. 86–87

Parry, William S.

b. 1826

In 1850, John Werge, a Newcastle native then just starting his career as a daguerreotypist, met Parry in his hometown. Parry was then a glass dealer and an amateur calotypist, Werge later wrote, although not yet very successful in the latter field, for his negatives suffered from decomposition. Parry kept working at the process, however, and eventually became "one of the best Calotypists in the neighborhood." Parry opened his own photographic studio in Newcastle. Half a century later, Werge still owned some of Parry's negatives, which were still in excellent condition, and regarded them as "some of the finest Calotype negatives he ever produced."

REFERENCE: John Werge, *The Evolution of Photography* (London: Piper & Carter, 1890), pp. 39–40

Penney, George S.

b. 1820

A dentist in Cheltenham, Dr. Penney has been listed in various publications as G. S. Penny, G. Penny, Geo. S. Penny, and George S. Penney (with both variations of the surname) from Cheltenham. While there might have been a Penny and a Penney active at the same time, these appear to have been one and the same person. In his first publication on photography, in 1855, he described the calotype as his "favourite process" and, "in order to induce others to take up the subject," outlined his own working practices. In 1857 Penney showed two waxed-paper views in the Photographic Society exhibition in London, and the following year he showed two calotypes. He then turned to glass-negative processes, exhibiting at least through the 1865 Dublin International Exhibition. In 1873 he proposed a process for printing botanical specimens, using special tissue from the Autotype Company.

EXHIBITED: 1858, London, Photographic Society

REFERENCES: George S. Penny, "The Calotype Process," *LPJ* 2 (October 13, 1855), pp. 130–31; Penny, "Correspondence," *Photographic Notes* 1 (December 1, 1856), p. 255; Penny, "Pigment Printing Applied to Botanical Specimens, &c.," *BJPA*, 1873, pp. 74–76

Penrice, John

1818–1892

A major in the Norfolk Artillery, Penrice exhibited calotypes and waxed-paper architectural and landscape views in the 1854 and 1855 Photographic Society exhibitions in London and in the 1855 London Photographic Institution exhibition. His work after that was in collodion. A complex character, Penrice eventually became a justice of the peace in Norfolk. In 1844, on the death of his father, he sent twenty-five major paintings from Wilton House, the family home near Yarmouth in Norfolk, to Messrs. Christie and Manson. Some of these are in the National Gallery, London, and The Metropolitan Museum of Art, New York.

In 1861 he published *The Valley of the Nile*, a series of one hundred stereoscopic views taken in Egypt and Nubia. Although Penrice's photographs are now virtually unknown, his 1873 *Dictionary and Glossary of the Kor-ân* was such a substantial piece of scholarship that an edition of it is still in print.

Exhibited: 1854 and 1855, London, Photographic Society

Reference: John Penrice, *A Dictionary and Glossary of the Kor-ân, with Copious Grammatical References and Explanations of the Text* (London: H. S. King, 1873)

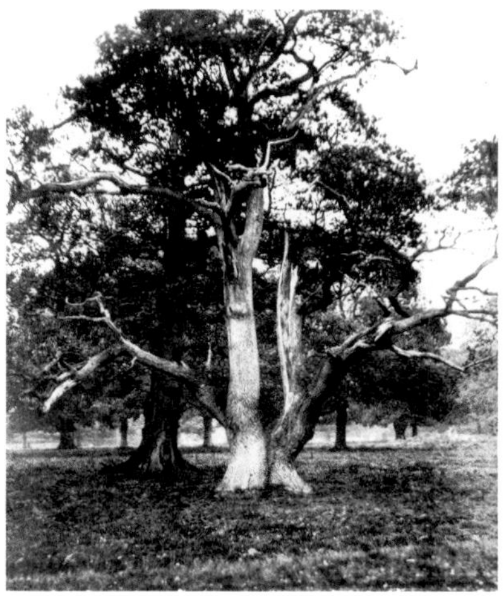

87. John Percy

Percy, John *ill. 87*

1817–1889

Trained as a medical doctor at Edinburgh, Percy received his degree in 1839, the same year photography was introduced to the public. Additional medical training in Paris brought him into contact with leading French chemists, at just the time when interest in the processes of photography was developing rapidly. Percy then practiced in Birmingham, an industrial center dependent on the metals that were to shape Percy's life. Although his 1847 fellowship in the Royal Society was granted in recognition of his medical research, Percy's interests had already turned toward metallurgy. In 1848 he devised a process for extracting silver from low-grade ores, using the same hypo so crucial to photography. Percy's treatise was the first and for some time the standard one on this important subject. Birmingham was also a center of photographic activity, and by the time of the 1852 exhibition at the Society of Arts, Percy had become an enthusiastic calotypist. He contributed two calotypes of trees to the Photographic Exchange Club in 1855. Percy was a pivotal figure in the formation of the Photographic Society, and at its very first ordinary meeting in February 1853 he read a paper, "Upon the Waxed-Paper Process as Applicable to Hot Climates." In 1855, the problem of prints fading had become widely recognized, and Percy played a leading role in the Photographic Exchange Club's Positive Printing Committee, whose recommendations alleviated this devastating shortcoming. By 1856 Percy had mastered large wet-collodion plates and photographed North Devon locations that had been painted by his friends Edwin Landseer, George Fripp, and Frederick Henshaw; he often duplicated exact viewpoints, making for illuminating comparisons in subsequent exhibitions. His interest in metals eventually lured him away from active photography. He was an avid collector of watercolors, minerals, and metallurgical examples. Two days before Percy died, the Prince of Wales conferred on him the Albert Medal of the Society of Arts. In receiving this award, Percy said, "My work is done." More than 3,700 of his carefully labeled specimens were purchased from his estate by the Science Museum, London.

References: John Percy, "Upon the Waxed-Paper Process as Applicable to Hot Climates," *JPS* 1 (March 3, 1853), pp. 9–12; *Photographic News* 33 (June 28, 1889), pp. 418–19 (obituary); *Proceedings of the Royal Society of London* 46 (1889), pp. xxxv–xl (obituary); *Nature* 40 (June 27, 1889), p. 206 (obituary)

Petley, Robert

b. 1813

Born in Gibraltar, Lieutenant Petley was an instructor in military surveying at Sandhurst College by the time photography was introduced to the public. The army took great interest in the potential of photography, and Petley's talent for surveying would have encouraged him in this direction as well. Curiously, his only known public showing of calotypes was in the 1852 Society of Arts exhibition, where he displayed a portrait and a copy of an engraving. In subsequent exhibitions he turned to collodion but kept portraits as his main subject.

Exhibited: 1852, London, Society of Arts

Philpot, Giovanni [John] Brampton

1812–1878

A native of Maidstone in Kent, John Philpot adopted the name Giovanni when he moved to Florence. Originally a copperplate printer, he became a professional studio photographer about 1850. In the 1856 Photographic Society of Scotland exhibition in Edinburgh, JAMES DRUMMOND of the Royal Scottish Academy submitted two of Philpot's waxed-paper views of Florence. Philpot then turned to stereoscopic photography, sometimes sharing credit with another photographer by the name of Jackson. Philpot's one known literary work was his 1854 *Sabina: A Sicilian Tale of the Thirteenth Century*, a novel the *Athenaeum* found to be "full of fine writing and modern antique phraseology."

Exhibited: 1856, Edinburgh, Photographic Society of Scotland

References: Giovanni [John] Brampton Philpot, *Sabina: A Sicilian Tale of the Thirteenth Century* (London: Saunders & Otley, 1854); Geraldine E. Jewsbury, review of *Sabina*, by Philpot, *Athenaeum*, September 23, 1854, p. 1138; Marilena Tamassia, ed., *Firenza ottocentesca nelle fotografie di J. B. Philpot* (Florence: Sillabe Edizione, 2002)

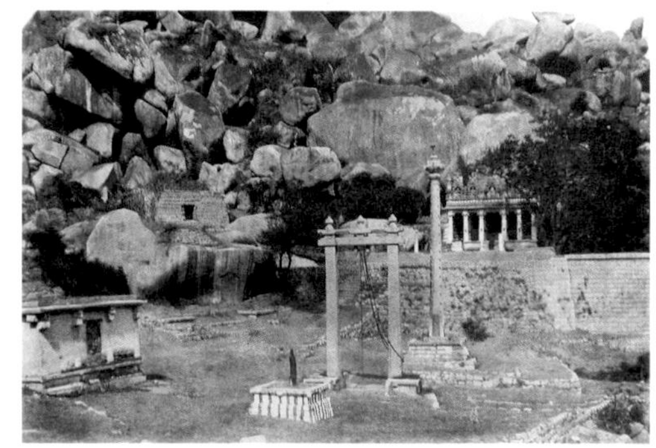

88. William Harry Pigou

Pigou, William Harry *ill. 88*

1818–1858

When Captain THOMAS BIGGS recommended Dr. Pigou, of the Indian Medical Service (Bombay), to replace him as official photographer for the Bombay Presidency in 1855, he pointed out that "besides professing a good knowledge of chemistry, Pigou has the advantage of several years experience in Photography in this country," a familiarity essential for coping with the demands of the hot climate. In his new position Pigou struggled with the bureaucracy over equipment and supplies but began producing high-quality waxed-paper negatives. Records of his service in India show that the Court of Directors was very pleased with his work, praising the photographs as "of the highest merit as works of Art." Facing a serious shortage of artillery officers, the army commanded his return to service in May 1857. This order was temporarily suspended, but Pigou's health had suffered during two summers of photographic expeditions. At forty-one he died from a "disease of the brain." His estate was ordered to relinquish his hundreds of waxed-paper negatives to the government.

References: William Harry Pigou, records of military service, India Office Records, British Library; Meadows Taylor and James Fergusson, *Architecture in Dharwar and Mysore* (London: John Murray, 1866); Janet Dewan, "Captain Biggs and Dr Pigou," *Photoresearcher*, no. 5 (December 1993), pp. 6–13

Pinyon, Peter
b. 1831
Virtually nothing is known about Dr. Pinyon except for an album of seventeen views from waxed-paper negatives that was auctioned in the 1970s. Its cover was inscribed "Peter Pinyon, Dec'r 20th 1858," possibly making him the compiler but more likely the photographer. The views ranged from Sussex (his birthplace) to Norwich and, unusually, even included Tasmania. Pinyon married a widow in 1859 and was still alive at the time of the 1871 census, when he was listed as a surgeon and apothecary.

Reference: Sale cat., Sotheby's, London, October 20, 1976, lot 52

Piper, John Dixon
b. 1818
Piper was a printer and stationer in Ipswich when he first came to notice in the 1856 Norwich Photographic Society exhibition. Most of his work in this and subsequent exhibitions was realized in collodion, but in the 1858 Photographic Society exhibition in London, Piper showed one Talbotype architectural view. At the 1859 Photographic Society of Scotland, it was noted that "a new name . . . demands notice—that of Mr. J. Dixon Piper of Ipswich, who contributes some subjects, both architectural and of general nature, which are of a very high class . . . on a large scale, and most effective photographs." Piper disappears from photographic circles after 1865. He remained in Ipswich, in 1881 listing himself in the census as a "retired bookseller and printer," and was still alive at the time of the 1891 census.

Exhibited: 1858, London, Photographic Society; 1860, Edinburgh, Photographic Society of Scotland

Reference: "Exhibition of the Photographic Society of Scotland," *Photographic Journal* 6 (February 15, 1860), p. 157

Pitter, Mr.
In December 1850 the *Hastings & St Leonards News* carried notice that on Monday, December 23, at the Mechanics' Institution, "Mr Pitter delivered his second lecture on the 'Science of the Sunbeam' . . . the photographic processes were explained, and some daguerreotypes and talbotypes were exhibited." Pitter was possibly an itinerant lecturer, for no likely candidates have been traced to the Hastings area.

Playfair, Hugh Lyon
1786–1861
Always known as Colonel Playfair, although he attained the rank of lieutenant general, Playfair was a larger-than-life character and a natural leader. The son of the principal of United College at St. Andrews, Playfair entered the East India Company army in 1804 and served brilliantly in the field. Considered "the most efficient officer in his regiment," he advanced through the ranks of the artillery before retiring to his native St. Andrews in 1834. He was elected provost of United College in 1842 and held that post until his death, thus being well positioned to influence the early course of photography in Scotland. The ancient city of St. Andrews had fallen into serious decay by the time of the invention of photography. Playfair rapidly instituted radical and far-reaching reforms to both the political and physical structure of the city. Within a decade he had improved the sanitation and the roads, built a library, baths, and a town hall, and developed leisure opportunities. A "ruthlessly efficient" golfer, he saved the failing course at St. Andrews. He worked with Dr. John Adamson to improve physical health and with Sir David Brewster to improve the intellectual side of the city. According to his obituary, "the Major was never known to have tried anything which he did not accomplish," and possessed of boundless energy. Playfair actively participated in the evolution of the calotype at St. Andrews. His obituary described him as "a good mechanic, with a special leaning towards photography, which he was the first (being initiated by his friend Claudet) to introduce into St. Andrews, now celebrated as a chief home of the art." While Playfair's first introduction to photography was more likely from Brewster, the connection with Antoine Claudet was undoubtedly a useful one. A contemporary recalled those early days, when Playfair and his associates "might be seen almost every day calotyping or being calotyped." Playfair's only formal photographic exhibition was of collodion views contributed to the meeting of the British Association for the Advancement of Science in Glasgow in 1855.

References: *Gentleman's Magazine* 210 (March 1861), pp. 333–36 (obituary); *Oxford Dictionary of National Biography*, s.v. "Playfair, Sir Hugh Lyon (1786–1861)" (by Ian Edward Wareham)

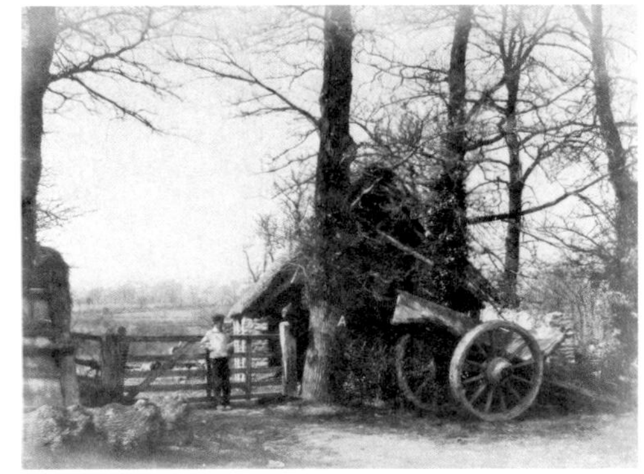
89. Thomas Cadby Ponting

Ponting, Thomas Cadby *ill. 89*
b. 1819
Born in Devizes, not far from Talbot's Lacock Abbey, Ponting started his career as a druggist's assistant in London. By 1852 he had his own chemist's shop in Bristol. He does not appear in the 1851 census. He may have been in Ireland, for his calotype contributions to the 1854 Photographic Society exhibition in London were all of Ireland. His only other known surviving calotype was taken in Wales about 1850. By 1856 Ponting was styling himself as chemist to the queen and had a booming business manufacturing collodion. He claimed he had spent three years developing the formula and that many amateur and professional photographers in the west of England had used it for two years. Ponting continued to exhibit and to photograph; not surprisingly, all his subsequent work is in collodion.

Exhibited: 1854, London, Photographic Society

Ponton, Mungo
1802–1880
Trained as a lawyer and grounded in ancient religious beliefs, Ponton helped found the National Bank of Scotland and eventually became its secretary. The pressures of business proved to be too much for his frail health, and he was forced to retire early. This freedom from commercial responsibilities was fortunate, for Ponton was at heart an amateur scientist. A fellow of the Royal Society of Edinburgh since 1834, he published scientific papers on optics, spectroscopy, polarization, and improvements to the electric telegraph. It was through a single communication in 1839 that Ponton was to revolutionize photography. He suggested the use of potassium bichromate to make a simple and cheap photographic

paper. While as he conceived it the method created only a muddy greenish image, still it could be made permanent with a mere wash of water. It was immediately adopted by botanists. Three years later, JOHN HERSCHEL would use bichromate in conjunction with iron salts to invent the blueprint. TALBOT and others were to use the method as the fundamental basis of the photomechanical processes that would eventually allow ink to supplant silver in photographic book illustration, an idea Talbot freely credited to Ponton. Ponton conceived of using photography to automatically record fluctuations of thermometers and other instruments, an idea that won him a silver medal from the Royal Scottish Society of Arts in 1845. He was a staunch advocate of the wave theory of light. Moving from Edinburgh to Clifton in 1854, Ponton became more and more engaged in religion and philosophy. His crowning publication was his 1871 book *The Beginning: Its When, and Its How,* skillfully illustrated with his drawings, which blends religion and science, with a particular emphasis on the influence of solar light.

REFERENCES: Mungo Ponton, "Notice of a Cheap and Simple Method of Preparing Paper for Photographic Drawing, in which the Use of Any Salt of Silver Is Dispensed with [dated May 18, 1839]," *Transactions of the Royal Scottish Society of Arts* 1 (May 29, 1839), pp. 336–38; Ponton, *The Beginning: Its When, and Its How* (London: Longmans Green & Co., 1871); *BJP* 27 (August 27, 1880), p. 420 (obituary); *Photographic News*, 24 (August 20, 1880), pp. 402–3 (obituary); Alison Morrison-Low, "Photography in Edinburgh in 1839: The Royal Scottish Society of Arts, Andrew Fyfe and Mungo Ponton," *Scottish Photography Bulletin*, 1990, pp. 26–35

Pooley, Charles
1817–1890
Pooley, a complex figure, was a medical practitioner in Weston-super-Mare and taught at the University of Bonn but then returned to his native England. A fellow of the Royal Chemical Society, he found mastering the technical aspects of photography quite easy. In his 1854 book, *Notes on the Cross of Amney Holyrood, Gloucestershire,* he explained, "the Views were taken by myself, in Calotype, from which the Frontispiece, in coloured lithography, and the Cross in the Church-yard, are executed by Adlard." The likely basis for one of these plates turned up in a 1970s auction: a print titled *At Amney Crucis* and inscribed "C. Pooley, Calotype, 1853." In 1856 Pooley published *On Engraving Collodion Photographs, by Means of Fluoric Acid Gas.* It is almost certain that he continued to use photography in his antiquarian publications. The lithographs in his 1868 *Notes on the Old Crosses of Gloucestershire* are signed "C.P. del" and have the look of illustrations based on camera images. The one of Amney Holyrood is clearly derived from his 1853 calotype. In his 1877 *Old Stone Crosses of Somerset* the illustrations are very similar but by then are signed simply "C. Pooley F.S.A." Pooley wrote a number of related books on ancient crosses. While antiquarian studies were clearly his passion, other books by him covered a wide range of topics, including mesmerism, spiritual doctrines, and the causes of salubrity in Weston-super-Mare.

REFERENCES: Charles Pooley, *Notes on the Cross of Amney Holy-Rood, Gloucestershire* (London: Hamilton, Adams & Co., 1854); Pooley, *On Engraving Collodion Photographs, by Means of Fluoric Acid Gas* (London, 1856); Pooley, *An Historical and Descriptive Account of the Old Stone Crosses of Somerset* (London, 1877); sale cat., Sotheby's, London, October 24, 1979, lot 351

Prichard, John
The editor of the *British Journal of Photography* was unusually impressed by the qualities of the negatives that Prichard showed him in 1863. In presenting his "Improved Calotype Process," Prichard said he was "practically alive to the inconvenience of working with collodion, either wet or dry, when on a photographic excursion." Nothing further is at present known of the man or his work.

REFERENCE: John Prichard, "Improved Calotype Process," *BJP* 10 (May 15, 1863), pp. 203–4

Pumphrey, William A. *ill. 90*
1817–1905
The son of a Quaker glover, Pumphrey moved to York in 1845 to take a position as a science teacher. The new art of photography intrigued him so much that in 1849 he established his Photographic Portrait Gallery, York's first such business. Pumphrey found the daguerreotype process that he employed for portraiture too limiting and in 1852 began using calotype. The following year he published *Photographic Views of York and Its Environs,* marking the start of an extensive documentation project. Probably for financial reasons, Pumphrey sold his studio in 1854 to become the director of a lunatic asylum. He continued to lecture on science. On November 7, 1854, the *Yorkshire Gazette* observed (as an author noted in 1986), "Mr. Pumphrey . . . entered at some length into the origin and progress of the art during the last 30 years and discussed the merits and demerits of the several processes, the daguerreotype and the calotype. He illustrated his remarks with some interesting experiments and a large collection of very beautiful photographic pictures." Pumphrey showed collodion work in the 1856 Photographic Society exhibition in London. It was his only participation in these exhibitions, but he continued to photograph both at home and abroad throughout the rest of his life.

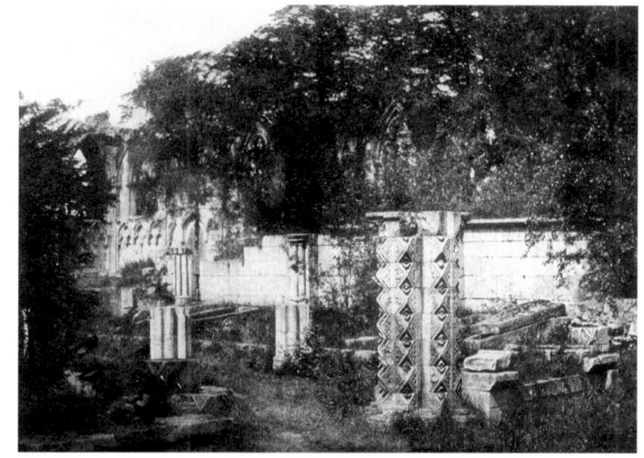
90. William A. Pumphrey

REFERENCES: Adrian Budge, *Early Photography in Leeds, 1839–1870,* exh. cat. (Leeds: Leeds City Art Galleries, 1981), p. 7; Hugh Murray, *Photographs & Photographers of York: The Early Years, 1844–1879* (York: Yorkshire Architectural and York Archaeological Society, 1986), pp. 21–22

Radcliffe, Elizabeth
d. 1855
In the 1970s a calotype portrait described as "of a middle-aged gentleman seated and holding a book on his lap" was auctioned at Sotheby's. It was "attributed to E. Radcliffe of Rudding Park." In 1807, Joseph Pickford Radcliffe of Rudding Park had married his third wife, Elizabeth, née Creswick. By the 1850s, when this image was taken, some of Radcliffe's children by previous wives had reached middle age; this might be a portrait of one of her stepchildren. There is no other likely "E. Radcliffe" in the area.

REFERENCE: Sale cat., Sotheby's, London, May 24, 1973, lot 116

Rae, Alexander
b. 1811
A chemist in Banff, in the remote north of Scotland, Rae displayed four calotype portraits in the 1853 Mechanics' Institution exhibition in Aberdeen. He also showed collodion portraits, groups on glass, and a frame containing eight daguerreotypes. At the British Association for the Advancement of Science meeting in Aberdeen in 1859, Rae submitted a wide range of collodion material,

including stereo views. Such a range indicated either that he was a very dedicated and inquisitive amateur or that as a supplier he felt the need to keep up with the evolving technology of his clients. He then became a dentist, and his son, Alexander Jr. (b. 1846), became both his apprentice dentist and his apprentice chemist. From 1877 to 1908 they operated the studio of Alexander Rae & Son.

Exhibited: 1853, Aberdeen, Mechanics' Institution

Reference: D. Richard Torrance, *Photographers in Northern Scotland to 1914* (Edinburgh: Scottish Genealogy Society, 2001), p. 8

Ralfs, William
b. 1819
In the 1856 Norwich Photographic Society exhibition, a "W. Ralfs" showed two waxed-paper views of architecture in Bury St. Edmunds. The only W. Ralfs traced in the area was William Ralfs, a goldsmith's shopman. The reviewer for the *Norfolk News* found these views "pleasing" but obviously did not know the photographer, so it is probable that he was not from the area. Another possibility is William Ralfs of Tonbridge, who had a circulating library and later was a newspaper proprietor.

Exhibited: 1856, Norwich, Photographic Society

Reference: *Norfolk News*, January 3, 1857

Ralston, J.
The Glasgow Post Office Directory reveals that J. Ralston had a studio on Argyle Street from 1856 to 1857, but nothing else is known about him. He wrote to the *Liverpool and Manchester Photographic Journal* in 1857, suggesting helpfully that "in my experience of photography, I generally find the simplest methods of doing things to be the best. In salting paper for calotypes . . . for a long time back I have used nothing but *pure sea water*, by which method I never fail in getting good results."

Reference: J. Ralston, letter in *LMPJ*, n.s., 1 (March 15, 1857), p. 65

Ramsay, William
1806–1865
In the 1856 Edinburgh exhibition of the Photographic Society of Scotland, Ramsay showed a waxed-paper view of the Capitoline Hill in Rome, taken from the Forum. It is the only time he is known to have exhibited and his only known photograph; most likely it represents a much more significant body of work, at present lost. Ramsay experimented with photolithography and was a friend of Robert Macpherson and a member of the Photographic Society of Scotland. Virtually all of his professional life was based in Glasgow, where he held the Chair of Humanity at the university until his death. His obituary stated, "Few teachers have ever left upon their pupils—of whatever class or type of mind—so deep and clearly-cut an impress of their personality as Professor William Ramsay." He published extensively on mathematics and classics. Ramsay was remembered in the *Scotsman* as "an accomplished man of the world, full of human sympathies and interests," who "had considerable practical knowledge of chemistry, and was one of the first amateurs to practise photography in this country." He died during a visit to San Remo.

Exhibited: 1856, Edinburgh, Photographic Society

References: *Scotsman* (Edinburgh), February 15, 1865 (obituary); *Proceedings of the Numismatic Society*, n.s., 5 (June 15, 1865), pp. 18–20 (summary of article in *Edinburgh Courant*); *Memoirs and Portraits of One Hundred Glasgow Men Who Have Died in the Last Thirty Years* (Glasgow: James Maclehose and Sons, 1886), vol. 2, pp. 265–66

Ramsden, John William
1834–1894
Born the son of a tavern owner just five years before the discovery of photography, Ramsden took up the art at a young age while apprenticed to a bookseller. Wanting to be an artist, he was entranced by some daguerreotypes displayed in an optician's window and resolved to take up the new art. His camera was a cigar box, fitted with a spectacle glass, and the space under his bed served as his darkroom. Ramsden's earliest work was in a waxed-paper process that he devised himself. WASHINGTON TEASDALE, in his 1854 analytical chart of various approaches to formulating waxed paper, failed at Ramsden's formula but confessed, "in other hands, the best negatives I have ever seen." In 1852, at eighteen, Ramsden was one of the founders and the first vice president of the Leeds Photographic Society. The following year he opened his first studio, later going into partnership with THOMAS HENRY BRIGGS. Ramsden specialized in architectural and landscape photographs, using the waxed-paper process, and exhibited several in the 1856 Photographic Society exhibition in London. He also took portraits and other types of photographs in his studio. When the wet-collodion process asserted itself he became the first and foremost seller of collodion in Britain. His "Ramsden's Tourist Camera," lightweight and ideal for field photography, was widely marketed and versatile enough to take paper or glass-plate negatives.

Exhibited: 1856, London, Photographic Society

References: John William Ramsden, "Modification of M. Le Gray's Waxed-Paper Process," *JPS* 1 (October 21, 1853), p. 121; Washington Teasdale, "Photographic Processes," *JPS* 1 (January 21, 1854), pp. 161–62; *BJP* 41 (February 2, 1894), pp. 73–74 (obituary)

Ranking, James Lancaster
1817–1897
Dr. Ranking spent most of his professional career in India and eventually rose to be surgeon general of the Indian Medical Service. In 1887 he looked back in the *Amateur Photographer*, to the time when "in 1857, while serving in Burmah, I took up the Calotype process, under the tuition of the late Colonel Greenlaw, of the Madras Army." ALEXANDER JOHN GREENLAW's waxed paper had important advantages over collodion in India, being both more readily handled in a hot climate and far more portable than glass plates. When Ranking wrote in 1887, glass was just being supplanted by more flexible supports—first paper and soon plastic films. In this period of a new upheaval in the technology of the medium, Ranking recalled, "I was one of the earliest of the great army of amateur photographers to suggest the use of gelatino-bromide paper as a substitute for glass plates for negative work in the Camera." Ranking adapted some of the early commercially made papers, intended for printing but in his hands the precursors of film, for making negatives. In addition to greater portability, paper did not suffer from the halation problems inherent in glass plates and thus rendered highlights more accurately. Ranking was also a fan of the new tricycles then emerging, seeing them as "good weight-carriers" for a variety of photographic equipment and possibly even for a dark tent. He displayed prints from some of his paper negatives in the 1886 Photographic Society exhibition.

References: James Lancaster Ranking, "Paper Negatives," *BJPA*, 1883, pp. 69–72; Ranking, "Paper Negatives," *BJPA*, 1886, pp. 180–83; Ranking, "Negative Films," *Amateur Photographer* 4 (January 21, 1887), pp. 29–30

Ranking, William Harcourt
1814–1867
As a surgeon in Norwich, Ranking was well placed to join the newly formed Norwich Photographic Society. In its 1856 exhibition he showed twelve waxed-paper views of architecture and scenery in the Norwich area.

According to the *Norfolk News*, his "many specimens by this process . . . display alike artistic and photographic skill." One of his entries was of Costessey Hall, suggesting a possible connection with JOHN BLOWERS, an amateur photographer and the manager of the estate. The few surviving examples of Ranking's work indicate that he was a master of the waxed-paper process, employing it successfully even for church interiors. He was to become the second president of the society. He is best known in medical circles for his editorship of *The Half-Yearly Abstract of the Medical Sciences.*

EXHIBITED: 1856, Norwich, Photographic Society

REFERENCES: *Norfolk News*, January 3, 1857; *Gentleman's Magazine* 223 (August 1867), pp. 252–53 (obituary); Richard Denyer and Andrew Moore, eds., *A Period Eye: Photography Then and Now*, exh. cat. (Norwich: Norfolk Museums and Archaeology Service, 2003), pp. 60–61

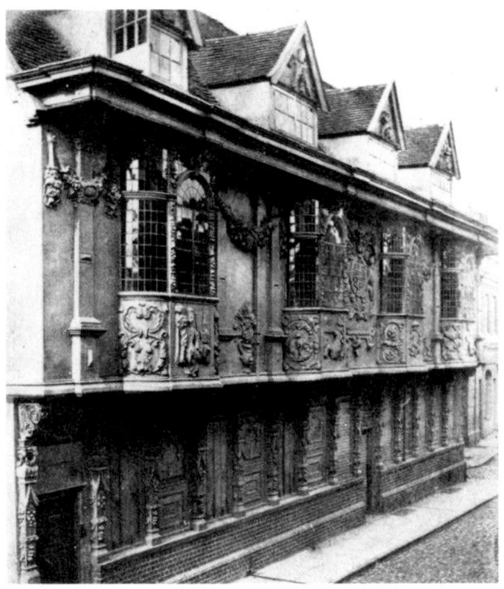

91. Robert Charles Ransome

Ransome, Robert Charles *ill. 91*

1830–1886

The Ransome family of Ipswich made its fortune in the discovery of chilled cast iron, a hardened metal important to early-nineteenth century agriculture; then expanded into metalworking and eventually into steam engines. Educated at Quaker schools and entering his grandfather's business at the age of sixteen, Ransome stood out, as noted in *Public Men of Ipswich . . .*, for his "marked individuality" and for being "less of a specialist" within this estimable family. Early in his career he acted as the representative for its Orwell Works, traveling both to the Continent and to the colonies. By the time Ransome became a full partner, the firm had more than a thousand employees. He specialized in developing the overseas business, giving him ample opportunity to travel. In the 1854 and 1855 exhibitions of the Photographic Society in London, Ransome displayed Talbotypes of architectural views in the Ipswich region. For his contribution to the 1857 *Photographic Album* he remained devoted both to the calotype and to Ipswich. In spite of an early judgment by *Public Men of Ipswich and East Suffolk* that in Ransome "geniality did not seem to come by nature," at thirty-seven he was elected the mayor of Ipswich and went on to take an active role in encouraging education for artisans.

EXHIBITED: 1854, Norwich, Photographic Society; 1856, London, Photographic Society

REFERENCES: *Public Men of Ipswich and East Suffolk: A Series of Personal Sketches* (Ipswich: W. J. Scopes, 1875), pp. 283–89; *Proceedings of the Institution of Mechanical Engineers* 37 (February 1886), pp. 122–23 (obituary)

Raven, E.

The 1856 exhibition of the Photographic Society of Scotland in Edinburgh contained seven calotypes by "E. Raven." Four of these were contributed by E. Raven himself, or herself, and the remaining three by the Reverend THOMAS MILVILLE RAVEN, almost certainly a relation. They were all taken in Surrey. The photographer might have been Rev. Raven's brother Eustace, a twenty-year-old destined for the ministry. Or perhaps the photographer was Rev. Raven's wife, Eliza, née Jaques, whom he had married in 1849. Neither Eustace nor Eliza Raven had a documented connection with Surrey. No further work by this photographer is known, although a 1980s auction listed a print attributed to "Rev'd E. Millville Raven." That could have been Eustace Raven (although he was never Milville) or could have been a typographical error or misreading of "Rev'd T. Millville Raven."

EXHIBITED: 1856 and 1858, Edinburgh, Photographic Society of Scotland

REFERENCES: Sale cats., Christie's, London, March 26, 1981, lot 149, and April 24, 1984, lot 478

Raven, Thomas Milville *ill. 92*

1828–1896

Shortly after joining the Photographic Society of Scotland, Rev. Raven recalled in the *Journal of the Photographic Society* of December 21, 1858, "it was after reading Dr. Keith's admirable paper on the waxed-paper process that

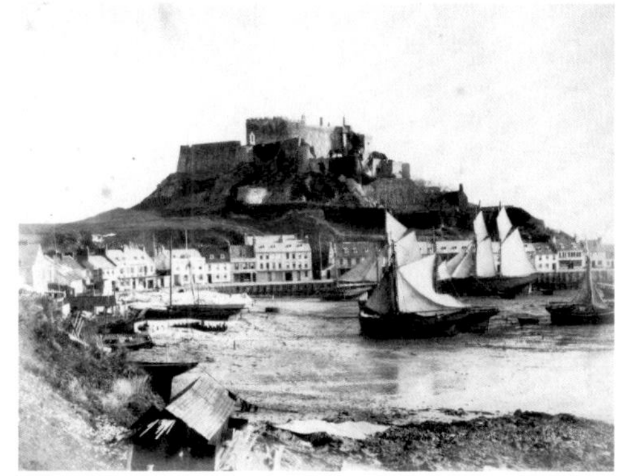

92. Thomas Milville Raven

I determined to adopt it. I was at that time living in a country parish in Yorkshire, and had to fight my way through photographic difficulties and troubles unaided and unadvised by any one. I had been working some little time with various processes before I came to Edinburgh." Raven was elected a fellow of the Royal Society of Edinburgh, and thus had a scientific background. One brother was a painter, and his brother-in-law was Henry Holiday, a prominent member of the Pre-Raphaelite circle. THOMAS KEITH, himself a masterful photographer, had adapted the waxed-paper process to the needs of the British amateur, and Raven probably had the opportunity to discuss photography with him. Raven began exhibiting as soon as he joined the society in 1856, contributing dozens of calotype and waxed-paper views, mostly of architecture and archaeological sites. By the time of their 1858 exhibition, his subject matter had broadened to include the Pyrenees, where he did a substantial amount of waxed-paper work. Raven submitted more than two dozen waxed-paper views of French architecture and scenery to the 1859 exhibition of the Glasgow Photographic Society. His published account of his photographic journey through the Pyrenees is instructive about photography but reveals nothing of himself. He and his wife, Eliza (possibly the mysterious photographer E. RAVEN), arrived in Pau with a daughter in December 1857. The daughter is not recorded on a subsequent visit, and no daughter is registered in either the 1851 or 1861 census. One might conclude that the Ravens went to Pau hoping to find a cure for their young daughter but left childless. Whatever transpired, Raven used the time there to good photographic advantage, and his narrative, "Account of a Photographic Tour from Jersey to the Pyrenees," illuminates the experience of a dedicated amateur photographer. After his success with waxed paper in

France, Raven returned to calotype in the cooler climate of Britain, finding it, as he wrote in *Photographic Notes* in 1858, "unrivalled" for "landscape portraiture." He also experimented with a dry collodion view of Stirling Castle. His contributions to the 1861 Photographic Society exhibition in London were a mix of waxed-paper and collodion, including views, portraits, and studies of busts. Raven continued to show some waxed paper in 1864 and made his final contribution to the 1865 International Exhibition in Dublin, again a mix of collodion and waxed paper. In 1860, in *Photographic Notes*, Raven cheerfully challenged THOMAS SUTTON, the outspoken editor of *Photographic Notes*, having "so often told you 'that the success of all out-door work in photography must eventually depend on paper, and that to *paper* all collodion men would have to turn.'" Raven was elected a member of the Photographic Society in London on June 7, 1864, the same day that Julia Margaret Cameron was admitted.

EXHIBITED: 1856, Norwich, Photographic Society; 1856, Edinburgh, Photographic Society of Scotland; 1857, Birmingham, Photographic Society; 1858, London, Photographic Society; 1858, Edinburgh, Photographic Society of Scotland; 1859, London, Photographic Society; 1859, Glasgow, Photographic Society; 1861 and 1864, London, Photographic Society, 1865, Dublin, International Exhibition

REFERENCES: Thomas Milville Raven, letter in *Photographic Notes* 1 (December 15, 1856), pp. 272–73; Raven, "Account of a Photographic Tour from Jersey to the Pyrenees," *Photographic Notes* 1 (February 1, 1858), pp. 42–45; Raven, "Pau and the Pyrenees, with a Slight Sketch of a Photographic Tour Made to Them through the West of France," *JPS* 5 (December 21, 1858, and January 8 and 21, 1859), pp. 104–8, 131–32, 155–57; "Mr. Raven's Waxed Paper Process," *JPS* 5 (March 5, 1859), p. 219; Raven, "On the Preparation of Paper for the Waxed-Paper Process," *JPS* 6 (May 15, 1860), pp. 233–35; Raven, "Paper Photography," *Photographic Notes* 5 (December 15, 1860), p. 347

Reade, Joseph Bancroft *ill. 93*

1801–1871

Born into a strongly religious family but one that mixed mercantile with evangelical interests, Reade was destined for the clergy. As a curate in Halifax in the 1830s, he forged a close friendship with the amateur meteorologist John Waterhouse (whose "Waterhouse stops" would later contribute to photographic lens structure). In December 1839, shortly after photography was announced, Reade accepted the post of vicar of Stone, Buckinghamshire, where there was a small school and an observatory. He had published his first scientific paper, on the relationship between solar rays and heat, in 1836. Reade took a particular interest in the microscope and was an important innovator with this instrument. His interest in chemistry led to an 1846 patent for a metallic salt-based ink. It is certain that Reade began experimenting with photography in 1839 and was an early adopter of Sir JOHN HERSCHEL's hypo fixing. What is less clear is his work with gallic acid and how it related to TALBOT's autumn 1840 discovery of the calotype, the development of which depended on this derivative of oak galls. Counterclaims between Reade and Talbot were acrimonious but never proven on either side; in 1854 Reade testified against Talbot in the patent trial. In 1855 he joined the Photographic Society, becoming a vice president in the 1860s. His imagination and experimental nature were impressive, and undoubtedly he influenced many early photographers. He was reported to have had an early exchange with the father of CHARLES PIAZZI SMYTH. The *British Journal of Photography* recounted on December 16, 1870, that Admiral Smyth, whose wife was an accomplished artist, dismissed Reade's early photographs as "a quick mode of taking bad pictures," to which Reade responded, "True, Admiral; but even *you* were born a *baby*." Very few of Reade's own photographs survive, and he is not known to have exhibited. His obituary of December 23 noted, "As an astronomer and a naturalist his reputation was of the highest."

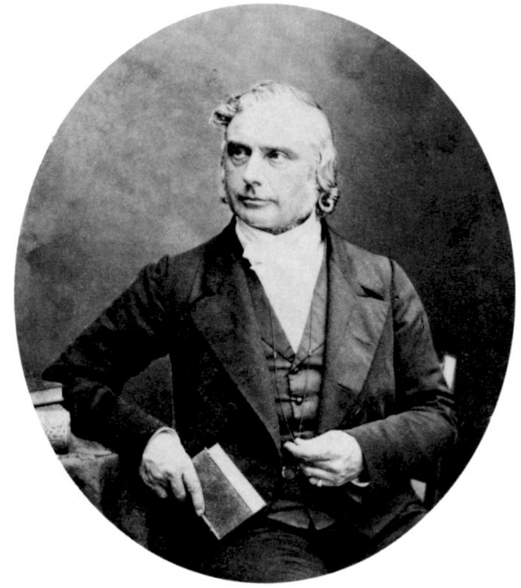

93. Portrait of Joseph Bancroft Reade

REFERENCES: *BJP* 17 (December 16 and 23, 1870), pp. 588–89, 607 (obituaries); *Photographic Journal* 15 (February 18, 1871), pp. 57–58 (obituary); Rupert Derek Wood, "J. B. Reade, F.R.S., and the Early History of Photography," *Annals of Science* 27 (March 1971), pp. 13–45 (pt. 1, "A Re-Assessment on the Discovery of Contemporary Evidence"), 47–83 (pt. 2, "Gallic Acid and Talbot's Calotype Patent")

Redman, Theodore Smith

b. 1811

In a letter to Sir JOHN HERSCHEL in March 1840, Redman, a chemist in Peckham, outlined his own methods of preparing photogenic paper and fixing the results in a letter he had been prompted to write by JOSEPH BANCROFT READE. Herschel was apparently interested in knowing more about Redman's techniques. In the summer of 1839 Redman had conducted an extensive series of tests and had finally concluded that silver nitrate and ammonium chloride produced a paper both sensitive and capable of deep blacks. Herschel, immersed in his own extensive photographic studies, wrote back that he was "surprised . . . how . . . you have been able to get a depth of shadow sufficient for such a very sharp re-transfer is to me marvellous." John Werge, a daguerreotypist and author then living in Peckham, might have been one of Redman's customers but in any case took credit for teaching him photogenic drawing. When his pupil excelled with his own methods, Werge, according to his own memory, was the one who suggested he write to Herschel. Four of Redman's 1839 photogenic drawings and a later calotype portrait are included in RICHARD WILLAT's album. By 1846 Redman had moved to Fleet Street and was not only advertising daguerreotype portraits but also giving lessons in the calotype and supplying chemicals for the process. He began selling packets of iodized paper for the waxed-paper process. His Fleet Street studio was taken over by Jane Nina Wigley, London's first woman daguerreotypist. Redman continued in a succession of London photographic studios well into the 1860s.

REFERENCES: Theodore Smith Redman to Herschel, March 31, 1840, The Royal Society, London, HS 14:474; John Werge, *The Evolution of Photography* (London: Piper & Carter, 1890), p. 17

Reeve, James

1833–1920

In 1913, Reeve presented a waxed-paper negative of the west end of Norwich Cathedral to the Norwich Library. It was presumed to be an example of his own work, and this, given his talents, seems entirely plausible. Reeve was a geologist and, even at an early age, also an amateur artist. He received a medal from the Norwich Government School of Design in 1856 for his artwork. Reeve then went on to being a museum curator and art historian. The Norwich Cathedral negative appears to have been destroyed in a 1980s fire.

Reeves, Walter Waters
b. 1819
Reeves submitted numerous photographs to the 1852 Society of Arts exhibition in London, including several of Tunbridge Wells done from paper negatives. In the 1840s he was a chemist there and may well have been introduced to photography by his customers. After 1852 he became a professional photographer and gilder of picture frames in Berkley, Sussex. By 1871 he was a lodger in Greenwich and assistant secretary of the Royal Microsocopal Society, a position he held for many years.

EXHIBITED: 1852, London, Society of Arts

Reid, David Boswell
1805–1863
Reid was responsible for the very first public showing in Scotland of TALBOT's new art. As organizer of the 1839 Exhibition of Arts, Manufactures, and Practical Science in Edinburgh, Reid accepted Sir WALTER TREVELYAN's entry of photogenic drawings sent by Talbot. Reid also attempted photography himself. PAULINE TREVELYAN recalled in her diary that in one of his 1840 lectures he demonstrated "photogenisizing" to the audience. Reid was the son of a doctor, and his mother was the daughter of an antiquarian. A promising medical doctor himself, he started a popular course of chemical lectures in 1827. He probably would have been more involved in the progress of photography in Scotland had he not moved to London in 1840. In 1836, after the Houses of Parliament burned, Reid was hired as a consultant on the ventilating and acoustics of the replacement buildings. This increasingly took over his time, although his plans eventually proved impractical. In 1856 Reid moved to New York, then Wisconsin, and finally, in 1863, to Washington, D.C., to accept the post of inspector of military hospitals. He died within weeks of arriving in Washington.

REFERENCES: *Proceedings of the Royal Society of Edinburgh* 5 (November 23, 1863), pp. 133–36 (obituary); Larry J. Schaaf, "Henry Talbot's First Exhibition in Scotland," *Studies in Photography*, 1998, pp. 25–28

Rimmer, Richard
1826–1905
Rimmer was born in Scotland but educated in England. In 1856 he became the vice president of the Dumfries and Galloway Photographic Society. Rimmer first exhibited in the Photographic Society of Scotland exhibition in 1858 and remained a member of the society for five years. In the 1859 exhibition of the Glasgow Photographic Society, he turned from collodion to waxed paper. None of his photographic work is known to have survived. Rimmer became a fellow of the Linnean Society in 1879, and in 1888 he was elected president. He still kept his Dumfriesshire roots, however, and took over from Patrick Dudgeon as president of the Observatory Museum. In 1880 his *Land and Freshwater Shells of the British Isles* became a pioneering scientific reference work. It was illustrated with photographs and printed by the Albertype process (a version of the collotype) under his personal supervision.

EXHIBITED: 1859, Glasgow, Photographic Society

Robertson, Archibald David
Archibald David Robertson was a businessman with offices in Bombay. Joining the Photographic Society in London in December 1853, he continued as a member, but resident in Bombay, until 1859. Robertson was soon elected to the council of the Photographic Society of Bombay and was consulted in the choice of candidates for the position of instructor of photography at the Elphinstone Institution. Robertson published views of India made from his waxed-paper negatives, some of which survive, but nothing else is known of him or his photography.

REFERENCE: "Inaugural Meeting of the Photographic Society of Bombay," *Journal of the Photographic Society of Bombay*, no. 1 (January 15, 1855), pp. 1–7

Robertson, James D.
1813–1888
Prominent among the few facts known about Robertson are his position as chief engraver to the Royal Mint at Constantinople and his accomplishments as a photographer. Robertson is most closely associated with views of the Crimea, taken in collaboration with his partner, Felice Beato. We know from official records that his father was English. Robertson has been variously identified, most convincingly as a London-based gem engraver who exhibited at the Royal Academy during the 1830s. In 1839 a new sultan decided to modernize the mint. New equipment was purchased from London, and a team of experts, mostly British and including Robertson, was hired to install and use it. Just when or why he took up photography is unknown; a claim that he calotyped in 1850 is unsubstantiated but not impossible. In 1853 the *Athenaeum* reviewed twenty of his photographs, published by JOSEPH CUNDALL under the title *Photographic Views of Constantinople*. In 1854 Robertson's photographs of "Grecian Antiquities" were exhibited by the Society of Arts in London. While their process was unspecified, his contributions to two of the society's touring exhibitions in 1854 were made using paper negatives. Three of these, simply titled *Pyramid*, were presumably but not necessary taken in Egypt; the other eight were views of architecture in Constantinople. In 1855 Robertson again contributed to the touring exhibition of the Society of Arts, showing mostly views of Athens, done from paper negatives. His last known public showing of paper photography was the contribution of two Talbotypes of ruins in Greece to the 1857 Birmingham Photographic Society exhibition. In 1856 Robertson married Maria Matilde, the sister of Felice Beato. Robertson then turned to the wet-collodion process, and photographs by "Robertson & Beato" became known. Robertson seems to have given up photography not long after. He retired from the Constantinople mint in 1881 because of ill health and moved with his family to Japan.

EXHIBITED: 1854, second touring exhibition, Society of Arts (London); 1855–56, third touring exhibition, Society of Arts (London); 1857, Birmingham, Photographic Society

REFERENCES: Walter Chappell, "Robertson, Beato & Co. Camera Vision at Lucknow," *Image* 7 (February 1958), pp. 35–40; B. A. Henisch and H. K. Henisch, "James Robertson of Constantinople: A Chronology," *History of Photography* 14 (January–March 1990), pp. 23–32; Colin Osman, "The Later Years of James Robertson," *History of Photography* 16 (Spring 1992), pp. 72–73

Robertson, James Walker
Nothing is known of Robertson except his membership in the Photographic Society of Bombay starting in 1856. He showed both calotypes and waxed paper in its exhibition that year. Although the members felt he would prove eventually to be among the "waxed paper men," the *Liverpool Photographic Journal* commented, Robertson's calotypes of "the lake and other views at Oorun, with native coasting vessels . . . were very beautiful, both as regards execution as photographs, tone as prints, and in artistic effect, and were deservedly admired by all." Robertson's studies sound from these descriptions well out of the ordinary, but none of his work is known to have survived.

EXHIBITED: 1856, Bombay, Photographic Society

REFERENCE: "Exhibition of Photographs at Bombay," *LPJ* 3 (October 11, 1856), pp. 141–42

Robinson, R.

Robinson has yet to be identified, and although his Talbotype contributions to the 1856 Photographic Society exhibition in London were numerous, they covered too large a geographical range to provide much of a clue. He submitted views of Monmouthshire, Ledbury, Leicester, Warwickshire, Stratford-on-Avon, and Chepstow Castle.

EXHIBITED: 1856, London, Photographic Society

Rodger, Thomas, Jr.

1833–1883

The St. Andrews studio of "Thomas Rodger, Calotypist" was a commercial manifestation of the fertile photographic experimentation that had taken place in this university town. A native of St. Andrews, Rodger apprenticed to a chemist at fourteen and then became an assistant to JOHN ADAMSON in the chemical classes at the university. Adamson taught him calotypy, and he experimented on his own with the daguerreotype. Not seeing a financial future in photography, Rodger spent two sessions at Glasgow studying medicine. He returned to St. Andrews just after Adamson's younger brother, Robert, died, and Adamson persuaded Rodger to give up medicine to become a calotypist. Rodger had become known as "the adept," who "to all capable of understanding it, explained the wonderful art," the *St. Andrews Citizen* later wrote. With his social contacts established and his reputation secure, Rodger set up his own photographic studio, at the young age of sixteen. Curious artists who visited his studio to see the new art freely disclosed their own secrets, and Rodger's artistic sensibilities grew to match his chemical mastery. In 1853, at the Mechanics' Institution exhibition in Aberdeen, Rodger showed a number of calotype views of St. Andrews and many calotype portraits, for which he received a medal. Starting with the 1854 Photographic Society exhibition in London, he showed work entirely in collodion. He exhibited profusely and regularly in all the major exhibitions through 1864. Rodger proudly carried on with the label "calotypist," surely out of respect for his early roots in the art. Nearly three hundred townsfolk turned out for his funeral. "His manners were as pleasing as his photographs were admirable," according to his obituary in the *British Journal of Photography:* Rodger had been "gifted with very refined tastes and high intellectual powers," ones he used well as "from early boyhood a great admirer of all that was grand, noble, and beautiful, both in nature and art."

EXHIBITED: 1853, Aberdeen, Mechanics' Institution

REFERENCES: *The Kingdom of Fife, Calotyped by Thomas Rodger, St. Andrews*, published in parts by subscription (Cupar: John Cunningham Orr, n.d.); *St Andrews Citizen*, January 13, 1883, p. 4 (obituary); *BJP* 30 (January 26, 1883), p. 53 (obituary)

Rogerson, John

b. 1816

Rogerson seems to have had an interest in the production of large photographs. Frustratingly, in the myriad references made to him he is always "Mr. Rogerson." Given his location and personal accomplishments, he seems most likely to have been John Rogerson, an engineer and millwright in Manchester who advanced through his skills to the title of mechanician. Rogerson was a member of the Chorlton Photographic Association from at least 1857 and was clearly an experimenter. He attempted to apply electricity to the photographic plate, with no success, and commented frequently in journals on the approaches of others. Rogerson was elected a member of the larger Manchester Photographic Society in 1860 and remained active throughout that decade. He experimented with enlarging small negatives, writing in 1859 that his "attention was first drawn to the subject by being called upon to make large negatives, at times when it was utterly impossible to do so, from the feebleness of the light." However, he was primarily a master of the large waxed-paper negative, an accomplishment for which he was highly praised. At an 1860 meeting of the Manchester Photographic Society, according to *Photographic News*, Rogerson "exhibited several very large pictures—23 by 18 inches—taken by the turpentine waxed-paper process, which were very much admired, being remarkably sharp, and full of half-tone, and force." In 1860 he built an "exceedingly small and compact" stereo camera, and in 1865 he was commissioned by JOSEPH SIDEBOTHAM to make a camera. None of Rogerson's large photographs are known to have survived.

REFERENCES: John Rogerson, "The Enlargement of Photographic Pictures, Either Positive or Negative," *BJP* 6 (April 1, 1859), p. 83; "Manchester Photographic Society," *Photographic News* 4 (August 31, 1860), p. 213

Rose, Caleb Burrell

1790–1872

As a long-established surgeon in a small market town, Dr. Rose had the opportunity to develop his youthful interest in natural science, finally concentrating on geology. The local men who worked the gravel pits and brickyards soon supplied him with interesting finds, especially fossils. As early as 1810 Rose was making drawings by employing the camera obscura. In 1839, Charles Lyell, a friend of TALBOT's, visited Rose to study the local geology, and perhaps it is through Lyell that Rose had his first contact with photography. His one known surviving example is a photogenic drawing negative, carefully labeled and preserved in the Royal Society in London. Rose modestly titled it *An early attempt at photography from Norwich.* He may well have made further photographs, for when Rose's widow died in 1908, the picture collection was sold at Christie's. A grandson, C. E. R. Sherrington, recalled frequent trips to London and a "house literally full of pictures—on chairs, on tables—for there was no room to hang them . . . there were endless collections—fossils, shells, coins, stones, minerals and like."

REFERENCES: Horace B. Woodward, *Memoir of Caleb B. Rose* (Norfolk: Norfolk and Norwich Naturalist's Society, 1893); C. E. R. Sherrington, "Charles Scott Sherrington (1857–1952)," *Notes and Records of the Royal Society of London* 30 (July 1975), pp. 45–63; Richard Denyer and Andrew Moore, eds., *A Period Eye: Photography Then and Now*, exh. cat. (Norwich: Norfolk Museums and Archaeology Service, 2003), frontispiece and p. 20

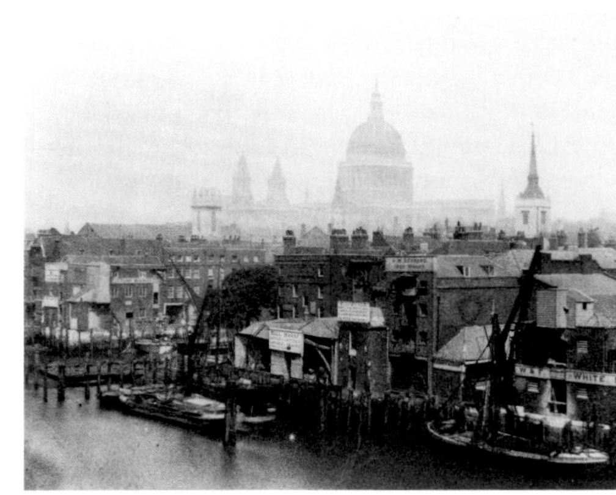

94. Alfred Rosling

Rosling, Alfred

ills. 94, 95

1802–1892

As soon as amateur photographers began organizing in the early 1850s, Alfred Rosling, a timber merchant in Reigate, became one of the most active and innovative. He was on the first council for the Photographic Society and, presumably because of his Quaker probity, was elected its first treasurer. For the 1852 Society of Arts exhibition in London Rosling submitted two dozen images, the majority made using paper negatives. His biggest sensation in that pioneering exhibition was made by collodion, however, and consisted of microscopic

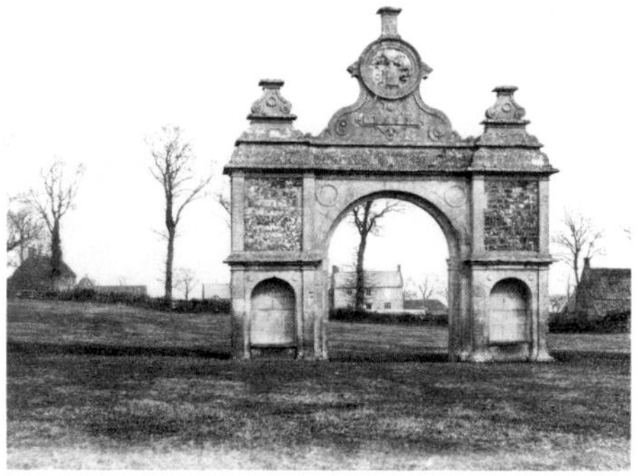

95. Alfred Rosling

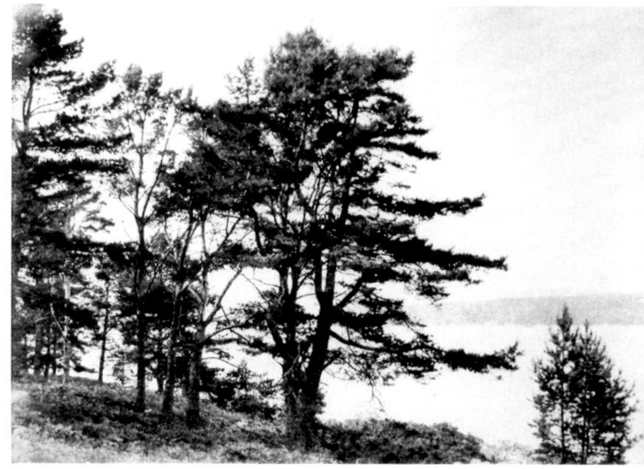

96. Horatio Ross

reproductions of pages of the *Illustrated London News* that could only be read with a magnifying glass. In the 1854 Photographic Society exhibition in London his contributions were all calotypes, including five sets of pictures for the Wheatstone stereo viewer. His BUCKLE-process calotypes shown in the 1854 photographic exhibition at the Royal Institution in Liverpool were described in the *Liverpool Photographic Journal* as "exquisite." Although Rosling continued to exhibit until 1860, his last calotypes were shown in the 1855–56 touring exhibition of the Society of Arts. Rosling's daughter married the commercially successful photographer Francis Frith.

EXHIBITED: 1852, London, Society of Arts; 1853, London, Photographic Institution; 1853–54, first touring exhibition, Society of Arts (London); 1854, London, Photographic Society; 1854, Dundee, Royal Infirmary Fund; 1854, Liverpool, Photographic Society; 1854, second touring exhibition, Society of Arts (London); 1855, London, Photographic Society; 1855–56, third touring exhibition, Society of Arts (London)

REFERENCE: "Photographic Exhibition at the Royal Institution," *LPJ* 1 (October 14, 1854), p. 139

Ross, Horatio *ill. 96*

1801–1886

Ross had a reputation as the deadliest and most enthusiastic shooter in Scotland. That was for game, but in many ways it applied to photography as well. Ross sat beside TALBOT in the 1833 Reform Parliament. His parish minister was James Brewster, brother of Sir DAVID BREWSTER, and the men were exceptionally close. However he first heard about photography, Ross recalled making his first daguerreotypes in 1843 or 1844. He was one of the few British landscape daguerreotypists. Financial problems set in, and Ross had to give up his home, Rossie Priory, and take up residence northwest of Stonehaven, near the royal family's Balmoral Castle. Ross, apparently, began to see the limitations of the metal-plate daguerreotype, and on March 26, 1849, he paid for a series of calotype lessons from the firm of Ross & Thomson (no relation). He became disillusioned with the paper process when he found that the texture of his beloved mountain subjects was rendered almost as flat planes, and he moved on to the waxed-paper negative process. Ross entered a large number of collodion views in the 1856 Photographic Society of Scotland exhibition, but in that of the 1857 Birmingham Photographic Society he exhibited more waxed paper than collodion. Most of his fifteen paper entries were scenes taken on his estate, but one was a portrait, *A Very Old Highlander*, and another a view of the Sir Walter Scott Monument in Edinburgh. After that Ross exhibited waxed paper extensively, including at the 1859 Glasgow Photographic Society exhibition. He became one of the founding members of the Photographic Society of Scotland and in 1857 read a paper there, "On the Comparative Merits of the Different Processes of Photography in Taking Views in Mountainous Districts." In 1859 Ross took delight in presenting the society's gold medal to Talbot, as he wrote to the inventor on March 9, 1859, "as a mark of their respect, & of gratitude to you as the great discoverer of photography." The *Scotsman*'s reviewer of the 1861 exhibition of the Photographic Society in Edinburgh noted on February 4, 1861, "Mr. Horatio Ross is celebrated for his love of and proficiency in field sports, and displays the same taste in his selection of subjects for photographic representation. He may be termed the Landseer of amateur photography." Ross maintained his dual interests of photography and hunting until the end of his life.

EXHIBITED: 1857, Birmingham, Photographic Society; 1858, Edinburgh, Photographic Society of Scotland; 1859, Glasgow, Photographic Society; 1859, Aberdeen, British Association for the Advancement of Science

REFERENCES: Horatio Ross, "On the Comparative Merits of the Different Processes of Photography in Taking Views in Mountainous Districts, and on the Photographic Exhibitions Now Open in London and Paris," *Photographic Notes* 2 (March 15, 1857), pp. 95–97; Ross to Talbot, March 9, 1859, Talbot Collection, British Library, London, LA59-12 (Talbot Correspondence Project, http://foxtalbot.dmu.ac.uk, doc. no. 07826); *Scotsman* (Edinburgh), February 4, 1861; James Ross, "A Few Extracts from a Photographer's Old Ledger," *BJP* 20 (February 14, 1873), p. 75; *Scotsman* (Edinburgh), December 7, 1886, p. 5 (obituary); *BJP* 33 (December 10, 1886), p. 786 (obituary); Chris Titterington, *Photographs by Horatio Ross, 1801–1886*, exh. cat. (New Haven: Yale Center for British Art, 1993); Paschal Downs, "'The Delight of Their Existence': The Photography of Horatio Ross of Rossie (1801–86)," *Studies in Photography*, 2006, pp. 35–43

Ross, James

b. 1816

The Edinburgh firm of Ross & Thomson was among the most widely admired photographic businesses in the 1850s. However, Ross had made his own reputation before he met JOHN THOMSON. A native of Aberdeenshire, Thomson established himself as a portrait painter in Edinburgh about 1840, and by 1844 he had expanded his offerings to landscapes. In about 1842 Ross began experimenting with the calotype in conjunction with ROBERT BISHOP, a chemist friend, and was appalled to find his first print literally fading in his hands soon after he developed it. Months of hard work followed until he had mastered the process. In 1846, just as ROBERT ADAMSON was nearing the end of his short life, Ross established his calotype studio in the National Monument on Calton Hill in Edinburgh. Ross then formed a partnership with Thomson, offering calotype and daguerreotype portraits, plain and colored, and views of gentlemen's mansions, as well as instructions, apparatus, and supplies. At first the two men retained separate identities, with Thomson listed as the daguerreotypist and Ross as the calotypist. By 1848 they had moved to Princes Street and from that point their firm flourished, especially after being appointed in 1849 "Photographers to the Queen in Scotland," the first to be so named. By 1851, Ross & Thomson was simply listed as a firm of calotypists. This can be misleading in the literature, for by then, although it paid a proud nod to the Talbotype label, it employed mostly albumen on glass negatives to great public acclaim. The firm exhibited prolifically and constantly, starting with the Great

Exhibition in 1851 through to the 1864 Photographic Society exhibition in London, but none of the exhibited work was from paper negatives. Ross was a genial fellow who had a reputation among his peers for an intense love of art and constant striving for perfection. He was appointed a member of the council of the Photographic Society of Scotland and participated actively in their meetings. In later years, because Ross had kept his old financial ledgers, he was able to recall in detail orders from printsellers, CHARLES PIAZZI SMYTH and many others; in 1849 Ross had paid for a series of lessons in calotype. As Thomson started to ease himself into retirement, the firm took on Thomas Pringle and eventually became Ross & Pringle. Ross retired in 1878, turning his business over to Pringle, and disappeared from the photographic scene.

EXHIBITED: 1853, Aberdeen, Mechanics' Institution

REFERENCES: James Ross and John Thomson, *A Few Plain Answers to Common Questions Regarding Photography* (Edinburgh, 1853); "The Substance of a Paper Read by Mr. J. Ross before the Photographic Society of Scotland, April 14th, 1857," *Photographic Notes* 2 (October 1, 1857), pp. 361–64; Ross, "A Few Extracts from a Photographer's Old Ledger," *BJP* 20 (February 14, 1873), pp. 75–77; John Nicol, "Notes from the North," *BJP* 25 (December 27, 1878), p. 617

Ross, Justine Henrietta

1815–1894

The wife of HORATIO ROSS, Henrietta, née Macrae, may not have shared his passion for shooting but was more enthusiastic about photography. In the 1858 Photographic Society of Scotland exhibition in Edinburgh she showed *A Photographer in His Studio*, presumably a study of her husband. In the British Association for the Advancement of Science exhibition in Aberdeen the following year she submitted a waxed-paper landscape of her native Scottish Highlands. She outlived her husband by eight years.

EXHIBITED: 1859, Aberdeen, British Association for the Advancement of Science

REFERENCE: Paschal Downs, "'The Delight of Their Existence': The Photography of Horatio Ross of Rossie (1801–86)," *Studies in Photography*, 2006, pp. 35–43

Ross, Thomas

In the 1857 exhibition of the Birmingham Photographic Society, a Captain Oakes submitted three Talbotype views of architectural details taken in Portugal, credited only to "Major Ross." The lender was probably the calotypist, THOMAS OAKES. In this period the only navy captain named Ross was Sir James Clark Ross of Antarctic fame, an unlikely candidate. However, the army listed Major Thomas Ross in its 73rd Regiment of Foot. In 1852 the regiment was dispatched to reinforce the army in the Kaffir War in South Africa, but its ship struck rocks just outside Cape Town and sank in less than ten minutes. The soldiers established the practice of women and children first into the lifeboats, and the loss of life was great. The remnants of the 73rd finally returned to their base in England in 1860, and Ross may well have had the opportunity to calotype in Portugal. That may not have been his last photography. In the 1860 Photographic Society of Madras exhibition, Major Thomas Ross of the 73rd exhibited sixteen large views from collodion negatives. The reviewer in Madras was critical of the blurred figures in some of Ross's photographs, but conceded that "the atmospheric effect . . . is well rendered."

EXHIBITED: 1857, Birmingham, Photographic Society; Madras, 1860, Photographic Society

REFERENCE: *Madras Journal of Literature and Science*, no. 11 (May 1861), pp. 192–93

Rosse, Mary

1813–1885

In nineteenth-century Europe, serious amateur scientific installations were highly valued, especially in the field of astronomy. Birr Castle, in Ireland, contained one of the most important. William Parsons, the Earl of Rosse, had built there the largest telescope in the world, one familiarly known as "The Leviathan," and his wife, Mary, née Field, had participated in its design and construction. Lord Rosse had started daguerreotyping in 1842 and had known TALBOT through scientific circles. In 1853, when Mary, Countess of Rosse, was expecting her eleventh child, she decided it was time to take up photography herself. Earl Rosse wrote to Talbot on February 2, 1854, "Lady Rosse has just commenced photography, and I enclose a few specimens of her first attempts." Talbot replied that he was highly impressed with her "details of the telescope which are all that can be desired." Lady Rosse's work was from waxed-paper negatives, a process in which she was soon to be an expert and one she continued to favor. She became a member of the Dublin Photographic Society in 1856 and received a silver medal "for the best paper negative" from the Photographic Society of Ireland in 1859. Mary Rosse's library contained at least three books on the waxed-paper process and an original of Talbot's *The Pencil of Nature*. Birr Castle is unusual in that large parts of its heritage, including significant relics from Mary Rosse's photographic activities, survive to this day.

EXHIBITED: 1865, Dublin, International Exhibition

REFERENCES: William Parsons (Earl of Rosse) to W. H. F. Talbot, February 2, 1854, Talbot Collection, British Library, London, LA54-05 (Talbot Correspondence Project, http://foxtalbot.dmu.ac.uk, doc. no. 06909); Talbot to Parsons, February 5, 1854, Birr Scientific Heritage Foundation / Earl of Rosse Ireland (Talbot Correspondence Project, doc. no. 06914); David H. Davidson, *Impressions of an Irish Countess: The Photography of Mary, Countess of Rosse, 1813–1885* ([Birr]: Birr Scientific Heritage Foundation, 1989)

Rowe, Josiah

1809–1871

When Josiah Rowe displayed some of his early works at an 1856 meeting of the Photographic Society of Bengal, they were cited in the society's *Journal* as "creditable specimens of the rare skill of the oldest photographer in Calcutta." Rowe moved to India sometime before 1839 and began making daguerreotypes in the 1840s. In the 1856 exhibition of the Photographic Society of Madras he showed, as noted by the *Indian Journal of Art, Science and Manufacture*, five "calotype views of different parts of Calcutta, all of them clearly focused, well printed and of a good tone." Rowe might have been darkly amused at the article's criticism that he placed his horizon too high in these photographs—"the lines of perspective in consequence too sudden and angular in the foreground to be pleasing"—for that same year he had been appointed professor of drawing and surveying at Presidency College, Calcutta. Surprisingly, he continued to employ the daguerreotype throughout the 1850s alongside his paper and collodion work, including panoramas and views of shipping. Rowe was elected to the committee of the Photographic Society of Bengal in 1862.

EXHIBITED: 1856, Madras, Photographic Society

REFERENCES: *Indian Journal of Art, Science and Manufacture*, 2nd ser., 1 (1856), p. 175; *Journal of the Photographic Society of Bengal*, no. 2 (January 21, 1857), p. 26

Ruck, William

b. 1812

When LEWIS GRIFFITHS wrote to the *Journal of the Photographic Society* in 1857 about the calotype process, he credited "Mr. Ruck, photographic artist, Cheltenham" with having the experience to solve his problems. In the 1859 directory Ruck listed himself as an artist, but by the time of the 1861 census he proudly styled himself a photographer. None of Ruck's work has been identified to date.

REFERENCE: Lewis R. Griffiths, "Calotype Process," *JPS* 3 (February 21, 1857), p. 225

S., T. W.

This photographer has yet to be identified. Five waxed-paper negatives were auctioned in 1976. Three were views of Whitby, annotated and dated September 1854 and two were studies of trees. "T.W.S." was written in ink on one of the group.

REFERENCE: Sale cat., Christie's, London, June 10, 1976, lot 37

Saddler, Mr.

In an 1854 meeting of the Liverpool Photographic Society, "the Chairman called attention to a beautiful slide for the calotype process by Mr. Saddler. It was made of ruby glass, and in exposing papers, the great advantage was that the slide was so made as to turn first one side and then the other, and thus take a second impression without removing the papers." In addition to this slide (a holder for the sensitized paper that was placed in the back of the camera just before use), Saddler "also exhibited a number of very successful wet-paper landscape photographs and explained the process by which they were taken." His identity has not been established nor any of his work traced.

REFERENCE: "Liverpool Photographic Society," *LPJ* 1 (June 10, 1854), p. 72

St. John, Jane Martha

1803–1882

Jane St. John, née Beach, who married a landed proprietor in Hampshire, became a distant relative of photographer JOHN DILLWYN LLEWELYN through the marriage of her eldest brother. He was the grandfather of Carolyn Beach, who married John Talbot Dillwyn Llewelyn, the eldest son of the family. Through that connection, she met TALBOT's relatives. This tangled family tree brought her regularly into the country houses that served as centers of amateur photography. St. John worked in both calotype and collodion, taking portraits, views in Italy, and scenes of the grounds of the houses. In an undated letter to Talbot's cousin, EMMA LLEWELYN, she commented on her Italian negatives; some were fine and some so bad they were worthless to print from. Unlike many amateurs, she prided herself on making her own prints. Dashing to and from the camera during a long exposure, she attempted a self-portrait in front of the Colosseum. St. John was particularly fond of her "picturesque" view of Salerno.

REFERENCE: Jane St. John to Emma Llewelyn, undated letter, Llewelyn family archives

Sanford, John Charlie

b. 1812

Sanford was originally a partner in the London wholesale and retail stationers firm of Bowen & Sanford. By the time of the Great Exhibition of 1851 he had established his own business, and soon he turned to the blossoming trade of supplying specialty papers to photographers. By 1853, according to an advertisement, Sanford stocked "some of the best papers" for photographers, including Whatman's and Turner's and ones of his own make. He offered papers iodized for the Talbotype, waxed for Gustave Le Gray's process, and salted by John Stewart's air-pump process; he also established a separate printing establishment for making positives. His offerings continued to expand, and by 1856 he listed himself solely as a "photographic stationer." Sanford actively used his own products, undoubtedly bringing him both personal satisfaction and credibility with his customers. In the 1852, 1854, and 1855 Society of Arts exhibitions he submitted many of his own waxed-paper architectural views, along with prints from negatives by others (presumably his customers). Similarly, in the Photographic Society of London's exhibitions in 1854 and 1855 he displayed his personal mastery of the art. His waxed-paper views shown in the 1854 exhibition of the Liverpool Photographic Society were admired, as the society's journal wrote, for their "large size and elaborate detail." Obviously, he was in a position to chose any process he wanted, but waxed-paper was his favorite. The heyday of paper photography coincided with the peak years of his firm. By the time of the 1861 census he called himself a "paper manufacturer."

EXHIBITED: 1852, London, Society of Arts; 1854, London, Photographic Society; 1854, 1854, Dundee, Royal Infirmary Fund; 1854, second touring exhibition, Society of Arts (London); 1854, Liverpool, Photographic Society; 1855, London, Photographic Society; 1855–56, third touring exhibition, Society of Arts (London); 1858, London, Photographic Society

REFERENCE: *LPJ* 1 (October 14, 1854), p. 139

Sawyer, John Robert Mather

1828–1889

The Norwich Photographic Society, founded in 1854, was one of the first and among the most active of the early associations of photographers. It attracted early photographers like Sawyer, a surgical instrument maker. Starting his photographic work in 1853, Sawyer became one of the few carte-de-visite photographers to actively seek quality rather than low cost. In the society's 1856 exhibition, Sawyer displayed collodion portraits and three waxed-paper architectural views. By 1869, Sawyer, who was concerned by the lack of permanence in photography, had taken up collotype. In 1871 he moved to London and joined the Photographic Society, publishing frequently in its *Transactions*. Sawyer's contemporaries remembered him not so much for his original research as for being an "earnest and indefatigable worker" who delighted in adapting photographic science to practical use. In recognition of his dedication, he was named the director of the Autotype Company, the premier publisher of photographs in permanent ink.

EXHIBITED: 1856, Norwich, Photographic Society

REFERENCE: *Photographic Journal* 18 (February 21, 1890), p. 105 (obituary)

Scott, Charles

1824–1892

The son of a purser in the Royal Navy, Scott received a classical and mathematical education, went to a military seminary, and was accepted by the Royal Engineering Establishment at Chatham for field instruction in the arts of sapping and mining. He arrived in Bombay in 1844 and rose through the ranks of military engineering in several posts through 1870. His travels left him well placed to observe the landscape and architecture of India. By the 1850s, like many British based in India, Scott had turned to amateur photography. His work, little known today, seems to have been extensive. In 1860 the London publisher J. Hogarth began issuing original prints made from Scott's paper negatives. Seven prints were in the series *Views in the Island of Bombay*, five in *Views of the Caves of Karlee . . . and of the adjacent Temple of Ambernath*, nine in *Views in the Old Fort of Bassein*, and ten in *Views on the Bhore Ghaut, shewing some of the Railway Cuttings*. The last group implies a strong, logical link between his professional work and the opportunity to observe photographic subjects.

Scott, William Elliot

1811–1901

The descendant of an ancient Scottish clan at Arkleton and an Edinburgh-based Writer to the Signet (a member of a distinguished legal society), Scott was an early member of the Photographic Society of Scotland and showed two calotypes in its 1856 exhibition. One was a view of North Street in St. Andrews, and the other was of cottages in Dumfriesshire. Nothing else is known of his photographic work.

EXHIBITED: Edinburgh, 1856, Photographic Society of Scotland

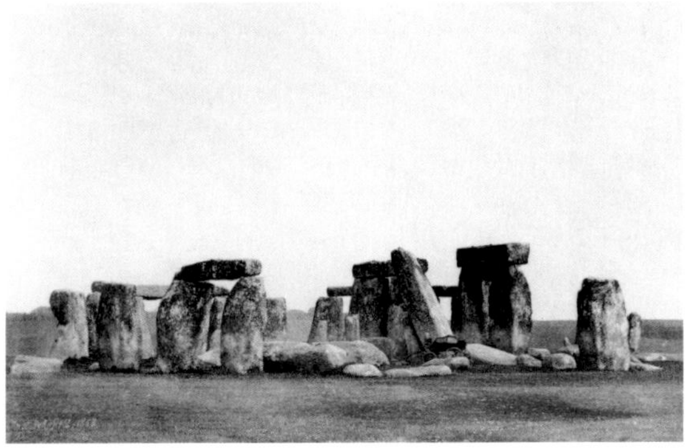

97. William Russell Sedgfield

Sedgfield, William Russell *ill. 97*

1826–1902

Sedgfield was born in Devizes, just a few miles from Lacock Abbey, shortly before TALBOT moved back into his family home. There is no evidence they ever met, but later Russell Sedgfield (as he styled himself) would remember his unhappy brush with the calotype patent at age sixteen. About 1842 he started making photographs with MUNGO PONTON's bichromate process and asked ROBERT HUNT about using the calotype as an amateur. On Hunt's advice, Sedgfield wrote to Talbot, but in reply he got a demand from Talbot's solicitor that he apply for an expensive license. Two decades later Sedgfield confessed that after observing some more prominent figures "refusing to have a license, I straightaway went and got a camera, and proceeded in my experiments, hoping that, as I was scarcely safe for costs, Mr. Talbot would begin with some of those more distinguished amateurs." Sedgfield established himself in London as an engraver on wood but continued to practice his photography. Sometime after 1851 he shifted professions. At the start of 1854, Samuel Highley (soon to become the first editor of the *British Journal of Photography*) advertised a "Photographic Exhibition" of Sedgfield's views. Highly soon published four parts of Sedgfield's *Photographic Delineations of the Scenery, Architecture and Antiquities of Great Britain and Ireland*, and a lifelong career was launched. Sedgfield showed ten waxed-paper architectural views in the 1854 exhibition of the Royal Infirmary Fund in Dundee and twice that number in the exhibition of the Photographic Society of London that year. From that point on, Sedgfield exhibited with regularity, continuing to use waxed paper for his architectural views through at least 1858. He was so accomplished in waxed paper that during an 1854 meeting of the Liverpool Photographic Society, as reported in its journal that March, a debate broke out between two members who could not believe the quality of Sedgwick's view of a church at Salisbury; it was so sharp that "the doggerel poetry could be read on the tomb-stones." Sedgwick became a member of the Norwich Photographic Society, bringing him into contact with some of the most active amateurs. However, Sedgfield had firmly committed to a photographic studio in London, and commercial realities began to influence his art. He began taking portraits on collodion, a technique that would soon dominate his business. In the 1860s he turned to the newly popular stereo views, photographing some of his favored architecture in this medium. Sedgfield, who had been deaf since childhood, remained a professional photographer until about 1890.

EXHIBITED: 1854, London, Photographic Society; 1854, Dundee, Royal Infirmary Fund; 1854, second touring exhibition, Society of Arts (London); 1855, London, Photographic Society; 1855, London, Photographic Institution; 1855–56, third touring exhibition, Society of Arts (London); 1856, Manchester, Photographic Society; 1856, Edinburgh, Photographic Society of Scotland; 1858, London, Photographic Society

REFERENCES: *LPJ* 1 (March 11, 1854), p. 38; William Russell Sedgfield, "The Recent Meeting of the Photographic Society," *Photographic News* 5 (February 15, 1861), pp. 81–82; Hardwicke Knight, "Russell Sedgfield: The Complete Photographer," *History of Photography* 1 (October 1977), pp. 301–12

Shadbolt, George

1830–1901

As a youth, Shadbolt was captivated by the announcements of Daguerre and TALBOT. Finding the daguerreotype too expensive to attempt, he remembered in his 1864 "Valedictory and Introduction" in the *British Journal of Photography*, his "gratification of being enabled to repeat the experiments of the latter." With a smattering of chemistry, he "entered enthusiastically into the idea of investigating the phenomena of photogenic action." His first darkroom was his father's wine cellar, which was illuminated by a candle. Shadbolt vividly recalled "the subsequent triumph when . . . the first impressions of leaves and lace and flowers were produced, and fixed (!) . . . how they were shown to admiring friends, and preserved as 'pearls of great price.'" Shadbolt entered his father's timber business but remained active as an amateur photographer, taking a great interest in lenses and becoming a pioneer in microphotography. In both the 1854 Royal Infirmary Fund exhibition in Dundee and the Photographic Society exhibition in London he showed waxed-paper and calotype architectural views and portraits. He continued to exhibit frequently, turning to collodion. However impressive his photographs were, more important was the role Shadbolt played in the acceptance of photography. He was one of the founders of the Photographic Society in London and in 1857 became the first editor of the *London and Manchester Photographic Journal*, which evolved into the widely influential *British Journal of Photography*. In his editorial capacity Shadbolt finally made actual his youthful ambition of "reading every scrap that was published relative" to photography. Ill health and the demands of his commercial business forced him to give up research in photography. In 1864, in one of his last acts as editor, Shadbolt wrote to TALBOT, addressing him as "one to whom photographers owe in eternal debt of gratitude." On his retirement from the *British Journal of Photography* he was widely praised in its pages (July 1865) as "a scholar and a man of science" and was given a silver epergne by his friends. On his death thirty-six years later, pronounced the same journal in his obituary, there were "photographers still living who speak in terms of the highest appreciation of the late Mr. Shadbolt's great ability as an editor and a student of photographic science."

EXHIBITED: 1854, London, Photographic Society; 1854, Dundee, Royal Infirmary Fund

REFERENCES: George Shadbolt to W. H. F. Talbot, April 7, 1864, Talbot Collection, British Library, London, LA64-26 (Talbot Correspondence Project, http://foxtalbot.dmu.ac.uk, doc. no. 08817); Shadbolt "Valedictory and Introduction," *BJP* 11 (June 15, 1864), pp. 199–200; "Presentation to Mr. Shadbolt," *BJP* 12 (July 7, 1865), p. 350; *BJP* 48 (June 21, 1901), p. 391 (obituary); *BJPA*, 1902, pp. 688–89 (obituary)

Shaw, A.

d. ca. 1854

Sometimes an early photographer's record hangs by a thread. In September 1854, FRANCIS EDMOND CURREY, the Duke of Devonshire's land agent for estates in Ireland, received a letter from a friend, known only as "A. Shaw," from Waterford, Ireland. Shaw wrote that he had trouble with collodion and was going to "iodise some paper & try calotype again." Apparently, this was in preparation for a journey, one he never made. Currey annotated the letter with a note about Shaw's tragic death not long after.

REFERENCE: Sale cat., Sotheby's, London, March 27, 1981, lot 168 (letter from A. Shaw to Francis Edmond Currey, September 3, 1854)

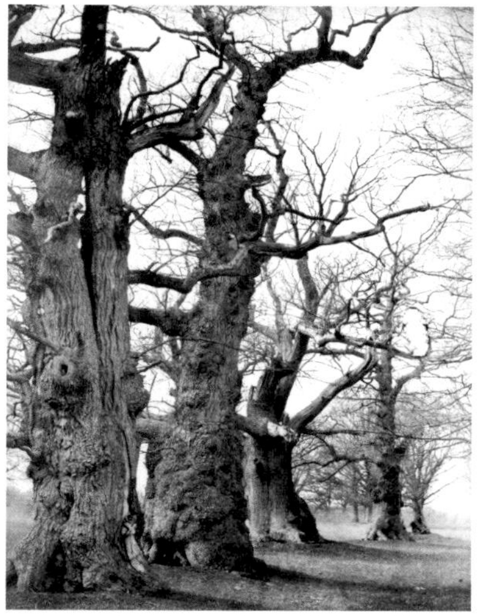

98. George Shaw

Shaw, George *ill. 98*
1818–1904
Shaw was an exceptional character in the thriving industrial city of Birmingham. The son of a glass seller and sickly in his youth, he was largely self-taught. He was so successful that at the age of twenty he was appointed the professor of chemistry at Queen's College in that city. Shaw's vocation was working as a patent agent, which brought him into contact with all the latest scientific and technical advances. He became widely known to the scientists of his day and was fascinated by archaeology. His *Manual of Electro-Metallurgy*, a pioneering publication, went through several editions. Possessed of an intense interest in art, he formed a collection of engravings by J. W. M. Turner and was a capable watercolorist. In early 1844 Shaw undertook a series of lectures on photography at the Birmingham Philosophical Institution. He wrote to TALBOT, explaining that he had tried calotype earlier and asking permission to make a public demonstration of the process. Talbot was fully supportive and sent him two groups of his latest photographs to exhibit. Shaw wrote that he found them "particularly beautiful" and noted that although he himself had made some "excellent negative pictures," good prints from them eluded him. In 1849 he was joint secretary of the Arts and Industrial Exhibition held in Birmingham, and he served as a juror in both the 1851 Great Exhibition and the 1862 International Exhibition. By the time of the 1852 Society of Arts Exhibition in London, Shaw was able to exhibit a number of scenic views made with paper negatives. In 1853, JOSEPH CUNDALL published two volumes of Shaw's *Photographic Studies*; they did not impress the *Athenaeum*. Shaw continued to contribute to exhibitions, showing seven Talbotype views as late as 1857 at the Birmingham Photographic Society. His calotypes of trees are outstanding examples. Shaw was remembered in his obituary as "a brilliant conversationalist . . . always willing to impart information to others, and he possessed the marvellous faculty of being able to render abstruse subjects clear to the understanding of uninstructed persons."

EXHIBITED: 1852, London, Society of Arts; 1853, London, Photographic Institution; 1855, London, Photographic Institution; 1857, Birmingham, Photographic Society

REFERENCES: George Shaw to Talbot, January 29, 1844, Talbot Collection, British Library, London, LA44-02 (Talbot Correspondence Project, http://foxtalbot.dmu.ac.uk, doc. no. 04926); "Fine Arts," *Athenaeum*, December 24, 1853, p. 1559; *Birmingham Daily Post*, August 15, 1904 (obituary)

Shaw, T.
Nothing is presently known of T. Shaw other than the exhibition of three waxed-paper views of India shown in 1860 at the Photographic Society in London. They were listed as "specimens of the Tinting Printing Process, printed in 1854."

EXHIBITED: 1860, London, Photographic Society

Shelley, Blanche Henrietta Johnes
1841–1898
The extent to which photography rapidly became parlor entertainment is not fully appreciated. One young practitioner was Blanche Shelley. She was very distantly related to TALBOT through his half sister, Caroline Mount Edgcumbe. Shelley's family was drawn into this circle in 1834, so her childhood years were ripe with the possibility of being exposed to the new art. At thirteen she made her one known surviving photograph, *Ferns and Daffodil*, dated 1854. Two decades later, under her married name of Pechell, she published a children's story, *Fernseed; or, The Woodland Fairy*.

REFERENCE: Blanche Pechell [Blanche Henrietta Johnes Shelley], *Fernseed; or The Woodland Fairy*, in *Stories for Our Girls, by Friendly Writers*, no. 3 (London: Hatchards, 1876)

Shepherd, G.
In the early 1980s dozens of highly competent waxed-paper negatives emerged in several auctions, many of them signed "G. Shepherd." Taken in Dover, Canterbury, and Hastings, they depicted urban scenes, ecclesiastical architecture, and coastal views. The tentative attribution made at the time was to George Sidney Shepherd (1802–1861), a watercolor artist. He, however, signed his paintings "Geo. Sidney Shepherd," "George Sidney Shepherd," "Geo. S. Shepherd," or "G.S.S." There were a number of other painters at the time named George Shepherd, and of course, the photographer may have been an amateur who was not a painter. The only other clues at present are that one view of Hastings (printed in albumen from a paper negative) was dated 1851 and one street scene September 8, 1854.

REFERENCES: J. F. C. Phillips, *Shepherd's London* (London: Cassell, 1976); sale cat., Sotheby's, London, March 27, 1981, lots 358, 359; sale cats., Christie's, London, October 29, 1981, lot 159, March 28, 1985, lot 136, June 27, 1985, lot 131, and October 31, 1985, lot 177

Sheridan, James Peter
d. 1861
In April 1861 the *British Journal of Photography* noted the death, "suddenly, at his residence, the Estanci de los Sajoues, Buenos Ayres, James Peter Sheridan, Esq., formerly a member of the Liverpool Photographic Society, and an ardent photographer in the waxed-paper process." Sheridan was born in Ireland and married an English woman in 1845. In 1851 he got his first instruction in waxed-paper photography from JAMES HOW, manager of the London firm of Knight's. In 1854 Sheridan was active in the newly formed Liverpool Photographic Society. He favored subjects of ecclesiastical architecture, ranging from Glasgow to Chester and using How's process. In the 1854 exhibition at the Royal Institution in Liverpool he showed *Skipton Station*, *Ilkley Castle*, *Bolton Abbey*, and other waxed-paper views. James Alexander Forrest, a fellow photographer, observed in 1888 that Sheridan "was a great lover of nature" and "was home in this country for some years, during which time he visited every place of note in England." At one meeting of the Liverpool Photographic Society, Sheridan good-naturedly said he "would be happy to break a lance with Mr. Berry, and I will undertake to take more pictures on wax-paper within a given time than he by collodion." HENRY HELE praised Sheridan's loyalty to the medium, asserting that "the followers of the wax-paper process must feel themselves greatly indebted" to him. Sadly, Sheridan died on a steamer that caught fire on the way to Argentina. Forrest remembered him as "greatly respected by every member of the Society—a gifted Irishman, and one of 'nature's noblemen.'"

Exhibited: 1854, Liverpool, Photographic Society

References: Henry Hele, letter in *LPJ* 1 (October 14, 1854), p. 129; *LJP* 8 (April 1, 1861), p. 135 (obituary); James Alexander Forrest, "Historical Notes of What Liverpool Has Done in the Art-Science of Photography," *BJP* 35 (February 3, 1888), pp. 72–74

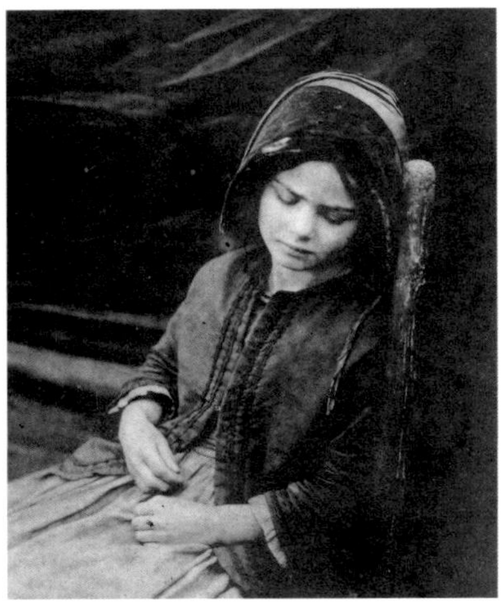

99. William Sherlock

Sherlock, William *ill. 99*

b. 1813

In 1842, Sherlock approached TALBOT to secure a license to practice the calotype commercially in London. Talbot was still supporting HENRY COLLEN, to whom he had granted a commercial license with exclusive rights, so the negotiations failed. On September 15, 1843, Sherlock sent along with a letter various examples to Talbot "taken in from 20 to 25 seconds with a favorable light but bad apparatus." Sherlock was learning on his own, for, as he wrote on November 15, he was "quite unaware of the time usually occupied in taking a portrait never having exchanged a word with anyone acquainted with the art or derived any knowledge upon the subject except from the Edinburgh Review and my own perseverance but I feel confident that at another season of the year I could take a portrait in from 5 to 10 seconds." By November his technique had advanced to the point where he could enclose three calotype portraits. Since Talbot refused to license him in London, Sherlock suggested Bristol, Liverpool, and Dublin as possible alternative locations, all without success. Persisting, in September 1844 he sent Talbot a two-print panorama. Sherlock then tried to join in business with NICOLAAS HENNEMAN in London, writing to Talbot in March 1846, "In the formation of your projected Establishment I yet hope there may be some situation in which I may be found useful." Nothing came of this, unless some of the unidentified negatives in Talbot's archives are by him. Having been a solicitor in London in the early 1840s, Sherlock moved to Devon later in the decade. At the time of the 1851 census he was visiting his father-in-law (a professor of music) in London and still listed his profession as attorney at law. About this time, like ROGER FENTON before him, Sherlock decided to give up on the law and to make his life in photography. In the 1852 Society of Arts exhibition in London, Sherlock was one of the major contributors, showing more than forty paper views of architecture, landscape, and portraiture. He was so well known by 1853 that PAULINE TREVELYAN referred to him in her diary as "Sherlock the Calotypist." Sherlock was a regular contributor of paper negative views in various exhibitions through 1855, at which point he converted to collodion and continued to exhibit prolifically, forging a relationship with the London publisher J. Hogarth. The catalogue of the 1856 Norwich Photographic Society exhibition described one of his entries as "a pure photograph." It was shown in both its original form and a hand-colored version, and was proclaimed the "best in the room." Likewise, his cloud studies were called "extraordinary." In 1878 Sherlock's photographs won bronze, silver, and gold medals at the Paris International Exhibition. He continued to live in Devon through the 1881 census, where at sixty-eight he still identified himself as an active photographer. That is the last known record of him.

Exhibited: 1852, London, Society of Arts; 1853, London, Photographic Institution; 1853–54, first touring exhibition, Society of Arts (London); 1854, second touring exhibition, Society of Arts (London); 1855–56, third touring exhibition, Society of Arts (London)

References: William Sherlock to Talbot, September 15 and November 15, 1843, and March 2, 1846, Talbot Collection, British Library, London, LA43-79, LA43-86, and LA46-34 (Talbot Correspondence Project, http://foxtalbot.dmu.ac.uk, doc. nos. 04879, 04896, and 05593); Ken Jacobsen, *Étude d'après Nature: 19th Century Photographs in Relation to Art* (Petches Bridge: Ken & Jenny Jacobson, 1996), pp. 179–81; Larry J. Schaaf, *Sun Pictures, Catalogue Fifteen: From Talbot to Turner* (New York: Hans P. Kraus, Jr., 2006), pp. 42–43

Sherrington, John

Sherrington, who was from a prominent Catholic family in Preston, Lancashire, was ruined in a bank failure and emigrated to Rotterdam with his family in 1838. His daughter, Helen Lemmens-Sherrington (1834–1906), became a well-known singer. Twenty calotypes, some signed in the negative "J. Sherrington/fecit," survive in the RICHARD WILLATS album; about half are portraits and half are architectural views of Rotterdam. Some are dated 1845 and 1847, and one is titled *Ruins after a Fire of a Theatre, Rotterdam.* Those signed "Sherrington, esq." may be by him or by W. SHERRINGTON. Nothing further is known about their photographic work.

References: Richard Willats Photograph Album, Princeton University Library; "Memorabilia," *Notes and Queries*, September 29, 1934, p. 217

Sherrington, W.

Although this photographer's identity has not been firmly established, he was possibly a brother of the famous singer Helen Lemmens-Sherrington (1834–1906), whose father, JOHN SHERRINGTON, moved his family to Rotterdam in 1838. Two calotype views of the docks of Rotterdam carry inscriptions that date them to 1845 and credit them to W. Sherrington. There are Sherrington photographs in the RICHARD WILLATS album without an initial, so it is possible that some work attributed to John was actually done by W. Sherrington. Nothing further is known of his work.

Shipperdson, Edward

Within the wide-ranging displays in the 1843 Polytechnic Exhibition hosted by the Durham Mechanics' Institute, Shipperdson contributed a *Photogenic Portrait.* The most likely candidate by this name was a mining engineer and coal entrepreneur in South Bailey, Durham, but at present nothing else is known about him or about any other of his photographic works.

Exhibited: 1843, Durham, Mechanics' Institute

Shortt, John Macourtrie

b. 1803

The son of a solicitor, Shortt came from landed gentry in a well-established Dumfriesshire family and received a classical education. Very little else is known about him except for his service as a major general in the Bombay

Army. At least four waxed-paper negatives and two albumen prints from other waxed-paper negatives, accompanied by an 1867 manuscript, survive in the Museum of the History of Science, Oxford. The subjects are all architecture in India. Shortt attended the funeral of Patrick Dudgeon of Cargen, and it is possible that his interest in photography was nurtured when he was back in his native Dumfries.

Sidebotham, Joseph

1824–1885

The son of a mill manager, Sidebotham was apprenticed to a calico printer in Manchester. He began to demonstrate his many talents early in life, making a working steam engine at fifteen and then taking classes in natural history at the Manchester Mechanics' Institute. It was there that Sidebotham met the celebrated optician J. B. Dancer, and it is likely that through him became interested in photography. About 1846, Sidebotham became close friends with the engineer James Nasmyth, and the relationship mutually reinforced not only their astronomical interests but also their photographic ones. That same year Sidebotham became a partner in a calico printing firm that specialized in a particular shade of red. Sidebotham's comprehensive and practical understanding of chemistry was very useful in his photographic experiments. In 1852 Sidebotham was elected to membership in the prestigious Manchester Literary and Philosophical Society, further strengthening his ties with Dancer and Nasmyth. Sidebotham's earliest known calotypes are from the mid-1840s, but he is best known for his exquisite mastery of the waxed-paper process in the 1850s. When the Manchester Photographic Society was formed in 1855, Sidebotham was elected its honorary secretary. He contributed eighteen waxed-paper architectural views to its first exhibition. About 1856 Sidebotham formed a close working relationship with JAMES MUDD, and the two men photographed together. Not long afterward, like many amateurs, Sidebotham converted to collodion. He had made his first ambrotype in 1853. In the 1860s Sidebotham contributed a variety of articles to the photographic journals, ranging from technical treatises to a commentary on perspective. In 1865 he was an important conduit for information from his friend CHARLES PIAZZI SMYTH, then engaged in a controversial study of the Great Pyramid. Before Smyth's departure, Sidebotham had worked with him on problems of measurement and illumination. In ill health, Sidebotham retired from calico printing in 1877 and lived off the proceeds of a colliery.

EXHIBITED: 1856, Manchester, Photographic Society

REFERENCES: *BJP* 32 (June 5, 1885), pp. 358–59 (obituary); Joseph Sidebotham, "On the Waxed Paper Process," *Photographic Notes* 1 (February 25, 1856), p. 5; Leo H. Grindon, *Joseph Sidebotham: A Memoir* (Manchester: Palmer and Howe, 1886)

Simpson, Alexander

b. 1823

The son of a merchant in Aberdeen, Lieutenant Simpson received a classical and mathematical education from Marischal College and from the Edinburgh Military Academy. He entered the Bengal Artillery in 1842. How his interest in photography was stimulated is not known, but in 1862 he joined the Photographic Society of Bengal. He collaborated with JOHN BURNIE DICKSON in photographically copying paintings for the geologist Sir Henry Yule's *Narrative of the Mission Sent by the Governor-General of India to the Court of Ava in 1855*, a critical work in Burmese historical studies.

REFERENCE: Henry Yule, *A Narrative of the Mission Sent by the Governor-General of India to the Court of Ava in 1855, with Notices of the Country, Government, and People* (London: Smith, Elder and Co., 1858)

Sims, Thomas

1826–1910

Inspired by the new art growing up around him but short on financial resources, Sims made a camera with cigar boxes and fitted it with a simple meniscus lens. On September 20, 1847, after many trials, he finally recorded his first successful negative. Sims met ROBERT HUNT and heard Antoine Claudet lecture at the British Association for the Advancement of Science meeting in his hometown of Swansea in 1845. Four years later he married Frances, the sister of Alfred Wallace, the famous naturalist, and later did photographic work for him. Wallace owned a whole-plate daguerreotype apparatus purchased in Paris, to which Sims, as quoted by Ernest Ashton, "became literally a slave for years." He attempted opening a daguerreotype studio in Weston-super-Mare, found it unproductive, and moved his studio to the grounds of the Natural History Museum in Swansea. During the 1840s the calotype and the daguerreotype both interested him, but, starting with his entry in the 1852 Society of Arts exhibition, he turned to collodion negatives in order to combine the detail of the metal process with the convenience and versatility of paper. Sims opened a studio near Regent's Park in London in 1853 and promptly heard from TALBOT's attorneys that he was infringing on Talbot's patent and would be prosecuted. Sims closed his studio, and his own case never made it to court. The acquittal of Sylvester LaRoche, who worked in collodion, effectively broke Talbot's patent, and Sims soon reopened his studio. In 1868 he moved to Tunbridge Wells, continuing as a photographer until the end of his life. As Ashton wrote in his 1930 memoir, "Sims was a man of great energy in worldly affairs, and was also an exceedingly active experimenter in the photographic processes of the very earliest days." The memoir drew on Sims's manuscript autobiography and a "large quantity of manuscripts . . . together with many specimens of photographic work." Sadly, this archive, potentially a rich source of information on early photography, is not known to have survived past this point.

REFERENCES: Ernest R. Ashton, "Memoirs of a Photographic Pioneer," *BJP* 77 (June 13, 1930), pp. 353–55; Edgar Yoxall Jones, "The Calotype," *Photography* 4 (May 1969), p. 537; "Thomas Sims (1826–1910)," *Photohistorian*, no. 94 (Autumn 1991), pp. 82–83

Sisson, Joseph Lawson, Jr.

b. 1816

In 1861 the editor of the *Photographic News* wrote an unusual "Valedictory" for the Reverend Joseph Lawson Sisson, "a gentleman whose name has been honourably connected with photography from the very first. His waxed paper process has yielded some of the finest results that have ever been produced in that direction." The editor quoted Sisson: "I have ceased to be a photographer, finding that the art demands more time than I have now at my disposal." One is tempted to assume that the writer was the Reverend Sisson, born in 1793 and the Gloucester author of several historical books. However, there are clues strongly suggesting that it was Joseph Lawson Jr., his son. Rev. Sisson exhibited collodion views of Edingthorpe, Norfolk, to the 1854 Photographic Society exhibition in London and the Royal Infirmary Fund Exhibition in Dundee that year. In the 1858 and 1861 architectural photographic exhibitions in London, Sisson's contributions were all views of Lausanne. Joseph Jr. was rector of Edingthorpe in the 1850s. He then took charge of the British Chapel at Lausanne. In 1858, Marion, the London photographic suppliers, published his booklet *The Turpentine Waxed-Paper Process, Described and Illustrated by the Rev. J Lawson Sisson.* His article on the turpentine waxed-paper process was written in Lausanne on March 15, 1860.

References: Joseph Lawson Sisson Jr., in *Photographic Notes* 4 (May 1, 1859), p. 123; Sisson, letter of March 15, 1860, in *Photographic News* 3 (March 23, 1860), pp. 351–52; "Valedictory," *Photographic News* 5 (October 25, 1861), p. 504; [Sisson], *The Turpentine Waxed-Paper Process, Described and Illustrated by the Rev. J Lawson Sisson* (London: Marion, 1858)

Smee, Alfred
1818–1877
Based in London, Smee took an early interest in chemistry and electricity, activities that remained a major part of his life even after he became a medical doctor in 1840. In the first months of 1839, Smee mastered the new art of photogenic drawing, using ammonio-nitrate of silver both in printing and in the camera obscura. His detailed account in the *Literary Gazette* was a critical step in bringing Talbot's first process into the wider range of chemistry. It was Smee's reduction of iron salts that inspired Sir John Herschel to pursue a line of experimentation that led to the invention of the cyanotype and related processes. Smee's father had been an accountant for the Bank of England, and perhaps that influence inspired Alfred's interest in bank notes. The bank started using his long-lasting black ink in 1842, and Smee's electroplating technique was adopted by the bank in 1853 to increase the longevity of the finely engraved printing plates. Smee's interest in photography was always more concerned with process than production, but he maintained his interest in the art. In 1854 Smee hosted a soiree for scientists and artists, displaying a wide range of stereoscopic views, including paintings, daguerreotypes, and paper photographs.

References: Alfred Smee, "Photogenic Drawing," *Literary Gazette*, May 18 and 25, 1839, pp. 314–16, 332; Elizabeth Mary Smee Odling, *Memoir of the Late Alfred Smee, F.R.S.* (London: George Bell and Sons, 1878)

Smith, James Cullen
Smith wrote to the newly established *Liverpool Photographic Journal* in 1854, describing his waxed-paper process that "gives most splendid blacks, and the half tints are very soft and fine, and incomparably quicker than any I have seen published." Three months later the astonished editor said he had heard from Smith that the process was a hoax. No motivation for this stunt was ever revealed, but Smith clearly understood the process of waxed-paper well enough to have been a practitioner.

References: James Cullen Smith, letters in *LPJ* 1 (October 14 and December 9, 1854), pp. 140, 153

Smith, John Buchanan
1805–1878
Smith was a drawing master in Blackheath, in the Greenwich area of London. He contributed waxed-paper views to the exhibitions of the Photographic Society in London in 1856 and 1857 and became a member by 1859. In 1846 Smith married a widow, Charlotte Melhuish, thereby gaining a stepson in Arthur James Melhuish. They lived together for some time, and Melhuish went on to become an important photographer. None of Smith's work is known to have survived.

Exhibited: 1856 and 1857, London, Photographic Society

Reference: Neal Rhind, *Blackheath Village and Environs, 1790–1870* (Blackheath: Bookshop Blackheath, 1983), vol. 2, p. 87

Smith, John Shaw *ills. 100, 101*
1811–1873
Smith is a true enigma. Born to Anglo-Irish landed gentry, he lived north of Dublin. He left few traces of his life, yet during a Grand Tour in 1850–52 he created one of the largest and best-documented bodies of calotype negatives, many of which survive. There is no record of how or why Smith learned the calotype process. His preparations for his 1850 trip were extensive, and it is apparent that he followed the newly developed guidebooks for tourists. His photographic work started in Paris and carried on in Italy, Malta, Greece, Egypt, Palestine, and Syria. His diaries map out everything except his personal experiences. Nearly 350 of his calotype negatives survive from this trip, and they are the work of a master with a mature command of the art. Photo historian Helmut Gernsheim claimed rightly that Smith's Egyptian work was "technically and artistically superior" to that of the well known master French calotypist Maxime Du Camp. Like many photographers, Smith opaqued the sky areas of his negatives to mask off the mottled appearance of the paper base. He then used this neutral ground to record extensive notes directly on the negative, preserving a historical record in ink on the originals that would not deface the prints. The negatives and prints were then carefully assembled in labeled groups. Not much more is known about Smith after he returned to Ireland. About 1854 he became a member of the Photographic Society in Dublin. Smith's only known publication was a brief article in 1857 in which he explained his "modifications of the wet-paper process by which I have been enabled with great certainty to obtain negatives of excellent quality in Eastern climes. . . ." His only known public showing, in

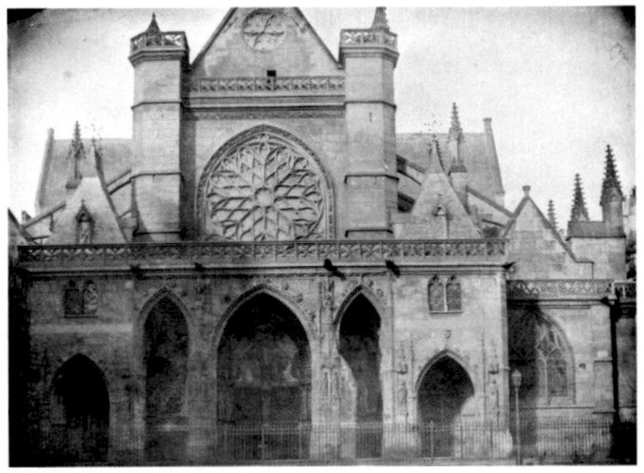

100. John Shaw Smith

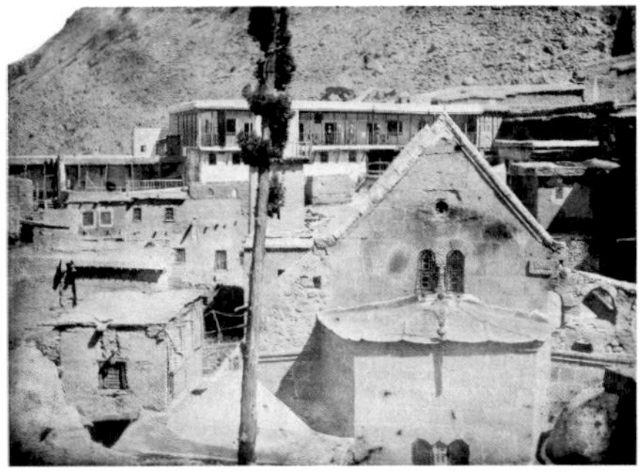

101. John Shaw Smith

the 1865 Dublin International Exhibition, received an honorable mention for "photographs from paper negatives." Smith's photographic work and journals were preserved by his descendants, but they made no attempt to preserve his memory. The *Times* reported at the beginning of 1873, "Mr. John Shaw Smith, who was possessed of considerable landed property in the county of Cork, committed suicide by shooting himself with a revolver at his residence."

Exhibited: 1865, Dublin, International Exhibition

References: John Shaw Smith, "Calotype or Wet-Paper Process," *JPS* 3 (April 21, 1857), p. 257; "Dublin Photographic Society," *LMPJ*, n.s., 1 (May 15, 1857), p. 101 (abstract of Smith's paper detailing his modifications of the calotype or wet paper process); *Times* (London), January 30, 1873, p. 10, col. E; Maria Antonella Pelizzari, "The Inclusive Map of John Shaw Smith's 1850–1852 Photographic Tour," *Visual Resources* 16 (2000), pp. 351–75

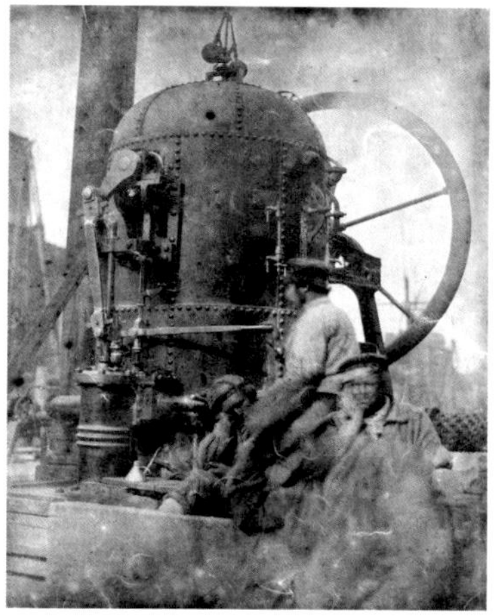

102. Samuel Smith

Smith, Samuel *ill. 102*
1802–1892
Born into a farming family, Smith rose from his humble beginnings through the textile trade. An inheritance from his father-in-law in 1847 freed him from a career in commerce, allowing him to pursue many interests. Known locally as "Philosopher Smith," he was a collector of natural history and a numismatist. Skilled with a lathe, he built microscopes and other instruments. Smith took up waxed-paper photography in 1852, documenting extensively the countryside and ruined abbeys of East Anglia for a period of at least twelve years. Active in his community, he was a director of the gasworks and a member of the committee set up to bring water to Wisbech. Smith's photographs of the river Nene were shown to Parliament as persuasive evidence of how this should be done.

References: Michael Millward and Brian Coe, *Victorian Townscape: The Work of Samuel Smith* (Woodstock, N.Y.: Overlook Books, 1977); William P. Weston, ed., *Samuel Smith's Wisbech: Then and Now, 1852–1992* (Wisbech: Friends of the Wisbech & Fenland Museum, 1992)

Smith, William Lyndon
1837–1865
Smith went by his middle name of Lyndon, probably to avoid confusion with his father, William W. Smith, his partner in a Leeds woolen firm. At the age of eighteen he began contributing to the photographic journals, already showing a mastery of the waxed-paper process. In 1855 he published his thoughts, in case "there are any photographers who still practise the wax-paper process, notwithstanding the current mania for tents and collodion," explaining how he practiced during a seven-month residence in France. It is not known what processes he used for his contributions to the 1857 Birmingham Photographic Society exhibition, but the numerous views of Heidelberg Castle and the Black Forest would have been more easily made with paper negatives. However, by the time of the 1857 Photographic Society exhibition in London, he, too, had succumbed to the lure of collodion. From that point forward, Smith was a regular contributor to the photographic exhibitions and, according to his obituary in *Photographic News*, "an amateur of much skill and artistic feeling." He received the first medal given by the Photographic Society of Scotland, for his *Rising Mist*, described in the *British Journal of Photography*'s obituary for him as a "striking advance in originality of conception on anything previously attempted." In January 1865 Smith gallantly went to the rescue of a young couple who had fallen through the ice while skating. He saved one of them but perished in the attempt. The photographic world remembered, in the last-mentioned obituary, his contributions to photographic science: "His style was clear and forcible, and the subjects which he treated were imbued with much interest."

References: William Lyndon Smith, "The Waxed-Paper Process," *JPS* 2 (July 21, 1855), p. 200; Smith, "Pyrogallic Acid in the Waxed-Paper Process," *JPS* 2 (January 21, 1856), p. 297; *Photographic News* 9 (January 27, 1865), pp. 47–48 (obituary); *BJP* 12 (January 27, 1865), p. 38 (obituary); Adrian Budge, *Early Photography in Leeds, 1839–1870*, exh. cat. (Leeds: Leeds City Art Galleries, 1981), p. 9

Smyth, Charles Piazzi
1819–1900
Piazzi Smyth, as he was universally known, would probably have rebelled at the thought of a being a laboratory experiment, but he is an ideal case study in the early history of the calotype. Born in Naples to Admiral William Henry Smyth, a close friend of Sir John Herschel, Smyth was able to balance this scientific heritage with the artistic sensibilities he got from his mother, Arabella, a fine painter. He was a clever sketch artist, devastating in his observations of his fellow man; a talented inventor of scientific instruments; and a tireless and careful researcher. His sister's scandalous marriage to the very much older scientist Baden Powell produced Robert Baden Powell, perhaps best remembered for founding the Boy Scouts. Smyth was a brilliant young man but a shy one with a stutter. Posted to South Africa as an astronomer's assistant, he was given the opportunity to be in close communication with Herschel during the late 1830s. Sir John returned to England on the eve of the public introduction of photography. As the events of 1839 unfolded, he sent examples and instructions to Smyth in the Cape, carefully compensating for what he knew would be the absence of certain materials in the colony. Herschel also opened up direct lines of communication between Talbot and other pioneers with Smyth. Thus, Smyth worked with the most complete instructions, both published and directly from the inventors, although isolated by three months and thousands of miles from other practitioners. He experimented on his own, following these directions, but without the interactions that influenced the course of photography in Europe. His calotypes produced around Cape Town are certainly the earliest ones made in Africa and also in many ways preserve the purest intent of the original inventors in Europe. In 1845 the young man was appointed to the prestigious but frustrating position of astronomer royal for Scotland, posted on Calton Hill immediately above Robert Adamson's calotype studio. In 1856, on the eve of his departure for Tenerife in the Canary Islands on an expedition designed to carry an astronomical telescope "above the clouds," Herschel recommended Smyth as "an excellent photographer" and suggested he document his trip. Smyth quickly learned wet-collodion photography from Joseph James Forrester and accomplished his goal. Although his scientific reputation will always be shadowed by his research in Egypt, which bore fruit in many publications on the Great Pyramid, Smyth was an innovative photographer throughout his life, constantly assisted by his wife, Jessie. Together they made metal cameras, designed high-speed shutters, enlarged miniature negatives, published photographically illustrated works, and ended life photographing clouds, much in a manner later popularized by Alfred Stieglitz. Although Smyth exhibited his scientific instruments, he never participated in photographic exhibitions.

References: *Men and Women of the Time*, 14th ed. (London: G. Routledge and Sons, 1895), pp. 783–84; *Monthly Notices of the Royal Astronomical Society* 56 (February 8, 1901), pp. 189–97 (obituary); Larry J. Schaaf, "Piazzi Smyth at Teneriffe," *History of Photography* 4 (October 1980), pp. 289–307 (pt. 1, "The Expedition and the Resulting Book"), and 5 (January 1981), pp. 27–50 (pt. 2, "Photography and the Disciples of Constable and Harding"); Hermann Alexander Brück and Mary T. Brück, *The Peripatetic Astronomer: The Life of Charles Piazzi Smyth* (Bristol: Adam Hilger, 1988)

Spackman, Benjamin L.
b. 1834
Spackman, a sergeant in the Royal Engineers, benefited from a peculiar arrangement between the military and the museum world. Thurston Thompson had been hired as the official photographer for the South Kensington Museum, now the Victoria and Albert Museum in London. His appointment grew out of the 1851 Great Exhibition, where the sappers of the Royal Engineers had been involved in the construction and documentation of the Crystal Palace. A detachment was posted to act as firemen for the new museum, where courses of instruction were set up in 1856 to keep them from idleness. One of the courses was in photography, and Spackman excelled. As a corporal he began producing waxed-paper negatives of the construction site. In 1856 and 1857 Spackman was posted to accompany Charles Newton in his excavations at Halicarnassus on the coast of what is now Turkey. In 1862 at the London International Exhibition, Spackman displayed his photographs of the progress of the building and also of the gardens of the Royal Horticultural Society. For nearly two decades Spackman remained a royal engineer, while acting primarily as a photographer for the museum. The sappers' quarters were behind the north cloister of the museum.

References: John Physick, *Photography and the South Kensington Museum* (London: Victoria & Albert Museum, 1975), pp. 3–4; Anthony J. Hamber, *"A Higher Branch of the Art": Photographing the Fine Arts in England, 1839–1880* (Amsterdam: Gordon and Breach, 1996), pp. 412, 418, 428

Spencer, John A.
1827–1878
Spencer succeeded his father in the family's chemical business in London and in 1851 received a bronze medal at the Great Exhibition. This award led to an appointment as demonstrator of applied chemistry at the Royal Panopticon of Science and Art, an exhibition palace designed to highlight the universality of knowledge. With this background, it is not surprising that he entered photographs in the 1852 Society of Arts exhibition. They were predominantly collodion but included a calotype street view. Whereas plain salted paper had generally been made by the individual photographer, the newly introduced albumen paper was a much more complex product and demanded professional manufacture. Spencer moved quickly to capture this market. Starting from his base in London, he built the business into a dedicated manufactory, where, the firm advertised, quality Rives and Saxe papers were "prepared with Pure and Fresh Albumen Only," and "Rolled exclusively upon Plates of Silver." In the 1850s it was not unusual for photographers to take pride in making their negatives but to have no talent or interest in making prints. Spencer printed many of the plates for the Photographic Club albums and routinely provided printing services to Photographic Society members. Spencer opened outlets in Glasgow, Dublin, and Paris, and his firm's consumption of fresh eggs for the albumen prints must have been enormous. Although commercially successful, Spencer recognized that albumen silver prints would one day be overtaken by photomechanical printing. Much of his later life was devoted to making carbon tissues for the Autotype Company. He died from esophageal cancer in 1878.

Exhibited: 1852, London, Society of Arts

Reference: *BJP* 25 (April 26, 1878), pp. 194–95 (obituary)

Spencer, Thomas
In April 1839 Spencer wrote to the *Liverpool Mercury*, "Since Brewster invented the kaleidoscope, I know of nothing that has occupied so much attention as Mr. Talbot's ingenious mode of photogenic painting. . . . I am half ashamed to confess I have been led away with the mania." Spencer went on to detail his own photographic method, similar to Talbot's but using ammonia as a fixer, and offered help to a correspondent in a subsequent article. In 1840 Spencer published *Instructions for the Multiplication of Works of Art in Metal, by Voltaic Electricity*, a subject that interested Talbot greatly and is reflected in his correspondence. Electroplating became a major force in industry, but Spencer gained little from it. Predictably, the metal plate of the daguerreotype appealed to him more than Talbot's paper, and he opened a daguerreotype portrait studio in Liverpool. He found that his exposure times were getting longer and longer, and fellow photographer and glass merchant James Alexander Forrest came to his rescue. The manganese in the glass of his skylight was turning it pink, blocking the actinic rays of sunlight.

References: Thomas Spencer, "The New Art," *Liverpool Mercury*, April 26, 1839, p. 5; James Alexander Forrest, "Historical Notes of What Liverpool Has Done in the Art-Science of Photography," *BJP* 35 (February 3, 1888), pp. 72–74

Spicer, Mr.
Spicer exhibited "A Series of Indian Views by the Calotype Process" at a meeting of the North London Photographic Association on April 28, 1858. Nothing further is known about him.

Reference: "North London Photographic Association," *JPS* 4 (May 21, 1858), p. 215

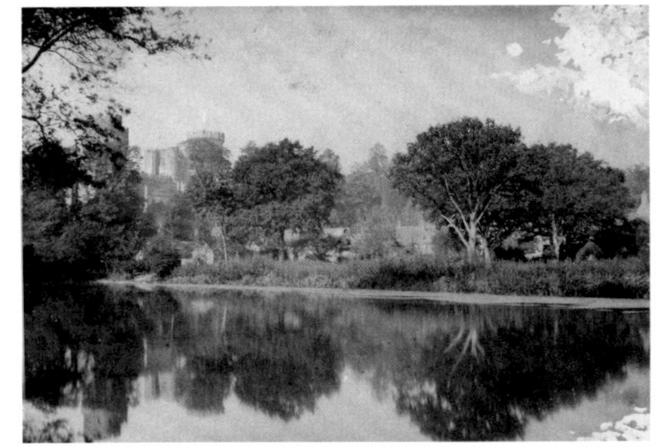

103. Mr. (John?) Stanton

Stanton, Mr. (John?) *ill. 103*
1799–1888
Stanton's negatives and prints are in a number of collections, but in all the known inscriptions he is simply "Mr. Stanton of Warwick." For some time historians speculated, without any evidence, that he might have been George Stanton, a bookbinder in Warwick. An inscription on a print in the Smithsonian Institution reads: "I got this from Mr. Stanton Longbridge nr. Warwick (who took it some years 15 or 20 before) in March 1867." William Staunton (a common variation of Stanton) of Longbridge died in 1848. His eldest son and heir was John Staunton, who trained as an M.D. but was an enthusiastic author and collector. In 1875 he donated his "very fine collection of books, pamphlets, pictures, engravings, newspapers, old charters, pedigrees and autographs" to the Birmingham Central Free Library. Tragically, the library burned to the ground four years later. Among Staunton's published books was his 1873 *The Persians*, illustrated with albumen prints by C. W. Smartt.

Reference: Larry J. Schaaf, *Sun Pictures, Catalogue Ten: British Paper Negatives, 1839–1864* (New York: Hans P. Kraus, Jr., 2001), pp. 48–49

Stevenson, George D.
In 1978 a group of architectural studies made in Spain and Italy about 1860 was sold at auction. At least one albumen print was printed from a waxed-paper negative. Most were only monogrammed "G.D.S.," but one bore the ink inscription "Geo. D. Stevenson." Nothing else is presently known about him. The label on the verso must have been that of the subsequent owner, Henry Joseph Mills, a London photographer born in 1849 and active later in the nineteenth century.

Reference: Sale cat., Sotheby's, London, 27 October 27, 1978, lot 157

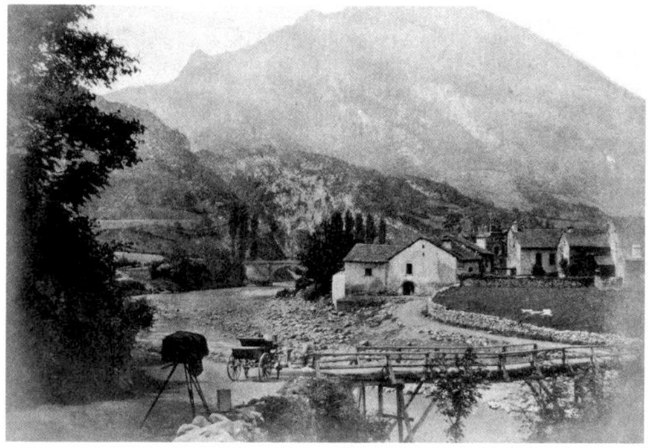

104. John Stewart (1814–1887)

Stewart, John *ill. 104*
1814–1887
In the summer of 1829, JOHN HERSCHEL (later Sir John), drawing with a camera lucida in the Pyrenees, wrote to his mother: "Johnny & I are running a race which shall sketch most—he draws very nicely & with practice from Nature will acquire 'freedom of hand' in abundance." Johnny was the younger brother of Herschel's new Scottish wife, Margaret ("Maggie") Stewart. Two decades later John Stewart had acquired that "freedom of hand," not with a pencil, but rather with the photographic camera. Together with his brothers, he entered the printing business in London, and in 1839 he married a childhood Scottish friend, a resident of France in delicate health. This was one factor in his living mainly in Pau in southwest France, a favored area for recuperation and also a hotbed of photographic activity. It is not known when or why Stewart first took up photography, but his close relationship with Herschel could have encouraged him. Once in Pau he fell into the circle of unusually active amateurs who employed waxed paper. Stewart's entries in the London exhibitions of the Society of Arts in 1852, the Photographic Institution in 1854, and the Photographic Society in 1855 were all views taken in the Pyrenees. They were done with a variety of waxed-paper processes, both wet and dry, using largely the special system that he devised based on advice from Henri-Victor Regnault, the French physicist who was director of the Sevres porcelain works. Stewart used a vacuum pump to force the chemicals into the fibers of the paper, leading to better uniformity, and Herschel proudly published this process for him in the *Athenaeum* in 1853. Stewart was an excellent photographer, taking not only landscapes in the Pyrenees but also views on visits to England. He submitted his portrait of Herschel to the 1857 Manchester "Art Treasures" exhibition. In a paper on photography's relation to art published in the *Journal of the Photographic Society* in 1853, Sir WILLIAM NEWTON felt that photographic prints "ought not to be so *chemically*, as *artistically* beautiful. The nearest approach in this respect . . . were the excellent Photographs exhibited by Mr. Stewart." At Pau, Stewart teamed up with Maxell Lyte and others to form an active photographic society and a printing establishment. Later in the 1850s his commercial activities began to overwhelm his amateur photography. A banker, Stewart died a wealthy man, in Pau, where he had enriched the photographic scene.

EXHIBITED: 1852, London, Society of Arts; 1855, London, Photographic Society; 1855, London, Photographic Institution

REFERENCES: John Herschel to Mary Herschel, June 15, 1829, Herschel Collection, Harry Ransom Humanities Research Center, The University of Texas at Austin, LO521; William J. Newton, "Upon Photography in an Artistic View, and in Its Relations to the Arts," *JPS* 1 (March 3, 1853), p. 6; John Stewart, letter in John Herschel, "New Photographic Process," *Athenaeum*, July 9, 1853, p. 831; John Stewart, "The Paper Process," *JPS* 1 (June 30, 1854), pp. 225–30; *Times* (London), August 3, 1887, p. 1, col. A (obituary)

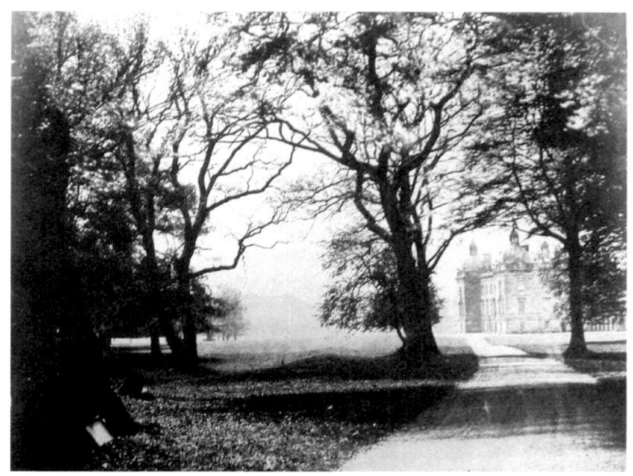

105. John Stewart (d. 1867)

Stewart, John *ill. 105*
d. 1867
Stewart was born in Scotland and educated at Edinburgh University. He became a fellow of the Society of Antiquaries in Scotland and a member of the Edinburgh Calotype Club. In the 1853 exhibition at the Mechanics' Institution in Aberdeen, ROSS & THOMSON submitted Stewart's work as a "Stereoscopic Group, Taken from Life, by an amateur." The process was not specified. Through marriage, Stewart inherited property in Lancashire. He became a merchant in Liverpool and joined the Norwich Photographic Society. In 1856 he entered a substantial group of waxed-paper and collodion views, including *Trees Laden with Snow*, which the reviewer for the *Norfolk News* found to be "as beautiful as they are unique." Stewart also exhibited a two-part collodion panorama, but the reviewer marveled more at his waxed-paper view, *Carrow Bridge*, as being "nearly as sharp in definition and equally fine as a landscape." Stewart also became a founding member of the Photographic Society of Scotland. None of his photographs are known to have survived.

EXHIBITED: 1856, Norwich, Photographic Society

REFERENCES: *Norfolk News*, January 3, 1857; "A Reminiscence of the Calotype Club," *BJP* 21 (August 14, 1874), p. 385; Richard Denyer and Andrew Moore, eds., *A Period Eye: Photography Then and Now*, exh. cat. (Norwich: Norfolk Museums and Archaeology Service, 2003), pp. 52, 62–63, 68, 71

Stewart, S. A.
An engineer in India, Stewart joined the Photographic Society of Bengal in 1862, clearly already experienced in photography. In the 1856 Photographic Society of Scotland exhibition in Edinburgh, Lady Baillie contributed two of his calotypes, *Bungalow, with Cotton Trees* and *River Boat of the Ganges, under repair*. Stewart was also an inventor and showed a panoramic camera of his design to the Bengal society. In its 1864 exhibition Stewart was praised as a mechanical engineer but chastised as one who "works smugly and scarcely does himself justice."

EXHIBITED: 1856, Edinburgh, Photographic Society of Scotland

REFERENCE: *Journal of the Bengal Photographic Society* 2 (March 1864), p. 76

Stokes, George
b. 1805
There were two George Stokeses listed as members of the Photographic Society in the 1850s, one the well-known Sir George Gabriel Stokes of Cambridge, the other an architect and surveyor living in London. It was the latter who was the more active photographer. (He was not the more famous architect George Henry Stokes, 1826–1871, who married Joseph Paxton's daughter.) By the time of the 1861 census, George Stokes the photographer had retired, living off his property investments. In 1852 Stokes entered the first great photographic exhibition in London, which was sponsored by the Society of Arts, submitting all waxed-paper views. Predictably, most

were of architecture, although one, intriguingly, was called *Beehives*. He joined the Photographic Society of London and in 1855 was a member of the Photographic Exchange Club. At least in his public work, Stokes had converted to collodion by 1854, when his contributions to the Photographic Society exhibition included vernacular architecture and genre studies. In the 1855 and 1858 exhibitions he continued with collodion.

EXHIBITED: 1852, London, Society of Arts

Stone, J.

In the 1856 exhibition of the Photographic Society in London, Stone showed two calotypes, one of the Pontoise Station, on the Paris & Boulogne Railway, the other of St. Gervais, Paris. No further photographic activity nor any personal information has been traced.

EXHIBITED: 1856, London, Photographic Society

Streeter, E. (Edward?)

In 1855, at the third meeting of the newly established Brighton and Sussex Photographic Society, a Mr. E. Streeter made a presentation "On the Waxed Paper Process." The only person with that initial traced in the Brighton area was Edward, a baker, an occupation that might at first seem unlikely to yield a candidate. However, a baker often worked at night and thus had precious daylight hours available for photography. It appears that this was a substantial bakery, employing several men, and that Streeter had retired by the end of the 1850s.

REFERENCE: "Brighton and Sussex Photographic Society," *LPJ* 2 (October 13, 1855), p. 122

Sutton, Thomas

1819–1875

The son of a famous London numismatist, Sutton emerged as an excellent mathematician at Cambridge. He posed for a daguerreotype by Antoine Claudet in 1841 and immediately became intrigued by photography. Sutton secured a daguerreotype camera and dabbled in calotypy following instructions in ROBERT BINGHAM's manual. Becoming a tutor, Sutton followed his student to Jersey in 1847 and there soon began serious photographic researches. Struck by the beauty of calotypes he saw in a shop window, he arranged for lessons from their creator, JOHN NICOLAS LAVERTY, a locally based naval instructor. Sutton's first serious calotypes were taken during a visit to Italy in 1851. He began a collaboration with the Frenchman Louis Blanquart-Evrard and established a photographic printing plant in Jersey, asserting, "I solemnly believe that the best paper work for views is absolutely finer than the best collodion work." Sutton displayed calotypes of Jersey, Italy, and France in the 1855 Photographic Institution exhibition in London, in the 1856 Photographic Society of Scotland exhibition in Edinburgh, and in the Manchester Photographic Society exhibition that same year. Also in 1856 Sutton started *Photographic Notes*, a highly personal and lively journal, the columns of which reflected the enthusiasm and combative nature of their editor. Entranced by collodion, Sutton began to rail against his former passion, the calotype, leading Reverend THOMAS MILVILLE RAVEN to remind him in 1860 in *Photographic Notes* "that the success of all out-door work in photography must eventually depend on paper, and that to *paper* all collodion men would have to turn. I never could get you to listen to me when I was in Jersey, for you were always calling it ugly names." Raven credited Sutton's invention of a panoramic camera with bringing him back into the circle of paper photographers, for the camera required a curved negative plate, expensive in glass but easily accomplished in waxed paper. In 1858 the *Jersey Times* reported that Sutton was "thrown among some neighboring furze" by an explosion of ether that destroyed his photographic laboratory, but he survived. In 1861 he briefly held the post of lecturer of Photography at King's College in London, but he so disliked his hometown that he quit after a few months and moved to Brittany, becoming the French correspondent for the *British Journal of Photography*. Sutton died after a lingering illness. Despite his ascerbic comments, his contemporaries greatly regretted the loss of one of their most influential colleagues.

EXHIBITED: 1855, London, Photographic Institution; 1856, Manchester Photographic Society; 1856, Edinburgh, Photographic Society of Scotland

REFERENCES: *Jersey Times*, November 5, 1858; Thomas Milville Raven, letter in *Photographic Notes* 5 (December 15, 1860), p. 347; "Thomas Sutton, "Reminiscences of an Old Photographer," *BJP* 14 (August 30, 1867), pp. 413–14; *Photographic News* 19 (April 2, 1875), pp. 162–63 (obituary); *BJP* 22 (April 30, 1875), pp. 210–12 (obituary)

T., G . J.

In 1842, "G.J.T." submitted a paper to the *Annals of Electricity, Magnetism and Chemistry; and Guardian of Experimental Science*. The author had been inspired by TALBOT's publication of the calotype and ROBERT HUNT's subsequent improvements to devise a process of his own. G. J. T. added an iron compound to the formula, yielding a paper that would darken in two or three minutes from the light of a single candle. Nothing else is known of the photographer's identity or location.

REFERENCE: G.J.T., "Preparation of Calotype Paper," *Annals of Electricity, Magnetism and Chemistry; and Guardian of Experimental Science* 8 (June 1842), pp. 414–15

Talbot, Christopher Rice Mansel

1803–1890

Kit Talbot, as he was known to family and friends, was recognized as "the wealthiest commoner" in Britain. His wealth extended beyond the monetary realm, for he was the favorite cousin of W. H. F. TALBOT and a member of an interesting scientific and artistic family. In the world of art, his father, Thomas Mansel Talbot, was primarily remembered for making collecting tours on the Continent to acquire paintings and especially antique sculpture, some from the famed excavator Gavin Hamilton. It was his son Kit who built Margam Castle in Wales, a suitable home for this outstanding collection. Kit was slightly younger than his cousin and came under his wing at Harrow. He read mathematics at Oxford, becoming deeply engaged by science, and there met his future lifelong friend, the Reverend CALVERT R. JONES. They were to share not only mathematics and science but also a love of art and particularly of travel, the latter financed by Kit and the former enhanced by Jones. When he attained his majority in 1824, Kit Talbot came into an immense fortune, a small portion of which he put into his beloved yacht, *Galatea*. Travel was to be the core of his life. Remaining close to his cousin, Kit was one of the first to learn of photography and observed, if he did not participate in, the photographing of Margam Castle by W. H. F. Talbot in late 1839. Kit Talbot's opportunity to become a photographer himself stemmed from adversity. His wife, Charlotte, began a fatal decline in 1845, and Kit resolved to take her to the Mediterranean on his yacht in the hope of a cure in the warm climate. As was typical, Calvert Jones came along; by this time he was fired with enthusiasm for the calotype. Kit Talbot calotyped in Malta along with Reverend Jones and the Reverend GEORGE BRIDGES. Perhaps because he had no particular ambition to be a photographer, Kit's few calotypes were charmingly informal and in their own way very modern. His wife died at the beginning of 1846, and by then his daughter was ill. The journey home was a slow one, giving Kit more opportunities to take calotypes throughout northern Europe. His cousin published at least one of his photographs taken in Germany. Perhaps Kit's greatest contribution to the calotype was the financial and travel support he gave to his friend Jones, who produced an extraordinary body of early negatives that served to validate the invention. W. H. F. Talbot purchased many of these.

Reference: John Vivian Hughes, *The Wealthiest Commoner: C. R. M. Talbot, M.P., F.R.S. (1803–1890)* (Port Talbot: Talbot Printing Company, 1978)

Talbot, Constance

1811–1880

It is not surprising that Constance Talbot, née Mundy, the wife of the inventor of photography, herself became involved in the new art. Indeed, the only surprise is that she did not become more involved. It was really her mother-in-law, the formidable Lady Elisabeth Feilding, who exercised the most influence over TALBOT's progress in the art: she suggested ideas for Talbot's photographs, critiqued them, supervised photographic sessions, and promoted her son's work through her extensive social contacts. But she is not known to have taken any photographs. While Constance Talbot was publicly much less enthusiastic about her husband's work, she did some photographic printing and made some photographs. Perhaps her most insightful contribution was the concept that eventually led to photographic typesetting. In the autumn of 1843 she set to work with the first few lines of her friend Thomas Moore's *Irish Melodies.* She reported in a letter to her husband on December 1, 1843, "I have composed a little frame with the 4 first lines of the 'Last rose of Summer' & it is now waiting for brighter weather." Sometime shortly after that, Constance arranged her cutout letters in front of the camera and produced a negative of the text that is still printable today.

Reference: Constance Talbot to W. H. T. Talbot, December 1, 1843, Talbot Collection, British Library, London, LA45-155 (Talbot Correspondence Project, http://foxtalbot.dmu.ac.uk, doc. no. 05454)

Talbot, William Henry Fox *ill. 106*

1800–1877

Photography on paper—photography as we know it—exists because of Talbot. A brilliant only child born into the financially strapped branch of a well connected family, he was brought to his full and considerable potential through the efforts of his mother, the Lady Elisabeth Fox-Strangways, later Feilding. His half sister Horatia provided intellectual inspiration and close support, while his other half sister Caroline, later Lady Mount Edgcumbe, provided an artistic model and access to the

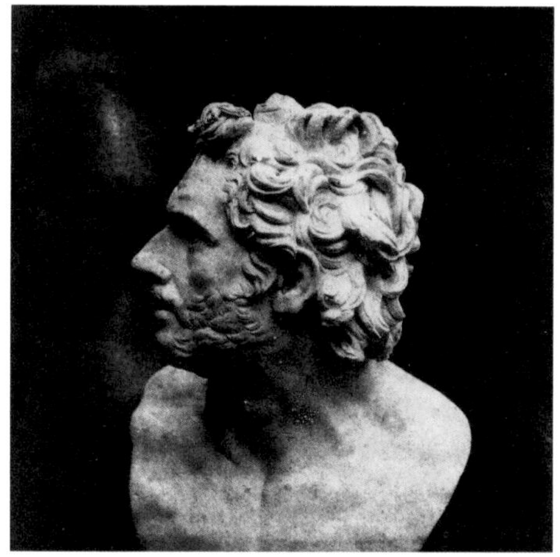

106. William Henry Fox Talbot

royal court. The resonant name "Fox Talbot" so beloved of historians was actually anathema to him. Professionally he was H. F. Talbot, and to his family he was Henry. Talbot took an early interest in botany, mathematics, and travel. He had published six papers on mathematics before he met JOHN (later, Sir John) HERSCHEL in Munich in 1824. More than anything else, their meeting changed the direction of Talbot's scientific life, moving it in the direction of the physical sciences and toward the work of his later close friend Sir DAVID BREWSTER. By 1839, the year that photography was announced to the public, Talbot was a fellow of the Royal Society, had given their Bakerian lecture, and had published nearly thirty scientific papers and two books. More were to follow, but they were overshadowed by his invention of photography.

In 1832, while a member of the Reform Parliament, Talbot had married. In 1833 he and his new wife, CONSTANCE MUNDY TALBOT, commenced a Continental tour, and in the autumn they had reached Bellagio on the banks of Lake Como, where they were joined by Talbot's sister Caroline. Talbot was frustrated by watching her and Constance happily sketching, for, with all his talents he could not draw, and even turning to Wollaston's camera lucida only proved that science could not substitute for artistry. Talbot considered the problem with his analytical mind and realized that the light entering a camera obscura could affect physical entities. Back at his home, Lacock Abbey in Wiltshire, Talbot by the summer of 1834 had managed to harness light to produce an image on silver-nitrate-coated paper. He called this skiagraphy, the depiction of objects through their shadows: the light darkened the paper, producing what we now call a negative. Talbot improved this process in 1835 to the point of being able to take pictures of nature in Lilliputian cameras. He then put these primitive photographs into a drawer, having triumphed over the immediate problem and with much work to do in mathematics and crystals.

When Daguerre made his surprise announcement in 1839, Talbot was caught completely off guard and hastened to make his first presentation of photogenic drawings (as he now styled them) before the Royal Institution in London on January 25, 1839. His photographs on paper, capable of producing multiple prints, were viewed unfavorably compared to the unique daguerreotypes with their crisp detail. Talbot continued to work at his process, observing how Nature translated herself onto his paper. His autumn 1840 discovery of the latent image culminated in his 1841 calotype process, a developed paper negative with a realistic exposure time. While many refinements would follow, photography was complete at this point. Between 1844 and 1846 Talbot issued the fascicles of his *The Pencil of Nature*, each copy illustrated with pasted-in photographic prints. Talbot submitted a good deal of work to the 1852 Society of Arts exhibition in London, but his most significant entry was a precious album, inscribed in his own hand: *The Specimens sent by H.F. Talbot are intended to exhibit an Early Period of the Art from 1841 to 1846. None of them are of a more recent date.* Talbot had already moved on from photography based on silver, realizing that it could never be permanent. In 1852 he introduced photographic engraving, the first successful merger between the image of nature and the time-tested ink of the printer. In 1858 he revealed his improved photoglyphic engraving, a significant step on the path toward photogravure. Talbot spent the last thirty-five years of his life, three times as long as that of his photographic involvement, perfecting a method of bringing the photographic image to the printed page. The true dimensions of his vision were as clear as they had been in 1833.

Exhibited: 1839, Birmingham, British Association for the Advancement of Science; 1839, Edinburgh, Exhibition of Arts, Manufactures, and Practical Science; 1840, Newcastle, Exhibition of Arts, Manufactures, and Practical Science; 1852, London, Society of Arts; 1854, first touring exhibition, Society of Arts (London); 1854, second touring exhibition, Society of Arts (London); 1856, London, Photographic Society

References: H. J. P. Arnold, *William Henry Fox Talbot: Pioneer of Photography and Man of Science* (London: Hutchinson Benham, 1977); Larry J. Schaaf, *The Photographic Art of William Henry Fox Talbot* (Princeton, N.J.: Princeton University Press, 2000)

Tanner, Mr.

In 1857 the editor of the *Liverpool and Manchester Photographic Journal* recalled, "upon the first appearance of Mr. Talbot's calotype patent, the late Mr. Robert Murray sent a brief account of the specification to his friend, Mr. Tanner, who was at that time on the continent. Mr. Tanner soon found that with foreign paper it was not possible to adhere to the directions given by Mr. Talbot, whose experiments had of course been made on English paper. Mr. Tanner, being a chemist, was soon enabled to modify Mr. Talbot's process in such a way that French and German papers could be used." Tanner's adaptation was claimed to be more sensitive to light than TALBOT's original, but, frustratingly, no further personal details are revealed. The account continued, "portraits were taken from time to time and sent to England, to the astonishment of some few who considered the calotype to have become of doubtful utility, as far as portraiture was concerned." Tanner's identity may have been buried: the same editorial claimed that Tanner taught Louis Blanquart-Evrard his process and was later surprised to see Blanquart-Evrard publish it as his own.

REFERENCE: "Tanner's Wet Paper Process," *LMPJ*, n.s., 1 (September 15, 1857), pp. 202–3

Taylor, Mrs.

In the 1856 exhibition of the Norwich Photographic Society, a Mrs. Taylor showed two calotypes, both of local architecture. They were *Burnham Rectory*, reputed to be the birthplace of Lord Nelson, and *North Creake Abbey*. No further identification was given about the photographer.

EXHIBITED: 1856, Norwich, Photographic Society

Taylor, Alfred Swaine *ill. 107*

1806–1880

Taylor's father was an East India Company captain, and his maternal grandfather was a manufacturer of gunflints. Nothing in his background suggests that Taylor might emerge as the leading forensic doctor of his generation. Apprenticed to a doctor in London at sixteen, he excelled in anatomy and took an extended Continental tour upon completion of his medical studies. In 1831 he was appointed England's first professor of medical jurisprudence at Guy's Hospital, London. Taylor had proven to be an enthusiastic if not talented draftsman during his Continental tour, and perhaps that skill and chemistry were equal draws for him when photography was announced in 1839. He took it up right away and carried

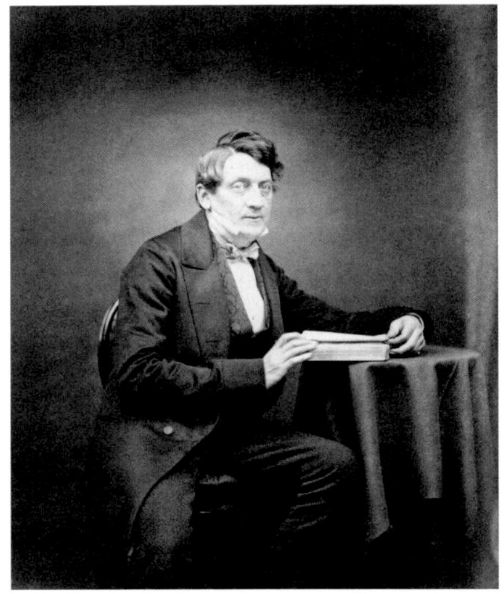

107. Portrait of Alfred Swaine Taylor

out his own experiments on TALBOT's process for more than a year, publishing his findings in 1840 in *On the Art of Photogenic Drawing*. Taylor, like many others, found Talbot's original process "capricious" and he devised his own, based on ammonio nitrate of silver. He worked with HENRY COLLEN to improve Collen's prints and to gain access to the artist's fine Ross camera. Taylor particularly liked copying prints by photography, and one early example (published in 1987 by Stephen White) was captioned by its owner *Photogenic before photography by Faraday and Dr. Alfred Taylor*. In April 1839 Taylor explained his entire process to the chemist and physicist Michael Faraday, loaning some of his photographs for exhibition at the Royal Institution and mentioning that he did not copy directly from engravings but rather from lampblack tracings of them. An album preserved by his daughter Edith indicates that Taylor's interest in photography extended beyond his 1840 book: it includes a salted paper print of the back of his house and a caricature drawn and titled by Taylor *Cambridge Photography Saloon*, a reference to the house on Cambridge Place near Regent's Park that he occupied until 1854.

REFERENCES: Alfred Swaine Taylor, *On the Art of Photogenic Drawing* (London: Jeffery, 1840); Samuel Wilks and G. T. Bettany, *A Biographical History of Guy's Hospital* (London: Ward, Lock, Bowden & Co., 1892), pp. 392–95; Stephen White, "Alfred Swaine Taylor: A Little Known Photographic Pioneer," *History of Photography* 11 (July–September 1987), pp. 229–35; Laurence Alt, "Alfred Swaine Taylor (1801–80): Some Early Material," *History of Photography* 16 (Winter 1992), pp. 397–98

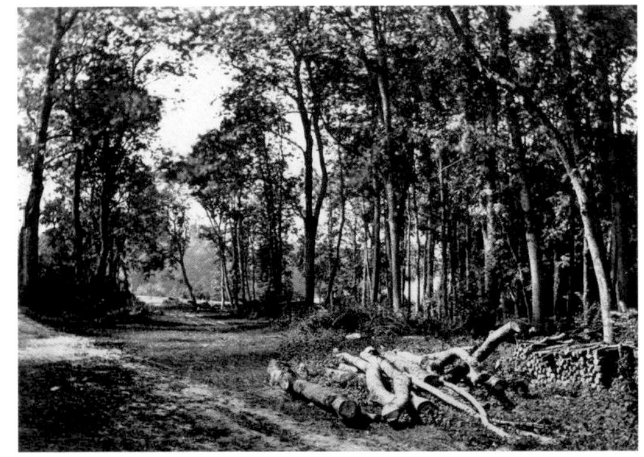

108. Arthur A. Taylor

Taylor, Arthur A. *ill. 108*

d. 1873

Taylor is known only through his work in Marseilles, where he resided and was referred to as an "able amateur" by the editor of *Photographic News* and as "the English photographer." He monogrammed some of his negatives "AAT." Taylor was a founding member of Photographic Society of Marseilles and in 1866 was appointed to its Special Committee because of his "great experience in waxed paper." He served as president from 1867 to 1868. In 1867 he displayed his waxed-paper negatives to the society, and seven more were hung in the 1869 exhibition of the Société Française de Photographie. Surviving prints show that Taylor favored views of parks and trees in urban settings, much in the style of later work by Eugène Atget. In 1866 Taylor gave a detailed aesthetic analysis of the features of the waxed-paper camera that he invented. Designed to make 10 x 14 inch negatives, it had a wide-angle lens that he felt better embraced the vista that artists painted. In order to place the vanishing point off center, he enabled the lens to rise and fall and shift left to right. Taylor took a special interest in the problems of fading prints and in 1863 devised his own paper coated with shellac. After a test period of three years, the prints remained strong in tone. But this was not just a technical triumph: the *Photographic News* of August 10, 1866, found the works to be "some of the most charmingly artistic landscape pictures we have seen for some time. They are chiefly printed on rough drawing-paper, and possess much of the quality for which water-colour artist prise this kind of paper." While admiring the rich tones, the writer gave equal credit to Taylor's mastery of the waxed-paper process, finding an "admirable selection of light, and the artistic feeling, which have characterized the negatives, materially assist in producing this impression." In

1868 Taylor visited England and there was impressed by the Woodburytype process. He also had some of his photographs reproduced in photogravure. In 1869 Gustave Arosa, a tutor to Paul Gauguin, sold prints from Taylor's negatives made by his own variant of the collotype, a photomechanical process dependant on bichromated gelatine. Sadly, the only prints known today are these and not the shellac ones that so impressed his contemporaries. Taylor died in Marseilles, where he had lived and made his reputation.

EXHIBITED: 1869, Paris, Société Française de Photographie

REFERENCES: Arthur A.Taylor, "Shellac Printing Process," *Photographic News* 10 (June 1, 1866), pp. 256–57; "The Shellac Printing Process," *Photographic News* 10 (August 10, 1866), p. 374

Taylor, C. Johnson

Taylor exhibited a waxed-paper view of Broomhill Mill, near Tunbridge Wells, in the 1857 exhibition of the Photographic Society in London. The following year he showed three collodion views of architecture in Oxford, described in the exhibition catalogue as "developed on the spot in an Archer's Camera, without any Dark Tent." There was a Reverend Charles J. Taylor in nearby Folkestone who graduated from Oxford. However, his "J" stood for Joseph, and there are no other obvious candidates for the identity.

EXHIBITED: 1857, London, Photographic Society

Taylor, Henry D.

b. 1814 (alive at 1891 census)

Taylor was a chemist, druggist, and bookseller in Surrey when he was introduced to photography by ARTHUR KERR. In 1853 Kerr stayed near Taylor and was fresh from taking calotype lessons from SAMUEL BUCKLE. Taylor bought a fine camera from the optical firm of Andrew Ross and produced his first successful calotype on August 1, 1853, using, of course, a Buckle brush to coat his papers. Starting with the 1855 Photographic Society exhibition in London, Taylor contributed dozens of calotypes through 1858 in both England and Scotland. At the 1856 Photographic Society of Norwich exhibition, Taylor's photographs were found by the *Norfolk News* to "have as much harmony and breadth as it is possible to obtain from paper negatives." The reviewer of the *Edinburgh Evening Courant* commented on Taylor's studies of "ferns, water lilies, bind-weed and nettles, hedge with brambles, &c. The process is calotype, and yet these studies have all the sharpness of collodion, and, we venture to say, more of the half tints and gradations of light and shade than collodion is generally capable of." By 1855 Taylor had merged his hobby and his profession, offering instructions, materials, and apparatus. Taylor manufactured iodized paper for use by amateurs, counting Rev. T. MILVILLE RAVEN among his best customers. Taylor provided a rare insight into the early days of photography when he published his reminiscences near the end of the nineteenth century. Although he had always exhibited some collodion, Taylor remembered the calotype process with particular fondness as being clean to use and versatile in the field. He had a 12 x 15 inch camera made and took four sheets of paper out at a time. The calotype was slow enough in developing for local areas to be controllable. Taylor was especially appreciative of the fact that the calotype could be developed under reduced light rather than in total darkness: "I have frequently had quite a bevy of ladies looking on during the development of my day's work."

EXHIBITED: 1854 and 1855, London, Photographic Society (both under single name of "Taylor"); 1856, London, Photographic Society; 1856, Manchester, Photographic Society; 1856, Norwich, Photographic Society; 1856, Edinburgh, Photographic Society of Scotland; 1857, London, Photographic Society; 1857, Manchester, "Art Treasures" Exhibition; 1858, London, Photographic Society

REFERENCE: *Norfolk News*, January 3, 1857; *Edinburgh Evening Courant*, December 19, 1857; Henry D. Taylor, "The Calotype Process, and How We Photographed in the 'Fifties,'" *International Annual of Anthony's Photographic Bulletin*, June 1889, pp. 242–46

Taylor, Isaac Weld

1812–1891

Born in Liverpool to Philip Meadows Taylor, an Anglo-Indian agent, artist, and author, Isaac used the professional name Weld Taylor. He was a painter and lithographer in London. None of his photographs are known to have survived, but in 1853 he began a series of contributions on waxed paper to the discussion journal *Notes and Queries*. In the spirit of many early photographers, he was eager to share his approach, and he commented in that publication, "as I have experienced the excellence of these preparations, I hope they may be useful to your photographic students." His formulation involved using Canson Frères paper, potassium cyanide, and walnut oil. Revealing another common quality of early photographers, contentiousness, GEORGE SHADBOLT immediately declared Taylor's process "perfectly unintelligible." Taylor vigorously defended his method, touching on another common problem of photographers of the period, the inconsistencies of papers, and pointing out that Canson's was much thinner and harder than Whatman's, which Shadbolt employed. Taylor's last published communication was in February 1853. Shortly afterward he became a drawing teacher, living in Wimborne Minster, Dorset, for the rest of his life.

REFERENCES: Isaac Weld Taylor, "Ready Mode of Iodizing Paper," *Notes and Queries*, January 8, 1853, pp. 48–49; George Shadbolt, "Mr. Weld Taylor's Process," *Notes and Queries*, January 22, 1853, pp. 92–93; Taylor, "Mr. Weld Taylor's Iodizing Process," *Notes and Queries*, February 19 and 26, 1853, pp. 187, 218–19

Taylor, John Traill

1827–1895

Taylor, born in the Orkney Islands, moved to Edinburgh at eighteen. His own photographs are less important than the tremendous influence he had on the new art. Originally destined for the ministry, he instead followed in the footsteps of his watchmaker father. Optics was a part of that business, and seeing a daguerreotype for the first time "exerted so great an influence" on Taylor that photography was to be his main interest in life. Forty years later, during one of his frequent and popular talks, published in the *British Journal of Photography* in 1885, Taylor recalled this period, of which, he said, "I now submit a few of the negatives themselves, some of which are by Mr. Talbot, the others being by various experimentalists who at once rushed into the field, including myself." Taylor first became active in the emerging photographic journals by circulating the *Photographer*, a manuscript magazine frequently quoted in the published journals (fortunately, for the unique originals were lost in an 1859 burglary). He then became a regular contributor to the *British Journal of Photography*, and his 1861 article on the waxed-paper process displayed a mastery of that method. That same year Taylor was responsible for the foundation of the Edinburgh Photographic Society. He recalled, in the *Photogram* in March 1895, that "it was in the little workroom at the back of my shop that four or five friends interested in the progress of photography used to meet and have what we called 'a photographic chat.' From these meetings arose the Edinburgh Photographic Society, which we started with seven members. We took a small room in the coffee-house, and drew the first subscription of five shillings from James Valentine, the founder of the present firm of view publishers." In 1864 Taylor moved to London to accept the editorship of the *British Journal of Photography*, an influential position that he held until 1879. Taylor then moved to the United States, briefly dabbling in commerce before starting the

Photographic Times in New York. In 1886 he returned to London, again taking up the editorship of the *British Journal of Photography* and also of its companion, the *Annual*. Taylor was one of the few consistent supporters of TALBOT, and some accounts have him actively experimenting with the inventor, most likely a confusion resulting from his correspondence with Talbot. Taylor was an honorary or full member of numerous photographic organizations and the cofounder of the Photographic Convention. The *Journal* explained in his obituary, "the popularity Mr. Taylor enjoyed among the many thousands of photographers with whom he came into contact during the course of his long career is not difficult to understand. He was ever genial, communicative, and kind-hearted, ready to help with advice, counsel, or information, the *beau-idéal*, in fact of natural *bonhomie* and good humour." He died of dysentery while visiting the orange grove that he owned in Florida.

REFERENCES: John Traill [Taylor], "The Waxed-Paper Process," *BJP* 8 (July 1, 1861), p. 233; Taylor, "Paper Negatives," *BJP* 32 (December 11, 1885), p. 790; "Brief Biographies: J. Traill Taylor, F.R.P.S.," *Photogram* 2 (March 1895), pp. 57–58; *BJP* 42 (November 15, 1895), p. 725 (obituary); *Photogram* 2 (December 1895), p. 272 (obituary); *Practical Photographer* 6 (December 1895), pp. 371–72 (obituary)

Teasdale, Washington
1831–1903
In late 1853, at a time when experimental variations on processes were proliferating at a dizzying pace, Teasdale presented his thoughts "On the Waxed-paper Process" to the members of the Leeds Philosophical Society. He was only twenty-two at the time, but, as noted in his obituary, "from boyhood his mind showed a scientific bent." The chart that Teasdale published in connection with his talk was the first tabulation of the various formulas and a courageous attempt to make sense of the process. Teasdale joined the fledgling Photographic Society and was briefly active in photographic publishing. As a civil engineer he could not resist the lure of major public works projects, and he soon moved to India to take a job on the railways. In 1858 he married his English fiancée in the Bombay Cathedral, but, tragically, she died in childbirth. Although the experience in India profoundly influenced him, and, as his obituary commented, "even up to his death he preserved the habit of thinking in Hindustani," he returned to his native village of Headingley, near Leeds. He retired there sometime in the 1860s. It was also remembered that in Leeds, as "the doyen of local scientists, Mr. Teasdale was well known and welcomed wherever men of science most do congregate." Teasdale developed new types of microscopes and was the driving force behind the reestablishment of the Leeds Astronomical Society in 1892. "His love of science amounted to a passion. His home . . . was a veritable treasure house of scientific apparatus, works of art, interesting curios. . . . In astronomy and photography he found his chief delights. In photography he was among the pioneers."

REFERENCES: Washington Teasdale, "Photographic Processes," *JPS* 1 (January 21, 1854), pp. 161–62; Teasdale, "Hints on Positive Printing," *JPS* 1 (February 21, 1854), pp. 170–71; Teasdale, "On the Waxed-Paper Process," *JPS* 1 (March 21, 1854), pp. 182–84; *BJP* 50 (September 25, 1903), p. 773 (obituary)

Tenison, Edward King *ills. 109, 110*
1805–1878
A captain in the 13th Dragoons, Tenison came from aristocratic Irish stock. His 1833 marriage to Lady Louisa Anson brought not only a handsome dowry but also a strong artistic influence. Lady Louisa was independent in means and equally so in spirit, and soon after their marriage she traveled alone through the Holy Land and Egypt. Her *Sketches in the East* established her reputation as a travel writer and as an artist. Just when Tenison first started in photography is not known, but it must have been quite early, for in 1860 he stated in the *British Journal of Photography* that "he had tried almost every process of photography, from its first introduction by Daguerre on the silvered plate, up to the present time, on both waxed and unwaxed paper, together with the albumen and collodion processes on glass." The ample mountain water supply and the practical resources of an Irish castle undoubtedly facilitated his experimentation. Tenison emerged as a strong advocate for paper negatives, making the revealing observation in the *Journal* that "it was true the development of a paper negative was slow, but that prolonged the pleasure to an amateur." Tenison taught himself the calotype, which he told the *Journal* worked "best on old English paper." However, he then took lessons from Gustave Le Gray in the waxed-paper process. Tenison's photography first emerged seriously in Spain in 1850–51. They had moved there for Lady Louisa's health, and she sketched and painted while he photographed. In 1852 he became a pupil of Édouard Baldus, captivated by his approach, as he commented in 1860 in the *British Journal of Photography*, "because of its simplicity and general success." Baldus used his own modification of the calotype process employing gelatine, but most significantly delayed waxing his negatives until after fixing. With this technique, Tenison was able to scale his negatives up to 12 x 15 inches. This impressive size made Tenison's work stand out in the 1853 Dublin International Exhibition. In the 1854 and 1855 exhibitions of the Photographic Society in London, he submitted a mixture of waxed-paper and calotype views, drawing on subjects in Spain, Belgium, and Normandy. Although these were the only exhibitions in which Tenison participated, he became an active member of the Photographic Society of Ireland and also photographed in Algeria and in his native Ireland. By 1860 he had so mastered Baldus's technique that he could make up a two-year supply of paper, finding it superior, as he noted in the *Photographic Journal* that year, "over any other for taking large pictures on a foreign tour." However, he also confessed to the *British Journal of Photography* that he had "almost given up the science altogether."

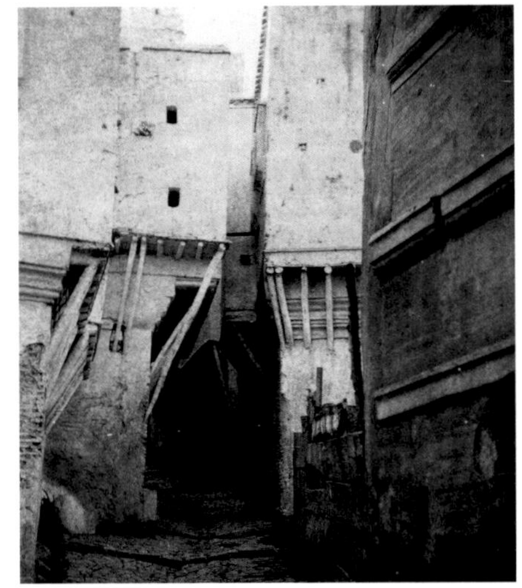

109. Edward King Tenison

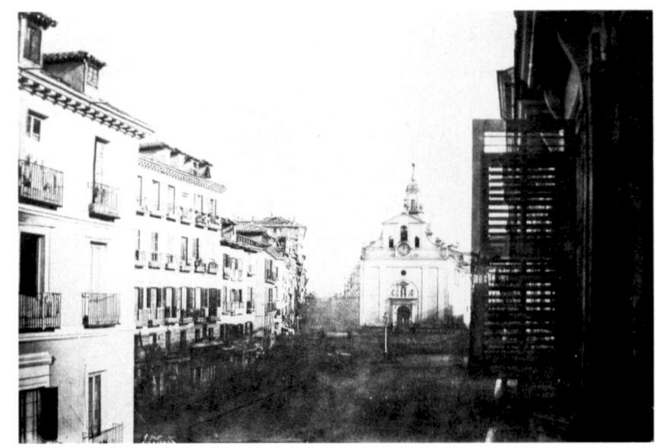

110. Edward King Tenison

Exhibited: 1853, Dublin, International Exhibition; 1854 and 1855, London, Photographic Society

References: Edward King Tenison, in "Photographic Society of Ireland," *BJP* 7 (March 1, 1860), pp. 67–68; "Photographic Society of Ireland," *Photographic Journal* 6 (March 15, 1860), pp. 182–83; *Times* (London), June 27, 1878, p. 5, col. F (obituary)

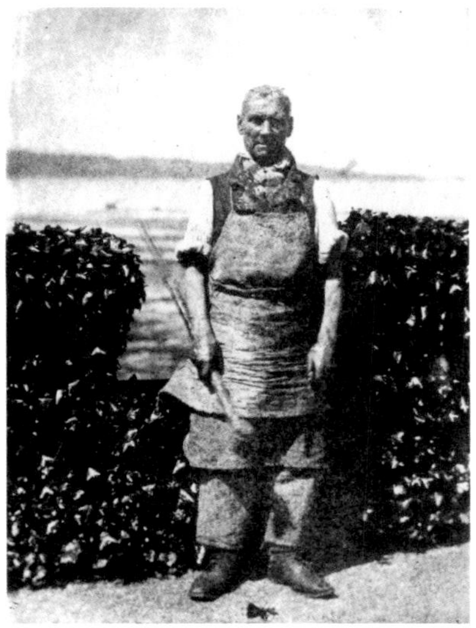

111. Hugh Lyon Tennent and Robert Tennent

Tennent, Hugh Lyon *ill. 111*

1817–1874

Several of Tennent's calotypes survive, just enough to confirm his mastery, but it was in his support of the new art that his reputation lies. Tennent and his brother ROBERT TENNENT became members of the Edinburgh Calotype Club. One of their albums has long been a justly famous holding of the Edinburgh Central Library, but in 2001 a second album was discovered and purchased by the National Library of Scotland. Its captions are in Tennent's hand, and the album appears to have been assembled by him. He eagerly joined the Photographic Society of Scotland when it was established in 1856. An advocate and a sheriff, Tennent was well liked and highly respected by all who knew him. His philanthropic activities included supporting the Discharged Prisoners' Aid Society. He was a keen sailor and a member of the Royal Clyde Yacht Club. His fifteen-ton yacht, *Seaward*, was sold after his death. An account of his family's cruise around the Western Isles in 1838 is still preserved in a private collection.

References: "A Reminiscence of the Calotype Club," *BJP* 21 (August 14, 1874), p. 385; *Scotsman* (Edinburgh), January 24, 1874, p. 6 (obituary)

Tennent, Robert *ill. 111*

1813–1890

Tennent was connected to the Tennent brewing family of Glasgow, and like his brother HUGH TENNENT he became a member of the Edinburgh Calotype Club in the 1840s. He had land holdings in Tasmania and appears to have spent most of the 1840s and early 1850s there. However, in volume 1 of the club's albums (now at the National Library of Scotland) the photographs initialed "T" are by Hugh and Robert working together. By the late 1850s Robert had returned to Scotland, marrying and living in Fife, but no photographs by him are known from this period.

Reference: "A Reminiscence of the Calotype Club," *BJP* 21 (August 14, 1874), p. 385

Thomas, Iltid

1812–1889

Little is known of this Welshman beyond his showing of a Talbotype, *Chateau de Pau, the Birth-place of Henri Quartre*, in the 1856 exhibition of the Photographic Society in London. Thomas's work preserved in a J.W. GUTCH album was also taken in France and included views of Cauterets, the Baths of Rulliere, and Eaux Bonnes, as well as *The Hill in Swansea*. Thomas's future wife, Dulcie Eden, was a photographic subject for JOHN DILLWYN LLEWELYN, so it is possible that Thomas had a connection to photography in this way.

Exhibited: 1856, London, Photographic Society

Thomas, Richard Williams

1823–1881

Thomas was a London chemist, one of the first to specialize in supplying the growing ranks of photographers. He was an early member of the Photographic Society when it was formed in the 1850s. Thomas became the premier supplier of collodion later in the 1850s, and his name is mainly associated with negatives on glass. However, in 1852 Thomas made a four-month journey to Italy, and his report to the *Art-Journal* makes clear that photography was foremost in his attentions. Thomas wrote, "When I left England I could make a good negative on paper by the usual method introduced by Mr. Fox Talbot, and, consequently, with much expectation of success, prepared a large quantity of iodised paper." One can imagine his chagrin as the paper failed time after time, until Thomas tore up fifty unsatisfactory negatives. He had gone to see "Mr. Robinson, well known to all artists and amateurs of every denomination in Rome. I cannot speak too highly of his courteous bearing towards a stranger who introduces himself as a follower of his favourite pursuit." Robinson and others in Frédéric Flacheron's circle said they had not succeeded with the dry process. Thomas then went to Tivoli and worked for ten days with Giacomo Caneva. Adopting his damp-paper process, Thomas succeeded in every negative, especially at Pompeii. The generous "Mr. Robinson" has yet to be identified and may have been a British calotypist. Thomas returned to a London that soon demanded all of his time in the manufacture of collodion. His son, also Richard Williams, became a London photographer and a fellow of the Photographic Society.

References: "Photography in Rome," *Art-Journal*, May 1, 1852, pp. 159–60; *BJP* 28 (July 15 and 22, 1881), pp. 368, 377 (obituaries)

Thomas, William F.

1829–1920

Thomas wrote to the *Journal of the Photographic Society* in 1856, saying he had used a particular method "for some years for applying the exciting and developing solutions to calotype paper." He mixed his solutions in paper cups and used paper spreaders, thus avoiding contamination by having fresh utensils each time. Thomas also had a suggestion for ARTHUR MELHUISH's paper-holding slide, indicating that he did indeed have a good deal of experience. Thomas had mastered the daguerreotype process in 1845 and gone on to be a sewing machine manufacturer in London. When he died, the *British Journal of Photography* called him the "oldest amateur photographer in the United Kingdom." None of his photographs are known to have survived.

References: W. F. Thomas, "Method of Exciting and Developing Calotypes," *JPS* 3 (July 21, 1856), p. 89; "Death of the Oldest Amateur Photographer," BJP 67 (June 4, 1920), p. 350

Thompson, Stephen

b. 1831

In the 1861 exhibition of the Photographic Society in London, Thompson showed mostly collodion but also four waxed-paper architectural views. That same year he displayed similar subjects in the Architectural Photographic Association exhibition, and while the processes were not specified, it seems likely that at least some of them were from paper negatives as well. After

ROGER FENTON's acrimonious separation from the British Museum, that institution relied on a number of photographers. Thompson was the most important of these, carrying out a number of projects for the museum in the 1860s and 1870s. In the end, however, the museum refused to make a permanent appointment for a photographer. That was not the first of Thompson's problems. In the early 1850s he was the partner of William Wagstaff in the London studio of Wagstaff & Thompson. Wagstaff brought suit against him in 1856, trying to reclaim the 200 pounds he had paid for instruction. He had locked Thompson out of the studio and had hidden the cameras to hold for ransom, but Thompson broke in and retrieved them. The judge wisely ruled that, whereas the partnership should be dissolved, Wagstaff could not collect his tuition. Thompson's lot improved after this incident. He received an award in the 1862 International Exhibition for his landscapes, architectural subjects, and reproductions of art. He later did contract work for the Autotype Company.

EXHIBITED: 1861, London, Photographic Society

REFERENCES: "Rolls Court," *Times* (London), January 25, 1856, p. 8, col. E; Anthony J. Hamber, *"A Higher Branch of the Art": Photographing the Fine Arts in England, 1839–1880* (Amsterdam: Gordon and Breach, 1996), pp. 385–86

Thompson, William

While staying with a Mr. Hitchman in Yarmouth in 1841, Thompson sent examples of his earliest attempts at calotypy to TALBOT. The inventor replied with encouraging advice, pointing out that he held a patent but did "not wish it to interfere with amateurs practising the art for their own amusement." In 1844, writing from Tavern Street in Ipswich, Thompson expressed continuing frustration over the quality of paper and modestly assuring Talbot that "I practise the art entirely for my amusement & edification, & that I do not derive the smallest advantage from it, as you will readily believe, from the specimens." In 1845, then staying with Mr. Howes in Happisburgh, Norfolk, Thompson again wrote to Talbot, saying that he had purchased a copy of *The Pencil of Nature.* He observed that *Leaf of a Plant,* the contact copy of a leaf, was a simple thing to make and respectfully hoped that Talbot would include more camera images in the next part (mirroring the advice that Talbot's mother had already given him!). The only known surviving photograph by Thomson is *Houses in Ipswich,* a calotype dated March 1846 and preserved in one of THOMAS DAMANT EATON's albums. William Thompson was too common a name to trace without further identification. However, it was unusual for Talbot to carry on a detailed correspondence with an amateur, and that he did in this case suggests one possibility. William Thompson (1823–1893), a baker's son in Ipswich, was plagued by poor health and turned to the study of botany, cultivating a small but sophisticated garden behind his father's shop. He soon became known as the "baker botanist." Passionate about botany himself, Talbot is perhaps more likely to have corresponded with such a person. Thompson & Morgan seeds are now one of the leading British brands.

REFERENCES: W. H. T. Talbot to William Thompson, December 18, 1841, Talbot Collection, British Library (Talbot Correspondence Project, http://foxtalbot.dmu.ac.uk, doc. no. 04391); Thompson to Talbot, March 18, 1844, Talbot Collection, British Library, LA44-20 (Talbot Correspondence Project, doc. no. 04968); Thompson to Talbot, Talbot Collection, British Library, LA45-29 (Talbot Correspondence Project, doc. no. 05203)

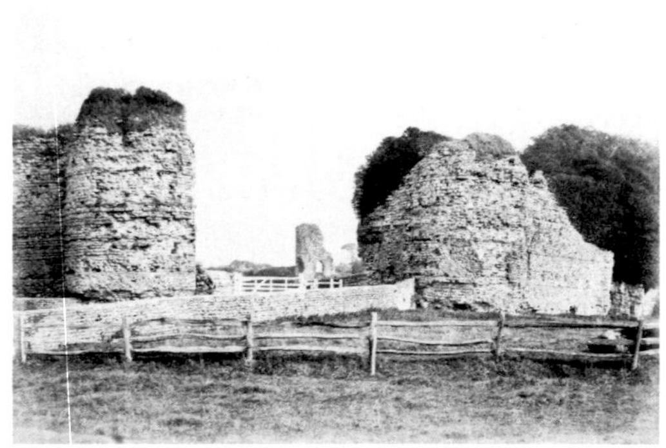

112. William John Thoms

Thoms, William John *ill. 112*

1803–1885

Although Thoms's first job was as a clerk in a hospital, his real passion was literature and especially bibliography. At twenty-four, still a clerk, he published *Early Prose Romances,* and he was elected a fellow of the Society of Antiquaries in 1838. He finally left the hospital in 1845 to take a position as clerk at the House of Lords, bringing him in regular contact with influential people. After several publication ventures, he realized his dream in 1849, establishing the journal *Notes and Queries.* Primarily designed to serve the needs of antiquarians and historians, this periodical was a vehicle not only for news about what was old but also for correspondence on what was new. Many important photographic contributions and speculations first appeared in its pages. Perhaps this is what stimulated Thoms's interest in photography. His first exhibited work was a collodion portrait in 1852, but at the 1854 Photographic Society exhibition in London he also showed calotypes of architectural subjects. All of his entries in the society's 1855 exhibition were Talbotypes. He contributed others, including a calotype of Stonehenge, to the 1855 and 1856 Photographic Exchange Club albums.

EXHIBITED: 1854 and 1855, London, Photographic Society

Thomson, John

1804–1881

A pioneering photographer in Edinburgh, Thomson was self-taught in the daguerreotype. He was one of the legion of photographers who remembered starting with a camera made from a cigar box and a spectacle lens, although in his case using a polished silver coin as the plate. His later partner, JAMES ROSS, was very specific in describing a paper photograph taken by Thomson in 1841, so he must have experimented with calotypy early on. In 1844 Thomson went into partnership with a case manufacturer to form the short-lived daguerreotype practice of Macmillan & Thomson. In 1847 Thomson met Ross, a portrait painter who had mastered the calotype, and the resulting firm of Ross & Thomson quickly emerged as the finest Edinburgh calotypists. In a symbiotic partnership similar to that of HILL & ADAMSON, Thomson was the technical underpinning of the firm and Ross its artistic director. By 1849 they had largely converted to the underrated but splendid albumen-on-glass-negative process, but in the 1853 Mechanics' Institution exhibition in Aberdeen they showed a large number of calotype landscapes. In 1855 Thomson published his *Progress of Heliochromy, or Painting in Colours by Light.* Ross & Thomson had been exhibiting their glass negative images widely, but, curiously, in the 1856 Photographic Society of Scotland exhibition in Edinburgh they included many daguerreotype portraits. Perhaps the book and the daguerreotypes signaled the start of a change in Thomson's thinking about photography. By the end of the 1850s Ross had acquired a new partner. Thomson had made his fortune and retired quite happily into obscurity.

EXHIBITED: 1853, Aberdeen, Mechanics' Institution

REFERENCES: John Thomson, *The Progress of Heliochromy, or Painting in Colours by Light* (Edinburgh: James Wood, 1855); "The Substance of a Paper Read by Mr. J. Ross before the Photographic Society of Scotland, April 14th, 1857," *Photographic Notes* 2 (October 1, 1857), p. 361; John Nicol, "Notes from the North," *BJP* 28 (March 25, 1881), p. 148 (obituary)

Thomson, T.

In the enormous and groundbreaking 1852 exhibition of photographs at the Society of Arts in London, "T. Thomson" contributed three paper negative views, all of Versailles and the surrounding area. Nothing further is known about him or her, and T. Thomson does not appear to have shown in any subsequent exhibitions. Although the subjects were French, Thomson is more likely to be a British name, and perhaps these views were taken by a tourist engaging in the new art of photography.

Exhibited: 1852, London, Society of Arts

Tibbits, Richard

b. 1806

Little is known of Tibbits, a Brighton brewer, who contributed five calotypes to the 1857 exhibition of the Photographic Society in London. They were all architectural views, including ones of Lichfield Cathedral and Alton Castle. Tibbits seemed particularly interested in details, photographing the *Porter's Lodge at Willersloy Castle*, the *Terrace at Haddon Hall*, and *Gray's Cenotaph*. None of his photographs are known to have survived.

Exhibited: 1857, London, Photographic Society

Todd, Thomas

Todd is known to have exhibited only once, submitting three calotypes to the 1853 Mechanics' Institution exhibit in Aberdeen. His subjects were all of Aberdeen, two studies of the Old Town cathedral and one of the thirteenth-century Brig o' Balgownie. Thomas Todd was a common name in Scotland, but, curiously, no one by that name has been traced to Aberdeenshire for this period. He listed himself as "Esquire," so it is likely that he had independent means.

Exhibited: 1853, Aberdeen, Mechanics' Institution

Todd, William(?) (or Austin?)

b. 1828

In the 1856 Norwich Photographic Society exhibition, the society member W. A. Todd displayed four waxed-paper views, all of architecture in Norwich and Bury St. Edmunds. He also exhibited some small portraits done in collodion, which, according to the *Norfolk News*, "leave nothing to be desired." Although the identification is tentative, Todd appears to have been a tailor's assistant living in Norwich who eventually rose to being a master tailor.

Exhibited: 1856, Norwich, Photographic Society

Reference: *Norfolk News*, December 6, 1856

Tose

Nothing is known of Tose. He or she showed one Talbotype, *Glenade, County Leitrim, Ireland*, in the 1854 exhibition in Dundee supporting the Royal Infirmary Fund. No further identification was given. Tose is a common name in England but virtually unknown in Ireland and Scotland.

Exhibited: 1854, Dundee, Royal Infirmary Fund

Townshend, Frederick

While there is some uncertainty over the identity of this photographer, there is no uncertainty over his mastery of waxed paper. An "F. Townsend" contributed six waxed-paper views to the 1855 exhibition of the Photographic Society in London. They were landscapes and architecture taken in Sussex and on the Isle of Wight. In the 1856 exhibition Townsend contributed three waxed-paper views of Tintern Abbey. The 1854 membership list of the Photographic Society included "F. Townshend of 6 Adelaide Crescent, Brighton," which in the directories was a "furnished house," so it may have been a temporary address. Frederick Townsend was on the 1859 list, living at 37 Lansdowne Place, Leamington. All of these listings are assumed to be the same Frederick Townshend who presented a talk "On the Waxed-Paper Process" to the Photographic Society in 1854. Townshend related that he started with Gustave Le Gray's waxed-paper process but found it too tedious and too slow in exposure. During the photographically dead winter season he analyzed and tried "nearly all the formulae given by the various practitioners" and was amazed at the variation in ingredients and proportions. At the meeting Townshend exhibited a wide range of experimental examples demonstrating many different approaches to waxed paper. In the end, he advocated a very simple formula with few ingredients, forgiving in its exposure time, stable enough to make several days ahead, and producing a good density for printing. The following year Townshend gave another talk, "On the Quality of Paper Required for Photographic Purposes." Once again he laid a range of experimental examples on the table. He found the English papers excellent as long as he did not wax them, for their gelatine sizing resisted the wax. Townshend ended by recommending most German and French papers (save for Canson's), but he felt that better results could be had by working with the more uniform fibers of the English papers. None of Townshend's photographs, experimental or exhibition, are known to have survived.

Exhibited: 1855 and 1856, London, Photographic Society

References: *List of Members of the Photographic Society* (London: Photographic Society, 1854), p. 11; Frederick Townshend, "On the Waxed-Paper Process," *JPS* 1 (June 21, 1854), pp. 218–20; *LPJ* 1 (July 8, 1854), p. 81; Townshend, "On the Quality of Paper Required for Photographic Purposes, More Particularly for the Wax-Paper Process," *JPS* 2 (May 21, 1855), pp. 166–69

Trevelyan, Pauline Jermyn

1816–1866

Pauline Trevelyan (christened Paulina), née Jermyn, was the daughter of a clergyman, antiquarian, and naturalist who was more inclined than many to allow a seventeen-year-old girl to accompany him to the 1833 British Association for the Advancement of Science meeting at Cambridge. Her agile brain and retentive memory greatly impressed the gathered scientists, none more so than the geologist Walter (later Sir Walter) Trevelyan. Two years later they were married, and most of the first decade of this union was spent in traveling on the Continent, where they studied scientific subjects and purchased art, and Pauline sketched with the camera lucida. While her husband had a connection with Talbot, meeting him was not her first exposure to photography. In May 1839 Alan Maconochie showed her his first photogenic drawings, contact prints of botanical specimens. In 1840 she learned the chemical and optical principles of photography from lectures by David Reid. Pauline examined the daguerreotypes at the 1840 British Association for the Advancement of Science exhibition, where she discussed the reproduction of daguerreotypes with "Capt. Ibbotson" (Levett Ibbetson). Sir David Brewster showed her photographs, and while in Rome in 1843, she marveled at the daguerreotypes that Maconochie had taken in the Pyrenees. In 1843, David Octavius Hill and Robert Adamson's calotypes impressed her greatly, reminding her (and others) of Rembrandt's sketches. Sir Thomas Phillipps proudly showed her his copy of Talbot's *The Pencil of Nature*. Nevertheless, Trevelyan seemed content to draw with her camera lucida while observing the photographic progress of others. It was not until April 1844 that she finally admitted to helping her husband make some calotypes. The day Talbot announced his invention of photography, January 25, 1839, happened to be her birthday. For her birthday in 1845, her husband presented her with his own calotype camera, signaling the end of his photographic endeavors and the serious start of hers. All of her previous artistic and scientific training was brought to bear on the effort, and she was immediately successful, recording photographic triumphs in her diaries. Pauline Trevelyan was an acerbic critic of art and literature, publishing largely in *Chamber's Edinburgh Journal*, and she became a close friend of and correspondent with John Ruskin. She was a patron of the Pre-Raphaelites, particularly in conjunction with the renovation of her home at Wallington. She designed lace patterns for the lace makers near her home in Devonshire and also designed the capitals for the Oxford University Museum. The artist William Bell Scott described her as "light as a feather and as quick as a kitten." In 1866 the Trevelyans joined Ruskin on a trip to Switzerland, where she finally succumbed to the cancer she had been fighting for years and was buried at Neuchâtel. Her photographs might illuminate the link between photography and the Pre-Raphaelites, but very few of her works have survived.

References: *Selections from the Literary and Artistic Remains of Paulina Jermyn Trevelyan*, ed. David Wooster (London: Longmans, Green, and Co., 1879); *Autobiographical Notes of the Life of William Bell Scott*, ed. W. Minto (New York: Harper & Brothers, 1892), vol. 2, p. 3; Larry J. Schaaf, "Henry Talbot's First Exhibition in Scotland," *Studies in Photography*, 1998, pp. 25–28; John Batchelor, *Lady Trevelyan and the Pre-Raphaelite Brotherhood* (London: Chatto & Windus, 2006)

Trevelyan, Walter Calverley

1797–1879

At Harrow, no two classmates were closer intellectually and spiritually than Trevelyan and Talbot, who shared a passion for botany. Trevelyan went on to study geology at Oxford under William Buckland and became a dedicated antiquary. He was also a social reformer, abstainer, a sincere believer in phrenology, and a promoter of concrete structures. Trevelyan discarded his first choice of a potential wife after a phreneological examination; at the 1833 meeting of the British Association for the Advancement of Science he met seventeen-year-old Pauline Jermyn, who was to become his wife and his artistic inspiration. In September 1839, the first batch of photogenic drawings sent by his childhood friend Talbot caught up with Trevelyan in Arbroath. On Christmas Day 1839 Trevelyan entered these into David Reid's exhibition in Edinburgh, thus giving Talbot his first public showing in Scotland. The Treveylans' contact with photography was frequent, first in Glasgow, then in St. Andrews with Sir David Brewster and John Adamson. In Rome in 1842 Trevelyan worked in daguerreotype with Alan Maconochie, assisting especially in the compounding of chemicals, and he took a special interest in photographic engraving. In 1843 Trevelyan saw Hill & Adamson's "capitol Calotypes" and by April 1844, he wrote in his diary, had "made some tolerably successful essays with Calotype" himself. He kept at it, becoming fairly adept. However, Sir Trevelyan's largest accomplishment in photography was interesting his wife, Pauline Trevelyan, in the art.

References: Larry J. Schaaf, "Henry Talbot's First Exhibition in Scotland," *Studies in Photography*, 1998, pp. 25–28; John Batchelor, *Lady Trevelyan and the Pre-Raphaelite Brotherhood* (London: Chatto & Windus, 2006)

Tripe, Linnaeus *ill. 113*

1822–1902

The son of surgeon and blessed with a wonderfully evocative name, Linnaeus Tripe opted for a career in the army of the East India Company. Educated in mathematics and the classics, he was sent to India in 1839. Tripe's earliest calotypes were taken in 1853 while he was on furlough in England. Returning to India, he photographed temples in 1855. In the 1855 exhibition of the Photographic Society of Madras, although this was early in his photographic career, Tripe's extensive contribution stood out. He showed sixty-eight photographs, printed from massive 14 x 12 inch waxed-paper negatives. According to the *Reports by the Juries* of the Madras exhibition, "the majority of these are clear, sharp, and well defined in the details. . . . The half tints and reflected lights are also well brought out. . . . As studies for the artist, the antiquary, or the engraver, these are invaluable." Tripe was appointed the official photographer for the government of Madras from 1857 to 1860. He traveled hundreds of miles, carting his heavy photographic equipment and exotic supplies, to photograph not only public works but also the region's ancient temples and palaces and exotic landscapes. Many of Tripe's photographs were published in grand albums and as stereograph cards. In 1859 Charles Trevelyan (the cousin of Walter Trevelyan), the new governor of Madras, shut down the photographic endeavor in an economy move. In 1860 Tripe sold his cameras and returned to his regiment; he eventually retired to England. No further photography by him is known.

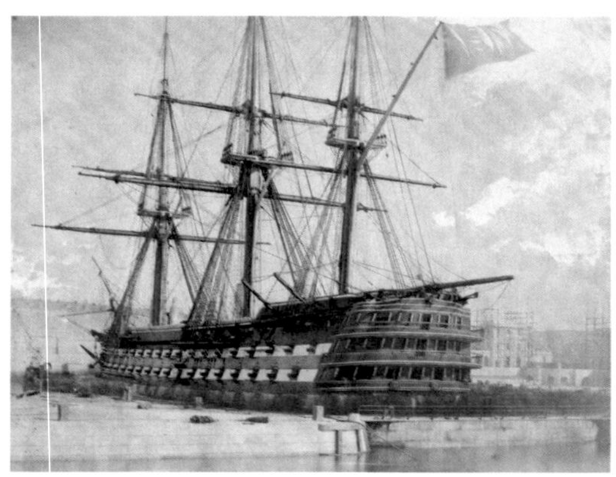

113. Linnaeus Tripe

Exhibited: 1855 and 1857, Madras, Exhibition of Raw Products, Arts, and Manufactures of Southern India; 1857, Calcutta, Bengal Photographic Society; 1858, Edinburgh, Photographic Society of Scotland; 1859, Madras, Photographic Society; 1860, Madras, Photographic Society

References: *Madras Exhibition of Raw Products, Arts, and Manufactures of Southern India, 1855: Reports by the Juries on the Subjects in the Thirty Classes into which the Exhibition Was Divided* (Madras: General Committee of the Madras Exhibition, 1856), pp. 133–34; G. Thomas, "Linnaeus Tripe in Madras Presidency," *History of Photography* 5 (October 1981), pp. 329–37; Janet Dewan, *The Photographs of Linnaeus Tripe: A Catalogue Raisonné* (Toronto: Art Gallery of Ontario, 2003)

Tucker, Harriet Ann

b. 1809

When the Will Weissberg Collection was sold in 1967, it contained three prints intriguingly inscribed on the mounts "H. A. Tucker, Calotype taken by Herself." Two of these were dated 1845. With this little information, the identity of Tucker must remain speculative. The most likely candidate is Harriet Ann, the wife of John Tucker, the highly successful Honiton lace manufacturer who gained prominence in 1839 by making the lace flounce for Queen Victoria's wedding dress. At its peak the Tucker firm employed an astonishing two thousand workers. In the census Harriet Tucker was listed both as a wife and as "occupied in the above business," almost certainly in a managerial role. She was known to Pauline Trevelyan and would have had the means and, apparently, the technical skills to master photography. Two of Tucker's calotypes were auctioned in 1977; most likely they were the two from the earlier sale.

Reference: *The Will Weissberg Collection of Rare Photographs, Cameras & Related Devices*, sale cat., Parke-Bernet Galleries, New York, May 16, 1967, lot 58; sale cat., Sotheby's, London, February 9, 1977, lot 273

Tuely, Nathaniel C.

b. 1833

A fundholder and landowner in London, Tuely's photographic work is known only through a single waxed-paper view, *The King's Stone and Old Houses, Kingston on Thames*, shown at the 1860 Photographic Society exhibition in London. However, he must have produced much more. In 1859 he wrote in reply to an appeal made by the *Photographic Journal* for more practical information on waxed paper: "I am surprised that waxed paper is so much neglected in England. I have had considerable experience in almost all the processes on glass; and, in my humble opinion, where the amateur does not wish to make a toil of a pleasure by practising the wet-collodion process out of doors, there is nothing like waxed paper for large views. It gives good definition, is very little liable to the objectionable snowy appearance so common in photographic pictures, and is more certain than any dry process on glass, to say nothing of its superior convenience."

Exhibited: 1860, London, Photographic Society

Reference: Nathaniel C. Tuely, "Waxed Paper," *Photographic Journal* 6 (October 15, 1859), pp. 59–60

Tunny, James Good
1820–1887
In 1869 Tunny was remembered as "one of the oldest and most advanced photographers in this country, having been professionally engaged in the art long anterior to the introduction of the collodion process." He started as a shoemaker in his native Scotland but was intrigued by chemistry, finding "every new discovery is the unlocking of another of Nature's boundless storehouses." In the autumn of 1839 an English friend sent Tunny a newspaper account of Talbot's fixing an image on paper. The young man immediately dissolved a silver sixpence in nitric acid, made some paper, and went to his neighbor, a Mr. Milne, to use his sketching camera obscura. His first negative took a two-day exposure, but the image of the geranium was captivating, and Milne promptly exhibited it during a natural philosophy lecture. Tunny further observed, in "Reminscences," "the enthusiasm with which I returned to repeat my experiment can only be appreciated by those who have just soiled their fingers for the first time, in the development of their first negative." Recalling Hill & Adamson's calotype studio, Tunny added, "time after time have I gone and stood on the projecting rock below Playfair's monument on the Calton Hill, and drawn inspiration from viewing Mr. Adamson placing a large square box upon a stand, covering his head with a focussing-cloth, introducing the slide, counting the seconds by his watch, putting the cap on the lens, and retiring to what we now know to be the dark room." Tunny exhibited a calotype portrait in the 1854 Royal Infirmary Fund exhibition in Dundee and in 1855 was still advertising "Calotype Portraits and Views of Edinburgh." But both the calotype and the daguerreotype were to give way to wet collodion, of which he was one of the earliest adopters. Tunny became one of the founding members of the Photographic Society of Scotland and was later on the council of the Edinburgh Photographic Society. He was very successful commercially and traveled widely to the Continent, the Middle East, and America. He taught many a Scottish gentleman amateur. Tunny's third wife, Margaret Wilson, was his photographic assistant; her early death in 1877 was widely lamented in the photographic community. A decade later, when he died, Tunny was remembered as being "thorough and enthusiastic in everything he undertook . . . he contributed . . . both by papers on practical topics and *vivâ voce* utterances."

Exhibited: 1855, Dundee, Royal Infirmary Fund

References: *Scotsman* (Edinburgh), May 26, 1855, p. 1 (advertisement); James Good Tunny, "Early Reminiscences of Photography," *BJP* 16 (November 12, 1869), pp. 545–46; *Scotsman*, September 26, 1887, p. 6 (obituary); *BJP* 34 (September 30, 1887), pp. 610–11 (obituary)

Turner, Benjamin Brecknell *ill. 114*
1815–1894
"I beg to say, that I do not employ the *waxed-paper process*, but the *original process* of Mr. Fox Talbot." Turner's emphatic statement, published in the *British Journal of Photography* in 1859, was occasioned by some flattering remarks in the *Photographic Journal* in the same year, typical praise for one who had emerged as one of the finest photographers of his generation. Turner's family were tallow chandlers (their products are still available today). His day job throughout his life was with this firm, but it was a financially successful venture and gave him ample opportunity to pursue his love of photography. And pursue it he did. Turner's own recollection is that he started in photography about 1849, taking up and never putting aside the calotype. He later claimed to have contributed to Talbot's *The Pencil of Nature* and by then had become a proud owner of one of the scarce originals. Certainly none of the plates in the album are credited to him, but the publication collapsed when fewer than half of Talbot's projected fifty plates had been published, so Turner's authorship is not totally implausible. In fact, in 1876, Turner donated a lens, labeled as the one used to take the plates in *Pencil*. Turner's earliest calotypes were of typical size, but in 1852 he undertook an ambitious 10 x 15 inch image, and most of his subsequent work was done in that format. Some of his earliest mature photographs date from 1852 and are poignant views of the Crystal Palace being dismantled for its move from Hyde Park. Starting with the pivotal 1852 exhibition at the Society of Arts in London, Turner was a prolific and consistent exhibitor. He had shown at least twenty-five calotypes in the London exhibitions by 1855, always entrancing the public and critics alike with his boldly and well-composed views of architecture and nature. Turner briefly dabbled in collodion in 1856, but by the time of the 1857 Manchester "Art Treasures" exhibition he had returned to the calotype. Between then and 1862 he was more prolific than ever, filling both English and Scottish exhibitions with his work. Turner found the plain paper of the calotype to be quite versatile and did not hesitate to reinforce details in pencil or to opaque out uneven skies. However, he did so with a grace that in no way undermined the truthfulness to nature for which he was known. In 1858 William Crookes declared, "Turner's 'calotype' old oaks, &c., equal anything of the same size that we meet with, whether glass or paper." In the 1875 exhibition by the Photographic Society of Great Britain, Turner's negatives were given an unusual treatment. Two of them that he had exhibited in the 1854 exhibition of the Photographic Society in London, including *Scotch Firs, Hawkhurst*, were enlarged to 20 x 24 inches and printed in carbon. Their beauty remained.

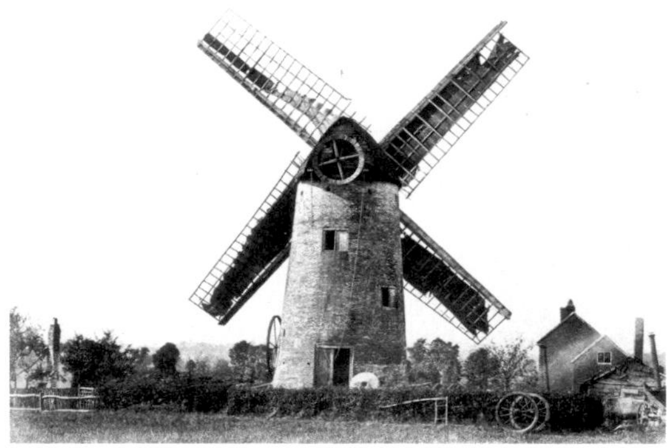

114. Benjamin Brecknell Turner

Exhibited: 1852, London, Society of Arts; 1853–54, first touring exhibition, Society of Arts (London); 1854, London, Photographic Society; 1854, second touring exhibition, Society of Arts (London); 1855, London, Photographic Society; 1857, Manchester, "Art Treasures" Exhibition; 1858, London, Photographic Society; 1858, Edinburgh, Photographic Society of Scotland; 1859, London, Photographic Society; 1859, Glasgow, Photographic Society; 1862, London, International Exhibition

References: William Crookes, "On the Calotype Process," *Photographic News* 1 (October 1, 1858), p. 38; Benjamin Brecknell Turner, "Calotype Pictures, &c.," *BJP* 6 (May 15, 1859), p. 137; *Photographic Journal*, n.s., 19 (February 26, 1895), p. 159 (obituary); Martin Barnes, *Benjamin Brecknell Turner: Rural England through a Victorian Lens*, with a biography by Mark Haworth-Booth (London: V&A Publications, 2001)

Tytler, George
1789–1849
Tytler was a successful artist, a draftsman to the Duke of Gloucester and the illustrator of the *Pictorial Alphabet* favored by the royal family. He traveled widely and "was

well known to the *literati* in London and abroad." In April 1839, having heard about Daguerre and the English photographers, Tytler "made some paper to be sensitive to a Camera obscura's glass." He sent several examples of his early photography printed on the paper he used to write a letter to his artist friend Barron Graham, in Edinburgh. The letter survives in a private collection, and although it is all that is known of Tytler's work, it is a graphic demonstration of an independent photographic invention inspired by the idea being made public. Always an eccentric, Tytler, in spite of his wide connections, would never admit anyone to his lodgings. His friends raised an annuity to sustain him in old age, but he died in crushing poverty in London. It is unlikely that any other photographic examples by him were saved, for in the end his room "resembled a dung-heap more than the habitation of a human being."

REFERENCE: *Times* (London), September 6, 1849, p. 5, col. F (obituary)

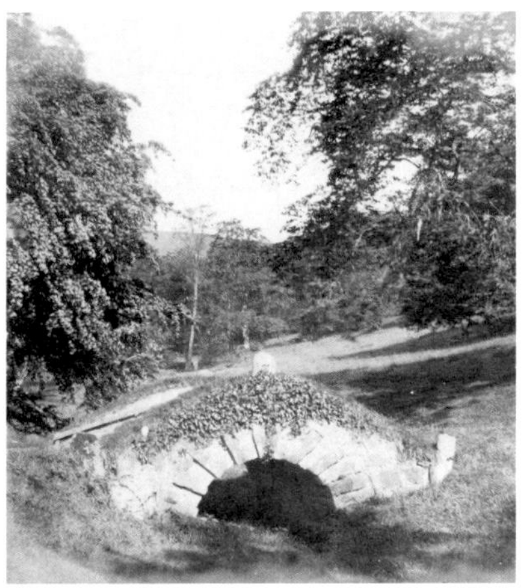

115. George Michael Tytler

Tytler, George Michael *ill. 115*

1822–1905

Tytler hailed from the Fraser-Tytler family of Woodhouselee, on the river Esk near Roslin, just south of Edinburgh, but as the fourth son, he did not acquire the Fraser title. His grandfather, Alexander Fraser Tytler, was a lawyer, writer on translation, and friend of Robert Burns, but George seems to have left no record of activity in publishing, in any sort of commercial activity, or in the legal and banking worlds, and even managed to elude every census. When Tytler joined the Photographic Society of Scotland in 1856 he gave the address of his Edinburgh bank for correspondence, but when he joined the Edinburgh Photograph Exchange Club three years later he listed Woodhouselee as his address. If that was his normal residence, the idea that he lived off family income is reinforced. In the 1859 album of the Exchange Club, Tytler showed six views of Woodhouselee done in collodion and seven views titled *Scots Firs at the Bush* done in waxed paper. In the 1856 exhibition of the Photographic Society of Scotland in Edinburgh, Tytler displayed four collodion views of Woodhouselee. He was elected a member of the society's council in 1858.

Tytler, Harriet Christina

1828–1907

In 1848 Harriet Earle became the second wife of ROBERT TYTLER, a major for the East India Company. Although British and educated in London, she was born and died in India. As a young woman she displayed unusual courage and pluck, traits that were to serve her well during the Great Mutiny in Delhi in 1857. Among the few to escape the uprising, she was the only British woman present during the subsequent siege and gave birth to her third child under a donkey cart. Her husband had been taught the rudiments of photography by Felice Beato and JOHN MURRAY. It had always seemed surprising that he was able to produce at least five hundred waxed-paper negatives after the siege, even though he was on leave part of the time. In the 1980s, quantities of these emerged at auction, many bearing the monogram "H.C.T." In fact, in the *Englishman* Tytler is described as crediting his wife with being "a most successful photographer." Hearing a rumor that part or all of the city was to be knocked down, Harriet wrote in her memoirs that she decided to preserve "what the home of the Emperors of Delhi was like," even though she had never painted a landscape in her life. She arranged a six-foot-high circle of paper six feet in diameter supported by bamboo rods, and set up threads within to insure correct perspective. A departing artist gave her a six-by-eighteen-foot canvas and paints, and thus she begun her cyclorama. She hoped to sell it to Barnum, but a long delay in getting home made the mutiny old news. An audience with the queen to show it and the couple's photographs was frustrated by Harriet's ill health. She did not complete the cyclorama until after her husband's death in 1872. Always loyal to India, she then founded an orphanage, which carried on after her death as an industrial school. Her contributions to photography have yet to be fully recognized. In 1986 a mammoth paper negative was auctioned and credited on the basis of a later inscription to "Stanley Tytler." This in fact was Stanley Delhi-force Tytler, her son born during the siege.

REFERENCES: "Report of the Photographic Society of Calcutta," *Englishman* (Calcutta), March 31, 1859; G. Thomas, "Indian Mutiny Veterans: The Tytlers," *History of Photography* 9 (October–December 1985), pp. 267–73; sale cat., Christie's, London, April 24, 1986, lot 454; *An Englishwoman in India: The Memoirs of Harriet Tytler, 1828–1858*, ed. Anthony Sattin, with an introduction by Philip Mason (Oxford: Oxford University Press, 1986)

Tytler, Robert Christopher

1818–1872

Tytler was born in Cawnpore, his father being an Irish-born surgeon stationed in India. Tytler received a classical education from Leith High School in Edinburgh and became a cadet in the East Indian Army in 1834. Later, as Major Tytler, he was present at the Great Mutiny in Delhi in 1857 and was assigned duties in the siege to retake the city. At some time, Tytler had received instruction in photography from Felice Beato and from JOHN MURRAY and had mastered the waxed-paper process. Tytler was credited with producing at least five hundred negatives of the siege and its aftermath, supposedly as records for his wife, HARRIET TYTLER, to use in painting her cyclorama. However, recent discoveries indicate that at least a number of these calotypes were in fact taken by her. When some of the negatives were exhibited at a meeting of the Photographic Society of Bengal in Calcutta in 1859, they were judged by the *Englishman* to be "perhaps the finest series that has ever been exhibited to the Society" and "clearly shewed the eye of the artist." Tytler "wished it to be understood that the full merit of his photographs did not lie with himself; that Mrs. Tytler, who is a most successful photographer, not only selected many of the subjects, but even developed the pictures herself."

REFERENCES: "Report of the Photographic Society of Calcutta," *Englishman* (Calcutta), March 31, 1859; G. Thomas, "Indian Mutiny Veterans: The Tytlers," *History of Photography* 9 (October–December 1985), pp. 267–73

Verschoyle, Catherine

1802–1882

Catherine Verschoyle, née Curtis, was the wife of Robert Verschoyle, a barrister in London descended from a branch of the Dutch family who began settling in Ireland in the early seventeenth century. In 1839 Catherine's portrait was included in *Heath's Book of Beauty*, and she was praised not only for her face but also for her sweet singing voice. She was an accomplished watercolorist before photography. She became one of the earliest members of the

Photographic Society in London, especially notable for a woman, being accepted for membership in April 1853. In the society's 1854 exhibition, she contributed three collodion views of Holland Park and one calotype, *Cedars in Holland Park*. *Cedars* was her only known calotype, although it is probably representative of a larger body of work. It was the first of many botanical and tree studies that she exhibited. Catherine Verschoyle continued to exhibit a wide variety of subjects until at least 1863, at which time the *British Journal of Photography* placed her "amongst our landscape photographists of repute." She also continued to exhibit her watercolor landscapes at least this late. Her son, Colonel Henry William Verschoyle (1835–1870), acquired her drawing and photographic skills. He served in the Crimea and became an exhibiting member of the Photographic Society. His early demise came not in battle but from "heat apoplexy" while racing a yacht.

Exhibited: 1854, London, Photographic Society

References: "The Ninth Annual Exhibition of the Photographic Society (London)," *BJP* 10 (January 15, 1863), p. 32; Virginia Mason, *Gens Van der Scuylen: 600 Years of the Verschuijl and Verschoyle Family* (Whitehill: Verschoyle Mason Publishers, 2001)

W., H.

This author of "Rambles and Recollections" signed it with only initials, revealing few personal clues and no hint of his or her occupation. But H. W. was clearly a dedicated amateur photographer. Resident in London in 1853, H. W. was inspired by photographic exhibitions but could not afford to take lessons from Thomas Malone at the Polytechnic Institution and thus was self-taught from a handbook. The following year H. W. was in the country, with more time and enough money to buy the entire (then) nine-month run of the fledgling *Photographic Journal*. It was Robert Hunt's *Manual of Photography and* his *Researches on Light*, however, that most inspired H.W., who favored Hunt's chromatype process for copying engravings and Thomas Wood's iron-based catalisotype for making paper negatives in the camera. About 1855, H.W. converted to collodion and was still active in photography two decades later.

Reference: H.W., "Rambles and Recollections of an Amateur Photographer," *BJP* 22 (August 13, 1875), pp. 389–91

W., T.

In a 1985 auction catalogue, four 1850s studies of Jerusalem were offered. Salt prints from waxed-paper negatives, they were monogrammed in the negative "T.W.," the W contained within a barbed circle. Nothing else is presently known of this photographer, but the distinctive monogram may some day be identified.

Reference: Sale cat., Sotheby's, London, March 29, 1985, lot 78

Walker, William *ill. 116*

1814–1885

Dr. Walker's "ripe experience assured to him the position of a mentor in all professional questions," making him popular with both the younger and older members of the medical community. An eye surgeon in Edinburgh, he became surgeon oculist to the queen for Scotland and served the last fifteen years of his life as president of the Royal College of Surgeons. The *Lancet* remembered "his commanding figure, which was well known in the streets of the Scottish metropolis" and that he was "gifted with a ready wit and a dry vein of humour." The *Edinburgh Medical Journal* noted that he was "distinguished by his robust common sense." All of these were useful traits for an early amateur in photography. Walker became a member of the Edinburgh Photographic Exchange Club and was a friend of Thomas Keith. Compared with the work of such a masterful colleague, Walker's photography was perhaps more enthusiastic than aesthetically accomplished. He was a clever experimenter, and in 1856 he published his design for a portable camera that had a cloth body over a collapsing wooden frame. That same year Walker gave a presentation on his approach to the calotype process, acknowledging his debt to Hugh Diamond. In common with an important minority of photographers, Walker, as he explained in *Photographic Notes*, "thought that the best prints were always obtained from an unwaxed negative, as the shadows were not so transparent, and the half tints much more delicate." He also stressed the need for "the strictest attention to cleanliness in the different stages." The reviewer of the 1859 exhibition of the Photographic Society of Scotland singled out Walker's work, feeling that his "'Dalhousie Castle,' and views on the 'Esk,' by the calotype *(old school)* process, are very good."

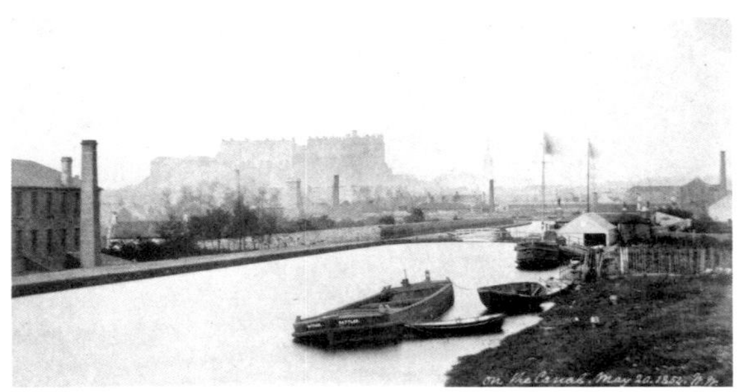

116. William Walker

Exhibited: 1856 and 1858, Edinburgh, Photographic Society of Scotland; 1859, Glasgow, Photographic Society; 1859, Aberdeen, British Association for the Advancement of Science

References: William Walker, "On the Calotype Process," *Photographic Notes* 1 (June 17, 1856), pp. 77–78; *Scotsman* (Edinburgh), August 17, 1885, p. 4 (obituary); *Lancet* (London), August 22, 1885, p. 369 (obituary); *Edinburgh Medical Journal* 31 (October 1885), pp. 399–400 (obituary); Julie Lawson, "William Walker: An Early Amateur Photographer," *Scottish Photography Bulletin*, Autumn 1988, pp. 3–13; Larry J. Schaaf, *Sun Pictures, Catalogue Six: Dr. Thomas Keith and John Forbes White* (New York: Hans P. Kraus, Jr., 1993), p. 11

Wardley, George

About 1861, when James Mudd separated his business from that of his brother, he hired George Wardley as an assistant in his Manchester studio. Wardley already had considerable experience in photography. In the 1856 Manchester Photographic Society exhibition he displayed nineteen views from waxed-paper negatives, all of them taken in Wales. Wardley became a member of the Chorlton Photographic Society and in an 1858 presentation to the members noted "that the waxed paper process is one specially suitable for use in localities destitute of the convenience of railways for the transport of heavy masses of glass, while it is peculiarly adapted for producing softness and delicacy of effect, particularly with bold rustic subjects." Wardley stayed with Mudd for six years, opening his own studio in nearby Salford about 1867.

Exhibited: 1856, Manchester, Photographic Society

Reference: "Chorlton Photographic Society," *LMPJ* 2 (June 1, 1858), p. 136

Waring, Charles Henry *ill. 117*

1818–1887

Waring was the works' agent for the Neath Abbey Ironworks, part of the great Quaker industrial holdings in Wales. His grandfather was Joseph Tregelles Price, a founder of the Peace Society, a humanitarian, and an industrialist, whose daughter was Waring's mother. Waring attended a Quaker school in Bristol, excelling in Latin, Greek, and mathematics. He became an apprentice at the ironworks in 1832, and there he likely gained mechanical skills later valuable for his amateur photography. Injured in a colliery explosion in 1834, Waring recovered to become manager of the ironworks 1845–51. When he took up photography is not recorded, but his first known public display, possibly in support of a charity, was in the 1854 Royal Infirmary Fund exhibition in

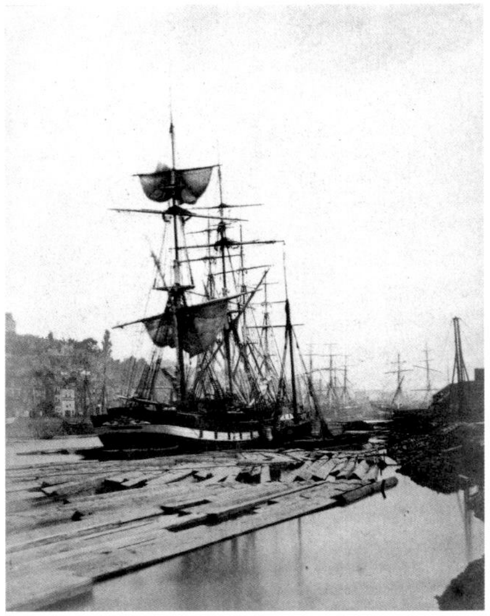

117. Charles Henry Waring

Dundee. Waring entered one collodion portrait and ten calotypes of landscape and architecture around Bristol and South Wales. He entered a dozen similar calotypes in the 1854 exhibition of the Photographic Society in London. In its 1855 exhibition Waring entered another dozen calotypes, all from Wales, including *Stream in Winter*, *A Quiet Pond*, and *The Fallen Tree*. He also displayed collodion views of a landscape and of an aqueduct, perhaps signaling a departure from his paper negatives for fieldwork. Waring may have given up photography after this. In 1864 he wrote the descriptions for *Views in Wales. The Vale of Neath—Photographed by the British and Foreign Portrait Company.* The collodion views in this publication were taken by Robert Peter Napper, a member of the Blackheath Photographic Society. No further photographic work by Waring is known. He became managing partner of another iron company and a member of the Institute of Civil Engineers.

Exhibited: 1854, London, Photographic Society; 1854, Dundee, Royal Infirmary Fund; 1855, London, Photographic Society

Reference: Laurence Ince, *Neath Abbey and the Industrial Revolution* (Stroud: Tempus, 2001)

Warren, John Neville
1818–1861

Warren exhibited only once, in the 1854 Photographic Society exhibition in London. In addition to five collodion views he showed two calotypes of Chichester Cathedral. A civil engineer and an agent of the Scinde Railway Company in India, Warren built railways in India and in Germany. It is likely that he took up the calotype process for its ease of use in the field. Warren perished in a steamer accident on the Red Sea in 1861.

Exhibited: 1854, London, Photographic Society

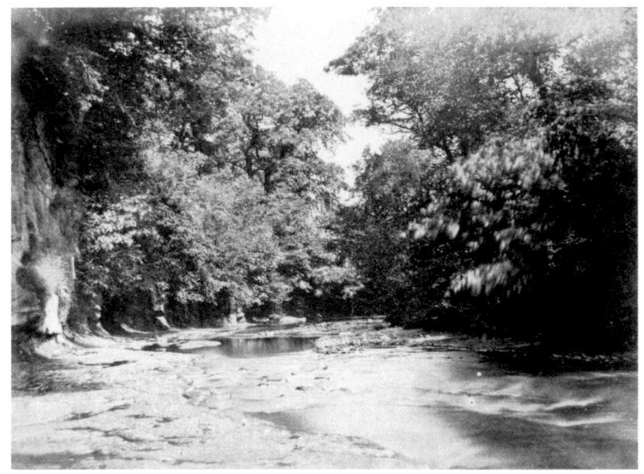

118. Henry George Watson

Watson, Henry George *ill. 118*
1796–1879

An Edinburgh accountant, Watson had two calotypes accepted for the 1855 Photographic Exchange Club album, both views of St. Andrews, hinting at a likely influence from that cradle of photography in Scotland. In 1856 he became one of the founding members of the Photographic Society of Scotland, accepting the post of honorary treasurer. In their exhibition that year Watson showed mostly collodion copies of his brother's paintings, along with a portrait of his brother, Sir John Watson Gordon. Gordon (who had assumed the extra surname in 1826) was the president of the Royal Society of Arts and undoubtedly another influence on his brother's photography. In the 1858 exhibition of the society, Watson returned to calotypy, showing three architectural views. Upon his death in 1879, Watson honored his brother by endowing the chair of Fine Art at Edinburgh University.

Exhibited: 1856, Edinburgh, Photographic Society of Scotland; 1858, Edinburgh, Photographic Society

Reference: *Times* (London), July 8, 1879, p. 8, col. b (obituary)

Watson, William Frederick Wilcocks
d. 1869

At the inaugural meeting of the Brighton and Sussex Photographic Society in June 1855, Rev. Watson read a paper titled "On Calotype." In the exhibition of the Photographic Society in London that year he showed nine calotypes, architectural and scenic views in Derby, Sussex, and Hertfordshire. Not surprisingly, his photographic subjects seem to have been inspired by where he lived. Watson was curate at Rye in Sussex 1841–50 and of Brighton 1851–55, and rector of Ickleford, at Hitchin in Hertfordshire, 1854–59. Neither his text nor any of his photographs are known to have survived.

Exhibited: 1855, London, Photographic Society

Reference: "Brighton and Sussex Photographic Society," *LPJ* 2 (October 13, 1855), p. 122

Wells, G. G.

Resident in Ireland and an army captain, possibly retired, Wells showed "Specimens of Talbotype drawings" in the 1853 Dublin International Exhibition, according to its catalogue.

Exhibited: 1853, Dublin, International Exhibition

West, James

In the 1854 exhibition of the Photographic Society in London, according to the exhibition record, West showed a Talbotype, *View of Town of Montrechaud* (most likely this is a cataloguing misspelling of the historic Loire Valley market town of Montrichard). Nothing else is known about West.

Exhibited: 1854, London, Photographic Society

West, William
1801–1861

A landscape painter in Bristol, West exhibited in the Royal Academy from 1845 and was elected a member of the Society of British Artists. In 1828 he had acquired the rights to an eighteenth-century windmill, spectacularly sited overlooking the Clifton Gorge. By the following year he had installed an astronomical observatory complete with a camera obscura (still available to the public today). In April 1839 West started exhibiting "various kinds of photogenic drawing" and was selling "superior photogenic paper" at the observatory. In December 1842 he wrote to Talbot, explaining that "having been for some time as an Amateur engaged in photographic pursuits," he would like to obtain a license to practice it commercially. No surviving examples of his work are known.

References: William West to W. H. F. Talbot, December 21, 1842, British Library, London, LA42-84 (Talbot Correspondence Project, http://foxtalbot.dmu.ac.uk, doc. no. 04678); John Latimer, *The Annals of Bristol in the Nineteenth Century* (Bristol: W. & F. Morgan, 1887), pp. 124–25

West, William A.
b. 1808
It was not unusual for amateurs to experiment with diverse photographic processes, many of them with a culinary connection. West's first known photograph, shown in the 1854 Photographic Society exhibition in London, was made using "Everard's Milk Process." In the following year's exhibition, however, he became more conventional, showing some collodion and several Talbotypes. A fundholder (that is, investor in public funds) living in Sussex, West divided his subjects between local sites and several areas in France.

Exhibited: 1855, London, Photographic Society

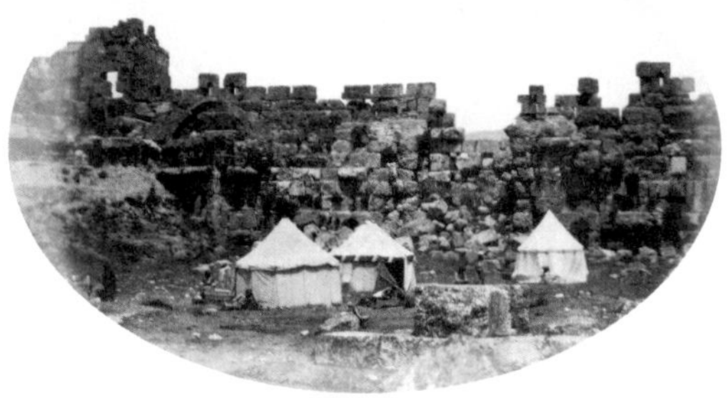

119. Claudius Galen Wheelhouse

Wheelhouse, Claudius Galen *ill. 119*
1826–1909
Wheelhouse was born in Yorkshire, began working at Christ's Hospital in London at ten, and was apprenticed to a doctor in Newark at sixteen. He finished his medical training in 1849, and his first practice was an unusually interesting one as the medical officer aboard a private yacht touring the Mediterranean. It is not known when Wheelhouse had first taken up photography, but this sojourn offered ample leisure time, good production facilities, and fascinating subjects. He later explained in a note, now in the National Media Museum, Bradford, that "the photographs were taken by what was then called the Talbot-type process . . . they were taken on simple paper . . . and, when completed were made as transparent as possible by being saturated with white wax, with the aid of a warm flat iron and blotting paper, by which means they were also made tough and durable." Wheelhouse took calotype negatives in Spain, Greece, Egypt, and the Holy Land, including masterful ones of the Parthenon and of the temple at Karnak. The only exhibition that Wheelhouse is known to have participated in was at the Leeds Photographic Society in 1857. He appears to have given up photography after this tour in favor of his medical practice. Dr. Wheelhouse established hospitals in Leeds, where he was a prominent philanthropist, and eventually became president of the British Medical Association. Although durable in handling, Wheelhouse's negatives and many of his prints were destroyed in a fire in 1879.

References: Claudius Galen Wheelhouse, signed manuscript note, RPS Collection, National Media Museum, Bradford; *Times* (London), April 12, 1909, p. 9, col. c (obituary); Richard Pare, *Photography and Architecture, 1839–1939* (Montreal: Canadian Centre for Architecture, 1982), p. 78; Adrian Budge, *Early Photography in Leeds, 1839–1870*, exh. cat. Leeds (Leeds: Leeds City Art Galleries, 1981), p. 8; Wheelhouse, *Narrative of a Yacht Voyage in the Mediterranean, 1849/1850*, ed. Badr El-Hage (London: Folios, 2006)

White, J. P.
White started as a daguerreotypist on fashionable Buchanan Street in Glasgow, but by 1852 he was styling himself in Post Office directories and on daguerreotype cases as a "photographist." In the 1855 exhibition celebrating the British Association for the Advancement of Science meeting in Glasgow, his versatile firm showed a mixture of collodion, albumen, and waxed-paper views. It even exhibited the original waxed-paper negative of a view of Alloway Kirk.

Exhibited: 1855, Glasgow, British Association for the Advancement of Science

White, John Forbes *ill. 120*
1831–1904
White and Thomas Keith, who married sisters, had already shared a passion for waxed-paper photography. Born in Aberdeen, White was identified as an exceptional student by the age of thirteen—his classics professor, as a 1918 biography of him records, gave him a Greek name meaning "the shining one." White moved to Edinburgh to

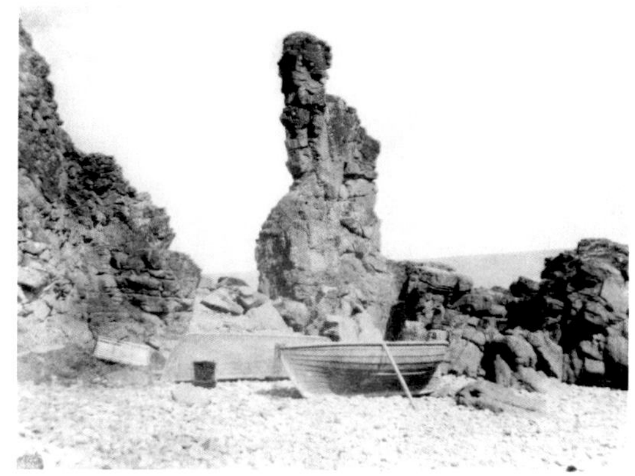

120. John Forbes White

study medicine, and by the summer of 1853 he and Keith were photographing together. Their landscapes and architectural subjects are virtually indistinguishable in selection and mastery. Both of their views of Melrose Abbey were singled out for praise in the 1853 Aberdeen exhibition. In the 1857 exhibition of the Photographic Society of Scotland, White showed views from a photographic expedition in England and was praised for his "artistic skill & handling." White was the driving force behind the 1859 exhibition in Aberdeen that was held in connection with the meeting of the British Association for the Advancement of Science, where he showed nine of his own waxed-paper views. But this exhibition was to be his last public showing and the last one for his friend Thomas Keith as well. The death of White's missionary brother had forced him to give up medicine in order to take over the family milling business in Aberdeen. White's real devotion, however, was to the world of art. He became an important collector of paintings, particularly of Dutch art, and White's home in Aberdeen was a regular gathering place for Scottish artists. The editor of the *Enclyclopedia Britannica*, accepting his extensive essays on Vermeer, Rembrandt, and Velázquez, wrote, "Mr. White is not a scholar, he doesn't pretend to be one, but he is one of the most scholarly men I know."

Exhibited: 1853, Aberdeen, Mechanics' Institution; 1857, Edinburgh, Photographic Society of Scotland; 1859, Aberdeen, British Association for the Advancement of Science

References: Ina Mary Harrower, *John Forbes White* (Edinburgh: T. N. Foulis, 1918), p. 25; C. S. Minto, *John Forbes White: Miller, Collector, Photographer, 1831–1904* (Edinburgh: Library and Museums Committee, 1970); Larry J. Schaaf, *Sun Pictures, Catalogue Six: Dr. Thomas Keith and John Forbes White* (New York: Hans P. Kraus, Jr., 1993)

Wiggin, Henry

In her personal 1848 album, "Photogenic Drawings of Various Objects," BESSIE RAYNER PARKES included only one photograph by another person. It was a salt print labeled "Executed & given to me by Mr. Henry Wiggin" and titled *Bridge near Coventry*. Nothing else is known of Wiggin or any other photographic work that he might have produced.

REFERENCE: Larry J. Schaaf, *Sun Pictures, Catalogue Ten: British Paper Negatives*, 1839–1864 (New York: Hans P. Kraus, Jr., 2001), pp. 36–41

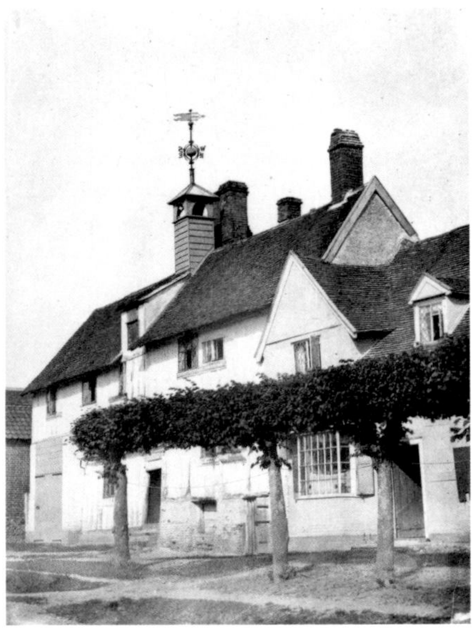

121. John Wiggin

Wiggin, John *ill. 121*

b. 1819

Wiggin was an enterprising pharmaceutical and analytical chemist in Ipswich. By 1869 he was offering scientific apparatus, patent medicines, oils, and colors. Wiggin seems to have established his firm just about the time that his interest in photography became public. In the 1855 exhibition of the Photographic Society in London, Wiggin showed three waxed-paper views, two taken in Ipswich and one of Baylham Hall in Suffolk, formerly a residence of Anne Boleyn. In the 1856 exhibition Wiggin again showed waxed paper views, one listed in the exhibition catalogue as being "near Ipswich," and the other of the cathedral in his native Peterborough. An undated broadside in a private collection written by him lists "pure photographic chemicals, lenses, and apparatus of every description." Wiggin also offered to take views of gentleman's seats, landscapes, and statuary, and was prepared to give full instructions in "the various processes." Curiously, Wiggin mentioned nothing about collodion or glass in this otherwise complete advertisement. He did advertise "waxed, albumenized, iodized, and other papers of the best French and English makers." Albumen paper and wet collodion were introduced almost simultaneously in the early 1850s, so the exclusion of glass processes must have been a deliberate choice.

EXHIBITED: 1855 and 1856, London, Photographic Society

Wilkinson, A.

Wilkinson's connection with photography is known solely through a single "photogenic portrait" that he or she contributed to the 1843 Polytechnic Exhibition of the Durham Mechanics' Institute. No further details were given in the catalogue.

EXHIBITED: 1843, Durham, Mechanics' Institute

Wilkinson, W. T.

Nothing is at present known of Wilkinson's life or work other than his 1898 presentation titled "Paper Negatives." He told the members of the London and Provincial Photographic Association, "to the photographer of forty years' experience the above title recalls almost endless trouble, first in the difficulty of procuring paper at all suitable for the purpose, then the mess and trouble of waxing, iodising, sensitising, etc. After all this trouble the tedious operations of exposure and development had to be faced, but after an expenditure of time and trouble a present-day amateur would shirk; the process gave negatives leaving little to be desired, as may be seen by the example No. 1, a waxed paper negative made in 1855."

REFERENCE: W. T. Wilkinson, "Paper Negatives," *BJP* 45 (January 21, 1898), p. 41

Willats, Richard

b. 1820

Along with his brother Thomas, Willats was a partner in the firm of T. & R. Willats, a leading London philosophical instrument maker and one of the first significant dealers in photographic apparatus and supplies. In 1898 a photographer named Edward Foxlee gave a presentation on the early history of photography to the Photographic Club in London, illustrating it with actual examples in a significant album compiled many years before by the Willats brothers. The Photographic Club members were so delighted by the opportunity of seeing the old examples that "a vote of thanks was passed to him and to Mr. Willats." Miraculously, this album survives today, purchased at the historic 1952 Albert E. Marshall sale and preserved at Princeton University. It still contains 255 of the prints seen by the Photographic Club. The album is a uniquely valuable resource in the earliest history of the art and the sole repository of the memory of photographers such as JOHN SHERRINGTON. Its earliest dated examples were made by THEODORE REDMAN in 1839, and nearly all the others are from the 1840s. In addition to designing and building cameras, selling supplies, and giving instructions, the Willats firm was also an important publisher of photographic books, including the influential manual written by John Croucher, a parliamentary agent, owner of an academy, studio photographer, and author. Willats was not only a supplier and a collector but also admitted to at least one photogenic drawing, done in 1840 and included in his album. He almost certainly produced others, and perhaps some of the presently unattributed photographs in the album are by him.

REFERENCES: "An Album of Old Prints," *BJP* 45 (December 2, 1898), pp. 776–77; *A Panoramic History of the Art of Photography as Applied to Book Illustration, from Its Inception Up to Date*, sale cat., Swann Galleries, New York, February 2, 1952

Williamson, A.

In 1857 the Calcutta Volunteer Infantry Guards, commanded to form a square to fend off a cavalry charge, must have been surprised when they learned this was not for bloodletting, but rather for the purpose of a photograph to be taken by a Mr. Williamson. A merchant in Calcutta, Williamson contributed thirty prints from both calotype and collodion negatives to the 1857 Photographic Society of Bengal exhibition. In 1858 Williamson photographed the reading of the royal proclamation that ended the rule of the East India Company. In 1859 Williamson exhibited "a number of his very beautiful landscape views, amongst which was a very fine panorama of Calcutta." These were to be the last of his Indian views, for Williamson "announced that as he was about to go to England, his camera and lenses were for sale." No trace of him has been found after that.

EXHIBITED: 1857, Calcutta, Bengal Photographic Society

REFERENCE *Englishman* (Calcutta), January 22, 1859

Wilson, Charles
b. 1814
Wilson was a prosperous tailor and draper established in Preston. His earliest known photographs, taken in 1852, include both glass and calotype negatives. They document the commercial architecture and grand homes of Preston. There is a possibility that much more could be learned about Wilson's photography. In 1977 a now untraced album containing work by several photographers was auctioned. It included annotated calotypes and experiments with the honey-collodion process by Wilson, dated from about 1850 to 1853. Some idea of Wilson's interests can be divined from the titles of his pictures—*Mechanics Institute Building*, and also portraits of his relatives. One portrayed *Thomas Wilson & his telescope*. Also in the album were leaflets from Howard Wilson, an optician and instrument maker in Garstang in Lancashire.

References: Sale cat., Sotheby's, London, November 18, 1977, lot 239; Emma Heslewood and John Garlington, *Robert Pateson, a Scientific Philosopher: The Life and Work of an Early Photographer*, exh. cat. (Preston: Harris Museum and Art Gallery, 2004), p. 13

Wilson, Thomas Maryon *ill. 122*
1800–1869
Wilson is best known in some circles for having been thwarted in his efforts to build houses on Hampstead Heath, a cherished London park. However, he was also an avid photographer and an early calotypist. When he died, the *Photographic Journal* lamented that the Photographic Society had lost "one of its best and earliest supporters." Wilson had taken part in the formation of the society in 1853 and served as a member of its first council. Just when he took up calotypy as an amateur is not clear, but the *Liverpool Photographic Journal* reported that he practiced "the calotype process at a very early date." Wilson contributed twenty-one Talbotypes and calotypes to the 1854 exhibition of the Photographic Society in London. His impressive range included copies of paintings, formal portraits, genre portraits, architecture, landscape, and some very ambitious attempts not typical of his contemporaries. One was *Forest Scene—taken during a storm*. The *Builder* enthused, "Sir Thomas Wilson's 'Snow-storm' (692) is excellent: it is really a snow storm." The *Photographic Journal*, comparing his copies of paintings with other attempts, reported, "Sir Thomas M. Wilson has been more successful in his calotype and talbotype copies of pictures by McIan." When PAULINE TREVELYAN and her husband, Sir Walter, visited Wilson in 1852, she noted in her diary that they found Wilson "busy making calotype portraits in a glass house he has built on the roof

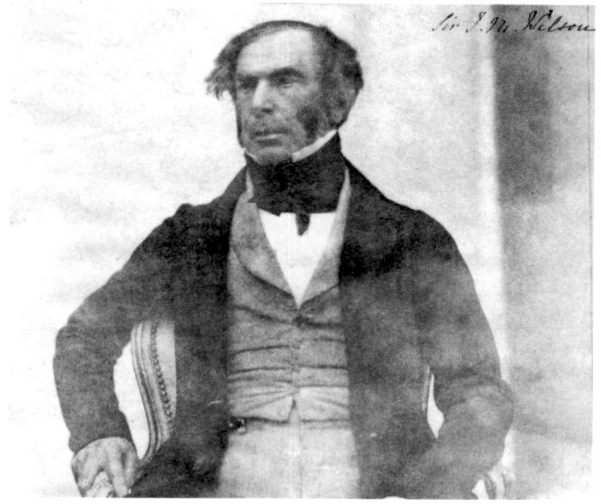
122. Portrait of Thomas Maryon Wilson

of their house." Wilson became one of Dr. HUGH DIAMOND's first students, learning the new collodion process from him. In the 1858 exhibition of the Photographic Society, Wilson was still showing calotypes, but after that he turned to collodion. He continued to exhibit up to the year of his death.

Exhibited: 1854, London, Photographic Society

References: "The Photographic Club," *Almanac of the Fine Arts* (London: G. Rowney, 1852), p. 155; "Photography and the Photographic Exhibition," *Builder* 12 (January 21, 1854), p. 28; "The Exhibition of Photographs and Daguerreotypes, by the London Photographic Society," *LPJ* 1 (February 11, 1854), p. 17; *Photographic News* 13 (May 14, 1869), p. 239 (obituary); *Photographic Journal* 14 (May 15, 1869), pp. 45–46 (obituary)

Winter, John Saumarez *ill. 123*
1807–1875
Rev. Winter presented his "Observations on the Calotype Process" to the members of the North London Photographic Association in 1858, exhibiting a number of his "excellent negatives" to illustrate the talk. Sadly, this was read during a time when the photographic journals were beginning to tire of the older paper processes, and his text seems not to have been published. However, at least two albums preserve the memory of his early photography. His younger brother, James (1813–1856), lived in Tasmania but visited the Vicarage at Tottenham in 1854. As a departure present, John presented him with an album, dated November 18, 1854, that contained diverse architectural and scenic views taken across the north of London. In 1976 a second Winter album emerged at auction, this one with the bookplate of another brother, Thomas Le Mesuier Winter (1809–1876), who spent much of his life as a merchant in Australia but moved to

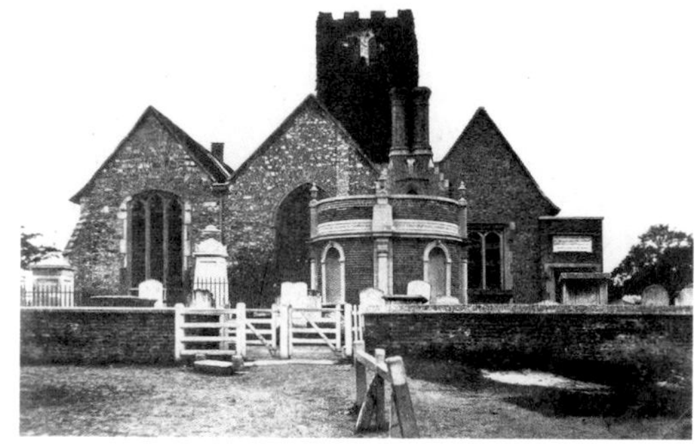
123. John Saumarez Winter

London in retirement. It contained both collodion and calotype views, all dated from 1853 to 1855 and showing a wide range of subjects, including portraits, architectural views, still lifes, and landscapes. There is no evidence that Thomas was a photographer, so this album must be assumed to have been a gift from his brother.

References: "North London Photographic Association," *JPS* 4 (May 21, 1858), p. 231; sale cat., Christie's, London, June 10, 1976, lot 38; Rupert Derek Wood, "John S. Winter's Family, Friends, and Places in 1854," *New Zealand Journal of Photography*, no. 19 (May 1995), pp. 12–15

Wood, John Muir
1805–1892
Born into an Edinburgh family of piano makers and music publishers, Wood first began to take an interest in scientific topics when he studied in Paris and Vienna in the 1820s. He returned to Edinburgh and was there when photography began to be introduced during the 1840s. He was friends with GEORGE SMITH CUNDELL and many other figures involved in early calotypy and of course would have been well aware of the work of HILL & ADAMSON. Wood's earliest known photographs, calotype groups and portraits, date from the mid-1840s. In 1847 he made calotypes on a journey that started in York and went on to Belgium and Germany. Wood then photographed Melrose Abbey and, extensively, the landscape of Scotland. Highly competent as an amateur photographer, Wood was also an experimentalist who annotated many of his prints and negatives. His descendants carefully preserved his photographic archive, making it one of the most important study collections available today.

Reference: Sara Stevenson, Julie Lawson, and Michael Gray, *The Photography of John Muir Wood, 1805–1892: An*

Accomplished Amateur (Edinburgh: Scottish National Portrait Gallery; London: Dirk Nishen, 1988)

Woods, Thomas
1815–1905
Dr. Woods was appointed vaccinator for Parsonstown, adjacent to Lord Rosse's Irish estate in 1841, and by 1890 he was the longest-serving medical practitioner in the area—he remained in service for some time after that. While we do not know when Woods first took an interest in photography, he was a friend of Lord and Countess Rosse, and their interest in daguerreotypy dates to at least 1842. In 1844 Woods presented the first of his new photographic processes. His awkwardly but descriptively named Electrolysotype and Catalysotype papers produced photographic negatives on paper using iron salts. TALBOT felt these were functionally the same as his calotype, and he and Woods battled verbally in the scientific press. Woods is not known to have ever exhibited his photographs, but he continued his researches into the collodion period. In 1861 he developed a method for producing precise micrometers photographically. Woods dedicated his 1860 book, *The Existence of the Deity, Evidenced by Power and Unity in Creation, from the Results of Modern Science*, to Lord Rosse.

REFERENCES: Thomas Woods, "On the Electrolysotype: A New Photographic Process," *Report of the British Association for the Advancement of Science*, 1844, sec. 2, pp. 36–37; "Catalysotype," *Proceedings of the Royal Irish Academy* 3 (May 12, 1845), pp. 97–98; "Photography," *Athenaeum*, January 3, 1852, pp. 22–23

Worden, J.
J. Worden of Hull has yet to be identified, but he gave some very interesting advice "On Getting Good Distances in Calotype Landscapes," in *Photographic Notes* for 1857. Worden was struck by Sir DAVID BREWSTER's observation that the distances never looked right in camera lucida drawings, even though he knew them to be optically correct, for the eye and brain combined to expect a different effect. Worden had been "perplexed in taking Calotype views, because the far objects did not appear to be as far off as they ought, nor so remote as they would look in a good painting or engraving." He concluded that only stereo calotypes would give the correct impression of nature. A late entry in the 1854 exhibition of the Photographic Society in London was credited simply to "Worden." This may or may not be by the letter writer, for a Newcastle bookseller, Thomas Worden, became a professional photographer by 1857.

REFERENCE: J. Worden, "On Getting Good Distances in Calotype Landscapes," *Photographic Notes* 2 (January 1, 1857), pp. 14–15

Wyatt, Thomas
1799–1859
Wyatt was a portrait painter in the Midlands, practicing in Birmingham, Liverpool, and finally Manchester. His younger brother, Henry, was the more promising of the two artists, but he died at an early age. In Birmingham Wyatt's portraiture was highly regarded, and he was elected secretary to the Birmingham Society of Artists. In an April 1845 letter Wyatt completed negotiations with TALBOT and purchased the exclusive calotype portrait license for Manchester and the surrounding locality. Wyatt had been disappointed with the portraits produced at Antoine Claudet's establishment but was inspired by what he had seen in Talbot's *The Pencil of Nature* and was determined to persist. Wyatt was so entranced by the new art that he neglected his regular painting practice. A bequest from an old friend in Birmingham gave him several hundred pounds more to put into calotypy. Then bad fortune came his way as he started to lose his sight. Wyatt returned to his birthplace and tried to continue painting, but he had to give up even that when he became paralyzed. He died a lingering death, and the *Art-Journal* launched an appeal for his widow and child. Few of Wyatt's paintings and none of his photographs are known to have survived.

REFERENCES: Thomas Wyatt to W. H. F. Talbot, April 14, 1845, Talbot Collection, British Museum, LA 45-38 (Talbot Correspondence Project, http://foxtalbot.dmu.ac.uk, doc. no. 05229); *Art-Journal*, September 1859, p. 288 (obituary)

Young, W. J.
Young has the distinction of having taken the earliest known views in the north of Ireland. At least two of his calotypes survive, both views in Belfast. One is dated March 1854 and the other November 1855. He used Turner's "Patent Talbotype" paper for his negatives. Young's images preserve Belfast architecture in transition, and perhaps this interest influenced his nephew, Robert, who was to go on to become a noted antiquarian.

REFERENCE: W. A. Maguire, *A Century in Focus; Photography and Photographers in the North of Ireland, 1839–1939* (Belfast: Blackstaff Press, 2000), pp. 11–12

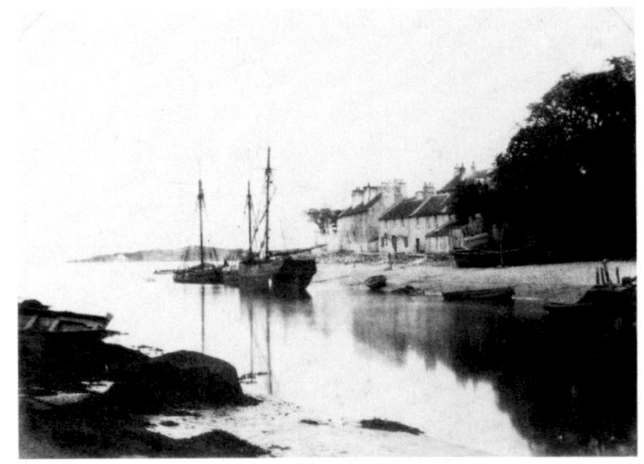

124. John Ziegler

Ziegler, John *ill. 124*
Although Ziegler's identity has not been firmly established, the address he used was that of William Ziegler, one of a long line of Edinburgh silversmiths. John Ziegler was one of the founding members of the Edinburgh Photographic Exchange Club in 1859. Earlier, in 1855, he had joined the Photographic Society of Scotland. Ziegler displayed six waxed-paper architectural and scenic views in the society's 1858 exhibition. In 1859 he placed five waxed-paper views with the same titles, along with a collodion architectural study, in the Photographic Society of Glasgow exhibition. Ziegler remained a member of the Photographic Society of Scotland until it was disbanded in 1873.

EXHIBITED: 1858, Edinburgh, Photographic Society of Scotland; 1859, Glasgow, Photographic Society

List of Illustrations in the Biographical Dictionary of British Calotypes

Titles in *italics* were given by the photographer. Those in roman type are modern descriptive titles.
All photographs are from paper negatives unless stated otherwise.

1. Alexander Forsyth Adam, *Sweetheart Abbey*, Kirkcudbright, ca. 1855. Albumen silver print from waxed-paper negative, 25.7 x 20.4 cm (10 1/8 x 8 in.). National Media Museum, Bradford

2. John Adamson, *Part of South Street, Pulled Down for Improvement*, St. Andrews, March 1844. Salted paper print, 14.3 x 19.3 cm (5 5/8 x 7 5/8 in.). Hans P. Kraus, Jr., New York

3. Attributed to Richard Dykes Alexander, View of Ipswich Docks, ca. 1855. Image digitally created from a paper negative, 30.2 x 37.5 cm (11 7/8 x 14 3/4 in.). Hans P. Kraus, Jr., New York

4. Attributed to Alexander Todd Anderson, *Niagara Falls*, 1851. Salted paper print, 10.7 x 17.7 cm (4 1/4 x 7 in.). Hans P. Kraus, Jr., New York

5. Benjamin Herschel Babbage, *Banksia. The Honeysuckles of Colonists*, Australia, 1851–57. Salted paper print, 14.5 x 17.2 cm (5 3/4 x 6 3/4 in.). Scottish National Photography Collection, National Galleries of Scotland, Edinburgh, PGP 127(1)

6. Alfred Backhouse, *Genoa*, 1854. Albumen silver print, 21.3 x 27.4 cm (8 3/8 x 10 3/4 in.). Paula and Robert Hershkowitz, Sussex

7. Edward Backhouse, Jr., *Sunderland Cast Iron Bridge*, December 31, 1853. Albumen silver print, 20.8 x 25.6 cm (8 1/4 x 10 1/8 in.). Paula and Robert Hershkowitz, Sussex

8. Thomas James Backhouse, *Portico: West Hendon House, 1853. Residence of Thomas J Backhouse*. Albumen silver print, 20.5 x 25.7 cm (8 1/8 x 10 1/8 in.). Paula and Robert Hershkowitz, Sussex

9. William Robert Baker, A Mountain Road, ca. 1855. Image digitally created from a paper negative, 25.8 x 30.4 cm (10 1/8 x 12 in.). Collection Musee d'Orsay, Paris, PHO 1987 21 28

10. William Robert Baker, Town View with Bell Tower, ca. 1855. Image digitally created from a paper negative, 16.8 x 22 cm (6 5/8 x 8 5/8 in.). Hans P. Kraus, Jr., New York

11. Arcangelo Corelli Collard Bere, Rural Scene, early 1850s. Image digitally created from a paper negative, 17.3 x 22.4 cm (6 7/8 x 8 7/8 in.). The Royal Photographic Society Collection at the National Media Museum, Bradford

12. Thomas Biggs, *Iwullee, East Front of the Temple*, ca. 1855. From Meadows Taylor and James Fergusson, *Architecture in Dharwar and Mysore* (London, 1866). Albumen silver print, 27.5 x 39.5 cm (10 7/8 x 15 1/2 in.). The Metropolitan Museum of Art, New York, Rogers Fund, 1920, transferred from the Library, 1991, 1991.1073.98 (74)

13. Golding Bird, *Fac-simile of a Photogenic Drawing*. Engraving from photogenic drawing, 15.3 x 11.3 cm (6 x 4 1/2 in.). From the *Mirror*, April 20, 1839, p. 241. Private collection

14. John Cooke Bourne, *Dnieper Bridge, looking towards the Lavra Heights, with the decking loaded with sand for load testing*, September 19, 1853. Salted paper print, 32 x 42.5 cm (12 5/8 x 16 3/4 in.). National Museum of the History of the Ukraine, Kyiv

15. George Wilson Bridges, *Mount Etna*, 1846. Image digitally created from a paper negative, 16.7 x 21.8.cm (6 5/8 x 8 5/8 in.). National Media Museum, Bradford

16. George Wilson Bridges, *The gulph* [sic] *of fire at the bottom of the crater, Etna, taken between explosions*, 1846. Image digitally created from a paper negative, 16.4 x 21.5 cm (6 1/2 x 8 1/2 in.). National Media Museum, Bradford, 1937/2180

17. Charles Brittan, *On the Downs, Clifton*, ca. 1854. Salted paper print, 17.4 x 22.3 cm (6 7/8 x 8 3/4 in.). The Royal Photographic Society Collection at the National Media Museum, Bradford, RPS 16766

18. Benjamin Browning, *The Dewerstone near Bickleigh, Devon*, 1850s. Albumen silver print, 26.7 x 20.3 cm (10 1/2 x 8 in.). Collection of Charles Isaacs and Carol Nigro, New York

19. Samuel Buckle, *Buckle's Laboratory, Leamington*, late 1850s. Albumen silver print from collodion negative, half of a stereoscopic pair. Warwick County Record Office, Warwick, PH 480/61

20. Robert Burrows, A Landscape Study, 1850s. Albumen silver print, 30.5 x 40.6 cm (12 x 16 in.). Collection of Charles Isaacs and Carol Nigro, New York

21. Miss Bush, *The Observatory*, ca. 1855. Salted paper print, 9.8 x 15.6 cm (3 7/8 x 6 1/8 in.). The Metropolitan Museum of Art, New York, Gilman Collection, Gift of The Howard Gilman Foundation, 2005, 2005.100.382 (4a)

22. William George Campbell, *Part of the old walls, Southampton*, 1854. Salted paper print, 17.8 x 22.6 cm (7 x 8 7/8 in.). The Royal Photographic Society Collection at the National Media Museum, Bradford, C10/56

23. Henry Collen, *Mr. Traherne*, ca. 1843. Salted paper print from a calotype negative, with modern intensification, 10.4 x 7.9 cm (4 1/8 x 3 1/8 in.). Hans P. Kraus, Jr., New York

24. William Collie, Woman with Baskets of Produce, 1850. Salted paper print, 18.8 x 15.2 cm (7 3/8 x 6 in.). The Royal Photographic Society Collection at the National Media Museum, Bradford

25. William Collie, Girl Knitting Socks, ca. 1850. Salted paper print, 19.9 x 14 cm (7 7/8 x 5 1/2 in.). The Royal Photographic Society Collection at the National Media Museum, Bradford

26. William Collie, Portrait of Woman Smelling Flowers, ca. 1850. "The negative of this picture was taken in twenty seconds." Salted paper print, 19.4 x 14.9 cm (7 5/8 x 5 7/8 in.). The Royal Photographic Society Collection at the National Media Museum, Bradford

27. Unknown photographer, Portrait of George Smith Cundell, early 1850s. Salted paper print, 8 x 5.5 cm (3 1/8 x 2 1/8 in.). Victoria and Albert Museum, London, Ph 184–1982

28. Alfred Capel Cure, *Shrubland*. Albumen silver print, 17.2 x 21.9 cm (6 3/4 x 8 5/8 in.). Hans P. Kraus, Jr., New York

29. Thomas Davies, *Lyme Gardens, Winter*, Lyme Park, Cheshire, ca. 1855. Albumen silver print, 11 x 16 cm (4 3/8 x 6 1/4 in.). Warrington Museum and Art Gallery, Warrington Borough Council

30. Hugh Welch Diamond, *Roman Bridge, Ardoch, Perthshire*, 1854. Salted paper print, 15.8 x 19.9 cm (6 1/4 x 7 7/8 in.). The Royal Photographic Society Collection at the National Media Museum, Bradford, 11497

31. James Matthews Duncan, *On the Aber Water, Invernesshire*. Albumen silver print, 20.3 x 26.9 cm (8 x 10 5/8 in.). National Media Museum, Bradford

32. James Dunlop, Strada Britannica, Valletta, Malta. Salted paper print, 15.8 x 14.6 cm (6¼ x 5¾ in.). National Library of Scotland, Edinburgh, Phot.med.33

33. Thomas Damant Eaton, The Erpingham Gate, Norwich, ca. 1850. Albumen silver print, 21.1 x 16.4 cm (8¼ x 6½ in.). The Royal Photographic Society Collection at the National Media Museum, Bradford, 11519

34. William Ellis, Portrait of a Man, Madagascar, ca. 1853. Salted paper print, 18.2 x 22.8 cm (7⅛ x 9 in.). Thomas Walther, New York

35. Walter Evans, *Lichfield*, ca. 1855. Salted paper print, 16.4 x 21.5 cm (6½ x 8½ in.). Hans P. Kraus, Jr., New York

36. Roger Fenton, Bridge over the Dnieper at Kiev under Construction, 1852. Albumen silver print. Acervo da Fundação Biblioteca Nacional–Brasil, Rio de Janeiro

37. Thomas Hatton George Fermor, *Interior of the Hall of Karnack*, 1853–54. Albumen silver print, 20 x 25 cm (7⅞ x 9⅞ in.). Hans P. Kraus, Jr., New York

38. Joseph James Forrester, *The Convent Bell, Portugal*, ca. 1856. Albumen silver print, 21.1 x 15.9 cm (8¼ x 6¼ in.). The Royal Photographic Society Collection at the National Media Museum, Bradford, 11552

39. Edward Fox, Jr., Farm Scene, late 1850s. Image digitally created from a waxed-paper negative, 11.9 x 10 cm (4⅝ x 4 in.). © Philippe Garner, London

40. Unknown photographer, Portrait of Peter Wickens Fry, 1850s. Albumen silver print from collodion negative, 13.6 x 11.2 cm (5⅜ x 4⅜ in.). Victoria and Albert Museum, London, Ph 137-1982

41. Peter Wickens Fry, Panorama of a Farmhouse and Trees, late 1840s. Images digitally created from a pair of waxed-paper negatives, 18.6 x 22.5 (7⅜ x 8⅞ in.) and 18.8 x 23.8 cm (7⅜ x 9⅜ in.). Hans P. Kraus, Jr., New York

42. Cecilia Louisa Glaisher, *Study of Ferns № 36 (Adiantum capillus-veneris L,* true maidenhair fern), 1854. Paper negative, 44.4 x 28 cm (17½ x 11 in.). Fitzwilliam Museum, Cambridge, SL 7735

43. James Graham, *The Street called Straight, Damascus*, 1856. Salted paper print, 26 x 19.7 cm (10¼ x 7¾ in.). Collection of Charles Isaacs and Carol Nigro, New York

44. Alexander John Greenlaw, *Vitthala Temple, Interior of Mahamandapa*, 1856. Image digitally created from a paper negative, 40.7 x 45.5 cm (16 x 17⅞ in.). The Alkazi Collection of Photography

45. Francis Robert Griffith, Malabar Point, Bombay, ca. 1855. Image digitally created from a paper negative, 23.8 x 31.7 cm (9⅜ x 12½ in.). Collection of the Prentice and Paul Sack Photographic Trust, ST1998.0201.4

46. John Moyer Heathcote, Sr., Round Tower and Cart Sheds, ca. 1855 Image digitally created from a paper negative, 14.6 x 19.3 cm (5¾ x 7⅝ in.). Collection of the Prentice and Paul Sack Photographic Trust, ST1998.0219

47. Unknown photographer, Portrait of Charles Heisch, 1850s. Salted paper print from collodion negative, 18.8 x 14.6 cm (7⅜ x 5¾ in.). Victoria and Albert Museum, London, Ph 181-1982

48. Thomas Henry Hennah, *Wool Bridge, Dorsetshire*, September 1854. Albumen silver print, 15.2 x 22.6 cm (6 x 8⅞ in.). The Royal Photographic Society Collection at the National Media Museum, Bradford

49. Nicolaas Henneman, *Foxbury Hill, Reading*, 1845. Salted paper print, 10.1 x 8.2 cm (4 x 3¼ in.). National Gallery of Art, Washington, Paul Mellon Fund, 2007.29.21

50. Alexander Young Herries, View in Guernsey, 1855. Albumen silver print, 21.4 x 27.8 cm (8⅜ x 11 in.). National Media Museum, Bradford

51. Alexander Young Herries, *Roslin Chapel*, 1857. Albumen silver print, 27.7 x 20.5 cm (10⅞ x 8⅛ in.). National Media Museum, Bradford

52. David Octavius Hill and Robert Adamson, *Oyster Dredging*, Newhaven, ca. 1845. Salted paper print. Gernsheim Collection, Harry Ransom Humanities Research Center, The University of Texas at Austin

53. David Octavius Hill and Robert Adamson, *Lady Ruthven*, ca. 1845. Salted paper print, 19.9 x 15 cm (7⅞ x 5⅞ in.). The Metropolitan Museum of Art, New York, The Rubel Collection, Purchase, Manfred Heiting and Lila Acheson Wallace Gifts, 1997, 1997.382.18

54. Richard Barton Hill, *Garden in Indigo Districts*. Albumen silver print, 18.3 x 24.1 cm (7¼ x 9½ in.). The Metropolitan Museum of Art, New York, Gilman Collection, Museum Purchase, 2005, 2005.100.948.2 (20)

55. Alfred Huish, *A Sikh Howitzer*, 1849. Salted paper print, 14.1 x 17.5 cm (5½ x 6⅞ in.). Private collection, London

56. William Howes Hunt, Figure Seated in Yard, ca. 1845. Salted paper print, 13.6 x 9.9 cm (5⅜ x 3⅞ in.). Norfolk County Council Library and Information Service, Norwich

57. Cosmo Nelson Innes, *Villa Guilini, Lago di Como*. Albumen silver print, 22.3 x 26.9 cm (8¾ x 10½ in.). National Media Museum, Bradford

58. Albert Augustus Isaacs, *The Wailing Place*, 1856. Albumen silver print, 21.9 x 27.5 cm (8⅝ x 10⅞ in.). Collection Centre Canadien d'Architecture / Canadian Centre for Architecture, Montréal, PH1983:0517.01:013

59. Thomas Brumby Johnston, *Old Bridge, Stirling, Twilight*, 1858. Albumen silver print, 18.5 x 21.6 cm (7¼ x 8½ in.). National Media Museum, Bradford

60. George Fowler Jones, *Rievaulx Abbey, 1895*. Image digitally created from a collodio-gelatin paper negative, 25 x 20 cm (9⅞ x 7⅞ in.). The Royal Photographic Society Collection at the National Media Museum, Bradford, RPS 18495

61. Edward Kater, *Old English House*, ca. 1856. Albumen silver print, 14.7 x 18.4 cm (5¾ x 7¼ in.). The Royal Photographic Society Collection at the National Media Museum, Bradford, RPS 1150

62. Thomas Keith, *Reid's Close, Canongate, Edinburgh*, 1856. Salted paper print, 27.8 x 24.6 cm (11 x 9¾ in.). Royal Scottish Academy, Edinburgh, 1994.040

63. Arthur Schomberg Kerr, *Eashing Village*, September 1854. Salted paper print, 19.5 x 24.5 cm (7⅝ x 9⅝ in.). The Royal Photographic Society Collection at the National Media Museum, Bradford

64. Charles George Hood Kinnear, *West Door, St. Sebalds, Nurnberg*, 1855. Albumen silver print, 27.1 x 20.9 cm (10⅝ x 8¼ in.). National Media Museum, Bradford

65. John Kirk, *Ward № V, Renkioi*, Crimea, ca. 1854–56. Albumen silver print, 15.5 x 18.8 cm (6⅛ x 7⅜ in.). J. Paul Getty Museum, Los Angeles, 84.XA.618.20

66. John Kirk, Mary Livingstone's Grave, Zambezi, 1862. Albumen silver print, 14.5 x 19.8 cm (5¾ x 7¾ in.). National Library of Scotland, Edinburgh, PGP 203.27

67. James Peter Knight, *A Peep in Leigh Woods*. Salted paper print, 18 x 22 cm (7⅛ x 8⅝ in.). The Metropolitan Museum of Art, New York, Gilman Collection, Gift of The Howard Gilman Foundation, 2005, 2005.100.382 (20)

68. James Peter Knight, *A very pretty house*. Salted paper print, 17.8 x 22.4 cm (7 x 8⅞ in.). The Metropolitan Museum of Art, New York, Gilman Collection, Gift of The Howard Gilman Foundation, 2005, 2005.100.382 (19)

69. William Law, Study of Trees, ca. 1855–56. Image digitally created from a paper negative, 21.7 x 27.3 cm (8 ½ x 10¾ in.). Courtesy of Mrs. C. Allington and Leicestershire Heritage Services, M.H.113.1985.21

70. Henry Ledger, Landscape Study in Parkland, ca. 1854. Albumen silver print, 20.3 x 25.7 cm (8 x 10⅛ in.). Collection of Charles Isaacs and Carol Nigro, New York

71. John Dillwyn Llewelyn, *St. Govan's Chapel, Pembrokeshire*, ca. 1852. Albumen silver print, 17.5 x 21.6 cm (6⅞ x 8½ in.). Hans P. Kraus, Jr., New York

72. Robert Wilfred Skeffington Lutwidge, *Stonehenge*, ca. 1857. Albumen silver print, 13.9 x 19.6 cm (5½ x 7¾ in.). The Royal Photographic Society Collection at the National Media Museum, Bradford, RPS 11579

73. James Calder Macphail, Colosseum, Rome, 1840s. Salted paper print, 15.7 x 20.2 cm (6⅛ x 8 in.). Edinburgh City Libraries and Information Services

74. John Richardson Major, Jr., *The Priory Farm, Thetford*, 1854. Albumen silver print, 17.6 x 22.1 cm (6⅞ x 8¾ in.). National Media Museum, Bradford, K-K 2/24

75. John McCosh, Great Pagoda at Prome, ca. 1852. Salted paper print, 17 x 20 cm (6¾ x 7⅞ in.). Courtesy of the Council of the National Army Museum, London, NAM1963-04-3-146

76. Arthur James Melhuish, *Thames Street, Windsor*, 1853. Salted paper print, 37.9 x 48.8 cm (14⅞ x 19¼ in.). The Royal Collection, © Her Majesty Queen Elizabeth II, RCIN 2100376

77. George Moir, Door of Belleisle House, Ayshire, 1840s. Salted paper print, 13.3 x 11.4 cm (5¼ x 4½ in.). National Library of Scotland, Edinburgh, Phot.med.33

78. James Francis Montgomery, Self-Portrait with James Coventry at right, 1840s. Salted paper print, 16.3 x 15.6 cm (6⅜ x 6⅛ in.). National Library of Scotland, Edinburgh, Phot.med.33

79. Henrietta Augusta Mostyn, *Allington Castle, Kent*, 1854. Albumen silver print, 17.9 x 20.3 cm (7 x 8 in.). The Royal Photographic Society Collection at the National Media Museum, Bradford, RPS 11507

80. James Mudd and Robert Mudd, Conway Castle and Bridge, 1855. Image digitally created from a paper negative, 28 x 37.3 cm (11 x 14⅝ in.). National Media Museum, Bradford

81. Robert Murray, *Village of Ekhmim*, Egypt, ca. 1855. Albumen silver print, 13.7 x 22.6 cm (5⅜ x 8⅞ in.). Wilson Centre for Photography, London

82. Andrew Charles Brisbane Neill, *The Hunooman at Beejanggur*. Albumen silver print, 33 x 26.3 cm (13 x 10⅜ in.). Frontispiece of Meadows Taylor and James Fergusson, *Architecture in Dharwar and Mysore* (London, 1866). Wilson Centre for Photography, London

83. Caroline Emily Nevill, *Allington Castle, Kent*, ca. 1854. Albumen silver print, 17.9 x 19.8 cm (7 x 7¾ in.). The Royal Photographic Society Collection at the National Media Museum, Bradford, RPS 11527

84. William John Newton, Windsor Castle, ca. 1854. Salted paper print, 16.9 x 22.3 cm (6⅝ x 8¾ in.). National Media Museum, Bradford K-K2/34

85. Unknown photographer, Portrait of Sir William Newton, 1850s. Salted paper print from collodion negative, 13.3 x 10.3 cm (5¼ x 4 in.). Victoria and Albert Museum, London, Ph 167-1982

86. Bessie Raynor Parkes, *Leaf Specimen*, 1848. Photogenic drawing negative, 16.3 x 11.5 cm (6⅜ x 4½ in.). Hans P. Kraus, Jr., New York

87. John Percy, *Oak*, 1854. Albumen silver print, 26.4 x 16.4 cm (10⅜ x 6½ in.). The Royal Photographic Society Collection at the National Media Museum, Bradford, RPS 11520

88. William Harry Pigou, *Chittuldroog. Temple of Chamoondee*, 1855–56. Albumen silver print, 27.9 x 39.4 cm (11 x 15½ in.). From Meadows Taylor and James Fergusson, *Architecture in Dharwar and Mysore* (London, 1866). The Metropolitan Museum of Art, New York, Rogers Fund, 1920, transferred from the Library, 1991, 1991.1073.98 (79)

89. Thomas Cadby Ponting, Scene in the Vale of Neath, ca. 1855. Salted paper print, 17.9 x 22.8 cm (7 x 9 in.). Collection of the Prentice and Paul Sack Photographic Trust, ST1998

90. William A. Pumphrey, *The Chapter House, St. Mary's Abbey, York*, 1853. Albumen silver print, 21.6 x 16.6 cm (8½ x 6½ in.). Collection of Charles Isaacs and Carol Nigro, New York

91. Robert Charles Ransome, *Sparrowe's House*, Ipswich, 1853. Blanquart-Evrard print, 19.8 x 16.8 cm (7¾ x 6⅝ in.). The Metropolitan Museum of Art, New York, The Elisha Whittelsey Collection, The Elisha Whittelsey Fund, 1963, 63.606.1.32

92. Thomas Milville Raven, *Mont Orgueil, Jersey*, Albumen silver print, 24.5 x 29.7 cm (9⅝ x 11¾ in.). National Media Museum, Bradford

93. Unknown photographer, Portrait of Rev. Joseph Bancroft Reade, 1850s. Salted paper print from collodion negative, 12.6 x 10.6 cm (5 x 4⅛ in.). Victoria and Albert Museum, London, Ph 180-1982

94. Alfred Rosling, *St. Paul's on a Misty Morning*, 1853. Albumen silver print, 17.6 x 23.2 cm (6⅞ x 9⅛ in.). The Royal Collection, © Her Majesty Queen Elizabeth II, RCIN 2906195

95. Alfred Rosling, *Gateway at Holdenby, Northamptonshire, a palace of Queen Elizabeth*, ca. 1854. Salted paper print, 16.1 x 17.1 cm (6⅜ x 6¾ in.). The Royal Photographic Society Collection at the National Media Museum, Bradford, RPS 11533

96. Horatio Ross, *Fir trees on the banks of Dornoch Firth between Ardgay and Fearn*, ca. 1858. Albumen silver print, 25.4 x 33.7 cm (10 x 13¼ in.). Janet Lehr, Inc., New York

97. William Russell Sedgfield, *Stonehenge*, 1853. Albumen silver print, 22.3 x 15.3 cm (8¾ x 6 in.). The Royal Collection, © Her Majesty Queen Elizabeth II, RCIN 2906077

98. George Shaw, Ancient Oak Trees, ca. 1852. Image digitally created from a paper negative, 31.2 x 23.2 cm (12¼ x 9⅛ in.). Collection Musee d'Orsay, Paris, PHO 1981 55

99. William Sherlock, Girl Asleep in Chair, ca. 1854. Salted paper print, 24.7 x 20 cm (9¾ x 7⅞ in.). Ken and Jenny Jacobson, Essex

100. John Shaw Smith, *Church of Saint Germain L'Auxerrois, Paris*, ca. 1850. Image digitally created from a paper negative, 16.6 x 22 cm (6½ x 8⅝ in.). George Eastman House, Rochester, 81:1683:0028

101. John Shaw Smith, *Convent of Sinai*, 1852. Image digitally created from a paper negative, 16.7 x 22.1 cm (6⅝ x 8¾ in.). George Eastman House, Rochester, 81:1683:0167

102. Samuel Smith, Dockside Machinery, Wisbech, ca. 1856. Image digitally created from a paper negative, 22.3 x 16.7 cm (8¾ x 6⅝ in.). National Media Museum, Bradford

103. John(?) Stanton, *Distant view of Warwick Castle over the Osier marshes along the Avon*. Image digitally created from a paper negative, 21.5 x 29.1 cm (8½ x 11½ in.). Hans P. Kraus, Jr., New York

104. John Stewart (1814–1887), *La Vieux pont à Laruns, Basses Pyrénées*, ca. 1852. Blanquart-Evrard print, 22.5 x 31 cm (8⅞ x 12¼ in.). Bibliotheque National de France, Paris

105. John Stewart (d. 1867), Houghton Hall from the North-West Drive, ca. 1855. Salted paper print, 18.8 x 22.8 cm (7⅜ x 9 in.). Norfolk County Council Library and Information Service

106. William Henry Fox Talbot, *Bust of Patroclus*, 1843. Salted paper print, 14.9 x 14.5 cm (5⅞ x 5¾ in.). The Metropolitan Museum of Art, New York, Gift of Hans P. Kraus Jr., 1988, 1988.1159

107. Unknown photographer, Portrait of Alfred Swaine Taylor, 1850s. Albumen silver print from collodion negative, 13.2 x 10.6 cm (5¼ x 4⅛ in.). Victoria and Albert Museum, London, Ph 191-1982

108. Arthur A. Taylor, View in a Forest, 1865–69. Arosa process photolithograph, 24.7 x 33 cm (9¾ x 13 in.). Collection of Charles Isaacs and Carol Nigro, New York

109. Edward King Tenison, *Rue de la Porte Neuve, Alger*, ca. 1852. Albumen silver print, 20 x 17.1 cm (7⅞ x 6¾ in.). J. Paul Getty Museum, 84.XP.368.24

110. Edward King Tenison, *Puerta del Sol, Madrid*, ca. 1852. Salted paper print, 27.6 x 38.1 cm (10⅞ x 15 in.). Bibliothèque Nationale de France, Paris, Res.Vf 268 Fol

111. Hugh Lyon Tennent and Robert Tennent, Portrait of an Unknown Laborer, 1840s. Salted paper print, 14.5 x 10.5 cm (5¾ x 4⅛ in.). Edinburgh City Libraries and Information Services

112. William John Thoms. *Pevensey Castle, Sussex*, 1854. Albumen silver print, 15.7 x 19.6 cm (6⅛ x 7¾ in.). The Royal Photographic Society Collection at the National Media Museum, Bradford, RPS 11534

113. Linnaeus Tripe, *H.M.S. Duke of Wellington*, 1854. Albumen silver print, 27.8 x 35.6 cm (11 x 14 in.). J. Paul Getty Museum, Los Angeles, 85.XM.391

114. Benjamin Brecknell Turner, *Windmill, Kempsey, Worcestershire*, 1852–54. Albumen silver print, 26.8 x 38.9 cm (10½ x 15⅓ in.). Victoria and Albert Museum, London, Ph.10-1982

115. George Michael Tytler, *Bridge at Woodhouselee*. Albumen silver print, 19.9 x 23.9 cm (7⅞ x 9⅜ in.). National Media Museum, Bradford, KK1/42

116. William Walker, *On the Canal, May 20, 1854*, Edinburgh. Albumen silver print, 9.8 x 18.4 cm (3⅞ x 7¼ in.). Royal Scottish Academy, Edinburgh, 1994.040

117. Charles Henry Waring, *Bristol Docks*, 1853. Albumen silver print, 19.8 x 15.7 cm (7¾ x 6⅛ in.). Private collection, London

118. Henry George Watson, *View on the Esk, Dalhousie*. Salted paper print, 16.5 x 21.6 cm (6½ x 8½ in.). National Media Museum, Bradford, KK1/09

119. Claudius Galen Wheelhouse, *Baalbeck – Our encampment within the walls*, May 31, 1850. Albumen silver print, 14.6 x 19.8 cm (5¾ x 7¾ in.). The Royal Photographic Society Collection at the National Media Museum, Bradford

120. John Forbes White, A Rocky Outcrop Near Aberdeen, ca. 1854–57. Image digitally created from a paper negative. Scottish National Photography Collection, National Galleries of Scotland, Edinburgh

121. John Wiggin, House in Lavenham, Suffolk, ca. 1855. Image digitally created from a waxed-paper negative, 39 x 28 cm (15⅜ x 11 in.). Hans P. Kraus, Jr., New York

122. Attributed to William John Newton, *Thomas Maryon Wilson*, 1850s. Salted paper print, 13.2 x 15.5 cm (5¼ x 6⅛ in.). The Metropolitan Museum of Art, New York, Gift of Paul F. Walter in memory of Christopher Hemphill, 1987, 1987.1183.38.17

123. John Saumarez Winter, *Tottenham Church*, early 1850s. Salted paper print, 16.5 x 21.6 cm (6½ x 8½ in.). Stephen White, Los Angeles

124. John Ziegler, Estuary with Shipping, ca. 1856. Albumen silver print, 16 x 20.4 cm (6¼ x 8 in.). National Media Museum, Bradford, KK1/41

Notes to the Chapters

The following abbreviations are used in the notes.

BJP	*British Journal of Photography***
BJPA	*The British Journal Photographic Almanac and Photographer's Daily Companion*
ILN	*Illustrated London News*
JPS	*Journal of the Photographic Society**
JSA	*Journal of the Society of Arts*
LMPJ	*Liverpool and Manchester Photographic Journal***
LPJ	*Liverpool Photographic Journal***

*The *Journal of the Photographic Society*, published by the Photographic Society beginning in 1853, changed its name in 1859 to *Photographic Journal.*
Citations to *Photographic Journal* refer to this publication.

***The Liverpool Photographic Journal*, begun in 1854, changed its name in 1857 to *Liverpool and Manchester Photographic Journal* and in 1859 to *Photographic Journal.*
Citations to *Photographic Journal (BJP)* refer to the 1859 issues of this publication.
In 1860 the name was changed again, to *British Journal of Photography.*

1. *Photography and an Age of Paradox*
pages 1–11

1. *Times* (London), January 9, 1839, p. 6, col. F. The phrase "Age of Paradox" is, sadly, not my own; it comes from the title of an excellent book on the cultural history of Britain during the 1840s. See Dodds 1953.
2. "Effects of the Storm," *Times*, January 9, 1839. The report, dated January 8, 1839, includes accounts from Liverpool and Manchester.
3. "Melancholy Shipwrecks and Loss of Life," *Times*, January 10, 1839. This comprehensive account of the storm first appeared on January 9 (second ed.) and was reprinted the following day.
4. Arago 1839, translated in H. Gernsheim and A. Gernsheim 1956, pp. 79–81 (quotation on p. 79).
5. Gaucheraud, *Literary Gazette*, January 12, 1839, reprinted from the *Gazette de France*, January 6, 1839. It seems likely that Talbot learned of Daguerre's process from the report by Gaucheraud in the *Literary Gazette*. See also "Foreign Correspondence," *Athenaeum*, January 26, 1839.
6. "Daguerotype [*sic*]," *Literary Gazette*, January 19, 1839, p. 43, reprinted from *Le Commerce*, January 16, 1839.
7. Others as well had previously attempted to fix images made by light. Most failed, but a notable exception was Joseph-Nicéphore Niepce, whose experiments in Chalon-sur-Saône had yielded a camera image as early as circa 1826. Two years later he went into partnership with Daguerre, and until Niepce's early death in 1833 the two men worked together to improve the process. On Niepce's life and achievements in photography (and much else besides), see Maison Nicéphore Niépce (website). The best account of Daguerre's life and achievements is still H. Gernsheim and A. Gernsheim 1956.
8. The most detailed and thorough account of Talbot's "invention" of photography and his subsequent struggle for recognition is given in Schaaf 1992. An earlier but excellent and well-illustrated account is Buckland 1980.
9. According to Vernon Heath, Faraday invited the audience to inspect Talbot's handiwork with the words, "No human hand has hitherto traced such lines as these drawings display; and what man may hereafter do, now that Dame Nature has become his drawing mistress, it is impossible to predict." See Heath 1892, pp. 48–49. Heath's is the only known eyewitness account of Talbot's presentation at the Royal Institution, and since it was published some fifty years after the event, its accuracy is open to question.
10. Lady Elisabeth Feilding to Talbot, February 3, 1839, Talbot Collection, British Library (archival source), LA39-04; Talbot Correspondence Project (website), doc. no. 03787.
11. In the 1830s the camera obscura was most often used by artists working outdoors to help them draw in accurate perspective.
12. Two detailed studies of the daguerreotype process are Barger and White 1991 and B. Lowry and I. B. Lowry 1998.
13. A technically informed account of the photogenic drawing process is given in Ware 2001.
14. Talbot fixed his photogenic drawings by immersing the exposed image in a solution of potassium iodide or sodium chloride; this did not remove the unexposed silver salts but stabilized them sufficiently to prevent their responding readily to light. This method is now known to have sown the seeds of self-destruction in photogenic drawings, ultimately causing them to change irrevocably. The problem was explained for the first time in Ware 1994.
15. Talbot to Sir John Herschel, February 11, 1839, The Royal Society, London, HS 17:282; Talbot Correspondence Project (website), doc. no. 03803. The Royal Society holds an extensive archive of Herschel material.
16. Talbot's discoveries prompted others to experiment, most notably Sir John Herschel, who, ignorant of the process details, created his own process from scratch in late January 1839. See Schaaf 1992, p. 49. Others less eminent than Herschel also tried their hand. As early as February 1839, an individual from Norfolk signing himself "Clericus" wrote that on hearing of Daguerre's success he had devised a way of making photographic images that used writing paper; he called them lucigraphs. See Clericus, *Times*, February 21, 1839. In May 1839, simple instructions were published encouraging housewives and children to make photogenic drawings; the method recommended was based on Sir John Herschel's procedures, in which only pure silver nitrate was employed and the resulting image fixed in pure water. See "Familiar Instructions in Photography," *Magazine of Domestic Economy*, May 1839.
17. Longford 1964, p. 61.
18. The phrase is that of John Bright (1811–1888), manufacturer, politician, and social reformer; quoted in Mather 1965, p. 20.
19. For a thorough account, see Pearce 2004.
20. Changes in the social order and their effects on the working classes throughout the 1830s and 1840s are discussed at length in Himmelfarb 1984.
21. Since coal was vital to practically every process of industrialization, the industry thrived. When the demand for low-paid labor outstripped the supply, women and children were employed to work underground in appalling circumstances. See "Children's Employment Commission," *Athenaeum*, May 7, 1842.
22. On this pattern of migration, see Prince 1981.
23. "Ninth Meeting of the British Association for the Advancement of Science," *Athenaeum*, August 31, 1839. In the opening of the report (p. 641) is the statement, "The recent disturbances had rendered it doubtful whether the meeting might not be adjourned to another time and place." A report on Talbot's paper is on pp. 643–44.
24. The six points of the charter were universal male suffrage, vote by ballot, equal electoral districts, the abolition of property qualifications for members of Parliament, payment for MPs, and the annual election of Parliament. See Ashton, Fyson, and Roberts 1995, which contains a succinct history.
25. A month-by-month account of events in Britain and Europe as they unfolded is given in Postgate 1955.
26. For an account of the Chartist meeting as seen from the perspective of the monarchy, see Taylor 1987.
27. On the Corn Laws and their effect on diet, see Drummond and Wilbraham 1939, pp. 331–56.
28. "Sanitary Condition of the Labouring Population of Great Britain" 1843, pp. 22–23. For a contemporary fictional account, see Mrs. Elizabeth Gaskell's novel *Mary Barton: A Tale of Manchester Life*, published in 1848, which exposes the

appalling slum conditions in which Manchester mill workers were compelled to live. In her description of the conflict between workers and masters, the author drew heavily on the plight of the Chartists.

29. "The Contagion of Numbers" is the title of an essay by J. A. Banks (see Banks 1973). The same theme is addressed in Porter 1995, p. 205.
30. See "Cholera Morbus," in Haydn 1853, p. 141. The traditional use of the term "visitation" for an outbreak of cholera disease was laden with religious connotations, including a reflection of the widespread belief that cholera was God's punishment of a sinful society.
31. The introduction of the Penny Post throughout Britain in January 1840 reformed the existing system and within two years dramatically increased the numbers of letters handled by the Post Office, from 75 to 196.5 million annually. For a concise account of these reforms, see *Encyclopaedia Britannica*, 11th ed., s.v. "Post, and Postal Service: Sir Rowland Hill's Reforms (1836–1842)" (by Thomas Allan Ingram).
32. This represented a 172 percent increase over the mileage in 1844, the first year for which accurate figures are available. By 1860 the figure had grown to just over 9,000 miles. A good account of the early development of the railway system in Britain is Hoppen 1998, p. 289.
33. Ibid., p. 291. Between 1844 and 1851, the peak years of railway building, a high percentage of all pig iron manufactured in Britain was for the railway. In 1845 some 740 million bricks were used in its building works, and 44 million pounds were invested in its further expansion in 1847.
34. A contemporary account is given in Evans 1848. For a modern analysis of railway investment and speculation, see "The Wider Culture of Capital," in Freeman 1999, pp. 99–105.
35. Jack Simmons, "Royal Travelling," in *Oxford Companion to British Railway History* 1997, pp. 427–28.
36. Hoppen 1998, p. 289.
37. The coronation took place on June 28, 1838, amid much pomp and splendor, although in fact the ceremony was unrehearsed; see Hobsbawm and Ranger 1984.
38. A notice describing the function and scope of the commission appeared in "Royal Commission of Fine Arts," *Athenaeum*, April 30, 1842.
39. On Eastlake's appointment as secretary to the commission, see Robertson 1978, pp. 58–62.
40. Its full name was "Society for the Encouragement of Arts, Manufactures and Commerce." There are two books on the society: Wood 1913 and Hudson and Luckhurst 1954.
41. Wood 1913, pp. 286–311.
42. An excellent account of the historical context in which the Great Exhibition was created is given in Davis 1999, pp. 1–31.
43. "Retrospect of the Year," *ILN*, December 29, 1849, p. 434.

2. *The Formative Years: The Calotype in the 1840s*

pages 12–29

1. Creating an image by the actinic power of light alone required an exposure a million times longer than that needed for an image chemically developed into visibility. An explanation of the chemistry underlying the process is given in Ware 1994, p. 17.
2. Talbot, Notebook Q (archival source), entry for September 23, 1840, transcribed in Schaaf 1996, n.p.
3. Talbot, "Calotype (Photogenic) Drawing," *Literary Gazette*, February 27, 1841. See also Talbot Correspondence Project (website), doc. no. 04195.
4. Talbot, "Calotype (Photogenic) Drawing," *Literary Gazette*, February 27, 1841, p. 139. See also Talbot, Notebook Q (archival source), entry for September 23, 1840, transcribed in Schaaf 1996, n.p.
5. February 8, 1841, Patent no. 8842, Patent Office Library, British Library, London. See also Woodcroft 1854.
6. Talbot, "Calotype (Photogenic) Drawing," *Literary Gazette*, February 13, 1841. See also Talbot Correspondence Project (website), doc. no. 04191. In one of the many parallel occurrences that dogged Talbot's photographic career, the French Academy of Sciences had met on January 11, 1841, to hear Jean-Baptiste Biot read a paper by Edmund Becquerel on the chemical action of rays of solar light. In it Becquerel described the existence of the latent image as the "fundamental fact on which the two principle operations of the Daguerreotype depend," effectively preempting Talbot's announcement soon thereafter. On Becquerel's paper, see "Chemical Action of Light," *Magazine of Science and School of Arts*, February 6, 1841.
7. Talbot, "Calotype (Photogenic) Drawing," *Literary Gazette*, February 13, 1841.
8. Lady Elisabeth Feilding to Talbot, February 2, 1841, Talbot Collection, British Library (archival source), LA40-12; Talbot Correspondence Project (website), doc. no. 04014. Lady Elisabeth spotted the word's derivation: "I suppose Calotype is derived from To Kalon—is it?" Defined as "the (morally) beautiful—the ideal good—the 'summum bonum,'" *kalon* crops up in literature, for instance in works by Henry Fielding and Lord Byron. *Oxford English Dictionary*, s.v. "Kalon."
9. For the first recorded use of the term "Talbotype," see Sir John Frederick Herschel to Talbot, March 16, 1841, Talbot Collection, National Media Museum (archival source), 1937-4873; Talbot Correspondence Project (website), doc. no. 04213.
10. Talbot, "Calotype (Photogenic) Drawing," *Literary Gazette*, February 13, 1841.
11. Ibid.
12. Klonk 1996.
13. Talbot, "Calotype (Photogenic) Drawing," *Literary Gazette*, February 27, 1841, p. 140.
14. On this sorry episode, and the more successful discovery and launch of the calotype process, see Schaaf 1992, pp. 75–102.
15. Ibid., pp. 112–22. Despite this apparently auspicious start, Talbot again ran into trouble with the Royal Society when its Committee of Papers ruled that his paper would not be published in the society's lead journal *Transactions* but in its less prestigious *Proceedings*, on the grounds that the French Academy had already published an account of the process. Talbot, "An Account of Some Recent Improvements in Photography," *Proceedings of the Royal Society*, 1841.
16. Talbot, "Calotype (Photogenic) Drawing," *Literary Gazette*, June 12, 1841; "Royal Society," *Athenaeum*, July 17, 1841. Later in 1841 Talbot had the entire text of his paper privately printed for personal distribution as *The Process of Calotype Photogenic Drawing* (printed by J. L. Cox & Sons, 75 Gt. Queen Street, London). It was subsequently reprinted in 1845 under the title *The Process of Talbotype (Formerly Called Calotype) Photogenic Drawing* (printed by J. & H. Cox Brothers, 74 & 75 Gt. Queen Street, London).
17. In this photograph the pose of the figure and the use of backlighting strikingly recall Caspar David Friedrich's *Wanderer above the Sea of Fog*, 1818 (Kunsthalle, Hamburg). Although it is unlikely that Talbot knew the work, his enjoyment of fine views and the sublime mountain scenery of the Alps on his frequent visits to Europe during the 1820s encouraged an affinity to the German Romantic movement. See Talbot to Charles Feilding, September 4, 1822, Talbot Collection, British Library (archival source), LA22-47; Talbot Correspondence Project (website), doc. no. 1005.
18. As a further precaution Talbot also recommended treating the negative in a 2 percent solution of potassium bromide, which further stabilized it. The negative could still be "revived," although the procedure was now less straightforward chemically than in the previous stage.
19. Talbot's term "calotype" refers strictly to a negative made by his process. But even during his lifetime the term was used indiscriminately to describe both negatives and prints, a practice that continued until recently. In the present narrative, Talbot's original definition is used throughout.
20. Although Talbot initially recommended fixing positives in the same way as the calotypes themselves, the following year he noted that "the best method of fixing Copies seems to be, to wash them with one part hyposulphite of soda + one part carbonate of soda." Talbot, Notebook Q (archival source), entry for September 20, 1842, transcribed in Schaaf 1996, n.p.
21. Robert Hunt, one such frustrated beginner, explained to Talbot in 1842 after many trials, "I have not succeeded in producing one so clear as that you sent me. . . . I cannot secure the light parts from some slight smuttiness and this interferes sadly with the transfer." Robert Hunt to Talbot, September 9, 1842, Talbot Collection, British Library (archival source), LA42-73; Talbot Correspondence Project (website), doc. no. 04608.

22. [E. Eastlake], *Quarterly Review*, April 1857, p. 451.
23. On the commercial potential of the daguerreotype in portraiture and the costs to Beard and Claudet, see Wood 1979, pp. 305–9. See also B. Heathcote and P. Heathcote 1979, for a detailed account of Beard's entrepreneurial activities. Mention of daguerreotype studios being established in Plymouth, Bristol, Cheltenham, and Liverpool by September 1841 is made by H. Gernsheim 1982, p. 130.
24. "To William Henry Fox Talbot, of Locock [*sic*] Abbey, in the County of Wilts," *London Journal of Arts and Sciences*, 1842, p. 194. Talbot also described the ideal lens for portraiture as having a focal length not more than three to four times the aperture and recommended that for portraits taken in full sunlight a screen of blue glass be used to protect the eyes of the sitter.
25. Collen said he received his first payment for a calotype portrait on August 16, 1841. See West Awdry (Talbot's solicitor) to Talbot, August 17, 1842, Talbot Collection, British Library (archival source), LA42-59; Talbot Correspondence Project (website), doc. no. 04580. On Collen's work, see Schaaf 1982 and Schaaf 1983.
26. Collen wrote to Talbot at that time asking him to give "an assurance of not having a competitor in London," as he had worked hard "without any reward, and shall consider it very hard if I am interfered with just as [I] am commencing to reap the fruits of my labour." Henry Collen to Talbot, March 18, 1842, Talbot Collection, British Library (archival source), LA42-15; Talbot Correspondence Project (website), doc. no. 04456.
27. Eleven letters between Beard and Talbot discussing the terms of licensing have survived. See Talbot Correspondence Project (website).
28. Advertisement, "Claudet's Talbotype (or Calotype) Portraits," *Athenaeum*, July 6, 1844. On the same page Claudet advertised his "Daguerréotype Portraits" for prices that started at 1 guinea. For a Londoner at that time, a guinea (21 shillings) would buy a ton of the best quality coal; 5 shillings bought ten substantial loaves of bread, enough to feed a family for a week. "London Markets (Corrected to January 24)," *Magazine of Domestic Economy*, February 1843.
29. Even Talbot's mother was pleased, telling her son that "Claudet having the stimulus of his own interest will spread your Fame by his success." Lady Elisabeth Feilding to Talbot, September 13, 1844, Talbot Collection, British Library (archival source), LA44-60; Talbot Correspondence Project (website), doc. no. 05066.
30. Henry Collen to West Awdry, August 16, 1842, forwarded to Talbot, August 17, 1842, Talbot Collection, British Library (archival source), LA42-59; Talbot Correspondence Project (website), doc. no. 04580. Collen's gross income in his first year was 233 pounds, 70 shillings.
31. Henry Collen to West Awdry, May 30, 1844, forwarded to Talbot, June 1, 1842, Talbot Collection, British Library (archival source), LA44-31; Talbot Correspondence Project (website), doc. no. 05010. Collen received forty-five requests for portraits during the whole of 1844. West Awdry to Talbot, forwarding a letter from Henry Collen, January 9, 1845, Talbot Collection, British Library (archival source), LAM-122; Talbot Correspondence Project (website), doc. no. 05133.
32. Antoine Claudet to Talbot, July 15, 1845, Talbot Collection, British Library (archival source), LA45-101; Talbot Correspondence Project (website), doc. no. 05326. Claudet's takings for the year were 25 pounds, 1 shilling and 6 pence; Talbot's share came to a little over 6 pounds.
33. "Photography," *Blackwood's Edinburgh Magazine*, April 1842.
34. For a sense of the range of daguerreotypes and their presentations, see Wood 1989 and B. Lowry and I. B. Lowry 1998.
35. For the best discussion of Henneman and his role at the Reading Establishment, see Schaaf 1989, pp. 16–20.
36. At the end of his first eight months at the Reading Establishment, Henneman billed Talbot for 10,400 prints. Henneman to Talbot, invoice, September 5, 1844, Talbot Collection, British Library (archival source), LA44-45; see also Schaaf 1989, p. 19.
37. December 1, 1843, Patent no. 9753, Patent Office Library, British Library. See also Woodcroft 1854; *Photography: Talbot's Specification* 1856. The patent was filed June 1, 1843, and issued December 1, 1843.
38. "Improvements in Photography," *Magazine of Science and School of Arts*, 1844.
39. Ibid., p. 323.
40. Ibid., p. 324; see also *Oxford Dictionary of National Biography*, s.v. "Fortnum, Charles (1738–1815)" (by T. A. B. Corley).
41. Talbot, prospectus for *The Pencil of Nature*, illus. in Schaaf 1989, p. 22, fig. 12.
42. See, for example, "New Publications," *Athenaeum*, January 6, 1844, p. 19, with references to the second part of J. D. Harding's *Baronial Halls* and the twentieth and final part of William Brockedon's *Italy*.
43. The history and background of this publication are covered in detail in Schaaf 1989.
44. Ibid., p. 27. These figures are extrapolated from a table drawn up by Schaaf from sales records at Longman's, the London publishers who distributed *The Pencil of Nature*. Since they reflect only sold fascicles, the actual number of prints was likely much higher. It took twelve separate, hand-performed stages to make a single print.
45. Ibid. Schaaf estimates that of the last four fascicles, a combined total of only 553 were sold. The four were issued between May 1845 and April 1846.
46. Talbot, *Pencil of Nature* 1989 (repr. of 1844–46 ed.), fasc. 2, plate X, *The Haystack*.
47. When Scott's *Rob Roy* first appeared in 1817, ten thousand copies sold within a fortnight, and between 1829 and 1849 more than 78,000 sets of the Waverley Novels were sold. See Altick 1957, pp. 383, 386.
48. This popular guidebook, filled with romantic facts and telling quotations from Scott's works, was generally regarded as the standard work for aspiring tourists throughout the 1840s. The third edition was published in 1844 and offered twenty-three itineraries for visitors. *Black's Picturesque Tourist of Scotland* 1844.
49. On the royal family at Balmoral, see Millar 1985.
50. Several manuscript lists of subscribers to *Sun Pictures in Scotland* survive. The most complete is in the National Media Museum, Bradford, and earlier versions are in the British Library, London.
51. The private character of the publication makes it unlikely that copies would have been submitted for review, and so far no reviews from 1845–46 have been found.
52. The early circulation figure of 750 is given in Hall 1883, p. 195. For the mention of 7,000 plates, see Talbot to the Editor of the *Art-Union*, March 1, 1848, Talbot Collection, British Library (archival source); Talbot Correspondence Project (website), doc. no. 06116.
53. The first of these, which appeared in February 1844, was a "Specimen Plate of the Illustrated Edition of the Works of Robert Burns," published by Blackie and Son, Glasgow. See "Works of Robert Burns," *Art-Union*, February 1844. The inserts were usually printed on heavy, fine-quality paper or mounted on thin card, presentations that set them off against the letterpress pages of the magazine.
54. Talbot to the Editor of the *Art-Union*, March 1, 1848, Talbot Collection, British Library (archival source); Talbot Correspondence Project (website), doc. no. 06116.
55. Hall 1883, p. 3.
56. *Oxford Dictionary of National Biography*, s.v. "Holloway, Thomas (1800–1883)" (by T. A. B. Corley).
57. Talbot, "Introductory Remarks," in *Pencil of Nature* 1989 (repr. of 1844–46 ed.), fasc. 1, n.p.
58. Lady Elisabeth Feilding to Talbot, July 29, 1845, Talbot Collection, British Library (archival source), LA45-109; Talbot Correspondence Project (website), doc. no. 05339.
59. "The Talbotype.—Sun-Pictures," *Art-Union*, June 1, 1846, p. 143. Although the article was published anonymously, it has been assumed that Hall, as editor, was the author.
60. William Thompson to Talbot, December 13, 1841, Talbot Collection, British Library (archival source); Talbot Correspondence Project (website), doc. no. 04391.
61. See "Learned Societies" 1851.
62. The Scottish educational system was looked upon with envy by the rest of Britain, for even in the remotest agricultural districts many village schools employed university graduates as teachers. See Taylor 1981, pp. 2–4, for one example. For an excellent account of the educational movement in Scotland and Edinburgh in particular, see Secord 2000.
63. The patent system in Britain was medieval in its complexity. Ten individual stages had to be authorized by ten different officials ranging from a master in chancery to the secretary of state. Unless the matter were placed in the hands of a specialized patent agent at additional expense, delays occurred at every stage. The average cost of taking out a patent was about 120 pounds for England, 100 pounds for Scotland, and

125 pounds for Ireland. A contemporary discussion is "Law of Patents," *Magazine of Science and School of Arts*, July 3 and 17, 1841. See also Dutton 1984.

64. David Brewster advised Talbot that it would be unprofitable to extend his patent to Scotland. Sir David Brewster to Talbot, February 4, 1841, Talbot Collection, National Media Museum (archival source), 1937-4870; Talbot Correspondence Project (website), doc. no. 04190.
65. Sir David Brewster to Talbot, October 27, 1841, Talbot Collection, National Media Museum (archival source), 1937-4891; Talbot Correspondence Project (website), doc. no. 04349.
66. Ibid.
67. Furlong's contribution to the chemical evolution of the calotype process is described in Taylor and Ware 2003, p. 310.
68. Of the many accounts of the Hill and Adamson partnership, by far the best are those by Sara Stevenson; the most recent is *The Personal Art of David Octavius Hill* (Stevenson 2002).
69. For a sense of the extraordinary range and scope of early photography in St. Andrews, see Smith 1990.
70. After a visit to Brewster in St. Andrews, one member of the group recalled, they became "smitten with the photographic mania, and set about the work as if their very existence depended upon it." "Reminiscence of the Calotype Club," *BJP*, August 14, 1874.
71. On the Edinburgh Calotype Club and the photographs it produced, see Pencils of Light (website).
72. See Taylor 1999.
73. See "Photogenic Drawings," *Literary Gazette*, May 16, 1840, p. 315. On these early works, see Schaaf 2000.
74. Reports of the Graphic Society's monthly meetings were regularly published in the *Art-Union*, *Literary Gazette*, and *Athenaeum*, but for some reason only two reports were published between 1841 and 1847, so we have no information on this period. The archives of the Graphic Society are held by the Royal Academy of Arts, London.
75. Notable among these submissions was "a volume of Talbotypes of a very superior description, done by D. O. Hill of Edinburgh, brought by Mr. [Clarkson] Stanfield." "Fine Art Gossip," *Athenaeum*, April 24, 1847. This album is now in the Gernsheim Collection, Harry Ransom Humanities Research Center, University of Texas at Austin (acc. no. 964:0048:0001-0109).
76. Graphic Society, "Annual Prospectus, 1848" (archival source).
77. Cundall was nominated for membership in the society on December 25, 1846; see Graphic Society, "Lists of Members, 1840–1850" (archival source). On Cundall, see McLean 1976. On his presentation to the Graphic Society, see "Graphic Society," *Athenaeum*, December 11, 1847.
78. "Calotype Society," *Athenaeum*, December 18, 1847. The author was probably the journal's editor, William Jerdan, a keen supporter of Talbot and photography.
79. "Gentleman," in *Imperial Dictionary* 1850, vol. 1, p. 829.
80. See Taylor and Ware 2003.
81. Cundell, *London, Edinburgh, and Dublin Philosophical Magazine*, May 1844, pp. 321–22. Cundell was a banker and, along with his brother Henry, an enthusiastic amateur photographer.
82. Ibid., p. 328. Two years later Cundell suggested that the gallo-nitrate solution could be diluted anywhere between ten and forty times: see Cundell, *London, Edinburgh, and Dublin Philosophical Magazine*, August 1846.
83. [E. Eastlake], *Quarterly Review*, April 1857, p. 452.
84. *Plain Directions for Obtaining Photographic Pictures* 1845, p. 9.
85. "Cundell's Improved Camera for Calotype Drawing" 1845, p. 2.
86. Blanquart-Evrard 1847. He followed this with additional publications, the most comprehensive in 1851: *Traité de photographie sur papier* (Blanquart-Evrard 1851).
87. The Blanquart-Evrard affair is discussed in Taylor and Ware 2003, pp. 311–12.
88. Guillot-Saguez 1847.
89. Many subsequent modifications were proposed, but they are all of relatively little consequence. See Taylor and Ware 2003, in which Table 2 lists thirty-seven different formulations for the calotype process that were published between 1841 and 1869. There were undoubtedly more.
90. The best account of Le Gray's photographic career is Aubenas 2002.
91. Le Gray 1851.
92. On Le Gray's waxed-paper process, see Taylor and Ware 2003, p. 313.
93. *Plain Directions for Obtaining Photographic Pictures* 1851.
94. Fenton, "Photography on Waxed Paper," 1852. Fenton had visited Paris in October 1852 and there met Le Gray and Auguste Mestral, who showed him several hundred waxed-paper negatives they had recently made for *La Mission héliographique*, a state-sponsored photographic survey of architectural monuments in France. The quality of the negatives convinced Fenton that pre-waxed paper "superseded in practical employment all the other kinds of prepared paper." Fenton, "Photography in France," *Chemist*, February 1852, p. 221; see also Mondenard 2002.

3. *The Great Exhibition of 1851*

pages 30–43

1. "Mr. Babbage on the Exposition of 1851," *North British Review*, May–August 1851, p. 529, a review of Charles Babbage's *The Exposition of 1851; or, Views of the Industry, the Science, and the Government, of England*, 2nd ed. (London: John Murray, 1851).
2. See Luckhurst 1951.
3. "National Exposition," *Art-Journal*, August 1 and September 1, 1849. In 1849 the *Art-Union* became the *Art-Journal*. See Hall 1883, pp. 194–209.
4. See Auerbach 1999.
5. By the end of the year, "nearly 5000 persons registered themselves as promoters of the proposed Exhibition." Timbs 1851, p. 18.
6. A list of the royal commissioners is given in Auerbach 1999, pp. 28–29. The commission, with Prince Albert as president, included many powerful and influential figures drawn from the fields of science, industry, and the arts; among its notables were the Earl of Rosse, president of the Royal Society; Robert Peel, first lord of the Treasury; Charles Barry, architect of the Houses of Parliament; Charles Lock Eastlake, director of the National Gallery; and Richard Westmacott, sculptor.
7. On the economic crisis of the late 1840s, see Levi 1872, pp. 292–315.
8. "Society would run great risk of having their minds tainted with revolutionary doctrines": W. Temple, quoted in Fay 1951, p. 7.
9. *The Crystal Palace: Its Injustice, Impolicy, and General Evil Tendency* was one pamphlet that expressed many of these general anxieties in exaggerated and provocative terms. See *Crystal Palace* 1851.
10. "Design by Joseph Paxton," *ILN*, July 6, 1850, which has a woodcut illustration of the building.
11. Dickens, *Household Words*, January 18, 1851, p. 386. Here Dickens is describing the greenhouse Paxton built at Chatsworth to house the Victoria Regina water lily. This extraordinary building, now demolished, was a prototype for the Crystal Palace, which was built with similar construction techniques but on a much larger scale.
12. Work commenced on August 3, 1850, with 30 men, but by early November the number had risen to 1,538. In the following weeks the workforce grew steadily, reaching a peak of over 2,000 in April 1851, immediately prior to the opening on May 1. *First Report of the Commissioners* 1852, app. no. XI, p. 70, "Return Showing the Number of Men Paid Each Week in Hyde Park, in the Erection of the Exhibition Building."
13. *Times* (London), October 26, 1850, p. 4, col. A. Illustrations of the building under construction appeared regularly in the *Illustrated London News*, which offers the best all-round source of information and visual material relating to the exhibition.
14. W. H. F. Talbot to Constance Talbot, April 30, 1851, Talbot Collection, British Library (archival source), LA51-14; Talbot Correspondence Project (website), doc. no. 06407.
15. The Duke of Wellington suggested using sparrow hawks to clear the sparrows, a story recounted in full in French 1950, pp. 174–75.
16. Editorial, *Times* (London), May 2, 1851, p. 4, cols. C–D. For a detailed account of the inauguration and a double-page woodcut, see *ILN*, May 3, 1851, pp. 348–52, and suppl., pp. 359–74.
17. He returned home that night, however, a "little overfatigued with walking, pushing & being pushed, and gazing at a thousand Sights." W. H. F. Talbot to Constance Talbot, May 2, 1851, Talbot Collection, British Library (archival source),

LA51-16; Talbot Correspondence Project (website), doc. no. 06410. In his firsthand account of the opening ceremony Talbot comments on minutia as well as the overall pomp and grandeur. See also Talbot to Henrietta Horatia Maria Gaisford, May 1, 1851 (Talbot Collection, British Library [archival source], LA51-15; Talbot Correspondence Project [website], doc. no. 06409), another letter describing the same event.

18. The most comprehensive statistical analysis of everything associated with the Great Exhibition is in *First Report of the Commissioners* 1852.
19. Ibid., app. no. XXXVI, p. 163.
20. The idea was to make it possible systematically to trace the conversion of raw materials into finished articles: from raw cotton, for instance, into printed fabric. (The principle was also applied to some photography exhibits and accounts for the decision to display photographs alongside cameras and equipment in Class 10.)
21. *Official Descriptive and Illustrated Catalogue* 1851; *Official Descriptive and Illustrated Catalogue. Supplementary Volume* 1852. These four volumes list every British exhibitor and exhibit following the system of classification, and non-British entries only by place of origin.
22. *First Report of the Commissioners* 1852, p. xlii.
23. See entries listed under Class 30, *Official Descriptive and Illustrated Catalogue* 1851, vol. 2, pp. 819–46.
24. For a complete list of the local committees with details of the subscriptions they raised and the number of exhibitors proposed by each, see *First Report of the Commissioners* 1852, pp. xxiv–xxvi.
25. For example, the local committee of the city of Birmingham was made up of eighty-one elected members "consisting of leading manufacturers in principal trades, merchants, professional men, &c." Ibid., p. 51.
26. For a list of the exhibits of these three photographers, see Taylor 2002 and Photographic Exhibitions in Britain, 1839–1865 (website).
27. W. H. F. Talbot to Constance Talbot, October 1851, Talbot Collection, British Library (archival source), LA51-45; Talbot Correspondence Project (website), doc. no. 06470.
28. "Arrangements with Foreign Powers," in *First Report of the Commissioners* 1852, p. 15.
29. Drew 1852, pp. 320, 331.
30. The figure has been calculated from Queen Victoria's journal, which is reprinted in Fay 1951, pp. 44–71.
31. Jerrold 1851.
32. Hunt 1851.
33. For a comprehensive listing of photographers and those exhibiting photographic equipment, see Photographic Exhibitions in Britain, 1839–1865 (website), and follow the links.
34. These were Richard Beard, Richard Beauford, Antoine-François-Jean Claudet, Griffiths & Le Beau, William Edward Kilburn, Martin Laroche, John Jabez Edwin Mayall, Matthew John Rippingham, Ross & Thomson, Tyree Brothers, and Voigtlander, Evans & Co. There were also photographs taken in the new collodion process by Peter Wickens Fry, which, shortly after the opening of the exhibition, were added to the philosophical instrument exhibits of Horne & Thornthwaite. This is the first recorded occasion on which photographs made by the process were exhibited. "Light and Its Applications," *ILN*, May 17, 1851.
35. See chapter 2, p. 28, and, for the background to Blanquart-Evrard's claim, Taylor and Ware 2003.
36. Hunt 1851, vol. 1, p. 398.
37. Ibid., p. 399.
38. Talbot to Sir David Brewster, October 20, 1851, National Media Museum (archival source), 1937-4989; Talbot Correspondence Project (website), doc. no. 06484. Additional details of this episode are given in Sir David Brewster to Talbot, October 23, 1851, National Media Museum (archival source), 1937-4990; Talbot Correspondence Project (website), doc. no. 06487.
39. Talbot complained of this in a letter to Sir David Brewster, October 20, 1851, National Media Museum (archival source), 1937-4989; Talbot Correspondence Project (website), doc. no. 06484.
40. Ibid.
41. "Decisions Regarding Juries" 1852; "Classification of Subjects" 1852.
42. Editorial, *Times* (London), October 17, 1851, p. 4, col. F–p. 5, col. A.
43. "Return Showing the Number of Awards of Different Kinds Made by Juries" 1852.
44. Glaisher 1852.
45. The jury report and the awards treat photography as a single subject but indicate in which class each specific work had been exhibited. "List of Jury Awards: Class X" 1852; Glaisher 1852, pp. 275–79.
46. These figures are based on the listing for "List of Jury Awards: Class X" 1852.
47. Glaisher 1852, p. 244.
48. The total attendance was given as 6,063,986, with the revenue from ticket sales an impressive 429,000 pounds. The income created a large surplus fund that was subsequently used to develop the museums in South Kensington, London. For details of visitor and revenue statistics, see Timbs 1851, app., pp. 337–41.
49. *Account of the Proceedings at the Dinner Given by Mr. George Peabody to the Americans Connected with the Great Exhibition* 1851.
50. *Official Descriptive and Illustrated Catalogue* 1851; *Official Descriptive and Illustrated Catalogue. Supplementary Volume* 1852; *Reports by the Juries* 1852. See also Keeler 1982. A more recent account, based on research in the archives of the royal commissioners, is Asser 2005. For this presentation set, the single volume of *Reports by the Juries* was rebound as four volumes to accommodate the photographic plates, and the first and second reports of the royal commissioners, extracted from the *Supplementary Volume* of the *Official Catalogue*, were reissued as *Reports to the Crown*. I am extremely grateful to Saskia Asser for her generous help, which added much to my understanding of the circumstances surrounding the publication of *Reports by the Juries*.
51. Edgar A. Bowring to Colonel Grey, November 8, 1851, Archives, Royal Commission for the Exhibition of 1851, Imperial College, London, vol. 9, item no. 21. The £60 cited did not include the additional cost of the medals. Translation into contemporary values is difficult; the equivalent today is probably in the region of £9,000–£12,000 ($17,000–$23,000) per set.
52. A list of 122 recipients was prepared for distribution, but this did not include the fifteen sets subsequently promised to Talbot. See Asser 2005, p. 166 and n. 80.
53. G. Francis Duncombe (for the Executive Committee) to Talbot, August 20, 1851, Talbot Collection, British Library (archival source), LA51-40; Talbot Correspondence Project (website), doc. no. 06456.
54. Talbot did not specifically mention Owen; he wrote of "sundry gentlemen" who had been taught by Henneman and had broken their agreement. But the context and dates of the relevant correspondence support the hypothesis that his reference was meant to include Owen. Talbot to Nicolaas Henneman, July 15, 1851, private collection; Talbot Correspondence Project (website), doc. no. 00863.
55. G. Francis Duncombe (for the Executive Committee) to Talbot, August 20, 1851, Talbot Collection, British Library (archival source), LA51-40; Talbot Correspondence Project (website), doc. no. 06456.
56. Matthew Digby Wyatt to Talbot, September 10, 1851, Talbot Collection, British Library (archival source), LA51-42; Talbot Correspondence Project (website), doc. no. 06462.
57. Talbot to Matthew Digby Wyatt, September 13, 1851, Talbot Collection, British Library (archival source), LA51-43; Talbot Correspondence Project (website), doc. no. 06464.
58. Robert Bingham had been a chemical assistant in the laboratory of the London Institution and was the author of *Photogenic Manipulation* (London: Charles Knight and Sons, 1848). On Bingham's photography of works of art in France, see Bann 2001.
59. Talbot to Matthew Digby Wyatt, September 29, 1851, Talbot Collection, British Library (archival source), LA51-45; Talbot Correspondence Project (website), doc. no. 06468.
60. W. H. F. Talbot to Constance Talbot, October 1, 1851, Talbot Collection, British Library (archival source), LA51-53; Talbot Correspondence Project (website), doc. no. 06471.
61. W. H. F. Talbot to Constance Talbot, October 15, 1851, Talbot Collection, British Library (archival source), LA51-61; Talbot Correspondence Project (website), doc. no. 06480.
62. The complete passage in Talbot's letter to his wife reads: "The Ex^{ve} Comm^{ee} altho' rolling in riches want to make Henn^{n} work for next to nothing, indeed with respect to one set of pictures they require him to furnish them at a loss to himself as he is to procure them from a Mr Owen & they will not reimburse him the whole of his outlay. Henn^{n} is desirous

of obliging them & of finishing the work but their own vexatious conduct makes it doubtful. He thinks they wish it not to be completed—Why then order it? The fact is there are endless intrigues among the ranks of the Ex[ve] Comm[ee] they are opposing each other and offending everybody who has the misfortune to have any dealings with them." Ibid.

63. Talbot to Great Exhibition Committee, November 1, 1851, Talbot Collection, British Library (archival source), LA51-69; Talbot Correspondence Project (website), doc. no. 06498. The new procedure called for an additional stage in which every print was dipped in boiling caustic potash to remove all traces of residual sulphur. Despite the drastic sound of this treatment, I am assured by Dr. Mike Ware, my chemistry confidant, that as long as the print was not immersed for too long the procedure was workable, although it shrank the prints.
64. Talbot to Lyon Playfair, November 6, 1851, Talbot Collection, British Library (archival source), LA51-75; Talbot Correspondence Project (website), doc. no. 06505.
65. Charles Thurston Thompson to Talbot, November 8, 1851, Talbot Collection, British Library (archival source), LA51-80; Talbot Correspondence Project (website), doc. no. 06510.
66. Talbot to Lyon Playfair, November 6, 1851, Talbot Collection, British Library (archival source), LA51-75; Talbot Correspondence Project (website), doc. no. 06505.
67. Henry Cole to Talbot, November 14, 1851, Talbot Collection, British Library (archival source), LA51-82; Talbot Correspondence Project (website), doc. no. 06513.
68. Asser 2005, pp. 164–65 and n. 70.
69. Talbot to John Henry Bolton, November 16, 1851, Royal Photographic Society Collection, National Media Museum (archival source); Talbot Correspondence Project (website), doc. no. 06514. Talbot to William Carpmael, November 16, 1851, Royal Photographic Society Collection, National Media Museum (archival source); Talbot Correspondence Project (website), doc. no. 06515.
70. Talbot to Granville George Leveson-Gower, November 21, 1851, Talbot Collection, British Library (archival source), LA51-85, LA51-86; Talbot Correspondence Project (website), doc. no. 06519.
71. W. H. F. Talbot to Constance Talbot, November 17, 1851, Talbot Collection, British Library (archival source) LA51-84; Talbot Correspondence Project (website), doc. no. 06518.
72. Talbot to Granville George Leveson-Gower, November 21, 1851, Talbot Collection, British Library (archival source), LA51-85, LA51-86; Talbot Correspondence Project (website), doc. no. 06519. This letter is the fullest account of the whole affair, as understood by Talbot. While Talbot was negotiating with Granville, the Foreign Office, acting for the Royal Commission, was negotiating with the French Foreign Office and with French and British Customs for the duty-free export of negatives and imminent import of Bingham's prints from France, an arrangement that was confirmed on December 4. The following day the Executive Committee wrote to Talbot agreeing to settle the long-running affair. Asser 2005, pp. 163–64, nn. 62, 64.
73. Executive Committee to Talbot, December 5, 1851, Talbot Collection, British Library (archival source), LA51-91; Talbot Correspondence Project (website), doc. no. 06529.
74. Talbot received his fifteen sets of *Reports by the Juries* toward the end of April 1854. With typical generosity, he gave many sets away to friends and relatives. W. H. F. Talbot to Constance Talbot, April 26, 1854, Talbot Collection, British Library (archival source), LA54-20; Talbot Correspondence Project (website), doc. no. 06948.
75. For a wonderful example of colored lithographic printing, see *Dickinson's Comprehensive Pictures of the Great Exhibition* 1854.
76. They were placed where relevant, as follows: 5 prints in volume 1, 45 prints in volume 2, 45 prints in volume 3, and 59 prints in volume 4.
77. Owen's prints are warmer in tone and have a slightly rough surface texture, while those from Ferrier's negatives have a neutral greenish tone and are on paper with a smoother texture. These subtly distinct characteristics match those of British and French prints, respectively, from this period. The theory that British printers were involved gains further credence from the fact that when Talbot negotiated with the Executive Committee he offered to forgo his royalty payments in an effort to bring the price down and retain the printing work in Britain. See Talbot to Lyon Playfair, November 6, 1851, Talbot Collection, British Library (archival source), LA51-75; Talbot Correspondence Project (website), doc. no. 06505, and Talbot to George Knight, November 16, 1851, Royal Photographic Society Collection, National Media Museum (archival source); Talbot Correspondence Project (website), doc. no. 06516.
78. Editorial, *Times* (London), January 1, 1852, p. 4, col. B, reprinted in *Annual Summaries* 1893, vol. 1, p. 2.

4. *Battling Patents and Gaining Legitimacy*

pages 44–55

1. "Photographic Club," *Art-Union*, April 1, 1848, p. 130. In a later article Hall pronounced that Talbot could "no more patent a right to *tracing paper*, than he can to writing or other paper, for receiving photographic images." "Patent of Mr. Fox Talbot," *Art-Journal*, August 1, 1850, p. 262.
2. A report on the albumen process of Niepce de Saint-Victor appeared in the *Comptes rendus* of the French Academy of Sciences in October 1847, and that of Blanquart-Evrard in the *Comptes rendus* in August 1849. See Niepce de Saint-Victor 1847 and Blanquart-Evrard 1849. Also see Eder 1945, p. 339.
3. "Scientific Gossip," *Athenaeum*, September 8, 1849.
4. Hunt, *Art-Journal*, February 1, 1850, p. 39. Hunt had already employed proto-sulphate of iron as a developing agent in his Energiatype process, introduced in 1844; see Hunt, *Athenaeum*, June 1, 1844.
5. Hunt, *Art-Journal*, February 1, 1850, p. 40.
6. For a succinct outline of British patent history, see Gomme 1946.
7. Talbot to Robert Hunt, November 7, 1851, Royal Photographic Society Collection, National Media Museum (archival source), 141(a); Talbot Correspondence Project (website), doc. no. 06507.
8. "Photography and Its Patents," *Art-Journal*, June 1, 1852.
9. Talbot and Thomas Malone filed a patent specifying three different applications of the albumen-on-glass process: Patent no. 12,906, Patent Office Library, British Library, London; see also Woodcroft 1854; *Photography* [Patent no. 12,906] 1857. In 1851, Talbot filed a further patent in which he set out detailed improvements to the process: Patent no. 13,664, Patent Office Library, British Library, London; see also Woodcroft 1854; *Photography* [Patent no. 13,664] 1857.
10. Archer, *Chemist*, March 1851.
11. Once dry, however, the collodion formed a skin that repelled all solutions. This meant photographers had to coat, sensitize, expose, and develop the plate before it dried; hence the name "wet-collodion" process.
12. Negotiations of some sort may have begun previously, as early as March 1851; Hunt mentions submitting a letter by Talbot to "some of the more influential movers in the Photographic Club." Robert Hunt to Talbot, March 23, 1851, Talbot Collection, British Library (archival source), LA51-09; Talbot Correspondence Project (website), doc. no. 06399.
13. Robert Hunt to Peter Wickens Fry, March 5, 1852, in Johnston 1946, p. 2.
14. "Proposal for the Formation of a Photographical Society," *Art-Journal Advertiser*, April 1, 1852. The advertising pages of the journal were meant to be removed and few have survived intact; one copy is in the British Library, London. See also "Photographical Society," *Art-Journal*, April 1, 1852. A draft manuscript outlining the aims and objectives of the proposed photographic society exists and has been reprinted; see Kamlish 2002. On the authorship of this document, see Taylor 2003 and Kamlish 2003. On Roger Fenton's role in the formation of the Photographic Society, see Roberts 2004.
15. Robert Hunt to Talbot, March 19, 1852, Talbot Collection, British Library (archival source), LA52-15; Talbot Correspondence Project (website), doc. no. 06580.
16. Talbot to Robert Hunt, March 24, 1852, Royal Photographic Society Collection, National Media Museum (archival source), T/2 1279; Talbot Correspondence Project (website), doc. no. 06585.
17. Ibid.
18. Frederick Berger was a color pigment manufacturer; Roger Fenton, Peter Wickens Fry, and Peter Le Neve Foster were lawyers; Thomas Goodeve was a tutor at King's College, London; Robert Hunt was a chemist and author on photography; and Sir William Newton was miniature painter to Queen Victoria. All were amateur photographers. "Resignation of the Photographic Patents," *Art-Journal*, September 1, 1852, p. 270.

19. Roger Fenton, in "Inaugural Meeting of the Photographic Society," *JPS*, March 3, 1853, p. 3.
20. Hunt communicated the feelings of the provisional committee to Talbot: "Every one is quite disposed to give you all honour as the discoverer of the Calotype—but every one also says you are pushing your claims too far in claiming *Iodised paper*—[and] any developing agent beyond *Gallic Acid*—and there is a common feeling that the Collodion process is entirely beyond any of your specifications." Robert Hunt to Talbot, April 28, 1852, Talbot Collection, British Library (archival source), LA52-23; Talbot Correspondence Project (website), doc. no. 06600.
21. Talbot to Robert Hunt, April 30, 1852, Royal Photographic Society Collection, National Media Museum (archival source), 141(c); Talbot Correspondence Project (website), doc. no. 06602.
22. A detailed account of the trial, complete with highlights of statements by witnesses and the judge's summing-up, is in "Photographic Patent Right," *Art-Journal*, February 1, 1855. The amount of space Hall dedicated to covering this trial is perhaps an indication of his determination to bring down Talbot and his patents.
23. On Foster's appointment to the Society of Arts, see Wood 1913, pp. 364–65.
24. Society of Arts, Minutes of Council (archival source), vol. 4, p. 29, report of meeting, June 9, 1852.
25. "Letter to Mr. Talbot," *Weekly Proceedings*, June 26, 1852.
26. Talbot to William Parsons [Lord Rosse], May 30, 1852, Royal Photographic Society Collection, National Media Museum (archival source), T/2 1274A; Talbot Correspondence Project (website), doc. no. 06624.
27. Both letters were published in full; see "Photographic Patent Right," *Times*, August 13, 1852, and "Resignation of the Photographic Patents," *Art-Journal*, September 1, 1852. See also Charles Lock Eastlake to Talbot, July 1852, Royal Photographic Society Collection, National Media Museum (archival source), T/2 1273, and Talbot to William Parsons [Lord Rosse], July 30, 1852, Birr Scientific and Heritage Foundation / Earl of Rosse Ireland; Talbot Correspondence Project (website), doc. nos. 06653 and 06668.
28. For a summary of the act, see "Patent Law Amendment" 1853.
29. A survey of cultural institutions in London, Edinburgh, and Dublin appeared annually in *The British Almanac* (London: Charles Knight) from 1827 to 1888.
30. A history of the society's formation is given in *Jubilee of the Chemical Society of London* 1896, pp. 115–292.
31. Society of Arts, Minutes of Council (archival source), vol. 4, p. 127, report of meeting, November 17, 1852. "Photography," *ILN*, January 1, 1853, with woodcut illustration of the soiree.
32. Cundall and Delamotte were professional colleagues with close ties to the Society of Arts. In 1850 they had jointly published *Choice Examples of Art-Workmanship*, a portfolio of sixty engravings after objects in the exhibition of ancient and medieval art at the society; it was advertised in the *Athenaeum*, March 30, 1850, p. 331.
33. For the notice of the extended run, see "Photographic Exhibition," *JSA*, January 21, 1853.
34. *Catalogue of an Exhibition of Recent Specimens of Photography* 1852. The revised edition included a reprinting of the paper read by Roger Fenton at the opening soiree and expanded notes on various photographic processes. A copy of this edition can be found in the National Art Library, Victoria and Albert Museum, London.
35. This analysis of exhibits comes from Taylor 2002; see also Photographic Exhibitions in Britain, 1839–1865 (website).
36. Edward Solly to Talbot, December 6, 1852, Talbot Collection, British Library (archival source), LA52-52; Talbot Correspondence Project (website), doc. no. 06709.
37. British Library, London, Album NB1: LA2000–LA2058. I am grateful to my colleague Professor Larry J. Schaaf for this information and for the detailed listing of the album's contents that he prepared as part of his projected catalogue raisonné of Talbot's photographic output.
38. The album may have had additional significance for Talbot because this was the last occasion on which he exhibited photographs. After 1852 he concentrated increasingly on perfecting his photoglyphic engraving process; see Schaaf 2003.
39. One of the earliest and most influential publications to examine the emergence of amateur photography during the 1850s is Seiberling and Bloore 1986. I am indebted to both authors but especially to Carolyn Bloore, whose continuing research in the field has added much to my understanding.
40. Boase 1965, vol. 1, col. 129, entry for Hippolyte Baillière.
41. It seems likely this was William Little, publisher of the *Illustrated London News*, which had used photography as a basis for its wood-block illustrations beginning in 1842. A William Little was elected a member of the Photographic Society on April 7, 1853. Photographic Society, Minutes of General Meetings (archival source), "Third Ordinary Meeting."
42. The exhibition was widely reviewed and generally well received; see "Photographic Exhibition at the Society of Arts," *Art-Journal*, February 1, 1853; "Exhibition of Photographic Pictures at the Society of Arts," *Athenaeum*, January 1, 1853; "Photography," *ILN*, January 1, 1853, with half-page woodcut illustration; "Exhibition of Photography," *Literary Gazette*, January 15, 1853.
43. "Exhibition of Photographs," *Times*, December 31, 1852.
44. "Inaugural Meeting of the Photographic Society," *JPS*, March 3, 1853. See also Photographic Society, Minutes of Council, and Minutes of General Meetings (archival sources).
45. Eastlake's long-standing relationship to the royal family had begun in 1841, when, as secretary to the Royal Commission of Fine Arts, he worked alongside Prince Albert. Somers had just been appointed lord-in-waiting to Queen Victoria in January 1853 and shared an interest in photography with Dr. Ernst Becker, tutor to the princes in the royal household.
46. For a list of the council members, see Roberts 2004, pp. 216–17.
47. "Photographic Society. Anniversary Meeting, Thursday, February 2nd, 1854," *JPS*, February 21, 1854, where it is reported that the society had received the considerable income of 645 pounds from subscriptions.
48. Martin Laroche and Thomas Richard Williams, both commercial photographers, became members on May 5, 1853. Photographic Society, Minutes of General Meetings (archival source), "Fourth Ordinary Meeting."
49. "Photographic Society. Anniversary Meeting, Thursday, February 2nd, 1854," *JPS*, February 21, 1854.
50. Reported at the "Photographic Society. Fifth Ordinary Meeting. Thursday, June 2nd, 1853," *JPS*, June 21, 1853, p. 69.
51. The dispersal of the surplus funds from the Great Exhibition greatly exercised the minds of the royal commissioners and prompted numerous appeals for financial support from institutions throughout the country. For details of these considerations, see *Second Report of the Commissioners* 1852, pp. 9–41, 44–59, appendices A–D.
52. These figures were cited in a review of *Mechanics' Institutes*, by A. Kilgour, *Athenaeum*, November 12, 1853, pp. 1348–49.
53. For insight into the scope and purpose of this movement, see Society for the Diffusion of Useful Knowledge, *Manual for Mechanics' Institutions*, 1839.
54. Harry Chester was also assistant secretary to the Committee of Privy Council for Education from 1848 to 1858; his proposal may even have been informally suggested by the Privy Council, a select body of senior politicians chosen by the monarch to advise on matters of state. Chester's letter on the subject, dated November 28, 1851, was published in *Weekly Proceedings*, February 21, 1852. On discussion of the idea in council, see "Society of Arts," *Times*, February 27, 1852.
55. An account of the conference held in London to discuss Chester's proposal, where the scheme was formally accepted, and a list of delegates attending are given in the *Weekly Proceedings*, May 22, 1852. The term "Institutions in Union" was adopted later.
56. "Society of Arts," *Times*, September 29, 1853.
57. George Sanders, Hon. Sec., Stafford Mechanics' Institute, to the Secretary, Society of Arts, November 9, 1855; Society of Arts, Correspondence files (archival source), A/RSA/12/E/17.
58. "Photographic Exhibition," *JPS*, March 3, 1853.
59. "Photography," *JSA*, March 4, 1853.
60. "Notice to Institutions," *JSA*, August 5, 1853.
61. For a list of the photographers and their exhibited works, see Taylor 2002 and Photographic Exhibitions in Britain, 1839–1865 (website).
62. On the tour, see "Collection of Photographs," *JSA*, September 16, 1853, p. 522. See also Taylor 2002 and Photographic Exhibitions in Britain, 1839–1865 (website).
63. These difficulties become apparent from the correspondence between exhibiting institutions and the Society of Arts. Society of Arts, Correspondence files (archival source), A/RSA/7/B/1-67, A/RSA/7/E/1-219, A/RSA/12/F/1-48.

64. These were not photographs but delicate casts made from the imprint on a soft metal plate of natural objects such as ferns, mosses, and seaweeds. See *Ure's Dictionary of Arts* 1860, vol. 2, pp. 234–37.
65. One exhibition contained 129 prints, the other 121. See Taylor 2002 and Photographic Exhibitions in Britain, 1839–1865 (website).
66. A full list of exhibition venues and dates is in "Collection of Photographs," *JSA*, March 24, 1854.
67. The venues of this tour were never published. A list of its exhibits shows that examples of various types of photomechanical printing were shown alongside the photographs. Society of Arts, Correspondence files (archival source), A/RSA/12/G/37.
68. Advertisement, "Photographic Exhibition, Mechanics' Institution," *Aberdeen Journal*, December 7, 1853.
69. "School of Arts—Lecture on Photography," *Stirling Journal and Advertiser*, November 17, 1853.
70. "Lynn Conversazione and Society of Arts," *Lynn Advertiser*, January 14, 1853.
71. "Literary Institute. Fine Collection of Photographs," *Wrexham and Denbigh Weekly Advertiser*, June 3, 1854.
72. "Photographic Exhibition," *Burnley Advertiser*, August 12, 1854.

5. *The Calotype Finds Its Place*
pages 56–73

1. Fenton, in "Inaugural Meeting of the Photographic Society," *JPS*, March 3, 1853, p. 3. It has been suggested that Fenton himself took up photography because of the Great Exhibition; see Greenough 2004, p. 11.
2. A.H.R., *Notes and Queries*, August 28, 1852.
3. C.P.S., *Notes and Queries*, September 11, 1852.
4. On William John Thoms, editor of *Notes and Queries*, see *Oxford Dictionary of National Biography*, s.v. "Thoms, William John (1803–1885)" (by Arthur Sherbo).
5. William J. Thoms, in "Photography and Manuscripts," *Notes and Queries*, October 9, 1852.
6. Diamond's first article appears in *Notes and Queries*, September 18, 1852. Crookes's account is "Wax-Paper Process," *Notes and Queries*, November 6, 1852.
7. Archer, *Notes and Queries*, December 25, 1852.
8. For a detailed account, see Budge 1981. In November 1850, Claudius Galen Wheelhouse gave a lecture on the calotype and showed examples of his work recently taken during his cruise around the Mediterranean.
9. "Copy of the Rules of the Leeds Photographic Society" 1952.
10. Only three issues of "Productions of the Leeds Photographic Society" are known to have survived. They carry dates between July and September 1852, and, given the ephemeral nature and tiny circulation of "Productions," it seems likely that these three were the only issues completed. Department of Photographs, The Metropolitan Museum of Art, New York. A contemporary reference to this "Illustrated Photographic Journal" occurs in "Correspondence," *JPS*, June 21, 1854.
11. In 1842, the spiritual needs of Leeds were served by the established Church of England and also by places of worship for "Baptists, the Society of Friends, Independents, Wesleyans, Primitive Methodists, Methodists of the New Connexion, Female Revivalists, members of the Scottish Church, Southcotians, Swedenborgians, and Unitarians, and two Roman Catholic chapels." Lewis 1842, vol. 3, p. 50.
12. With the exception of George Fowler Jones, an architect, and William Pumphrey and John William Ramsden, both photographers, little is known about the members of the Leeds Photographic Society or their occupations. These names are gleaned from "Productions of the Leeds Photographic Society." See, in the Dictionary of British Calotypists in the present volume, entries for William Fieldhouse (president), John Birch, Thomas Henry Briggs, Thomas Dixon, William Gardam, E. Holliday, Thomas Alfred Hope, George Fowler Jones, William Pumphrey, and John William Ramsden (vice president).
13. See Taylor 2002 and Photographic Exhibitions in Britain, 1839–1865 (website).
14. The Liverpool Royal Institution was founded in 1814 when a group of like-minded individuals decided to establish a society "for promoting the increase and diffusion of Literature, Science and the Arts." The institution housed a rich variety of collections and in 1826 was the venue for John Audubon's first European exhibition. Ormerod 1953.
15. "Liverpool Photographic Society," *JPS*, May 2, 1853. The speaker was James Allanson Picton (d. 1889), an architect, surveyor, historian, and active promoter of the public library system, who was knighted in 1881.
16. Good 1953, pp. 9–10. The society was renamed the Liverpool Amateur Photographic Association in 1859.
17. For the names of the retailers, see *LPJ*, January 14, 1854, title page.
18. *Literary Gazette; and Journal of the Belles Lettres, Arts, Sciences, &c.*, February 24, 1855, p. 122. In 1857 the *Liverpool Journal* became the *Liverpool and Manchester Photographic Journal*; in January 1860 it transmuted into the *British Journal of Photography*, which is still published today. The history of the journal is outlined in Gernsheim 1984, p. 131.
19. The Leeds Photographic Society submitted papers read at its meetings to the journal of the London Photographic Society and a paper or excerpt was occasionally printed, but the proceedings of the Leeds society were never reported. For an example, see Ramsden, *JPS*, October 21, 1853. Some members of the Leeds Photographic Society who regularly submitted prints to the annual exhibitions in Birmingham, Edinburgh, London, and Manchester gained a wider reputation than the society itself.
20. For an account of these societies with dates of their founding, see Jaeger 1995.
21. For society history and membership, see, for Scotland, Edinphoto (website), and for Dublin, Chandler 2001, pp. 65–70.
22. Jaeger 1995.
23. Diamond, *JPS*, November 21, 1853; Percy, *JPS*, March 3, 1853.
24. For a description of the cameras under discussion, see "Photographic Society. Third Ordinary Meeting. Thursday, April 7, 1853," *JPS*, April 21, 1853. An article on lenses is Hunt, *JPS*, April 1, 1853.
25. These were the photograph societies of Birmingham, Manchester, and Scotland. See Gernsheim 1984, p. 132.
26. The wider context of advertising in the nineteenth century is discussed in Nevett 1982, pp. 25–109.
27. Advertisement, "Photogenic Drawing-Paper," *Athenaeum*, March 16, 1839.
28. That Britain constituted a mass market was underlined by the sale by Schweppes of over a million bottles of mineral water and other nonalcoholic beverages during the six months of the Great Exhibition. While before 1851 manufacturers either distributed their goods locally or exported them to overseas markets, the expansion of the railway network in the 1840s made possible the rapid transport of goods throughout Britain. See Freeman 1999, pp. 140–47.
29. These figures should be treated with caution, since occasionally a single business is cited more than once, under different headings. *Post Office London Directory* (London: Frederick Kelly) for 1853, 1855, 1856, and 1860. This rapid expansion is graphically revealed in Pritchard 1994, which is also available online: see Directory of London Photographers, 1841–1908 (website). I am especially grateful to Michael Pritchard for generously helping me obtain information on a wide range of subjects over many years.
30. For one aspect of this, see Pritchard, "Rise of British Photographic Manufacturing, 1839–*c.* 1862," 1990.
31. A reviewer wrote, "We have had a vast number of those small books, all professing to simplify the Photographic art, but we have not had one which deals so thoroughly with a special process as does this 'Handbook' of Mr. Sutton." [Hunt], review of *The Calotype Process*, by Thomas Sutton, *Athenaeum*, July 14, 1855.
32. Sutton, *Calotype Process*, 1855, preface.
33. The Photographic Institution occupied premises previously used by the photographer Richard Colls, who was taken to court by Talbot in January 1852 after patent infringements. His premises and camera were sold four months later, suggesting that he was put out of business by the costs involved. Advertisement, "Photography.—To Be Let or Sold . . . Mr. [Richard] Colls," *Athenaeum*, May 15, 1852. See also correspondence in the Talbot Collection, British Library (archival source), LA48-36, LA50-05, LA50-09, LA50-12, LA50-16, LA52-05 (Talbot Correspondence Project [website], doc. nos. 06158, 06290, 06300, 06303, 06308, 06556), for the context of this dispute.
34. Advertisement, "Photographic Institution," *Athenaeum*, April 16, 1853, which contains a full-page list of services and photographic publications available.
35. For photographers and titles of work, see Taylor 2002 and

Photographic Exhibitions in Britain, 1839–1865 (website).

36. See the advertisements, "Venice.—Sixty Large and Highly-Interesting Views . . . by M. Bresolin," *Athenaeum*, April 30, 1853, and "Marten's Views in Switzerland and the Pyrenees," *Athenaeum*, May 7, 1853.
37. "Court Circular," *Times* (London), August 4, 1853, p. 5, col. B, and July 17, 1854, p. 8, col. F. In early 1854 the royal family commissioned Cundall and Delamotte to take photographs in Windsor and Buckingham Palace, and they continued sporadically to request this work until 1869. For early instances, see Privy Purse Accounts (archival source), PP2/4/4035, PP2/5/4343, PP2/8/5060.
38. The list of camera outfits, chemicals, and materials advertised in the back of Sutton's handbook gives an idea of prices. For example, one fluid ounce of silver nitrate—a very small amount—cost 4 shillings 6 pence, and the same amount of potassium iodide cost 3 shillings. The price of a packet of iodized photographic paper, 19 x 15 inches, was 1 pound, or more than the weekly cost of feeding a family (see note 39 below).
39. For a contemporary discussion of the cost of living, see "Where to Live with a Small Income" 1854, in which weekly household expenses are tabulated and from these the annual cost of living estimated. For example, a family with an annual income of 100 pounds could rent a house, hire a good servant, and "live in a comfortable and even genteel style." The annual wage for the servant was 5 pounds.
40. This figure is for England and Wales only. It includes photographic artists and their assistants, of whom just 163 were women. "England and Wales.—Occupations of the People," in *Census of England and Wales* 1863, p. xxxvi, table XVII.
41. [E. Eastlake], *Quarterly Review*, April 1857, p. 443. Although Lady Eastlake's numbers may have been fanciful, her observations were undoubtedly accurate.
42. Sutton, *Calotype Process*, 1855, p. 3.
43. Ibid., p. 7.
44. Ibid., pp. 7, 23.
45. The early-nineteenth-century development of mackintosh cloth, which blocked light and was waterproof, proved a real boon to photographers. It was also used to wrap delicate equipment during travel, as a dark cloth when focusing the camera, and as a protective covering for tables and furniture during processing. See *Oxford Dictionary of National Biography*, s.v. "Macintosh, Charles (1766–1843)" (by R. B. Prosser, rev. Geoffrey V. Morson).
46. Sutton suggested it not be used "when there are any cuts or scratches upon the hands." Sutton, *Calotype Process*, 1855, p. 88.
47. Delamotte 1853, p. 48. Other ways to hold the negative in the dark slide were proposed; for one using pins, see Davies, *Photographic News*, November 5, 1858.
48. Before wide-angle lenses were introduced during the 1860s, photographers chose lenses that gave an angle of view and perspective roughly comparable to human vision, approximately 53 degrees. The focal length of the lens had to correspond to the size of the chosen negative format. A 6½ inch lens was ideal for a 5 x 4 inch negative, and a 12 inch lens for the 10 x 8 format. A lens of shorter focal length transmits correspondingly more light than one of longer focal length in a ratio governed by the inverse square law, which states that the intensity of light is inversely proportional to the square of the distance from the source (i.e., the lens).
49. Sutton, *Calotype Process*, 1855, p. 31.
50. Ibid., p. 36.
51. Ibid., p. 37.
52. If the photographer was working away from home, fixation could be deferred provided the negatives were thoroughly washed, dried, and stored in the dark. Ibid., p. 39.
53. On French and British papers, see Taylor and Ware 2003.
54. Crookes 1857. Based on Crookes's practical experience with the process at the Radcliffe Observatory at Oxford, the handbook was generally well received. One reviewer, however, wished that Crookes "had spoken with more modesty of his own labours, and in a less depreciating tone of the labours of others." [Hunt], *Athenaeum*, August 29, 1857.
55. Crookes, *JPS*, September 21, 1855.
56. Crookes 1857, p. 25.
57. Waxed Canson paper was three times more expensive than plain paper. See the advertisement for "Photographic Papers" by John Sanford, *JPS*, October 21, 1853, n.p. (facing p. 117).
58. In contrast, see the recipes proposed by George Dawson, which called for up to eight separate ingredients including potassium cyanide, sugar of milk, and gum-arabic, and, for one variant, "calf's stomach, quite fresh . . . cut up into small pieces." Dawson, *JPS*, October 21 and November 21, 1857. See also the useful table of variants in Teasdale, *JPS*, January 21, 1854.
59. Hannavy 1993, pp. 233–43, and n. 14, where Hannavy suggests that the presence of free iodine assisted in this bonding, although this is not accepted in Taylor and Ware 2003. The matter will only be resolved when the research with an electron scanning microscope has established the precise location of the silver salts within the paper fibers.
60. The deep purple color resulted from the combination of iodine with the starch size used in French papers.
61. Crookes 1857, p. 38.
62. Ibid., p. 40.
63. For a range of approaches to the process, see How, *Chemist*, 1854; Keith, *Photographic Notes*, July 17, 1856; Sutton, *Photographic Notes*, October 1, November 1, and December 1, 1856.
64. According to the Reverend William Law, the process could be made to rival in sensitivity the exquisitely sensitive collodion process by increasing the strength of the iodizing solution, within certain limits. Law, *LMPJ*, October 1, 1857.
65. "Waxed-Paper Processes," *Photographic News*, March 8, 1861.
66. Fitt, *LPJ*, January 12, 1856, p. 8.
67. There is little written evidence directly linking choices of paper to aesthetic goals, but surviving collections of paper negatives suggest that photographers worked with papers in a variety of thicknesses ranging from very thin to heavy. The negatives of Dr. John Murray, Benjamin Brecknell Turner, and Linnaeus Tripe in the collections of the Royal Photographic Society, National Media Museum, Bradford, offer a wide range of examples.
68. However, although they offer useful information on individual activity and processes employed, nineteenth-century exhibition catalogues should be interpreted with caution, as errors abound. See Taylor 2002 and Photographic Exhibitions in Britain, 1839–1865 (website).
69. On silver printing-out processes and the exposure times required, see Ware 1994, p. 17. Blanquart-Evrard's printing process, which relied on the chemical development of a latent image, required only a brief exposure time. This allowed prints to be made rapidly. Although his method was commercially successful, the predominantly neutral tones of the resulting prints never found wide favor with amateurs. See Eder 1945, pp. 327–28.
70. Sutton, *Calotype Process*, 1855, p. 52.
71. Ibid.
72. Ibid., p. 68.
73. Ibid., p. 53.
74. For an excellent discussion of photographic papers and printing during the nineteenth century, with contemporary woodcut illustrations, see Reilly 1980.
75. Sutton, *Calotype Process*, 1855, p. 57.
76. Ibid., p. 64.
77. To create an effective toning bath, silver nitrate, iodine, or ferric chloride was added.
78. Delamotte 1853, pp. 58–59.
79. Sutton, "Gold *versus* Old Hypo," *JPS*, February 21, 1855, p. 122. A lively exchange followed between Sutton and Thomas Frederick Hardwich, author of the well-respected *Manual of Photographic Chemistry*, in the pages of the *Journal of the Photographic Society*. See Hardwich, *JPS*, April 21, 1855; Sutton, "On the Chemistry of Mr. Sutton's Negative Printing Process," *JPS*, August 21, 1855; and Sutton, "On the Hyposulphite of Gold," *JPS*, September 21, 1855.
80. See "Photographic Society. Committee on Positive Printing," *JPS*, May 21, 1855; Delamotte et al., *JPS*, November 21, 1855. A discussion aimed at the general public was Hunt, "On the Fading of Photographic Pictures," *Art-Journal*, July 1, 1855.
81. See Sutton, "The French Violet Tints," in Sutton, *Calotype Process*, 1855, pp. 67–72.
82. See Ware, *Gold in Photography*, 2006.
83. Bede [Edward Bradley] 1855, p. 54. Bradley's comic narrative is littered with dreadful puns, but his observations are sharply drawn.
84. Ibid., p. 47.
85. Glaisher was responsible for distilling the judges' opinions into an official report. See Glaisher 1852; the report on photography is on pp. 274–79. On Glaisher, see *Oxford Dictionary of National Biography*, s.v. "Glaisher, James (1809–1903)" (by H. P. Hollis, rev. J. Tucker).
86. Glaisher, *JSA*, January 28, 1853.
87. Ibid.

88. Knight 1860, cols. 396–97. In 1850, the manufacture of sheet glass still relied on the skill of the glassblower, who created cylinders of glass up to five feet long. These were cut open and laid on metal sheets in a hot oven, where they flattened. The method, introduced from France during the 1830s, was perfected by Chance Brothers to create the 300,000 panes, each 49 x 10 inches, that roofed the Crystal Palace. Antoine Claudet acted as an intermediary between Robert Lucas Chance and the French manufacturer Georges Bontemps when Chance Brothers was establishing new techniques at its factory in Birmingham. See Chance 1919, pp. 5–6.
89. Prior to the introduction of sheet glass, flat panes of glass were made by taking a pontil of molten glass and spinning it with great force to create a large disc that when cool was cut into rectangles. Glass produced this way had numerous bubbles and ripples that rendered it useless for photography.
90. The society never stated its policies except in the broadest terms, for which see Sir Charles Eastlake in "Inaugural Meeting of the Photographic Society," *JPS*, March 3, 1853, p. 2. The nearest thing to a policy statement was a paper that Fenton delivered at the inaugural meeting, "Upon the Mode in which It Is Advisable the Society Should Conduct Its Labours." Fenton, *JPS*, March 3, 1853.
91. Photographic Society, Minutes of Council (archival source), p. 84, report of meeting, December 1, 1853, in which Fenton reports that he has secured the exhibition space at a rental of 25 pounds per month. In subsequent years the society used the rooms of the Society of Painters in Water Colour, Pall Mall, and, on one occasion, the South Kensington Museum for its annual exhibitions. See Taylor 2002 and Photographic Exhibitions in Britain, 1839–1865 (website).
92. See *Exhibition of the New Society of Painters in Water Colours* 1853.
93. "Court Circular," *Times* (London), January 4, 1854, p. 6, col. E. Sir Charles Eastlake was invited to join the royal couple at Windsor Castle the following day. "Court Circular," *Times* (London), January 6, 1854, p. 6, col. E.
94. Taylor 2004.
95. The Privy Purse Accounts (archival source) contain the original invoices and receipts for photographs purchased privately by the queen and Prince Albert, confirming that 1853 marked the start of their collecting and commissioning activities. Prince Albert visited the exhibition of the Photographic Society again in early March. "Court Circular," *Times* (London), March 3, 1854, p. 9, col. D.
96. *JPS* 1 (January 21, 1854), p. 153.
97. See Taylor 2002 and Photographic Exhibitions in Britain, 1839–1865 (website).
98. "Photographic Society. Anniversary Meeting. Thursday, February 2nd, 1854," *JPS*, February 21, 1854.
99. "Photography and the Photographic Society," *Builder*, February 11, 1854. This published report differs widely from the one that appeared in the *Journal of the Photographic Society*, where the heated discussion was condensed into a few carefully phrased sentences, and the outcome was reported but the wider implications left unaddressed.
100. "Photography and the Photographic Society," *Builder*, February 11, 1854.
101. Ibid. When Eastlake realized that three members of his council had resigned, he tried to persuade Rippingham to recall his proposal; when this failed, a poll was taken and the original motion negated. This meant that the eight professional photographers about to join the society would indeed be eligible for council, and to avoid that possibility the entire original council was reelected for a further year.
102. "Occupations of the People" 1854. Any attempt to interpret the occupational returns of the 1851 census is surrounded by pitfalls. The fifty-one photographers and daguerreotypists cited in the official returns (*Census of Great Britain* 1854, app., p. 138, table XXXII, no. 102) must be understood in the wider context of the census; see Higgs 1996.
103. "Occupations of the People" 1854, p. 63.
104. Ibid., p. 72. Two final, anomalous classes, the only ones not directly pertaining to an occupation, stood slightly apart from the overall system: Class 15, laboring classes who worked seasonally or occasionally and had no fixed employment; and class 16, persons of rank and property, characterized in the census as "gentlemen" or "men of independent means."
105. Ibid., p. 63.
106. Ibid., p. 67.
107. Submissions to the 1855 annual exhibition came mostly from amateur photographers, with only a only a sprinkling of commercial portraits on show. By 1859, submissions from portrait studios and professional photographers dominated the exhibition. For details of both, see Taylor 2002 and Photographic Exhibitions in Britain, 1839–1865 (website).
108. See *Oxford Dictionary of National Biography*, s.v. "Newton, Sir William John (1785–1869)" (by V. Remington).
109. Newton, *JPS*, March 3, 1853. See also Zillman 1986.
110. Newton, *JPS*, March 3, 1853, p. 6.
111. Robinson 1896, chap. 12, "The Question of Focus."
112. Newton, *JPS*, March 3, 1853.
113. The retouching of a negative often appeared intrusive, but when skillfully done it could subtly enhance the image. Deep shadows were lightened by the addition of yellow pigment to these areas, which inhibited light from passing through the negative. Skies, often troublesome, were sometimes made completely white by filling in the corresponding area of the negative with solid black pigment or graphite pencil. In other instances clouds were added for visual effect. Chemicals were infrequently applied, since they were difficult to control and gave uncertain results.
114. Newton, *JPS*, March 3, 1853, p. 6.
115. Leighton, *JPS*, June 21, 1853, p. 74, reprinted in *Builder*, October 1, 1853. John Leighton was a distinguished and prolific artist who joined the Photographic Society in 1854.
116. These figures come from Taylor 2002; see also Photographic Exhibitions in Britain, 1839–1865 (website).

6. *Subjects Fit for the Camera*
pages 74–87

1. Editorial, *Times* (London), January 1, 1856, p. 6, col. B, reprinted in *Annual Summaries* 1893, vol. 1, p. 26.
2. Fenton, *JPS*, January 21, 1856.
3. The fleet sailed to the Baltic for action against Russia on March 11, 1854, and the treaty was signed the following day, with war being declared on March 27, 1854. For a contemporary chronology of the war, see "Russo-Turkish War," in *Haydn's Dictionary of Dates* 1866, pp. 637–39.
4. The entire sequence of Fenton's eight prints is included in *Calotypes*, vol. 2, Photograph Archives, Royal Collection, Windsor Castle. For the titles of the five works exhibited in 1855, see Taylor 2002 and Photographic Exhibitions in Britain, 1839–1865 (website).
5. Two examples: "Launch of the 'Royal Albert,' at Woolwich Dockyard," *ILN*, May 20, 1854, an illustrated article covering the launch of *The Royal Albert*; and "Royal Regiment of Artillery," *ILN*, June 3, 1854, with a double-page spread portraying the officers and men striking noble postures. The technology did not yet exist to incorporate photographic images into newspapers, except by translating them into woodcuts.
6. On the decision to exhibit at these galleries and the consequent rise in attendance, see "Report of the Council," *JPS*, February 21, 1855, p. 116.
7. An excellent and detailed study is Black 1992.
8. Said over supper with James Boswell and the Corsican patriot Pasquale Paoli, April 11, 1776. *Travellers' Dictionary of Quotation* 1983, p. 525.
9. *Oxford Dictionary of National Biography*, s.v. "Gilpin, William (1724–1804)" (by Malcolm Andrews).
10. Gilpin 1792, p. 42. See also Gilpin 1768.
11. Gilpin 1782, pp. 1–2.
12. Ibid., pp. 7–8.
13. Ibid., pp. 12–13.
14. Gilpin 1792, pp. 47–48.
15. For one of the best accounts of the cult of the Picturesque, see Andrews 1989.
16. Twining 1846, p. 2.
17. Ibid., pp. 83–84.
18. Ibid., pp. 168, 170.
19. Quoted in Twining 1849, pp. 51–52. For the original passage, see Johann Joachim Winckelmann, *Geschichte der Kunst des Alterthums* (Dresden, 1764), book 4, chap. 2, sec. 9. The work has been translated into English and many other languages.
20. Twining 1849, pp. 51–52.
21. Talbot appreciated the value of the Sublime and offered this advice in a letter: "Take a guide & walk for a distance of half a mile thro' a wood, which takes you out upon a meadow on the brow of the Jura, where you discover the celebrated view: — The best time for seeing it is near sunset, & it is of the greatest sublimity." Talbot to Charles Feilding,

July 16, 1834, Talbot Collection, British Library (archival source), LA(H)34-08; Talbot Correspondence Project (website), doc. no. 02950.
22. Jack Simmons, "System, Development of the," in *Oxford Companion to British Railway History* 1997, pp. 492–93.
23. Lardner 1850, p. 33.
24. See Freeman 1999.
25. An entertaining account of the guidebook is given in Sillitoe 1995.
26. *Black's Picturesque Guide to the English Lakes* 1854, advertisement, front flyleaf.
27. Good examples of this type of descriptive text are found in *Black's Picturesque Tourist of Scotland* 1845. While this approach may seem quaint or even questionable today, it is not so different from the present-day phenomenon of the *Da Vinci Code*, which has devotees scurrying around European cities, book and map in hand, in search of revelations.
28. See William H. Scheuerle, "Amusements and Recreation: Middle Class," pp. 17–19, and Chris Waters, "Amusements and Recreation: Working Class," pp. 19–21, in *Victorian Britain* 1988.
29. One manual of the period cites these as elegant recreations for young women: geology, mineralogy, conchology, entomology, ornithology, and photography. *Young Lady's Book* 1859.
30. Excellent discussions of the Victorian enthusiasm for natural history are given in Allen 1976 and Barber 1980.
31. For a detailed description of use of the Claude glass, see Andrews 1989, chap. 4. The critic William M. Rossetti described the effects of Claude Lorraine's painting technique that the Claude glass sought to emulate: "His skies are aerial and full of lustre, and every object harmoniously illumined. His distances and colouring are delicate, and his tints have a sweetness and variety till then unexampled." *Encyclopaedia Britannica*, 11th ed., s.v. "Claude of Lorraine."
32. The popularity of sketching was greatly advanced by technical advances in the manufacture of the lead pencil, for which see Petroski 1990.
33. A variety of sketches and travel diaries are reproduced in Gard 1989.
34. Harding 1834, pp. 4–5.
35. For the source of "Knowledge of drawing," see n. 36. For a large group of camera lucida drawings by Sir John Herschel and a history of the instrument, see Schaaf, *Tracings of Light*, 1989.
36. Talbot, "Brief Historical Sketch of the Invention of the Art," in Talbot, *Pencil of Nature* 1989 (reprint of 1844–46 ed.), fasc. 1, n.p.
37. Ibid.
38. These figures are if anything low, since there are exhibitions known to have taken place but for which no catalogue survives. For more on this, see Taylor 2002 and Photographic Exhibitions in Britain, 1839–1865 (website).
39. Rev. Thomas Milville Raven is a good example. During the course of nine years of activity as an amateur photographer he submitted over 170 prints to exhibitions throughout Britain, and he won a prize medal at the 3rd Annual Exhibition of the Photographic Society of Scotland for *Pierrefitte*, a study made during his tour of the French Pyrenees. Despite extensive searches for Raven's work, only two surviving examples are known. They are in the "Photographic Exchange Club Album" in the collection of the National Media Museum, Bradford.
40. "Photographic Society. Annual General Meeting. Feb. 7th, 1856," *JPS*, February 21, 1856, p. 302.
41. Quoted in *Rules of the Photographic Society Club* 1856, n.p. Four copies of this publication are in the archives of the Royal Photographic Society Collection at the National Media Museum, Bradford.
42. Sir Frederick Pollock had been elected president of the Photographic Society following the resignation of Sir Charles Eastlake in February 1855. "Photographic Society. Special General Meeting. Feb. 20th, 1855," *JPS*, April 21, 1855.
43. The only member of the Photographic Club who may not have been a photographer was Joseph Durham (1814–1877); at the last minute he took the place of John McCosh, who was in India at the time (see Chapter 9). For a complete listing, see "Members of the Photographic Society Club," in *Rules of the Photographic Society Club* 1856, n.p.
44. Ibid.
45. Each album measured 45 x 31 centimeters (17¾ x 12¼ inches) and was fully bound in black leather, with a gilt title and decorative borders on the cover and raised bands on the spine. The endpapers were of apricot paper stamped to look like polished silk. Each photograph was presented alone on the page, protected by a thin paper cover sheet, with the title and descriptive text on the facing page. These albums occupy a unique place in the history of nineteenth-century photographically illustrated published books. The size of the edition is unknown but must have been small. A number of copies are still extant and in major collections in Europe and North America; the largest group by far belongs to the Royal Photographic Society Collection at the National Media Museum, Bradford.
46. Announcement, "Notices to Members," *JPS*, April 1, 1853, n.p. (facing p. 13).
47. "Photographic Exchange Society," *Notes and Queries*, February 24, 1855. The editor of *Notes and Queries*, W. J. Thoms, was a member of the Photographic Exchange Club.
48. A printed list of members along with operational details for the Photographic Exchange Club dated May 12, 1855, is in the Royal Photographic Society Collection at the National Media Museum, Bradford, RPS 301/P/1.
49. They were Phillip Delamotte, Dr. Hugh Diamond, Joseph J. Forrester, Rev. John Major, Dr. John Percy, Henry Pollock, and William J. Thoms.
50. See letters from Rev. J. R. Major Jr., July 9, 1855, and September 29, 1855, Royal Photographic Society Collection, National Media Museum (archival source), RPS 353/M1, RPS 350/P/1.
51. This is known from a surviving Photographic Exchange Club album that contains prints from all three exchanges. It was presented to the Royal Photographic Society in November 1943 by Miss Margaret Robinson, the granddaughter of H. P. Robinson. Royal Photographic Society Collection at the National Media Museum, Bradford, RPS 11,495–11,580.
52. For an example, see the notice "Rules and Regulations of the Liverpool and National Photographic Exchange Club," *Photographic Notes*, January 1, 1856. Of variant exchanges proposed, one was the Stereoscopic Exchange Club; see Bell, *JPS*, January 21, 1857; Hannaford, *BJP*, June 15, 1860; "Stereoscopic Exchange Club," *Photographic News*, October 10, 1860; and "Photographic Exchange Club," *Photographic News*, October 18, 1861.
53. See Edinburgh Photograph Exchange Club, "Rules of the Edinburgh Photograph Exchange Club" (archival source). The thirteen members listed are H. Ross, G. Moir, C. Innes, H. G. Watson, Rev. T. M. Raven, W. Walker, C. G. H. Kinnear, A. F. Adam, J. Duncan, T. B. Johnston, A. Y. Herries, G. M. Tytler, and J. Ziegler. I am especially grateful to Peter Stubbs for detective work at the National Archives of Scotland that he undertook on my behalf, on the Edinburgh exchange club and much else besides. See Edinphoto (website) for the invaluable website created by Peter Stubbs.
54. Rule 9, in *Rules of the Photographic Society Club* 1856, n.p. It seems likely that activity of the Photographic Society Club gradually dwindled rather than coming to a decisive stop, and that this is the reason nothing was ever presented to the British Library.

7. *British Sensibilities 1855–1857*

pages 88–103

1. From a review of William Powell Frith's *Life at the Sea-Side* in "Royal Academy," *Art-Journal*, June 1, 1854, p. 161. The painting is now known as *Ramsgate Sands: "Life at the Seaside"* (The Royal Collection).
2. Rates of life expectancy and mortality are difficult to discuss, for the statistics vary widely according to region, occupation, and nutrition. The figures cited here are those for the Whitechapel area of London; see Rosa Lynn B. Pinkus, "Health," in *Victorian Britain* 1988, pp. 355–56. Various other regions, especially in the manufacturing districts of the North, experienced even higher mortality rates. A useful treatment is Woods and Shelton 1997.
3. More than 100,000 infants died before their first birthday, constituting a quarter of all deaths each year nationally. Once a child had survived past five, his life expectancy greatly increased. Jalland 1996, pp. 120–21, 143–44.
4. First published anonymously, *Vestiges of the Natural History of Creation* was later revealed to be the work of the Scottish publisher and author Robert Chambers. The book challenged

the established belief that the universe had been created in a single act by God, arguing instead that scientific laws and principles account for the development of life and the evolution of species. It sparked a national debate. For an excellent account of the book's reception, see Secord 2000.

5. Taylor and Baldwin 2004, pp. 232, 238.
6. 1851 census, entry for Hugh Owen, HO 107/1945, fol. 536, p. 37, schedule 179; visible on a commercial website, www.ancestry.com.
7. Tuberculosis was the real killer of the Victorian period, accounting by some estimates for 75 percent of all deaths by disease. Intimately linked with malnutrition, overcrowding, and the ill-ventilated living quarters of the poor, it nevertheless affected all classes of society and became widely feared. See Jalland 1996, pp. 39–51.
8. The population density in London, on average 19,000 individuals for every square mile, was approximately twenty-four times greater than that anywhere else in Britain. "Census of Great Britain, 1851" 1854, p. 33.
9. In doing so they utterly ignored the hardships and deprivations endured by those who worked the land. For an idea of the extent and nature of rural poverty during this period, see Digby 1981.
10. Editions of Keats's *Poetical Works* were published with great frequency during the early 1850s. Most notable was the edition published by Edward Moxon with illustrations by George Scharf, which appeared in 1856. See *English Catalogue of Books* 1864, p. 421. Endymion is portrayed in Greek myth as a shepherd boy who chose eternal sleep so that he might remain youthful forever.
11. Runcorn's industries were numerous and included iron foundries, forges, tanneries, soap works, chemical works, and distilleries for making turpentine. Tall factory chimneys 200 to 300 feet high, intended to lift the fumes above the town, were commonplace. See the entry for "Runcorn" in *National Gazetteer of Great Britain* 1868, vol. 10, p. 369.
12. In his technical caption Davies notes that the photograph was "Taken by the calotype process, May 29, 1856, about 11am; weather sunny; Exposure twenty-five minutes (usually five), owing to the foliage." *Photographic Album for the Year 1857* 1857, pl. 11.
13. Noted in Thomas 1983, p. 218.
14. These qualities are cited in *English Forests and Forest Trees* 1853, chap. 3, pp. 40–79.
15. *Knight's Excursion Companion* 1851, no. 7, p. 23. The Great Western Railway ran from Paddington to Slough, and from there it was just a short coach ride to Burnham. The site is now owned by the Corporation of London and managed as a conservation area by English Nature.
16. See Taylor 2002 and Photographic Exhibitions in Britain, 1839–1865 (website) for Newton's and Fenton's exhibiting activities during the early 1850s and for others who also photographed Burnham Beeches.
17. All the beeches at Burnham were pollarded; that is, most of the branches were cut off, initially when the tree was still young, leaving only the trunk. It usually took between five and twenty years for the branches to grow back, at which time the tree could be pollarded anew. This ancient, now long-forgotten craft allowed timber to be harvested on a regular basis without killing the tree. The timber was taken to nearby High Wycombe, a center for chair making.
18. Edward Jesse, quoted in *English Forests and Forest Trees* 1853, p. 107.
19. Act 4, scene 4, lines 24–30.
20. For a lucid explanation of this phenomenon, see Ware 2004.
21. For the history of Badger Hall, see P. A. Stamper, "Badger," in *History of the County of Shropshire* 1998, pp. 213–20.
22. See "Robert Cheney," in *Royal Military Calendar* 1820, vol. 3, p. 29, no. 289.
23. For the history of Blake Hall and the estate, see Audrey M. Taylor, "Bobbingworth," in *History of the County of Essex* 1956, pp. 9–10.
24. Burke 1906, p. 410.
25. See *Watercolours of the Grand Tour* 2005, an auction catalogue of drawings and watercolors by the three Cheneys. It contains an essay on the Cheney family and their activities as artists and collectors. I am indebted to Mr. Ronnie Capel Cure for his generous help while I was researching the Cure and Cheney families.
26. See Bermingham 2000, pp. 77–85.
27. See *Oxford Dictionary of National Biography*, s.v. "Cheney, Edward (1803–1884)" (by Charles Sebag-Montefiore, rev.). On Cheney's place as a collector, see Haskell 1976, p. 80. After Edward's death in 1884, part of his collection was sold by Christie's, London, April 29–May 5, 1885. On a subsequent dispersal, see "Sales of the Past Season" 1905, pp. 44–45.
28. Cheney to Cromek, May 8, 1846, Department of Literary and Historical Manuscripts, Morgan Library & Museum, New York, MA 3172, quoted in Lambert 1982, p. 9. Some of Cheney's correspondence with Cromek is now in the collection of the Morgan Library.
29. Rodwell to Talbot, September 5, 1845, National Media Museum, Bradford; Talbot Correspondence Project (website), doc. no. 05382.
30. As recorded in the 1851 census, three Cheney brothers were living at Badger Hall supported by a staff of ten domestic servants, and their two gardeners employed a further seven men, three boys, and two women to look after the extensive grounds. See 1851 census, HO 107/1987, fol. 11, p. 1, schedule 1; visible on a commercial website, www.ancestry.com.
31. This date is derived from a note inscribed in an album: "The negatives of these Photos were taken by my uncle RHCheney on Paper between 1850–60, the Positives were printed by me, in 1859–60, *ACC*." See Anninger and Mellby 1999, p. 23, no. 17.
32. Detailed information on the regiment's travels, activities, and military engagements is given in Noakes, "Records of the Services of the Fifty Fifth or Westmoreland Regiment" (archival source). I am very grateful to Stuart Eastwood and Tony Goddard, curators at the Regimental Museum, Carlisle, for their generous help and access to the museum's archives.
33. Cure's bravery at Sebastopol is recalled in Hume 1894, pp. 127–36.
34. Cure's military appointments are recorded in Noakes, "55th Westmoreland Regiment: Roll of Officers, 1756–1881" (archival source), p. 80, entry 645. According to Noakes, Cure joined the 55th as an ensign on July 25, 1845, became lieutenant on April 9, 1847, captain on August 17, 1852, major on May 25, 1855, brevet lieutenant-colonel on November 2, 1855, and lieutenant colonel (unattached) on January 18, 1856, having served the regiment for ten years and five months. At this point he transferred to the Grenadier Guards, the regiment of his maternal grandfather, where he held the rank of colonel until his retirement in November 1863.
35. The dated print of *Badger, N E*, is in an album in the Department of Special Collections, Charles E. Young Research Library, University of California, Los Angeles, no. 94/22 v. 2.
36. A rather poor photograph, *Bloomfield, 1st Collodion, 10 March 1854*, is in the album cited in note 35.
37. Many of the photographs in the Cure albums owned by the Canadian Centre for Architecture, Montreal, are dated; those in the albums of other collections are not.
38. *Black's Picturesque Guide to Yorkshire* 1862, pp. 269–70.
39. See Taylor 2002 and Photographic Exhibitions in Britain, 1839–1865 (website).
40. *Photographic Tour among the Abbeys of Yorkshire* 1856, with 24 photographs by Philip H. Delamotte and Joseph Cundall, and descriptive notices by John Richard Walbran and William Jones.
41. The fence at Rievaulx has all four rails in the studies made by Fenton and Turner; see Baldwin et al. 2004, pl. 11; and Barnes 2001, p. 122, pl. 45.
42. A print in the collection of the Canadian Centre of Architecture, Montreal, is dated on the mount "December 11, 1856," though whether this refers to the storm or the making of the photograph is unclear. However, the meteorological records for Nottingham, a city not too distant from Badger, reveal there was a severe thunderstorm with "much lightning" on September 19. No storms are recorded for early December. See "Country News," *ILN*, September 27, 1856, p. 320.
43. According to official statistics, just over twenty thousand British officers and men lost their lives in the Crimean War. Of these, fewer than four thousand fell in battle or died from wounds received in warfare. The remaining thirteen thousand died from other causes, most commonly cholera, which was endemic in the Crimea. In addition, almost three thousand men were discharged as incapacitated. Cited in "Close of the Russian War" 1857, p. 104. For a personal account, see Roger Fenton's Letters from the Crimea (website).
44. A study of Blake Hall, *My Last Photo, ACC, 1860*, concludes the Cure album owned by the Museum of Modern Art, New York (acc. no. EL 79.339.186).
45. *Times* (London), July 31, 1896, p. 5, col. F.

8. *Echoes of the Grand Tour*
pages 104–117

1. Talbot to Lady Elisabeth Feilding, July 24, 1821, Talbot Collection, British Library (archival source), LA21-26; Talbot Correspondence Project (website), doc. no. 00933.
2. Despite attempts to bring stability to Europe through the Congress of Vienna, held during the winter of 1814–15, peace only became a reality after the battle of Waterloo on June 18, 1815, and Napoleon's subsequent exile to St. Helena.
3. Lady Caroline Augusta Edgcumbe to Talbot, September 1833, Talbot Collection, British Library (archival source); Talbot Correspondence Project (website), doc. no. 02738.
4. "Sketches by a Travelling Architect," *Library of the Fine Arts*, June 1831, p. 393, the first installment of an entertaining anonymous account of a twelve-month trip through France and Italy.
5. The experiences "Kit" Talbot described were typical: "I did a few Talbotypes for you, but did not find out till after a great many failures a very simple fact which ought to be known by every experimenter, namely that the solutions will not keep, and ought to be made fresh at least once a fortnight. Gallic acid especially decomposes." Christopher Rice Mansel Talbot to W. H. F. Talbot, May 3, 1846, Talbot Collection, British Library (archival source), LA46-56; Talbot Correspondence Project (website), doc. no. 05643.
6. Christopher Rice Mansel Talbot to W. H. F. Talbot, January 14, 1822, Talbot Collection, British Library (archival source), LA22-05; Talbot Correspondence Project (website), doc. no. 00954.
7. On Jones and his photography, see Schaaf 1990. A comprehensive illustrated list of Jones's photographs appears in Buckman 1990.
8. A group portrait of the Bridges family was painted by John Constable in 1804 and is now in the collection of the Tate Gallery, London.
9. Bridges 1827–28.
10. Lady Elisabeth Feilding to Talbot, December 18, 1845, Talbot Collection, British Library (archival source), LA45-174; Talbot Correspondence Project (website), doc. no. 05482.
11. Bridges to W. H. F. Talbot, March 30, 1846, Talbot Collection, British Library (archival source), LA46-42; Talbot Correspondence Project (website), doc. no. 05617.
12. Jones to W. H. F. Talbot, March 15, 1846, and Bridges to W. H. F. Talbot, March 30, 1846, Talbot Collection, British Library (archival source), LA46-40, LA46-42; Talbot Correspondence Project (website), doc. nos. 05606, 05617. In 1852 Bridges began publishing *Selections from Seventeen-Hundred Genuine Photographs . . . Taken around the Shores of the Mediterranean between the Years 1846–52*. The photographs were to be issued "occasionally, in numbers, or in sheets" under the pseudonym "A Wayworn Wanderer." A copy of an advertisement for them is in the photographic collections of the Canadian Centre for Architecture, Montreal. Probably very few were actually published.
13. Larry Schaaf suggests that the photograph was a collaboration between Jones and Bridges and makes his case in Schaaf 2006, p. 48.
14. Bridges to Talbot, March 30 and April 23, 1846, Talbot Collection, British Library (archival source), LA46-42, LA46-52; Talbot Correspondence Project (website), doc. nos. 05617, 05632.
15. Bridges to Talbot, October 25, 1846, Talbot Collection, British Library (archival source), LA46-111; Talbot Correspondence Project (website), doc. no. 05759.
16. Jones sent a batch of negatives to Talbot from Malta, asking for printed copies to be sent him so "that I may see how my handywork has answered." Jones to Talbot, February 13, 1846, Talbot Collection, British Library (archival source), LA46-26; Talbot Correspondence Project (website), doc. no. 05563.
17. Valery 1842, p. 440. Valery describes how the gardens were "open to the common people, peasants, and servants in livery only one day a year."
18. Letters that Bridges and Jones sent from Malta to W. H. F. Talbot during the opening months of 1846 contain frequent references to the invalid Lady Charlotte; Talbot Collection, British Library (archival source), LA45-151, LA45-154, LA45-177, LA46-15, LA46-40, LA46-42, LA46-54 (Talbot Correspondence Project [website], doc. nos. 05448, 05453, 05488, 05531, 05606, 05617, 05639). Although the child pictured is most likely to be Emily, it is possible that she is Jones's daughter, who was traveling with Kit Talbot at the time. In either case, the wearing of black would have been a social requirement.
19. For their correspondences during the 1840s, see the Talbot Correspondence Project (website).
20. For the collodion process, see Price 1858, with very helpful line illustrations. Although the book was written chiefly for portrait photographers, the underlying principles outlined apply to landscape photography as well.
21. Percy, *JPS*, March 3, 1853.
22. "Liverpool Photographic Society," *LPJ*, March 11, 1854, p. 38.
23. Ibid.
24. Prints made from waxed-paper negatives are often difficult to distinguish from those made by collodion. Even Fenton found it impossible to distinguish between the two when called upon at a meeting of the Graphic Society in 1854. Ibid., p. 39.
25. As one leading maker described its offerings. *Horne & Thornthwaite's Descriptive Catalogue of Scientific Instruments* 1855, p. 95.
26. Ottewill registered his design for the camera; see National Archives, Kew, Design Registration, May 25, 1853, no. 3570.
27. Lewis Carroll, "Hiawatha's Photographing," in Carroll 1869, reprinted in Carroll 1939, pp. 856–60.
28. *Horne & Thornthwaite's Descriptive Catalogue of Scientific Instruments* 1855, p. 94.
29. Pritchard, "Tropical Cameras," 1990.
30. Virtually every exhibition in Britain included a significant number of works by European photographers. In many cases these were submitted by British printsellers who sold foreign photographs, to promote sales. For more on photographers and exhibitors, see Taylor 2002 and Photographic Exhibitions in Britain, 1839–1865 (website).
31. The Wheatstone mirror stereoscope is explained and illustrated in Coe 1978, chap. 14, pp. 155–68.
32. Tenison 1846. The large-format publication, a lavish affair, was offered in black-and-white at 5 pounds, 5 shillings and at 10 pounds, 10 shillings for the colored version.
33. In the book published in 1853 by Lady Louisa Tenison, *Castile and Andalucia* (London: Bentley), Tenison's photography is briefly mentioned. The book was reviewed in the *Athenaeum*, July 30, 1853, pp. 910–11.
34. Tenison used the process published by the French photographer Édouard Baldus in 1852, in which the paper was coated with gelatin prior to iodizing. For those traveling abroad it was, in Tenison's opinion, far superior to and more certain than any other process. See "Photographic Society of Ireland," *JPS*, March 15, 1860. For a translation of Baldus's 1852 treatise on photography, see Daniel 1994, app. 12, pp. 250–54.
35. W. K. Sullivan, "Class X: Philosophical, Musical, Surgical, and Horological Instruments," in *Resources and Manufacturing Industry of Ireland* 1854, p. 234. Although published after the exhibition had closed, this detailed and comprehensive volume functioned as both catalogue and reports of the juries.
36. At the Dublin International Exhibition, just fourteen exhibitors showed photographs. For this and the Photographic Society exhibits, see Taylor 2002 and Photographic Exhibitions in Britain, 1839–1865 (website).
37. The works shown by Clifford and Tenison are noted in "Exhibition of the Photographic Society," *Art-Journal*, February 1, 1854. Bird's studies of Cadiz and Seville were most likely taken en route to Egypt, where he photographed extensively; for a list of his Egyptian studies, see Taylor 2002 and Photographic Exhibitions in Britain, 1839–1865 (website). Only one print by Bird has been located; otherwise his photographs remain unknown.
38. The most comprehensive account of Clifford's career, including an inventory of his known photographs, is Fontanella 1999. I am extremely grateful to Lee Fontanella for sustained help and for answers to my numerous inquiries about Clifford over many years.
39. Clifford 1860, pp. 5–6.
40. Ibid., p. 3.
41. The chapel has now been restored and was recently designated a World Heritage Monument.
42. A good biography of Saint Bruno, with links to information about the Carthusian order, is in *The Catholic Encyclopedia* available online at www.newadvent.org/cathen. See also *New Catholic Encyclopedia*, 2nd ed., s.v. "Bruno the Carthusian, St." (by B. Bligny).
43. St. John's album of photographs, now in the collections of

the J. Paul Getty Museum, Los Angeles, is undated. But a date is suggested by her photograph of the Tartarughe Fountain, Rome, where a poster that bears the date "Mercoledi 16" can be seen on the wall of a civic building. A perpetual calendar shows that only a few Wednesdays fell on the 16th during the 1850s and even fewer in the spring, which, to judge from the leafless trees and bare vines visible in some photographs, is the probable season of their visit. These factors considered together narrow the year to 1856.

44. After Jane Beach married Edward St. John in 1848, the couple moved to Oakley Cottage, close to her father's home at Oakley Hall. Her mother's forebears dated back to the sixteenth century. Jane's family was closely related to the Hicks-Beach dynasty that in the later years of the nineteenth century produced some notable politicians, such as Sir Michael Hicks Beach, twice chancellor of the Exchequer—although her father, William, had changed his name from Hicks-Beach to Beach by royal license in 1838. For more on the family, see Burke 1878, pp. 622–23, and Hicks-Beach 1932.
45. I am extremely grateful to Richard Morris for generously sharing his research files on Jane St. John, which added significantly to my understanding of her relationship with the Llewelyn family.
46. Valery 1842, p. 437.

9. *Under an Indian Sky*
pages 118–131

1. Of the numerous histories of early photography in India, two of the most notable are John Falconer, "Pioneers of Indian Photography," in Falconer 2001, pp. 8–36, and Pelizzari 2003. I am deeply indebted to John Falconer on two counts: firstly for the generous access he gave me to his personal research notes and files, and secondly for sharing his encyclopedic knowledge of photography in India. Both of them materially assisted my understanding of the subject.
2. A photographer living in Ceylon (Sri Lanka) wrote, "Not only is the weather trying to photographic apparatus, but the insect world is often anxious to find out holes and corners in boxes. I fear therefore that any cameras of the bellows form or cloth funnel shape might become a prey to white ants, cockroaches, &c." "Camera for Hot Climates," *JPS*, April 21, 1857, p. 266.
3. "Address," *Journal of the Photographic Society of Bombay*, February 15, 1855, p. 16.
4. A richly illustrated survey of the British in India is *Raj* 1990.
5. For historical coherence, the Indian place-names cited in this chapter are generally those in use during the nineteenth century and much of the twentieth; in some cases the spelling has been modernized. The present-day name appears in parentheses after the first relevant mention when it differs significantly from the older one. While the names Bombay and Madras now have modern replacements, here they refer not to cities but to regions for which there is no present-day equivalent.
6. P. J. O. Taylor 1996, p. 252. The cost of maintaining the army in India was calculated to be almost 9.5 million pounds per annum, a fabulous sum of money for the time.
7. "Our Anglo-Indian Army," *ILN*, July 11, 1857.
8. A trichinopoly chain was woven of fine silver wire in a way that imparted flexibility. The technique had its origins in the Anglo-Saxon and Viking periods, but by the nineteenth century it had been appropriated by the gold- and silversmiths of Trichinopoly in southern India and applied to a wide range of jewelry and decorative objects for export to Britain.
9. "India Supplement," *ILN*, November 28, 1857, p. 537. This supplement presents a detailed, if biased, overview of Britain's relationship with India. Issues of the periodical throughout the second half of 1857 are a rich source of illustrations and articles on the history and culture of India and on the mutiny.
10. For a full account of India under company rule, see *Encyclopaedia Britannica*, 11th ed., s.v. "India," pp. 407–15 (by William Wilson Hunter and James Sutherland Cotton).
11. There were six major conflicts between 1800 and 1850: the Pindaree War, 1817–18, Burmese War, 1824, Afghan War, 1838–42, Scinde War, 1843, Gwalior War, 1845, and Sikh Wars, 1845–50.
12. Gubbins 1858 is a detailed treatment of the mutiny, with maps and illustrations. For succinct contemporary accounts of the events and underlying causes, see the entries for 1857 and 1858 in *Annual Summaries: Reprinted from "The Times"* 1893, vol. 1, pp. 39–67.
13. "India Supplement," *ILN*, November 28, 1857, p. 537.
14. "Photographs of Indian Cities," *Art-Journal*, December 1, 1857. Thirty views by Dr. John Murray were exhibited by Joseph Hogarth to promote their publication as a portfolio.
15. The only account of O'Shaughnessy's work is Ware, "Herschel's Chrysotype," 2006. By the early 1840s O'Shaughnessy was successfully making daguerreotypes.
16. An anonymous album of photogenic drawing positives made in India in 1843–45 is in the collections of the J. Paul Getty Museum, Los Angeles (96.XA.319).
17. Little has been written about McCosh and his pioneering photography in Bengal and Burma. The most comprehensive account is McKenzie 1987. See also Russell-Jones 1968.
18. On the Playfair family network, see *Oxford Dictionary of National Biography*, vol. 44, pp. 552–67. On the family's contributions to early photography and the Calotype Club of Edinburgh, see Pencils of Light (website).
19. Evidence of this early start is a portrait of Lieutenant Stewart in the album of McCosh's photographs owned by the National Army Museum, London (NAM 1962-04-3-169). The original titles of the photographs were written in the paper negatives; when McCosh assembled the album in 1859 he added further inscriptions beneath the prints. The inscription for Stewart reveals that he was killed in action at Gwalior in 1843.
20. In a letter to his wife dated November 6, 1849, Dr. John Login, the guardian for Maharaja Dalip Singh and other prisoners, wrote, "Dr. McCosh is anxious to take daguerreotypes here, and begs to be allowed to come to-morrow to take likenesses of all the notabilities collected here, myself included among the number, he says! I have told him he cannot take any of the prisoners." Login 1890, p. 179, quoted in Patel 1999, p. 194. I am grateful to Divia Patel for her generous help with my research into the collections in her care.
21. See Martin 1985.
22. See Hall 1950, p. 51.
23. Father Abbona remained in Amarapura, where he acted as the king's emissary when the British mission was sent to the Court of Ava in 1855 to secure a treaty with Mindon Min. An account of the mission was subsequently published with illustrations in 1858, and republished in 1968: Yule 1858 (repr., Yule 1968). The 1968 edition contains additional plates, one of which is a pencil sketch of Father Abbona made by Colesworthy Grant, the artist sent with the mission. There is a strong resemblance between the subject of McCosh's earlier portrait and Father Abbona as portrayed in Grant's sketch. See Yule 1968, pl. III.
24. McCosh 1856, pp. 5–6, quoted in McKenzie 1987, p. 117, n. 10. *Advice to Officers in India* is a revised and expanded version of his early work *Medical Advice to the Indian Stranger*; see McCosh 1841.
25. McCosh 1856, p. 7, quoted in McKenzie 1987, p. 109.
26. This inscription was written by McCosh on the flyleaf of the album now at the National Army Museum (see note 19 above).
27. "Introductory Address," *Journal of the Photographic Society of Bombay*, January 15, 1855, p. i.
28. The list of honorary members included Hugh Welch Diamond, Robert Hunt, Roger Fenton, John Llewelyn, John Percy, and T. Frederick Hardwich of London, and the president, secretary, and four other members of the Liverpool society. "General Meeting,—January 17, 1855," *Journal of the Photographic Society of Bombay*, February 15, 1855, p. 21.
29. Ibid.
30. "Inaugural Meeting of the Photographic Society of Bombay," *Journal of the Photographic Society of Bombay*, January 15, 1855, pp. 2–3.
31. A succinct but informative account of Murray's life and career is given in Fraser 2000. In addition to publishing works on cholera, Murray was the author of *On the Topography of Meerutt* (1839) and *Topography and Diseases of Futtehpore Seekree* (1853). He was also an ardent ornithologist and collected some 1,700 specimens (skins) during his time in India. Obituary, *Aberdeen Evening Express*, July 30, 1898.
32. This information comes from the agreement drawn up between Joseph Hogarth and John Murray and dated October 3, 1857; manuscript, private collection.
33. Hogarth, *JPS*, January 21, 1857, p. 207.
34. Agreement between Hogarth and Murray, October 3, 1857

(see note 32 above). Perhaps mindful of the dangers he would face on his return to India, Murray also named his brother Andrew, an advocate in Aberdeen, to act on his behalf.
35. "Photographs of Indian Cities," *Art-Journal*, December 1, 1857. The date of publication for *Photographic Views in Agra and Its Vicinity* is given as 1858 (it appears on the title page of the accompanying descriptive text written by J. Middleton, principal of the Honourable East India Company's school in Agra). Although the photographs were exhibited in November 1857, the publication of the descriptive text was delayed. Photographic publishing was a speculative venture, and Hogarth was probably unwilling to commit further capital to the project until after he had tested the market with an exhibition.
36. Good examples of this type of illustration are the four woodcuts of Delhi based on photographs taken by George Beresford, secretary of the Delhi Bank, in "Mutiny in India," *ILN*, July 18, 1857, pp. 56, 57.
37. Viscountess Canning to Queen Victoria, November 25, 1857, The Royal Archives, Windsor Castle, RA Z502/24, quoted by Frances Dimond in Dimond and Taylor 1987, p. 124.
38. In a letter to C. Beadon, secretary to the Government of India, Calcutta, January 4, 1858, Murray sought further clarification of the subjects to be photographed and asked for a carriage and a servant to move his equipment and baggage, as well as a cash advance to help defray expenses. In reply he received specific instructions from Canning about subjects to be photographed: C. Beadon to John Murray, January 22, 1858, India Office Records, British Library (archival source), IOR/P/188/49.
39. Editorial, *Times* (London), September 17, 1857, p. 8, col. A.
40. To get some sense of how these events were reported, see "Massacre at Cawnpore," *Times*, September 2, 1857, and October 2, 1857, and "Cawnpore," *Times*, October 16, 1857. For a recent account compiled from primary source material, see Ward 1996.
41. It is impossible to calculate how often Murray photographed the Taj Mahal, as there are large numbers of duplicate negatives, some in different formats, suggesting that he made pictures there numerous times over the course of his stay in India. The most comprehensive record of his activity is found in *Early Photographs of India* 1999, lots 125–86.
42. Few authors have tackled the subject of the panorama, photographic or in other media. The most detailed and authoritative is Hyde 1988.
43. Jones described and illustrated the camera in a paper he read to the Photographic Society on May 5, 1853, subsequently published: Jones, *JPS*, May 21, 1853.
44. *Catalogue of Pictures in the Exhibition of the Photographic Society of Bengal* 1857.
45. I am deeply indebted to Janet Dewan's invaluable work on Tripe's photographic oeuvre, which gave me the historical and contextual understanding on which this discussion depends. In addition to detailing Tripe's photographic campaigns it provides maps, plans, and diagrams of the sites of individual photographs. Dewan 2003.
46. Yule 1858.
47. Dewan 2003, pp. 207–13.
48. *Madras Exhibition of Raw Products, Arts, and Manufactures of Southern India* 1856, p. 134, reprinted in ibid., p. 167.
49. India and Bengal Despatch, no. 22 of 1855 (February 7), para. 3, India Office Records, British Library, IOR/E/4/829, quoted in Dewan 2003, p. 6.
50. The official report drawn up by Henry Yule, an engineer, artist, and the official secretary of the mission to the Court of Ava, contains architectural studies of temple buildings, plans of the Irrawaddy River, and maps of Amarapura and the whole of Burma, as well as numerous illustrations taken from the drawings and photographs of Grant and Tripe. Yule's own narrative offers a richly detailed account of Burmese life and customs and, unlike other government reports of the period, makes entertaining reading. Yule 1858.
51. The catalogue raisonné lists 219 Burmese images and illustrates most of them. Dewan 2003, pp. 214–312.
52. Henry Yule was a skilled draftsman, and his drawings of Burmese temples are closer in feel and level of detail to Tripe's photographs than Grant's more evocative impressions. See Yule 1858.
53. The "placid and eternal smile" of this statue recalled to the British "as no other Buddhist figure did, the characteristic expression of the colossi of the Nile." Ibid., p. 161.
54. The archive of Tripe's negatives and prints was donated by his family in 1948 to the permanent collections of the Royal Photographic Society, which are now in the care of the National Media Museum, Bradford. Dewan 2003, p. 745.
55. Tripe's note is reproduced in Dewan 2003, p. 211, fig. 9.
56. Tripe to F. A. Murray, July 22, 1856, India Office Records, British Library (archival source), IOR/F/4/2725 198.065, quoted in ibid., p. 40.
57. See Dewan 2003 pp. 94–124, where many original documents that offer valuable insights into Tripe's photographic activities for the Madras Presidency are reprinted. Among them are lists of the types of cameras, equipment, and photographic materials in use and the cost of each.
58. Charles Trevelyan, memorandum, March 30, 1859, no. 46, India Office Records, British Library (archival source), IOR/P/249/69, quoted in ibid., p. 16.
59. Dewan 2003, pp. 16–19.

10. *Commercialism Advances, the Calotype Declines*
pages 132–143

1. [E. Eastlake], *Quarterly Review*, August 1857, p. 443.
2. Ibid.
3. Ibid., p. 444.
4. The Royal Charter of Incorporation granted to the Chemical Society in 1848 is reprinted in *Jubilee of the Chemical Society of London* 1896, pp. 135–39.
5. *JPS* 4 (September 21, 1857), p. 33. The first announcement for a meeting at New Coventry Street appeared in *JPS* 4 (October 21, 1857), n.p. (advertisement). The cost of refurbishing the rooms was subsequently revealed in "Photographic Society. Annual General Meeting, Tuesday, 2nd February, 1858," *JPS*, February 22, 1858, p. 159, to be 700 pounds.
6. [E. Eastlake], *Quarterly Review*, August 1857, p. 444.
7. See chapter 5, page 74 and note 99.
8. "'Touched-up or Coloured' Photographs," *JPS*, April 21, 1856.
9. The rules stated, "Coloured photographs will be admitted only when accompanied by untouched copies of the same pictures," and "Positive Pictures, printed from touched or painted negatives, and also touched or painted positive proofs must be described accordingly." "Photographic Society of London," *JPS*, January 21, 1858.
10. *JPS* 5 (August 21, 1858), p. 1.
11. *JPS* 5 (October 21, 1858), pp. 35–36.
12. [E. Eastlake], *Quarterly Review*, August 1857, p. 443.
13. "Holywell-Street Revived," *JPS*, September 21, 1858 (reprinted from the *Saturday Review*).
14. Ibid. An excellent account of the Strand and Holywell Street where photographs such as these would have been found is given in Nead 2000, "Streets and Obscenity," pp. 150–203.
15. See Taylor 2002 and Photographic Exhibitions in Britain, 1839–1865 (website).
16. "Photographic Society of London. Annual General Meeting, Tuesday, February 7, 1860," *Photographic Journal*, February 15, 1860, p. 149.
17. "Photographic Society of London. Annual General Meeting, King's College, February 5, 1861," *Photographic Journal*, February 21, 1861. King's College, London, had long enjoyed a close if informal relationship with the Photographic Society. In 1856 it began offering courses in photography taught by the eminent chemist and photographer Thomas Frederick Hardwich, who was replaced in 1860 by Thomas Sutton and later by George Dawson. Delamotte had been appointed a professor of drawing in 1854. See Hearnshaw 1929, p. 259.
18. The decline can be charted through the president's reports and accounts presented to annual general meetings of the society, which were published in the *Journal of the Photographic Society* and other photographic journals, notably *Photographic News*.
19. These figures come from the original database used to create the website Photographic Exhibitions in Britain, 1839–1865. The exhibition of the Photographic Society of 1858 included a significant body of work sent in by the Société Française de Photographie; these have been excluded from the table given here. Interestingly, 22 percent of the work submitted by the French came from paper negatives.
20. "Photographic Society," *Photographic News*, June 24, 1859.
21. "Society of Arts and the Exhibition of 1862," *Times*, November 17, 1859.
22. At the close of the Great Exhibition the commissioners had been granted a royal charter to manage the considerable

profits and acquire land, with the goal of increasing the influence of science and art on industry. See *Third Report of the Commissioners* 1856. The Royal Commission for 1851 is still in existence and playing an active role.

23. It was widely believed that the Civil War would soon be over and peace restored.
24. Hollingshead 1862.
25. See Redgrave 1856. A complete list of paintings and sculpture submitted is in "British Pictures and Works in Sculpture," *Art-Journal*, April 1, 1855.
26. "Exposition des Beaux Arts," *Art-Journal*, December 1, 1855. Despite the number of medals awarded to British artists, many claimed that the jury was prejudiced against historical painting and sculpture, which received no prizes.
27. See "Fine Art Department" 1863; *Cassell's Illustrated Family Paper Exhibitor* 1862, pp. 14–15.
28. Frederick Pollock to F. R. Sandford, April 26, 1861, in "International Exhibition, 1862," *Photographic Journal* 7 (May 15, 1861), p. 174. See also *Report of the Commissioners* 1863, pp. 2–4.
29. M. Laulerie to Dr. Hugh W. Diamond, July 12, 1861, in *Photographic Journal* 7 (August 15, 1861), pp. 240–41.
30. A. Claudet to Dr. Hugh W. Diamond, in "On the Classification of the International Exhibition of 1862 as Regards Photography," *Photographic Journal* 7 (August 15, 1861), p. 242. This letter is part of a heated exchange between Claudet and the fashionable London portraitist Camille Silvy that had been triggered by the classification issue.
31. Fenton, *JPS*, January 21, 1858; "Artistic Copyright," *Art-Journal*, July 1, 1858. For a legal interpretation, see Duncan, *Photographic Journal*, February 22, 1859.
32. "Copyright in Works of Fine Art," *Photographic News*, May 3, 1861. For the complete act, see "New Copyright Act," *Photographic News*, August 8, 1862; for instructions about how to protect photographs, see "Registering Photographs," *Photographic News*, August 22, 1862.
33. An unanticipated consequence of the new law, which was enacted in 1862, was that any photograph, whatever its quality or level of artistic integrity, could be registered for copyright protection. The Copyright Registers are held at the National Archives, Kew. For an alternative history of photography drawn exclusively from this resource, see Hiley 1983.
34. Dr. Hugh W. Diamond to F. R. Sandford, August 8, 1861, in *Photographic Journal* 7 (August 15, 1861), p. 240.
35. "Forthcoming International Exhibition," *Photographic News*, September 27, 1861, p. 455.
36. "Memorial of the South London Photographic Society," *Photographic News*, October 11, 1861.
37. "Photographic Society," *Photographic Journal*, December 16, 1861; *Photographic Journal* 7 (April 15, 1861), p. 149.
38. "International Exhibition," *Times*, May 10, 1862.
39. The protocols of state mourning meant none of the immediate royal family attended the official opening. Instead the duty fell on the duke of Cambridge, a grandson of George III. For an account of the opening with transcripts of the addresses, see *Cassell's Illustrated Family Paper Exhibitor* 1862, pp. 18–122.
40. *Catalogue of the Photographs Exhibited in Class XIV* 1862. On the title page it is noted that the catalogue was "published under the sanction of Her Majesty's Commissioners and allowed by them to be sold in the building."
41. However, the first and subsequent exhibitions of the Photographic Society contained roughly comparable numbers of exhibits: 980 at the first annual exhibition, for which see Taylor 2002 and Photographic Exhibitions in Britain, 1839–1865 (website).
42. This bold initiative on the part of the South London Photographic Society was warmly welcomed by the photographic fraternity, many of whom were unrepresented at the International Exhibition. See "Proposed Additional Photographic Exhibition," *Photographic News*, February 7, 1862; "Supplementary Photographic Exhibition," *Photographic News*, March 14, 1862; "South London Photographic Exhibition," *Photographic News*, April 17, May 23, June 13, June 20, and July 4, 1862.
43. "France: Class XIV" 1862.
44. Figures on the United States exhibitors in 1851 are set out in "Space by Countries and Classes" 1852. This report was incorporated into the *Official Descriptive and Illustrated Catalogue. Supplementary Volume* 1852. The figure of ninety-five exhibitors in 1862 is cited by the United States commissioner B. P. Johnson in Johnson 1863, p. 9. Johnson called the photographic displays "quite extensive" (p. 74), but this is not borne out by other contemporary reports or the sole award of an honorable mention to Dexter & Co. for a photographic series of busts of "Governors of States in America." See "Class XIV: Photography and Photographic Apparatus" 1863, p. 17.
45. The chairman was the French senator Baron Gros. "Class XIV: Photography and Photographic Apparatus" 1863. The judges listed are: Baron Gros (France), Dr. Hugh W. Diamond (London), A. J. F. Claudet (London), Lord Henry Lenox (London), Charles Thurston Thompson (London), B. Delessert (France), and Lieutenant-Colonel Demanet (Belgium).
46. These figures are drawn from "Return of the Number of Awards Made by the International Juries" 1863.
47. "Awards of Jurors in the Exhibition," *Photographic News*, July 18, 1862, p. 337.
48. "British Photographic Gallery," *Photographic News*, May 30, 1862, p. 255. The reporter also criticized the hanging of the British displays.
49. "Damp Walls in the Exhibition," *Photographic Journal*, July 15, 1862.
50. "Miscellanea," *Photographic Journal*, September 15, 1862, p. 137.
51. Receipts, expenditures, and attendance figures are detailed in *Report of the Commissioners* 1863, app. nos. XVII, XVIII, and XIX, pp. 86–91. The surplus amounted to 783 pounds.
52. "Year 1862," *Times*, December 31, 1862, p. 6, col. B–p. 7, col. D, reprinted in *Annual Summaries* 1893, vol. 1, pp. 127–52.
53. Ellison, *JSA*, March 7, 1862.
54. The figure of 2,534 photographers recorded in the 1861 Census is cited in "Photography: Its Social and Economic Position," *Photographic News*, January 25, 1867, p. 44. It was believed that this figure fell short of the real number. By 1867 the number had doubled or even trebled and rose to five times that figure when individuals associated collaterally were included.
55. "Photographs of the Exhibition," *Times*, August 13, 1862. The figure was later increased to 2,000 guineas to secure additional privileges.
56. "Photography: Its Social and Economic Position," *Photographic News*, January 25, 1867, p. 44.
57. The increasing commercialization of photography was further underlined by the inclusion in the commissioners' report of a "Classified List of the Trades" represented in each class. Under Class 14 eight trades are named, ranging from albumenized paper makers to photographic printers. See "Classified List of the Trades in the United Kingdom" 1863, p. 120.
58. It was initially called the Amateur Photographic Publishing Association, but this name was dropped after Arthur J. Melhuish, secretary to the association, gave up his connections with the photographic publishing company of McLean, Melhuish & Co. following claims of conflicts of interest. See Melhuish 1871.
59. "Amateur Photographic Association," *Photographic Journal*, August 15, 1862.
60. "Amateur Photographic Association," *Photographic News Almanac* 1862, n.p. (advertisement).
61. Melhuish, *Photographic Journal*, July 15, 1862.
62. "Amateur Photographic Association," *Photographic News*, July 18, 1862.

Epilogue: Revivals of the Paper Negative after the 1860s

pages 144–149

1. The annual general meeting of 1864 revealed that the expenses of the society "far exceeded its income" and placed the blame on the timing and poor location of the 1863 annual exhibition. See "Photographic Society of London. Annual General Meeting. King's College, London. Tuesday, February 2, 1864," *Photographic Journal*, February 15, 1864, pp. 449–50.
2. For their annual exhibitions the Amateur Photographic Association relied on members' sending in their negatives. These were then printed, exhibited, and sold commercially for the benefit of the association and individual members. "Amateur's Photographic Association," *Photographic News*, May 17, 1861. See also "Amateur Photographic Association," *Photographic News*, November 15, 1867.
3. Very little has been written about the Amateur Photographic Association, probably because the surviving

presentation albums are now widely dispersed and the records of the association lost. The most comprehensive article is McCauley 1978–79.

4. Prize albums of the Amateur Photographic Association are held in a number of collections, principally the Royal Photographic Society Collection at the National Media Museum, Bradford; the J. Paul Getty Museum, Los Angeles; George Eastman House, Rochester, N.Y.; and the University Art Museum, University of New Mexico, Albuquerque.
5. In 1870, annual exhibitions of the Photographic Society were revived, but the convention of regularly citing the negative process in the catalogues had been dropped. Details of negative and print processes were included only intermittently, most likely at the request of the photographer.
6. Dawson, "Negatives on Paper," *BJP*, June 17 and July 15, 1870, p. 278.
7. Dawson, "Attempts at a New Paper Process," *BJP*, October 7, 1870, p. 471.
8. Maddox, a medical man and amateur photographer, experimented widely with albumen on glass before turning to gelatin as an emulsion. See Maddox, *BJP*, September 8, 1871.
9. *BJP* 18 (September 8, 1871), p. 422.
10. "Summarised Notes of Progress during the Past Year" 1886, p. 49.
11. Whaite, *BJP*, October 16, 1885, p. 665.
12. "Another Advance in Photography," *Times*, August 11, 1885.
13. "International Inventions Exhibition," *BJP*, August 28, 1885, p. 546. A detailed description of the "Walker-Eastman System of Film Photography" follows (on pp. 547–48).
14. Eastman's American film, known technically as a stripping film, is described fully in Jenkins 1975, pp. 100–105. The concept of stripping was not new and had first been introduced in Britain in 1875 by Leon Warnerke. See Warnerke, *BJP*, June 25, 1875; see also "Development of Paper Negatives," *BJP*, July 2, 1875.
15. Quoted in Jenkins 1975, p. 98.
16. "Kodak," *BJP*, September 14, 1888.
17. According to *Kodak* 1888, anyone "who has sufficient intelligence to point a small box straight and press a button" was capable of taking a photograph.
18. The phrase "You push the button and we do the rest" became synonymous with the Eastman Dry Plate Company and subsequently with Eastman Kodak Ltd. and was one of the most memorable advertising slogans of the nineteenth and twentieth centuries.
19. "Photographic Societies of the United Kingdom" 1893. This comprehensive listing includes the founding date of each society, its officers, and its address. See also the announcement for the "Royal Photographic Society of Great Britain," *BJP*, August 10, 1894.
20. The *British Journal of Photography* for 1892 reviewed nineteen exhibitions in Britain, from one in Aberdeen, Scotland, to the Royal Cornwall Polytechnic Society in the south.
21. "Societies which Manage the Exhibitions" 1900.
22. The only detailed account of the Pictorialist movement in British photography (1892–1910) is Harker 1979.
23. Coburn also collected prints by Julia Margaret Cameron and Lewis Carroll, making enlarged copy negatives from these and printing them by the platinum process. He reprinted the calotype negatives of Hill & Adamson and Keith as well, using the same process, and showed a selection at the annual exhibition of the Royal Photographic Society in 1914. The following year he organized "Old Masters of Photography" at the Albright Art Gallery, Buffalo, a show that included works by all these photographers. See *Catalogue of an Exhibition of the Old Masters of Photography* 1915. I am extremely grateful to Pam Roberts for her help, based on encyclopedic knowledge, on the subject of Coburn.
24. McKenzie 1993, p. 14.
25. Ibid.
26. The history of photographic enlargers has yet to be written. A good sense of their development from the horizontal magic-lantern style to the more sophisticated vertical enlarger, commonplace in darkrooms until recently, can be obtained by tracing the copiously illustrated advertisements of the *British Journal Photographic Almanac.*
27. MacLean 1898, pp. 60–63.
28. A. T. Newton, *BJP*, February 2, 1900.
29. On the carbon process, see Maskell, *BJP*, November 9 and 16, 1894.
30. Willis, "New Process of Photo-Chemical Printing," *BJP*, August 23, 1878, and Willis, "Notes on the Plainotype Process," *BJP*, December 20, 1878.
31. To celebrate the seventy-fifth anniversary and its own Diamond Jubilee, the *British Journal of Photography* published a special supplement tracing the history of photography from its earliest days to the most recent color photography and half-tone reproduction. "Photography: Past and Present," *BJP*, June 19, 1914.
32. By way of a codicil to this history, it should be noted that the paper negative reappeared twice more. During the Depression in the 1930s, the High Street portrait studios of Jerome used paper negatives, which were significantly cheaper than conventional materials. The postcard-size paper negative could be processed, dried, retouched, and printed within ninety minutes. These very low prices and quick turnaround created a healthy trade, with up to four hundred customers passing through on an average Saturday. The same technology was employed when a company called Gratispool offered a "free" roll of film as part of its developing and processing service, much of which was conducted by mail. Here too the cost of the paper negatives was very low, bringing photography within the reach of many households for whom it would otherwise have been a luxury. Both companies remained in business well into the 1950s. They were the last to use paper negatives commercially in Britain. On this subject I am indebted to Maurice Fisher for his help.

Bibliography

Published sources are arranged according to year of publication.

The *Journal of the Photographic Society*, published by the Photographic Society beginning in 1853, changed its name in 1859 to *Photographic Journal*.
Citations to *Photographic Journal* refer to this publication.

The *Liverpool Photographic Journal*, begun in 1854, changed its name in 1857 to *Liverpool and Manchester Photographic Journal* and in 1859 to *Photographic Journal*.
Citations to *Photographic Journal (BJP)* refer to the 1859 issues of this publication.
In 1860 the name was changed again, to *British Journal of Photography*.

Archival Sources

Edinburgh Photograph Exchange Club. "Rules of the Edinburgh Photograph Exchange Club." Records of the Photographic Society of Scotland. National Archives of Scotland, Edinburgh, GD 356/28.

Graphic Society. "Annual Prospectus, 1848." Graphic Society Records, 1833–1891. Royal Academy of Arts, London, GS 1-9.

———. "Lists of Members, 1840–1850." Graphic Society Records, 1833–1891. Royal Academy of Arts, London, GS 1-9.

India Office Records, British Library, London. Documentary archives of the administration in London of the pre-1947 government of India.

National Media Museum, Bradford. William Henry Fox Talbot correspondence, notebooks, and additional manuscript materials.

Noakes, George. "Records of the Services of the Fifty Fifth or Westmoreland Regiment." [Also known as the "Digest of Service."] MS. 1875. Regimental Museum, Carlisle.

———. "55th Westmoreland Regiment: Roll of Officers, 1756–1881." MS. 1875. Regimental Museum, Carlisle.

Photographic Society. Minutes of Council. Royal Photographic Society Collection, National Media Museum, Bradford.

———. Minutes of General Meetings. Royal Photographic Society Collection, National Media Museum, Bradford.

Photographic Society of Scotland. Records of the Photographic Society of Scotland. National Archives of Scotland, Edinburgh, GD 356.

Privy Purse Accounts. The Royal Archives, Windsor Castle.

Royal Photographic Society Collection, National Media Museum, Bradford. William Henry Fox Talbot correspondence.

Society of Arts. Correspondence files. Archives, Royal Society of Arts, London.

———. Minutes of Council. Vol. 4, May 1852–June 1853. Archives, Royal Society of Arts, London.

Talbot, William Henry Fox. Notebook Q. National Media Museum, Bradford. [Transcribed in Schaaf 1996.]

Talbot Collection, British Library, London. William Henry Fox Talbot correspondence, notebooks, and additional manuscript materials formerly at the Fox Talbot Museum, Lacock Abbey, and now in the Department of Manuscripts, British Library.

Websites

Directory of London Photographers, 1841–1908
A Directory of London Photographers, 1841–1908. Compiled by Michael Pritchard.
http://www.photolondon.org.uk/directory.htm

Edinphoto
Information on photographers, professional organizations, publications, and other areas of interest related to the history of photography in Edinburgh. Site created by Peter Stubbs.
http://www.edinphoto.org.uk/

Maison Nicéphore Niépce
Reference site on the photographer Joseph-Nicéphore Niepce (1765–1833).
http://niepce.com

Pencils of Light
Pencils of Light: The Albums of the Edinburgh Calotype Club. Site produced by the National Library of Scotland, in association with the Edinburgh City Libraries.
www.nls.uk/pencilsoflight

Photographic Exhibitions in Britain, 1839–1865
Photographic Exhibitions in Britain, 1839–1865: Records from Victorian Exhibition Catalogues. Individual records from Victorian exhibition catalogues for over 20,000 photographic exhibits, listed by exhibition, photographer, title, process, exhibitor, and original prices, where known. [Online version of Taylor 2002.]
http://www.peib.org.uk

Roger Fenton's Letters from the Crimea
Transcriptions of letters from Roger Fenton to Grace Fenton, Joseph Fenton, and William Agnew in the collections of the Harry Ransom Humanities Research Center, University of Texas at Austin, and the National Media Museum, Bradford. Site initiated by De Montfort University, Leicester.
http://www.rogerfenton.org.uk

Talbot Correspondence Project
The Correspondence of William Henry Fox Talbot Project. Project Director and Correspondence Editor, Larry J. Schaaf. Transcriptions of nearly 10,000 letters to and from William Henry Fox Talbot. Project initiated at the University of Glasgow and now housed at De Montfort University, Leicester.
http://foxtalbot.dmu.ac.uk

Published Sources

1768
Gilpin, William. *Essay upon Prints; Containing Remarks upon the Principles of Picturesque Beauty, etc.* London: J. Robson, 1768.

1782
Gilpin, William. *Observations on the River Wye, and Several Parts of South Wales, &c. Relative Chiefly to Picturesque Beauty; Made in the Summer of the Year 1770.* London: R. Blamire, 1782.

1792
Gilpin, William. *Three Essays: On Picturesque Beauty; on Picturesque Travel; and on Sketching Landscape: To which is Added a Poem, on Landscape Painting.* London: R. Blamire, 1792.

1802
Annual Register; or, A View of the History, Politics, and Literature for the Year 1798. 2nd printing. London: J. Dodsley, 1802.

1820
The Royal Military Calendar; or, Army Service and Commission Book. Edited by John Philippart. 3rd ed. 5 vols. London: Printed by A. J. Valpy, 1820.

1827–28

Bridges, George Wilson. *The Annals of Jamaica.* 2 vols. London: John Murray, 1827–28.

1831

"Sketches by a Travelling Architect." *Library of the Fine Arts* 1 (June 1831), pp. 393–403.

1834

Harding, James Duffield. *Elementary Art; or, The Use of the Lead Pencil Advocated and Explained.* London: Charles Tilt, 1834.

1839

Arago, François. "Fixation des images qui se forment au foyer d'une chambre obscure." [Presented at a séance held January 7, 1839.] *Comptes rendus hebdomadaires des séances de l'Académie des Sciences* 8 (January–June 1839), pp. 4–7. [English translation in H. Gernsheim and A. Gernsheim 1956, pp. 79–81.]

Clericus [pseud.]. "M. Daguerre's Discovery." *Times* (London), February 21, 1839, p. 6, col. C.

"The Daguerotype [*sic*]." *Literary Gazette; and Journal of the Belles Lettres, Arts, Sciences, &c.*, January 19, 1839, pp. 43–44. [Reprinted from *Le Commerce*, January 16, 1839.]

"Effects of the Storm." *Times* (London), January 9, 1839, p. 5, col. A.

"Familiar Instructions in Photography; Preliminary Step for Young Persons." *Magazine of Domestic Economy* 4 (May 1839), pp. 339–40.

"Foreign Correspondence. Paris, 16th January." *Athenaeum*, January 26, 1839, p. 69.

Gaucheraud, H. "The Daguerotype [*sic*]." *Literary Gazette; and Journal of the Belles Lettres, Arts, Sciences, &c.*, January 12, 1839, p. 28. [Reprinted from the *Gazette de France*, January 6, 1839.]

"Melancholy Shipwrecks and Loss of Life." *Times* (London), January 10, 1839, p. 5, cols. C–D.

Murray, John. *On the Topography of Meerutt, and the Principal Diseases which Prevailed in the First Brigade of Horse Artillery.* Calcutta: G. H. Huttmann, 1839.

"Ninth Meeting of the British Association for the Advancement of Science." *Athenaeum*, August 31, 1839, pp. 641–64.

"Photogenic Drawing-Paper . . . Prepared by J. T. Cooper, jun., Chemist, &c." *Athenaeum*, March 16, 1839, p. 193. [Advertisement.]

Society for the Diffusion of Useful Knowledge [England]. *A Manual for Mechanics' Institutions.* London: Longman, Orme, Green, & Longmans, 1839.

1840

"Photogenic Drawings." *Literary Gazette; and Journal of the Belles Lettres, Arts, Sciences, &c.*, May 16, 1840, pp. 315–16.

1841

"Chemical Action of Light." *Magazine of Science, and School of Arts* 2 (February 6, 1841), pp. 358–59.

"The Law of Patents." *Magazine of Science, and School of Arts* 3 (July 3 and 17, 1841), pp. 106–8, 122–25.

McCosh, John. *Medical Advice to the Indian Stranger.* London: William H. Allen & Co., 1841.

"Royal Society. 'An Account of Some Recent Improvements in Photography.' By H. F. Talbot, Esq." *Athenaeum*, July 17, 1841, pp. 540–41.

Talbot, William Henry Fox. "An Account of Some Recent Improvements in Photography." *Proceedings of the Royal Society* 4 (1841), pp. 312–15.

———. "Calotype (Photogenic) Drawing." *Literary Gazette; and Journal of the Belles Lettres, Arts, Sciences, &c.*, February 13, 1841, p. 108.

———. "Calotype (Photogenic) Drawing." *Literary Gazette; and Journal of the Belles Lettres, Arts, Sciences, &c.*, February 27, 1841, pp. 139–40.

———. "Calotype (Photogenic) Drawing." *Literary Gazette; and Journal of the Belles Lettres, Arts, Sciences, &c.*, June 12, 1841, p. 379. [Abstract of a paper read before the Royal Society, London, June 10, 1841.]

———. *The Process of Calotype Photogenic Drawing: Communicated to the Royal Society, June 10th, 1841.* [London]: Printed by J. L. Cox & Sons, 1841. [Reprinted as *The Process of Talbotype (Formerly Called Calotype) Photogenic Drawing: Communicated to the Royal Society, June 10th, 1841.* (London): Printed by J. & H. Cox Brothers, 1845.]

1842

"Children's Employment Commission." *Athenaeum*, May 7, 1842, pp. 395–401.

Lewis, Samuel. *A Topographic Dictionary of England.* 5th ed. 4 vols. London: S. Lewis & Co., 1842.

"Photography." *Blackwood's Edinburgh Magazine* 51 (April 1842), pp. 517–18.

"Royal Commission of Fine Arts, Whitehall, April 25, 1842." *Athenaeum*, April 30, 1842, p. 369. [Announcement.]

"To William Henry Fox Talbot, of Locock [*sic*] Abbey, in the County of Wilts, Esq., for Improvements in Obtaining Pictures or Representations of Objects.—[Sealed 8th February, 1841.]." *London Journal of Arts and Sciences; and Repertory of Patent Inventions* 19 (1842), pp. 189–97.

Valery [pseud., Antoine-Claude Pasquin]. *Historical, Literary, and Artistical Travels in Italy: A Complete and Methodical Guide for Travellers and Artists.* Translated by C. E. Clifton. Paris: Baudry's European Library, 1842.

1843

"London Markets. (Corrected to January 24.)." *Magazine of Domestic Economy, and Family Review*, n.s., 1 (February 1843), p. 384.

"Sanitary Condition of the Labouring Population of Great Britain." In *Companion to the Almanac; or, Year-Book of General Information for 1843*, pp. 21–39. London: Charles Knight & Co., 1843.

1844

Black's Picturesque Tourist of Scotland. 3rd ed. Edinburgh: Adam and Charles Black, 1844.

"Claudet's Daguerréotype Portraits, Royal Adelaide Gallery, Lowther Arcade, Strand." *Athenaeum*, July 6, 1844, p. 609. [Advertisement.]

"Claudet's Talbotype (or Calotype) Portraits, Adelaide Gallery." *Athenaeum*, July 6, 1844, p. 609. [Advertisement.]

Cundell, George S. "On the Practice of the Calotype Process of Photography" *London, Edinburgh, and Dublin Philosophical Magazine*, May 1844, pp. 321–32.

Hunt, Robert. "Energiatype. A New Photographic Process." *Athenaeum*, June 1, 1844, pp. 500–501.

"Improvements in Photography." *Magazine of Science, and School of Arts* 5 (1844), pp. 323–24.

"New Publications." *Athenaeum*, January 6, 1844, pp. 18–19.

Webster, Thomas. *An Encyclopaedia of Domestic Economy: Comprising Such Subjects as Are Most Immediately Connected with Housekeeping* . . . London: Longman, Brown, Green and Longmans, 1844.

"The Works of Robert Burns." *Art-Union*, February 1844, p. 36.

1844–46

Talbot, William Henry Fox. *The Pencil of Nature.* 6 fascicles. London: Longman, Brown, Green, & Longmans, 1844–46. [Facsimile edition, with commentary volume by Larry J. Schaaf. New York: Hans P. Kraus, Jr., 1989.]

1845

Black's Picturesque Tourist of Scotland. 4th ed. Edinburgh: Adam and Charles Black, 1845.

"Cundell's Improved Camera for Calotype Drawing, with Divided Ivory Scale." In *Horne, Thornthwaite, & Wood's Condensed Catalogue of Optical, Chemical, Nautical, Astronomical, Philosophical, Surveying, and Photographic Instruments.* London: Horne, Thornthwaite, and Wood, 1845.

Plain Directions for Obtaining Photographic Pictures by the Calotype, Energiatype, and Other Processes on Paper; including the Chrysotype, Cyanotype, Chromotype, etc., etc., with All the Latest Improvements. Edited by John H. Croucher. Willats's Scientific Manuals, no. 1. London: T. & R. Willats, 1845.

Talbot, William Henry Fox. *The Process of Talbotype (Formerly Called Calotype) Photogenic Drawing: Communicated to the Royal Society, June 10th, 1841.* [London]: Printed by J. & H. Cox Brothers, 1845. [Originally published as *The Process of Calotype Photogenic Drawing: Communicated to the Royal Society, June 10th, 1841.* (London): Printed by J. L. Cox & Sons, 1841.]

1846

Cundell, George S. "On the Gallo-Nitrate of Silver of Mr. Fox Talbot, and Its Action upon Iodized Paper." *London, Edinburgh, and Dublin Philosophical Magazine,* August 1846, pp. 101–3.

"The Talbotype.—Sun-Pictures." *Art-Union,* June 1, 1846, pp. 143–44. [Although the article was published anonymously, it has been assumed that Samuel Carter Hall, the editor of the *Art-Union,* was the author.]

Tenison, Lady Louisa. *Sketches in the East.* London: Dickinson & Co., 1846.

Twining, Henry. *On the Elements of Picturesque Landscape, Considered with Reference to Landscape Painting.* London: Printed for private distribution, 1846.

1847

Blanquart-Evrard, Louis-Désiré. *Procédés employés pour obtenir les épreuves de photographie sur papier.* Paris: C. Chevalier, 1847.

"The Calotype Society." *Athenaeum,* December 18, 1847, p. 1304. [The author was probably William Jerdan, the editor of the *Athenaeum.*]

"Fine Art Gossip." *Athenaeum,* April 24, 1847, p. 440.

"The Graphic Society." *Athenaeum,* December 11, 1847, p. 1278.

Guillot-Saguez. *Méthode théorique et pratique de photographie sur papier.* Paris: Victor Masson, 1847.

Claude-Félix-Abel Niepce de Saint-Victor. "De la photographie sur verre." [Presented at a séance held October 25, 1847.] *Comptes rendus hebdomadaires des séances de l'Académie des Sciences* 25 (July–December1847), pp. 586–89.

1848

Bingham, Robert. *Photogenic Manipulation . . . Containing the Theory and Plain Instructions in the Art of Photography.* London: Charles Knight and Sons, 1848.

Evans, D. Morier. *The Commercial Crisis, 1847–1848: Being Facts and Figures Illustrative of the Events of That Important Period . . .* London: Letts, Son & Steer, 1848. [2nd ed., 1849. Reprint of 2nd ed., Newton Abbott: David & Charles, 1969.]

Gaskell, Elizabeth Cleghorn. *Mary Barton: A Tale of Manchester Life.* 2 vols. London: Chapman and Hall, 1848.

"Photographic Club." *Art-Union,* April 1, 1848, pp. 130–31. [The unsigned article is presumed to have been written by Samuel Carter Hall, the editor of the *Art-Journal.*]

"Scientific Gossip." *Athenaeum,* September 8, 1848, p. 914.

1849

Blanquart-Evrard, Louis-Désiré. "Recherches photographiques." [Presented at a séance held August 20, 1849.] *Comptes rendus hebdomadaires des séances de l'Académie des Sciences* 29 (July–December 1849), pp. 215–17.

"National Exposition." *Art-Journal,* August 1, 1849, pp. 233–48; September 1, 1849, pp. 273–86.

"Retrospect of the Year." *Illustrated London News,* December 29, 1849, pp. 433–34.

"Scientific Gossip." *Athenaeum,* September 8, 1849, p. 914.

Twining, Henry. *On the Philosophy of Painting: A Theoretical and Practical Treatise.* London: Longman, Brown, Green, and Longmans, 1849.

1850

"Choice Examples of Art-Workmanship, Selected from the Exhibition of Ancient and Mediaeval Art at the Society of Arts." *Athenaeum,* March 30, 1850, p. 331. [Advertisement for a portfolio of sixty engravings drawn by Joseph Cundall and published by Philip H. Delamotte.]

"Design by Joseph Paxton, F.L.S., for a Building for the Great Exhibition of 1851." *Illustrated London News,* July 6, 1850, p. 13.

Hunt, Robert. "Photography on Glass Plates." *Art-Journal,* February 1, 1850, pp. 38–40.

Imperial Dictionary, English Technological and Scientific: Adapted to the Present State of Literature, Science, and Art on the Basis of Webster's English Dictionary. Edited by John Ogilvie. 2 vols. Glasgow: Blackie and Son, 1850.

Lardner, Dionysius. *Railway Economy: A Treatise on the New Art of Transport, Its Management, Prospects, and Relations, Commercial, Financial, and Social.* London: Taylor, Walton, and Maberly, 1850.

"The Patent of Mr. Fox Talbot." *Art-Journal,* August 1, 1850, pp. 261–62. [The unsigned article is presumed to have been written by Samuel Carter Hall, the editor of the *Art-Journal.*]

1851

An Account of the Proceedings at the Dinner Given by Mr. George Peabody to the Americans Connected with the Great Exhibition, at the London Coffee House, Ludgate Hill, on the 27th October 1851. London: William Pickering, 1851.

Archer, Frederick Scott. "On the Use of Collodion in Photography." *Chemist,* March 1851, pp. 257–58.

Babbage, Charles. *The Exposition of 1851; or, Views of the Industry, the Science, and the Government, of England.* London: John Murray, 1851.

Blanquart-Evrard, Louis-Désiré. *Traité de photographie sur papier.* Paris: Librairie Encyclopédique de Roret, 1851.

The Crystal Palace: Its Injustice, Impolicy, and General Evil Tendency. London: John Robinson, 1851.

Dickens, Charles. "The Private History of the Palace of Glass." *Household Words,* January 18, 1851, pp. 385–91.

Hunt, Robert. *Hunt's Hand-Book to the Official Catalogues: An Explanatory Guide to the Natural Productions and Manufactures of the Great Exhibition of the Industry of All Nations, 1851.* 2 vols. London: Spicer Brothers and W. Clowes & Sons, 1851.

Illustrated London News, May 3, 1851, pp. 348–52, 359–74. [Issue and supplement devoted to the Great Exhibition.]

Jerrold, William Blanchard. *How to See the Exhibition: In Four Visits.* 4 vols. London: Bradbury and Evans, 1851.

Knight's Excursion Companion: Excursions from London, 1851. London: Charles Knight, 1851.

"Learned Societies." In *Knight's Cyclopaedia of London,* pp. 363–84. London: Charles Knight, 1851.

Le Gray, Gustave. *Nouveau Traité théorique et pratique de photographie sur verre.* Paris: Lerebours et Secretan, 1851.

"Light and Its Applications." *Illustrated London News,* May 17, 1851, suppl., pp. 424–25.

"Mr. Babbage on the Exposition of 1851." *North British Review* 15 (May–August 1851), pp. 529–68. [Review of Charles Babbage, *The Exposition of 1851; or, Views of the Industry, the Science, and the Government, of England.* 2nd ed. London: John Murray, 1851.]

Official Descriptive and Illustrated Catalogue [of the Great Exhibition of 1851]. 3 vols. London: Spicer Brothers and W. Clowes and Sons, 1851.

Plain Directions for Obtaining Photographic Pictures by the Calotype, Energiatype, and Other Processes on Paper; including the Chrysotype, Cyanotype, Chromotype, etc., etc., with All the Latest Improvements. Edited by John H. Croucher. 4th ed. Willats's Scientific Manuals, no. 1. London: T. & R. Willats, 1851.

Timbs, John. *The Year-Book of Facts in the Great Exhibition of 1851.* London: David Bogue, 1851.

Times (London), May 2, 1851, p. 4, cols. C–D. [Editorial on the opening of the Great Exhibition.]

Times (London), October 17, 1851, p. 4, col. F–p. 5, col. A. [Editorial on the awards made by the juries at the Great Exhibition.]

1852

A.H.R. "Photography in the Open Air." *Notes and Queries,* August 28, 1852, p. 193.

Archer, Frederic Scott. "Collodion Process." *Notes and Queries,* December 25, 1852, p. 612.

Bridges, George Wilson. *Selections from Seventeen-Hundred Genuine Photographs: (Views—Portraits—Statuary—Antiquities.) Taken around the Shores of the Mediterranean between the Years 1846–52. With, or without, Notes, Historical, and Descriptive. By a Wayworn Wanderer.* N.d., [ca. 1852].

A Catalogue of an Exhibition of Recent Specimens of Photography. Exh. cat. London: Society of Arts, 1852. [The revised edition, also 1852, included a reprinting of the paper read by Roger Fenton at the opening soiree and expanded notes on various photographic processes; a copy can be found in the National Art Library, Victoria and Albert Museum, London.]

"Classification of Subjects in the Thirty Classes into which the Exhibition is Divided." In *Reports by the Juries on the Subjects in the Thirty Classes into which the Exhibition Was Divided,* app. A 1, pp. v–xxii. London: Printed for the Royal Commission by William Clowes & Sons, 1852.

C.P.S. "Photography in the Open Air." *Notes and Queries,* September 11, 1852, pp. 251–52.

Crookes, William. "The Wax-Paper Process." *Notes and Queries,* November 6, 1852, pp. 443–44.

"Decisions Regarding Juries." In *Reports by the Juries on the Subjects in the Thirty Classes into which the Exhibition Was Divided,* app. A, pp. iii–v. London: Printed for the Royal Commission by William Clowes & Sons, 1852.

Diamond, Hugh Welch. "Photography Applied to Archaeology, and Practised in the Open Air." *Notes and Queries,* September 18, 1852, pp. 276–78.

Drew, William A. *Glimpses and Gatherings, during a Voyage and Visit to London and the Great Exhibition, in the Summer of 1851.* Augusta: Homan & Manley, 1852.

"Exhibition of Photographs." *Times* (London), December 31, 1852, p. 5, col. F.

Fenton, Roger. "Photography in France." *Chemist,* February 1852, pp. 221–22.

———. "Photography on Waxed Paper." In *A Guide to Photography,* pp. 86–92. 5th ed. London: W. H. Thornthwaite, 1852.

First Report of the Commissioners for the Exhibition of 1851. London: Printed by W. Clowes and Sons for Her Majesty's Stationery Office, 1852.

Glaisher, James. "Class X: Philosophical Instruments and Processes Depending on Their Use." In *Reports by the Juries on the Subjects in the Thirty Classes into which the Exhibition Was Divided,* pp. 243–316, 317–23 (index). London: Printed for the Royal Commission by William Clowes & Sons, 1852.

"Letter to Mr. Talbot." *Weekly Proceedings* (Society of Arts, Manufactures, and Commerce), n.s., no. 18 (June 26, 1852), n.p.

"List of Jury Awards: Class X." In *Reports by the Juries on the Subjects in the Thirty Classes into which the Exhibition Was Divided,* pp. lxiii–lxv. London: Printed for the Royal Commission by William Clowes & Sons, 1852.

Official Descriptive and Illustrated Catalogue. Supplementary Volume. London: Spicer Brothers, 1852. [Bound into many editions of this volume are the *First Report of the Commissioners for the Exhibition of 1851* (1852) and *Second Report of the Commissioners for the Exhibition of 1851* (1852).]

"The Photographic Patent Right." *Times* (London), August 13, 1852, p. 4, col. F.

"The Photographical Society." *Art-Journal,* April 1, 1852, p. 103. [The unsigned article is presumed to have been written by Samuel Carter Hall, the editor of the *Art-Journal.*]

"Photography.—To Be Let or Sold. . . . . Mr. [Richard] Colls." *Athenaeum,* May 15, 1852, p. 529. [Advertisement.]

"Photography and Its Patents." *Art-Journal,* June 1, 1852, pp. 193–94.

"Photography and Manuscripts." *Notes and Queries,* October 9, 1852, p. 347.

"Proposal for the Formation of a Photographical Society." *Art-Journal Advertiser,* April 1, 1852, n.p.

Reports by the Juries on the Subjects in the Thirty Classes into which the Exhibition Was Divided. London: Printed for the Royal Commission by William Clowes & Sons, 1852.

"Resignation of the Photographic Patents." *Art-Journal,* September 1, 1852, pp. 270–71.

"Return Showing the Number of Awards of Different Kinds Made by Juries of Each Class and Group to Each Country Represented in the Exhibition." In *First Report of the Commissioners for the Exhibition of 1851,* app. no. XLI, pp. 196–203. London: Printed by W. Clowes and Sons for Her Majesty's Stationery Office, 1852.

Second Report of the Commissioners for the Exhibition of 1851. London: Printed by W. Clowes and Sons for Her Majesty's Stationery Office, 1852.

"The Society of Arts." *Times* (London), February 27, 1852, p. 3, col. F.

"Space by Countries and Classes." In *First Report of the Commissioners for the Exhibition of 1851,* app. no. XXXIX, pp. 172–79. London: Printed by W. Clowes and Sons for Her Majesty's Stationery Office, 1852.

Times (London), January 1, 1852, p. 4, col. B. [Review of events of 1851.] [Reprinted in *Annual Summaries: Reprinted from "The Times,"* vol. 1, p. 2. London: Macmillan and Co., 1893.]

Weekly Proceedings (Society of Arts, Manufactures and Commerce), February 21, 1852. [Letter to the Editor from Harry Chester, November 28, 1851.]

1853

Athenaeum, July 30, 1853, pp. 910–11. [Review of *Castile and Andalucia,* by Lady Louisa Tenison.]

"Collection of Photographs." *Journal of the Society of Arts* 1 (September 16, 1853), pp. 522–24.

Delamotte, Philip H. *The Practice of Photography: A Manual for Students and Amateurs.* London: Joseph Cundall, 1853.

Diamond, Hugh Welch. "On the Simplicity of the Calotype Process." *Journal of the Photographic Society* 1 (November 21, 1853), pp. 129–32.

English Forests and Forest Trees, Historical, Legendary, and Descriptive. London: Ingram Cooke, and Co., 1853.

"Exhibition of Photographic Pictures at the Society of Arts." *Athenaeum,* January 1, 1853, pp. 23–24.

"Exhibition of Photography." *Literary Gazette; and Journal of the Belles Lettres, Arts, Sciences, &c.*, January 15, 1853, pp. 68–69.

Exhibition of the New Society of Painters in Water Colours. Nineteenth Annual Exhibition. Exh. cat. London: New Society of Painters in Water Colours, 1853.

Fenton, Roger. "Upon the Mode in which It Is Advisable the Society Should Conduct Its Labours." *Journal of the Photographic Society* 1 (March 3, 1853), pp. 8–9.

Glaisher, James. "On the Chief Points of Excellence in the Different Processes of Photography, as Illustrated by the Present Exhibition." *Journal of the Society of Arts* 1 (January 28, 1853), pp. 109–11.

Haydn, Joseph. *Dictionary of Dates, and Universal Reference, Relating to All Ages and Nations.* 6th ed. London: Edward Moxon, 1853.

How, James. "On the Production of Waxed Paper Negatives." *Chemist*, n.s., 1 (1854), pp. 529–36.

Hunt, Robert. "On the Principles upon which the Construction of Photographic Lenses Should Be Regulated." *Journal of the Photographic Society* 1 (April 1, 1853), pp. 14–23.

"Inaugural Meeting of the Photographic Society." *Journal of the Photographic Society* 1 (March 3, 1853), pp. 2–5. [Includes the "Address" given by Sir Charles Lock Eastlake and the "Report of the Provisional Committee" read by Roger Fenton at the meeting, held January 20, 1853.]

Jones, Calvert. "On a Binocular Camera." *Journal of the Photographic Society* 1 (May 21, 1853), pp. 60–61.

Leighton, John. "On Photography as a Means or an End." *Journal of the Photographic Society* 1 (June 21, 1853), pp. 74–75. [Reprinted in the *Builder*, October 1, 1853, pp. 615–16.]

"Liverpool Photographic Society." *Journal of the Photographic Society* 1 (May 2, 1853), p. 54.

"Lynn Conversazione and Society of Arts." *Lynn Advertiser*, January 14, 1853.

"Marten's Views in Switzerland and the Pyrenees." *Athenaeum*, May 7, 1853, p. 545. [Advertisement.]

Murray, John. *Topography and Diseases of Futtehpore Seekree in the Agra District during the Years 1859, 1850 and 1851.* Agra: Printed at the Secundra Orphan Press, 1853.

Newton, William J. "Upon Photography in an Artistic View, and in Its Relations to the Arts." *Journal of the Photographic Society* 1 (March 3, 1853), pp. 6–8.

"Notice to Institutions." *Journal of the Society of Arts* 1 (August 5, 1853), p. 449.

"Notices to Members." *Journal of the Photographic Society* 1 (April 1, 1853), n.p. (facing p. 13). [Announcement.]

"Patent Law Amendment." In *Companion to the Almanac; or, Year-Book of General Information for 1853*, pp. 139–41. London: Charles Knight, 1853.

Percy, John. "On the Waxed-Paper Process as Applicable to Hot Climates." *Journal of the Photographic Society* 1 (March 3, 1853), pp. 9–11.

"Photographic Exhibition." *Journal of the Photographic Society* 1 (March 3, 1853), p. 12.

"Photographic Exhibition." *Journal of the Society of Arts* 1 (January 21, 1853), p. 100.

"Photographic Exhibition at the Society of Arts." *Art-Journal*, February 1, 1853, pp. 54–56.

"Photographic Exhibition, Mechanics' Institution." *Aberdeen Journal*, December 7, 1853, p. 4. [Advertisement.]

"The Photographic Institution." *Athenaeum*, April 16, 1853, p. 485. [Advertisement for services and publications available from the Photographic Institution.]

"Photographic Papers." *Journal of the Photographic Society* 1 (October 21, 1853), n.p. (facing p. 117). [Advertisement for photographic papers by John Sanford.]

"Photographic Society. Fifth Ordinary Meeting. Thursday, June 2nd, 1853." *Journal of the Photographic Society* 1 (June 21, 1853), pp. 69–70.

"Photographic Society. Third Ordinary Meeting. Thursday, April 7, 1853." *Journal of the Photographic Society* 1 (April 21, 1853), pp. 33–42.

"Photography." *Illustrated London News*, January 1, 1853, pp. 11–12.

"Photography." *Journal of the Society of Arts* 1 (March 4, 1853), p. 175.

Ramsden, John William. "Modification of M. Le Gray's Waxed-Paper Process." *Journal of the Photographic Society* 1 (October 21, 1853), p. 121.

"School of Arts—Lecture on Photography." *Stirling Journal and Advertiser*, November 17, 1853.

"Society of Arts." *Times* (London), September 29, 1853, p. 8, col. D.

Tenison, Lady Louisa. *Castile and Andalucia.* London: Bentley, 1853.

"Venice.—Sixty Large and Highly-Interesting Views . . . Calotyped by M. Bresolin." *Athenaeum*, April 30, 1853, p. 513. [Advertisement.]

1854

Black's Picturesque Guide to the English Lakes. 6th ed. Edinburgh: Adam and Charles Black, 1854.

"Census of Great Britain, 1851." In *Companion to the Almanac; or, Year-Book of General Information for 1854*, pp. 16–39. London: Charles Knight, 1854.

The Census of Great Britain in 1851; Comprising an Account of the Numbers and Distribution of the People, Their Ages, Conjugal Condition, Occupations and Birthplace. London: Longman, Brown, Green, and Longmans, 1854.

"Collection of Photographs." *Journal of the Society of Arts* 2 (March 24, 1854), p. 319.

"Correspondence." *Journal of the Photographic Society* 1 (June 21, 1854), p. 224.

Dickinson's Comprehensive Pictures of the Great Exhibition of 1851, from the Originals Painted for H.R.H. Prince Albert by Messrs. Nash, Haghe, and Roberts, R.A. London: Dickinson Bros., 1854.

"The Exhibition of the Photographic Society." *Art-Journal*, February 1, 1854, pp. 48–50.

"Launch of the 'Royal Albert,' at Woolwich Dockyard." *Illustrated London News*, May 20, 1854, pp. 469–70.

"Literary Institute. Fine Collection of Photographs, (Received from the Society of Arts London,) which Will Be Exhibited in the New Music Hall London." *Wrexham and Denbigh Weekly Advertiser*, June 3, 1854, p. 1, col. 2. [Advertisement.]

"Liverpool Photographic Society." *Liverpool Photographic Journal* 1 (March 11, 1854), pp. 32–39.

"Occupations of the People." In *The Census of Great Britain in 1851; Comprising an Account of the Numbers and Distribution of the People, Their Ages, Conjugal Condition, Occupations and Birthplace*, pp. 56–78. London: Longman, Brown, Green, and Longmans, 1854.

"Photographic Exhibition." *Burnley Advertiser*, August 12, 1854.

"Photographic Society. Anniversary Meeting. Thursday, February 2nd, 1854." *Journal of the Photographic Society* 1 (February 21, 1854), pp. 165–67.

"Photography and the Photographic Society." *Builder* 12 (February 11, 1854), p. 73.

The Resources and Manufacturing Industry of Ireland, as Illustrated by the Exhibition of 1853: Being a Series of Essays on Raw Materials, Machinery, and Manufactures of Various Kinds; to which is Appended the Official Catalogue of the Exhibition. Edited by John Sproule. Manchester: James Ainsworth, 1854.

"The Royal Academy: The Exhibition, 1854." *Art-Journal,* June 1, 1854, pp. 157–75.

"The Royal Regiment of Artillery." *Illustrated London News,* June 3, 1854, suppl., pp. 535, 536–37.

Teasdale, Washington. "Photographic Processes." *Journal of the Photographic Society* 1 (January 21, 1854), pp. 161–62.

"Where to Live with a Small Income. The Isle of Man." In *Family Economist; and Entertaining Companion for Town & Country,* vol. 2, pp. 65–69. London: Groombridge and Sons, 1854.

Woodcroft, Bennet. *Alphabetical Index of Patentees of Inventions from March 2, 1617 (14 James I) to October 1, 1852 (16 Victoriae).* London, 1854. [Reprint, New York: Evelyn, Adams & Mackay, 1969.]

1855

"Address." *Journal of the Photographic Society of Bombay,* no. 2 (February 15, 1855), pp. 15–19.

Bede, Cuthbert [Edward Bradley]. *Photographic Pleasures: Popularly Portrayed with Pen and Pencil.* London: Thomas McLean, 1855.

"The British Pictures and Works in Sculpture, in the Great French Exhibition." *Art-Journal,* April 1, 1855, pp. 128–30.

Crookes, William. "On Wax and Waxing Paper." *Journal of the Photographic Society* 2 (September 21, 1855), pp. 231–32.

Delamotte, Philip H., Hugh Welch Diamond, Thomas Frederick Hardwich, T. A. Malone, John Percy, Henry Pollock, and George Shadbolt. "First Report of the Committee Appointed to Take into Consideration the Question of the Fading of Positive Photographic Pictures upon Paper." *Journal of the Photographic Society* 2 (November 21, 1855), pp. 251–52.

"The Exposition des Beaux Arts: Honours to British Artists." *Art-Journal,* December 1, 1855, p. 317.

"General Meeting,—January 17, 1855." *Journal of the Photographic Society of Bombay,* no. 2 (February 15, 1855), pp. 20–22.

Hardwich, Thomas Frederick. "On the Use of Salts of Gold in Photographic Printing." *Journal of the Photographic Society* 2 (April 21, 1855), pp. 145–50.

Horne & Thornthwaite's Descriptive Catalogue of Scientific Instruments. Pt. 2, *Photographic Apparatus and Chemicals.* 4th ed. London: For the manufacturer, 1855.

Hunt, Robert. "On the Fading of Photographic Pictures." *Art-Journal,* July 1, 1855, pp. 210–11.

[Hunt, Robert]. Review of *The Calotype Process. A Handbook to Photography on Paper,* by Thomas Sutton. *Athenaeum,* July 14, 1855, p. 811. [The anonymous reviewer is identified in Athenaeum Index of Reviews and Reviewers, 1830–1870, http://www.soi.city.ac.uk/~asp/v2/home.html.]

"Inaugural Meeting of the Photographic Society of Bombay." *Journal of the Photographic Society of Bombay,* no. 1 (January 15, 1855), pp. 1–7.

"Introductory Address." *Journal of the Photographic Society of Bombay,* no. 1 (January 15, 1855), pp. i–iv.

The Photographic Album for the Year 1855: Being Contributions from the Members of the Photographic Club. London: Printed by Charles Whittingham for the Photographic Society Club, 1855.

"Photographic Exchange Society." *Notes and Queries,* February 24, 1855, p. 151.

"The Photographic Patent Right. Talbot v. Laroche." *Art-Journal,* February 1, 1855, pp. 49–54.

"Photographic Society. Committee on Positive Printing." *Journal of the Photographic Society* 2 (May 21, 1855), pp. 159–60.

"Photographic Society. Special General Meeting. Feb. 20th, 1855." *Journal of the Photographic Society* 2 (April 21, 1855), p. 144.

"Report of the Council." *Journal of the Photographic Society* 2 (February 21, 1855), pp. 115–18.

Sutton, Thomas. *The Calotype Process. A Hand Book to Photography on Paper.* London: Joseph Cundall, 1855.

———. "Gold *versus* Old Hypo." *Journal of the Photographic Society* 2 (February 21, 1855), pp. 121–22.

———. "On the Chemistry of Mr. Sutton's Negative Printing Process." *Journal of the Photographic Society* 2 (August 21, 1855), pp. 212–14.

———. "On the Hyposulphite of Gold." *Journal of the Photographic Society* 2 (September 21, 1855), pp. 226–28.

1856

"Country News." *Illustrated London News,* September 27, 1856, p. 320.

Fenton, Roger. "Narrative of a Photographic Trip to the Seat of War in the Crimea." *Journal of the Photographic Society* 2 (January 21, 1856), pp. 284–91.

Fitt, George R. "Mode of Working the Wax-Paper Process." *Liverpool Photographic Journal* 3 (January 12, 1856), pp. 4–10.

Hardwich, Thomas Frederick. *Manual of Photographic Chemistry, including the Practice of the Collodion Process.* 3rd ed. London: J. Churchill, 1856.

Keith, Thomas. "Dr. Keith's Paper on the Waxed Paper Process." *Photographic Notes* 1 (July 17, 1856), pp. 101–4. [Reprinted in Schaaf 1993, pp. 61–63.]

"The Liverpool and National Photographic Exchange Club." *Photographic Notes,* January 1, 1856. [Announcement.]

Madras Exhibition of Raw Products, Arts, and Manufactures of Southern India, 1855: Reports by the Juries on the Subjects in the Thirty Classes into which the Exhibition Was Divided. Madras: General Committee of the Madras Exhibition, 1856.

McCosh, John. *Advice to Officers in India.* London: William H. Allen & Co., 1856.

"Photographic Society. Annual General Meeting. Feb. 7th, 1856." *Journal of the Photographic Society* 2 (February 21, 1856), pp. 299–304.

A Photographic Tour among the Abbeys of Yorkshire. With photographs by Philip H. Delamotte and Joseph Cundall and descriptive notices by John Richard Walbran and William Jones. London: Joseph Cundall; Bell and Daldy, 1856.

Photography: Talbot's Specification. Patent no. 9753. London: Printed by Eyre & Spottiswoode for the Patent Office, 1856.

Redgrave, Richard. "Report on the Arrangements for Contributing a Collection of Works of Fine Art to the Paris Universal Exhibition." In *Reports on the Paris Universal Exhibition,* pt. 1, pp. 73–88. London: George E. Eyre and William Spottiswoode, 1856.

Rules of the Photographic Society Club with the Portraits of the Members. London: Imprinted by and for members of the Photographic Society Club, 1856.

Sutton, Thomas. "The Waxed-Paper Process." *Photographic Notes* 1 (October 1, 1856), pp. 188–90; (November 1, 1856), pp. 217–20; (December 1, 1856), pp. 253–55.

Third Report of the Commissioners for the Exhibition of 1851. London: George E. Eyre and William Spottiswoode, 1856.

Times (London), January 1, 1856, p. 6, cols. A–E. [Review of events of 1855.] [Reprinted in *Annual Summaries: Reprinted from "The Times,"* vol. 1, p. 26. London: Macmillan and Co., 1893.]

"'Touched-Up or Coloured' Photographs." *Journal of the Photographic Society* 3 (April 21, 1856), p. 33.

1857
Bell, Christopher. Letter to the Secretary of the Photographic Society. *Journal of the Photographic Society* 3 (January 21, 1857), p. 191.

"Camera for Hot Climates." *Journal of the Photographic Society* 3 (April 21, 1857), pp. 265–66. [Signed "One from 'Ceylon's Isle.'"]

Catalogue of Pictures in the Exhibition of the Photographic Society of Bengal. Calcutta: P. M. Cranenburgh and Bengal Military Orphan Press, 1857.

"Cawnpore." *Times* (London), October 16, 1857, p. 7, col. E.

"The Close of the Russian War." In *Companion to the Almanac; or, Year-Book of General Information for 1857*, pp. 100–109. London: Charles Knight, 1857.

Crookes, William. *A Hand Book to the Waxed Paper Process in Photography*. London: Chapman & Hall, 1857.

Dawson, George. "The Waxed-Paper Process." *Journal of the Photographic Society* 4 (October 21, 1857), pp. 53–56; (November 21, 1857), pp. 95–96.

[Eastlake, Lady Elizabeth]. "Photography." *Quarterly Review* 101 (April 1857), pp. 442–68.

Hogarth, Joseph. "Catalogue of Photographs." *Journal of the Photographic Society* 3 (January 21), 1857, p. 207.

[Hunt, Robert]. Review of *A Hand Book to the Waxed Paper Process in Photography*, by William Crookes. *Athenaeum*, August 29, 1857, p. 1084. [The anonymous reviewer is identified in Athenaeum Index of Reviews and Reviewers, 1830–1870, http://www.soi.city.ac.uk/~asp/v2/home.html.]

"India Supplement." *Illustrated London News*, November 28, 1857, pp. 537–52.

Law, William. "The Waxed Paper Process." *Liverpool and Manchester Photographic Journal*, n.s., 1 (October 1, 1857), pp. 210–12.

"The Massacre at Cawnpore." *Times* (London), September 2, 1857, p. 5, col. D.

"The Massacre at Cawnpore." *Times* (London), October 2, 1857, p. 6, col. F.

"The Mutiny in India." *Illustrated London News*, July 18, 1857, pp. 56–58.

"Our Anglo-Indian Army." *Illustrated London News*, July 11, 1857, p. 27.

The Photographic Album for the Year 1857. London: Printed by Charles Whittingham for the Photographic Society Club, n.d. [ca. 1857].

"Photographs of Indian Cities." *Art-Journal*, December 1, 1857, p. 386.

Photography. Patent no. 12,906. London: Printed by Eyre & Spottiswoode for the Patent Office, 1857. [Patent filed by William Henry Fox Talbot.]

Photography. Patent no. 13,664. London: Printed by Eyre & Spottiswoode for the Patent Office, 1857. [Patent filed by William Henry Fox Talbot.]

1858
"Artistic Copyright." *Art-Journal*, July 1, 1858, pp. 205–9.

Davies, Thomas S. "To Hold the Sensitive Calotype Paper in the Dark Slide." *Photographic News* 1 (November 5, 1858), p. 107.

Fenton, Roger. "The Law of Artistic Copyright." *Journal of the Photographic Society* 4 (January 21, 1858), p. 151.

Gubbins, Martin R. *An Account of the Mutinies in Oudh and the Siege of the Lucknow Residency; with Some Observations on the Condition of the Province of Oudh and on the Causes of the Mutiny of the Bengal Army*. 2nd ed. London: Richard Bentley, 1858.

"Holywell-Street Revived." *Journal of the Photographic Society* 5 (September 21, 1858), p. 33. [Reprinted from the *Saturday Review*.]

"Photographic Society. Annual General Meeting. Tuesday, 2nd February, 1858." *Journal of the Photographic Society* 4 (February 22, 1858), pp. 154–59.

"The Photographic Society of London." *Journal of the Photographic Society* 4 (January 21, 1858), p. 132.

Price, William Lake. *Manual of Photographic Manipulation, Treating of the Practice of the Art; and Its Various Applications to Nature*. London: John Churchill, 1858.

Yule, Henry. *A Narrative of the Mission Sent by the Governor-General of India to the Court of Ava in 1855, with Notices of the Country, Government, and People*. London: Smith, Elder and Co., 1858. [Facsimile edition, *A Narrative of the Mission to the Court of Ava in 1855*, with an introduction by Hugh Tinker and additional illustrations by Colesworthy Grant and Linnaeus Tripe. Kuala Lumpur and London: Oxford University Press, 1968.]

1859
Duncan, J. M. "On the Law of Copyright, as Applied to Photographic Works." *Photographic Journal* 5 (February 22, 1859), pp. 187–97.

"The Photographic Society." *Photographic News* 2 (June 24, 1859), p. 185.

"The Society of Arts and the Exhibition of 1862." *Times* (London), November 17, 1859, p. 7, col. F.

The Young Lady's Book: A Manual of Elegant Recreations, Arts, Sciences, and Accomplishments. London: Henry G. Bohn, 1859.

1860
Clifford, Charles. *A Photographic Scramble through Spain*. London: A. Marion & Co., n.d. [ca. 1860].

Hannaford, Michael. "Exchange Club (in Connexion with the South London Photographic Society)." *British Journal of Photography* 7 (June 15, 1860), p. 179.

Knight, Charles. "Glass Manufacture." In *The English Cyclopaedia: A New Dictionary of Universal Knowledge, Arts and Sciences*, vol. 4, cols. 390–400. London: Bradbury and Evans, 1860.

"Photographic Society of Ireland." *Photographic Journal* 6 (March 15, 1860), pp. 182–83.

"Photographic Society of London. Annual General Meeting. Tuesday, February 7, 1860." *Photographic Journal* 6 (February 15, 1860), pp. 145–50.

"Stereoscopic Exchange Club." *Photographic News* 4 (October 10, 1860), p. 300.

Ure's Dictionary of Arts, Manufactures, and Mines, Containing a Clear Exposition of Their Principles and Practice. Edited by Robert Hunt. 5th ed. 3 vols. London: Longman, Green, Longman, and Roberts, 1860.

1861
"The Amateur's Photographic Association." *Photographic News* 5 (May 17, 1861), p. 229.

"Copyright in Works of Fine Art." *Photographic News* 5 (May 3, 1861), pp. 205–6.

"The Forthcoming International Exhibition." *Photographic News* 5 (September 27, 1861), pp. 455–56.

"International Exhibition, 1862." *Photographic Journal* 7 (May 15, 1861), pp. 172–74.

"The Memorial of the South London Photographic Society to Her Majesty's Commissioners for the International Exhibition of 1862." *Photographic News* 5 (October 11, 1861), p. 488.

"On the Classification of the International Exhibition of 1862 as Regards Photography." *Photographic Journal* 7 (August 15, 1861), pp. 241–44. [Letter from Antoine Claudet to Hugh Welch Diamond.]

"The Photographic Exchange Club." *Photographic News* 5 (October 18, 1861), pp. 491–92.

"Photographic Society." *Photographic Journal* 7 (December 16, 1861), p. 319.

"Photographic Society of London. Annual General Meeting. King's College, February 5, 1861." *Photographic Journal* 7 (February 21, 1861), pp. 98–102.

"Waxed-Paper Processes." *Photographic News* 5 (March 8, 1861), p. 119. [Signed "A Waxed-Paper Man."]

1862

"Amateur Photographic Association." *Photographic Journal* 8 (August 15, 1862), pp. 105–6.

"The Amateur Photographic Association." *Photographic News* 6 (July 18, 1862), p. 338.

"Amateur Photographic Association." In *Photographic News Almanac*, n.p. London: Cassell, Petter, & Galpin, 1862. [Announcement.]

"Awards of Jurors in the Exhibition." *Photographic News* 6 (July 18, 1862), pp. 337–38.

Black's Picturesque Guide to Yorkshire, with a Map of the Country and Numerous Plans and Views. 2nd ed. Edinburgh: Adam and Charles Black, 1862.

"The British Photographic Gallery." *Photographic News* 6 (May 30, 1862), pp. 255–56.

Cassell's Illustrated Family Paper Exhibitor . . . with Letter-Press Descriptions of All the Principal Objects in the International Exhibition of 1862. London: Cassell, Petter, & Galpin, 1862.

Catalogue of the Photographs Exhibited in Class XIV. London: Her Majesty's Commissioners, 1862.

"The Damp Walls in the Exhibition." *Photographic Journal* 8 (July 15, 1862), p. 97.

Ellison, Thomas. "On the Progress of the Commerce of Great Britain during the Ten Years, 1850 to 1860." *Journal of the Society of Arts* 10 (March 7, 1862), pp. 239–54.

"France: Class XIV." In *Illustrated Catalogue of the Industrial Department*, vol. 3, pp. 99–102. London: Printed for Her Majesty's Commissioners, 1862.

Hollingshead, John. "A Concise History of the International Exhibition of 1862: Its Rise and Progress, Its Building and Features, and a Summary of All Former Exhibitions." In *Illustrated Catalogue of the Industrial Department*, vol. 1, pp. 1–183. London: Printed for Her Majesty's Commissioners, 1862.

"The International Exhibition." *Times* (London), May 10, 1862, p. 14, col. B.

Melhuish, Arthur J. "Amateur Photographic Association." *Photographic Journal* 8 (July 15, 1862), p. 93.

"Miscellanea." *Photographic Journal* 8 (September 15, 1862), pp. 137–38.

"New Copyright Act." *Photographic News* 6 (August 8, 1862), pp. 380–81.

Photographic News Almanac. London: Cassell, Petter, & Galpin, 1862.

"Photographs of the Exhibition." *Times* (London), August 13, 1862, p. 8, col. D.

"Proposed Additional Photographic Exhibition." *Photographic News* 6 (February 7, 1862), p. 61.

"Registering Photographs." *Photographic News* 6 (August 22, 1862), p. 397.

"The South London Photographic Exhibition." *Photographic News* 6 (April 17, 1862), p. 181; (May 23, 1862), p. 241; (June 13, 1862), pp. 277–78; (June 20, 1862), pp. 290–91; (July 4, 1862), p. 319.

"Supplementary Photographic Exhibition." *Photographic News* 6 (March 14, 1862), p. 121.

"The Year 1862." *Times* (London), December 31, 1862, p. 6, col. B–p. 7, col. D. Reprinted in *Annual Summaries: Reprinted from "The Times,"* vol. 1, pp. 127–52. London: Macmillan and Co., 1893.

1863

Census of England and Wales for the Year 1861. Vol. 2, pt. 1, *Population Tables.* London: Her Majesty's Stationery Office, 1863.

"Class XIV: Photography and Photographic Apparatus." In *Reports by the Juries on the Subjects in the Thirty-six Classes into which the Exhibition Was Divided*, pp. 1–17. London: Printed for the Society of Arts by William Clowes & Sons, 1863.

"Classified List of the Trades in the United Kingdom." In *Report of the Commissioners for the Exhibition of 1862*, app. no. XXIII, pp. 114–30. London: George E. Eyre and William Spottiswoode, 1863.

Diamond, Hugh Welch. "Photography and Photographic Apparatus." In *The Record of the International Exhibition, 1862*, pp. 564–78. Glasgow: William MacKenzie, 1863.

"Fine Art Department." In *Report of the Commissioners for the Exhibition of 1862*, pp. xxxi–xxxvii. London: George E. Eyre and William Spottiswoode, 1863.

Johnson, Benjamin P. *Report on International Exhibition of Industry and Art, London, 1862.* Albany: C. van Benthuysen, 1863.

Report of the Commissioners for the Exhibition of 1862. London: George E. Eyre and William Spottiswoode, 1863.

Reports by the Juries on the Subjects in the Thirty-six Classes into which the Exhibition Was Divided. London: Printed for the Society of Arts by William Clowes & Sons, 1863. [Each class was given a separate pagination.]

"Return of the Number of Awards Made by the International Juries, in Every Class, to Each Country." *Report of the Commissioners for the Exhibition of 1862*, app. no. XXXVII, pp. 170–84. London: George E. Eyre and William Spottiswoode, 1863.

1864

English Catalogue of Books Published from January, 1835, to January, 1863; Comprising the Contents of the "London" and the "British" Catalogues, and the Principal Works Published in the United States of America and Continental Europe. London: Sampson Low, Son and Marston, 1864.

"Photographic Society of London. Annual General Meeting. King's College, London. Tuesday, February 2, 1864." *Photographic Journal* 8 (February 15, 1864), pp. 447–54.

1866

Haydn's Dictionary of Dates Relating to All Ages and Nations: For Universal Reference. London: Edward Moxon and Co., 1866.

1867

"Amateur Photographic Association." *Photographic News* 11 (November 15, 1867), p. 553.

"Photography: Its Social and Economic Position." *Photographic News* 11 (January 25, 1867), pp. 43–44.

1868

The National Gazetteer of Great Britain and Ireland. 12 vols. London: James S. Virtue, 1868.

1869

Carroll, Lewis. *Phantasmagoria, and Other Poems.* London: Macmillan and Co., 1869.

1870

Dawson, George. "Attempts at a New Paper Process." *British Journal of Photography* 17 (October 7, 1870), pp. 469–71.

———. "Negatives on Paper." *British Journal of Photography* 17 (June 17 and July 15, 1870), pp. 278–79, 325.

1871

Maddox, Richard Leach. "An Experiment with Gelatino-Bromide." *British Journal of Photography* 18 (September 8, 1871), pp. 422–23.

Melhuish, Arthur J. "The Amateur Photographic Association." *The British Journal Photographic Almanac and Photographer's Daily Companion*, 1871, pp. 120–22.

1872
Levi, Leone. *The History of British Commerce and of the Economic Progress of the British Nation, 1763–1878*. London: John Murray, 1872.

1874
"A Reminiscence of the Calotype Club." *British Journal of Photography* 21 (August 14, 1874), p. 385.

1875
"The Development of Paper Negatives." *British Journal of Photography* 22 (July 2, 1875), pp. 313–14.

Warnerke, Leon. "A New Method of Using Paper in Place of Glass for Negatives in Dry-Plate Photography." *British Journal of Photography* 22 (June 25, 1875), pp. 306–7.

1878
Burke, Bernard. *A Genealogical and Heraldic Dictionary of the Peerage and Baronetcy of the British Empire*. 40th ed. London: Harrison, 1878.

Willis, W., Jr. "A New Process of Photo-Chemical Printing in Metallic Platinum." *British Journal of Photography* 25 (August 23, 1878), p. 400.

———. "Notes on the Platinotype Process." *British Journal of Photography* 25 (December 20, 1878), pp. 605–6.

1883
Hall, Samuel Carter. *Retrospect of a Long Life, from 1815 to 1883*. New York: D. Appleton and Company, 1883.

1885
"Another Advance in Photography." *Times* (London), August 11, 1885, p. 3, cols. A–B.

"International Inventions Exhibition." *British Journal of Photography* 32 (August 28, 1885), pp. 545–46.

"The Walker-Eastman System of Film Photography." *British Journal of Photography* 32 (August 28, 1885), pp. 547–48.

Whaite, T. G. "Paper Negatives." *British Journal of Photography* 32 (October 16, 1885), pp. 664–65.

1886
"Summarised Notes of Progress during the Past Year." *The British Journal Photographic Almanac and Photographer's Daily Companion*, 1886, pp. 49–50.

1888
Kodak. Rochester, N.Y.: Eastman Dry Plate and Film Co., 1888. [Manual issued with "The Kodak" camera.]

"The Kodak." *British Journal of Photography* 35 (September 14, 1888), pp. 585–86.

1890
Login, Lena Campbell (Lady Login). *Sir John Login and Duleep Singh*. London: W. H. Allen & Co., 1890.

1892
Heath, Vernon. *Vernon Heath's Recollections*. London: Cassell & Company, 1892.

1893
Annual Summaries: Reprinted from "The Times." 2 vols. London: Macmillan and Co., 1893.

"Photographic Societies of the United Kingdom." *The British Journal Photographic Almanac and Photographer's Daily Companion*, 1893, pp. 448–85.

1894
Hume, John Richard. *Reminiscences of the Crimean Campaign with the 55th Regiment*. London: Unwin Brothers for the author, 1894. [Reprint, Uckfield, East Sussex: Naval and Military Press, 2003.]

Maskell, Alfred. "Carbon Printing without Transfer." *British Journal of Photography* 41 (November 9 and 16, 1894), pp. 709–11, 728–29.

"The Royal Photographic Society of Great Britain." *British Journal of Photography* 41 (August 10, 1894), p. 501.

1896
The Jubilee of the Chemical Society of London: Record of the Proceedings Together with an Account of the History of the Development of the Society, 1841–1891. London: Chemical Society, 1896.

Robinson, H. P. *The Elements of a Pictorial Photograph*. London and Bradford: Percy Lund & Co., 1896.

1898
MacLean, Hector. *Popular Photographic Printing Processes: A Practical Guide to Printing with Gelatino-Chloride, Artigue, Platinotype, Carbon, Bromide, Collodio-Chloride, Bichromated Gum and Other Sensitised Papers*. London: L. Upcott Gill, 1898.

1900
Newton, A. T. "Plain Salted Printing Papers: Their Treatment and Permanency." *British Journal of Photography* 47 (February 2, 1900), pp. 71–72.

"The Societies which Manage the Exhibitions." In *Photograms of the Year: 1900*, p. XXII. London: Dawbarn & Ward, 1900.

1905
"The Sales of the Past Season." *Burlington Magazine* 8 (October 1905), pp. 44–46.

1906
Burke, Ashworth P. *A Genealogical and Heraldic History of the Landed Gentry of Great Britain and Ireland*. 11th ed. London: Harrison & Sons, 1906.

1911
Jones, Bernard Edward, ed. *Cassell's Cyclopaedia of Photography*. London: Cassell and Co., 1911. [Reprint, New York: Arno Press, 1973.]

1913
Wood, Henry Trueman. *A History of the Royal Society of Arts*. London: John Murray, 1913.

1914
"Photography: Past and Present." *British Journal of Photography* 61 (June 19, 1914), suppl., pp. i–xxiv.

1915
Catalogue of an Exhibition of the Old Masters of Photography. Exh. cat. Buffalo: Albright Art Gallery, Buffalo Fine Arts Academy, 1915.

1919
Chance, J. F. *History of the Firm of Chance Brothers and Co.: Glass and Alkali Manufacturers*. London: Spottiswoode, Ballantyne & Co., 1919.

1929
Hearnshaw, F. J. C. *The Centenary History of King's College, London, 1828–1928*. London: George G. Harrap & Co., 1929.

1932
Hicks-Beach, Lady Victoria Alexandrina. *Life of Sir Michael Hicks Beach (Earl St. Aldwyn)*. 2 vols. London: Macmillan and Co., 1932.

1939
Carroll, Lewis. *The Complete Works of Lewis Carroll*. London: Nonesuch Press, 1939.

Drummond, Jack Cecil, and Anne Wilbraham. *The Englishman's Food: A History of Five Centuries of English Diet*. London: Jonathan Cape, 1939.

1945
Eder, Josef Maria. *History of Photography*. Translated by Edward Epstein (from the 4th ed. of *Geschichte der Photographie*). New York: Columbia University Press, 1945. [Reprint, New York: Dover Publications, 1978.]

1946
Gomme, Arthur Allan. *Patents of Invention; Origin and Growth of the Patent System in Britain*. London: Published for the British Council by Longmans, Green and Co., 1946.

Johnston, Dudley J. "The Story of the R.P.S." N.p.: Privately printed, 1946.

1950
Ffrench, Yvonne. *The Great Exhibition: 1851*. London: Harvill Press, 1950.

Hall, Daniel George Edward. *Burma*. London: Hutchinson's University Library, 1950.

1951
Fay, Charles Ryle. *Palace of Industry, 1851: A Study of the Great Exhibition and Its Fruits*. Cambridge: Cambridge University Press, 1951.

Luckhurst, Kenneth W. *The Story of Exhibitions*. London: Studio Publications, 1951.

1952
"Copy of the Rules of the Leeds Photographic Society." In *Centenary Souvenir Brochure*, p. 9. Leeds: Leeds Photographic Society, 1952.

1953
Dodds, John W. *The Age of Paradox: A Biography of England, 1841–1851*. London: Victor Gollancz, 1953.

Good, George. *The History of the Liverpool Amateur Photographic Association from 1853 to 1953*. Liverpool: Liverpool Amateur Photographic Association, 1953.

Ormerod, Henry Arderne. *The Liverpool Royal Institution: A Record and a Retrospect*. Liverpool: University Press, 1953.

1954
Hudson, Derek, and Kenneth W. Luckhurst. *The Royal Society of Arts, 1754–1954*. London: John Murray, 1954.

1955
Postgate, Raymond. *Story of a Year: 1848*. London: Jonathan Cape, 1955.

1956
Gernsheim, Helmut, and Alison Gernsheim. *L. J. M. Daguerre (1878–1851): The World's First Photographer*. Cleveland and New York: World Publishing Company, 1956.

A History of the County of Essex. Edited by W. R. Powell. Vol. 4, *Ongar Hundred*. The Victoria History of the Counties of England. London: Oxford University Press for the Institute of Historical Research, 1956. [Online version available at http://www.british-history.ac.uk.]

1957
Altick, Richard Daniel. *The English Common Reader: A Social History of the Mass Reading Public, 1800–1900*. Chicago: University of Chicago Press, 1957.

1964
Longford, Countess of (Elizabeth Harman Pakenham). *Victoria R.I.* London: Weidenfield and Nicolson, 1964.

1965
Boase, Frederic. *Modern English Biography: Containing Many Thousand Concise Memoirs of Persons Who Have Died between the Years 1851–1900, with an Index of the Most Interesting Matter*. 6 vols. London: Frank Cass & Co., 1965. [Reprint of the 1892–1921 edition.]

Mather, Frederick Clare. *Chartism*. Historical Association (Great Britain) General Series, no. 61. London: Historical Association, 1965.

1968
Russell-Jones, Peter R. "John MacCosh's Photographs of the 2nd Sikh War, 1848–49, and of the 2nd Burma War, 1852–53." *Photographic Journal* 108 (January 1968), pp. 25–27.

Yule, Henry. *A Narrative of the Mission to the Court of Ava in 1855*. Facsimile of the 1858 edition, with an introduction by Hugh Tinker and additional illustrations by Colesworthy Grant and Linnaeus Tripe. Kuala Lumpur and London: Oxford University Press, 1968. [Originally published as *A Narrative of the Mission Sent by the Governor-General of India to the Court of Ava in 1855, with Notices of the Country, Government, and People*. London: Smith, Elder and Co., 1858.]

1973
Banks, J. A. "The Contagion of Numbers." In *The Victorian City: Images and Realities*, edited by H. J. Dyos and Michael Wolff, vol. 1, pp. 105–22. London and Boston: Routledge & Kegan Paul, 1973.

1975
Jenkins, Reese V. *Images and Enterprise: Technology and the American Photographic Industry, 1839 to 1925*. Baltimore and London: Johns Hopkins University Press, 1975.

1976
Allen, David Elliston. *The Naturalist in Britain: A Social History*. London: Allen Lane, 1976.

Haskell, Francis. *Rediscoveries in Art: Some Aspects of Taste, Fashion, and Collecting in England and France*. Ithaca, N.Y.: Cornell University Press, 1976.

McLean, Ruari. *Joseph Cundall, a Victorian Publisher: Notes on His Life and a Check-List of His Books*. Pinner: Private Libraries Association, 1976.

1978
Coe, Brian. *Cameras: From Daguerreotypes to Instant Pictures*. London: Marshall Cavendish, 1978.

Robertson, David. *Sir Charles Eastlake and the Victorian Art World*. Princeton, N.J.: Princeton University Press, 1978.

1978–79
McCauley, Elizabeth Anne. "Evasion in Victorian Landscape Photography: The Amateur Photographic Association Album." *Bulletin* (Art Museum, University of New Mexico), no. 12 (1978–79), pp. 3–13.

1979
Harker, Margaret F. *The Linked Ring: The Secession Movement in Photography in Britain, 1892–1910*. London: Heinemann, 1979.

Heathcote, Bernard V., and Pauline F. Heathcote. "Richard Beard: An Ingenious and Enterprising Patentee." *History of Photography* 3 (October 1979), pp. 313–29.

Wood, R. Derek. "The Daguerreotype in England: Some Primary Material Relating to Beard's Lawsuits." *History of Photography* 3 (October 1979), pp. 305–9.

1980
Barber, Lynn. *The Heyday of Natural History, 1820–1870*. London: Jonathan Cape, 1980.

Buckland, Gail. *Fox Talbot and the Invention of Photography*. London: Scolar Press, 1980.

Reilly, James M. *The Albumen and Salted Paper Book: The History and Practice of Photographic Printing, 1840–1895*. Rochester: Light Impressions, 1980.

1981
Budge, Adrian. *Early Photography in Leeds, 1839–1870*. Exh. cat. Leeds: Leeds Art Galleries, 1981.

Digby, Anne. "The Rural Poor." In *The Victorian Countryside*, edited by G. E. Mingay, vol. 2, pp. 591–602. London: Routledge & Kegan Paul, 1981.

Prince, Hugh. "Victorian Rural Landscapes." In *The Victorian Countryside*, edited by G. E. Mingay, vol. 1, pp. 17–29. London: Routledge & Kegan Paul, 1981.

Taylor, Roger. *George Washington Wilson: Artist and Photographer, 1823–93*. Aberdeen: Aberdeen University Press, 1981.

1982
Gernsheim, Helmut. *The Origins of Photography*. 3rd ed. London and New York: Thames & Hudson, 1982.

Keeler, Nancy B. "Illustrating the 'Reports by the Juries' of the Great Exhibition; Talbot, Henneman, and Their Failed Commission." *History of Photography* 6 (July 1982), pp. 257–72.

Lambert, Phyllis. Introduction to *Photography and Architecture, 1839–1939*, edited by Richard Pare, pp. 7–11. Exh. cat. Montreal: Canadian Centre of Architecture, 1982.

Nevett, Terry R. *Advertising in Britain: A History.* London: Heinemann, 1982.

Schaaf, Larry J. "Henry Collen and the Treaty of Nanking." *History of Photography* 6 (October 1982), pp. 353–66.

1983

Hiley, Michael. *Seeing through Photographs.* London: Gordon Fraser, 1983.

Schaaf, Larry J. "Addenda to Henry Collen and the Treaty of Nanking." *History of Photography* 7 (April–June 1983), pp. 163–65.

Thomas, Keith. *Man and the Natural World: Changing Attitudes in England, 1500–1800.* London: Allen Lane, 1983.

The Travellers' Dictionary of Quotation: Who Said What, about Where? Edited by Peter Yapp. London and Boston: Routledge & Kegan Paul, 1983.

1984

Dutton, H. I. *The Patent System and Inventive Activity during the Industrial Revolution, 1750–1852.* Manchester: Manchester University Press, 1984.

Gernsheim, Helmut. *Incunabula of British Photographic Literature: A Bibliography of British Photographic Literature, 1839–75, and British Books Illustrated with Original Photographs.* London and Berkeley: Scolar Press, in association with Derbyshire College of Higher Education, 1984.

Himmelfarb, Gertrude. *The Idea of Poverty: England in the Early Industrial Age.* London and Boston: Faber & Faber, 1984.

Hobsbawm, Eric J., and Terence O. Ranger, eds. *The Invention of Tradition.* Past and Present Publications. Cambridge: Cambridge University Press, 1984.

1985

Martin, Jane. "Krumen 'Down the Coast': Liberian Migrants on the West African Coast in the 19th and Early 20th Centuries." *International Journal of African Historical Studies* 18 (1985), pp. 410–23.

Millar, Delia. *Queen Victoria's Life in the Scottish Highlands Depicted by Her Watercolour Artists.* London: Philip Wilson, 1985.

1986

Seiberling Grace, with Carolyn Bloore. *Amateurs, Photography, and the Mid-Victorian Imagination.* Chicago: University of Chicago Press, 1986.

Zillman, Linda Goforth. *Sir William Newton: Miniature Painter and Photographer, 1785–1869.* History of Photography Monograph Series, special issue, no. 2. Tempe: School of Art, Arizona State University, 1986.

1987

Dimond, Frances, and Roger Taylor. *Crown & Camera: The Royal Family and Photography, 1842–1910.* Harmondsworth: Penguin Books, 1987.

McKenzie, Ray. "'The Laboratory of Mankind': John McCosh and the Beginnings of Photography in British India." *History of Photography* 11 (April–June 1987), pp. 109–18.

Taylor, Roger. "The Chartist Meeting, 10 April 1848." In Dimond and Taylor 1987, pp. 26–29.

1988

Hyde, Ralph. *Panoramania! The Art and Entertainment of the "All-Embracing" View.* London: Trefoil, in association with the Barbican Art Gallery, 1988.

Victorian Britain: An Encyclopedia. Edited by Sally Mitchell. New York and London: Garland Publishing, 1988.

1989

Andrews, Malcolm. *The Search for the Picturesque: Landscape Aesthetics and Tourism in Britain, 1760–1800.* Aldershot: Scolar Press, 1989.

Gard, Robin, ed. *The Observant Traveller: Diaries of Travel in England, Wales, and Scotland in the County Record Offices of England and Wales.* London: Her Majesty's Stationery Office, 1989.

Schaaf, Larry J. *H. Fox Talbot's The Pencil of Nature: Anniversary Facsimile. Introductory Volume, Historical Sketch, Notes on the Plates, Census.* Published with a facsimile edition of William Henry Fox Talbot, *The Pencil of Nature* [1844–46]. New York: Hans P. Kraus, Jr. 1989.

———. *Tracings of Light: Sir John Herschel & the Camera Lucida.* San Francisco: Friends of Photography, 1989.

Talbot, William Henry Fox. *The Pencil of Nature.* 6 fascicles. Facsimile edition, with commentary volume by Larry J. Schaaf. New York: Hans P. Kraus, Jr., 1989. [1st ed., London: Longman, Brown, Green, & Longmans, 1844–46.]

Wood, John, ed. *The Daguerreotype: A Sesquicentennial Celebration.* Iowa City: University of Iowa Press; London: Gerald Duckworth, 1989.

1990

Buckman, Rollin. *The Photographic Work of Calvert Richard Jones.* Introduction by John Ward. London: H.M.S.O. for the Science Museum, 1990.

Petroski, Henry. *The Pencil: A History of Design and Circumstance.* London: Faber & Faber, 1990.

Pritchard, Michael. "The Rise of British Photographic Manufacturing, 1839–*c.* 1862: Sources and Trends." In *Technology and Art: The Birth and Early Years of Photography—The Proceedings of the Royal Photographic Historical Group Conference, 1–3 September 1989,* edited by Michael Pritchard, pp. 57–65. Bath: Royal Photographic Society Historical Group, 1990.

———. "Tropical Cameras." *Photographica World,* no. 54 (September 1990), pp. 11–13.

The Raj: India and the British, 1600–1947. Exh. cat. London: National Portrait Gallery Publications, 1990.

Schaaf, Larry J. *Sun Pictures, Catalogue Five: The Reverend Calvert R. Jones.* New York: Henry P. Kraus, Jr., 1990.

Smith, Graham. *Disciples of Light: Photographs in the Brewster Album.* Malibu, Calif.: J. Paul Getty Museum, 1990.

1991

Barger, M. Susan, and William B. White. *The Daguerreotype: Nineteenth-Century Technology and Modern Science.* Washington, D.C.: Smithsonian Institution Press, 1991.

1992

Black, Jeremy. *The British Abroad: The Grand Tour in the Eighteenth Century.* Stroud: Alan Sutton; New York: St. Martin's Press, 1992.

Schaaf, Larry J. *Out of the Shadows: Herschel, Talbot, & the Invention of Photography.* New Haven and London: Yale University Press, 1992.

1993

Hannavy, John. "Roger Fenton and the Waxed Paper Process." *History of Photography* 17 (Autumn 1993), pp. 233–43.

McKenzie, Ray. "Pictorialism and Its Malcontents." In *Photography 1900: The Edinburgh Symposium,* pp. 13–17. Edinburgh: National Museums of Scotland and National Galleries of Scotland, 1993.

Schaaf, Larry J. *Sun Pictures, Catalogue Six: Dr. Thomas Keith and John Forbes White.* New York: Hans P. Kraus, Jr., 1993.

1994

Daniel, Malcolm R. *The Photographs of Édouard Baldus.* With an essay by Barry Bergdoll. Exh. cat. New York: The Metropolitan Museum of Art, 1994.

Pritchard, Michael. *A Directory of London Photographers, 1841–1901.* Rev. ed. Watford: PhotoResearch, 1994. [Online version available at http://www.photolondon.org.uk/directory.htm.]

Ware, Mike. *Mechanisms of Image Deterioration in Early Photographs: The Sensitivity to Light of W. H. F. Talbot's Halide-Fixed Images, 1834–1844.* London: Science Museum; Bradford: National Museum of Photography, Film & Television, 1994.

1995

Ashton, Owen, Robert Fyson, and Stephen Roberts, eds. *The Chartist Movement: A New Annotated Bibliography.* London: Mansell, 1995.

Jaeger, Jens. "Photographic Societies in Britain in the Nineteenth Century." In *"Darkness and Light": The Proceedings of the Oslo Symposium, 25.–28. August 1994,* ed. Roger Erlandsen and Vegard S. Halvorsen, pp. 133–40. Oslo: National Institute for Historical Photography and the Norwegian Society of the History of Photography, 1995.

Porter, Roy. *London: A Social History.* Cambridge, Mass.: Harvard University Press, 1995.

Sillitoe, Alan. *Leading the Blind: A Century of Guidebook Travel, 1815–1914.* London: Macmillan, 1995.

1996

Higgs, Edward. *A Clearer Sense of the Census: The Victorian Censuses and Historical Research.* Public Record Office Handbooks, no. 28. London: Her Majesty's Stationery Office, 1996.

Jalland, Patricia. *Death in the Victorian Family.* Oxford: Oxford University Press, 1996.

Klonk, Charlotte. *Science and the Perception of Nature: British Landscape Art in the Late Eighteenth and Early Nineteenth Centuries.* New Haven and London: Published for the Paul Mellon Centre for Studies in British Art by Yale University Press, 1996.

Schaaf, Larry J. *Records of the Dawn of Photography: Talbot's Notebooks P & Q.* Cambridge: Cambridge University Press, with the National Museum of Photography, Film & Television, Bradford, 1996.

Taylor, P. J. O., ed. *A Companion to the "Indian Mutiny" of 1857.* Delhi and New York: Oxford University Press, 1996.

Ward, Andrew. *Our Bones are Scattered: The Cawnpore Massacres and the Indian Mutiny of 1857.* New York: Henry Holt; London: John Murray, 1996.

1997

Oxford Companion to British Railway History from 1603 to the 1990s. Edited by Jack Simmons and Gordon Biddle. Oxford: Oxford University Press, 1997.

Woods, Robert, and Nicola Shelton. *An Atlas of Victorian Mortality.* Liverpool: University of Liverpool Press, 1997.

1998

A History of Shropshire. Edited by G. C. Baugh. Vol. 10, *Wenlock, Upper Corve Dale, and the Stretton Hills.* The Victoria History of the Counties of England. London: Oxford University Press for the Institute of Historical Research, 1998. [Online version available at http://www.british-history.ac.uk.]

Hoppen, K. Theodore. *The Mid-Victorian Generation, 1846–1886.* The New Oxford History of England. Oxford: Clarendon Press, 1998.

Lowry, Bates, and Isabel Barrett Lowry. *The Silver Canvas: Daguerreotypes Masterpieces from the J. Paul Getty Museum.* Los Angeles: J. Paul Getty Museum, 1998.

1999

Anninger, Anne, and Julie Mellby. *Salts of Silver, Toned with Gold: The Harrison D. Horblit Collection of Early Photography.* Edited by Victoria Alexander. Exh. cat. Cambridge, Mass.: Houghton Library, Harvard University, 1999.

Auerbach, Jeffrey A. *The Great Exhibition of 1851: A Nation on Display.* New Haven and London: Yale University Press, 1999.

Davis, John R. *The Great Exhibition.* Stroud: Sutton Publishing, 1999.

Early Photographs of India. Sale cat. Sotheby's, London, June 18, 1999.

Fontanella, Lee. *Clifford en España: Un fotógrafo en la corte de Isabel II.* Madrid: Ediciones El Viso, 1999.

Freeman, Michael J. *Railways and the Victorian Imagination.* New Haven and London: Yale University Press, 1999.

Patel, Divia. "Photography and the Romance of the Panjab." In *Arts of the Sikh Kingdoms,* edited by Susan Stronge, pp. 192–207. London: V&A Publications, 1999.

Taylor, Roger. "The Graphic Society and Photography, 1839: Priority and Precedence." *History of Photography* 23 (Spring 1999), pp. 59–67.

2000

Bermingham, Ann. *Learning to Draw: Studies in the Cultural History of a Polite and Useful Art.* New Haven and London: Published for the Paul Mellon Centre for Studies in British Art by Yale University Press, 2000.

Fraser, John. "Dr John Murray of Agra." *Photohistorian,* no. 132 (November 2000), pp. 13–15.

Nead, Lynda. *Victorian Babylon: People, Streets and Images in Nineteenth-Century London.* New Haven and London: Yale University Press, 2000.

Schaaf, Larry J. *The Photographic Art of William Henry Fox Talbot.* Princeton, N.J.: Princeton University Press, 2000.

Secord, James A. *Victorian Sensation: The Extraordinary Publication, Reception, and Secret Authorship of Vestiges of the Natural History of Creation.* Chicago: University of Chicago Press, 2000.

2001

Bann, Stephen. *Parallel Lines: Printmakers, Painters and Photographers in Nineteenth Century France.* New Haven and London: Yale University Press, 2001.

Barnes, Martin. *Benjamin Brecknell Turner: Rural England through a Victorian Lens.* With a biography by Mark Haworth-Booth. London: V&A Publications, 2001.

Chandler, Edward. *Photography in Ireland: The Nineteenth Century.* Dublin: Edmund Burke, 2001.

Falconer, John. *India: Pioneering Photographers, 1850–1900.* London: British Library and the Howard and Jane Ricketts Collection, 2001.

Ware, Mike. "Invento *en cámara*: Los logros técnicos de W. H. F. Talbot / Invention in Camera: The Technical Achievements of WHF Talbot." In *Huellas de luz: El arte y los experimentos de William Henry Fox Talbot,* pp. 25–35, 343–46. Exh. cat. Madrid: Museo Nacional Centro de Arte Reina Sofia, 2001.

2002

Aubenas, Sylvie. *Gustave Le Gray, 1820–1884.* With contributions by Anne Cartier-Bresson et al. Edited by Gordon Baldwin. Los Angeles: J. Paul Getty Museum, 2002.

Kamlish, Marian. "Claudet, Fenton and the Photographic Society." *History of Photography* 26 (Winter 2002), pp. 296–306.

Mondenard, Anne de. *La Mission héliographique: Cinq Photographes parcourent la France en 1851.* Paris: Monum, Éditions du Patrimoine, 2002.

Stevenson, Sara. *The Personal Art of David Octavius Hill.* New Haven and London: Published for the Paul Mellon Centre for Studies in British Art by Yale University Press, 2002.

Taylor, Roger. *Photographs Exhibited in Britain, 1839–1865: A Compendium of Photographers and Their Works / Photographies exposées en Grande-Bretagne de 1839 à 1865: Répertoire des photographes et de leurs oeuvres.* Library and Archives, Occasional Paper / Bibliothèque et Archives, document hors série, 5. Ottawa: National Gallery of Canada, 2002. [Online version available at http://www.peib.org.uk.]

2003

Dewan, Janet. *Photographs of Linnaeus Tripe: A Catalogue Raisonné.* Toronto: Art Gallery of Ontario, 2003.

Kamlish, Marian. "A Response to Roger Taylor." *History of Photography* 27 (Winter 2003), pp. 389–90. [See Taylor 2003.]

Pelizzari, Maria Antonella, ed. *Traces of India: Photography, Architecture, and the Politics of Representation, 1850–1900.* Exh. cat. Montreal: Canadian Centre for Architecture; New Haven: Yale Center for British Art, 2003.

Schaaf, Larry J. *Sun Pictures, Catalogue Twelve: Talbot and Photogravure.* New York: Hans P. Kraus, Jr., 2003.

Taylor, Roger. "Claudet, Fenton and the Photographic Society: A Response." *History of Photography* 27 (Winter 2003), pp. 386–88. [See Kamlish 2002 and Kamlish 2003.]

Taylor, Roger, and Mike Ware. "'Pilgrims of the Sun': The Chemical Evolution of the Calotype, 1840–1852." *History of Photography* 27 (Winter 2003), pp. 308–19.

2004
Baldwin, Gordon, Malcolm Daniel, and Sara Greenough, with contributions by Richard Pare, Pam Roberts, and Roger Taylor. *All the Mighty World: The Photographs of Roger Fenton, 1852–1860.* Exh. cat. New York: The Metropolitan Museum of Art; Washington, D.C.: National Gallery of Art; Los Angeles: J. Paul Getty Museum; New Haven and London: Yale University Press, 2004.

Greenough, Sarah. "'A New Starting Point': Roger Fenton's Life." In Baldwin et al. 2004, pp. 2–31, 245–49.

Pearce, Edward. *Reform! The Fight for the 1832 Reform Act.* London: Pimlico, 2004.

Roberts, Pam. "'The Exertions of Mr. Fenton': Roger Fenton and the Founding of the Photographic Society." In Baldwin et al. 2004, pp. 211–20, 260–61.

Taylor, Roger. "'Mr. Fenton Explained Everything': Queen Victoria and Roger Fenton." In Baldwin et al. 2004, pp. 74–81, 255–56.

Taylor, Roger, and Gordon Baldwin. "A Chronology of the Life and Photographic Career of Roger Fenton." In Baldwin et al. 2004, pp. 231–39, 262–66.

Ware, Mike. "Prolegomena to a 'Skiology' of Photogenic Drawing." *History of Photography* 28 (Autumn 2004), pp. 237–46.

2005
Asser, Saskia. "*A Handsome & Highly Finished Present:* Foto's voor de juryrapporten van de Great Exhibition, 1851." *Bulletin van het Rijksmuseum* 53 (2005), pp. 141–77, 229–33 (summary in English).

Watercolours of the Grand Tour. Sale cat. Christie's, London, October 12, 2005. With an essay by Huon Mallalieu, "Following the Grand Tour: The Cheneys of Badger Hall," pp. 2–7. [Sale of drawings and watercolors by the Cheney family.]

2006
Schaaf, Larry J. *Sun Pictures, Catalogue Fifteen: From Talbot to Turner.* New York: Hans P. Kraus, Jr., 2006.

Ware, Mike. *Gold in Photography: The History and Art of Chrysotype.* Brighton: Ffotoffilm Publishing, 2006.

———. "Herschel's Chrysotype: A Golden Legend Re-Told." *History of Photography* 30 (Spring 2006), pp. 1–24.

Index

Page numbers for figures (figs.) and Biographical Dictionary illustrations (ills.) are shown in *italic* type. Plates (pls.) can be located by plate number. Photographic subjects located in cities are indexed under the name of the city. From the Biographical Dictionary, only the names of the featured calotypists are included here; page numbers for main entries are shown in **boldface** type.

Photograph Credits

Photographs were in most cases provided by the institutions or individuals owning the works and are published with their permission; their courtesy is gratefully acknowledged. Additional information on photograph sources follows.

© Art Gallery of Ontario: figs. 31, 33, 34, 36, 41; pls. 20, 21, 22

© Copyright The Trustees of The British Museum: fig. 67

Photograph by R. H. Hensleigh: fig. 13b

Digital Image © The Museum of Modern Art/Licensed by SCALA/Art Resource, NY: figs. 76, 87; pls. 58, 59, 78

Photograph by Garth Olsen: fig. 63

The Royal Collection © 2007, Her Majesty Queen Elizabeth II: figs. 9, 11; pl. 47; dictionary ills. 76, 94, 97

Photograph by Bruce M. White, © 2001 Trustees of Princeton University: fig. 62